Constitutional and Administrative Law

Hilaire Barnett's *Constitutional and Administrative Law* has consistently provided students with reliable, accessible and comprehensive coverage of the Public Law syllabus. Mapped to the common course outline, the Fourteenth Edition equips students with a thorough understanding of the UK constitution's past, present and future by analysing and illustrating the political and socio-historical contexts that have shaped the major rules and principles of constitutional and administrative law, as well as ongoing constitutional reform.

This edition has been fully updated and includes discussion of the consequences of the United Kingdom's withdrawal from the European Union, including the impact on the legislative supremacy of Parliament and the relationship between EU and domestic law after departure. It also features discussion of the 2020 Coronavirus Act, with its implications for state power, and ahead of the forthcoming new SQE qualification, revised multiple choice questions on the Companion Website.

Ideal for students studying constitutional and administrative law for the first time, this is an indispensable guide to the challenging concepts and legal rules in public law.

Hilaire Barnett is a former Senior Lecturer in Law, Queen Mary, University of London.

Constitutional and Administrative Law

FOURTEENTH EDITION

Hilaire Barnett

Routledge
Taylor & Francis Group
LONDON AND NEW YORK

First published 2021
by Routledge
2 Park Square, Milton Park, Abingdon, Oxon OX14 4RN

and by Routledge
605 Third Avenue, New York, NY 10158

Routledge is an imprint of the Taylor & Francis Group, an informa business

First edition published by Cavendish Publishing 1995.
Thirteenth edition published by Routledge 2020.

British Library Cataloguing-in-Publication Data
A catalogue record for this book is available from the British Library

Library of Congress Cataloging-in-Publication Data
A catalog record has been requested for this book

ISBN: 978-0-367-72627-0 (hbk)
ISBN: 978-0-367-56632-6 (pbk)
ISBN: 978-1-003-15563-8 (ebk)

Typeset in Joanna
by Deanta Global Publishing Services, Chennai, India

Visit the companion website:www.routledge.com/cw/barnett

Printed and bound by CPI Group (UK) Ltd, Croydon, CR0 4YY

For Matthew and Essie, George, Amy and Toby

Outline Contents

Detailed Contents

Preface

The United Kingdom's constitution, while of ancient origins, remains both dynamic and vibrant. As every public lawyer is only too aware, the boundaries of constitutional and administrative law are both increasingly wide and subject to debate. In compiling any textbook on this subject, one of the principal preliminary tasks lies in defining the scope of material to be included and the approach to be adopted in relation to that material. The task of writing is made more problematic by the many and varied depths in which, and the means by which, the subject is taught both in the United Kingdom and overseas. Full-time students, part-time students, students on long-distance learning programmes and students combining both constitutional and administrative law within a one-year course all have differing needs. The aim in this book has been to provide sufficient detail to meet all such needs in a user-friendly manner.

As emphasised in the introductory chapters, the study of the United Kingdom's constitutional and administrative law involves rather more than a learning of rules of law, and necessarily encompasses – over and above an understanding of legal rules – an understanding of history, government, politics and conventional practices which form the foundations of the contemporary constitution. As a result, any constitutional and administrative law textbook must incorporate sufficient information relating to such matters so as to enable students to view the constitution in its historical, political and conventional context. In this book, I have addressed the subject in this manner in order to provide a rounded, contextual explanation of the United Kingdom's constitution, which goes beyond pure law while also adequately covering the law.

The text is divided into eight main parts. Part 1 provides a general introduction to the scope of constitutional law, the sources of the constitution and the structure of the United Kingdom. In Part 2, the fundamental concepts of the constitution are considered: the rule of law, separation of powers, the royal prerogative and parliamentary sovereignty. In Part 3, the European Union is discussed. The material is divided into two chapters. Chapter 7 considers the evolution, aims and structure of the Union and the principal institutions and their respective powers, together with the sources of EU law. In Chapter 8, the relationship between national and European Union law is discussed. In 2016 the people of the UK voted in a referendum, by a slim majority, to leave the EU ('Brexit') and, after much delay, this was accomplished on 31 January 2019. A transition period ran until the end of December 2020, during which the ongoing relationship between the UK and the EU was negotiated. Although no longer a member state of the EU, the European Union and EU law will remain an important area of study, not least because during over 45 years' membership of the EU so much of domestic law has its origins in the EU and will be retained post-Brexit. It will also remain important because whatever future relationship between the UK and the EU is eventually agreed, there will remain close economic and political ties between the UK and EU. In Part 4, the structure of government in the UK is discussed, Chapter 9 considering the role of Prime Minister, Cabinet and the Civil Service, Chapter 10 discussing the concept of ministerial responsibility and Chapter 11, the devolution of power to the Northern Ireland Assembly, Scottish Parliament and Welsh Assembly and local government.

Part 5 is devoted to the United Kingdom Parliament: Westminster. Chapter 12 discusses the electoral system, and Chapter 13 introduces the reader to the House of Commons. Chapters 14 and 15 are devoted to parliamentary procedures for the scrutiny of legislative proposals and scrutiny of government administration. With the Coronavirus pandemic of 2019–2021, the government considered that new and additional measures were necessary to deal satisfactorily with the outbreak. The Coronavirus Act 2020 and associated legislation and Regulations was the outcome, fast-tracked through Parliament, and ushering in draconian restrictions on individual freedoms in the effort to control the virus. The House of Lords, its role, functions and the current reform proposals are considered in Chapter 16. Parliamentary privilege is discussed in Chapter 17.

Part 6 focuses on the individual and the state, covering civil liberties and the protection of human rights. The subject of state security, including emergency powers, is discussed in Chapter 21. Part 7 covers judges and the legal system. Part 8 introduces administrative law. Judicial review of administrative action comprises three chapters, the first dealing with the role and scope of judicial review and procedural matters, and the second and third analysing the grounds for judicial review. Tribunals and Inquiries are discussed in Chapter 26, and the role, functions and powers of Commissioners for Administration (Ombudsmen) are considered in Chapter 27.

The Fourteenth Edition, like its predecessor, has been prepared and published under the shadow of the 2016 decision of the British people to leave the European Union. That decision and the process of withdrawing from the Union represents the most profound constitutional change in decades. The process of leaving has been far from smooth. On the day on which the UK was originally to leave the EU – 29 March 2019 – the House of Commons rejected the Withdrawal Agreement – the formal treaty regulating the terms of leaving – for the third time. A change in Prime Minister, a further General Election, and further delay ensued. While the UK formally left the EU on 31 January 2020, the question of the future relationship between the UK and EU remained undecided, and an agreement only reached at the last minute before the end of the transition period in December 2020, although many issues remain unresolved.

My thanks to Chloe James, Russell George and the team at Routledge and to Lillian Woodall of Deanta Global Publishing Services for all their input and support.

Hilaire Barnett
May 2021

Table of Cases

Table of UK and International Legislation

Table of Statutory Instruments

Table of Decisions, Directives, Regulations, Treaties and Conventions

Part 1

General Introduction

Chapter 1

Introducing Constitutional Law

Chapter Contents

Learning Objectives

By the end of this chapter you should be able to:

☐ explain the term 'constitution';
☐ discuss the major categories of constitutions and their characteristics;
☐ discuss the evolutionary development of the UK constitution;
☐ explain the principal characteristics of the UK constitution.

PART A: THE CONSTITUTION

Introduction

Constitutional law is concerned with the role and powers of the institutions within the state and with the relationship between the citizen and the state. The constitution is a living, dynamic organism which at any point in time will reflect the moral and political values of the people it governs, and, accordingly, the law of the constitution must be appreciated within the socio-political context in which it operates.

The study of the constitution of the United Kingdom involves acquiring an understanding of a variety of historical, legal, philosophical and political factors which have, over the centuries, shaped the organisation of the state. The United Kingdom appears to be almost unique in not having a constitution which is conveniently set out in a single written document. Israel and New Zealand share this constitutional feature. However, not too much weight should be given to the 'unwritten' nature of the constitution. Under all constitutions, not all of the rules will be written, and still less will they be collected within a single document.

In the United Kingdom, by contrast with most other states, the constitution is the product of many centuries of continuous and, mostly, gradual, peaceful evolution. With the exception of the constitutional turmoils of the seventeenth century,[1] the United Kingdom's constitutional development has an unbroken history dating from 1066. Accordingly, historical origins form the background for the study of the contemporary constitution, and no meaningful appreciation of the present constitution can be acquired without understanding this historical backcloth which reveals the moral and political influences that have shaped the constitution as it exists today. That said, it must always be remembered that the principal emphasis of study is on the contemporary constitution of the United Kingdom rather than on the many centuries of development which underlie it. With that point in mind, it is necessary to draw on historical sources and events with a view to understanding the contribution made to an evaluation of the many constitutional issues which present themselves today.

It is particularly true of the United Kingdom's constitution, which is more the product of evolution than conscious rational thought, that it is difficult to see clearly the demarcation lines between constitutional law, history, philosophy and political science. In order, therefore, to study the United Kingdom's constitution successfully, it is necessary to gain an insight into the history, politics and political philosophy which underpin the constitution. This task is not easy, particularly as many students will come to constitutional law without a background in history, politics or political philosophy. It is, however, an essential component of constitutional study, without which the structure, law and policies of the state cannot be understood. More than any other area of legal study except jurisprudence, constitutional law in the United Kingdom involves far more than a learning of legal rules. Indeed, it may be said, without exaggeration, that the non-legal rules and practices within the constitution

---

1 See in particular Chapters 2, 5 and 6.

are at least as important – if not more important on many occasions – as the legal rules. For example, in analysing and evaluating the extent to which the individual citizen enjoys constitutional protection of individual rights, it is necessary to appreciate the timeless and tireless quest to ensure the legal protection of the rights of individuals. This study involves, *inter alia*, an appreciation of natural law and social contract theories[2] which underpin the constitutional limitations on government power in order that the rights of individuals are protected against the power of the state.

Also, by way of example, the study of the constitutional relationship between the government and the legislature – the United Kingdom Parliament today encompasses a knowledge of the political backcloth, the rules of parliamentary practice and the non-legal or conventional rules which apply in a given situation. By way of further illustration, when studying the legislative supremacy of Parliament, it is of fundamental importance to grasp that, in terms of classical constitutional legal theory, the power of Parliament – in the absence of a written constitution – is omnipotent or sovereign.[3] However, the constitutional and legal fact that Parliament has the ultimate law-making power within the state does not mean that there are no restraints on what Parliament may do. The law-making powers of Parliament, while theoretically and legally unlimited, are in fact constrained by the electorate to which Parliament is accountable, and by economic, moral and political necessities. In terms of accountability to the electorate and the limits which this imposes on Parliament's powers, it is necessary to appreciate the philosophical and historical foundations of democracy and the idea of individual rights. Notwithstanding the lack of a codified constituent document, under the constitution of the United Kingdom, the principles on which the government operates today are precisely those which govern the relationship between the government and the people under a written constitution. Here, an understanding of the idea of 'social contract'[4] makes it possible to understand the complex relationship between 'sovereign power' and the power of the people to determine who holds that sovereign power and the manner in which it may – and may not – be exercised.

To illustrate further the distinction between absolute legal power and practical power, in terms of law, the Crown has the right to appoint the Prime Minister of its choice, to summon Parliament and to enter into Treaties. To know these rules, however, is not to know very much, for the legal powers of the Crown are restricted – constrained – by non-legal, 'conventional' rules which determine the conditions under which the Crown has a discretion to exercise its powers. In order, therefore, to understand how the constitution works, it is necessary to understand the conventional rules which have developed over time and have taken on binding force.

What is a Constitution?

In lay terms, a constitution is a set of rules which governs an organisation. Every organisation, whether social club, trade union or nation state, which has defined objectives and departments or offices established to accomplish those objectives, needs a constitution to define the powers, rights and duties of the organisation's members. This set of rules, in addition to regulating the internal working of the organisation, will make provision for the manner in which the organisation relates to outside bodies. It can therefore be said that a constitution looks to both internal and external regulation of the body to which it relates.

---

2 See Chapters 3 and 18.
3 See Chapter 6.
4 See Chapter 3.

In addition to the function of allocating powers and duties and determining the relationships between the institutions of the state, a constitution fulfils two related purposes – those of definition and evaluation. In its defining function, the constitution is both descriptive and prescriptive (or normative). Differently expressed, the constitution will both define the manner in which the rules in fact operate and dictate what ought to happen in a given situation. As such, the rule or normative statement in question sets a standard of conduct or behaviour which is regarded as correct and which is expected to be adhered to by those to whom the rules are addressed. These constitutional rules – whether written or unwritten – facilitate the stability and predictability of behaviour. Further, when such normative rules exist, they provide a standard against which actual conduct can be judged or evaluated. If the accusation is made that members of an organisation have acted 'unconstitutionally', the speaker is claiming that those accused have acted in a manner which breaches the required standards of behaviour as laid down in the body of generally accepted pre-determined normative rules. In this sense, a constitutional rule, in addition to being descriptive, normative and predictive, is evaluative and judgmental.

When examining the rules of any organisation, it becomes apparent that individual rules have differing levels of importance and, moreover, that rules may have differing degrees of specificity or generality. The manner in which the rules are expressed may also differ; some may be written down, whereas some may be discernible only through observation of actual conduct. And thus it is with the constitution of a state, and particularly that of the United Kingdom, in which the sources of constitutional law are varied. The legal sources are represented by a mixture of statute and judicial precedent, and these legal sources are supplemented by the binding, non-legal, conventional rules and practices. The rules of constitutional law will also reveal differences in the manner in which they may be changed to adapt to changing circumstances. Under a written constitution, the constitution will itself define the procedure for amendment and may provide for varying degrees of ease or difficulty in amendment in relation to particular rules. The rules regarded as the most important are characterised by the greatest degree of difficulty in the process of amendment. Under the United Kingdom's constitution, by way of contrast, the manner in which constitutional change is effected will be dependent not upon clearly defined written rules but, rather, on accepted constitutional practice which has evolved over time.

Defining Constitutions

Professor KC Wheare defines the constitution of a state as: 'the whole system of government of a country, the collection of rules which establish and regulate or govern the government' (1966, page 1).

An older definition, that of Thomas Paine, reveals a more complex set of ideas:

A constitution is not the act of a government, but of a people constituting a government, and a government without a constitution is power without right … A constitution is a thing antecedent to a government; and a government is only the creature of a constitution. [1792, Part II, page 93]

From this second definition, it can be seen that a constitution is something which is prior to government, or, as Paine expresses it, 'antecedent' to government, giving legitimacy to the government and defining the powers under which a government may act. As such, the constitution sets limits both to the powers which can be exercised and to the manner in which they may be exercised. Accordingly, the constitution defines the legality of power. This notion is particularly apposite in a country with a written constitution and a Supreme Court which is conferred with jurisdiction to rule on the legality of government action.

Under such a constitutional arrangement, it can be said that everything which the government does is either lawful or unlawful depending upon whether the contested conduct is held to be 'constitutional' or not. Under a largely unwritten constitution, the position is less clear-cut, and it may often be the case that conduct will be adjudged to be 'unconstitutional' and yet not be 'unlawful'. This distinction will be returned to in a subsequent discussion of the legal and non-legal sources of the constitution. At this introductory stage, it need only be noted that the unwritten nature of the United Kingdom's constitution has given rise to argument as to whether or not a constitution – as generally understood in the majority of states – exists. Sir Ivor Jennings, author of *The Law and the Constitution*, offers a balanced evaluation of this apparent paradox:

> If a constitution means a written document, then obviously Great Britain has no constitution. In countries where such a document exists, the word has that meaning. But the document itself merely sets out rules determining the creation and operation of governmental institutions, and obviously Great Britain has such institutions and such rules. The phrase 'British constitution' is used to describe those rules.[5]

See Chapter 2.

A 'CONSTITUTION'

---

5 Jennings, 1959b, p. 36. See also McIlwain, 1958; Ridley, 1988.

Classifying Constitutions

When looking for the salient characteristics of the constitution, it is helpful to bear in mind the range of possible classifications which can be applied to any constitution. Professor KC Wheare identifies the following classifications (1966, Chapter 1):

(a) written and unwritten;
(b) rigid and flexible;
(c) supreme and subordinate;
(d) federal and unitary;
(e) separated powers and fused powers; and
(f) republican and monarchical.

Written and unwritten constitutions

A written constitution is one contained within a single document or a series of documents, with or without amendments, defining the basic rules of the state. The origins of written constitutions lie in the American War of Independence (1775–1783) and the French Revolution (1789). More recent written constitutions derive from the grant – or devolution – of legislative power from previously imperial powers to former colonies and dominions,[6] whether secured as a result of peaceful settlement or violent revolution.[7]

As noted above, the feature which characterises all states with a written constitution is that there has been a clear historical break with a previously pertaining constitutional arrangement, thus providing the opportunity for a fresh constitutional start. As Wheare explains:

> If we investigate the origins of modern constitutions, we find that, practically without exception, they were drawn up and adopted because people wished to make a fresh start, so far as the statement of their system of government was concerned ... The circumstances in which a break with the past and the need for a fresh start come about vary from country to country, but in almost every case in modern times, countries have a constitution for the very simple and elementary reason that they wanted, for some reason, to begin again ... This has been the practice certainly since 1787 when the American constitution was drafted, and as the years passed, no doubt imitation and the force of example have led all countries to think it necessary to have a constitution. [1966, page 4]

The absence of any such break in continuity in British history, from 1066 to the current time,[8] more than any other factor, explains the mainly unwritten nature of the United Kingdom's constitution.

The characterisation of constitutions into 'written' and 'unwritten' is, however, too limited, for such classification tells neither the whole constitutional story nor necessarily makes the constitution accessible to those seeking to understand it. A written constitution will provide the basic rules, but, for an understanding of the whole constitutional picture, it is also necessary to examine subsequent interpretations of the constitution contained in case law and the political practices which reveal the actual operation of the constitution. At the heart

---

6 See e.g. the South Africa Act 1909, the British North America Act 1867 (now the Constitution Act 1867) and the Canada Act 1982.
7 See e.g. the Nigeria Independence Act 1960 and the Zimbabwe Act 1979. See also de Smith, 1964, Chapter 5.
8 With the exception of the seventeenth-century constitutional upheavals (see Chapters 5 and 6).

of this matter lies one simple fact: all constitutions – howsoever defined and categorised – are dynamic organisms. They are dependent for much of their meaning and relevance on the societal framework which surrounds them. Nowhere is this more apparent than in relation to individual rights and liberties. The vast majority of states have adopted both written constitutions and Bills of Rights stipulating the inviolable rights of citizens – nevertheless, the political reality for many citizens' rights around the world is very different from the formally drafted constitution. Irrespective of whether or not a state has a written constitution and a Bill of Rights, it must be recognised that the actual protection of individual rights, as with so much of the constitution, is explained not solely by reference to written rules. Regardless of the form in which rights are protected, in any society, it will be the democratic political process, political practice and norms of acceptable governmental conduct that, while not having the force of law, provide constitutional standards which determine the respect accorded to individual rights.[9] These constitutional features also establish standards against which the probity of official conduct may be measured. It is for this reason that a true understanding of constitutions and the concept of constitutionalism requires a deeper understanding than that provided for by an analysis of the formal written rules.

Rigid and flexible constitutions

This classification rests primarily on the question whether or not constitutions can be amended with ease. The framers of a written constitution, endeavouring to provide a comprehensive legal framework for the state, will naturally seek to protect its constitutional provisions from subsequent repeal or amendment. Towards this end, all or many of the rules will be 'entrenched', that is to say the constitution will stipulate stringent procedures to be followed in any attempt to amend the provision in question. As will be seen later, entrenchment may take several forms, but its central characteristic is that it either prevents, or makes difficult, amendment or repeal. By way of example, the federal Commonwealth of Australia Constitution Act of 1900 specifies the procedure to be adopted for its own alteration. An amending Bill must pass through at least one House of Parliament by a specified majority and the proposed amendment must be endorsed in a referendum which approves the measure by an overall majority in at least four of the six states.[10] Between 1900 and 1990, 42 proposals for constitutional amendment had been put forward. Of these, only eight were approved by a majority of electors nationally and a majority of electors in a majority of states. In this regard, it has been observed that 'constitutionally speaking, Australia is a frozen continent'.[11] As a further example, under the United States' constitution, constitutional amendments may be proposed either by a two-thirds majority of both Houses of Congress or, following a request by the legislatures of two-thirds of the states, by the convention summoned by Congress. To be accepted, the proposed amendments must then be approved by the legislatures of three-quarters of the states, or by conventions in three-quarters of the states. Between 1813 and 1913, only three amendments had been accepted; between 1913 and 1933 six amendments; and by 1951, only one further amendment.[12]

The United Kingdom's constitution, by comparison with the constitutions of the United States and Australia, represents the height of flexibility. Under the doctrine of parliamentary sovereignty examined in Chapter 6, Parliament is the supreme law-making body and can pass any law, by a simple majority vote in Parliament, on any subject matter whatsoever.

9 See Bogdanor, 1988.
10 Commonwealth of Australia Constitution Act 1900 (UK), s. 128.
11 Sawer, 1967, p. 208. See Lee, 1988.
12 See Wheare, 1963, Chapters 4 and 12.

Moreover, no court may hold an Act of Parliament to be void.[13] Note for now, therefore, that under the United Kingdom's constitution, no legal constraints can – under the traditional doctrine of sovereignty – fetter Parliament's powers.[14] Of particular importance in this regard is the fact that no Parliament may lay down irreversible rules regulating future legislative procedures which must be followed. The constitutional importance of this lies in flexibility. It has been argued, controversially, that the legislative supremacy of Parliament is constrained by various constitutional devices and Acts of constitutional importance. However, it is significant that none of these challenges has yet succeeded in limiting Parliament's theoretical power. On this point see Chapter 6.

It is clear that the absence of a written constitution, allied to the doctrine of parliamentary sovereignty, enables constitutional change to be brought about within the United Kingdom with the minimum of constitutional formality. The constitution has evolved in a pragmatic and gradual manner over the centuries. At the current time, however, the constitution is undergoing more major change than in previous decades. The last and greatest constitutional change occurred in 1973 when the United Kingdom joined the European Communities (now the European Union). Joining the European Union involved not only entering into an agreement which affected the economic life of the country, but also joining a unique legal order under which rights and obligations in matters regulated by the Treaties are ultimately defined and enforced by the Court of Justice of the European Union (CJEU). Moreover, the Treaties on European Union marked new and significant developments within the European Union in relation to economic, monetary and political union and the evolution of common policies in relation to cooperation in judicial and policing matters, home affairs and security and foreign affairs policies. However, in June 2016, the people of the United Kingdom voted in a referendum to leave the European Union. This again raised a number of constitutional questions as the government negotiated the terms on which the UK left the EU and how relations with the EU are to be governed in the future. This development is discussed in more detail in Chapter 8.

It was the general election of 1997 which presaged further significant constitutional change. The incoming Labour government had committed itself to several constitutional reforms. Devolution of wide-ranging law-making powers to Scotland and Wales was the first issue to be addressed by the government.[15] An elected 'strategic authority' for London was also on the agenda, as was regional devolution in England. Reform of the membership of the House of Lords, the 'upper House' of the United Kingdom's bicameral Parliament, was achieved in 1999 when most of the hereditary peers were removed from membership, although the ultimate role and powers of the Lords still remain to be determined. The settlement reached in April 1998 with regard to Northern Ireland culminated in devolved powers to a new Northern Ireland Assembly. The government was also committed to the better protection of rights and freedoms, and, in order to achieve this objective, the Human Rights Act 1998 'incorporated' rights protected under the European Convention on Human Rights into domestic law, thereby for the first time providing a 'code' of human rights which is enforceable in the domestic courts. The Human Rights Act marked a change in perception about freedoms and rights among the British people who, by contrast with citizens living under written constitutions and Bills of Rights, had previously been largely unaware of their rights and freedoms.

---

13 *Edinburgh and Dalkeith Railway v Wauchope* (1842); **Sillars v Smith** (1982).
14 Complications arise in relation to the European Union, to be examined in Chapters 7 and 8.
15 On devolution to Northern Ireland, Scotland and Wales, see Chapter 11.

Further reform was effected by the Constitutional Reform Act 2005, which reformed the office of Lord Chancellor, established a new Supreme Court physically separated from Parliament and provided for the House of Lords to elect its own Speaker, an office formerly held by the Lord Chancellor. The Act is discussed further in Chapters 2 and 4.[16]

In 2009 it was revealed that a number of Members of Parliament had been abusing the system of parliamentary allowances and expenses. This prompted the rapid introduction of the Parliamentary Standards Act 2009 which, for the first time, established a body outside Parliament – the Independent Parliamentary Standards Authority – to regulate the system of pay and allowances. The Constitutional Reform and Governance Act 2010 effected further constitutional reform. This wide-ranging Act covers a number of different areas including the introduction of a statutory basis for the management of the civil service and the introduction of a new procedure for the approval (ratification) of treaties.

In 2010 a Coalition government (formed of the Conservative Party and Liberal Democrat Party) was established. Included in its plans for constitutional reform were the introduction of fixed-term Parliaments, abolition of the Crown's power to dissolve Parliament and reform of the voting system for general elections. The Fixed-Term Parliaments Act 2011 achieved the first two objectives. The issue of reform of the voting system for general elections, however, was subject to a referendum of the people, who rejected the proposal by a significant majority. Reform of the organisation of the police, reform of parliamentary oversight of the security services and reform of the law relating to terrorism have been effected. In 2014 a referendum was held in Scotland to decide whether or not Scotland should leave the United Kingdom and become an independent state. The people rejected independence, but further powers have been devolved to Scotland and the question of independence remains live. The issue of constitutional flexibility should not be exaggerated. That there are no legal restraints on what Parliament does, does not mean that there are no non-legal constraints. In practical terms, such 'extra-legal' constraints may be as important as legal controls. By way of illustration of the distinction between legal and non-legal constraints, Sir Ivor Jennings offers the example of Parliament passing an Act which bans smoking in the streets of Paris. As he states, there is nothing in the constitution which prevents Parliament from doing precisely that: 'If it enacts that smoking in the streets of Paris is an offence, then it is an offence' (1959b, page 170). The relevant Act so passed would be valid and recognised by the English courts. However, the Act would be totally ineffective and ignored by the courts and everyone else in France. Equally, as Jennings states, 'if Parliament enacted that all men should be women, they would be women so far as the law is concerned'. Sir Leslie Stephens, writing in the nineteenth century,[17] asks what restrains Parliament from passing an Act providing that all blue-eyed babies be put to death? The response to this question is that in legal–theoretical terms, of course Parliament could pass such a law, but in political terms, it neither could nor would do so because, ultimately, Parliament is dependent upon the support of the people.

Supreme and subordinate constitutions

This constitutional category overlaps in many respects, although not totally, with the classification into federal and unitary states. A 'supreme' constitution refers to a state in which the

---

16 In 2007 the government announced further constitutional reforms designed to strengthen the accountability of Ministers to Parliament in part through transferring a number of powers now exercised by the government under the royal prerogative. See further Chapter 5.

17 See Stephens, 1882.

legislative powers of the governing body are unlimited. Conversely, a subordinate constitution is one whose powers are limited by some higher authority.[18]

Federal and unitary constitutions

In many states, for example in the United States of America, Canada, Australia and Malaysia, there exists a division of powers between central government and the individual states or provinces which make up the federation. The powers divided between the federal government and states or provinces will be clearly set down in the constituent document. Some powers will be reserved exclusively for the federal government (most notably, such matters as defence and state security); some powers will be allocated exclusively to the regional government (such as planning and the raising of local taxation); and others will be held on the basis of partnership, powers being given to each level of government, with overriding power, perhaps, reserved for central government. The common feature of all federal states is the sharing of power between centre and region – each having an area of exclusive power, other powers being shared on some defined basis. Equally common to all federations is the idea that the written constitution is sovereign over government and legislature and that their respective powers are not only defined by the constitution but are also controlled by the constitution, which will be interpreted and upheld by a Supreme Court.

The constitution of the United Kingdom presents a very different arrangement from that outlined above. The state is in theory unitary and there is no defining written constitution controlling the powers of central government or of the United Kingdom Parliament. Instead of a written constitution, there exists a sovereign legislative body, which represents the ultimate law-making power in the state. Power is given to the Northern Ireland, Scottish and Welsh legislatures and to local government, under Acts of the United Kingdom Parliament, to fulfil defined functions such as the provision of services and raising of local revenue to finance such services. However, no power is given to the nations or to local government other than that decreed by Parliament. Regional Parliaments and assemblies and local authorities are entirely creatures of Acts of Parliament, and any power given can subsequently – subject only to political acceptability to the electorate – be withdrawn. An illustration of this point can be seen in relation to the statutory abolition of the Greater London Council and other Metropolitan Borough Councils in 1985, under the Local Government Act of that year. An example on a larger scale can be seen in the grant of limited legislative authority to the Northern Ireland Assembly under the Government of Ireland Act 1920. The law-making power given in 1920 was later revoked by the United Kingdom Parliament by the Northern Ireland Constitution Act 1973. In 1998, however, devolution of power was again on the constitutional agenda. The Northern Ireland Act 1998, Scotland Act 1998 and Government of Wales Act 1998 each involved a decentralisation of power, although ultimate sovereign power remains with the Westminster (i.e. the United Kingdom) Parliament.[19]

However, although the United Kingdom Parliament is legally 'sovereign', the transfer of wide-ranging law-making powers to the Northern Ireland Assembly, Scottish Parliament and the National Assembly of Wales represents a significant dispersal or diffusion of power. It is for this reason that nowadays it is less realistic than formerly to label the United Kingdom constitution 'unitary'. It is better and more accurately described as 'multi-layered'.

---

18 See Chapter 6 for discussion in relation to New South Wales (Australia) and South Africa.
19 The Northern Ireland Act 2000 temporarily suspended the operation of the Northern Ireland Assembly and Executive. See further Chapter 11.

Separated powers and fused powers

The separation of powers is a fundamental constitutional concept which will be discussed more fully in Chapter 4. With respect to the classification of constitutions, the concept here requires outline consideration. The doctrine is of great antiquity, dating back at least to Aristotle.[20] John Locke, Viscount Bolingbroke and Baron Montesquieu gave further expression to the idea.[21]

The essence of the doctrine is that the powers vested in the principal institutions of the state – legislature, executive and judiciary – should not be concentrated in the hands of any one institution.[22] The object of such separation is to provide checks on the exercise of power by each institution and to prevent the potential for tyranny which might otherwise exist. A constitution with clearly defined boundaries to power, and provisions restraining one institution from exercising the power of another, is one in conformity with the doctrine of separation of powers. This arrangement is most readily achievable under a written constitution, although it is arguable whether, under any constitution, a pure separation of powers is possible, or indeed desirable, a point which will be returned to later. At the other end of the spectrum of constitutional arrangements from a nearly 'pure' separation of powers is a totalitarian state or a purely monarchical state. Under such a constitution will be found a single figure, or single body, possessed with the sole power to propose and enact law, to administer the state and both to apply and to adjudicate upon the law.

Under the largely unwritten constitution of the United Kingdom, the separation of powers is difficult to ascertain and evaluate. There is undeniably a distinct legislative body, executive and judiciary, each exercising differing powers. On further examination, however, it will be found that, in practice, there are so many exceptions to the 'pure' doctrine that the significance of separation of powers is called into question. Suffice to say at this introductory stage that it is a doctrine which is respected under the constitution, despite many apparent anomalies.

Republican and monarchical constitutions

A republic is a state having as its figurehead a (usually) democratically elected President, answerable to the electorate and to the constitution. Presidential office is both a symbol of statehood and the repository of many powers. In the name of the state, the President will enter into treaties, make declarations of war and represent the state on formal international and domestic occasions. Additionally, as with the President of the United States of America, the President has responsibility for proposing legislation to give effect to the political programme which gave him the mandate of the people. The President, however, has no formal power to initiate legislation, and it is the Congress of the United States which will ultimately determine the acceptability of legislative proposals. It may well be that the elected President is from a different political party from that which dominates Congress.[23] When that political situation pertains, the prospect of successful implementation of presidential election promises is weakened, and although the President has a veto power over legislation passed by Congress, that veto can be overridden by Congress voting with a two-thirds majority.

Looking at the United Kingdom as an example of a sophisticated Western democracy based on constitutional monarchy, the position of the head of state is very different.[24] Queen

---

20 384–323 BC; see *The Politics*.
21 Locke, 'Second treatise of civil government', 1690, Chapter XII, para. 143; Bolingbroke, 1748; Montesquieu, 1748, Bk XI.
22 See Vile, 1967, Chapter IV.
23 As was the position under President Clinton (Democrat) and Congress (Republican).
24 See Chapter 9.

Elizabeth II is the head of state, and all acts of government are undertaken in the name of the Crown. This statement implies that great power is accorded to the Queen. In reality, however, and with the exception of important residual powers, this is not the case. As with the President of the United States of America, the Queen is the figurehead – the symbol of nationhood – on a domestic and international level. The Crown also represents the continuity of the state. From an historical constitutional viewpoint, it matters little which leader of which political party at any one time occupies the office of Prime Minister, or whether he or she is a Labour or Conservative Prime Minister, for he or she will be exercising all powers in the Queen's name. Unlike the position of the head of state under the United States' constitution, however, the Queen is, by definition, unelected and unaccountable to the electorate in any democratic sense. The Crown enjoys enormous legal–theoretical power but little practical power, save in exceptional circumstances.

The legal powers held by the Crown are, for the most part,[25] exercised in her name by the elected government of the day. The rules which restrict the monarch's powers are for the most part non-legal. The restrictions comprise the all-important conventional rules of constitutional practice which regulate so much of the United Kingdom's constitution. Thus, for example, the Crown has the legal power to withhold Royal Assent from Bills passed by Parliament but, by convention, this assent will never be withheld (and has not been withheld since 1708) unless so advised by the government.

In addition to representing the symbolic figurehead, the role of the Crown may be said to be protective. The Queen, it has been said, has the power to 'warn and advise' the Prime Minister of the day.[26] Queen Elizabeth II, since her accession in 1952, has seen many Prime Ministers, both Conservative and Labour, enter and leave office. Throughout her 69-year reign, the Queen has quietly influenced government,[27] and garnered vast experience in domestic, international and particularly Commonwealth affairs. That experience represents a wealth of knowledge at the disposal of the government in power. While the role of the monarchy is a matter for contemporary debate, the continuity and longevity of monarchy remains a distinguishing feature of the United Kingdom's constitution.

Summarising the characteristics of the UK constitution

From the discussion of classification above, some conclusions can now be reached about the characteristics of the United Kingdom's constitution. In summary, it can be said that it:

(a)   is largely written, but is not codified;
(b)   is flexible in nature;
(c)   is supreme;
(d)   is formally unitary in structure, but with powers devolved to Northern Ireland, Scotland and Wales and to local government;
(e)   exhibits mainly but not completely separated powers; and
(f)   is monarchical.

Each of these features will become clearer as we examine the constitution in more detail.

---

25 See, however, Chapter 5 for discussion of the circumstances under which this theoretical power may become real power.
26 Bagehot, 1867, Chapter II.
27 See Macmillan, 1961–1963; Wilson, 1971.

The Concept of Constitutionalism[28]

'Constitutionalism' is the doctrine which governs the legitimacy of government action. By constitutionalism is meant – in relation to constitutions written and unwritten – conformity with the broad philosophical values within a state. Constitutionalism implies something more important than the idea of 'legality', which requires official conduct to be in accordance with pre-fixed legal rules. A power may be exercised on legal authority; however, that fact is not necessarily determinative of whether or not the action was 'constitutional'. The doctrine of constitutionalism suggests, at least, the following:

(a)   that the exercise of power is kept within the legal limits conferred by Parliament – the concept of *intra vires* – and that those who exercise power are accountable to law;

(b)   that the exercise of power – irrespective of legal authority – must conform to the notion of respect for the individual and the individual citizen's rights;

(c)   that the powers conferred on institutions within a state – whether legislative, executive or judicial – be sufficiently dispersed between the various institutions so as to avoid the abuse of power; and

(d)   that the government, in formulating policy, and the legislature, in legitimating that policy, are accountable to the electorate on whose trust power is held.

In summary, constitutionalism suggests the limitation of power,[29] the separation of powers,[30] the doctrine of responsible accountable government and the protection of individual rights and freedoms. It is against these conceptual and practical requirements that the constitution of the United Kingdom must be studied and evaluated.

Constitutionalist theorists take two approaches to the concept: the legal and the political. Legal constitutionalists emphasise the role of the courts in controlling power and protecting rights. It is the law which, if there is an alleged abuse of power, will control executive power through judicial review. Furthermore, the rights of individuals stem ultimately from the common law as developed by the judges. Political constitutionalists, on the other hand, emphasise the importance of the political process in controlling power, and are markedly less trusting of the judiciary. Central to the political constitutionalists is the idea of democracy: the representation of the people in Parliament and the ability of the political process to control executive power and ensure the accountability of the executive to the people, through Parliament.

Professor JAG Griffith (1918–2010) of the London School of Economics was a leading political constitutionalist. In *The Politics of the Judiciary*,[31] Griffith argued that the judiciary, appointed from the legal profession, is predominantly white, male and middle class. As a result the senior judiciary is comprised, as the inadvertent but direct consequence of the socio-economic profile of the profession, of a social elite which broadly corresponds with other establishment institutions: the armed forces, civil service, Church of England, House of Lords. It follows, for Griffith, that there is an understandable empathy between government and judiciary which is a natural consequence of shared backgrounds. The conservative mindset of the judges, he argued, meant that the judges regularly ruled against certain groups in society – notably trade unions and students. On the judiciary see further Chapter 22.

---

28 See Bogdanor, 1988 'Introduction'; McAuslan and McEldowney, 1985, pp. 11 ff.
29 See Chapter 3.
30 See Chapter 4.
31 Griffith, 1977. See also Griffith, 1979.

Adam Tomkins is a contemporary political constitutionalist. In *Our Republican Constitution*, Tomkins stresses the democratic legitimacy of elected politicians and argues that 'politics really can stop governments from abusing their authority'.[32] By contrast judges cannot match that democratic legitimacy.

Legal constitutionalists, however, doubt the faith placed by political constitutionalists in democracy and the political process through the democratically elected Parliament. First, Parliament is not representative of all of society. The system of election – the simple majority system – is a majoritarian system which usually returns governments with a majority of seats but a minority of the popular vote. In terms of representativeness, the composition of Parliament also falls far short on the basis of ethnicity and gender. Second, it is the government which controls the parliamentary timetable, and the majority of Bills presented to Parliament are government Bills. If a government has a strong majority it is guaranteed, because of that majority, to get its legislation through.

Judges are not empowered, under the UK constitution, to invalidate Acts of Parliament: the doctrine of parliamentary sovereignty is respected by the courts. This doctrine, however, it has been argued, is coming under strain. In *Jackson v Her Majesty's Attorney General* (2005) Lord Steyn refuted the Attorney General's claim that there is an 'uncontrolled constitution'. He went on to outline the changing concept of sovereignty – and the role of the courts. Lord Steyn stated that in addition to the decision in *Factortame* (1991) which required the court to 'disapply' an Act of Parliament in favour of EU law:

> The settlement contained in the Scotland Act 1998 also point to a divided sovereignty. Moreover the European Convention on Human Rights as incorporated into our law by the Human Rights Act 1998, created a new legal order ... The classic account given by Dicey of the doctrine of the supremacy of Parliament, pure and absolute as it was, can now be seen to be out of place in the modern United Kingdom. Nevertheless, the supremacy of Parliament is still the general principle of our constitution. It is a construct of the common law. The judges created this principle. If that is so, it is not unthinkable that circumstances could arise where the courts may have to qualify a principle established on a different hypothesis of constitutionalism. In exceptional circumstances involving an attempt to abolish judicial review or the ordinary role of the courts, the Appellate Committee of the House of Lords or a new Supreme Court may have to consider whether this is a constitutional fundamental which even a sovereign Parliament acting at the behest of a complaisant House of Commons cannot abolish.[33]

However, as Sir Jeffrey Jowell QC has argued, if parliamentary sovereignty were 'to be discarded as our prime constitutional principle', the '"last word" would pass from the legislature to the courts – but only on the question whether the legislature has strayed beyond the line of its democratic confines'.[34] Vast areas of law and policy would remain in Parliament's domain, and outside that of the courts. Nevertheless, Lord Steyn's dictum raises the potential for a shift further in favour of legal constitutionalism and an adjustment to the traditional concept of parliamentary sovereignty. Sovereignty, and the idea of shared or bi-polar sovereignty, is discussed in Chapter 6.

---

32 Tomkins, 2005, p. 3.
33 At para. 102. Note that this view is contested. See further Chapter 6.
34 See Jowell, 2006.

Pause and Reflect

Does the United Kingdom need a written constitution? Why? Why not?

 SELF-TEST QUESTIONS

What is the principal reason behind countries adopting a written constitution?
List at least four characteristics that constitutions may have (for example, a constitution may be *federal* or *unitary*).
What are the primary characteristics of the British constitution?

PART B: A VERY LITTLE HISTORY

Introduction

The majority of constitutions around the world are in written form and their origins can be traced to a specific date in history. The United Kingdom's constitution, by contrast, is one that has never been rationally constructed and formally written down, but has gradually evolved over the centuries. To study public law successfully, it is not essential to have an in-depth knowledge of constitutional history, but having an appreciation of some of the issues and the most important periods of development does make the contemporary constitution and its different elements easier to understand.

The UK today comprises the four nations of England, Northern Ireland, Scotland and Wales. It was not always that way. It was Henry VIII (reigned 1509–1547) who claimed the island of Ireland as his own. It was to remain united with England until 1922 when the island was divided – six counties in the north remaining united with England while the south became the independent Republic of Ireland. Scotland was united with England through the Acts of Union 1706/07,[35] which created Great Britain. Wales on the other hand was conquered in the twelfth century and has been united with England since that time.

Early Origins: 1066–1500

As every schoolchild is supposed to know, at the Battle of Hastings in 1066, the Norman King William beat the English King Harold and claimed the English Crown. William set about unifying the differing areas of England (any union with Ireland, Scotland and Wales lay far in the future). He also undertook a nationwide survey of the land and property: the *Domesday Book*, a clear record of where wealth and influence lay.

It was in the reign of Henry II (1154–1189) that a legal system common to all of England developed. The King installed a system of courts staffed by the King's judges, with the task of establishing common procedures and a law common to all: the English common law.

From these early days of a united England, Kings and Queens held near absolute power. That power supposedly derived from God, the 'divine right of Kings'. In order to keep their power, however, Kings and Queens were dependent upon their supporters, who not only

---

35 The difference in dates being explained by the two countries using different calendar years.

provided financial support but also men to fight in support of the King. It was a two-way relationship: in exchange for support the King or Queen granted land and titles – the origins of the contemporary honours system.

In the reign of King John (1199–1216), discontent with the system of taxation and complaints about the criminal justice system administered by the Crown led to the first formal limitation of royal power: Magna Carta 1215. Magna Carta was an agreement between the aristocracy and the Crown. It established the right to jury trial, thereby ensuring that a citizen's liberty could only be removed by a legal process rather than by the arbitrary exercise of royal power. Furthermore, Magna Carta proclaimed that the King was accountable to law, laying the foundation for the idea of government under – rather than over – law.

The King's loyal supporters and advisers made up the House of Lords, the earliest of the two chambers of Parliament to be established. Gradually it became the practice for the King to summon representatives of the common people to advise him: it was in the thirteenth century that the House of Commons came into being. By Edward III's reign (1327–1377) members of the House of Commons were elected to represent local areas. The system was far from democratic. It was not the 'ordinary' men and women who voted but rather those who owned property (it was to be the twentieth century before the right to vote was fully extended to all men and women, irrespective of property).

1500–1700

In the reign of Henry VIII (1509–1547), a situation arose which was to have a profound consequence for the future. England at the time was a Roman Catholic country, its religious head being the Pope in Rome. Henry VIII had first married his deceased brother's widow, Catherine of Aragon. Catherine gave Henry a daughter, later Queen Mary, but not a male heir. Henry turned his attentions to Anne Boleyn. The Roman Catholic Church did not recognise divorce and marriages could only be formally set aside by a decree of nullity issued by the Church. Henry sought an annulment, claiming that his first marriage was not valid on account of Catherine being his deceased brother's widow. The Pope refused Henry's request. Determined to get his way, Henry declared that England would no longer follow the Catholic Church, but rather establish its own church, the head of which would be the King. And so the Church of England came into being. Henry's marriage to Catherine was annulled and Henry married Anne.[36]

The break with Rome ushered in a period of severe religious repression. Mary Tudor, Henry's daughter by Catherine of Aragon (reigned 1553–1558), was an ardent Roman Catholic. She married the Catholic heir to the Spanish throne, Philip, and was intent on re-establishing Catholicism in England. Elizabeth I (reigned 1558–1603), Henry VIII's daughter by Anne Boleyn, by contrast, firmly established the Church of England. The political situation at home was complicated by the fact that England was now a Protestant country while her sometime allies (sometime enemies) to the south – France, Italy and Spain – remained Catholic.[37] Nevertheless, Elizabeth I's long reign was characterised by religious tolerance and a flourishing of the arts. Furthermore, England was now established as an international power. The Tudor era ended with Elizabeth's death in 1603, the crown being assumed by

---

36 Anne Boleyn was beheaded and Henry would go on to marry Jane Seymour, Anne of Cleves, Catherine Howard and Catherine Parr.
37 The Protestant Reformation took hold in Northern Europe and also in Scotland.

James VI of Scotland, who assumed the title of James I of England, thereby uniting the two countries under a common crown.[38]

James' reign was characterised by a shortage of money. When Parliament denied him funds he resorted to issuing proclamations to achieve his objective, thereby making law without Parliament's consent. When a judge had the impertinence to challenge the King's use of the prerogative to make new law, the King dismissed the judge – Coke CJ.[39]

The reign of Charles I (1625–1649) was also one marked by tensions between the Crown and Parliament. Charles I was autocratic and made full use of his royal powers. When Parliament displeased him, he dismissed it and assumed the power to rule under the prerogative. This abuse of power was, however, to lead to civil war, which first broke out in 1641. Charles I was tried for treason and executed in 1649. England was now under military rule. Oliver Cromwell declared himself Protector of England. The monarchy was abolished, as was the House of Lords and the Church of England.

Under Cromwell, Britain became a republic. A period of puritanical rule commenced, with music, dancing and all forms of entertainment banned and acts of immorality met with harsh punishment. In 1653, Cromwell drafted a written constitution – the Commonwealth Constitution – for England, Scotland and Ireland, but it was never to come into being. By the end of the 1650s England had had enough of military rule. Following Oliver Cromwell's death and the inability of his son to assert the same authority as his father, the monarchy was restored.

While civil war raged in England, Charles I's heir was in France. His return to England as Charles II (reigned 1660–1685) not only restored the monarchy, but also ushered in a period in which culture, science and the arts flourished and international trade expanded. During this period also, the seeds of what would later become the two main political parties – Conservative and Liberal (although going by different names) – were sown.

When Charles II died he was succeeded by his brother James II (reigned 1685–1688). Although Charles II was suspected of remaining sympathetic to Roman Catholicism, he gave little outward sign of it. James II, however, was blatantly Catholic, appointing Catholics to public posts and the army, and suspending laws that penalised Catholics. He sought complete religious toleration and issued Declarations of Indulgence to secure that end. Concern grew that James and Mary would produce a male heir to the throne who would return England to the Catholic Church and, indeed, in 1688 a son was born. Having lost the support of those he relied on, James fled the country. While James had been abusing his position and using powers to reintroduce Catholics to public life, negotiations had been entered into with James' Protestant son-in-law, William of Orange, with the intent that William and his wife Mary should seize the throne. With James fleeing, their arrival was peaceful.

Kings and Queens were no longer to enjoy the wide-ranging powers of the past. William (reigned 1689–1702) and Mary assumed the throne under the conditions provided for in the Bill of Rights 1689. The right to suspend Parliament's laws, the right to raise taxation without Parliament's consent and the right to raise and keep an army without Parliament's consent were abolished. Article 9 of the Bill of Rights provided absolute protection for freedom of speech in parliamentary proceedings – a protection that remains today. The right for Parliament to meet regularly was asserted. The right to trial by jury, first provided for by Magna Carta, was reaffirmed. However, while the Bill of Rights restricted some of the powers of the Crown, it left many prerogative powers intact. Moreover, it did not address the

---

38 James succeeded under the terms of the Treaty of Berwick, 1586, agreed by Elizabeth and James.
39 See the Case of Proclamations (1610) 12 Co Rep 74; 2 St Tr 723.

succession to the Crown or the position of the judges: it was to be 1701 before those issues were tackled under the Act of Settlement.

1700–1901

The Act of Settlement provided that succession to the throne should be restricted to Protestant heirs and, moreover, that no heir to the throne could marry a Roman Catholic.[40] The Act of Settlement also protected the independence of judges by providing that senior judges could only be removed from office by a successful address to both Houses of Parliament.[41]

William and Mary were succeeded by Queen Anne (reigned 1702–1714) – the younger daughter of James II. It was during Anne's reign that the union between England and Scotland was secured. Although united with England under the same Crown (from the reign of James I), Scotland retained its own sovereign law-making Parliament. Under the Acts of Union of England and Scotland, both the English and Scottish Parliaments were effectively abolished, giving rise to the single Parliament of Great Britain.

When Queen Anne died in 1714 the Crown passed from the House of Stuart to the House of Hanover – to George I, the son of Anne's named (but now deceased) successor. By this time Britain was established as a world military power with a large army and expanding navy. Maintaining Britain's international power was expensive and the King required Parliament's and the people's support. George I (reigned 1714–1727), however, was not a popular King. His English was poor and he had little interest in England. George appointed a 'first minister' – Sir Robert Walpole – who served for over 20 years – in effect the first Prime Minister of Britain.

The emergence of the Cabinet – the innermost circle of contemporary central government – came in the reign of George II (1727–1760).[42] Society was also undergoing change. While the majority of the population remained involved in agriculture, new production techniques led to industrial expansion. Allied to that came greater urbanisation and the development of the road system. In 1760, George III came to the throne (reigned until 1820). Britain's empire was growing: under the Treaty of Paris Britain acquired Canada, parts of south-eastern America and islands of the Caribbean from the French. However, unrest in the North American colonies was on the increase. In 1765, under the Stamp Act, the British imposed direct taxation on the colonies for the first time. The sentiment of 'no taxation without representation' fuelled revolt and the government abolished the Act. Import duties on goods continued to be levied, as did rebellion, which culminated in the Boston Tea Party of 1773 in which 342 chests of tea were dumped in the sea. Full-scale revolution started in 1775, and the Congress of 13 colonies formally passed the Declaration of Independence on 4 July 1776. War with Britain escalated, ending in 1783 with the British acceptance of American independence and the signing of the Treaty of Paris in 1783.

In 1789 the French revolution swept away centuries of aristocratic rule. In 1793 France declared war on Britain and Holland, and conflict in Europe was to endure until 1815. The French revolution and years of war brought change. While Britain now had a vast empire, at home there was economic depression and mass unemployment. Amidst the hardship came demands for political reform and universal male suffrage. Reform came in 1832. The Representation of the People Act 1832 reformed constituencies and extended the conditions that qualified adult males to vote and introduced a register of voters. The right to vote was

---

40 A restriction that still remains in place.
41 See, now, the Supreme Court Act 1981. Also see, the Constitutional Reform Act 2005.
42 Note that local government predated central government by some centuries. Today the system is entirely statutory.

confined to those with property: men without property and women were still not entitled to vote. By this time the Industrial Revolution was moving apace. Cities were developing around the centres of industrial production. Workers organised into unions to press for better conditions.[43] Economic and industrial change forced the government into a massive extension of legal regulation into such areas as health, factories, housing and employment.

By the time Victoria came to the throne in 1837 (reigned until 1901), the constitution was much changed. The office of Prime Minister and the Cabinet were now established as the executive. Over the eighteenth century, two distinctive political parties (Tories and Whigs) had become established, each offering voters political choice. The House of Commons had acquired greater legitimacy due to the reformed electoral system. The role of the monarch had also changed. No longer exercising autocratic power, the Crown was perceived as being above politics. As the political journalist Walter Bagehot expressed it, she had the 'right to be consulted, the right to encourage and the right to warn'.[44] The monarchy had been transformed into a 'constitutional monarchy'. In George III's reign (1760–1820) the Civil List had been introduced. This agreement between Parliament and the Crown provided for the public funding of the official work of the monarch in exchange for the surrender of much of the hereditary revenues of the Crown.[45]

Constitutional conventions had developed alongside the evolution of the executive, which was now perceived to be accountable to Parliament. While the Crown retained the formal power to summon and dissolve Parliament, the convention had developed that Parliament would be dissolved only at the request of the Prime Minister. The Crown also retained the formal right to reject a Bill when it had passed through both the House of Commons and House of Lords. However, the convention had developed that the Crown would grant the necessary Royal Assent (without which a Bill cannot become law) to a Bill that had duly passed both Houses. No formal legal rules existed regarding the choice of Prime Minister or in which House of Parliament s/he should sit. However, by convention, the Crown appointed the leader of that political party which won the majority of seats in a general election and could command a majority in the House of Commons.[46] In the early nineteenth century, the Duke of Wellington (Prime Minister 1828–1830) commented that it would be more appropriate for the Prime Minister to sit in the House of Commons – the elected House – rather than the Lords. The last Prime Minister to sit in the House of Lords was Lord Salisbury (1886–1892) and it is now a firm convention (but not law) that the Prime Minister is a Member of the Commons.

It was towards the end of the nineteenth century that the origins of today's Labour Party are found, coming into being with the objective of providing representation in Parliament for ordinary working men and women.[47] Whereas Members of Parliament had hitherto regarded their parliamentary work as public service for which no payment was made, for those who were to become representatives of the working class, sponsorship was needed to help meet the costs, not only of standing for Parliament, but also to enable them to carry out their parliamentary duties. It was in 1911 that salaries first became payable to Members of the House of Commons.[48]

---

43 A former ban on unionisation was repealed in 1824.
44 The English Constitution, 1867.
45 See the Civil List Acts 1952, 1972 and 1975. The Queen first became liable to income tax on her private income in 1993.
46 A personal decision had to be made when there was no obvious candidate. This ended only in the 1960s, when the major parties introduced their own system of electing their leader.
47 The right to vote having been considerably extended by the Reform Act 1867. Women did not get the right to vote until 1928.
48 Members of the House of Lords are not salaried. They receive a daily allowance for attendance.

1902–Present

Victoria died in 1901, to be succeeded by Edward VII (1901–1910). It was in this decade that a protracted struggle took place between the House of Commons and House of Lords over their respective legislative powers. As the Commons grew in democratic legitimacy, so the convention became established that the House of Lords would give way to the Commons over matters of national finance.[49] However, the Liberal government's budget proposals were controversial, and the House of Lords, in breach of convention, rejected them. A general election later, and a threat by the King (now George V) to create enough new peers to force the legislation through, the House of Lords gave way. The Parliament Act 1911 was enacted to avoid future conflicts, setting a strict timetable in which the Lords could reject a proposal and allowing the Commons to seek the Royal Assent without agreement from the Lords at the end of the specified period, thereby ensuring the ultimate legislative supremacy of the Commons.[50]

That decade also saw a battle over the future status of Ireland, which had become united with England, Scotland and Wales under the Act of Union 1800. The nineteenth century had brought economic disaster to Ireland and thousands emigrated. In addition, there was discrimination in the provision of education and in property rights against the majority of the population, who were Roman Catholics. Dissatisfaction with British rule turned to violence and the demand for home rule grew. However, one of the obstacles to home rule lay in the significant minority of Protestants who had settled in Ireland over the centuries and who vehemently rejected any idea of being ruled by an independent Irish state. The solution lay in separating a part of Ireland off from the rest. As the situation worsened and Civil War looked imminent, the First World War (1914–1918) erupted, postponing any settlement over Ireland.

In 1920 the Government of Ireland Act was passed, partitioning the country, with six of the northern counties being separated from the remainder. In 1921 an Anglo-Irish Treaty was signed, giving the Irish Free State (southern Ireland) the right to self-governance within the British Commonwealth. The Constitution of the Irish Free State was published in 1937, declaring independence from Britain. It was not to be until 1949 that the United Kingdom formally accepted Irish independence.

Electoral reform continued with women finally being given the right to vote in 1928. Meanwhile, the pressure on Parliament's time and energy had led to a massive growth in delegated, or secondary, legislation. This in turn gave rise to increased legal challenges by way of applications for judicial review to test whether the powers conferred by Parliament had been correctly interpreted and applied by those bodies on which they were conferred.

The Second World War, 1939–1945, tore Britain and Europe apart, with millions of people killed or displaced and economies ruined. But out of this devastation came two developments of profound constitutional importance. The first was the founding of the Council of Europe in 1949 with the express objective of improving the protection of civil rights and freedoms on a European-wide basis. Britain played a key role in drafting the European Convention on Human Rights, which came into being under the auspices of the Council of Europe. However, the idea of allowing citizens to apply to a court outside the UK for the protection of their rights was something that the government was not prepared to allow. That right only came into being in the 1960s. Nevertheless, the case law from the Court of Human Rights in Strasbourg has had a major influence, not only in findings against the British government for having breached citizens' rights, but also in promoting the idea that a Bill of

---

49 There is a further convention that requires that the Lords give way to legislation that gives effect to a government's policies which were put to the electorate at a general election on the ground that the electorate had 'mandated' the policy(ies).
50 The 1911 Act was amended by the Parliament Act 1949, which reduced the permitted period of delay by the Lords.

Rights that could be enforced before the local courts should be introduced. That was not to happen until the Human Rights Act 1998.

The second European development was the signing of treaties that would lead, ultimately, to the introduction of the European Union (EU). Initially, the objective was to ensure that the raw materials of war – coal, steel and atomic energy – should be placed beyond the control of nation states and regulated by 'supranational organisation'. Towards this end the European Coal and Steel Community (ECSC) and the Atomic Energy Community (Euratom) were introduced in treaties of 1951 and 1957. The next development was economic: the desire to create a tariff-free trading block that would make Europe more competitive on the world stage and also raise standards of living within its Member States. This was achieved, with six original Members, in 1957, under the Treaty of Rome. Britain again stood aloof, only to have her first application for membership blocked by the French government. It was 1972 before Britain signed the Treaty of Rome and Community law entered into domestic law under the European Communities Act 1972, with effect from January 1973. The three Communities were subsequently merged and nowadays the European Community represents the largest component of the EU, which was introduced in 1992 and now has 27 Member States. As already noted, and discussed in detail in Chapter 8, in 2016 the people of the United Kingdom decided to leave the EU. Under the terms of the European Union (Withdrawal) Act 2018, formal withdrawal from the EU was effected in January 2019.

By 1996 a Conservative government had been in power for 18 years. The Labour Party, then under the leadership of Tony Blair, pledged significant constitutional reform if elected to office. The general election of 1997 brought in a Labour government with a majority of 179 seats in the House of Commons. Among the promised reforms were reform of the still unelected House of Lords, reform of electoral law, the introduction of a Human Rights Act, devolution of power to the nations of Scotland and Wales and re-devolution of power to Northern Ireland. In addition, there was to be established a London-wide form of government and London Mayor. Devolution was the first reform to be effected.[51] In relation to the House of Lords, the government decided on a two-stage process. First, there would be the removal of all the hereditary peers, to be followed by reform aimed to increase the democratic legitimacy of the House. The House of Lords Act 1999 managed to remove all but 92 hereditary peers. In 2021, further reform is still awaited.

On the electoral front, a Commission was established to consider the voting system used for general elections. In the event, the Report proposed a 'mixed system' – retaining the present system but adding to it an element of proportional representation. No further action has been taken. Legal regulation of political parties, however, has been increased. The Political Parties, Elections and Referendums Act 2000 introduced an Electoral Commission with the task of overseeing the democratic process. Political parties are now required to register all financial donations to the Party in order to achieve greater transparency in the political process. Furthermore, there is now a fixed limit to the amount of money that can be spent by the political parties at a general election.[52]

The Human Rights Act 1998 made the majority of European Convention Rights enforceable before the local courts. It is now unlawful for any public authority to act in contravention of Convention rights, unless an Act of Parliament makes it impossible for them to act otherwise. Carefully drafted, the Act ensures that Parliament's supremacy is maintained and

---

51 See the Scotland Act 1998, Government of Wales Act 1998, Northern Ireland Act 1998, Greater London Authority Act 1999. Note that devolution to Northern Ireland was suspended due to breaches of the terms of the peace settlement between the various parties. A re-devolution of power once again occurred in 2007.
52 There have been strict legal controls over individual candidates' expenditure during an election campaign for a long time, but until the recent Act, there was no control over national party expenditure.

that the separation of powers between the judiciary and Parliament is preserved by ensuring that judges cannot challenge the validity of an Act of Parliament, but rather declare that the Act is incompatible with Convention rights.

It was in part the European Convention on Human Rights that brought about reform of the ancient office of Lord Chancellor. The Lord Chancellor formerly held positions in each of the three major institutions of the state. He sat as Speaker of the House of Lords. He was a political appointment with a seat in Cabinet. He was also head of the judiciary, with powers of appointment. Challenges in the courts questioned this breach of separation of powers. The end result was the Constitutional Reform Act 2005, which provided for most of the Lord Chancellor's functions in relation to the judges to be transferred to the Lord Chief Justice. The office of Lord Chancellor remains, but the Chancellor no longer acts as Speaker of the House of Lords and need no longer be a Member of that House. The first Lord Chancellor following reform was a Member of the House of Commons and held the office of Lord Chancellor in conjunction with the newly established office of Secretary of State for Justice.

The Constitutional Reform Act 2005 provided for a new Supreme Court to be established. Prior to 2009 when the Supreme Court started work, the highest domestic court was the Appellate Committee of the House of Lords. The judges of the House of Lords, in addition to their judicial functions, were also Members of the legislative part of the House of Lords. With the introduction of the Supreme Court, the formal separation of powers between the legislature and the judiciary is enhanced.

In *The Governance of Britain*, Cm 7170, the government proposed to surrender or limit a number of the Crown's prerogative powers to parliamentary control. The Governance and Constitutional Reform Act 2010 gave effect to the proposal with Parliament having to approve Treaties, and introducing a statutory framework for the civil service. Further reforms included the Fixed-term Parliaments Act 2011, which introduced fixed five-year Parliaments and placed the dissolution of Parliament on a statutory basis, and the Equality Act 2010, which consolidated the law on equality and discrimination.

In 2016 a referendum was held on the question of whether the UK should remain a member of the EU. By a small majority, the decision was taken to leave the EU. A Withdrawal Agreement (an international treaty) was negotiated and ratified by Parliament under the terms of the 2010 Constitutional Reform and Governance Act. As noted above, the UK left the EU in 2019.

PART C: THE UNITED KINGDOM

Introduction

The United Kingdom comprises the four nations of England, Northern Ireland, Scotland and Wales. The United Kingdom has a population of over 60 million, of which approximately 84 per cent live in England, three per cent in Northern Ireland, eight per cent in Scotland and five per cent in Wales.[53]

The terms 'United Kingdom' and 'Great Britain' are often used interchangeably. In law, however, there is a distinction. The United Kingdom – formally the United Kingdom of Great Britain and Northern Ireland – comprises the four nations. 'Great Britain', however, refers to Scotland, England and Wales but not Northern Ireland. The term 'the British Islands' refers to the United Kingdom, the Channel Islands and the Isle of Man (on which see further below).

---

53 Office for National Statistics, August 2006: www.statistics.gov.uk.

The United Kingdom comprises England, Wales, Scotland (which together comprise Great Britain) and Northern Ireland.[54] The Channel Islands and the Isle of Man, while not forming part of the United Kingdom other than for the purposes of nationality law,[55] are represented by the United Kingdom Government in international affairs.

While it is correct to speak of the constitution of the United Kingdom, it should not be assumed that there is a single legal system within the constitutionally defined area. The English legal system extends to England and Wales. Scotland has its own system of private law which is distinct from English law. Equally, in Northern Ireland there exists a quite distinct legal system. Nevertheless, it is the United Kingdom Parliament (otherwise referred to as the Westminster Parliament) which has hitherto legislated for each jurisdiction, and been supreme or 'sovereign'. As noted above, change came about in 1998, with devolution of law-making powers to a Scottish Parliament, to a Northern Ireland Assembly and to a Welsh Assembly.[56] Each enjoys limited legislative powers, which must be considered alongside the legislative powers which remain with Westminster. The United Kingdom will remain in being: the object of devolution is to provide more representative and accountable regional government, and to strengthen rather than undermine the union with England.[57]

The devolution of law-making powers to Northern Ireland, Scotland and Wales raises the question of the governance of England, for England alone remains without its own central legislative body. As will be seen from Chapter 11, London now has its own form of devolved government. Plans to introduce regional assemblies in England, however, failed to attract popular support.

The United Kingdom also has a system of local government. Local government is made up of democratically elected local authorities with wide-ranging powers and responsibilities, and represents the most localised form of democratic governance. Local government pre-dates central government by many centuries. Local authorities are entirely creatures of statute: accordingly, the only powers they have are those conferred by the sovereign Westminster Parliament.

The British Islands

The United Kingdom, the Channel Islands and the Isle of Man together comprise the British Islands.[58] Accordingly, while the islands are not part of the United Kingdom, they are part of Her Majesty's dominions. Citizens of the islands are treated as citizens of the United Kingdom for the purposes of the British Nationality Act 1981.

The Channel Islands[59]

The Channel Islands comprise the islands of Jersey, Guernsey, Alderney and Sark. Historically part of the Duchy of Normandy, the Channel Islands remained in allegiance to the King of England when Normandy was lost by the English in 1204. The islands are organised under two separate Bailiwicks: the Bailiwick of Jersey and the Bailiwick of Guernsey, which includes Alderney and Sark. Each Bailiwick enjoys its own legislature, court structure and system of

---

54 Interpretation Act 1978, Sched. 1.
55 British Nationality Act 1981, s. 50(1).
56 Legislative power is conferred under the Government of Wales Act 2006.
57 Devolution is discussed in Chapter 11.
58 Interpretation Act 1978, s. 5 and Sched. 1.
59 See, inter alia, Report of the Royal Commission on the Constitution, Cmnd 5460, 1973, London: HMSO, Vol. 1, Pt XI.

law. Alderney and Sark, whilst part of the Guernsey Bailiwick, enjoy a large measure of independence, having their own legislative assemblies.

The States of Jersey comprises 52 elected Members and five non-elected Members. The States of Guernsey comprises 61 Members. Official links between the Crown and the United Kingdom Government are through the Lieutenant Governor of the Bailiwicks. The legislature – the States – is headed by the Bailiff and Deputy Bailiff.

The European Convention on Human Rights applies to the Channel Islands. Because the Channel Islands are not part of the United Kingdom but are Crown Dependencies, the Convention takes effect not under the Human Rights Act 1998 but under separate distinctive legislation. That legislation was passed by the legislatures of Jersey, Guernsey, Alderney and Sark but did not become law until given the Royal Assent. Once in force, the English courts had no jurisdiction to rule on challenges in relation to the Convention. The Supreme Court so ruled in **R (Barclay) v Lord Chancellor and Secretary of State for Justice (No 2)** (2014).

The Isle of Man

The Isle of Man became formally linked with England in 1405. From that time until 1765, it was ruled by 'Kings' or 'Lords' of Man. Under Acts of Parliament of 1765[60] and 1825,[61] the Westminster Parliament assumed, in the name of the Crown, the rights of the Lords. In 1958, under the Isle of Man Act of that year, much control over the Isle was relinquished by Westminster. The Isle enjoys full powers of self-government and has its own system of courts and law. The head of the Executive, the Lieutenant Governor of the Isle of Man, is the formal link between the local administration and the Crown and United Kingdom Government. The Parliament (the Court of Tynwald) has executive and legislative functions. It comprises the Lieutenant Governor, the Legislative Council and the House of Keys. The lower House – the House of Keys – has 24 Members elected on a constituency basis for a five-year term of office. The Legislative Council comprises the senior Bishop, the Attorney General, a judge and seven Members elected by the House of Keys.

The constitutional relationship between the islands and the United Kingdom

See Chapter 11.

'The constitutional position of the islands is thus unique. In some respects, they are like miniature States with wide powers of self-government'.[62] The Crown has ultimate responsibility for the islands. Under international law, the United Kingdom Government is responsible both for the islands' international relations and for their defence. Where legislative measures are to extend to the islands, these are effected through the Privy Council. Acts of Parliament extend to the islands only if the statute expressly so provides, or where the Act applies to all Her Majesty's dominions 'by necessary implication'.[63] The Bailiwicks of Jersey and Guernsey do not accept that either the United Kingdom Parliament or the Queen in Council have the power to legislate for them without the consent of the local legislatures and registration in the Royal Court. Contrary to the accepted doctrine of parliamentary supremacy, the Channel Islands deny that Acts of Parliament or prerogative acts, under Orders in Council, can take effect without local registration.

---

60 Isle of Man Purchase Act 1765.
61 Duke of Atholl's Rights, Isle of Man Act 1825.
62 *Report of the Royal Commission on the Constitution*, Cmnd 5460, 1973, London: HMSO, Vol. 1, para. 1360.
63 **Sodor and Man (Bishop) v Derby (Earl)** (1751).

The Islands and Europe

The European Union

When the United Kingdom signed the Treaty of Rome, special arrangements had to be effected for the islands.[64] Under Article 227(4) of the Treaty of Rome, the Treaty extends to all territories for which Member States have responsibility for their international relations. Were the Treaty to extend automatically to the islands, it would confer power on the institutions of the European Community (as it then was known, now the European Union) to legislate for the islands in matters such as taxation – which the United Kingdom Parliament, consistent with the convention, would have no *de facto* power to legislate. Accordingly, the islands sought special terms in relation to membership of the Community. The resulting solution was that the United Kingdom Government negotiated special status for the islands in relation to the Union: the islands are part of the Union for the purpose of free movement of industrial and agricultural goods but not for the purpose of free movement of persons or taxation provisions. The Withdrawal Agreement between the EU and the UK applies to the Channel Islands and the Isle of Man to the extent that EU law was applicable to them before the date of the Agreement coming into force.

The European Convention on Human Rights

While the position of the Channel Islands and the Isle of Man vis-à-vis the European Union is the same, the position is different in relation to the Convention. Initially, the Convention on Human Rights extended to both the Channel Islands and the Isle of Man, and nowadays it continues to apply to the Channel Islands.[65] While the Convention initially applied to the Isle of Man, the case of **Tyrer v United Kingdom** (1978) brought about a change. In this case, the European Court of Human Rights held that judicial birching in the Isle of Man of a juvenile amounted to degrading punishment in violation of Article 3 of the Convention. As a result, the Isle of Man government requested that the right of individual petition under the Convention be withdrawn. The United Kingdom Government acceded to the request.

The United Kingdom and the Commonwealth[66]

From Empire to Commonwealth

In the sixteenth and seventeenth centuries, Britain embarked on empire building, although the original expansion of British interests overseas was essentially undertaken by private commercial companies. Where territory was taken over by conquest, it became the property of the Crown.[67] Legal authority over such territories vested in the Crown and political control lay with the Privy Council.

The earliest 'revolution' against colonisation came with the American Declaration of Independence in 1776 in which Britain was deprived of 13 North American colonies. By the end of the nineteenth century, vast swathes of the world's map were 'coloured pink' – that is to say, under British power and control. The relationship between Britain and its colonies may be characterised as the movement from full British sovereignty over the territories through to increasing self-government and independence. In 1865, the Colonial Laws Validity

---

64 See Simmonds, 1970, 1971.
65 See **Gillow v United Kingdom** (1986).
66 See, *inter alia*, Roberts-Wray, 1966; Dale, 1983; Wheare, 1960; de Smith, 1964.
67 **Calvin's Case** (1608).

Act was passed by the British Parliament in order to clarify the relationship between British law and colonial law and the capacity of colonial legislatures for self-regulation. While the Act confirmed self-regulating legislative capacity, it also affirmed the principle that such devolved powers were subject to the overriding sovereignty of the imperial Parliament.

In 1867, Canada became the first self-governing Dominion (a status implying equality with rather than subordination to Britain), to be followed by Australia in 1900, New Zealand in 1907, South Africa in 1910 and the Irish Free State in 1921. The recognition that the Empire was being transformed into a Commonwealth of Nations came in 1884.

The desire for formal recognition and explication of the constitutional relationship between Britain and the Dominions led to four-yearly Prime Ministerial conferences, which commenced in 1887. The Imperial Conference of 1926 adopted the Balfour Report, which defined the Dominions as:

> autonomous communities within the British Empire, equal in status, in no way sub-ordinate one to another in any aspect of their domestic or external affairs, though united by common allegiance to the Crown, and freely associated as members of the British Commonwealth of Nations.

The Statute of Westminster 1931 gave formal recognition to this definition. Section 2 of the Act extended the powers of Dominion legislatures to amend or repeal Acts of the United Kingdom Parliament, although this power did not extend to going against the limits on the Dominion's legislative capacity as laid down in the Acts containing that country's constitution.[68]

By the end of the Second World War in 1945, much of the remaining British power had been repossessed by its rightful owners, either through direct resistance to British rule (as in India) or by way of negotiated constitutional settlements between the British Crown and the formerly dependent territory.[69] From this time, what remained of the British Empire was transformed into a loosely defined, voluntary Commonwealth of nations, of which the British monarch represents the formal Head.[70] While the Commonwealth was originally characterised by its members' allegiance to the British Crown, the movement towards repub-licanism forced a change in direction for the Commonwealth. It was Indian independence that represented the catalyst for change. India had remained a Dominion under the India Act of 1935, until independence in 1947. In 1949, India's desire to become a republic and yet remain within the Commonwealth posed a novel question concerning allegiance to the British Crown. The London Declaration of 1949 revised the position and enabled India to enter as the first republican member. Heads of government also agreed, however, that members would continue to recognise the Crown as the 'symbol of their free association and thus Head of the Commonwealth', the position which still pertains.

---

68 See *Harris v Minister of the Interior* (1952); *British Coal Corporation v R* (1935); *Ndlwana v Hofmeyer* (1937); and, further, Chapter 6. The constitutional position in relation to Canada was defined by the British North America Act 1867, which contained no amendment provisions. Accordingly, it remained for the United Kingdom Parliament to amend the Canadian Constitution. This anomalous position was resolved in 1982 by the Canada Act which 'repatriated' the Canadian Constitution. For a challenge to the Act, see *Re Amendment of the Constitution of Canada* (1982), discussed in Chapter 2.

69 The constitutional relationship between the United Kingdom Parliament and Australia was finally resolved in 1986 under the Australia Act, which severed the legislative links with Westminster and terminated appeals from the Australian courts to the Privy Council.

70 See further Dale, 1983; Roberts-Wray, 1966.

The Commonwealth today

The Commonwealth is made up of 54 countries, many of them small, ranging from monarchies – either under Queen Elizabeth II or national monarchs – to republics.[71]

Nowadays, 32 members are republics and five have national monarchies of their own, while 16 recognise Queen Elizabeth II as Head of State.[72] The shared history and traditions of Britain and other Commonwealth members, including legal traditions, provides the basis for this voluntary association of states, which spans six continents and five oceans, and has a population of some 2.4 billion – almost one-third of the world's population.

The Commonwealth was defined in 1971 at the Commonwealth Heads of Government Meeting (CHOGM) as: 'a voluntary association of independent sovereign States, each responsible for its own policies, consulting and cooperating in the common interests of their peoples and in the promotion of international understanding and world peace'.[73]

In 2013 the Commonwealth adopted its first formal Charter. The Charter affirms the Commonwealth's commitment to democracy; human rights; international peace and security; tolerance, respect and understanding; freedom of expression; separation of powers; the rule of law; good governance; sustainable development; protection of the environment; access to health, education, food and shelter; gender equality; the importance of young people in the Commonwealth; the recognition of the needs of small and vulnerable states; and the role of civil society.

The Commonwealth Secretariat

The Commonwealth is headed by a Secretary General. Under her stewardship, the Commonwealth Secretariat has been refashioned to enable it better to achieve Commonwealth objectives. The Secretariat was formed in 1965 and now has 12 separate divisions.

A Commonwealth Ministerial Action Group (CMAG) was established in 1995 to deal with serious or persistent violations of the Harare Declaration. Its task is to assess the nature of alleged infringements and recommend measures for collective Commonwealth action. The CMAG has authority to suspend a member country.

Appeals from Commonwealth courts to the Privy Council

The Judicial Committee of the Privy Council has jurisdiction to hear appeals from 'dependencies of the Crown'. Deriving from the royal prerogative, the jurisdiction was given statutory force under the Judicial Committee Acts of 1833 and 1844. Appeals may be with special leave of the Privy Council, or without leave. Appeals with special leave are predominantly criminal cases. Appeals against the death penalty represent the majority of appeals.

While before independence colonies had no power to abolish appeals to the Privy Council, on independence, this power arose. As a result, a majority of Commonwealth countries have abolished the right of appeal. The jurisdiction of the Judicial Committee of the Privy Council is now exercised by the Supreme Court (on which see Chapter 4).

---

71 See the website for a full list of Member States.
72 In 2020 Barbados announced that it intended to become a Republic, but remain within the Commonwealth.
73 Commonwealth Declaration, 22 January 1971. CHOGMs take place every two years.

📖 Further Reading

Allan, TRS, 'Law, democracy and constitutionalism: reflections on *Evans v Attorney General*' (2016) 75 *Cambridge Law Journal* 38.

Barendt, E, 'Is there a United Kingdom constitution?' (1997) 17 *Oxford Journal of Legal Studies* 137.

Beatson, J, 'Reforming an unwritten constitution' (2010) 126 *Law Quarterly Review* 48.

Bogdanor, V and Vogenauer, S, 'Enacting a British constitution: some problems' [2008] *Public Law* 38.

Eleftheriadis, P, 'On rights and responsibilities' [2010] *Public Law* 31.

Le Sueur, A, 'Gordon Brown's new constitutional settlement' [2008] *Public Law* 21.

Leigh, I, 'Local government and political constitutionalism' [2014] *Public Law* 43.

Loughlin, M, 'Constitutional theory: a 25th anniversary essay' (2005) 25 *Oxford Journal of Legal Studies* 183.

McIlwain, CH, *Constitutionalism Ancient and Modern*, 1947, London: Cornell University Press, Chapter 1.

Munro, CR, *Studies in Constitutional Law*, 2nd edn, 1999, London: Butterworths, Chapter 1.

Murkens, JEK, 'The quest for constitutionalism in UK public law discourse' (2009) 29 *Oxford Journal of Legal Studies* 427.

Oliver, D, *Constitutional Reform in the United Kingdom*, 2003, Oxford: Oxford University Press.

Poole, T, 'Tilting at windmills? Truth and illusion in "the political constitution"' (2007) 70 *Modern Law Review* 250.

Walker, D, 'The idea of constitutional pluralism' (2002) 65 *Modern Law Review* 317.

Chapter **2**

Sources of the Constitution

Chapter Contents

Learning Objectives

By the end of this chapter you should be able to:

☐ explain why an understanding of the different sources is so important under the UK constitution;
☐ list the legal (statutory and common law) and non-legal sources;
☐ give examples of both statutory and common law sources, including the royal prerogative;
☐ give a definition of constitutional conventions;
☐ discuss the range of conventions and their varying degrees of certainty;
☐ give illustrations of both certain and less certain conventions;
☐ consider whether conventions should be 'codified';
☐ evaluate the extent to which the UK constitution is 'written' or 'uncodified'.

Introduction

As has been seen in Chapter 1, the United Kingdom's constitution is classified as 'unwritten' or 'uncodified'. It is the result of gradual evolutionary development over centuries rather than a consciously constructed document drafted to meet the needs and aspirations of a country at a particular time and intended to remain largely unaltered in the future. As a result of this, in order to understand its content and scope it is necessary to study the various legal 'sources' which make up the constitution.

These include:

- statutes (Acts of Parliament);
- the powers of the Crown (the royal prerogative);
- the law relating to the working of Parliament (the law and custom of Parliament); and
- judicial decisions.

In addition, there are numerous non-legal, but binding, rules which surround and give meaning to the legal rules of the constitution, the most important of which are constitutional conventions. Basic principles also form a part of the constitution, and in addition to the formal sources it is necessary to understand the concepts of:

- the rule of law (Chapter 3);
- separation of powers (Chapter 4); and
- parliamentary sovereignty or supremacy (Chapter 6).

This approach is very different from that which applies to studying a written constitution where the original document – the constitution – represents the principal document for analysis, supplemented by the judicial decisions of a Supreme Court which (usually) has the final say over the interpretation of the constitution.

One key feature of the British constitution which results from its evolution is its *flexibility*. Constitutional change can be achieved with the minimum of formality with the passage of an ordinary Act of Parliament, involving no special procedures. By contrast, a written constitution is essentially one which is rigid or *inflexible*, with special procedures laid down for its amendment to ensure that the constitution is only altered in exceptional circumstances.

Definitional Difficulties

Defining the scope of sources which are correctly labelled 'constitutional' under an unwritten constitution is an inherently difficult exercise. Were the United Kingdom to have a written constitution, all of the rules now contained within various sources would be contained within it. By this means, a clear picture would be obtained as to those rules which the framers of the constitution regarded as being of 'constitutional importance'. In the absence of such a document, matters are less clear-cut and doubt exists as to precisely which rules – statutory, common law or conventional – are correctly defined as 'constitutional' rules. As Geoffrey Marshall explains: '[N]o easy logical limit can be set to the labour of the constitutional lawyers ... any branch of the law, whether it deals *prima facie* with finance or crime or local government, may throw up constitutional questions' (1971, page 6).

The disadvantage of such a lack of precision may be illustrated in relation to the legal protection of civil liberties and human rights before the Human Rights Act 1998. Having neither a written constitution nor a comprehensive enforceable Code, or Bill of Rights, an individual seeking to discover precisely what legal rights he or she had was obliged to scrutinise the statute book, the text of the European Convention on Human Rights and case law, both domestic and European. Furthermore, because rights protected under the European Convention on Human Rights were not enforceable before the domestic courts, the aggrieved individual had to seek a remedy by applying to the Court of Human Rights in Strasbourg – a lengthy procedure. The Human Rights Act 1998 remedied this deficiency by conferring jurisdiction on domestic courts to rule on and protect Convention rights.

In the absence of a written constitution, it is also difficult for the individual citizen to decide what is and what is not a 'constitutional' issue. As Marshall observes, all legal issues in the United Kingdom are potentially capable of being interpreted as constitutional issues. That fact is not, however, reassuring to the student of the constitution who is trying to define its scope and limits.

To illustrate this definitional difficulty, questions as to the status of many and differing statutes may be briefly examined.

Employment law

Statutes regulating relations between workers and employers define the extent to which an employee is free to withdraw his or her labour, to act in support of a dispute between him or herself and his or her employer and to act in support of other workers in support of a dispute with employers. Such matters raise the fundamental question of the individual's right to withdraw his or her labour and the conditions under which this is lawful. Are such statutes 'constitutional' in nature?

Pornography

Also by way of illustration, in the United Kingdom, the Obscene Publications Act 1959 (as amended), an ordinary Act of Parliament having no particular 'constitutional status', provides the legal rules relating to pornographic literature. In contrast, in the United States of America, legal challenges to the availability of and access to allegedly pornographic material fall under the First Amendment to the Constitution.[1] The subject of pornography in the United States may accordingly be classified as a clearly constitutional issue, being regarded as a question of 'freedom of speech'.

Abortion

In the United Kingdom, the right to abortion is defined under the Abortion Act 1967 (as amended). In the United States of America, by contrast, the right to abortion falls under the constitutional right to privacy provisions of the constitution. The constitution of the Republic of Ireland prohibits abortion under its right-to-life provisions, and a challenge to that prohibition was launched under the guise of restrictions on equal access to information and the right to free movement to receive services under the law of the European Community.[2]

These examples are not intended to lead to an analysis of the substantive legal and constitutional issues, but rather demonstrate a very real and important point of principle. That point is that under a written constitution, a particular issue may be defined as a 'constitutional' issue. Under an unwritten constitution, matters are far less certain. Pornography and abortion are clearly regarded as constitutional matters in some jurisdictions.

---

1 **Roth v US** (1957).
2 **The Society of the Unborn Children Ireland Ltd v Grogan** (1991). See Spalin, 1992.

SELF-TEST QUESTION

What are the principal characteristics of a 'constitutional statute'? Do employment laws, obscenity laws and the law relating to abortion meet these characteristics?

There are obvious limitations to the utility of merely listing statutory and common law sources of the constitution. It is, however, important at an early stage of study to be familiar with the major statutory sources of the constitution.

Legal Sources

The Magna Carta

One starting point is the Magna Carta of 1215.[3] Historically, the Magna Carta represented a formal settlement between the Crown and the barons. The Charter represented settlement of the grievances of citizens and challenged the untrammelled powers of the King. The settlement provided for freedom of the Church, and the right of merchants to be free from exorbitant taxation. Today, the document's importance lies in its declaration of the confirmation of the liberties enjoyed by 'freemen of the realm' and their future protection, and in the protection to be given to the enjoyment of these liberties by the requirement for trial by jury:

> No freeman shall be taken or imprisoned, or be disseised of his freehold, or liberties, or free customs, or be outlawed, or exiled, or any other wise destroyed; nor will we pass upon him, nor condemn him, but by lawful judgment of his peers, or by the law of the land. We will sell to no man, we will not deny or defer to any man either justice or right. [Holt, 1965, Chapter XXIX]

While of little legal importance today – for much of the original Magna Carta has been repealed – the document has symbolic value as an early assertion of the limits of monarchical power and the rights of individuals.

The Petition of Right 1628

The Petition of Right 1628 arose as a result of **Darnel's Case** (the **Five Knights' Case**) (1627), where the defendants had been convicted and imprisoned for refusing to pay a loan imposed by King Charles I. The Petition forbade such loans, taxes and other monetary demands without the consent of Parliament. The Petition, while still in force, was superseded by the Bill of Rights 1689.

The Bill of Rights 1689

The background

The Bill of Rights 1689 is of greater contemporary constitutional importance than Magna Carta and the Petition of Right. The source of the Bill of Rights lies, in large measure, in the tensions between Roman Catholicism and the state, originating with the conflict between

---

3 Magna Carta, Statute 25 Edw I (1297). See Holt, 1965.

the Holy See of Rome and Henry VIII (1509–1547). The Succession Act, the Act of Supremacy and the Treason Act 1534 had established the supremacy of the King as head of the Church of England and destroyed formal papal authority in England. Catholicism did not die out, but over the next 150 years, suspicion and fear of 'popery' remained high at a public level. The death of Charles II in 1685 heralded the succession of James II, an avowed Roman Catholic, who nevertheless publicly declared himself bound 'to preserve this government both in Church and state as it is now by law established'.[4] Despite such assurances, in subsequent years, James II strove to remove discrimination against Catholics and to place Catholics in prominent public administrative offices at both central and local level. Prominent Anglicans, dismayed by James' promotion of Catholicism, entered into negotiations with William of Orange, the Protestant husband of James' daughter Mary, with a view to their seizing the throne. In the absence of a male heir, Mary was next in line to the English Crown. However, in 1688, James' wife gave birth to a son, thus providing a Catholic heir. In July of that year, James dissolved Parliament. William of Orange landed in England with his army on 5 November 1688 and James II fled the country, landing in France in December 1688.

William and Mary's accession was not to be unconditional.[5] The Declaration of Right sought to resolve the actual and potential tensions between Crown and Parliament, Church and state. The terms of the Bill of Rights marked a sharp alteration in the balance of power between Crown and Parliament – in Parliament's favour.[6]

The major provisions of the Bill of Rights
The principal provisions of contemporary importance are:

Article I	the pretended power of suspending ... or executing laws by the Crown without parliamentary consent is illegal;
Article IV	the levying of money for use of the Crown under the prerogative without parliamentary consent is illegal;
Article VI	the raising or keeping of an army in peacetime without parliamentary consent is illegal;
Article VIII	elections of Members of Parliament ought to be free;
Article IX	freedom of speech and debates in proceedings in Parliament ought not to be impeached or questioned in any court or place out of Parliament;
Article X	excessive bail ought not to be required, nor excessive fines imposed, nor cruel and unusual punishments inflicted;
Article XI	jury trial is available; and
Article XIII	for the redress of grievances, Parliament ought to meet frequently.

Subsequent to the Bill of Rights – and to give effect to its provisions – the Crown and Parliament Recognition Act 1689 gave statutory force to the Bill of Rights, and the Meeting of Parliament Act 1694 provided that Parliament must be summoned to meet at least once in three years.

---

4 Quoted in Lockyer, 1985, p. 351.
5 As had been that of Charles II in 1660.
6 In Scotland, the Claim of Right 1689.

The Act of Settlement 1700

The Act of Settlement 1700 clarified the line of succession to the throne. The Act also provided for security of tenure for the judiciary 'during good behaviour',[7] thus ending the power of the Crown to dismiss judges at will. In relation to succession to the throne, the Act tied the succession to Protestant heirs and gave precedence to male heirs. The succession to the Crown Act 2013 reforms the law (see page 226).

The Treaty of Union 1706

The Treaty of Union also has enduring constitutional effect. The Treaty united England and Scotland under a single Parliament of Great Britain. Prior to the Treaty, each country enjoyed independent sovereign status. Scotland had its own Parliament and its own system of private law. Decades earlier, James VI, King of Scotland and subsequently King of England (as James I (1603–1625)), had attempted but failed to bring about a union between Scotland and England. By the late seventeenth century, negotiations were continuing with a view to ending the historical conflicts between the two countries,[8] and the Treaty of Union represented the culmination of this process. See further Chapter 6.

The major provisions of the Treaty of Union 1706

For current purposes, the most important provisions are as follows:

Article I	that the two kingdoms of England and Scotland shall be united in one kingdom by the name of Great Britain;
Article II	that succession to the united throne be according to the Act of Settlement 1700;
Article III	that there be a single Parliament;
Article XVIII	that no alteration be made in laws which concern Scottish private rights except for the evident utility of the subjects; and
Article XIX	that the Court of Session in Scotland remain 'in all time being as now constituted', and that lower courts remain subject to alteration in their powers by Parliament.

The European Communities Act 1972

The European Communities Act 1972, as amended, together with the European Treaties, regulated the United Kingdom's membership of the European Union and continues to have significance for the constitution of the United Kingdom. The law of the European Union (EU) represented a significant source of constitutional law. By acceding to the European Community (now the European Union), the United Kingdom undertook the obligation to accept the law of the Union. To understand the constitutional implications of membership of the European Union, it is necessary to understand the scope of the Treaties and the law-making institutions, and the manner in which laws are made and enter into force within the legal systems of the Member States. It is also necessary to understand clearly the relationship between European law and domestic law and, during the UK's membership of the EU, the question of which law had supremacy should a conflict between them arise. Under the

---

7 On the independence of the judiciary, see Chapter 4.
8 For a succinct account of the history, see Maitland, 1908, pp. 331–332.

traditional doctrine of parliamentary sovereignty, the United Kingdom Parliament alone has sovereign law-making power. The perception of the Court of Justice of the European Union – the highest court of the European Union – is very different. As will be seen, the European Court has long asserted the supremacy of EU law[9] over the laws of Member States, thus providing a fertile source for constitutional speculation about Parliament's sovereignty.

In 2016, in a UK-wide referendum, the people voted to leave the EU. The details of this decision, and its constitutional implications, are discussed in Chapter 6 (on parliamentary sovereignty) and Chapter 8 (the European Union). Note, however, that the European Communities Act 1972 will be repealed at the end of the transition period in 2020. Under the terms of the EU (Withdrawal) Act 2018, on departure from the EU, EU law will be transposed into domestic law, enabling Parliament to retain, amend or repeal the law.

Acts establishing devolution

The Acts establishing a Scottish Parliament and Welsh Assembly and re-establishing a Northern Ireland Assembly have decentralised the process of government and law making, giving greater national autonomy to Northern Ireland, Scotland and Wales.

See Chapter 11.

The Human Rights Act 1998

The Human Rights Act 1998, which incorporates the rights enshrined in the European Convention on Human Rights and Freedoms into domestic law, represents a fundamental change in the domestic protection of rights. The impact of the Human Rights Act 1998 has been felt across wide areas of domestic law and provides citizens for the first time with a code of rights which are enforceable in the domestic courts rather than in the European Court of Human Rights in Strasbourg.

See Chapter 18.

The Constitutional Reform Act 2005

The Constitutional Reform Act 2005 introduced changes in three principal areas. The Act reformed the office of Lord Chancellor, transferring his powers as head of the judiciary to the Lord Chief Justice and providing for the House of Lords to elect its own Speaker. In addition the Appellate Committee of the House of Lords – formerly the highest domestic court in the United Kingdom – has been replaced by a Supreme Court which is physically separate from Parliament.

Further illustrations

Further statutes of major constitutional importance – and the list is by no means exhaustive – include the following:

(a) Acts extending and regulating elections and the right to vote (the franchise);[10]
(b) the Statute of Westminster 1931 gave statutory force to the conventions regulating relations between the sovereign United Kingdom Parliament and legislatures of the Dominions;

---

9 **Costa v ENEL** (1964).
10 1832, 1867, 1884, 1918, 1928, 1948, 1969, 1983, 2000, 2006.

(c)   His Majesty's Declaration of Abdication Act 1936 varied the succession to the throne established under the Act of Settlement 1700;

(d)   the Regency Acts 1937–1953 provided that if the Sovereign is under the age of 18, regal powers shall be exercised through a Regent appointed under the Acts;

(e)   the Royal Titles Act 1953, which founded a challenge from Scottish lawyers to its compatibility with the Act of Union,[11] provided that the Sovereign may by Proclamation adopt such a style and titles as she may think fit;

(f)   the Treaty of Union with Ireland Act 1800, the Government of Ireland Act 1920, the Ireland Act 1949 and the Northern Ireland Constitution Act 1973 have all reflected the changing constitutional relationship between Ireland, Northern Ireland and the United Kingdom;

(g)   the Representation of the People Acts from 1832 to the present date, setting out the right to vote and the law relating to elections;

(h)   the Parliament Acts 1911 and 1949 restricting the powers of the House of Lords in relation to legislation. The House of Lords Act 1999 reforming the membership of the House of Lords;

(i)   the Acts devolving power to national Assemblies: the Northern Ireland Act 1998, the Scotland Act 1998 and 2012, the Government of Wales Act 1998, 2006, 2014 and 2017;

(j)   the Parliamentary Standards Act 2009, the Constitutional Reform and Governance Act 2010, the Parliamentary Voting System and Constituencies Act 2011 and the Fixed-term Parliaments Act 2011;

(k)   the Equality Act 2010 consolidating the law relating to freedom from discrimination;

(l)   the Localism Act 2011 reforming the structure and powers of local government;

(m)   the Police Reform and Social Responsibility Act 2011 introducing elected Police and Crime Commissioners;

(n)   the Fixed-term Parliaments Act 2011 introducing fixed five-year parliamentary terms;

(o)   the European Union (Withdrawal) Act 2018; European Union (Withdrawal Agreement) Act 2020 and European Union (Future Relationship) Act 2020.

The royal prerogative

See further Chapter 5.

The prerogative powers of the Crown are those powers which arise out of the common law and which are unique to the Crown. Two definitions may be given by way of introduction. To Dicey, the prerogative powers were 'the residue of arbitrary and discretionary powers legally left in the hands of the Crown' which, being exercised by the government in the name of the Crown, entails 'every act which the executive government can do without the authority of an Act of Parliament' (1885, page 425).

Blackstone, in his *Commentaries*, offers a more limited definition: 'that special pre-eminence which the King hath over and above all persons, and out of the ordinary course of the common law … And … only applied to those rights and capacities which the King enjoys in contradistinction to others'. The prerogative will be discussed in detail in Chapter 5.

Judicial decisions

See further Chapter 22.

Throughout history, the judiciary has, through case law, defined the relationship between the institutions of the state – the Crown, the executive, Parliament and the judiciary – and defined the relationship between the state and the individual. As with statutory sources of

11 **MacCormick v Lord Advocate** (1953). See further Chapter 6.

the constitution, the study of constitutional and administrative law concerns the examination and analysis of judicial precedents. The judiciary today has no power to question the validity of an Act of Parliament.[12] However, whilst Acts of Parliament are unchallengeable as to their validity, delegated or secondary legislation is not immune from such review. Furthermore, the judges have the power to review the legality of acts of persons and organisations acting under powers conferred by an Act of Parliament in order to ensure that they act within (*intra vires*) the powers conferred by Parliament.

The extent to which judges have been able to protect individual rights under the common law – in the light of Parliament's supremacy – has been limited. Traditionally, the United Kingdom had no Bill of Rights in so far as such a document provides a written source of protection for certain fundamental rights and freedoms. In the absence of such guaranteed protection – protection which would prevail even against an Act of Parliament – the citizen remained dependent either upon ad hoc statutory provisions – such as the Habeas Corpus Acts (1679, 1816, 1862), the Race Relations Act 1976 or the Sex Discrimination Act 1975 – or upon judicial protection under the common law (see Chapters 18 and 22). By way of introductory illustration, the contrasting cases of **Entick v Carrington** (1765) and **Liversidge v Anderson** (1942) may be cited. In the former case, the court ruled that a general warrant issued by a Home Secretary for the entry into private property and seizure of allegedly seditious material was contrary to law and amounted to a trespass to property. This bold assertion of judicial power to rule on the legality of acts of the executive and to control such acts is in stark contrast to the ruling in **Liversidge v Anderson**. Here, in the context of a challenge to the legality of detention without warrant under the order of the Home Secretary, the House of Lords held that the courts could not, in times of emergency, review the Home Secretary's belief that detention was justified. Such conflicting outcomes demonstrate that reliance on judicial protection from executive action, under common law, is by no means certain, let alone guaranteed. The Human Rights Act 1998, however, now enables citizens to challenge the legality of government action against the provisions of the Convention. As will be discussed in Chapter 18, the Act does not empower the courts to challenge the validity of Acts of Parliament, but rather preserves Parliament's traditional sovereignty by empowering the courts to make declarations of incompatibility between a statute and Convention requirements. Thereafter, it is for the government and Parliament to change the law if it wishes to comply with the Convention requirements.

A 'third source' of power?

In 1945, in a memorandum to the government drafted by Sir Granville Ram, then First Parliamentary Counsel, it was stated that an agent of the Crown had the right, under common law, to exercise any powers that the Crown has power to exercise, except where precluded from doing so by statute. This suggested that there was a 'third source' of power beyond statute and prerogative. The memorandum remained unpublished until 2003. The 'Ram doctrine', as it became known, is an attractive proposition to government, suggesting that it can do anything unless prohibited by statute.[13] The so-called doctrine was relevant in **Malone v Metropolitan Police Commissioner** (1979). In that case, the Home Secretary issued a warrant authorising the police to intercept Malone's telephone. The 1969 Post Office Act provided that it was a defence to various offences if the act 'was done in obedience to a warrant under the

---

12 **Edinburgh and Dalkeith Railway v Wauchope** (1842); **Pickin v British Railways Board** (1974). But see Chapters 6 and 8 on the position in relation to the law of the European Union.
13 See HL Deb 24 February 2003, vol. 645, cc.12-3WA.

hand of the Secretary of State'. The Act therefore assumed that the Home Secretary had such a power, and gave it legal effect. However, in **Malone** Sir Robert Megarry stated that 'the tapping of telephones … does not require any statutory or common law power to justify it: it can lawfully be done simply because there is nothing to make it unlawful'.

The House of Lords' Select Committee on the Constitution examined this so-called 'third source of power' in its Thirteenth Report of 2012–2013.[14] On Ram, the Committee robustly stated that: 'The Ram memorandum is the source of another, more troubling, legal fallacy (namely that ministers can do anything a natural person can do, unless limited by legislation)'. The Report cited the evidence of Sir Stephen Sedley, a retired Lord Justice of Appeal:

> What appears to be being made in Whitehall, out of Ram, is a fabrication. Ram never said what is attributed to him. His proposition that government can do anything reasonably ancillary to its explicit functions is completely unobjectionable, but it is nowhere near the proposition that appears to have derived from it in Whitehall that Government can do anything that a private individual can do. The converse is the case. [At paragraph 56]

Sir Jeffrey Jowell expressed his view that: '[the doctrine is] … a constitutional heresy. Even if it were a settled convention, it would be overridden by a constitutional principle, which has higher authority: namely, the rule of law' (at paragraph 57).

The Committee concluded that:

> The Ram memorandum is not an accurate reflection of the law today. In addition to statutory restraints, ministers' ability to exercise common law powers is constrained by: the public law limitations on Government action as enforced through judicial review; human rights law; the pre-existing rights and significant interests of private persons; and rules on financial propriety;

and furthermore that: 'The description of the common law powers of the Crown encapsulated by the phrase "the Ram doctrine" is inaccurate, and should no longer be used' (at paras 54 and 60 respectively).

Non-Legal Sources of the Constitution

Constitutional conventions

'The short explanation of the constitutional conventions is that they provide the flesh which clothes the dry bones of the law; they make the legal constitution work; they keep it in touch with the growth of ideas'.[15]

Constitutional conventions form the most significant class of non-legal constitutional rules.[16] A clear understanding of their nature, scope and manner of application is essential to the study of the United Kingdom's constitution. Conventions supplement the legal rules of the constitution and define the practices of the constitution. Conventions, as Jennings states, 'provide the flesh which clothes the dry bones of the law' and represent the 'unwritten maxims' of the constitution. Conventions apply to virtually all aspects of the constitution, and for

---

14 The Pre-emption of Parliament, HL 165.
15 Jennings, 1959a, pp. 81–82.
16 See, *inter alia*, Dicey, 1885, Chapter 14; Jennings, 1959a, Chapter 3; Marshall and Moodie, 1971, Chapter 2; Marshall, 1984, esp. Chapters 1 and 13; Munro, 1999, Chapter 3.

this reason it is, in part, unrealistic and unsatisfactory to attempt adequately to consider their role in a 'vacuum'. Nevertheless, given their central importance, conventions must be considered at this early stage, while bearing in mind that many and varied further illustrations will emerge throughout the course of study.

Conventions defined

Conventions are defined by AV Dicey as: 'conventions, understandings, habits or practices which, though they may regulate the … conduct of the several members of the sovereign power … are not in reality laws at all since they are not enforced by the courts' (1885, page clii).

Marshall and Moodie offer an alternative definition: 'rules of constitutional behaviour which are considered to be binding by and upon those who operate the constitution but which are not enforced by the law courts … nor by the presiding officers in the Houses of Parliament' (1971, pages 23–24). A number of important questions arise concerning these non-legal rules, namely:

(a)   what are the characteristics of a conventional rule?
(b)   what is the source or origin of the rule?
(c)   in what manner are conventions distinguishable from laws?
(d)   who is bound by the conventional rules?
(e)   what is the consequence of a breach of the rule?
(f)   does the distinction between law and convention really matter?
(g)   what is the attitude of the courts to conventional rules?
(h)   how do conventions change?
(i)   how best can these rules be analysed and understood?
(j)   should conventions be codified?
(k)   Each of these questions, many of which overlap, must be addressed and answered.

Conventions illustrated

Before turning attention to the task of further analysis, some examples of constitutional conventions will aid understanding. Each of these conventions will be discussed in greater detail later in this book:

(a)   Acts of Parliament are technically enacted by the Queen in Parliament – the Crown, Commons and Lords. The Queen has the legal right to refuse to give Royal Assent to Bills passed by the House of Commons and Lords. By convention, the Queen must assent to such Bills unless advised to the contrary by her government (Chapter 5).
(b)   The Queen will appoint as Prime Minister the leader of the political party with the majority of seats in the House of Commons (Chapter 5).
(c)   The Prime Minister must be a Member of the House of Commons (Chapter 5).
(d)   The government must maintain the confidence of the House of Commons. If a 'vote of confidence' on a matter central to government policy is lost, the government must resign (Chapter 5).
(e)   Ministers of the Crown are individually and collectively responsible to Parliament (Chapter 10).
(f)   Ministers must be Members of either the House of Commons or the House of Lords (Chapter 9).
(g)   Parliament must be summoned to meet at least once a year (Chapter 13).
(h)   The House of Lords will not reject Bills which reflect government policies put to the electorate before a General Election (Chapters 14 and 16).

(i) Judges shall not play an active part in political life (Chapter 4).
(j) Members of Parliament shall not criticise the judiciary (Chapter 4).
(k) The opinion of the law officers of the Crown is confidential (Chapter 10).

This list is not intended to be exhaustive, but is sufficient to give a flavour of the nature and scope of constitutional conventions.

One important example of an emerging convention relates to the deployment of British troops in action overseas. This has hitherto been a power exercised by the Prime Minister, in the name of the Crown, under the royal prerogative. When Prime Minister Margaret Thatcher sent troops to the Falkland Islands to repel Argentinean forces, she acted without debating the matter in Parliament beforehand. The same situation existed when Prime Minister Tony Blair committed British troops to supporting the United States' invasion of Iraq in 2003. In both cases parliamentary debate took place after the event. However, in 2013 Prime Minister David Cameron decided that he should seek the consent of Parliament before committing troops to fight in Syria. The House of Commons voted decisively against such action. In 2014 the United States took the lead in forming a coalition of troops to act in Syria and Iraq against the forces of Islamic State, which had taken control of vast areas in both countries. Before committing British troops, the Prime Minister regarded it as a convention that Parliament had to be consulted before taking action. Parliament voted in favour of action in Iraq but rejected the proposal to act in Syria. Arguably, there is now a convention that Parliament must be consulted and must vote on any proposal to deploy troops overseas, and that Parliament's decision binds the government. The only situation in which the government could act (in the name of the Crown) would be in an emergency situation in which national interests and/or security would be damaged by a prior debate on action (on this see further Chapter 5).

The binding nature of conventions

The characteristics of conventions are suggested both by Dicey and by Marshall and Moodie. The latter authors correctly introduce the concept of a 'rule', and it is this concept which is central to our understanding and which requires further analysis. What is a rule? A rule may be defined as a statement prescribing the conduct which is required in a given situation and which imposes an obligation on those who are regulated by the rule.[17] The idea of obligation is of prime importance here, for if a person is under an obligation which is recognised by observers of the constitution, and that person fails to act in accordance with the obligation, then that failure will give rise to legitimate criticism which will invariably be phrased in terms of 'constitutionality'. To reiterate, the obligation imposes a standard of conduct which is expected to be followed. The obligation is 'normative' or 'prescriptive' – that is, it dictates the appropriate form of action in a particular situation. As Sir Ivor Jennings states, conventions 'not only are followed but have to be followed' (1959a, page 2).

Dicey's definition suggests that conventions are of the same quality as 'understandings, habits or practices'. This view is inaccurate in so far as none of these words conveys the idea of obligation – the normative (or prescriptive) – the idea of what ought to be done in particular circumstances.

Conventions distinguished from habits

Conventions are conceptually different from 'habits' or 'practices' in that these concepts do not prescribe or dictate what ought to happen but are merely descriptive of what in fact does happen. To offer a simple but possibly outdated example, consider the statement that 'the

---

17 Hart, 1961, pp. 79–88.

English drink tea in the afternoon'. Drinking tea is a habit: the statement is simply reflective of actual observable conduct. There is nothing in the statement which requires that conduct, or which states that it ought to happen. Accordingly, it is a descriptive and not a normative statement. If the English fail to drink tea in the afternoon, or drink coffee instead, that action is not going to give rise to any criticism because a mere habit imposes no obligation. The observation is a statement of what 'is', and not what 'ought to be'. There is no obligation imposed on the English to drink tea and hence no criticism will follow from failure to do so. It is very different with a breach of a constitutional convention, which will invariably give rise to adverse criticism. Conventions are thus distinguishable from habits.

Conventions distinguished from understandings

To what extent is Dicey correct in equating conventions with 'understandings'? Once more, it is helpful to resort to definitions. The word 'understanding' connotes a mutual agreement between relevant actors as to the pertinent subject matter, or the manner in which it is appropriate to respond or react to a given situation. As such, any understanding rests on a meeting of minds, and is capable of being the subject of misunderstanding, as in cases where the actors, through a lack of understanding of the situation (or as a result of a differing interpretation of the situation), fail to be 'of one mind'. An 'understanding' may well be relied on by the parties, as are conventions. Understandings may also be brought about by some form of previous, or precedent, conduct or mutual recognition: but this is not a prerequisite for their existence or nature. Most importantly, an understanding, while imposing some weak form of moral obligation, will not, in the case of failure to comply with its terms, give rise to a sanction in the form of criticism of the same magnitude as that of a breach of a constitutional convention. The explanation for this lies in the fact that an understanding – as opposed to a convention – does not amount to a rule, and accordingly is not obligation-imposing to the same degree as a convention.

Conventions distinguished from practices

The concept of a practice remains for consideration. A practice may be defined as being 'a usual or customary action or proceeding'.[18] A practice, therefore, is the normal manner in which a person or body will react to a factual situation on the basis of some precedent form of conduct. In everyday life – whether in commercial offices or in the professions of medicine or law – it is a commonplace assertion that 'it is our practice to do'. That statement conveys the message that past experience of doing something in a particular way is the correct way of proceeding, and that – unless there are justifiable reasons for not so doing – the practice will be adhered to. A practice, therefore, may be distinguished from a mere habit on the basis that it imports a notion of reflectiveness, the idea of the 'right' way of reacting to a situation. How, then, is a practice distinguishable from a convention? The borderline between the two is admittedly fine. It may be, however, that the correct dividing line is drawn on the basis of the concept of obligation and rule, and that it is legitimate to argue that whilst a practice imposes some form of weak obligation – and requires some justification for departure from the practice – the practice is no more than an emergent or potential convention and has not yet acquired the binding characteristic of a rule.

Conventions distinguished from laws

Conventions are distinguishable from laws in a number of important respects. First, the source of a legal rule is, for the most part, identifiable and certain. In searching for a legal rule,

---

18 Collins *English Dictionary*.

its source will normally be found within a judicial decision or within an Act of Parliament. Conventions are far less certain in their origins, and it may at times be difficult to see whether a particular form of conduct is, for example, one of practice or convention. Second, the core content of a legal rule will generally have a settled meaning.[19] Conventions, however, are again less certain, and the obligations imposed by a convention may be varied – as illustrated by the discussion of collective ministerial responsibility below.

The foregoing discussion can be presented – albeit with recognition of overlaps between, and ambiguities in, the concepts – in the tabular form below.

	Habits	Understandings	Practices	Conventions	Laws
Regularity of conduct	Yes	Not necessarily	Yes	Yes	Yes
Reflectiveness	No	Yes	Yes	Yes	Yes
Degree of obligation imposed	None	Weak	Strong	Theoretically absolute	Absolute
Sanction attending breach	None	Justification required	Justification required	Charge of unconstitutional conduct	Unlawful conduct

Summary of the meaning of constitutional conventions

A constitutional convention is a non-legal rule which imposes an obligation on those bound by the convention, breach or violation of which will give rise to legitimate criticism; and that criticism will generally take the form of an accusation of 'unconstitutional conduct'.

The source of conventions

The question concerning the source of the constitutional convention is in part interwoven with the characteristics of the convention. A conventional rule may be said to exist when a traditional practice has been consciously adopted and recognised by those who operate the constitution as the correct manner in which to act in a given circumstance. A practice will be seen to have become a convention at the point at which failure to act in accordance with it gives rise to legitimate criticism.

Sir Ivor Jennings once suggested that three questions must be asked in order to determine whether a convention exists. First, are there any precedents for the convention? 'Mere practice', he tells us, 'is not enough. The fact that an authority has always behaved in a certain way is no warrant for saying that it ought to behave in that way'. What more, then, is required? According to Jennings, that turns on the normativity of the practice: 'if the authority itself and those connected with it believe that they ought to do so [behave in a certain way], then the convention does exist ... Practice alone is not enough. It must be normative' (1959a, page 135).

Finally, Jennings argues that neither practice nor precedent is sufficient. In addition, there must be a reason for the rule: 'the creation of a convention must be due to the reason of the thing because it accords with the prevailing political philosophy'.

---

19 See the analysis of a rule in Hart, 1961, Chapter 7.

The effects of breaching constitutional conventions

The question of consequences that flow from a breach of a conventional rule constitutes both a simple and a complex issue. If – as a starting point for discussion – the consequence of breaking a rule of law is examined, two basic points must be recognised. The first point is that a breach of law normally, but not invariably, leads to enforcement of the rule by the courts. The second point is that when a rule of law is breached, the rule remains valid and in force, unless repealed by Parliament or overruled by the judges. With conventional rules, the situation is very different. Being non-legal rules, there is no question of a breach of convention being enforced by the courts: the courts do not have the jurisdiction to enforce conventional rules, although they may give recognition to them.[20] However, it is also the case, as Dicey argued, that breach of a convention may lead to a breach of law. The most often cited example offered is that if Parliament, in breach of convention, did not meet annually, the consequence would be that money granted on an annual basis by Parliament for the maintenance of the armed forces would not be forthcoming. Accordingly, maintenance of the army would become unlawful by virtue of Article VI of the Bill of Rights 1689, which provides that the raising and keeping of an army in peacetime, without Parliament's consent, is unlawful. Such consequences are the exception. For the most part, the consequence of violating a conventional rule is political rather than legal.

That said, it is not possible to offer a single consequence. Much will turn on the particular convention 'broken', the extent of the 'breach' and the political mood of the country at the time. Conventions are obeyed because of the potential political difficulties which would arise if a firmly established convention was departed from without constitutional justification.

One illustration of the effect of breaching conventional rules is provided by the House of Lords.[21]

Collective ministerial responsibility

The doctrine of collective ministerial responsibility provides an example of the uncertainties entailed in the scope and binding nature of conventional rules. The convention of collective ministerial responsibility has two main elements. The first is that when a decision has been reached in Cabinet (the highest decision-making body of government) that decision is binding on all government Ministers, who must – irrespective of their personal feelings about the matter – support the decision in public. The second rule is that Cabinet discussions are absolutely confidential and may never be disclosed without prime ministerial authority. In two situations the doctrine has been 'waived' in order to respond effectively to political circumstances. In 1932, a Coalition government was in office.[22] Following Cabinet disagreements over economic policy, the government adopted an 'agreement to differ', whereby members of Cabinet were free to express their divergent views both in Parliament and in public. Within months, the dissident members resigned from the Cabinet and collective responsibility was reinstated. In 1975, the Labour government was divided as to the benefits of continued membership of the European Community. It was decided that the matter should be put to the electorate in a referendum. The Cabinet itself was deeply divided on the question and the Prime Minister decided to 'lift' the convention of collective responsibility in order to facilitate full and free public debate. Thus, a convention was set aside for a particular purpose, for a defined period of time and for a specific matter. A similar situation arose in 2010. The general election resulted in the first Coalition government in nearly 70 years

---

20 *Attorney General v Jonathan Cape Ltd* (1976); **Manuel v Attorney General** (1983).
21 Discussed more fully in Chapters 10 and 16, respectively.
22 See Marshall, 1984, Chapter 4; and see further Chapter 10.

(between the Conservative Party and Liberal Democrat Party). Policy differences between the two parties have necessitated an agreement to differ over a range of issues, without which conflict in Cabinet would occur and the stability of government would be threatened. Above all, these situations demonstrate the point that conventions can be adjusted, under certain circumstances which are undefined, to suit the exigencies of a particular situation.

The House of Lords 1908–1910

See Chapters 10 and 16.

A very different consequence followed a breach of convention by the House of Lords between 1908 and 1910.[23] Prior to the Parliament Act 1911, one major conventional rule regulated the relationship between the House of Lords and the House of Commons in legislative matters and most particularly in financial matters: namely, that the Lords would ultimately give way to the will of the elected House. This convention broke down in 1908 when the House of Lords rejected the Finance Bill of the Commons. After a deadlock between the two Houses, and a threat by the King to 'flood' the House of Lords with sufficient new peers to secure a majority for the Bill, the government introduced the Parliament Bill 1911. The Parliament Act, which will be looked at in detail in Chapter 16, provided that the House of Lords would no longer enjoy equal powers to approve or reject legislative proposals and that its power would be restricted to a power to delay legislation, subject to strict time limits.[24] It can be seen from this that where the breach of a convention is deemed to be sufficiently grave, Parliament can – in the exercise of its sovereign power – place a convention on a statutory basis.

See Chapter 16.

Further illustrations will present themselves throughout the course of this book: conventional rules are of such fundamental importance that they regulate virtually every aspect of constitutional law. The main point to be understood here is that breaches of conventions have no automatic or defined ramifications.

The differing importance of individual conventions

A related factor which should also be understood is that not all conventions are of equal certainty or importance, and it is in part for this reason that the consequences of a breach will vary. For example, in legal terms, the right to assent or to refuse to assent to Bills passed by Parliament rests with the Crown. However, by convention, the Crown must assent to Bills passed by Parliament whenever so advised by the Prime Minister. So settled is the convention that the Crown must assent to Bills passed by Parliament that it is difficult to foresee circumstances under which it would be broken.[25] Perhaps a political situation could present itself where a Bill had been duly passed by Parliament and where the government had a change of heart and, despite parliamentary opposition, refused to present the Bill for assent. Would this represent a breach of convention? Arguably not, for the convention requires that the monarch give assent on the advice of her government. A situation such as this would undoubtedly cause a political furore; but it is doubtful that it would represent unconstitutional conduct on the part of the government, and still less so by the Crown. It could also be asked, speculatively, what the position would be if a Bill was duly passed by Parliament, the Bill was presented for Royal Assent and was refused on the basis that public opinion was so firmly set against the Bill that to assent would amount to defeating the rights of the electorate. Such a situation raises some fundamental questions about democracy and the relationship between the electorate and the elected government. Geoffrey Marshall questions whether the power to refuse assent to legislation is 'now a dead letter', and states that, 'under present

23 See Jennings, 1969, Chapter 12.4.
24 Money Bills, one month; non-Money Bills, two years over three parliamentary sessions.
25 See Marshall, 1984, p. 22.

constitutional arrangements, it may well be so' (1984, page 22), while recognising that the issue is not closed.

At the other end of the spectrum of the certainty of conventions and their meaning is the doctrine of individual ministerial responsibility, discussed in detail in Chapter 10. As will be seen, in essence, individual ministerial responsibility requires that Ministers of the Crown are accountable to Parliament, and through Parliament to the electorate, for their personal conduct and for the conduct of their Departments.[26] In practical terms, the doctrine is expressed at Parliamentary Question Time, in debates and in committee proceedings, whereby Parliament ensures that Ministers explain and, if necessary, defend their actions.[27] In theory, if a Minister's personal conduct falls below the high standard required of public figures, he or she should resign. Equally, if the government Department under a Minister's authority is found to have misused or mismanaged its powers, it is the Minister who takes the responsibility in Parliament. If the matter is of sufficient gravity and the Minister loses the support of his party and Prime Minister, he or she may be forced to resign. But, as with responsibility for personal conduct, there are no hard and fast rules. There exist no fixed criteria from which it can be predicted in advance the consequence which will flow from a breach of convention. In terms of consequences, this convention is the most uncertain of all conventional rules.

See Chapter 10.

 Pause and Reflect

It is sometimes suggested that because some conventions are uncertain in their scope and application, there should be some form of 'codification' of conventions. Examine this suggestion and explain the arguments for and against codification. What form (if any) could, and should, codification take?

Evolution and change

It has been seen that conventions come into being, unlike legal rules, when a habit or practice becomes so established that it imposes obligations on those to whom it applies, and takes on the characteristics of a rule. And so it is with changes in conventions. A convention may change with changing circumstances: individual ministerial responsibility is a prime example of this feature of conventions. Conventions may adapt to meet particular needs, as with collective responsibility in relation to the European Community (now European Union) in 1975, discussed above. Conventions may be breached and placed on a statutory basis, as with the House of Lords in 1911. A legal rule has a relatively fixed and certain quality while in existence. If a legal rule is changed, either by judicial decision or by Parliament, the previous rule will be superseded by the new: it will 'go out with a bang'. The same cannot be said of conventions. For the most part, they evolve, adapting in amoeba-like fashion to meet the constitutional needs of the time. It is for this reason that they present the student of the constitution with such a fascinating challenge.

The courts and conventions

Given that conventional rules are non-legal rules, the attitude of the courts towards constitutional conventions is inevitably different from their attitude to legal rules. The courts

---

26 See Chapter 9.
27 See Chapter 15.

do not have jurisdiction to adjudicate upon conventions. This is not to say that a court must take no cognisance of conventional rules, but rather, as Dicey asserted, conventions are not 'court enforceable'. The courts will give recognition to conventions, although they are rarely called upon to do so. Two cases are illustrative. The first is that of ***Attorney General v Jonathan Cape Ltd*** (1976). In 1976, the executors of the late Richard Crossman, a former Cabinet Minister, decided to proceed with publication of the diaries he had kept while in government. The diaries included records of Cabinet discussions which, under the doctrine of collective ministerial responsibility, may never be revealed other than under the conditions specified by law or on the authority of the Cabinet Secretary. The government sought an injunction to restrain publication on the basis that Cabinet meetings are, by convention, confidential, and that the diaries, accordingly, represented a breach of confidentiality. The court ruled in favour of the government in relation to the doctrine of confidentiality. In the event, however, the court declined to suppress 'secrets' which were over ten years old. The court ruled that, unless national security was involved, an eight-to-ten-year embargo was the maximum period that such material would be protected.

In 1982, in the Canadian case of ***Reference re Amendment of the Constitution of Canada***, the principal question for decision by the Supreme Court of Canada was whether, as a matter of law, the constitution of Canada could be amended without the consent of the Provinces. A second question was whether the consent of the Provinces was required as a matter of convention. The British North America (No 2) Act 1949 conferred substantial powers on the Canadian Federal Parliament relating to the distribution of power between the Federal and Provincial legislatures.[28] One of the accepted principles regulating constitutional amendments was that there had to be consultation with and the agreement of the Provinces. By a majority the Supreme Court ruled that as a matter of law the consent of the Provinces was not required. The Court also ruled, however, that as a matter of constitutional convention, consent was required. Recognising the distinction between convention and law, the Court ruled that the convention was unenforceable. However, the Court emphasised the importance of conventions, stating that 'some conventions may be more important than some laws' and that 'constitutional conventions plus constitutional law equal the total constitution of the country'.

 SELF-TEST QUESTIONS

Write a brief definition of a constitutional convention.
What are the key differences between a legal rule and a constitutional convention?

Should conventions be codified?

One question asked earlier was whether or not constitutional conventions should be codified. Again, no straightforward or simple answer to this question presents itself. Much will turn on the perception of the value of the status quo. Much also turns on the constitutional implications of attempting to provide a comprehensive, binding code of constitutional conventions.

---

28 The British North America Act 1867 could be amended only by an Act of the United Kingdom Parliament. The Statute of Westminster 1931 provided, in part, that there should be no change to the 1867 Act which affected the competence of the federal or provincial legislatures.

The Australian experiment

In Australia, a constitutional crisis in 1975 contributed to the experiment in codification of conventions into an authoritative but non-legally binding text. The crisis involved the prerogative power of the Crown in the person of the Governor General to dismiss the Prime Minister and appoint a caretaker Prime Minister on the condition of ensuring the passage of financial legislation and the holding of a general election. One outcome of the crisis – in which the inherent vagueness of the conventional rules was revealed – was formal consideration of the 'codification' of conventions, albeit in a non-legal form. In 1983, a plenary session of the Constitutional Convention adopted a set of 34 practices which were to be 'recognised and declared' as conventions of the Australian constitution. Among those 'recognised' were the powers of the Crown in relation to the Governor General, and his powers in relation to the dismissal of Ministers and powers over Parliament, and the relationship between the Prime Minister and the Governor General in relation to the dissolution of Parliament.[29]

Professor Charles Sampford analysed the merits and demerits of the codification of conventions. Among the many unanswered questions raised are the following. Under what authority did the Constitutional Convention act? What is the effect of the resolution? Is it merely declaratory of the existing rules? If there is a conflict with the restatement and actual practice, which should be authoritative? Professor Sampford contends that there exist three possibilities here. If the code is followed in preference to conventional practice, then the codification goes beyond clarification and becomes a source of the rules themselves. This raises the question 'why should the old rules and old sources give way to the new?' The second approach is that the 'declaration' has whatever force the constitutional actors accord to it: it would be absurd if the declaration were to have no authority. Third, it could be argued that the declaration is merely evidence of the rule. This latter possibility, however, is unsatisfactory in so far as the declaration was intended to be 'sole and conclusive evidence for the existence of the recognised convention. This effectively makes the Constitutional Convention a new source for conventions'. Furthermore, what is the position where a convention was agreed to only by a small majority? What then happens to its authority? To what extent will the new conventions be observed? What is the status of those pre-existing conventions which were not 'recognised and declared'? As can be seen, codification is – even if desirable – by no means a simple matter.

It is clear from the analysis thus far that conventions comprise a set of binding rules, non-legal in nature, which supplement and inform the legal rules of the constitution and which can adapt to meet changing circumstances. Viewed in that light, their primary importance lies in their flexibility. On the other hand, it may be argued cogently that for rules of such importance to be ill-defined, uncertain in application and unenforceable by the courts is, at best, anomalous, and, at worst, a threat to the principle of government according to law.

Further considerations intrude upon the discussion. It has been seen that conventions are flexible. In this feature lies much of their value, and it is to be doubted whether, in relation to such a dynamic organism as the constitution, it would be possible to identify, define and formalise conventions in such a manner both to provide a comprehensive code and to allow for subsequent constitutional development. It may prove to be the case that codification would stultify the growth of the constitution. On the other hand, such codification would undoubtedly provide greater insight into the rules regulating government and thereby act as some check on the power of government. Professor SA de Smith[30] states that codification of

---

29 A previous convention in 1983 had adopted resolutions relating to the conventions regulating the powers of the Queen and the Governor General.
30 de Smith and Brazier, 1998, Chapter 2.

conventions would purchase certainty at the expense of flexibility, and this point must carry great weight in evaluating the desirability of codification.

The relationship between the government and the courts must also be weighed in the balance in this regard. It has been seen that the courts give recognition to, but cannot enforce, conventions. If the effect of codification were to give jurisdiction to the courts, this would represent a very real and problematic shift in the balance of authority and power between the government and the courts. In Chapter 4, the doctrine of the separation of powers is considered in detail. Enough has been said by way of introduction for it to be apparent that if the courts were to be given jurisdiction to adjudicate upon and enforce, by way of legal sanction, the conventional rules of the constitution, this would impinge greatly upon the concept of the separation of powers.

For these reasons, the loss of flexibility and the separation of powers doctrine, it can be argued that conventions should not be codified.

Authoritative works

Finally and in brief, mention should be made of the writings of eminent jurists such as Blackstone, Dicey, Jennings and later commentators to whose works the actors on the constitutional stage, including the judges, may make reference for elucidation of matters of constitutional law.

 SELF-TEST QUESTIONS

To what extent is it accurate to describe the British constitution as 'unwritten' or 'uncodified'?
Give five examples of statutes of constitutional importance.
What do you understand by the term 'common law'? What is the relationship between common law and statute?

Summary

In order to understand the United Kingdom's constitution, which is largely but not wholly unwritten, it is necessary to examine the various legal and non-legal sources. The legal sources include Acts of Parliament and judicial decisions regulating the relationship between institutions of the state and the state and individual citizen. They also include the Royal Prerogative: acts of government undertaken under the authority of the Crown without an Act of Parliament. The law of the European Union and case law under the European Convention on Human Rights are also important sources. The principal non-legal sources of the constitution are constitutional conventions which are binding on those who operate the constitution and give rise to the accusation of unconstitutional (but not unlawful) conduct if not observed.

Underpinning or underlying these sources are the constitutional principles of democracy and responsible government, the separation of powers and the rule of law and the doctrine of parliamentary sovereignty or supremacy.

📖 Further Reading

Barber, NW, 'Laws and constitutional conventions' (2009) 125 *Law Quarterly Review* 294.

Dicey, AV, *Introduction to the Study of the Constitution*, (1885) 1959, London: Macmillan.

Hennessy, P, 'Helicopter crashes into Cabinet: Prime Minister and constitution hurt' (1986) 13 *Journal of Legal Studies* 423.

Jaconelli, J, 'The nature of constitutional conventions' (1999) 19 *Legal Studies* 24.

Jaconelli, J, 'Do constitutional conventions bind?' (2005) 64 *Cambridge Law Journal* 149.

Jennings, Sir I, *Cabinet Government*, 1959, 3rd edn, Cambridge: Cambridge University Press.

Jennings, Sir I, *The Law and the Constitution*, 1959, 5th edn, London: Hodder & Stoughton.

Munro, CR, 'Laws and conventions distinguished' (1975) 91 *Law Quarterly Review* 224.

Munro, CR, *Studies in Constitutional Law*, 1999, 2nd edn, London: Butterworths, Chapter 3.

White Paper, *The Governance of Britain*, 2007, Cm7170.

Wilson, R, 'The robustness of conventions in a time of modernisation and change' [2004] *Public Law* 407.

Part 2

Fundamental Constitutional Concepts

Chapter 3

The Rule of Law

Where laws do not rule, there is no constitution.

Aristotle, *The Politics*, Bk iv, para 1292a31

Chapter Contents

Learning Objectives

By the end of this chapter you should be able to:

☐ explain the different philosophical and political approaches to the rule of law;

☐ explain the constitutional importance of the rule of law in relation to (a) the government and (b) the individual citizen;

☐ evaluate the differing approaches to the rule of law by AV Dicey, Lon Fuller, Joseph Raz, Ronald Dworkin and Lord Bingham;

☐ discuss the ways in which the rule of law is evidenced in the contemporary system of law and governance, with reference to both case law and specific examples of political practice;

☐ offer your own view of the rule of law.

Introduction

The rule of law represents one of the most challenging concepts of the constitution. The rule of law is a concept which is capable of different interpretations by different people, and it is this feature which makes an understanding of the doctrine elusive. Of all constitutional concepts, the rule of law is also the most subjective and value laden. The apparent uncertainties in the rule of law and its variable nature should not cause concern, although, inevitably, they will cause some insecurity. In the study of the rule of law, it is more important to recognise and appreciate the many rich and varied interpretations which have been given to it, and to recognise the potential of the rule of law for ensuring limited governmental power and the protection of individual rights, than to be able to offer an authoritative, definitive explanation of the concept.

The rule of law may be interpreted either as a *philosophy* or *political theory* which lays down fundamental requirements for law, or as a *procedural device* by which those with power rule under the law. The essence of the rule of law is that of the sovereignty or supremacy of law over man. The rule of law insists that every person – irrespective of rank and status in society – be subject to the law. For the citizen, the rule of law is both *prescriptive* – dictating the conduct required by law – and *protective* of citizens – demanding that government acts according to law. This central theme recurs whether the doctrine is examined from the perspective of philosophy, or political theory, or from the more pragmatic vantage point of the rule of law as a procedural device. The rule of law underlies the entire constitution and, in one sense, all constitutional law is concerned with the rule of law. The concept is of great antiquity and continues to exercise legal and political philosophers today.

The rule of law cannot be viewed in isolation from political society. The emphasis on the rule of law as a yardstick for measuring both the extent to which government acts under the law and the extent to which individual rights are recognised and protected by law, is inextricably linked with Western democratic liberalism.[1] In this respect, it is only meaningful to speak of the rule of law in a society which exhibits the features of a democratically elected, responsible – and responsive – government and a separation of powers, which will result in a judiciary which is independent of government. In liberal democracies, therefore, the concept of the rule of law implies an acceptance that law itself represents a 'good'; that law and its governance is a demonstrable asset to society.

---

1 See, *inter alia*, Fine, 1984; Hutchinson and Monahan, 1987; Neumann, 1986.

Contrasting Attitudes to the Rule of Law

It should not be assumed that this acceptance of law as a benevolent ruling force is universally accepted. In differing societies, subscribing to very different political philosophies, the insistence on the rule of law – in the Western liberal sense – has little application. For example, from a Marxist perspective (on which see below) the law serves not to restrict government and protect individual rights but rather to conceal the injustices inherent in the capitalist system. Accordingly, the concept of the rule of law – denoting some form of morality in law – represents no more than a false idealisation of law designed to reinforce the political structure and economic status quo in society. Echoes of this thesis dominate the more moderate socialist conceptions of the rule of law and the critique of liberalism. It can be argued – from the socialist perspective – that liberalism pays too little regard to true equality between persons and too great attention to the protection of property interests. The liberal domain thus becomes one which, again, masks true social and economic inequality while at the same time proclaiming equality and justice under the rule of law.[2]

The rule of law, as understood in liberal democracies, also has little relevance in a totalitarian state. While it is true that such a state will be closely regulated by law, there will not be government under the law – as adjudicated upon by an independent judiciary – which is insisted upon under the liberal tradition.

In traditional Oriental society, the Western preference for law is an alien notion. By way of example, in relation to traditional Chinese society, David and Brierley write:

> For the Chinese, legislation was not the normal means of guaranteeing a harmonious and smooth-working society. Laws, abstract in nature, could not take into account the infinite variety of possible situations. Their strict application was apt to affect man's innate sense of justice. To enact laws was therefore considered a bad policy by traditional Chinese doctrine. The very exactitude which laws establish in social relations, and the way in which they fix the rights and obligations of each individual, were considered evils, according to the Chinese, not benefits. The idea of 'rights', an inevitable development of the laws themselves, ran counter to the natural order. Once individuals think of their 'rights' there is, it was thought, some form of social illness; the only true matter of concern is one's duty to society and one's fellow men.

> The enactment of laws is an evil, since individuals, once familiar with them, will conclude that they have rights and will then be inclined to assert them, thereby abandoning the traditional rules of propriety and morality which should be the only guides to conduct. Legal disputes become numerous, and a trial, by reason of its very existence, is a scandalous disturbance of the natural order which may then lead to further disturbances of the social order to the detriment of all society. [1966, page 442; and see 3rd edn, 1985, Title III, Chapter 1 for the persistence of traditional ideas]

In Japan, despite the nineteenth-century adoption of codes based on French and German models,[3] law, in the Western sense, remained largely irrelevant to traditional Japanese life:

---

2 For a critical account of the liberal tradition see Lustgarten, 1988.
3 Penal Code and Code of Criminal Procedure enacted in 1882; Codes on Judicial Organisation and Civil Procedure 1890; Commercial Code 1899.

> Still essential for the Japanese are the rules of behaviour (*giri-ninjo*) for each type of personal relation established by tradition and founded, at least in appearance, on the feelings of affection (*ninjo*) uniting those in such relationships. A person who does not observe these rules is seeking his own interest rather than obeying the nobler part of his nature; he brings scorn upon himself and his family. Apart from the contracts arising between important but depersonalised business and industrial concerns, one does not attempt to have one's rights enforced in a court of law even though this is permitted by the various codes. [David and Brierley, *Major Legal Systems* 1966, page 458; see 3rd edn, Title III, Chapter 2]

As the notion of the rule of law is dependent upon the political foundations of a state, so, too, it is dependent – according to the approach adopted to the concept – upon a nation's economic resources. It may be that law, as a mere regulator of individual behaviour, is perfectly feasible in an impoverished state, and, accordingly, a state which maintains law and order, and no more, can conform to a narrow interpretation of the rule of law which insists simply on a citizen's unquestioning compliance with rules of the law. However, if the rule of law implies more than mere regulation by law and is elevated to a theory guaranteeing freedom from hunger and homelessness and entitlement to a basic decent standard of life, then economic conditions are of paramount importance to conformity with the rule of law. Such an approach is adopted by the International Commission of Jurists, which in the New Delhi Declaration of 1959 included – alongside traditional civil and political rights – the realisation of social, economic, cultural and educational standards under which the individual could enjoy a fuller life within the ambit of the rule of law. On the other hand, reasoning such as this is anathema to radical conservatives such as Friedrich von Hayek (1944), who viewed the correct role of government as being best confined to establishing clear, fixed rules of law which ensure maximum economic freedom for individuals, unimpeded either by planning controls or ideas of redistributive justice. From von Hayek's perspective, the rule of law requires no more than the existence of a stable set of minimum rules which are to be applied in a uniform, non-discretionary manner. A legal system is viewed as just – and in conformity with the rule of law – if it exhibits both these features and an absence of discretionary rules or practices.

Uncertainty in the Western Rule of Law

An understanding and appreciation of the rule of law is both politically and culturally dependent. Moreover, it is also clear that the rule of law has more than one meaning, even within the Western liberal tradition. To some theorists, the rule of law represents an aspirational philosophy; to others, it is no more than a device under which compliance with law – good or bad in content – is secured. It has been remarked that: 'It would not be very difficult to show that the phrase "the rule of law" has become meaningless thanks to ideological abuse and general over-use'.[4] Partly as a result of such 'over-use', some writers have refuted the claim that the rule of law represents anything other than a purely procedural or formalistic device. By way of example, Raz writes that the rule of law: 'says nothing about how the law is to be made: by tyrants, democratic majorities, or any other way. It says nothing about fundamental rights, about equality, or justice'.[5]

---

4 Shklar, 'Political theory and the rule of law', in Hutchinson and Monahan, 1987, p. 1.
5 See Raz, 1979, p. 210. On Dicey's influence see below, pp. 64 ff.; de Smith and Brazier, 1998.

Contrast such views with that expressed in the following statement:

> The rule of law is a rare and protean principle of our political tradition. Unlike other ideals, it has withstood the ravages of constitutional time and remains a contemporary clarion-call to political justice. Apparently transcending partisan concern, it is embraced and venerated by virtually all shades of political opinion. The rule of law's central core comprises the enduring values of regularity and restraint, embodied in the slogan of 'a government of laws, not ... men'. [Hutchinson and Monahan, 1987, page ix]

In light of such divergent assessments, it must be recognised that any attempt to align the rule of law with a broad philosophical doctrine – or indeed with any other interpretation – is likely to meet with opposition from some quarters. Notwithstanding such criticisms, the rule of law retains a secure grasp on political and legal thinking: in the words of Raz (1979), it has 'enduring importance as a central artefact in our legal and political culture'.

Natural Law and the Rule of Law

The rule of law is an aspect of ancient and modern natural law thought.[6] In essence, the natural law tradition – of which there are many strands – insists that the authority of law derives not from the power of any political ruler, but from a higher source, either theological or secular. The laws of man must be evaluated against the dictates of this 'higher' form of law. It is impossible to provide more than a mere sketch of the rich history of natural law in Western philosophy and political thought and the legacy it gives to modern constitutions. Nevertheless, a basic understanding of its nature and evolution is instructive, for it reveals the manner in which the requirements of good law – morally worthwhile law – have been stipulated over centuries.

Natural law in Ancient Greece and Rome

Aristotle stated in *The Politics* that 'the rule of law is preferable to that of any individual'. The appeal to law as a control over naked power has been apparent throughout history. At a philosophical level, the natural law tradition, whether theological or secular, instructs that the power of man is not absolute, but is rather controlled and limited by the requirements of a higher law. To the ancient Greeks, man was under the governance of the laws of nature – the natural forces which controlled the universe – although this view is more closely aligned to the 'law of nature' than 'natural law' as it came to be understood in later times. However, from the time of Socrates (470–399 BC), Plato (427–347 BC) and Aristotle (384–322 BC), the quest for virtue – or goodness or justice under the law – has been a recurrent theme. Socrates, a teacher and philosopher, was accused, tried and convicted by the grand jury of Athens for corrupting youth with his teachings. Despite the possibility of escape, Socrates chose to accept the verdict of death which had been imposed upon him, in order to demonstrate his fidelity to law. When pressed by Crito to escape, Socrates considered the questions which would be put to him by the laws and constitution of Athens were he to succumb to the temptation to escape the penalty of the law:

> Can you deny that by this act [of escaping] which you are contemplating you intend, so far as you have the power, to destroy us, the laws, and the whole state as well?

---

6 On natural law, see d'Entrèves, 1970; and Finnis, 1980.

> Do you imagine that a city can continue to exist and not be turned upside down, if the legal judgments which are pronounced in it have no force but are nullified and destroyed by private persons? [Crito, in Hamilton and Cairns, 1989, page 50b]

In submitting to death, Socrates was doing nothing other than giving recognition to the supremacy of law: to the rule of law. An early – and famous – formulation of the dictates of natural law was offered by Cicero (106–43 BC):

> True law is right reason in agreement with nature; it is of universal application, unchanging and everlasting; it summons to duty by its commands, and averts from wrongdoing by its prohibitions. And it does not lay its commands or prohibitions upon good men in vain, though neither have any effect on the wicked. It is a sin to try to alter this law, nor is it allowable to attempt to repeal any part of it, and it is impossible to abolish it entirely. We cannot be freed from its obligations by Senate or People, and we need not look outside ourselves for an expounder or interpreter of it. And there will not be different laws at Rome and at Athens, or different laws now and in the future, but one eternal and unchangeable law will be valid for all nations and for all times, and there will be one master and one ruler, that is, God, over us all, for He is the author of this law, its promulgator, and its enforcing judge. [De Republica, cited in d'Entrèves, 1970, page 25]

It is from ancient Greek philosophy that natural law enters into Roman law. From the *Corpus Iuris Civilis* (AD 534) are derived *ius civilis*, *ius gentium* and *ius naturale*. *Ius civilis* denotes the law of the state, *ius gentium* the law of nations and *ius naturale* 'a law which expresses a higher and more permanent standard'. It is the law of nature (*ius naturale*) which corresponds to 'that which is always good and equitable' (d'Entrèves, 1970, page 24).

Christian natural law thought

The scriptures and gospel provided the basis for Christian natural law thought which developed in the Middle Ages. Natural law was perceived as God-given, communicated to man by Revelation and remaining absolutely binding upon man and unchanging in its content. As a result, the dictates of natural law take precedence over man-made laws. If the demands of the state conflict with the laws of God, the obligation to God must prevail. Undoubtedly, the most powerful writing of the Middle Ages comes from St Thomas Aquinas (1225–1274):

> This rational guidance of created things on the part of God ... we can call the Eternal Law.

> But, of all others, rational creatures are subject to divine Providence in a very special way; being themselves made participators in Providence itself, in that they control their own actions and the actions of others. So they have a share in the divine reason itself, deriving therefrom a natural inclination to such actions and ends as are fitting. This participation in the Eternal Law by rational creatures is called Natural Law. [Summa Theologica, cited in d'Entrèves, 1970, page 43]

In the thirteenth century, Bracton proclaimed that 'the King himself ought not be subject to man but subject to God and to the law, because the law makes him King' (1968–1977, f.5 b). In 1534, Thomas More (1478–1535) – at the cost of his life – refused to recognise Henry VIII as head of the Church, thereby acknowledging the higher duty of obedience to God rather than the rule of his temporal King.

Natural law and international law

On an international level, natural law thought played a significant role in establishing the over-arching dictates of international law. Grotius (1583–1645), for example, maintained that natural law was discernible by man by virtue of his rationality and that a system of natural law would accordingly exist independently of theological perceptions and dictates. In short, natural law would exist even if God did not exist. In addition to the insistence on rationalism, the emphasis of natural law at this time started to focus on the individual, and from this period is discerned the origins of assertions of the rights of man. AP d'Entrèves writes:

> when we read the American or the French Declarations we know that we are confronted with a complete architecture, about the style of which there can be no mistake. It is a political philosophy based upon a particular notion of the individual, of society and of their mutual relationship. [1970, page 57]

Natural law and common law

In the West, the sovereignty of law became inextricably linked with the Christian faith. In England, the break with the Roman Catholic Church in 1535 established Henry VIII as head of the English Church. By assuming supreme power over both spiritual and secular matters, Henry VIII ostensibly broke the logical separation of duty towards God and the duty owed to the King: obedience to the sovereign now became a religious as well as a political duty. The execution of Sir Thomas More in 1535 is illustrative of the King's reaction to an individual refusal to recognise the absolute supremacy of the King. Nevertheless, natural law thought continued to permeate the common law of England before the settlement of 1688 and the rise of parliamentary sovereignty.

One of the classic exponents of the demand for the King to be subject to the law – rather than above it – was Sir Edward Coke (1552–1634), whose struggle with the King led to his dismissal as Chief Justice in 1616. James I[7] viewed himself as imbued with ultimate power, derived from God under the prerogative. To Coke, laws derived from Parliament, and the power of Parliament was subject to the common law, and accordingly Coke took the view that: 'when an Act of Parliament is against the common right or repugnant or impossible to be performed the common law will control it and adjudge such Act to be void'.[8]

When, in 1608, Coke told the King that the common law protected the King, the King regarded his speech as traitorous. Nevertheless, Coke's view expresses an idea which is central to natural law thought, namely that there is a higher authority – based on moral judgment – than the law of man. With the settlement of 1688 and the Bill of Rights 1689, the doctrine of parliamentary supremacy over the King, the prerogative and common law was established. Thereafter, there were to be no assertions of any overriding higher law. The judges bowed to the sovereignty of Parliament.

---

7 King of Scotland 1567–1625; King of England and Scotland 1603–1625.
8 **Dr Bonham's Case** (1610). But see the contrary explanation offered by Thorne, 1938.

Social Contract Theory

See Chapter 6.

It is from natural law principles that the theories of social contract and the rights of man derive. The writings of John Locke and Thomas Paine are infused with the doctrine of the inalienability of individual human rights – rights which transcend the law of the state, which cannot be overridden by the state and which affirm the supremacy of the law of the state with the important proviso that the law of the state is in compliance with natural law.[9]

Thomas Hobbes[10] offered the most extreme version of the social contract theory, arguing that man by nature is incapable of regulating his life in peace and harmony with his fellow man. Hobbes' view of man in a society lacking a restraining all-powerful sovereign was inherently pessimistic, an attitude encapsulated in the often quoted phrase that life is 'solitary, poor, nasty, brutish and short'. In order for there to be civil order, it was necessary for each man to surrender to the state his own sovereignty in exchange for security. Such a surrender was revocable only if the state abused its trust. The requirement of obedience to law is strict; and yet there are limits:

> If the Soveraign command a man (though justly condemned) to kill, wound, or mayme himselfe; or not to resist those that assault him; or to abstain from the use of food, ayre, medicine, or any other thing, without which he cannot live; yet hath that man the Liberty to disobey.

Further, Hobbes states that:

> The Obligation of Subjects to the Soveraign, is understood to last as long, and no longer, than the power lasteth, by which he is able to protect them. For the right men have by Nature to protect themselves, when none else can protect them, can by no Covenant be relinquished.

According to Jean-Jacques Rousseau,[11] the citizen enters into a 'contract' with the state, surrendering to the state individual rights in exchange for the protection of the state. The state, according to Rousseau, is thus embodied in the 'general will' of the people and becomes both the agent and ruler of the people in the people's name. Rousseau's vision of man differs markedly from that of Thomas Hobbes – far from living in a state of 'war' with one another, men in the 'natural state' of primitive society would have nothing to fight over and would be united in a community of endeavour to secure the essential provisions of life. Man comes together – from necessity – within civil society, and, through participation in the decision-making processes, produces a democratic society. Rousseau distinguishes between supreme power – sovereignty – and the government. Sovereignty lies with the people, and is absolute and inalienable. The government's power is less absolute, established to implement the will of the people and accountable to the people. The government is dependent upon the sovereign people for the continuation of its power, and the people retain the right to revoke the power devolved.

Thus, for Rousseau, sovereignty is a concept which entails moral approval and acceptance by the people whose 'collective will' sovereignty represents.[12] Indeed, for Rousseau:

> the sovereign, being formed wholly of the individuals who compose it, neither has nor can have any interest contrary to theirs; and consequently the sovereign power

---

9 Locke, 1690; Paine, 1791, Pt I.
10 *The Leviathan*, 1651.
11 *The Social Contract and Discourses*, p. 176.
12 *Ibid.*, Bk I, Chapter VII, and Bk II.

need give no guarantee to its subjects, because it is impossible for the body to wish to hurt all its members. We shall also see later on that it cannot hurt any in particular. The sovereign, merely by virtue of what it is, is always what it should be. [page 177]

Thomas Paine advances a social contract theory in which the rights of the individual are given central importance.[13] Paine both influenced and was influenced by the French and American Revolutions. In *Rights of Man*, Paine argued that the citizen gives up his rights to the state, but on a conditional basis. The state is placed in the position of trustee of the rights of man, and should that trust be broken, the citizen has the ultimate – or sovereign – right to depose the government. Paine argues that man has natural rights, 'those which appertain to man in right of his existence'. These rights are both individualistic and civil. The former category includes: 'all the intellectual rights, or rights of the mind, and also all those rights of acting as an individual for his own comfort and happiness, which are not injurious to the natural rights of others'. By way of distinction: 'Civil rights are those which appertain to man in right of his being a member of society. Every civil right has for its foundation, some natural right pre-existing in the individual' (page 90).

These natural and civil rights are held by government on trust for the people, and should – under an ideal constitution – be protected from governmental abuse by a Bill of Rights. Such an approach is also taken by John Locke, who regards the people, as a collectivity, as holding the sovereign power which is in some sense delegated to the government on trust, and who may accordingly exert their sovereign power to remove the government if it violates its sacred trust.

In *Two Treatises of Government*, John Locke advances powerful arguments for the limits of governmental power and the ultimate political sovereignty of the people. In Book II,[14] Locke argues that men come together in civil society and tacitly consent to be ruled by government directed to 'the peace, safety, and public good of the people'. Hence, the power accorded to government is not absolute, but whilst in existence, the legislative power is the 'supreme power'. Nevertheless, Locke concludes that if the people:

have set limits to the duration of their legislative, and made this supreme power in any person or assembly only temporary, it is forfeited; upon the forfeiture of their rules, or at the determination of the time set, it reverts to the society, and the people have a right to act as supreme, and continue the legislative in themselves or place it in a new form, or new hands, as they think good. [page 242]

Sovereignty, then, is limited and conditional: government holds supreme power on trust for the people. On this view, the authority of the constitution will be dependent upon its conformity with a higher law. As KC Wheare explains:

This view of government limited by the natural rights of man lies at the basis of the American Constitution and finds a place ... in many modern constitutions. It provides a moral basis upon which a government's actions can be judged and, what is more, upon which the validity of a constitution can be tested. A constitution binds in so far as it is in accordance with natural law. Neither a government nor a citizen may disregard the authority of a constitution except in so far as the action can be justified by the law of nature. This is indeed a 'higher law' than a constitution. [1966, page 65]

---

13 *Rights of Man*, 1791, Pt 1.
14 'An essay concerning the true original extent and end of civil government'.

Law and Order: The Obligation to Obey Law

A very different approach to the rule of law may be labelled the 'law and order' model. In legal philosophy, the idea of obedience to law is compatible with the analytical, positivist school of thought which dominated much jurisprudential thought from the nineteenth century until after the Second World War. In the nineteenth-century analysis of John Austin, for example, law is the command of a sovereign (or sovereign body), whose authority and law-making power is exemplified by the 'habit of obedience' of the people.[15] Positivism is the antithesis of natural law (discussed above). The primary quest for positivists is to separate legal and moral issues: to distinguish between the 'is' (that which exists as fact) and the 'ought' (that which is desirable). This does not make morality irrelevant to the law; far from it. First, much of law is explained by reference to society's moral values: the law relating to murder, assaults, the protection of the young and vulnerable is grounded in morality. Second, from an analytical perspective, having a clear distinction between law and morals enables the law to be evaluated and criticised from a moral standpoint.

On the plus side, the 'law and order' model emphasises the desirability of the peaceful settlement of disputes without recourse to violence, armed force or terrorism. However, taken to its logical conclusion, the 'law and order' view can lead to the suppression of freedom and accordingly it must be tempered with other considerations. A fundamental question here is the extent to which individuals are expected to obey laws which, although valid on the basis that they have been formally enacted by Parliament, are nevertheless perceived to be 'unjust' when judged against different criteria: namely morality.

Is there an absolute obligation to obey, irrespective of the moral quality of the law? Or is the duty only *prima facie*? Is there ever a duty to disobey the law in pursuit of a higher ideal? Each of these vast and timeless philosophical questions underpins the concept of the rule of law.

Both natural law and social contract theory, discussed above, in differing ways imply that there are limits to the obligation to obey law.

Is there a duty to obey law?

To be balanced against the arguments for strict obedience to law is the legitimacy of protest against unjust law. Since the time of Aristotle, it has been argued that the law must be tempered with equity, which dictates the standards of justice and rightness in society. Law derives its authority from the obedience of the people.[16] Laws must be directed to the 'good', not only to comply with the dictates of morality, but also for the more pragmatic reason of ensuring voluntary compliance with law. It may be argued that nowadays in a responsive, democratic state, any dispute as to the rights of individuals and grievances against government action will be dealt with through the provided channels of complaint, for example through the individual's Member of Parliament or through an investigation by the Commissioners for Administration.[17] Alternatively, it may be argued that if many citizens are commonly aggrieved, the media can be employed to influence government and that, ultimately, at least once every five years,[18] the electorate can express its views through the ballot box. None of these avenues, however, may yield the desired result, particularly if the aggrieved individual or group is a minority without popular support.

---

15 See *The Province of Jurisprudence Determined*, 1865.
16 Aristotle, *The Politics*, 1269a.
17 See Chapter 28.
18 Under the Parliament Act 1911, the maximum life of a Parliament is five years. See further Chapter 13.

Is there a right to disobey law?

The question that then arises is whether the individual has a 'right' to disobey the law.[19] A government true to democratic precepts of representativeness and fairness must be sensitive to demands for change. If it fails in that regard, it is at least arguable that demands for change, while entailing technical breaches of the law, should be accommodated within the constitutional framework.

In 1848, Henry Thoreau refused to pay taxes to support the slavery laws and declared: 'the place for a just man in such a community is in jail'.

In the same century, the suffragette movement resorted to unlawful behaviour in the ultimately successful pursuit of the right to enfranchisement – the right to vote.[20] Mahatma Gandhi's peaceful civil disobedience campaign led to the independence of India in 1947. The Civil Rights movement in the United States in the 1950s, led by Martin Luther King, resulted in reforms of the law concerning racial segregation.[21] The tide of protest over American involvement in the Vietnam war had a direct impact on government policy and further raised legal and political interest in civil disobedience. Major social changes of such magnitude would have been impossible without recognition that under certain limited conditions there exists a right of legitimate protest, however inconvenient and uncomfortable this is for governments.

John Rawls concedes a right to disobedience in pursuit of changing a society's 'sense of justice', but confines civil disobedience to peaceful protest.[22] Rawls' thesis is founded on the notion of social contract. That concept, as has been seen above, involves the mutual recognition, *inter alia*, of the rights of citizens and the rights of the state. The extent to which citizens participate in the law-making process is critical to an understanding of the extent to which there exists an obligation to obey the law. Participation in the democratic process may, however, be used as a means to deny any right to disobey. That is to say, it may be argued that democratic participation implies the individual's acceptance of all laws within the state. Here we must consider what it is that citizens consent to when electing a government. It seems implausible to argue that we each consent to every action of government throughout a possible five-year term of office, irrespective of its merits. However, Professor Plamenatz states that when a vote is cast:

> you put yourself by your vote under an obligation to obey whatever government comes legally to power under the system, and this can properly be called giving consent. For the purpose of an election is to give authority to the people who win it and if you vote, knowing what you are doing and without being compelled to do it, you voluntarily take part in the process, which gives authority to those people. [1963, Volume 1, page 239]

This argument surely is contentious and represents a very limited view of the requirement that a government should have moral authority to govern. Richard Wasserstrom (1963), on the other hand, argues that, by the participatory democratic process, a prima facie obligation to obey law is imposed, but this prima facie duty can be overridden by the demands of conscience.

The appropriate response of the state to acts of civil disobedience is a difficult matter. Professor Ronald Dworkin, for example, argues for official tolerance in the face of dissent and

19 See Rawls, 1973, Chapter 7.
20 See, inter alia, Kent, 1987.
21 **Brown v Board of Education of Topeka** (1954); and see King, 1963.
22 Rawls, 1973, Chapter 6.

law breaking which is undertaken in pursuit of rights – even where violence is employed.[23] In *Taking Rights Seriously*, Dworkin argued that the state should act with caution in prosecuting civilly disobedient acts. First, the state should respect the stand taken in the defence of rights, even if that stand should prove misguided when the matter ultimately comes before the Supreme Court for a ruling on the validity of the contentious legislation. The decision to prosecute should be decided on the basis of utilitarianism.[24] As Dworkin stated in *A Matter of Principle*:

> Utilitarianism may be a poor general theory of justice, but it states an excellent necessary condition for just punishment. Nobody should ever be punished unless punishing him will do some good on the whole in the long run all things considered. [1985, page 114]

By prosecuting disobedience to law, the state upholds the positive law and reinforces it. On the other hand, in prosecuting, the state may reveal the defects in the law and may be seen to be enforcing that for which there exists little or no popular support. It may also be argued that by rigid enforcement the state enhances the moral claims advanced by one alleging injustice. In part, this was the view adopted by Socrates (c.470–399 BC) in submitting to his fate. A critic of the state, Socrates was falsely accused and convicted of corrupting the minds of the youth of Athens and of 'impiety'. He was sentenced to death to be caused by drinking a mixture containing poison. He drank the poison to show respect to the law and constitution of Athens, although he must have known that in so doing he would bring the law of the state into disrepute. What he could not foresee was the timeless example that Athens, in executing Socrates, set for humanity.[25]

Is there a duty to disobey?

The converse position must also be considered: if a state violates the requirements of the rule of law, to what extent is it the duty of citizens to disobey the law? Furthermore, what justification, if any, is there for another state or the international community taking action against the 'guilty' state? The Nazi regime in Germany provides the most obvious – but not unique – example (see the discussion at pages 72 to 73, below). On individual duty, Professor Lon Fuller maintained that the citizen is under no obligation to obey unjust law: 'A mere respect for constituted authority must not be confused with fidelity to law'. Fuller goes further and asserts that an evil regime, which grossly violates the basic precepts of morality, is incapable of creating law at all.[26] In HLA Hart's view, this represents confused thinking on Fuller's part. His preferred approach is to recognise the validity of Nazi laws – however abhorrent in moral terms – but also to recognise that moral obligations can outweigh the legal obligation to obey.[27] In addition to facilitating clarity about law, this approach enables the regime to be held to account for its actions. Simply to deny – as does Professor Fuller – that there was any law during Nazi rule is to remove the basis for international legal sanctions.

---

23 Dworkin, 1977, Chapters 7 and 8; and see MacGuigan, 'Obligation and obedience', in Pennock and Chapman, 1970.
24 The doctrine which assesses the justification for a particular action according to the overall increase in the sum of benefit to society as a whole.
25 See Plato, 'Socrates' defence and "Crito"', in Hamilton and Cairns, 1989.
26 Fuller, 1958.
27 Hart, 1958, p. 593 – a view echoing that of St Thomas Aquinas.

Pause and Reflect

1. How should the state react to people who break the law with the intention of bringing about a reform of a 'bad' law? Giving reasons for your answer, should the state:

   (a) ignore the unlawful behaviour;
   (b) prosecute the offender and apply the normal sanction;
   (c) prosecute but ensure that a minimal or no sanction is applied?

2. In a democracy such as the United Kingdom, individuals have an elected representative in Parliament to whom they can complain, a free press, the right to freedom of expression and peaceful demonstration. In light of these factors, under what circumstances, if any, can an individual be morally justified in engaging in civil disobedience?
3. What is the justification for stating that citizens are 'obliged' to obey law?

Marxism and the Rule of Law

Arguments against a formalistic perception of the rule of law adopted by, *inter alia*, Dicey and von Hayek present a formidable target for attack from a Marxist perspective. Where liberalism insists that law is neutral as between persons and classes and favours maximum liberty for all under the law, Marxism insists that law represents the interests of the powerful within society. Law is an ideological device engaged by those with power to mask the reality of that power in society, and the correlative powerlessness of the ordinary citizen. The rule of law is thus portrayed as a means of subterfuge: it is a mere pretence which hides injustice. Marxism stands in opposition to liberalism and yet, paradoxically, seeks as its end result the complete liberty of man. Law, from a Marxist perspective, is the reflection of economic power within society, a power which is used to exploit the powerless. Thus it is that, under capitalism, the worker is not rewarded with the full value of his labour: rather, he receives a price for his labour to which is added production costs and profits, and together these comprise the final price of a product. The laws which regulate factories and employment terms are all underpinned by the acceptance of the capitalist ideal. Laws which ameliorate the conditions of the poor do not represent – as appears at first sight – real social justice, but rather they represent a calculated means by which the poor are kept compliant within their powerlessness.[28] Accordingly, the welfare state is but a cynical mask for maintenance of the status quo which defeats the movement towards revolutionary economic and social change:

> Far from hastening the revolution, the welfare state undermines efforts to create working class solidarity. By preventing the fullest development of the material degradation of the working class and by providing a limited immunity from the vicissitudes of economic crises, a welfare state delays the formation of class consciousness and thus prevents a revolutionary situation from arising. [Collins, 1982, pages 126–127]

Whether law serves to oppress or merely to uphold the economic status quo – and there exists dispute on this matter between Marxists themselves – law, from a Marxist perspective does not serve the interest of all in society. The rule of law thus becomes a grand slogan under which is hidden the reality of oppression and absence of liberty. The capitalists' insistence on

---

28 See Cain and Hunt, 1979.

the rule of law is seen as a 'fetishism' which must be removed along with economic oppression (Cain, 1979, Chapter 5). Only when the capitalist system breaks down and the law which serves it 'withers' will society become truly free. When that occurs, there will be no need for law and man will achieve true freedom.

Dicey and the Rule of Law

In *Introduction to the Study of the Law of the Constitution*, AV Dicey offered a prosaic explanation of the rule of law. Here, there are none of the ringing proclamations of the theological or political philosophers. Nevertheless, Dicey's views have continued to exert their influence, despite many challenges, and it is this influence which requires examination.

Dicey argued that the rule of law – in its practical manifestation – has three main aspects:

- no man is punishable or can be lawfully made to suffer in body or goods except for a distinct breach of law established in the ordinary legal manner before the ordinary courts of the land. In this sense, the rule of law is contrasted with every system of government based on the exercise by persons in authority of wide, arbitrary, or discretionary powers of constraint;
- no man is above the law; every man and woman, whatever be his or her rank or condition, is subject to the ordinary law of the realm and amenable to the jurisdiction of the ordinary tribunals; and
- the general principles of the constitution (as, for example, the right to personal liberty, or the right of public meeting) are, with us, the result of judicial decisions determining the rights of private persons in particular cases brought before the courts.

Each of these points requires examination.

Lack of arbitrariness and retrospectivity

The first element of this analysis is self-explanatory. It requires that no one be punished except for conduct which represents a clear breach of law.[29] Designed to deny governments any right to make secret or arbitrary laws, or retrospective penal laws, and to limit the discretionary powers of government, the rule protects the individual. In order to comply fully with this requirement, laws should be open and accessible, clear and certain. In part, this idea ties in with that of the 'social contract' and the reciprocal relationship between the state and the individual. Under social contract theories, the individual citizen transfers his autonomous individual rights to the government, to be held by that government on trust. To express the matter differently, the citizen owes allegiance to the Crown in return for which he is under the protection of the Crown.[30] The doctrine of allegiance incorporates the idea of obedience to law – both on the part of the citizen and on the part of government. Laws which are arbitrary or secret are incapable of justification on the basis of the mandate of the people and, accordingly, offend against the reciprocal relationship on which constitutional democracy depends. Where wide discretionary powers are conferred on the executive – whether they be in the form of granting power to a Minister of the Crown to act 'as he thinks fit' or on civil servants administering the social welfare system – it will be impossible for the individual

---

29 The principle of *nulla poena sine lege*.
30 See Chitty, 1820, discussed in Chapter 6.

to know what rights he or she has. Moreover, the delegation of broad discretionary power – albeit on the authority of the sovereign Parliament – renders such power difficult, if not impossible, to challenge before a court of law or other adjudicatory tribunal.[31]

If retrospective penal liability is imposed, the individual is placed in the position where his conduct was lawful at the time of his action but, subsequently, he is held responsible as if his conduct was then unlawful. An examination and evaluation of the relevance of this first proposition entails drawing on relevant illustrations from both statute and case law. For example, the courts construe penal statutes narrowly and will be slow to find that Parliament intended to impose retrospective liability. So important is the concept of *mens rea* in the criminal law[32] that it will rarely be appropriate for a prosecution to succeed in its absence, and it is for this reason that the courts employ the presumption of statutory interpretation against retrospectivity:

> Perhaps no rule of construction is more firmly established than this – that a retrospective operation is not to be given to a statute so as to impair an existing right or obligation, otherwise than as regards matters of procedure, unless that effect cannot be avoided without doing violence to the language of the enactment. If the enactment is expressed in language which is fairly capable of either interpretation, it ought to be construed as prospective only.[33]

In **Waddington v Miah** (1974), the House of Lords interpreted the Immigration Act 1971 in a manner which denied retrospective effect in relation to criminal offences, using, as an aid to construction, Article 7 of the European Convention on Human Rights, which guarantees freedom from retrospectivity. Nonetheless, the presumption will not be available where Parliament expressly provides for retrospectivity, as, for example, in the War Damage Act 1965 and the War Crimes Act 1991.[34] In **Burmah Oil v Lord Advocate** (1965), where the House of Lords had awarded compensation for the destruction of oil installations in wartime, the government speedily introduced legislation nullifying the effect of the decision under the War Damage Act 1965. This case demonstrates clearly the subordination of the judiciary to parliamentary supremacy and the limits thereby imposed on the judges' capacity to uphold rights.

Notwithstanding the general prohibition against retrospectivity, there may be instances where a decision which imposes, for example, criminal liability may be upheld by the courts. For example, until 1990, there existed a time-honoured exemption from the law of rape for husbands who raped their wives. In the case of **R v R** (1991), however, the House of Lords (then the highest court in the domestic legal system) upheld the conviction of a husband for the rape of his wife, arguing that the rule against liability for rape within marriage was anachronistic. In a challenge to this decision under the European Convention on Human Rights, on the basis that it infringed Article 7 of the Convention, which makes retrospectivity unlawful, the Court of Human Rights ruled that the sweeping away of husbands' immunity from criminal prosecution and conviction for rape represented an evolution towards greater equality between the sexes and was consistent with that equality.[35]

---

31 See Smith, 1985.
32 *Sweet v Parsley* (1970).
33 Wright J in *Re Athlumney* (1898), pp. 551–552.
34 See Chapter 6.
35 *SW v United Kingdom; CR v United Kingdom* (1995).

Equality before the law: government under the law

Dicey's second limb emphasises the notion that government itself is subject to law and that everyone, irrespective of rank, whether official or individual, shall be subject to the law,[36] and subject to the same courts. Dicey viewed the French system of special courts to deal with complaints against government as abhorrent, fearing that specially constituted courts would unduly favour the government over the citizen. Dicey has often been interpreted as requiring that there be actual equality in terms of legal rights, powers and capacities. Such an interpretation is, however, misguided. The idea of equality before the law, irrespective of status, is subject to so many exceptions 'that the statement is of doubtful value'.[37] In so far as equal powers are concerned, it must be recognised that the police have powers over and above the citizen,[38] that Ministers have power to enact delegated legislation (but subject to parliamentary approval), that the Crown enjoys immunities under the law, that the government acting in the name of the Crown may exercise prerogative powers which may defeat the rights of individuals, that Members of Parliament have immunity from the law of defamation under the privileges of Parliament[39] and that diplomats enjoy immunities not available to citizens. And, as Sir Ivor Jennings points out, no two citizens are entirely equal: 'pawnbrokers, money lenders, landlords, drivers of motor cars, married women, and indeed most other classes have special rights and duties' (1959b, Appendix II, page 11).

Against this catalogue, which is not exhaustive, must be set the extent to which government and public officials are subject to law in the sense of being accountable for their actions before the ordinary courts, for this, indeed, was Dicey's real argument. The doctrine acknowledges the need of a consistent application of the law irrespective of status. No one is immune from criminal prosecution (other than the monarch: 'Against the King law has no coercive power').[40]

Official accountability to law is one of the foundations of the rule of law. Following a detailed analysis of Dicey's writing, Professor Jeffrey Jowell concludes that:

> its ghost has refused to rest. It rises still to haunt a minister who publishes 'guidelines' that cut across the powers of the statute under which he operates, the minister who penalises local authorities for overspending without giving them a fair hearing, a government department which decides in accordance with a secret code not available to the public, or a Prime Minister who seeks to deprive civil servants of their rights to remain members of a trade union. ['The rule of law and its underlying values', in Jowell and Oliver, 2011]

Sir Ivor Jennings criticises Dicey's emphasis on government according to law on the basis that it is too narrow an interpretation: 'it is a small point upon which to base a doctrine called by the magnificent name of "rule of law", particularly when it is generally used in a very different sense' (1959b, page 312).

Sir Ivor Jennings also criticises Dicey for being motivated by his conservative views. Dicey, in expressing his preference for clear and stable rules and the minimum of discretion within the legal process, was, according to Jennings, revealing his preference for certainty within law rather than concern for the law being directed towards social justice, which necessarily entails much discretionary power in the application of broad rules.

---

36 See Zellick, 1985.
37 Jackson and Leonard, 2001.
38 Under common law and the Police and Criminal Evidence Act 1984.
39 See Chapter 17.
40 Maitland, 1908, p. 100.

Jennings (1959b, page 311) writes that Dicey was 'concerned not with clearing up the nasty industrial sections of the towns, but with the liberty of the subject'. For Jennings, Dicey's view that '"Englishmen are ruled by the law, and by the law alone" is not enough'.

For Jennings, the doctrine implies, first, that the state as a whole must be regulated by law; second, that the separation of powers is implied within the doctrine in order to prevent dictatorship or absolutism. Accordingly, there are incorporated certain basic requirements[41] of the law: equality before the law; clearly defined police powers; clear general rules adjudicated upon by the courts; non-retrospectivity in penal statutes; and the strict construction of penal statutes. Third, the doctrine incorporates the principle of equality, a notion which Jennings concedes is as vague as that of the rule of law itself (1959b, page 49). Moreover, and of prime importance, the rule of law implies the notion of *liberty*.

TRS Allan subjects Dicey's analysis to detailed scrutiny, focusing on Dicey's second principle: that of equality before the law.[42] Allan seeks a solution to the apparent paradox presented by Dicey's insistence that both parliamentary sovereignty and the rule of law comprise the fundamental doctrines of the constitution − given that the former concept is inherently capable of damaging the latter. Towards this end, Allan presents a wealth of evidence directed to establishing a middle way between the formalism of the 'principle of legality' and the vagueness of the 'broad political ideal'. In other words, what is sought is an explanation of the means by which the power of sovereignty is restrained or restricted without expounding a 'complete social philosophy' (1985a, page 114). The key to such an understanding, according to Allan, lies in the role of the judiciary and in an acceptance that it is the judges who − in applying the 'juristic principle' of the rule of law − limit the power of Parliament. To summarise, Allan draws on the principles of statutory interpretation (non-retrospectivity, clarity, *mens rea* in penal statutes, etc.), on the independence of the judiciary as ensured by the separation of powers, on the right of access to the courts for all citizens and on the judiciary's reluctance for the jurisdiction of judicial review to be limited. By these and other means, Allan seeks to demonstrate that: 'the rule of law strengthens democracy by ensuring that government operates only within rules adopted or sanctioned by Parliament' and that:

> The constitutional principle of the rule of law serves, however, to bridge the gap between the legal doctrine of parliamentary sovereignty and the political doctrine of the sovereignty of the people. In interpreting statutes in conformity, so far as possible, with general notions of fairness and justice − in seeking to apply those common standards of morality which are taken for granted in the community − the judge respects the natural expectations of the citizen.
>
> The rule of law therefore assists in preventing the subversion of the political sovereignty of the people by manipulation of the legal sovereignty of Parliament. [1985a, page 130]

The protection of rights under common law?

The third limb of Dicey's description of the rule of law reveals his preference for common law protection of human rights over and above a specially formulated code of rights, thus demonstrating a faith in the judiciary which is arguably not sustainable nowadays. Evaluation

---

41 Cf. Raz, 1979, Chapter 11; and Fuller, 1964.
42 Allan, 1985a; 1993, Chapter 2; 2001.

of this aspect of the definition must await analysis of the Human Rights Act 1998 in Chapter 18 and the scope of the protection which it gives to individual citizens.

The Human Rights Act 1998 'incorporated' rights protected under the European Convention on Human Rights into domestic law. Accordingly, citizens no longer have to undertake the lengthy process of applying to the Court of Human Rights in Strasbourg, but are able to seek a remedy in the domestic courts. The method of incorporation adopted, however, fell far short of enabling the judges to invalidate or set aside domestic legislation.

Notwithstanding the Act's status, the rule of law is undoubtedly buttressed by the Act: every public body – by no means a simple concept[43] – is required to comply with Convention rights, and to fail to do so is to act unlawfully save where there is no available alternative form of action because of the requirements of primary legislation.

Fuller and the Rule of Law

Professor Lon Fuller of Harvard University provided a very different perspective on the rule of law. There is, for Fuller, an essentially moral quality in law, which presents itself in two forms. First there is the 'morality of duty', which leads Fuller to identify the necessary qualities that a good legal system will have if it is to serve the people. These qualities are analogous to the foundations of a house. For a house to be safe and to endure, it must be built on sound foundations; so too the legal system. The basic requirements of the legal system are that:

- the law operates prospectively, non-retrospectively;
- the law is clear and relatively certain;
- the law is publicised, not secret;
- laws must be non-contradictory;
- there must be an accessible legal system, which is
- staffed by independent judges.

Over and above these basic requirements there is the 'morality of aspiration', an intangible concept which nevertheless directs the law to serve the people by allowing them the means to pursue their own legitimate life goals. A legal system that fails to serve the people is, for Fuller, no legal system at all: it lacks an essential defining quality – that of morality.

Fuller's morality of law gives rise to difficult questions concerning the criteria for holding a law to be valid or invalid. It also raises important questions about a citizen's obligation to obey the law, discussed above. The question of whether an immoral law should be regarded as valid or not was explored in the dialogue between Fuller and Professor HLA Hart of the University of Oxford.[44] A key difficulty is shown in one example from their debate. Under German law, during the Nazi regime, it was a criminal offence to criticise Hitler. As Hart explains, in 1944 a woman reported her husband to the authorities for insulting remarks he made about Hitler. The wife was under no legal duty to report his acts. The husband was arrested and sentenced to death, although he was not executed but sent to the eastern war front. In 1949 the wife was prosecuted for unlawfully depriving a person of his freedom (under a law that remained in force throughout the period). She pleaded in her defence that

---

43 For discussion see Chapter 18, but note here that s. 6(3)(a) and (b) includes courts and tribunals, and 'any person certain of whose functions are functions of a public nature, but does not include either House of Parliament or a person exercising functions in connection with proceedings in Parliament'.

44 See Hart, 1958.

she acted under a valid law and therefore committed no crime. She was convicted, the Nazi statute being declared by the court to be 'contrary to the sound conscience and sense of justice of all human beings'.

Hart objects to this approach on the basis that it involved a court declaring a statute to be invalid. The alternative outcomes were either to let the woman go free or to punish her but recognise that in doing so retrospective law was being applied. Hart preferred the retrospectivity approach, arguing that:

> It would have made plain that in punishing the woman a choice had to be made between two evils, that of leaving her unpunished and that of sacrificing a very precious principle of morality (i.e. prospectivity) endorsed by most legal systems.

The central difficulty that arises from the differing approaches to immoral law is that it becomes impossible to decide which 'law' is valid. To claim that a law that has been enacted according to the rules of the constitution is invalid because it is immoral involves the imposition of personal subjective values on to law. On the most difficult moral dilemmas facing society there may well be little or no agreement on which constitutes the 'correct' interpretation of morality, and confusion will arise as to whether or not a law is valid.

From Hart's perspective, it is preferable to accept that a law – however immoral – is valid, and then to decide what to do about it. To say that it is invalid is to invite argument and doubt, which itself is contrary to the clarity and certainty demanded by the rule of law.

Raz and the Rule of Law

There are echoes of Fuller's morality of duty – the basic requirements of a legal system – in the writings of Professor Joseph Raz. Raz, however, approaches the rule of law from a morally neutral standpoint, and asserts that:

> The rule of law is a political ideal which a legal system may lack or may possess to a greater or lesser degree. That much is common ground. It is also to be insisted that the rule of law is just one of the virtues which a legal system may possess and by which it is to be judged. It is not to be confused with democracy, justice, equality (before the law or otherwise), human rights of any kind or respect for persons or for the dignity of man. A non-democratic legal system, based on the denial of human rights, on extensive poverty, on racial segregation, sexual inequalities, and religious persecution may, in principle, conform to the requirements of the rule of law better than any of the legal systems of the more enlightened Western democracies. [1979, page 211]

Raz acknowledges that his claim will 'alarm many', but insists that it presents 'a coherent view of one important virtue which legal systems should possess'. In seeking to elucidate the ideal of the rule of law, Raz draws the analogy between the rule of law and a knife. One quality of a good knife is sharpness. However, the quality of sharpness says nothing as to the use to which the knife might be put: beneficial surgery or murder. Sharpness is morally neutral. And thus it is with the rule of law. However, the purpose of law is to enable citizens to live within the law. Accordingly, there are certain principles that must be respected if that goal is to be fulfilled. For the rule of law to exist in society, certain qualities must be present. The law must be clear if it is to be capable of being obeyed. In **Merkur Island Shipping Corporation v Laughton** (1983), for example, Lord Donaldson MR stated that:

> The efficacy and maintenance of the rule of law, which is the foundation of any parliamentary democracy, has at least two pre-requisites. First, people must understand that it is in their interests, as well as in that of the community as a whole, that they should live their lives in accordance with the rules and all the rules. Secondly, they must know what those rules are.

Lord Donaldson's view was endorsed by Lord Diplock in the House of Lords: 'Absence of clarity is destructive of the rule of law; it is unfair to those who wish to preserve the rule of law; it encourages those who wish to undermine it' (1979, page 612). The law must be publicised in order that citizens are aware of its demands; reasonably stable in order that citizens can plan their lives according to law; prospective so that the law does not require the impossible;[45] non-contradictory for the same reason; and, in addition, the courts must be accessible and staffed by an independent judiciary. Compliance with each of these requirements will indicate that a society respects the rule of law. To make such a statement is not to say that the legal system is one which is necessarily morally 'good'. As seen in Raz's illustration with the quality of sharpness in relation to the knife, the fact of sharpness does not dictate the morality of the purposes to which the knife will be put. It is possible, therefore, for Raz (in contrast to Fuller) for the rule of law to exist without the legal system necessarily pursuing morally good ends.

Dworkin and the Rule of Law

Ronald Dworkin (1931–2013) was one of the pre-eminent liberal legal and moral philosophers of the twentieth century. In *A Matter of Principle* 1985, Dworkin criticised formalistic, 'content-free' interpretations of the rule of law, labelling them 'rule-book conceptions'. For Dworkin, law is a moral enterprise inextricably linked to political morality.[46] His interpretation of the rule of law focuses on individual rights: it is therefore a 'substantive', or 'content rich' or a 'thick' (as opposed to 'thin') version of the rule of law. Dworkin recognises that the state must be bound, as are citizens, by rules of law. However, this rule-book conception is very narrow: it says nothing whatsoever about the content of the rules. The rule-book version of the rule of law does not deny that individuals have rights. However, it regards those rights as a part of substantive justice which is a concept quite separate (on this analysis) from the rule of law. His rights conception is both more complex and ambitious than the rule-book conception and makes no distinction between the rule of law and individual rights. Conversely, individual rights are entailed in the rules. As Dworkin expresses it:

> The rule of law on this conception is the ideal of rule by an accurate public conception of individual rights. It does not distinguish, as the rule-book conception does, between the rule of law and the substantive justice; on the contrary it requires, as part of the ideal of law, that the rules in the rule book capture and enforce moral rights.

---

45 A principle endorsed in **Phillips v Eyre** (1870) and **Waddington v Miah** (1974). See, however, the War Damage Act 1965 and the War Crimes Act 1991 for illustrations of Parliament's power to legislate retrospectively.
46 Dworkin, 2011.

Dworkin argues that the rule-book conception and the rights conception have differing dimensions. Under the formal version of the rule of law, an officer of the state may use his or her powers wrongly and thus be accountable to law: there is just one way in which the official can misuse his or her powers. Under the substantive, thick, content-rich Dworkinian rule of law, the state may fail in several ways. It may fail in the scope of rights it purports to confer on individuals, or fail to enforce rights against itself, or may fail to recognise certain important rights. It might fail also in enforcing, or not enforcing, rights in a discriminatory manner. In terms of measuring justice in society, a society will be just if it 'achieves a high rating in each of the dimensions of the rights conception'.[47]

Bingham and the Rule of Law

Lord Bingham (1933–2010), a British judge, held the highest judicial offices, serving as Master of the Rolls, Lord Chief Justice and Senior Law Lord. His book, *The Rule of Law*, was published in 2010, and represents an authoritative contemporary analysis of the rule of law.

As a starting point, Lord Bingham states that:

> The core of the existing principle is, I suggest, that all persons and authorities within the state, whether public or private, should be bound by and entitled to the benefit of laws publicly made, taking effect (generally) in the future and publicly administered in the courts.

From this broad analysis, Bingham develops eight key characteristics of a system conforming to the rule of law. These are that:

(1)   The law must be accessible and so far as possible intelligible, clear and predictable. The individual citizen needs to know what the law is — both criminal and civil — in order to plan and undertake his or her actions within the legal framework. In terms of commercial transactions also, the economy depends on there being a clear system of rules to which all can comply and thereby be sure that their dealings are lawful.

(2)   Questions of legal right and liability should ordinarily be resolved by application of the law and not the exercise of discretion. Recognising Dicey's opposition to unfettered discretion, Lord Bingham accepts that officials and judges need some leeway in decision making and the application of rules, but insists that the discretion granted must be limited so that its exercise does not become arbitrary. Discretion must not be unconstrained.

(3)   The laws of the land should apply equally to all, save to the extent that objective differences justify differentiation. This is equality before the law, a concept with a history stretching back to ancient Greece and a key component of Dicey's rule of law. What is important is that the law applies equally to all: like cases must be treated alike but different cases must be treated differently. Hence children are not to be treated as adults in relation to the law, and the mentally ill, prisoners and those with no right of abode within the country are justifiably treated differently. What is important is that the different treatment is objectively justified on the basis of difference.

---

47   *A Matter of Principle*, p. 12.

(4)   Ministers and public officers at all levels must exercise the powers conferred on them in good faith, fairly and for the purpose for which the powers were conferred, without exceeding the limits of such powers and not unreasonably.

Although inherent in the principle of equality before the law, there is a need to emphasise the requirement that government be conducted under the law. Judicial review is the mechanism by which the actions and decisions of officials are scrutinised by the courts to ensure that they are within the scope of power granted by Parliament (*intra vires*). Public officials must also respect the rules of fairness and natural justice and powers must be exercised reasonably and rationally (on this see further Chapters 23–25 on Judicial Review).

(5)   The law must afford adequate protection for fundamental human rights. Lord Bingham discusses Raz's proposition that a legal system may comply with the rule of law despite denying human rights. Referring to this as a 'thin' definition of the rule of law, Bingham states his preference for a 'thick' definition, one which 'embraces the protection of human rights within its scope'. Law, for Bingham (as for natural lawyers) 'cannot be simply what is dictated by political authority or issued by the state'.

(6)   Means must be provided for resolving, without prohibitive cost or inordinate delay, *bona fide* civil disputes which the parties themselves are unable to resolve. Prohibitive costs and delays both offend against the principle and hence the rule of law. Legal aid must be available to those who in the interests of justice need access to the courts but cannot afford the cost. Lord Bingham cites Gladstone 'justice delayed is justice denied'. Delay is undesirable in itself but also exacerbates costs.

(7)   Adjudicative procedures provided by the state should be fair. This is the principle of the right to fair trial, now enshrined in Article 6 of the European Convention on Human Rights. Under this heading comes the need for an independent and politically impartial judiciary and an independent legal profession. Lord Bingham refers to the Act of Settlement 1700 which protected judges against dismissal by the executive, and the Constitution Reform Act 2005 with its statutory references to the rule of law, section 1 requiring the Lord Chancellor and other Ministers to uphold the independence of the judiciary and section 3(5) providing that neither the Lord Chancellor nor other Ministers may seek to influence the decision of the judges. In relation to criminal trials, these must be held in public, and procedures in place to ensure equality between prosecution and defence. Also in this connection, Bingham discusses the difficult case of terrorist trials which cannot, without risk to state security, be held in open court with all the evidence before the court. On this see Chapter 22.

(8)   The rule of law requires the same compliance by the state with its obligations under international law as under national law. Here Lord Bingham discusses a number of issues. The need for the international protection of human rights; the regulation of trade and commerce under international law; the resort to war, the conduct of war and rights and duties of an occupying power after a war are all fundamental to the rule of law.

 Pause and Reflect

Drawing on the discussion above, critically examine the following statements.

'The core of the existing principle is, I suggest, that all persons and authorities within the state, whether public or private, should be bound by and entitled to the benefit of laws publicly made, taking effect (generally) in the future and publicly administered in the courts'. [Bingham, 2010]

'It [the rule of law] may well have become just another one of those self-congratulatory rhetorical devices that grace the public utterances of Anglo-American politicians. No intellectual effort need therefore be wasted on this bit of ruling class chatter'. [Shklar, 1987]

The Rule of Law and the Legal System

Various interpretations of the rule of law have been discussed above. In the following section, aspects of the legal system which have particular relevance to the rule of law are considered.

Judicial review

The means by which, and grounds upon which, judicial review may be granted are considered in Chapters 23 to 25. It is sufficient for current purposes to note that judicial review is the means by which administrative authorities – whether Ministers of the Crown, government Departments, local authorities or others with law-making and administrative powers – are confined within the powers granted to them by Parliament by the courts. It is for a court to determine – following the granting of an application for judicial review – whether the body in question has acted *intra vires* or *ultra vires* (that is, inside or outside its powers).

Actions for judicial review of administrative action, employing concepts of *intra* and *ultra vires* and the rules of natural justice, ensure that the executive acts within the law. Judicial review – in its infancy in Dicey's time – represents the means by which the sovereignty of Parliament is upheld and the rule of law applied. Dicey, writing in 1915, analysed the significance of **Board of Education v Rice** (1911) and **Local Government Board v Arlidge** (1915), claiming that:

> each case finally lays down, as far as the courts of England are concerned, a clear and distinct principle by which any department of the government, such for example as the Board of Education, must be guarded in the exercise of powers conferred upon it by statute.[48]

Judicial review is confined to matters of public, rather than private law. Thus, where a relationship between an aggrieved citizen and a body is based, for example, on the law of contract, judicial review will not lie.[49] It is also necessary – in the interests of good administration – that aggrieved individuals have 'sufficient interest' – or *locus standi* – in the matter to bring it to court.[50] There are numerous grounds on which judicial review may be sought. By way of illustration, a body may act *ultra vires* if it uses its powers for the wrong purpose,[51] or if it abuses its powers,[52] or if it adopts a policy which is so rigid that it fails to exercise a discretion with which it has been invested.[53] The law imposes standards of reasonableness upon administrative bodies, and failure to act in a reasonable manner may cause a body to

---

48 Dicey, 1885, Appendix 2, p. 493.
49 See e.g. **R v City Panel on Takeovers and Mergers ex parte Datafin plc** (1987); **O'Reilly v Mackman** (1983).
50 See, inter alia, **Inland Revenue Commissioner v National Federation of Self-Employed and Small Businesses Ltd** (1982).
51 **Attorney General v Fulham Corporation** (1921).
52 **Webb v Minister of Housing and Local Government** (1965); **Westminster Bank v Minister of Housing and Local Government** (1971).
53 **Padfield v Minister of Agriculture Fisheries and Food** (1968).

act *ultra vires*.[54] A body may act *ultra vires* if it is conferred with delegated powers but delegates them further to another.[55]

Statute may require that administrators adopt particular procedures in the exercise of these powers; should they not do so, and the procedures are judicially deemed to be 'mandatory' (compulsory) rather than 'directory' (advisory), a body will be held to be acting *ultra vires*. If a public body under a duty to act fails to act at all, the court can order it to do so by a mandatory order. The rules of natural justice must also be observed in decision making: where an individual has a right or interest at stake because of an administrative decision, he is entitled to fair treatment.[56] All of these grounds for review were rationalised by the Judicial Committee of the House of Lords (now the Supreme Court) into three principal categories: irrationality, illegality and procedural impropriety.[57] These categories were not regarded as exhaustive, and it was recognised that the European concept of 'proportionality' might emerge as a distinctive category. This has happened, most particularly in relation to the Human Rights Act 1998, which enables rights protected under the European Convention on Human Rights to be enforced in the domestic courts. The essence of proportionality is that a public body must only do what is necessary to achieve a legitimate objective, and no more. An early (pre-Human Rights Act) example of proportionality being applied is **R v Barnsley Metropolitan Borough Council ex parte Hook** (1976). In this case a market stall holder had his licence revoked by the Council for urinating in public. Lord Denning MR quashed the decision, partly on the basis that the penalty was disproportionate to the 'offence'.

The powers of the court can only be exercised over a matter which it is competent to determine. This introduces the concept of justiciability, and it is this latter doctrine which most particularly undermines the concept of the rule of law. In **Council of Civil Service Unions v Minister for the Civil Service**, the House of Lords identified the categories of decision which would be immune from judicial review – that is to say non-justiciable. Amongst these – and the list is not exhaustive – are the making of treaties, the dissolution of Parliament, the appointment of Ministers, declarations of war and peace and matters relating to the granting of honours. What unites these categories is the fact that each involves matters of high policy which is most appropriately determined – in the eyes of the judiciary – not by the courts but by the executive. Where this applies, it may be said that the rule of law is undermined by respect for the doctrine of the separation of powers: an ironic consequence.

The doctrine of judicial review nevertheless represents a bedrock for the application of the rule of law, keeping those with law-making and discretionary powers within the law. From **Entick v Carrington** (1765) to **R v Secretary of State for the Home Department ex parte Fire Brigades' Union** (1993), wherein Kenneth Baker, the Home Secretary, was held to be acting *ultra vires* when attempting to introduce a new tariff for compensation under the Criminal Injuries Compensation Scheme under the royal prerogative rather than under power conferred by statute, the principle is established and reiterated.

The legal process

For the rule of law to be respected and applied, the legal process – civil and criminal – must exhibit certain features. These features may be categorised as accessibility and procedural fairness.

---

54 *Associated Provincial Picture Houses Ltd v Wednesbury Corporation* (1948).
55 *Barnard v National Dock Labour Board* (1953); *Vine v National Dock Labour Board* (1957).
56 *R v IRC ex parte Preston* (1985); *Wheeler v Leicester City Council* (1985).
57 *Council of Civil Service Unions v Minister for the Civil Service* (1985).

Accessibility

The law must be accessible to all if rights are to be enforced. As Lord Phillips of Worth Matravers PSC stated: '[A]ccess to a court to protect one's rights is the foundation of the rule of law'.[58] Accordingly, there must not only exist a system of courts available locally but the cost of having recourse to the courts must be such that there is real – rather than symbolic – access to the courts. For the law to be attainable, adequate legal advice and assistance must be provided at a cost affordable by all.[59]

The right to a fair trial is protected under Article 6 of the European Convention on Human Rights, and includes the right of the citizen: 'to defend himself in person or through legal assistance of his own choosing or, if he has not sufficient means to pay for legal assistance, to be given it free when the interests of justice so require'.

In **Granger v United Kingdom** (1990), the defendant had been denied further legal aid to pursue an appeal against conviction. Granger, unable to afford legal representation, acted in person. Representing the Crown were senior government counsel. On an application under the Convention, Granger alleged that he had been denied the protection of law. The Court of Human Rights ruled that the denial of legal aid infringed Granger's rights.

Habeas corpus

The ancient writ of habeas corpus is available to test the legality of a person's detention by the state.[60] The writ can be issued either by the person imprisoned or by someone acting on his behalf. If it is established that there is a prima facie ground for believing the detention to be unlawful, the writ will be issued. Habeas corpus is used in several areas of law where acts of the executive result in detention. Its use can be seen in, for example, immigration and asylum law and mental health law. In **Nikonovs v Governor of Brixton Prison** (2005), the Court of Appeal stated that the right to habeas corpus could only be restricted by express statutory language and could not be implied into an Act.

Originally a common law power, the right to a writ was placed on a statutory basis under the Habeas Corpus Act 1679. The Act of 1679 relates to persons imprisoned on a criminal charge. The Habeas Corpus Act 1816 relates to persons detained other than on a criminal charge.[61] AV Dicey instructed that:

> if, in short, any man, woman, or child is deprived of liberty, the court will always issue a writ of habeas corpus to any one who has the aggrieved person in his custody to have such person brought before the court, and if he is suffering restraint without lawful cause, set him free.[62]

In the case of **Wolfe Tone** (1798), Tone was tried and found guilty of high treason by a court martial and sentenced to death. A writ was issued on the basis that, since Wolfe Tone was not under commission to the English army, but rather held a commission from the French Republic, there was no jurisdiction for his trial by court martial in Ireland. The Lord Chief Justice instructed the sheriff to go immediately to the army barracks and demand that Tone not be executed. When the officers refused to comply with the order, the Lord Chief Justice ordered that Tone, and the detaining officers, be taken into the custody of the sheriff. On

---

58 **A v HM Treasury** (2010), at para. 146.
59 See, inter alia, Slapper and Kelly, 2015; Zander, 2003, Chapters 6 and 9.
60 The use of habeas corpus now needs to be considered in light of the development of the European arrest warrant. See van Sliedregt, 2007. And **re Hilali (respondent) (application for a writ of Habeas Corpus)** (2008).
61 The Habeas Corpus Act 1862 prohibits the courts from issuing writs in respect of colonies or dominions where those jurisdictions have power to issue the writ.
62 Dicey, 1885, p. 219.

seeking to recover Tone from detention, it was found that he had cut his throat and could not be moved. On this case, Dicey wrote, seemingly without irony, that 'it will be admitted that no more splendid assertion of the supremacy of law can be found than the protection of Wolfe Tone by the Irish Bench'.[63]

The writ has also been used to test the legality of detention of slaves: **Sommersett's Case** (1771) and of students: **Ex parte Daisy Hopkins** (1891). In **Board of Control ex parte Rutty** (1956), a writ was issued to test the legality of the detention of a mentally defective patient who had been detained for eight years without an order of a court.

Nowadays, the writ of habeas corpus is most often used to test the legality of the detention of immigrants. However, in **R v Home Secretary ex parte Mughal** (1974) and **R v Home Secretary ex parte Zamir** (1980), the court refused to allow habeas corpus to be used to question the decision to remove an illegal immigrant from the country. Conversely, in **R v Home Secretary ex parte Khawaja** (1984), the House of Lords ruled that the question as to whether a person was an illegal immigrant was not within the exclusive jurisdiction of the Home Secretary to decide. Rather it was a matter of fact, which the courts would decide. Before Khawaja could be removed from the country, the court had to be satisfied on the evidence that he was in fact an illegal immigrant. Only if he was an illegal immigrant would the court permit deportation.

See Chapter 21.

In **Yunus Rahmatullah v Secretary of State for Foreign and Commonwealth Affairs; Secretary of State for Defence** (2011), the Court of Appeal granted a writ of habeas corpus against the respondents, requiring the government to secure the release of Mr Rahmatullah and produce him for trial before a British court within seven days, or release him without trial. The appellant had been captured by British forces in Iraq in 2004 and handed over to US forces. The Secretary of State for Defence claimed that Rahmatullah was a member of a proscribed organisation with links to Al-Qaeda. He was detained in Afghanistan from 2004 to 2011, in a detention centre, and without any charges being brought against him. The appellant claimed that his detention was unlawful, and applied (through a relative) for a writ of habeas corpus. The government resisted the application on the basis that it did not have sufficient control over the applicant (he being in the custody of US forces), and that the issue of a writ would require the UK government making a request to the US government for his release – thereby involving the law stepping into the area of foreign relations. The Court of Appeal, unanimously, agreed to the grant of the writ.

See Chapters 7 and 8.

On appeal to the Supreme Court, the decision of the Court of Appeal on the issue of the writ was upheld: see **Rahmatullah v Secretary of State for Defence** (2012). The Court rejected the government's argument that the issue of the writ would represent an intrusion on foreign policy. It would not; the Court was merely requiring the Secretary of State to explain whether the state had control over the applicant.

See also Chapter 23.

There exists an overlap between habeas corpus and judicial review which causes uncertainty. In **R v Home Secretary ex parte Cheblak** (1991), the Court of Appeal held that habeas corpus is not a substitute for judicial review proceedings. However, where an application for judicial review is pending, a writ may be used to ensure that the applicant is not prematurely removed from the country.[64]

---

63 Dicey, 1885, p. 294. See also Heuston, 1964, Chapter 2; **Stockdale v Hansard** (1839); and **Sheriff of Middlesex's case** (1840), discussed in Chapter 17.
64 **R v Home Secretary ex parte Muboyayi** (1991).

Procedural fairness

Justice and the rule of law demand that, in the conduct of legal proceedings, procedural fairness be observed. Subsumed within this requirement are many subsidiary conditions. The judge must be impartial: *nemo iudex in sua causa*. Where jurors are involved, they, too, must be free from bias. In addition, jurors should be reasonably representative of the society they serve. Evidence gathered by the police must be acquired by lawful means. The evidence admitted into court must be both of an admissible nature and fairly presented. The proceedings should be conducted in such a manner as to be intelligible to the parties, witnesses and jurors.[65]

The jury

The precise origins of trial by jury in its modern form are shrouded in mist.[66] It is thought that by the end of the fifteenth century, the jury, as triers of fact, was established in what today would be a recognisable form. Trial by jury for serious criminal offences, and in civil cases where defamation, malicious prosecution, false imprisonment and allegations of fraud are at issue,[67] is regarded as the 'bulwark of our liberties'.[68] The decision of the jury is regarded as conclusive and unimpeachable. Criticisms have long been made of the lack of representativeness of the jury. Several factors militate against representativeness: the accuracy of the electoral register from which jurors are selected; the relative lack of randomness in jury selection; the vetting of jurors;[69] and challenges to members of the jury. Moreover, a wide range of persons are either ineligible for jury service, or disqualified from sitting or may be excused from jury service. When a jury is summoned, the presence of a juror may be challenged 'for cause' – that is, where some fact relating to the juror is known and gives rise to a challenge. Little is known about the individual juror – only the names and addresses are given.[70] This relative anonymity of jurors contrasts starkly with the position in the United States of America, where the selection of a jury entails a prolonged inquiry into the lives and attitudes of prospective jurors. While the process is protracted,[71] it is designed to ensure that the jury ultimately selected will be one free from bias in relation to the defendant. In the United Kingdom, a person may be excused from service on the basis of personal knowledge of the case, bias, personal hardship or conscientious objection to jury service. A juror should not be excused on general grounds such as race, religion, political beliefs or occupation.[72]

Evidence

For the rule of law to be observed, it is of central importance that the evidence before the court be both complete and reliable. Contravention of this requirement undermines the concept of a fair trial. Subsumed within this question is the complex and controversial matter of the manner in which evidence is obtained and the question of admissibility. While the Police and Criminal Evidence Act 1984[73] went some way to improving the safeguards for the

---

65 See, *inter alia*, Kafka, 1956; and Keedy, 1951 for illustrations of breaches of this requirement.
66 See Maitland, 1908, pp. 115–130. See also Denning, 1982, Pt 2.
67 Supreme Court Act 1981, subject to the proviso in s. 69(1) which permits the court to refuse trial by jury in cases of complexity or impracticality.
68 *Ward v James* (1966), p. 295, *per* Lord Denning MR.
69 *R v Mason* (1980); *Attorney General's Guidelines on Jury Checks* (1988).
70 Prior to 1973, jurors' occupations were made known.
71 Jury selection for the trial of John de Lorean took five weeks.
72 *Practice Direction* (1988).
73 See, *inter alia*, Zander, 2003.

accused and was introduced, in part, to rectify deficiencies which had come to light,[74] the cases of the Birmingham Six,[75] the Guildford Four and the Maguire Seven[76] illustrated the deficiencies in the criminal justice system. In each of these cases, the defendants had served long terms of imprisonment for alleged Irish Republican Army (IRA) terrorist acts. In each case, the evidence relied upon was unreliable. Their convictions were quashed by the Court of Appeal following years of campaigning by relatives and friends for a review of their cases. In each case, a serious miscarriage of justice had occurred and as a result the integrity of the criminal justice system was tarnished.

At common law, a confession which is improperly obtained is inadmissible.[77] The Police and Criminal Evidence Act 1984 places this rule on a statutory basis, providing that if a confession has been obtained 'by oppression', the court shall not allow the confession to be given in evidence unless satisfied beyond reasonable doubt that the confession – even if true – has not been obtained improperly (section 76).

Whereas the rules on the admissibility of improperly obtained confessions are relatively clear, the admissibility of other evidence obtained by either dubious or unlawful means has proved less clear and less satisfactory. Until 1979, the judges exercised their discretion as to whether or not evidence improperly acquired would be admissible.[78] However, in **R v Sang** (1979) the House of Lords ruled that no discretion existed to exclude evidence which had been obtained by unlawful or improper means. The only basis on which evidence could be excluded would be where the effect of admitting it would prove unduly 'prejudicial' to the defence or 'unfair' to admit it. The fact that the evidence was unlawfully acquired does not amount to 'unfairness' per se.[79] The admissibility of such evidence is now governed by section 78 of the Police and Criminal Evidence Act 1984, which provides that a court may refuse to allow evidence if:

> it appears to the court that, having regard to all the circumstances, including the circumstances in which the evidence was obtained, the admission of the evidence would have such adverse effect on the fairness of the proceedings that the court ought not to admit it.

The cost of law

> To no one will we sell, or no one deny or delay right or justice. (Magna Carta, 1215, Article 40)

The accessibility of the law is a characteristic which features in the majority of theoretical approaches to the rule of law. By accessibility is meant the availability of both legal advice and, where necessary in the interests of justice and fairness, legal representation. As successive governments strive to reduce public spending, legal aid has been a consistent target for cuts. The current position is that only the very poor and the very rich have access to justice, with an estimated 70 per cent of the population being ineligible.

---

74 See McConville and Baldwin, 1980.
75 **R v McIlkenny** (1992).
76 See May, 1990–1991, On fair trial see Robertson, G, 2015.
77 **Marks v Beyfus** (1890).
78 **Kuruma Son of Kaniu v R** (1955); **Jeffrey v Black** (1978).
79 See Heydon, 1973; Ashworth, 1977.

The Legal Aid, Sentencing and Punishment of Offenders Act 2012 (LASPO) introduced significant reductions to legal aid, with the objective of saving some £350 million per year. Overall, expenditure in 2013–2014 was down by 24 per cent from 2009–2010. Criminal legal aid expenditure was down by 14 per cent, while civil justice legal aid expenditure was down by nearly two-thirds. In relation to civil legal aid, divorce, personal injury, debt, housing, employment and immigration (unless a person is detained) cases are now excluded, unless certain criteria are met.[80] Legal aid will be available for serious cases such as domestic violence, forced marriage or child abduction, mental health cases, asylum cases and debt cases where a person's home is at risk.

In Lord Bingham's words, 'denial of legal protection to the poor litigant who cannot afford to pay is one enemy of the rule of law'.[81]

Compliance with International Obligations

International law regulates relationship between states and sets standards to be complied with in the international community. Individual states, or associations of states such as the EU, enter into agreements with other states. It is a fundamental principle of international law that states comply with the obligations undertaken through a treaty.

Under most constitutions in the world, international law takes precedence over domestic law, entering automatically into a country's legal system once a treaty has been formally approved (ratified) according to the country's constitutional requirements. In the UK, however, as explained further in Chapter 8, treaties have no automatic or immediate impact on the domestic legal system – and therefore do not create enforceable rights – unless and until the treaty is formally incorporated into domestic law by an Act of Parliament. For example, when the UK joined the EU in 1973 by signing the Treaty of Rome, in order for EU law to enter into the domestic legal system, it was necessary to pass the European Communities Act 1972. A further example is the Human Rights Act 1998. The UK signed up to the European Convention on Human Rights – an international treaty – in 1953. However, none of the rights guaranteed by the Convention were enforceable in the domestic courts until Parliament passed the Human Rights Act 1998. Prior to that time, if a Convention right was violated an individual had to make an application under the Convention to the institutions in Strasbourg and the case would ultimately be heard by the Court of Human Rights, whose judgment was binding on the UK government.

In the course of leaving the EU, the government signed the Withdrawal Agreement -- an international treaty -- with the EU and Parliament passed the European Union (Withdrawal Agreement) Act. However, problems arising over future arrangements for Northern Ireland during the transition/implementation period led the government – contrary to the basic principle of international law that Treaties must be respected – to introduce the Internal Market Bill, a Bill which violated part of the Withdrawal Agreement. Having an 80-strong majority in Parliament, the government passed the Bill through its initial stages in spite of the widespread condemnation of the violation of international rule of law and the resignation of two senior government legal advisers. On the outcome of this development see further Chapter 8.

---

80 Ministry of Justice Annual Legal Aid Statistics 2013–2014.
81 The Rule of Law, at p. 88.

The Rule of Law in International Dimension

The Universal Declaration of Human Rights of the United Nations, published in 1948, declares that: 'It is essential, if man is not to be compelled to have recourse, as a last resort, to rebellion against tyranny and oppression, that human rights should be protected by the rule of law'.

The European Convention also recognises the concept of the rule of law. The preamble states that: 'The governments of European countries which are like-minded and have a common heritage of political traditions, ideals, freedom and the rule of law ... have agreed as follows'.

On an international level, the rule of law is also advanced by the International Commission of Jurists, which strives to uphold and improve the rule of law within the legal systems of its members. The Declaration of Delhi, issued under the auspices of the International Commission of Jurists, affirms the rule of law and its value in promoting the protection of civil and political rights and linked such rights with the development and protection of social and economic rights. The Congress of the International Commission of Jurists met in 1959 in order to 'clarify and formulate a supranational concept of the rule of law'.[82] The Declaration of Delhi 1959 recognised that:

> the rule of law is a dynamic concept for the expansion and fulfilment of which jurists are primarily responsible and which should be employed not only to safeguard and advance the civil and political rights of the individual in a free society, but also to establish social, economic, educational and cultural conditions under which his legitimate aspirations and dignity may be realised.

Such aspirational statements recognise the need for the economic foundations to be such that the dignity of man can be a reality in society. It is meaningless to speak of the rule of law as insisting on decent, or even minimal, standards of living within the context of poverty and disease. In order to secure any such standards, a sufficient level of economic wealth must be achieved. Even where such standards do exist, there will remain resistances to any formulation of social and economic rights as enforceable positive legal rights, for such formulations require the allocation of resources within society. Whereas governments may be willing – indeed obliged – to respect civil and political rights in a democracy, the protection of such rights generally will be effected without significant national resource implications. The protection of freedoms, such as freedom of speech and association, requires no more than a restraint on government. The protection of social and economic rights requires positive action, at a high cost.[83]

Summary

The rule of law – in its many guises – represents a challenge to state authority and power, demanding both that powers be granted legitimately and that their exercise is according to law. 'According to law' means both according to the legal rules and something over and above purely formal *legality* and imputes the concepts of *legitimacy* and constitutionality. In its turn, legitimacy implies *rightness* or *morality* of law. The law is not autonomous but rests on the support of those it governs. The law is the servant of the sense of rightness in the

---

82 Marsh, 'The rule of law as a supranational concept', in Guest, 1961, p. 240, and Marsh, 1959.
83 See Aubert, 1983, Chapters 2 and 7.

community, and whilst the rule of law places law above every individual – irrespective of rank and station – it remains, paradoxically, subject to the ultimate judgment of the people.

Further Reading

Allan, T, 'The rule of law as the rule of reason: consent and constitutionalism' (1999) 115 *Law Quarterly Review* 221.

Allan, T, *Constitutional Justice: A Liberal Theory of the Rule of Law*, 2001, Oxford: Oxford University Press, Chapters 1–4.

Bingham, Lord, 'The rule of law' (2007) 66 *Cambridge Law Journal* 67.

Bingham, Lord, *The Rule of Law*, 2010, London: Penguin.

Dworkin, R, *Taking Rights Seriously*, 1978, Cambridge, MA: Harvard University Press.

Dworkin, R, *A Matter of Principle*, 1985, Oxford: Oxford University Press.

Dworkin, R, *Justice for Hedgehogs*, 2011, Cambridge, MA: Harvard University Press.

Hutchinson, AP and Monahan, P (eds), *The Rule of Law: Ideal or Ideology*, 1987, Toronto: Carswell.

Jowell, J, 'The rule of law and its underlying values' in J Jowell and D Oliver (eds), *The Changing Constitution*, 7th edn, 2011, Oxford: Oxford University Press.

Raz, J, 'The rule of law and its virtue' [1977] *Law Quarterly Review* 93.

Raz, J, *The Authority of Law*, 1979, Oxford: Oxford University Press.

Steyn, Lord, 'Civil liberties in modern Britain' [2009] *Public Law* 228.

Wasserstrom, R, 'The obligation to obey the law' [1963] *California University Law Review* 780.

Chapter 4

The Separation of Powers

Chapter Contents

Learning Objectives

By the end of this chapter you should be able to:

☐ explain the early origins and constitutional importance of the separation of powers;
☐ discuss the three principal institutions of the state, their personnel and functions;
☐ explain the difference between written and 'uncodified' constitutions in relation to separation of powers;
☐ discuss the importance of judicial independence and the manner in which law and convention upholds it;
☐ explain why the judges insist that separation of powers is a fundamental concept under the UK constitution, using case law to support your argument;
☐ critically assess the separation of powers in relation to (a) the legislature and executive, (b) legislature and judiciary and (c) the executive and judiciary;
☐ offer an evaluation of the extent to which the UK constitution does or does not conform to separation of powers.

Introduction

The separation of powers, together with the rule of law and parliamentary sovereignty, runs like a thread throughout the constitution of the United Kingdom. It is a doctrine which is fundamental to the organisation of a state – and to the concept of constitutionalism – in so far as it prescribes the appropriate allocation of powers, and the limits of those powers, to differing institutions. The concept has played a major role in the formation of constitutions. The extent to which powers can be, and should be, separate and distinct was a central feature in formulating, for example, both the American and French revolutionary constitutions. In any state, three essential bodies exist: the executive, the legislature and the judiciary. It is the relationship between these bodies which must be evaluated against the backcloth of the principle. The essence of the doctrine is that there should be, ideally, a clear demarcation of personnel and functions between the legislature, executive and judiciary in order that none should have excessive power and that there should be in place a system of checks and balances between the institutions. However, as will be seen, there are significant departures from the pure doctrine under the United Kingdom's constitution, and it must be conceded that, while the doctrine is accorded respect, it is by no means absolute.

In order to evaluate the extent to which the separation of powers applies – and the many exceptions to the pure doctrine – it is necessary first to define the major institutions of the state and evaluate the relationship between them. In order to do this the following relationships will be examined:

- the executive and the legislature;
- the legislature and the judiciary;
- the executive and the judiciary.

Historical Development

The identification of the three elements of the constitution derives from Aristotle (384–322 BC). In *The Politics*, Aristotle proclaimed that:

> There are three elements in each constitution in respect of which every serious lawgiver must look for what is advantageous to it; if these are well arranged, the constitution is bound to be well arranged, and the differences in constitutions are bound to correspond to the differences between each of these elements. The three are, first, the deliberative, which discusses everything of common importance; second, the officials; and third, the judicial element. [Bk iv, xiv, 1297b35]

The constitutional seeds of the doctrine were thus sown early, reflecting the need for government according to and under the law, a requirement encouraged by some degree of a separation of functions between the institutions of the state.

The constitutional historian FW Maitland traces the separation of powers in England to the reign of Edward I (1272–1307): 'In Edward's day all becomes definite – there is the Parliament of the three estates, there is the King's Council, there are the well known courts of law' (1908, page 20).

Viscount Henry St John Bolingbroke (1678–1751), in *Remarks on the History of England*, advanced the idea of separation of powers. Bolingbroke was concerned with the necessary balance of powers within a constitution, arguing that the protection of liberty and security within the state depended upon achieving and maintaining an equilibrium between the Crown, Parliament and the people. Addressing the respective powers of the King and Parliament, Bolingbroke observed that:

> Since this division of power, and these different privileges constitute and maintain our government, it follows that the confusion of them tends to destroy it. This proposition is therefore true; that, in a constitution like ours, the safety of the whole depends on the balance of the parts. [1748, pages 80–83]

Baron Montesquieu (1689–1755, living in England from 1729 to 1731) stressed the importance of the independence of the judiciary in *De l'Esprit des Lois* (1748):

> When the legislative and executive powers are united in the same person, or in the same body of magistrates, there can be no liberty ... Again, there is no liberty if the power of judging is not separated from the legislative and executive. If it were joined with the legislative, the life and liberty of the subject would be exposed to arbitrary control; for the judge would then be the legislator. If it were joined to the executive power, the judge might behave with violence and oppression. There would be an end to everything, if the same man, or the same body, whether of the nobles or the people, were to exercise those three powers, that of enacting laws, that of executing public affairs, and that of trying crimes or individual causes.

Here is the clearest expression of the demand for a separation of functions. It has been remarked that Montesquieu's observations on the English constitution were inaccurate at the time, representing more a description of an idealised state than reality.[1] Moreover, it should not be assumed that Montesquieu's preferred arrangement of a pure separation of powers is uncontroversial. Throughout history, there has been a tension between the doctrine of separation of powers and the need for balanced government – an arrangement depending more on checks and balances within the system (as emphasised by Bolingbroke) than on a formalistic separation of powers. Sir Ivor Jennings has interpreted Montesquieu's words to mean not that the legislature and the executive should have no influence over the other, but rather that neither should exercise the power of the other.[2] Sir William Blackstone, a disciple of Montesquieu, adopted and adapted Montesquieu's strict doctrine, reworking his central idea to incorporate the theory of mixed government. While it was of central importance to Blackstone that, for example, the executive and legislature should be sufficiently separate to avoid 'tyranny', he nevertheless viewed their total separation as potentially leading to dominance of the executive by the legislature.[3] Thus, partial separation of powers is required to achieve a mixed and balanced constitutional structure.

The Contemporary Doctrine

The separation of powers doctrine does not insist that there should be three institutions of government each operating in isolation from each other. Indeed, such an arrangement would be unworkable, particularly under a constitution dominated by the sovereignty of Parliament.

Under such an arrangement, it is essential that there be a sufficient interplay between each institution of the state. For example, it is for the executive, for the most part, to propose legislation for Parliament's approval. Once passed into law, Acts of Parliament are upheld

---

1 Vile, 1967, pp. 84–85.
2 Jennings, 1959b, Appendix I.
3 *Commentaries on the Laws of England* (1765–1769), Vol. I.

by the judiciary. A complete separation of the three institutions could result in legal and constitutional deadlock. Rather than a pure separation of powers, the concept insists that the primary functions of the state should be allocated clearly and that there should be checks to ensure that no institution encroaches significantly upon the functions of the other. If hypothetical constitutional arrangements within a state are considered, a range of possibilities exists:

(a) absolute power residing in one person or body exercising executive, legislative and judicial powers: no separation of powers;

(b) power being diffused between three separate bodies exercising separate functions with no overlaps in function or personnel: pure separation of powers; and

(c) powers and personnel being largely – but not totally – separated with checks and balances in the system to prevent abuse: mixed government and weak separation of powers.

It is to this third category that the constitution of the United Kingdom most clearly subscribes.

Defining the Institutions

The executive

The executive may be defined as that branch of the state which formulates policy and is responsible for its execution. In formal terms, the sovereign is the head of the executive. The Prime Minister, Cabinet and other Ministers, for the most part, are elected Members of Parliament.[4] In addition, the Civil Service, local authorities, police and armed forces, consti- tute the executive in practical terms.

 See Chapters 9–10.

With devolution to Northern Ireland, Scotland and Wales, each of those countries has established its own form of government. In Northern Ireland the executive comprises the First Minister and Deputy First Minister, who jointly appoint other Ministers. Together they form an Executive Committee, the equivalent of the United Kingdom Cabinet. In Scotland the executive comprises the First Minister and such Ministers as the First Minister appoints. In Wales, the executive is made up of the First Minister and such other Ministers as he or she appoints. For further detail see Chapter 11.

 See Chapters 13–16.

The legislature

The Queen in Parliament is the sovereign law-making body within the United Kingdom. Formally expressed, Parliament comprises the Queen, House of Lords and House of Commons. All Bills[5] must be passed by each House and receive Royal Assent.

Parliament is bicameral, that is to say there are two chambers, each exercising a legislative role – although not having equal powers – and each playing a part in ensuring the accountability of the government. By way of introduction, it should be noted that membership of the House of Lords is not secured by election and is accordingly not accountable in any direct sense to the electorate.[6] The House of Commons is directly elected, and a parliamentary term is limited under the Parliament Act 1911 to a maximum of five years. Under the Fixed-term Parliaments Act 2011, each Parliament (with limited exceptions) lasts for five years.

---

4 Note that some ministers are drawn from the unelected House of Lords. See further Chapter 16.
5 With the exception provided by the Parliament Acts 1911–1949.
6 But note that there are proposals under consideration for reforming the composition of the House of Lords.

The House of Commons is made up of the governing party: the political party which secures the highest number of seats at the election, and the opposition parties. The opposition parties comprise the remainder of the now 650 Members of Parliament. The official Opposition is the party which represents the second largest party in terms of elected Members. In principle, the role of the official Opposition is to act as a government in waiting, ready at any time to take office should the government be forced out of office.[7] The General Election of 2010 produced an unusual result with no one political party having a sufficient majority of seats to form a government. A Coalition government made up of the larger Conservative Party and the Liberal Democrat Party was formed, with the Labour Party forming the official Opposition.

Northern Ireland, Scotland and Wales each has its own legislative body – in Scotland the Parliament, in Northern Ireland and Wales the Assembly. See further Chapter 11.

The judiciary

The judiciary is that branch of the state which adjudicates upon conflicts between state institutions, between state and individual, and between individuals. The judiciary is independent of both Parliament and the executive. Judicial independence is of prime importance both in relation to government according to law and in the protection of the rights and freedoms of the citizen against the executive. As Blackstone observed in his *Commentaries*:

> in this distinct and separate existence of the judicial power in a peculiar body of men, nominated indeed, but not removable at pleasure by the Crown, consists one main preservative of the public liberty which cannot subsist long in any state unless the administration of common justice be in some degree separated both from the legislative and from the executive power. [Volume 1, page 204]

It is apparent, however, that, whilst a high degree of judicial independence is secured under the constitution, there are several aspects of the judicial function which reveal an overlap between the judiciary, Parliament and the executive.

As discussed in Chapter 22, England and Wales share a common legal system, while Northern Ireland and Scotland each has its own distinctive legal system. The separation of powers is a common feature of each legal system.

The appointment of judges and other aspects of judicial independence is discussed in Chapter 22.

The Office of Lord Chancellor

The office of Lord Chancellor derives from the Norman Conquest when the King's secretary became known as the royal 'chancellor'. The first Chancellor is recorded in 1068. In the Middle Ages, the primary role of the Chancellor was to preside over Parliament. From the fourteenth century, his functions have been both parliamentary and judicial, in the latter role presiding over the Court of Chancery until 1875.

Prior to the Constitutional Reform Act 2005, the office of Lord Chancellor spanned all three institutions of the state – the executive, legislature and judiciary. The Lord Chancellor was a politically appointed member of the Cabinet, the Speaker of the House of Lords and the head of the judiciary. Furthermore, as a senior judge the Lord Chancellor was entitled to participate in judicial proceedings, although by convention he would not adjudicate in cases

---

7 For consideration of the role of the Opposition, see Chapters 13–15.

which involved the government or were overtly political in nature. As head of the judiciary, with wide-ranging powers relating to the appointment of judges, the Lord Chancellor acted as the spokesperson for the judges and defended their independence from interference by the executive.

However, whatever perceived advantages flowed from the close relationship between the executive and Lord Chancellor, these were outweighed by the criticism that the office of Lord Chancellor represented a major breach in the separation of powers, and could not withstand the allegation that the office raised doubts about the independence of the judiciary.[8] As discussed below, the Constitutional Reform Act 2005 reformed the office of Lord Chancellor in a manner which establishes a clearer separation of powers between the executive, legislature and judiciary. The office of Lord Chancellor is retained in name but the powers of the office are radically curtailed. The post is combined with that of the Secretary of State for Justice. The office holder must be 'qualified by experience'[9] but need not be a lawyer, and the Lord Chancellor no longer exercises any judicial functions or acts as Speaker of the House of Lords. Section 1 of the Act makes explicit reference to the rule of law, stating that the Act does not adversely affect that principle or the Lord Chancellor's existing role in protecting the rule of law. Section 3 imposes a statutory duty on the Lord Chancellor and other Ministers of the Crown and those with responsibility for matters relating to the judiciary to uphold the continued independence of the judiciary.

The Supreme Court

One constitutional curiosity which represented a challenge to the separation of powers was the existence of the highest court in the United Kingdom, the Appellate Committee of the House of Lords, sitting in Parliament. Judges elevated to the highest court were made Life Peers under the Appellate Jurisdiction Act 1876, and known as Lords of Appeal in Ordinary, or Law Lords. The Court was physically located in committee rooms of the House of Lords, and judgments were delivered in the chamber of the House of Lords where its legislative work is carried out. The judges also contributed to the legislative work of the House of Lords, further blurring the line between the judiciary and the legislature. The arrangement can only be understood by reference to the constitutional convention which regulated the relationship between the judges sitting in their judicial capacity and the judges participating in the law-making work of the House of Lords. Convention dictated that – in order to protect their independence and impartiality – judges would not participate in party political debate.

The Constitutional Reform Act 2005 remedied this anomalous situation by creating a Supreme Court physically removed from the Houses of Parliament.[10] Housed in Middlesex Guildhall, opposite the Houses of Parliament, the Supreme Court represents an improved separation of powers between Parliament and the judiciary and complements the reformed office of Lord Chancellor. Although the name 'Supreme Court' was adopted, the Court was not given additional powers and is not comparable to a Supreme Court under a written constitution. Accordingly, it has the same powers as the Appellate Committee of the House of Lords, and – as previously – has no power to invalidate Acts of Parliament.

The Justices of the Supreme Court sit in panels of five, seven, nine or 11 Justices. Proceedings are open to the public.

---

8 The requirements of judicial independence were considered by the European Court of Human Rights in **Findlay v United Kingdom** (1997) and **McGonnell v United Kingdom** (2000): see further Chapter 18.

9 Section 2 provides that relevant experience may include experience as a minister, as a Member of either House of Parliament, as a practitioner, as a teacher of law in a university and any other experience that the Prime Minister considers relevant.

10 The Supreme Court commenced work on 1 October 2009.

The Relationship Between Executive and Legislature; Legislature and Judiciary; Executive and Judiciary

> In the field of constitutional law the delicate balance between the various institutions ... is maintained to a large degree by the mutual respect which each institution has for the other. [Lord Hope of Craighead, *Jackson v Attorney General* (2005) at paragraph 125]

In order to evaluate the separation of powers under the contemporary constitution, it is necessary to evaluate the manner in which, and the extent to which, separate functions are allocated between the differing bodies and kept separate. This task is most conveniently undertaken by examining the relationship between first, the executive and legislature; second, the legislature and judiciary; and, third, the executive and judiciary.

Executive and legislature
The personnel of government

Parliament provides the personnel of government. Ministers of the Crown, including the Prime Minister, must be Members of either House of Parliament. By convention, the Prime Minister must be a Member of the House of Commons. It is thus immediately apparent that the executive, far from being separated from the legislature, is drawn from within its ranks. It is for this reason that Walter Bagehot in *The English Constitution* denounced the theory of the separation of powers under the English constitution. For Bagehot, this feature of the constitution, however, far from being a dangerous divergence from an ideal separation of powers, had clear merits. To Bagehot, the close relationship between executive and Parliament represented 'the efficient secret of the English constitution', which:

> may be described as the close union, the nearly complete fusion, of the executive and legislative powers. No doubt by the traditional theory, as it exists in all the books, the goodness of our constitution lies in the entire separation of the legislative and executive authorities, but in truth its merit consists in their singular approximation. The connecting link [between the executive and parliament] is the Cabinet. [1867, pages 67–68]

There are, however, opposing views. Lord Hailsham, the Lord Chancellor in the 1979–1987 Parliament, asserted[11] that the current electoral process which, generally, but not invariably, returns a government with a large majority of seats in Parliament, contributes to what he termed an 'elective dictatorship' – that is to say, a situation in which the executive controls the legislature. While Bagehot's view may have been tenable at the time in which he wrote, it is nowadays too simplistic and inaccurate a description of the working of the constitution.[12]

Prima facie, this close union of executive and legislature would suggest that the potential for abuse against which Montesquieu warned exists at the heart of the constitution. This would be so if it were to be demonstrated that the executive controls Parliament. Judgment on that matter must be suspended until the working of Parliament has been examined in detail. There exist, however, tenable grounds for such an argument, but these must be set

See Chapters 13–15.

---

11 (1976) 120 SJ 693.
12 Richard Crossman (1993) states that Bagehot provides a correct description of Cabinet government as it was between 1832 and 1867; but see the opposing view expressed by Vile, 1967.

against the extent to which procedural mechanisms in Parliament avoid an actual or potential abuse of power by the executive. The constitutional principle entailed in this close union between executive and legislature, deriving from historical practice, is that of 'responsible government': that is to say that the powers of government are scrutinised adequately by a democratically elected Parliament to whom every member of government is individually and collectively responsible.

Statutory limits on membership

There exist statutory limits on the extent to which the executive can dominate Parliament. The House of Commons Disqualification Act 1975 preserves the separation between the executive and legislature by providing that certain categories of people are disqualified from holding parliamentary office. Under section 2, holders of judicial office, civil servants, members of the armed forces and the police and members of foreign legislatures are debarred from office.

The Act also limits the number of government Ministers in the House of Commons to 95 (section 2). Despite this limitation, 95 Ministers, when considered together with their loyal Parliamentary Private Secretaries,[13] ensures that the government will generally enjoy the automatic support of some 120 Members of Parliament. Where the government has been elected with a strong majority of seats – as in 1983, when the Conservative Party had a majority of 144, and in 1997, when the electorate returned a Labour government with a majority of 179 – it must be conceded that the potential for dominance exists. An evaluation of this matter depends upon the adequacy of parliamentary procedures.

Political and procedural checks on government

The government, it must be recognised, irrespective of the size of its majority of seats in Parliament, is dependent upon Parliament for its continuance in office.[14] The loss of a vote of confidence on a matter of policy central to a government's programme will cause the government to fall, as occurred in 1979 when the Labour Prime Minister, James Callaghan, was forced to seek a dissolution of Parliament and call a general election. Furthermore, parliamentary procedures are devised to secure adequate scrutiny for legislative proposals, and it cannot merely be assumed that the government will always get its legislation through in the form which it envisaged. By way of example, in 1983–1984, the Police and Criminal Evidence Bill was substantially amended following pressure from politicians of all parties, pressure groups, academics and lawyers. Furthermore, in 1986 the government – despite having a strong majority in Parliament – was forced to abandon its plans for legislation to deregulate Sunday trading due to parliamentary pressure. In 2012 the Coalition government was forced to modify its plans for reform of the House of Lords in light of opposition from Conservative Party MPs.

The Opposition

The role of the official Opposition must also be considered. Her Majesty's Loyal Opposition is, constitutionally speaking, a 'government in waiting'. Not only is it the function of the Opposition to question, challenge and oppose the government, but it also puts forward alternative policies and solutions to problems. In order to ensure that there is adequate opportunity for the Opposition to fulfil its constitutional role, 20 days per session are set aside for debate on subjects chosen by the Opposition.

---

13 Who are elected Members of Parliament.
14 Note that this remains the case when fixed-term parliaments are introduced under the Fixed-term Parliaments Act 2011.

Question Time, debates and Select Committees

Question Time and debates in Parliament ensure the accountability of government to Parliament. The administration of the state is scrutinised by a system of Select Committees in Parliament with wide powers of inquiry.

The House of Lords

See Chapter 15.

In addition to checks within the House of Commons, the House of Lords may cause government to modify or abandon proposed legislation. The House of Lords has the power to amend and delay non-Money Bills for approximately a year before the Bill can receive Royal Assent under the Parliament Acts 1911 and 1949. Rather than risk the delay of legislation, the government may prefer to compromise its proposals and accept proposed amendments from the Lords.

The electorate

Finally, the electorate, in addition to its role in a general election, can also express its displeasure with government policies during a parliamentary term at by-elections and local government elections and, albeit rarely, referendums.

Delegated legislation and the separation of powers

Delegated – or secondary – legislation raises important questions relating to the separation of powers. Delegated legislation refers to laws, rules and regulations, made by government Departments, local authorities and other public bodies, under the authority of an Act of Parliament: 'every exercise of a power to legislate conferred by or under an Act of Parliament'.[15]

The principal justification for the delegation of such law-making power is efficiency. By granting delegated power, Parliament is freed from scrutinising every technical detail of a Bill. Delegated power also enables Ministers and others to 'fill in the details' after the parent Act has been passed. AV Dicey approved of delegated powers on this basis.[16] Delegated power has, however, been questioned. In 1929, Chief Justice Hewart[17] criticised delegated legislation as being an abuse of power. An Interdepartmental Committee of Inquiry on Ministers' Powers[18] exonerated Ministers from this charge and defended both the necessity and desirability of delegated legislation.

In any parliamentary year, some 40 to 50 Acts of Parliament will be passed. The volume of delegated legislation, however, may amount to some 3,000 statutory instruments per year. While general Bills – public and private – are subjected to full parliamentary scrutiny, it will be seen in Chapter 14 that delegated legislation receives far more cursory examination by Parliament as a whole. The implication of delegated legislation in constitutional terms is that a legislative function is being exercised by the executive and not Parliament. The delegation of law-making power is a necessity given the heavy legislative programme and the modern complexity of legal regulation. Provided that parliamentary scrutiny is adequate, and that the courts are vigilant and effective in ensuring that delegated powers are exercised consistently with the law – *intra vires* – it may be concluded that this ostensible breach of the separation of powers is unavoidable, although whether it is subject to adequate scrutiny and control remains questionable.

In addition to the delegation of power to make secondary legislation, Acts of Parliament may on occasion confer on Ministers the power to amend primary legislation. Such powers are known as Henry VIII powers and are discussed at pages 375 to 376 below.

See Chapter 14.

---

15 *Joint Committee on Delegated Legislation*, HL 184, HC 475 (1971–1972), London: HMSO, para 6. See further Chapter 14.
16 Dicey, 1885, p. 52.
17 Hewart, 1929.
18 Donoughmore-Scott Committee, Cmnd 4046, 1932, London: HMSO.

Pause and Reflect

In *The English Constitution* (1861) Walter Bagehot stated that the 'near fusion' of the executive and legislature was the 'efficient secret' of the constitution. What did he mean by this statement? Does it reflect the relationship between the executive and Parliament now, and if so in what ways?

Legislature and judiciary

It has been stated above that Parliament is sovereign and that the judiciary is subordinate to Parliament, but that the independence of the judiciary is protected. At the head of the judiciary is the Crown. The Crown appoints senior judges and represents the 'fountain of justice': all judicial acts are carried out in the name of the Crown.

Rules against criticism of the judiciary

To reinforce the independence of judges, convention dictates that there should be no criticism levelled at them from members of the executive – but not from other Members of Parliament. Parliamentary practice prohibits the criticism of judges other than under a motion expressing specific criticism or leading to an Address to the Crown for the removal of a judge. It was not, however, regarded as a breach of conventional rules when the then Prime Minister, Mrs Thatcher, in Parliament, criticised the light sentence imposed on a child molester.[19] There have, however, been other incidents where judges have been criticised in Parliament. The manner in which Members of Parliament are controlled in terms of what they may, or may not, say is through the powers of the Speaker of the House of Commons (see further Chapter 14).

The *sub judice* rule

Where proceedings are either before a court or awaiting trial, Members of Parliament are barred from raising them in debate. If the matter has not yet reached the courts, debate may be barred if the Speaker considers that there would result a real and substantial danger of prejudice to the trial arising as a consequence. No reference may be made to criminal proceedings from the time of the charge being made until the final appeal is determined.

Parliamentary supremacy and the judicial function

The doctrine of parliamentary supremacy entails the necessary constitutional subordination of judges to Parliament and has several implications. First, it is well established that the sovereign Parliament can overturn any court decision by way of legislation.[20] Second, the judiciary's primary role in relation to the interpretation of statutes is to give effect to the latest expression of the will of Parliament.[21]

See Chapter 6.

The Human Rights Act 1998 was consciously drafted in such a manner as to preserve the balance of power – and separation of power – between the judiciary and Parliament. As will be seen more fully in Chapter 19, this is accomplished by providing that primary (but not secondary) legislation remains immune from being declared invalid even where that legislation is ruled to be incompatible with Convention rights. Where judges in the higher

19 HC Deb Vol. 34 Cols 123–125, 285–286.
20 For example, the War Damage Act 1965.
21 **Vauxhall Estates Ltd v Liverpool Corporation** (1932); **Ellen Street Estates Ltd v Minister of Health** (1934).

courts make 'declarations of incompatibility', the matter is referred back to the executive to determine whether, and in what form, amending primary legislation should be enacted by Parliament.

The separation of powers is also reflected in the rules relating to parliamentary privilege, discussed in Chapter 17. Parliamentary privilege is designed to protect Parliament from outside interference or influence and is inextricably linked to parliamentary sovereignty. One of the rules of both privilege and sovereignty is that judges will not consider the procedures followed by Parliament or in any way criticise Parliament's procedures. This rule came under consideration in **R (HS2 Action Alliance Ltd) v Secretary of State for Transport and others** (2013). An EU Directive (Directive 2001/42/EC) requires that major infrastructure projects should entail a Strategic Environmental Assessment (SEA). One of the issues before the Supreme Court in HS2 was whether the government's decision to go ahead with the high-speed rail line from London to the north should have been preceded by an SEA under the Directive. In judicial review proceedings, the appellants argued that the Directive, as interpreted by the Court of Justice of the European Union, required the courts to be satisfied that the information on which Parliament reached its decision was adequate and that the court should scrutinise Parliament's procedures to ensure that Members of both Houses understood the issues.

On this argument Lords Neuberger and Mance stated clearly that:

> Scrutiny of the workings of Parliament and whether they satisfy externally imposed criteria clearly involves questioning and potentially impeaching (i.e. condemning) Parliament's internal proceedings, and would go a considerable step further than any United Kingdom court has ever gone. [at paragraph 206]

On this aspect of HS2 Lord Neuberger stated extra-judicially that:

> The observations [made in the CJEU] appeared to suggest that, in a case where the environmental impact had been considered by Parliament, it would be the duty of the national court to examine the quality of the debate, how much parliamentary time was allowed, whether the vote was free and so on. In our view this raised the point, namely whether the European Communities Act 1972, which effectively imported EU law into this country, had the effect of overriding section 9 of the Bill of Rights 1689, which, for over 300 years, had ensured that the courts in no circumstances get involved with what goes on in Parliament. We were concerned about the notion that what we regard in this country as a fundamental aspect of the separation of powers was being questioned, indeed undermined, almost by a European sidewind.[22]

Judges as legislators

One of the most debated aspects of the relationship between the legislature and the judges lies in the question: 'Do judges make law?' In constitutional terms, the issue is whether by making law – either by virtue of the doctrine of precedent or through the interpretation of statutes – the judges are usurping the legislative function or, in other words, violating the separation of powers.[23]

The role of judges as law-makers must be understood against the backdrop of the long history of the common law – the law common to the whole country, developed by the judges rather than by Act of Parliament. In terms of the volume of law, Parliament only became the principal law-maker in the nineteenth century when the effects of industrialisation required

22 Conkerton Lecture, Liverpool Law Society, 9 October 2014, The Supreme Court and the Rule of Law, at para. 24.
23 This issue is complex. See Reid, 1972.

major programmes of legislation, much of it relating to safety at work and employment law, housing, health and relief from poverty. As discussed in Chapter 6, Acts of Parliament are supreme and may overturn the common law, as occurred for example in **Burmah Oil v Lord Advocate** (1965), in which the House of Lords awarded compensation for property loss and Parliament overruled the decision by enacting the War Damage Act 1965. However, when judges make law, Parliament may also 'tacitly' approve the decision by not interfering with it: when this occurs it can be said that the judges and Parliament are acting in a form of constitutional partnership. Parliament may also expressly endorse a judicial decision by incorporating it into statute, as occurred with the amendment to the statutory definition of rape following the House of Lords' decision in **R v R** (1991).[24]

The rules of precedent have been developed by the judges in order to ensure certainty and uniformity in decisions.[25] The need for certainty is expressed in the words *stare decisis*: 'stand by the decided cases'. In essence, decisions of the highest court – the Supreme Court – are binding on all the courts lower in the hierarchy. Furthermore, the Supreme Court is very slow to go against a previous decision of its own, although the House of Lords has had the power to do so since 1966.[26] Decisions of the next highest court – the Court of Appeal – are binding on courts lower in the hierarchy, and the Court of Appeal may only depart from its own previous decisions under limited circumstances.[27] There is thus a structure in place by which the lower courts are controlled by the decisions of the higher courts.

It is of course essential that while the law is certain, it is also able to reflect changes in society. The requisite flexibility is provided within the rules that structure the extent to which judges may depart from previous decisions. Taken together, the rules relating to being bound by the higher courts and to the *ratio* and distinguishing produce a high degree of stability, while also allowing for necessary flexibility. For further detail, see Chapter 22.

The rules of statutory interpretation, devised by the judges themselves, are also designed to limit judicial creativity. Statutory interpretation is not straightforward, even though Acts of Parliament are couched in detailed language in order to maximise clarity and minimise vagueness or obscurity. Despite this attempt to achieve clarity in statutory language, it is artificial to deny that judges 'make law'. Every new meaning conferred on a word, every application of a rule to a new situation, whether by way of statutory interpretation or under common law, 'creates' new law. Judges have themselves abandoned the fiction of the 'declaratory theory' which asserts that they do not 'make' law but merely discover its true meaning. From the separation of powers perspective, judicial law making should cause disquiet only if judges display overtly dynamic law-making tendencies. By way of illustration, in **Magor and St Mellons Rural District Council v Newport Corporation** (1965), Lord Denning MR was accused by Lord Simonds in the House of Lords of 'naked usurpation of the legislative function'.

The traditional techniques of statutory interpretation contrast markedly with the European method of interpretation. Civil Codes are, for the most part, phrased in broad language which indicates the objective(s) being sought. The interpretative technique – the teleological or purposive approach – is accordingly designed to guide the judge towards the desired outcome and involves far less detailed construction of the statutory words than is customary within the English legal system. The scope for 'creative' interpretation has been enlarged by the Human Rights Act 1998, section 3 of which requires the judges to 'read and give effect to' primary and subordinate legislation 'in a way which is compatible with Convention rights'. Even here, however, Parliament has restricted this requirement by the preceding words 'so far as it is possible to do so', and as we shall see in Chapter 18, the judges

---

24 See the Criminal Justice and Public Order Act 1994.
25 The detailed rules are outside the scope of this text.
26 See *Practice Statement* [1966] WLR 1234.
27 As defined in **Young v Bristol Aeroplane Ltd** (1944).

recognise and respect this limitation. The rules of statutory interpretation and the doctrine of precedent are discussed in more detail in Chapter 22.

 Pause and Reflect

Look up each of the following cases and explain, from a separation of powers perspective, why the courts reached the decision. You will find the full report of each case on the British and Irish Legal Information Institute website at www.bailii.org.

Do you agree with the decisions reached? Why? Why not?

Shaw v Director of Public Prosecutions (1962)

The defendant was prosecuted for conspiracy to corrupt public morals, a criminal offence not previously known to law. Parliament allowed the decision to stand.

Burmah Oil v Lord Advocate (1965)

Parliament overturned the decision of the House of Lords ordering compensation to be paid for the destruction of property by British troops in wartime.

R v R (1991)

The House of Lords overturned the historic immunity from the law of rape. Parliament endorsed the decision by redefining rape in statute.

Bellinger v Bellinger (2003)

The House of Lords issued a Declaration of Incompatibility in relation to section 11 of the Matrimonial Causes Act 1973. Parliament passed the Gender Recognition Act 2004 in response.

R (Nicklinson) v Ministry of Justice (2014)

The Supreme Court declined to issue a Declaration of Incompatibility in relation to the Suicide Act 1961 on the ground that it was for Parliament to consider the issue first. Four of the nine Justices wanted the matter resolved by Parliament; five of the nine Justices held that the Court could grant a Declaration, but three of those five held that Parliament should have the opportunity to rule on the matter first.

The High Court of Parliament

The United Kingdom Parliament has the sovereign power to regulate its own composition and procedure. Under parliamentary privilege – derived from the law and custom of Parliament and thus part of the common law – Parliament, and not the courts, has jurisdiction to rule on its own powers. Parliament cannot, however – other than by an Act of Parliament – extend its own privileges.[28]

The role of the judges in relation to privilege is to rule on its existence and extent. Once the court is satisfied that a particular matter falls within Parliament's domain, it will defer to Parliament. Accordingly, if, for example, a citizen is defamed by the absolute privilege of free speech in parliamentary proceedings,[29] there is no legal redress. Privilege will thus protect

---

28 *Stockdale v Hansard* (1839).
29 Bill of Rights 1689, Article IX.

the Member of Parliament from the law of defamation and leave the aggrieved individual without a legal remedy.

Privilege also extends to regulating the legislative process. It is for Parliament alone to determine the procedure by which an Act of Parliament should come into being. It is clearly established that, in order to become an Act of Parliament, a Bill must pass its legislative stages in the Commons and Lords (except where the Parliament Acts apply) before receiving Royal Assent. Once that process is complete, it is not for the judiciary to inquire behind the parliamentary roll.[30]

Executive and judiciary

With regard to the relationship between the executive and the judiciary, several matters having implications for the separation of powers require examination: the attitude of the courts in matters entailing the exercise of the royal prerogative, parliamentary privilege, judicial review, the role of judges in non-judicial functions and the role of the Law Officers of the Crown.[31]

The royal prerogative

Detailed consideration of the royal prerogative will be undertaken in Chapter 5. The royal prerogative has significant implications for the separation of powers. Being the residue of monarchical power, the prerogative is part of the common law and thus amenable to the jurisdiction of the courts. Today, the vast majority of prerogative powers are exercised by the government in the name of the Crown. As will be seen later, the substance of many prerogative powers is political, entailing matters of policy on which the judges are not competent to decide – in other words, matters which, if ruled on by the judges in a manner inconsistent with the interpretation of the executive, would place the judges in a sensitive constitutional position and leave them open to accusations of a violation of the separation of powers. That is not to suggest, however, that the courts have no role to play with respect to the royal prerogative. The traditional role of the courts is to rule on the existence and scope of the prerogative, but – having defined its existence and scope – to decline thereafter to rule on the exercise of the power. However, in **Council of Civil Service Unions v Minister of State for Civil Service** (1985) (the **GCHQ** case), the House of Lords made it clear that the courts have jurisdiction to review the exercise of executive power irrespective of whether the source of power is statutory or under the prerogative. Having seemingly extended the jurisdiction of the courts in relation to the prerogative, the House of Lords, nevertheless, proceeded to rule that there exists a wide range of 'non-justiciable' matters which should be decided by the executive rather than the courts: a clear expression of the separation of powers.

Law Officers of the Crown

The Law Officers of the Crown – the Attorney General and the Solicitor General – are members of the government. The Attorney General may also be a member of Cabinet. The Attorney General is bound by conventions which serve to limit the overlap in functions. Thus, where his consent to prosecution is required, by convention the Attorney General must avoid party political considerations, and may not take orders from government. This is a particularly delicate matter when essentially political prosecutions are being contemplated.[32] The Law Officers are advisers to government and its Ministers, and, by convention, this advice must never be

---

30 **Pickin v British Railways Board** (1974).
31 On the Home Secretary's former powers to determine the length of prison sentences and judicial review of his decisions, see the Fourth Edition of this book, pp. 893–896.
32 See **R v Ponting** (1985).

disclosed. In 1986, this convention was breached when Leon Brittan, then Secretary of State for Trade and Industry, revealed advice given on the Westland Helicopter rescue plan.[33]

Two recent matters have renewed concern over the office of Attorney General. The first relates to the legal advice given to the government on the legality of the war in Iraq, and allegations that the Attorney General's initial advice differed from that which was eventually disclosed to Parliament in 2003, and – following controversy and leaks to the media – ultimately published in 2005.

The second issue relates to the legality of the decision by the Director of the Serious Fraud Office (for whom the Attorney General had constitutional responsibility) to discontinue a criminal investigation into allegations of corrupt payments allegedly made by BAE Systems Plc. One aspect of the investigation concerned a valuable arms contract between the British government and the Kingdom of Saudi Arabia, for which BAE was the main contractor. The Director announced that the investigation would be discontinued in light of representations made to the Attorney General and Director concerning the need to safeguard national and international security. In Parliament the Attorney General stated that while there was a strong public interest in upholding and enforcing the criminal law, he also had to take into account the public interest in the security of the United Kingdom which would be harmed by the threats of the Saudi Arabian government that it would withdraw from the existing bilateral counter-terrorism cooperation arrangements with the United Kingdom, withdraw cooperation from the UK in relation to its strategic objectives in the Middle East and end negotiations for the procurement of Typhoon aircraft.

See
Chapters 23–25.

In **R (Corner House Research and Others) v Director of the Serious Fraud Office** (2008), the Appellate Committee of the House of Lords ruled that the decision of the Director was lawful. Lord Bingham of Cornhill referred to the Director's judgment that 'the public interest in saving British lives outweighed the public interest in pursuing BAE to conviction'. That was a decision that the Attorney General was lawfully entitled to make, and his decision 'involves no affront to the rule of law, to which the principles of judicial review give effect'.

The office of Attorney General, as the Iraq War and BAE Systems investigation illustrate, gives rise to allegations that his legal and political roles are insufficiently separated.

Judicial review

Judicial review of administrative action is designed to keep those persons and public bodies with delegated powers within the scope of the power conferred upon them by Parliament: the doctrine of *intra vires*. Thus, if a Minister of the Crown or a local authority or other public body exceeds the power granted, the courts will nullify the decision taken and require that the decision maker reach a decision according to the correct procedure. Judicial review is concerned with the process by which decisions are made, not with the merits of the decision itself, nor with the merits of the legal rules which are being applied by the administrator. From this perspective, it may be said that the judges are upholding the will of Parliament in controlling the exercise of powers delegated by it to subordinate bodies. The scope of judicial review has increased considerably – and the rule of law enhanced – since the coming into force of the Human Rights Act 1998.[34] The Human Rights Act, section 6, makes it unlawful for any public body – excluding Parliament but including the courts – to act in a way which is incompatible with the Convention rights protected under the Act. A person who claims that a public authority has acted or proposes to act in a manner incompatible with Convention rights may bring proceedings – including an application for judicial review – against that body.[35]

---

33 See further Chapter 15.
34 On which see Chapter 18.
35 Section 7. Alternatively, Convention rights may be used as a defence against action taken by a public body which is incompatible with Convention rights.

Summary of the United Kingdom's Separation of Powers

	The Executive	The Legislature	The Judiciary
Composition	Crown, Prime Minister, Cabinet and non-Cabinet ministers, civil service. Other institutions: devolved and local government, public bodies, police, armed forces, Revenue and Customs.	Crown, House of Commons, House of Lords. Other law-making bodies: the European Union; devolved legislatures (Northern Ireland, Scotland, Wales).	Judges and magistrates staffing courts and tribunals. The independence of the judiciary is guaranteed by the Act of Settlement 1700 which provides security of tenure for senior judges.
Functions and powers	• Government exercises royal prerogative powers on behalf of the Crown. • Makes policy. • Initiates legislation. • The civil service administers the law.	• Makes laws. • Scrutinises government policy and administration. • Holds government to account.	• Interprets and applies common law and statute. • Ensures the legality of the exercise of government powers through judicial review proceedings.
'Checks and balances' Composition	• By law, civil servants, serving police officers and members of the armed forces cannot be Members of either House of Parliament. • By convention, Ministers must be Members of either the House of Commons or House of Lords.	• By law, the number of salaried government Ministers in the Commons is limited to 95.	
Functions and powers	• Ministerial responsibility is the key concept in accountability of executive to Parliament. • A successful vote of 'No Confidence' in the House of Commons will lead to a government's resignation.	• The life of a Parliament is limited to five years. • Parliament's law-making powers are theoretically unlimited, in practice they are restricted by EU law, by devolution of law-making power to Northern Ireland, Scotland and Wales and by the political need to retain the support of the people. • The exercise of statutory powers may be reviewed by the courts in judicial review proceedings to ensure its compatibility with the power granted.	• Judges may not question the validity of Acts of Parliament. • The concept of justiciability restricts the role of judges to matters of law and prevents them ruling on matters of high policy. • By convention, judges must be politically neutral. • Parliament scrutinises government and holds it to account: the government must maintain the confidence of the House of Commons on key areas of policy or resign.

SEPARATION OF POWERS: THE UK AND USA COMPARED

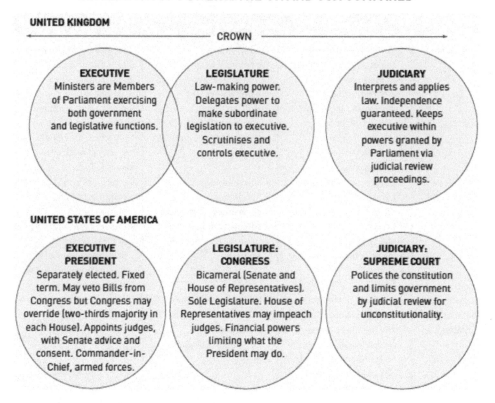

UNITED KINGDOM

— CROWN —

EXECUTIVE
Ministers are Members of Parliament exercising both government and legislative functions.

LEGISLATURE
Law-making power. Delegates power to make subordinate legislation to executive. Scrutinises and controls executive.

JUDICIARY
Interprets and applies law. Independence guaranteed. Keeps executive within powers granted by Parliament via judicial review proceedings.

UNITED STATES OF AMERICA

EXECUTIVE PRESIDENT
Separately elected. Fixed term. May veto Bills from Congress but Congress may override (two-thirds majority in each House). Appoints judges, with Senate advice and consent. Commander-in-Chief, armed forces.

LEGISLATURE: CONGRESS
Bicameral (Senate and House of Representatives). Sole Legislature. House of Representatives may impeach judges. Financial powers limiting what the President may do.

JUDICIARY: SUPREME COURT
Polices the constitution and limits government by judicial review for unconstitutionality.

Judges as fact finders

It has become increasingly common for the executive to appoint judges as chairmen of tribunals of inquiry.[36] That this should be so is unsurprising. Judges are equipped by training and experience to review evidence with impartiality and rigour and to present findings in a logical manner. Inquiries have been conducted by judges into such diverse matters as state security,[37] civil unrest and terrorism,[38] football club disasters,[39] BSE in cattle,[40] Arms to Iraq[41] and the 2003 inquiry into the circumstances surrounding the death of the government weapons inspector Dr David Kelly.[42]

Many of these inquiries involve sensitive political issues. As a result, it is inevitable that judges will attract criticism from one quarter or another. There exists the potential for charges of political bias in the report, or that the judge has avoided the issue and effected a 'whitewash' or that the inquiry has not been conducted properly. To place judges in the position where criticism is likely to ensue is to create the possibility that their independence and impartiality will be damaged.

---

36 See Drewry, 1996.
37 Cmnd 1681, 1962; Cmnd 2009, 1963; Cmnd 2125, 1963.
38 Cmnd 566 (NI), 1972; Cmnd 4801, 1972; Cmnd 5158, 1972; HC 220 (1971–1972) (see Boyle, Hadden and Hillyard, 1975, pp. 126–129); Cmnd 5847, 1975.
39 Cmnd 9710, 1986; Cmnd 962, 1990.
40 Lord Phillips.
41 See further Chapters 10 and 15.
42 Lord Hutton.

The Inquiries Act 2005 goes some way to meet such concerns. The Act provides that a Minister may establish an inquiry into events which 'have caused' or 'are capable of causing public concern'. Section 10 of the 2005 Act provides that where a Minister proposes to appoint a judge, the Minister must consult, as appropriate, the President of the Supreme Court, Lord Chief Justice of England and Wales, Lord President of the Court of Session and Lord Chief Justice of Northern Ireland. Inquiries are discussed in Chapter 26.

Summary

Some academic constitutional authorities either deny, or minimise, the relevance of the doctrine of separation of powers under the United Kingdom's constitution. Geoffrey Marshall, for example, writes: 'the principle is infected with so much imprecision and inconsistency that it may be counted little more than a jumbled portmanteau of arguments for policies which ought to be supported or rejected on other grounds' (1971, page 124).

On the other hand, it has been judicially asserted by Lord Diplock that: 'it cannot be too strongly emphasised that the British constitution, though largely unwritten, is firmly based on the separation of powers: Parliament makes the laws, the judiciary interprets them'.[43]

Equally, Sir John Donaldson MR has stated that: 'it is a constitutional convention of the highest importance that the legislature and the judicature are separate and independent of one another, subject to certain ultimate rights of Parliament over the judicature'.[44] As Professor Munro has said, 'there is something of a puzzle here'.

The separation of powers is certainly neither an absolute nor a predominant feature of the British constitution. Nevertheless, it is a concept which is firmly rooted in constitutional tradition and thought. Judicial assertions of the importance of the doctrine can be explained in light of the constitutional position of judges in relation to Parliament. The concept of separation of powers offers the judiciary a device both for the protection of the independence of the judiciary and against allegations of judicial intrusion into matters more appropriate to Parliament or the executive. The reluctance of judges to be drawn into such matters is reflected particularly strongly in relation to matters of the royal prerogative and parliamentary privilege.[45] Accordingly, to deny the relevance of some form of separation of powers would be to misconstrue the evidence. The separation of powers is a principle respected under the constitution which exerts its influence on each of the fundamental institutions of the state. While the separation of powers is ill defined, and is not accorded absolute respect, it ought not to 'be lightly dismissed'.[46]

Further Reading

Barendt, E, 'Separation of powers and constitutional government' [1995] *Public Law* 599.

Bradley, AW, 'Relations between Executive, Judiciary and Parliament: an evolving saga?' [2008] *Public Law* 470.

Cooke, Lord, 'The law Lords: an endangered heritage' [2003] 119 *Law Quarterly Review* 49.

Gee, G, 'What are Lord Chancellors for?' [2014] *Public Law* 11.

---

43 *Duport Steels Ltd v Sirs* (1980), p. 157.
44 *R v HM Treasury ex parte Smedley* (1985), p. 306.
45 See Chapters 5 and 17, respectively.
46 Munro, 1999, pp. 195, 328–332.

Hope of Craighead, Lord, 'Voices from the past: the law lords' contribution to the legislative process' (2007) 123 *Law Quarterly Review* 547.
House of Lords Select Committee on the Constitution, 6th Report of 2014–2015, 'The Office of Lord Chancellor', HL Paper 75, London: TSO.
Legal Studies Special Issue, 'Constitutional innovation: the creation of a supreme court for the United Kingdom' [2004] *Domestic, Comparative and International Reflections* 2, 3, 5, 7, 8, 9, 10.
Munro, CR, *Studies in Constitutional Law*, 2nd edn, 1999, London: Butterworths, Chapter 9.
Reid, Lord, 'The judge as law-maker' [1972] *Journal of the Society of Public Teachers of Law* 22.
Steyn, Lord, 'The case for a supreme court' (2002) 118 *Law Quarterly Review* 382.
Tomkins, A, *Public Law*, 2003, Oxford: Clarendon Press.

Chapter 5

The Royal Prerogative

The King should not be over man, but under God and the law.

Bracton (1200–1268)

Chapter Contents

Learning Objectives

By the end of this chapter you should be able to:

- ☐ explain Blackstone's and AV Dicey's definition of the royal prerogative;
- ☐ give illustrations of prerogative powers to demonstrate the broad range of powers;
- ☐ explain the rise of parliamentary sovereignty and the curtailment of the prerogative under the Bill of Rights 1689;
- ☐ discuss both parliamentary and judicial controls over the prerogative and the limits of those controls;
- ☐ discuss whether the prerogative is in need of reform.

Introduction

Under the constitution of the United Kingdom, all actions of government are undertaken in the name of the Crown. Any account of the prerogative is an account of power, and the prerogative, historically and contemporarily, concerns the power of the Crown.[1] The prerogative today represents one of the most intriguing aspects of the unwritten constitution. In order fully to appreciate the meaning of the term 'the Crown', an analysis of both who in fact exercises various powers in the name of the Crown, and the source of the power exercised, needs to be examined. The question to be asked is this: is the power (to be exercised) a prerogative power or is it the outcome of statute? As will be seen, there is no certainty as to either the existing prerogative powers or the manner in which these may be extinguished. It is, however, clear that no new prerogative powers can be created.

The Prerogative Defined

Blackstone defines the prerogative in his *Commentaries* (1765–1769) as:

> that special pre-eminence which the King hath over and above all other persons, and out of the ordinary course of the common law, in right of his regal dignity. It signifies, in its etymology (from *prae* and *rogo*) something that is required or demanded before, or in preference to, all others.

Dicey, on the other hand, describes the prerogative in the following manner:

> the residue of discretionary or arbitrary authority, which at any time is legally left in the hands of the Crown ... Every act which the executive government can lawfully do without the authority of an Act of Parliament is done in virtue of this prerogative. [1885, page 424]

---

1 On the distinctions between the monarch and the Crown, see Marshall, 1971, pp. 17–24.

From these differing definitions, the following can be deduced:

(a)   that these are powers which are inherent in, and peculiar to, the Crown;
(b)   that the powers derive from common law;
(c)   that the powers are residual;
(d)   that the majority of the powers are exercised by the executive government in the name of the Crown; and
(e)   that no act of Parliament is necessary to confer authority on the exercise of such powers.

Joseph Chitty, whose work remains the most comprehensive account of the prerogative, explains the need for prerogative power in the following manner: 'The rights of sovereignty, or supreme power, are of a legislative and executive nature, and must, under any form of government, be vested exclusively in a body or bodies, distinct from the people at large' (1820, page 2). In Chitty's analysis, the power of the King is but part of a reciprocal relationship between monarch and subject. To the King is owed a duty of allegiance on the part of all subjects; to the subjects is owed the duty of protection.

The Prerogative Before 1688

Before 1688, the King exercised powers relating to Parliament, law making and the administration of the courts, the regulation of trade, taxation and defence of the realm and miscellaneous other prerogatives. Principal among these powers were the following:

- The King would summon Parliament and prorogue it. The King could suspend Parliament's sittings and dissolve it. The absoluteness of the King's power came to a head in the reign of Charles I (1625–1649) when Charles confronted Parliament over taxation to meet the cost of war, imprisoning over 70 people who refused to pay the forced loan, including the 'five knights'[2] who sought a writ of habeas corpus against the King. The conflict between the King and Parliament came to a head when in 1629 Charles dissolved Parliament and there commenced an 11-year period of personal monarchical rule. In 1641, under the leadership of Pym, the 'Grand Remonstrance' was drafted – listing the grievances of the country under the rule of prerogative. While the Commons was divided over the Remonstrance, it represented a starting point in history, one which was to lead to the Civil War, Charles' execution and the rule of Oliver Cromwell under the only Republican constitution Britain has ever experienced.[3]
- The King claimed the right to legislate by 'proclamation', thereby usurping Parliament's law-making role. This power was challenged in the reign of James I (1603–1625) in the Case of Proclamations (1611), in which Sir Edward Coke CJ declared that:

> the King by his proclamation or other ways cannot change any part of the common law, or statute law, or the customs of the realm ... the King cannot create any offence by his prohibition or proclamation, which was not an offence before, for that was to change the law, and to make an offence which was not ... Also, ... the King hath no prerogative but that which the law of the land allows him.

---

2 *Darnel's Case* (1627).
3 See Lockyer, 1985, Chapters 12–13.

- The King's assent was needed for the enactment of statutes, but he also had the power to dispense with statutes and suspend their application.[4] The conflict between Crown and the courts in the seventeenth century is illustrated by the cases of **Thomas v Sorrell** (1674) and **Godden v Hales** (1686). In **Thomas v Sorrell**, it was declared that the King could not dispense with a penal law made for the good of the public. However, in **Godden v Hales**, the court accepted that the King could dispense with a penal law – under specific circumstances – where that law fell within his jurisdiction.

- It was within the King's prerogative to establish new courts of justice. The Court of Star Chamber, exercising extensive criminal jurisdiction with little of the formality of judicial proceedings and without the use of juries, was established either under the Statute of 1487 or under the Crown's inherent prerogative; doubt exists as to its source. Unlike the ordinary courts, the Court of Star Chamber used torture. It became one of the most feared and powerful weapons under the control of the Crown until its abolition in 1641.

- The King's claim to dispense justice in his own right and without the judges was dispelled in 1607. In Prohibitions Del Roy (**Case of Prohibitions**) (1607), the King sought to settle a dispute concerning land. In the Resolution of the Judges, Coke declared:

> that the King in his own person cannot adjudge any case, either criminal, as treason, felony, etc, or betwixt party and party, concerning his inheritance, chattels, or goods, etc, but this ought to be determined and adjudged in some Court of Justice, according to the law and custom of England; and always judgments are given ... so that the Court gives the judgment.

When, in 1617, the King ordered the Court of King's Bench to adjourn proceedings until he had been consulted, Chief Justice Coke refused, declaring that: 'Obedience to His Majesty's command to stay proceedings would have been a delay of justice, contrary to the law, and contrary to oaths of the judges'.[5]

Coke was dismissed from the Bench.

- The King claimed the power to detain a subject free from interference by the courts. Whether a writ of habeas corpus would lie against the King was determined in 1627. In **Darnel's Case** (the Five Knights' Case) (1627), it was held that, where the King detained a prisoner under special order, the court would not look behind the order. Thus, while the King could not determine cases, he could nevertheless hold a subject free from interference by the judges. The Petition of Right 1628 declared such power to be unlawful and, in 1640, the Habeas Corpus Act guaranteed that habeas corpus would lie against the Crown.

- Historically, much of the commerce and trade of the country was under the prerogative of the Crown, but such a power was effectively abolished by statute.

- The King had a duty to protect the realm, a duty which encompassed the powers to restrict imports of raw material of war and the right to erect ports and havens, beacons and lighthouses.

- The Crown's power of taxation is inextricably linked to the notion of the King as ultimate lord of all land. The King was the largest landowner in the Kingdom and exercised his right to collect revenues from the land. In addition, the King received profits from legal

---

4 *Case of Proclamations* (1611).
5 *John Colt and Glover v Bishop of Coventry and Lichfield* (the **Commendam Case**) (1617).

proceedings in the form of fees paid by litigants and fines. Pardons were also sold. The granting of supply to the King by Parliament from direct taxation had been established in 1215, from which time it was accepted that the King had no power to levy direct taxation without parliamentary consent.[6] The position of indirect taxation was, however, unclear. The power to regulate trade, including the power to establish, open and close ports, was within the royal prerogative. Accordingly, it could be argued that the correlative power to levy taxes on imports and exports was within the power of the Crown. Indirect taxation was in issue in the **Case of Ship Money (R v Hampden)** (1637). Hampden had refused to pay taxes levied by Charles I to raise money for the navy in times of emergency. The King argued that it was for the Crown to determine whether or not an emergency situation existed and that this determination was conclusive of his right to exercise his prerogative power to raise revenue. The courts upheld the power of the Crown. The Shipmoney Act of 1640 reversed the decision, and Article IV of the Bill of Rights 1689 declared it illegal for the Crown to raise money without parliamentary approval.

The Bill of Rights 1689, provided, *inter alia*, that there should be regular meetings of Parliament, that elections should be free, that the Crown's power to raise taxation[7] was subject to Parliament's approval (as was the power to maintain an army), that the powers of suspending or dispensing with laws by the Crown[8] were illegal and, of the greatest significance, that the 'freedom of speech and debates or proceedings in Parliament ought not to be impeached or questioned in any court or place out of parliament'.[9]

From this time, the supremacy of Parliament over the Crown was established and the prerogative powers of the Crown continued in existence or were abolished or curtailed as Parliament determined. No new prerogative powers may be claimed by the Crown: as Diplock LJ stated in **BBC v Johns** (1965): 'it is 350 years and a civil war too late for the Queen's courts to broaden the prerogative'.

Miscellaneous prerogatives included the right to raise revenue from the demesne lands of the Crown,[10] to the ownership of tidal riverbeds and to the land beneath a non-tidal riverbed – provided that it had not become a dry riverbed, whereupon the soil is equally owned by the owners of the adjoining banks. Equally, the King, by virtue of his prerogative, was owner of the shores of seas and navigable rivers within his dominions. The ancient right of the King to wild creatures, to franchises of forest, 'free chase', park or free warren have been abolished[11] with the exception of the right to royal fish (sturgeon) and swans, which is expressly reserved by the 1971 Act. Additionally, the Crown had the right to treasure trove, now regulated under the Treasure Act 1996.[12]

The Prerogative Today

The constitutional questions requiring answer include those relating to the relationship between statute and prerogative and the control, judicial or political, of the prerogative. The

---

6 In the reign of Edward I, 1271–1307.
7 **R v Hampden** (1637).
8 *Godden v Hales* (1686).
9 Bill of Rights, 1689, Article IX, discussed in Chapter 17.
10 Chitty, 1820, p. 206.
11 Wild Creatures and Forest Laws Act 1971.
12 See MacMillan, 1996, and **Attorney General of Duchy of Lancaster v GE Overton (Farms) Ltd** (1982). Treasure found must be reported within 14 days to the local coroner. Failure to do so will be a criminal offence. A Treasure Valuation Committee has been established which has the duty to value treasure and advise on *ex gratia* payments to the finder.

most significant question which continues to intrigue and concern constitutional theorists today relates to the very existence and scope of the powers themselves, together with the constitutional implications of this ill-defined reservoir of power. As Maitland observed, and as remains true in the twenty-first century, examination of the prerogative is 'set about with difficulties, with prerogatives disused, with prerogatives of doubtful existence, with prerogatives which exist by sufferance, merely because no one has thought it worthwhile to abolish them' (1908, page 421).

Under the United Kingdom's constitutional monarchy, the Queen is part of the legislature: Parliament comprises the Crown, Lords and Commons. The Queen is the 'fountain of justice' – and while the Queen has no power to make laws or suspend laws or to act in a judicial capacity,[13] the entire administration of justice is conducted in the name of the Crown.[14] The Queen is Supreme Head of the Church of England.[15] The Queen is Head of State in relation to foreign affairs. The Queen is head of the executive, and all acts of government, whether domestic or foreign, are conducted in the name of the Crown. The right to summon Parliament remains a legal power vested in the Crown. The Queen is the Fountain of Honour, and all honours in the United Kingdom are conferred by the Crown.

While regal powers are exercised in the name of the Crown by the government of the day, the Crown nevertheless retains important residual powers which are discussed below. It must also be recognised that a few powers remain the personal prerogative of the Crown. Illustrations include the grant of honours such as the Order of Merit and the Orders of the Garter and Thistle. More importantly, there still remains the prerogative notion that the Crown never dies and that the Crown is never an infant (thus ensuring continuity of monarchy), and that the Crown can 'do no wrong', thus placing the Queen outside the jurisdiction of the courts and guaranteeing immunity from prosecution in her own courts. Beyond these limited powers and immunities, the sovereign has, in the words of Bagehot (1867), 'under a constitutional monarchy such as ours, three rights – the right to be consulted, the right to encourage, the right to warn'. In legal theory, however, the position is much different. As Bagehot stated:

> Not to mention other things, she could disband the army (by law, she cannot engage more than a certain number of men, but she is not obliged to engage any men); she could dismiss all the officers, from the General Commander in Chief downwards; she could dismiss all the sailors too; she could sell off all our ships of war and all our naval stores; she could make a peace by the sacrifice of Cornwall, and begin a war for the conquest of Brittany. She could make every parish in the United Kingdom a 'university'; she could dismiss most of the civil servants; she could pardon all offenders. In a word, the Queen could by prerogative upset all the action of civil government within the government, could disgrace the nation by a bad war or peace, and could, by disbanding our forces, whether land or sea, leave us defenceless against foreign nations. [1867, 'Introduction' and pages 287–288]

In order to understand the power of the Crown, it is necessary to look beyond the superficial phrase 'in the name of the Crown'. The actual power which is exercisable by the Crown is limited in two ways. First, by convention, the majority of powers are exercised by Her Majesty's government or Her Majesty's judges in her name. Second, the existence and scope

---

13 *Case of Proclamations* (1611); Bill of Rights 1689; *Case of Prohibitions* (1607), respectively.
14 See Blackburn, 2004.
15 Act of Supremacy 1558. See Leigh, 2004.

of a purported prerogative power is subjected to the scrutiny of the courts: 'The King has no power save that allowed by law'.[16] However, that should not be considered as equivalent to a power to control the prerogative.[17]

The Prerogative Illustrated

Before examining the nature, scope and constitutional significance of the prerogative, some examples are necessary to indicate the areas of power which fall under the prerogative. Under the United Kingdom's unwritten constitution, there exists no formal and agreed text as to the prerogative. In order, therefore, to ascertain the contents of the prerogative, an examination of the historical attributes of the Crown and the attitude of the courts to the prerogative is required. It is paradoxical – but undeniable – in a modern democracy that there is no comprehensive, authoritative 'catalogue' of prerogative powers.[18]

To make an analysis of prerogative powers manageable, they may be separated into two categories:[19] those relating to domestic affairs and those relating to foreign affairs.

Within the domestic category fall:

- the summoning and (previously) the dissolution of Parliament although this is due to be revived under the Draft Fixed-term Parliaments Act 11 (Repeal) Bill 2021;[20]
- the appointment of Ministers;
- Royal Assent to Bills;
- the granting of honours;
- defence of the realm and national security;
- the issuing, refusal or withdrawing of passports;
- the protective jurisdiction of the courts in relation to children – *parens patriae*;
- the prerogative of mercy;
- the power to establish non-statutory agencies;
- regulation of the civil service;
- regulation of the armed forces;
- the right to royal fish and swans.

Under foreign affairs can be subsumed:

- Act of state;
- the power to make declarations of war and peace;
- the recognition of foreign states;
- diplomatic relations;
- the annexation and cession of territory;
- the regulation of colonial territories;
- the disposition of the armed forces overseas.

It can be seen from this list, which is by no means exhaustive, that the powers are wide and diverse.

---

16 **Case of Proclamations** (1611)
17 See **Council of Civil Service Unions v Minister for Civil Service** (1985), discussed below, p. 110.
18 The most recent authoritative account remains that of Chitty, 1820.
19 As does Blackstone, in his *Commentaries*.
20 Note that prior to the Fixed-term Parliaments Act 2011, the dissolution of Parliament was regulated under the royal prerogative, a power which is to be restored under the 2021 Draft Fixed-term Parliaments Act 2011 (Repeal) bill.

The Prerogative and Domestic Affairs

The summoning and dissolution of Parliament

Prior to a general election being held, it is necessary to bring the life of the existing Parliament to an end. This is done through the dissolution of Parliament. Prior to the Fixed-term Parliaments Act 2011, the Crown dissolved Parliament under the royal prerogative at the request of the Prime Minister. This power gave rise to many doubts and criticisms. The main political criticism was that the Prime Minister could choose the date of a general election when it most favoured the re-election of the government. The Coalition government formed in 2010 introduced a fixed five-year parliamentary term. The Fixed-term Parliaments Act 2011 placed the dissolution of Parliament on a statutory basis. The Crown's power to summon Parliament remains unaffected.

The rules relating to the dissolution of Parliament under the Fixed-term Parliaments Act 2011 are discussed in Chapter 12. Note, however, that dissatisfaction with the rigidity caused by the 2011 Act has prompted further reform and as of February 2021 there is a Draft Fixed-term Parliaments Act 2011 Bill under consideration by a pre-legislative scrutiny committee.[21] It is the government's intention to revive the prerogative power to dissolve Parliament, enabling it to call a general election at the time of its choosing.

Appointment of Prime Minister

In constitutional theory, the Queen – under the royal prerogative – may appoint whomsoever she pleases to the office of Prime Minister.[22] In practice, the position is governed by convention and the Queen must appoint the person who can command a majority in the House of Commons; this, under normal circumstances, will be the leader of the political party which secures the greatest number of parliamentary seats at a general election. Several differing situations present themselves: the government of the day may be returned by the electorate with a majority and the Prime Minister will remain in office. Alternatively, the government may lose the election, and the incoming Prime Minister will be the leader of that political party which commands a majority of seats in the House of Commons. More difficult is the position where the election produces no outright winner, resulting in no one party having an overall majority. Here, the spectre of a 'hung parliament' arises (as in 2010). The situation may also arise where a Prime Minister resigns due to old age or ill health during the course of his term of office – as was the case in 1935 (Ramsey MacDonald), 1955 (Winston Churchill) and 1957 (Anthony Eden) – or dies in office (Campbell-Bannerman, 1905–1908). Finally, it may be the case that a Prime Minister chooses to resign, as occurred in 1937 (Stanley Baldwin), in 1976 (Harold Wilson), in 2007 (Tony Blair) and in 2019 (Theresa May).

Appointment of Prime Minister following a general election

In a general election the electoral system usually returns a single party with an overall majority of seats in the House of Commons, and no question arises as to whom the Queen should appoint as Prime Minister. It is not out of the question, however, for a different political scenario to present itself. Should the Queen send for the leader of the party having the largest

---

21 On pre-legislative scrutiny see Chapter 14.
22 See, *inter alia*, Jennings, 1959a; Marshall and Moodie, 1971; Laski, 1951; Brazier, 1990, Chapters 1 and 2; Marshall, 1984, Chapter II.

number of seats, or the leader of the party which will hold the balance of power? There has been much debate over the issue,[23] but once again no clear-cut answer.

In February 1974, the Conservative Party lost the general election by a small number of seats and could command no overall majority in the House of Commons. Following the election results, the Prime Minister, Edward Heath, did not tender his resignation immediately but rather entered into negotiations over the following weekend with the Liberal Party, with a view to forming a political pact which would ensure a majority over the opposition parties. When those negotiations broke down, Mr Heath immediately resigned, and the Queen invited the Leader of the Labour Party to become Prime Minister.[24]

A similar result occurred in 2010, with no political party winning a clear majority of seats. The Labour Party, which had been in office since 1997, won fewer seats than the Conservative Party. The incumbent Labour Prime Minister remained in post until an agreement was reached between the Conservatives and Liberal Democrats, resulting in a full Coalition government. Once that agreement was reached, the Prime Minister resigned office and the Crown appointed the Leader of the Conservative Party, David Cameron, as Prime Minister, with the Leader of the Liberal Democrat Party being appointed Deputy Prime Minister.

See Chapter 10.

Appointment of Prime Minister following retirement/resignation of the incumbent

When the Prime Minister retires, the government still retains the mandate of the people and hence the choice of the new Prime Minister will be dictated by the wishes of the Party. It may be that there is a 'Prime Minister in waiting' who commands the support of the Party and will hence be appointed without delay.[25] Under such circumstances, it is unrealistic to speak of the Crown having any choice in the matter. Where no Party consensus as to a successor exists, the political process will come into play. Nowadays, each of the major political parties utilises a method of election of its leader, and it is that process which will determine the successor; again, the Queen has no practical 'say' in the matter. However, in the past there were instances where the Queen did have a role in the selection of a Prime Minister.

In 1957, Sir Anthony Eden resigned office, and there was no obvious successor – nor was there in place at that time an electoral process within the governing Conservative Party which would produce a successor. The Queen was thus left with a choice. The Queen consulted elder statesmen of the Conservative Party and acted upon their advice that Harold Macmillan be appointed. Had she not acted upon impartial advice, the Crown could have been damaged by charges of political decision making. One consequence of the 1957 dilemma was that the Labour Party announced its intention to introduce a selection procedure for its leader, a move designed to remove any discretion from the Crown. The Conservative Party did not react in this manner until after the difficulties revealed in 1963. The resignation of Harold Macmillan fell at a time when there were several contenders for leadership of the Party. The matter was resolved by the appointment of Lord Home, a Conservative peer who relinquished his peerage and took a seat in the House of Commons as Sir Alec Douglas-Home. However, the saga emphasised the uncertainties in the choice of Party Leader, and an electoral system for the leadership of the Party was subsequently introduced.

---

23 See, *inter alia*, Jennings, 1959a, Chapter II; Marshall, 1984, pp. 29–35; Marshall and Moodie, 1971, pp. 44–51; Brazier, 1982.
24 See, *inter alia*, Bogdanor, 1983, Chapters 5–8; Butler, 1983.
25 As in 2007 when the Chancellor of the Exchequer, Gordon Brown, succeeded Tony Blair as Prime Minister.

The Royal Assent

As discussed in Chapter 14, to become an Act of Parliament a Bill needs to be approved by the House of Commons and House of Lords (with the exception of the Parliament Act procedure) and receive the Royal Assent. In law, the Crown may refuse the Royal Assent but, by convention, the Royal Assent will not be withheld if the government supports a Bill.[26]

The Granting of Honours

Whilst legally still in the hands of the Crown, the effective control over the granting of the majority of honours lies with the executive. The Queen has the personal right to confer the Order of the Garter, the Order of the Thistle, the Royal Victorian Order and the Order of Merit. Otherwise, the conferment of honours is by the Queen, acting on the advice of the Prime Minister who is, in turn, advised by a Political Honours Scrutiny Committee comprising three Privy Counsellors.[27] The link between the granting of honours and the financing of political parties has been a matter of concern for decades. This issue is discussed in Chapter 12.

Defence and National Security

One of the key duties of government is the protection of the state from internal or external threats. As will be seen in Chapter 21, the statutory regulation of the security and intelligence agencies is relatively recent, and the law relating to terrorism is now contained in several Acts of Parliament. Nevertheless, national or state security remains within the royal prerogative. It is also an aspect of power in relation to which the judges will defer to the executive, thus preserving the separation of powers between the unelected, democratically unaccountable judiciary and the elected, democratically accountable government. Where national security is pleaded, for example in **Council of Civil Service Unions v Minister of State for the Civil Service** (1985) (the **GCHQ** case), discussed below at page 116, the courts were unable to protect the right of workers to belong to a trade union once the executive had argued that the withdrawal of the right to belong to a union was necessitated by considerations of state security.

Issuing, Refusal or Withdrawal of Passports

Consistent with the Crown's power to regulate its boundaries and those who enter and leave is the power to issue passports; again, under Blackstone's definition, this is a questionable prerogative power, for the government is doing no more than what it is free to do under statute and the power has no legal effect as such. Nevertheless, the conventional classification of the right to issue and withhold passports is that of the prerogative. At common law, citizens have the right to enter and leave the realm. It is nevertheless extremely difficult in practice to travel without a passport, which is issued under the prerogative. In **R v Foreign Secretary ex parte Everett** (1989), the court for the first time held that the granting and withholding of passports was subject to review by the courts. The position in the United Kingdom – both uncertain

---

26 See Wheeler, 2016.
27 Cmnd 1789, 1922, London: HMSO; see **Parkinson v Royal College of Ambulance** (1925), which led to the passing of the Honours (Prevention of Abuses) Act 1925; and see Wagner and Squibb, 1973. It has been proposed that the Scrutiny Committee be merged with the Independent Appointments Commission to ensure greater scrutiny.

and unsatisfactory – may be contrasted with that in the United States of America, where the Supreme Court has held that freedom of travel is a basic constitutional liberty.[28] The ancient right to issue the writ *ne exeat regno* – forbidding a person from leaving the realm – is declared by Jackson and Leonard (2001), relying on **Felton v Callis** (1969), to be 'obsolescent'. The doctrine of obsolescence has never been one accepted in English law. The rationale for such acceptance in relation to the writ *ne exeat regno*, and that of impressment into naval service, is that offered by Lord Simon of Glaisdale in **McKendrick v Sinclair** (1972) to the effect that:

> a rule of English common law, once clearly established, does not become extinct merely by disuse … but may 'go into a cataleptic trance' … and revive in propitious circumstances … but not revive if it is 'grossly anomalous and anachronistic'.

That it is not obsolete is confirmed by two cases. In **Al Nahkel for Contracting Ltd v Lowe** (1986), the writ was used to prevent a defendant leaving the country to avoid a judgment of the court. In **Parsons v Burk** (1971), an unsuccessful attempt was made to prevent the New Zealand rugby team from leaving the country to play in South Africa. Executive control over the issuing, refusal or withdrawal of passports is an important aspect of national security on which see Chapter 21.

The Protective Jurisdiction of the Courts in Relation to Minors

The modern law relating to children is now largely statutory. However, there remains an important residual prerogative jurisdiction to protect children. This prerogative power underlies the law relating to wardship, where the protection of the child is placed in the hands of the courts.

The Prerogative of Mercy

Nowadays, the prerogative of mercy entails two aspects: the power to grant pardons and the power to enter a *nolle prosequi*.

Pardons and commutation of sentence

A complete pardon is used to remove the 'pains, penalties and punishments' which flow from a conviction for a criminal offence, but does not eliminate the conviction itself.[29] The right of pardon does not extend to civil matters. The power is exercisable in England and Wales on the advice of the Secretary of State for the Home Department, who is accountable to Parliament. The Crown therefore has no personal involvement in its exercise. Commutation of sentence is a limited – or conditional – form of pardon. The sentence will be reduced on conditions: 'a condemned murderer is pardoned on condition of his going into penal servitude'. As Maitland comments (1908, page 480): 'It is a nice question whether he might not insist on being hanged'. Commutation is distinguishable from remission of sentence. The latter reduces the sentence imposed but does not alter its form.

---

28 See, inter alia, **Aptheker v Secretary of State** (1964); **Kent v Dulles** (1958).
29 **R v Foster** (1985).

The prerogative of mercy has traditionally been regarded as unreviewable by the courts. In 1976, in **De Freitas v Benny** (1976), Lord Diplock was to state that:

> At common law, this has always been a matter which lies solely in the discretion of the sovereign, who by constitutional convention exercises it in respect of England on the advice of the Home Secretary to whom Her Majesty delegates her discretion. Mercy is not the subject of legal rights. It begins where legal rights end.[30]

In **Council of Civil Service Unions v Minister for the Civil Service** (1985), Lord Roskill confirmed that the prerogative of mercy was not 'susceptible to judicial review'. However, the case of **Bentley** (1993) suggests a different approach. In 1952, Derek Bentley, aged 19, and with the mental age of an 11-year-old, was convicted of the murder of a policeman. At the time, the death penalty was the mandatory sentence for murder. Derek Bentley was hanged in 1953, a mere three months after the murder. His co-defendant, Christopher Craig, who fired the fatal shot at the police officer who died, was also convicted of murder, but escaped execution because he was aged only 16. Despite a recommendation by the jury that mercy be exercised, the Home Secretary decided not to exercise the prerogative. In an application for judicial review brought by Derek Bentley's family, the court considered the question whether the prerogative of mercy was amenable to judicial review.[31] The applicant sought a declaration that the Home Secretary had erred in law in declining to recommend a posthumous free pardon, and mandamus to require the Home Secretary to reconsider the matter.

Counsel for the Home Secretary argued that the exercise of the royal prerogative of mercy was not reviewable in the instant case, on the basis that the criteria upon which the pardon should be granted was a question of policy, which was not justiciable. The court ruled that the view that 'the formulation of the criteria for the exercise of the prerogative by the grant of a free pardon was entirely a matter of policy which is not justiciable' was 'probably right' (page 453). However, it ruled that the Home Secretary failed to recognise that the prerogative of mercy is 'capable of being exercised in many different circumstances and over a wide range', and should have considered the form of pardon which might be appropriate to the facts of the case.[32] This the Home Secretary did not do, and this failure was reviewable by the courts. The court expressed the view that the prerogative of mercy is now 'a constitutional safeguard against mistakes'. The court also ruled, however, that it had no power to direct the way in which the prerogative of mercy should be exercised, but that it had a role to play by way of judicial review. The court declined to make any formal order, but invited the Home Secretary to reconsider the matter 'in light of the now generally accepted view that this young man should have been reprieved' (page 455).

In 1998, the Court of Appeal, Criminal Division[33] quashed Derek Bentley's conviction for murder. The Court ruled that the conviction had been unsafe (**R v Bentley** (1998)). Thus, 45 years after the event, Bentley's name was cleared by the courts on the basis that his conviction had been unsafe, the royal prerogative of mercy in the hands of the politicians having failed to provide a remedy.

---

30 At p. 247. See also **R v Allen** (1862); **Hanratty v Lord Butler** (1971).
31 **R v Secretary of State for the Home Department ex parte Bentley** (1993).
32 On the power to issue a pardon, see **R (Shields) v Secretary of State for Justice** (2008).
33 On a reference by the Criminal Cases Review Commission under s. 9 of the Criminal Appeal Act 1995.

Nolle prosequi

On proceedings on indictment, the Attorney General, in the name of the Crown, can enter a *nolle prosequi*, the effect of which stops the legal proceedings. The power is not subject to the control of the courts: **R v Comptroller of Patents** (1899). The grant of a *nolle prosequi* does not amount to an acquittal, and accordingly, the accused may be brought before the court on the same charge. The effect of this would be to invite a further application for a *nolle prosequi*.

Power to Establish Non-Statutory Agencies

The Criminal Injuries Compensation Board was established under the prerogative in 1964. Its objective was to provide compensation for the victims of criminal offences[34] through *ex gratia* payments calculated on the same principles as compensation paid to victims of tort. The Board was reconstituted under statute in 1988,[35] although the provisions had not been brought into force. Was the setting up of the Board in 1964 the exercise of a true prerogative? Reverting to Blackstone's definition, the answer must be negative. The power to establish such a scheme clearly fell within Parliament's jurisdiction, as the Criminal Justice Act 1988 proves. However, under Dicey's definition, the government is effectively given a choice in the manner of establishing such bodies – a surely questionable prerogative?

Regulation of the Civil Service[36]

Prior to the Constitutional Reform and Governance Act 2010, on which see below, the control of the Civil Service was vested in the Crown. Appointments were based on merit and permanent. A civil servant would not be dismissed other than for misconduct.[37] Civil servants had no contractual relationship with the Crown.[38] Salaries and other benefits were prescribed by statute, but for the most part, the Civil Service was governed under the prerogative.[39]

The government's 2007 Green Paper, *The Governance of Britain*, envisaged legislation 'enshrining the core values and principles of the Civil Service'. The Constitutional Reform and Governance Act 2010 places the Civil Service on a statutory basis for the first time. Section 2 provides for the establishment of the Civil Service Commission with functions relating to the appointment of civil servants. The management of the Civil Service remains with the Minister for the Civil Service (usually the Prime Minister), with the exception of the Diplomatic Service, which remains under the control of the Foreign and Commonwealth Office. It also provides for a Code for Special Advisers (on whom see further Chapter 9), defines their role and provides an overall limit on the number of Special Advisers to be made by Order.

Section 1(2) of the Constitutional Reform and Governance Act 2010 provides that the Act does not apply to the Secret Intelligence Service, the Security Service, the Government Communications Headquarters, the Northern Ireland Civil Service or the Northern Ireland Court Service. The Act also does not apply to the appointment of civil servants outside the United Kingdom whose duties are carried out wholly outside the United Kingdom.

---

34 See Newburn, 1989, p. 41.
35 Criminal Justice Act 1988, ss 108–117 and Scheds 6–7.
36 See further Chapter 9. The structure and conditions of employment are outside the scope of this work: see Jackson and Leonard, 2001, Chapter 17.
37 Fulton Committee Report, Cmnd 3638, 1971, London: HMSO.
38 **CCSU v Minister for the Civil Service** (1985), p. 419.
39 For a detailed and critical analysis of the Civil Service, see Hennessy, 1990. On proposed reforms, see further Chapter 9.

Regulation of the Armed Forces

As with the Civil Service, members of the armed forces are regulated under the royal prerogative, and statutory protection of employment in, for example, the Employment Protection (Consolidation) Act 1978 does not apply to members of the armed forces.[40]

The sovereign is Commander in Chief of the armed forces. The Bill of Rights 1689 prohibits the maintenance of an army by the Crown in peacetime without the consent of Parliament. The control, organisation and disposition of the forces are within the prerogative and cannot be questioned in a court of law.[41]

The Prime Minister, acting in the name of the Crown, has hitherto had the ultimate say in committing British troops to military action. For example in 1939 (following months of an attempt to reach a peaceful agreement with Germany), when German troops invaded Poland on 1 September, the British Prime Minister declared that Britain was at war with Germany. More recently, in 2003 the British Prime Minister backed the United States' invasion of Iraq by committing British troops without prior parliamentary approval. In practical terms, the deployment of troops cannot be effected without Parliament's approval of finance – accordingly Parliament must (albeit belatedly) approve the government's decision.

Interventions by armed forces in another sovereign state may involve either the use of military force or humanitarian aid. Interventions have to be seen within the context of the UK's membership of both the United Nations and North Atlantic Treaty Organization (NATO). Since the early 1990s, UK armed forces have been involved in military interventions including Bosnia (1992), Kosovo (1999), Sierra Leone (2000), Afghanistan (2001), Iraq (2003), Libya (2011) and Mali (2012).

The wide-reaching power relating to the deployment of troops, exercised without Parliament's prior consent, is controversial. The Constitutional Reform and Governance Bill 2009–2010 provided that in relation to war, international armed conflict and international peace-keeping activities, prior approval must be given by each House, by Resolution, except where the Prime Minister considers that exceptional considerations require immediate action. The provision, however, did not survive the passage of the Bill and accordingly the prerogative power relating to the deployment of troops remained in the hands of the government. It is, however, accepted that there now exists a constitutional convention that Parliament should have the opportunity to debate the issue, and that Parliament's decision binds the government.

In 2011 the Foreign Secretary committed the government to 'enshrine in law for the future the necessity of consulting Parliament on military action'.[42] On 29 August 2013 the government was defeated on a proposal to authorise the use of military force in response to the situation in Syria and the use by the Syrian government of chemical weapons. Following the vote (332 to 220), the Prime Minister stated that: 'It is very clear tonight that … the British Parliament, reflecting the views of the British people, does not want to see military action. I get that, and the Government will act accordingly'. Professor Malcolm Chambers of the Royal United Services Institute was to comment that: 'It is now hard to see how any UK

---

40 For details of the organisation and control of the armed forces see Jackson and Leonard, 2001, Chapter 18.
41 **China Navigation Company Ltd v Attorney General** (1932); **Chandler v Director of Public Prosecutions** (1964). See also the Crown Proceedings Act 1947, s. 11.
42 HC Deb Col. 799, 21 March 2011.

Government could undertake significant military action without the support of Parliament, or indeed the wider public'.[43,44]

The establishing of a new convention concerning prior parliamentary approval for the deployment of British troops overseas curtails the exercise of the prerogative. In practical terms it would now appear that the prerogative could only be exercised without prior parliamentary approval in a situation where the national interest and/or security were threatened if immediate action were not taken.[45]

Royal Fish and Swans and Treasure Trove

This is a residual prerogative entitling the Crown to certain fish and swans. Rather more relevant until recently was the right of the Crown to treasure trove. This latter prerogative has now been placed under statute with the Treasure Act 1996.

 Pause and Reflect

In 2014 the Prime Minister sought the prior approval of the House of Commons for the involvement of British troops in military action in Syria. The House rejected the proposal and the Prime Minister accepted that decision.

What is the significance of this development?

Is there now a convention that Parliament will be consulted prior to any future military action? Are there any exceptions to this requirement?

Is there now a convention that Parliament must approve any future military action?

What would be the constitutional consequence of the government failing to consult Parliament in advance?

The Prerogative and Foreign Affairs

Act of state[46]

Act of state doctrine has a long history, its origins lying in the seventeenth century.[47] Act of state was examined in **Yukos Capital Sarl v OJSC Rosneft Oil Co (No 2)** (2014), where it was explained that the essence of the doctrine is that the courts of law will not adjudicate on the validity, legality, lawfulness, acceptability or motives of state foreign actors. It is founded on the principle of the comity of nations. The doctrine has limitations. Among these are that the act of state must, generally speaking, take place within the territory of the foreign state itself, although exceptionally borders may be crossed. A second limitation is that the doctrine will

---

43 RUSI Analysis: Parliament's Decision on Syria: Pulling our Punches, August 2013, cited in the House of Commons' Defence Committee 14th Report, 'Intervention: Why, When and How?' April 2014.
44 See the Political and Constitutional Affairs Select Committee of the House of Commons: Twelfth Report of 2013–2014, *Parliament's role in conflict decisions: a way forward.*
45 Note that the Overseas Operations (Service Personnel and Veterans) Bill 2019–2021 provides greater protections to armed service personnel and veterans serving on military operations overseas.
46 See Anson, 1933, Vol. II, Pt I, Chapter 6.8.
47 **Blad v Bamfield** (1674); **Duke of Brunswick v King of Hanover** (1844).

not apply to acts which are contrary to international law, or English public policy, or where there are serious violations of human rights.

Act of state was central to **Belhaj & Anor v Straw & Ors** (2014). In this case, the claimants sought a declaration of illegality and damages arising out of the alleged involvement of the respondents in their unlawful abduction, kidnapping and removal to Libya in 2004. Their claim included false imprisonment, trespass to the person, conspiracy to torture, conspiracy to use unlawful means, negligence and misfeasance in public office. The High Court, with reluctance, concluded that examination by the court would involve ruling on the legality of the conduct of US officials acting outside the United States, and that this would be damaging to the national interest. Accordingly the Court ruled that the act of state doctrine operated as a bar to the claim and that the claims were non-justiciable.

On appeal, however, the Court of Appeal ruled that the English courts had jurisdiction to rule on the claims. The claim was not barred by the act of state doctrine because it fell within the limitation on grounds of public policy in cases of violations of international law and fundamental human rights. There was a 'compelling public interest' in the investigation of the allegations, and if the court declined jurisdiction the 'grave allegations' would remain uninvestigated and the appellants left without any legal remedy. The 'risk of displeasing our allies or offending other states' could not justify declining jurisdiction on the basis of act of state. In **Rahmatullah (No 2) v Ministry of Defence; Mohammed v Ministry of Defence** (2017)[48] the claimant, an Afghan national, had been captured by British troops and transferred to Afghan custody. He alleged mistreatment and unlawful detention and claimed damages from the British government. The Supreme Court ruled that the treatment complained of amounted to Crown acts of state for which the government could not be liable. However, the Court also held that the definition of acts of state must be narrowly confined to a class of acts which are governmental in nature, committed abroad and so closely related to policy as to be necessary. It could not apply to acts of torture or mistreatment of detainees.

Declarations of war and peace

As with national security, declarations of war and peace remain within the royal prerogative and are not justiciable before the courts.

Recognition of foreign states

The recognition of foreign states is within the prerogative of the Crown. Several statutes regulate the privilege and immunities enjoyed by heads of foreign states[49] and their diplomatic representatives.[50]

Diplomatic relations

In 1708, the Diplomatic Privileges Act was passed after a Russian Ambassador had been arrested for debt. The Russian Czar, Peter the Great, regarded this action as a criminal offence. The Court of Queen's Bench was uncertain as to the legal position.[51] The Act of 1708 provided that no judicial proceedings could be brought against diplomats or their servants and that it was an offence to commence proceedings.

---

48 See also **Belhaj v Straw** (2017).
49 State Immunity Act 1978. On state immunity and its effect on the protection of human rights, see Chapter 18.
50 Diplomatic Privileges Act 1964. On immunities and privilege accorded to international and commonwealth organisations, see the International Organisations Acts 1968 and 1981; Diplomatic Immunities (Conferences with Commonwealth Countries and Republic of Ireland) Acts 1952 and 1961; International Headquarters and Defence Organisations Act 1964.
51 **Mattueof's Case** (1709).

Under the Diplomatic Privileges Act 1964, diplomatic staff enjoy full immunity – both civil and criminal – whereas administrative and technical staff have immunity for actions taken in the course of their duties but are otherwise civilly – but not criminally – liable for other acts. Members of service staff are immune only in respect of official acts. Whether a particular member of diplomatic staff falls within a certain category is determined by the Foreign Secretary by means of a certificate. The court will determine whether the action performed is within – or without – the individual's official duties.[52] Diplomatic immunity extends to diplomatic special missions, defined as a temporary mission sent by one state to another state with consent of the latter for the purpose of dealing with a specific question or matter. The Court of Appeal so ruled in **R (Freedom and Justice Party) v Secretary of State for Foreign and Commonwealth Affairs** (2018). Accordingly members of a special mission were granted immunity from arrest or detention and from criminal proceedings.

Where an individual enjoys immunity from the courts, the only redress will be for the Foreign Secretary to request the diplomat's government to recall him as *persona non grata*.

Annexation and cession of territory

In 1955, the Crown exercised its prerogative power to take possession of the island of Rockall, which subsequently was incorporated into the United Kingdom as part of Scotland.[53] Once territory has been annexed, the Crown has a discretion as to the extent to which it will take over the liabilities of the former government of the state.[54]

The Crown also has the power to alter the limits of British territorial waters.[55] However, while this prerogative seems firmly established, there are doubts as to the power of the Crown – without parliamentary approval – to cede territory and thereby deprive British citizens of their nationality and other rights under United Kingdom law.[56] When the Crown sought to cede Heligoland to Germany in 1890, parliamentary approval was sought. While the law may be doubtful, there is at least a convention that Parliament's approval will be sought and granted.

The regulation of colonial territories

Colonies and dependent territories are regulated by Orders in Council made in the exercise of the prerogative powers of the Crown. The control of Crown power in relation to such territories – exercised by the government – has been considered by the courts.[57]

In **R (Bancoult) v Secretary of State for Foreign and Commonwealth Affairs (No 2)** (2007), the Court of Appeal ruled that the use of Orders in Council to frustrate a ruling of the court was an unlawful abuse of power.[58] Under the British Indian Ocean Territory Ordinance No 1 of 1971, the inhabitants of the Chagos Islands were compulsorily removed from their home on the basis that, pursuant to a Treaty with Britain, the principal island was required for use by the United States of America as a military base. In 2000, the Divisional Court quashed the 1971 Immigration Ordinance on the ground that it fell outside the purpose of the British

---

52 In *Aziz v Aziz, Sultan of Brunei intervening* (2007), the Court of Appeal ruled that the head of a foreign state had no right to anonymity in court proceedings.
53 Island of Rockall Act 1972.
54 *West Rand Central Gold Mining Company v The King* (1905).
55 *Ibid.*
56 Anson, 1933, pp. 137–142; Holdsworth, 1942. See further Chapter 21.
57 See in particular **R (Quark Fishing Ltd) v Secretary of State for Foreign and Commonwealth Affairs** (2005) and references therein.
58 See also the earlier cases of **R v Secretary of State for Foreign and Commonwealth Affairs ex parte Bancoult** (2001); **Chagos Islanders v Attorney General** (2003).

Indian Ocean Territory Order in Council.[59] However, Orders subsequently drafted declared that no person had the right of abode in the territory, or the right without authorisation to enter and remain there; these were declared unlawful.

The House of Lords, however, in **R (Bancoult) v Secretary of State for Foreign and Commonwealth Affairs** (2008), allowed the government's appeal by a majority of three to two. Lord Hoffmann placed great emphasis on the practicalities of the situation. The islanders would be unable to exercise their 'right of abode' without financial support from the government, and the policy as to expenditure of public resources (and diplomatic interests of the Crown) were 'peculiarly within the competence of the executive'. It was impossible to say that the decision had been unreasonable or an abuse of power. Lord Rodger of Earlsferry and Lord Carswell agreed. Lord Rodger emphasised that there was here no breach of legitimate expectations: the government had not made any 'clear and unambiguous promise' to the islanders on which they could rely. Lord Carswell stated that where there was 'an overriding public interest' behind a change in policy there will 'not be an abuse of power'.[60]

The **Bancoult** case returned to the courts in 2016. In **R (Bancoult (No 2)) v Secretary of State for Foreign and Commonwealth Affairs** (2016) the Supreme Court, by a majority of three to two, dismissed the appeal of the islanders. The appellants sought to have the 2008 House of Lords' decision set aside on the basis that it had been reached without consideration of documents (the 'Rashid documents') which should have been disclosed prior to the 2008 ruling and that new evidence had come to light which amounted to justification for setting aside the 2008 decision. By a majority the Supreme Court dismissed the appeal, holding that even if the documents had been disclosed they would have made no material difference to the outcome of the case.

Treaty-making powers

The power to enter into treaties under international law is a feature of the sovereignty of a state. In the United Kingdom, it is generally accepted that such power is an emanation of the prerogative. As such, the entry into treaties is regarded as a matter solely for the executive and not for Parliament. A treaty is defined as a written agreement between states governed by international law.[61] It will be seen in Chapter 6 that under the doctrine of parliamentary sovereignty, an Act of Parliament alone can alter domestic law. Accordingly, a treaty – being a creature of international law – cannot alter national law without being given effect by an Act of Parliament.[62] It is for this reason that, *inter alia*, the European Communities Act 1972 was enacted to provide for the entry and application of European Community law into the United Kingdom.

The treaty-making power of the executive was challenged in **R v Secretary of State for Foreign and Commonwealth Affairs ex parte Rees-Mogg** (1994). In February 1991, the Heads of Government of the Member States of the European Community signed the Treaty on European Union – the Maastricht Treaty (see Chapter 7). The Treaty was to come into effect on ratification by the Member States. In some countries, ratification was dependent upon the approval of the majority of the people voting in a referendum, as for example in France and Denmark. Under the constitution of the United States of America, treaties are ratified by the President with the advice and consent of two-thirds of the Senators present and voting.

---

59 SI 1965 No 1920.
60 See para. 135.
61 Vienna Convention on the Law of Treaties, Cmnd 4848, 1969, London: HMSO.
62 **Walker v Baird** (1982); The Parlement Belge (1879); **JH Rayner (Mincing Lane) Ltd v Department of Trade and Industry** (1990).

In the United Kingdom, no such constitutional arrangements exist. Under constitutional practice, a treaty need only be approved by Parliament if it requires a change in legislation or the grant of public money. Under the Ponsonby Rule,[63] a constitutional convention, the government undertook first to lay every treaty, when signed, for a 21-day period before ratification; and second, to inform the House of all other 'international agreements and commitments which may bind the nation to specific action in certain circumstances'. The Ponsonby undertaking also included a commitment on the part of government to make time for debate on a treaty if there is a formal demand from the Opposition or other party. The issue raised in **Rees-Mogg** was whether the government had the power to ratify the Maastricht Treaty without the approval of the House of Commons. It was clear that there was substantial opposition to the Treaty on all sides of the House, and the government was not confident that any vote would approve the Treaty. As a result, or as a failsafe device, the Prime Minister announced that, if necessary, the Treaty would be ratified under the prerogative, thus avoiding the risk of parliamentary disapproval. The Queen's Bench Division refused to grant an application for judicial review: the matter was within the prerogative of the Crown. In the long run, the Bill bringing the Treaty into legal effect was passed by both Houses of Parliament.

The Constitutional Reform and Governance Act 2010, section 20, provides that a treaty is not to be ratified unless a Minister has laid a copy of the treaty before Parliament and neither the House of Commons nor the House of Lords has resolved, in a period of 21 sitting days, that the treaty should not be ratified. If the House of Commons has resolved (whether or not the House of Lords has also resolved), the treaty may still be ratified if a Minister lays before Parliament a statement of reasons why the treaty should be ratified and a period of 21 sitting days has expired without the House of Commons resolving that it should not be ratified. If the House of Lords (but not the House of Commons) resolves that the treaty should not be ratified, the treaty may be ratified if a Minister has laid before Parliament a statement indicating, with reasons, that he or she is of the opinion that it should be ratified.

 ## SELF-TEST QUESTIONS

Write a definition of the royal prerogative.

What are the principal differences between Blackstone's definition and that of AV Dicey? Do these differences matter, and if so, why?

What are the 'personal prerogatives' of the Crown?

List four prerogative powers relating to foreign affairs and four relating to domestic affairs.

Judicial Control of the Prerogative

'[T]he King hath no prerogative, but that which the law of the land allows him'.[64] This bold statement by Sir Edward Coke above, however, did not entitle the courts at that time to question the *manner* in which the prerogative was exercised – rather its role was limited to enquiring whether a particular prerogative power existed, and its scope.

---

63 Under Secretary of State for Foreign Affairs 1924. See HC Deb Vol. 171 Cols 2001–2004.
64 *Case of Proclamations* (1611).

That limitation, as recognised by Lord Scarman in **Council for Civil Service Unions v Minister for the Civil Service** (1985),[65] had now gone, 'overwhelmed by the developing modern law of judicial review'. The courts' modern power to review the exercise of the prerogative was forcefully expressed by Lord Parker CJ in **R v Criminal Injuries Compensation Board ex parte Lain** (1967),[66] in which he stated that the fact that the Board had been established under the prerogative rather than statute did not make it immune from review. This approach is reflected in the dicta of Sedley LJ in **Bancoult** (2007):

> an Order in Council is an act of the executive and as such is amenable to any appropriate form of judicial review, whether anticipatory or retrospective. What determines the constitutional status of a measure – a statute, a judgment or an order – is not its formal authority, which is always that of the Crown,[67] but its source in the interlocking but unequal limbs of the state.[68]

Although there is a degree of certainty as to the existence and scope of the prerogatives discussed above, the discussion of all prerogatives must be regarded as overlain with a degree of doubt. Consistent with the doctrine of parliamentary sovereignty, Parliament has the right and power to abolish, restrict or preserve prerogative powers.

Where an Act of Parliament seeks to regulate a matter previously falling under the prerogative but does not expressly abolish the prerogative, the statute will prevail. In **Attorney General v de Keyser's Royal Hotel Ltd** (1920), the court was faced with a claim for compensation by the owners of the hotel, under the Defence of the Realm Act 1914, for compensation due as a result of occupation by the armed forces in wartime. The government sought to rely on the prerogative under which a lesser, discretionary sum of compensation would be payable. The House of Lords rejected the government's right to rely on the prerogative, holding that, once a statute had been enacted, the prerogative power fell into 'abeyance', that is to say, it was set aside for the duration of the life of the statute. Should the statute be repealed, the prerogative would once more come into operation.

In **Laker Airways v Department of Trade** (1977), statute and prerogative were considered once again. The facts involved regulation of the transatlantic air route. Under the Bermuda Agreement of 1946, the United States and United Kingdom governments agreed that air carriers should be approved by both governments: the 'designation' requirement. In 1971, the Civil Aviation Act was passed by Parliament, providing for the licensing of airlines by the Civil Aviation Authority (the CAA). The Act provided that the Secretary of State could give 'guidance' to the CAA as to the policy to be followed in the consideration of licence applications. Mr Freddie Laker had both applied for designation under the Bermuda Treaty and been granted a licence under the Civil Aviation Act 1971.

A change in government led to a change in policy, and it was decided that British Airways should have a monopoly on the transatlantic route. Accordingly, the Secretary of State issued 'guidance' to the CAA to the effect that Mr Laker's licence should be withdrawn. The Secretary of State also requested that the United States Government did not proceed to grant designation to Laker Airways under the Treaty. In an application for judicial review by Mr Laker, it was argued that the Secretary of State's 'guidance' was *ultra vires*. The court agreed, regarding the instruction given to the CAA as beyond the normal meaning of the word 'guidance'. The

---

65 On which see further below.
66 A case described by Lord Scarman as a 'landmark case ... comparable in its day to the *Proclamations Case*' of 1611.
67 On the distinction between the Crown and the Executive see **R (Quark Fishing Ltd) v Secretary of State for Foreign and Commonwealth Affairs** (2005).
68 At para. 35.

court also rejected the government's argument that it had the right, under the prerogative, to deny Laker Airways' right to fly the Atlantic route. The government could not, it was held, defeat a statutory right by use of a prerogative power.

In **Council of Civil Service Unions v Minister of State for Civil Service** (1985), the prerogative returned to the courts. The Prime Minister, as the Minister for the Civil Service, by a prerogative order (an Order in Council) terminated the right of workers at the Government Communications Headquarters (GCHQ) to belong to trade unions. The order followed industrial unrest which threatened to disrupt the interception of signals intelligence. The unions challenged the order under judicial review proceedings, claiming that they had a legitimate expectation to be consulted prior to their rights to membership being withdrawn. The unions won at first instance, but lost before both the Court of Appeal and the House of Lords.

The House of Lords accepted that the terms and conditions of employment of civil servants were within the prerogative powers of the Crown.[69] Their Lordships likewise accepted that the employees had a legitimate expectation to be consulted before their rights were adversely affected. Nevertheless, the government's plea of national security trumped the interests of the union members.[70]

The significance of the **GCHQ** case in relation to prerogative power is twofold. On the question of the reviewability of the royal prerogative, the House of Lords declared that the exercise of the prerogatives of the Crown were, in principle, as reviewable as powers exercised under statute. However, having boldly declared the principle, the court proceeded to qualify the approach by stating that a number of matters would not be subjected to review. Utilising the concept of 'justiciability', the court held that matters such as the appointment of Ministers, dissolution of Parliament, grant of honours, treaties and *par excellence* matters of national security were not appropriate subjects for review by the courts.[71] Each of these matters was regarded as involving matters of high policy which it should be for Ministers to decide and, by implication, for Parliament to control.[72] It remains the case after **GCHQ** that many significant attributes of the prerogative remain immune from judicial review.[73]

The case of **R v Secretary of State for the Home Department ex parte Northumbria Police Authority** (1988) reveals a far less robust judicial attitude towards the control of the prerogative than did the **Laker Airways** case. Once again, the issue involved was the relationship between statute and the prerogative. The Police Act 1964 sets out the respective powers of the Home Secretary, the police authorities and the Chief Constables of police with regard to, *inter alia*, the supply of equipment to police forces (sections 4 and 5).

The Secretary of State, by way of a Circular, advised that the Secretary of State would be making available supplies of riot control equipment to police forces, irrespective of approval by the police authorities. The Northumbria Police Authority sought judicial review of the legality of the Circular. The Home Secretary argued that, as a matter of statutory interpretation, he had power to issue the equipment, and that, independent of the statutory power which he claimed, he had the power under the prerogative to issue the weapons. On the point of statutory interpretation, the Court of Appeal held that no monopoly was reserved to the Police Authority and that, accordingly, the Secretary of State had not acted *ultra vires*.

---

69 On HWR Wade's doubts concerning the accuracy of this classification, see Wade, 1985, p. 180.

70 A Labour government subsequently reinstated the right of workers to join trade unions.

71 In **R v Jones (Margaret)** (2006) the House of Lords ruled that the legality of the Iraq war could not be pleaded in defence to various statutory charges.

72 See also *Patriotic Front – ZAPU v Minister of Justice, Legal and Parliamentary Affairs* (1986), discussed by Walker, 1987.

73 Note, however, that in **R v Ministry of Defence ex parte Smith** (1995), Simon Brown LJ stated, *obiter*, that the question of whether homosexuals were allowed to serve in the armed forces – a matter falling within the prerogative – was not immune from review. There were no operational considerations or security implications: the courts were qualified to rule on the matter.

On the prerogative aspect, the court's reasoning was both surprising and interesting. First, the Court of Appeal accepted that the Police Act 1964 left unaffected the prerogative powers to keep the peace. Little evidence was adduced as to the existence of such a prerogative but, nevertheless, Croom-Johnson LJ felt able to hold that he had 'no doubt' that the Crown had such a prerogative. Nourse LJ stated that there was no historical or other basis for denying that a prerogative to keep the peace could be viewed as a 'sister' prerogative to the power to declare war, without making any reference to Blackstone's division of prerogatives into 'foreign' and 'domestic' categories. Recalling that it had never been possible to identify all the prerogatives of the Crown and that their existence could be ascertained only by means of piecemeal decisions, Nourse LJ declared that there had never been 'a comparable occasion for investigating a prerogative of keeping the peace within the realm':

> The Crown's prerogative of making war and peace, the war prerogative, has never been doubted ... it is natural to suppose that it was founded, at least in part, on the wider prerogative of protection ...
>
> The wider prerogative must have extended as much to unlawful acts within the realm as to the menaces of a foreign power. There is no historical or other reason for denying to the war prerogative a sister prerogative of keeping the peace within the realm.

More surprisingly, the judge argued that the fact that no evidence existed was almost conclusive proof that it did exist. In the seminal case of **Entick v Carrington** (1765), Lord Camden had asserted that, if there existed authority for the lawful exercise of power, it would be found 'in the books'. It might be thought that in passing the Police Act, Parliament considered that it was providing comprehensive regulation of the terms and conditions under which each regulatory body could act. It cannot have been contemplated that, by plea of a previously unconsidered prerogative, the provisions of the Act could be circumvented. Nevertheless, Purchas LJ was clear that:

> the prerogative powers to take all reasonable steps to preserve the Queen's peace remain unaffected by the Act and these include the supply of equipment to police forces which is reasonably required for the more efficient discharge of their duties.

The **Northumbria Police Authority** case is indicative of the fine line to be drawn between updating a prerogative and creating a new prerogative. Prerogatives, being a feature of monarchical power are, as Dicey stated, residual. Accordingly, for the judges to give recognition to an alleged prerogative, it must be shown that the prerogative claimed existed before 1688. In **BBC v Johns** (1965), Lord Diplock gave judicial expression to this in the statement 'it is 350 years and a civil war too late for the Queen's courts to broaden the prerogative'.

In **R v Secretary of State for the Home Department ex parte Fire Brigades' Union** (1995), the matter in issue was whether the Secretary of State, having failed to implement the statutory scheme provided in the Criminal Justice Act 1988, was free to implement a different scheme under the royal prerogative.[74] The scheme introduced a 'tariff' for compensation for injuries at a substantially lower rate than provided for under the statute.

---

74 As announced in the White Paper, *Compensating Victims of Violent Crime: Changes to the Criminal Injuries Compensation Scheme*, Cmnd 2434, 1993, London: HMSO. The scheme was implemented on 1 April 1994.

The Master of the Rolls accepted that the Home Secretary had the power to invite Parliament to repeal the provisions or to seek enactment of the tariff provisions in statute, or, alternatively, to seek to have the statutory provisions abolished and then implement the tariff provisions under the royal prerogative. But 'what he could not do, so long as the 1988 provisions stood unrepealed as an enduring statement of Parliament's will, was to exercise prerogative powers to introduce a scheme radically different from what Parliament had approved'. Accordingly, the Secretary of State could not avoid the requirements of the 1988 Act and introduce – by means of the prerogative – a different scheme.

The House of Lords ruled, by a majority (Lord Keith of Kinkel and Lord Mustill dissenting), that the decisions of the Secretary of State not to implement the statutory scheme, and to introduce an alternative scheme under the prerogative, were unlawful. The House of Lords refused, however, to rule that the Secretary of State was under a legally enforceable duty to bring the statutory scheme into effect at a particular date.

However, the Secretary of State did not enjoy an unfettered discretion as to whether to bring the scheme into effect, and he could not, through use of the prerogative, defeat the purpose of the statute. Lord Keith, dissenting, argued that the court should not become involved in a matter which was for Parliament to determine.

Here, within one case, are seen differing considerations weighing on the judges in the House of Lords. The majority decision rests squarely on the rule of law and the preference for statute over the prerogative. The minority view, however, leans far more clearly in favour of the doctrine of separation of powers and the supremacy of Parliament in regulating its own affairs and in calling Ministers to account.

Two of the most significant cases to reach the Supreme Court on the control of the royal prerogative and its relationship with statute arose over the decision of the people of the United Kingdom, voting in a referendum in 2016, to leave the European Union (EU) (on which see further Chapter 8). The background to these cases is Article 50 of the EU Treaty, which provided the legal foundation for leaving, and required any Member State which wished to leave the EU to notify the EU Council of its intention. As foreign affairs are a matter for the royal prerogative, the then Prime Minister decided that she would initiate the Article 50 process using the royal prerogative.

This decision was immediately challenged in the courts on the basis that such a major constitutional change could only be effected by an Act of Parliament, and not under the prerogative. Two cases – one heard in the High Court of Northern Ireland, one heard in the High Court in England – led to different results. In **McCord, Re Judicial Review; Agnew and Others v Same** (2016) the applicants' principal grounds for judicial review were that the prerogative power had been displaced by the Northern Ireland Act 1998 (and other devolution provisions) and that an Act of Parliament was required to trigger Article 50. Furthermore, if an Act of Parliament was required then there is a requirement that the Northern Ireland Assembly give its consent through a Legislative Consent Motion (LCM).[75] It was further argued that Article 50 could not be triggered without the consent of the people of Northern Ireland because the Good Friday Agreement (reflected in section 1 of the Northern Ireland Act 1998, see Chapter 11) had created a 'legitimate expectation' that there would be no change in the constitutional status of the people of Northern Ireland without their consent.

The High Court ruled that there were no statutory provisions which expressly (or by necessary implication) limited or altered the Crown's prerogative power in relation to notification under Article 50. Maguire J for the Court ruled that (contrary to the position taken

---

75 On Legislative Consent Motions, see Chapter 11.

by the High Court in London in the **Millar** case discussed below) giving notification under Article 50 did not initiate an irreversible process and as such did not alter the law of the United Kingdom or the rights of individual citizens.

In **R (Gina Miller and Others) v Secretary of State for Exiting the European Union** (2016) the English High Court considered the question whether 'as a matter of the constitutional law of the United Kingdom, the Crown – acting through the executive government of the day – is entitled to use its prerogative powers to give notice under Article 50 for the United Kingdom to cease to be a member of the European Union' [at paragraph 3]. Both parties accepted that triggering the Article 50 process was irreversible and would inevitably lead to the UK leaving the EU at the end of the two-year period.

The principal argument for the claimants was that the Crown's prerogative powers could not be used by the government to 'diminish or abrogate rights under the law of the United Kingdom' unless Parliament has given authority to the Crown to do so. Leaving the EU inevitably 'diminishes or abrogates' rights conferred under EU law and the giving of notice under the royal prerogative would remove the real decision over rights from Parliament.

For the government it was argued that Parliament could choose to leave prerogative power in the hands of the Crown, even if its use would result in a change to common law and statutory rights. To remove or abrogate the prerogative required express words in a statute (or words which led to a necessary implication that this was intended), and no such words could be found in the ECA 1972 or any other statute.

The High Court recognised that the ECA 1972 was a statute of 'special constitutional significance' and 'the wide and profound extent of the legal changes in domestic law created by the ECA 1972'. That, the Court ruled, made it especially unlikely that Parliament intended to leave their continued existence 'in the hands of the Crown'. Moreover, Parliament having legislated to accept the direct effect of EU law, it was 'not plausible to suppose that it intended that the Crown should be able by its own unilateral action under its prerogative powers to switch it off again' (see paragraph 87). Accordingly, having interpreted the ECA in light of the constitutional background and principles, the Court concluded that 'the Crown ... has no prerogative power to effect a withdrawal from the relevant Treaties by giving notice under Article 50 of the TEU' (at paragraph 92).

These conflicting decisions were considered by the Supreme Court in **Miller v Secretary of State for Exiting the European Union** (2017). Eleven Justices considered the case, three of whom (Lords Reed, Carnwath and Hughes) dissented. The Supreme Court ruled that Notice could not be given under the Prerogative, and that the UK's 'constitutional arrangements' required the authority of an Act of Parliament before Article 50 could be triggered.

This conclusion centred on the European Communities Act 1972 (ECA). Section 2 of the ECA does more than give effect to the EU treaties by enabling EU law to enter domestic law. The effect of section 2 is that EU law not only becomes a source of UK law, but also takes precedence over 'all domestic sources of UK law, including statutes'. The 1972 Act also operates as a partial transfer of law-making powers. In constitutional terms, the Court ruled, the 'effect of the 1972 Act was unprecedented' (see paragraph 60). Withdrawal marks a fundamental constitutional change which is inevitable once Notice is given. Under the 1972 Act, Parliament 'endorsed and gave effect to the United Kingdom's membership of what is now the European Union under the EU treaties in a way which is inconsistent with the future exercise by ministers of any prerogative power to withdraw from such Treaties' (at paragraph 77).

Lord Neuberger PSC for the majority, at paragraph 81, stated that:

It would be inconsistent with long-standing and fundamental principle for such a far-reaching change to the UK constitutional arrangements to be brought about by ministerial decision or ministerial action alone. All the more so when the source in question [the European Communities Act 1972] was brought into existence by Parliament through primary legislation, which gave that source an overriding supremacy in the hierarchy of domestic law sources.

Accordingly, at paragraph 82, it followed that:

a major change to UK constitutional arrangements … must be effected in the only way that the UK constitution recognises, namely by Parliamentary legislation.

In response to the **Miller** case, Parliament passed the EU (Notification of Withdrawal) Act 2017 authorising the Prime Minister to give notice under Article 50.

The second case is that of **R (Miller) v The Prime Minister** (2019). As discussed in Chapter 8, having given notice to the EU of the intention to leave, the government entered into negotiations over the terms on which the UK would leave following a two-year transition period. The Prime Minister, Theresa May, decided to hold a new general election which took place on 8 June 2017, with the result that she lost the slender majority of seats in the House of Commons. A Withdrawal Agreement was negotiated with the EU, but was rejected on three occasions by the House of Commons (its agreement being a constitutional requirement before the Agreement could be passed into law). In June 2019 the Prime Minister resigned and, following a leadership election, Boris Johnson became Prime Minister. By that time, Parliament had been in session for the longest time since records began; there was little legislative business to be concluded and no new legislation could be introduced without prolonging the session further. In light of this, and the fact that the Commons would not approve the Withdrawal Agreement in its then-current form, the Prime Minister decided to hold a further general election, his central election slogan being 'to get Brexit done'.

In order to hold the election, Parliament had to be prorogued, and in August 2019 an Order in Council was made signifying the approval of the Crown, the Queen having acted on the advice of the Prime Minister. Prorogation was to run from between 9 and 12 September to 14 October when a new session would begin, a five-week period in which Parliament would not be sitting.

Earlier, on 30 July, an application had been made to Court of Session in Scotland for a declaration (interdict) that prorogation would be unlawful. This was firstly dismissed as non-justiciable (outside the jurisdiction of the courts), but on appeal the Inner House ruled that the issue was justiciable and that the request for prorogation was motivated by the improper purpose of 'stymying Parliamentary scrutiny of the executive' and that the prorogation would therefore be unlawful and of no effect.[76]

When prorogation was announced at the end of August, Mrs Gina Miller started proceedings in the High Court, seeking a declaration that the Prime Minister's advice to the Crown

---

76 **Cherry v Advocate General for Scotland** (2019).

was unlawful. The Court ruled that the issue was non-justiciable, but granted leave to appeal to the Supreme Court.[77]

The appeals went to the Supreme Court. The issues to be decided were:

- whether the advice given to the Queen was justiciable;
- if so, whether the advice was lawful; and
- if not, what remedy should be granted.

On the question of justiciability, the Supreme Court ruled that it was necessary first to determine whether the exercise of the prerogative in the case before it fell within the legal limits of the power. The Court acknowledged that establishing the legal limits of a prerogative power was not straightforward, but that in doing so the Court was guided by common law principles. The relevant principles in this case were firstly the sovereignty of Parliament, and secondly the accountability of the executive to Parliament.

On sovereignty, the longer the prorogation, the longer Parliament was prevented from exercising its sovereign power of holding the executive to account. The Court explained that:

> a decision to prorogue Parliament (or to advise the monarch to prorogue Parliament) will be unlawful if the prorogation has the effect of frustrating or preventing, without reasonable justification, the ability of Parliament to carry out its constitutional functions as a legislature and as the body responsible for the supervision of the executive.

The Court ruled that the issue was justiciable. Was the advice lawful? The Court turned to the foundations of the constitution. In a representative democracy, the Government exists because it had the confidence of the House of Commons (on this see further Chapter 14). The task of governing is for the executive; the task of Parliament is a hold the Government to account. Did 'the Prime Minister's action have the effect of frustrating or preventing the constitutional role of Parliament in holding the Government to account'? Yes it did: this was not a normal prorogation and it denied the Commons its constitutional role for five weeks. The question then had to be asked whether there was any justification for this. As the Court said, it was not concerned with the Prime Minister's *motive*, but with whether there was a good reason for the prorogation. The Government had claimed that it needed the time to develop its legislative programme for the coming session, but a former Prime Minister giving evidence to the Court stated that the necessary planning could be done within a matter of days, not weeks. The Court concluded that there was no good reason for the advice to prorogue for five weeks. Accordingly, the decision was unlawful and of no effect.

It followed that Parliament had not been prorogued, and the Court granted a declaration to that effect. Since Parliament had not been prorogued, it could resume as soon as could be arranged. Parliament then passed the Early Parliamentary General Election Act 2019, in accordance with section 2 of the Fixed-term Parliaments Act 2011, in order to hold a general election.

---

77 On 3 September, Parliament returned from the summer recess and MPs decided to take control of the business of the House. The European Union (Withdrawal) (No 2) Act 2019 was passed, requiring the Prime Minister to seek an extension of three months to the negotiating period. The Bill was passed by the Commons in one day; two days later the Lords approved it, and the Royal Assent was given on 9 September.

Political Control of the Prerogative

Political control over the exercise of the prerogative, while preserving the separation of powers between the executive and judiciary, may in practice prove to be inadequate. In theory, the prerogative, as is the case with any other act of government, is capable of being subjected to the full range of parliamentary procedure.[78] Thus, Question Time, debates and Select Committees may be utilised in order to scrutinise prerogative acts. However, under parliamentary practice, there exist a number of issues on which Ministers conventionally decline to provide information, and many of these matters are precisely those which fall within the scope of the prerogative. The grant of honours, for example, is a matter not for parliamentary discussion. On matters of the disposition of the armed forces, weaponry for the armed forces, government contracts, judicial appointments and investigations by the Director of Public Prosecutions, the government will decline to answer questions. Aside from such specific matters, the government may plead such wide notions as national security, confidentiality or the public interest in order to avoid scrutiny.

The royal prerogative and the Human Rights Act 1998

The Human Rights Act 1998 – discussed in detail in Chapter 18 – enables the rights protected under the European Convention on Human Rights to be enforced before the domestic courts. Section 6(1) of the Act makes it unlawful for a public authority to act in a way which is incompatible with Convention rights, thereby extending protection to actions taken under the prerogative. However, section 21 of the Act protects the prerogative by raising the status of Orders in Council made under the prerogative to that of primary legislation. As a result, although the courts may make a declaration that an action is incompatible with Convention rights, the Orders in Council cannot be annulled by the courts and will remain valid in the same way as Acts of Parliament.

Reform of the Prerogative?

It has been seen from the above discussion that prerogative powers have been the subject of much discussion and proposals for reform. The Constitutional Reform and Governance Act 2010 provides for parliamentary scrutiny of treaties, and a statutory basis for the civil service and the Fixed-term Parliaments Act 2011 which brings the dissolution of Parliament under statutory authority, thereby removing the power of the Crown over the dissolution of Parliament represents significant reform to the prerogative.[79]

All reform of the prerogative, however, entails constitutional and legal challenges. First, the extent to which placing the prerogative under statutory authority would clarify questions as to the scope of the power in question, and its control, is necessarily a matter for speculation. In relation to the scope of power, the case of the **Northumbria Police Authority** (1988), discussed above, illustrates the difficulty. It was seen there that the prerogative 'to keep the peace' was pleaded as an alternative to the existence of power under the Police Act 1964 – seemingly a 'reserve power' claimed as insurance against the court finding that the Minister had acted outside the power granted by the Act.

---

78 This is to be discussed in more detail in Chapters 14 and 15.
79 The Act preserves the Crown's role in the summoning of Parliament.

There are two principal approaches to reforming the prerogative. The first is to place individual prerogatives under statutory authority on an individual basis. The second would be to attempt comprehensive reform involving all known prerogatives. As has been seen, hitherto the first approach has held sway. Examples discussed above include the Treasure Act 1996 (treasure trove), the Constitutional Reform and Governance Act 2010 (treaties and civil service).

In 2004, the Public Administration Select Committee labelled these two approaches the 'pragmatic' and the 'principled'. In its report, *Taming the Prerogative*,[80] the Committee called for greater parliamentary control over 'all the executive powers enjoyed by Ministers under the royal prerogative', and that reform is 'unfinished constitutional business'.[81] As has been seen, nearly two decades later, that constitutional business remains largely unchanged.

In terms of the control over the exercise of the prerogative – judicial and political – the limits of such control must be remembered. While an application for judicial review of the exercise of power may be granted, it has been seen in relation to the **GCHQ** case that the courts have developed a category of non-justiciable matters. The concept of non-justiciability protects the judges from encroaching on decisions which – in light of separation of powers – are within the proper sphere of decision of the democratically accountable executive. That protective concept is unlikely to change if and when such non-reviewable matters are placed under statutory authority. In light of that, the extent to which governments demonstrate their real commitment to openness and transparency and allow parliamentary scrutiny of their actions becomes all the more important. It is by no means certain that placing such powers under statutory authority, even if they were correctly identified and defined, would guarantee the degree of control which the rule of law requires.

Summary

Under all constitutions, written or unwritten, there will be a number of powers reserved to the executive, powers which are exercisable without the passage of legislation. Such powers may include entering into treaties, declarations of war and peace and recognition of foreign states and diplomats. Such powers are referred to as 'inherent executive powers', or 'prerogative powers'.

Under the United Kingdom constitution, it may be concluded, quite reasonably, that parliamentary control over the exercise of prerogative power is less than adequate. Set alongside or juxtaposed with the excluded areas of judicial review under the concept of justiciability, it can be seen that there exists a reservoir of power, much of which is undefined or at best ill defined, which is not amenable to either judicial or parliamentary control.

Further Reading

Blackburn, R, 'Monarchy and the personal prerogatives' [2004] *Public Law* 546.
Blackburn, R, *King and Country: Monarchy and the Future King Charles II*, 2007, London: Politico's Publishing.
Blackburn, R, 'The prerogative power of dissolution of parliament: law, practice and reform' [2009] *Public Law* 766.
Blom-Cooper, L and Drabble, R, 'GCHQ revisited' [2010] *Public Law* 18.

---

80 Taming the Prerogative, Strengthening Ministerial Accountability to Parliament, Fourth Report, 2003–2004, HC 422.
81 *Ibid.*, paras 60, 61.

Butler, D, 'The Australian crisis of 1975' (1976) 29 *Parliamentary Affairs* 201.

Chitty, J, *Law of the Prerogatives of the Crown*, 1820, London: Butterworths.

Daly, P, 'Justiciability and the "political question" doctrine' [2010] *Public Law* 160.

Hadfield, B, 'Judicial review and the prerogative powers' in M Sunkin and S Payne (eds), *The Nature of the Crown*, 1999, Oxford: Oxford University Press, Chapter 8.

Markesinis, BA, *The Theory and Practice of Dissolution of Parliament*, 1972, Cambridge: Cambridge University Press.

Munro, C, *Studies in Constitutional Law*, 2nd edn, 1999, London: Butterworths, Chapter 8.

Sunkin, M and Payne, S (eds), *The Nature of the Crown: A Legal and Political Analysis*, 1999, Oxford: Clarendon Press.

Chapter 6

Parliamentary Sovereignty

Chapter Contents

Learning Objectives

By the end of this chapter you should be able to:

☐ explain the essential difference between a 'written' and 'uncodified' constitution in relation to the ultimate source of law;

☐ offer a definition of parliamentary sovereignty and explain its constitutional importance;

☐ explain the essential difference between a 'written' and 'uncodified' constitution in relation to the ultimate source of law;

☐ understand the difference between political and legal sovereignty;

☐ discuss AV Dicey's three-part explanation of sovereignty, with reference to illustrative case law;

☐ discuss contemporary academic debates concerning sovereignty;
☐ explain the challenges to sovereignty posed by:
    the Acts of Union;
    'manner and form' and 'redefinition' theory;
    the UK's membership of the European Union;
    the Devolution Acts;
    the Human Rights Act 1998.

Introduction

Under any constitution – whether written or unwritten – there must be a source of ultimate authority: one supreme power over and above all other power in the state. Under a written constitution the highest source of power is the constitution as interpreted by the Supreme Court. Under the British constitution, in theory if not in practice, the highest source of authority is the United Kingdom Parliament and Acts of Parliament are the highest form of law.

Writing in the late nineteenth century, AV Dicey took the view that the supremacy of Parliament is 'the dominant characteristic of our political institutions'.[1] However, the concept of sovereignty has long caused controversy and is one which assumes differing interpretations according to the perspective being adopted. For example, international lawyers are concerned with the attributes which identify a state as independent and sovereign within the international community. Political scientists on the other hand are concerned with the source of political power within a state. From the perspective of legal theorists and constitutional lawyers, the focus is on the ultimate legal power within a state.

To categorise Britain as a sovereign independent state with the ultimate source of legal authority vesting in its Parliament was accurate in the nineteenth century. However, in today's world of increasing economic, legal and political interdependence, the traditional theory of sovereignty has an air of unreality about it. International relations and obligations, membership of the European Union from 1973 to 2020, devolution of law-making powers away from Westminster to Northern Ireland, Scotland and Wales and other factors all restrict what Parliament can in fact do: theory and practice are increasingly separated. In this chapter we examine the various aspects of sovereignty, and the challenges posed to the orthodox view.

Legal and Political Sovereignty

Political sovereignty refers to the supreme political authority within a state. Legal sovereignty – from the standpoint of sovereignty within the state as opposed to sovereignty as understood in international law – refers to the supreme legal authority within a state.[2]

It is often difficult to distinguish clearly between legal and political sovereignty. The distinction is nevertheless one insisted upon by authorities such as Sir Edward Coke, Sir William Blackstone and AV Dicey. In large measure, this clear demarcation between the political and the legal is explained by the unwritten nature of the United Kingdom's constitution. In the majority of states having a written constitution, the constitution defines the limits of governmental power. In the United Kingdom, by way of contrast, the powers of government – whilst ultimately dependent upon the electoral 'mandate' – remain unconstrained by any

---

1 Dicey, 1885, p. 39.
2 For a more elaborate categorisation, see Rees, 'The theory of sovereignty restated', in Laslett, 1975, Chapter IV.

fundamental written document and subject only to Parliament's approval. All law-making power thus derives, not from a power-conferring and power-delimiting constitutional document, endorsed by the people, but from the sovereignty of the legislature: Parliament.

Social contract theory underpins the political sovereignty of the people. Two early theorists may briefly be considered here. In *Two Treatises on Government* (1690)[3] John Locke advances powerful arguments for the limits of governmental power and the ultimate political sovereignty of the people. Locke argues that men come together in civil society and tacitly consent to be ruled by government directed to 'the peace, safety and public good of the people'.[4] Accordingly, the power conferred on government is not absolute, but whilst in existence, is supreme power. However, Locke concludes that if the people:

> have set limits to the duration of their legislative, and made this supreme power in any person or assembly only temporary, it is forfeited; upon the forfeiture of their rules, or at the determination of the time set, it reverts to the society, and the people have a right to act as supreme, and continue the legislative in themselves or place it in a new form, or new hands, as they think good.[5]

Sovereignty – the supreme power – is limited and conditional: government holds power on trust for the people.

A century later Thomas Paine advanced a social contract theory in which the rights of the individual are given central importance. Paine both influenced and was influenced by the French and American Revolutions. In *Rights of Man* (1791)[6] Paine argued that the citizen gives up his rights to the state, but on a conditional basis. The state is placed in the position of trustee of the rights of man, and should that trust be broken, the citizen has the ultimate – or sovereign – right to depose the government. Paine argues that man has natural rights, 'those which appertain to man in right of his existence'. These rights are both individualistic and civil. The former category includes: 'all the intellectual rights, or rights of the mind, and also all those rights of acting as an individual for his own comfort and happiness, which are not injurious to the natural rights of others'. By contrast: 'Civil rights are those which appertain to man in right of his being a member of society. Every civil right has for its foundation, some natural right pre-existing in the individual'.[7] In the writings of both Locke and Paine[8] are found the theoretical foundations for the rule of law, government limited by law, the political sovereignty of the people and the idea of human rights.

Legal sovereignty

Professor HLA Hart analyses the source of ultimate power in *The Concept of Law* (1961). Hart argues that law is a system of rules, each rule being validated by a higher rule. In practical terms, for example, a local authority bylaw is valid because a higher form of law – an Act of Parliament – conferred power on the authority to pass the bylaw. In the United Kingdom (and ignoring for current purposes the European Union and Council of Europe) an Act of Parliament is the highest form of law. The question then arises: but what rule validates the Act of Parliament? Here we reach what Hart calls the 'ultimate rule of recognition'. This ultimate

---

3 Locke, 1977, Book II.
4 At p. 182.
5 At p. 242.
6 **Part I.**
7 At p. 90.
8 But see also Thomas Hobbes, *Leviathan* (1651); Jean Jacques Rousseau, *The Social Contract and Discourses* (1762).

rule of recognition lies outside the system of legal rules, as it must. For Hart it lies in the sociologically observable fact of official acceptance of Acts of Parliament. By this, Hart means that the officials' – and most importantly the judges' – acceptance of authority can be seen in operation whenever one observes a court of law. A judge may perhaps personally disapprove of a precedent case or of a statutory provision, but his or her acceptance of its validity is demonstrated by his or her application of the law. Expressed differently, it is the judges who uphold and reinforce the sovereignty of Parliament – the ultimate rule of recognition of the constitution.

The key to understanding parliamentary sovereignty therefore lies in its acceptance – but not necessarily moral approval – by the judges within the legal system. For as long as the judges accept the sovereignty of Parliament, sovereignty will remain the ultimate rule of the constitution. As Salmond explains:

> All rules of law have historical sources. As a matter of fact and history they have their origin somewhere, though we may not know what it is. But not all of them have legal sources ... But whence comes the rule that Acts of Parliament have the force of law? This is legally ultimate; its source is historical only, not legal ... It is the law because it is the law, and for no other reason that it is possible for the law to take notice of. No statute can confer this power upon Parliament, for this would be to assume and act on the very power that is to be conferred.[9]

Accordingly, the rule that confers validity on legislation is 'logically superior to the sovereign'. The logical consequence of this is stated by HWR Wade:

> if no statute can establish the rule that the courts obey Acts of Parliament, similarly no statute can alter or abolish that rule. The rule is above and beyond the reach of statute ... because it is itself the source of the authority of statute.[10]

The sovereignty of Parliament will only be lost under two conditions. The first condition would be where Parliament decided – perhaps on the authority of the people, tested in a referendum – to abolish its sovereignty and to place its residual authority under that of a written constitution to be adjudicated upon by the judiciary. The second condition would be where the judiciary itself underwent a 'revolution' in attitude, and accepted that Parliament was no longer the sovereign law-making body and that the judges owed allegiance to an alternative – or different – sovereign power. These points will be returned to when considering challenges to the traditional view of sovereignty.

In the United Kingdom, in the absence of a written constitution which asserts the sovereignty of the people and the sovereignty of the constitution – as interpreted by the judiciary – over the legislature and executive, the vacuum is filled by the doctrine of parliamentary sovereignty, or supremacy. Under this doctrine, political sovereignty vests in the people; legal sovereignty vests with Parliament over which no legal controls are exerted, but which remains responsible to the electorate for the continued, and regularly renewed, grant of law-making and executive authority. The constitution is renewed through the democratic process and the concept of a responsive responsible government, rather than through the means of a Supreme Court reinterpreting the constitution according to judicial perceptions of the mores in society. This is not to suggest that under a written constitution,

---

9 Williams (ed.), *Jurisprudence*, 10th edn, p. 155, cited by Wade, 1955, p. 187.
10 Wade, 'Introduction', in Dicey, 1885, 1959 edn.

there is no responsive, accountable and democratic government or that the evolution of the constitution lies solely within the domain of the judges. Rather, the point to be emphasised is that, under a written constitution, there is an additional element in effecting constitutional change. Depending upon the independence, integrity and motivation of the courts, acts of the executive and legislature can be subjected to the control of the constitution.

 SELF-TEST QUESTIONS

What is the distinction between political and legal sovereignty? How, if at all, do they relate to one another?

'Sovereignty lies in the breast of the judges' (HLA Hart, *The Concept of Law*, 1961). What does Hart mean by this statement? In what way(s), if at all, is his view verifiable?

Sovereignty and Written Constitutions

Where a written constitution exists, it will have come into being either by a grant of independence from a previously sovereign power or through a revolution – peaceful or otherwise. Where the constitution arises from the authority of the native people, it is 'autochthonous': '[the people] assert not the principle of autonomy only; they assert also a principle of something stronger, of self-sufficiency, of constitutional autarky ... of being constitutionally rooted in their own soil' (Wheare, 1960, Chapter 4).

Where autochthony[11] exists, the authority for the constitution arises from the people. The phrase 'We the People' has powerful psychological – and legal – force, and the resultant document, the constitution, will be supreme. All power entrusted to government comes from the people; it is accordingly understandable that, under such a constitutional arrangement, there is a strongly held belief that government holds its power on 'trust' for the people. It may be said, as a result, that both law-making and executive powers are conditionally conferred on those who hold public office, subject to the doctrine of trust which will be enforced by the courts in the name of the people. All constitutions – written and unwritten – exist against the backcloth of historical, political and moral evolution: none exists in a vacuum. However, under a written constitution, this background has a particular significance. The constitution, being the expression of the political morality of its age – updated by the judiciary through interpretative methods – is a constant reflection and reminder of the will of the people and the restraints which that will imposes on government.

Chief Justice Marshall, in **Marbury v Madison** (1803), explained the power of the constitution:

It is a proposition too plain to be contested that the constitution controls any legislative act repugnant to it; or, that the legislature may alter the constitution by an ordinary act. Between these two alternatives, there is no middle ground. The constitution is either a superior, paramount law, unchangeable by ordinary means, or it is on a level with ordinary legislative acts, and, like other acts, is alterable when the legislature shall please to alter it. If the former part of the alternative is true, then a legislative act contrary to the constitution is not law; if the latter part be true, then written constitutions are absurd attempts, on the part of the people, to limit a power in its own nature illimitable.

11 See Marshall, 1971, Chapter III.4.

It is possible, accordingly, under such a constitutional arrangement, for the constitutional court[12] effectively to redefine the relationship between the governors and the governed, the state and its citizens. By this means, the constitution is renewed and reinvigorated. By way of example, the American Bill of Rights, enacted as amendments to the 1787 Constitution, provides that:

> All persons born or naturalized in the United States, and subject to the jurisdiction thereof, are citizens of the United States and of the state wherein they reside. No state may ... deprive any person of life, liberty, or property, without due process of law; nor deny to any person within its jurisdiction the equal protection of the laws.[13]

This 'equal protection' clause has been the focus of the development of equal civil and political rights in the United States of America. In 1896, the Supreme Court was called upon to determine whether the policy of segregation of black and white citizens was lawful under the Constitution. The court ruled that 'separate but equal treatment' laws did not amount to a denial of the equal protection of law.[14] When, however, in 1954, the question of 'equal protection' came before the Supreme Court concerning segregation in the schools of the states of Kansas, South Carolina, Virginia and Delaware, the court was to rule that such 'treatment' violated the Fourteenth Amendment of the Constitution.[15]

The origins of parliamentary sovereignty

In Chapter 5, the manner in which the near absolute powers of the Crown[16] were reduced by the courts and Parliament was discussed. With the reduction in the King's prerogative powers, there came about the correlative rise in the sovereignty of Parliament. From 1688, the supremacy of Parliament over the Crown was established. From this time, the prerogative powers of the Crown continued in existence or were abolished or curtailed as Parliament determined. No new prerogative powers may be claimed by the Crown, as Diplock LJ stated in **BBC v Johns** (1965).

Dicey and Sovereignty

The classical definition of sovereignty, offered from a constitutional law rather than a jurisprudential perspective, is that of AV Dicey (1885). Dicey insisted that it was essential to separate the political from the legal and to recognise that, as matters stand, legal sovereignty remains with the United Kingdom Parliament, although there may be political restraints which effectively inhibit the exercise of those powers. On sovereignty, Dicey stated:

> The principle of parliamentary sovereignty means neither more nor less than this: namely, that Parliament thus defined has, under the English constitution, the right to make or unmake any law whatever; and, further, that no person or body

---

12 Howsoever labelled: in the United States of America, the Supreme Court; in Australia, the High Court.
13 Bill of Rights, Article XIV, s. 1, ratified 9 July 1868.
14 *Plessey v Ferguson* (1896).
15 **Brown v Board of Education of Topeka** (1954). The ruling did not end segregation on other grounds. See King, 1963; see further the Civil Rights Acts 1964 and 1968.
16 To make laws by proclamation, to rule under the prerogative without Parliament and to participate in the judicial process.

is recognised by the law of England as having a right to override or set aside the legislation of Parliament.

A law may, for our present purpose, be defined as 'any rule which will be enforced by the courts'. The principle, then, of parliamentary sovereignty may, looked at from its positive side, be thus described: any Act of Parliament, or any part of an Act of Parliament, which makes a new law, or repeals or modifies an existing law, will be obeyed by the court. The same principle, looked at from its negative side, may be thus stated: there is no person or body of persons who can, under the English constitution, make rules which override or derogate from an Act of Parliament, or which (to express the same thing in other words) will be enforced by the courts in contravention of an Act of Parliament. [1885, page 39]

From this description can be deduced three basic rules:

(a)   Parliament is the supreme law-making body and may enact laws on any subject matter;
(b)   no Parliament may be bound by a predecessor or bind a successor;
(c)   no person or body – including a court of law – may question the validity of Parliament's enactments.

It is the correctness of this definition which must be tested and evaluated. Having considered the concept of sovereignty in theoretical terms, examination of the manner in which this is translated into a practical legal doctrine is required. Dicey's description of sovereignty will provide the framework for discussion.

Parliament's unlimited law-making power

This aspect of sovereignty is the easiest both to explain and to understand: the rule means that there is no limit on the subject matter on which Parliament may legislate. Thus Parliament may legislate to alter its term of office. In 1716, the life of a Parliament was limited to three years under the Act of 1694. Fearing the effects of an election, the government introduced, and Parliament passed, the Septennial Act, extending the life of Parliament to seven years. The consequence of this Act was to confer authority on the Commons to legislate without the express consent of the electorate, thus usurping the rights of the people.[17] The Septennial Act, under a written constitution such as that of the United States, would be legally invalid. Nevertheless, as Dicey argued, 'Parliament made a legal though unprecedented use of its powers' (1885, page 47). Parliament also extended its own life between 1910 and 1918, and the Parliament elected in 1935 was to endure until 1945.[18] Parliament may also legislate to alter the succession to the throne, as with the Act of Settlement 1700 and His Majesty's Declaration of Abdication Act 1936. Parliament may 'abolish' itself and reconstitute itself as a different body, as occurred with the Union with Scotland Act 1706. Parliament may also legislate to alter its own powers, as with the Parliament Acts 1911 and 1949, whereby the powers of the House of Lords in respect of legislation were curtailed. Parliament may grant independence to dependent states, whether dominions or colonies, as with the Nigeria Independence Act 1960 and the Zimbabwe Independence Act 1979. Furthermore, Parliament may legislate to

---

17 See Priestley, 1771, cited in Dicey, 1885, p. 47.
18 Dicey, 1885, p. 47.

limit its own powers in relation to dependent territories, as shown by the Colonial Laws Validity Act 1865 and the Statute of Westminster 1931.[19]

Parliament may also legislate with retrospective effect, as with the War Damage Act 1965. The War Damage Act effectively overruled the decision of the House of Lords in **Burmah Oil Company v Lord Advocate** (1965). In 1942, British troops had destroyed oil installations in Rangoon, with the intention of preventing them from falling into the hands of the Japanese. The British government made an *ex gratia* payment of some £4 million to the company. Burmah Oil sued the government for some £31 million in compensation. The House of Lords held that compensation was payable by the Crown for the destruction of property caused by the exercise of the prerogative power in relation to war. The government immediately introduced into Parliament the War Damage Bill to nullify the effect of the decision.

Parliament may legislate with extra-territorial effect; that is to say, it may enact laws affecting the rights and duties of citizens and non-citizens outside the territorial jurisdiction of the United Kingdom. For example, certain offences committed in a foreign state will be triable in this country. Thus, murder, manslaughter, treason, bigamy and tax offences committed abroad will not render the accused immune from prosecution in this country.[20] Parliament may expressly legislate for overseas territory, as in the Continental Shelf Act 1964, under which exploration and exploitation rights of the continental shelf vest in the Crown. However, it is a presumption of statutory interpretation that statutes will not be given extra-territorial effect other than where it is expressly or impliedly provided for under the Act.[21] Such statutes will normally be passed in order to give effect to obligations undertaken under an international treaty.[22] The Hijacking Act 1971, for example, gave legislative effect to the Convention for the Suppression of the Unlawful Seizure of Aircraft. Section 1 of the Aviation Security Act 1982, which succeeded the Hijacking Act 1971, provides that the crime of hijacking is committed when a person on board an aircraft in flight unlawfully seizes control of the aircraft and exercises control over it by the use of force or by threats. The jurisdiction of the United Kingdom courts, with limited exceptions, extends to an act of hijacking, wherever it occurs, and irrespective of the nationality of the hijacker.[23] Similarly, the Terrorist Asset-Freezing Act 2010, section 33, provides that a criminal offence may be committed by British citizens or incorporated bodies, by act or omission wholly or partly outside the United Kingdom. The most often quoted and best remembered examples of Parliament's theoretically untrammelled legislative powers are those offered by Sir Ivor Jennings (1959) – Parliament can legislate to ban smoking on the streets of Paris; Parliament can legally make a man into a woman – and Sir Leslie Stephens (1882) – Parliament could legislate to have all blue-eyed babies put to death. These extreme, hypothetical examples illustrate the distinction between what is theoretically possible and what is practically possible, or, to express it differently, the distinction between *validity* and *effectiveness* discussed above. The distinction is important and helps to explain the apparent paradox of unlimited legislative power.

An Act of Parliament will be valid if it has passed through the requisite parliamentary stages and received Royal Assent. The manner in which the judges deal with this 'enrolled Bill' rule is discussed further below. All that need be noted for now is that, provided an Act of Parliament is 'on the parliamentary roll', it will be held to be good law.

---

19 Prolongation of Parliament Act 1944.
20 Law Com No. 91, *Territorial and Extra-territorial Extent of Criminal Law*, 1978, London: HMSO.
21 **Treacy v DPP** (1971); **R v Kelly** (1982).
22 Parliament may, however, legislate contrary to the requirements of international law. See **Mortensen v Peters** (1906); **Cheney v Conn** (1968).
23 See also the Taking of Hostages Act 1982 giving effect to the International Convention Against the Taking of Hostages.

Acts of Parliament alone are supreme
Resolutions of Parliament
Resolutions of either House of Parliament – for example, decisions of the House of Commons – do not have the force of law and cannot alter the law of the land and thereby affect individual rights and duties.[24] For a resolution to have the force of law, it must be placed on a statutory basis.

Proclamations
Proclamations of the Crown, issued under the royal prerogative, do not have the force of law. To understand the status of proclamations, it is necessary to turn to the reign of Henry VIII. Under the Statute of Proclamations 1539, the King was given wide – though not unlimited – power to make law without Parliament's consent. The Act was repealed in 1547, although monarchs continued to 'legislate' by proclamation. The **Case of Proclamations** (1611) clarified the constitutional position. The most significant aspects of the case lay in the findings, first, that the King could not by proclamation create an offence previously unknown to law, and, second, that the King had only such prerogative power as was granted under law.

Treaties
Treaties entered into under the royal prerogative cannot alter the law of the land. The courts have made it clear that treaties can take legal effect only under the authority of an Act of Parliament.[25] This point will be returned to when the constitutional relationship between the United Kingdom and the European Union is examined in Chapters 7 and 8. It is sufficient to note here that a treaty has no legal force under domestic law unless and until its provisions are incorporated into law by way of statute.

Resolutions, proclamations and treaties are but three species of 'law making' which are distinguishable from statute, and it is the statute alone which will be valid, provided that the required parliamentary procedures have been followed.

Intrinsic and extrinsic limits on Parliament's power
As seen above, the criterion of effectiveness underlies the supremacy of Parliament and represents one important – albeit extra-legal – constraint on Parliament's power. As Dicey says, sovereignty 'is limited on every side by the possibility of popular resistance' (1885, page 79). Leslie Stephens makes the same point and is quoted at length by Dicey:

> Lawyers are apt to speak as though the legislature were omnipotent, as they do not require to go beyond its decision. It is, of course, omnipotent in the sense that it can make whatever law it please, in as much as a law means any rule which has been made by the legislature. But, from the scientific point of view, the power of the legislature is of course strictly limited. It is limited, so to speak, both from within and from without; from within, because the legislature is the product of certain social conditions, and determined by whatever determines the society; and from without, because the power of imposing laws is dependent upon the instinct of subordination, which is itself limited. If a legislature decided that all blue eyed babies should be murdered, the preservation of blue eyed babies would be illegal; but legislators

24 *Stockdale v Hansard* (1839); *Bowles v Bank of England* (1913).
25 See, *inter alia*, The Parlement Belge (1879); *AG for Canada v AG for Ontario* (1937); *McWhirter v AG* (1972); *Blackburn v AG* (1971).

must go mad before they could pass such a law, and subjects be idiotic before they could submit to it. [page 81]

These views are indicative of the constitutional role of government today. In a representative democracy, the proper purpose of government is to serve the people. In former times, when government was conducted by the King in Council, this was not necessarily the case. But even then, there were limits on monarchical and aristocratic power: ultimately, law cannot be enforced against the will of the governed. Compliance – in the absence of a military or police state – depends for the most part on voluntary acquiescence, not on the application of power. Nowadays, with a more or less democratic House of Commons, the internal and external constraints discussed by Dicey and Stephens coalesce. As Dicey explains:

The aim and effect of such (representative) government is to produce a coincidence, or at any rate diminish the divergence, between the external and the internal limitations on the exercise of sovereign power.

Where a Parliament truly represents the people, the divergence between the external and the internal limit to the exercise of sovereign power can hardly arise, or if it arises, must soon disappear. [1885, pages 82–83]

No Parliament may be bound by its predecessor or bind its successor

The rationale for this aspect of Dicey's definition of sovereignty lies in the recognition that for a body to be sovereign it must be, in Austin's word, illimitable. For a sovereign body to be subordinate to another body would be a logical contradiction:

The logical reason why Parliament has failed in its endeavours to enact unchange-able enactments is that a sovereign power cannot, while retaining its sovereign character, restrict its own powers by any particular enactment ... 'Limited sover-eignty', in short, as in the case of a parliamentary as of every other sovereign, is a contradiction in terms. [1885, page 68]

It follows, therefore, that each Parliament must enjoy the same unlimited power as any Parliament before it. No Parliament can enact rules which limit future Parliaments. It is this aspect of Dicey's definition which gives rise to the most argument and which requires the most careful analysis.

The doctrine of implied repeal

The doctrine of implied repeal provides the mechanism by which the judge gives effect to the rule against Parliament being bound by previous Parliaments or being able to bind subsequent Parliaments, and thereby guarantees contemporary sovereignty. Parliament may, of course, repeal any previous law by expressly declaring that law to be repealed. The position of the judiciary is then clear: they must give effect to the latest expression of sovereign will and judges are not free to apply the earlier statute. The position, however, may not always be so clear cut. Parliament may pass, perhaps through inadvertence, a statute which, while not expressly repealing an earlier Act, is inconsistent with it. When the judges are thus faced with two apparently conflicting statutes, the doctrine of implied repeal will come into play, the judges applying the latest statute in time and deeming the earlier provisions to be impliedly repealed.

Two cases which illustrate the principle in operation are **Vauxhall Estates Ltd v Liverpool Corporation** (1932) and **Ellen Street Estates Ltd v Minister of Health** (1934), each of which entailed similar facts. Section 7(1) of the Acquisition of Land (Assessment of Compensation) Act 1919 provided that:

> The provisions of the Act or order by which the land is authorised to be acquired ... shall ... have effect subject to this Act and so far as inconsistent with this Act those provisions shall cease to have or shall not have effect.

The Housing Act 1925 provided for a less generous scheme for compensation on the compulsory acquisition of land than the 1919 Act. In both cases, the plaintiffs argued that section 7(1) of the 1919 Act was binding on the courts and should be applied in preference to the Housing Act 1925. If that claim were to succeed, the constitutional position would be that the provisions of the 1919 Act were effectively 'entrenched' – that is to say, have a superior legal status to that of other Acts of Parliament and therefore binding – on a future Parliament. In the **Vauxhall Estates** case, the Divisional Court held that the 1925 Act impliedly repealed the conflicting provisions in the 1919 Act and, in the **Ellen Street Estates** case, the Court of Appeal again ruled that the 1919 Act must give way to the 1925 legislation. Maugham LJ stated that:

> The legislature cannot, according to our constitution, bind itself as to the form of subsequent legislation, and it is impossible for Parliament to enact that in a subsequent statute dealing with the same subject matter there can be no implied repeal. If, in a subsequent Act, Parliament chooses to make it plain that the earlier statute is being to some extent repealed, effect must be given to that intention just because it is the will of the legislature.[26]

While the implied repeal rule still applies in relation to most statutes, it has been regarded by some senior judges as inapplicable to statutes of major constitutional importance. This view has been expressed in relation to the European Communities Act 1972 and the Human Rights Act 1998; see below for further discussion.

With the doctrines of express and implied repeal firmly in mind, consideration must now be given to the special problems allegedly posed for legislative supremacy by grants of independence, the Acts of Union with Scotland and Ireland, 'manner and form' and 'redefinition' theories. The impact of membership of the European Union (and the 2016 referendum decision to leave the EU) also requires careful consideration, as does the recent devolution of power to the Scottish Parliament and the Northern Ireland and Welsh Assemblies, and the Human Rights Act 1998.

---

26 See, however, the earlier case of **Nairn v University of St Andrews** (1909), in which the House of Lords ruled that the Universities (Scotland) Act 1889, which empowered commissioners to make ordinances, *inter alia*, to enable universities to confer degrees on women, did not impliedly repeal the Representation of the People (Scotland) Act 1868, s. 27, which provided the right to vote for, *inter alia*, 'every person whose name is for the time being on the register, ... if of full age, and not subject to any legal incapacity'. In **Jex-Blake v Senatus of the University of Edinburgh** (1873), following **Chorlton v Lings** (1868), the court ruled that 'women' were not 'persons' within the meaning to be applied to the right to vote. The House of Lords in **Nairn** ruled that only Parliament, in the most express terms, could 'effect a constitutional change so momentous and far-reaching', and it could not be taken to have done so by 'so furtive a process' as this later Act (1909, *per* Lord Loreburn LC). Given the date of this case, and its positioning in the continuing struggle for women's right to vote, which was so consistently obstructed by the courts, the decision is perhaps best understood within the political climate of the time rather than as an illustration of objective legal analysis.

Grants of independence

The Statute of Westminster 1931 was enacted to give statutory force to the constitutional convention that the United Kingdom Parliament would not legislate for Dominions without their consent. Section 4 provides:

> No Act of Parliament of the United Kingdom passed after the commencement of this Act shall extend, or be deemed to extend, to a Dominion as part of the law of that Dominion unless it is expressly declared in that Act that that Dominion has requested, and consented to, the enactment thereof.

Where Parliament confers partial competence on a subordinate legislature, the question arises as to whether the United Kingdom Parliament can revoke that grant of power. The principle that Parliament cannot be bound by the acts of its predecessor has already been established. The issue here is the relationship between the sovereign Parliament and a Parliament dependent for its powers upon Westminster. This issue arose in **British Coal Corporation v The King** (1935). The Judicial Committee of the Privy Council had to determine whether or not the Canadian legislature had the power to regulate or prohibit appeals in criminal matters to the King in Council. A determination of that matter entailed consideration of the scope of legislative competence of the legislature. The relevant Acts were the British North America Act 1867, the Colonial Laws Validity Act 1865, the Statute of Westminster 1931 and the Canadian Criminal Code, which prohibited appeal to the courts of the United Kingdom. The Statute of Westminster had removed any legislative incompetence from the Canadian legislature and accordingly the legislature had full power to enact the section in question. It was accepted by the Judicial Committee of the Privy Council that, whilst the power of the Imperial Parliament remained 'in theory unimpaired' and that, 'as a matter of abstract law', section 4 of the Statute of Westminster could be repealed by the Parliament of the United Kingdom, in practice it could not be: 'legal theory must march alongside practical reality'. **British Coal Corporation v The King** is, however, no more than a recognition of the extrinsic or practical limitations on the exercise of sovereignty, and not of any legal limitations on Parliament's supremacy.

In **Ndlwana v Hofmeyer** (1937),[27] the Appellate Division of the South African High Court adopted the view that such a restriction amounted to a fetter on Parliament's powers. Again, however, it is to be noted that such judicial utterances do no more than recognise the practical political restraints which are imposed on Parliament, not its legal powers. It is correct, therefore, to view such *obiter* as reflecting the distinction between legal and political sovereignty, a point emphasised by Dicey himself.

The question of the status and effect of section 4 of the Statute of Westminster arose once more in **Manuel v Attorney General** (1982). The issue was whether the Canada Act 1982, passed by the United Kingdom Parliament at the request and with the consent of Canada, was a valid enactment. The plaintiffs' argument was that the United Kingdom Parliament had no power to amend the Constitution of Canada to the detriment of the native population without their consent. It was argued that section 4 of the Statute of Westminster required not just the consent of the federal Parliament but also that of all the provincial legislatures and the native minority population. The application failed. The Statute of Westminster required only that the 1982 Act declared that Canada had requested and consented to the Act.

---

27 See also **Ibralebbe v R** (1964); **Blackburn v AG** (1971).

The Acts of Union with Scotland 1706/1707 and Ireland 1800[28]

The Acts of Union, their status and their effect on Parliament's sovereignty have provided a fertile source for academic debate which represents a powerful argument against the unlimited freedom of any Parliament at any time to legislate as it pleases. The whole debate centres on the notion that the new United Kingdom Parliament was, in the words of Professor JDB Mitchell, 'born unfree'.[29] The idea being conveyed here is that the Acts of Union have some form of 'higher law' status which binds and limits the powers of Parliament.

The Union with Scotland

Prior to the accession to the throne of James I (James VI of Scotland), England and Scotland were both independent sovereign states, each having its own monarch and Parliament. With James' accession to the English throne in 1603, the two countries were united under one monarch but retained their sovereign Parliaments until 1706. The Treaty of Union 1706 effected, conceptually, the abolition of both Parliaments and the birth of the Parliament of Great Britain.

Article I of the Act of Union provides:

> That the two kingdoms of England and Scotland shall upon the first day of May which shall be in the year one thousand seven hundred and seven and for ever after be united into one Kingdom by the name of Great Britain.

The sovereignty issue has been argued in three cases concerning the Act of Union with Scotland. In **MacCormick v Lord Advocate** (1953), MacCormick sought an injunction against the Lord Advocate, as representative of the Crown, preventing the use of the title Queen Elizabeth II of the United Kingdom of Great Britain. The objection to the use of the title was based on historical inaccuracy[30] and a contravention of Article I of the Treaty of Union which provided for the union of the two countries from 1707. The petition was dismissed, as was the subsequent appeal. Lord Cooper, the Lord President, however, proceeded to discuss the doctrine of sovereignty:

> The principle of the unlimited sovereignty of Parliament is a distinctively English principle which has no counterpart in Scottish constitutional law ... Considering that the Union legislation extinguished the Parliaments of Scotland and England and replaced them by a new Parliament, I have difficulty in seeing why it should have been supposed that the new Parliament of Great Britain must inherit all the peculiar characteristics of the English Parliament but none of the Scottish Parliament, as if all that happened in 1707 was that Scottish representatives were admitted to the Parliament of England. That is not what was done ...

> I have not found in the Union legislation any provision that the Parliament of Great Britain should be 'absolutely sovereign' in the sense that that Parliament should be free to alter the Treaty at will.

---

28 As the Union with England Act 1707.
29 Mitchell, 1963; and see Munro, 1999.
30 Queen Elizabeth I was Queen of England, not of Scotland.

In **Gibson v Lord Advocate** (1975), the issue tested was whether allowing fishermen of Member States of the European Community to fish in Scottish coastal waters infringed Article XVIII of the Act of Union. Article XVIII provides that: 'no alteration be made in laws which concern private right except for the evident utility of the subjects within Scotland'. The claim was dismissed, Lord Keith ruling that the European Community Regulations did not confer rights or obligations on individual citizens and accordingly were matters of public and not private law and, accordingly, that Article XVIII could not be invoked. On the sovereignty question, Lord Keith, however, stated:

> Like Lord President Cooper, I prefer to reserve my opinion what the position would be if the United Kingdom Parliament passed an Act purporting to abolish the Court of Session or the Church of Scotland or to substitute English law for the whole body of Scots law. I am, however, of the opinion that the question whether a particular Act of the United Kingdom Parliament altering a particular aspect of Scots private law is or is not 'for the evident utility' of the subjects within Scotland is not a justiciable issue in this court. The making of decisions upon what must essentially be a political matter is no part of the function of the court, and it is highly undesirable that it should be.

In **Sillars v Smith** (1982), a similar challenge was lodged over the validity of the Criminal Justice (Scotland) Act 1980, on the basis that the United Kingdom Parliament, which had passed the Scotland Act 1978, which created a legislative Assembly for Scotland, had no power to repeal that Act – as had been done – and accordingly, Parliament, it was argued, had no power to pass the Criminal Justice (Scotland) Act. The claim was dismissed, the court adopting the classical view expressed in **Edinburgh and Dalkeith Railway Company v Wauchope** (1842) by Lord Campbell:

> All that a court of justice can look to is the parliamentary roll; they see that an Act has passed both Houses of Parliament, and that it has received the royal assent, and no court of justice can enquire into the manner in which it was introduced into Parliament, what was done previously to its being introduced, or what passed in Parliament during the various stages of its progress through both Houses of Parliament.

Despite the questioning *dicta* of Lords Cooper and Keith on sovereignty, the evidence to date goes clearly against the notion that the Act of Union is legally unalterable. To take but one example, the Protestant Religion and Presbyterian Church Act 1707 provision that 'the true Protestant religion and the worship, discipline and government' of the established church were 'to continue without any alteration to the people of this land in all succeeding generations' was incorporated into the Treaty of Union and declared to be 'a fundamental and essential condition of the ... Union in all times coming'. The Act also required that teachers in universities and schools had to subscribe to the faith. Yet, in 1711, the Scottish Episcopalians Act and the Church Patronage (Scotland) Act were passed to reflect greater religious toleration, and by the Universities (Scotland) Act 1853 and the Parochial and Burgh Schoolmasters (Scotland) Act 1861, the requirement that teachers must subscribe to the Protestant faith was removed. Further changes in the organisation of the Church were made in the Church of Scotland Act 1921.

The Union with Ireland

The Act of Union with Ireland 1800 has given rise to similar arguments, although these arguments are even less convincing than those addressed to the Act of Union with Scotland. The Act of Union was declared to 'last forever'. Article 5 provided for a United Church of England and Ireland that 'shall be and shall remain in full force for ever, and that this be deemed and taken to be an essential and fundamental part of the Union'. Nevertheless, in 1869 the Irish Church was disestablished under the Irish Church Act of that year. In **Ex parte Canon Selwyn** (1872), a clergyman sought an order of mandamus against the Lord President of the Council ordering him to petition the Queen for adjudication of the question of whether the giving of Royal Assent to the Irish Church Act 1869 was contrary to the coronation oath and the Act of Settlement. The coronation oath contained a commitment to maintain a unified and established Church of England and Ireland. The court dismissed the petition on the basis that the statute was supreme and could not be questioned in a court of law.

The Acts of Union[31] provided for the permanent union between Ireland and Great Britain. However, the Ireland Act 1949 recognised the republican status and independence of southern Ireland, thereby terminating the union. The 1949 Act also provided that Northern Ireland:

> remains part of His Majesty's dominions and of the United Kingdom and it is hereby affirmed that in no event will Northern Ireland or any part thereof cease to be part of His Majesty's dominions and of the United Kingdom without consent of the Parliament of Northern Ireland. [section 1(2)]

That commitment is reiterated in section 1 of the Northern Ireland Act 1998. However, such assurances, whilst morally and politically binding on the government, do not amount – under Diceyan theory – to a legal restriction on Parliament's powers. Parliament remains free, in legal theoretical terms, to legislate contrary to such undertakings, although the political implications of so doing guarantee that Parliament will not do so.

AV Dicey had argued that the Acts of Union had no greater legal status than the Dentists Act 1878, or indeed any other unimportant Act.[32] Moreover, as has been seen, Dicey viewed the Acts of Union as being ordinary Acts of Parliament by which – in the case of the Union with Scotland – the English and Scottish Parliaments 'abolished' themselves, to be reconstituted as the Parliament of Great Britain, and in the case of the Act of Union with Ireland, were reconstituted as the Parliament of the United Kingdom.

Alternative interpretations of the Acts of Union

The power of Parliament to 'abolish itself' and be reconstituted as a 'new parliament' is one of the principal matters to which opponents to Diceyan theory address their arguments. Professor JDB Mitchell (1963), for example, questions Dicey's insistence on the equal legal status of Acts of Parliament, distinguishing between rules which create and represent the foundation of the state, and other derivative rules of law: 'the one set of rules creates or is the legal foundation of the state, the other is built upon that foundation'.

The Acts of Union of Scotland and England creating the unified Parliament of Great Britain represents a 'fresh starting point'. In Mitchell's view, the Acts of Union, being antecedent to the Parliament of Great Britain, imposed valid legal limitations on its powers.

---

31 The Act of Union (Ireland) 1800; the Act of Union with Ireland 1800.
32 Dicey, 1885, p. 145.

Conceding that many legislative changes have been made to the provisions of the Acts of Union, Mitchell nevertheless argues that the provisions, at least in relation to the Church of Scotland and the Court of Session, are essential limitations on Parliament's powers.

Professor Neil MacCormick also challenges Diceyan orthodoxy.[33] In MacCormick's view, the Acts of Union amounted to a rudimentary written constitution: the Anglo-Scottish Treaty of 1706 and the Union with Ireland 1800 represent the 'historically first constitution' of Great Britain and the United Kingdom respectively, and accordingly have a very special status in constitutional law. Harry Calvert (1968) specifically rejects Dicey's view of the effects of the Acts of Union as 'untenable'. Calvert adopts Professor RVF Heuston's arguments (1964a, pages 20–30) regarding the legal status of the Acts of Union and proceeds to argue that Royal Assent could be denied – in a departure from constitutional convention – to a Bill purporting to sever the union between Northern Ireland and the rest of the United Kingdom against the wishes of the people, the expression of which has been provided for by statute. Such a severance would, in Calvert's view, be unconstitutional. Accordingly, it would be for the Crown to defeat any attempt to act unconstitutionally:

> [A]t all events, it cannot readily be conceded that a constitutional monarch has no constitutional power to resist being implicated in unconstitutionality by his ministers. The bounds of the British constitution are very widely drawn. There is very little that a Prime Minister, supported by his Cabinet and a majority of the House of Commons, cannot do. But if there is nothing that he cannot do, there is no constitution at all. [1968, page 32]

These differing arguments about the status of the Acts of Union, and the future of the Union with Scotland in particular, continue to have constitutional relevance. As discussed in Chapter 11, in 2014 a referendum was held in Scotland on the question of its union with the rest of the United Kingdom. Although a majority of voters decided that Scotland should remain a part of the UK, the question of Scotland's independence was reignited in 2016 when a majority of the people in Scotland voted (in a UK-wide referendum) to remain part of the European Union – a decision which contradicted that of voters in England, the majority of whom voted to leave the EU. On this issue, see further Chapter 11.

Manner and form and redefinition theories

Parliament, in the exercise of its sovereign power, may specify particular procedures which must be undertaken in order to enact legislation. It has been seen, for example, that the Northern Ireland Constitution (Amendment) Act 1973 provided that the six counties of Northern Ireland shall not cease to be part of the United Kingdom unless the proposed separation is approved by a majority of the electorate in a border poll (referendum). This may be interpreted to mean either that Parliament has specified the procedure – or manner and form – for enacting laws, or that Parliament has 'redefined' itself for the purposes of enacting laws, by including in the definition of Parliament the electorate of Northern Ireland. Any provision relating solely to procedure but not affecting the composition of Parliament may be termed a 'manner and form' provision; whereas when the actual composition of Parliament is altered, the appropriate term is 'redefinition'. The Northern Ireland Constitution (Amendment) Act straddles both theories.

---

33 1978; see also 2001.

The essential question to be asked is whether such provisions, however labelled, are capable of binding a future Parliament. If that were to be the case – and, as will be seen, there are supporters for that view – two possible conclusions would follow: first, that Parliament has unlimited power – exercisable only at one single point in time, for ever after to limit the sovereignty of future Parliaments; and, second, that future Parliaments would be less than sovereign – a contradiction in terms, for it would not then be correct to speak of Parliament having unlimited sovereignty.

A seminal case illustrating manner and form theory is that of **Attorney General for New South Wales v Trethowan** (1932). In 1929, the government of New South Wales, Australia, sought to prevent a subsequent government from abolishing the Legislative Council (the upper chamber). An Act of Parliament was passed, amending the Constitution Act 1902, providing that any Bill purporting to abolish the upper House must have the approval of both legislative chambers and of two-thirds of the Members of each chamber. Further, there had to be popular electoral support for the abolition, to be determined in a referendum. In addition, to prevent a subsequent Parliament ignoring the provisions of the 1929 Act, it was provided that any Bill attempting to repeal the 1929 Act must follow the same procedure – a device known as 'double entrenchment'. In 1930, following an election, the incoming government decided to abolish the upper chamber and to do so by ignoring the provisions of the 1929 Act. Members of the Legislative Council sought an injunction restraining the grant of Royal Assent to the Bill, and a declaration that such a grant of assent would be unlawful, being *ultra vires* the lower House. The High Court of Australia ruled that the provisions of the 1929 Act could not be avoided, and that Royal Assent could not be given to the Bill. The matter was referred to the Privy Council, which affirmed the judgment of the High Court of Australia.

The constitutional reason underlying the court's rejection of the government's claim that the 1932 Bill could lawfully receive Royal Assent was that the Parliament in New South Wales was a legislative body having subordinate and not supreme power. Such powers as the legislature enjoyed were derived from the sovereign United Kingdom Parliament under the Constitution Acts 1902–1929 and the Colonial Laws Validity Act 1865. The Colonial Laws Validity Act 1865 represented a landmark in the clarification of powers between the sovereign United Kingdom Parliament and subordinate colonial legislatures. The Act gave statutory affirmation to the non-legal conventional rule that laws enacted in the colony which were contradictory to statute or the common law of the United Kingdom would not be held to be invalid by the courts of the United Kingdom. The Act further clarified the extent to which the colonial legislature had power to amend its own composition and procedure. Section 5 is the all-important provision for current purposes. It provides that:

> every representative legislature shall ... have and be deemed at all times to have had, full power to make laws respecting the constitution, power, and procedure of such legislature; provided that such laws shall have been passed in such manner and form as may from time to time be required by any Act of Parliament, letters patent, Order in Council, or colonial law, for the time being in force in the said colony.

It is this section which dictated the decision in **Attorney General for New South Wales v Trethowan** (1932). The government of New South Wales was not free to introduce the 1932 Bill and attempt to enact it other than in conformity with the requirements of section 5. Section 5 required that the legislature complied with the 'manner and form' provisions in force. The specific 'manner and form' provisions were those laid down in the 1929 Constitution Act, and these requirements could not merely be ignored by the subordinate legislature.[34] In the High Court of Australia in the **Trethowan** case, Rich J denied the proposition that the New South Wales Parliament had unlimited sovereign power.

A similar constitutional arrangement can be seen demonstrated by the South African case of **Harris v The Minister of the Interior** (1952) and that of **Bribery Commissioner v Ranasinghe** (1965) from Sri Lanka (Ceylon, as it then was). These cases demonstrate one fundamental principle: that legislative bodies do not necessarily enjoy full sovereign power, and that some form of 'higher law' may control their powers. In each of these cases, the powers of the legislatures of New South Wales, South Africa and Ceylon (as it then was) had been established under an Act of the sovereign United Kingdom Parliament. That being so, the legislative bodies had to comply with the constitutional laws in force, and failure to do so would give the courts the jurisdiction to declare a legislative act void.

No one may question the validity of an Act of Parliament

'True it is, that what the Parliament doth, no authority on earth can undo'.[35] As has been seen, an Act will be accepted as valid by the courts provided that it has passed through the requisite legislative stages and received Royal Assent.[36] Regardless of the subject matter of the Act, it will be upheld by the judges.[37] In the time before the 1688 settlement, it was not uncommon for judges to proclaim that an Act of Parliament could be held to be invalid because it conflicted with some higher form of divine law.

In **Dr Bonham's Case** (1610), there is the often-cited *obiter dictum* of Coke CJ to the effect that: 'When an Act of Parliament is against common right and reason, or repugnant, or impossible to be performed, the common law will control it, and adjudge such act to be void'. Such views, while appealing to the senses, were of doubtful validity when expressed and have no authority today. The opinion of Lord Reid expressed in **Pickin v British Railways Board** (1974) represents the correct contemporary judicial view on the authority of statute:

> In earlier times many learned lawyers seem to have believed that an Act of Parliament could be disregarded in so far as it was contrary to the law of God or the law of nature or natural justice, but since the supremacy of Parliament was finally demonstrated by the revolution of 1688 any such idea has become obsolete.[38]

---

34 The Australia Act 1986 (Commonwealth and UK), s. 3(1), provides that the Colonial Laws Validity Act 1865 shall not apply 'to any law made after the commencement of this Act by the Parliament of a State'.
35 Blackstone's *Commentaries on the Laws of England* (1765–1769), Vol. I.
36 See **The Prince's Case** (1606).
37 But see further below and Chapter 8, on the complexity arising by virtue of membership of the European Union.
38 The case of **Jackson v Attorney General** (2005) represents a recent challenge to the validity of a statute – the Hunting Act 2004. The case is discussed in detail in Chapter 16.

LIMITATIONS ON PARLIAMENTARY SOVEREIGNTY

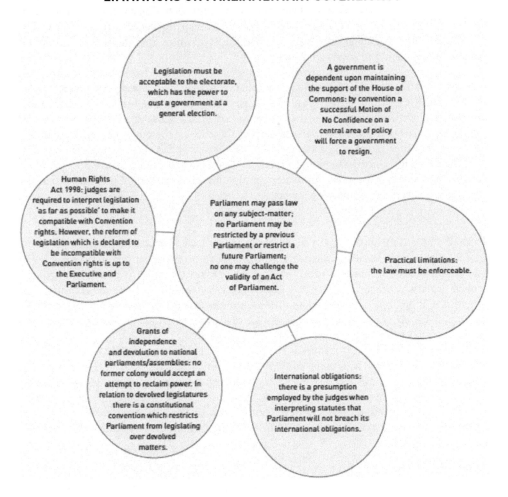

Non-legal constraints on Parliament's powers

Political acceptability to the electorate represents the strongest external basis of restraint. All governments are accountable to the electorate, albeit in terms of a direct vote only periodically. But elections do not of themselves always provide the means of sanctioning governments, nor do they guarantee that government invariably acts in accordance with the electorate's wishes. Still less can the electorate be regarded as exercising any power to enact law. Whilst the electorate may be correctly regarded as politically sovereign, and can, at the end of the day, oust a government which violates its trust, on the exercise of the franchise the electorate conditionally transfers sovereign legislative power to Parliament.

Whereas, therefore, the power of the electorate is great at the time of a general election, it is a more limited power during a government's term of office – most particularly where the government has a strong majority in Parliament. It is the task of Parliament as a whole, both Commons and Lords, to scrutinise government policy and legislative proposals, and a range of procedural devices exists which facilitate such inquiry. It is through Parliament that the will or wishes of the electorate for the most part find expression.[39] No government can afford to ignore Parliament and, ultimately, a government can be brought down if its policies are such that it loses the confidence of the House as a whole. If Parliament is truly the 'sounding board of the nation', Parliament must reflect the political morality within society.[40]

A further political restraint imposed on governments relates to international relations. No state today exists in isolation from its neighbours. The United Kingdom, as with most states, is bound by numerous treaties under international law which impose restrictions on the freedom of government action. Across virtually every aspect of government, such restraints are visible: environmental protection, protection of human rights, the protection of children from abduction, the regulation of currency exchanges, agreements on trade and tariffs and so on. In addition to such treaties, the United Kingdom is bound in practical terms by membership of the European Union (until Britain's membership of the EU ceased) and the United Nations. In theoretical terms, therefore, Parliament may remain free to enact laws violating any or all of the United Kingdom's international obligations; in practice, it would not and could not.

Alternative Views on Sovereignty

We have seen above that there are a number of arguments concerning the traditional doctrine of sovereignty. In this brief section, the differing approaches are brought together for further consideration.

In **Bribery Commissioner v Ranasinghe** (1965), Lord Pearce had asserted that:

> The proposition which is not acceptable is that a legislature, once established, has some inherent power derived from the mere fact of establishment to make a valid law by the resolution of a bare majority which its own constituent instrument has said shall not be a valid law unless made by a different type of majority or by a different legislative process.

Geoffrey Marshall seizes upon this dictum and argues that Lord Pearce: 'seemed to imply equally that both non-sovereign and sovereign legislatures may be made subject to procedural rules entrenching parts of the law from simple majority repeal'.

Sir Ivor Jennings has also questioned the orthodox view. In *The Law and the Constitution*, Jennings distinguishes two situations:

> If a prince has supreme power, and continues to have supreme power, he can do anything, even to the extent of undoing the things which he has previously done. If he grants a constitution, binding himself not to make laws except with the consent of an elected legislature, he has power immediately afterwards to abolish the legislature without its consent and to continue legislating by his personal decree.

> But if the prince has not supreme power, but the rule is that the courts accept as law that which is in the proper legal form, the result is different. For when the prince enacts that henceforth no rule shall be law unless it is enacted by him with

---

39 See JS Mill, 1861, Chapter V.
40 See Allan, 1985b; and Lee, 1985.

the consent of the legislature, the law has been altered, and the courts will not admit as law any rule which is not made in that form. Consequently a rule subsequently made by the prince alone abolishing the legislature is not law, for the legislature has not consented to it, and the rule has not been enacted according to the manner and form required by the law for the time being.

The difference is this. In the one case, there is sovereignty. In the other, the courts have no concern with sovereignty, but only with the established law. 'Legal sovereignty' is merely a name indicating that the legislature has for the time being power to make laws of any kind in the manner required by law. That is, a rule expressed to be made by the Queen, 'with the advice and consent of the Lords spiritual and temporal, and Commons in this present Parliament assembled, and by the authority of the same', will be recognised by the courts, including a rule which alters this law itself. If this is so, the 'legal sovereign' may impose legal limitations upon itself, because its power to change the law includes the power to change the law affecting itself. [page 152]

Sir Ivor Jennings then illustrates his thesis by reference to **Attorney General for New South Wales v Trethowan** (1932), **Ndlwana v Hofmeyer** (1937) and **Harris v The Minister of the Interior** (1952). Jennings concedes that the decisions do not necessarily 'determine the law as it applies in the United Kingdom', and leaps from that proposition to one which claims that Dicey 'failed to prove that that law made the King in Parliament a sovereign law making body' (1959b, page 156). Such a view is unconvincing. The constitutional justification for the decisions examined lay precisely in the fact that the legislatures of both New South Wales and South Africa had legislative powers conferred upon them by a fully sovereign superior sovereign body – the United Kingdom Parliament. Only once such complete sovereignty was conferred would the legislative fetters be removed. No such controlling device pertains to the Parliament of the United Kingdom itself.

Arguing from the proposition that Parliament may redefine itself – as in the Parliament Act 1911[41] – and may alter its own composition – as in the Life Peerages Act 1958 – Professor JDB Mitchell turns to 'the purported self-limitations of Parliament' (1968, page 78). On section 4 of the Statute of Westminster, Mitchell argues that there are two possible interpretations when looked at from the point of view of the United Kingdom judges. The first is that section 4 amounts to a rule of construction directed to the courts, which does not raise the problem of limitation on Parliament. If, however, section 4 is understood to mean that Parliament has forfeited its legislative capacity – by conferring that capacity on the recipient legislature – then there 'is quite clearly a purported limitation of the United Kingdom Parliament' (page 79). Parliament has redefined itself in a manner which excludes its power to legislate for the Dominion.

Mitchell cites in support of the argument the dictum of Lord Radcliffe in **Ibralebbe v The Queen** (1964) in which Lord Radcliffe argues that while the United Kingdom Parliament has the legal power to legislate for Ceylon (as it then was), to use such power would be 'wholly inconsistent' with the powers of legislation conferred on the legislature of Ceylon.

Further authorities could be offered in support of this view. As seen above, in **British Coal Corporation v The King** (1935), Lord Sankey LC said, in relation to section 4, that: 'indeed, the Imperial Parliament could, as a matter of abstract law, repeal or disregard section 4 of the statute. But that is theory and has no relation to realities' (page 20). Further, in **Ndlwana v Hofmeyer**

---

41 The Parliament Act 1911 reduced the powers of the House of Lords with respect to legislation. See Chapter 16.

(1937), Lord Denning asserted that 'freedom once given cannot be revoked'. How should such claims be evaluated? First, as Dicey made clear, the United Kingdom Parliament – in the exercise of its sovereign power – clearly has the power to abolish itself, or to surrender its sovereignty in favour of another legislature, as in grants of independence. In political terms, it is, of course, unthinkable that Parliament would attempt to revoke such independence. The more troublesome question is whether Parliament retains the capacity to revoke such grants of freedom in legal terms. On this, Dicey was very clear: '"Limited sovereignty", in short, is, in the case of a Parliamentary as of every other sovereign, a contradiction in terms' (1885, page 68).

Professor RVF Heuston has put forward a 'new view' of sovereignty. This view is summarised as follows:

(a) sovereignty is a legal concept: the rules which identify the sovereign and prescribe its composition and functions are logically prior to it;
(b) there is a distinction between rules which govern, on the one hand, (i) the composition and (ii) the procedure, and, on the other hand, (iii) the area of power, of a sovereign legislature;
(c) the courts have jurisdiction to question the validity of an alleged Act of Parliament on grounds b(i) and b(ii), but not on ground b(iii); and
(d) this jurisdiction is exercisable either before or after the Royal Assent has been signified – in the former case by way of injunction, in the latter by way of declaratory judgment.[42]

To what extent is it correct to state that the judiciary may 'question the validity of an alleged Act of Parliament' on the grounds of the composition and the procedure adopted within Parliament? Clearly, as demonstrated by **Attorney General for New South Wales v Trethowan** (1932) and other comparable cases, under certain circumstances, it is within the jurisdiction of the courts to question whether or not an Act is valid. Those circumstances usually arise within jurisdictions having subordinate rather than supreme legislatures. More recently, with devolution to Northern Ireland and Scotland, the courts are given the power to invalidate Acts of the devolved legislatures if they fall outside the scope of their legislative competence.[43]

In this regard, it may be said that the judges are protecting the sovereignty of the United Kingdom Parliament by keeping subordinate legislatures within the powers conferred. In the United Kingdom, however, Parliament is distinguishable by the absence of any such controlling powers. The orthodox position is that expressed in **British Railways Board v Pickin** (1974), where the House of Lords, affirming its earlier decision,[44] endorsed the 'enrolled Bill rule'. Thus, once the Bill has proceeded through Parliament, either under the normal legislative process or under the Parliament Acts 1911 and 1949, and received Royal Assent, the Bill becomes a validly enacted Act of Parliament and will not be impugned by the courts. The courts have jurisdiction to determine what is an Act of Parliament. As has been seen earlier, the courts have held, by way of illustration, that mere resolutions of the House of Commons are incapable of having legal effect in the same manner as an Act; **Stockdale v Hansard** (1839) and **Bowles v Bank of England** (1913) are clear authorities for that view.

The central distinguishing feature between the jurisdictions concerned in the 'manner and form' cases and the United Kingdom lies in the existence of a higher legislative authority. In each case, it was the United Kingdom Parliament which defined and limited the powers of

---

42 Heuston, 1964a, Chapter I. See also Munro, 1999, Chapter 4. Professor Heuston is supported in his approach by Jennings, 1959b, Chapter 4, Appendix III; Cowen, 1951; Marshall, 1957, Chapters 2–4.
43 For the case law see Chapter 11.
44 **Edinburgh and Dalkeith Railway Co v Wauchope** (1842).

a subordinate legislative body. Only once a Parliament enjoys full sovereignty can it be free of such constraints. The United Kingdom Parliament, by contrast, is 'uncontrolled': there exists no higher source of legal authority than Parliament itself. For this reason, to draw an analogy between the legislatures of New South Wales or South Africa and the United Kingdom misses the vital dimension of unlimited power which is enjoyed by the United Kingdom Parliament.

The last words on the manner and form arguments shall be left to Professors Wade (1989) and Munro (1999). Professor Wade summarises his views on manner and form theorists as follows:

> But, in the end, what is the substance of their argument? It is simply their prediction, made with varying degrees of dogmatism, that the judges will, or should, enforce restrictions about manner and form and abandon their clear and settled rule that the traditional manner and form is what counts. But if it is vain for Parliament to command the judges to transfer their allegiance to some new system of legislation if the judges are resolved to remain loyal to the old one, it is still more vain for professors to assert that they should. The judicial loyalty is the foundation of the legal system and, at the same time, a political fact.

Professor Munro finds the arguments as to manner and form equally unconvincing, stating that 'the cases cited by the "manner and form" school do not, in the end, seem very helpful'.

 SELF-TEST QUESTION

Outline AV Dicey's view on sovereignty and offer case law in support of your answer.

Parliamentary Sovereignty and the European Union during UK Membership

See
Chapters 7 and 8

In 2016 the people voted to leave the European Union (EU) in a referendum. The following discussion relates to the period in which the UK was a member of the EU. In Chapters 7 and 8, the aims, organisation and law-making power of the institutions of the EU are considered, and the relationship between the law of the United Kingdom and EU law during membership of the EU will become clearer after those chapters have been studied. Nonetheless, it is necessary to consider here, in outline, the impact of membership of the EU on the doctrine of parliamentary supremacy during UK membership from 1973 to 2020.

The United Kingdom became a Member of the European Communities (now EU)[45] in 1973. The original Communities had their own constitutional structure as defined in the Treaties. The Court of Justice of the European Union (CJEU) has, since the 1960s, asserted the supremacy of EU law over the laws of any Member State.[46] As will be seen later, the Court of Justice has adopted the view that, by becoming signatories to the Treaties, Member States

---

45 European Economic Community, European Coal and Steel Community, European Community for Atomic Energy.
46 See the early cases of **Costa v ENEL** (1964); *Van Gend en Loos* (1963); **Simmenthal** (1977); *Internationale Handelsgesellschaft* (1972). Note that under the Lisbon Treaty 2007 the Court was renamed the 'Court of Justice of the European Union' and from 2009 the term 'Community law' became 'European Union law'.

have limited their own legislative competence in EU matters, conferring the supreme power to legislate on these matters on the law-making institutions of the Union.[47]

The laws of the Union – the Treaties, laws enacted by the Council of Ministers and the European Parliament together with the judicial decisions of the European Court – are binding on all Member States. In the United Kingdom, the acceptance of EU law was under the European Communities Act (ECA) 1972 – an Act of the United Kingdom Parliament. Accordingly, all EU law derived its force and authority under this Act, which, as with any Act, had no special legal status within the constitution (under the EU (Withdrawal) Act 2018 the ECA is repealed at the end of the transition period in 2020). However, membership of the EU raised some unique questions for the sovereignty of Parliament.

The principal issue for consideration was the attitude of the judges – both domestic and European – towards EU law during the UK's period of membership. It is clear, from the perspective of the Court of Justice of the EU (CJEU), that EU law prevailed over domestic law, and that domestic legislatures had no power to enact binding legislation contrary to the requirements of EU law. From the domestic perspective, however, the issue was not so clear-cut. The issues which require explanation are:

(a)   the extent to which the judges were prepared to accept and apply EU law and
(b)   the manner in which, and extent to which, inadvertent or deliberate parliamentary Acts were reconciled with the requirements of EU law.

The application of European Union (formerly Community) Law

Section 2 of the European Communities Act 1972 provided that Community (now EU) law shall have direct applicability in the United Kingdom:

> 1. All such rights, powers, liabilities, obligations and restrictions from time to time created or arising by or under the Treaties, and all such remedies and procedures from time to time provided for by or under the Treaties, as in accordance with the Treaties are without further enactment to be given legal effect or used in the United Kingdom shall be recognised and available in law, and be enforced, allowed and followed accordingly; and the expression 'enforceable Community right' and similar expressions shall be read as referring to one to which this sub-section applies.

Section 2(4) provided for the primacy of Community (now EU) law, without expressly stating that the law of the European Union is supreme:

> The provision that may be made under sub-section (2) above[48] includes, subject to Schedule 2 of this Act, any such provision (of any such extent) as might be made by Act of Parliament, and any enactment passed or to be passed, other than one contained in this part of this Act, shall be construed and have effect subject to the foregoing provisions of this section.

---

47 Under the proposed Reform Treaty (Treaty of Lisbon) the Union shall 'replace and succeed the Community' – see further Chapter 7.
48 Which provides for implementation of Community obligations by secondary legislation.

Accordingly, all the rights, powers, liabilities, obligations and restrictions provided for under section 2(1) were to be given effect by the courts, and section 2(4) operated as a rule of construction to the courts to interpret law in accordance with the requirements of EU law. The manner in which the courts achieved the objectives expressed in the European Communities Act 1972 are considered in Chapters 7 and 8, as is the view of the CJEU on the supremacy of EU law. However, it would be misleading to leave this chapter on the traditional theory of sovereignty without giving some introductory overview of the challenge which EU law posed. The CJEU adopts as its guiding principle the supremacy of the law of the European Union. In the CJEU's view, a new legal order has been founded, a sovereign legal order within its sphere of competence. The sovereignty of EU law must, according to the CJEU, be respected by Member States, because through accession to the European Union, Member States have 'surrendered' their sovereign power in relation to those matters now regulated by the Union.

There are two differing approaches which may be taken to the sovereignty issue. First, it may be argued that the traditional theory remained unimpaired, despite all appearances and arguments to the contrary, on the basis that the United Kingdom voluntarily acceded to the European Union, the force of EU law within domestic law deriving from the 1972 European Communities Act. That Act, as seen, is consistent with constitutional law and convention – not entrenched (nor could it be) – and remained subject to repeal (as occurred at the end of 2020). From this perspective, parliamentary sovereignty remained the fundamental rule of the common law, and the key to the source of sovereignty lay with the judges. While the judges continue to cling to the rationale that EU law was given effect – even to the point of setting aside legislation[49] – because of the rule of construction provided under section 2 of the European Communities Act 1972, judicial loyalty remained unaffected. The clearest evidence for this view was expressed by Lord Bridge in **R v Secretary of State for Transport ex parte Factortame (No 2)** (1991), when he stated that:

> By virtue of section 2(4) of the Act of 1972, Part II of the [Merchant Shipping Act 1998] is to be construed and take effect subject to enforceable Community rights – this has precisely the same effect as if a section were incorporated in Part II of the Act 1988.

Alternatively, it has been argued[50] that for the first time in constitutional history, Parliament succeeded in 'entrenching' a provision (section 2(4) of the 1972 Act), so as to bind future Parliaments. This position, Professor HWR Wade submitted, is more than evolutionary: it represents more than a rule of construction to be applied by the courts, and is rather an illustration of the Parliament of 1972 imposing 'a restriction upon the Parliament of 1988' (page 570). If this argument had substance, there would indeed have been a 'revolution' in the constitution. However, the argument is unconvincing in light of the dicta of the judges, exemplified by that of Lord Bridge cited above, which confirms the conventional allegiance of the judiciary to the United Kingdom Parliament. Moreover, successive cases raising questions on EU law have come before senior courts in which the courts found the requisite interpretative mechanisms to accommodate the requirements of EU law as interpreted by the Court of Justice. Judicial interpretative techniques are the essence of the common law, and the essence of the common law is its capacity to evolve in accordance with the socio-political and legal domain within which it resides. In this light, the insistence on the part of the domestic

---

49 This issue being central to the *Factortame* cases, discussed in Chapter 8.
50 See Wade, 1996, but see the counter-arguments put forward by Allan, 1997, responding to Wade's analysis.

courts that section 2(4) of the European Communities Act 1972 was a rule of construction to be applied to future legislation is hardly 'revolutionary' but rather more a recognition of the requirements of the European legal order and the overriding force of EU law for which the 1972 Act provided during the UK's membership of the EU.

The preoccupation with parliamentary sovereignty is understandable given that sovereignty has conventionally, in the absence of a written constitution, represented the 'cornerstone' or foundation of the British constitution. Membership of the European Union, and the insistence of the CJEU on the supremacy of EU law, inevitably challenged traditional understandings of that concept, and raised hitherto unforeseen questions. While traditional Diceyan theory could accommodate membership of the Union, it could do so only by clearly demarcating, as did its author, the realms of the legal and political. Legal theory resides against the backcloth of the political. Political sovereignty, while the United Kingdom remained a Member of the Union, may (arguably) lie in the institutions and law-making processes of the Union, in which every Member State participates, and which is supported by the political will of the citizens of the Member States. That political sovereignty, while membership continued, had a profound impact on the extent to which the domestic legislature may legislate over areas within the ambit of the Treaties establishing the Union. Thus, as Dicey himself argued, back in the nineteenth century under fundamentally different socio-economic and political conditions, the extra-legal may *de facto* limit the exercise of sovereign power. This *de facto* limitation on *legal sovereignty* remains ultimately conditional on the political commitment of the United Kingdom Government and people to continued membership of that unique legal order which it voluntarily joined in 1972. The decision to end membership of the EU brings to an end the debate over where sovereignty lies.[51]

The question of the UK's future relationship with the EU is discussed in Chapter 8.

Devolution and the Human Rights Act

As noted above, the devolution of power to regional assemblies (in the case of Wales and Northern Ireland) and the Scottish Parliament and the Human Rights Act 1998, which 'incorporates' the European Convention on Human Rights into domestic law, both raise the issue of sovereignty. While full discussion of these matters is found in Chapters 11 and 18 respectively, it is useful here to consider the sovereignty issue.

See Chapter 11.

Devolution

The Scotland Act, Government of Wales Act and Northern Ireland Act 1998 each establish a system of self-government, in differing degrees, for the nations of the United Kingdom other than England. In London, a new layer of government was introduced with the Greater London Authority and the office of Mayor of London. Since the powers devolved are the will of Parliament, the continued existence of such power remains dependent upon Parliament's will. This ultimate power to confer and rescind powers granted to subordinate bodies is nothing new: at a lower governmental level, there is the granting of limited autonomy, defined by Act of Parliament and controlled by the courts, whereby local authorities have

---

51 In 2010 the government undertook not to transfer any further powers from the United Kingdom to the European Union without holding a referendum seeking the approval of the people. This commitment is reflected in the European Union Act 2011 (on which see further Chapter 8). On the question of sovereignty, section 18 of the 2011 Act makes an unequivocal statement of constitutional principle that EU law is recognised and available in law in the United Kingdom **only by virtue of that Act** or where it is required to be recognised and available in law by virtue of any other Act.

long enjoyed a measure of self-governance. This statement, however, and the legal provisions which give it expression, disguise a fundamentally important factor in the devolution debate: the dependence of legal-theoretical sovereignty upon the political sovereignty of the people of the nations.

It is the devolution of legislative power to the Scottish Parliament which illustrates the complexity of the sovereignty issue most starkly. By contrast with Northern Ireland and Wales, Scotland has retained a strong sense of national identity since the Union with England in 1707, and has a memory of national independence and a distinctive identity expressed through its own legal system.

The Labour government of 1997–2010, while enthusiastic about devolution to the regions, was also intent on preserving the United Kingdom and the sovereignty of the United Kingdom Parliament. This was expressed strongly in the government's 1997 White Paper, *Scotland's Parliament*:[52] 'the United Kingdom Parliament is and will remain sovereign in all matters'. Section 28(7) of the Scotland Act gives clear expression to this intention: 'this section does not affect the power of the Parliament of the United Kingdom to make laws for Scotland'. The Northern Ireland Act 1998 and the Government of Wales Act 1998 repeat this assertion.

However, while Westminster retains the right to legislate over 'reserved matters', which are adjudged to be of United Kingdom–wide concern rather than national concern, the legislative powers devolved are considerable. The theoretical stance that Westminster remains free to legislate for Scotland over such matters must be in doubt. While Northern Ireland enjoyed devolved power, the convention developed that Westminster would not legislate over areas devolved and, moreover, that domestic affairs of Northern Ireland would not even be debated at Westminster. Were the United Kingdom Parliament to attempt to legislate over Scottish domestic affairs which have been devolved to Edinburgh, against Scottish wishes, real conflict would arise – and no assertions of the sterile sovereignty of Westminster would quell political dissent from north of the border.

See
Chapters 8 and 12.

This adds up to considerable legislative and political autonomy for Scotland and its people. What, then, is left of 'the sovereignty of the United Kingdom Parliament' in conventional terms? *Theoretically*, two aspects of sovereignty remain. The first is the ability – notwithstanding the political unreality – to legislate for Scotland contrary to Scottish wishes. The second is the power to abolish the Scottish Parliament and to reclaim the powers devolved. Given that the government chose first to seek the endorsement of the people for devolution before devolving power, the likelihood of either theoretical power being exercised, *without the support and consent of the people of Scotland*, is negligible. It will be recalled that, in **MacCormick v Lord Advocate** (1953), Lord Cooper questioned the notion that the Treaty of Union resulted in the adoption of the 'distinctively English principle [of sovereignty] which has no counterpart in Scottish constitutional law'. Under Scottish constitutional law, it has always been the case that it is the people, and not a Parliament, which is sovereign: the Scottish people exercised their sovereignty in choosing to have their own Parliament.

The use of referendums[53]

The use of referendums raises the question of whether or not Parliament redefines itself to include the people – in a direct expression of their views – for the purpose of legislating. The referendum has been used in relation to constitutional matters in Northern Ireland in

---

52 Cm 3648, para. 42.
53 See Butler and Ranney, 1994; Marshall, 1997; Munro, 1997.

1973 and 1998; in relation to devolution to Scotland and Wales in 1977 and 1997 and in Wales in 2011; in London in 1998 in relation to the re-establishment of a London-wide elected authority; and in the United Kingdom as a whole in 1975 in relation to the United Kingdom's continued membership of the European Communities and again in 2016 the UK's membership of the European Union. Under the UK constitution, referendums are regarded as morally binding on government, but do not affect Parliament's sovereignty.

The European Union Act 2011 introduced a complex system of 'control mechanisms' to be employed when further transfers of power are to be made from the United Kingdom to the European Union. One of these is a UK-wide referendum. In 2014, a referendum in Scotland was used to decide whether or not Scotland should become independent. The government accepted that the result would be binding. In the event, the people of Scotland voted against independence. On this see further Chapter 11.

The Human Rights Act 1998

As with the devolution of power to the nations, the manner in which the government chose to 'incorporate' the rights protected under the European Convention on Human Rights into domestic law is based on the premise of ensuring that Parliament retains its sovereignty over law making. See Chapter 18. Whereas under most constitutions which include fundamental guarantees protecting human rights, those rights are protected from encroachment by the legislature, and the legislature is thereby limited in what it may enact – and is subject to the rulings of a constitutional court – the Human Rights Act 1998 utilises a peculiarly British device which preserves Parliament's theoretical sovereignty. The Act provides that judges in the higher courts may issue 'declarations of incompatibility' between statute and the Convention rights incorporated under the Act. Where such a declaration is made, the matter is then referred to the executive, which may choose whether and how to amend the law to bring it into line with Convention rights. Further, where proposals for legislation are introduced into Parliament, the relevant Minister must declare whether the Bill in question accords with Convention rights. If it does not, an explanation as to the necessity for the legislation must be given. While both of these measures undoubtedly improve the protection of rights and generate a more rights-conscious society, they fall far short of making individual rights and freedoms immune from legislative change.

However, the traditional theory of sovereignty, as applied to the Human Rights Act 1998, disguises the importance of the constitutional change which the Act represents. All aspects of policy and practices of public and quasi-public bodies now fall for scrutiny in accordance with Convention requirements. The Human Rights Act has quickly become established at the heart of the legal system, providing a yardstick against which all actions of government and other public bodies may be judged.

While the government adopted a constitutional mechanism which preserves Parliament's sovereignty, and maintains the conventional (and subordinate) role of the judiciary, the working of the Act is more subtle than the restatement of sovereignty implies. The judges are under a duty to interpret legislation in a manner which gives effect to Convention requirements, save where such an interpretation is impossible. Here, there is a significant shift in the process of judicial reasoning which traditionally focuses on interpreting the 'latest will of parliament' as expressed in legislation. The requirement that Ministers must state that legislative proposals are in compliance with Convention requirements, coupled with the directive to judges to interpret in line with Convention rights, gives rights a special constitutional and moral status. That the ultimate decision to amend the law in line with a declaration of incompatibility rests with the executive and Parliament does not suggest a lessening in the importance of rights so much as an ingenious device by which to keep constitutional fundamentals

– sovereignty and separation of powers – intact, rather than turning the constitution on its head by reversing the balance of power between judges and Parliament. Nevertheless, the Act does give to judges an unprecedented scope for statutory interpretation and development of the common law in line with Convention rights.

 Pause and Reflect

With reference to case law, assess the impact on parliamentary sovereignty on:

(a) membership of the European Union;
(b) the Human Rights Act 1998; and
(c) the Devolution Acts.

The Emergence of the 'Constitutional Statute'

It has been seen above that – however significant the subject matter – no Act of Parliament has any formal special status. The effect of this is that no Act may be entrenched; there are no special mechanisms necessary for amendment or repeal of any Act; and that all Acts are subject to implied repeal. However, the courts have long recognised that the European Communities Act 1972, at least, had a special status and that the principle of implied repeal did not apply to the Act.[54]

The constitutional reform programme undertaken since 1997, and most particularly the Human Rights Act 1998, has revived the question whether implied repeal applies to all statutes, or whether some – because of their constitutional importance – may only be expressly repealed. Two cases illustrate this view: **R v Secretary of State for the Home Department ex parte Simms** (2000) and **Thoburn v Sunderland City Council** (2002).

The case of **ex parte Simms** concerned a prisoner's right (under Article 10 of the European Convention) to communicate with journalists with a view to challenging his conviction for a crime. On parliamentary supremacy and the status of the Human Rights Act, Lord Hoffmann was to state that:

> Parliamentary sovereignty means that Parliament can, if it chooses, legislate contrary to fundamental principles of human rights. The Human Rights Act 1998 will not detract from this power. The constraints upon its exercise by Parliament are ultimately political, not legal. But the principle of legality means that Parliament must squarely confront what it is doing and accept the political cost. Fundamental rights cannot be overridden by general or ambiguous words ... In the absence of express language or necessary implication to the contrary, the courts therefore presume that even the most general words were intended to be subject to the basic rights of the individual. In this way the courts of the UK, through acknowledging the sovereignty of Parliament, apply principles of constitutionality little different from those which exist in countries where the power of the legislature is expressly limited by a constitutional document.

The case of **Thoburn v Sunderland City Council** (2002) concerned the Weights and Measures Act 1985, which authorised both metric and imperial measures for the purposes of trade, and

---

54 See *Garland v British Rail Engineering Ltd* (1983); Lord Denning in *Macarthys Ltd v Smith* (1981).

subsequent regulations made under section 2(2) of the European Communities Act 1972, which prohibited dual use and gave priority to the metric system. It was argued that the regulations were inconsistent with the 1985 Act and that this later Act must be taken as having impliedly amended section 2(2) of the European Communities Act 1972. The court held that there was no inconsistency between the 1985 Act and the 1972 Act, so there was no need to discuss implied repeal. Laws LJ, however, chose to consider the issue:

> We should recognise a hierarchy of Acts of Parliament: as it were 'ordinary' statutes and 'constitutional' statutes. The two categories must be distinguished on a principled basis. In my opinion a constitutional statute is one which (a) conditions the legal relationship between citizen and state in some general, overarching manner, or (b) enlarges or diminishes the scope of which we would now regard as fundamental constitutional rights. (a) and (b) are of necessity closely related: it is difficult to think of an instance of (a) that is not also an instance of (b). The special status of constitutional statutes follows the special status of constitutional rights. Examples are the Magna Carta, the Bill of Rights 1689, the Act of Union, the Reform Acts which distributed and enlarged the franchise, the Human Rights Act 1998, the Scotland Act 1998 and the Government of Wales Act 1998. The European Communities Act clearly belongs to this family ...
>
> Ordinary statutes may be impliedly repealed. Constitutional statutes may not. For the repeal of a constitutional Act or the abrogation of a fundamental right to be effected by statutes, the court would apply this test: is it shown that the legislature's actual – not imputed, constructive or presumed – intention was to effect the repeal or abrogation? I think that this could only be met by express words in the later statute, or by words so specific that the inference of an actual determination to effect the result contended for was irresistible. The ordinary rule of implied repeal does not satisfy this test. Accordingly, it has no application to constitutional statutes.[55]

Shared, or Bi-Polar, Sovereignty?

In addition to judicial recognition of the constitutional statute and its implications for sovereignty, in recent years a small number of influential judges in the higher courts have questioned Parliament's ultimate law-making power, suggesting that there might be limits to that power. It must be stressed, however, that the statements made in the course of giving judgment are *obiter dicta* – something said 'by the way' and not part of the *ratio decidendi* which is the essential element in the doctrine of binding precedent. It should also be noted that the judicial comments questioning parliamentary sovereignty are by no means representative of the views of all judges, and far more judicial statements can be found in the case law expressing the courts' traditional acceptance of Parliament's sovereignty than those which appear to question it. Nevertheless, coming from such respected judicial figures, notice must be taken of judicial statements which query Parliament's sovereign power with a view to asking the question whether there is, or may be in future, a reappraisal of parliamentary sovereignty as the fundamental concept of the UK constitution. In essence, the *dicta* in differing ways are suggesting that Parliament's sovereignty is dependent upon its acceptance by the judges, and that therefore the judges can determine the limits of that sovereign power. In suggesting that there can be limits to Parliament's power the judges are also suggesting that the courts share

---

55 See Campbell and Young, 2002.

in sovereignty. In this debate there are reflections of the debate on constitutionalism discussed in Chapter 1. It was seen there that constitutional theorists fall into two main camps – the political constitutionalists and the legal constitutionalists. For the former, Parliament is the body which holds sovereign power on behalf of the people. Parliament, unlike the judges, is elected and accountable. For legal constitutionalists on the other hand, the idea that Parliament has unlimited power and that the judges as guardians of the common law are powerless to restrain that power is unacceptable. The common law underpins parliamentary supremacy, and if a government with a strong majority in Parliament should act unconstitutionally and attempt to undermine fundamental constitutional principles such as the rule of law, it would be for the courts to restrain Parliament. The judicial statements given below reflect the idea of shared, or bi-polar, sovereignty.

Over 20 years ago, Lord Bridge of Harwich in **X Ltd v Morgan Grampian Ltd** (1991)[56] stated that:

> The maintenance of the rule of law is in every way as important in a free society as the democratic franchise. In our society the rule of law rests upon twin foundations: the sovereignty of the Queen in Parliament in making the law and the sovereignty of the Queen's courts in interpreting and applying the law.

The idea that there could be two, rather than one, sovereign powers was suggested by Lord Woolf in **Hamilton v Al-Fayed** (1999)[57] when he referred to the 'wider constitutional principle of mutuality of respect between two constitutional sovereignties'. In **R v Secretary of State for the Home Department ex parte Simms and O'Brien** (1999)[58] Lord Hoffmann considered sovereignty in light of the Human Rights Act 1998 and stated that:

> In the absence of express language or necessary implication to the contrary, the courts therefore presume that even the most general words were intended to be subject to the basic rights of the individual. In this way the courts of the United Kingdom, though acknowledging the sovereignty of Parliament, apply principles of constitutionality little different from those which exist in countries where the power of the legislature is expressly limited by a constitutional document.

In **Thoburn v Sunderland City Council** (2002) Sir John Laws argued that: 'the traditional doctrine [of parliamentary sovereignty] has in my judgment been modified. It has been done by the common law, wholly consistent with constitutional principle' (at paragraph 59). Furthermore in **International Transport Roth GmbH v Secretary of State for the Home Department** (2002), Sir John Laws stated that: 'Not very long ago, the British system was one of Parliamentary supremacy pure and simple … In its present state of evolution the British system may be said to stand at an intermediate state between parliamentary supremacy and constitutional supremacy' (at paragraph 71).

In **Jackson v Attorney General** (2005) Baroness Hale of Richmond considered sovereignty in the following terms:

> The concept of Parliamentary sovereignty which has been fundamental to the constitution of England and Wales since the seventeenth century (I appreciate that Scotland may have taken a different view) means that Parliament can do anything.

---

56 At para. 48.
57 At para. 320.
58 At p. 131.

The courts will, of course, decline to hold that Parliament has interfered with fundamental rights unless it has made its intention crystal clear. The courts will treat with particular suspicion (and might even reject) any attempt to subvert the rule of law by removing governmental action affecting the rights of the individual from all judicial scrutiny. Parliament has also, for the time being at least, limited its own powers by the European Communities Act 1972 and, in a different way, the Human Rights Act 1998. It is possible that other qualifications may emerge in due course. In general, however, the constraints upon what Parliament can do are political and diplomatic rather than constitutional.

Lord Steyn, in **Jackson**, questioned sovereignty in the following manner:

> The classic account given by Dicey of the doctrine of the supremacy of Parliament pure and absolute as it was, can now be seen to be out of place in the modern United Kingdom. Nevertheless, the supremacy of Parliament is still the general principle of our constitution. It is a construct of the common law. The judges created this principle. If that is so, it is not unthinkable that circumstances could arise where the courts may have to qualify a principle established on a different hypothesis of constitutionalism. In exceptional circumstances involving an attempt to abolish judicial review or the ordinary role of the courts, the Appellate Committee of the House of Lords or a new Supreme Court may have to consider whether this is a constitutional fundamental which even a sovereign Parliament acting at the behest of a complaisant House of Commons cannot abolish.[59]

Similar observations were made in **AXA General Insurance Ltd v HM Advocate** (2011), Lord Hope stating that 'The question whether the principle of the sovereignty of the United Kingdom Parliament is absolute or may be subject to limitation in exceptional circumstances is still under discussion'.

Lord Steyn's *dicta* that sovereignty is a construct created by the judges goes against accepted theoretical explanations of sovereignty which – epitomised by HLA Hart – insist that the source of sovereignty lies *outside* or *beyond* legal rules. Hart's thesis is echoed in Lord Bingham's analysis. Lord Bingham rejects the notion that sovereignty was the creation of the judges and common law. In *The Rule of Law* (2010) Lord Bingham states:

> I cannot for my part accept that my colleagues' observations are correct. It is true of course that the principle of parliamentary sovereignty cannot without circularity be ascribed to statute, and the historical record in any event reveals no such statute. But it does not follow that the principle must be a creature of the judge-made common law which the judges can alter: if it were, the rule could be altered by statute, since the prime characteristic of any common law rule is that it yields to a contrary provision of statute. To my mind, it has been convincingly shown that the principle of parliamentary sovereignty has been recognized as fundamental in this country not because the judges invented it but because it has for centuries been accepted as such by judges and others officially concerned in the operation of our constitutional system. The judges did not by themselves establish the principle and they cannot, by themselves, change it.[60]

---

59 At para. 102.
60 At p. 167.

From the above extracts from judgments it can be seen that the idea that parliamentary sovereignty might be subject to change is one which attracts increasing, although still limited, judicial support. With membership of the European Union from 1973 to 2020, the introduction of the Human Rights Act 1998 and devolution to Northern Ireland, Scotland and Wales, the constitutional landscape has changed from that of a unified, centralised state governed under a single Parliament to one characterised by the dispersal, or sharing, of law-making power and the idea of constitutionally guaranteed rights. The constitution has evolved and with that evolution comes the argument that the 'foundational principle' of parliamentary sovereignty should be re-examined and re-stated to reflect the new constitutional order.

There are two main areas of contemporary focus. The first is the increasingly recognised view that Convention rights protected under the Human Rights Act 1998 are rooted in the common law, not statute, and that it is for the judges to give such rights protection (on this see Chapter 18). The second focus is on judicial review of administrative action, with the view being expressed that if a government with a significant majority tried, and Parliament agreed, to severely restrict or abolish judicial review, the courts might not recognise such a statute as valid. Do statements such as these – albeit coming from a minority of judges – suggest that there is a fundamental shift in the relationship between Parliament and the judiciary, with the power moving away from Parliament and towards the judges, or to a form of dual, or bi-polar, sovereignty shared by Parliament and the courts?

Such a change was suggested by Sir Stephen Sedley LJ. Sir Stephen wrote of a new 'constitutional paradigm' that was:

> no longer of Dicey's supreme parliament to whose will the rule of law must finally bend, but of a bi-polar sovereignty of the Crown in Parliament and the Crown in its courts, to each of which the Crown's ministers are answerable – politically to Parliament, legally to the courts.[61]

Shared or 'bi-polar' sovereignty gives rise to many difficult questions and there is a need for caution. Where bi-polar sovereignty is suggested it is within the context of *fundamental rights*, rights now enforceable in the domestic courts under the Human Rights Act 1998, and rights derived from common law. What is, or is not, *fundamental*, is a matter for debate, and one which will be determined by the judges. For the most part, when judges are questioning sovereignty, they are considering extreme situations such as Parliament enacting legislation which runs counter to the democratic values enshrined in the constitution. Examples of such legislation would include restricting freedom of expression without justification, permitting torture by state agents or denying the right of access to a court of law. As **Anisminic v Foreign Compensation Commission** (1969) demonstrates, the judges, under the guise of statutory interpretation, may find ways to frustrate an attempt by Parliament to oust the jurisdiction of the courts.

It must be emphasised that the idea that sovereignty might be undergoing change and moving away from Parliament towards the courts is one expressed by a minority of, albeit influential, judges and that currently the traditional relationship between Parliament and the courts – namely that the judges will interpret and apply the latest expression of Parliament's will – prevails.

---

61 Sedley, 1994, p. 282.

Pause and Reflect

Discuss the differing contemporary academic approaches to sovereignty.
Is 'limited sovereignty' a contradiction in terms?

Summary

In any state there must be an ultimate source of authority. Under a written constitution this will be the Constitution itself, as interpreted by the Supreme or Constitutional Court. Under an unwritten constitution such as the United Kingdom, this ultimate source of legal authority is parliamentary sovereignty, or legislative supremacy, which rests on the political sovereignty of the people.

The traditional doctrine states that Parliament may legislate on any subject-matter, that no Parliament may be bound by a previous Parliament or bind a further Parliament and that no one, including a court of law, may challenge the validity of an Act of Parliament. Each of these principles is subject to qualification by non-legal – economic or political – factors. The most significant recent challenge to Parliament's legal authority was membership of the European Union, which required that domestic law complied with the requirements of European Union law. However, while this restricted what Parliament may in fact do, membership of the EU was voluntary and any restrictions were accepted by Parliament under the European Communities Act 1972. The repeal of the European Communities Act 1972 restores Parliament's sovereignty. The Human Rights Act 1998 and the Devolution Acts of that year also have an impact on sovereignty by limiting the UK Parliament's law-making role. None of these Acts, however, is immune from amendment or repeal should the right political climate exist.

 Further Reading

Ahmed, F and Perry, A, 'The quasi-entrenchment of constitutional statutes' [2014] *Cambridge Law Journal* 514.

Allison, JWF, *The English Historical Constitution: Continuity, Change and European Effects*, 2007, Cambridge: Cambridge University Press.

Bellamy, R, 'Political constitutionalism and the Human Rights Act' (2011) 9 *International Journal of Constitutional Law* 86.

Bingham, T, *The Rule of Law*, 2010, London: Penguin.

Bradley, A, 'The sovereignty of parliament: form or substance?' in J Jowell and D Oliver (eds), *The Changing Constitution*, 7th edn, 2011, Oxford: Oxford University Press.

Craig, P, 'Constitutional foundations, the rule of law and supremacy' [2003] *Public Law* 92.

Elliott, M, 'United Kingdom: parliamentary sovereignty under pressure' (2004) 2 *International Journal of Constitutional Law* 545.

Gordon, M, 'The conceptual foundations of parliamentary sovereignty: reconsidering Jennings and Wade' [2009] *Public Law* 519.

Griffith, JAG, 'The brave new world of Sir John Laws' (2000) 63 *Modern Law Review* 159.

Griffith, JAG, 'The common law and the political constitution' (2001) 117 *Law Quarterly Review* 42.

Hart, HLA, *The Concept of Law*, 1961, Oxford: Clarendon Press.

Joseph, P, 'Parliament, the courts, and the collaborative enterprise' [2004] *King's College Law Journal* 321.

Jowell, J, 'Parliamentary sovereignty under the new constitutional hypothesis' [2006] *Public Law* 562.

Knight, CJS, 'Bi-polar sovereignty restated' (2009) 68 *Cambridge Law Journal* 361.

Munro, CR, *Studies in Constitutional Law*, 2nd edn, 1999, London: Butterworths, Chapters 5, 6.

Sedley, Sir Stephen, 'The sound of silence: constitutional law without a constitution' (1994) 110 *Law Quarterly Review* 270.

Sedley, Sir Stephen, 'Human rights: a twenty-first century agenda' [1995] *Public Law* 386.

Wade, HWR, 'The basis of legal sovereignty' [1955] *Cambridge Law Journal* 172.

Wade, HWR, 'Sovereignty: revolution or evolution?' (1996) 112 *Law Quarterly Review* 568.

Wade, Sir William, 'What has happened to the sovereignty of parliament?' (1991) 107 *Law Quarterly Review* 1.

Part 3

The European Union

Chapter 7

Structures and Institutions of the European Union

A day will come when all the nations of this continent, without losing their distinct qualities or their glorious individuality, will fuse together in a higher unity and form the European brotherhood. A day will come when there will be no other battlefields than those of the mind – open marketplaces for ideas. A day will come when bullets and bombs will be replaced by votes.

Victor Hugo, address to Parliament, 1849

Chapter Contents

Learning Objectives

By the end of this chapter you should be able to:

- [ ] explain the aims of the European Union;
- [ ] explain the concepts of subsidiarity and proportionality;
- [ ] discuss the principal institutions of the EU, their personnel and functions;
- [ ] explain the procedure and importance of references to the Court of Justice of the European Union;
- [ ] explain the sources of EU law;
- [ ] discuss direct and indirect effect and vertical or horizontal effect.

Introduction

The European Union (EU) now comprises 27 Member States with a population of around 500 million people. As will be seen below, the original three Communities arose from the desire to put the raw materials of war beyond the control of the nation state once and for all and to unite previously warring nations within a community which would foster not only peace and security but also economic growth and raised standards of living for all its peoples. The European Union – of which the European Community was the largest and most developed part – is based on the rule of law, the protection of individual human rights and a common European Union citizenship. For over half a century, the European project has fostered political and economic integration, while retaining respect for the individuality and identity of its Member States. Economically nowadays the Union represents a major trading power – a position which could not be achieved by any of the Member States acting alone. A common currency – the euro – was introduced in 1999. The ambitions of the Union have extended far beyond the original objectives of a common market for goods and services and now include common foreign and security policy and extensive cooperation between the police and authorities of the Member States. Citizens of all Member States have EU citizenship. Freedom of movement and rights of establishment are a central feature of the European Union. The elimination of border controls between Member States further extends the freedom of movement for persons within the territorial boundaries of the European Union.[1] In addition to rights of residence, every citizen of the Union has the right to stand as a candidate and to vote in municipal elections in the Member State in which he or she resides, and to stand as a candidate and vote in elections for the European Parliament. Union citizens are entitled to protection from the diplomatic or consular authorities of any Member State. Citizens of the EU have the right to petition the European Parliament, and have the right also to apply to the European Union Ombudsman.[2]

To understand the origins of the Union, it is necessary to look back to 1945 and a Europe that had been devastated by war – economically, politically and socially. In the desire to attain some form of harmony in order to guarantee peace and to rebuild Europe, the movement towards the integration of European countries was started. The movement took several forms. In 1948, the Organisation for Economic Co-operation and Development (OECD) was established with financial aid from the United States of America in order to restructure the European economies. In 1949, the North Atlantic Treaty Organization (NATO) was formed as a military alliance between the United States, Canada and Europe. In 1950, under the leadership of the French Foreign Minister, Robert Schuman, a plan was devised whereby the raw materials of war – coal and steel – would be placed under the control of a supranational organisation and, thus, the European Coal and Steel Community (ECSC) was established under the Treaty of Paris, signed in 1951. The original Member States were Germany, France, Belgium, Italy, Luxembourg and the Netherlands. Initiatives were being introduced to provide supranational regulation of the non-military use of atomic energy. At the same time, the move towards greater economic cooperation and the creation of a European trading area was under way. The results of these developments took the form of the Treaties of Rome signed in 1957, establishing the European Economic Community (EEC) and the European Atomic Energy Community (Euratom).

The EEC had the broadest aims of the three communities, seeking to create a European common market and close cooperation between Member States. The common market (now

---

1 The United Kingdom, however, retains its border controls.
2 On which see further below.

called the internal market) is based on four basic freedoms: persons, goods, capital and services.

The law relating to the European Union is now a wide-ranging subject. European Union law intrudes upon, and affects, a substantial volume of domestic law. This will remain the case after leaving the EU as most EU law created prior to the date of leaving the EU will be retained in domestic law unless subsequently repealed and/or amended (this is discussed in Chapter 8).

The original Treaties establishing the three European Communities have been much amended. Moreover, in 1992, the Treaty on European Union was signed by the Member States. The 1992 Treaty brought into being the European Union, the aims of which go far beyond the original objectives of the European Economic Community and seek to provide the further integration of the laws and policies of Member States. The 1992 Treaty also extended the competence of the EU institutions.

The Treaty of Amsterdam 1997 confirmed the Union's 'attachment to the principles of liberty, democracy and respect for human rights and fundamental freedoms and of the rule of law'. The political objectives of the Union are extensive, seeking to achieve European economic and monetary union, the promotion of economic and social progress, 'taking into account the principle of sustainable development and within the context of the accomplishment of the internal market and of reinforced cohesion and environmental protection', common defence and foreign policy,[3] and the complete elimination of border controls within the Union.[4]

The United Kingdom stood aloof from the early development of the Community, rejecting the call of Sir Winston Churchill in 1949 for a 'United States of Europe'.[5] Instead, Britain formed the European Free Trade Area (EFTA) together with Austria, Denmark, Norway, Portugal, Sweden and Switzerland. In part, EFTA was formed as a defensive action to fend off the potentially adverse effects of the free trading area established under the EEC.

By 1961, the Conservative government of Harold Macmillan had decided to seek entry to the Community, an application which was initially blocked by France. It was not until 1972 that the United Kingdom (along with Ireland, Denmark and Norway) was admitted with effect from January 1973.[6] Membership of the EU always gave rise to political disputes in the United Kingdom. The Conservative government elected in May 2015 was committed to holding a referendum on Britain's membership of the EU before the end of 2017, the outcome of which was the decision to leave the EU with effect originally from 2019 but ultimately in 2020. The current membership of the Union, with dates of accession, is as follows: Austria (1995), Belgium (1957), Denmark (1972), Finland (1995), France (1957), Germany (1957), Greece (1981), Ireland (1972), Italy (1957), Luxembourg (1957), Netherlands (1957), Portugal (1985), Spain (1985), Sweden (1995), United Kingdom (1973), Cyprus, the Czech Republic, Estonia, Hungary, Latvia, Lithuania, Malta, Poland, Slovakia, and Slovenia (2004),[7] Romania and Bulgaria (2007), Croatia (2013).

---

3 Article 11 TEU.5.
4 Article 2 TEU.
5 Speech at University of Zurich, 19 September 1946.
6 The people of Norway rejected EC membership in a referendum.
7 See the European Union (Accessions) Act 2003.

The European Union

Note that the Treaty of Lisbon 2007 provides that the term 'European Union' (EU) replaces the term 'European Community'. Further, all references to the European Community in the Treaties are to be removed and replaced by the term 'European Union'.

Aims and objectives

Article 3 of the Treaty on European Union (TEU) provides that the activities of the Union include, *inter alia*:

- the establishment of an internal market free of all internal tariffs;
- the abolition of measures obstructing the free movement of goods, persons, services and capital;
- common policies relating to agriculture and fisheries, commerce and transport;
- environmental protection;
- strengthening consumer and health protection;
- forming associations with overseas countries to increase trade and jointly promote economic and social development;
- strengthening economic and social cohesion;
- the promotion of research and technological development.

A unique legal order

The European Union is the creation of the original EEC Treaty, as amended. European Union law, however, is not international law as normally understood in the sense of merely establishing mutual obligations between contracting states. In addition to creating mutual obligations between Member States, EU law also involves the transfer of sovereign rights to the institutions of that system and the creation of rights and obligations for their citizens which are enforceable in their local courts. The EU is, therefore, a unique constitutional entity, having its own institutions and law-making powers, capable of creating rights and duties within the legal systems of the Member States. The law-making powers of the EU institutions, as will be seen below, are far-reaching. When duties are imposed on Member States, these may imply rights for individuals which may be enforced in the domestic courts and ultimately in the Court of Justice of the European Union (CJEU, formerly European Court of Justice [ECJ]), the EU's judicial forum.

In constitutional terms, the European Union is not a 'state', neither is it a 'federation'; rather it is a unique supranational organisation. When new Member States are admitted to the Union, they became automatically bound by the entire law of the Union – in European terminology, the *acquis communautaire*.[8] Under international law, when a state becomes a signatory to a treaty, it becomes bound by the provisions of that treaty, but it is not bound by any acts done under the treaty before that state's accession. It is different with the European Union, and new Member States become automatically committed to the Treaties, all secondary legislation, judicial and non-judicial decisions made by the institutions of the Union, together with non-binding opinions and resolutions of institutions.

---

8 Which, literally translated, means 'Community patrimony'. See TEU 1992, Articles 2 and 3.

The major constitutional issues

From the constitutional law perspective, the issues which require scrutiny are:

(a) the nature of the European Union (EU), the institutions and their law-making powers;
(b) the nature and sources of EU law;
(c) the effect of membership of the EU on the constitution of the United Kingdom from 1973 to 2020;
(d) the relationship between EU law and the domestic law of Member States.

The allocation of functions between the institutions and Member States

In any federal or quasi-federal state or organisation, the functions of the federal government and the regional governments must be allocated. As discussed in Chapter 1, the concept of federalism involves the allocation of powers which may reserve some powers to the exclusive competence of the federal government, some powers which will be concurrently held by the federal and regional governments, and some powers over which the regional government has exclusive competence. In the European Union, the manner in which powers are allocated and exercised is largely determined by the Treaty provisions.

The principle of subsidiarity[9]

Subsidiarity is a fundamental concept designed to achieve an appropriate balance between the institutions of the EU and Member States. Designed to determine the appropriate level of action across the whole spectrum of public activity, international (in the widest sense), national, regional and local, it has been invoked in the European context to assist in determining the exercise of powers. In this context, it has been described, variously, as 'the principle of necessity, or proportionality, of effectiveness, an elementary principle of good government, or simply a principle of good sense'. It has been interpreted as meaning that the EU should act only:

(a) where the objective cannot be achieved by regulation at national level;
(b) where the objective can be better, or more effectively, achieved by action at EU level (the 'efficiency by better results' criterion); or
(c) where the matter in question can be more effectively regulated at EU level (the 'administrative efficiency' criterion).[10]

The closely related principles of subsidiarity and proportionality are both provided for in the Treaties. The Protocol on the Application of the Principles of Subsidiarity and Proportionality restates the principles, listing guidelines to be followed in reaching decisions as to whether action should be taken at European Union level or at national level. Now a legal concept, it will be for the Court of Justice of the EU (CJEU) to adjudicate on its scope and application. Subsidiarity is a concept which is dynamic and flexible, allowing decisions on the appropriate level at which action should be taken to develop on a case-by-case basis. The doctrine of proportionality requires that measures taken must not be more extensive than is necessary to achieve the desired result.

---

9 See Emiliou, 1991, and 'Subsidiarity: panacea or fig leaf?' in O'Keefe and Twomey, 1994, Chapter 5; Toth, 1992.
10 Steiner, 'Subsidiarity under the Maastricht Treaty', and references therein, in O'Keefe and Twomey, 1994.

Categories of competence

Exclusive competence

Article 5 TEU makes it clear that where the EU has 'exclusive competence', the subsidiarity principle has no application. The EU has sole power of decision and therefore no question arises as to whether others share that power, or the extent to which they should be entitled to act. Article 3 TFEU now provides a catalogue of areas in which the EU has exclusive competence, which includes customs, monetary policy, rules necessary for the functioning of the internal market, aspects of common fisheries policy and common commercial policy.[11]

Shared concurrent powers

Where a Member State has a concurrent power, the power to act remains, so long as the EU has not exercised that power. Once the EU takes action itself, the power of the Member State is pre-empted, and the power to act – once pre-empted – remains with the EU.[12] Where the EU has exclusive power, the Member State has no power to act unless the legislation in question contains a specific authorisation by the EU in favour of the Member States.[13] However, the Court has ruled that, where the EU has exclusive competence to act but has not so acted and urgent action is needed, the Member States may act as 'trustees of the common interest'.[14]

Issues of subsidiarity inevitably fall to the Court to consider. For example, if the EU legislates on a particular area, a Member State may wish to resist that legislation by invoking subsidiarity, and thus the Court will be obliged to make a decision.

On subsidiarity, the Treaty of Lisbon provides that:

- competences not conferred upon the Union in the Treaties remain with the Member States;[15]
- the use of Union competences is governed by the principles of subsidiarity and proportionality;[16]
- under the principle of subsidiarity, in areas which do not fall within its exclusive competence, the Union shall act only if and in so far as the objectives of the proposed action cannot be sufficiently achieved by the Member States, either at central level or at regional and local level;
- under the principle of proportionality, the content and form of Union action shall not exceed what is necessary to achieve the objectives of the Treaties;
- the Protocol on Subsidiarity, Article 8, provides that the CJEU shall have jurisdiction to rule on allegation of infringement of the principle of subsidiarity by a legislative act.

 Pause and Reflect

Explain the constitutional function of the concepts of subsidiarity and proportionality. What is their constitutional significance in the relationship between the EU and Member States? How do these concepts interact, if at all?

---

11 See Communication to the Council and Parliament outlining proposals for the Subsidiarity Principle Bulletin EC 10-1992, Pt 2.2.1, cited in *op cit.*, Steiner, fn. 34.
12 See Weatherill, 'Beyond pre-emption', in O'Keefe and Twomey, 1994.
13 Article 2 TFEU; *Donckerwolcke v Procureur de la Republique* (1976).
14 *Commission v United Kingdom* (1981).
15 See Communication to the Council and Parliament outlining proposals for the Subsidiarity Principle Bulletin EC 10-1992, Pt 2.2.1, cited in *op cit.*, Steiner, fn. 34.
16 See Communication to the Council and Parliament outlining proposals for the Subsidiarity Principle Bulletin EC 10-1992, Pt 2.2.1, cited in *op cit.*, Steiner, fn. 34.

The Institutions of the European Union

The European Commission[17]

Originally called the High Authority, the Commission is centrally concerned with all aspects of decision making at all levels and on all fronts; the Commission is the very heart of the EU, exercising both powers of initiative and powers of enforcement. As envisaged by the authors of the original Treaties, the Commission, while acting independently of governments and in pursuit of the objectives of the Community, would help preserve the interests of individual Member States. The Commission was intended to be the engine which drives Europe forward.

Article 17 TEU provides (in part) that the Commission shall:

- promote the general interest of the Union and take appropriate initiatives to that end;
- ensure the application of the Treaties and of measures adopted by the institutions;
- oversee the application of Union law under the control of the Court of Justice of the European Union;
- execute the budget;
- exercise coordinating, executive and management functions as laid down in the Treaties;
- ensure the Union's external representation (with the exception of common foreign and security policy and other cases provided in the Treaties).

Commissioners are appointed by the European Council upon the consent of the European Parliament (Article 17(7) TEU). Commissioners must be nationals of one of the Member States.[18] Commissioners are appointed for a renewable five-year term of office, and cannot be dismissed during their term of office by governments.[19] The appointment of Commissioners is subject to the approval of the European Parliament. Commissioners remain in office until replaced, or compulsorily retired.[20] Decisions in the Commission are reached by majority voting.

Once appointed, Commissioners must act independently of government: they are not representatives of government. Article 17(3) TEU provides that:

> the Commission shall be completely independent ... members of the Commission shall neither seek nor take instructions from any Government or other institution, body, office or entity. They shall refrain from any action incompatible with their duties or the performance of their tasks.

The Commission is headed by a President, nominated by the European Council, and subject to the approval of the European Parliament. Following the Lisbon Treaty, the nomination for the head of the Commission must reflect the results of the European elections, thereby reflecting the voters' political preference.

The European Parliament has the power to pass a motion of censure to remove the Commission en bloc. However, when, in 1999, allegations of waste and mismanagement in the Commission surfaced, the Parliament failed to pass a motion of sanction. In the event, the entire Commission, including the President, resigned.

---

17 See new Article 17 TEU and Articles 244–250 TFEU.
18 Note that under the Lisbon Treaty, there will be a reduction in the number of Commissioners.
19 Commissioners can, however, have their reappointment blocked by a government, as occurred in 1989 when the Prime Minister felt that Lord Cockfield had been over-zealous in his support of the Community.
20 Article 247 TFEU provides that, if a Commissioner no longer fulfils the conditions required for the performance of his duties, or if he has been guilty of serious misconduct, the CJEU may, on an application of the Council or the Commission, compulsorily retire him.

Organisationally, the Commission is divided into Directorates General, each headed by a Director responsible to the relevant Commissioner. Each Commissioner holds one or more portfolios, that is to say, special responsibility for some area of EU policy, and is assisted by a Cabinet of six.

The broad and ill-defined power conferred under the Treaty and the role of the Commission can only be understood within the framework of the European Union as a whole. It is clear that it is the Commission which is charged with the duty to act in the interests of the objectives of the Union as expressed in the Treaties. It is the Commission which puts forward proposals for decision by the Council of the EU (see below), having negotiated widely with representatives of Member States' governments and with interest groups within the EU. The Council of the EU may, in some instances, request the Commission to draft proposals, and the European Parliament has the right to request the Commission to submit a proposal for legislation. Where the Commission is under an obligation to submit legislative proposals within a certain time laid down in the Treaty, failure to act within that time will render the Commission liable to a challenge before the CJEU. When such proposals assume the force of law, it is again the Commission which is charged primarily with the task of law enforcement.

The Commission's broad powers of initiative should not be understood to mean that the Commission has total freedom of action. The working of the EU depends on a variety of factors, actors and forces. In the final analysis, the EU can only be effective in achieving the goals set out in the Treaties if its proposals can carry the support of the Member States. The effectiveness of EU law within the legal systems of all Member States is ultimately dependent upon the political acceptability of that law. It is for this reason that the role of the Commission is so important, for the Commission – having the sole power to formulate proposals for the implementation of Treaty objectives – is responsible for ensuring that proposals have the support of Member States before they are hardened into law. As originally envisaged by the drafters of the original Treaties, only a body acting with complete independence was competent to negotiate with Member States and formulate acceptable policies. The European Union comprises 27 states of vastly differing sizes and populations, and within these states there are regions with differing interests and needs. It is vital, therefore, that there is some guarantee that the interests of the smaller Member States, and regions in all Member States, are protected against the power of the larger states. Accordingly, in the process of formulating policies, one of the Commission's principal tasks is to reconcile the differing interests at stake and to make the resulting law acceptable to all.[21]

Where a Member State is in default of Treaty obligations, the Commission has the power to deal with the breach. If the Commission considers that a Member State has failed to fulfil an obligation under the Treaties, it shall deliver a reasoned opinion on the matter after giving the state concerned the opportunity to submit its observations. If the state concerned does not comply with the opinion within the period laid down by the Commission, the latter may bring the matter before the Court of Justice (Article 258 TFEU).

Most matters are settled at an early stage – infringements being due not to wilful disregard of the law, but rather arising from genuine differences of opinion as to the meaning of requirements, or from administrative delay. Where, however, a Member State fails to fulfil its EU obligations, the Commission may take the case to the CJEU. Where the Court rules that the Member State is in default of its obligations and the Member State fails to comply with its

---

21 Temple-Lang, J, 'The European Commission: safeguard for Member States', European Law Lecture (Queen Mary, University of London, 5 June 1995).

judgment, the Court, at the request of the Commission, may impose a financial penalty on the Member State.[22]

In **Commission v United Kingdom** (2000), the Commission sought a declaration that the United Kingdom had failed fully to comply with a Directive[23] concerning the protection of waters against pollution caused by nitrates from agricultural sources. The United Kingdom authorities had identified only surface waters intended for extraction of drinking water, whereas the Directive also required the identification of surface freshwaters not intended for the abstraction of drinking water which contained excessive nitrate concentrations or could do so. The fact that the authorities were now taking action to remedy the failure did not exclude the state's liability for breach of its obligations under the Directive.[24] Failure to transpose a Directive into national law by the stipulated date will not be excused on the basis that transposition required revision of provisions of a Member State's constitution.[25]

The Council of the European Union

The Council of the European Union (formerly the Council of Ministers) has legislative and executive powers and functions. The Council should not be confused with the European Council in which the heads of government meet regularly to discuss the EU's political priorities (see further below). The Council of the EU:

- passes EU law (jointly with the European Parliament);
- coordinates the broad economic policies of the EU Member States;
- signs agreements between the EU and other countries;
- approves the annual EU budget;
- develops the EU's foreign and defence policies;
- coordinates cooperation between courts and police forces of member countries.

The Council is headed by a President. The Presidency changes every six months, rotating between Member States. It is the Council which defends the interests of Member States. The Council has no fixed membership and its composition varies depending upon the subject matter under discussion. Each Member State is represented in Council by a government Minister. Accordingly, when the subject on the agenda is agriculture, the Council will consist of the Ministers of Agriculture from all Member States; when the subject is transport, the membership will be made up of the respective Ministers of Transport. Article 16 TEU now provides that the Council is to exercise 'legislative and budgetary functions'. It shall also carry out 'policy making and coding functions laid down in the Treaties'. When the Council meets to deliberate and vote on draft legislation, it must meet in public.

The voting system for decision making[26]

Central to EU development is the voting system used in the Council. The Treaty provides for three basic methods by which the Council can reach a decision: unanimously, by qualified majority vote or by a simple majority vote. Unanimity is normally required where a new policy is to be initiated or the existing policy framework is to be developed or modified.

---

22 See Article 258 TFEU.
23 Council Directive 91/676/EC of 12 December 1991.
24 See also **Commission of the European Union v United Kingdom** (2002).
25 See **Commission v Kingdom of Belgium** (1998).
26 See Morner, 'The conflicts inherent in enlargement: is history catching up with the European Union?' in Butterworths, 1994.

Unanimity is also required when the Council wishes to amend a Commission proposal against the wishes of the Commission. While the Union rests on consensus, and there is little point in adopting a procedure which will cause national Parliaments resentment or reluctance on the part of state authorities to implement decisions, a balance is needed between respecting the interests of the Member States while not impeding EU development.

Article 16(3) TEU states that, unless otherwise provided in the Treaty, that is to say under specific articles, the Council shall act by qualified majority vote. In some specific cases the Council is required to act by a qualified majority, for which purpose the votes of Member States are weighted, the largest states having a weighting of ten, the remaining, according to size, eight, five, four, three or two. Where the Council adopts a matter on a proposal from the Commission, 62 votes are required. Where unanimity is required, the abstention of a Member State shall not prevent the Council adopting a matter. The voting system was designed in order to minimise the circumstances in which one state could block EU progress. It became clear in the 1960s, however, that this was unworkable – most notably when France refused to cooperate in any decisions and caused a constitutional crisis.

The outcome of the crisis was an agreement contained in what is known as the *Luxembourg Accord* of 1966, which provided that:

> Where in the case of decisions which may be taken by majority vote on a proposal from the Commission, very important interests of one or more partners are at stake, the Members of the Council will endeavour, within a reasonable time, to reach solutions which can be adopted by all Members of the Council while respecting their mutual interests and those of the Community in accordance with Article 2 of the Treaty. [Bulletin of the European Community 3/66, page 5]

The French government insisted that where very important state interests are at stake, the discussion should continue until unanimous agreement is reached.

This *Accord* had no formal legal status. It was an informal agreement, and probably unlawful. However, the *Accord* profoundly affected decision making, and the French amendment has been interpreted to mean that any state has the right to exercise a veto on questions which affect its vital national interests, and it is for the states themselves to determine when such interests are at stake. Under the Treaty of Amsterdam, the issue of important national interests was resurrected and formalised in the EC Treaty. It has been noted that

> predictions of the demise of the Luxembourg Compromise were thus distinctly premature: it has been given a new lease of life, no longer in the demi-monde of political deals but as part of the legal machinery of the EC Treaty.[27]

Article 16 TEU provided that, with effect from 2014, a new system of qualified majority voting in Council (of Ministers) has been adopted. The new system is based on a 'double majority of Member States and people' and provides that a vote is passed if:

(a)   55 per cent of Member States are in favour (15 of 28 countries); and
(b)   these Member States represent 65 per cent of the EU's population.[28]

---

27 Editorial, Common Market Law Review, 1997, p. 769.
28 See also the Protocol on Transitional Provisions, Article 3 which, *inter alia*, specifies the number of votes per country until 2014: Article 16 TEU.

To block a decision, at least four countries representing at least 35 per cent of the total EU population are needed. Sensitive issues such as foreign policy and taxation require a unanimous vote. For procedural and administrative issues, a simple majority vote is required.

The Council, together with the European Parliament, represents a major law-making body within the EU. Because the Council has a fluctuating membership and is not permanently in session,[29] the Committee of Permanent Representatives (COREPER) acts as the permanent body engaged in Council work (Article 240 TFEU). The Committee is supported by more than 150 committees and working groups consisting of delegates from Member States. Many of these committees have a specific role of providing coordination and expertise in a particular area.

Votes in Council

Country	Votes	Country	Votes
Austria	10	Italy	29
Belgium	12	Latvia	4
Bulgaria	10	Lithuania	7
Croatia	7	Luxembourg	4
Cyprus	4	Malta	3
Czech Republic	12	Netherlands	13
Denmark	7	Poland	27
Estonia	4	Portugal	12
Finland	7	Romania	14
France	29	Slovakia	7
Germany	29	Slovenia	4
Greece	12	Spain	27
Hungary	12	Sweden	10
Ireland	7	**Total**	**316**

The European Parliament[30]

Members of the Parliament were initially delegates designated by the Parliaments of Member States. In constitutional terms, the delegates had a dual mandate: that of membership of both the domestic and European Parliaments. The Treaty, however, envisaged that the Parliament should be directly elected by the people. The first direct elections to the European Parliament took place in 1979. The European Parliament agreed to end the dual mandate for elected representatives with effect from 2004.

Seats in the European Parliament are allocated according to the size of population of the Member States, although there is no absolute equality in voting powers. The current number of MEPs is 705. No Member State can have fewer than six seats or more than 96 seats. Representatives are elected for a term of five years. The Members of Parliament do not sit in groupings organised by nationality but rather by political party groupings.[31]

The European Parliament is required to hold an annual session, and may meet in extraordinary session at the request of a majority of its Members or at the request of the Council or of the Commission. In practice, the Parliament meets approximately 12 to 14 times a year for a

---

29 Some 80 Council meetings take place each year.
30 Articles 189–210 EC. See now Articles 11 and 14 TEU and Articles 223–236 TFEU.
31 See Article 11 TEU and Article 224 TFEU.

few days per session. Members of the Commission may attend all parliamentary meetings and are entitled to address the Parliament. The Parliament holds plenary sessions in Strasbourg and committee meetings and additional plenary sessions in Brussels, and it has its secretariat based in Luxembourg. Much of the work of Parliament is undertaken by committees on, for example, agriculture, legal affairs and so on. Before a matter goes before Parliament sitting in plenary session, it will normally be considered by the relevant standing committee. Unless otherwise provided for under the Treaties, the Parliament acts by an absolute majority of the votes cast.

The original intention in relation to Parliament's function was that it would be a 'supervisory and advisory' body, with no legal effect being attached to its deliberations. Under specific Treaty articles, the Council of the EU is obliged to seek the advice of the Parliament, and failure to consider Parliament's view would cause the Council to be in violation of an essential procedural requirement of Community law, and could cause the decision of the Council to be declared void by the CJEU.[32] As will be seen, the powers of the European Parliament have been increasing since 1986 (under the Single European Act 1986), but even now it remains a very different constitutional institution from that of domestic Parliaments.

The European Parliament can adopt its own ideas and try to persuade the Commission to adopt them. Usually this takes the form of an initiative report – around 100 a year are approved by the European Parliament. However, Parliament has no power to insist that the Commission adopt a proposal from Parliament – the right of initiative is firmly in the hands of the Commission itself, other than where the European Parliament or the Council requests a proposal from the Commission.

The European Parliament has decision-making powers regarding the annual budget. This power in relation to the EU budget has always been of significance. The revenue of the EU comes primarily from agricultural levies, customs duties on imports from outside the EU and value added tax (VAT) levied within the EU. When the draft budget is drawn up by the Council, after receiving proposals from the Commission, it is then submitted to Parliament, which has power to accept, amend or reject the budget.

Parliament has the power to reject the EU budget in total if there are 'important reasons to do so': Article 314 TFEU. There must be a majority of votes in Parliament and also two-thirds of the votes cast. Rejection of the budget occurred in 1979, when a new budget was subsequently drawn up. The Treaty of Lisbon extends Parliament's powers over all categories of expenditure.

Parliament has the right to question the Commission and Council, and replies are given both orally and in writing, and published in the *Official Journal of the European Communities*. Parliament also has the power to dismiss the entire Commission on a vote of censure if the vote is carried by a two-thirds majority of the votes cast, a vote which must represent an overall majority of the votes in Parliament. If the vote is carried, the Commission resigns as a body. However, in one sense, the power is too great to be effective, for Parliament has no power to force the incoming Commission to adopt a different policy from that of its predecessor.

Extension of Parliament's powers

The powers of the European Parliament have been extended significantly. The Lisbon Treaty 1997 extended Parliament's legislative power to more than 40 new areas, including agriculture, energy security, immigration, justice and EU funds. The Parliament also has the power to approve or reject international agreements.

---

32 *Roquettes Frères SA v Council* (1980); *Maizena GmbH v Council* (1980).

The Ordinary Legislative Procedure (formerly co-decision procedure)

The TEU 1992 and the 1997 Treaty further extended Parliament's role in the legislative process.[33] The Treaty of Lisbon extends the Parliament's powers of co-decision with the Council to the extent that the Parliament now has an equal role in law making.[34] The co-decision procedure is now the Ordinary Legislative Procedure (OLP).

The ordinary legislative procedure is as follows:[35]

- the Commission puts forward a proposal to Council;
- Council submits this to Parliament for its opinion (first reading stage);
- Parliament submits its opinion to Council which adopts – by a qualified majority of votes – a 'common position';
- the common position is considered by Parliament (second reading stage) and:
    - if approved the measure is adopted by Council;
    - if Parliament rejects the measure or proposes amendments which the Council will not accept a Conciliation Committee comprising Council members and MEPs is established to draft an agreed text;
    - if a majority in Parliament and qualified majority in Council approve the text, it is adopted;
    - if no agreement is reached, Council may reinstate its original common position by majority vote;
    - the measure may then be adopted unless vetoed by a majority in Parliament.

According to Juan Mayoral the co-decision procedure has been undermined by the organisation of informal meetings between the Council Presidency, the Commission's representatives and the European Parliament's Rapporteur. These 'trilogues' are designed to reduce delays by avoiding second readings and the need to resort to the Conciliation Committee.[36]

The TEU 1992 provided that Parliament shall appoint an ombudsman to inquire into allegations of maladministration within the EU. Parliament may also establish committees of inquiry to investigate allegations of maladministration. It was a committee of inquiry which led to the downfall of the Santer Commission in 1999. The SEA gave the Parliament power to agree or to veto special trade agreements. It also extended Parliament's role in the admission of new Member States, whose admission must be approved by a majority, thus giving the Parliament a power of veto.

The Lisbon Treaty introduced the citizens' initiative.[37] Article 11.4 provides that

> not less than one million citizens who are nationals of a significant number of Member States may take the initiative of inviting the European Commission, within the framework of its powers, to submit any appropriate proposal on matters where citizens consider that a legal act of the Union is required for the purpose of implementing the Treaties.

---

33 On Parliament's powers under the TEU, see Bradley, '"Better rusty than missing?" The institutional reforms of the Maastricht Treaty and the European Parliament', in O'Keefe and Twomey, 1994.

34 Article 294 TFEU.

35 And is further extended under the 2007 Treaty of Lisbon.

36 Democratic improvements in the EU after the Lisbon Treaty, Robert Schuman Centre for Advanced Studies, European University Institute, February 2011.

37 Articles 10 and 11 TEU.

The special legislative procedure

Special legislative procedures replace the former consultative, cooperation and assent procedures. Under the special legislative procedure the Council of the EU is the sole legislator. These procedures therefore are a departure from the normal ordinary legislative procedure. Under the special legislative procedures the European Parliament is limited to consultation or approval. The Treaty on the Functioning of the EU does not give a precise definition of the special legislative procedures; the rules are to be found in specific Treaty Articles.

Passerelle clauses

A passerelle clause is a clause in the EU Treaties that allows for the alteration of legislative procedures without a formal amendment of the treaties. Their use requires unanimity in Council or the European Council, thereby ensuring that all Member States agree. A passerelle clause, unlike a revised Treaty, does not require ratification by Member States. Following the Treaty of Lisbon, there are two general passerelle clauses. The first provides that the European Council can replace unanimous voting in the Council of the EU with qualified majority voting, and the second is to move from the special legislative procedure to the ordinary legislative procedure. Before these measures can be implemented, two preconditions must be met:

- the European Parliament must approve the measure by an absolute majority of its Members, i.e. 376 of 751 MEPs; and
- national Parliaments must be notified of the intended use of the clause. If anyone objects within six months, the proposal fails.

In addition there are six other passerelle clauses relating to specific EU policies and facilitating different decision-making procedures.

Relations with national Parliaments

The Lisbon Treaty conferred new rights and powers on national Parliaments in order to improve the democratic legitimacy of the EU institutions. First, national Parliaments have the right to receive information on legislative proposals. Second, national Parliaments have the right to scrutinise draft legislation with a view to assessing whether it conforms to the principle of subsidiarity. A period of eight weeks is given in which to submit a reasoned opinion on subsidiarity to the EU institutions. Third, the European Parliament and national Parliaments must be informed of measures relating to Freedom, Security and Justice, and have the right to scrutinise activities of Europol and Eurojust (on which see below). National Parliaments also ratify Treaty changes in accordance with their own constitutional procedures. In addition, national Parliaments have the right to be notified of applications for accession to the EU. National Parliaments also have the right to participate in cooperation between national Parliaments and the European Parliament. All Member States have a parliamentary committee dedicated to the scrutiny of EU matters.

Implementing EU law

The primary responsibility for implementing EU law lies with EU Member States. Where implementation needs to be uniform, the EU law will confer implementing powers on the Commission, or exceptionally the EU Council. In relation to most EU laws, before the law can be implemented the Commission must consult a committee where every EU country is represented, thereby giving control to Member States. This implementing process is known as *comitology*.[38] Comitology was given a legal base under the Single European Act. Comitology is not compulsory for all EU laws. Four types of committee may be formed. Advisory committees give their opinion to the Commission which must take it into account but the Commission retains the power of implementation. Management committees are formed when implementing measures relate to the management of programmes and when they have budgetary implications, and they may block implementation by a qualified majority. Regulatory committees are formed when the measures relate to legislation applicable to the whole of the EU; a qualified majority is needed to approve a measure. Regulatory committees with scrutiny give to Council and the Parliament the right to carry out a check prior to the adoption of a measure and to block a proposed measure.

Where a proposed implementing measure is rejected by a committee, the Commission may take the matter to an appeal committee. The appeal committee is made up of representatives of the EU Member States. The decision of the appeal committee is binding.

The European Parliament pressed for reform of the comitology process, in part on the basis that it excluded the role of the Parliament. The Parliament and the EU Council now have the power to check the Commission's implementing powers. All proposed Commission action discussed in the committees must be disclosed to Parliament and Council. Where measures are passed through co-decision, the Parliament and/or Council have a right of scrutiny and to notify the Commission that implementation as proposed would exceed the Commission's powers. In this case the Commission is obliged to review its proposed action.

The concept of institutional balance

Under any constitution there must be a separation of powers in order to ensure that power is dispersed among the major institutions of the state rather than concentrated in one institution. However, as has been seen above, the separation of powers among the EU institutions differs markedly from conventional arrangements. In the first place, it may be noted that the principal institutions – the Council, Commission and Parliament – represent different interests: the Council representing the interests of the Member States, the Commission representing the interests of the EU and the Parliament representing the interests of EU citizens through the political parties. Second, there is no 'government' in the normal sense of that word; rather, executive powers are shared between the Council and Commission, and the law-making powers shared by the Commission, Council and Parliament. As a result, the arrangements are governed not so much by the concept of separation of powers but by the concept of 'institutional balance'. This is a dynamic concept which has changed over the years – most notably with the increase in power of the European Parliament, but also in the move away from unanimity in decision making in Council and towards Qualified Majority Voting.[39]

The principle of institutional balance is both political and legal. The case of **Roquettes Frères SA v Commission** (1976) illustrates the principle, the Court of Justice ruling that the requirement of consultation laid down in the EC Treaty 'represents an essential factor in the institutional balance intended by the Treaty'. The failure to consult resulted in a distortion of balance which would be remedied by declaring the relevant measure void. Institutional balance was also central to the case of **Parliament v Council**, the **Chernobyl** case (1990). In that case, although the (former) EC Treaty did not provide that the European Parliament had the right to challenge acts adopted in breach of the Treaty before the Court of Justice, the

---

38 Regulation (EU) No. 182/2011 of the European Parliament and of the Council.
39 Which in turn affects the ability of a Member State to obstruct developments. See further below.

Court nevertheless ruled that its duty to ensure that the law is observed entailed the duty to maintain the institutional balance. Accordingly, it ruled that the absence of a right to bring an action was a procedural gap which the Court would not allow to 'prevail over the fundamental interest in the maintenance and observance of the institutional balance laid down in the Treaties'.

Under the Treaty of Lisbon, the institutional balance is altered:

- The European Council is to propose a candidate for election to the Presidency of the Commission. The Parliament elects the President.
- The Parliament acquires the right of co-decision with the Council over a majority of legislative proposals.
- The Parliament's powers over the annual Budget are enhanced.
- Parliament acquires the right to initiate Treaty revision.

The European Council[40]

The year 1974 saw the formalisation of an informal arrangement which had pertained from the 1960s, with a communiqué providing that Heads of Government and their Foreign Ministers would meet at least three times a year to further political cooperation in the development of the Community (now Union). The first official recognition of the communiqué is found in the SEA 1986, which specified the membership of the European Council and reduces the minimum number of annual meetings from three to two. The TEU confirms this arrangement and Article 15 TEU states that: 'The European Council shall provide the Union with the necessary impetus for its development and shall define the general political guidelines thereof'.

The Heads of Government and Foreign Ministers accordingly meet at least twice a year, together with the President of the Commission, two Members of the Commission and officials. A primary purpose of the meetings is to review economic and social matters such as inflation, economic growth, unemployment, the European monetary system, international political issues, reform of the Common Agricultural Policy and constitutional issues such as applications for membership of the Union and political integration.

The Treaty of Lisbon provides for the election of a President of the European Council by a qualified majority, for a term of two-and-a-half years, renewable once. The President 'shall not' hold national office. The functions of the President of the European Council are defined as:

- chairing Council;
- ensuring the preparation and continuity of the work of the European Council;
- endeavouring to facilitate cohesion and consensus with the European Council;
- reporting to the Parliament after each meeting of the European Council;
- ensuring the representation of the Union on issues concerning its common foreign and security policy.

---

40 Not to be confused with the Council of the EU, which comprises Ministers of national governments, or with the Council of Europe.

Pause and Reflect

It is sometimes said that the European Union has a 'democratic deficit'.

What do you understand by this term? In what ways is it or is it not an accurate reflection of the institutions of the EU?

The Court of Auditors

The Court of Auditors comprises one member from each Member State, appointed under similar terms and conditions to judges of the CJEU. The term of years is six, and Members are under a duty to act completely independently in the performance of their duties and to act in the general interests of the EU. A President of the Court, appointed for a renewable term of three years, heads the Court of Auditors. It is the Court of Auditors which has responsibility for monitoring the expenditure of the EU. It carries out audits, examining the accounts of all revenue and expenditure of the EU. At the end of each financial year, the Court of Auditors is under a duty to draw up an Annual Report which is forwarded to the other institutions of the EU and published, with replies from these institutions, in the *Official Journal of the European Union*.

The Court of Auditors has the full range of legal remedies available to other institutions, thus reinforcing the safeguards which ensure that it is able to perform effectively. The Court of Auditors' task is to assist the European Parliament and the Council in exercising their powers of control over the implementation of the budget. The Court may also submit observations on specific questions and deliver opinions at the request of one of the European institutions.

The Court of Auditors is required to provide the Council and Parliament with a Statement of Assurance relating to the reliability of accounts and the legality of the underlying transactions. In its auditing function, the Court of Auditors may examine records in the European institutions and the Member States. The Court of Auditors examines the accounts of EU revenue and expenditure and considers whether these have been received and incurred in a lawful manner and whether the financial management has been sound. The Court of Auditors is independent and has the power to carry out its audits at any level. In addition to monitoring the internal revenues and expenditure of the Union, the Court of Auditors also monitors cooperation agreements between the European Union and many developing countries, and the system of EU aid to Central and Eastern Europe.

The Economic and Social Committee

The Economic and Social Committee is appointed by the Council, the number of members being based on the populations of Member States. The Member States submit lists of nominees for appointment, and are required to nominate twice as many persons as will be appointed. Members of the Committee are representative of different occupational and social groups. The Committee has advisory status. The Committee comprises representatives of producers, farmers, carriers, workers, dealers, craftsmen, professional occupations and representatives of the general public.

The Committee provides a forum for representatives of Europe's socio-occupational groups to express their points of view, and thus play a role in the EU's decision-making process. Members of the Committee are nominated by national governments and appointed by the Council for a renewable five-year term of office. The Committee issues advisory documents and opinions. Opinions are forwarded to the Council, Commission and European Parliament and published in the EU's *Official Journal*.

The Committee of the Regions

The Committee of the Regions comprises representatives of regional and local bodies and has advisory status (Articles 305–307 TFEU). It advises the Council and Commission on education, culture and regional development. The Committee, headed by a Chairman, meets at the request of the Council or Commission, and may also meet on its own initiative. The Committee must be consulted by the Council or the Commission where the Treaty so provides.

The European Investment Bank

Established under the TEU 1992, the European Investment Bank is charged with the task of promoting the 'balanced and steady development of the common market in the interest of the Community (EU)'. The Bank operates on a non-profit making basis, and grants loans and can give guarantees which facilitate the financing of a number of projects, including projects for developing less developed regions, modernising or conversion projects and projects of common interest to several Member States.

Court of Justice of the EU (CJEU), formerly European Court of Justice (ECJ)[41]

The Treaty of Lisbon provides that:[42]

- the Court of Justice of the European Communities is renamed the 'Court of Justice of the European Union';
- the Court comprises the Court of Justice, the General Court and specialised courts;
- the Court consists of one judge from each Member State;
- the Court has jurisdiction to rule on actions brought by Member States, an institution or a natural or legal person;
- the Court has jurisdiction to give preliminary ruling on the interpretation of Union law or the validity of acts adopted by institutions;
- the Court has jurisdiction where otherwise provided for by the Treaties;
- the Court of Justice has no jurisdiction relating to common Foreign and Security Policy or in relation to operations of the police and other law-enforcement agencies.[43]

On penalties, the Treaty of Lisbon provides that:[44]

- if the Commission considers that a Member State has failed to comply with the judgment of the Court, it 'shall specify', after giving the Member State the opportunity to make observations, the penalty to be paid;
- where a Member State has failed to fulfil its obligations relating to the notification of domestic measures designed to implement a Directive to the Commission, the Commission may specify the penalty to be paid and the Court may impose a penalty not exceeding the amount specified by the Commission.

The judges of the CJEU are appointed by 'common accord of the governments of Member States'. Each state makes one nomination. Unlike superior judges in the United Kingdom,

---

41 EC Treaty, Article 19 TEU, Articles 251–255 TFEU.
42 Treaty of Lisbon, Article 9F.
43 Article 24 TEU.
44 Article 260 TFEU.

the qualification for appointment to judicial office in the CJEU is that candidates are 'persons whose independence is beyond doubt and who possess the qualifications required for appointment to the highest judicial offices in their respective countries or who are jurisconsults of recognised competence'. Under the Treaty of Lisbon, judges will henceforth be appointed following consultation with a panel responsible for giving an opinion on candidates' suitability. The panel comprises seven persons from among former members of the Court, members of national supreme courts and lawyers of recognised competence. Judges are appointed for a six-year term of office (Article 253 TFEU).

The Court is presided over by a President, who holds office for a three-year term. Assisting the judges are Advocates General. It is the Advocates General who will examine each case and present the legal arguments to the Court for its decision.

Pressure on the CJEU resulted in a Court of First Instance (now called the General Court) being introduced under the SEA 1986. The majority of cases are heard in Chambers comprising three or five judges. The General Court is not empowered to hear and determine questions referred for a preliminary ruling under Article 267 TFEU, on which see further, Chapter 8.

The role of the CJEU is provided for in the most general terms by Article 19 TEU: 'The Court of Justice shall ensure that in the interpretation and application of the Treaties, the law is observed'. At first sight, given that the jurisdiction of the Court is derived solely from the Treaties, this would seem to confine the CJEU to consideration of EU law, a point reinforced by the wording of Article 267 TFEU. In the early days, the Court adopted this narrow interpretation of its jurisdiction and rejected any invitation to draw on the law of Member States in the forming of decisions. From the 1970s at least, a change in attitude can be discerned in the reasoning of the Court. From that time, judges felt able, indeed compelled, to make recourse to domestic law of Member States in order to ensure both the effectiveness of EU law within a particular Member State and to produce harmony between the laws of all Member States. The Court accordingly draws particularly on fundamental concepts existing in the laws of Member States in order to enable common legal concepts to be incorporated into EU law.[45] However, the CJEU can only rule on the interpretation and legality of EU law: it has no power to rule on the domestic laws of Member States. It is the need for uniformity of the law within the legal systems of Member States which represents a major function of the Court. It must also be recognised, however, that in its interpretation of the Treaties and pursuit of the uniform application of EU law, the CJEU has proved itself to be extremely creative – the concepts of direct effect, indirect effect, the supremacy of Community (now EU) law and state liability all being 'judge-made'.

Preliminary rulings: Article 267 TFEU[46]

The single most important jurisdiction in terms of ensuring that EU law is uniformly interpreted within national legal systems is that conferred on the Court to give preliminary rulings under Article 267 TFEU. The Court may rule on the interpretation of the Treaty, and on the validity and interpretation of acts of the institutions of the EU. Article 267 provides that:

> The Court of Justice shall have jurisdiction to give preliminary rulings concerning:
>
> (a) the interpretation of this Treaty;
> (b) the validity and interpretation of acts of the institutions, bodies, offices or agencies of the Union;

---

45 See Mendelsen, 1981; Dauses, 1985.
46 See Arnull, 1988b, 1989 and 1990.

> Where such a question is raised before any court or tribunal of a Member State that court or tribunal may, if it considers that a decision on the question is necessary to enable it to give judgment, request the Court to give a ruling thereon.
>
> Where any such question is raised in a case pending before a court or tribunal of a Member State against whose decision there is no judicial remedy under national law, that court or tribunal shall bring the matter before the Court.
>
> If such a question is raised in a case pending before a court or tribunal of a Member State with regard to a person in custody, the Court of Justice of the European Union shall act with the minimum of delay.

It is this Article which raises directly the nature of the legal system of the EU and the relationship between EU law, the CJEU and domestic law and the role of judges in national courts. The power to interpret the Treaty gives the CJ a dynamic function, and the CJEU has a role in the creation of law at least as important as the legislative powers of the Council and Parliament. This power, as utilised, is a matter of some controversy with the CJ, being both criticised and praised for adopting a deliberate policy-making stance which goes beyond that of interpretation of the Treaty.[47]

Article 267 envisages a partnership approach between the domestic courts and the CJ. It is important both as a matter of principle and as a practical matter that the domestic courts are actively involved in the application of EU law, and that a measure of discretion is left to domestic courts in the matter of referring a matter to the CJ. It must also be recognised, however, that the discretion left to domestic courts carries with it the potential for a distortion of the meaning of EU law within the different legal systems. A particular difficulty faced the courts in the United Kingdom, whose traditional approach to the interpretation of statutes has been one very much constrained by the detailed wording of statutes and the literal, golden and mischief rules. By contrast, in civil law systems,[48] the judges are experienced in interpreting broadly phrased statutory provisions, using the teleological interpretative method which seeks the interpretation which most closely fits the objective sought by the legislature, if necessary departing from the literal interpretation. On Article 267 see further Chapter 8.

In order to understand the relationship between the CJ and national courts, and the issue of the supremacy of EC (now EU) law, it is first necessary to examine the sources of EC/EU law, and the manner in which EU law comes into effect in domestic law. These issues are discussed in the next chapter.

Under Article 259 TFEU one Member State may bring a fellow Member State before the Court. Again, a procedure is specified which gives the Commission a quasi-judicial function. Before an action is brought before the Court, the aggrieved Member State must bring the matter to the attention of the Commission. The Commission must give a reasoned opinion, the Member State having been given the opportunity to make oral and written submissions on the allegation. Once this procedure has been completed, the Member State has a discretion whether or not to bring the matter before the Court. If the Commission fails to deliver its opinion within three months from the date of the allegation, then the aggrieved state may proceed with the action before the Court.

---

47 See Rasmussen, 1988; Slynn, 1984.
48 Defined as those deriving primarily from Roman law.

Penalties for failure to comply with rulings of the European Court

Article 260 TFEU provides that, if the CJEU finds that a Member State has failed to fulfil its obligations, the state shall be required to take the necessary measures to comply with the judgment of the Court.

As with Article 259, the Commission plays a role:

> If the Commission considers that the Member State concerned has not taken the necessary measures to comply with the judgment of the Court, it may bring the case before the Court after giving that State the opportunity to submit its observations. It shall specify the amount of the lump sum or penalty payment to be paid by the Member State concerned which it considers appropriate in the circumstances.

> If the Court finds that the Member State concerned has not complied with its judgment it may impose a lump sum or penalty payment on it.

Actions against EU institutions

Article 263 TFEU provides the CJEU's jurisdiction to review the legality of acts adopted 'jointly by the European Parliament and the Council, of acts of the Council [and] of the Commission'. Actions may be brought by Member States, the Council, the Commission or the European Parliament on grounds of 'lack of competence, infringement of an essential procedural requirement, infringement of the Treaties or of any rule of law relating to its application, or misuse of powers'. If an action is well founded, the Court may declare the act concerned to be void.[49] It is by these means that the CJEU controls the exercise of powers by the institutions of the EU.[50]

However, EU law did not impose any obligation on a Member State to bring, for the benefit of one of its citizens, an action against an EU institution under Article 263 TFEU for annulment of an act adopted by the institution, or under Article 265 TFEU for failure to act. That did not in principle preclude national law from providing for such an obligation. The Court of Justice so ruled in **Staat der Nederlanden (Ministerie van Landbouw, Natuurbeheer en Visseril) v Ten Kate Holding Musselkanaal BV** (2005).

In **Kadi and Al Barakaat International Foundation v Council and Commission** (2008) Regulations relating to the seizure of terrorist funds and their legality under EU law were challenged. The Court in **Kadi** ruled that respect for property was a general principle of EU law, and that for guidance the court had to take into account Article 1 of the European Convention on Human Rights Protocol which enshrines that right. The question to be asked was whether a freezing measure provided by contested Regulations amounted to 'disproportionate and intolerable interference impairing the very substance of the fundamental right to respect for ... property'.[51] The Regulation would be annulled. In **Kadi v EU Council** (2011) the CJEU ruled that the Council's response to its former ruling again breached the rights of the defence and therefore the principle of effective judicial protection. The contested Regulation was annulled.[52]

---

49 Article 264 TFEU.
50 See Steiner, 1995, and references therein. See **European Parliament v Council of the European Union** (1999); **Re Cosmetic Products Directive: France v European Parliament, Council** (2005).
51 At para. 357.
52 See also **UK v EU Council** (2011).

Europol

In 1991 the German Chancellor, Helmut Kohl, called for a European police agency. The Maastricht Treaty of 1992, Article K1(9) provided for police cooperation between Member States to combat terrorism, drug trafficking and other international crime. The Convention regulating Europol came into force in 1998. Each Member State is required to designate a national unit to liaise between its own authorities and Europol. Joint Investigation Teams (JITs) were set up to combat trafficking in drugs and people as well as terrorism, money laundering, organised fraud, counterfeiting and cybercrime. Europol's headquarters are in The Hague. Europol officers have no powers of arrest but support EU law enforcement officers by gathering, analysing and disseminating information and coordinating operations. There are 145 Europol Liaison Officers seconded to Europol by Member States and non-EU partners.

Eurojust

Eurojust was established in 2002 to facilitate judicial cooperation. It is composed of national prosecutors, magistrates and police officers drawn from Member States. Council Decision 2002/187/JHA established Eurojust as a judicial coordination unit. Eurojust is based in The Hague. Article 85 of the Lisbon Treaty defines the role of Eurojust as being 'to support and strengthen coordination and cooperation between national investigating and prosecuting authorities in relation to serious crime affecting two or more Member States'.

In order to investigate and prosecute EU fraud, the European Public Prosecutor's Office (EPPO) has been proposed by the Commission. The EPPO will be able to tackle cross-border crime. The EPPO will have a decentralised structure to conduct investigations, working closely with Member States' investigative and prosecutorial offices. Investigations affecting individuals' fundamental rights will require prior authorisation by a national court. The EPPO's investigations will be subject to judicial review.

Sources of EU Law

Primary and secondary sources

Every act and decision of the EU must have a basis in law, and if there is no such base, a decision or provision will be annulled by the Court of Justice of the EU.[53] The primary sources of EU law are the Treaties, as amended. Secondary legislation is law made by the EU institutions, and includes the interpretation of both primary and secondary sources by the CJEU. Secondary legislation comprises Regulations, Directives and Decisions. Article 288 of the Treaty on the Functioning of the European Union (TFEU) defines these terms as follows:

> To exercise the Union's competences, the institutions shall adopt regulations, directives, decisions, recommendations and opinions.
>
> - a regulation shall have general application. It shall be binding in its entirety and directly applicable in all Member States;
> - a directive shall be binding, as to the result to be achieved, upon each Member State to which it is addressed, but shall leave to the national authorities the choice of form or methods;

---

53 See **European Commission v European Council** (2010).

- a decision shall be binding in its entirety. A decision which specifies those to whom it is addressed shall be binding only on them;
- recommendations and opinions shall have no binding force.

It is clear from Article 288 TFEU that Regulations and Directives have 'binding effect' in all Member States, but, as discussed below, this takes different forms. Decisions and recommendations, on the other hand, have more limited effect, the former binding those to whom they are addressed, the latter having 'no binding force'. There are, however, other 'sources' which, while not having legally binding force, nevertheless have a significant impact on the working of the Union. The institutions of the Union, for example, formulate their own procedures for self-regulation. As will be seen below, the Council has the power to enter into international agreements between the Union and non-EU states on behalf of the Member States of the Union. In addition, there are measures which are labelled 'soft' (as opposed to 'hard') law. As well as recommendations and opinions under Article 288, Jo Shaw (2000) cites 'communications, conclusions, declarations, action programmes and communiqués' as examples of soft law. Joint actions taken by Member States in pursuit of Union objectives also fall within soft law.[54] While the principal concern in this chapter is with the 'hard law' of the EU, it must also be recognised that these disparate mechanisms exist in order to further European objectives across wide-ranging fields of policy on which it may not be possible always to secure complete agreement between all Member States, which would enable the translation of a soft law measure into hard law with binding legal effect.

Direct Applicability and Direct Effect

Direct applicability: an EU provision/measure is automatically legally effective from the relevant date, without any legislative action on the part of the Member State's legislature.

Direct effect: an EU provision automatically confers legal rights on individuals which are enforceable against the Member State government and other bodies. Direct effect may be vertical or horizontal (see below). Where a provision does not have direct effect, it may be indirectly effective as a result of a national court's duty to interpret law in a manner which gives effect to EU law.

As can be seen from the text of Article 288 TFEU, a Regulation is 'binding in its entirety' and has direct applicability. By 'direct applicability' it is meant that the measure leaves no discretion to the Member States but, rather, confers rights and duties within the Member States without further legislative participation. In other words, the provision is self-executing. On the other hand, a Directive, whilst binding in its objective, leaves the Member State some leeway in its introduction and the manner in which a Member State implements and achieves the objectives set by the Council, Commission and European Parliament.

In order to understand the way in which EU law operates within Member States' legal systems, the principle of direct effect must be examined. The basic principle of direct effect of EU measures is that individuals may invoke certain provisions as conferring direct rights,

---

54 The Court of Justice has ruled that the principle that national law must be interpreted in line with EU law applies as much to framework decisions as to other sources: **Criminal Proceedings against Pupino** (2005).

which may be relied on in the national courts. While Article 288 TFEU states specifically that Regulations are directly applicable, the Article is silent as to the legal *consequence* of this applicability, and as to whether a Treaty provision itself, or Regulations or Directives, can have direct legal effect on individuals.[55]

The principle of direct effect is linked to the principle of 'loyal cooperation' or 'fidelity' enshrined in Article 4.3 TEU (formerly Article 10 EC), which provides, in part, that:

> Pursuant to the principle of sincere cooperation, the Union and the Member States shall, in full mutual respect, assist each other in carrying out tasks which flow from the Treaties.
>
> The Member States shall take any appropriate measure, general or particular, to ensure fulfilment of the obligations arising out of the Treaties or resulting from the acts of the institutions of the Union.
>
> The Member States shall facilitate the achievement of the Union's tasks and refrain from any measure which could jeopardise the attainment of the Union's objectives.

As can be seen from Article 4.3 TEU, Member States are under a legal duty both to take action to ensure compliance with EU law and to refrain from any action which might impede the application and effectiveness of EU law. Article 4.3 TEU forms the basis of much of the jurisprudence of the CJEU, and the foundation for the enforcement of individual rights against Member States.

Direct effect and Treaty (TFEU) provisions

In 1963, the CJEU articulated the theoretical basis for the principle of direct effect in **Van Gend en Loos** (1963), a case which involved a reference to the CJEU from the Dutch courts. From this case many significant later developments of EU law can be seen to originate. Under Article 25 of the EC Treaty (formerly Article 12 EEC Treaty; now Article 30 TFEU): 'Customs duties on imports and exports and charges having equivalent effect shall be prohibited between Member States. This prohibition shall also apply to customs duties of a fiscal nature'.

Before 1958, and the coming into force of the EEC Treaty, the Dutch firm of Van Gend en Loos had been importing glue from Germany, applying a customs duty of 3 per cent. In 1959, the Dutch government ratified an agreement with other countries establishing an 8 per cent duty. The company protested to the Customs Court, relying on the direct effect of Article 12 of the EEC Treaty. The Court referred the matter to the CJEU. The principal question for the court was whether, as claimed, Article 12 had direct effect on the legal position of the company. The Treaty Article did not stipulate its legal effect, and Article 189 of the EEC Treaty (later Article 249, now Article 288 TFEU) refers only to Regulations having direct applicability. The CJEU held that if a Treaty provision is to confer individual enforceable rights, it must:

(a) indicate that it applies not just to Member States but also to individuals within the state;
(b) be clear and precise;
(c) be unconditional and unqualified and not subject to any further measures on the part of Member States;
(d) be one which does not leave any substantial latitude or discretion to Member States.

---

55 See **Consorzio del Prosciutto di Parma v Asda Food Stores Ltd** (1999), in which the Court of Appeal ruled that a regulation did not have direct effect, *inter alia*, since it was not sufficiently clear and precise and itself indicated that it was not intended to have direct effect.

Specifically in relation to Article 12, as it then was, the CJEU held that the text was clear and unconditional, that it required no legislative intervention by the Member State and that the Member State had no power to subordinate Article 12 to its own law. Thus, it can be seen that both provisions in the Treaty and Regulations are capable of having direct effect if they satisfy the requirements laid down by the CJEU.

Regulations and direct effect

It was noted above that Article 288 TFEU provides, in part, that a Regulation shall 'be binding in its entirety' and 'directly applicable in all Member States'. The Regulation becomes directly applicable in domestic law from the date on which it is brought into force. Any domestic legislation which is needed to bring it into effect may not obstruct or change the Regulation. The clear wording of Article 288 suggests that Regulations should have direct effect and that individuals can rely on the Regulation and have it enforced in his or her domestic courts. In **Commission v Italy** (1973) the Court of Justice confirmed this view: Regulations – provided that they are sufficiently precise, clear and unconditional – have direct effect, stating that:

> it cannot be accepted that a Member State should apply in an incomplete or selective manner provisions of a Community (now EU) Regulation so as to render abortive certain aspects of Community (now EU) legislation which it has opposed or which it considers contrary to its national interests.

Directives and direct effect[56]

A further question which arises is whether Directives are similarly capable of having direct effect. It has been seen from Article 288 TFEU that Directives leave no discretion as to their objectives, but do leave some discretion as to manner of implementation. Nevertheless, the CJEU has found provisions of Directives to be capable of having direct effect. The reasoning of the CJEU is revealed in **Van Duyn v Home Office** (1975). Article 45 TFEU provides (in part) that:

(1) Freedom of movement for workers shall be secured within the Union.
(2) Such freedom of movement shall entail the abolition of any discrimination based on nationality ... as regards employment, remuneration and other conditions of work and employment.
(3) It shall entail the right, subject to limitations justified on grounds of public policy, public security and public health to accept offers of employment.

Yvonne Van Duyn, a Dutch national, arrived in England in May 1973, having accepted a job as a secretary with the Church of Scientology. Immigration officials refused Ms Van Duyn admission to the United Kingdom on the basis that the Secretary of State considered employment with the Church undesirable. In an action against the Home Office, Ms Van Duyn sought to rely on Article 48 of the EEC Treaty (now Article 45 TFEU) and a reference was made to the ECJ (now CJEU).

The Directive in question was that of the Council[57] which set out the objective of coordinating measures concerning movement and residence. The public policy issue, relied on by

---

56 See Craig, 1997.
57 64/221/EEC, Article 3.

the Home Office, was then regulated by Article 3(1) of Directive 64/221, which stipulated that: 'measures taken on grounds of public policy and public security shall be based exclusively on the personal conduct of the individual concerned'. The CJEU held that since the Directive laid down an obligation which was not subject to any exception or condition, and by its nature did not require intervention on the part of the Community or Member States, it followed that the Directive was to be regarded as directly effective and conferred enforceable individual rights which national courts must protect.

Thus, it can be seen that, in some cases, Directives, as well as Regulations and Treaty provisions, may have direct effect – depending on their wording and clarity and whether or not Member State action is required as a prerequisite to implementation. The deadline for implementation of the Directive must, however, have passed.[58] Where a Directive is not precise, and a right insufficiently defined, it will not have direct effect.[59] Note that in the period allowed for the implementation of a Directive, a Member State must not take any action which would frustrate or undermine the objective sought by the Directive: **Inter-Environnement Wallonie** (1997).

Vertical and horizontal effect of EU law

The concept of direct effect utilises the concepts of vertical and horizontal effect of legal provisions. In essence, the concept of vertical effect means that a measure – whether a Treaty provision, Regulation or Directive (depending on whether the qualifying criteria are met) – is directly enforceable by an individual against the Member State and its institutions. In other words, the rights conferred and obligations imposed are enforceable at the suit of an individual against his or her own Member State and its agents, which are responsible for giving effect to the provision. For example, in **Van Duyn v The Home Office** (above), the citizen was challenging the decision of a government Minister; the action was thus vertical in nature and the Directive could be invoked. Of greater difficulty is the question of whether an enforceable obligation exists which entitles an individual to pursue his or her rights, not directly against the Member State and its agencies but horizontally against private institutions, organisations or individuals other than the government of the state and public bodies.

With vertical effect, the law imposes a duty on the Member State to comply and confers an enforceable right on the citizen. The Member State is thus responsible to the citizen for the enforcement of his or her rights under EU law. Directives enjoy vertical, but not horizontal, effect and can only be invoked against the state and emanations of the state. The CJEU denies the possibility of horizontal direct effect of Directives,[60] which would extend the liability for failure to comply with EU law requirements to non-state bodies or individuals. However, the concept of indirect effect (on which, see below) of Directives complicates this theoretically straightforward position. Under the concept of indirect effect, the CJEU insists that national courts as public bodies have a duty to interpret national law in a manner consistent with EU Directives so far as possible. This doctrine applies even in actions between two individuals, and regardless of whether the Directive or national law is earlier in time. Where indirect effect applies, therefore, a Directive appears to have been given horizontal effect.

---

58 See **Pubblico Ministero v Ratti** (1979).
59 See **Gibson v East Riding of Yorkshire Council** (2000).
60 See **Marshall v Southampton and SW Hampshire AHA** (1986); **Faccini Dori** (1994).

THE VERTICAL EFFECT OF EU LAW   **THE HORIZONTAL EFFECT OF EU LAW**

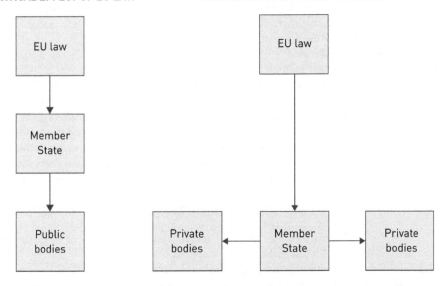

In securing the uniformity of the application of EU law within Member States, the CJEU has utilised Article 10 EC (now Article 4.3 TEU) to great effect. National courts are required to interpret all national law in light of EU law, and that duty exists irrespective of whether a measure has direct effect.

In **Defrenne v SABENA** (1978), the CJEU confirmed the principle of horizontal direct effect of Treaty provisions. Gabrielle Defrenne, an air hostess with the Belgian airline SABENA, was required, under her contract of employment, to retire at the age of 40, whereas men did not have to retire at that age. Moreover, she was paid less than male employees, and would receive a smaller state pension than men. The state pension question went to the CJEU, which ruled that Article 119 of the EEC Treaty (now Article 157 TFEU) did not cover state pension rights.[61] Ms Defrenne then commenced actions against her employer, on the issue of equal pay and on the discriminatory retirement ages. In relation to the question of equal pay (but not retirement age), the action was successful.[62] The matter was referred to the CJEU, which ruled that Member States were obliged to implement Article 119 EEC by the end of a transitional period, and that the principle of direct effect of the Article entitled individuals to rely on Article 119 EEC, against both public and private sector employers, even where the provisions implementing the principle of equal pay had not been implemented by the state.

The question of whether a Directive could be relied on by individuals against employers was tested in the English courts in **Marshall v Southampton and South West Hampshire Area Health Authority** (1986). The Sex Discrimination Act 1975 enabled differing retirement ages to be fixed for men and women. Mrs Marshall challenged the legality of the requirement for women to retire at the age of 60, alleging that the Act was contrary to the European Community's Equal Treatment Directive.[63] Two issues, therefore, fell for consideration by the court. First, were different retirement ages in breach of the Directive and, second, if so, could an individual rely on the Directive to challenge an Area Health Authority? In other words, the issue was whether the Directive was directly effective against an employer in its contractual

---

61 **Defrenne v Belgian State** (1971). See now State Social Security Directive 79/7/EEC.
62 **Defrenne v SABENA** (1978).
63 Directive 76/207/EEC.

relationship with an employee or, alternatively, whether the Area Health Authority was an 'emanation of the state'. An Area Health Authority was deemed to be a public (as opposed to a private) body, and accordingly bound by EU law. The CJEU made clear that in principle a Directive could not, of itself, create obligations for non-state actors.

In **Foster v British Gas plc** (1991), however, which also entailed differing retirement ages for employees, the Court of Appeal had held that British Gas, a statutory corporation, was not a public body against whom the Directive could be enforced. The House of Lords sought clarification on this issue from the CJEU. The CJEU refused to accept British Gas's argument that there was a distinction between a nationalised undertaking and a state agency and ruled that a Directive might be relied on against organisations or bodies which were 'subject to the authority or control of the state or had special powers beyond those which result from the normal relations between individuals'. The Court accordingly ruled that a Directive might be invoked against 'a body, whatever its legal form, which has been made responsible, pursuant to a measure adopted by the state, for providing a public service under the control of the state and has for that purpose special powers beyond those which result from the normal rules applicable in relations between individuals'. Therefore, British Gas was a public body against which a Directive might be enforced, a ruling which the House of Lords subsequently accepted. In **Doughty v Rolls Royce plc** (1992), however, the Court of Appeal distinguished **Foster** and held that Rolls-Royce plc, although 'under the control of the state', had not been 'made responsible pursuant to a measure adopted by the state for providing a public service'. Rolls-Royce was at the time a nationalised body, responsible for providing defence equipment. However, the court distinguished between services for the public and services provided to the state, and thereby ruled Rolls-Royce not to be a public body for the purposes of the effectiveness of Directives. A different result was reached by the Court of Appeal in **National Union of Teachers v Governing Body of St Mary's Church of England (Aided) Junior School** (1997). The court ruled that the governors of a voluntary aided school who had chosen to enter it into the state system were a public body. The powers and duties of the Secretary of State for Education and the local education authority amounted to control of the school while it remained in the state system. The school, therefore, was a public body.

The CJEU, in **Faccini Dori v Recreb srl** (1994), re-examined the principle of the horizontal effect of Directives. An EC consumer Directive,[64] which had not yet been implemented by the Italian authorities, founded a claim against a private undertaking. The Advocate General argued that the CJEU should extend the principle of direct effect of Directives to claims against all parties (irrespective of their public or private nature). The CJEU declined to do this, and reasserted its view that Directives could not be invoked directly against private bodies. However, the CJEU referred to the possibility that Directives could be deemed to be indirectly effective and also that they might be enforceable via the principle of state liability to give effect to Community measures, as seen in **Francovich and Bonifaci v Italy** (1992) (on which, see below).

In relation to Directives, the CJEU has ruled that these can, at best, have vertical effect against an emanation of the state – as laid down in **Marshall v Southampton Area Health Authority (No 1)** and subsequently confirmed, as in **Faccini Dori v Recreb srl** (1994) – and not horizontal effect. The role of Directives in ensuring the harmonisation and approximation of laws within the legal systems of the Member States of the Union, and the manner in which direct effect ensures harmonisation, is illustrated by the case of **CIA Security International SA v Signalson SA and Securitel SPRL** (1996),[65] which also has significant implications on the direct effect of

---

64 85/577/EC.
65 See Slot, 1996; Coppel, 1997.

Directives. Involved in this case was the interpretation of Article 28 of the EC Treaty (now Article 34 TFEU) (free movement of goods) and of Directive 83/189/EEC.

Articles 8 and 9 of Directive 83/189 lay down procedures for the provision of information in the field of technical standards and Regulations. Under these provisions, Member States must notify the Commission of all draft technical Regulations, and, except in particularly urgent cases, suspend their adoption and implementation for specified periods until the requirement of notification has been complied with. The provisions are unconditional and sufficiently precise in terms of their content to have direct effect and so enable an individual to rely on them before a national court, which must decline to apply a national technical Regulation which has not been notified in advance in accordance with the Directive. The purpose of making such Regulations inapplicable is in order to ensure the effectiveness of EU control for which the Directive is made. The CJEU ruled that:

> It is settled law that, wherever provisions of a directive appear to be, from the point of view of their content, unconditional and sufficiently precise, they may be relied on against any national provision which is not in accordance with the directive. [judgment, paragraph 42]

This decision appears to undermine the clear rule against the horizontal effect of Directives as expressed in **Faccini Dori**.[66]

The principle of indirect effect

Whereas the principle of direct effect entails rights which are directly enforceable against the Member State or an emanation of the state, indirect effect provides a more subtle mechanism for ensuring compliance with EU law. Indirect effect involves the application of the duty imposed on Member States, including courts of law under Article 4.3 TEU discussed above.

In **Von Colson v Land Nordrhein-Westfalen** (1984), Article 5 of the EEC Treaty (now Article 4.3 TEU) and the Equal Treatment Directive 76/207 fell for consideration by the CJEU. Ms Von Colson's application for employment in the prison service was rejected. The rejection was based on gender, and was justifiable according to the German court. Under German law, the only compensation payable to Ms Von Colson was her travelling expenses. The question arose as to whether such compensation gave effect to the requirements of Article 5, as it then was. On a reference, the CJEU examined Article 5 of EEC Treaty (now Article 4.3 TEU). The CJEU ruled that Article 5 imposed a duty not just on the governments of Member States, but on all national authorities, including the courts. It is therefore the duty of the domestic courts to interpret national law in such a way as to ensure that the obligations imposed by EC law are achieved. The result is that, although a provision is not directly effective, it may be applied indirectly as law by means of interpretation.[67]

The question of the relationship between domestic law and subsequently introduced EU law came before the CJEU in **Marleasing SA v La Comercial Internacional de Alimentacion SA** (1992).[68] The CJEU had ruled that, whereas a Directive cannot of itself impose obligations on private parties, national courts must as far as possible interpret national law in order to achieve a result pursued by a Directive, and that this must be done whether the national provisions in question were adopted before or after the Directive. In **Marleasing**, no legislation had been passed to comply with the Directive; the duty was nevertheless on the courts to give effect to the **Von Colson** principle, that is to say, the court must interpret domestic law

---

66 See also **Unilever Italia v Central Food** (2000).
67 See Drake, 2005.
68 See also **Criminal Proceedings Against Arcaro** (1997); and **Perceval-Price v Department of Economic Development** (2000).

in accordance with EU law. This principle enables Directives to have horizontal effect 'by the back door'. A gap in protection, however, still remained. Where there was no domestic law on an EU matter and where, as a result, there was no domestic provision to construe in line with EU law, a problem would remain. The CJEU reaffirmed the interpretative duty in **Centrosteel Srl v Adipol GmbH** (2000), in which the Court stated that it was well settled that 'in the absence of proper transposition into national law, a Directive cannot of itself impose obligations on individuals'. However, it went on to state that:

> when applying national law, whether adopted before or after the directive, the national court that has to interpret that law must do so, as far as possible, in the light of the wording and the purpose of the directive so as to achieve the result it has in view.[69]

 SELF-TEST QUESTIONS

List the primary and secondary sources of EU law.
What is the difference between direct applicability and direct effect?
What is vertical effect? What is horizontal effect?

The liability of the state

As seen above, Article 4.3 TEU imposes an obligation on Member States to facilitate and not to impede the objectives of the European Union. Where a Member State has failed to undertake its duty, the concept of state liability arises. In **Francovich and Bonifaci v Italy** (1991), employees were seeking compensation against Italy for failure to implement a Directive which was designed to guarantee the payment of arrears of wages to employees in the event of their employer's insolvency. The time limit set down for implementation of the Directive had expired and, as a result, Italy was held to be in breach of its EC obligations under Article 5 EEC Treaty (now Article 4.3 TEU).[70]

The CJEU held that, while the Directive was not sufficiently clear to be directly effective against the state, as regards the identity of institutions responsible for payments, Italy was under an obligation to implement the Directive under Article 5 of the EEC Treaty. Accordingly, since Italy had failed in its obligation, it was under a duty to compensate individuals for damage suffered as a result of its failure.[71] The CJEU laid down three conditions which applied to the issue of compensation for loss, namely that:

(a)   the Directive confers individual rights;
(b)   the content of those rights can be identified on the basis of the provisions of the Directive; and
(c)   there is a causal link between the state's failure and the damage suffered by individuals affected.[72]

---

69   In **Aannemersbedrijf PK Kraaijeveld BV ea v Gedeputeerde Staten van Zuid-Holland** (1996) and **World Wildlife Fund (WWF) v Autonome Provinz Bozen** (2000) the CJEU considered the question of whether Directives could be invoked by individuals in their national courts in the context of judicial review applications, and accepted that this could be the case, without enquiring into their capacity for direct effect. The implication of this is that Directives may have an effect distinct from direct effect, which is labelled the 'public law effect'. See Scott, 1998, pp. 123, 157.
70   See **Gibson v East Riding of Yorkshire DC** (1999).
71   Cf. **Evans v Motor Insurers Bureau** (1999).
72   See also **Marks & Spencer plc v Customs and Excise Commissioners (No 1)** (2000); and **R v Durham County Council ex parte Huddleston** (2000).

Under such conditions, an individual may proceed directly against the state. Accordingly, the importance of the principle of direct effect diminishes, and liability falls not on the employer – whether public or private – but on the state, by virtue of its obligations under the Treaty.

In **Brasserie du Pêcheur SA v Federal Republic of Germany** (1996)[73] and **R v Secretary of State for Transport ex parte Factortame Ltd (No 4)** (1996), the CJEU ruled on the principles which regulate the grant of compensation to bodies suffering damage as a result of Member States' breach of EU law. Member States are obliged to make good the loss suffered by individuals when:

- the national legislature, executive or judiciary is responsible for the breach;
- the rule of law breached is intended to confer rights on individuals;
- the breach is sufficiently serious, defined as a manifest and grave disregard of the limits on the Member State's discretion; and
- there is a direct causal link between the breach of the obligation and the damage suffered.

As to the degree of seriousness of the breach, the considerations to be taken into account by the court considering the issue of compensation, as stipulated by the CJEU, are:

> the clarity and precision of the rule breached; the measure of discretion left by that rule ...; whether the infringement and the damage caused was intentional or involuntary; whether any error of law was excusable or inexcusable; the fact that the position taken by a Community institution may have contributed towards the omission, and the adoption or retention of national measures or practices contrary to Community law.

> On any view, a breach of Community law will clearly be sufficiently serious if it has persisted despite a judgment finding the infringement in question to be established, or a preliminary ruling or settled case law of the court on the matter from which it is clear that the conduct in question constituted an infringement. [**Ex parte Factortame (No 4)** (1996)]

Note that **Brasserie** and **Factortame** concerned loss suffered as a result of breaches of Treaty provisions that are directly effective. In other words, the scope of state liability is neither limited to the failure to implement Directives nor to the absence of direct effect. Member States must compensate individuals at a level which is commensurate with the loss or damage suffered. Further, if damages could be awarded under English law to similar claims based on domestic law, it is possible to award exemplary damages for the breach of EU law.

The question of compensation was also considered by the CJEU in **R v HM Treasury ex parte British Telecommunications plc** (1996). The United Kingdom had incorrectly transposed a Directive into domestic law. The CJEU ruled that compensation for loss caused was only payable under the circumstances laid down in **Factortame (No 4)** (above). In the instant case, no reparation was payable because the breach was not sufficiently serious. The Directive was imprecisely worded and was reasonably capable of being interpreted in the manner adopted by the United Kingdom.[74]

In **Dillenkofer v Federal Republic of Germany** (1996), the CJEU ruled, once again, that if a Member State failed to take 'timeous' (timely) action to implement a Directive, individuals injured by that failure were entitled to seek reparation from the Member State. Member

---

73 For the development of this case, see **R v Secretary of State for Transport ex parte Factortame Ltd (No 1)** (1989); **(No 2)** (1991); **(No 3)** (1992); **(No 5)** (2000).
74 By contrast see **R v Ministry of Agriculture, Fisheries and Food ex parte Hedley Lomas (Ireland) Ltd** (1996).

States had been required to bring a Directive[75] into effect before 31 December 1992. Germany brought the Directive into effect as from July 1994. Travellers adversely affected by this delay sought compensation for their loss. Reciting the precedents, the Court stated that individuals who had suffered damage were entitled to compensation where the three conditions set out above were met. Germany had argued in its defence that the time allowed for full implementation of the Directive was too short. This argument, however, did not succeed, and the Court ruled clearly that failure to implement a Directive within the specified time period per se constituted a sufficiently serious breach of EC law.

In **Haim v Kassenzahnärztliche Vereinigung Nordrhein** (2000), the CJEU made it clear that a public body – as well as the state itself – could be liable for damages for breaches of EU law. Citing **Hedley Lomas**, the Court stated that the same principles applied when considering the liability of the public body as when considering the liability of the state. The question of whether a court of law could be liable to individuals for loss suffered as a result of an error in interpretation was considered by the CJEU in **Köbler v Republic of Austria** (2004). The Court ruled that a Member State's highest court was in principle liable, but only where the court had 'manifestly infringed the applicable law'. All state authorities – legislative, executive and judicial – incurred liability for breach of EU law.

The concept of state liability was examined in **Traghetti del Mediterraneo SpA (in liq) v Italy** (2006). The Court stressed the exceptional nature of state liability:

> state liability can be incurred only in the exceptional case where the national court adjudicating at last instance has manifestly infringed the applicable law.
>
> Manifest infringement is to be assessed, inter alia, in the light of a number of criteria, such as the degree of clarity and precision of the rule infringed, whether the infringement was intentional, whether the error of law was excusable or inexcusable, and the non-compliance by the court in question with its obligation to make a reference for a preliminary ruling under the third paragraph of Article 234 EC.[76]

Note that having left the EU, an action for damages for a breach of EU law under the **Francovich principle** will no longer be available within the UK.[77]

Fundamental principles

The application and enforcement of EU law has been extended by the CJEU enforcing the fundamental principles of EU law. The starting point is the case of **Werner Mangold v Rudiger Helm** (2005). In this case, a Directive (2000/78) laid down a 'general framework for combating discrimination on the grounds of religion or belief, disability, age or sexual orientation as regards employment and occupation, with a view to putting into effect in the Member States the principle of equal treatment'. Differences of treatment on grounds of age would not constitute discrimination if they were 'reasonably justified by a legitimate aim' and if the means of 'achieving that aim are appropriate and necessary'. A German national law introduced a difference of treatment on the grounds directly of age.

As discussed above, Directives are not legally enforceable horizontally, and Directive 2000/78 could not therefore be relied on by Mr Mangold against Mr Helm. Furthermore,

---

75 Council Directive 90/314/EEC of 13 June 1990, Article 9.
76 See also **TUSGAL v Administracion del Estado** (2011).
77 See EU (Withdrawal) Act 2018, Schedule 1, paragraph 4.

the date for implementing Directive 2000/78 had not yet expired. Notwithstanding these difficulties, the Court of Justice of the EU ruled that any provision of national law which may conflict with EU law was to be set aside by the national court. It did so by resorting to the *source of the principle underlying the prohibition on forms of discrimination*. That source lay in various international instruments and in the constitutional traditions common to the Member States: 'the principle of non-discrimination on grounds of age must thus be regarded as a general principle of Community law' (see paras 74 and 75).

This controversial decision was followed in **Kukukdeveci v Swedex GmbH** (2009). This case involved a factual situation similar to **Mangold**, and the action involved two private parties. As in **Mangold**, the time for implementing the Directive had not yet expired. The CJEU once again stated that Directives could not have horizontal effect. Nevertheless, the Court ruled that national law conflicting with the fundamental principles of EU law should be disapplied.[78]

 Pause and Reflect

Making reference to case law, explain the constitutional significance of the CJEU's extension of the concepts of vertical and horizontal effect, indirect effect and state liability. What explains the CJEU's reluctance to extend horizontal effect to Directives?

Summarising direct and indirect effect

Article 288 of the Treaty on the Functioning of the European Union (TFEU)

TREATY PROVISIONS	Direct effect if clear and unconditional: ***Van Gend en Loos*** (1963)	Vertical and horizontal effect
REGULATIONS	Direct effect if clear and unconditional: Article 288 and ***Commission v Italy*** (1972)	Vertical and horizontal effect
DIRECTIVES	Direct effect if: the date for implementation has passed: ***Marshall*** (1984); and the text is clear and unconditional: ***Van Duyn*** (1975)	Vertical effect only

---

78 In **Dominguez v Centre informatique du Centre Ouest Atlantique** (2012), the CJEU was asked for a preliminary ruling in respect of a Directive (2003/88) relating to the right to annual paid leave. The CJEU did not follow the cases of **Mangold** and **Kucukdeveci** (above), but stated that if an individual was unable to rely on a Directive and if the party concerned was injured as a result of domestic law not being in conformity with European law, he or she could rely on **Francovich** (1991) in order to obtain compensation for the loss sustained.

Exceptions to the Rule that Directives Have Only Vertical Effect

Indirect effect	TEU A 4(3) imposes a duty on Member States, including national courts, to apply EU law: *Von Colson* (1984)
State liability	(i) the Directive confers an individual right; (ii) the failure of the State causes damage/loss which is causally related to the failure: *Francovich* (1992)

Understanding Human Rights in Europe

There is frequently confusion as to the source of rights within continental Europe, and it is essential to distinguish between the different legal bases which underpin rights. The principal distinction to be drawn is between rights protected under the Council of Europe and the European Union. The two organisations are formally distinct and separate, although as will be seen, the European Union is founded on the rights and freedoms guaranteed by the Convention on Human Rights which exists under the umbrella of the Council of Europe, which predates the European Union.

The Council of Europe was founded in 1949 with the express purpose of protecting individual rights and freedoms. The Council has a membership of some 47 states and is quite separate and distinct from the European Union. It was under the authority of the Council of Europe that the European Convention on Human Rights and Fundamental Freedoms (ECHR) was drafted and implemented. The rights are ultimately interpreted and enforced by the Court of Human Rights and the Committee of Ministers of the Council of Europe.

See Chapter 18.

Accordingly, the European Convention on Human Rights is the principal treaty under which rights and freedoms are protected throughout Europe. However, as the European Community and Union have developed, there has emerged a separate, parallel, mechanism for the protection of rights, enforced not by the European Court of Human Rights in Strasbourg, but by the CJEU in Luxembourg. As a result, rights in Europe are protected under domestic law, the law of the ECHR and the law of the EU. This may be portrayed as follows:

The protection of rights and freedoms stems from:

- the domestic (or national) law of Member States;
- the European Convention on Human Rights and Fundamental Freedoms (ECHR);
- the law of the European Union, with specific Treaty articles stipulating rights (e.g. the right to equal pay etc.);
- the EU's Charter of Fundamental Rights and Freedoms;
- the law of the European Union which regards the rights protected under the ECHR as part of the general principles of EU law, and accordingly enforceable by the Court of Justice of the EU (see Article 6(2) TEU).

In order to understand human rights law, therefore, it is necessary to understand the various sources of law and the relationship/interaction between them.

National law

- All European States which are members of the European Union have written constitutions. Human rights are a key feature of written constitutions, and all domestic laws must comply with the constitution, as interpreted by the Supreme (Constitutional) Court.

- With membership of the Council of Europe and the European Union, domestic laws must conform to the requirements of the European Convention on Human Rights and European Union law.

The Council of Europe
- All Member States of the EU are members (High Contracting Parties) of the Council of Europe, membership of which is a condition of membership of the EU.
- The European Convention on Human Rights, promulgated by the Council of Europe, sets out the civil and political rights which all European states are obliged to respect and protect.

The European Union
- The European Union is founded on respect for the rights set out in the European Convention on Human Rights (Article 6(2) Treaty on European Union 1992), which provides that:

> The Union shall respect fundamental rights, as guaranteed by the European Convention for the Protection of Human Rights and Fundamental Freedoms signed in Rome on 4 November 1950 and as they result from the constitutional traditions common to the Member States, as general principles of Community law.

- Specific rights are provided for in the Treaties, for example the right to equal pay and equal treatment in employment (Article 157 TFEU).
- Under the Lisbon Treaty 2007, the Charter of Fundamental Rights and Freedoms, which covers civil and political and economic and social rights, comes into effect. Note that the United Kingdom has opted out of the Charter.
- The Court of Justice of the EU (CJEU) does not have jurisdiction to rule on rights protected by the national law of Member States or the ECHR. However the CJEU has – through its case law – incorporated into EU law those fundamental rights and freedoms which are common to Member States (see for example **Internationale Handelsgesellschaft** (1970); **Simmanthal** (1979); **Kadi** (2008); **FIAMM** (2008)).

It is inevitable that situations will arise where the relationship between the Charter and the ECHR falls for consideration, particularly since the Lisbon Treaty provides for the EU to become a signatory to the ECHR.[79]

The original Treaties made no explicit reference to the protection of individual rights in their entirety, although Treaty articles such as Article 141 EC provide for equal treatment of men and women in matters of employment. The manner in which the CJEU has developed the jurisprudence on rights is linked inextricably with its insistence on the supremacy of Community law over the domestic law of Member States. **Internationale Handelsgesellschaft mbH v EVST** (1970) clarified the relationship between domestic constitutional law and Community law in the protection of rights. The CJEU expressed its opinion that respect for fundamental rights

> forms an integral part of the general principles of law protected by the Court of Justice. The protection of such rights, whilst inspired by the constitutional

---

79 An early example of a case concerning rights under EC law and the ECHR was **Bosphorus Hava Yollari Turizm ve Ticaret AS v Minister for Transport, Energy and Communications** (1996).

traditions common to the Member States, must be ensured within the framework of the structures and objectives of the Community.[80]

On a piecemeal, case-by-case basis, the CJEU has gradually and steadily incorporated the protection of individual rights into its case law. However, while all Member States of the Union are signatories to the ECHR, the Union is not a party to the ECHR, and the relationship between the Union and ECHR remains indistinct. The CJEU accepts the significance of the ECHR, and regards the ECHR provisions as part of the general principles of EU law. If and when the EU accedes to the ECHR as envisaged by the Treaty of Lisbon, the ECHR will become a central, integral part of EU law.[81]

The Treaty of Amsterdam 1997, reiterating the fundamental commitment of the Union to human rights and fundamental freedoms, introduced the power to issue penalties to Member States who are in breach of rights. Aware of the potential problems entailed in the enlargement of the Union, the Treaty provides for a penalty falling short of expulsion from the Union, a penalty which itself could undermine the protection of rights of that Member State's citizens. The principle of respect for human rights is also binding on Member States when acting within the scope of EU law, namely when implementing an EU measure,[82] or seeking to derogate from a fundamental freedom.[83]

The Charter of Fundamental Rights

The European Union's Charter of Fundamental Rights originated in 2000. The Treaty of Lisbon declares that the Charter has 'legally binding value'. The Charter does not replace either the human rights laws of Member States or the ECHR, but rather reinforces the EU's commitment to the protection of individual rights.

The Charter contains civil, economic, political and social rights which must be respected by the institutions of the EU and by Member States when implementing EU law. Because of its potentially wide-ranging implications, the Czech Republic, Poland and the United Kingdom negotiated exemptions from the Charter, creating uncertainty regarding the uniform application of EU law throughout the European Union. The Charter is not part of the EU law which will be retained at the end of the UK's leaving process.

Summary

The origins of the European Union lie in the Treaties establishing the European Coal and Steel Community (the Treaty of Paris 1951), the Atomic Energy Community and the European Economic Community (the Treaty of Rome 1957). Originally having six Member States, the European Union now has a membership of 27 States.

Under the Treaties there are now five principal institutions:[84]

- the European Council, headed by a President and having a High Representative for Foreign Affairs;
- the Council (formerly known as the Council of Ministers), representing the interests of Member States;

---

80 See also **Nold v Commission** (1974).
81 On this see Schermers, 1990 and 1987; Dremczewski, 1981.
82 *Wauchauf v Bundescourt für Ernährung und Fortwistschalt* (1989).
83 **ERT v Dimotiki** (1991).
84 Other institutions include the Court of Auditors, the European Ombudsman, specialist institutions such as the Economic and Social Committee.

- the European Commission (independent of nominating governments and representing the interests of the EU);
- the European Parliament, directly elected and representing the interests of the citizens of Europe;
- the Court of Justice of the European Union, the highest court in the Union with the task of interpreting and applying European Union law.

The European Union (EU) came into being in 1993 with the Treaty on European Union (the Maastricht Treaty). With the expansion in membership, the organisation of the EU required adaptation. The Treaty of Lisbon 2007, ratified in 2009, effects this. The two principal Treaties are now the Treaty on European Union and the Treaty on the Functioning of the European Union, which replaces the EC Treaty.

The sources of EU law include the Treaties, Regulations, Directives and Decisions. EU law takes effect within the legal systems of Member States through the concepts of direct and indirect effect and the liability of the state.

Further Reading

Birkinshaw, P, 'Constitutions, constitutionalism and the state' (2005) 11 *European Public Law* 31.

Craig, P, 'The Treaty of Lisbon, process, architecture and substance' (2008) 33 *European Law Review* 137.

Craig, P, 'Britain in the European Union' in J Jowell and D Oliver (eds), *The Changing Constitution*, 7th edn, 2011, Oxford: Oxford University Press.

Dougan, M, 'The Treaty of Lisbon 2007: winning minds, not hearts' (2008) 45 *Common Market Law Review* 617.

Doukas, D, 'The verdict of the German federal constitutional court on the Lisbon Treaty: not guilty, but don't do it again' (2009) 34 *European Law Review* 866.

Harlow, C, 'European governance and accountability' in M Bamforth and P Leyland (eds), *Public Law in a Multi-Layered Constitution*, 2003, Oxford: Hart Publishing.

Harlow, C and Rawlings, R, 'Accountability and law enforcement: the centralised EU infringement procedure' (2006) 31 *European Law Review* 447, 226 and 228 EC.

Lenaerts, K, 'The rule of law and the coherence of the judicial system of the EU' (2007) 44 *Common Market Law Review* 1625.

Peers, S, 'Finally "fit for purpose"? The Treaty of Lisbon and the end of the third pillar legal order' (2008) 27 *Yearbook European Law* 47.

Rasmussen, H, 'Present and future European judicial problems after enlargement and the post-2005 ideological revolt' (2007) 44 Common *Market Law Review* 1661.

Sadurski, W, 'Solange, chapter 3: constitutional courts in Central Europe – democracy – European Union' (2008) 14 *European Law Journal* 1.

Schutze, R, 'Cooperative federalism constitutionalised: the emergence of complementary competences in the EU legal order' (2006) 31 *European Law Review* 167.

Schutze, R, 'From Rome to Lisbon: "executive federalism" in the (new) European Union' (2010) 47 *Common Market Law Review* 1385.

Shaw, J, 'Europe's constitutional future' [2005] *Public Law* 132.

Snyder, F, 'Enhancing EU democracy, constituting the EU' (2005) 11 *European Law Journal* 131.

Somek, A, 'Postconstitutional treaty' (2007) 8 *German Law Journal* 1121.

Walker, N, 'European constitutionalism and European integration' [2005] *Public Law* 266.

Chapter **8**

European Union Law and National Law

Chapter Contents

Learning Objectives

By the end of this chapter you should be able to:

- [ ] discuss the interaction between the Court of Justice of the EU and national courts;
- [ ] with reference to case law, discuss the CJEU's view on the supremacy of EU law;
- [ ] with reference to case law, explain the English courts' view on supremacy during membership of the EU;
- [ ] explain the constitutional issues involved in withdrawing from the EU.

Introduction

Having examined the structure, institutions and sources of EU law, it is now necessary to turn attention to the interaction between EU law and the domestic law of Member States. From 1973 until its departure from the EU in 2020, a vast body of EU law had entered the domestic law of the UK. This body of law remains relevant after the UK has left the EU ('post Brexit'), as will be discussed below.

With the membership of the European Union at 27 Member States, the task of ensuring that the law is interpreted and applied in a uniform manner is complex. As discussed in Chapter 7, the differing forms of law – principally Treaty Articles, Regulations and Directives – have differing effects and leave to the Member States differing degrees of discretion relating to their implementation. For the law to be uniform it is essential that the domestic courts work in partnership with the Court of Justice of the EU (CJEU) and that – where necessary – the domestic courts seek the advice of the CJEU on the correct interpretation of the law. It will be seen that the CJEU has, since the 1960s, insisted on the supremacy of EU law over domestic law. From the Court's point of view, what has been created is nothing less than a new legal order: a **supranational** organisation which imposes legal duties on Member States and creates enforceable legal rights for citizens. In order to achieve this supremacy, the Court insists that Member States have, in signing the Treaties, surrendered or transferred part of their sovereign law-making powers over matters governed by the Treaties to the institutions of the EU. Furthermore the Court, in its role as 'guardian of the Treaties', has to ensure that EU law is given priority over domestic law.

The Interaction Between National Courts and the Court of Justice of the EU (CJEU)[1]

Article 267 of the Treaty on the Functioning of the EU (TFEU) represents a vital means by which the harmony of laws between Member States is achieved. The CJEU is insistent both that EU law has supremacy and that it be uniformly applied within Member States. The task of uniformity is problematic as all nation states adopt and adapt to the requirements of EU law. Article 267 enables the courts in Member States to refer a question of EU law for interpretation by the CJEU. Once that interpretation has been undertaken, the issue is returned to the domestic courts to reach a decision in accordance with the CJEU's interpretation of EU law. For optimum effectiveness, a balance needs to be struck between making references to the CJEU where necessary and the domestic courts being able to apply EU law without undue delay or cost. The obligation to refer applies equally to adversarial and inquisitorial legal systems.[2]

The text of Article 267 is set out on pages 189 to 190, and from this it can be seen that courts or tribunals may refer a question, provided that it is a question of EU law – and not national law – which requires interpretation, and provided also that a decision of the CJEU is necessary to enable the national court to reach a decision in the case. A reference becomes mandatory when the question of law is before a court or tribunal of last resort, that is to say, a court or tribunal from which there is no further appeal. This does not always mean the Supreme Court: in many cases, the appeal structure will end lower in the hierarchy, or leave to appeal may be needed and be refused. Accordingly the court of last resort may effectively be at any level in the judicial hierarchy. If no appeal is possible and the other criteria of a question of EU law and the necessity for interpretation exist, a reference must be made. In **Costa v ENEL** (1964), the reference was from a magistrates' court and involved a claim of less than £2 in value; no right of appeal existed because the amount in issue was so small.

---

1 See Watson, 1986; Winter, 1972; Curtin, 1990; Pescatore, 1983.
2 See **Kelly v National University of Ireland** (2012).

The English Court of Appeal, in **Bulmer v Bollinger** (1974), considered the question of when references to the CJEU should be made, and Lord Denning laid down the following guidelines for English courts to apply when a reference was a matter of discretion:

(a) the decision must be necessary to enable the court to give judgment – a court must feel that it cannot reach a decision unless a reference is made;
(b) the decision of the question must be conclusive to the case – not just a peripheral issue;
(c) even if the court considers a reference to be necessary, regard must still be paid to the delay involved, the expense, the difficulty of the point of law, and the burden on the CJEU.

These 'guidelines' were questionable in so far as they could impede the willingness of a court to refer matters to the CJEU, and they represented a gloss on the wording of Article 267 TFEU. Note that from the end of 2020 the UK courts will no longer make reference to the CJEU.

An impediment to referral may arise from the European doctrine of *acte clair* – the concept which states that if a matter is so obvious in its meaning to the domestic court, then no reference need be made. As with the **Bulmer v Bollinger** guidelines, the doctrine of *acte clair* can lead to distortions in interpretation within domestic legal systems. The CJEU has itself considered the circumstances under which courts should refer, and the doctrine of *acte clair*,[3] in the **CILFIT** case of 1982.[4] The Court was asked to consider the meaning of Article 177(3) (now 267) which relates to mandatory references from a court of last resort. The Court ruled that:

(a) there is no duty to refer where a question of Community law was irrelevant – that is, if the interpretation can have no effect on the outcome of the case;
(b) there is no duty to refer when the question is one substantially the same as one previously answered by the CJEU;
(c) there is no need to refer where no real doubt about the law exists. The national court must, however, be satisfied that the matter is equally obvious to courts of other Member States and to the CJEU. To this limited extent, the doctrine of *acte clair* is endorsed.

In **CILFIT**, the CJEU emphasised that the purpose of Article 177 EEC Treaty (now Article 267 TFEU), in general, was to ensure the proper application and uniform interpretation of EC law in all Member States and to prevent divergencies occurring within Member States.[5] This objective, however, may be frustrated if domestic courts within any one or more of the now 28 Member States' legal systems misinterprets the meaning of EU law. In **Kobler v Republik Österreich** (2003) the CJEU returned to the doctrine of *acte clair* and the duty imposed on national courts of last resort to refer questions to the CJEU. The Austrian Court held that a question arising under Article 39 EC (now Article 45 TFEU) had been settled by an earlier decision of the CJEU and decided it was *acte clair* and stopped the reference procedure. The applicant sought compensation from the Austrian government, arguing that he had suffered financial loss as a result of the national court's decision. The CJEU held that the Austrian Supreme Administrative Court had been wrong to hold that the matter was *acte clair*, in that the precedent case had not decided the issue in question and that where a national court incorrectly interpreted and applied EU law that could give rise to state liability, which under certain circumstances entitles the applicant to compensation.

---

3 The concept derives from French law.
4 [1982] ECR 3415; [1983] 1 CMLR 337.
5 See **Grattan plc v Revenue and Customs Commissioners** (2011).

The CJEU returned once more to *acte clair* in **Traghetti del Mediterraneo SpA v Italy** (2006). In this case concerning EU competition law, Traghetti brought an action for damages against the state based on the court of last instance's wrongful interpretation of EU law and its failure to refer to the CJEU. The CJEU ruled that failure to refer could be classified as an infringement of EU law which gives rise to state liability.

Whereas national courts have some discretion as to whether to refer a matter to the CJEU, the position is different in relation to matters of validity – as opposed to interpretation – of EU law. It is clear that the CJEU has the sole power to rule on whether a measure of EU law is invalid. It is not for national courts to rule on that question. National courts only have the power to uphold the validity of EC legislation.

As seen from the text of Article 267 TFEU, the questions which may be referred are:

(a)   interpretation of the Treaties;
(b)   the validity and interpretation of acts of institutions of the Community: Regulations, Directives, etc.

Once the CJEU accepts jurisdiction – and a discretion is conferred on the CJEU over whether or not to accept jurisdiction – and gives a ruling, the matter is then returned to the domestic court for application, thus preserving the partnership ideal.

The Court of Justice considered the duty of a national court to refer a question under the discretionary second paragraph of Article 234 (as it then was; now Article 267) in **R (International Air Transport Association and European Low Fares Airline Association) v Department of Transport** (2006). Where a party had raised questions on the validity of an EU instrument which the court considered arguable and not unfounded, that court had a duty to stay proceedings and refer the matter to the Court of Justice for a preliminary ruling on validity.

In **Kelly v National University of Ireland (University College, Dublin)** (2012), the CJEU considered whether the obligation to make a reference to the CJEU, under Article 267 TFEU, differed in a Member State with an adversarial, rather than an inquisitorial, legal system. The CJEU explained that the preliminary ruling mechanism was one designed to avoid differences in the interpretation of European Union law and to eliminate difficulties in the application of EU law. The reference procedure represents 'direct co-operation' between the Court of Justice and the national courts. In the CJEU's view, it is for the national courts to decide whether an interpretation of EU law by the CJEU is necessary to enable it to reach a decision, and it is also for the national court to decide how to frame the question. In relation to differing legal systems within the EU, whether a system was adversarial or inquisitorial made no difference to the obligation to refer.

What is the legal position when a higher court establishes a precedent which is binding on a lower court, but which conflicts with a decision of the CJEU? In **Rheinmullen-Dusseldorf** (1973), the CJEU ruled that national procedures could not prevent a lower court from making further preliminary references to the CJEU to clarify the law. Furthermore,[6] a lower court is under a duty to depart from the precedent of a higher court where that precedent conflicts with EU law.

---

6 **Elchinov v NZOK** (2009).

SELF-TEST QUESTIONS

Under what circumstances **may** a domestic court make a reference under Article 267?

Under what circumstances **must** a domestic court make a reference under Article 267?

The Question of Legal Supremacy

The question of legal supremacy can be examined both from the standpoint of the EU and from that of national law.

The Court of Justice of the EU's view

The CJEU claims that EU law is supreme over national law. This claim carries the following implications:

(a)   EU law confers rights on individuals to which national law must give effect;

(b)   national law cannot prevail over EU law;

(c)   the effectiveness of EU law must be the same in all Member States – it cannot vary in effect from one Member State to another;

(d)   courts of Member States must follow the interpretation of laws given by the CJEU or, where there is no authority, and under certain conditions, they must refer the matter to the CJEU under Article 267 of the Treaty;

(e)   where the CJEU gives a ruling, Member States are under an obligation to amend their national laws so as to conform to EU law.

The CJEU has asserted the supremacy of EC/EU law on many occasions. The early cases lay the foundations for the current relationship between domestic law and EU law. The starting point is once again the case of *Van Gend en Loos v Nederlandse Tariefcommissie* (1963), in which the CJEU enunciated the view that, by signing the Treaties, the Member States had created a new legal order, in which individual states had limited their sovereign rights. In **Costa v ENEL** (1964), this view was reaffirmed by the CJEU:

> The transfer by the states from their domestic legal system to the Community (now EU) legal system of the rights and obligations arising under the Treaty carries with it a permanent limitation of their sovereign rights against which a subsequent unilateral act incompatible with the concept of Community law cannot prevail.

Internationale Handelsgesellschaft mbH v EVST (1970) took the principle of EC supremacy further. Under EC law, in order to export produce, the company was required to obtain a licence, for which a 'permanent deposit' had to be paid. If the goods were not exported within the licence period, the deposit was to be forfeited. The company paid the deposit and failed to complete the export, and forfeiture was made. The firm sued the agency involved for return of the deposit, arguing that the forfeiture was contrary to the Constitution of the Federal Republic of Germany. The matter was referred to the CJEU.

The CJEU declared that giving effect to rules or concepts of national law contained even within the constitution of a state, for the purposes of judging the validity of EC measures, would have an adverse effect on the uniformity and efficacy of EC law. The validity of EC measures could be judged only in the light of EC law and could not be affected by allegations that the measures ran counter to fundamental rights as formulated by the constitution of the Member State. Having made this unequivocal and controversial statement, the CJEU softened its tone, ruling that the respect for fundamental rights forms an integral part of the 'general principles of law' protected by the CJEU, and that the protection of such rights, inspired by traditions common to Member States, must be ensured within the framework of the structure and objectives of the EC.

The **Simmenthal** case (1979) further developed the jurisprudence of the CJEU in relation to supremacy. Simmenthal imported beef from France into Italy. Under Italian legislation of 1970, fees for veterinary and health checks had to be paid by the importer at the frontier. Simmenthal sued the Italian Minister of Finance for return of the money, arguing that the fee was equivalent to a customs duty and was contrary to Article 12 of the Treaty and Community Regulations on the common organisation of beef imports. The national court ordered the Ministry to return the money. The Minister pleaded that the domestic 1970 Act was binding unless and until set aside by the Italian Constitutional Court.

The Italian court was thus faced with a conflict between Article 12, as it then was, of the Treaty and a later Italian statute. A reference was made, the question at issue being whether directly applicable Regulations required national courts to disregard subsequently passed domestic legislation, without waiting for the Constitutional Court to declare it invalid. The CJEU held that Regulations take precedence over previous and subsequent domestic legislation and that a national court, whatever its position or role in the national judicial hierarchy, must set aside any provision which conflicts with EC law and apply EC law in its entirety, without waiting until the domestic legislation had been set aside by the Constitutional Court.

The **European Road Transport Agreement (ERTA)** case (**Commission v Council**) (1971) offers another perspective.[7] In 1962, several European states, five of which were EC Member States, others being Eastern European states, signed the European Road Transport Agreement, which sought to establish common rules concerning conditions of work of long-distance lorry drivers crossing several state boundaries. As such, the Agreement was not an EC agreement. In 1969, the EC had acted for the (then) six Member States by issuing a Regulation covering the same issue. In 1970, the matter was further complicated by the Council meeting to attempt to find a common basis for a new transport agreement. The Commission attempted to have the proceedings of the Council annulled on the basis that the Council was not competent to reach agreements of this kind.[8]

At the heart of the matter lay the question as to who had the power – Member States, the Council or the Commission – to make such 'international' agreements. If Member States retained the power to enter into international agreements (and such a power is a basic attribute of sovereignty), then the Council proceedings were merely recommendatory; if the Council had power then the proceedings took on more of a law-making character, which deprived the Member States of competence to act either unilaterally or collectively. The Court held that, having regard to the legal personality of the Community (now EU), the sole power to enter into such agreements would, by implication, vest in the Community (now EU) institutions, thus depriving Member States of any capacity in this regard.[9]

In summary, the effect of these early cases is that, since 1962, the CJEU has declared the existence of a new legal order, one to which Member States have limited their sovereign rights

7 See Mancini and Keeling, 1991.
8 Article 217 TFEU. The power to enter treaties is conferred under Article 310 EC Treaty. In 2006, the Court of Justice reaffirmed the Community's exclusive competence to conclude treaties: see Press Release No. 10/06, 7 February 2006, Opinion 1/03.
9 See also **Commission v Finland** (2002).

by transferring these to the EU. These rights include even the protection of constitutionally guaranteed individual rights. Further, it matters not whether a domestic law in conflict with EU law was passed prior to accession to the Union or subsequently; neither can prevail over EU law. Third, where the EU has the power to act on behalf of Member States in the making of international agreements, Member States have lost that capacity.

Before examining the position of the English courts during membership of the EU, it is necessary to consider the means by which EU law was received into domestic law.

MONISM AND DUALISM

The Reception of EU Law into the United Kingdom from 1973 to 2020

The concepts of monism and dualism

At a conceptual level, the manner in which international law, of which EU law may be regarded as a *sui generis* (that is to say, unique) example, is dependent upon whether a particular state adopts a monist or dualist approach to international law. Monism is the doctrine whereby international law and national law form a single whole, or part of the same conceptual structure, in which international law takes precedence. Under this doctrine, adhered to by, *inter alia*, France and Italy, the obligations of international law, once assumed, enter automatically into the legal system, needing no domestic legislative acts. Once entered, the obligations take precedence over national law.

Dualism, on the other hand, regards the systems of international law and national law as separate: in order for international law to enter into national law, some domestic legislation must be enacted by the national Parliament. This is the view adopted by the United Kingdom and is one consistent with the sovereignty of Parliament. Treaties are part of international law, and can have no effect in domestic law unless and until a statute of the sovereign United Kingdom Parliament is enacted to give them effect.

In 1972, Lord Denning MR confirmed this view in **Blackburn v Attorney General** (1971):

> Even if a Treaty is signed, it is elementary that these courts take no notice of trea-
> ties as such. We take no notice of treaties until they are embodied in laws enacted
> by Parliament, and then only to the extent that Parliament tells us. [page 1382]

Accordingly, the signing of the EC Treaties, without any further parliamentary action, had
no effect in English law. In order to have effect, it was necessary for Parliament to pass the
European Communities Act 1972.

The European Communities Act 1972

Note that the European Union (Withdrawal) Act 2019 repeals the European Communities Act
1972 with effect from the end of the transition period after leaving the EU (December 2020).
What follows is a discussion of the legal position during the UK's membership of the EU.

The most fundamental provisions of the Act can be found in sections 2 and 3(1). Here
it is specified that rights and duties which are directly applicable or effective are to be given
legal effect within the United Kingdom; that the executive has the power to give effect to EU
obligations; that existing and future enactments are to be interpreted and have effect; and that
the meaning or effect of Treaty provisions is to be decided according to EU law.

The view of the United Kingdom courts

The manner in which, and extent to which, the United Kingdom courts have accommodated
EU obligations requires consideration. First, it should be noted that nothing in the European
Communities Act (ECA) 1972 represented an attempt to entrench its provisions, that is to say,
to make them immune from amendment or repeal. There was no statement in the Act that
EU law is a 'higher form of law', or that the Act could not be repealed, or could be repealed
but only by some specified 'manner and form'. As discussed in Chapter 6, however, it is clear
that the doctrine of implied repeal did not operate in relation to the ECA 1972.

Two early challenges were made to the signing of the Treaty on the basis of the potential
or actual loss of parliamentary sovereignty. In **Blackburn v Attorney General** in 1971, the plaintiff
sought a declaration that the government, by signing the Treaty of Rome, would surrender
part of Parliament's sovereignty which it could not lawfully do, as no Parliament could bind
another. In **McWhirter v Attorney General** (1972), the plaintiff adduced that joining the EC (now
EU) was contrary to the Bill of Rights 1689, which declared that all powers of government
are vested in the Crown and Parliament could not, therefore, by means of a Treaty, transfer
those rights. In both cases, the arguments were disposed of with speed. In **Blackburn**, Lord
Denning MR emphasised that even if a treaty is signed, the courts take no notice of it until it
is embodied in an Act of Parliament.

Conflicts between EU law and UK domestic law[10]

One area of law which gave rise to an instructive array of case law concerning the relationship between domestic law and EU law is that of sex discrimination. In **Macarthys v Smith**

---

10 See, *inter alia*, Szyszczack, 1990; de Búrca, 1992a and 1992b.

(1981), Mrs Smith was employed by Macarthys as a stockroom manageress. The man who had previously held the position had been paid a higher wage than Mrs Smith. The applicable domestic legislation was the Equal Pay Act 1970, as amended by the Sex Discrimination Act 1975, which provided, *inter alia*, that men and women employed in the same job should be paid equal amounts. The Act was silent, however, as to whether employers were required to pay the same wage to a woman who came to the job after the man had left their employment. The relevant point for interpretation, therefore, was whether men and women, employed at differing times for the same job, were required to be paid equally.[11]

Article 141, now Article 157 TFEU (formerly Article 119) of the EC Treaty provides for equal pay for men and women. This Article is couched in far broader terms than those used by the Equal Pay Act 1970. The CJEU held that Article 119 required equal pay for men and women whether they were employed contemporaneously or in succession. On receiving the judgment of the ECJ (now CJEU), the Court of Appeal ruled in favour of Mrs Smith. Lord Denning's judgment was of particular significance:

> In construing our statute, we are entitled to look to the Treaty as an aid in its con-struction: and even more, not only as an aid, but as an overriding force. If on close investigation it should appear that our legislation is deficient – or is inconsistent with Community law – by some oversight of our draftsmen – then it is our bounden duty to give priority to Community law. Such is the result of section 2(1) and (4) of the European Communities Act 1972.

> Thus far, I have assumed that our Parliament, whenever it passes legislation, intends to fulfil its obligations under the Treaty. If the time should come when our Parliament deliberately passes an Act with the intention of repudiating the Treaty or any provision in it – or intentionally of acting inconsistently with it – and says so in express terms – then I should have thought that it would be the duty of our courts to follow the statute of our Parliament.

Article 141 fell for further consideration in **Garland v British Rail Engineering Ltd** in 1983, this time by the House of Lords. British Rail made concessionary travel facilities available to the children of male employees reaching retirement, but not to the children of women reaching retirement. The question was whether this policy amounted to discrimination contrary to EC law and whether the courts in England should construe the Sex Discrimination Act 1975 in a manner so as to make it compatible with the requirements of EC law. The House of Lords referred the matter to the CJEU, which ruled that the policy amounted to discrimination contrary to EC law, and that EC law must prevail.

In **Duke v GEC Reliance Ltd** (1988), the House of Lords considered the construction of section 6(4) of the Sex Discrimination Act 1975. In the **Duke** case, the plaintiff's claim for damages based on unequal treatment was for a period prior to Parliament's amendment of the Sex Discrimination Act to bring English law into line with the requirements of European law. The House of Lords declined to give retrospective effect to the amendment in light of Parliament's express decision not to amend the Act retrospectively. One interpretation of **Duke** is that, being a pre-**Marleasing** case – which makes it clear that the Article 10 (now Article 4.3

---

11 Where women whose work was of equal value to men when employed by a local authority were transferred to another employer by the local authority, the new employer was not obliged to pay the women the same rate as previously. There was no violation of Article 141(1) of the EC Treaty since there was no one body which was responsible for the irregularity and could bring about equal treatment: **Lawrence v Regent Office Care Ltd** (2000).

TEU) duty is imposed on national courts – the House of Lords was in line with the CJEU's interpretation of the law at the time.

In **Litster v Forth Dry Dock Ltd** (1990), however, the House of Lords interpreted a domestic Regulation contrary to its clear meaning in order to comply with a Directive as interpreted by the CJEU. The domestic Regulation had been introduced for the purpose of complying with the Directive and, accordingly, the House of Lords was complying with its duty under section 2(4) of the ECA 1972 to give effect to Community law.[12]

In **Webb v EMO Cargo (UK) Ltd** (1992), the issue of dismissal on the basis of pregnancy was considered in relation to the Directive on Equal Treatment. The English Trades Union Reform and Employment Rights Act 1993 provides that dismissal on the grounds of pregnancy is unfair.[13] However, in **Webb v EMO Cargo (UK) Ltd** (1992), the Court of Appeal ruled, and the House of Lords affirmed, that a woman who was dismissed from employment because of her pregnancy was not unlawfully dismissed, since – comparing her to a man with a temporary physical disability who would also have been unable to work – the man would also have been dismissed. The CJEU ruled that English law was inadequate and held, first, that pregnancy was not a pathological condition to be compared with illness and, second, that a pregnant woman's inability to work was temporary and not permanent. Accordingly, the dismissal had amounted to sex discrimination.[14]

The House of Lords, in **Webb v EMO Air Cargo (UK) Ltd (No 2)** (1995) ruled that sections 1(1)(a) and 5(3) of the 1975 Act were to be construed in accordance with the ECJ's (now CJEU) ruling.[15]

In **Grant v South West Trains Ltd** (1998), the CJEU apparently reached the limits of its respect for equality. A Southampton employment tribunal had referred a question to the CJEU concerning whether the female partner of a lesbian woman was entitled to the same employment benefits enjoyed by married or cohabiting heterosexual couples. The CJEU ruled that there had been no violation of the Treaty on the basis of sexual inequality.[16,17,18]

Undoubtedly, the most constitutionally significant British case revealing the relationship between European law and domestic law during the UK's membershiip of the EU was that of **R v Secretary of State for Transport ex parte Factortame** (1991). In 1970, the Council of Ministers passed a Regulation relating to the common organisation of the market in fishery products. The basic principle employed was that, subject to certain exceptions, there should be equal access for the fishing vessels of all Member States to the fishing grounds of fellow Member States. In 1983, due to fears of over-fishing caused by such open access, the Council established, by way of Regulation, a system for the conservation and management of resources. This entailed, in part, setting limits to the amount of fish to be caught in certain periods by way of 'total allowable catches' – the allocation of total allowable catches being fairly distributed among the Member States by way of national quotas. The quotas were based on the number of ships flying the flag of a Member State or registered in a Member State.

Spain acceded to the EC in 1986. Before 1986, the extent to which Spanish vessels could ship in British waters was determined under agreements between the Spanish and United

---

12 See further below on the 1972 Act. See also **Finnegan v Clowney Youth Training Programme Ltd** (1990).

13 Trades Union Reform and Employment Rights Act 1993, ss 23–25 and Scheds 2 and 3; EC Pregnancy Directive 92/85.

14 **Dekker v VJV Centrum** (1991).

15 In **Strathclyde Regional Council v Wallace** (1998), the House of Lords ruled that an objectively justifiable employment practice which was not 'tainted' by sexual discrimination, which resulted in unequal pay, did not contravene the Equal Pay Act 1970, relying on **Bilka-Kaufhaus GmbH v Weber von Hartz** (1987), EC Treaty, Article 119 (now Article 141).

16 Note that discrimination on the basis of sexual orientation is now unlawful. See **KB v National Health Service Pensions Agency** (2004).

17 See also **Cadman v Health and Safety Executive, Equal Opportunities Commission, intervenor** (2006) and **Rutherford v Secretary of State for Trade and Industry** (2006).

18 See also **Palacios de la Villa v Cortfiel Servicios SA** (2007).

Kingdom governments. Under English law, the Merchant Shipping Act 1894 prohibited non-British nationals from owning British fishing vessels but did permit corporate ownership by British companies. Thus, directors/shareholders of Spanish vessels were able to register under the 1894 Act. Some 96 Spanish fishing boats were registered under the Act, and each of these vessels counted as part of the United Kingdom's quota under European law.

The United Kingdom government, understandably alarmed at the restrictions imposed on the domestic fishing industry and the ability of foreign companies to register and therefore take up part of the United Kingdom's quota, imposed additional conditions for registration which came into force in 1986. The three principal conditions for registration were to be that a proportion of the catch was to be sold in the United Kingdom; that 75 per cent of the crews were to be EC nationals ordinarily resident in the United Kingdom; and that all crew were to be required to contribute to the National Insurance Scheme.

In 1988, the United Kingdom Parliament passed the Merchant Shipping Act and enacted fresh merchant shipping Regulations. The new system of registration[19] entailed qualification on the basis of a 'genuine and substantial connection with the United Kingdom'. The revised conditions required that not less than 75 per cent of vessels be owned by United Kingdom citizens resident in the United Kingdom; or wholly owned in the United Kingdom, with 75 per cent of shareholders and directors in the United Kingdom; or part owned, with 75 per cent of owners in the United Kingdom; and, further, that vessels be effectively operated from the United Kingdom. Registration would be lost with effect from 31 March 1989 until vessel owners could satisfy the government that they were eligible for registration.

As a result, Factortame, which did not comply with these more stringent requirements, challenged the domestic requirements as incompatible with European law, claiming discrimination on the grounds of nationality contrary to Article 14 of the Treaty and the rights of companies to establishment under Articles 43–48 (now Articles 49–52 TFEU). The Divisional Court, in 1990, granted an interim injunction against the government restraining it from applying the Merchant Shipping Act regulations until final judgment was made following a reference to the CJEU. The government appealed to the Court of Appeal, which ruled that the court had no jurisdiction to grant interim relief disapplying an Act of Parliament. On appeal to the House of Lords, the decision of the Court of Appeal was upheld: injunctive relief against the Crown was not within the court's jurisdiction.

Three constitutionally significant factors arose in **Factortame**: first, whether the court could protect alleged rather than established rights under European law; second, whether the English courts could grant injunctive relief against the Crown; and, third, the conditions under which such relief could be granted.

The CJEU, in its preliminary ruling on the first point (Case 213/89), held that the offending provisions of the Merchant Shipping Act should be suspended, pending a full determination of Factortame's claim, stating that:

> The full effectiveness of Community [now EU] law would be impaired if a rule of national law could prevent a court seized of a dispute governed by Community law from granting interim relief in order to ensure the full effectiveness of the judicial decision to be given on the existence of rights claimed under Community law.

The CJEU reverted to its decision in **Simmenthal** (1979), reiterating that directly applicable rules were to be fully and uniformly applied in all Member States in accordance with the principle of precedence of European law over national law. Article 5 of the EEC Treaty (see

---

19 SI 1988/1926.

now Article 4.3 TEU) imposes an obligation, as has been seen above, to ensure the legal protection which is provided for under the principle of direct effect. The House of Lords in **R v Secretary of State for Transport ex parte Factortame Ltd (No 2)** accepted the CJEU's ruling and granted interim relief.

In **R v HM Treasury ex parte British Telecommunications plc** (1993) (the **BT** case), the applicant sought an interim injunction which would have had the effect – as in **Factortame** – of causing national legislation to be disapplied while the substantive issue was being considered by the ECJ (now CJEU). In **Factortame**, great weight was attached to the very strong prima facie case put forward by the applicants. In the **BT** case, the Court of Appeal cautioned against over-reliance on the likelihood of success in the CJEU as a basis for granting relief. In part, this caution was based on the fact that a reference had been made to the CJEU, and that to give great weight to the prognosis for success was to prejudge the interpretation to be given by the CJEU. The fact that a reference had been made meant that the English court was uncertain as to the question in issue. Accordingly it would be inappropriate to prejudge the issue by granting relief at an interim stage. The Court of Appeal also warned of the difficulties in disapplying domestic legislation. As the court stated, there should be a distinction drawn between a 'major piece of primary legislation' and a 'minor piece of subordinate legislation'. In relation to the former, the court ruled that it would be far more circumspect than in relation to secondary legislation. In the instant case, unlike **Factortame**, the issues were not clear-cut. The court, ruling that it would only grant an interim order 'in the most compelling circumstances', declined to grant the injunction.[20]

The question of the compatibility of domestic law with EU law arose once more in the case of **R v Secretary of State for Employment ex parte Equal Opportunities Commission** (1995) (the **EOC** case). There, the Equal Opportunities Commission had brought an action challenging allegedly discriminatory employment protection provisions in English law, arguing that these contravened European Community legislation. The House of Lords, in a bold decision, granted a declaration to the effect that national law was incompatible with European law. However, the House of Lords did not go so far as to rule that the English provisions were void; rather, it confined its ruling to the compatibility issue – thus avoiding any potential conflict with Parliament and the concept of sovereignty.

 SELF-TEST QUESTION

Explain the concepts of monism and dualism. To which concept does the United Kingdom adhere and why?

'Brexit': The UK's Withdrawal from the EU

As discussed, in June 2016 the people of the United Kingdom voted in a referendum to leave the European Union, a decision which has major constitutional and legal implications for the UK. The referendum was regulated under the EU Referendum Act 2015. Under the UK constitution a referendum is advisory rather than binding. However, as the extract from **Shindler v Duchy of Lancaster** (2016) below shows, the 2016 referendum was judicially recognised as having rather more than 'advisory' status.

---

20 See also **R v Secretary of State for Health ex parte Imperial Tobacco Ltd** (2001) and **Lawrence v Regent Office Care Ltd** (2003); **Armstrong v Newcastle upon Tyne NHS Hospital Trust** (2005).

I accept that Parliament is sovereign and that it does not need the mandate of a referendum to give it the power to withdraw from the EU. But by passing the 2015 Act, Parliament has decided that it will not withdraw from the EU unless a withdrawal is supported by referendum. In theory, Parliament could decide to withdraw without waiting for the result of the referendum despite the passing of the 2015 Act. In short, by passing the 2015 Act, Parliament decided that one of the constitutional requirements that had to be satisfied as a condition of a withdrawal from the EU was a referendum. [at paragraph 19]

 Pause and Reflect

Revisit the discussion of *Attorney General for New South Wales v Trethowan* (1932) in Chapter 6. Compare the status of the Colonial Laws Validity Act 1865 in relation to the attempt to abolish the New South Wales Upper House with the dicta above on the EU Referendum Act 2015.

The process of withdrawing from the European Union – first formally provided for under the Lisbon Treaty of 2007 – centres on Article 50 of the Treaty on European Union (TEU).

Article 50 TEU provides that any Member State may decide to withdraw from the Union 'in accordance with its own constitutional requirements'.

Initiating the withdrawal process

Article 50 represents the only means by which a Member State can leave the EU. It is for the Member State wishing to withdraw from the EU to start the process by a formal notification to the European Council (comprising the Heads of Government of Member States); there is no time frame for when this must be done. Only the state wishing to leave the Union may trigger Article 50; other Member States cannot force that state to instigate the withdrawal process.

Article 50: royal prerogative or Act of Parliament?

As discussed in Chapter 5, the royal prerogative is the legal base for conducting foreign affairs. It was clear at an early stage following the referendum that the Government intended to initiate the Article 50 process under the royal prerogative, rather than an Act of Parliament. However, the Supreme Court ruled in **Miller v Secretary of State for Exiting the European Union** (2017)[21] that an Act of Parliament was required and that the process could not be initiated under the prerogative.

The European Union (Withdrawal) Act 2018 (as amended and on which see further below) regulated the withdrawal process. The 2018 Act repealed the European Communities Act 1972 at the end of the transition period following leaving the EU. Secondly, the Act preserved EU law as it was at the time immediately prior to leaving the EU, making it part of domestic law. The UK Parliament and devolved administrations can then decide which laws should be preserved, amended or repealed. Thirdly, the Act provides for secondary legislation to make necessary changes to laws that would otherwise not function effectively after leaving the EU.

---

21 See page 129.

The negotiating period

Following notification, Article 50 provides for a two-year period in which negotiations of the terms of exit take place, leading to a formal agreement. However, there is no requirement that an agreement is reached.[22] There is no explicit provision in Article 50 for renouncing the notification, and the CJEU ruled that a Member State could do so and remain a member, with the effect that the UK could have stopped the withdrawal process and remained in the EU.[23]

The role of EU institutions in the negotiations

Once notification was given, the formal negotiating process began. The European Council issued guidelines to the Council of the EU (Ministers from EU Member States) which then conferred negotiating powers on the Commission. Once negotiations were completed, a draft Withdrawal Agreement (an international treaty) was drawn up and had to be approved by the European Parliament, following which it would be ormally signed and concluded by the Council. The Agreement required an 'enhanced qualified majority' of Member States which could prevent any one Member State from vetoing the agreement. The majority required was agreement by 20 of the 27 remaining Member States, representing 65 per cent of the population of the EU. The Agreement also had to be ratified (formally approved according to their constitutional requirements) by each of the Member States and required the approval of the UK Parliament under the terms of the Constitutional Reform and Governance Act 2010 and an Act of Parliament giving legal effect to the Agreement within the UK.[24]

Brexit and devolution

The UK government negotiated the EU Withdrawal Agreement on behalf of the whole of the United Kingdom. Accordingly the devolved governments of Northern Ireland, Scotland and Wales did not have any formal role in the negotiations.

Northern Ireland and Scotland had voted to remain in the EU. In Northern Ireland 56 per cent voted to remain while 44 per cent voted to leave. In Scotland the figures were 62 per cent remain and 38 per cent leave. In Wales, by contrast, the vote was 53 per cent in favour of leaving and 47 per cent for remaining. The passage of the EU (Withdrawal) Bill caused considerable disagreements between the UK government and the devolved administrations. Negotiations between the UK government and the Welsh Ministers over Brexit resulted in the Welsh Assembly passing a Legislative Consent Motion, but negotiations with the Scottish government did not, giving rise to concerns over when the Sewel Convention did, and did not, operate.[25]

Following the referendum, the Scottish First Minister, Nicola Sturgeon, made it clear that she wished Scotland to remain in the EU. However, it was the United Kingdom as a whole which was the Member State; individual nations within the UK had no independent status which could be asserted to enable them to remain within the EU. Consequently, once the UK left the EU, so too did the nation states within the UK. The only option from the perspective of a devolved nation wishing to remain would be to seek independence from the rest of the UK and then, as an independent nation, apply for membership of the EU.[26] This would

---

22 As per the German Constitutional Court in **Re Ratification of the Treaty of Lisbon** (2010).
23 See **Wightman and Others v Secretary of State for Exiting the European Union** (2018).
24 The EU (Withdrawal Agreement) Act 2020 fulfilled this rquirement.
25 The Sewel Convention refers to Legislative Consent Motions, the requirement that devolved legislatures must approve proposed legislation relating to them: on this see page 289.
26 As discussed in Chapter 11, a referendum on Scottish independence was held in 2014 in which voters rejected independence.

involve a lengthy accession process and agreement by all Member States. The terms of accession would not be as favourable as those enjoyed by the UK, which had 'special status' as a Member. This special status included a rebate on payments to the EU budget, opt-outs from the euro (the single currency) and the Schengen border-free area, and the right to choose which Justice and Home Affairs arrangements to join.

In relation to Northern Ireland, a major complexity involved the border with the Republic of Ireland, which is a member of the EU. On leaving the EU, the border between the Republic of Ireland and Northern Ireland became the border between the EU and the rest of the UK. The Prime Minister stated that there was no intention to erect a physical border between the two countries. This, however, led to difficulties in the negotiating process, with the EU insisting that a guarantee – the 'backstop' – was inserted into the Withdrawal Agreement to ensure that if no frictionless trade agreement between the EU and the UK was secured within the transition period, Northern Ireland would remain in a customs union with the EU. This in turn would require some mechanism to ensure that goods crossing the border between the Republic of Ireland and Northern Ireland did so on EU terms and that the correct customs tariffs etc. were paid.

Politically the backstop was unacceptable to the Democratic Unionist Party of Northern Ireland (on which at the time the British government depended for a majority in Parliament) on the basis that it would be treating Northern Ireland differently from the rest of the United Kingdom and would violate the terms of the Good Friday (Belfast) Agreement of 1998, which finally secured peace in Northern Ireland after decades of sectarian violence (on this see Chapter 11). The EU (Withdrawal) Act 2018 contains a specific provision in relation to Northern Ireland, stating that no regulations could be made under the Act which diminished North–South cooperation; or created or facilitated a hard border between Northern Ireland and the Republic of Ireland.[27,28] The European Union (Withdrawal) Act 2018, section 12, provides that the devolved legislatures may amend retained EU law, provided that the subject matter was within their legislative competence immediately prior to the end of the transition/implementation period (31 December 2020).[29,30]

The Brexit Process and Legislation

Withdrawing from the EU (Brexit) proved a tortuous process. The timeline and legislative framework for Brexit was as follows:

23 June 2016: in a referendum, leaving the EU was approved by 52 per cent of the voters;

On 24 January 2017 the Supreme Court ruled that the government needed the authority of an Act of Parliament (rather than the royal prerogative) to initiate the Article 50 process: see **Miller v Secretary of State for Exiting the European Union** [2017] UKSC 5;

The EU (Notification of Withdrawal) Act 2017 gave authority to the government to initiate the Article 50 TEU process which triggered the negotiations for the terms under which the UK would leave the EU and the future EU/UK relationship;

27 2018 Act, section 10; see also the European Union (Withdrawal Agreement) Act 2020, section 21.
28 On the special circumstances of Northern Ireland see Chapter 11 and further below.
29 Defined in section 39 of the EU (Withdrawal Agreement) Act 2020 as the 'implementation completion day'.
30 In 2020 the government introduced the UK Internal Market Act, designed to facilitate the smooth passage of goods between the nations of the UK. The Bill proved controversial from the devolution perspective in that it applied to the whole of the UK without having the consent of the devolved administrations and furthermore provided that the Act cannot be amended by the national legislatures, despite the fact that trade falls within their competence. The First Minister for Scotland, Nicola Sturgeon, described the Bill as an 'assault on devolution'.

The EU (Withdrawal) Act 2018 (as amended) provided the framework for the relationship between the EU and domestic law and providing that the European Communities Act 1973 would be repealed at the end of the transition/implementation period;

In November 2018 a Draft Withdrawal Agreement was published and agreed by EU leaders. Under section 13 of the EU (Withdrawal) Act 2018, the Agreement required the approval of Parliament (a vote in the House of Commons and 'take note' motion in the House of Lords);

In March 2019 the Draft Agreement was rejected by the House of Commons;

On 22 March 2019 the EU agreed to the extension of the Article 50 period until 31 October 2019;

On 24 May 2019, the then Prime Minster, Theresa May, resigned with effect from 7 June 2019;

On 23 July 2019 Boris Johnson won the leadership election for the Conservative Party and became Prime Minister;

In September 2019, fearing that the government would fail to reach agreement on the future relationship between the EU and UK, members of the House of Commons took control of the order paper[31] for 4 September and introduced a Bill – the EU Withdrawal (No 2) Act 2019 (the 'Benn Act') – providing that if MPs had not approved an agreement between the EU and UK, or approved leaving without an agreement, by 19 October 2019, the Prime Minister had to write to the President of the EU Council seeking an extension to Article 50 until 31 January 2020;

On 17 October 2019 a new Withdrawal Agreement was agreed and approved by the European Council but on 21 October failed to win the approval of the House of Commons;

On 12 December 2019 an early general election was held, which returned the government with a majority of 80;[32]

On 19 December 2019 a new EU (Withdrawal Agreement) Bill was introduced, implementing the Withdrawal Agreement as agreed by the EU and UK;

On 31 January 2020 the UK formally left the EU, with a transition period running until 31 December 2020;

On 30 December 2020 the Withdrawal Agreement was finally approved by the House of Commons;

On 31 December 2020 the EU (Future Relationship) Act 2020 received the Royal Assent;

On 31 December 2020 the transition period came to an end;

On 1 January 2021 the new relationship between the EU and UK commenced.

EU law and domestic law post-Brexit

The European Union (Withdrawal) Act 2018 (as amended) repeals the European Communities Act 1972 from the end of the transition/implementation period.[33] EU law which has been incorporated into domestic law continues to have effect after that date, while EU regulations, decisions and tertiary legislation are converted into domestic law.[34,35] All rights, powers, liabilities, obligations, restrictions, remedies and procedures which were recognised and available under section 2(1) of the ECA 1972 immediately before 31 December 2020 continue to be recognised and available in domestic law on and after that date.[36]

---

31 Under Standing Order No 24, a motion for an emergency debate.
32 Under the terms of the Early Parliamentary Election Act 2019.
33 EU(W)A 2018, section 1.
34 Subject to section 5 and Schedule 1, which lists exceptions to savings and incorporation.
35 European Union (Withdrawal) Act 2018, sections 2 and 3.
36 Ibid., section 4.

The Act sets out exceptions to the saving and incorporation of EU law. Section 5(1) provides that the principle of the supremacy of EU law does not apply to any enactment or rule of law passed on or after the end of the transition/implementation period. An Act of Parliament passed on or after that date will therefore take precedence over any saved or incorporated EU law. However, the principle will continue to apply to the interpretation, disapplication or quashing of enactments or rules of law passed or made before that date 'so far as relevant'. Accordingly, if there is a conflict between prior domestic law and retained EU law, the principle of the supremacy of EU law will continue to apply. It may also continue to apply to any modification of previously made law, if the modification is consistent with the intention of the modification.

Section 6 of the 2018 Act explains the relationship between the CJEU and the domestic courts and tribunals from the end of the transition/implementation period on 31 December 2020. The jurisdiction of the CJEU ended at the end of the transition period. Until that time, the UK had the same rights as Member States to resort to the CJEU. Firstly, section 6(1) of the 2018 Act provides that domestic courts and tribunals are not bound by any decisions made by the CJEU on or after the end of the transition period. Secondly, no court or tribunal may refer questions to the CJEU under Article 267 TEU. However, a court or tribunal may consider decisions of the CJEU made on or after that date, 'so far as it is relevant' to the matter before the court. Considering CJEU decisions does not mean that they take precedence as this is prohibited by section 6(1).

See Chapter 22.

In relation to retained EU law (i.e. EU law which has been saved and incorporated into domestic law), any questions about its validity or meaning must be interpreted in accordance with retained general principles of EU law. However the Supreme Court and Scottish High Court of Justiciary (the latter with exceptions) are not bound by any retained EU case law.[37] When considering whether to depart from any CJEU case law, the Supreme Court and High Court of Justiciary must apply the same principles as when considering whether to depart from their own decisions.

Where problems arise in relation to retained EU law, as a result of withdrawing from the EU, section 8 confers powers on Ministers to make secondary legislation to correct the problem/defect. Problems may arise where EU law requires, for example, the EU Commission to be consulted on a proposal for legislation or provisions relating to functions carried out on behalf of the UK by an EU agency during the UK's membership of the EU, a process made irrelevant by the UK's exit from the EU.

Section 8(5) of the 2018 Act provides that, within the transition period and with stated exceptions, the secondary legislation made to correct a problem can do anything that an Act of Parliament may do, including altering an Act of Parliament. The exceptions to this wide-ranging power were that it could not be used to impose or increase taxes or fees, make retrospective provisions, create criminal offences, establish a public authority or amend the Devolution Acts (other than in specific ways stated in Schedule 7 to the Act or the Human Rights Act 1998).

In September 2020 the government introduced the UK Internal Market Bill. The Act was designed to facilitate free trade between the nations of the UK, based on the twin principles of mutual recognition and non-discrimination. However, the Bill proved highly controversial. Neither the Scottish Parliament nor the Welsh Senedd Cymru consented to the Bill and it was rejected by the House of Lords. Under the Bill Ministers were given wide-ranging powers, including the power – in relation to Northern Ireland – to disapply or modify the effect of Article 10 of the Northern Ireland Protocol, including the power to disapply it

---

37 EW(W)A 2018, section 6(4).

completely. Section 45 provided that the powers given under Sections 42, 43 and 45 will be legally effective notwithstanding any incompatibility with any relevant international or domestic law. This was intended to ensure that domestic courts would give effect to domestic Regulations even if they conflicted with domestic or international law (including the Withdrawal Agreement). The EU called on the government to withdraw the draft Bill and following negotiations with the EU the controversial provisions were removed.

The Trade and Cooperation Agreement (TCA)

The Trade and Cooperation Agreement (TCA) (the Withdrawal Agreement) provides that there will be no tariffs or quotas on the movement of goods produced in the UK between the UK and the EU. The Agreement is in seven Parts:

- Part 1 covers common and institutional provisions;
- Part 2 covers trade and other economic aspects of the UK/EU relationships such as aviation, energy, fishing, road transport and social security;
- Part 3 covers cooperation on law enforcement and criminal justice;
- Part 4 covers 'thematic issues' such as collaboration on health;
- Part 5 covers participation in EU programmes;
- Part 6 covers dispute resolution;
- Part 7 sets out final provisions.

The TCA provides for a Partnership Council to supervise the operation of the Agreement at a political level. Decisions made by it must be by mutual consent. The Council will be supported by other specialist committees. The Agreement includes procedures for dispute resolution which do not involve the Court of Justice of the EU.[38] Consultation followed by independent arbitration is provided for in cases of disagreement over areas of cooperation. Arbitration will also be available if there are differences over participation in EU programmes. As a 'safeguarding measure', in the event of serious economic, societal or environmental difficulty which 'arises and is likely to persist', the UK or the EU may unilaterally take 'strictly proportionate and time-limited measures to remedy the situation'.[39]

EU (Withdrawal Agreement) Act 2020

The EU (Withdrawal Agreement) Act 2020 implements the Withdrawal Agreement as agreed between the UK and the EU.[40] Where the provisions of these Agreements are capable of having direct effect, legal or natural persons are able to rely on the provisions in the UK courts. The 2020 Act works alongside the 2018 EU (Withdrawal) Act 2018.

The conversion of existing EU law into 'retained EU law' and the retention of past decisions of the CJEU took place at the end of the transition period.[41]

Retained law includes:

- EU Regulations, Decisions and aspects of the EEA Agreement as they existed on exit day;
- domestic legislation passed to implement EU Directives etc.;
- most general principles of EU law (but not the supremacy of EU law);

---

38 Part 6, Title I.
39 Title III, Article 177.
40 It also implements the EEA–EFTA Separation Agreement and the Swiss Citizens' Rights Agreement.
41 EU (Withdrawal Agreement) Act 2020, sections 25 and 39.

- rights and obligations already existing under the ECA, as at exit day;
- decisions of the CJEU issued before exit day (but note that the Supreme Court and High Court of Justiciary may depart from CJEU decisions).

Retained law does **not** include:

- the EU Charter of Fundamental Rights;
- EU Directives (other than those that have already been transposed into domestic law);
- the supremacy of EU law; and
- the **Francovich principle** of state liability (on which see pages 200–201 above).

On the role of the courts in interpreting retained EU law, the 2020 Act provides that a Minister may, during the transition/implementation period, make regulations concerning the extent to which named courts or tribunals are not bound by retained EU law, and the test to be applied in deciding whether to depart from existing EU case law.[42] Before making the regulations, the Minister must consult senior members of the judiciary. The Act includes special provisions in relation to Northern Ireland in order to ensure that rights enshrined in the Good Friday Agreement (the Belfast Agreement) of 1998, which was central to the peace settlement in Northern Ireland, will not be diminished or that the arrangements for North–South cooperation set out in the 1998 Agreement will not be altered.[43]

The 'four freedoms' – of movement of people, capital, goods and services – are fundamental principles of the EU. Freedom of movement came to an end at the end of the transition period, to be replaced by domestic legislation.[44]

Summary

During the UK's membership of the EU, the law of the European Union entered into the legal systems of the United Kingdom[45] via the European Communities Act 1972. The legal effect of EU law on domestic law depended on the type of law: whether a Treaty Article, Regulation, Directive, Recommendation or Opinion. While the Treaty stipulates that Regulations shall have 'direct effect', it has been the Court of Justice which has developed the concepts of vertical and horizontal direct effect and indirect effect of EU provisions which determine their legal significance. In addition the Court has developed the concept of state liability, which requires that Member States which fail in their duty to implement/apply EU law correctly, and by that failure directly causes loss, must compensate the party which has suffered loss. The domestic courts of Member States are under a duty to apply and give effect to EU law to ensure that it has supremacy over domestic law. In doing so the courts act in a form of partnership with the Court of Justice of the European Union. In order that EU law is given priority over incompatible national law, the Treaty provides for references to be made to the CJEU requesting clarification of the meaning of EU law. Once the CJEU has ruled, it is for the domestic court to apply the correct interpretation of EU law to the case in question, thereby ensuring the supremacy of EU law.

---

42 Ibid., section 26.
43 Ibid., section 21.
44 EU citizens, EEA/ EFTA nationals and Swiss nationals and their families who have been continuously resident in the UK for five years are eligible for settled status, which confers indefinite leave to remain in the UK. Those who have been in the UK for less than five years are entitled to 'pre-settled status'. This confers a right to remain for five years and the right to apply for settled status at the end of that period.
45 Note that Northern Ireland and Scotland have separate legal systems from England and Wales.

Following the referendum result of June 2016, the UK gave formal notice of its intention to leave the EU under Article 50 TEU. The negotiation process was protracted and the Withdrawal Agreement was three times rejected by the House of Commons, principally on the basis of the Northern Ireland 'backstop'. A change of Prime Minister in 2019 was the impetus for reaching a settlement acceptable to the House of Commons. The Trade and Cooperation Agreement was approved by Parliament in December 2020. The UK formally left the EU on 31 January 2020; the transition period ended on 31 December 2020.

Further Reading

Convery, J, 'State liability in the United Kingdom after *Brasserie du Pecheur*' (1997) 34 *Common Market Law Review* 603.

Craig, P, 'Sovereignty after Factortame' (1991) 11 *YNEL* 221.

Craig, P, 'Directives: direct effect, indirect effect and the construction of national legislation' (1997) 22 *European Law Review* 519.

Craig, P, 'Britain in the European Union' in J Jowell and D Oliver (eds), *The Changing Constitution*, 8th edn, 2015, Oxford: Oxford University Press.

Craig, P and de Búrca, G, EU Law: *Text Cases and Materials*, 6th edn, 2015, Oxford: Oxford University Press.

de Búrca, G, 'Giving effect to European Community directives' (1992) 55 *Modern Law Review* 215.

Drake, S, 'Twenty years after Von Colson: the impact of "indirect effect" on the protection of the individual's community rights' (2005) 30 *European Law Review* 329.

Hartley, T, 'The European Court, judicial objectivity and the constitution of the European Union' (1996) 112 *Law Quarterly Review* 411.

House of Lords' European Union Report, Withdrawing from the EU, HL Paper138, 2016.

Miller, V, Lang, A and Simson-Caird, J, 'Brexit: how does the Article 50 process work?' House of Commons Library, Briefing Paper No. 7551, 16 January 2017.

Murphy, C, 'An effective right to cross-border healthcare? Comment on *Elchinov*' [2011] *European Current Law Yearbook* cxv.

Nugent, N, *The Government and Politics of the European Union*, 2010, Basingstoke: Macmillan.

Peterson, J and Shackleton, M (eds), *The Institutions of the European Unions*, 3rd edn, 2012, Oxford: Oxford University Press.

Public Law, *Special Brexit Edition*, 2018.

Part 4

Central, Regional and Local Government

Chapter 9

Central Government

Chapter Contents

Learning Objectives

By the end of this chapter you should be able to:

☐ explain the constitutional role of the Crown;
☐ discuss the composition and jurisdiction of the Privy Council;
☐ explain the powers of the Prime Minister;

- [ ] discuss the composition and functions of Cabinet;
- [ ] explain the constitutional principles underpinning the Civil Service;
- [ ] in outline discuss the liability of the Crown;
- [ ] in outline explain the concept of public interest immunity.

Introduction

In this chapter, the structure and roles of the institutions of central government – the Crown, Privy Council, Prime Minister, Cabinet, Ministers and government Departments – are examined. If government is to be conducted under the law, and in line with the principles of democracy and constitutionalism, it is of the utmost importance that those holding power should be accountable to citizens through their elected legislature. The responsibility of Ministers of the Crown is thus fundamental to the constitution, and the more so in the absence of an authoritative constitutional document which defines the scope and limits of ministerial power. Note that the procedural means by which Parliament scrutinises government action is considered in Chapter 15.

The Crown

> It is commonly hidden like a mystery, and sometimes paraded like a pageant, but in neither case is it contentious. The nation is divided into parties, but the Crown is of no party. Its apparent separation from business is that which removes it both from enmities and from desecration, which preserves its mystery, which enables it to combine the affection of conflicting parties – to be a visible symbol of unity to those still so imperfectly educated as to need a symbol.[1]

See Chapter 5.

While the Monarch is titular head of the government and all government acts are carried out in the name of the Crown, the role of the Queen is largely, but not completely, formal and ceremonial. In the study of the government it is necessary to bear in mind that the United Kingdom remains a constitutional monarchy and that the Crown is the symbolic head of the executive, legislature and judiciary. The remaining prerogatives of the Crown have been discussed in Chapter 5, which should be referred to for discussion of the Crown's role in the appointment of the Prime Minister.

Succession to the Crown

The Act of Settlement 1700 provides that succession to the throne is confined to members of the Protestant religion and specifically excluded Roman Catholics, or those married to Roman Catholics, from succession.[2] Succession to the Crown traditionally devolves according to the principles of *primogeniture*, that is to say that male heirs, and their children (irrespective of sex), take precedence over female heirs. The succession to the Crown Act 2013 changes the rules so that the line of succession is based on date of birth, rather than gender, and the prohibition against marrying a Roman Catholic is removed.

---

1 Bagehot, 1867, p. 90.
2 For this reason, Prince Michael of Kent was excluded from the line of succession upon his marriage to a Catholic in 1978.

The Regency Acts

Should the Crown fall 'vacant', through death or (more rarely) abdication, or the Monarch becomes too ill to fulfil his or her constitutional duties,[3] and the successor has not yet reached the age of majority, there will be a need for the appointment of an adult with responsibility for the Crown's duties during the successor's minority. This situation is regulated under the Regency Acts 1937–1953.

The Regency Act 1937 provides that the Sovereign may appoint Counsellors of State, charged with the responsibility of carrying out the Sovereign's duties whenever he or she is either absent from the United Kingdom, or suffering from temporary physical or mental illness. Those eligible to be appointed include the Monarch's spouse and the next four persons in line of succession.

Where there is the need to appoint a Regent, the Regency Act 1937 provides that, until the heir to the throne reaches the age of 18, his or her duties will be carried out by a Regent.[4] The appointment of a Regent continues until it is declared to be no longer necessary by the wife or husband of the Monarch, the Lord Chancellor, the Speaker, the Lord Chief Justice and the Master of the Rolls.

The Royal Titles Act 1953

By statute, the Monarch may assume whatever title she thinks fit, with the assent of member governments of the Commonwealth. The Royal Titles Act provides the title:

> Elizabeth II by the Grace of God of the United Kingdom of Great Britain and Northern Ireland and of her other Realms and Territories Queen, Head of the Commonwealth, Defender of the Faith.

Within the Commonwealth, it was agreed in 1952 that the title of the Monarch within the Commonwealth was for each state to determine.[5] Accordingly, the only title of the Monarch which is uniform throughout the Commonwealth is that of 'Head of the Commonwealth'. Prince Charles has made it known that he would prefer, on succession, to be known as 'Defender of Faith', rather than Defender of the (Protestant) Faith.

The role of the Monarch in the United Kingdom's constitutional democracy

In Walter Bagehot's often-quoted phrase, the Monarch has the right to 'be consulted, the right to encourage, the right to warn' (1867). As such, the Queen must be fully informed of the actions of her government, and given adequate opportunity to express her views.

If the role of the Monarch is to remain respected by governments of all political persuasions, and the nation, it is axiomatic that the Queen be seen formally to be immune from party-political differences and to fulfil her duties in an even-handed manner. This is not to suggest that the Queen has no views on her government's policies or that she should not express them to the Prime Minister. What is required, however, is the absolute confidentiality of discussions between herself and the Prime Minister, and, should there be a disagreement

---

3 As occurred in the reigns of George III (in 1811) and George VI (in 1938).
4 The 1953 Regency Act provided that if one of Queen Elizabeth II's minor children succeeded to the throne, the Queen and the Duke of Edinburgh would be appointed Regent.
5 At a meeting of Commonwealth Prime Ministers. See Cmd 8748, 1952, London: HMSO.

over policy, it is required that, once the Monarch's views are made known, irrespective of her approval or otherwise, she follows the advice of her Prime Minister on policy matters.[6]

Queen Elizabeth II, since her accession to the throne in 1952, has presided over 69 years of government and accumulated a wealth of experience in political matters unmatched by her individual Prime Ministers.

The State Opening of Parliament

At the start of each new parliamentary session, the Monarch formally opens Parliament. The Queen's Speech is formally delivered to the House of Lords with Members of the House of Commons having been summoned to the Lords by Black Rod. The Speech outlines the government of the day's proposals for legislation in the forthcoming session. Thereafter, there is a four- or five-day debate on the Speech in the Commons.

The Channels of Communication Between Crown and Government

Government papers

The Monarch receives copies of all significant government papers. She also receives copies of reports from ambassadors abroad and Commonwealth High Commissioners. All Cabinet papers and the minutes of Cabinet meetings are received by the Queen.

The weekly prime ministerial audience

Whatever the pressure of work, the Prime Minister attends a weekly half- to one-hour audience with the Queen. It is at this weekly meeting that issues will be discussed and the Queen's views made known to the Prime Minister.[7] Channels of communication are facilitated by the Queen's Private Secretary, whose appointment is the choice of the Queen, and who on appointment will become a Member of the Privy Council. The Private Secretary may not belong to any political party. Very rarely will the Queen's Private Secretary be drawn into public debate, although in 1986, the then Private Secretary, Sir William Heseltine, wrote to The Times (following public claims that the Queen and the Prime Minister – then Margaret Thatcher – disagreed on policy matters). In his letter, Sir William Heseltine spelled out three main points concerning the relationship between the Crown and the Prime Minister:

(a) the Sovereign has the right and duty to counsel, encourage and warn her government. She is thus entitled to have opinions on government policy and to express them to the Prime Minister;

(b) whatever the Queen's personal opinions may be, she is bound to accept and act on the advice of her Ministers;

(c) the Sovereign is obliged to treat communications with the Prime Minister as entirely confidential.[8]

---

6 See the letter to The Times by the Queen's Press Secretary, Sir William Heseltine, 29 July 1986.
7 See further Brazier, 1990, Chapter 8 and 1999, Chapter 9.
8 The Times, 29 July 1986; see also Marshall, 1986b.

Pause and Reflect

It is said that the Crown 'reigns but does not rule'. What do you understand by this phrase?

The Privy Council
Historical origins
The Privy Council is traceable to the thirteenth century. It was through the Privy Council that monarchs would rule without recourse to Parliament. With the Glorious Revolution of 1688 and the rise of parliamentary sovereignty, the role of the Council changed. Under William, the inner circle of the Council became known as the Cabinet Council. Through this Cabinet, the King could exercise all his powers, although he had to have recourse to the wider membership of the Privy Council in order to undertake acts which required Orders in Council, the formal means by which such prerogative acts came into effect. It was the Privy Council which determined the summoning and dissolution of Parliament, although it seems clear that the King would act through Orders in Council published after consultation with an inner circle of the Privy Council. The early origins of Cabinet government can be seen here.

While King William and Queen Anne attended Council meetings regularly, a change of practice occurred with the reign of George I (1714–1727) and George II (1727–1760). Neither could speak English, and nor were they particularly concerned with English matters. Accordingly, the Cabinet began to meet without the King. Under George III (1760–1820), the same situation prevailed, the Cabinet meeting without the King and communicating its decision to the King. Again, we find the origins of today's Cabinet, with the three principles of Cabinet government becoming apparent: those of 'political unanimity, common responsibility to Parliament and a common leader'.[9] With the rise of the Cabinet system of government in the eighteenth century, the Privy Council gradually lost much of its power.[10]

Composition of the Privy Council
The Privy Council has around 600 members. There is no fixed number of members. Appointments are made by the Crown, on the advice of the Prime Minister. By convention, all present and past Cabinet members are appointed to the Privy Council. Also included in the membership are members of the Royal Family, senior judges, two Archbishops, British Ambassadors, the Speaker of the House of Commons, present and former leaders of the Opposition and leading Commonwealth spokesmen and judges. On appointment, a new member of the Council takes the oath of allegiance, or affirms loyalty. The Privy Council oath binds the member to secrecy in relation to any matters discussed in the Council.[11]

Meetings of the Privy Council
The Privy Council may meet wherever the Queen so decides, although normally, the Council will meet at Buckingham Palace. The quorum is three.

---

9 Maitland, 1908, p. 395.
10 See Mackintosh, 1977, Chapter 2. On the constitutional struggles between King, courts and Parliament, see Chapter 5.
11 Privy Councillors would in any event be prevented from disclosing confidential information by virtue of the Official Secrets Acts 1911–1989.

Functions of the Privy Council

Proclamations and Orders in Council

Proclamations are used for the summoning of Parliament and declarations of war and peace. Orders in Council give effect to decisions reached under the royal prerogative and under statute. Orders in Council may be legislative, executive or judicial.

Committees of the Privy Council

The majority of Privy Council functions are undertaken in committees. Miscellaneous committees have been established. These include committees dealing with scientific research, universities and the granting of charters. The most important committee is the Judicial Committee.

The Judicial Committee was established under statute by the Judicial Committee Act 1833. The Judicial Committee Act 1844 provided that the Queen may, by Order in Council, admit appeals from courts of British colonies or overseas territories. In addition, under the Devolution Acts[12] the Judicial Committee has jurisdiction to determine disputes relating to devolved or reserved powers of the Scottish Parliament, the Northern Ireland Assembly and the Welsh Assembly.

The Constitutional Reform Act 2005 amended the composition and jurisdiction of the Judicial Committee of the Privy Council. In terms of composition, the Lord Chancellor and Lord President of the Council are no longer entitled to sit as members of the Privy Council which comprises Justices of the Supreme Court. In relation to jurisdiction, the power to determine devolution issues is transferred from the Privy Council to the Supreme Court.[13]

The Office of Prime Minister[14]

As with so much of the United Kingdom's constitution, the office of Prime Minister is one which developed by convention rather than by law. The office dates from the early eighteenth century,[15] and had become firmly established as a necessary and inevitable post in the latter half of the nineteenth century, when the extension of the franchise combined with the growth of political parties to produce both a (reasonably) accountable government and an opposition party. The first official recognition of the post of Prime Minister derives from the Treaty of Berlin 1878, and statutory and other formal references to the office remain scant.[16]

In 1889, Lord Morley[17] stated that:

> the Prime Minister is the keystone of the Cabinet arch. Although in Cabinet all its members stand on an equal footing, speak with an equal voice, and, on the rare occasions when a division is taken, are counted on the fraternal principle of one man, one vote, yet the head of the Cabinet is primus inter pares, and occupies a position which, so long as it lasts, is one of exceptional and peculiar authority.

---

12 Government of Wales Act 1998, Government of Wales Act 2006, Northern Ireland Act 1998, Scotland Act 1998.
13 See the Constitutional Reform Act 2005, ss 40, 138 and Sched. 9.
14 See Blake, 1975.
15 Sir Robert Walpole, 1721–1742.
16 *Inter alia*, the Chequers Estates Act 1917, Chevening Estate Act 1959, the Parliamentary and Other Pensions Act 1972, the House of Commons Disqualification Act 1975, Ministerial and Other Pensions and Salaries Act 1991.
17 Cited in Gwynn, 1932.

Little has changed over the intervening years, and Lord Morley's view remains true today. Contemporary interest focuses on the power of the office, the relationship between the Prime Minister and the Cabinet and the occasional dominance of the Prime Minister over Cabinet colleagues.[18] One question which inevitably arises is whether government has changed from being parliamentary government, through to being best described as Cabinet government and now through to prime ministerial government.[19] The extent to which there exists prime ministerial dominance depends very much upon the individual personality of the incumbent Prime Minister: there can be no broad generalisations. It must also be recognised that, whatever the personal power of the Prime Minister, he or she is ultimately dependent upon the support of Cabinet, party and Parliament; and, in turn, that support is dependent upon the support of the electorate expressed not just through the vote at a general election, but continually expressed in that amorphous concept 'the mood of the people'. As the resignation of Margaret Thatcher in 1990 demonstrated, even a seemingly invincible Prime Minister, who had enjoyed success at three general elections, can fall victim to the loss of the vital support of Cabinet and consequently the loss of office. The resignation of Prime Minister Theresa May in 2019 is also an example of loss of Cabinet support and then office.

The powers of the Prime Minister

The role and powers of the Prime Minister are not set down in any code or statute, but include the following:

- the Prime Minister holds office as Prime Minister and First Lord of the Treasury;[20]
- the Prime Minister as First Lord of the Treasury has responsibility for the Civil Service and assumes the title of Minister for the Civil Service;
- by convention the Prime Minister must be a Member of the House of Commons and is an elected constituency Member of Parliament;
- the Prime Minister has powers of appointment and dismissal of Ministers (formally this is undertaken by the Crown);
- the Prime Minister determines the size of Cabinet (on Cabinet see further below);
- the Prime Minister determines which Ministers sit in Cabinet;
- the Prime Minister controls the agenda for Cabinet;
- the Prime Minister controls the number and role of Cabinet Committees;
- the Prime Minister has special responsibility for national security and receives intelligence data from the security services;
- the Prime Minister has the power to declare war and peace and to send troops to war (but see Chapter 5 on recent developments in relation to military action);
- the Prime Minister has a weekly audience with the Queen;
- the Prime Minister represents the Crown in foreign affairs;
- the Prime Minister, together with the Secretary of State for Foreign Affairs, participated (during the UK's membership of the EU) in European Union Heads of State Summit (the European Council) Meetings;
- the Prime Minister is accountable to Parliament through weekly Prime Ministerial Question Time and the convention that the government must maintain the confidence of the House of Commons.

---

18 See Hennessy, 1986b, Chapter 3.
19 See Wolf-Phillips, 1984; Brazier, 1991.
20 Ministerial and Other Salaries Act 1975. As First Lord of the Treasury, the Prime Minister has responsibility for the Civil Service, which is controlled by the Treasury.

The Prime Minister has significant powers and influence over the appointment of persons to senior positions. For example, it is the Prime Minister who is responsible for the appointment of a Commission to oversee the work of the Security Service, and his or her consent is required for the appointment of most senior civil servants. Prime Ministerial nomination leads to the appointment of, *inter alia*, bishops and the Parliamentary Commissioner for Administration. His or her advice is given to the Queen on honours and on appointments to the Privy Council.

The Prime Minister and membership of the House of Commons

Between 1837 and 1902, six Prime Ministers were peers.[21] However, as early as 1839, the Duke of Wellington expressed the view that:

> I have long entertained the opinion that the Prime Minister of this country, under existing circumstances, ought to have a seat in the other House of Parliament, and that he would have great advantage in carrying on the business of the Sovereign by being there.[22]

With the extension of the franchise in 1832, 1867 and 1884, the supremacy of the Commons over the Lords was firmly established and the role of the House of Lords in legislation was reduced significantly by the Parliament Acts of 1911 and 1949. There are good reasons – aside from the office of First Lord of the Treasury – for arguing that the Prime Minister must be a Member of the House of Commons. First, he or she is today the elected leader of the parliamentary party and must lead that party into a general election for an affirmation – or denial – of the party's, and hence his or her own, mandate. Second, the doctrine of individual and collective ministerial responsibility applies to the Prime Minister as it does to all other holders of office. Above all, the doctrines require that a Minister is accountable to the electorate through Parliament. For the Prime Minister not to be accountable to the democratically elected House of Commons would effectively defeat the concept of collective responsibility and would be an affront to democracy and the very idea of constitutionalism.

The choice of Prime Minister[23]

A change in Prime Minister will be brought about by either resignation or death or – rarely – dismissal of the office holder. Resignation from office may stem from electoral defeat at a general election, from conflict within the government, from losing the support of the party, from losing a vote of confidence in the House, from a challenge to the leadership of the party, from illness or old age, from death, from voluntary retirement or from loss of support of the Cabinet.[24]

Whatever the explanation for a change in Prime Minister, it is for the Monarch to appoint the succeeding Prime Minister. It was seen in Chapter 5 that it is the prerogative right of the Crown to appoint whomsoever she pleases, but that by convention rather than law the Queen

---

21 Lords Melbourne, John Russell, Derby, Aberdeen, Beaconsfield and Salisbury.
22 Parl Debs 3rd Ser Vol. 47 Col. 1016, cited in Jennings, 1959a, p. 21.
23 See, *inter alia*, Jennings, 1959a, Chapter II; Mackintosh, 1977, Chapter 20; Brazier, 1982 and 1990, Chapter 4.
24 Defeat: 1945, 1951, 1964, 1970, 1974, 1979, 1997, 2010. Conflict: as in 1931. Loss of Cabinet support: Thatcher's resignation in 1990 and that of May in 2019. Loss of confidence vote: 1895, 1923, 1979. Leadership challenge: Thatcher, 1990. Illness: Campbell-Bannerman, 1908; Bonar Law, 1923; Eden, 1957; Macmillan, 1963. Old age: Salisbury, 1902; MacDonald, 1935; Churchill, 1955. Voluntary retirement: Baldwin, 1937; Wilson, 1976; Blair, 2007; Cameron 2016.

appoints as Prime Minister the leader of the political party who can command a majority in the House of Commons. In the days before the major parties chose their leaders by some form of election, some discretion was left to the Queen as to the choice of Prime Minister. Nowadays, such discretion is all but dead, other than where a general election produces a situation where there is no overall majority party in the House of Commons (as occurred in 2010; see further below). The actual choice of Prime Minister will thus be dictated by the election process within the major political parties and, where relevant, by the result of a general election.[25]

Formation of Cabinet

Once in office, the first task of the Prime Minister is to form his or her Cabinet. Constitutionally, the appointment of all Ministers is a decision for the monarch but, in practice, it is the Prime Minister who determines who shall be appointed. The Prime Minister decides which government Departments should be represented in Cabinet, although by convention, certain Departments are always represented. Thus, the Chancellor of the Exchequer, the Secretary of State for Foreign and Commonwealth Affairs, the Home Secretary, the Secretary of State for Justice and Lord Chancellor, the Secretary of State for Defence, the Secretary of State for Scotland and the Leader of the House of Commons always hold a seat in Cabinet. Further constraints on membership exist. For example, under the Ministers of the Crown Act 1975, certain Cabinet positions are allocated to Members of the House of Lords. Further, under the House of Commons Disqualification Act 1975, the size of Cabinet is effectively controlled – if indirectly – by limiting the number of Ministers who may draw a ministerial salary.

It is also for the Prime Minister to decide whether Cabinet members should remain in office, and he or she has the right to require a member to resign and, if they refuse, to request the Queen to dismiss them. This form of control was most strikingly seen in 1962 when Harold Macmillan in 'the night of the long knives' removed seven Ministers (from a Cabinet of 20) overnight. The Cabinet normally comprises approximately 20 senior members of the government of the day. The actual membership is not fixed, and is (subject to convention) for the Prime Minister to determine.

 Pause and Reflect

The office of Prime Minister exists by convention and his or her powers are not formally defined.
Should the office and powers of the Prime Minister be placed under an Act of Parliament?

The role and functions of Cabinet[26]

A Cabinet is a combining committee – a hyphen which joins, a buckle which fastens the legislative part of the state to the executive part of the state. In its origins, it belongs to the one and in its functions, it belongs to the other.[27]

25 As in 1906, 1918, 1922, 1931, 1935, 1950, 1955, 1959, 1966, October 1974, 1983, 1987, 1992 where the government was returned with a clear majority in the House of Commons.
26 See, inter alia, Jennings, 1959a; Mackintosh, 1977; Hennessy, 1986b.
27 Bagehot, 1867, p. 68; see also Jones, 'Cabinet government since Bagehot', in Blackburn, 1992.

The Cabinet represents the nucleus of government. It is the Cabinet as a whole which, at least in theoretical terms, formulates, initiates and implements the policy of the government. The use and working of Cabinets will vary with different governments and the different style and personality of the Prime Minister of the day.

As the central decision-making body, the Cabinet has great power in relation to Parliament as a whole, in relation to the political party it represents and in relation to the Prime Minister. While the Prime Minister may control the composition and working of Cabinet, no Prime Minister can ultimately survive in office without the support of Cabinet and party. The style of leadership will depend upon the personality of the premier, and an evaluation of whether it is parliamentary government, Cabinet government or Prime Ministerial government will also depend upon the strength of the Prime Minister vis-à-vis his or her colleagues.

Cabinet committees

In order to facilitate efficiency, the Cabinet is supported by a system of committees which, again, is largely determined by the Prime Minister.[28] Some of these are standing committees which will exist for the life of the government. Ad hoc committees may be established to consider particular matters. In addition, a whole range of official committees staffed by civil servants exist to complement the work of Ministers.

While the use of committees is both necessary and inevitable, it raises important constitutional questions concerning the doctrine of collective responsibility. Collective responsibility requires that each member of Cabinet, and all government Ministers and Parliamentary Private Secretaries, are bound by the decisions of the Cabinet. The extent to which the doctrine will in practice be binding will depend upon the extent government members are prepared to maintain confidentiality and unanimity over decisions in which they may have played no part.

The Cabinet Manual

The Cabinet Manual, *A Guide to the Laws, Conventions and Rules on the Operation of Government*,[29] is a guide to those working in government. It was first published in 2011 as a preliminary step in the then Prime Minister's (Gordon Brown) interest in developing a written constitution. The status of the Cabinet Manual has given rise to debate. Considering this issue, the Political and Constitutional Reform Select Committee has stated that:

> One thing that is clear is that the Manual is not itself a written constitution.[30] Nevertheless, the Committee stated that the Cabinet Manual is a 'highly significant document' and that it represents one of the first attempts to codify some of the practices in British Governance and politics.[31]

The Prime Minister's private office

While it has often been mooted, and its absence is an apparent anomaly in a sophisticated system of government, there has never been a 'Prime Minister's Department' dedicated to

---

28 See www.cabinetoffice.gov.uk.
29 First Edition published in 2011.
30 Constitutional Implications of the Cabinet Manual, 2011, para. 45.
31 Ibid., para. 2.

the task of organising, coordinating and liaising on behalf of the Prime Minister. Instead, a British Prime Minister's team comprises civil service support and non-civil service political support in the form of a specially appointed team of advisers. Heading the Prime Minister's support system is his or her Chief of Staff and Principal Private Secretary, who heads the Private Office and who has close relations with both the Cabinet Secretary and the Queen's Private Secretary. A civil servant, usually seconded from the Treasury for a three-year period, it is the Chief of Staff who coordinates the work of the Prime Minister. In addition there is the Director of Communications and Spokesman for the Prime Minister.

The announcement in August 2020 that the Prime Minister's Private Office, policy unit and key staff at No. 10 Downing Street will be relocated to the Cabinet Office site in Whitehall was an effort to ensure 'maximum efficiency in delivering the government's agenda' and is the closest that government has come to creating a Prime Minister's Office.

The Cabinet Office[32]

The daily working of Cabinet is assisted by the Cabinet Office, established in 1917, headed by the Secretary to the Cabinet, the Prime Minister's most senior policy adviser. It is the Secretary to the Cabinet who is responsible for the recording of Cabinet meetings and circulation of the agreed conclusions. Within the Cabinet Office there exist a number of secretariats, including the Economic and Domestic Affairs Secretariat, Defence and Overseas Secretariat, European Secretariat and Government Communication Network Unit and Strategy Unit.

 Pause and Reflect

The Prime Minister is formally *primus inter pares* – first among equals. Does this represent the reality of the contemporary relationship between the Prime Minister and other Ministers? What powers does the Prime Minister have which suggest that it is not an accurate reflection of the relationship?

The Civil Service

A civil servant has been defined as: 'a servant of the Crown, other than holders of political or judicial offices, who is employed in a civil capacity and whose remuneration is paid wholly and directly out of monies voted by Parliament'.[33]

Some doubt exists as to the precise number of personnel in the Civil Service, doubts which arise from the difficulties concerning the appropriate classification of some occupations within the public service. For example, employees of the National Health Service are not technically employees of the Crown – and therefore not civil servants – although responsibility for the Health Service lies with the Secretary of State.

One further difficulty in evaluating the operation of the Civil Service arises from the disparity in size between government Departments, with some Departments having a staff of over 100,000, while others may have fewer than 10,000. The size of a Department has a practical bearing on the extent to which Ministers can realistically be said to be making decisions. Added to that difficulty is the preference of some governments for large Departments of state.

---

32 See Wilson, 1976, Chapter 4; Mosley, 1969; Jennings, 1959a, Chapter 9; Mackintosh, 1977, Chapter 21.
33 Report of the Royal Commission on the Civil Service, 1929–1931, Cmd 3909, 1931, London: HMSO.

Moreover, recent changes to the structure of the Civil Service to enhance its efficiency have led to a proliferation of government agencies (see below).

When considering responsibility for the Civil Service and accountability to Parliament, a further feature of political life must be borne in mind: that of ministerial mobility. The average tenure of responsibility for a Department is two years. The Department of Education and Science, between 1944 and 1986, had 21 ministerial heads. During the Thatcher administration (1979–1990), Cabinet reshuffles were frequent, with several Ministers holding a number of portfolios during that government.

A final practical preliminary point to consider is the sheer volume of work entailed in government. An estimated[34] two-thirds of a Minister's working week is taken up by non-departmental business: Cabinet meetings, Cabinet committees, parliamentary party meetings, debates and questions in the House, official visits and constituency duties. The task of heading a major Department of state in addition to all the other duties is a major one, and the practical impact of regular government 'reshuffles', the size of Departments and non-departmental duties is great.

Improving efficiency in the Civil Service

Much of the work of government Departments is carried out by agencies.[35] The (Social Security) Benefits Agency is the largest. Others include the Driver and Vehicle Licensing Agency, Stationery Office, Land Registry, Ordnance Survey, Patent Office and United Kingdom Passport Agency. Issues of responsibility of Ministers are also raised in respect of non-departmental public bodies – 'quangos' – whereby state enterprises are privatised.[36] A non-departmental public body is defined as a body 'which has a role in the processes of national government but is not a government department'.[37] The movement towards increased government involvement in commerce and industry stems from 1945, although public corporations had been established earlier.[38] More recently, the movement has been towards privatisation, with, among others, British Rail, British Gas, British Telecom, The Stationery Office and the Naval Dockyards being sold into private ownership. Accountability for such organisations, when publicly owned, was weak. Today the question is to what extent these organisations are truly private; to what extent Ministers exert control over them, whether via financial power or the power to issue policy guidance; and, more importantly, the extent to which Parliament assures that Ministers are accountable for the implementation of policies.

Appointment and Management

The Constitutional Reform and Governance Act 2010, section 2, provides for the establishment of the Civil Service Commission with responsibility for the appointment of civil servants. Recruitment is based on 'merit on the basis of fair and open competition'.[39]

---

34 Headey, 1974.
35 Report to the Prime Minister, *Improving Management in Government: The Next Steps*, 1988, London: HMSO. See also the Agency Policy Review, *Better Government Services: Executive Agencies in the 21st Century*, 2002.
36 See, *inter alia*, Lewis, 'Regulating non-governmental bodies: privatization, accountability and the public–private divide', in Jowell and Oliver, 2000, Chapter 9.
37 *Non-Departmental Public Bodies: Guide for Departments*, 1986, Cabinet Office/MPO, London: HMSO.
38 For example, the Port of London Authority 1908; Central Electricity Board 1926; London Passenger Transport Board 1933; British Overseas Airways Corporation and British European Airways 1939.
39 Constitutional Reform and Governance Act 2010, s. 10.

The management of the civil service (with the exception of the Northern Ireland civil service, diplomatic service and the security services) lies with the Minister for the Civil Service.[40] The prerogative is retained in relation to the management of the diplomatic service and the security services.

Constitutional Principles and the Civil Service

The role of the Civil Service must be considered against the constitutional features of permanence, political neutrality and anonymity.

Permanence

In many countries, such as the United States of America, the Civil Service is a semi-permanent body, the most senior posts of which change hands with a change in government. A variation on this model, which is employed in Germany and France, involves incoming Ministers bringing into the Department a small body of hand-picked professional advisers. The constitutional significance of permanency lies in the development of expertise and the natural growth of a Civil Service 'ethos'. Most importantly, permanency ensures the availability of such expertise to governments of differing political persuasions. The Private Secretary is a Minister's closest contact with a Department, and his adviser.

Political neutrality

The Civil Service owes its loyalty to the government of the day, irrespective of political party, and it is imperative that the Civil Service avoids creating the impression of political bias.

The anonymity and political neutrality of civil servants is reinforced by the rules restricting political activity. If the Civil Service is to serve governments of all political persuasions, it is imperative that civil servants, whatever their private political views, should not be seen to be politically active in a manner which would inevitably compromise their neutrality under one political party or another.

The Civil Service is divided, for the purpose of control over political activity, into three groups:

(a)   the 'politically free' category, which comprises industrial staff and non-officer grades, who may freely engage in either national or local politics;

(b)   the 'politically restricted' category, comprising higher staff grades who are debarred from participating in national political activities, but may be permitted to engage in local politics;

(c)   an intermediate group which comprises those who are employed in neither the highest nor lowest grades.

Political activities which are subject to restriction are divided into activities at both national and local level. Those activities subject to restriction at national level include standing as a candidate for election to the European Parliament; holding office in party political organisations which relate to party politics in relation to the United Kingdom or the European Parliament; and speaking on matters of national political controversy, or expressing such

---

40 A role normally undertaken by the Prime Minister.

views to the press or in books, articles or leaflets. Canvassing on behalf of a candidate for election to the United Kingdom Parliament or the European Parliament, or on behalf of a political party in respect of such elections, is also prohibited. At local level, civil servants in the restricted category may not stand as candidates for local elections; hold office in party political organisations relating to local government; speak on local politically controversial matters or express such views in the media or other publications; or canvass on behalf of either a candidate or a political party in the course of local elections.[41]

Anonymity

In order that the Minister be seen to be responsible and accountable for the working of his or her Department, the Civil Service has traditionally been shielded from the public gaze and protected from public inquiry. By protecting the Civil Service, its impartiality and integrity are enhanced. Further, if civil servants become public figures scrutinised in Parliament or the media, their capacity for maintaining the appearance of political impartiality, so important to the concept of permanence, would be damaged.

It has been seen that the Minister in charge of a particular government Department is absolutely responsible to Parliament for the conduct of civil servants, and that this responsibility in turn involves two aspects. The first of these is that the Minister has an obligation to explain and answer for the work of his Department to Parliament; the second is that the Minister is responsible in constitutional terms for any failure of departmental policy and administration. As a corollary to ministerial responsibility, the Civil Service is not accountable to Parliament and is protected by the concept of anonymity. The *Departmental Evidence and Response to Select Committees* (the 'Osmotherley Rules') states: 'Civil servants are accountable to Ministers and are subject to their instruction ... It is for this reason that when civil servants appear before Select Committees they do so on behalf of their Ministers and under their directions'.

While, in theoretical constitutional terms, the anonymity of civil servants is important in buttressing the responsibility of Ministers of the Crown, it is becoming an increasingly less notable feature of the Civil Service. The explanations for the decrease in anonymity are manifold: the vagaries of individual ministerial responsibility, the increasing strength of departmental Select Committees and the televising of those proceedings and recent developments in the management of government Departments. The Coalition government is committed to reviewing the Osmotherley Rules as part of its Civil Service Reform Plan. New guidelines published in 2014 affirm the principle of ministerial accountability but confirm that Senior Responsible Officers of the government's major projects are now directly accountable to Parliament for the implementation of projects.

The Civil Service Code[42]

Civil servants working in England are governed by the Civil Service Code.[43] Civil servants working in the Scottish Executive, the National Assembly for Wales and the Northern Ireland Civil Service have their own versions of the Code. As long ago as 1854, the Northcote-Trevelyan Report set out the key principles that underpin the role and governance of the

---

41 *Pay and Conditions of Service Code.*
42 HC 27-I (1993–1994), London: HMSO; Nolan Report, *Standards in Public Life*, Cm 2850-I, 1995, London: HMSO. See the Civil Service Management Code issued under the Civil Service Order in Council 1995, as amended by the Civil Service (Amendment) Order 1995 and the Civil Service (Amendment) Order 1996.
43 See: www.civilservice.gov.uk/about/values.

Civil Service: integrity, honesty, impartiality and objectivity. The Constitutional Reform and Governance Act 2010, section 5, provides that the Minister for the Civil Service must publish a code of conduct for the Civil Service (excluding the diplomatic service), and that separate codes may be published for civil servants serving the Scottish Executive or the Welsh Assembly government.

Special advisers

The appointment of special advisers to Ministers blurs the lines of responsibility between Ministers and civil servants. The Committee on Standards in Public Life examined a whole tranche of issues in 1999, including the role of special advisers, lobbying, sponsorship and public appointments. The Committee accepted that there was no evidence that special advisers were 'politicising the civil service' but expressed the concern that 'the considerable increase in numbers, particularly at Number 10, where influential roles are played by special advisers, raises the question of whether their authority outweighs that of objective advisers' and that 'any future growth in numbers would raise questions about a move towards the establishment of a "cabinet system" within departments'.[44]

The Constitutional Reform and Governance Act 2010 regulates the appointment of special advisers. Section 15 provides that special advisers are persons appointed to assist a Minister after being selected by that Minister personally and the appointment approved by the Prime Minister under terms and conditions approved by the Minister for the Civil Service. Appointments are to end either when the Minister who appointed the adviser ceases to be a Minister, or on the day after a general election following his or her appointment. Similar provisions apply to advisers serving the Scottish Executive and Welsh Assembly government.

A special adviser (Spad) holds a temporary position in the civil service, being appointed 'to assist Minister of the Crown after being selected for appointment by that Minister personally'. The appointment must be approved by the Prime Minister.

Whilst governments have always employed political and policy advisers, the increase in numbers stems from the Wilson Government in 1964. The Constitutional Reform and Governance Act 2010 requires that the number of Spads is reported annually,[45] and provides for a Special Advisers Code. As of November 2019 there were 109 Spads, 44 of whom were advisers to the Prime Minister.

The appointment of Spads to Ministers blurs the lines of responsibility between Ministers and civil servants. In 2015, in a controversial extension of their powers, under a revised Special Advisers Code of Conduct, Spads were allowed not only to convey 'Ministers' views and priorities' but also to give instructions to civil servants. The Code of Conduct for Spads states that:

> Special advisers are a critical part of the team supporting Ministers. they add a political dimension to the advice and assistance available to Ministers while reinforcing the political impartiality of the permanent Civil Service by distinguishing the source of political advice and support.[46]

---

44 See *Reinforcing Standards*, the Report of the Committee on Standards in Public Life, 2000.
45 As of November 2019, there were 108.4 full time equivalent Spads. The total Civil Service has 413,910 full time equivalent civil servants.
46 Code of Conduct for Special Advisers, paragraph 1.

The Special Adviser Code lists the activities of Spads as being:

- to give assistance on any aspect of departmental business, and give advice (including expert advice as a specialist in a particular field;
- to undertake long-term policy thinking and contribute to policy planning within the department;
- to write speeches and undertake research, including adding party political content to material prepared by permanent civil servants;
- to liaise with the party, briefing the party representatives and parliamentarians on issues of government policy;
- to represent the view of their Minister to the media (including a party viewpoint), where they have been authorised by the Minister to do so; and
- to liaise with outside interest groups (including those with a political allegiance).

In 2020 the Prime Minister's Chief Adviser, Dominic Cummings, launched a website dedicated to the recruitment of Spads, thereby potentially undermining the role of Ministers to appoint their preferred advisers. The matter came to a head when one of the Chancellor of the Exchequer's Spads was dismissed summarily and it was proposed to merge his Spads with those of No. 10, thereby giving control to the Prime Minister and his Chief Adviser. The Chancellor resigned.

The Government and the Courts

Liability of the Crown[47]

The government, acting in the name of the Crown, has a historic right to privileges and immunities.[48] Before the Crown Proceedings Act 1947, two main principles governed the question of the legal liability of the Crown. The first principle was that 'the King could do no wrong' and, accordingly, could not be held liable for any actions which would be unlawful if committed by individuals. The second rule was that the King could not be sued in his own courts. Designed to protect the unique constitutional position of the Crown, as state regulation increased, Crown privilege extended to a wide range of central government activities, thereby weakening the legal protection given to individuals aggrieved by government action. In 1947, the Crown Proceedings Act extended the liability of the Crown to areas of tort and contract. European Community law, the European Convention on Human Rights and the Human Rights Act have all had an impact on this area of law.

The Crown Proceedings Act 1947, section 17, provides that civil proceedings against the Crown must be instituted against the relevant government Department, or, if there is no government Department which has clear responsibility, the proceedings must be brought against the Attorney General. In Scotland, actions against United Kingdom Departments may be instituted against the Advocate General for Scotland, and actions against Scottish devolved bodies instituted against the Lord Advocate.[49]

Section 21 relates to remedies, section 21(1) providing that the court may make such orders as could be made in proceedings between subjects. This is subject to the restriction that the court may not issue injunctions or order specific performance, but may instead grant

---

47 The law is complex and outside the scope of this text. See de Smith, Woolf and Jowell, 1995; Hogg and Monahan, 2000. See also Fairgrieve, 2002; Sunkin, 2003; Andenas and Fairgrieve, 2003.
48 An aspect of the royal prerogative. See Chapter 5.
49 See the Scotland Act 1998, Sched. 8.

a declaration. In **M v Home Office** (1994), the House of Lords ruled that an injunction could be granted in an action against a Minister personally. Lord Woolf stated:

> There appears to be no reason in principle why, if a statute places a duty on a specified minister or other official which creates a cause of action, an action cannot be brought for breach of statutory duty claiming damages or for an injunction, in the limited circumstances where injunctive relief would be appropriate, against the specified minister personally by any person entitled to the benefit of the cause of action ...

> ... I do not believe there is any impediment to a court making such a finding [of contempt], when it is appropriate to do so, not against the Crown directly, but against a government department or a minister of the Crown in his official capacity.

The House of Lords also ruled in **M v Home Office** that applications for judicial review are not 'proceedings against the Crown' for the purposes of the Crown Proceedings Act 1947; accordingly, injunctive relief against a Minister or officer of the Crown is available in judicial review.

The European Convention on Human Rights, Article 13, requires that everyone whose rights have been violated 'shall have an effective remedy before a national authority notwithstanding that the violation has been committed by persons acting in an official capacity'. Moreover, Article 41 provides that where the Court finds a violation of a Convention right or Protocol and the internal law of a Member State allows only partial reparation to be made, the Court 'shall, if necessary, afford just satisfaction to the injured party'. Section 8 of the Human Rights Act 1998 reflects these provisions, requiring a court which has the power to award damages to make an award where this is necessary to achieve 'just satisfaction' and to have regard to the principles applied by the Court of Human Rights.[50]

See Chapter 18.

Liability in tort

In relation to tortious liability, the Crown is placed in the same legal position as any other adult individual, and has the same liability for the tortious acts of its employees and agents as do private persons and organisations. Two important exceptions to liability remained: liability in respect of actions of members of the armed forces while on duty or on premises used for the purposes of the armed forces, and liability for tortious actions committed by the Post Office.[51] In relation to the armed forces exception, the Crown Proceedings (Armed Forces) Act 1987 abolished the immunity. The Act was not, however, retrospective, and the immunity can be revived in times of war or national emergency. In **Matthews v Ministry of Defence** (2002), the Court of Appeal ruled that the immunity was not incompatible with Article 6 of the Convention. These exceptions aside, the Crown is placed in the same position as a private person.

Liability in contract

In principle, the liability of the Crown under contract is the same as that of a private person. In practice, however, special considerations apply. The legal status of the Crown has been

---

50 Note also the EU concept of state liability which applied during the UK's membership of the EU. This is discussed in Chapter 8.
51 The Post Office ceased to be a government Department and became a public corporation in 1969. The restrictions on liability were nevertheless retained.

considered and explained by the judiciary. For example, in **BBC v Johns** (1965) Lord Diplock was to state that the Crown 'personifies the executive government of the country'. In **Town Investments Ltd v Department of the Environment** (1978) Lord Simon of Glaisdale described the Crown as a 'corporation aggregate': a corporation comprising many persons and offices. That description was echoed in part by Lord Woolf in **M v Home Office** (1994) when he said – citing Lord Diplock and Lord Simon of Glaisdale in **Town Investments** – that 'the Crown has a legal personality. It can be appropriately described as a corporation sole or a corporation aggregate. ... The Crown can hold property and enter into contracts'.

One distinction between contracts between private parties and a contract involving the Crown lies in the sheer scale of government contracts for the procurement of goods and services and the use of standard conditions in government contracts. A further distinction lies in the responsibility of the Crown to act in the public interest. It has been held judicially that: 'the Crown cannot put itself in a position where it is prevented from performing its public duty ... If it seeks to make an agreement which has that consequence, that agreement is of no effect'.[52]

Two cases illustrate this rule of 'executive necessity'.[53] The first concerns exceptional wartime conditions. A Swedish shipping company had obtained an undertaking by the British government[54] that its ship would be allowed – contrary to government policy – to leave a British port into which it had entered to deliver its cargo without being replaced by a ship of the same tonnage: the 'ship for ship' policy. In breach of this undertaking, the ship *Amphitrite* was detained. The owners sold the ship to avoid further loss and claimed damages for breach of contract. The court ruled that, while the government could bind itself through a contract, and be liable for damages for breach of contract, the arrangement in question was not a commercial contract.[55] Rowlatt J stated:

> it is not competent for the Government to fetter its future executive action, which must necessarily be determined by the needs of the community when the question arises. It cannot by contract hamper its freedom of action in matters which concern the welfare of the State.

The second case is that of **Crown Lands Commissioners v Page** (1960), in which the Court of Appeal ruled that the exercise of the Crown's discretionary powers in relation to land could not be fettered by an implied covenant in favour of the tenant. Devlin LJ stated the principle:

> When the Crown, in dealing with one of its subjects, is dealing as if it too were a private person, and is granting leases or buying and selling as ordinary persons do, it is absurd to suppose that it is making any promise about the way in which it will conduct the affairs of the nation.

Public interest immunity[56]

The phrase 'Crown privilege' has been superseded by the term 'public interest immunity'. One aspect of the immunity which is of contemporary and continuing concern is the extent

---

52 Woolf J in **R v IRC ex parte Preston** (1983), p. 306.
53 *Rederiaktiebolaget Amphitrite v The King* (1921).
54 Sweden being neutral during the First World War.
55 Contrast this case with that of *Attorney General v De Keyser's Royal Hotel* (1920), discussed in Chapter 5, in which the liability of the Crown to award compensation arose out of statute, and not the royal prerogative.
56 See, *inter alia*, Jacob, 1993; Simon Brown, 1994; Zuckerman, 1994.

to which governments – and agencies of government – may be required to disclose information to a court of law. While the immunity from disclosure of information relates principally to the government, it extends to other persons and organisations. The rules regulating the disclosure of documents in civil and criminal cases vary, but in each case there are common features. First, a document may or may not fall within a category of documents which prima facie must be disclosed. Second, disclosure may be denied on the basis that the contents of the documents fall within a particular category of disclosure or non-disclosure,[57] or that the documents fall within a class of documents which may or may not be disclosed.[58] Third, disclosure involves the evaluation of the relevance of the information or documents, which in some cases will be clear, but in other cases less clear until disclosed and evaluated by counsel and the court. Over and above these rules is the public interest immunity certificate. The certificate may be used to claim that it is contrary to the public interest for information or documents to be disclosed irrespective of the first two rules, and may be claimed on the basis of either contents or class. Where the government would prefer not to disclose information, and the information falls into a 'grey area', there is a temptation to claim public interest immunity to protect the information.

Public interest immunity was raised, for example, in **D v NSPCC** (1978)[59] in order to protect the sources of information given to the National Society for the Prevention of Cruelty to Children.

The need for confidentiality was also accepted in **Bookbinder v Tebbit** (1992) in relation to sources of information given to the Audit Commission, which was investigating alleged irregularities in the financial dealings of a local authority. The court must, however, be satisfied that there is a real need to prevent the disclosure of an informant's identity.[60]

Under the Crown Proceedings Act 1947, a court may order the disclosure of documents in the interests of justice. Section 28, however, also provides that the power of the court in civil proceedings does not extend to disclosures which it would not be in the public interest to make.

There are two aspects of public interest entailed within this area of the law: the public interest in the administration of justice and the public interest in non-disclosure of damaging information. The questions which arise are: who has the power to decide whether disclosure would or would not be in the public interest, and on what basis is the 'public interest' to be evaluated?

In **Duncan v Cammell Laird** (1942), dependants of victims who died in the submarine Thetis, which sank during trials, sued the builders of the submarine. Disclosure was sought of documents relating to contracts between the Admiralty and the building contractors, and salvage reports on the submarine. The Admiralty refused to disclose the information, relying on national security, and the Minister certified that disclosure was against the public interest. The House of Lords held that the Minister's certificate was conclusive and could not be questioned. Accordingly, the rule emerged that a court of law could never question a claim of Crown privilege (or public interest immunity), irrespective of the type of documents being sought. The House of Lords ruled that public interest immunity could lie in respect of the contents of a particular document, or to a class of documents which ought to be withheld in the interests of the proper functioning of the public service. This decision altered the law

---

57 For example, non-disclosure is in the public interest if the contents reveal the identity of a police informer, or the workings of the security services.

58 For example, non-disclosure of Cabinet proceedings, or intergovernmental negotiations, or documents relating to military operations. See **Duncan v Cammell Laird** (1942); **Conway v Rimmer** (1968); **Burmah Oil v Bank of England** (1980); **Air Canada** (1983); **R v Chief Constable of West Midlands Police ex parte Wiley** (1995), discussed above.

59 And see **Alfred Crompton Amusement Machines Ltd v Customs and Excise Commissioners (No 2)** (1974).

60 See **Norwich Pharmaceutical Co Ltd v Customs and Excise Commissioners** (1974).

and, in the words of Professor Wade, gave the Crown the right to withhold information and thereby 'to override the rights of litigants not only in cases of genuine necessity but in any case where a government department thought fit'.[61]

In 1956, the Lord Chancellor, Lord Kilmuir, issued a statement.[62] He drew a distinction between documents which were absolutely necessary to protect the 'proper functioning of the civil service', and documents which are relevant to litigation but which do not require 'the highest degree of confidentiality ... in the public interest', and stated that privilege relating to medical and other documents relevant to the defence in criminal proceedings should not be routinely claimed.[63] The rule in **Duncan v Cammell Laird**, however, prevailed until 1967. In **Conway v Rimmer** (1968), the House of Lords took a more robust attitude to a claim of public interest immunity, reversing its own decision in **Duncan v Cammell Laird**. In an action for malicious prosecution against his former Superintendent of Police, the Home Secretary objected to the disclosure of reports made on the former police probationary officer. The court refused to follow the broad ruling in **Duncan v Cammell Laird** and ruled that it was for the court – and not the person seeking to prevent disclosure – to rule on the competing public interests in the administration of justice and confidential information. Accordingly, it is for the person seeking to withhold information to assert – through the use of a public interest immunity certificate – the right to non-disclosure, and for the court to determine whether or not non-disclosure is in the public interest. Lord Reid, in rejecting the claim that the power of decision lay solely with Ministers of the Crown, stated that he did not doubt that:

> There were certain classes of documents[64] which ought not to be disclosed whatever their content may be ... To my mind the most important reason is that such disclosure would create or fan ill informed or captious public or political criticism. The business of government is difficult enough as it is, and no government could contemplate with equanimity the inner workings of the government machine being exposed to the gaze of those ready to criticise without adequate knowledge of the background and perhaps with an axe to grind.

In **Burmah Oil Co v Bank of England** (1980), the oil company sought disclosure of information relating to the rescue of the company by the bank, in exchange for low-priced stock in the company. The Attorney General produced a public interest immunity certificate from the Chief Secretary to the Treasury, in which objection was made against producing documents sought on the basis that they related to government policy. The House of Lords inspected the documents, but felt that their disclosure was unnecessary.

A question relating to public interest immunity certificates which assumed particular importance in the Arms to Iraq affair was whether the Minister was under a duty to sign the certificate when advised to do so by the Attorney General. The notion of duty arose in **Air Canada v Secretary of State for Trade** (1983), in which Lord Scarman (in the minority) stated that, whilst it was for the court to accept or deny the claim, in claiming public interest immunity the Crown was not 'claiming a privilege but discharging a duty'. In the **Air Canada** case, the House of Lords ruled, by a majority, that the government was entitled to immunity. At issue were the circumstances under which, in judicial review proceedings, the court would examine documents for which immunity was claimed. No order for disclosure can be made unless the documents are inspected by the court. The majority in the House of Lords ruled that the

61 Wade and Forsyth, 2004.
62 HL Deb Cols 741–748, 6 June 1956.
63 On guidelines issued by the Court of Appeal in relation to disclosure in criminal proceedings, see **R v Keane** (1994).
64 Lord Reid refers here specifically to Cabinet minutes.

party seeking disclosure of documents had to show that 'the documents are very likely to contain material which would give substantial support to his contention on an issue which arises in the case' (*per* Lord Fraser, page 917e). It was not sufficient that the documents might reveal information relevant to the case; it had to be established by the person seeking disclosure that it was 'very likely' that the information would assist his case.

The distinction between a right and a duty was also considered in **Makanjuola v Metropolitan Police Commissioner** (1992). In that case, Bingham LJ stated that: 'where a litigant asserts that documents are immune from production or disclosure on public interest grounds he is not (if the claim is well founded) claiming a right but observing a duty'. Bingham LJ went on to state that:

> it [the distinction between a right and a duty] does, I think, mean: (1) that public interest immunity cannot in any ordinary sense be waived, since, although one can waive rights, one cannot waive duties; (2) that, where a litigant holds documents in a class prima facie immune, he should (save perhaps in a very exceptional case) assert that the documents are immune and decline to disclose them, since the ultimate judge of where the balance of public interest lies is not him but the court; and (3) that, where a document is, or is held to be, in an immune class, it may not be used for any purpose whatever in the proceedings to which the immunity applies, and certainly cannot (for instance) be used for the purpose of cross-examination.

Woolf LJ, while endorsing much of this analysis, noted that **Makanjuola** did not involve a Department of State, represented by a Secretary of State. He stated that:

> If a Secretary of State on behalf of his department, as opposed to any ordinary litigant, concludes that any public interest in the documents being withheld from production is outweighed by the public interest in the documents being available for purposes of litigation, it is difficult to conceive that, unless the documents do not relate to an area for which the Secretary of State was responsible, the court would feel it appropriate to come to any different conclusion from that of the Secretary of State. The position would be the same if the Attorney General was of the opinion that the documents should be disclosed.

However, that situation did not pertain to other bodies or persons, and it could not be left to individuals to decide that documents should be disclosed. The court retained the ultimate right to determine disclosure and would 'intervene to protect the public interest'. The decision in **Neilson v Laugharne** (1981), and those cases in which it had been applied, was wrong and could no longer be justified. It was not, Woolf LJ stated, that 'there had been a change in attitudes since the **Neilson** decision' but rather that 'establishing a class of public interest immunity of this nature was never justified'. In **Wiley**, the House of Lords ruled that in **Neilson** and the subsequent cases in which it had been applied, the law was incorrectly stated. The House of Lords did not, however, go so far as to say that material which came to light in investigations against the police could never be entitled to class immunity.

The House of Lords had the opportunity to re-examine the issue in **R v Chief Constable of West Midlands Police ex parte Wiley; Chief Constable of Nottinghamshire Police ex parte Sunderland** (1995). In that case, the defendant, Mr Wiley, was charged with robbery, but at his trial the prosecution offered no evidence. He subsequently made formal complaints against the police and commenced a civil action against the Chief Constable. Mr Sunderland had been charged with assault but, again, no evidence was offered at trial by the prosecution. He also made a formal complaint against the police. He alleged assault by the police and indicated that he would institute civil proceedings against them. The problem faced by both complainants was that the police had documents which it was thought would attract public interest immunity on behalf of the police, thereby making them unavailable to the complainants. The Chief Constables concerned refused to give undertakings that the documents would not be used to the detriment of the complainants, and the complainants secured a declaration that the Chief Constables had acted unlawfully in refusing to give the undertakings. The Chief Constables appealed against the declarations to the House of Lords. In the earlier case of **Neilson v Laugharne** (1981),[65] the House of Lords had ruled that public interest immunity attached to police complaints documents, on the basis that if it did not, the complaints procedure would be damaged. However, the House of Lords ruled that, in principle, documents which are relevant to litigation should be disclosed, unless that disclosure would cause 'substantial harm'. In particular, Lord Templeman stated that 'a rubber stamp approach to public interest immunity by the holder of a document is neither necessary nor appropriate'.[66]

On recent developments relating to the disclosure of evidence in court and national security, see Chapter 21.

Summary

All acts of government are undertaken in the name of the Crown. Central government comprises the Prime Minister and Cabinet and non-Cabinet Ministers backed by the Civil Service. The office of Prime Minister is conventional and unregulated by statute. The respective powers and duties of government are set out in the Cabinet Manual, the First Edition of which was published in 2011.

The Prime Minister, by convention, must be a Member of the House of Commons, and the majority of Ministers will also sit in the Commons, although a few will be Members of the House of Lords.

The Civil Service is largely administered under the Royal Prerogative (see Chapter 5). The Constitutional Reform and Governance Act places the Civil Service under the authority of Act of Parliament. Note that the government announced in 2020 that significant reforms to the Civil Service are being considered.

Further Reading

Blackburn, R, 'The 2010 General Election outcome and formation of the Conservative–Liberal Democrat coalition government' [2011] *Public Law* 30.

Daintith, T and Page, A, *The Executive in the Constitution*, 1999, Oxford: Oxford University Press, Chapters 1–6.

Drewry, G, 'The executive: towards accountable government and effective governance?' in J Jowell and D Oliver (eds), *The Changing Constitution*, 7th edn, 2011, Oxford: Oxford University Press.

Hennessy, P, *The Hidden Wiring*, 1995, London: Gollancz, Chapters 3, 4, 5, 8.

Twomey, A, 'Changing the rules of succession to the throne' [2011] *Public Law* 378.

---

65 Applied in **Halford v Sharples** (1992) in proceedings alleging unlawful sexual discrimination; distinguished in **Peach v Metropolitan Police Commissioner** (1986) on the basis that the allegation is of a serious crime committed by the police, and **Ex parte Coventry Newspapers Ltd** (1993).

66 At p. 281. In **Rowe v United Kingdom** (2000) the European Court of Human Rights has ruled that the use of Public Interest Immunity Certificates which prevent a judge from considering whether or not evidence should be disclosed in the court of a murder trial violates Article 6 of the Convention.

Chapter 10

Ministerial Responsibility

Chapter Contents

Learning Objectives

By the end of this chapter you should be able to:

- ☐ explain the constitutional importance of ministerial responsibility;
- ☐ discuss the rules relating to Cabinet responsibility;
- ☐ discuss the requirements of individual ministerial responsibility in relation to both the Department and personal conduct;
- ☐ explain the consequences of breaching ministerial responsibility and whether these are adequate;
- ☐ discuss whether ministerial responsibility is really a constitutional convention or not.

Introduction

The idea of responsible government is inextricably linked with constitutionalism and the rule of law: government *under* or *subject to* the law. However, as has been seen, much of the United Kingdom's constitution is regulated not under formal legal rules but by non-legal, but obligatory, constitutional conventions. A key convention in relation to responsible government is that of ministerial responsibility.

The convention of ministerial responsibility is central to the constitution, and plays a fundamental role in the relationship between the executive and Parliament. For the doctrine of government under the law to be observed, it is essential that government is accountable to both Parliament and the electorate, and that government is conducted in a manner sufficiently open, subject to the requirements of the national interest, to inspire public confidence. The origins of ministerial responsibility are traced by FW Maitland to the principle that 'for every exercise of royal power some minister is answerable' (1908, page 203).

The doctrine has two limbs – individual and collective responsibility. As with so much of the constitution, there is vagueness on occasion as to the distinction between the two limbs, which are both closely related and also complementary of one another. In order to facilitate analysis, the topic may be broken down into three aspects:

(a) the collective responsibility of the Cabinet to Parliament, and ultimately the electorate, for policy and administration;
(b) the individual responsibility of Ministers for the policy and administration of his or her Department;
(c) the individual responsibility of Ministers for their personal conduct.

Collective Cabinet Responsibility[1]

See Chapter 2.

The convention of collective Cabinet responsibility emphasises the unanimity of government and its accountability to Parliament. The classic expression of collective responsibility remains that of Lord Salisbury:

> For all that passes in Cabinet every member of it who does not resign is absolutely and irretrievably responsible and has no right afterwards to say that he agreed in one case to a compromise, while in another he was persuaded by his colleagues ... It is only on the principle that absolute responsibility is undertaken by every member of the Cabinet, who, after a decision is arrived at, remains a member of it, that the joint responsibility of Ministers to Parliament can be upheld and one of the essential principles of parliamentary responsibility established. [Official Report, HC Cols 833–834, 8 April 1878]

The rationale for the convention lies in the need for government to present a united front to Parliament and the public in order to maintain confidence. A government which exhibits public disagreements over policy matters is one which will be regarded as weak, and will be subjected to challenges to its authority to continue in office.

---

1 See Mackintosh, 1977, Chapter 2; Marshall, 1984, Chapter IV.

Two principal sub-rules underlie collective responsibility. The first rule is that, once an agreement is reached in Cabinet, all members of Cabinet – and many outside Cabinet – are bound to speak in support of the decision. There should be no criticism or dissent from the decision in public – irrespective of whether or not the particular member of Cabinet was party to the discussion. Equally, if a decision is reached by the Prime Minister in Cabinet Committee or the Inner Cabinet when only a small handful of members are present, the decision binds all. The second supporting rule is that records of Cabinet discussions are absolutely secret. The knowledge that Cabinet records are protected by confidentiality enhances the opportunity for members of Cabinet to discuss matters freely, secure in the knowledge that their personal point of view, whatever the decision, will be protected from the public gaze.

These principles are expressed in the Ministerial Code in the following manner:

> The principle of collective responsibility requires that ministers should be able to express their views frankly in the expectation that they can argue freely in private while maintaining a united front when decisions have been reached. This in turn requires that the privacy of opinions expressed in Cabinet and Ministerial Committees should be maintained. [Cabinet Office, 2018, para 2.1]

An example of a breakdown in collective responsibility is seen with the Westland Helicopter saga in 1986.[2] Westland, a helicopter manufacturing company, was threatened with closure. The government sought to promote a rescue bid for the company. Two alternative plans were put forward, one from an American consortium, the other from Europe. Mr Heseltine, Secretary of State for Trade and Industry, wanted the European option to be taken up. Mrs Thatcher, however, favoured the American plan. Mr Heseltine had been informed that he would be able to put his preferred plan to a Cabinet meeting. In the event, however, Mrs Thatcher cancelled that meeting. Mr Heseltine resigned.[3]

The Iraq War in 2003 resulted in two resignations from Cabinet. The Leader of the House of Commons and former Foreign Secretary, Robin Cook, resigned in March 2003 on the basis that he could not support the government's decision to go to war. The International Development Secretary, Clare Short, resigned in May 2003 on the basis that she could not accept the government's position on establishing a legitimate Iraqi government after the war. In 2014 Baroness Warsi resigned from the Foreign and Commonwealth Office over the government's failure to denounce Israeli attacks on Gaza. It was the first ministerial resignation on a point of principle since those of Robin Cook and Clare Short. In 2016 the Work and Pensions Secretary, Iain Duncan Smith, resigned in protest against the Chancellor's proposed cuts in disability benefits, and Lord O'Neill of Gatley resigned over government economic policy. Leaving the EU, following the referendum result of 2016, resulted in numerous ministerial resignations, including two Secretaries of State for Leaving the EU (on 'Brexit' see Chapter 8). Furthermore, Cabinet Ministers voted against the government in Parliament without either resigning or the sanction of dismissal being applied. This is perhaps best explained as a manifestation of the divisions over leaving the EU, in society, in Parliament and at the heart of government.

As with the convention of individual responsibility, there is dispute about the status and scope of collective responsibility. So many exceptions to the classic doctrine can be discerned

---

2 See Oliver and Austin, 1987; Hennessy, 1986a; Marshall, 1989, Chapter 18.
3 Leon Brittan also resigned from government for breaching the convention that the advice of Law Officers to the Crown should not be disclosed.

that it is possible to question whether it is a convention at all within the classical definition, or whether the term 'convention' should be discarded and replaced by the words 'practice or usage'. Alternatively, it may be argued that the variations which can be observed in the working of the convention merely illustrate one of the greatest strengths of conventional rules – their flexibility.

Agreements to differ

See Chapter 9.

It is possible for the convention of collective responsibility to be waived when the circumstances are such that the political disagreements within Cabinet are of such magnitude that the Prime Minister finds it more expedient to set aside the convention than to have the convention broken by members of Cabinet. In 1931–1932, the national (coalition) government contained bitterly opposing views over economic policy, in particular over the levy of tariff duties. Four members of Cabinet handed in their resignations, and withdrew them only after the Prime Minister, Ramsey MacDonald, decided to waive the convention and allow the dissident members to express their views publicly. In 1975, the Labour government of Harold Wilson was faced with an equally intransigent faction in Cabinet on the matter of the United Kingdom's continued membership of the European Community. Mr Wilson announced a limited waiver of the convention, in the guise of an 'agreement to differ'.[4] The waiver was limited to the single issue of continued membership of the European Community and did not extend to any other areas of government policy. During the period of coalition government from 2010 to 2015 it was necessary to relax the rules on unanimity to accommodate the differing views of Conservative and Liberal Democrats. A waiver was once again in place prior to the 2016 referendum on membership of the European Union.

Cabinet papers[5]

The confidentiality of Cabinet discussion is protected by the prohibition against disclosure by members of Cabinet. In addition, the rules regarding the confidentiality of Cabinet papers include the rule that the government of the day may not release the papers of a previous government without the consent of the former Prime Minister.[6] Furthermore, the papers of the previous government may not be disclosed to a government of a different political persuasion. It may at first sight appear curious that an incoming government cannot gain access to the papers of the previous government, and it may be wondered how the government is supposed to act effectively in any policy area if denied so much data. Nevertheless, the rule is justified on the basis that an outgoing government might be tempted to remove politically sensitive documentation if it feared that a new government would make political capital out of it.

Three categories of papers are excepted from the convention:[7]

(a)   papers which, even if not publicly available, can be deemed to be in the public domain, for example letters sent by former Ministers to trade associations, trade unions, etc., or to Members of Parliament about constituency cases, or to members of the public;

---

4 HC Deb Col. 1745, 23 January 1975; Col. 351, 7 April 1975; Cmnd 6003, 1975; Wilson, 1976, pp. 194–197.
5 On secrecy in government, see further below.
6 HC Deb Col. 1039, 1 July 1982; Cols 468, 8 July 1982; 474; Hunt, 1982.
7 Hunt (Lord), 'Access to a previous government's papers', in Marshall, 1989.

(b) papers, other than genuinely personal messages, dealing with matters which are known to foreign governments, for example, messages about intergovernmental negotiations;

(c) written opinions of the Law Officers, which are essentially legal rather than political documents.

Ministerial memoirs

The publication of a former Minister's memoirs of his political life poses problems for the rules relating to Cabinet secrecy. In 1976, the Radcliffe Committee Report[8] stated that:

> The author should be free to use his ministerial experience for the purpose of giving an account of his own work, subject to restrictions on three separate categories of information:
>
> (a) he must not reveal anything that contravenes the requirements of national security operative at the time of his proposed publication;
> (b) he must not make disclosures injurious to this country's relations with other nations;
> (c) he must refrain from publishing information destructive of the confidential relationships on which our system of government is based.
>
> The final restriction relates to opinions or attitudes of Cabinet colleagues, advice given to him by colleagues and criticism of those working for him in office.

The Ministerial Code prohibits the writing and publication of memoirs by a Minister still in office. In relation to former Ministers, the Code requires that the draft manuscript is submitted to the Cabinet Secretary before publication.[9]

In *Attorney General v Jonathan Cape Ltd* (1976), the issue of the publication of the diaries of Richard Crossman, a former Labour Cabinet member, was considered. Executors of the estate of Richard Crossman sought to publish his *Diaries*; the government sought an injunction restraining publication. Recognising the convention of collective responsibility, Lord Widgery CJ stated:

> I find overwhelming evidence that the doctrine of joint responsibility is generally understood and practised, and equally strong evidence that it is on occasion ignored.

Having given such ambivalent recognition to the convention, which in any event was not court-enforceable, the injunction was denied.

Individual Ministerial Responsibility[10]

The Ministerial Code provides that the Minister in charge of a Department is solely accountable to Parliament for the exercise of the powers on which the administration of the Department depends.

---

8 *Report of the Committee of Privy Councillors*, Cmnd 6386, 1976, London: HMSO, Appendix 2.
9 Ministerial Code, 2016, paras 8.9 and 8.10.
10 See Turpin, 'Ministerial responsibility: myth or reality?' in Jowell and Oliver, 2000, Chapter 3.

Ministerial responsibility for the Department

HIERARCHICAL STRUCTURE OF A TYPICAL GOVERNMENT DEPARTMENT

Secretary of State – Cabinet Minister in charge of whole Department; ultimate departmental authority and responsibility

Junior Ministers – Ministers of State (below Cabinet level) with responsibility for specific aspects of the work of the given Department

Principal/Permanent Private Secretary

Permanent Secretary – senior departmental civil servant in charge of its day-to-day administration

Special Advisers – expert 'outsiders' brought in to drive government priorities

Agencies – still within the control of the given government Department, these have been given some budgetary and day-to-day operational autonomy to run specific areas of departmental work

The classic doctrine of this limb of ministerial responsibility states that a Minister is responsible for every action of his Department. As AV Dicey expressed it, the responsibility of Ministers means, where used in its strict sense, the legal responsibility of every Minister for every act of the Crown in which he takes part.

Ministerial responsibility is governed by parliamentary Resolutions, the Codes of Conduct of both Houses of Parliament, the Seven Principles of Public Life and the Ministerial Code.[11] The general principle governing Ministers of the Crown is that:

> Ministers of the Crown are expected to behave in a way that upholds the highest standards of propriety.[12]

The Ministerial Code also provides, in part, that:

- Ministers must uphold the principle of collective responsibility;
- Ministers have a duty to Parliament to account, and be held to account, for the policies, decisions and actions of their Departments and agencies;
- Ministers must give 'accurate and truthful information to Parliament' – Ministers who knowingly mislead Parliament will be expected to offer their resignation to the Prime Minister;

---

11 Cabinet Office, 2018.
12 Ibid., para. 1.1.

- Ministers must be as 'open as possible with Parliament and the public' – refusing to provide information only when disclosure would not be in the public interest;
- Ministers must ensure that no conflict arises, or appears to arise, between their public duties and their private interests.[13]

The Code also makes clear the role and power of the Prime Minister in relation to Ministers:

> Ministers are personally responsible for deciding how to act and conduct themselves in the light of the Code and for justifying their actions and conduct to Parliament and the public. However, Ministers only remain in office for as long as they retain the confidence of the Prime Minister. She is the ultimate judge of the standards of behaviour expected of a Minister and the appropriate consequences of a breach of those standards.[14]

It is the Minister who represents the public face of the Department and who speaks for the Department in Parliament. The doctrine is underpinned by Parliamentary Question Time and in debates in Parliament and in committees. During the passage of legislation relating to a particular Department's responsibilities, it is the Minister who will introduce the Bill and who will defend the Bill throughout its passage through the House of Commons. The Minister thus stands as the link between the Civil Service and Parliament, assuming full responsibility for the Department. As seen in Chapter 9, the conventionally recognised characteristics of the Civil Service are permanence, political neutrality and anonymity. The civil servant owes his or her duty to the government of the day, and is directly accountable to his or her Secretary of State. The principle of ministerial responsibility to Parliament not only underpins the doctrine of democratic responsibility of Ministers to the people through Parliament, but also facilitates the distinction between the responsibility of elected representatives and the civil servants who are responsible for the practical implementation of policy.

In practical terms nowadays, several factors diminish the extent to which a Minister can assume responsibility for every action of the Department. The size of Departments, the usually short ministerial tenure of office in any one Department and the complexity of modern government have long made the pure doctrine unworkable. As a former Home Secretary, Mr Reginald Maudling, stated in 1973, the classic doctrine of responsibility must be viewed in the light of modern conditions, with large Departments of state. Furthermore, the complexity of defining the scope of ministerial responsibility must also be seen in light of the rapid and extensive administrative framework under the system of agencies which are designed to increase efficiency in administration by establishing specialist agencies, each with its own executive.

Crichel Down

The classic doctrine of individual ministerial responsibility was seen to operate most clearly in the Crichel Down affair in 1954.[15] Crichel Down, an area of some 725 acres in Dorset, had been compulsorily acquired by the Air Ministry in 1937 for use as a bombing range. After the Second World War, the land was no longer needed and it was transferred to the Ministry of Agriculture and administered by the Agriculture Land Commission. In 1950, the Commission

---

13 Ministerial Code.
14 Ibid. section 4.
15 Cmnd 9220, 1954, London: HMSO.

decided that the best way of disposing of the land was to equip it as a single farm unit and lease it.

A total of 328 acres of Crichel Down had been part of the Crichel Estates owned by a Mrs Marten. Her husband wanted to reclaim the land. In both 1950 and 1952 he asked the Commission whether he could buy back the land. The Commission wrongly thought that they had no power of sale and declined to investigate his request. Mr Marten raised the matter with his Member of Parliament, who referred the matter to the Parliamentary Secretary to the Minister of Agriculture, who requested a report from the Land Commission. The official in charge of making the report was instructed not to approach the previous owners or to inspect the land, and to treat the matter as one of great confidentiality. The resulting report was full of inaccuracies, and went unchecked by the Ministry, which decided to adhere to its original plan for the land.

Mr Marten was informed of the decision in 1953, and advised the Ministry that he would rent the whole of the land. Meanwhile, the Ministry had committed itself to another course of action. Mr Marten's letters to the authorities went unanswered and he pressed for a public inquiry. The inquiry found that there had been inaccuracies in the report on the land, confusion and inefficiency in handling the matter and hostility to Mr Marten. In July 1954, the Minister Thomas Dugdale accepted responsibility and resigned.[16]

Ministerial responsibility after Crichel Down

It is notable that, between 1954 and 1982, there were no instances of ministerial resignation following allegations of and inquiries into serious defects in departmental administration. In 1959, 52 people were killed by security forces in Nyasaland but the Colonial Secretary Mr Lennox-Boyd did not resign. In 1964, due to a lack of coordination within the Ministry of Aviation, an overpayment of some £4 million was made to the Ferranti company, but the Minister did not resign. In 1968, the Foreign Secretary, Mr George Brown, did not resign over the Sachsenhausen affair, in which 12 former detainees in a Nazi prison camp were wrongly denied compensation under a scheme set up to compensate victims of Nazi persecution.[17]

In 1971, the Vehicle and General Insurance Company collapsed, leaving over a million policyholders uninsured. The Department of Trade and Industry had supervisory responsibility for insurance companies. An inquiry report placed the blame on a civil servant, Mr Jardine, an Under Secretary in the Department, and the Minister did not resign.[18] In 1982, the Home Secretary, Mr William Whitelaw, did not resign over a breach of security at Buckingham Palace which resulted in an intruder entering the Queen's bedroom, nor did Mr James Prior (as he then was), the Northern Ireland Minister, resign in 1984, following the escape of terrorists from the Maze Prison. The exchange in Parliament revealed divergent views about accountability. In debate, Mr Prior distinguished carefully between responsibility for policy – for which he accepted responsibility – and the failure of officials to follow the correct orders and procedures – for which he denied responsibility:

> However, I do not accept – and I do not think it right for the House to accept – that there is any constitutional or other principle that requires ministerial resignations in the face of failure, either by others to carry out orders or procedures or by their supervisors to ensure that staff carried out those orders.

16 See, inter alia, Nicolson, 1986; Griffith, 1987.
17 Third Report of the Parliamentary Commissioner for Administration, HC 54 (1967–1968), London: HMSO; Select Committee Report, HC 258 (1967–1968); Fry, 1970.
18 HL Deb 80; HC Deb 133 (1971–1972), para. 344.

In 1994, the Home Secretary, Michael Howard, faced several calls for his resignation over escapes from Whitemore prison and over the finding of escape equipment and weapons in prisons. Mr Howard refused to resign, citing in his support the precedent set by Mr James Prior (as he then was) over escapes from the Maze prison in Ulster, and the distinction between responsibility for operational matters and matters of policy.[19]

The Falklands War in 1982 provided the scenario for three ministerial resignations. Lord Carrington, the Foreign Secretary, resigned following allegations, which he denied, over the lack of preparation of the British forces when the Argentineans attacked; Mr Luce and Mr Atkins also resigned from the Foreign Office.[20]

In 1989, Mrs Edwina Currie resigned over the furore caused by her claim that the majority of eggs in the United Kingdom were infected with salmonella and, in 1990, Mr Nicholas Ridley resigned from the Department of Trade and Industry, having accepted responsibility for making intemperate remarks about a fellow Member State of the European Community. In 2002, the Secretary of State for Transport, Stephen Byers, resigned. He had seemed unable to produce progress in transport revitalisation. He also, fatally, failed to dismiss his special adviser after a callous remark made on 11 September 2001. Also in 2002, the Secretary of State for Education resigned following sustained criticism over examinations. The Health Secretary, Alan Milburn, resigned office in 2003, not for any shortcomings in office, but on the basis that he wanted to have more time to spend with his family.

The Work and Pensions Secretary, David Blunkett, resigned office for the second time in November 2005. He had first resigned his post as Secretary of State for the Home Department in 2004, having had an affair with a married woman and allegedly having intervened to have her nanny's application to remain in Britain 'fast tracked' through the system. The reason given for the second resignation was a breach of the rule that former Ministers should consult the Advisory Committee on Business Appointments about any business appointments they intend to take within two years of leaving office. The Ministerial Code now makes it clear that Ministers must seek advice from the Committee and are expected to abide by the advice received.[21]

In 2011 the Secretary of State for Defence, Dr Liam Fox, resigned office following disclosures that a close friend, Adam Werritty, had gained access to high-level meetings by representing himself as Dr Fox's adviser. A report by the Cabinet Secretary stated that Dr Fox had put the security of his staff at risk by disclosing details of his overseas visits and had risked causing confusion overseas about Britain's foreign policy by allowing the impression that Mr Werritty represented the British government. Furthermore, Mr Werritty had accepted donations from Conservative supporters, which could have given rise to the perception of a conflict of interest.

In 2014, Mark Harper, Minister for Immigration, resigned after discovering that his cleaner was an illegal immigrant. In 2014 the Minister for Culture Media and Sport, Maria Miller, was forced to resign office following a public outcry over allegations concerning her expenses. The Secretary of State for International Development, Priti Patel, resigned in November 2017 following revelations that she had held unauthorised meetings with Israeli ministers and others in 2017. The Home Secretary, Amber Rudd, resigned in April 2018 over the Home Office's treatment of people who had come to Britain from the Commonwealth lawfully but who lacked the necessary documents proving their entitlement to remain. The 'Windrush scandal' came to light when some elderly residents were threatened with

---

19 In 2006 the Home Secretary, Charles Clarke, refused to resign over the Home Office failure to deport foreign criminals on the expiry of their sentences. Mr Clarke was sacked by the Prime Minister.

20 See Cmnd 8787, 1983, London: HMSO.

21 Ministerial Code, 2016, para. 7.25.

deportation on the basis that they were living in Britain illegally. It was then revealed that the Home Office had set targets for deporting illegal immigrants, a fact about which the Home Secretary claimed to be unaware and denied in Parliament, leading to claims that she had misled Parliament contrary to the Ministerial Code.

Evaluating the evidence

From the above evidence, how is the working of the doctrine of individual ministerial responsibility to be evaluated? First, it is arguable that the doctrine represents one of the most significant conventions of the constitution, enhancing the accountability of the government to Parliament and the electorate. However, as has been seen above, the existence and acceptance of responsibility does not inevitably lead to the consequence of the resignation of a Minister for the failures within his or her Department. No hard and fast rules exist which will determine whether and when a Minister should resign, and accordingly it cannot clearly be said that resignation forms a part of the convention itself. On the question of the circumstances under which a Minister will resign as a result of departmental mismanagement, Professor SE Finer (1956) considered that:

> whether a minister is forced to resign depends on three factors: on himself, his Prime Minister and his party.

For a resignation to occur, all three factors have to be just so: the minister compliant, the Prime Minister firm, the party clamorous. This conjuncture is rare, and is in fact fortuitous. Above all, it is indiscriminate – which ministers escape and which do not is decided neither by the circumstances of the offence nor by its gravity.

In recent years there have been considerable improvements in the system of monitoring the conduct of Ministers and Members of Parliament through the Register of Members' Interests, the Advisory Committee on Business Appointments, the Committee on Standards in Public Life and the Parliamentary Commissioner for Standards and the Independent Parliamentary Standards Authority and Compliance Officer. However, there is no automatic sanction for breach of the rules by Ministers – the issue of resignation remains firmly in the political arena.

The Morality of Public Office

Qualification for ministerial office

Given the fundamental importance of ministerial responsibility, it is perhaps surprising that there are neither formal qualifications for office nor formal means by which the suitability for office is scrutinised in advance. Sir Ivor Jennings states that: 'the most elementary qualification demanded of a Minister is honesty and incorruptibility. It is, however, necessary not only that he should possess this qualification but also that he should appear to possess it' (1959a, Chapter V, page 106). Lord Hailsham expresses the same sentiment as follows: 'A politician must be trustworthy, and if he is found out telling a lie or if he is discovered in even a small financial dishonesty, he can only bow himself out of public life' (1975, page 199).

If a Minister of the Crown or Member of Parliament conducts his personal or financial affairs in a manner that falls below an 'acceptable standard', the Minister may be required to resign. Finer (1956) describes such conduct as being: 'a personal misadventure of the Minister which raises such doubt about his personal prudence or integrity as to cause him to resign'.

Vetting of prospective Ministers?

In the United States of America, appointment to Cabinet office is undertaken only after the 'advice and consent' of the Senate has been obtained.[22] By this means, it is intended to test the suitability of candidates prior to appointment and to avoid the inevitable embarrassment which occurs when resignation is forced through disclosure of some financial, sexual or other impropriety. In the United Kingdom, by contrast, appointment is entirely at the discretion of the Prime Minister and will be made on the basis of information which is publicly available and from the personal and political reputation of the candidate. As has been seen above, the standard of conduct required for public life and the reality frequently part company. It is thus at least arguable that some form of 'vetting' – such as occurs with prospective holders of senior Civil Service posts – should be introduced. Professor Rodney Brazier has advocated this course of action,[23] favouring some form of pre-appointment formal inquiry into fitness for office. Such an approach has not found favour with others who have considered it. In the inquiry following the Profumo scandal, Lord Denning stated that there should be no inquiry into politicians' private lives by the security services other than where state security was under threat, a view endorsed by the Security Commission in its report following the resignations of Lords Lambton and Jellicoe.[24] Lord Hailsham expressed the view that, in a democracy, there should be no such invasive advance inquiries into the private lives of public figures (1975), while recognising the real risks of corruption in public life which 'is hard to define ... harder to detect, and almost as catching as smallpox' (page 201). It must, however, be conceded that when the standard of conduct is lowered and the esteem of a government damaged by lack of integrity, then some action is needed.

Individual Responsibility for Personal Conduct

Personal conduct

While responsibility for the implementation and execution of policy of course entails 'personal conduct', one aspect of ministerial responsibility which has also given rise to particular concern is the conduct of Ministers in relation to their private lives. The personal relationships of Ministers are also matters which fall under intense public scrutiny. In 1963, the Minister of War, Mr John Profumo, was found to have been having a sexual relationship with a prostitute, Christine Keeler. Ms Keeler, it was discovered, also enjoyed a close personal relationship with a Russian Naval Attaché at the Soviet Embassy. When questioned in the House of Commons about the affair, Mr Profumo lied to the House. When the truth emerged, Mr Profumo resigned office. The cause of his resignation was not so much the sexual affair, but contempt of the House committed through lying. The potential security aspects of the affair led to a judicial inquiry headed by Lord Denning MR.[25]

In 1973, Lords Lambton and Jellicoe resigned office. Earl Jellicoe, Lord Privy Seal and Leader of the House of Lords, resigned after it had been revealed that he had been associating with prostitutes. Lord Lambton, Parliamentary Under Secretary of State for Defence for the Royal Air Force, resigned over allegations of involvement with illegal drugs. The government requested an inquiry by the Security Commission into any security aspects of the affairs,

---

22 Constitution, Article II, s. 2.
23 Brazier, 1998, Chapter 3, and 1994.
24 Lord Denning's Report, Cmnd 2152, 1963, London: HMSO, para. 230; Report of the Security Commission, Cmnd 5367, 1973, London: HMSO, para. 42.
25 Statement to the House 674 HC Deb 809–810, 21 March 1963; Lord Denning's Report, Cmnd 2152, 1963, London: HMSO; Macmillan, 1973, pp. 436–441; Denning, 1980, Pt 2, Chapter II; Marshall, 1984, Chapter VI.

which resulted in the finding that no classified information had in fact been revealed either directly or indirectly to 'any potentially hostile power'.[26]

In 1983, Cecil Parkinson MP, the Secretary of State for Trade and Industry and Conservative Party Chairman, resigned following revelations about a long-standing relationship with his secretary, Sarah Keays, who became pregnant. For some time, the Prime Minister, Mrs Thatcher and the Party maintained their support for Mr Parkinson,[27] as did his wife throughout the public attention focused on the affair. When Sarah Keays published a series of articles in the national press about the matter, and alleged that Mr Parkinson had said that he wanted to marry her, public and political support began to wane, and Mr Parkinson resigned.

In 1992, Alan Amos MP resigned after allegations of indecency with another man. Also in 1992, the Heritage Secretary David Mellor was forced to resign following revelations of a sexual relationship with an actress (and the receipt of gifts). The majority of the revelations had been brought about through the illicit bugging of an apartment used by Mr Mellor. While this affair alone may not have caused his downfall, the revelation that Mr Mellor and his family had enjoyed the hospitality, while on holiday, of the wife of a Palestinian Liberation Organisation official sealed his fate. Despite his being regarded as an excellent Heritage Secretary, the intense and hostile coverage by the media ensured his resignation.[28] In January 1994, Tim Yeo MP, Minister of State for the Environment, resigned after admitting fathering a child out of wedlock, as did Alan Duncan MP after allegations that he had used the 'right to buy' legislation to make money in property deals with a neighbour. In February 1994, Hartley Booth MP resigned after a 'close relationship' with a research assistant; in May 1994, Michael Brown MP resigned following newspaper reports of a 'friendship' with a male civil servant. In 1998, Ron Davies, the Welsh Secretary, resigned immediately after being discovered in unexplained but curious circumstances on Clapham Common. In 2012 the Energy and Climate Change Secretary, Chris Huhne, resigned from Cabinet following criminal charges of perverting the course of justice. In 2012 the Conservative Chief Whip, Andrew Mitchell, resigned following a disputed argument with a police officer. The message is, if you are caught out, resign sooner rather than later in order to spare the government embarrassment and loss of public confidence. The Secretary of State for Defence, Michael Fallon, also resigned in November 2017 following allegations that he had behaved 'inappropriately' towards a female journalist several years previously. In December 2017 the Deputy Prime Minister, Damian Green, was forced to resign over making 'inaccurate and misleading' statements about pornography found by the police on his parliamentary computer. There were also allegations of 'inappropriate behaviour' towards a female journalist.

Financial probity

The personal financial probity of Ministers, their Parliamentary Private Secretaries and other Members of Parliament is regarded with seriousness. Under the law and custom of Parliament, Members must declare their financial interests in the Register of Members' Interests and make public declarations in debate or committee proceedings of any interests they hold which may affect their impartiality.[29] The holding of directorships, ownership of shares, consultancy positions and receipt of gifts all raise issues concerning integrity and fitness for office. The Ministerial Code states that 'Ministers must scrupulously avoid any dan-

---

26 *Report of the Security Commission*, Cmnd 5367, 1973, London: HMSO, para. 5; Marshall, 1984, Chapter VI. On the role of the Security Commission, see further Chapter 22.

27 Thatcher, 1993, pp. 310–311; Tebbitt, 1988, pp. 205, 208–211.

28 Statement of Resignation 212 HC Deb 139, 25 September 1992.

29 On alleged payments for parliamentary questions, see Chapter 17.

ger of an actual or apparent conflict of interest between their Ministerial position and their private financial interests'. The general principle is that a Minister must either dispose of an interest or take steps to prevent any conflict.[30] Where a financial interest is retained, processes must be put in place to ensure that the Minister is not involved in any decision making relating to that interest. The Ministerial Code also requires that Ministers consult the Advisory Committee on Business Appointments about any business appointments they intend to take up within two years of leaving office – a requirement breached by David Blunkett in 2005 (above). There is an inherent vagueness in such criteria, yet relatively few Ministers and other Members of Parliament have fallen from grace as a result of imprudent (or dishonest) financial dealings. In 1913, the issue of Ministers holding shares was raised in debate following allegations of improper ministerial involvement in the Marconi Company.[31] It was rumoured that Ministers[32] had used information received as Ministers for their own personal advantage. All three Ministers involved denied any share dealings. A Select Committee inquiry exonerated the Ministers from all charges of corruption and from charges that they had used their ministerial positions for personal gain.

Ministerial resignations involving allegations of financial imprudence – although in each case there were additional factors involved in the resignations – include, as noted above, David Mellor, the Heritage Secretary, who resigned following a mixture of allegations, one of which involved the receipt of a free holiday from a woman with Palestinian Liberation Organisation associations.[33] In 1992, it was revealed that the Chancellor of the Exchequer, Norman Lamont, had received £4,700 of public money for legal fees involved in the eviction of a tenant from his apartment.[34] In June 1993, the Minister for Northern Ireland, Michael Mates MP, resigned office after it had been revealed that Mr Mates gave to the fugitive businessman Asil Nadir, who faced prosecution on charges of theft and fraud, an inexpensive watch, shortly before Mr Nadir fled the United Kingdom. A subsequent allegation was made that Mr Mates accepted the loan of a car from Mr Nadir for his ex-wife's use, and he ultimately resigned despite claiming to have the full support of the Prime Minister.[35] Further embarrassment was caused to the government in 1994, when it was alleged that Jeffrey Archer, former Conservative Party Chairman, had been involved in share-dealing in Anglia Television, on whose Board of Directors his wife held a directorship. Also in 1994, allegations were made that Members of Parliament had accepted payment for asking parliamentary questions. This affair escalated into a full-scale judicial inquiry into 'standards in public life', and to a tightening of the rules regulating the financial interests of all Members of the House of Commons.[36] In 1998 came the culmination of the long-running inquiry into the financial affairs of Geoffrey Robinson, the former Paymaster General, when in December both Robinson and Peter Mandelson, Secretary of State for Trade and Industry, resigned. Peter Mandelson had been a leading architect in making the 'New' Labour Party 'electable' and a pivotal figure in the general election campaign. However, it was revealed that Mandelson had accepted a personal loan from Robinson to finance the purchase of a London home, and that the loan had not been disclosed. While protesting that he had done nothing 'wrong', Mandelson resigned. He returned to ministerial office in 1999 as Secretary of State for Northern Ireland, only to resign again over allegations that he interfered in a passport application of a wealthy Indian businessman who had contributed money to the Millennium Dome, for which Mandelson

---

30 A full list of interests which might give rise to an appearance of conflict must be provided.
31 54 HC Deb 5 Ser. 391–514, 543–664. See Donaldson, 1962.
32 Attorney General, Sir Rufus Isaacs, Chancellor of the Exchequer, D Lloyd George, and Postmaster General, Sir Herbert Samuel.
33 HC Deb Col. 139, 25 September 1992.
34 See Brazier, 1992 and 1993.
35 Interview, BBC News, 22 June 1993.
36 On this see Chapter 17.

had responsibility at the time.[37] In 2005 the resignation of the Work and Pensions Secretary, David Blunkett, discussed above, was in part prompted by allegations concerning shares in a company which was due to bid for a government contract.

See Chapter 17.

In 2009, it was disclosed that several government Ministers and numerous Members of Parliament had abused the system of parliamentary allowances and expenses, leading to many resignations. The matter is discussed in detail in Chapter 17.

Premature disclosure of confidential information

By convention, the contents of the Chancellor of the Exchequer's Budget are kept secret until revealed in Parliament. Traditionally, the rule about secrecy was so strict that the details would not even be revealed to Cabinet before Parliament. Nowadays, however, the rule is much relaxed and it is not uncommon for the Chancellor to discuss proposals prior to formal disclosure.

The Nolan Committee

The continued and intensive media interest in ministerial conduct has caused a loss of public confidence in Members of Parliament as a whole, and in the conduct and probity of Ministers. The Nolan Committee, appointed to inquire into standards in public life, examined in general the standards of conduct expected of Ministers. More specifically, the Committee has investigated the question of the rules relating to Ministers who retire from office and subsequently take up employment with organisations with whom they had dealings whilst in ministerial office. In addition, the Committee considered the organisation, regulation and personnel employed in non-departmental public bodies (NDPBs or 'quangos').[38]

The Nolan Committee endorsed the view that the 'public is entitled to expect very high standards of behaviour from Ministers, as they have profound influence over the daily lives of us all'.[39] The Committee distinguished between the need for clear enforceable rules regulating financial conduct and those regulating sexual conduct. In respect of the latter, the Committee, whilst recognising that sexual improprieties may on occasion be relevant to the performance of a Minister's public duties, took the view that it was not possible to lay down hard and fast rules to regulate such private conduct. The Committee recommended that the Prime Minister should be given explicit power to determine whether Ministers – who are responsible for complying with the standards of conduct – have in fact upheld the required standard (paragraph 13).

Public Inquiries into the Conduct of Government

Occasionally a situation arises which causes such political concern that it is considered appropriate to establish a public inquiry into the matter. The different types of public inquiries and their composition and procedures are discussed in Chapter 26. Here, four major inquiries are discussed to illustrate their role in ensuring the accountability of government.

---

37 An Inquiry chaired by former Treasury Secretary Sir Anthony Hammond cleared Mandelson of any wrongdoing.
38 Quasi-autonomous non-governmental organisations, on which see further below and Chapter 23.
39 Nolan Report, *Standards in Public Life*, Cm 2850-I, 1995, London: HMSO, Chapter 3, para. 4.

Matrix Churchill and Arms to Iraq[40]

Between 1987 and 1989, the Matrix Churchill company exported machine tools to Iraq. It was alleged by Customs and Excise (which brought the prosecution against the directors of the company) that those exports breached the export regulations in place at the time. In defence, it was argued that the government knew about the exports and had in fact authorised them, and that MI6 (the Secret Intelligence Service) was aware of the exports. When the matter came to trial, four government Ministers signed public interest immunity certificates (on which see further below) refusing disclosure of documents relating to, *inter alia*, records of meetings and communications between the Department of Trade and Industry and the Foreign and Commonwealth Office. The effect of the certificates was to deny to the court the evidence which might have led to the acquittal of the defendants, each of whom was facing a significant term of imprisonment if convicted. The trial of the directors of Matrix Churchill collapsed after a former government Minister, Alan Clark, revealed to the court that the government had — as the defence claimed — in fact known of the exports. The Prime Minister established a judicial inquiry, chaired by Sir Richard Scott, the day after the collapse of the trial.[41] The decision to establish a judicial inquiry was brought about in large measure through the failure of Select Committee inquiries to unravel the full facts surrounding the issue.[42]

In 'Ministerial accountability' (1996), Sir Richard Scott discussed the recently drawn distinction between ministerial *accountability* and ministerial *responsibility*, citing the evidence of a former Cabinet Secretary (Sir Robin Butler) as follows:

> I am using 'accountability' to mean that the Minister must always answer questions and give an account to Parliament for the action of his department, whether he is 'responsible' in the sense of attracting personal criticism himself, or not. So I am using 'accountability' to leave out, as it were, the blame element of it. The blame element is an open question. There are cases where he is accountable in which he may be personally blameworthy, and there will be occasions when he is not personally blameworthy.[43]

The 'divorce' between the acceptance of responsibility and the consequence of resignation was not, in Sir Richard's expressed view, the 'heart of an effective system of parliamentary accountability'. In Sir Richard's view, what does lie at the heart of the constitutional doctrine is rather the: 'obligation of ministers to give, or to facilitate the giving, of information about the activities of their departments and about the actions and omission of their civil servants'.[44]

In the Arms to Iraq affair, the obligation to provide information came into conflict with the government's insistence on following the practice of not disclosing to Parliament information concerning individual export licensing matters. The refusal to answer questions at all is but part of the problem of the duty to give information. A further cause for concern lay in the failure of Ministers to give full answers to questions and, in relation to the Scott Inquiry, in the failure of witnesses to provide the full picture. 'Commercial confidentiality' is an accepted reason for the denial of information, but that, in Sir Richard's view, did not excuse the refusal of information or the provision of information about weapons supply. National security is another justified exception to the duty to make full disclosure. Nevertheless:

---

40 See Leigh, D, 1993; Norton-Taylor, 1995; Tomkins, 1998.
41 See *Report of the Inquiry into the Export of Defence Equipment and Dual-Use Goods to Iraq and Related Prosecution*, HC 115 (1995–1996), 15 February 1996 (the Scott Report).
42 See the Trade and Industry Select Committee, *Second Report, Exports to Iraq: Project Babylon and Long Range Guns*, HC 86 (1991–1992), London: HMSO; see also Tomkins, 1993; Bradley, 1992a.
43 Evidence given to the Inquiry on 9 February 1994: transcript, pp. 22–23, cited in the Scott Report.
44 Scott Report, p. 415.

setting those rare cases aside, the proposition that it is acceptable for a Minister to give an answer that is deliberately incomplete is one which, in my opinion, is inconsistent with the requirements of the constitutional principle of ministerial accountability. Half the picture can be true ... But the audience does not know that it is seeing only half the picture. If it did know, it would protest.[45]

A strong democracy can only be a legitimate label if the electors are able to express their view on the basis of adequate knowledge of government activities: 'A failure by Ministers to meet the obligations of ministerial accountability by providing information about the activities of their departments engenders cynicism about government and undermines, in my opinion, the democratic process'.[46]

The Public Service Committee Report: ministerial accountability and responsibility[47]

Reviewing the doctrine of ministerial responsibility from the Crichel Down affair in 1954, the Committee produced 34 conclusions and recommendations. In the Committee's view, it was not possible to distinguish absolutely between areas in which a Minister is personally responsible (and blameworthy) and areas in which the Minister is constitutionally accountable.[48] Further, the Committee concluded that 'proper and rigorous scrutiny and accountability' is a more important feature of ministerial responsibility than Parliament's ability to force that Minister's resignation.[49] The Public Service Committee had been critical of the fact that the definition and scope of ministerial responsibility was formulated by the government of the day, via *Question of Procedures for Ministers*, rather than by Parliament, which alone had the right to demand and enforce ministerial responsibility. As a result, and after much inter-Party debate, the House of Commons resolved in 1997 that:

In the opinion of the House, the following principles should govern the conduct of ministers of the Crown in relation to Parliament:

(1) Ministers have a duty to Parliament to account, and be held to account, for the policies, decisions and actions of their departments and next step agencies;

(2) It is of paramount importance that ministers should give accurate and truthful information to Parliament, correcting any inadvertent error at the earliest opportunity. Ministers who knowingly mislead Parliament will be expected to offer their resignation to the Prime Minister;

(3) Ministers should be as open as possible with Parliament, refusing to provide information only when disclosure would not be in the public interest;

(4) Ministers should require civil servants who give evidence before parliamentary committees on their behalf and under their directions to be as helpful as possible in providing accurate, truthful and full information.[50]

---

45 Scott Report, p. 422. See Tomkins, 1996.
46 Ibid., p. 425.
47 *Second Report from the Public Service Committee*, HC 313 (1995–1996), London: HMSO.
48 See HC Deb Vol. 290 Col. 273, 12 February 1997; and *Government Response to the Report of the Public Service Committee on Ministerial Accountability*, HC 67 (1996–1997), London: HMSO, November 1996, p. vi.
49 See *Government Response to the Report of the Public Service Committee on Ministerial Accountability*, HC 67 (1996–1997), London: HMSO.
50 These principles are reflected in the Ministerial Code 2010, para. 1.2 b–e.

Pause and Reflect

1. Trace the changing concept of individual ministerial responsibility from the mid-twentieth century to the current day. What explains the changed approach? Is the distinction between 'responsibility' and 'accountability' convincing, and why do you think it is, or is not, constitutionally justifiable?
2. Constitutional conventions exist on a spectrum from uncertainty to certainty. Where would you place (a) collective ministerial responsibility and (b) individual ministerial responsibility on this spectrum?
3. The rule of law requires that government acts under the law. To what extent do the conventions of collective and individual ministerial responsibility promote the rule of law?

The Hutton Inquiry[51]

The Iraq War in 2003 was to lead to two judicial inquiries. The first, the Hutton Inquiry, was prompted by the suicide of Dr David Kelly CMG, a senior government scientist who, inter alia, had been one of the chief weapons inspectors in Iraq on behalf of the United Nations' Special Commission.

Central to the circumstances surrounding Dr Kelly's death was the intelligence relating to weapons of mass destruction (WMD) set out in a government dossier published in September 2002. In May 2003 a journalist, who had met with Dr Kelly, alleged in a radio programme that the government's dossier was wrong in that it claimed that Iraq had WMD which were deployable within 45 minutes and that the government had exaggerated the intelligence to bolster its case to attack Iraq. Dr Kelly acted as an adviser to the Ministry of Defence, the Defence Intelligence Staff and the Secret Intelligence Service (MI6), and part of his role was to speak to the media and other institutions on Iraq issues. The government complained to the BBC about the broadcast. The identity of the journalist's source of information then became of central importance.

Among the several issues which Lord Hutton considered in relation to the government dossier was whether the Prime Minister or officials in No. 10 Downing Street were responsible for intelligence being set out in the dossier which they knew or suspected was incorrect or misleading. The Inquiry's conclusions regarding the dossier exonerated the government from any attempt to embellish the data relied on. The 45-minute claim at the heart of the controversy had been received by the SIS from a source in Iraq which was regarded as reliable. The allegation that the government 'knew' that the claim was wrong was unfounded. Further, the Inquiry found that Downing Street recognised that nothing should be stated in the dossier which was inconsistent with the intelligence received.

The Butler Inquiry

In February 2004 the Prime Minister decided to establish a committee of inquiry to review intelligence on weapons of mass destruction. The Inquiry was chaired by the Rt Hon Lord Butler, a former Cabinet Secretary.[52] The terms of reference of the Inquiry were to investigate

---

51 See Blom-Cooper and Munro, 2004.
52 See Review of Intelligence on Weapons of Mass Destruction, Report of a Committee of Privy Counsellors, London: The Stationery Office, HC 898, July 2004.

the intelligence coverage available in respect of WMD programmes in countries of concern and on the global trade in WMD, taking into account what is now known about these programmes; as part of this work, to investigate the accuracy of intelligence on Iraqi WMD up to March 2003, and to examine any discrepancies between the intelligence gathered, evaluated and used by the government before the conflict, and between that intelligence and what has been discovered by the Iraq survey group since the end of the conflict; and to make recommendations to the Prime Minister for the future on the gathering, evaluation and use of intelligence on WMD, in the light of the difficulties of operating in countries of concern.

The Inquiry concluded that there had been no wrongdoing on the part of the government. On the '45-minute claim', the Inquiry found that the intelligence report itself was 'vague and ambiguous'.[53] On allegations that the government's motivation for going to war was a desire to control Iraq's oil supplies, the Inquiry found 'no evidence' to support such an allegation.

The Chilcot Inquiry

The Chilcot Inquiry was established to examine the United Kingdom's involvement in the Iraq War 2003, including the way in which decisions were made and actions taken. The Inquiry was chaired by Sir John Chilcot.[54] Public hearings began in November 2009.[55] The hearings were open to the public and televised. The hearings were not covered by parliamentary or other privilege, and witnesses were entitled to have a legal representative present during the hearing, although not to give evidence or ask questions. The Inquiry was not a court of law, and questions of guilt or innocence were not in issue.[56] Publication of the Report of Inquiry was delayed until July 2016.[57] The Report runs to 12 volumes and offers a highly critical and detailed account of the decision-making process in the run up to the 2003 war in Iraq. Among the many criticisms of the government's decision-making processes are the following:

- that the diplomatic options had not … been exhausted. Military action was therefore not a last resort;
- that the Attorney General changed his advice to the government from the view that military action would be unlawful to the view that there was a lawful basis for the use of force without a further Security Council Resolution but continued to have serious concerns about the legality of war;
- that the government knew it did not have the support of a majority in the UN Security Council, and that the UK's actions 'undermined the authority of the Security Council';
- one of the essential factors in whether action without a further Resolution would be lawful or not turned on whether or not the Iraqi government was in 'substantial compliance' with the requirement to allow inspections and reduce its arsenal of weaponry. The Prime Minister took the decision that there was not substantial compliance on his own, without consulting Cabinet or other Ministers;
- the US and UK governments sought to justify their proposed invasion of Iraq on the basis that Iraq had WMD which it could deploy against the West. On this the Report was damning:

---

53 *Review of Intelligence on Weapons of Mass Destruction*, para. 507.
54 A retired senior civil servant. All five members of the Committee are Privy Councillors.
55 For security reasons a number of hearings have been held in private.
56 www.iraqinquiry.org.uk.
57 See Report of a Committee of Privy Counsellors, *Report of the Iraq Inquiry*, HC 264, 6 July 2016.

> The lack of evidence to support pre-conflict claims about Iraq's WMD challenged the credibility of the Government and the intelligence community, and the legitimacy of the war. [Executive Summary, paragraph 577]

- that there were serious equipment shortfalls when the conflict began;
- that the UK planning and preparation for the post-conflict stage of operations was 'wholly inadequate', and that:

> The Government, which lacked both clear Ministerial oversight of post-conflict strategy, planning and preparation, and effective coordination between government departments, failed to analyse or manage those [post-conflict] risks adequately. [Executive Summary at paragraph 814]

- that the government failed to achieve its stated objectives in Iraq.

Coronavirus

The Coronavirus Pandemic of 2019–2020 gave rise to emergency legislation and to many questions concerning the competence of government in handling the issue. A public inquiry is expected to be undertaken in the near future.

 Pause and Reflect

1. Trace the changing concept of individual ministerial responsibility from the mid-twentieth century to the current day. What explains the changed approach? Is the distinction between 'responsibility' and 'accountability' convincing, and why do you think it is, or is not, constitutionally justifiable?
2. Constitutional conventions exist on a spectrum from uncertainty to certainty. Where would you place (a) collective ministerial responsibility and (b) individual ministerial responsibility on this spectrum?
3. The rule of law requires that government acts under the law. To what extent do the conventions of collective and individual ministerial responsibility promote the rule of law?

Summary

The accountability of government to Parliament and the people is essential in any democratic state. The constitutional conventions of collective and individual ministerial responsibility are central to ensuring this accountability. Collective responsibility refers to the requirements that decisions reached in Cabinet are binding on all Cabinet and non-Cabinet Ministers and that Cabinet discussions are confidential and may not be disclosed. Individual ministerial responsibility also has two aspects: the first is the responsibility of the Minister to account to Parliament for the operation of his or her Department; the second is responsibility for personal conduct.

Government must retain the confidence of the House of Commons, and failure to do so may result in a successful Motion of No Confidence, which by convention forces the government to resign.

📖 Further Reading

Allen, TRS, 'Law, democracy and constitutionalism: reflections on *Evans v Attorney General*' (2016) 75 *Cambridge Law Journal* 38.

Benn, T, 'The case for a constitutional premiership' (1980) 33 *Parliamentary Affairs* 7.

Blackburn, R, *King and Country: Monarchy and the Future King Charles III*, 2008, London: Politico's Publishing.

Brazier, R, *Constitutional Practice*, 3rd edn, 1999, Oxford: Oxford University Press, Chapters 5–7.

Craig, R, 'Black spiders weaving webs: the constitutional implications of executive veto of tribunal determinations' (2016) 79 *Modern Law Review* 166.

Drewry, G, 'The executive: towards accountable government and effective governance?' in J Jowell and D Oliver (eds), *The Changing Constitution*, 7th edn, 2011, Oxford: Oxford University Press.

Finders, M, 'The enduring centrality of individual ministerial responsibility within the British constitution' (2000) 6 *Journal of Legislative Studies* 73.

Hough, B, 'Ministerial responses to parliamentary questions: some recent concerns' [2003] *Public Law* 211.

Woodhouse, D, 'Ministerial responsibility in the 1990s: when do ministers resign?' (1993) 46 *Parliamentary Affairs* 277.

Woodhouse, D, 'Ministerial responsibility: something old, something new' [1997] *Public Law* 262.

Chapter 11

Devolution and Local Government

Chapter Contents

Learning Objectives

By the end of this chapter you should be able to:

- [ ] explain the aims and objectives of devolution;
- [ ] in outline, explain the differences between devolution to Northern Ireland, Scotland and Wales;
- [ ] discuss the relationship between the UK Parliament and the devolved legislatures;
- [ ] discuss the Sewell Convention;
- [ ] consider the issues entailed in independence for Scotland;
- [ ] explain the question of devolution to England;
- [ ] explain the role of the courts in settling devolution issues;
- [ ] discuss, in outline, the governance of London;
- [ ] explain the main features of local government in England.

Introduction

As discussed in Chapters 1 and 2, the constitution of the United Kingdom has traditionally been characterised by the unity of its several parts, with centralised government. The history of Ireland and the union of Northern Ireland with Britain is long and complex and is outlined below. Wales became united with England through being conquered in 1262, while the Acts of Union 1706 and 1707 marked the end of the separation of Scotland and England under two sovereign Parliaments. Despite the former attempt at devolution of power to both Wales and Scotland in 1978, the population of neither country then expressed – according to the terms of the referendum – the desire for greater separation from centralised government. Two decades later, however, the political position was much changed. A disenchantment with the extent to which the national Parliament reflected the views of the people of Scotland, in particular, and Wales, and a rising tide of nationalist regional sentiment, led to change and power being devolved from the centre to the nations. In addition, settlement reached in Northern Ireland under the 1998 Good Friday agreement facilitated the re-establishment of the Northern Ireland Assembly. The Scotland Act 1998 and the Government of Wales Acts 1998 gave effect to devolution of power with the establishment of a Scottish Parliament and the Welsh Assembly (now Senedd).[1]

In terms of constitutional structures, devolution may be compared and contrasted with unitary states and federal states. As discussed in Chapter 1, a unitary state is one with a centralised government and legislature which governs the whole territory. In practice none but the smallest of states could run on such lines: the need to delegate powers to local bodies or authorities will always arise. Nevertheless, in a unitary state, it will be the central government which will formulate policy and determine the scope of any delegated powers. Historically, since the uniting of the four nations of England, Northern Ireland, Scotland and Wales, this has been the predominant model of government, with the United Kingdom (UK) Parliament (Westminster) having sovereign law-making power under the uncodified constitution. In addition to being uncodified, the constitution is also inherently flexible, constitutional change being brought about by Acts of the UK Parliament under ordinary parliamentary procedures.

Federal states, such as Malaysia and the United States of America, are those in which governmental power is divided between the centre and the component states which make up the union. A written constitution will set out the division and allocation of powers, and any amendment to those powers will require the use of formal procedures as laid down in the constitution. Typically, powers relating to national security, defence and foreign policy will be reserved to central (federal) government, while matters such as education, transport and health are transferred to the states. The federal government does not have the power unilaterally to alter the allocation of powers.

Devolution has been defined as 'the delegation of central government powers without the relinquishment of sovereignty'.[2] It involves the establishment of national legislatures with law-making powers defined in the constituent Act of the United Kingdom Parliament: the Northern Ireland Act 1998, the Scotland Act 1998 and the Governance of Wales Act 1998. The UK Parliament retains its sovereign power to legislate for the nations: section 5(6) of the Northern Ireland Act 1998, section 28(7) of the Scotland Act 1998, section 107(5) of the Governance of Wales Act 1998. However, in practical terms the law-making power of the Westminster Parliament has diminished as increasing powers are devolved to the nations.

---

1 See also the Government of Wales Act 2006 and Scotland Act 2012.
2 Royal Commission on the Constitution 1967–1973, CM 5460, Vol. 1, para. 543.

Devolution to the nations of Northern Ireland, Scotland and Wales varies: it is asymmetrical. This is deliberate: each of the three devolution Acts has been drafted to reflect the appropriate form and scope of devolution for that nation. In addition to being varied, devolution is also a dynamic process, not a once-and-for-all event. In relation to each country, new Acts of the UK Parliament have been passed to adjust devolution. One of the constitutional consequences of devolution is that Members of the United Kingdom Parliament in London (Westminster) who represent constituencies in Northern Ireland, Scotland and Wales vote on matters which relate solely to England, whereas English MPs do not have any say in matters which have been devolved to the national Parliaments.[3] This is the 'West-Lothian Question'. The issue was considered by the Commission on the Consequences of Devolution for the House of Commons (the McKay Commission), which reported in 2013.

A Memorandum of Understanding (MOU)[4] set out the principles underpinning relations between the devolved governments and the UK Government. Good communication, consultation and cooperation are key principles. It also sets out the procedures for avoiding and resolving disputes between governments. The MOU establishes a Joint Ministerial Committee (JMC). The JMC is a consultative body designed to consider and advise on devolved issues, keep liaison between the UK Government and devolved administrations under review and to consider any disputes between the administrations.

Forms of local government – which reflect the needs and wishes of people living in local communities – have existed as long as communities have existed and pre-date central government by centuries. Local government represents both a form of decentralisation of power from central government and a basis for local democracy. The country is divided into local authorities – either county or district – each having law-making and administrative powers as delegated by Parliament. Local authorities nowadays are entirely creatures of statute; accordingly, the only powers which they have are those conferred by the sovereign United Kingdom Parliament.

In 2020 the Government announced that it intends to extend devolution and reform local government. The plans however, has been delayed by the need to deal with the Coronavirus pandemic and the publication of a White Paper has been delayed until 2021.

The combined effect of devolution to Northern Ireland, Scotland and Wales and local government is a constitution which is less 'unitary' and increasingly multi-layered.[5]

Northern Ireland

Ireland first came under the control of the English in the twelfth century. The province of Ulster – then the nine northern counties of Ireland – was largely unaffected by English rule until the sixteenth century. In the seventeenth century there was a considerable level of immigration into the north, principally from Scotland and Wales, resulting in a significant Protestant (non-Roman Catholic) population. Relations between Ireland (which adhered to the Roman Catholic faith) and England – fuelled by the issue of religion – worsened. In an attempt to quell unrest and reach a lasting settlement, negotiations took place which resulted in the Act of Union 1800. Intended to be a permanent union, it was not to survive the economic crises which led to famine and mass emigration from Ireland. The movement towards independence from England grew. In 1919, civil unrest escalated into war. In 1920 the United Kingdom Parliament passed the Government of Ireland Act under which the country was

---

3 The 'West Lothian Question': see below at p. 250.
4 September 2012.
5 See Schutz and Tierney 2018.

partitioned, with six of the original nine Ulster counties being separated from the remainder of Ireland. In the following year, the Anglo-Irish Treaty gave to southern Ireland (the Irish Free State) self-governing dominion status. In 1937 the Irish Prime Minister published the Constitution of the Irish Free State, proclaiming independence from the United Kingdom, a situation not formally accepted by the United Kingdom until 1949.

From the time of partition until 1972, Northern Ireland enjoyed a measure of self-government represented by the assembly at Stormont. However, the turbulent legacy of the past continued to exert its influence with the Irish Republican Army (IRA) seeking to rid Northern Ireland of British rule and reunite the province with the Republic of Ireland. The terrorist campaign was to last for 30 years.

In 1972, with the violence unabated and the civilian death toll mounting, the UK Government once again assumed responsibility for the province. The Northern Ireland Assembly – Stormont – was prorogued indefinitely and the powers of the Northern Ireland government transferred to a Secretary of State for Northern Ireland.

In 1973, following a referendum, a new system of power-sharing between the Northern Ireland Assembly and the Westminster Parliament was introduced. Under the Northern Ireland Assembly Act 1973 and the Northern Ireland Constitution Act 1973, an Assembly was to be established, having 78 members elected under the single transferable vote system. The Northern Ireland Constitution Act 1973 provided a statutory guarantee that Northern Ireland would remain part of the United Kingdom until the time at which a majority of the people, voting in a referendum, should determine otherwise.[6] Representation of Northern Ireland at Westminster was increased to 17 Members of Parliament.

However, the system broke down and in 1974 the Northern Ireland Act led to the restoration of direct rule of Northern Ireland by Westminster. Attempts were made to dismantle the significant discrimination which existed in fields of housing and employment. Section 17 of the Northern Ireland Constitution Act 1973 provided that any Northern Ireland legislation which discriminated against persons on the basis of religion or political belief was void. The attempts proved largely ineffective. Throughout the 1970s and 1980s a virtual civil war existed in Northern Ireland.[7] From 1971 to 1977 'an average of 252 persons were killed each year'.[8] In 1975 a further attempt to devolve power was made. The attempt failed as a result of the Ulster Unionists' insistence that they retain a majority of seats in any new Assembly. The Northern Ireland Act 1982 nevertheless provided for a new Assembly, to be elected by proportional representation, which was initially designed to be a debating and deliberative forum which would, in the future, propose plans for a new form of devolved government. The Social Democratic and Labour Party (SDLP) and Sinn Féin members refused to take their seats. Faced with political deadlock, the Assembly was once more dissolved. In 1983 the New Ireland Forum was established, in which the major political parties in the north and south were represented. The outcome of the deliberations was the Anglo-Irish Agreement, signed by the Prime Ministers of the United Kingdom and the Republic of Ireland.

The Anglo-Irish Agreement 1985
The Agreement endorsed the principle that no constitutional change concerning the relationship between the north and south could come about other than with the consent of the people of Northern Ireland. That majority did not exist. In the absence of such consent, it was agreed

---

6 See Hadfield, 1989.
7 See Gearty, 1991, Chapter 8.
8 Dickson, 1993.

that there should be closer cooperation in relation to security, economic, social and cultural matters and the promotion of reconciliation between the two parts of Ireland. An Inter-Governmental Conference was established to consider reforms, The Unionists of Northern Ireland opposed the Agreement regarding the involvement of the Republic of Ireland in the Intergovernmental Conference as an unwarranted interference in the affairs of the north and an indication that unification with the Republic remained on the agenda. In **Ex parte Molyneaux and Others**, a challenge was issued over the legality of the Agreement. It was claimed that the Agreement would fetter the powers and duties of the Secretary of State for Northern Ireland, that it created a distinction between the rights of citizens of Northern Ireland and those of the rest of the United Kingdom contrary to Article 6 of the Union with Ireland Act 1800 and that the Executive – as opposed to the Queen in Council – had no power to exercise the prerogative and enter into agreements with the Republic of Ireland. The application was dismissed.

In 1993 a Joint Declaration was signed between the British and Irish governments. While reiterating the commitment to preserving the union with the United Kingdom for as long as the majority of the people of Northern Ireland wanted it, it also for the first time indicated that the British government had no 'selfish, strategic or economic interest' in Northern Ireland, thus officially giving recognition to the neutrality of the government's position over the long-term future of the province. In 1995, the IRA announced a ceasefire of hostilities. Negotiations were to take place between Sinn Féin and the British government; these however were delayed in part over the terms for negotiation and in part over the refusal of the IRA to relinquish its armoury of weapons in advance of peace talks. The fragile hopes of 1995 were dashed when the IRA bombed Canary Wharf in London.

The election of the Labour government in 1997 led to renewed efforts to revitalise the peace talks. Success followed with the Good Friday Agreement of 1998.[9] Uniquely, the settlement required that former political opponents, the Ulster Unionist Party (now the Democratic Unionist Party) and Sinn Féin (the political wing of the republican movement) work together. In other words, cooperation between representatives of both communities was a prerequisite for the devolution of power. In 1999 the re-devolution of power was complete, the Assembly elected and a power-sharing executive in place. However, in 2002 power was recalled to Westminster.[10] The Northern Ireland (St Andrews Agreement) Act 2006, section 2, provided for the re-devolution of power to Northern Ireland, subject to three conditions being met before a specified date. These conditions were that:

- members of the Assembly would elect a First Minister and Deputy First Minister;[11]
- nominations would be made for other ministerial offices; and
- that those elected or nominated would affirm the pledge of office.

Once those conditions were met, the Secretary of State was obliged to make a restoration order under the 2000 Act, restoring devolution and ending direct rule.[12]

The devolution of powers to the Northern Ireland Assembly under the 1998 Act excluded powers in relation to policing and justice in Northern Ireland – a contentious political matter over which no agreement could be reached. However, in March 2010 agreement between

---

9 Cm 3883.
10 Under the Northern Ireland Act 2000.
11 Section 8 of the Northern Ireland (St Andrews Agreement) Act 2006 inserts new ss 16A–16C into the 1998 Act making detailed provision for the appointment of First and Deputy First Minister.
12 The 2000 Act was to be repealed automatically on the day after the restoration order took effect: Sched. 2, para. 3(1). The Northern Ireland (St Andrews Agreement) Act 2006 makes further provision relating to the restoration of devolved government.

the parties in Northern Ireland was finally reached, enabling the transfer of powers and the establishment of a Department of Justice for Northern Ireland.

The status of Northern Ireland

Section 1 of the Northern Ireland Act 1998 reiterates earlier pledges regarding the status of Northern Ireland, stating that:

> Northern Ireland in its entirety remains part of the United Kingdom and shall not cease to be so without the consent of a majority of the people of Northern Ireland voting in a poll held for the purposes of this section.

Giving recognition to long-held Republican ambitions for a united Ireland, section 1 commits the government of the United Kingdom to giving effect to the wishes of the people should a majority express the wish to cease to be part of the United Kingdom and form part of a united Ireland, following such agreement as may be made between the United Kingdom Government and the government of Ireland.

The Northern Ireland Act 1998 regulates the Northern Ireland Assembly and Executive. The Act includes many significant distinguishing features unique to the situation pertaining in Northern Ireland. In particular, the Act provides for a power-sharing executive, with offices allocated between differing political parties according to their electoral support. The Assembly has statutory power to exclude a Minister or Junior Minister, or a political party, from holding office for a 12-month period if the Assembly resolves that he, she or it no longer enjoys the confidence of the Assembly on the basis that he or she is not committed to non-violence and exclusively peaceful and democratic means. The Act also provides for the protection of all citizens of Northern Ireland from discrimination on the grounds of religious belief and introduces a Human Rights Commission and Equal Opportunities Commission.[13]

The executive

Part III of the Northern Ireland Act 1998 regulates the executive authorities. Within six weeks of the date of the first meeting of the Assembly, the Assembly elected the First Minister and Deputy First Minister. If either the First Minister or Deputy First Minister resigns or otherwise ceases to hold office, the other Minister must also cease to hold office at that time, but may continue in office until a new election is held.[14]

Suspension of devolution 2017–2020

As noted above, there is a shared executive in Northern Ireland. In 2017 the Deputy First Minister resigned, prompting the resignation of the First Minister. As required under the Northern Ireland Act 1998, the consequence was that there had been no Assembly business since January 2017 and no Northern Ireland Department had a Minister since March 2017. Essential administration is undertaken by civil servants and financial costs covered by Budget Acts passed by the UK Parliament.

---

13 The Act repeals, *inter alia*, in full, the Government of Ireland Act 1920, Northern Ireland (Temporary Provisions) Act 1972, Northern Ireland Assembly Act 1973, Northern Ireland Constitution (Amendment) Act 1973, Northern Ireland Act 1974 and, in part, the Northern Ireland Constitution Act 1973 and all of the Northern Ireland Act 1982 and the Northern Ireland (Elections) Act 1998.
14 Northern Ireland Act 1998, s. 16 subs by Northern Ireland (St Andrews Agreement) Act 2006, s. 8(1).

The problems posed for the conduct of government in the light of no Ministerial authority were considered in **Buick, Re Judicial Review** (2018). The Department of Infrastructure had power to grant planning permission. Article 4 of the Departments (Northern Ireland) Order 1999 stated that the functions of Departments 'shall at all times be exercised subject to the direction and control of the Minister'. The Court stated that to allow civil servants to make such decisions in the absence of a Minister would be a 'remarkable constitutional change' and one which would 'effectively turn civil servants into Ministers' and be 'profoundly undemocratic'. Furthermore, and most significantly, it was a controversial issue and one which therefore should be decided by the Executive Committee (see below).

Some of the issues raised in **Buick** came before the Supreme Court in a **Reference by the Attorney General for Northern Ireland** (2019). Among the questions asked were whether, in the absence of a Minister, a civil servant was bound by the Ministerial Code and whether Northern Ireland Ministers were empowered to take decisions in the absence of a Minister. The Supreme Court held that the questions being posed were theoretical and academic and that Parliament intended that references should be made by the Attorney General in the context of actual proceedings. Such proceedings existed, but had been stayed, in relation to an electricity issue in Northern Ireland. The Attorney General should apply to intervene in those proceedings and the reference considered in light of that issue rather than in the abstract.

The deadline for the restoration of devolution to Northern Ireland was 26 March 2019, which was later extended by a further five months. Negotiations on re-establishing the devolved institutions were hampered by two emotive issues: same-sex marriage and abortion rights, both of which remained illegal in Northern Ireland. Both had been decriminalised in the Republic of Ireland following referendums. The Northern Ireland (Executive Formation) bill 2017–2019 provided that the Secretary of State would be obliged to bring forward regulations changing the law in October 2019 unless a devolved Executive had been formed by that date; that date was later extended to March 2020. The Assembly and Executive were eventually restored on 11 January 2020.

The Executive Committee

The Executive Committee comprises the First Minister and Deputy First Minister and up to ten Ministers with Departmental responsibilities. The Committee provides a forum for the discussion of issues which cut across the responsibilities of two or more Ministers and for prioritising executive and legislative proposals.[15] It also considers significant or controversial issues.[16]

Ministerial offices

The number of ministerial offices is determined by the First Minister and Deputy First Minister acting jointly, but may not exceed ten, or such greater number as is approved by the Secretary of State. The allocation of ministerial offices provided for under the Act is designed to achieve power-sharing between the political parties, in proportion to the number of seats held in the Assembly. An Executive Committee is established, comprising the First Minister, the Deputy First Minister and the Northern Ireland Ministers. The First Minister and Deputy First Minister are chairmen of the Committee.[17] In addition to providing a forum for dis-

---

15 The Belfast Agreement 1998, paragraph 19.
16 Section 20 Northern Ireland Act 1998.
17 Ibid., s. 20 as amended Northern Ireland (St Andrews Agreement) Act 2006.

cussion of issues which cut across the responsibility of two or more Ministers, prioritising executive and legislative proposals and formulating an agreed position on various issues, the Northern Ireland (St Andrews Agreement) Act 2006 provides that the Committee is the forum for discussion and agreement on controversial matters which the First and Deputy First Minister have decided should be dealt with by the Committee.[18]

Ministers of Northern Ireland Departments have no power to make, confirm or approve any subordinate legislation, or do any act, so far as the legislation or act is incompatible with Convention rights or EU law, or discriminates against, or aids or incites another person to discriminate against, a person or class of person on the ground of religious belief or political opinion.[19]

Elections

The Representation of the People Act 2000, Schedule 2 extends the parliamentary franchise in relation to overseas voters, amending the Representation of the People Act 1985.

Prior to the Northern Ireland (Miscellaneous Provisions) Act 2014, Assembly elections were held every four years. Provision was made for extraordinary elections, whereby, if the Assembly passes a resolution that it should be dissolved, the Secretary of State was under a duty to propose a date for the election of the next Assembly. The 2014 Act, section 7, provides that the Assembly is to move to five-year fixed terms. The move will take effect from 2016, providing for the next election to take place in 2021 and so avoid a clash with elections to the UK Parliament. This brings Northern Ireland in line with elections to the Scottish Parliament and Welsh Assembly.

The Northern Ireland (Miscellaneous Provisions) Act 2014, section 7, provides for the Assembly to move to fixed five-year terms, to bring it into line with the electoral cycle for elections to the UK Parliament (Westminster).[20]

Constituencies are the same as those for parliamentary elections and each constituency returns six members. Voting is by single transferable vote.

The Northern Ireland (Miscellaneous Provisions) Act 2006 amends section 84(1) of the Northern Ireland Act 1998 to enable the anonymous registration of voters in situations where the voter would be at risk if he or she were identified.

Control over donations and loans to political parties are regulated under Political Parties, Elections and Referendums Act 2000 and Northern Ireland (Miscellaneous Provisions) Act 2006. The prohibition in relation to foreign donors is moderated in relation to Northern Ireland to enable donations to be made from Irish citizens and other Irish bodies.[21] Special provision is also made to protect the identity of donors, and the Electoral Commission is under a statutory duty not to disclose any information relating to donations, including the identity of donors. The Northern Ireland (Miscellaneous Provisions) Act 2014 provides that greater transparency may be gradually introduced, provided that there is no danger to the security of individuals or businesses. The Electoral Commission is under a duty to verify information submitted in donation reports but is also placed under a duty of confidentiality.[22]

---

18 The 2006 Act, s. 5 also makes provision for a statutory Ministerial Code, inserting s. 28A into the 1998 Act.
19 Northern Ireland Act 1998, s. 24.
20 Similar arrangements have been made in relation to elections for the Welsh Assembly and Scottish Parliament.
21 Section 12 Northern Ireland (Miscellaneous Provisions) Act 2006, inserting new ss 71A–71C into the 2000 PPER Act.
22 Schedule 1 ibid., inserting new ss 71D and 71E into the 2000 PPER Act.

The Assembly

The Assembly originally consisted of 108 elected Members, six from each of the 18 Westminster constituencies. With a population of some 1.8 million, the UK Government expressed the view that the size of the Assembly should be reduced. Such a reduction, however, was dependent upon the agreement of the political parties in Northern Ireland. Section 6 of the Northern Ireland (Miscellaneous Provisions) Act 2014 amends the Northern Ireland Act 1998 to insert the reduction in size of the Assembly as a reserved matter. The Assembly Members (Reduction of Numbers) Act (Northern Ireland) 2016 reduces the number of Assembly Members to 90.

The Northern Ireland (Miscellaneous Provisions) Act 2014 amends the Northern Ireland Assembly Disqualification Act 1975 (NIADA). Sections 3 and 4 end the practice of Members of the Northern Ireland Assembly being able also to sit as Members of the House of Commons (subject to the exception discussed below) or as Members of the Dáil Éireann (the lower house of the Irish Parliament). The exception relates to a person who is already a Member of the UK Parliament and who wishes to stand for election to the Assembly. If elected to the Assembly, he or she may then choose whether to sit in the UK Parliament or the Assembly. Sections 3 and 4 provide that a person is not disqualified during the eight-day period following a person's election to the Assembly or Parliament, thereby providing adequate time to make the choice between the two legislatures.

Proceedings of the Assembly are regulated under Standing Orders. The first task of the elected Assembly is to elect from among its Members a Presiding Officer and deputies, positions analogous to the Speaker of the House of Commons and his or her deputy.[23] Consistent also with the Scotland Act 1998, there is established a corporate body, known as the Northern Ireland Assembly Commission, comprising the Presiding Officer and Members of the Assembly, to perform the functions of providing property, staff and services, and other contractual functions.

Legislation

Section 5 of the Northern Ireland Act 1998 provides for the making of Acts of the Assembly, but reserves to the United Kingdom Parliament the right to make laws for Northern Ireland, subject to the right of the Assembly to modify provisions made by Act of Parliament in so far as it is part of the law of Northern Ireland. The legislative competence of the Assembly is regulated by sections 6 and 7, and section 6(1) states that a provision of an Act is not law if it is outside the legislative competence of the Assembly. A provision of an Act is outside the legislative competence of the Assembly if it:

- it is extra-territorial in nature;
- if it deals with excepted matters and is not ancillary to other provisions dealing with reserved or transferred matters;
- it is incompatible with Convention rights;
- it is incompatible with Community law (during membership of the EU);
- it discriminates against any person or class of person on the ground of religious belief or political opinion;
- it modifies an entrenched enactment.

A Bill passes through similar stages to those at Westminster. There is a formal first stage, a second stage at which the principles of the Bill are debated and a Committee stage to

---

23 Northern Ireland Act 1998, s. 39.

examine all the clauses of the Bill and consider amendments. The Bill then returns to the whole Assembly for a consideration stage (the equivalent of Report) and a further consideration stage which is the final opportunity to amend a Bill. The Bill is then referred to the Speaker who determines whether it should be sent to the final stage. The Bill must then be sent to the Attorney General and the Advocate General who will decide whether a provision of the Bill falls within the legislative competence of the Assembly. If there is doubt about this, the Bill will go to the Supreme Court. Once confirmed that the Bill does not need to go to the Supreme Court, the Secretary of State is notified and the Royal Assent may be given. There is also an Accelerated Passage procedure, under which a Bill may pass all its stages within ten days. For this to be adopted there must be cross-community support for fast-tracking the Bill.

Resolving disputes about devolution issues

Schedule 10 defines and regulates proceedings in relation to disputes over the legislative competence of the Assembly.

In **Robinson v Secretary of State for Northern Ireland** (2002), Peter Robinson, a Member of the Northern Ireland Assembly, challenged the appointment of the First Minister and Deputy First Minister, on the grounds that the Assembly had agreed their appointments two days after the deadline set for the election. The Ministers argued that their appointment was lawful.

Section 10 of the 1998 Act provides for the scrutiny of legislation by the Presiding Officer at both the introduction stage of a Bill and before it enters the final stage in the Assembly. If he or she considers that any provision deals with an excepted matter or other matters outside the competence of the Assembly, he or she may refer it to the Secretary of State. The Assembly may not proceed with the Bill unless the Secretary of State consents or informs the Assembly that the Bill does not contain any prohibited matter.

Section 11 provides for references to be made by the Attorney General for Northern Ireland to the Supreme Court to decide on whether a provision of a Bill falls within the legislative competence of the Assembly. The Supreme Court is not obliged to accept the reference and will firstly determine whether the provision being referred falls within one of the prohibited areas.

As noted above, the Northern Ireland Act 1998, section 24(1)(a) provides that a Department of Northern Ireland has no power to make, confirm or approve any subordinate legislation, or to do any act, so far as the legislation is incompatible with any of the rights guaranteed by the European Convention on Human Rights (ECHR).

The Supreme Court considered a devolution issue in **A Reference by the Attorney General for Northern Ireland** (2020). The Attorney General alleged that provisions in secondary legislation breached aspects of the European Convention on Human Rights and were therefore invalid under section 24 of the Northern Ireland Act 1998 (see above). The Supreme Court refused to accept the Attorney general's application to refer the issue. Acts of the Secretary of State for Northern Ireland, or of departments in Westminster did not come within section 24 of the 1998 Act: the act etc. had to be one carried out by a Northern Ireland minister or department. That was not the case here.

Members' interests

A register of Members' interests is provided for under section 43. Members having a financial or other interest must declare that interest before participating in Assembly proceedings, and standing orders may include a provision preventing or restricting participation in proceedings by a Member with a registrable interest. It is an offence to advocate or initiate any cause, or urge another Member to do so, in consideration of any payment or benefit in kind. A person guilty of an offence is liable to a fine not exceeding level five on the standard scale. Proceedings may only be brought with the consent of the Director of Public Prosecutions for Northern Ireland.

Privilege

For the purposes of the law of defamation, absolute privilege attaches to the making of a statement in Assembly proceedings, and to the publication of a statement under the Assembly's authority.[24]

Human rights and equal opportunities

The Act establishes a Human Rights Commission,[25] consisting of a Chief Commissioner and other Commissioners appointed by the Secretary of State.[26] The functions of the Commission include ensuring the adequacy and effectiveness of law and practice in relation to the protection of human rights, and reporting to the Secretary of State such recommendations as are considered necessary to improve law and practice. The Commission has a duty to advise the Assembly on the compatibility of Bills with human rights. The Commission is also under a duty to promote understanding and awareness of the importance of human rights in Northern Ireland. The Justice and Security (Northern Ireland) Act 2007 amends the Northern Ireland Act 1998 by granting new powers to the Northern Ireland Human Rights Commission, including the power to institute judicial proceedings in its own right. This will enable the Commission to bring test cases without the involvement of an individual victim.

The Act also establishes an Equality Commission for Northern Ireland, consisting of between 14 and 20 Commissioners appointed by the Secretary of State. The Equality Commission replaces bodies formerly promoting equal opportunities.[27] A statutory duty is imposed on all public authorities to have due regard to the need to promote equality of opportunity between persons of different religious belief, political opinion, racial group, age, marital status or sexual orientation; between men and women generally; between persons with a disability and those without; and between those with dependants and those without. It is unlawful for a public authority to discriminate, or aid or incite another to discriminate, against a person or class of persons on the grounds of religious belief or political opinion.[28]

North–South Ministerial Council and British–Irish Council

The Belfast Agreement established two new bodies designed to facilitate and promote cooperative relations between the United Kingdom and the Republic of Ireland. The North–South Ministerial Council comprises representatives of the Irish government and the Northern Ireland Executive with a view to fostering cross-community participation in the Council. The First Minister and Deputy First Minister acting jointly nominate Ministers to the Council. Agreements reached by meetings of the North–South Ministerial Council are given effect by

24 Northern Ireland Act 1998, s. 50.
25 See also ibid., Sched. 7.
26 Northern Ireland Act 1998, s. 68.
27 Ibid., s. 74.
28 Northern Ireland Act 1998, s. 76.

the Assembly, and no agreement entered into may come into effect without the approval of the Assembly.[29]

A British–Irish Council provides a forum for debate on matters of mutual interest between the British and Irish governments and representatives of the devolved institutions in Northern Ireland, Scotland and Wales, together with representatives from the Isle of Man and the Channel Islands.

Scotland

Scotland has a total area of some 30,000 square miles representing an area three-fifths the size of England, with a population of some 10 per cent of the United Kingdom total.

The historical relationship between Scotland and England is one marked by conflict and war resulting from English attempts at seizing sovereignty over Scotland. Scotland had been recognised as an independent state in 1328. One consequence of independence was a complete break between English and Scottish law. The Scots look to continental Europe for their training and law, and thus adopted the system based originally on Roman law, which had never been fully adopted in England. The Scottish legal system was protected under the Acts of Union which reunited the two countries, and remains separate and distinct.

Perhaps the original force uniting the two countries was the marriage, in 1503, of James IV of Scotland to Margaret, Henry VII's daughter. When Elizabeth I of England died in 1603 without leaving an heir to the throne, Henry VII's great-great-grandson – then James VI of Scotland – succeeded to the throne of England and James I.[30] Despite this union, each country retained its own constitution and Parliament and – separated by religious differences and economic rivalry – the two countries were to remain separate for a further century.

In *Calvin's Case* (1608) it was held that persons born in either of the kingdoms, after James' accession to the English throne, held dual nationality, all owing allegiance to the same Crown. James' accession was not, however, to lay past conflicts to rest. James ruled Scotland from London, much of government in practice being conducted by the Scottish Privy council acting on the King's orders. The Scottish Parliament seldom met and was dominated by the Lords of the Articles who were royal nominees. Within Scotland, conflict arose in the form of a religious dispute with the King, who attempted to curb the power of the Presbyterian Kirk, in 1606 exiling one of its leaders. In 1608, in the *Five Articles of Perth*, the King ordered certain religious practices to be undertaken which were regarded by the puritans as 'popery',[31] as was the Prayer Book drawn up at James' command in 1619.

It was in the reign of Charles I (1625–1649) that open conflict on the religious question emerged. Charles attempted to impose James' Prayer Book on the Scottish church. The end result, in brief, was that the Scots opponents of his attempted reforms – the Covenanters – played a significant role in Charles' defeat in the Civil War, which led to his trial, conviction and execution as 'a tyrant, traitor, murderer and public enemy to the good people of this nation'.[32]

From 1649–1660, during the interregnum (the period between the execution of Charles I and the restoration of the monarchy), Scotland was to be ruled by the military, whilst theoretically integrated into the Cromwellian united Republic of England and Scotland. On the restoration of the monarchy, religious persecution of the Scottish Presbyterians was rife.

---

29 Northern Ireland Act 1998, ss 52, 53.
30 See Wormald, 1983.
31 Adherence to the Roman Catholic faith.
32 Cited in Lockyer, 1985, p. 288.

The Scottish Parliament, under the control of the Lords of the Articles, proved impotent and was dissolved by Charles II. In 1666, provoked by persecution, the Pentland Rising against the Crown took place. While unsuccessful, it prompted Charles towards greater religious tolerance.

In 1688, when James II was forced to flee England, the Scots took the opportunity to assert their constitutional and religious liberties against William and Mary. The Claim of Right – the Scottish constitutional settlement with the Crown – went much further than its English counterpart, the Petition of Right. The Scots claimed that Parliament had the right to depose any King who violated the trust on which his powers were held, and William was not to establish his supremacy in Scotland without blood being shed. Rebellious highland chiefs, who refused to submit to William's authority, were massacred at Glencoe in 1692, as an example to others.

Scottish hostility towards the Crown was further exacerbated by the Navigation Acts, which treated Scotland and England as separate entities. As a response, acting alone and without royal support, the Scots raised revenues for an expedition to Panama. Three expeditions set out but failed, being decimated either by disease or military opposition from the Spanish Armada. The English, meanwhile, continued to exclude Scotland from its commercial empire. The Scottish response to such discrimination was to declare that Scotland would not be committed to either war or peace by English policy and that the succession to the Hanoverian Crown would not be accepted by Scotland unless and until constitutional, economic and religious liberties were guaranteed to the Scottish people.

The only long-term solution to such conflicts of interest was the full union of England and Scotland. The Union with Scotland Act 1706 and Union with England Act 1707 'abolished' the respective sovereign Parliaments, which became united under the title of the Parliament of Great Britain. The Union was subject to strict conditions and terms. In particular, the Act of Union protected the separate Scottish legal system and provided special protection for the Presbyterian Church. There was to be, however, a common Parliament, common taxation and coinage; by this, meaningful political and economic union was secured.

Following the union, Scottish interests were represented by a Secretary of State for Scotland. In 1885, the office of Secretary for Scotland was established, which from 1892 became a Cabinet post. Administrative devolution to Scotland included Boards created to administer agriculture, fisheries, local government, prisons, health and education, each operating under the supervision of the Scottish Secretary of State.

In 1952 a Royal Commission of Scottish Affairs was appointed to review government functions in relation to Scotland.[33] Further responsibilities were transferred to the Scottish Secretary of State: appointment of Justices of the Peace, animal health, highways and electricity. Subsequently, road passenger transport, ancient monuments, royal parks and palaces have been transferred. The Scottish Office was established in 1945 and based in Edinburgh.

Responsibility for the administration of the criminal law in Scotland lies with the Lord Advocate, who is normally a Member of the House of Commons but may, alternatively, be a Member of the House of Lords, having been conferred a life peerage. The Lord Advocate has responsibility for aspects of government business affecting Scotland. Scottish representation in Parliament was determined by the Act of Union at 45, but has since increased to 59.[34]

The Royal Commission on the Constitution (1969–1973) recommended the devolution of legislative power to Scotland. Devolution was dependent upon a referendum which returned

---

33 Report of the Royal Commission on Scottish Affairs 1952–1954, Cmnd 9212, 1954, London: HMSO.
34 Having risen to 72, and reduced under the Parliamentary Constituencies Act 1986 as amended by the Scotland Act 1998.

a majority of votes in favour, having secured a minimum of 40 per cent of all eligible voters.[35] The results in Scotland were 32.5 per cent in favour of devolution and 30.4 per cent against, with 37.1 per cent of voters abstaining. The statutory requirements for an electoral majority being unmet, the Scotland Act 1978 – which would have effected devolution – was repealed.

The General Election of 1997 presaged the devolution of power to a Scottish Parliament. The government's White Paper, Scotland's Parliament,[36] while retaining the ultimate sovereignty of the Westminster Parliament, envisaged devolution of law-making power to the Scottish Parliament, and a limited power to vary levels of taxation, while also reserving to the United Kingdom Parliament the legislative power in relation to certain matters. Whether or not the powers are devolved or reserved, the Scottish Parliament is entitled to debate all matters.

The referendum

The Referendums (Scotland and Wales) Act 1997 provided the mechanisms for testing the wishes of the people. The Scottish people were asked to vote both for or against a Scottish Parliament, and for or against the proposition that the Scottish Parliament should have tax-varying powers. In favour of the establishment of a Scottish Parliament were 74.3 per cent of voters, and in favour of tax-varying powers, 63.5 per cent.

Devolution and the Treaty of Union

The Union with Scotland Act 1706 and Union with England Act 1707 remain in force and have effect subject to the provisions of the Scotland Act 1998.[37]

The Scottish Parliament

The Scottish Parliament was established under section 1 of the Scotland Act 1998. The 129-seat Parliament is based in Edinburgh. The Parliament's first task was to elect a Presiding Officer and two deputies.[38] The Scottish Parliament is unicameral and originally had a fixed four-year term of office, subject to provisions made for the holding of extraordinary general elections under section 3. In 2011 the Scottish Parliament passed a Resolution calling for a five-year fixed-term Parliament and the rescheduling of elections to 2016. The Fixed Term Parliaments Act 2011, section 4, gave effect to this.

A Clerk of the Parliament, and Assistant Clerks, are appointed by the Scottish Parliamentary Corporate Body, comprising the Presiding Officer and four Members of Parliament. Parliamentary proceedings are regulated by standing orders.[39] The Scottish Parliament has the power to call for witnesses and documents, and provides for criminal penalties in the event of failure to comply with Parliament's directions.

The electoral process

In the White Paper, Scotland's Parliament, the government recognised the need both for a strong constituency link and for greater proportionality between votes cast and seats won to be achieved through the election of additional Members. Members of the Scottish Parliament

---

35 See Bogdanor, 1980.
36 Cmnd 3658, 1997, London: HMSO.
37 Scotland Act 1998, s. 37. Scotland's Parliament, Cm 3658, 1997, London: HMSO, para. 3.1.
38 Scotland Act 1998, s. 19 as amended by s. 4 of the Scotland Act 2012.
39 Ibid., s. 22.

(MSPs) are elected in two different ways. The majority are elected from individual constituencies. The remaining Members – 'additional members' – are selected from party lists drawn up for each of the current European Parliament constituencies.

Members' interests

Section 39 of the Scotland Act 1998, as amended by section 7 of the Scotland Act 2012, regulates Members' interests. It provides for a register of interests and requires Members to register financial interests, including benefits in kind, and declare interests before taking part in any proceedings in Parliament relating to that matter. A Member of Parliament who fails to comply with or contravenes the prohibition is guilty of an offence.

Parliamentary privilege[40]

Section 41 provides that for the purposes of the law of defamation any statement made in proceedings of the Parliament and the publication of any statement under the authority of Parliament is absolutely privileged.

Maladministration

Section 91 of the Scotland Act makes provision for the investigation of complaints made to Members in respect of the exercise of functions by the Scottish Executive.

Legislation

The Scottish Parliament has the power to make Acts of Parliament within the sphere of competence laid down in the Scotland Act. Section 28(7) makes clear that the legislative competence of the Scottish Parliament does not affect the power of the Parliament of the United Kingdom to make laws for Scotland. The Member of the Scottish Executive in charge of a Bill must state, on or before its introduction in Parliament, that the provisions of the Bill are within the legislative competence of Parliament,[41] and section 29 stipulates that an Act is not law if it is outside the Parliament's legislative competence.[42]

To become an Act of the Scottish Parliament, a Bill must pass through five stages. Before being introduced to Parliament, a Bill must undergo pre-legislative consultation, the outcome of which is attached to a draft Bill. The Bill is then sent to a Parliamentary Committee for consideration and report, following which the Bill will be debated and the Parliament will vote. If the Bill is not approved at this stage, it is lost. Stage 2 involves detailed scrutiny by a Committee, the whole Parliament or a combination of the two, and amendments considered. Stage 3 involves consideration by the whole Parliament which may refer up to half a Bill back to a Committee for reconsideration. If Parliament agrees the Bill, it is passed and a four-week period begins during which the Advocate General, Lord Advocate or Attorney General or the Secretary of State for Scotland may challenge the Bill on the basis that it is outside the competence of the Parliament. At the end of the four-week period the Bill may be submitted for the Royal Assent.

---

40 See Munro, 2000.
41 *Ibid.*, s. 31(1).
42 For a recent (unsuccessful) challenge over the competence of the Scottish Parliament see **Martin v HM's Advocate** (2010).

The Scotland Act 2012 extended the legislative competence of the Scottish Parliament as does the Scotland Act 2016, discussed below. The validity of Scottish Acts, on grounds of legislative competence (i.e. does the proposed legislation fall within the matters devolved to the Scottish Parliament under the Scotland Act 1998), is determined by the courts, the ultimate jurisdiction lying with the Supreme Court. Schedule 6, paragraph 1 of the Scotland Act 1998 includes the following:

- a question whether an Act of the Scottish Parliament, or a provision of an Act, is within the competence of the Parliament. An Act or provision will be outside that competence if it is a matter reserved to the UK Parliament, or if it is incompatible with either Convention rights or EU law;
- a question whether action by a member of the Scottish Government is or would be within devolved competence;
- a question whether an act or failure to act by a member of the Scottish Government is or would be incompatible with Convention rights or EU law.

In **AXA General Insurance Ltd v The Lord Advocate** (2011), the Supreme Court ruled that the Damages (Asbestos-related Conditions) (Scotland) Act 2009 was within the legislative competence of the Scottish Parliament. The Court held that the appellants were entitled to bring the proceedings under the Convention on Human Rights and that in order for the 2009 Act to comply with Article 1 of Protocol 1 (A1P1) of the Convention, it must be shown that the Act was pursuing a legitimate aim and the means adopted were proportionate to that aim. At issue was a question of social policy and the Supreme Court held that in such matters the Court should respect the judgment of the Scottish Parliament unless that was without reasonable foundation. In this case the Act pursued a legitimate aim and the means chosen to achieve that were proportionate. Accordingly, the 2009 Act was not outside the Scottish Parliament's legislative competence. In **The Withdrawal from the European Union (Legal Continuity) (Scotland) Bill – a Reference by the Attorney General and the Advocate General for Scotland** (2018) the Supreme Court ruled that while the whole of a Scottish Bill was not outside the legislative competence of the Parliament, parts of it were and were declared to be so. By contrast, in **Salveson v Riddell** (2013) the Supreme Court found that section 72 of the Agricultural Holdings (Scotland) Act 2003 was outside the legislative competence of the Scottish Parliament. At issue was a dispute over a tenancy, a fact which engaged the appellant's rights under A1P1 of the Convention. Those rights were violated by section 72 which did not pursue a legitimate aim, was discriminatory and violated A1P1 rights. The Court limited its decision about lack of competence to the offending section of the 2003 Act and made an order under section 102(2)(b) of the Scotland Act 1998 suspending the effect of its judgment for a period to allow the law to be reformed.

Challenges to the validity of Scottish legislation rarely succeed. According to Lord Hope DPSC in **Imperial Tobacco Ltd v The Lord Advocate** (2012), this is in part due to the care taken to ensure that Bills are within the legislative competence of the Scottish Parliament. It is also in part due to the use of Legislative Consent Motions (LCMs) passed by the Scottish Parliament to enable the United Kingdom Parliament to pass legislation on devolved issues (on which see below).

In the **Imperial Tobacco** case, Lord Hope laid down three principles which were to be followed when considering whether a measure was outside the legislative competence of the Scottish Parliament. These were:

(1)   that 'the question of competence must be determined in each case according to the particular rules that have been set out in section 29 of and Schedules 4 and 5 to the 1998 Act';

(2)   those rules 'must be interpreted in the same way as any other rules that are found in a UK statute';

(3)   the 'description of the Act as a constitutional statute cannot be taken, in itself, to be a guide to its interpretation'.[43]

Where there is an allegation of a breach of Convention rights, this will bring a matter within the definition of a 'devolution issue'. For example, in **Fraser v HM Advocate** (2011) the appellant had appealed against his conviction for murder, in part on the basis of new evidence and in part on the basis of an alleged breach of his right to fair trial under Article 6 of the Convention. The Scottish 'new evidence' rule was not within the jurisdiction of the UK Supreme Court. However, the Scottish Appeal Court had refused the appellant's claim regarding a devolution issue, and that amounted to a 'determination of a devolution issue'. The Supreme Court had jurisdiction to hear an appeal against that determination and granted him leave to appeal to the Court. The Supreme Court ruled that provisions of a Scottish Act were outside the legislative competence of the Scottish Parliament on the basis that the provisions of the Act would breach the right to privacy guaranteed under Article 8 of the European Convention in **Christian Institute and Others v Lord Advocate** (2016). The Children and Young People (Scotland) Act 2014 made provision of a named person service (NPS) in relation to children and young people in Scotland. The objective was to limit the intervention of public authorities after a risk to welfare had been identified in favour of early intervention to promote well being. Part of that scheme provided for information sharing between relevant authorities (for example, National Health Service; Police Authority). The appellants challenged the scheme by way of judicial review on the basis that it was outside the legislative competence of the Scottish Parliament on three grounds: first, that it related to matters reserved to the UK Parliament; second, that it was incompatible with Convention rights; and/or third, that it was incompatible with EU law. The Supreme Court allowed the appeal on the basis of the Convention challenge (and the EU challenge in so far as it mirrored the ECHR challenge). The provision could in practice result in a disproportionate interference with the right to privacy of many children.

The Sewel Convention: Legislative Consent Motions

The Sewel Convention – now known as Legislative Consent Motions (LCMs) – was a policy announced by Lord Sewel, then Parliamentary Under-Secretary for Scotland, during the passage of the Scotland Act 1998. In essence, the Convention provides that the UK Parliament (Westminster) would not legislate with regard to matters devolved to Scotland (or Wales or Northern Ireland) without the consent of the Scottish Parliament. Where the UK Parliament is considering legislation which extends to England and Wales alone, and Scotland wishes the legislation to apply to Scotland also, an LCM may be passed in which Scotland (or Northern Ireland or Wales) agrees that Westminster may legislate on a devolved issue. An LCM may also be passed where Westminster is considering legislation applying to a devolved legislature but which relates to both devolved and reserved matters, where it would otherwise be necessary for the devolved legislature to legislate separately.[44] The Scotland Act 2016 now gives statutory recognition to the Sewel Convention (section 2 adding subsection (8) to section 28 of the Scotland Act 1998).

---

43 At paras 13–15. See also Local Government Byelaws (Wales) Bill 2012 Reference by the Attorney General for England and Wales (2012).

44 By October 2013, the Scottish Parliament had passed 131 LCMs.

Schedule 5: reserved matters

Part I of Schedule 5 lays down five general categories of matters reserved to the United Kingdom Parliament: the constitution, the registration of political parties, foreign affairs, Civil Service, defence and treason. Part II lists specific reservations under 11 broad heads, namely: financial and economic matters; home affairs; trade and industry; energy; transport; social security; regulation of the professions; employment; health and medicines; media and culture; and miscellaneous. Matters reserved facilitate United Kingdom-wide uniformity, while devolving to the Scottish Parliament the power to regulate non-reserved matters according to national requirements. The Scotland Act 2016 devolves significant further powers to the Scottish Parliament to regulate itself and elections, over taxation and welfare policy.

The executive

The Scottish Executive, renamed the 'Scottish Government' under section 12 of the Scotland Act 2012, comprises the First Minister and such Ministers as the First Minister appoints, the Lord Advocate and the Solicitor General for Scotland. The First Minister is appointed by Her Majesty from among Members of the Parliament, and holds office at Her Majesty's pleasure.[45] Members of the Executive are responsible to the Scottish Parliament. The Scotland Act 2016 recognises that the Scottish Government is a permanent feature of the UK constitution and cannot be abolished without the consent of the Scottish people.

In **Davidson v Scottish Ministers** (2005) the House of Lords ruled that the Scottish courts had jurisdiction to make coercive orders against Ministers of the Scottish Government in judicial review proceedings. Section 21(1) of the Crown Proceedings Act 1947 should be interpreted so as to ensure that the protection Parliament intended they should have against government Ministers was the same as that available in the English courts.

Law officers

The Law Officers of the Scottish Government are the Lord Advocate and the Solicitor General for Scotland. The United Kingdom Government also needs advice on Scottish law, and the office of Scottish Law Officer to the United Kingdom Government was created to meet this need.[46]

Scottish representation at Westminster

The problematic issue of continued Scottish representation at Westminster after devolution, particularly in relation to matters exclusively English (the 'West Lothian question'),[47] was addressed by initially continuing the same level of Scottish representation as before. However, section 86 of the Scotland Act 1998 amends Schedule 2 to the Parliamentary Constituencies Act 1986 and provides for Scottish representation to be based on the same electoral quota as for England, the effect of which is to reduce the number of constituencies to 59.

Continuing unease over the anomaly caused by the current representation at Westminster of Northern Ireland, Scotland and Wales following devolution prompted the establishment in 2012 of an independent Commission, the McKay Commission, to examine the consequences of devolution for the House of Commons. The Terms of Reference of the Commission were to

---

45 Scotland Act 1998, ss 44 and 45 and also Scotland Act 2012, s. 12(2)(a).
46 Scotland Act 1998.
47 On which see the Fourth Edition of this book, pp. 381–384.

consider how the House of Commons might deal with legislation which affects only part of the United Kingdom, following the devolution of certain legislative powers to the Scottish Parliament, the Northern Ireland Assembly and the National Assembly for Wales. The Report is discussed below.

Financial arrangements[48]

Under the Scotland Act 1998, the Scottish Parliament had the power to increase or decrease the basic rate of income tax set by the United Kingdom Parliament by up to three pence in the pound. The Inland Revenue continues to administer tax variations. The Scotland Act 2012 removes this power, but transfers to the Scottish Parliament the power to set the basic and higher rate of income tax to be paid by Scottish taxpayers.

Since the 1970s, there has existed a 'block formula' (the 'Barnett formula') system of funding Scotland's public expenditure programmes. The Scotland Act 2012 reduces the block grant to reflect the power to set income tax rates. The Scotland Act 1998, as amended by the Scotland Act 2012, confers power on the Scottish Ministers to borrow funds from the UK Treasury.[49]

Debating powers

The Scottish Parliament is able to examine devolved matters, and debate all matters irrespective of whether they are devolved or reserved.[50]

Scotland and the European Union

During the UK's membership of the EU from 1973 to 2020, relations with Europe were the responsibility of the United Kingdom Parliament and government. However, the Scottish Parliament and government played an important role in relation to those aspects of European Union affairs which affected Scotland. The Scottish Parliament scrutinised European Union legislative proposals 'to ensure that Scotland's interests are properly reflected'. Responsibility for ensuring the implementation of European Union obligations lay with the Scottish Government.

Independence for Scotland?[51]

The Scottish Nationalist Party (SNP) is committed to the independence of Scotland. In 2012 the United Kingdom Government and Scottish Government signed the Edinburgh Agreement, providing for a referendum. In September 2014, the Scottish people rejected independence by 55 per cent to 45 per cent. That vote, however, does not end the debate over Scotland's future. Each of the main political parties committed themselves to further devolution – devomax – should Scotland vote 'no' to independence. With further devolution to Scotland comes the question of further devolution to Wales and the question of whether, and how, England

---

48 See the Scotland Act 1998, Pt III.
49 See s. 66 Scotland Act 1998, as amended by s. 32 Scotland Act 2012.
50 *Scotland's Parliament*, Cm 3658, 1997, London: HMSO, para. 2.5.
51 See HM Government, Scotland Analysis: Devolution and the Implications of Scottish Independence, Cm 8554, February 2013; House of Lords Select Committee on the Constitution, Scottish Independence: Constitutional Implications of the Referendum, 8th Report of Session 2013–2014, May 2014.

should have its own distinctive voice within the United Kingdom. That issue, the 'English question', has now been addressed by the government (on which see below).

Following the referendum, a Commission was established to reach agreement between the major political parties on further devolution to Scotland. Chaired by Lord Smith of Kelvin, the Commission reported in November 2014. The Scotland Act 2016 implements the Smith Commission Agreement. The major provisions of the Act are as follows:

- the Act provides that the Scottish Parliament and Scottish Government are permanent parts of the UK constitution and will not be abolished without the consent of the Scottish people (section 1 inserting section 63A of the Scotland Act 1998);
- the Act provides that the Sewel Convention is to be strengthened (section 2 adding subsection (8) to section 28 of the 1998 Act;
- the Act devolves matters relating to the arrangements and operation of the Scottish Parliament and Scottish Government including the overall number of MSPs and powers over the disqualification or removal of MSPs;
- the Act provides that the Scottish Parliament has the power to regulate elections to the Scottish Parliament and local government elections in Scotland. This includes the franchise, the voting system, spending limits and party political broadcasts. However, the Electoral Commission will continue to operate on a UK-wide basis and the Boundary Commission for Scotland will continue to operate as a UK public body. To avoid radical changes to electoral law, a 'super majority' of two-thirds of MSPs voting will be required;
- the Scottish Parliament will be able to set rates of Income Tax, but not National Insurance Contributions, Inheritance Tax, Capital Gains Tax, Corporation Tax and all aspects of taxation of oil and gas receipts;
- significant areas of welfare policy and delivery are devolved;
- the remaining block grant payable to Scotland will continue to be calculated under the Barnett formula.

Wales

Note that the Welsh Assembly is now renamed the Senedd. In this chapter, reference is made to the Assembly in relation to matters prior to 2020.

Wales covers an area of some 8,000 square miles, having a population approximately five per cent of that of the United Kingdom. Wales was conquered by the English in 1282, and from 1284 Wales was subject to English law. As with Scotland there was an attempt at devolution in 1978, but this failed due to lack of popular support. Accordingly it was in 1998 that devolution was effected with the passage of the Government of Wales Act.

Unlike devolution to Northern Ireland and Scotland, devolution to Wales was to be a three-stage process. Initially, the Government of Wales Act 1998 devolved executive powers. The Government of Wales Act 2006 then separated executive and legislative functions and gave the Assembly competence to make Assembly Measures which could amend UK primary legislation or take effect as primary legislation. Provision was also made for a future referendum on increasing Assembly powers. Whereas Northern Ireland and Scotland have legislative competence over all matters except those which are specifically reserved to the UK Parliament, Wales has been given legislative competence only in respect of those specified matters (a 'conferred powers' model). In 2011 the government established the Silk Commission to review devolution to Wales; in 2014 a further review – the St David's Day process – was established. The Wales Act 2014 implemented many of the Silk Commission's recommendations while the Wales Act 2017 introduced further changes, as discussed below.

Notwithstanding the evolution and extension of devolved power to Wales, the extent of devolution remains below that of Scotland and Northern Ireland, with a high number of powers being reserved to the UK Parliament under the Wales Act 2017. Schedule 7A of the Government of Wales Act reserves over 200 matters to Westminster. And as section 108A makes clear, matters listed in Schedule 7A fall outside the legislative competence of the Senedd (formerly Assembly). Furthermore, while Northern Ireland and Scotland have their own distinctive legal system, the legal systems of England and Wales have historically been united. This was the subject of the Commission on Justice for Wales Report (the Thomas Commission) of 2019, which concluded that major reform was needed to the current legal system and to devolution. Criticising the current system, the Commission argues that justice should be at the heart of government. Currently justice in Wales – unlike Scotland and Northern Ireland – is controlled by Westminster. The Commission states that there is no 'rational basis for Wales to be treated differently, particularly as Wales has its own long legal tradition'.[52]

The Government of Wales Act 1998

The Government of Wales Act 1998 devolved limited powers to a directly elected Welsh Assembly, which assumed the responsibilities formerly exercised by the Secretary of State for Wales. The law-making powers of the Assembly were restricted to secondary legislation ('Assembly Orders'), and the United Kingdom Parliament continued to legislate for Wales. While the executive powers were formally exercised by the Assembly as a corporate body, in practice the powers were exercised on its behalf by Assembly Ministers. The result was a lack of separation of powers between the legislature and executive.

The Government of Wales Act 2006 (GoWA)

The Government of Wales Act 2006 addresses this issue and confers additional legislative power on the Assembly (on which see below).[53]

The Wales Act 2014

Section 1 of the Act amends section 3(1) of the Government of Wales Act 2006 to provide for ordinary general elections to the Assembly to be held every five years (rather than four) in order to avoid elections coinciding with elections to the Westminster Parliament. Section 2(2) amends section 7 of the GoWA 2006 and removes the restriction on standing for election as both a constituency and regional candidate in an Assembly election.

Following a report by the Committee on Standards in Public Life, the practice of holding a dual mandate in both the House of Commons and a devolved legislature is brought to an end.[54] Section 3(1) provides that Members of the House of Commons are disqualified from being members of the Assembly.

Section 4(1) of the Wales Act 2014 renames the Welsh Assembly Government the Welsh Government. Part 2 of the Act deals with finance. The Assembly is given power to legislate about devolved taxation – principally tax in relation to property interests and landfill tax.

---

52 See the Commission on Justice for Wales Report: *Justice in Wales for the People of Wales*, October 2019.
53 See *The Report of the Commission on the Powers and Electoral Arrangements of the National Assembly for Wales (the Richard Report)*, 2004 and *Better Governance for Wales*, Cm 6582, 2004, London: The Stationery Office.
54 MPs' Expenses and Allowances: Supporting Parliament, Safeguarding the Taxpayer, Twelfth Report of Committee on Standards in Public Life, Cm 7724, 2009.

The Act also provides that, subject to a vote in favour in a referendum, the Assembly may also set Welsh rates for the purpose of calculating rates of income tax to be paid by Welsh taxpayers. Section 9(3) amends the Income Tax Act 2007, inserting a new section 6B into that Act. This provides that the UK basic, higher and additional rates will be reduced by 10 per cent, and the separate Welsh rates, set by the Assembly, will be added to each of the reduced rates. Section 12 of the Wales Act 2014 provides for a referendum to be held about whether the income tax provisions should come into force. The referendum may be held following an Order in Council or following a vote on an Assembly resolution passed by at least two-thirds of Assembly Members, which would require an Order in Council to be made.

The referendum

The result of the initial referendum on devolution was less clear-cut than that of the Scottish referendum. Only 50 per cent of the electorate voted, as compared with 60 per cent in the Scottish referendum, and 50.3 per cent voted in favour of the establishment of an Assembly.

The executive

The 2006 Act establishes a Welsh Assembly Government (now Welsh Government) as an entity separate from the National Assembly.[55] The First Minister and other Ministers and Deputy Ministers comprise the Government. The First Minister is nominated for appointment by the Assembly and the First Minister appoints Welsh Ministers from among the Assembly Members.[56] Under section 51, there is a limit of 12 on the number of Ministers and Deputy Ministers. Ministers must resign if the Assembly resolves that the Ministers no longer enjoy the confidence of the Assembly.[57]

The office of Counsel General is established. The Counsel General (or the Attorney General) may refer a question relating to the statutory powers of the Assembly to the Supreme Court for decision.[58]

The Assembly (now Senedd)

The Assembly has 60 Members and sits for a fixed four-year term. However, the 2006 Act gives the Assembly the right to dissolve itself earlier, provided that a two-thirds majority of Members approves the proposal. The Assembly elects committees the membership of which represents the political party composition of the Assembly as a whole.

The Wales Act 2014 provides, in part, that general elections to the Assembly will take place every five years, thereby bringing the Welsh Assembly in line with elections to the United Kingdom (Westminster) elections.

The electoral system

The additional member electoral system is employed for elections.[59] There are forty constituency members, elected on the simple majority system, and 20 additional members elected from the party list. Each voter has two votes – one for the constituency member and one for

---

55 Government of Wales Act 2006, Pt 2 and Sched. 3.
56 Ibid., ss 47 and 48. Appointments are subject to approval by Her Majesty the Queen.
57 Government of Wales Act 2006, s. 48(5).
58 Ibid., s. 96.
59 Government of Wales Act s. 4.

the additional member. The first elections took place in the spring of 1999. The Senedd and Elections (Wales) Act 2020 extends the right to vote to 16- and 17-year-olds for devolved elections.[60]

Welsh representation at Westminster

The Secretary of State for Wales and Welsh Members of Parliament play a full role at Westminster, but one which also involves a new partnership with the Senedd.[61] The number of Welsh MPs is 40.

The relationship between Westminster and the Senedd

Whereas under the 1998 Act, the Assembly (as it then was, now Senedd) had no power to make primary legislation, the Government of Wales Act 2006 conferred potentially more wide-ranging legislative power. The 2006 Act stipulates the matters on which the Assembly may legislate, and no Acts or Measures which are outside its legislative competence will be law. The 2006 Act preserves the ultimate right of the United Kingdom Parliament to legislate for Wales.

An Assembly Measure is a form of subordinate legislation. Section 94(1) provides that, subject to the restrictions laid down in the Act, an Assembly Measure may make any provision that could be made by an Act of Parliament.[62] Schedule 5, Part 1 specifies 20 'fields', ranging from Agriculture to the Welsh language, over which the Assembly has competence. Part 2 stipulates the general restrictions on competence and protects various Acts of the United Kingdom Parliament from amendment by the Assembly.[63] The general restrictions include amendment of ministerial functions, the creation of criminal offences carrying a stipulated level of punishment, legislation contradicting the Human Rights Act 1998 or legislation contrary to European Union law.

The power to pass primary legislation (an Assembly Act) was dependent upon a referendum being held in which the people approved the power.[64] A referendum was held in March 2011, with a majority voting in favour of increasing the Assembly's powers. Schedule 7 to the Government of Wales Act 2006 specifies the 'fields' over which the Assembly has competence which mirror those for Measures.[65] Disputes over competence are resolved by the courts.[66]

The procedure for passing proposed Measures and Bills reflects the Westminster procedure. There is a general debate on the principles equivalent to second reading. There is then detailed consideration of the matter, equivalent to the Committee stage, and finally there is a vote on whether the matter should be passed, equivalent to the third reading. Bills then require the Royal Assent. There is to be a four-week time lapse between completion of Assembly deliberations on a Bill and the submission for the Royal Assent. This period is designed to enable the Counsel General (or Attorney General) to refer the matter to the Supreme Court in order to determine whether the matter is within the legislative competence

---

60 And changes the name of the legislature from the Assembly to the Senedd.
61 *A Voice for Wales: The Government's Proposals for a Welsh Assembly*, Cm 3718, 1997, London: HMSO, para. 3.33.
62 The 2006 Act is amended by the Local Democracy, Economic Development and Construction Act 2009, s. 33, which extends the legislative competence of the Assembly.
63 These include the European Communities Act 1972, Data Protection Act 1998, Government of Wales Act 1998, Human Rights Act 1998 and Civil Contingencies Act 2004.
64 Government of Wales Act 2006, s. 105. See also the White Paper *Your Region, Your Choice, Revitalising the English Regions*, Cm 5511, May 2002, Cabinet Office/DTLR.
65 Government of Wales Act 2006, s. 103.
66 See for example *Attorney General v National Assembly for Wales Commission* (2012).

of the Assembly. Furthermore, the Secretary of State for Wales may intervene to prevent the Royal Assent being granted where he or she has reasonable grounds to believe that the matter is contrary to international obligations or contrary to the interests of defence or national security, would have an adverse effect on water resources or supply or would adversely affect the operation of law in England or on non-devolved matters.

Members' interests

A register of interests is established, requiring any Assembly Member who has a financial or other interest in any matter to be registered and requiring declarations of interests to be made before participating in Assembly proceedings. Under section 72, Members are prohibited from advocating any cause on behalf of any person in consideration of payments or benefits in kind. It is an offence to act in violation of the section 72 procedures, and a person found guilty of an offence is liable on summary conviction to a fine. Prosecutions may only be instituted by or with the consent of the Director of Public Prosecutions. Similar provisions to those in the Scotland Act relate to the attendance of witnesses, the giving of evidence and the production of documents.[67]

Privilege

The Government of Wales Act 2006, section 42 confers absolute privilege on any statement made in Assembly proceedings and on the publication of any statement made under the authority of the Assembly. Accordingly no actions for defamation may be taken in respect of such proceedings or publications.

Resolving disputes about devolution issues

Section 149 of the Government of Wales Act 2006 and Schedule 9 regulate devolution issues and make detailed provision concerning the courts with jurisdiction to resolve disputes.

In *Agriculture Sector (Wales) Bill – Reference by the Attorney General for England and Wales* (2014) the Welsh Assembly considered that it had competence to pass a Bill to regulate agricultural wages under section 108 of and Schedule 7 to the 2006 Act. The Attorney General, by contrast, considered that the Bill did not relate to agriculture but to employment and industrial relations, which were matters which had not been devolved. Under the 2006 Act, as amended, competence was conferred over 'agriculture, forestry animals, plants and rural development'. The Supreme Court ruled that the Assembly had legislative competence to pass the Bill. The purpose of the Bill was to support and protect the industry. Agriculture could not be interpreted solely as the cultivation of the soil or rearing of livestock. It 'should be understood in the broader sense as designating the industry or economic activity of agriculture in all aspects, including the business and other constituent elements of that industry'.[68]

The Welsh Assembly and the European Union

During the UK's membership of the EU, the Assembly scrutinised legislative proposals and other European documents. The Assembly also had responsibility for ensuring that European

---

67 Government of Wales Act 2006, ss 74, 75.
68 See also Local Government Byelaws (Wales) Bill 2012: Reference by the Attorney General for England and Wales (2012). The Bill was within the legislative powers of the Welsh Assembly.

Union obligations are implemented and enforced, and that any financial penalties which arose out of failure to implement or enforce Union obligations were met. Within the framework of the Council of Ministers, the Secretary of State for Wales participated in meetings of the Council. The Wales European Centre in Brussels acted as a facilitator and source of advice on European matters. Members of the Assembly represented Wales on the Committee of the Regions.

Further devolution to Wales

In February 2015 the government published its latest plans for further devolution to Wales.[69] This was in response to the recommendations of the independent Commission on Devolution in Wales (the Silk Commission).[70] Devolution to Wales has been incremental and more limited than the devolution of powers to Northern Ireland and Scotland; as the government recognised, 'it did not have the same breadth or depth as devolution elsewhere in the UK'.[71] The Wales Act 2017 gives effect to the recommendations.

The principal change is an amendment to the Government of Wales Act 2006 (GoWA) providing that the system of devolution to Wales changes from the 'conferred powers' model to the 'reserved powers' model. The conferred model lists the subjects devolved to the Assembly, other matters remaining the responsibility of the UK Parliament.[72] Moving to the reserved powers model entails setting out those powers which were to remain with the UK Parliament, everything else being devolved to the Welsh Assembly. This removes the potential for uncertainty and disagreement over the scope of power devolved.[73] Schedule 7 to the GoWA sets out the reserved matters, which are either general or specific. General reservations (from which there are listed exceptions) include the constitution, the Civil Service, political parties, the legal system of England and Wales, foreign affairs and defence.

On specific areas, the Assembly now has full powers over its organisation and operation, including its size and the power to rename itself the Welsh Parliament. The Wales Act 2017 recognises that the Assembly and Welsh Government are permanent institutions. Power over electoral matters including the number and boundaries of constituencies, voting age, electoral system and the conduct of elections are devolved. The regulation of political parties remains reserved. The Electoral Commission will continue to operate on a UK-wide basis. Control over local government elections will also be devolved.

Other areas devolved include the licensing of exploration and extraction of oil and gas. Offshore oil and gas extraction and the taxation of oil and tax receipts remain reserved. Transport, including ports, taxi and bus regulation, are devolved. There are guarantees relating to funding in order to promote economic growth.

Inter-governmental cooperation is improved and a revised Memorandum of Understanding drafted. Section 2 of the Act inserts subsection (6) into section 107 of GoWA, providing that although the sovereignty of the UK Parliament is unchanged by the legislative competence of the Welsh Assembly, the UK Parliament will not normally legislate for devolved matters without the Assembly's consent. Legislation on issues of constitutional importance, such as the franchise or electoral system, require a two-thirds majority (a 'super majority')[74] of all Assembly Members. The role of the Secretary of State for Wales is reduced

---

69 Powers for a Purpose: Towards a Lasting Devolution Settlement for Wales, Cm 9020, February 2015.
70 Second Report, Empowerment and Responsibility: Legislative Powers to Strengthen Wales, March 2014.
71 Powers for a Purpose, para. 2.1.6.
72 See Schedule 7 to the Government of Wales Act 2006.
73 For an example of the lack of clarity see *Recovery of Medical Costs for Asbestos Diseases (Wales) Bill* (2015).
74 See new ss 111A and 111B of GoWA.

and there is a general transfer of ministerial powers to Welsh Ministers. The Secretary of State no longer has the right to participate in Assembly proceedings, and the requirement to appear before the Assembly is removed.[75]

With effect from May 2020, the Welsh Assembly is renamed the Senedd Cymru/Welsh Parliament. The Welsh Parliament, however, lacks the level of law-making power when compared with Scotland and Northern Ireland.

Regulating Relations Between the Nations

The Memorandum of Understanding and Joint Ministerial Committee

The Memorandum of Understanding (MoU) between the United Kingdom Government, the Scottish Ministers, Welsh Ministers and Northern Ireland Executive Committee sets out the principles which govern relations between the four nations. The Memorandum provides for a Joint Ministerial Committee (JMC) and has three separate Concordats. The Concordats apply to EU policy and implementation, financial assistance to industry and international relations touching on responsibilities of the devolved administrations. The Memorandum is 'a statement of political intent, and should not be interpreted as a binding agreement'. The principals underpinning intergovernmental relations are good communication, cooperation on matters of mutual interest, the exchange of information and confidentiality.

The Joint Ministerial Committee meets in Plenary Session annually. The meeting is chaired by the Prime Minister and can cover any aspect of government relations. A Domestic Session of the JMC convenes two or three times a year. The European Session meets quarterly. The JMC publishes an Annual Report.

The Smith Commission on enhanced devolution to Scotland criticised the current system and called for improved inter-governmental communications.

 SELF-TEST QUESTION

What is meant by the statement that devolution to Northern Ireland, Scotland and Wales is 'asymmetrical'?

A Voice for England?

Of the four nations which make up the United Kingdom, only England lacks its own legislative body. Devolution to Northern Ireland, Scotland and Wales – in an asymmetrical fashion – has given to the people of those nations a greater say in the governance of their country. The issue which has increasingly been raised, post devolution, is how, if at all, the distinctive interests and concerns of England are to be addressed. In particular, there is dissatisfaction with the right of Members of Parliament who represent Northern Ireland, Scottish and Welsh constituencies to debate and vote on proposals which affect only England, while MPs representing English constituencies have no reciprocal right to debate and vote on proposals before the devolved legislatures: the 'West Lothian' question. The government established a Commission to examine the issue.

---

75 See Clause 24, repealing ss 32 and 33 GoWA.

The Commission's Report, *Report of the Commission on the Consequences of Devolution for the House of Commons*, was published in 2013.[76] The Commission considered survey research data on public attitudes in England.[77] The most striking evidence came from the 2011 Census, in which of 50.3 million respondents in England, 'some 60.4 per cent claimed an "English only" identity, while only 19.2 per cent claimed a "British only" identity'. The Commission also found that a majority of English respondents to research felt it wrong that Scottish MPs should be allowed to vote on laws that affect England only. The Commission recommended that the following constitutional principle should be adopted for England (and for England and Wales): 'decisions at the United Kingdom level with a separate and distinct effect for England (or for England-and-Wales) should normally be taken only with the consent of a majority of MPs for constituencies in England (or England-and-Wales)'.

The Commission did not recommend that MPs from outside England should be barred from voting on legislating. Rather it took the view that there should be special procedures to ensure that the English view could be expressed and taken into account in the legislative process. In particular, the Commission recommended that parliamentary procedures should ensure that sufficient information is available to permit clear identification of the English-only dimension; there is an opportunity, separately for views from England to be expressed; and such views are heard and considered.

In *The Future for England: Decentralisation and English Votes for English Laws*, the Conservative Party supported the guiding principle set out in the McKay Report, namely that:

decisions at the United Kingdom level with a separate and distinct effect for England, or for England and Wales, should normally be taken only with consent of a majority of MPs for constituencies for England, or for England and Wales.[78]

The Conservative Party did not support either the introduction of an English Parliament or a reduction in the number of Scottish MPs at Westminster. A new legislative procedure has been introduced to deal with Bills relating only to England or to England and Wales. The changes were introduced in 2015 under Standing Orders of the House of Commons. The procedure is discussed in Chapter 14.

 Pause and Reflect

What is 'the English question'? In what ways could the English question be addressed? What is your preferred solution to the problem?

London: The Greater London Authority and Mayor

In addition to the 1997 Labour government's firm commitment to devolution to Scotland and Wales, and the future consideration of devolution to the English regions, the government intended to introduce an elected 'strategic authority' for London. As noted below, the Greater London Council (GLC), which formerly represented a centralising focus for the capital city, was abolished in 1985. Many of the GLC's functions reverted to the individual London

---

76 The McKay Commission, see tmc.independent.gov.uk.
77 National Centre for Social Research, the Institute for Public Policy Research, and the Future of England Survey by Cardiff University and University of Edinburgh, and the 2011 Census.
78 December 2014.

councils. London was unique in being a capital city without an elected Mayor and central-ised area government. The government's White Paper, *A Mayor and Assembly for London*, pro-posed an elected Mayor and 25-seat Greater London Assembly. The Authority does not have direct tax-raising powers, but revenue is raised from congestion charging and parking fees. The Greater London Authority Act 1999 (as amended by the Greater London Authority Act 2007 and Localism Act 2011) establishes and regulates the Authority. The Authority comprises the Mayor and the London Assembly.

Elections

The first election was held in May 2000, electing an Assembly and Mayor for a four-year term of office.[79] Every eligible elector has one vote for the mayoral candidate, one vote for an Assembly Member and one vote – a 'London vote' – for a registered political party.

The simple majority voting system is used for the mayoral election unless there are three or more candidates. Where three or more candidates stand, the Mayor is elected under the supplementary vote system, a vote which indicates the voter's first and second preferences from among the candidates.[80] The Assembly Members are elected under the simple major-ity system.[81] 'London members' are elected on the party-list system. The qualifications for election to be Mayor or an Assembly Member are that the person must be a Commonwealth citizen, citizen of the Republic of Ireland or citizen of the European Union and must be over 21 years of age.[82] In addition, the candidate must have demonstrable links with Greater London, either by being a local government elector for Greater London, or through residency or principal employment in Greater London throughout the preceding 12 months.

The Greater London Authority

The general power of the Authority, as defined in Part II of the Act, is to 'do anything which it considers will further any one or more of its principal purposes', which are defined as:

(a)   promoting economic development and wealth creation in Greater London;
(b)   promoting social development in Greater London; and
(c)   promoting the improvement of the environment in Greater London.

The Secretary of State may issue guidance to the Authority in relation to the above general power.[83]

The Authority is required to consult with London councils and representative voluntary bodies (section 32).

The Authority is regulated by Standing Orders defining its procedures, which are made in consultation with the Mayor. The offices of Chair and Deputy Chair of the London Assembly are created. The Local Government Act 1972, Part VA, regulating access to meetings and documents, applies to the Assembly and its committees, with the exception of confidential information and exempt information which may be withheld from the press and the public.

The Assembly is under a statutory duty to keep under review the Mayor's exercise of statutory functions, and has the power to investigate and report on any actions and decisions

79 Greater London Authority Act 1999, s. 3.
80 Ibid., s. 4(2), (3) and Sched. 2, Pt 1.
81 Ibid., s. 4(4).
82 Greater London Authority Act 1999, s. 20.
83 Ibid., s. 30.

of the Mayor, actions and decisions of any member of staff of the Authority, matters relating to the principal purposes of the Authority and any other matters which the Assembly considers to be of importance to Greater London. The Assembly may submit proposals to the Mayor, but this function cannot be delegated to a committee or sub-committee.[84]

Bills in Parliament

The Authority may promote a local Bill in Parliament, or oppose any local Bill which affects the inhabitants of Greater London. The Mayor acts on behalf of the Authority, having consulted the Assembly. In addition, the Mayor on behalf of the Assembly, and following consultation with it, may request a London local authority to include provisions in local Bills. A local Bill promoted in Parliament by a London local authority may include provisions which affect the exercise of statutory functions by the Authority or any of the functional bodies, only if the Authority gives its written consent.[85]

The London Mayor

The Mayor is under a duty to prepare, keep under review and revise strategies relating to economic development, transport, spatial development (planning),[86] the London Biodiversity Action Plan, municipal waste management, air quality, ambient noise and culture.[87] In preparing or revising strategies, the Mayor must consult the Assembly, the functional bodies, each London borough council, the Common Council of the City of London and any other 'appropriate person or body'. Adequate publicity must be given to the strategies, and copies provided to the Common Council and each London borough council. The Secretary of State may issue directions to the Mayor to prepare and publish any strategy which the Mayor has not prepared and to stipulate the period in which the strategy must be prepared.[88] The Greater London Authority Act 2007 extends the duties and powers of the Mayor.[89] The Mayor is now under a duty to prepare and publish a Health Inequalities Strategy and a Housing Strategy.[90] The Mayor is also given additional powers in relation to planning. He or she is entitled to intervene in a local planning authority's development schemes and is empowered to determine planning applications which are of 'potential strategic importance', taking over the role of the local planning authority.[91] In addition, under the Further Education and Training Act 2007 the Mayor was given a new role in adult skills and employment in London.

The Police Reform and Social Responsibility Act 2011 abolished the Metropolitan Police Authority and conferred greater powers on the Mayor of London in relation to the Metropolitan Police (see further below).

Accountability

The Mayor is under a duty to report to the Assembly, not fewer than five clear working days before each meeting of the Assembly (section 3 Greater London Authority Act 2007, amending section 45 of the 1999 Act), on significant decisions taken and the reasons for them,

---

84 Greater London Authority Act 1999, ss 59, 60.
85 Ibid., ss 77–79.
86 Separate provision is made for revision of spatial development strategy under s. 340.
87 Greater London Authority Act 1999, ss 41, 142; Regional Development Agencies Act 1998, s. 7A(2); Greater London Authority Act 1999, Pt VIII; Greater London Authority Act 1999, ss 352, 353, 362, 370 and 376, respectively.
88 Greater London Authority Act 1999, ss 42–44.
89 The 2007 Act also makes detailed amendments to the Greater London Authority Act 1999.
90 Sections 22 and 28 Greater London Authority Act 2007 respectively.
91 Ibid., ss 30–34.

and his response to proposals submitted by the Assembly under section 60. The Mayor must attend every meeting of the Assembly and answer questions put to him about matters relating to his statutory functions.[92] Questions will be answered orally 'so far as practicable to do so', or in writing before the end of the third working day following the day on which the question was asked at the meeting. An Annual Report is to be prepared by the Mayor as soon as practicable after the end of each financial year, reporting on his mayoral activities during the year.

Once in each financial year the Mayor must hold and attend a 'State of London debate', open to all members of the public. In addition, twice in every financial year, a 'People's Question Time' is open to all members of the public, for the purpose of putting questions to the Mayor and Assembly Members. People's Question Time must be held within one month of the State of London debate.[93]

The Metropolitan Police[94]

The Police Reform and Social Responsibility Act 2011, discussed further in Chapter 21, established the Mayor's Office for Policing and Crime (replacing the former Metropolitan Police Authority).[95] The principal functions of the Mayor's Office for Policing and Crime are to ensure the maintenance of the Metropolitan Police force and ensure that the force is 'efficient and effective' and to hold the Commissioner of Police to account.

The Metropolitan Police force is under the operational direction and control of the Commissioner of Police of the Metropolis, appointed by Her Majesty on the recommendation of the Secretary of State following any recommendations made to him or her by the Mayor's Office for Policing and Crime.

London Fire and Emergency Planning Authority

The Fire and Emergency Planning Authority replaces the London Fire and Civil Defence Authority as established under the Local Government Act 1985. The reconstituted Authority is responsible to the Mayor. The Fire and Emergency Planning Authority consists of 17 members, of whom nine are Assembly Members appointed by the Mayor and the remainder are members of London borough councils appointed by the Mayor on the nomination of the London borough councils acting jointly. Members are appointed for a renewable one-year term of office. The Mayor is also responsible for appointing a chairman from among the members of the Authority.

Local Government: An Outline[96]

Introduction

Central government is ill equipped to deal with many matters which require special local knowledge and regulation on the basis of local needs. The devolution of power to directly elected local authorities enables those with local knowledge and expertise to regulate the

---

92 Should the Mayor be absent from six consecutive monthly Assembly meetings, he or she is disqualified from office: ibid., s. 13.
93 Greater London Authority Act 1999, ss 45–48.
94 See further Chapter 21.
95 Police Reform and Social Responsibility Act 2011, s. 3 and Sched. 3.
96 See, inter alia, Sharpe, 1970; Byrne, 2000; Stewart and Stoker, 1989; Newton and Karran, 1985; Leach, Stewart and Walsh, 1994; Jones, 1997. Note that local government in Scotland and Northern Ireland is differently arranged.

provision of services, such as public housing, public sanitation, educational and recreational facilities. Local government, therefore, is justified on the basis of efficiency. Local government also represents the citizen's closest contact with a democratic institution and enables individuals to play a role in the administration of their geographical area. The merits of local government were summarised by the Widdicombe Committee as follows:

The value of local government stems from its three attributes of:

(a) pluralism, through which it contributes to the national political system;
(b) participation, through which it contributes to local democracy;
(c) responsiveness, through which it contributes to the provision of local needs through the delivery of services.[97]

Local government represents the democratic form of government closest to the people. Successive governments have introduced reforms to both the structure and powers of local government, with major structural reforms during the 1960s, 1970s, 1980s and 1990s, the effect of which is a complex body of legislation.

The structure and powers of local government are determined by central government, and all powers exercised by local government are derived from Acts of Parliament, or, in the devolved administrations of Northern Ireland, Scotland and Wales, by Acts of the national assembly. Local authorities in the United Kingdom, therefore, do not have independence from central government. By contrast, Germany's Basic Law guarantees local authorities power to regulate all local affairs. Furthermore, the Council of Europe's European Charter of Local Self-Government commits Member States to guaranteeing the political, administrative and financial independence of local government.

The Local Government Act 2000, as amended, is currently the principal statute regulating local government in England. This Act has been substantially reformed by the Localism Act 2011, a key objective of which was to devolve further powers on local authorities and to give local communities greater control over local authority decisions. The 2011 Act also confers on local authorities in England a 'general power of competence'. This power gives local authorities the legal power to act in the same way as an individual may act, provided that the action does not contravene any existing statutory limitations or restrictions.

The structure of local government
England

In England there are over 400 local authorities, employing over two million people in the task of delivering, directly or indirectly, more than 700 different services. Under the Local Government Act 1972 there were two levels of local government in England: a County Council and a District Council. The County Council provided key services such as education, social services and transportation. District Councils covered smaller areas and provided day-to-day services such as leisure facilities, rubbish collection and recycling.

This two-tier arrangement made it difficult for the individual to understand which authority was responsible for which service, and weakened the accountability of local government. Voters were also confused over which council they were voting for.[98] In order to

---

97 *The Conduct of Local Authority Business*, Cmnd 9797, 1986, London: HMSO, p. 47, and see McAuslan, 1987. See also, *inter alia*, Keith-Lucas and Richards, 1979.
98 Electoral Commission, 2004b, p. 13.

improve clarity and accountability, two-tier authorities were replaced by unitary authorities that now operate in all metropolitan, and many other areas, in England. Unitary authorities are also established in Northern Ireland, Scotland and Wales.

The Conservative government's intention in the 1990s was to introduce unitary authorities across most of non-metropolitan England. However, political difficulties with the reform resulted in a mix of single tier – unitary – local authorities and two-tier authorities. Local authorities may be 'unitary' or single-tier, or two-tier.

In England there are:

Single-tier councils:
33 London Boroughs
36 Metropolitan districts
55 unitary authorities
1 Isles of Scilly

Two-tier councils:
27 County Councils
201 District Councils

Total: 353 Councils

Northern Ireland

Prior to 2015 there were 26 unitary District Councils. These were reduced to 11 from 2015. Elections are held every four years. Councils elect a chairman. In city and borough councils, the chairman is known as the Mayor. There have been attempts to reduce the number of councils in Northern Ireland, but failure to reach agreement over council boundaries caused these to be abandoned.

Northern Ireland is administered both by the UK Government and by the Northern Ireland Executive in Belfast. International relations, policing and justice are reserved to the UK Parliament, while the Northern Ireland Executive is responsible for health, education, industry, agriculture, environment and culture.

Scotland

In Scotland – which has its own directly elected Parliament with law-making powers – there are 32 unitary local authorities. Each local authority is governed by a council, made up of councillors directly elected by voters in council 'wards' (voting areas). Each ward will have three or four councillors. Elections are held every four years. The leader of the largest political party in the council will normally act as Leader of the Council. In addition, local authorities elect a Provost or Convenor who chairs council meetings and acts as the ceremonial figurehead.

Wales

In Wales – with its directly elected Assembly – there are 22 unitary local authorities. Elections are held every four years. Local authorities have a cabinet-style executive.

English local government: functions

Local government has no powers other than those conferred by Parliament. The powers conferred must be exercised according to law, and judicial review of local authority decisions may be made to ensure that the rule of law is respected.[99] Some discretion exists, however, as to the means by which local authorities achieve the goals set by central government.

Local authorities are required to put many services out to tender to the private sector, and may provide services themselves only if they can do so in a manner which is competitive with private companies and organisations. The provision of services is also undertaken in cooperation with private commercial organisations. In addition to taxation and the provision of services, local authorities have a regulatory and law-making role. Local councils have wide powers to regulate, for example, the granting of licences for taxis and market trading, and the approval of child care facilities and private welfare homes for the elderly, disabled or sick. In relation to law making, local authorities, acting under the authority of Acts of Parliament, have the power to make bylaws – local laws which regulate the area. For example, footpaths, parks and recreational facilities are controlled by local bylaws. In the exercise of all such power, the local authority is subject to control by the courts: all local authorities must act *intra vires* (within their powers), or their decisions will be declared null and void by the courts.

The Localism Act 2011

Section 1 of the Localism Act confers on local authorities in England (but not Northern Ireland, Wales or Scotland) a 'general power of competence'. This power confers on authorities the same competence to act as an individual may have. The power is subject to boundaries set out in section 2. In essence, the general power may only be exercised in accordance with any existing statutory limitations or restrictions. Where statutory restrictions are introduced subsequently, they will apply to the general power only where they are expressed to do so. Section 2(3) makes clear that the general power does not give local authorities the power to delegate or contract out of their functions, or to alter their government structure. The Secretary of State is given power to remove or change statutory provisions that prevent or restrict the capacity of local authorities to use the general power. This power to amend legislation is subject to statutory limits (see sections 5 and 6). The exercise of this power is subject to parliamentary procedures to be followed in relation to orders made under section 5.[100]

The allocation of functions between authorities in England

Functions are allocated between local authorities principally on the basis of 'operational efficiency and cost-effectiveness'.[101] The provision of certain services, for example education, is clearly a matter for regulation on a large scale, whereas the provision of local libraries and refuse collection may be appropriate for smaller councils to administer. However, there can be no generalisations about the distribution of functions: there are variations throughout. From the point of view of local democracy, and the accountability and responsiveness of local councillors, however, the larger the local government unit, and the more diffuse the provision of services between differing levels of local government, the more difficult it becomes for the individual to apportion responsibility. In Byrne's analysis, the allocation of responsibilities is made the more complex by the sharing of responsibilities, which of itself takes several forms. Shared responsibilities in this analysis may include *concurrent provision*, whereby all local authorities provide the same service in their area; *joint provision*, where two or more local

---

99 See Chapters 3 and 23–25.
100 On procedure, see Chapter 14.
101 Byrne, 2000, p. 80.

authorities combine to provide a common service to all within their common area; *shared but divided provision*, in which different levels of local authority provide differing aspects of the same service; *reserve powers*, under which larger authorities reserve the power to provide particular aspects of a service otherwise provided by smaller authorities; *claimed powers*, through which individual, small authorities assume responsibility for a service or function formally allocated to a larger authority; and *agency powers*, whereby one authority will act as the agent of another authority in the provision of a service or exercise of certain functions.[102]

In addition to the complexity in the allocation of functions between local authorities must be considered the requirement that services be provided in line with the principle of 'best value'.[103] As a result, local authorities nowadays are far less the actual providers of services and more bodies which, through contract, enable services to be provided by those in the private sector. Moreover, no picture of local government can be complete without recognition of the increased, and increasing, functions formerly undertaken by local authorities, which are now undertaken by boards and trusts under provisions introduced by the Conservative government in relation to education and housing, which further fragments local government, accountability and democracy.

English 'devolution deals'

The Conservative government elected in 2015 is committed to the decentralisation of power to local areas. The Cities and Local Government Devolution Act 2016 is an enabling Act providing for 'devolution deals' between central government and local areas in England. In its election manifesto the government stated that it intended to 'devolve far-reaching powers over economic development, transport and social care to large cities which choose to have elected mayors'. As of April 2016, ten 'devolution deals' had been agreed. Most of these cover areas in the north of England. In total, 34 bids were submitted to the government by the cut-off date in 2015. The deals 'transfer powers, funding and accountability for policies and functions previously undertaken by central government'. The substance of the deals varies, each being tailor-made to suit the locality. Aspects of transport, business support and further education are common themes, with housing and planning, employment support, health and social care featuring in some of the deals.[104] At central government level, negotiations are undertaken by HM Treasury and the Cities and Local Growth Unit,[105] which also has responsibility for implementing the deals.

The new arrangements give rise to accountability issues and the National Audit Office has called on the government to clarify 'the core purposes of devolution deals' and to clarify 'who will be responsible and accountable for devolved services and functions'.[106]

The election process

Section 10 of the Representation of the People Act 2000 makes provision for greater flexibility in the voting arrangements for local government elections. A local authority may submit to the Secretary of State proposals for a scheme relating to when, where and how voting is to take place; how the votes cast are to be counted; and the sending by candidates of election

---

102 Byrne, 2000, pp. 82–83.
103 Local Government Act 1999.
104 National Audit Office Report, *English Devolution Deals*, HC 948, April 2016, para. 8.
105 A joint unit of the Department for Communities and Local Government and the Department for Business, Innovation and Skills.
106 Report, *op cit.*, para. 21.

communications free of postage charges. The scheme may make provision for voting to take place on more than one day, and at places other than polling booths. The Secretary of State has power to approve the proposals either without modification or with such modifications as, after consulting the authority, he considers appropriate. Once elections under the scheme have taken place, the authority concerned must prepare a report on the scheme, detailing its provisions and assessing the scheme's success or otherwise in facilitating voting at the elections in question and, if relevant, the counting of votes, or in encouraging voting at the elections in question or enabling voters to make informed decisions at those elections.

A copy of the report must be sent to the Secretary of State, and published in the relevant area, by the end of a period of three months beginning with the date of the declaration of the result. If it appears to the Secretary of State that it would be desirable for provision to be made to apply generally and on a permanent basis to local government elections in England and Wales, he may by order make such provision as he considers appropriate.

The election of councillors

Councillors are elected for a four-year term of office and represent 'wards' within the local government area. In metropolitan districts, one-third of councillors retire each year, other than in a year in which there will be County Council elections. In other, non-metropolitan districts, councillors retire every four years, or they may choose to adopt the metropolitan model. The electoral system reflects that used for general elections, being the simple majority or 'first past the post' system.

Detailed rules regulate election expenditure and, as with general elections, a number of corrupt and illegal practices are proscribed. An election challenge may be presented by way of a petition to the Queen's Bench Division of the High Court.[107] The petition is heard by the election court, which consists of a commissioner appointed by the judges who are nominated to try election petitions.

Qualification and disqualification for election

A candidate must – unlike candidates for Parliament – be able to demonstrate a close connection with the locality. Accordingly, he or she must either be on the local register of electors, or have been resident or have occupied property or have had his or her place of employment within the local authority area for a 12-month period preceding 'nomination day'.[108] Bankruptcy, conviction for corrupt or illegal practices, a conviction and sentence of three months' imprisonment within five years of the election or the imposition of a surcharge by the Audit Commission for unlawful local government expenditure will all disqualify a person from standing for election.

Standards of conduct

The conduct of local government came under review from the Committee of Standards in Public Life, chaired by Lord Nolan.[109] The inquiry examined the 'seven principles of public life' – selflessness, integrity, objectivity, accountability, openness, honesty and leadership – identified by the Committee in its inquiries into parliamentary standards. Lord Nolan's frame

---

107 Representation of the People Act 1983, ss 127–163, as amended.
108 Local Government Act 1972, s. 79.
109 See Nolan (Lord), 'Lord Nolan's shopping list', in Jones, 1997, p. 58.

of reference included the issue of the manner in which, and extent to which, local government operates these principles.

Sections 27 and 28 of the Localism Act 2011 relate to standards of conduct in local government, and require all local authorities to adopt a code of conduct reflecting the Nolan principles. Every local authority maintains a register of members' interests.[110]

Forms of local government[111]

Prior to the reforms introduced by the Local Government Act 2000, the majority of local authority decision making was undertaken by committees, with their decisions being ratified by a meeting of the full council.[112] Committees operated on subject lines – education, transport and so forth – backed by departments staffed by Council officials. There were many criticisms of this system, not least that in reality most councils were dominated by one political party, and where the membership of committees reflected the party-political strengths of the council as a whole, opposition councillors had little impact. The Committee plus department model also encouraged specialisation, with councillors losing sight of the overall aims and objectives of the Council. To coordinate the work of the committees most councils established a Policy and Resources Committee. A further criticism was that the opportunities for holding the majority party to account were weak.

The Local Government Act 2000 aimed to end the perceived inefficiency and lack of transparency in local government and to provide for an identifiable figurehead. The 2000 Act, section 11, provided for new management structures in local government:

- an elected Mayor and Cabinet Executive;
- a Leader and Cabinet Executive; or
- a Mayor and Council Manager Executive.

The Localism Act 2011 reforms the 2000 Act and makes provision for three forms of local government. The permitted forms of local authority governance are executive arrangements, a committee system or 'prescribed arrangements'.

Executive arrangements

Executive arrangements must be either:

(a) a directly elected Mayor together with two or more councillors appointed to the executive by the mayor; or

(b) an executive Leader, elected by the full council from among the councillors, together with two or more councillors of the authority appointed to the executive by the Leader.

The Local Government Act 2000, new section 9H to 9HE, regulates elected Mayors. The Mayor is to be elected by local government electors in the local authority area. Elections are to take place on the same day as council elections. An elected Mayor's term of office is four years. The voting system to be used for electing a Mayor is the supplementary vote system, unless there are fewer than three candidates where the simple majority system will be used.[113]

---

110 Localism Act 2011, ss 29–34.
111 See Oliver, 2003, Chapter 16; Leach, Stewart and Walsh, 1994.
112 Local Government Act 1972, s. 101.
113 Section 9HC and Sched. 2 to the Local Government Act 2000.

Councils operating executive arrangements must establish overview and scrutiny committees to keep the work of the executive under scrutiny and to make reports and recommendations on any aspect of council business.[114]

The committee system

The committee system which had been the traditional form of local government for centuries was regulated under the Local Government Act 1972. As noted above, typically the committee form of local government operated on subject-based lines – for example, environment, children, family and education, housing, economy and business, social services and health. This system was abandoned under the Local Government Act 2000, which introduced the Executive style of governance.

The Coalition government's *Programme for Government* 2010 heralded a return to the committee system, if local authorities chose to adopt it.

Prescribed arrangements

These relate to local authorities which do not wish to operate an executive or committee system of governance. The Secretary of State may make regulations providing for arrangements proposed by a local authority. The regulations must include provisions about how, and by whom, the functions of the local authority are to be discharged. The conditions which must be satisfied before making regulations are: (a) that the operation of the proposed arrangements would be an improvement on current arrangements; (b) that the operation of the new arrangements would be likely to ensure that decisions are taken in an efficient, transparent and accountable way; and (c) that the proposed arrangements would be appropriate for all other local authorities to consider.[115]

Changes in the form of governance

The Localism Act 2011[116] provides that a local authority may change its form of governance and must pass a resolution to do so. The proposed change may be subject to a local referendum. The Secretary of State has the power to require a referendum to be held on forms of government.

Local authority constitution

Each local authority is required to maintain a constitution which is open to the public.[117]

Local authority meetings

The Secretary of State may specify in regulations the circumstances in which meetings of the executive or its committees must be open to the public and which must be held in private. Where there are no regulations governing the issue, the local authority executive may decide whether and which of its meetings are to be held in public or in private. Written records of meetings held in private must be kept and made available to the public[118] and must include reasons for the decisions to which they relate.

---

114 Localism Act 2011, s. 21 inserting new ss 9F–9FE to the Local Government Act 2000.
115 Schedule 2 to the Localism Act 2011, inserting s. 9BA to Local Government Act 2000.
116 Inserting new ss 9K and 9KA into the Local Government Act 2000.
117 Section 9P Local Government Act 2000.
118 Section 9G and 9GA Local Government Act 2000.

Standards of conduct

Section 26 of the Localism Act 2011 imposes a duty on local authorities to ensure that their members maintain high standards of conduct. The authority must adopt a Code of Conduct and establish a Register of Members' Interests.[119]

Central government and local government

Parliament is supreme and can control both the structure of local government and the extent of local government powers and functions. The major forms of control are through primary and delegated legislation. Local authorities have statutory power to make bylaws but these are subject to confirmation by the Minister. Central government policy and standard-setting control the manner in which local authorities may exercise their powers. Schemes for town planning, transport and education must have central approval and, in town planning, appeals will ultimately lie to the Secretary of State, and his/her approval will be needed in relation to compulsory purchase orders. In relation to fire, education and the police, regular inspections are made by central government inspectors.

English local government finance[120]

Some 30 per cent of local government revenue comes from or via central government; the remaining revenue coming from local taxes. In addition, local authorities may borrow money, subject to strict control by the Treasury.

The financial needs of local government are thus met by a mixture of local and central revenues. In terms of local revenue, from around 1600 until 1988, local domestic rates had been in existence. The rates, calculated according to the value of the property, were cheap and easy to collect, and the public were used to them. Rates applied to a property irrespective of the number of persons living in it.

By 1974, the Conservative Party was committed to abolishing local rates and introduced – under the Local Government Finance Act 1988 – the community charge, or poll tax. The same rate within a local authority area would apply to every person: it was a person-based rather than property-based tax. Accordingly, each resident in a local area would contribute to the costs of services which were enjoyed by all. In addition to that personal tax, the government was keen to reform business rates, and introduced the National Non-Domestic Rate, to be set by government and outside local authority control.

Since 1993, the Council Tax has been based on values of property within differing price bands and is payable irrespective of the number of people living within a house, although, to mitigate the perceived unfairness of the old rating system, a 25 per cent discount is allowable for single-person households.

The Coalition government, formed in 2010, was intent on conferring greater autonomy on local government. This in part is effected by enabling local government to retain a share of the Non-Domestic Rate (i.e. that of business, which formerly went to central government, which in turn redistributed it to local government) to encourage the local economy.[121] Local authorities also are able to determine the level of Council Tax payable. However, should this

---

119 Localism Act 2011 ss 28 and 29.
120 See *Report of the Layfield Committee of Inquiry into Local Government Finance*, Cmnd 6453, 1976, London: HMSO.
121 See the Local Government Finance Act 2012.

figure exceed the figure set by central government, a local authority is obliged to hold a referendum.[122]

In terms of expenditure, the majority goes to education, housing, social care, police and highways. Other services include court services, planning, parking and public transport. In 2012–2013 the total expenditure by local authorities in England was £154 billion. Local authority expenditure is subject to audit. Transparency in spending is encouraged, with the government requiring councils to publish items of spending over £500. The Local Audit and Accountability Act 2014 abolishes the Audit Commission and establishes a regulatory framework for local audit of authorities in England. The Northern Ireland Assembly, Scottish Parliament and Welsh Assembly regulate local authorities in their respective countries.

Complaints about local government

Complaints against local government may be made to the authority itself and, if such a complaint does not receive satisfactory treatment, a complaint may be made to the Commissioner for Local Administration. The jurisdiction, role and powers of Commissioners for Administration are considered in Chapter 26.

Local government and Europe

While the role and function of local government is defined, controlled and restrained by central government, local government must also be seen within the wider context of the European Union during the UK's membership from 1973 to 2020. An increasing volume of European law not only affects the legislative sphere of competence of Parliament in relation to matters within the competence of the Union, but also affects both national and local policies and standards. The original Economic Community was founded on the four freedoms – persons, goods, capital and services – which affect all levels of government. In addition, the Union has expanded its sphere of competence over the years to include such diverse matters as environmental protection, health and hygiene standards and weights and measures. Many of the EU laws on these areas fell on local authorities to implement.

The European Union's relationship to local government was not limited to the imposition of Regulations and Directives imposing duties on local authorities, but extended to the provision of regional aid. The Committee of the Regions of the European Union[123] provided the means by which the views and interests of local authorities could be taken into account. Furthermore, the provision of financial aids and grants through the Social Fund, European Investment Bank and Regional Development Fund provided an additional source of finance for local authorities, which ceases on leaving the EU.

Local government and the courts

Local authorities, being bodies to whom powers are delegated by Parliament, may exercise their powers and spend money only for the purposes authorised by statute. In order to ensure that bodies with delegated law-making, administrative and/or judicial powers act within those powers (*intra vires*), the courts are seized with jurisdiction to review any action challenged by a person or body aggrieved by that action. Applications for judicial review proceed by way of an application for leave to apply for judicial review. Applicants must have sufficient

See
Chapters 23–25.

---

122 Localism Act 2011.
123 Formerly, the Consultative Council of Regional and Local Authorities.

interest (*locus standi*) in the matter to apply, and the matter challenged must be one falling under public law as opposed to private law. Furthermore, the matter must be one which is justiciable, that is to say, a matter in which the courts deem themselves to be the appropriate body to adjudicate on the matter.[124]

Local government is a regular participant in judicial review proceedings. As seen earlier, all the powers exercised by them are powers delegated by statute; local authorities have no inherent jurisdiction. Accordingly, the courts may rule on the *vires* of their activities. Judicial review is considered in Chapters 23–25, and those chapters should be consulted for discussion of the case law. In relation to control over the exercise of local government powers, the courts employ the concept of fiduciary duty. Local government is in a fiduciary position of trustee of resources to be exercised for the benefit of the consumers of those resources, Council Tax payers.[125]

Reform of local government

In 2020 the government announced that it intended to bring forward proposals for reforming local government. The intention is to introduce more unitary authorities with directly elected mayors. The plans have been delayed as a result of the Coronavirus pandemic.

Summary

The United Kingdom comprises the nations of England, Northern Ireland, Scotland and Wales, which have long been united under central government in London. The establishment of national assemblies with law-making powers has been on the political agenda for many years, and in the case of Northern Ireland, a high degree of legislative autonomy existed between 1922 and 1974. In 1998 powers were devolved by statute to the newly established Scottish Parliament and Welsh Assembly and re-devolved to the Northern Ireland Assembly. The powers of these national assemblies derive entirely from statute, and remain conditional upon the support of the people. In theory, the legislative sovereignty of the United Kingdom Parliament is unaffected by the Devolution Acts; in practice, its powers are controlled by constitutional convention and politics.

A system of local government has existed for centuries and represents the most localised form of democracy. Local government is older than central government. The powers of directly elected local authorities in England are entirely statute based, and may be altered as Parliament so decides. Local government was devolved to Scotland and Wales under the devolution Acts of 1998.

 Further Reading

Bogdanor, V, *Devolution in the United Kingdom*, 2001, Oxford: Oxford University Press.
Bogdanor, V, 'Our new constitution' (2004) 120 *LQR* 242.
Brazier, R, 'The Scottish government' [1998] *Public Law* 212.
Byrne, A, *Local Government in Britain*, 7th edn, 2000, Harmondsworth: Penguin.

---

124 **Council of Civil Service Unions v Minister for Civil Service** (1985).
125 **Roberts v Hopwood** (1925); **Bromley London Borough Council v Greater London Council** (1982); **Hazell v Hammersmith London Borough Council** (1992).

Cornes, R, 'Devolution and England: what is on offer?' in N Bamforth and P Leyland (eds), *Public Law in a Multi-Layered Constitution*, 2003, Oxford: Hart Publishing.

English, R, *Irish Freedom: The History of Nationalism in Ireland*, 2006, London: Macmillan.

Hadfield, B, 'The Belfast agreement' [1998] *Public Law* 599.

Hadfield, B, 'The nature of devolution in Scotland and Northern Ireland: key issues of responsibility and control' [1999] *Edinburgh Law Review* 3.

Hadfield, B, 'Devolution, Westminster and the English question' [2005] *Public Law* 286.

Hazell, R, 'Reinventing the constitution: can the state survive?' [1999] *Public Law* 84.

House of Lords' Constitution Committee, *The Union and Devolution*, HL Paper149, 2016.

Hughes, M, *Ireland Divided: The Roots of the Modern Irish Problems*, 1994, Cardiff: Wales University Press.

Jones, T and Williams, J, 'The legislative future of Wales' (2005) 68 *MLR* 642.

Jones, T, Turnbull, J and Williams, J, 'The law of Wales or the law of England and Wales?' [2005] *Stat LR* 135.

Jowell, J and Oliver, D (eds), *The Changing Constitution*, 7th edn, 2011, Oxford: Oxford University Press, Chapters 7–9.

McCrudden, C, 'Northern Ireland and the British constitution since the Belfast Agreement' in J Jowell and D Oliver (eds), *The Changing Constitution*, 6th edn, 2007, Oxford: Oxford University Press.

McKittrick D and McVea, D, *Making Sense of the Troubles: A History of the Northern Ireland Conflict*, 2012, London: Penguin.

Rawlings, R, 'Hastening slowly: the next phase in Welsh devolution' [2005] *Public Law* 824.

Stanton, J, 'Local Democracy, Economic Development and Construction Act 2009: a reinvigorated local democracy?' [2010] *Public Law* 1.

Trench, A, 'The Government of Wales Act 2006: the next step in devolution for Wales' [2006] *Public Law* 687.

Walker, D, 'Beyond the unitary conception of the United Kingdom constitution' [2000] *Public Law* 384.

Walker, D, 'The idea of constitutional pluralism' (2002) 65 *Modern Law Review* 317.

Wicks, E, 'A new constitution for a new state? The 1707 union of England and Scotland' (2001) 117 *LQR* 109.

Part 5

Parliament

Chapter 12

The Electoral System

Chapter Contents

Learning Objectives

By the end of this chapter you should be able to:

☐ explain the scope of the franchise;
☐ discuss the importance of constituencies;
☐ explain the voting system used for general elections;

☐ discuss different voting systems used for different elections;
☐ discuss the legal rules relating to elections;
☐ explain the financing of political parties;
☐ evaluate whether state funding of political parties is desirable;
☐ evaluate the extent to which the principle of equality is promoted in the electoral process.

Introduction

In a democratic state, the electoral process determines who will hold political office. It is the electorate which confers the power to govern and calls government to account. If the electorate is to enjoy true equality in constitutional participation, it is of fundamental constitutional importance that the electoral system ensures four principles:

(a)   that there is a full franchise, subject to limited restrictions;
(b)   that the value of each vote cast is equal to that of every other vote;
(c)   that the conduct of election campaigns is regulated to ensure legality and fairness;
(d)   that the voting system is such as to produce both a legislative body representative of the electorate and a government with sufficient democratic support to be able to govern effectively.

It is against these four principal objectives that the law must be evaluated. However, it must be recognised that these elements are in large measure inseparable from each other. Each aspect of the electoral process combines to form a system:

> Any code of electoral law includes a number of essential sections of almost equal importance ... Each of these sections is meaningless in isolation from the others. A wide and equal suffrage loses its value if political bosses are able to gerrymander constituencies so as to suit their own interests; there is no point in having an elaborate system of proportional representation if the electors are all driven in one direction by a preponderance of bribes and threats; legal provisions mean nothing if enforcement is left wholly in the hands of those who profit by breaking it.

That is why it is right to speak of the 'electoral system'. Procedure for elections is systematic in that its parts are interdependent; it is impossible to advance on one 'front' without regard to others.[1]

The Electoral Commission

The Political Parties, Elections and Referendums Act 2000 established the Electoral Commission, comprising not fewer than five but not more than nine Electoral Commissioners, appointed by the Crown. The Commission is an independent body which regulates political party and election finances and set the standards for running elections. Schedule 1 makes detailed provision for the terms of office. The Commission regulates its own procedure, and may appoint a chief executive and such other staff as the Commission considers necessary.

---

1 Mackenzie, 1967, p. 19, cited in Rawlings, 1988, p. 2.

The Commission's functions include preparing and publishing reports relating to parliamentary general elections and elections to the European Parliament, Scottish Parliament,
National Assembly for Wales and Northern Ireland Assembly.[2] The Commission must keep
under review matters relating to elections and referendums, including the redistribution of
seats at parliamentary elections, the registration of political parties[3] and the regulation of
their income and expenditure and political advertising.[4] No nomination may be made in
relation to an election in the name of a party unless that party is registered, or the candidate
is a person who does not propose to represent any party.[5]

The Commission may provide advice and assistance in relation to elections.[6] The
Commission is under a duty to promote public awareness about electoral and democratic
systems, including the institutions of the European Union.[7] The Act provided for 69 offences,
with liability ranging from a fine at level five or six months' imprisonment on summary
conviction to a fine or one year's imprisonment on conviction on indictment.

There is a Speaker's Committee, consisting of the Speaker and the Chairman of the Home
Affairs Select Committee, the Secretary of State for the Home Department, the Minister with
responsibilities in relation to local government and five Members of the Commons who are
not Ministers.[8] The Speaker's Committee scrutinises the annual estimates of the Commission,
and decides whether the estimated level of income and expenditure is consistent with the
'economical, efficient and effective discharge' by the Commission of their functions. If
the Committee is not satisfied, it may modify the estimates. The estimates are laid before
the House of Commons. The Commission also submits to the Speaker's Committee a five-
year plan, setting out the aims and objectives for the period and estimated requirements for
resources. The Speaker's Committee is assisted by the Comptroller and Auditor General, who
each year carries out an examination into the economy, efficiency and effectiveness with
which the Commission has used its resources in discharging its functions, and reports to the
Speaker's Committee, including such recommendations as he considers appropriate.[9]

The Franchise[10]

Evolution of the franchise

Prior to the Reform Acts of 1832 and 1867, the right to vote was limited and based on rights
in property. The 1832 Act – the Representation of the People Act – increased the franchise by
50 per cent, which still represented only seven per cent of the population. The Reform Act of
1867 doubled the number of people entitled to vote.

The extension of the franchise in 1867 to skilled and unskilled male labourers was not
a matter greeted with universal approval. Walter Bagehot retorted that: 'no one will contend
that the ordinary working man who has no special skill, and who is only rated because he
has a house, can judge much of intellectual matters' ((1867) 1993, page 273). Bagehot feared
the potential power of the working class: should they combine as a class, the 'higher orders'

---

2 Political Parties, Elections and Referendums Act 2000, s. 5.
3 Introduced under the Registration of Political Parties Act 1998.
4 Political Parties, Elections and Referendums Act 2000, Pt II.
5 Ibid., s. 22.
6 Ibid., s. 10.
7 Ibid., s. 13.
8 Political Parties, Elections and Referendums Act 2000, s. 2.
9 For a critical assessment of the Electoral Commission see the Eleventh Report of the Committee of Standards and Privileges,
  January 2007.
10 For a full history of the franchise see, inter alia, Anson, 1933; Maitland, 1908, pp. 352–364.

might have to consider whether to concede to their demands or 'risk the effect of the working men's combination' (page 278).

Women and the right to vote

Women were to remain disenfranchised until 1928, but the movement for women's right to vote pre-dates the 1867 Act.[11] In 1851, Harriet Taylor Mill had published 'The Enfranchisement of Women' in the *Westminster Review*. In 1886, John Stuart Mill[12] presented a petition to Parliament calling for the enfranchisement of women. The following year, the Manchester Women's Suffrage Committee was formed, soon to be united in a National Committee based in London. When the Reform Bill was before Parliament, Mill introduced an amendment – changing the word 'man' to 'person' – thereby entitling women to vote. The amendment was defeated.

A legal challenge to disenfranchisement came in **Chorlton v Lings** (1868). It was argued before the Court of Common Pleas that the Representation of the People Act 1867 had conferred on women a right to vote. The argument centred on the use of the word 'man' in the Act. It was contended that Lord Brougham's Act which stipulated that the word 'man' included 'women' applied to an interpretation of the Representation of the People Act. The court rejected such a view. Willis J declared himself opposed to any view that women were excluded from the franchise on the basis of 'fickleness of judgment and liability to influence', which would be quite inconsistent 'with one of the glories of our civilisation – the respect and honour in which women are held'. However, concerning the prohibition of voting – and the prohibition against peeresses in the House of Lords – Willis J declared that

> out of respect to women, and a sense of decorum, and not from their want of intellect, or their being for any other reason unfit to take part in the government of the country, they have been excused from taking any share in this department of public affairs.

In 1869, JS Mill published *The Subjection of Women*. The right to vote was but one campaign. Women were also seeking equal rights in education, in politics and in the medical profession. In 1897, the differing suffrage movements were to be united under the National Union of Women's Suffrage Societies. By 1913, the number of affiliated societies had reached 400. The leadership of Emmeline and Christabel Pankhurst injected new energy into the campaign and the age of militancy in support of the right to vote began. The tide of public opinion started to turn in women's favour in 1909, when the authorities started to force feed hunger-striking suffragettes imprisoned as a result of their campaign. A Bill to give women the right to vote passed second reading in 1910, but was defeated by the Prime Minister, Asquith, acting in concert with Lloyd George, the Opposition Leader. The failure of a second Bill in 1911 sparked violent protest all over London: 217 women were arrested. A Bill of 1913 met with a similar fate and reaction. Fearful of the consequences of imprisonment and hunger strikes, the government passed the 'Cat and Mouse' Act,[13] which enabled the authorities to release hunger-striking prisoners who were in medical danger and re-arrest them on their physical recovery.

---

11 See Kent, 1987.
12 A Member of Parliament and radical reformer. See, *inter alia, Representative Government* (1861); see also *On Liberty* (1859) and *The Subjection of Women* (1869).
13 Prisoners (Temporary Discharge for Ill Health) Act 1913.

The persistence of the suffragettes, combined with the involvement of women in industry during the First World War, acted as catalysts for winning the right to vote. In 1916, an all-party conference on electoral reform was established under the chairmanship of the Speaker of the House of Commons.

The Representation of the People Act 1918, which implemented the conference's proposals, introduced a full franchise of all men in parliamentary elections and conferred the right to vote in Parliament on all women over the age of 30 who were either local government electors or the wives of local government electors.[14] Full equality with men was delayed until 1928. A full franchise, on the basis of equality, and respecting the principle of 'one person, one vote', was finally achieved under the Representation of the People Act 1948.

The current franchise

The right to vote is defined in the Representation of the People Act 1983, as amended. Prior to enactment of the Representation of the People Act 2000, eligibility was based solely on residency in a constituency at a 'qualifying date'.[15] The 2000 Act introduced greater flexibility, allowing registration once resident in a constituency at any date, and supplements the residency requirement with registration on the register of parliamentary electors for that constituency. In addition to residency, a person is eligible to vote once they have made a 'declaration of local connection'.[16] A declaration of local connection must state the name of the declarant and either give an address to which election correspondence can be delivered, or state that he or she is willing to collect such correspondence periodically from the registration officer's office. The declaration must state the required address and also be dated, and, on the date of declaration, the declarant must also be otherwise qualified to vote by virtue of relevant citizenship and age. A declaration of local connection may be cancelled at any time by the declarant. The declaration is of no effect unless it is received by the relevant registration officer within the period of three months beginning with the date of the declaration.[17] The Electoral Administration Act 2006 amends the 1983 Act and allows for anonymous entries to the register. Section 9B(10) provides that a person is eligible for anonymous entry if his or her safety (or that of any other person of the same household) would be at risk if the register revealed his or her name and/or address.

The right to vote is linked to citizenship, residence and entry on the electoral register. Under section 1 of the Representation of the People Act 1983, as amended, a person is eligible to vote in parliamentary elections if he or she:

- is 18 years of age at the date of the election;
- is a British citizen; a Commonwealth citizen who has the right to remain in the United Kingdom indefinitely; a citizen of the Republic of Ireland;
- is resident in or has a local connection with (see below) a constituency and is registered on the electoral register for the constituency.

A person is not allowed to vote more than once in the same parliamentary constituency or vote in more than one constituency. A person may, however, be eligible to vote in more

---

14 In addition, the Parliament (Qualification of Women) Act 1918 provided that: 'A woman shall not be disqualified by sex or marriage from being elected to or sitting or voting as a Member of the Commons House of Parliament'.
15 Representation of the People Act 1983, ss 1, 2.
16 2000 Act, s. 6.
17 The Representation of the People Act 2000, Sched. 2 extends the parliamentary franchise in relation to overseas voters, amending the Representation of the People Act 1985.

than one constituency but must choose in which to vote. In **Fox v Stirk** (1970), for example, it was held that a university student living in university halls of residence could register in that constituency provided that he or she was ordinarily resident there; there had to be a reasonable degree of permanence to the residency.

Persons who are not allowed to vote in general elections and by-elections include the following:

- persons under the age of 18;
- aliens;
- Commonwealth citizens who do not have the right to remain in the United Kingdom indefinitely;
- non-British EU citizens;[18]
- members of the House of Lords (other than Bishops sitting ex officio) – former Members of the House of Lords may now vote;[19]
- convicted prisoners in detention[20] (prisoners on remand may vote if they are on the electoral register);
- mental patients who are detained under statutory authority;[21]
- persons convicted of corrupt or illegal practices at elections.[22]

The European Convention on Human Rights: Protocol 1

The First Protocol to the European Convention on Human Rights, Article 3, guarantees the right to fair elections under conditions ensuring the free expression of the opinion of the people in the choice of the legislature. Those requirements were not breached by the existence of two unelected, but non-voting, members of the legislature of the Channel Island of Sark (on which see page 24). The Supreme Court so ruled in **R (Barclay) v The Lord Chancellor and Secretary of State for Justice** (2009). The Reform (Sark) Law 2008 provided for the replacement of unelected landowners with 28 democratically elected conseillers. It also provided that the Seigneur (an ancient office first appointed in 1565) lost his right to vote in the legislature (Chief Pleas) but retained his right to sit as an unelected member and to speak, and temporarily to veto ordinances. The Seneschal (President of Chief Pleas) also lost his right to vote and speak in Chief Pleas but continued to sit as an unelected member. Reviewing the Strasbourg jurisprudence, the Supreme Court ruled that it did not require that every member of a legislature should be elected, particularly where, as here, the unelected members did not have the right to vote. Even if Article 3 required non-voting members to be elected, it was well within the margin of appreciation allowed by Article 3 in light of the constitutional and political factors relevant to Sark.

In **Hirst v United Kingdom** (2004) the European Court of Human Rights ruled that the blanket restriction which deprives all prisoners of the right to vote – irrespective of the length of their sentence or the seriousness of the offence committed – was unlawful.[23] In **R (Chester) v Secretary of State for Justice** (2011) the Court of Appeal ruled that it was for Parliament, not the courts, to amend the law. The issue, Laws LJ stated, was controversial and a matter of

---

18 EU citizens resident in Britain are entitled to vote in elections to the European Parliament and local government elections but not to elections to the United Kingdom Parliament.

19 House of Lords Act 1999, s. 3.

20 Representation of the People Act 1983, s. 3, as amended by the Representation of the People Act 1985, Sched. 5. But see **Hirst v United Kingdom** (2004) and see HL Deb Vol. 687 Col. WS203, 14 December 2006.

21 Representation of the People Act 1983, s. 1.

22 Ibid., ss 51, 160. The disqualification is for a five-year period.

23 Article 3 of the First Protocol to the Convention provides for the holding of free elections under conditions ensuring 'the free expression of the opinion of the people in the choice of the legislature'. See also **Matthews v United Kingdom** (1999) and **Greens and MT v United Kingdom** (2010).

social policy. The Court of Human Rights returned to prisoner voting rights in **Scoppola v Italy (No 3)** (2012), ruling that there was no violation of human rights provided that the removal of a prisoner's right to vote was not automatic and indiscriminate. The Court accepted that restricting a prisoner's right to vote pursued a legitimate aim of preventing crime and enhancing civic responsibility and respect for the rule of law and democracy. The issue was whether the restriction was proportionate to the offence. Here the applicant had been sentenced to life imprisonment for murder and if he displayed good conduct was entitled to apply for rehabilitation and recover the right to vote. There was no violation of Article 3 of Protocol 1 (A3P1). In **Moohan v The Lord Advocate** (2014) the Supreme Court ruled (by a majority of five to two) that A3P1 is limited to periodic general elections and does not cover referendums. In **Millbank and Others v United Kingdom** (2016) the European Court of Human Rights reiterated its view that the United Kingdom remained in breach of the Convention by denying prisoners the right to vote.

In 2017 it was proposed that prisoners on Temporary Licence would be allowed to vote – a proposal welcomed by the Council of Europe as satisfying the demands of the Convention.

The responsibility for local and evolved elections in Scotland and Wales is a devolved matter and therefore for the Scottish and Welsh governments to decide. In 2020 the Scottish Parliament passed a Bill extending voting rights to prisoners serving 12 months or less. In Wales, the Local Government and Elections (Wales) Act 2019 lowered the voting age in Wales for local government elections to 16, and renamed the Assembly the Welsh Parliament, but it did not extend prisoner voting to the Welsh Parliament elections.

 Pause and Reflect

Why do you think the government was so opposed to prisoners having voting rights? What are the arguments for and against granting voting rights to prisoners? Should the right to vote be linked to the length of the prisoner's sentence?

Postal voting and voting by proxy

The majority of votes are cast by individuals attending designated polling stations in their constituency. However, circumstances may require that a person's vote be cast by post or by someone on his or her behalf. The Representation of the People Act 2000[24] introduced greater flexibility in the rules in the hope of encouraging more people to vote, and in anticipation of the possible introduction of electronic voting.

Postal voting, however, carries risks, and in the 2005 general election there was evidence of the misuse of postal votes. The Electoral Administration Act 2006 seeks to tighten the law and amends the Representation of the People Act 1983. Section 14 of the 2006 Act provides that applicants for proxy and postal votes must produce 'personal identifiers', namely their date of birth and a signature on their application forms. Furthermore, under section 37[25] postal voters are also required to provide their signature and date of birth on the postal voting statement, which must be completed and returned with the postal ballot paper.

Section 62A of the 1983 Act provides that it is both a corrupt practice and criminal offence to apply for a postal or proxy vote with the intention of stealing another's vote or gaining a vote to which the applicant is not entitled. If found guilty by an election court, a

---

24 See Scheds 1 and 4.
25 And para. 73 of Sched. 1.

person can be disqualified from standing for election or from being registered as a voter for five years. If found guilty in criminal proceedings, a person may be imprisoned for up to two years and fined. Section 13D of the 1983 Act is amended to make it an offence to provide false information for any purposes connected with registration.[26] The Political Parties, Elections and Referendums Act 2000 makes special provision for assistance with voting for persons with disabilities, whether by virtue of partial sight, blindness or other physical incapacity or inability to read.[27]

Reform

See Chapter 18.

Concerns over electoral fraud – in part the lack of checks on the identity of those registering to vote – have led to proposals for reform. The Electoral Registration and Administration Act 2013 introduced a system of individual electoral registration (IER).[28] The IER system provides that each elector must apply individually to be registered to vote. Regulations provide that registration offices may require a person who is applying to register to provide evidence of his or her identity.

Constituencies and the Boundary Commissions

The United Kingdom is divided for electoral purposes into 650 constituencies, or voting areas. Each constituency is represented in Parliament by just one member, who has secured a majority of votes in a general election or by-election.[29] The task of regulating constituency boundaries falls to the Boundary Commissions for England, Northern Ireland, Scotland and Wales. Under the Parliamentary Voting System and Constituencies Act 2011, section 10, the Boundary Commissions are to report every five years (rather than the previous eight to ten years).

Following a Review of constituency boundaries in 2018, the number of constituencies was reduced from 650 to 600.[30] Following a change of policy, however, the Parliamentary Constituencies Act 2020 (which applies to the whole of the UK) provides that the number of constituencies is to remain at 650.[31,32]

The constitutional principle of 'one man, one vote, one value' is given formal recognition in the rules regulating the work of the Boundary Commissions.[33] In the United States of America, the principle of equality in voting power was judicially considered by the Supreme Court in **Baker v Carr** in 1962. In that case, the principle was regarded as of such constitutional importance that the Supreme Court held that the Fourteenth Amendment of the Constitution – the 'equal protection' clause – required that electoral districts had to have an approximately equal number of electors to prevent over- or under-representation and inequality in voting power.

The Parliamentary Voting System and Constituencies Act 2011 gave priority to the principle of numerical equality. The electorate of all constituencies (with limited exceptions)

---

26 The more limited version of this section formerly applied only to Northern Ireland. It now applies to the whole of the United Kingdom.

27 Representation of the People Act 2000, s. 13, amending the 1983 Act, Sched. 1, the parliamentary elections rules. The Act also makes provision for the free delivery of election addresses by candidates at the first election for London Mayor: s. 14 of the 2000 Act amending the Greater London Authority Act 1999, s. 17, on which see Chapter 11.

28 For the background see the White Paper, *Individual Electoral Registration*, Cm 8108, 2011, London: TSO.

29 An election in a single constituency, conducted as a result of the seat falling vacant during the life of a Parliament.

30 The Parliamentary Voting System and Constituencies Act 2011 amending the Parliamentary Constituencies Act 1986.

31 Parliamentary Constituencies Act 2020, section 5.

32 The next Review is due to start in 2021 and to be completed by the Boundary Commissions by 1 July 2023.

33 Parliamentary Constituencies Act 1986, Sched. 2.

should be no less than 95 per cent and no more than 105 per cent of the electoral quota – the average number of electors in a constituency. Parliamentary constituencies are required to respect – as far as possible – local authority boundaries. While constituencies must respect the electoral quota, this may be departed from where there are special geographical considerations which must be respected.

Once a review by the Boundary Commissions is concluded, an Order in Council giving effect to the recommendations must be laid before Parliament 'as soon as practicable' and at the latest within a four month period from the date on which the Commissions' Report was laid before Parliament, unless there are 'exceptional circumstances'.[34] The Parliamentary Constituencies Act 2020 provides that Parliament will no longer vote to implement the Commissions' recommendations and that Ministers will no longer, as previously, have the power to alter recommendations of Boundary Commissions. This is designed to ensure that there is no political interference in the recommendations of the Commissions.

Legal challenges to Boundary Commission reports

The political difficulties – generally the loss of a number of 'safe' seats by one party – caused by boundary changes have in the past given rise to challenges in the courts. In **R v Home Secretary ex parte McWhirter** (1969), the Labour Party feared the loss of up to ten constituencies as a result of the Commission's recommendations. The Home Secretary laid the report before Parliament, without the draft Orders in Council which were necessary to implement the changes. The reason given for failure to produce the draft Orders was that it made little sense to implement changes, given that local government boundaries were under review at the time.

The Home Secretary introduced the House of Commons Redistribution of Seats Bill, implementing some of the recommendations regarding large urban areas, but not the remaining recommendations. The House of Lords introduced amendments, which the Home Secretary rejected. The Home Secretary then suggested compromise amendments, which the House of Lords rejected. Subsequently, the Home Secretary introduced the draft Orders in Council, leaving the Lords' amendments intact, but inviting the House of Commons to reject the Orders. The application for mandamus was withdrawn. In 1970, however, the incoming Conservative government reintroduced and passed the Orders.

In **R v Boundary Commission for England ex parte Foot** (1983), the Labour Party, having been aggrieved by the Boundary Commission's recommendations, sought an order of prohibition and injunctions to restrain the Commission from putting the recommendations to the Home Secretary, alleging that the Commission had misinterpreted the rules.[35] The court rejected the argument, relying on the considerable discretion built into the rules by the Parliamentary Constituencies Act. Sir John Donaldson MR, having referred to the constitutional role of judicial review and accepted that jurisdiction lay to review the decision of the Boundary Commission, stated that unless there was sufficient evidence that the Commission had made recommendations which no reasonable body could make, the court should not intervene.

The reluctant attitude of the courts towards controlling the Boundary Commission's exercise of power is understandable, given the politically charged nature of the subject matter. Judicial inquiry in this matter comes very close to questioning a matter which is more appropriately dealt with in Parliament, and to thereby infringing the privileges of Parliament.[36]

---

34 *Ibid.*, section 2.
35 Parliamentary Constituencies Act 1986, Sched. 2.
36 See Chapter 4 on separation of powers and Chapter 17 on privilege.

Nevertheless, such an attitude is thrown into sharp relief when compared with the position in the United States of America, where the constitutional guarantee of 'the equal protection of the law'[37] has been utilised to ensure real equality in voting power.

Initiating the Election Process

General elections

General elections must be held every five years, the maximum life of any Parliament.[38]

See Chapter 5.

Until 2010 the Prime Minister had control over the timing of general elections, the dissolution of Parliament being within the prerogative of the Crown. While a Parliament could run for a full five-year term, there were often political reasons against this, which resulted in Prime Ministers choosing a politically convenient date for his or her own party. Although there is a maximum time limit on the life of a Parliament, there was no minimum period which a government must serve before calling an election. In May 2010 the incoming Prime Minister announced that the Conservative/Liberal Democrat government would serve a fixed five-year term of office.

The Fixed-term Parliaments Act 2011 gave effect to this proposal. The Act provided that the next general election would take place on 7 May 2015, and general elections thereafter are to take place on the first Thursday in May in the fifth calendar year following the 2015 election.[39] To provide flexibility in the event of short-term crises, provision was made for the Prime Minister, by statutory instrument, to vary the election date by no more than two months earlier or later than the prescribed date. An early general election may take place if the House of Commons passes a motion 'That there shall be an early parliamentary general election'[40] or the House of Commons has passed a motion of no confidence in the government, and that a period of 14 days has ended without the House expressing confidence in the government.[41] Section 3 of the Act provides that Parliament dissolves automatically 17 working days before the date of the general election.[42] This removed the power of the Queen to dissolve Parliament under the royal prerogative. Note, however, that in 2020 the government announced plans to abolish the Fixed-term Parliament Act and to revive the prerogative power of dissolution.[43]

By-elections

By-elections take place following the death or retirement of a Member of Parliament. Any Member of Parliament may put down a motion to the House, which, if successful, requires the Speaker to issue a writ commencing the election procedure. In practice, the Chief Whip of the party which held the seat of the Member moves the motion for a writ. There is no limit laid down by law as to the time period in which a by-election must be held. In 1973, a Speaker's Conference recommended that the motion initiating the by-election process should be moved within three months of the vacancy arising.

---

37 The Fourteenth Amendment to the Constitution.
38 Fixed-term Parliament Act 2011, s. 1.
39 The Act repeals the Septennial Act 1715.
40 As occurred in 2019 under the Early Parliamentary General Election Act 2019.
41 Fixed-term Parliament Act 2011, section 2.
42 The Electoral Registration and Administration Bill 2012–2013, Clause 13, extends this period to 25 days.
43 See the Draft Fixed-term Parliaments Act (Repeal) Bill 2020–2021.

Eligibility of candidates

There is no statutory or other authority defining the qualifications for membership of the House of Commons. In order to promote a greater gender balance in Parliament, the Sex Discrimination (Election of Candidates) Act 2002 provides that the Sex Discrimination Act 1975 and Sex Discrimination (Northern Ireland) Order 1976 do not apply to the selection of candidates by political parties. The Equality Act 2010[44] replicates the provisions of the 2002 Act and extends its provisions until 2030.

Under the House of Commons Disqualification Act 1975, certain categories of persons are eligible for election and others are disqualified under the Act. Those disqualified include:

- members of the House of Lords;
- holders of judicial office specified in Part I of Schedule I;
- civil servants;
- members of the regular armed forces of the Crown or the Police Service of Northern Ireland;
- members of the police forces;
- members of legislative bodies outside the Commonwealth (other than Ireland);
- Commonwealth citizens who do not have a right of abode or indefinite leave to remain in the United Kingdom;[45]
- members of Boards of nationalised industries, Commissions, Tribunals and other bodies specified in Part II or Part III of Schedule I.

In addition, a number of general restrictions on eligibility apply:

Persons under the age of 18

The Electoral Administration Act 2006, section 17, reduced the age of qualification for election to the House of Commons or a local authority, and election to Mayor, Mayor of London and Assembly Members of the Greater London Authority from 21 to 18.

Persons suffering from mental illness

Formerly, if an elected Member of Parliament was authorised to be detained on grounds of mental illness for more than six months, the Member's seat was declared vacant. The Mental Health (Discrimination) Act 2013 reforms the law, repealing section 141 of the Mental Health Act 1983 and any common law rule that has the same effect.

Peers

Members of the House of Lords, or persons succeeding to a peerage, are not eligible for office. Under the Peerage Act 1963, a person succeeding to a peerage has a limited right to disclaim his peerage. If a Member of the House of Commons succeeds to a peerage, he has one month in which to disclaim his peerage or resign from the House of Commons.

Members of the clergy

Formerly, no person who had been ordained 'to the office of priest or deacon' or who was a Minister of the Church of Scotland could stand for election,[46] although a clergyman could relinquish his office and thereby become eligible to stand for election.[47] The House of

---

44 Sections 104–105.
45 Electoral Administration Act 2006, s. 18.
46 House of Commons (Clergy Disqualification) Act 1801; Roman Catholic Relief Act 1929; Welsh Church Act 1914.
47 Clerical Disabilities Act 1870.

Commons (Removal of Clergy Disqualification) Act 2001 removes the disqualification, other than for those who hold office as Lords Spiritual in the House of Lords.

Bankrupts

Persons declared bankrupt are ineligible for election to the House of Commons and, if already a Member, may not either sit or vote in Parliament until the bankruptcy is discharged by a court or the adjudication annulled.[48]

Treason

Persons convicted of treason are disqualified for election to the House and, if already a Member of the House, may not sit or vote until a pardon has been received or the sentence of the court has expired.[49]

The Conduct of Election Campaigns

The Representation of the People Act 1983 governs the law relating to election campaigns, controlling both the amount of expenditure and the manner in which it can lawfully be spent, proscribing certain unlawful practices and providing for challenges to the legality of a campaign. Corrupt practices include exceeding the lawful expenditure limits, bribery, treating and undue influence which includes making threats or attempts to intimidate electors.[50] A bribe is defined as 'any money, gift, loan or valuable consideration, office, place or employment, in order to influence how an elector will cast his or her vote'.[51] 'Treating' occurs where a candidate offers or gives food, drink or entertainment with a view to influencing how the elector will vote.[52] A corrupt practice may be committed by any person, not just the candidate or his or her election agent. While minor infringement of the strict rules may be excused by a court,[53] a finding of corrupt practices may cause the election of the candidate to be invalidated.[54]

On disputed elections, see below at pages 330 to 331.

Expenditure

Section 75 of the Representation of the People Act 1983 provides that no expenditure shall be made other than by the candidate or through his or her election agent. Each candidate is obliged to appoint an election agent.[55] The rationale for this rule lies in establishing and maintaining fairness between candidates and providing a mechanism for accountability as to election expenses. All accounts relating to election expenses must be reported, within 21 days of the election result, to the Returning Officer. Section 76 of the Act[56] permits the Secretary of State to set and raise the permitted amounts of expenditure, in line with inflation, by way of statutory instrument. The allowable amount comprises a fixed sum per constituency plus a sum calculated on the number of voters in a constituency. Any expenditure exceeding the

---

48 Insolvency Act 1986, s. 427.
49 Forfeiture Act 1870, ss 2 and 7.
50 Originally, the Corrupt and Illegal Practices Prevention Act 1883. See now the Representation of the People Act 1983, ss 72–75, 107, 109, 111, 115.
51 Ibid., s. 113.
52 Representation of the People Act 1983, s. 114.
53 Ibid., s. 167.
54 Ibid., s. 159.
55 Representation of the People Act 1983, s. 67(2).
56 As amended by the Representation of the People Act 1985.

prescribed limits amounts to a corrupt practice under section 75(1). Expenditure on national party election broadcasts is met by central party funds.

Several challenges to expenditure have been presented to the courts. In **R v Tronoh Mines Ltd** (1952), Tronoh Mines placed an advertisement in *The Times* newspaper urging voters not to vote socialist. The company and *The Times* were charged under the Act. The court held that the expenditure had been incurred with a view to promoting the interests of a Party generally, rather than an individual candidate; that any advantage incurred was incidental and not direct; and that accordingly the expenditure did not fall within section 75. Conversely, in **DPP v Luft** (1977), an anti-fascist group had distributed pamphlets in three constituencies urging voters not to vote for National Front (extreme right wing) candidates. The group was prosecuted under section 75 of the 1983 Act for incurring expenditure with a view to promoting the election of a candidate without the authority of an election agent. It was held that an offence had been committed, even though the promoters were seeking to prevent election of a candidate, rather than directly promote the election of a preferred candidate. In **Walker v Unison** (1995), the court ruled that section 75(1) of the Representation of the People Act 1983 had not been breached. During local elections in Scotland, Unison, a trade union, placed advertisements in national newspapers and on billboards, urging voters not to vote Conservative. The advertisements were placed without the authorisation of an election agent. Two Conservative candidates argued that there had been an illegal expenditure. The court ruled that the advertisements were a generalised attack on a political party, and not a direct attack on the candidates and, accordingly, the advertisements did not contravene the Act.[57]

In **Grieve v Douglas-Home** (1965), Alec Douglas-Home's election was alleged to be void on the basis that he had participated in a national Party Political Broadcast on behalf of the Conservative Party and had not declared the cost of this expenditure within his election expenses. The court held that no offence had been committed either by the candidate or by the broadcasters. The court accepted the contention that the intention behind the broadcast was not to promote the candidature of Douglas-Home in his own constituency but to provide general information about the Party to the general public. In **Finch v Richardson** (2008) the Court accepted that exceeding the permitted limits could be caused by an inadvertent ignorance of the law.

It may be noted that, before the Political Parties, Elections and Referendums Act 2000, while the law closely regulated the conduct of constituency campaigns, it virtually ignored regulation of the national political party campaigns. In an age of mass communication, and ever increasing personality politics in terms of political party leaders, the absence of regulation at national level – other than via broadcasting controls – was a matter for concern. On the 2000 Act, see below.

Broadcasting and Elections

Ofcom, the Office of Communications, which oversees broadcasting, telecommunications and postal industries in the United Kingdom, was established under the Office of Communications Act 2002. In relation to political party broadcasts, section 333 of the Communications Act 2003 imposes a duty on Ofcom to ensure that Party Political Broadcasts and Party Election Broadcasts and Referendum Campaign Broadcasts are included in every licensed public service television channel and radio services. The Broadcasters' Liaison Group, formed in 1997 and

---

57 On a challenge to the former £5 limit on expenditure not authorised by the candidate or his/her election agent, see **Bowman v United Kingdom** (1998). The limit operated as a restriction on freedom of expression and violated the Convention. The limit has been raised to £500: see the Representation of the People Act 1983, s. 75(1ZA).

comprising representatives of each of the broadcasters, works with the Electoral Commission to ensure a consistent approach to political broadcasts.

Broadcasts are allocated to the main parties, and to parties standing in at least one-sixth of seats in each of the four nations of the United Kingdom. Parties must be registered with the Electoral Commission to qualify for broadcasts. Broadcasts must comply with Ofcom's Broadcasting Code and the BBC Editorial Guidelines. All broadcasts must observe the law relating to libel, copyright, contempt, obscenity and incitement to racial hatred or violence.

Political advertisements and the European Convention on Human Rights

See further
Chapters 18 and 19.

Political advertisements are banned under the Communications Act 2003, section 321. The law was considered in **R (Animal Defenders International) v Secretary of State for Culture, Media and Sport** (2008). Animal Defenders International (ADI) is a non-profit-making campaign organisation. It submitted an advertisement to the Broadcast Advertising Clearance Centre which refused to clear it for broadcasting as being in breach of the ban on political advertising. ADI challenged the decision, arguing that the ban violated its right to freedom of expression as protected by Article 10 of the European Convention on Human Rights and seeking a Declaration that section 321 was incompatible with Article 10. The Court refused: the government had not certified the Communications Bill as compatible with the Convention (see section 19 Human Rights Act 1998). The ban was justified and the Court had to give great weight to Parliament's view on the matter. The European Court of Human Rights upheld the decision of the House of Lords in **Animal Defenders International v United Kingdom** (2013).[58]

The issue of freedom of speech protected under the Human Rights Act 1998 was considered by the House of Lords in **R (ProLife Alliance) v British Broadcasting Corporation** (2003). At issue was the right of a registered political party, the ProLife Alliance, to insist that the BBC and other terrestrial broadcasters transmit its party election broadcast, which contravened, in the BBC's opinion, the obligation to ensure that nothing in its programmes, inter alia, offended against good taste or decency.[59] In the Court of Appeal, Laws LJ had asserted that the court had a constitutional responsibility to protect political speech, and that while the film was 'graphic and disturbing', that could not justify any restriction. The House of Lords disagreed: the BBC and other terrestrial broadcasters had been entitled to refuse to televise the proposed election broadcast on the ground that it would be offensive to public feeling.

Disputed Elections

Any challenge to an election campaign must be made within three weeks of the result being declared. The complaint may be made by a registered elector, by unsuccessful candidates or by their nominees. Since 1868, such challenges go to the Election Court.

The Election Court has High Court status and comprises judges of the High Court.[60] The Election Court has jurisdiction to try parliamentary election petitions presented to the High Court in accordance with sections 120 and 121 of the 1983 Act. At the conclusion of the

---

58 See Lewis, 2014.
59 Under para. 5(1)(d) of the agreement between the BBC and Home Secretary, and in the case of independent broadcasters, the obligation is imposed by s. 6(1)(a) of the Broadcasting Act 1990.
60 Established under s. 123 of the Representation of the People Act 1983.

trial of a parliamentary election petition, the Election Court must certify its decision to the Speaker of the House of Commons, who will give directions as to the consequences.[61]

A decision of the Election Court can be subject to judicial review by the High Court: **R (Woolas) v Watkins** (2010). In that case it had been argued that there could be no judicial review of a decision of the Election Court on the basis that decisions of the High Court were not subject to review by the High Court. However, the Court ruled that High Court judges sitting as judges in the Election Court, although having the same powers as the judges of the High Court, exercised the more limited jurisdiction conferred under the Representation of the People Act 1983. Furthermore, the Court ruled that while Parliament intended that a lawful decision of the Election Court was to be final (and therefore not reviewable), Parliament could 'not have intended that a decision that had been made on a wrong interpretation of the law' could not be challenged.[62]

The court has the power to order a recount; declare corrupt or illegal practices; disqualify a candidate from membership of the House of Commons and declare the runner-up duly elected; or order a fresh election. In **Re Parliamentary Election for Bristol South East** (1964), Tony Benn MP, who had recently succeeded to a peerage as Viscount Stansgate, stood for re-election. The election was declared void and awarded to the runner-up. In **Ruffle v Rogers** (1982), the election papers were incorrectly counted, affecting the outcome of the election. The election was declared void, but the court made clear that had the miscount not affected the result, the election would have been upheld. In **Gough v Local Sunday Newspapers (North) Ltd** (2003), the Court of Appeal ruled that informal counts of ballot papers should not take place under any circumstances. The solicitor to Bedford Borough Council had approved an informal count – in the absence of the candidates and their agents – of postal votes which were discovered after the election had been declared. The rules governing local elections under section 36(2) of the Representation of the People Act 1983 did not provide for a situation where the ballot papers had been overlooked. A fresh election was ordered in 1997, following allegations concerning the accuracy of the count of the vote which returned a Member of Parliament with a majority of just two votes. In **Knight v Nicholls** (2004) it was held that a returning officer had fulfilled his duty to issue ballot papers by delivering them to a carrier (Royal Mail) chosen and paid for the purpose in good time for them to be delivered and returned before the election. At the local election Nicholls was elected by a majority of 40 votes over Knight. The Royal Mail had failed to deliver 110 papers on time for the election. However, since the returning officer had discharged his duty, the election was not invalid.[63]

In **Watkins v Woolas** (2010), the petitioner contested the result of the parliamentary election on the basis that the respondent had lied in his election literature in order to sway the vote, and was guilty of an illegal practice contrary to section 106 of the RPA 1983. Section 106 provides that it is an offence to publish, 'for the purpose of affecting the return of any candidate at the election', 'any false statement of fact in relation to the candidate's personal character or conduct' unless they believed it was true and had 'reasonable grounds' to do so. The Election Court ruled that the respondent had been personally guilty of an illegal practice, declared the election void (under section 159 of the RPA) and ordered that the respondent be disqualified from standing for election to Parliament for a period of three years.

---

61 Ibid., s. 144.
62 See para. 47.
63 In **R v Hussain** (2005) the Court of Appeal ruled that it was the duty of the courts to protect the UK's system of democracy and, therefore, those who committed electoral fraud could expect to receive sentences which were designed to deter others from such conduct.

The Registration of Political Parties Act 1998

This Act introduced for the first time a register of political parties. A political party is entitled to be entered on the Register of Political Parties if that party intends to have one or more candidates at parliamentary elections, elections to the European Parliament, Scottish Parliament, National Assembly for Wales, the Northern Ireland Assembly or local government elections. Registration is intended to clarify the identity of *bona fide* political parties and thereby make regulation more certain. Under section 14, no party political broadcast may be made by broadcasters other than on behalf of a registered political party. The responsibility for the register lies with the Electoral Commission.

 Pause and Reflect

With reference to the franchise, constituency boundaries and the legal rules relating to elections, evaluate the extent to which electoral law respects the constitutional principle of 'one person, one vote, one value'.

What demographic factors make achieving equality in the number of voters in each constituency so difficult? What are the legal rules regulating constituency boundaries? What effect does a disparity in voting numbers between constituencies have on the equality of voting power?

Political Party Funding[64]

In the United Kingdom, there is no provision for state aid for political parties for the conduct of election campaigns. Political parties do, however, receive public funds for their parliamentary work. In the House of Commons, under the system generally known as 'Short Money',[65] the money allocated is to be spent exclusively in relation to the party's parliamentary business, and not for election expenses. A similar scheme operates in the House of Lords. Introduced in 1996 by the then Leader of the House of Lords, Viscount Cranborne, 'Cranborne Money' is paid to the first two opposition parties. The Committee on Standards in Public Life has recommended that both the Commons and the Lords consider considerable increases of the amounts paid to opposition parties. In addition to financial support for parliamentary business, candidates at parliamentary elections or elections to the European Parliament are entitled to free postage for one election communication to every elector within the constituency. Candidates are also entitled to the free use of publicly funded premises for an election meeting. Indirect assistance is provided through party political broadcasts during election campaigns.

In addition, public funds in the form of Policy Development Grants (PDGs) are paid to political parties by the Electoral Commission.[66] There is a total grant of £2 million per year distributed to political parties on a formula based on performance at national and devolved legislature elections. In order to qualify for a PDG a political party must have two sitting MPs and have taken the Oath of Allegiance to the Crown. An application must be made by a

---

64 See the Electoral Commission, 2004b; Rowbottom, 2005.
65 After the Rt Hon Edward Short (later Lord Glenamara), the Leader of the House of Commons in 1975 when the system was introduced.
66 Under s. 12 of the Political Parties, Elections and Referendums Act 2000.

political party to the Electoral Commission outlining their policy development plans for the forthcoming year.

For election purposes, parties are dependent upon the support of the membership and, more importantly, from companies and trades unions. Concerns over party political funding led to an examination of the matter by the Committee on Standards in Public Life. Recognising that 'political parties are essential to democracy', the Committee identified three of the seven 'principles of public life', namely integrity, accountability and openness, as particularly relevant to the funding of political parties. Increasing election spending by the two main parties, who between them spent some £54 million on the 1997 general election, and the issue of large donations to political parties by persons known or unknown, gave rise to the public perception that election results can be affected by spending and that wealthy organisations or individuals could effectively influence public policy. Undisclosed foreign donations to the Conservative Party also caused concern.

In the Committee's view, it was 'undesirable that a political party should be dependent for its financial survival on funds provided by a few well-endowed individuals, corporations or organisations', irrespective of 'whether or not the suspicion [that he who pays the piper calls the tune] is justified'. The problem of public confidence in the political system was compounded when such donations came from undisclosed sources.[67]

The Political Parties, Elections and Referendums Act 2000

Part IV of the Political Parties, Elections and Referendums Act 2000 provides for the control of donations to registered parties and their members, defining permissible donors and providing rules regulating the acceptance or return of donations, and providing for the forfeiture of donations by impermissible or unidentifiable donors, under a court order on an application by the Electoral Commission. It is an offence to knowingly enter into, or do any act in furtherance of, any arrangement which facilitates or is likely to facilitate the making of donations by any person other than a permissible donor. The Act provides for a quarterly donations report to be made, and, in the period of general elections, for weekly reports.[68] Under section 69, the Commission is to maintain a register of donations. On the circumstances in which forfeiture should be ordered see **R (Electoral Commission) v City of Westminster Magistrates' Court** (2010). The Supreme Court ruled, by four to three, that the court had a discretionary power to order partial, rather than total, forfeiture of an impermissible donation. It was held that the object of the 2000 Act was primarily to prohibit the receipt of foreign funding by a political party and secondarily to provide a scheme which was easy to apply and police. Impermissible donors could be foreign or not (in the instant case the donor was eligible for entry on the electoral register, but was not so registered, and was therefore an impermissible donor). If the donor was not foreign, the circumstances of the donation might vary widely. Parliament intended that there should be a discretion with the intention that the court should discriminate between cases where full forfeiture was warranted and those where it was not. In some cases, total forfeiture would be disproportionate. The decision of the Court of Appeal was reversed.

Part V of the Act relates to campaign expenditure. No expenditure may be incurred by or on behalf of the registered party unless it is incurred with the authority of the treasurer or deputy treasurer of the party, or a person authorised by the treasurer or deputy treasurer. Section 74 and Schedule 8 impose limits on campaign expenditure in relation to

---

67 See further below for the 2011 Report of the Committee on Standards in Public Life.
68 Political Parties, Elections and Referendums Act 2000, ss 62, 63, respectively.

parliamentary general elections and general elections to the European Parliament, Scottish Parliament, National Assembly for Wales and the Northern Ireland Assembly.[69]

In relation to a general election, Part V of the Political Parties, Elections and Referendums Act 2000 provides that a political party may spend a specified sum per constituency it contests. The overall effect is that a party fielding candidates in every constituency is entitled to spend some £20 million. This figure is quite separate from the allowable expenditure that may be incurred by individual candidates in their constituencies.

In **R v Mackinlay** (2018) the Supreme Court considered the question of when expenditure incurred at a national level (by a political party) should be included in the returns on expenditure by the local candidate. For example, if the national party sent an election 'battlebus' into an individual constituency, that would be of benefit to the party's candidate. But did the cost of that bus have to be included in the candidate's declaration of election expenses? Under the statutory rules, the candidate had to declare expenses incurred by him or herself and/or incurred by another with the authorisation of the candidate (or agent). But did the law also require the candidate to declare 'benefits' (goods, property, services or facilities) provided by and at the cost of a third party? The answer was yes: if the services had been provided for the benefit of the candidate free of charge or at a discount, and were made use of by or on behalf of the candidate, and if the costs of the benefits – if not provided for by another – would have been incurred by the candidate, then those costs had to be declared.

The 2000 Act also regulates expenditure by bodies such as companies, trade unions and pressure groups. Section 85 of the Act allows such bodies to incur a fixed sum of money in each of Northern Ireland, Scotland and Wales for the production of election material. Any proposed expenditure over these limits requires the body to register with the Electoral Commission as a 'recognised third party'. Once registered, the body may expend prescribed amounts in England, Northern Ireland, Scotland and Wales. Following the election, details of expenditure must be submitted to the Commission.

The Political Parties and Elections Act 2009 amends the law relating to the Electoral Commission and the law relating to elections. The Act (which applies to the whole of the United Kingdom) is intended to strengthen the regulatory role of the Electoral Commission. Section 2 provides powers to enable access to information relating to donations. These include the power, under warrant, to enter premises and inspect and copy documents. Section 3 inserts a new section 147 to the 2000 Act, imposing civil sanctions for breach of the Act.

On the composition of the Commission, section 5 provides for four Commissioners to be nominated by the largest political parties. In order to ensure that the nominated Commissioners are in a minority, the Act increases the minimum number of Commissioners from five to nine and the maximum number of Commissioners from nine to ten.

Section 9 of the 2009 Act requires donors to make a formal declaration of donations over £7,500 to either national or local parties. It is a criminal offence to make a false declaration (Section 9(5)). Section 10 prohibits donations over £7,500 from non-resident donors. Donors must be resident and domiciled in the United Kingdom for income tax purposes in the tax year in which the donation was made. The same provisions relate to loans and other financial benefits/transactions.

A further inquiry into political party finance was undertaken by the Committee on Standards in Public Life in 2011. In its Thirteenth Report, *Political Party Finance: Ending the Big Donor Culture*,[70] the Committee recommended that there should be a cap on donations set at £10,000.

---

69 Part VII and Sched. 13 regulate expenditure at referendums.
70 Cm 8208, November 2011.

Recognising that this would represent a significant reduction in income for the major parties, the Committee recommended that there should be increased support for political parties from public funds. Estimated to cost £23 million per year, public funding would depend on the number of votes cast for a party in the previous election. The rate payable would be around £3 per vote in Westminster elections and £1.50 per vote in devolved and European elections. The Committee also recommended that the existing limits on campaign expenditure should be reduced by 'around 15 per cent'. As at November 2012 there was no cross-party agreement on the recommendations, and the Prime Minister was reported to have withdrawn support for the proposals, preferring a cap of £50,000.[71]

Financial support and granting of honours

The link between financial donations to political parties and the granting of honours has been a matter of concern since the early twentieth century. In 2006 – in spite of the reforms effected under the Political Parties, Elections and Referendums Act 2000 – fresh allegations of political impropriety were made. The 2000 Act did not regulate the granting of loans to political parties, and accordingly these were not declared. The allegation that the Labour government has been granting peerages to those who had made donations and loans to the Party came to light when the independent Appointments Commission, which scrutinises nominations for life peerages, blocked three nominees who allegedly made loans to the Party.

The Metropolitan Police investigated allegations that offences may have been committed under the Honours (Prevention of Abuse) Act 1925, which makes the granting of honours in exchange for financial support unlawful. In July 2007 it was announced that no charges would be brought under the Act. However, fresh concerns arose in November 2007 when it was disclosed that a wealthy donor to the Labour Party had disguised his identity by making donations under the names of other individuals.

The Electoral Administration Act 2006, section 61, amends the Political Parties, Elections and Referendums Act 2000 and now brings loans and other transactions formally within statutory regulation. Sections 71F to 71W of the 2000 Act provide that the granting of a loan, or the provision of credit, or the offer of any form of security which supports a financial transaction are 'regulated transactions'. Section 71G stipulates how regulated transactions are to be valued and with whom such transactions may be concluded.[72] The Electoral Administration Act 2006 introduces reporting requirements in relation to regulated transactions to bring them into line with the making of donations and specifies the frequency of reporting.[73] During a general election period (between the dissolution of Parliament and polling day), weekly transaction reports must be made by political parties.

State funding of political parties?[74]

Any limitation on the rights of parties to accept funds, disclosed or undisclosed, increases the arguments in favour of state funding of political parties. State funding in Europe is an accepted commonplace. Austria, Denmark, France, Germany, Greece, Italy, Portugal and Spain all have publicly funded political parties. This issue is, however, contentious in the United Kingdom on a number of grounds. First, it is argued that state funding potentially undermines the

---

71 See the *Independent*, 19 November 2012.
72 No transaction under £200 is a regulated transaction. See ss 71I–K.
73 Reporting is to the Electoral Commission.
74 See *Report of the Committee on Financial Aid to Political Parties*, Cmd 6601, 1976, London: HMSO (the Houghton Report); Hansard Society Commission, *The Financing of Political Parties*, 1981; Home Affairs Select Committee, *Funding of Political Parties*, HC 301 (1993–1994), London: HMSO.

cohesiveness of the party, and introduces the possibility of politically inspired changes to the bases of funding. Moreover, it is argued that state funding would encourage the formation and growth of extremist parties. Opposition is also voiced on the constitutional basis that to compel citizens to finance political parties through taxation, especially those with which they have no sympathy, would cause dissent. Set against these objections, however, are the benefits which would accrue from public funding. First, depending on the method used to calculate entitlement, greater equality and fairness would be achieved among the political parties. Second, party political finances would become most clearly a matter of open public record. Third, the elimination of contributions from individuals and organisations would eradicate the public's suspicions about the integrity of party political finance and thus enhance confidence in the political process. Fourth, the ability of parties to conduct their official duties would be enhanced by improving the level of contributions made.

In 2007, following an enquiry chaired by Sir Hayden Phillips, the Party Funding Review Report[75] made a number of recommendations. These included:

- a cap on donations and loans of £50,000;
- spending controls with an overall single limit on expenditure of £150 million to be spread over the life of a Parliament[76] and to include a £20 million general election 'premium';
- existing controls under the Representation of the People Acts to remain.

On the issue of public funding, the Report recommended that political parties should be entitled to receive an amount of public funding equivalent to the sum donated by an individual in any one year; thus for every £10 donated, the party would receive £10 state funding. The Report also recommended that the Electoral Commission should play a more investigative and tougher role in enforcing the law.[77]

 SELF-TEST QUESTIONS

What are the arguments in favour of state funding of political parties? What are the arguments against it? What is your view on state funding?

Voting Systems[78]

The first and foremost object of reforming zeal ought, in my opinion, to be the system of parliamentary representation, or rather misrepresentation.[79]

The Labour government came to power in 1997, committed to major electoral reform and to holding a referendum to ascertain the people's view. Substantial reform has taken place. The 1999 elections to the new Scottish Parliament employed the additional member system, as did election to the new National Assembly for Wales. The 1999 elections to the new Northern Ireland Assembly employed the single transferable vote system, one already utilised for elections

---

75 *Strengthening Democracy: Fair and Sustainable Funding of Political Parties*, March 2007.
76 On average a period of four years.
77 Inter-party talks on the Report broke down in October 2007.
78 See Finer, 1975; Bogdanor, 1981, 1983; Bogdanor and Butler, 1983; Chandler, 1982; Oliver, 1983; Butler, 'Electoral reform', in Jowell and Oliver, 2000.
79 Wade, 1989.

in Northern Ireland to the European Parliament and for local elections. The 1999 elections for the European Parliament in the rest of the United Kingdom saw the introduction of a new system of proportional representation based on party lists. Despite these reforms, no move has yet been made to reform the simple majority system employed for election to the United Kingdom Parliament. In this section, the merits and demerits of differing systems are considered.

Vernon Bogdanor categorises voting systems under three heads: plurality systems, majority systems and proportional systems. Under the heading of proportional systems, there exists a range of differing systems:

'Proportional representation' is in fact a generic term denoting a number of different systems sharing only the common aim of proportionality between seats and votes. This common aim, however, does not prevent the various proportional systems diverging considerably, one from another; and their political consequences, therefore, can be quite different. [Bogdanor and Butler, 1983, page 2]

Despite recent reforms, the United Kingdom is out of step with much of the rest of the world in terms of systems employed for electing its national Parliament. As a generalisation, it can be said that those countries influenced by English common law are the countries which retain the majority system of voting. The majority of states on the continent of Europe employ a list system; France by contrast employs a system which involves two ballots. In France, when no candidate wins an absolute majority of the vote in the first ballot, a second ballot is held to determine which of those candidates who have gained 12.5 per cent of the registered electorate in the first ballot are to be elected. In Australia, two electoral systems are employed. For election to the House of Representatives, a system of compulsory preferential voting is used. For election to the Senate, a proportional representation system is employed.

The Parliamentary Voting System and Constituencies Act 2011 provided, in part, for a referendum to be held in 2011 on whether the Alternative Voting system should be used for general elections. However, in a referendum held in May 2011 the proposal was rejected by a substantial majority.

The simple majority system

'If it is accepted that a democratic Parliament ought to represent so far as possible the preferences of the voters, this system is probably the worst that could be devised'.[80]

For elections to the United Kingdom Parliament, the system of election remains the simple majority (first past the post) system. The origins of the voting system lie in tradition, and the voting system is not a matter of law, but of past political practice. One principal merit of the system lies in its simplicity. The candidate who gains the largest number of votes in the election wins the seat – irrespective of the proportion of votes cast for himself or his opponents. To illustrate, if the votes cast for individual candidates at an election are Smith 3,200, Jones 2,700, Brown 2,500 (total votes 7,400), Smith wins the election, even though 5,200 voters, or 70 per cent, have voted for the other candidates. This lack of representativeness – when viewed from the perspective of proportionality of votes cast to seats won – is reflected in the results nationwide.

---

80 Wade, 1989, p. 9.

The 2019 general election

The result of the 2019 general election was as follows:

Party	Number of seats	Percentage of vote
Conservative	365	56.1
Labour	202	31.0
Scottish National Party	48	7.4
Lib Dem	11	1.7
Other	24	3.8
Total	**650**	**100**

The percentage of eligible voters voting (the 'turn-out') was 68.8 per cent.

In order to have a clear majority and the right to form a government, a political party needed to secure 326 parliamentary seats. As can be seen from the above table, the Conservative Party won 318 (down from 331 in 2015) seats. In order to have a majority in Parliament, the government entered into an agreement with the Northern Ireland Democratic Unionist Party (DUP), who hold ten seats.

Reform of the Voting System

The alternative vote

This system retains individual constituencies, but introduces the notion of multiple votes in order of preference. As noted above, it is a majoritarian system, not a proportional representation system. The voter marks his ballot paper with preferences expressed in numerical order. The candidate who wins 50 per cent of the first preference vote is declared elected. Should no candidate achieve 50 per cent, the votes of the candidate who achieves the lowest number of first preference votes are redistributed in accordance with that candidate's supporters' second preferences. The process is continued until one candidate achieves an overall majority of votes compared with all other candidates. Where the system fails is from the point of view of proportional representation, since the overall result will bear little or no resemblance to proportionality. It would also potentially have the effect of returning to Parliament candidates who have achieved no clear support (or mandate) from the people. The system does, however, ensure that, within each constituency, the candidate with most support overall is returned to Parliament. The advantages of the alternative vote are, first, that the traditional 'one member, one constituency' principle is retained and, second, that the elected candidate has a majority of votes, as compared with other candidates.

It is the Alternative Vote which was proposed for general elections under the Parliamentary Voting System and Constituencies Act 2011. However, as noted above, in a referendum held in May 2011 the proposal was rejected by a substantial majority.

The supplementary vote

This system is very similar to the alternative vote system, and is the system recommended by the working party on electoral systems set up by the Labour Party, under the chairmanship of Lord Plant, which reported in 1993.[81] The system allows voters to express a preference through voting for two candidates. If no candidate secures 50 per cent of the vote, the second preferences cast for all candidates other than the top two are redistributed between the two leading candidates until a clear winner emerges. Where there are only three candidates, this system would work smoothly. However, the system becomes more complex in constituencies where a greater number of candidates are standing for election, for the electorate would not be clear as to who the leading two candidates will be, and may therefore vote tactically in order to ensure, as far as possible, that a candidate whom they did not want elected would not be in either of the two top positions.

The additional member system (AMS)

This is the system adopted for elections to the Scottish Parliament and Welsh Assembly. The AMS seeks to combine the advantages of the single member constituency, with overall proportionality between votes and seats. The system is used in Germany. Under AMS, three-quarters of the United Kingdom's Members of Parliament would be elected in single member constituencies, using the first past the post system. The remaining quarter would be 'additional members', elected from party lists on a regional party basis, employing a formula based on the largest average of votes cast between the parties. The additional Members thus top up the total for each party in order to give overall proportionality.

Under AMS, each voter would thus have two votes: one for the candidate of his choice in the constituency, one for the party of his choice on a regional basis. It has the advantage of remaining close to the system which is currently in place, while departing from it sufficiently to ensure proportionality. The system would necessitate a reduction of the number of constituency Members of Parliament in order to accommodate the regionally elected Members. If the division between constituency and regional Members is to be equal, this would necessitate doubling the size of current constituencies. However, the AMS also confers wide powers on political parties who would control who is to be included on the regional list, and in what order of priority. For this reason, the Hansard Society Commission on Electoral Reform, chaired by Lord Blake, concluded that the German model of AMS was not suitable for Britain.[82]

A variant of this system is employed in local elections in Germany which avoids the problem of party control. Under this version of AMS, all candidates stand directly as constituency candidates, but only three-quarters, or some other proportion, are elected in single member constituencies. The remaining one-quarter of seats are allocated to those who were runners up in the election contest, who would sit as additional members.

Single transferable vote (STV)

Employed in the Republic of Ireland and in Northern Ireland for the European Parliament elections and elections to the Northern Ireland Assembly, the STV offers both proportionality between votes and seats and a constituency-based, but multi-member, system of election. The STV was recommended for introduction in urban constituencies as long ago as 1917. It would involve a rearrangement of the current single member constituencies into far larger regional

---

81 *Report of the Working Party on Electoral Systems*, 1993, London: Labour Party.
82 Hansard Society, *Report of the Commission on Electoral Reform*, 1976, London: Hansard Society, para. 93.

units, each returning several Members of Parliament. The method of calculation varies, but is based on a quota of the votes cast that is achieved either by first preference voting producing the required quota or the redistribution of votes cast for losing candidates. The STV offers both proportionality and the greatest range of choice to electors. The system used for local elections and elections to the European Parliament in Northern Ireland[83] requires that the total number of votes be divided by one more than the number of vacant seats, plus one. The current constituencies would require alteration in order to increase their size to accommodate three Members (or four or five, as favoured by the Liberal Democrats),[84] which would require a fresh look at the criteria for constituency boundaries. The current requirement to respect local authority boundaries is the most obvious criterion which would be compromised if such a system were to be adopted.

This is the most complex of alternative systems and, for that reason alone, is not favoured by many, although, despite the complexity, the system works well in Northern Ireland. The voter expresses his or her preferences for candidates in numerical order. A quota is predetermined. Thus, in a five-member constituency, the quota would be approximate to one-sixth of the votes cast. Successful candidates are those reaching the quota, and those who, on a redistribution of second, third and more remote preferences, reach the quota. If fewer than the required number of candidates reach the quota figure, then redistribution of second preferences will take place until the required number of elected Members is reached. If, on the other hand, the required number of elected Members is not achieved by the redistribution of second preferences, then a third stage comes into play. The candidate who polls the lowest number of votes is eliminated, and the votes for that candidate are distributed among the other remaining candidates in order of preferences expressed. This process of elimination continues until the quota is reached for all five required elected Members.

The party list system[85]

This system requires that a list of candidates be nominated by each political party. The votes for each party's list are calculated on a nationwide basis — rather than a constituency basis — and the parties obtain the number of seats in the legislature in direct proportion to the votes in the country. The party list system is not a serious contender for adoption in the United Kingdom. Two principal defects are perceived with the system: first, it destroys election on the basis of constituencies; and second, too much patronage is placed in the hands of party leaders. Within the two principal political parties in the United Kingdom — Conservative and Labour — there exists a broad spectrum of political opinion: from the political left to the political right in each party. To leave the power of nomination and the positioning of candidates on the 'list' to political leaders would potentially exclude some of the best candidates — most likely, those whose views are incompatible with, or troublesome to, the leadership.

The Case For and Against Reforming the Simple Majority System

Most of the arguments for reform of the electoral system centre on the alleged defects of the present system. Reformers argue that the status quo results in a government that does not

---

83 European Assembly Elections Act 1978, Sched. 1, para. 2(2)(b).
84 Liberal/SDP Alliance, 1982.
85 Employed in Belgium, Denmark, Greece, Netherlands, Portugal and Spain.

represent the majority of the voters' wishes. Since the Second World War, no government has been elected with a majority of votes overall.

The case for reform therefore centres on the principle of democracy and equality in voting power. For democracy to have real meaning, it is argued that the government of the day, and the composition of the legislature as a whole, must reflect the wishes of the electors. Under such a system, it can be argued that the government would have enhanced authority to pursue its electoral mandate. In answer to the charge that proportional representation can result in weak government, reformers argue that less extreme, rather than weak, government would be the result. Such an outcome would force a 'rethink' in radical politics, with governments being keenly aware that with a slim majority in Parliament, and possibly the balance of power being held by a third party (both outcomes being common to proportional representation systems), certain radical policies would have to be modified. Thus many of the more politically contentious subjects, such as education and health, might be largely removed from party political conflict; consensus would become the only way in which to make legislative progress.

Reformers also point to the inequity of the distribution of the vote between the parties under the current system. The simple majority system invariably favours a two-party system, and leaves little room for the adequate representation of smaller parties. The Liberal Democrat Party regularly achieves approximately 20 per cent of the popular vote at general elections (and has a high success rate at by-elections), but that overall popularity does not translate into a proportionally related number of parliamentary seats. One explanation for this result is that votes for the Liberal Democrats are spread fairly evenly over the United Kingdom, and not concentrated in one geographic area (although the southwest of England is becoming a Liberal Democrat stronghold).

The case for the status quo is linked to the point made above. The simple majority system generally, although not invariably, produces a government with a strong parliamentary majority which is able to implement its electoral programme without undue hindrance. This argument requires careful evaluation. One of the often experienced effects of proportional representation systems is that governments are returned with either a very small majority of seats or a minority of seats overall in the legislature. As a result, minority parties with few seats and relatively small electoral support may hold a disproportionate amount of power, making governments dependent upon their wishes in order to implement their legislative programme. As a consequence of this dependence, governments are also subject to the risk of defeats on motions of no confidence, thus producing general political insecurity and the potential for frequent elections.

A further, related effect is that a government may be required to compromise substantially upon its electoral promises in order to govern. Under the current system, it is generally the case that the elected government – always depending upon its majority in Parliament – is relatively free to implement its electoral programme. In other words, the voter knows what See Chapter 10. he or she is getting in terms of policies and proposals for legislation. Under proportional representation, where less strong government is the frequent result, voters can be far less certain either that the policies for which they are voting will be implemented or of the policies which will be pursued after the election.

There also exist doubts as to the effects of a reformed system on the convention of collective ministerial responsibility. Under current constitutional arrangements, the convention of collective responsibility requires that the Cabinet 'speaks with one voice' in order to maintain parliamentary, and electoral, confidence. The rule accordingly requires that, where a decision has been made by the Cabinet, each member of Cabinet and non-Cabinet Ministers and all their Parliamentary Private Secretaries adhere to the decision and do not speak out against it. Such a show of unity would prove difficult to sustain in coalition or minority governments.

The sister doctrine of individual ministerial responsibility might also prove more difficult to adhere to, particularly where a Minister felt unable to support and pursue a policy with which he or she disagreed on political principle. One consequence, therefore, that could flow from the introduction of some form of proportional representation is that governments become less cohesive and, as a result, less commanding of the confidence of the people.

A further argument is put for the status quo: that of the close links currently established between the constituency Member and his or her electorate. Irrespective of the proportion of votes won in an election, the Member of Parliament, once duly elected, and irrespective of political party, represents each and every one of his or her constituents in Parliament. Constituencies are relatively small and Members of Parliament are accessible – through surgeries and other contact – to the voters. A Member is thus able to gain a detailed knowledge of his or her constituency, its geography, industry and economy, environment and populace. With large constituencies, such a detailed working knowledge of an area becomes more difficult, with the attendant possibility that a Member is less effective in his representation of that constituency in Parliament.

As can be seen, the issue of electoral reform is by no means clear-cut, and real potential constitutional problems could be encountered as a result of its introduction. At the end of the day, the quest for an alternative system is rooted in the paramountcy of the principle of real democracy and equality of representation of the people in Parliament. Against that ideal must be set the constitutional implications of introducing reform.

As noted above, one of the manifesto pledges of the Labour Party before the 1997 election was a review of the electoral system for the Westminster Parliament and, once in office, the government appointed Liberal peer Lord Jenkins to review the system. The Jenkins Commission reported in October 1998, and recommended a novel, if complex, solution. The Commission, wanting to retain single-member constituencies but also inject a greater degree of proportionality into the system, opted for a 'mixed system' made up of the alternative vote and regional list systems. Constituency members would be elected on the alternative vote system, and comprise 80 to 85 per cent of members, with additional members, 15 to 20 per cent elected on the regional list basis. Greater proportionality would be achieved, while the traditional strong link between a member and his or her constituency would be retained. The system would also, the Commission claimed, avoid coalition governments and in its estimation would have produced a single-party majority government in three out of the four last general elections.[86]

The current position is that the United Kingdom now employs a number of systems: a system of proportional representation was used in May 1999 for elections to the European Parliament; for elections to the Scottish Parliament and National Assembly for Wales the additional member system has been used; and for elections to the Northern Ireland Assembly the single transferable vote system was used. In relation to elections to the United Kingdom Parliament, however, despite recommendations for reform, the voting system remains the simple majority system. Irrespective of constitutional arguments in favour of reform, the referendum result in May 2011 rejecting the alternative vote system for general elections makes reform in the foreseeable future very unlikely.

---

86 Cm 4090-I, para. 161. This claim has been disputed by M Pinto-Duschinsk, who calculates that coalition would have been the outcome in nine of the last 14 elections: *The Times*, 29 October 1998.

Reforming the Simple Majority System

Simple Majority System

Advantages	Disadvantages
Quick result, local and national	No (direct) proportionality between votes cast and seats won in Commons
Simple to understand and use	Many votes (even an overall majority in a constituency) 'wasted', only the winner relative to the second placed candidate being elected
Close link between MP and constituency	Two-party dominance, little representation of smaller parties (e.g. in the UK the 'third party', the Liberal Democrats)
Voting preference not watered down by transfer to different candidate	National result may effectively be determined by just a few 'marginal seats'
Usually clear result (a majority of seats in Commons to one political party), hence strong, stable government	Implements a mandate but not necessarily of the majority
Clear mandate, carried out without watering down by compromise derived from coalition	

Proportional Representation Systems

Advantages	Disadvantages
More votes count so greater, wider representation of views, especially where more than one candidate (with different politics) elected	Possibly less stable government
Better representation of minority interests and smaller parties	Small parties (in terms of voter support), perhaps of 'marginal' or 'extreme' stance, may hold disproportionate or even the balance of power
Coalition produces wider representation in government; encourages consensus and compromise	Majority mandate not implemented
Encourages voter participation by more votes counting	
Enables voter to express more than one (ranked) preference	Voter does not decide or know to whom his vote ultimately goes

 Pause and Reflect

In light of the alternative voting systems, evaluate the strengths and weaknesses of the simple majority voting system.

Summary

Electoral law comprises several aspects: the right to vote, the organisation of constituencies, the regulation of election campaigns, the voting system and the regulation of political parties.

The electoral system aims to ensure equality in terms of the size of constituencies, individual voting power and as between candidates for election. The regulation of constituency sizes, however, fails to produce formal equality because other statutory considerations come into play.

It has been seen above that there is a near-complete franchise (right to vote) and that the law regulating election campaigns at local level is strict. Until recently, however, there has been regulation of political parties – their funding and expenditure – at national level. The Political Parties, Elections and Referendums Act 2000 remedies this defect, establishing the Electoral Commission and requiring political parties to be formally registered and permissible donations to be recorded. The Act also sets a ceiling on election expenditure by political parties. The Political Parties and Elections Act 2009 amends the law and strengthens the powers of the Electoral Commission.

In relation to voting systems, it has been seen that there are several systems employed in the United Kingdom for different elections. For general elections, however, the system remains the easy to understand and administer but much-criticised simple majority system.

Further Reading

Blackburn, R, 'The 2010 General Election outcome and formation of the Conservative–Liberal Democrat coalition government' [2011] *Public Law* 30.

Easton, S, 'Electing the electorate: the problem of prisoner disenfranchisement' (2006) 69(3) *Modern Law Review* 443.

Electoral Commission, *The Funding of Political Parties: Report and Recommendations* (2004).

Ewing, K, *The Cost of Democracy: Party Funding in Modern British Politics*, 2007, Oxford: Hart Publishing.

Lardy, H, 'Prisoner disenfranchisement: constitutional rights and wrongs' [2002] *Public Law* 524.

Party Funding Review Report, *Strengthening Democracy: Fair and Sustainable Funding of Political Parties*, March 2007.

Report of the Independent Commission on the Voting System (Jenkins Report), *Cm*4090, 1998, London: HMSO.

Rowbottom, J, 'The Electoral Commission's proposals on the funding of political parties' [2005] *Public Law* 168.

Webb, P, 'Parties and party systems: modernisation, regulation and diversity' (2001) 54 *Parliamentary Affairs* 308.

Chapter 13

Introduction to the House of Commons

Chapter Contents

Learning Objectives

By the end of this chapter you should be able to:

- ☐ explain the constitutional functions of Parliament;
- ☐ define parliamentary terms such as summoning, dissolution and prorogation;
- ☐ explain the role of the Speaker of the House of Commons;
- ☐ explain the role of the political party Whips;
- ☐ discuss the constitutional importance of the Opposition.

Introduction

Parliament is composed of the Crown, the House of Lords and the House of Commons. Its origins lie in the King's Council – the assembly of advisers summoned by the King – and the term 'parliament' can be traced to the thirteenth century.[1]

In order to evaluate Parliament, it is necessary to examine its composition and procedure. The former task may be accomplished by either looking at the actual membership of Parliament by party allegiance at a fixed point in time or by looking at it in a more sociological manner in order to analyse the class and educational background of Members and their employment status. The undertaking is complicated by the bicameral nature of Parliament and the fact that the House of Commons is elected and the House of Lords unelected. The importance of procedure, particularly in the House of Commons, cannot be overemphasised. Only by acquiring an understanding of the procedural rules can sense be made of the functions of Parliament and its importance, or, otherwise, in the process of government. In the absence of a written constitution which clearly defines and allocates powers and functions, the manner in which the legislative proposals of government are examined, and the administration of the state scrutinised, assumes central importance to the notion of democratic control of the executive. The doctrine of constitutionalism can only be effective if the procedures adopted by Parliament are effective in controlling the government.

The Functions of Parliament

In *Representative Government* (1861), John Stuart Mill wrote of Parliament:

> Instead of the function of governing, for which it is radically unfit, the proper office of a representative assembly is to watch and control the government; to throw the light of publicity on its acts; to compel a full exposition and justification of all of them which anyone considers questionable; to censure them if found condemnable; and if the men who compose the government abuse their trust, or fulfil it in a manner which conflicts with the deliberate sense of the nation, to expel them from office, and either expressly or virtually appoint their successors.

> The House of Commons is the sounding board of the nation – an arena in which not only the general opinion of the nation, but that of every section of it can produce itself in full light and challenge discussion.

Very little has changed. Parliament is not there to govern; that is for the executive. Parliament exists to represent the views and opinions of the people and to influence, constrain and demand justification for the actions of government and to give them legitimacy.

Accordingly, the functions of Parliament may be summarised as being:[2]

(a) to provide the personnel of government;
(b) to legitimise government actions; and
(c) to subject matters of public policy to scrutiny and influence.

---

1 The role of the sovereign is discussed in Chapter 5. The House of Lords is discussed in Chapter 16.
2 Norton, 1985a and see 1993.

As discussed in Chapters 6 and 11, the devolution of legislative power to the Northern Ireland Assembly and Scottish Parliament and, to a lesser extent, the Welsh Assembly affects the scope of the United Kingdom Parliament's role and functions. In terms of debating and scrutinising government policy and administration and the passage of legislation, while the United Kingdom Parliament (Westminster) remains the sovereign legislature in the United Kingdom, there is now a diffusion of power – differing in nature and scope – between Westminster and the devolved institutions.

The Life of a Parliament

A Parliament is summoned by the sovereign to meet following a general election, and the life of the Parliament will run until the subsequent general election. Prior to 2010, the choice of date for a general election was at the Prime Minister's discretion (subject to the consent of the Crown). The incoming Coalition government of 2010 announced that the new Parliament would run until May 2015. The Fixed-term Parliaments Act 2011 gives five-year fixed-term Parliaments statutory effect. Note, however, that the current government intends to repeal the 2011 Act and revive the prerogative of dissolution.[3] In February 2021 the Draft Fixed-term Parliaments Act 2011 (Repeal) Bill was presented to Parliament for pre-legislative scrutiny.[4]

See Chapters 5 and 9.

The parliamentary session

A parliamentary session is the parliamentary year. At the end of the session, Parliament stands 'prorogued' until the new session begins. The significance of prorogation lies in the fact that all business is suspended until the new session. The number of sitting days per session varies from year to year. The average session length is 168 days.

Parliamentary sittings

The term 'parliamentary sitting' relates to the daily business of the House. The Commons meets daily from Monday to Friday but is adjourned for three weeks at Christmas, for one week at Easter, for the whole of August and for most of September. In emergency situations, the House may be recalled for urgent debate during a recess or at a weekend, as occurred in 1982 for debate on the invasion of the Falkland Islands.[5]

Westminster Hall

In addition to proceedings in the chamber of the Commons, since 1999 Westminster Hall has been used for backbench debates and debates on Select Committee reports (see Chapter 15). Any Member of Parliament may attend. In addition, Westminster Hall sittings are used for the questioning of junior Ministers generally on matters which affect more than one government Department.

---

3 On which see Chapter 5.
4 See Draft Fixed-term Parliament Acts (Repeal) Bill, CP 322.
5 3 April 1982.

Summoning, Adjournment, Prorogation[6] and Dissolution

Summoning

The Fixed-term Parliaments Act 2011, section 3, provides that once Parliament has been dissolved under section 1, the Queen may issue a proclamation summoning the new Parliament.

Adjournment

During a parliamentary session, Parliament will be adjourned on many occasions. The adjournment is no more than an 'interruption in the course of one and the same session'.[7] Up to a quarter of the time in the House of Commons is spent debating the question: 'that this House do now adjourn'.[8] The effect of adjournment is to suspend the sitting of the House for a period but leave unaffected the business of the House. Adjournments take place for a number of reasons and to effect a number of consequences.

A motion for adjournment can be used in debate to interrupt proceedings. The motion will take the form 'that the debate be now adjourned'. The device may be used as an alternative to moving an amendment to the question before the House, and will be used to determine consideration of the matter in question. The Speaker has a discretion whether to decline to put the matter to the House. The business which has been interrupted can be brought before the House at the next sitting day, provided that notice is given.

Daily adjournment debates

There is a daily motion for adjournment which suspends the day's sitting. Once the motion for adjournment has been moved, the daily adjournment debate takes place.[9] The adjournment debate enables one Member to speak on a topic, previously notified, for 15 minutes, and receive a ministerial reply. Topics may include any matter other than a request for legislation. There is a weekly ballot at which successful Members are chosen for the adjournment debate, other than for the debate on Thursdays, when the choice of Member is made by the Speaker.

Adjournment debates before holidays

Adjournment debates also take place before the House adjourns for holidays.[10] No ballot is held for participation: five backbenchers speak for half an hour each and the Leader of the House replies to the debate.

Adjournment debates following consideration of Consolidated Fund Bills

In any session, there will be three Consolidated Fund Bills before Parliament. Second reading consideration is purely formal, with no debate. When proceedings are finished, any Member of the government may move a motion 'that this House do now adjourn'.

Adjournments for emergency debates

Provision is made under Standing Orders for urgent matters to be brought to the attention of the House for early debate. A Member may, at the start of business of the day, propose that the House be adjourned for consideration of an urgent matter. It is within the discretion of the Speaker as to whether the matter should be discussed. If satisfied, it is then for the House to

---

6 From the Latin *prorogare*, literally to ask publicly, from *pro* in public, and *rogare* to ask.
7 Erskine May, 1997.
8 Silk and Walters, 1987, p. 210.
9 See further Chapter 15.
10 Four times a year.

give leave for the debate. If refused, the support of not more than 40 Members of the House is required in order for leave to be granted.[11] The debate will take place at the start of business the following day.

Prorogation

Prorogation is a prerogative power exercised by the Crown on the advice of the Privy Council. It is a formal process which precedes the dissolution of Parliament prior to a General Election. Prorogation has not been effected in person by the Crown since 1854. The effect of prorogation is that all business before Parliament is suspended. Parliament will be prorogued until a specified date. The power to prorogue Parliament is unaffected by the Fixed-term Parliaments Act 2011 (see section 6).

Prorogation has in the past been an uncontroversial formality. However, in 2019, it assumed considerable importance when the advice given to the Crown was subjected to a legal challenge in **R (Miller) v The Prime Minister** (2019)[12] The case is discussed in detail in Chapter 5. It should be noted here, however, that the advice given to the Crown in that case was held to be justiciable (i.e. within the competence of the courts to decide) and unlawful on the basis that it deprived Parliament, without justification, of its constitutional function of supervising the executive.

Dissolution

Parliament is dissolved prior to a general election, bringing the current Parliament to an end. Members of the House of Commons cease to be Members of Parliament. The Government remains in office but, because there is no Parliament to scrutinise its actions, there are conventions which restrict what it can accomplish during dissolution.

The Fixed-term Parliaments Act 2011 provides for five-year fixed-term Parliaments, with limited power to amend the date,[13] and provision made for an earlier general election where a vote of no confidence in the government is passed. Parliament will be dissolved 25 days before election day.

There have been criticisms of the five-year term and calls for the 2011 Act to be repealed. The dissatisfaction comes from the perception that the government does little business in the final year and that the political process works better when there is a degree of uncertainty about the date of the next general election. As noted above, in February 2021 the Draft Fixed-term Parliaments Act 2011 (Repeal) Bill was presented for pre-legislative scrutiny in the House of Commons.

See further
Chapter 6.

The Organisation of Business

The organisation of business in a typical parliamentary session is as follows. The session opens with the State Opening of Parliament and the Queen's Speech. The Queen's Speech outlines the government's proposals for legislation in the session. The following four to five days are spent in Debate on the Address, including two days on which the Opposition proposes – 'moves' – amendments to specific areas of policy. Following the summer recess (usually from mid-July to early September), and until Christmas, most of the time of the House will be spent on second reading debates of Government Bills. Between Christmas and Easter, the

---

11 If fewer than 40 Members but not fewer than ten Members support the motion, the House will determine the matter by a vote.
12 [2019] UKSC 41.
13 See, for example, the Early Parliamentary General Election Act 2019.

majority of the time of the House will be spent in second reading debates and the committee stage of Bills. Before the end of July, the remaining legislative stages of Bills take place, unless these are to be carried over to the next parliamentary year.[14]

Personnel of the House of Commons

The office of Speaker

The office of Speaker is traceable to 1377 and the appointment of Sir Thomas Hungerford, although from 1258 Parliaments had similar officers.[15] The Speaker of the House featured in the constitutional struggles between King and Parliament in the seventeenth century. When Charles I arrived in the Commons to arrest the Five Knights, the Speaker declared:

> May it please Your Majesty, I have neither eyes to see, nor tongue to speak in this place, but as the House is pleased to direct me, whose servant I am here, and I humbly beg Your Majesty's pardon that I cannot give any other answer than this to what Your Majesty is pleased to demand of me.

Henceforth, the independence of the Speaker from the Crown was established.

The Speaker regulates the proceedings of the House. The Speaker is a senior Member appointed by common agreement of all Members and is generally a Member of the Opposition Party. The election of the Speaker and Deputy Speakers is the first task undertaken by Parliament following a general election. The Speaker acts with political impartiality and controls the business of the House.[16]

The Speaker is the presiding officer of the House and ensures that the rules of conduct and order are observed. The Speaker is also the representative of the Commons in relations with the Crown – it is through the Speaker that the privilege of access to the Sovereign is effected – and the House of Lords and other bodies outside Parliament. When the House of Lords amends Commons' Bills, the Speaker checks the amendments to ensure that they do not infringe the financial privileges of the lower House. It is also the function of the Speaker to certify Bills under the Parliament Act 1911.

The Speaker has a discretion in relation to the granting of an application for an emergency debate, whether to allow urgent questions or grant requests for emergency debates and whether a *prima facie* case of a breach of the privileges of the House has been established. It is also for the Speaker to rule on matters of procedure. Furthermore, the Speaker will decide whether a proposed amendment to a motion will be accepted. The Speaker therefore has considerable power. This was felt acutely in 2019 during the debates on Brexit (the UK's leaving the EU). The Speaker first allowed MPs to amend a government motion for debate which shifted the control of parliamentary proceedings away from the government and towards Members of the House. This enabled MPs, against the wishes of the government, to put forward a variety of alternative proposals on leaving the EU for 'indicative' non-binding votes by MPs. Second, the Speaker subsequently proceeded to refuse to allow the government to bring forward its Withdrawal Agreement for a third vote (it having failed to pass on two previous votes), relying on a little-known precedent dating from 1604 which states that a proposal cannot be brought back to the House unless it is substantially different from a previous proposal.

---

14 On this see Chapter 14.
15 Known as 'parlour' or 'prolocutor'.
16 On the forced resignation of the Speaker in 2009, see Chapter 17.

Disciplinary powers of the Speaker

The control of debate lies with the Speaker, who chooses who is allowed to speak. Advance notice of the wish to participate in debate is given and the Speaker calls each side (Government and Opposition) alternately, and respects the rights of minority parties to participate. The Speaker has powers under Standing Orders to control the following:

See further Chapter 17.

(a) irrelevance or tedious repetition;
(b) minor breaches of order;
(c) the use of disorderly or unparliamentary expressions;
(d) grossly disorderly conduct;
(e) grave disorder;
(f) obstruction of the business of the House by other means.

Disorderly conduct – such as damaging the Mace[17] – may result in the Member, if a suitable apology is not given to the House, being suspended from the House for a period determined by the House on a motion. Suspension from the House in the first instance will be for five sitting days, on a second occasion for 20 days and, in the event of a further repetition, for the remainder of the session. Any Member refusing to withdraw from the chamber of the House may be forcibly removed by the Serjeant at Arms.[18] In such an event, the Member will be suspended for the remainder of the parliamentary session. In 2003 the House agreed the proposal that a Member could have his or her salary withheld for a defined period, without suspension.

If a Member persists in a speech after being ordered to discontinue on the basis of irrelevance or tedious repetition, the Speaker may direct him or her to withdraw from the House for the remainder of the sitting, or 'name' him or her for disregarding the authority of the Speaker's Chair. The same penalty may befall a Member who uses unparliamentary language. Unparliamentary language includes:

(a) the imputation of false or unavowed motives;
(b) the misrepresentation of the language of another and the accusation of misrepresentation;
(c) charges of uttering a deliberate falsehood;
(d) abusive and insulting language likely to create disorder.

The Leader of the House

The Leader of the House is responsible to the Prime Minister for the organisation of business in the Commons. It is the function of the Leader of the House to announce the parliamentary business for the following week. The Leader of the House is a Minister of the Crown.[19] When the Prime Minister is unavailable, it is the Leader of the House who represents the House of Commons.

The party Whips

The party political control of Members of Parliament is in the hands of the party Whips. Where an MP disagrees with his party line on a particular matter, the Whip may be withdrawn. This

---

17 The ceremonial staff of office of the Commons.
18 An officer of the House responsible for order.
19 House of Commons (Administration) Act 1978, s. 1.

has the effect of not only denying the MP vital information but also leaving him or her outside the party unless and until he or she is prepared to follow the party line.

On the government side, all Whips receive salaries[20] and are Ministers of the Crown. The Chief Whip[21] is assisted by up to 12 other Members. The Chief Whip organises the details of business of the House. The Opposition has a Chief Whip, two salaried assistants and between eight and ten non-salaried assistants. The task of the government Chief Whip is to act as contact between the Prime Minister, the Leader of the House (to both of whom he is responsible) and Members. The Whips (of all parties) keep Members informed about the House's business, and inform Members when they are obliged to attend the House. The degree of coercion of Members will depend on the importance of the matter in hand. When attendance is required – and when political consequences will flow from non-attendance – a 'three-line Whip' is announced. Where attendance is necessary, but not essential, a 'two-line Whip' is applied. In order that Members are not unduly pressured by the need for attendance in Parliament, 'pairing' is permitted. Pairing is the arrangement whereby Members of government and opposition parties will be linked together: if one is absent, the other may abstain from voting. Thus, the non-attendance of one Member will be offset – in the counting of votes – by the absence of the other. Pairing arrangements must be registered with the Party Whips. Pairing is not permitted in relation to divisions on the most important matters. It is this arrangement which is most frequently threatened when relationships between the government and Opposition break down.

Much of the organisation of the business of the House is in the hands of the Whips, including planning the parliamentary timetable and advising on practice and procedure. Whips of all parties are also responsible for recommending candidates for membership of parliamentary committees.

Members of Parliament

Front- and backbenchers

Business in the House is conducted on adversarial lines. The adversarial nature of the Commons is reflected in the layout of the House. The House is divided into two sections which face each other, separated by the Table of the House, behind which the Speaker sits. Each side has a front bench and several rows of back benches. On the side to the right of the Speaker sit Members of the government party, Ministers of the government occupying the front bench. Opposite, on the front bench, will sit the shadow Ministers of the Opposition party. All other Members of both the government and Opposition will sit on the back benches, hence the term 'backbenchers'.

The representation of women in the Commons

The Parliament (Qualification of Women) Act 1918 made women eligible to stand for election to Parliament. Of 1,613 candidates at the 1918 election, only 17 were women. The first female candidate to take her seat in the House of Commons was Lady Astor, elected in 1919 in a by-election. The representation of women has always been poor in the Commons. In 1918, there was just one woman Member; in 1945, 24 women were elected to Parliament. The figures remained between 17 and 29 until 1987, when 41 women were elected. All the major political parties are committed to increasing the representation of women in the Commons. The

---

20 Ministerial and Other Salaries Act 1975, s. 1(1)(a) and Sched. 1.
21 Who holds office as Parliamentary or Patronage Secretary to the Treasury.

2015 general election resulted in a significantly improved proportion of women Members of Parliament. Following the 2017 general election there were 208 (32 per cent).

The first woman to hold ministerial office was Margaret Bondfield. She became the first female Member of Cabinet in 1929. Only one woman has held the office of Speaker: Betty Boothroyd from 1992 to 2000. The first female Prime Minister was the Rt Hon Margaret Thatcher MP (as she then was), who held office from 1979 to 1990, the longest premiership in the twentieth century.

Salaries and allowances of Members of Parliament

As far back as the thirteenth century, representatives attending Parliament were paid – either in cash or in kind – and, in addition, could claim travelling expenses. Payment by electors had ceased by the end of the seventeenth century. In the eighteenth and nineteenth centuries, though unpaid, a seat in the House of Commons was valuable, and could attract large sums of money for its purchase. Members of Parliament remained formally unpaid until 1911, despite numerous previous attempts to introduce payment. Salaries are now the responsibility of the Independent Parliamentary Standards Authority (IPSA).[22] As of April 2018, the annual basic salary of an MP was £77,379. MPs' pay is linked to changes in average earnings in the public sector.

Members also receive allowances for secretarial and research assistance, car mileage and limited travel between the constituency and Parliament.

Members' Code of Conduct

Members of Parliament are governed by a Code of Conduct setting out general principles to guide members on the standards of conduct that the House and the public have a right to expect.

Complaints about MPs conduct

In 2017 the #MeToo scandal prompted a number of allegations concerning bullying and sexual harassment of staff in Parliament and led to a revised complaints system. In 2018 the Independent Complaints and Grievance System (ICGS) was established to receive complaints. In the first quarter of 2020, the ICGS received 201 calls and emails leading to 26 investigations into the conduct of MPs. Investigations are carried out by the Parliamentary Commissioner for Standards (on whom see Chapter 17).

If an MP has been arrested, it used to be the case that the Speaker of the House notified the House and the MP would have the party Whip suspended and be suspended from the House. As a result of some severe breaches of privacy, that system has now changed and the identity of the MP will remain private. Furthermore, the MP will not have the Whip with-drawn and will not be suspended until enquiries are completed.

See further Chapter 17.

The size of the House of Commons

For the 2010 general election there were 650 seats in the House of Commons. If the number of parliamentary representatives is compared with the total population of the country, it can be seen that there is a wide discrepancy in the representativeness of differing legislatures. In Ireland, for example, there are 166 Members of Parliament, each representing 24,000

---

22 See the Constitutional Reform and Governance Act 2010 amending the Parliamentary Standards Act 2009.

citizens. By contrast, in Australia, there are 147 Members, each representing 122,000 citizens. In the United Kingdom each Member of Parliament represents approximately 100,000 citizens.

 Pause and Reflect

The nineteenth-century parliamentarian and philosopher John Stuart Mill described the House of Commons as the 'sounding board of the nation'. What do you understand by this phrase, and what factors support this description and which factors detract from it?

Resignation and Recall of Members of Parliament

A Member, once duly elected, cannot relinquish his seat.[23] However, provision is made whereby a Member may retire under differing procedures,[24] each of which involves accepting office under the Crown, which obliges the Member to relinquish his seat on the basis of disqualification from membership[25] and a writ to be issued for a by-election. Application for the office is normally granted,[26] although power remains for the application to be refused. The offices are nowadays purely nominal and retained as a device to make up for the lack of a resignation procedure.

The Recall of the MPs Act 2015 provides for a process whereby voters in a constituency may 'recall' their MP and trigger a by-election. If an MP is convicted of an offence and receives a custodial sentence, or has been convicted of an offence relating to financial allowances, or has been suspended from the House of Commons for a period of ten days, the Speaker will notify the constituency. A recall petition will then be opened for signature. A petition will be successful if signed by ten per cent of eligible voters.

The political parties

The major political parties have a similar organisational structure in Parliament. The Conservative, Labour and Liberal Democrat Parties have a system of election for the party leader, and are organised into front- and backbench Members. The normal arrangement is that the Commons comprises the government, being the political party having a majority of seats and capable of securing the confidence of the House of Commons, elected on the basis of the simple majority vote; Her Majesty's Loyal Opposition, being the second largest party in the House; and minority parties – Liberal Democrat, Ulster Unionist, Scottish Nationalist, Plaid Cymru.

Government and Opposition

It is the government which controls the majority of Parliament's time. On 75 per cent of sitting days, government business takes priority and it is the government which determines the business to be undertaken (subject to established practices as to Opposition Days, days

---

23 *Commons' Journal* (1547–1628), p. 724.
24 Most usually accepting the office of steward or bailiff of Her Majesty's Three Chiltern Hundreds of Stoke, Desborough and Burnham or steward of the Manor of Northstead.
25 Under the House of Commons Disqualification Act 1975, s. 4.
26 By the Chancellor of the Exchequer.

set aside for Private Members' Bills, etc.). From scrutinising the work of Parliament, it may be tempting to underplay the importance of Parliament as a whole, and the Opposition in particular, in comparison with the power of the government. Such a view is implicit in the pejorative labelling of government as an 'elective dictatorship'.[27] Such charges need to be viewed with some caution. In 1947, Sir Ivor Jennings described the role of the Opposition as 'at once the alternative to the government and a focus for the discontent of the people. Its function is almost as important as that of the government'.[28]

In its constitutional role, the Opposition must constantly be questioning, probing and calling government to account. Viewed in this light, notwithstanding the government's control over the timetable and business of the House, it can be said that all parliamentary time is as much 'Opposition time' as 'Government time'.

The constitutional importance of the official Opposition is reflected in the fact that the Leader of the Opposition draws a substantial salary in both the House of Commons and Lords, which is drawn on the Consolidated Fund.[29] In addition, since 1975, financial assistance – Short Money – has been provided to all opposition parties to enable them to carry out their role effectively. Each party is entitled to a fixed sum per annum per seat won by the party, plus an amount for every 200 votes cast in the previous election.[30]

The Opposition is allocated 20 days per session in which it can determine the business of the day, representing in an average session 11.6 per cent of parliamentary time. The provision of Opposition Days ensures that the government is obliged to debate matters which it might prefer not to address. Following the Queen's Speech at the opening of a new parliamentary session, the Opposition has the right to determine the subjects for debate on the second of the six days set aside for debate on the speech.

In addition to normal parliamentary procedure for debate, questions, etc., and Opposition time, the Opposition has the weapon of the motion of censure – or vote of no confidence. The motion takes the form 'the House has no confidence in Her Majesty's Government'. The Fixed-term Parliaments Act 2011, section 2, places this on a statutory basis. See further Chapter 5 on the dissolution of Parliament.

 Pause and Reflect

The official Opposition is said to be a 'government in waiting'. What does this term mean and why is the idea constitutionally important?

Voting in the Commons

A 'division' is the name for the counting of votes on important issues where conflict is apparent. Not every debate will result in a division: divisions are reserved for instances when it is important to register formally the number of votes for and against a particularly important issue. For the observer, there is something archaic and humorous about the procedure. The Speaker orders 'Division: clear the lobbies'. Division bells sound throughout Parliament and in the division district immediately surrounding Parliament. Members will interrupt whatever they are doing in response to the bell and return to Parliament for the vote. Members

---

27 Hailsham, 1978, p. 21.
28 Jennings, 1959a, Chapter XV.
29 See Chapter 14.
30 Similar financial assistance, known as Cranbourn Money, is available to political parties in the House of Lords.

crowd into the 'Aye' or 'Noe' lobby, and as they exit the lobby their attendance is checked. The Speaker then announces the result of the division. Votes are recorded by name in the Official *Journal* of the House of Commons.

 SELF-TEST QUESTIONS

What is meant by the term 'adversarial politics'? How is it reflected in the working of the House of Commons?

Which political party forms the official Opposition? What effect did the formation of a Coalition government in 2010 have, if any, on this arrangement?

Parliamentary Publications and Papers

The House of Commons

- *The Commons' Journal*: contains the official record of the proceedings of the House. The Journal dates back to 1547 and is published annually. The Journal contains rulings from the Speaker on procedural matters.
- *The Commons' Official Report*: contains the records of speeches made in the House and written answers to Parliamentary Questions. It is a substantially verbatim report of the proceedings.
- *The Vote*: the collective name of a bundle of papers delivered to Members daily during a parliamentary session. It contains the record of the previous day's proceedings together with the Order Paper for the day which lists the business of the House.
- *The Order Book*: a daily publication setting out the future business of the House.

The House of Lords

- *Minutes of proceedings*: the record of the proceedings in the House of Lords together with details of forthcoming business.
- *The Lords' Journal*: since 1461, the Journals have been kept, providing details of attendance and voting.

Televised proceedings in Parliament

Radio broadcasting of Ministerial Question Time (see Chapter 15) began in 1978. Televised broadcasts of the House of Lords have been transmitted since 1985. In 1988, the House of Commons resolved: 'this House approves in principle the holding of an experiment in the public broadcasting of its proceedings by television'.[31] The Select Committee on Televising of Proceedings was established to make recommendations as to the rules of coverage.[32] Broadcasting commenced in 1989. The *Journals* of the House of Commons and Lords remain the official record of proceedings in Parliament.

---

31 HC 141 (1988–1989), London: HMSO, and *Votes and Proceedings 1988–1989*, 12 June 1989. And see Norton, 1991.
32 *Votes and Proceedings 1987–1988*, 7 February and 9 March 1988.

Public Petitions

The right of individual citizens to petition Parliament is a fundamental constitutional right. Recognised in Magna Carta 1215 and restated in the Bill of Rights 1689, 'it is the right of the subjects to petition the King, and all commitments and prosecutions for such petitioning are illegal'. Before the right to vote was extended to all citizens, petitioning was the only form of redress open to the vast majority of people: in the years 1837–1841 the average number of Petitions presented annually was almost 17,600.

A Petition must be addressed to the House of Commons, include the name and address of the petitioner and contain a 'prayer' (request) to the Commons, using 'respectful, decorous and temperate' language.[33] The Petition will be presented to the House by a Member of Parliament immediately before the half-hour adjournment debate at the end of each day's business. The usual practice is that Petitions will be sent to the relevant government Department for investigation. The Department will formally reply to the House and both the Petition and government response will be recorded in *Hansard*, the Official Journal of the House.[34] In the 2014–2015 session the total number of Petitions presented formally to the House of Commons was 104 (of a total of 166 Petitions). Of these, formal responses were published to 83 Petitions.

Summary

The House of Commons has 650 directly elected representatives of the people: Members of Parliament. The political party with the largest number of seats will generally be the governing party and the leader of that party will be appointed as Prime Minister. The second largest political party will form Her Majesty's Loyal Opposition: a 'government in waiting' should the government be forced out of office. The political party leaders are supported by a number of Whips who act as a channel of communication with ordinary Members and also have a role in ensuring attendance in the House as necessary.

Control of proceedings in the Chamber of the Commons is in the hands of the Speaker, an elected Member of Parliament who acts as the politically impartial Chair of proceedings. The House of Commons is self-regulating, its procedures being laid down in Standing Orders.

The three principal tasks of the House of Commons are to represent the people, to enact legislation and to scrutinise the administration of government.

 Further Reading

Blackburn, R and Kennon, A, *Parliament: Functions, Practice and Procedures*, 2nd edn, 2003, London: Sweet & Maxwell.

Brazier, R, Finders, M and McHugh, D, *New Politics, New Parliament? A Review of Parliamentary Modernisation Since 1997*, 2005, London: Hansard Society.

Cowley, P and Stuart, M, 'Parliament: a few headaches and a dose of modernisation' (2001) 54(3) *Parliamentary Affairs* 442.

Erskine May, T, *Parliamentary Practice*, 24th edn, 2011, London: Butterworths.

Rogers, R and Walters, R, *How Parliament Works*, 5th edn, 2004, London: Pearson, Chapters 6–11 and 13.

Tomkins, A, 'What is Parliament for?' in M Bamforth and P Leyland (eds), *Public Law in a Multi-Layered Constitution*, 2003, Oxford: Hart Publishing.

---

33 The Petition may be signed by one or many persons (the greatest number of signatures was an estimated 4.5 million in a Petition concerning an Ambulance Dispute presented in 1989).

34 Petitions and government responses are available on the *Hansard* homepage: www.parliament.uk/business/publications.

Chapter 14

The Legislative Process

Chapter Contents

Learning Objectives

By the end of this chapter you should be able to:

☐ explain the various origins of proposals for legislation and the differing types of Bills;

☐ discuss the differing parliamentary stages through which Bills must pass to become law, including both pre- and post-legislative scrutiny and procedures in the House of Lords;

☐ discuss the ways in which scrutiny of a Bill may be curtailed and recent reforms relating to the timetabling and carry-over of Bills;

☐ explain the relationship between the House of Commons and House of Lords as laid down in the Parliament Acts 1911 and 1949;

☐ discuss the need and justifications for secondary legislation and the procedures by which it is scrutinised in both the House of Commons and House of Lords;

☐ evaluate the adequacy of parliamentary scrutiny of Bills and secondary legislation.

Introduction

Approximately two-thirds of the time of the United Kingdom's House of Commons is devoted to the consideration of proposals for legislation. In order to effect changes in the law, any proposal must receive the authority of Parliament: Parliament legitimises policy objectives. A mere decision of Parliament, in the form of a Resolution of the Commons, cannot change the law of the land.[1] In order to become law, a legislative proposal must receive the consent of the three component parts of Parliament: the Commons, the Lords[2] and the Crown through the giving of Royal Assent. In this chapter the process of scrutiny in the House of Commons is considered. Discussion of the legislative role of the House of Lords is to be found in Chapter 16.

Before examining the process of scrutiny in the Commons, the various types of legislation must be considered. Legislative proposals fall under two main categories: primary and delegated (or secondary) legislation. Primary legislation refers to Acts of Parliament. Delegated or secondary legislation refers to legislation drafted by authorised persons or bodies under the authority of a 'parent' statute.

The United Kingdom Parliament and Devolution

As seen in Chapter 11, devolution to the Northern Ireland Assembly, Scottish Parliament and Welsh Assembly represents a diminution in the United Kingdom Parliament's (Westminster's) legislative role. Under devolution, in practical terms, the United Kingdom Parliament retains power to enact primary legislation only to the extent to which this power has not passed to the regional legislature.

Primary Legislation[3]

The classification of Bills

The majority of Bills will be those put forward by the government to implement its policy. Bills fall into seven categories: Public Bills, Private Bills, Hybrid Bills, Money Bills, Private Member's Bills, Consolidation Bills and Bills which are intended to affect only England (rather than the whole of the United Kingdom). The procedure for passing a Bill depends on its classification. Most attention is here devoted to the legislative procedure for Public Bills.

A Public Bill is one which has general application to all members of society, for example Road Traffic Acts, Environmental Protection Acts and National Health Service Acts. A Private Bill is one which affects only a particular locality or group or body of persons.

A Hybrid Bill is one of general application, that is to say a Public Bill which also affects particular private interests in a manner different from the private interests of other persons or bodies of the same category or class. The Bill regulating the development of the Channel Tunnel is an example of a Hybrid Bill, since it affected the private rights of landowners whose land would be compulsorily purchased.[4]

A Money Bill is one which is certified by the Speaker as such, and contains nothing other than financial measures.

---

1 *Stockdale v Hansard* (1839).
2 Other than where the Parliament Act procedure is employed. See Chapter 16.
3 See Rose, 1986; Hansard Society, 1993.
4 See also London (Transport) Bill 1968–1969; Norfolk and Suffolk Broads Bill 1986–1987.

A Private Member's Bill is one promoted by an individual Member of Parliament, as opposed to the government[5] or, alternatively, a matter which the government has been unable to fit into its legislative programme but will subsequently adopt and provide time – and support – for the passage of the Bill. Most often, such Bills involve sensitive issues of particular interest to their promoters. The Abortion Act 1967, for example, originated from a Private Member's Bill. Private Members' Bills follow the same legislative process as government Bills, but the time available for their consideration is restricted. Normally, ten (although occasionally more) Fridays each session will be set aside for Private Members' Bills, and it is rare for a Bill to succeed unless the government is prepared to provide additional time for its consideration.

Consolidation Bills represent a re-enactment of legislation in a comprehensive manner and they enable previous legislation – which will generally exist in several statutes – to be repealed. Consolidation Bills do not, for the most part, represent any change in the law; rather, they represent the chance to 'consolidate' all the law on a particular matter within one statute. Consolidation Bills are normally introduced in the House of Lords and then scrutinised by a Joint Committee on Consolidation Bills, composed of Members of both the House of Commons and the House of Lords. Since there is no change being made in the substantive law, parliamentary time devoted to Consolidation Bills is short, and it is rare for a Consolidation Bill to be debated more than briefly on the floor of the Commons. In 1994, the House of Commons agreed that, in order to save further time, Consolidated Bills would no longer require a committee stage. Finally, there are Consolidated Fund and Appropriation Bills which provide statutory authority for government expenditure and which are not debated in Parliament.

Bills which affect only England or England and Wales but not Scotland or Northern Ireland are subject to a special procedure. This was introduced in order to resolve the 'West Lothian problem', namely that it was perceived to be wrong for Scottish (and Northern Irish) MPs to vote on legislation which affects only England when English MPs have no equivalent right to vote on legislation passed by the devolved Parliament and Assembly.[6]

The legislative picture cannot be complete without consideration of delegated or subordinate legislation. In each parliamentary session an average of 62 Bills are enacted, while the average number of statutory instruments (see further below) amounts to 2,000 per session. In addition, administrative rules drafted by government Departments must be considered. These include Codes of Practice, Circulars and Guidances and, while they do not have the force of law, they nevertheless have an impact on the manner in which laws are implemented.[7]

The origins of legislation

The majority of Bills considered by Parliament will be introduced by the government of the day. This does not necessarily mean that the source of the proposal is one emanating from government policy, still less from the party manifesto on which the election was fought.

Consideration of the origins of legislative proposals is important in evaluating the extent to which government and the House of Commons interacts with the society it is elected to serve. JAG Griffith and M Ryle observe:

> It is a central feature of Parliament, however, that it performs a responsive rather than initiating function within the constitution. The government – at different

---

5 See Griffith and Ryle, 2003.
6 On this see further Chapter 11.
7 For example, Guidance to Local Authorities on the Provision of Sites for Gypsies under the Caravan Sites Act 1968; Guidance on Allocation of Local Authority Housing under the Housing Act 1985. See Baldwin and Houghton, 1986; Ganz, 1987.

levels – initiates policy, formulates its policy on legislation and other proposals, exercises powers under the prerogative or granted by statute and, in all these aspects, performs the governing role in the state. Both Houses of Parliament spend most of their time responding, in a variety of ways, to these initiatives, proposals or executive actions. [2003, page 5]

This 'responsive function' is seen most clearly in situations giving rise to the need for urgent legislation. This may arise in an emergency situation such as the 2019–2021 Coronavirus pandemic, which prompted legislation fast-tracked through Parliament within a matter of days. A law-making response may also be needed to reflect a recent decision of the courts, especially where the judges have ruled that the present law violates individual rights. One example of this is the case of **Bellinger v Bellinger** (2003), where the court ruled that the law preventing a person from marrying as a result of changing their gender breached their right to marry under the European Convention on Human Rights. The Government introduced the Gender Recognition Bill which became the Act of 2014.

The Opposition front bench and backbenchers on either side of the two Houses are also sources of parliamentary business. The inspiration for their input is largely found in general public opinion; outside pressures or interest groups; newspapers, radio and television; and in the minds and attitudes of millions of citizens represented in the Commons by Members.

Parliament therefore finds itself the recipient of a wide range of external pressures and proposals, broadly divided in origin between the government of the day on the one hand and the outside world – the public – on the other.

Professor Finer (1958) labels the forces external to Parliament which have an impact on its working the 'anonymous empire'. Finer is here referring to all those individuals and organisations, lobby groups and interest groups whose aim is to influence the content of legislation. Finer claims that the detailed programme of government legislation 'owes a great deal to sectional groups'. Amongst these groups we can include such organisations as the Confederation of British Industry, Trades Union Congress, National Farmers' Union, National Union of Teachers, British Medical Association and Law Society, each of which is engaged in promoting its own sectional interests. Other pressure groups pursue particular causes: for example, the Royal Society for the Prevention of Cruelty to Animals, JUSTICE (the International Commission of Jurists), Howard League for Penal Reform, Friends of the Earth (environmental issues) and Shelter (housing).

In addition to these and many other groups, the law reform bodies provide a source of legislation. The Law Commission, established under the Law Commissions Act 1965, is under a duty to keep the law under review with a view to its systematic development and reform, including codification of law, and simplification and modernisation of law. If we take, by way of example, the Law Commission's work on family law, the Commission has reviewed the law of legitimacy, custody, wardship, divorce, domestic violence and occupation of the matrimonial home. In conjunction with interdepartmental committees, the Law Commission has also been engaged in a comprehensive review of adoption law.

Commissions of inquiry may be established by the government to examine and report on particular issues, often culminating in a change in the law. For example, the Committee of Inquiry into Child Abuse in Cleveland resulted (in part) in changes implemented in the Children Act 1989, which represented a major overhaul of the law relating to children. The Criminal Law Revision Committee has examined the law relating, inter alia, to conspiracy, contempt, arrest and detention and criminal deception.

Each of these sources may result in proposals for changes in the law. The success of these proposals in terms of becoming law is largely dependent upon the government of the day and its willingness to provide parliamentary time for the consideration of Bills. In any parliamentary session, approximately 50 to 60 Bills will be introduced, the vast majority of which will reach the statute book.

 SELF-TEST QUESTION

Name the different types of Bills which come before Parliament. What are the principal characteristics of each type of Bill?

The preparation of a Bill

Once the government has decided to implement a particular measure, the aims of government must be translated effectively into language which will achieve those objectives. That task is entrusted to parliamentary draftsmen, or parliamentary counsel, attached to the Management and Personnel Office of the Treasury.[8] Drafting involves five stages: understanding, analysis, design, composition and revision.[9] Once a draft Bill is in being, it is examined by the Cabinet Home Affairs Committee before being formally submitted to Parliament for scrutiny and enactment.

The structure of a Bill

Each Bill has a short title, for example, the Transport Bill, which indicates the general area of policy involved, together with a long title which summarises the main objectives of the Bill. The Bill is made up of Chapters or Parts which encompass groups of related clauses, and Schedules which contain details supplementary to the primary clauses. The Bill may grant powers to make delegated legislation to Ministers or other specified bodies, such as local authorities. There is, necessarily, no uniformity as to the length of Bills, which may range from one clause (Abortion Amendment Bill 1988–1989) to 27 Parts, 747 clauses and 25 Schedules (Companies Bill 1985).

Pre-legislative scrutiny

In order to improve the quality of legislation, governments increasingly publish draft Bills for consideration before the Bill is presented in its proposed final form. Since 1997 there has been an increasing use of Select Committees to scrutinise draft Bills before they are formally presented to Parliament. As will be seen from the discussion in Chapter 15, Select Committees (unlike Public Bill Committees, which examine Bills) have the power to call witnesses and consider documentary evidence. This form of pre-legislative scrutiny enables specialist individuals and groups to contribute to the legislative process and thereby improve the quality of legislation.

Pre-legislative scrutiny may be undertaken by a departmental Select Committee, a specially convened Committee or a Joint Committee comprising Members of both the House of Commons and House of Lords.

---

8 SI 1981/1670.
9 Thornton, 1987, pp. 116–117.

The Joint Committee on Human Rights

The Joint Committee on Human Rights comprises six Members of the House of Commons and six Members of the House of Lords. The Committee examines every Bill which is presented to Parliament with a view to ensuring that the Bill is compatible with human rights.[10] It also examines Draft Bills which have been published for consultation prior to being formally presented to Parliament. The Committee reports to both Houses of Parliament.

The legislative stages: Public Bills
First reading

A Bill which is to be introduced will appear on the Order Paper of the relevant day. The Bill will be presented in 'dummy form' and is deemed to be read a 'first time'. Alternatively, a Bill may be introduced on order of the House, or after having been sent to the Commons following its passage by the House of Lords. Following the purely formal introduction into Parliament, a date will be set for second reading and the Bill will be printed and published.

Second reading

It is at the second reading that a Bill will receive its first in-depth scrutiny. The scrutiny occurs in the form of a debate, generally on the floor of the House, and is confined to matters of principle rather than detail. Exceptionally, the second reading debate may be referred to a committee for consideration, but may only be so referred if 20 or more Members of Parliament do not object and, accordingly, the procedure is reserved for non-controversial matters and not measures 'involving large questions of policy nor likely to give rise to differences on party lines'.[11] Public Bills which are to give effect to proposals contained in a report by either of the Law Commissions, other than a Private Members' Bill or a Consolidation Bill, when set down for second reading will be committed to a second reading committee, unless the House orders otherwise, or the Bill is referred to the Northern Ireland, Scottish or Welsh Grand Committee. If a Minister of the Crown moves a motion that a Bill not be referred to a second reading committee, the House will vote on the motion. Where a Bill has been committed to a second reading committee, the committee considers the principles of the Bill, but the vote on the Bill is taken on the floor of the House. It is at second reading stage that the Minister in charge of the Bill must explain and defend the contents of the Bill. The Opposition's task is to probe and question and set out reasons for opposing the Bill. It should not be assumed that the Opposition invariably opposes Bills. In many instances the proposed legislation is uncontroversial and may even be welcomed by the Opposition. The Dangerous Dogs Bill and the Child Support Bill 1990 are illustrations of this phenomenon. If the Bill is opposed, a vote will take place which determines the fate of the Bill. If the vote is lost, the Bill is rejected and the proposed legislation must either be abandoned or the Bill must be reintroduced at a later date.

Once a Bill has successfully completed the second reading stage, it 'stands committed' to a Public Bill Committee[12] unless, exceptionally, the House orders otherwise.[13]

---

10 As guaranteed under the European Convention on Human Rights, now enforceable in the domestic courts by virtue of the Human Rights Act 1998.
11 *First Report Select Committee on Procedure*, HC 149 (1964–1965), London: HMSO, para. 3.
12 Until the start of the 2006–2007 session known as Standing Committees.
13 In the 2000–2001 session, six Bills were considered by a Committee of the Whole House.

Committee stage

Once the second reading has taken place, Bills are sent to a committee for further and detailed consideration. Committee stage may be undertaken by:

- Public Bill Committee: this is the automatic procedure unless the Commons orders otherwise;
- Committee of the whole House: this is reserved for Bills of constitutional importance. The Human Rights Bill and Northern Ireland, Scotland and Wales devolution Bills were considered by the whole House;
- Committee of the whole House for some parts of the Bill with the remainder being sent to a Public Bill Committee. The Greater London Authority Bill was considered in this way;
- Select Committee;
- Joint Committee of both Houses.[14]

Public Bill Committees are designed to scrutinise Bills in detail. The committee will be established for the purpose of examining a particular Bill and will then stand down, a feature which, as will be seen, may have implications for the adequacy of scrutiny.

At any one time, there will be between eight and ten Public Bill Committees in operation. Committees may comprise between 16 and 50 Members of Parliament, and normally between 18 and 25.[15] Membership is drawn from Members of Parliament from all political parties and is proportionate to the overall strength of the party in the House, thus the larger the government's majority in the House, the larger its majority in the committee. Appointments are made by a Committee of Selection who will take advice from party Whips as to appropriate Members. The Speaker of the House appoints the Chairman of the committee, who may be a Member of either side of the House (government or Opposition). Once selected, the Chairman is impartial and enjoys the same powers as the Speaker of the House in relation to selection of amendments for discussion and imposition of the Closure Motion (see further below).

The function of the committee is to examine the Bill clause by clause. The Minister in charge of the Bill has the task of steering it successfully through committee, aided by his Parliamentary Private Secretary and civil servants. Amendments may be proposed by Members giving notice to the Public Bill Office of the House of Commons. These amendments may take the form of linguistic details, adding or subtracting a word here or there; alternatively, amendments may be of major substance. Once the clauses of the Bill have been considered, the committee moves to consider any proposed new clauses. Proposals for amendment may be ruled out of order if they are irrelevant, are beyond the scope of the Bill, conflict with other proposed amendments, conflict with the principle of the Bill or are unintelligible, ineffective, vague or spurious.[16]

The proceedings in Public Bill Committees are formal and ritualistic. A Member moves an amendment, the Minister responds, the Opposition speaks, other Members comment and debate continues until a decision on a clause – 'that the clause do stand part of the Bill' – is reached. The Minister's task is to ensure a smooth passage for the Bill in the fastest possible time. Richard Crossman, Minister of Housing and Local Government in the Labour government of 1974, commented that committee stage is tedious, with the Minister 'being pinned

---

14 See Griffith and Ryle, 2003, 6-128–6-129.
15 Complex Bills may warrant a larger committee membership, as with the Finance Bill 1992.
16 See Erskine May, 2004; Griffith and Ryle, 2003.

to the wall' throughout the process.[17] For the most part, deliberations will follow party politi-cal lines, and it follows that, provided the government has a majority on the committee, the chances of successfully moving amendments are slight.

The low success rate of back-bench proposals for amendment should not be given dis-proportionate weight. It has been seen above that Standing Orders set out a number of 'inad-missible' categories of proposed amendments. It must also be noted that Members may put forward amendments solely with a view to gaining a clearer picture of the Bill, or for more spurious reasons, such as delaying a Bill or embarrassing the government. Equally, it should be remembered that the composition of the committee reflects that of the House overall: governments with a firm majority will inevitably suffer fewer defeats in committee. Finally, recognition must be given to the fact that the government has gained a mandate in a general election and, whether or not a specific legislative proposal stems from that mandate, the government has a legitimate expectation of getting its legislative programme on the statute book. Equally, the principle of the Bill has been approved on second reading by the House. While Parliament as a whole, through its representative committee, has the equally legitimate expectation of being able to give adequate scrutiny to government proposals, that should not necessarily be understood to mean that Public Bill Committees should expect to be able to force their views on government.

At first sight, it appears anomalous that there is no committee system organised on spe-cialist lines. There is a *prima facie* case for committees to be geared to particular subjects, or groups of subjects. On this reasoning, a Public Bill Committee could be devised with the remit to consider transport matters, another to consider science and technology Bills, another to consider environmental issues and so on. If such committees were appointed for the life of the Parliament, or for a parliamentary session with Members appointed on the basis of their expertise and interests, the potential for improved scrutiny would be enhanced. However, there is a counter-argument to this. A specialist semi-permanent committee, while having the benefit of expertise, would lose the quality of the assortment of interests which is cur-rently brought to bear on proposals. Members of the committee might become too familiar with each other's attitudes, and Ministers and the committee could suffer from becoming inward looking and overly concerned with one subject at the expense of others. Committees are open to the public and their proceedings are recorded in the Official Report of the House, *Hansard*. For debate to become too narrow and technical might disadvantage other Members and the public in their capacity to understand proceedings.

One recognised shortcoming in the procedure of Standing Committees – the former Bill scrutiny committees – was the lack of power to send for 'persons and papers', in other words, witnesses and documents. Public Bill Committees now have the power to take written and oral evidence from officials and experts outside Parliament.

Report stage

Once the Bill has been considered in Public Bill Committee, the Bill is reported back to the House of Commons as a whole. If amendments have been made in committee, the Bill will be reprinted. Further amendments may be introduced at this stage, but the Speaker will be careful to avoid repetition of the debate in standing committee, so any proposed amendments previously considered will be rejected. The Speaker will accept amendments proposed by the government, proposals representing a compromise and amendments relating to new devel-opments. Generally, the debate at this stage will be brief but, again, this will depend on the importance of the Bill. The Police and Criminal Evidence Bill, for example, was debated for

17 Crossman, 1977.

18-and-a-half hours at report stage. Approximately nine per cent of time on the floor of the House is taken up with report.

Third reading

Third reading represents the last chance for the House of Commons to examine a Bill before it is passed to the House of Lords. At this stage, the Bill cannot be amended, other than to correct small mistakes such as grammatical or printing errors. A Bill may pass through the report and third reading stages at the same time.

 Pause and Reflect

Explain the parliamentary stages through which a Bill must pass before it becomes law. Which, if any, of these stages gives in-depth consideration to the contents of the Bill?

To which Committees of the House of Commons may Bills be sent for scrutiny? What advantages or disadvantages do these differing committees offer for the examination of Bills?

Bills affecting only England or England and Wales

A Bill which is certified by the Speaker to relate only to England or England and Wales will be considered at Committee Stage only by English, or English and Welsh, MPs. The Committee will reflect the party-political composition of English MPs, or English and Welsh MPs, in the Commons. Having been considered at Committee stage, the Bill then proceeds to the report stage as usual.

Following report, there is a new stage which involves a Grand Committee of English, or English and Welsh, MPs considering a 'consent motion'. In the case of a Bill which is entirely English or English and Welsh, the Grand Committee stage enables those MPs to consent to or veto the whole Bill. Where parts of a Bill relate to English only matters, or English and Welsh only matters, the Committee considers those clauses that the Speaker has certified as English, or English and Welsh only, and enables English, or English and Welsh, MPs to consent to or veto those clauses.

In the Grand Committee stage, no amendments may be made to the Bill. If the Committee vetoes clauses of a Bill, there then follows a reconsideration stage where amendments may be made to enable agreement to be reached.[18] All MPs are allowed to participate in this stage. A second Grand Committee of English, or English and Welsh, MPs will then consider the amendments made by the whole House. If no agreement is reached at this stage, and the Committee withholds consent to the whole Bill, the Bill may not be given a third reading and 'shall not pass'. If the Committee withholds consent to parts of the Bill, but not the whole Bill, the Bill will be amended.

Third reading then follows, in which all MPs can participate, and the Bill then goes to the House of Lords which follows its normal legislative procedure. If the House of Lords makes amendments to the Bill, any which are English only, or English and Welsh only, will have to be certified by the Speaker. The certified amendments are then subject to a 'double majority vote', which requires that the amendments must be supported by a majority of English, or English and Welsh, MPs in addition to a majority of all MPs.

---

18 Standing Order 83N.

The revised procedure was introduced in 2015 by Standing Order of the House of Commons.

Fast-Track Legislation

On occasion there is a need for legislation to be enacted with speed. The need may arise through an emergency of some sort – as in the case of the banking collapse in 2008 or the Coronavirus pandemic of 2019–2021 – or some phenomenon which is causing unusual public disquiet; anti-terrorism legislation, for example, has been fast-tracked in response to some terrorist events.

When an emergency, or fast-track, Bill is required, the normal parliamentary procedures are followed, but the time allowed for scrutiny is much reduced. The government will seek the agreement of the Opposition parties on the date by which the Royal Assent must be achieved, and the stages of the Bill will be tailored to achieve that objective.

While fast-track legislation is necessary on occasion, it gives rise to constitutional questions, not least the ability of Parliament as a whole to give adequate scrutiny to government proposals. Linked to this is the difficulty caused by the government tabling late amendments without providing adequate time for their debate and scrutiny. It is argued that the quality of the legislation may be reduced by the speed with which it has been processed. The need for speed also precludes valuable contributions being made by specialist interest groups.[19] For these reasons, the House of Lords Select Committee on the Constitution recommended that there should be a presumption in favour of 'sunset clauses' – a clause imposing a time limit on the operation of the Act following which it would need to be renewed or replaced, and that there should be a presumption in favour of early post-legislative scrutiny of fast-tracked Bills.

A recent example of fast-tracking is the Coronavirus Act 2020. The Bill was introduced in Parliament on 19 March; its stages passed within one day in each House and it received the Royal Assent on 25 March. The Act has to be read in conjunction with earlier emergency legislation: the Public Health (Control of Disease) Act 1984 and the Civil Contingencies Act 2004, together with the Coronavirus Regulations (the Health Protection (Coronavirus, Restrictions) (England) Regulations 2020) and corresponding regulations for Northern Ireland, Scotland and Wales.[20]

The Coronavirus Act 2020 is time-limited to two years, and its lifetime can be ended early. Should it prove necessary, the lifetime of the Act may be extended for a maximum of six months. The Act must be reviewed every six months.[21] Not all of the provisions came into force on Royal Assent; some may only come into force as and when needed. The Act applies to the whole of the United Kingdom, but – consistent with devolution arrangements – there are variations in the precise rules to be applied between the nations.

Questions were raised over the need for the 2020 Act, there being two previous Acts covering public emergencies. The first, the Public Health (Control of Disease) Act 1984, was specifically designed to deal with threats to public health. The second Act is the Civil Contingencies Act 2004, which also provides wide-ranging powers to deal with emergencies. However, Regulations made under the 2004 Act require parliamentary approval within seven

---

19 See the 15th Report of Session 2008–2009, *Fast-track Legislation: Constitutional Implications and Safeguards*, HL Paper 116-I, July 2009.
20 The Health Protection (Coronavirus, Restrictions) (Northern Ireland) Regulations 2020; the Health Protection (Coronavirus) (Restrictions) (Scotland) Regulations 2020; the Health Protection (Coronavirus, Restrictions) (No 2) (Wales) Regulations 2020.
21 Coronavirus Act 2020, section 98.

days of being made, and they expire after 30 days, unless renewed. The 2004 Act is therefore of limited utility unless Parliament is sitting most of the time.

Under the 1984 Act, as amended by the Health and Social Care Act 2008, magistrates were given wide-ranging powers to make orders to deal with threats to public health on the application of a local authority. Where a person 'P' is, or may be, infected or contaminated, and that presents or could present significant harm to human health because there is a risk that P might infect others and it is necessary to remove or reduce that risk, a justice of the peace may order that P summits to medical examination, be removed to and detained in, kept in isolation, be disinfected, wear protective clothing, answer questions, be subjected to restrictions on where P may go and with whom P may have contact and to abstain from working or trading.[22]

Other powers under the 1984 Act include powers to seize and retain 'things' that may be infected or contaminated and in relation to premises that may be infected or contaminated. Each of these powers includes the power to make an order in relation to a group of persons things or premises. While the individual has the protection of a judicial hearing, in an urgent situation this may not occur, and if 'necessary to do so' a justice of the peace may make these orders without giving notice to the person concerned.

An Order must specify the length of time it is to remain in force, but may be extended for up to 28 days.[23] Orders may be varied or revoked on the application of a local authority or the person affected.[24] A person who fails, without reasonable excuse, to comply with an Order is guilty of an offence carrying a fine of up to £20,000. However, these powers – which provide for judicial oversight of their exercise – were deemed to be inadequate to deal with an emergency situation such as Covid-19, hence the need for the Coronavirus Act and Regulations.

The 2020 Act confers broad powers and, read in conjunction with the 1984 Act,[25] provides for orders to be made to prevent, protect against and control the spread of an infection. The Act ensures that agencies and services – schools, hospitals, the police etc. – have the powers they need to deal with the pandemic. The 1984 Act, section 45C, provides for the making of Regulations.

Section 45C of the 1984 Act[26] authorises the Secretary of State to make Regulations 'for the purpose of preventing, protecting against, controlling or providing a public health response to the incidence or spread of infection or contamination in England and Wales'. The power may be exercised in relation to *infection or contamination generally* or *in relation to particular forms of infection or contamination*. In making Regulations under section 45C relating to a threat to public health, the Regulations **may not include any restrictions or requirements** '*unless the appropriate Minister considers, when making the regulations, that the restriction or requirement is* **proportionate** *to what is sought to be achieved by imposing it*' (emphasis added).[27]

The Health Protection (Coronavirus, Restrictions) (England) Regulations 2020[28] were made without a draft being laid and approved by each House of Parliament, the justification being that they were needed to respond to the serious and imminent threat to public health caused by the virus. The Regulations were required to be approved by each House of Parliament within 28 days and expire at the end of six months beginning on the day on which they came into force, unless renewed.[29] The Government must report to Parliament on

---

22 Public Health etc Act 1984, section 45G.
23 1984 Act, section 45L.
24 Ibid., section 45M.
25 As amended by the Health and Social Care Act 2008.
26 As inserted by the Health and Social Care Act 2008.
27 Public Health (Control of Disease) Act 1984, section 45D.
28 2020 SI 350.
29 Public Health etc. Act 1984, section 45R.

the working of the Act every two months.[30] The Secretary of State certified that in his view the Regulations were compatible with the European Convention on Human Rights (ECHR).[31] In times of war or other emergency threatening the life of a nation, it is possible for a state to derogate from aspects of the ECHR; this the Government did not seek to do.

The Regulations required the closure of drinking establishments, restaurants and cafes, cinemas, theatres, museums and galleries, all indoor leisure and sports facilities, playgrounds, funfairs, libraries, community centres and outdoor markets. Hotels were required to be closed, except for permanent residents and people moving home or attending a funeral, and those unable to return to their home country (e.g. overseas visitors) and key workers working away from home. It is an offence to contravene the Regulations. The police, Environmental Health and Trading Standards officers monitor compliance with the Regulations. Contravening the Regulations attracts a fixed penalty fine; if there are repeated breaches, the fine doubles each time to a maximum of £960.[32]

One of the most draconian measures was the restriction on people from leaving their homes 'without reasonable excuse': the 'lockdown'. Reasonable excuse included essential shopping, daily exercise, seeking medical help, the need to provide care and assistance to others, essential travel for work and access to critical public services. In addition, the Regulations provide powers for the police to disperse public gatherings which are prohibited. As with the stay-at-home rule, the police may direct people to return home, or if they refuse, to take them there. What is notable about these restrictions to individual freedoms and rights was that they were imposed on the entire population of the UK, without proof of infection or contamination, by Government order, with no judicial or other hearing.

Some of the powers which are available to magistrates under the 1984 Act have not been conferred on Ministers under the 2020 Act. These include the power to order a person 'P' to submit to a medical examination, to remove P to and detain P in a hospital or other suitable establishment and to keep P in isolation or quarantine.

Introducing a Private Member's Bill

In addition to Public (and Private and Hybrid) Bills, a number of legislative proposals will be introduced by individual Members of Parliament. In any one session, dozens of Private Members' Bills will be introduced, a minority of which will reach the statute book.

The success of a Private Member's Bill is largely dependent upon it receiving government support. As has been seen in Chapter 13, the government controls the parliamentary timetable and dominates parliamentary business. Since only six Fridays per session are allocated for consideration of Private Members' Bills, it will be necessary for the government to make additional time for the completion of such a Bill's parliamentary stages. Whether or not the government is willing to do this will depend upon the political support which the Bill acquires. However, even if a Bill does not successfully pass all its legislative stages, it may have served the useful purpose of heightening parliamentary and public awareness of a particular issue. For example, the Rt Hon Tony Benn MP introduced Private Member's Bills, *inter alia*, on placing the royal prerogative on a statutory basis,[33] and for enacting a written constitution.[34] Neither of these succeeded, but they represent matters in which there is widespread interest.

---

30 Coronavirus Act 2020, section 97.
31 Under the Human Rights Act 1998, section 19.
32 Health Protection (Coronavirus, Restrictions) (England) Regulations 2020, section/regulation 10(7)(b).
33 Crown Prerogatives (House of Commons Control) Bill 1988–1989.
34 Commonwealth of Britain Bill.

A Private Member's Bill may be introduced in one of four ways. The first procedure is that of the ballot.

Introduction by ballot
The House will agree, early in the session, for days to be appointed for the purpose of the ballot. Members of Parliament may put their names on the ballot paper on that day. Over 400 Members normally enter the ballot, although many will have no specific proposed legislation in mind. Twenty Members will be successful at the ballot. If successful, the Member must then, within nine days, table the subject matter for his or her Bill. Six Fridays per session are allocated to Private Members' Bills, on which days the Bills take precedence over other parliamentary business.

Introduction under Standing Order Procedure
Any Member may present a Bill under this procedure by placing the long and short title of the Bill on the Order Paper of the House. The Bill will not be considered, but will simply be deemed to have received a first reading and a date set for second reading.

Introduction under the 'Ten Minute Rule'
A Member may give notice of a motion for leave to introduce a Bill. The motions will be considered at specific times allotted by the House, which permits the Member to raise an issue after Question Time on Tuesdays and Wednesdays, thus guaranteeing media attention.[35] Several rules apply. The Member may give one notice at any one time. No notice may be given for leave to bring in a Bill which relates to taxation or expenditure, or to bring in a Bill which covers matters which are substantially the same as those contained in Bills on which the House has already reached a decision in that session.

'Ordinary presentation' of a Bill
Every Member is permitted to introduce a Bill after having given notice. These Bills, however, are not presented until after the Ballot Bills have been presented and put down for second reading. They therefore have little chance of success, nor do they enjoy the publicity given to Bills introduced under the Ten Minute Rule.

Introduction of a Bill after consideration in the House of Lords
Most Private Members' Bills are introduced in the House of Commons, but a small number in each session may have started their parliamentary life in the Lords. If the Bill passes the Lords, it then comes to the Commons. However, Bills introduced in the Lords are considered only after Bills introduced in the Commons, and, accordingly, given the severe time constraints, few are likely even to receive a second reading in the Commons.

'Carry-over' of Bills
It has been noted above that Bills which do not pass all legislative stages within one session will lapse and have to be reintroduced in the following session.[36] In order to avoid duplication of effort and time wastage, the House of Commons agreed[37] that government Bills could be

---

35 Usually on Tuesdays or Wednesdays before the start of public business.
36 There are two exceptions to this rule: Bills passed under the Parliament Acts and Private Bills. These may be suspended in one session and revived in the next.
37 Following the recommendation of the Modernisation Committee: Third Report, *Carry-over of Public Bills*, HC 543 of 1997–1998.

carried over from one session to the next. In 2002, the Commons approved a recommendation that no Bill should be carried over more than once.[38]

Curtailing debate on legislative proposals

As a result of the pressure on parliamentary time, and the need for a Bill to pass through all its legislative stages in a single session, procedures exist to limit consideration of a Bill.

Closure motions

The Closure Motion, introduced in 1881, is a means of stopping debate, usually by agreement between government and Opposition, in order to ensure that debates end at times agreed by the parties. The closure can be used in debate on the floor of the House or in Public Bill Committee. It is an instrument of control, and one which is used sparingly; rarely will it be used without agreement. In the 1987–1988 session, however (a long session), it was used 20 times without inter-party agreement.

In terms of procedure, the motion for closure is put to the Speaker, who has discretion whether or not to accept the motion. In addition, at least 100 Members of Parliament must vote in favour of closure.

Selection of amendments

This device is confined to legislative proposals and enables the procedure to be streamlined by the selection of amendments for discussion.

The Allocation of Time Motion

The most extreme form of control is the Allocation of Time Motion, colloquially called the Guillotine Motion, introduced in its present form in 1887. Erskine May (1997) describes Guillotine Motions as representing:

> the extreme limit to which procedure goes in affirming the rights of the majority at the expense of the minorities of the House, and it cannot be denied that they are capable of being used in such a way as to upset the balance, generally so carefully preserved, between the claims of business, and the rights of debate.

The device, if approved by the House, enables the government to set dates by which the various stages of scrutiny and debate must be completed. If the government puts forward a motion for an Allocation of Time, Standing Orders provide that a debate of up to three hours may take place (which may be extended), unless otherwise proposed in the motion or decided by the Business Committee of the House. Once agreed, the Business Committee of the House, or a business sub-committee of the Public Bill Committee will determine how many scrutiny sessions are to be held and the date by which the next procedural stage must be accomplished.

However, since the introduction of Programme Orders (see below), which have become a regular feature of the law-making process, Guillotine Motions are now reserved for the most difficult cases of delay through obstruction by the Opposition.[39]

---

38 See Standing Order No. 80A.
39 In the 2002–2003 session a total of 71 Programming Orders were made, with only three Guillotine Motions.

Programming of Bills

In the 2000–2001 session, Orders of the House provided that Programme Motions should be employed to facilitate efficiency in the legislative process. The Modernisation Committee stated that the basic requirements of the reformed system were to ensure that the government gets its legislation through in a reasonable time while allowing Members to have a full opportunity to debate and propose amendments. Further, it was essential that all parts of the Bill be properly considered, and that there should be an improvement in the preparation of Bills so as to reduce the need for amendments.[40]

A motion (request) for a Programme Order is moved directly after the second reading debate and sets out timetabling for further stages in the Commons.

Delegated Legislation

The picture of the law-making process would be incomplete without a consideration of delegated, or subordinate, legislation.

In 1972, Parliament's Joint Committee on Delegated Legislation described subordinate legislation as covering 'every exercise of power to legislate conferred by or under an Act of Parliament'.[41] Some examples will make the scope of delegated legislation clearer. Delegated legislation may be made by:

(a) *Ministers*, in the form of rules and regulations which supplement the provisions of an Act of Parliament;

(b) *local authorities*, in the form of bylaws to regulate their locality according to particular localised needs;

(c) *public bodies*, in the form of rules and regulations. Such bodies include the British Airways Authority, the British Railways Board and the Nature Conservancy Council;

(d) *judges*, in the form of rules of court made under the authority of section 75 of the Supreme Court Act 1981;

(e) *government Departments*, in the form of codes of practice, circulars and guidance. These do not contain legal rules, but have a substantive effect on the manner in which the legal rules operate;

(f) *the House of Commons*, in the form of Resolutions of the House. The Provisional Collection of Taxes Act 1968 makes possible the lawful imposition and collection of taxation between the Budget speech and the enactment of the Finance Bill in July/August. Whereas normal Resolutions of the House do not have the force of law, Resolutions enabling the impositions and collections of taxation – being authorised by statute – have legal effect.

The volume of delegated legislation also reveals its importance as a source of law: each year, approximately 3,500 pieces of delegated legislation are made.

The use of delegated law-making power is not a purely modern phenomenon, arising from increasing legal regulation of all aspects of life. The power to make subordinate legislation was exercised as early as the sixteenth century.[42] The increase in the volume of delegated legislation derives from the early nineteenth century.

---

40 See Standing Order No. 83A.
41 *Report of the Joint Committee on Delegated Legislation*, HL 184, HC 475 (1971–1972), London: HMSO, para. 6.
42 Statute of Proclamations 1539 (31 Hen 8 c. 26); and see Allen, 1965.

Delegated legislation raises questions about the supremacy of Parliament. In *The New Despotism* (1929), Hewart CJ argued that the increased use of delegated legislation, particularly during the First World War under the Defence of the Realm Act 1914, amounted to an effective usurpation of the sovereign law-making powers of Parliament. Such criticisms led to the appointment, in 1929, of a committee of inquiry[43] to consider the powers exercised by Ministers by way of delegated legislation and to report on safeguards that were desirable or necessary to secure the constitutional principles of the sovereignty of Parliament and the supremacy of the law.

The committee's report,[44] while recognising the need for improved parliamentary scrutiny of delegated legislation, nevertheless emphasised its necessity in terms of legislative efficiency. It is efficiency which is the principal justification for the delegation of law-making power. Put simply, Parliament, as currently constituted, struggles to give adequate scrutiny to primary legislation. To burden Parliament with the task of scrutinising every detail of legislation would overload the parliamentary timetable to the extent that the system would break under the strain. A related justification for delegated power lies in the need to supplement or amend the primary rules in light of new developments. Delegated legislation enables the fine tuning of the primary rules to take place, without encumbering Parliament as a whole. Further, it may be that the government is clear as to the broad policy to be pursued under an Act, and as to the primary legal rules necessary to achieve a particular goal. There may be less certainty as to the technical, detailed rules necessary; the delegation of law-making power enables such rules to be worked out, often in consultation with specialist interest groups outside Parliament.

The justifications for subordinate legislation can hold good only if the powers granted are sufficiently clear and precise as to be adjudicated upon by the courts by way of judicial review[45] and if the parliamentary scrutiny accorded to it is adequate. In 2015, the House of Lords rejected the government's Tax Credit Regulations, prompting a review of the relationship between the two Houses of Parliament and calls by two Committees of the House of Lords for there to be an in-depth examination of the use of, and the adequacy of scrutiny of, secondary or delegated legislation. On this issue see further below.

Under the doctrine of parliamentary sovereignty, the validity of Acts of Parliament cannot be questioned.[46] Subordinate legislation, however, can be reviewed, provided that the jurisdiction of the courts has not been excluded – or 'ousted' – in order to determine its compatibility with the enabling Act. Such exclusion of review is rare and, to ensure immunity from review, the exclusion clause would have to be unambiguous on the face of the parent Act. Of equal importance to the possibility of successful challenge in the courts is the breadth of discretion conferred on the delegate by the Act. If a statute conferred powers on a Minister to make regulations 'whenever the Minister thinks fit' or (say) to award compensation for injury 'under circumstances to be determined by the Minister', the grant of discretion is so wide as to be virtually unreviewable by the courts. Also important is that delegated legislation should not impose retrospective liability on citizens, or be so vague as to be unintelligible. Further, it is necessary that the power granted is conferred on an identifiable delegate in order that the exercise of power be challengeable. On this latter point, the Emergency Powers Act 1939 provided for differing levels of delegation. The Act provided that regulations might empower any authority on persons to make orders, rules and bylaws, for any of the purposes for which the Defence Regulations might themselves be made. Ministerial orders were issued

---

43 The Donoughmore-Scott Committee.
44 *Report on Ministers' Powers*, Cmnd 4060, 1932, London: HMSO.
45 See Chapters 23 to 25.
46 **Pickin v British Railways Board** (1974). See Chapter 6.

under the regulations, directions issued under the regulations and licences issued under the directions. Such sub-delegation breaches the rule that a person or body to whom powers are entrusted may not delegate them to another, *'delegatus non potest delegare'*.

The Statutory Instruments Act 1946

The vast majority of delegated legislation is in the form of statutory instruments governed by the Statutory Instruments Act 1946. Section 1 provides that where any Act confers power on His Majesty in Council or on any Minister of the Crown, where that power is expressed as a power exercisable by Order in Council or by statutory instrument, the provisions of the Act apply.

Parliamentary scrutiny of delegated legislation[47]

The Statutory Instruments Act 1946 lays down the means by which an instrument may come into effect, but the method adopted will depend on that which is stipulated in the particular enabling Act. First, the parent Act may provide that the instrument be laid before parliament[48] but that no parliamentary action is needed. Second, the parent Act may provide that the instrument is subject to the 'negative resolution procedure'.[49] Under this procedure, the instrument can be laid before Parliament in its final form and come into immediate effect subject only to there being a successful move to annul the instrument. This move takes the form of a motion, known here as a 'prayer', for annulment of the instrument, which can be made within 40 days of the instrument being laid. Third, the enabling Act may stipulate that the instrument be laid in draft form and that it will come into effect only if a prayer for annulment is not moved successfully. The Statutory Instruments Act also provides for an 'affirmative resolution procedure'. If this is adopted, the instrument may either come into immediate effect, subject to subsequent approval by Parliament, or be laid in draft form to come into effect if approved by Parliament.

Statutory Instruments are scrutinised by the following Committees:

- the Joint Committee on Statutory Instruments;
- the House of Commons Regulatory Reform Committee;
- the House of Lords Delegated Powers and Regulatory Reform Committee;
- the House of Lords Secondary Legislation Scrutiny Committee.

The choice of the procedure to be adopted lies with the government. The problem posed for Parliament is again one of time and opportunity. The affirmative resolution procedure is rarely adopted by government; the negative resolution procedure requires that Members of Parliament must be vigilant and astute if they (usually the Opposition) are to be aware that a particular instrument has been laid and are to be able to move a prayer for annulment within the 40-day period. Instruments made under the European Communities Act 1972 to give effect to Community law may be subject to either the affirmative or negative procedure. Since 1994–1995, instruments subject to affirmative resolution are automatically referred to a Public Bill Committee, unless the House orders otherwise. Instruments subject to the

---

47 See Beith, 1981; Hayhurst and Wallington, 1988; Hansard Society, 1993, Annex A.
48 Statutory Instruments Act 1946, s. 4.
49 Statutory Instruments Act 1946, s. 5.

negative resolution procedure, to which a prayer has been tabled, may be referred to a Public Bill Committee on a Motion by a Minister of the Crown.

Supplementing the above scrutiny methods is the Joint Select Committee on Delegated Legislation. The Joint Committee comprises seven Members of the House of Commons and seven Members of the House of Lords, and is chaired by a Member of the House of Commons. The committee is charged with examining all instruments laid before Parliament and those instruments for which there is no laying requirement. The grounds on which the committee will report to Parliament are:

(a)   that the instrument imposes a tax or charge;
(b)   that the parent Act excludes review by the courts;
(c)   that the instrument is to operate retrospectively;
(d)   that there has been unjustifiable delay in publication or laying;
(e)   that the instrument has come into effect in contravention of the rules of notice to the House;
(f)   that there is doubt as to whether the instrument is *intra vires*;
(g)   that the instrument requires clarification;
(h)   that the instrument's drafting is defective.

The committee examines over 1,000 instruments per session. Less than one per cent are reported to Parliament, and few are debated. The strength of the committee's work lies not in its reports to Parliament and any consequent action but rather in its scrutiny of instruments and drawing the relevant government Department's attention to defects in instruments.[50]

The Legislative and Regulatory Reform Act 2006 makes provision for a Minister to make amendments to primary or secondary legislation in order to remove or reduce burdens imposed on businesses or charities. A burden is defined as a financial cost; an administrative inconvenience; an obstacle to efficiency, productivity or profitability; or a sanction which affects the carrying on of any lawful activity. The burden must arise – directly or indirectly – from legislation.[51] The grant of power to Ministers to amend primary legislation is known as a 'Henry VIII power': the power to change the law without parliamentary action. These powers have become increasingly common and create concerns over the separation of powers and the reduction in parliamentary control. This problem has been addressed by the introduction of the 'super-affirmative procedure' which provides for greater parliamentary scrutiny.[52] Under this procedure, a proposal for a statutory instrument is laid in the form of a draft instrument, usually with an explanatory statement. A period of (usually) 60 days is then allowed for parliamentary scrutiny and report. Following the expiry of that period and consideration of any reports or representations made about the Draft, the Minister may amend the Draft, or if he or she wishes to proceed without making any amendments, a statement must be made to that effect. The Minister may then make the order, but only if it is approved by a resolution of each House of Parliament.[53]

An example of a Henry VIII power is section 10(3) of the Human Rights Act 1998, which provides that a Minister may – subject to certain conditions and restrictions – 'by order make such amendments to the primary legislation as he considers necessary'.

---

50 The House of Lords Scrutiny Committee for delegated legislation is discussed in Chapter 16. On delegated legislation and the Human Rights Act 1998, see Chapter 18.
51 See for example the Regulatory Reform Order 2007, No. 1889 which amends the Parliamentary Commissioner Act 1967, the Local Government Act 1974 and the Health Service Commissioner Act 1993 on which see Chapter 26.
52 Legislative and Regulatory Reform Act 2006, s. 18. See also the Localism Act 2011, s. 7.
53 See Erskine May, 2011, p. 672.

The courts will examine closely the grant of a Henry VIII power. For example in **R (Public Law Project) v Lord Chancellor** (2016) Lord Neuberger PSC cited with approval the dicta of Lord Donaldson MR in **McKiernon v Secretary of State for Social Security** (1989). Lord Donaldson stated in relation to Henry VIII powers that:

> Whether subject to the negative or affirmative resolution procedure, [subordinate legislation] is subject to much briefer, if any, examination by Parliament and cannot be amended. The duty of the courts being to give effect to the will of Parliament, it is, in my judgment, legitimate to take account of the fact that a delegation to the Executive of power to modify primary legislation must be an exceptional course and that, if there is any doubt about the scope of the power conferred upon the Executive or upon whether it has been exercised, it should be resolved by a restrictive approach.[54]

 Pause and Reflect

Do you consider that there is adequate scrutiny of secondary (or delegated) legislation? What improvements, if any, should be made to ensure that delegated legislation is confined to the purpose intended by the relevant Act of Parliament?

Scrutiny of Legislation by the House of Lords

Some Bills will start their life in the House of Lords and, once successfully passed in the Lords, will pass to the Commons for debate and scrutiny. Law Reform Bills, in particular, are regularly introduced in the House of Lords, under the aegis of the Lord Chancellor. The majority of Bills, however, start their parliamentary life in the Commons. Detailed consideration will be given to the House of Lords' role in legislation in Chapter 16. Note, however, that unless the Parliament Act procedure is used (which limits the role of the House of Lords in relation to legislation), Bills which have completed their passage in the Commons are passed to the House of Lords, which employs, with some notable differences, the same legislative stages as the House of Commons. The House of Lords may propose amendments to Bills, the acceptance or rejection of which will be a matter for negotiation between the two Houses. Note that by convention the House of Lords will not oppose a Bill which reflects government policy which has been endorsed by the people – 'mandated' – in a general election.

In relation to delegated legislation, as discussed in Chapter 16, the House of Lords participates in the Joint Committee on Statutory Instruments (JCSI), and has two committees which scrutinise delegated legislation: the Secondary Legislation Scrutiny Committee (SLSC) and the Delegated Powers and Regulatory Reform Committee. The JCSI checks that ministerial powers are being exercised in accordance with the parent Act and not in some unexpected or unusual way. The SLSC considers the merits of SIs and reports to the House on any which are legally or politically important, or which raise issues of public policy, or are in some way an inappropriate use of delegated legislation. The Delegated Powers Committee considers Bills going through the House and reports whether there are any powers being inappropriately delegated or whether they are subject to an inappropriate level of scrutiny by Parliament.

---

54 At para. 140.

The Parliament Acts 1911 and 1949 do not apply to delegated legislation. As a result, if the House of Lords rejects a Statutory Instrument, it cannot come into effect even if the House of Commons has approved it. However, there are constitutional conventions which regulate the relationship between the House of Lords and House of Commons. First, there is a convention (formalised by two Resolutions of the Commons in the seventeenth century) that the House of Lords, recognising the primacy of the Commons over finance, will not block financial measures in Bills. If there is an attempt by the House of Lords to amend a financial measure, the Commons will reject it on the grounds that it goes against the financial privilege of the Commons. There is also the Salisbury-Addison convention, by which the House of Lords will not block a Bill which gives effect to a commitment made by the government in its election manifesto. It is established that, with few exceptions, delegated legislation cannot be amended. There has, however, been debate and uncertainty over whether there is a convention that the Lords will not reject delegated legislation. There have been five occasions since 1968 on which SIs have been rejected by the House of Lords. The most recent example of rejection which caused a political and constitutional uproar, and calls for reform of the powers of the House of Lords, occurred in 2015.

As part of its cost-saving programme, the government intended to cut tax credits – benefits payable to those on low incomes. The Draft Tax Credits (Income Thresholds and Determination of Rates) (Amendment) Regulations 2015 were rejected by the House of Lords.[55] The government immediately established an inquiry, chaired by Lord Strathclyde, into the question of the balance of power between the two Houses. The Strathclyde Review suggested three options for reform.[56] The first was that the power of the House of Lords over delegated legislation should be removed. The second option was that the convention should be codified in a formal Resolution. The third was that there should be a new procedure, set out in statute, whereby the House of Lords could formally invite the House of Commons to 'think again' about a particular measure before insisting on passing the legislation. The first option would seriously reduce the ability of the Lords to scrutinise legislation, and would encourage governments to increase the use of delegated legislation, secure in the knowledge that it could not be challenged in the Lords. The second would not provide any certainty, given that Resolutions can be superseded. Accordingly it was the third option which Lord Strathclyde favoured.

These proposals have, however, met with criticism. The House of Lords Constitution Committee criticised the terms of reference of the Strathclyde inquiry.[57] In its view, rather than focusing on the balance of power between the two Houses, the inquiry should have focused on the wider issues relating to delegated legislation, and in particular the relationship between Parliament and the Executive which lies at the heart of concerns over delegated legislation. The Committee recommended that the government should initiate a more comprehensive review of delegated legislation rather than proceeding with the Strathclyde proposals. In relation specifically to the Tax Credit secondary legislation, the Committee called on the government to 'consider the extent to which it is appropriate to be making legislative changes with significant budgetary implications through delegated legislation'. The Delegated Powers and Regulatory Reform Committee of the House of Lords also responded to the Strathclyde Review. In its Report,[58] the Committee expressed concern over 'the extent to which government uses unamendable secondary legislation to achieve policy goals'. In particular the Committee criticised the use of 'skeleton bills', 'skeleton provisions in bills' and

See further Chapter 16.

---

55 The Labour and Liberal Democrat opposition parties united to defeat the Conservative government.
56 *Strathclyde Review: Secondary Legislation and the Primacy of the House of Commons*, Cm 9177, December 2015.
57 Constitution Committee, Ninth Report, 2015–16, HL Paper 116.
58 *Special Report: Response to the Strathclyde Report*, 25th Report, March 2016, HL Paper 119.

the use of Henry VIII powers and concluded that 'something needs to be done to re-set the boundary between primary and secondary legislation'. The Committee recommended that a Joint Committee should be established to undertake an in-depth examination of the scrutiny of delegated legislation.

The Royal Assent

See Chapter 5.

Receiving the Royal Assent represents the final stage in the enactment of legislation. The Royal Assent is a prerogative act; for further discussion of this, see Chapter 5. The giving of the Royal Assent is not a matter which involves the monarch personally. No monarch since 1854 has given the Royal Assent, although the power to do so still remains. When Royal Assent is required, the Lord Chancellor submits a list of Bills ready for the Assent. In the House of Lords, attended by the Commons with the Speaker, the Clerk of the Parliaments reads the title of the Bills for assent and pronounces the assent in Norman French. Once assent has been given, it is notified to each House of Parliament by the Speaker of the House.[59] It is a constitutional convention that the Royal Assent is granted once a Bill has passed both Houses of Parliament, or, where the Parliament Act procedure has been employed, once the Bill has been approved by the House of Commons.

See Chapter 8.

Parliament and European Union Legislation Under the terms of the EU (Withdrawal) Act 2018 at the end of the transition/implementation period (31 December 2020) existing EU law will be transposed into domestic law and Parliament will then be able to retain, amend or repeal that law. For further discussion, see Chapter 8.

Both Houses of Parliament had an EU Select Committee. The committees considered delegated legislation which was being introduced to give effect to European law and also scrutinised legislative proposals for future European law.

Summary

Parliament – the Crown, House of Commons and Lords – is the sovereign law-making body in the United Kingdom. It may make law on any subject matter, except where limited by obligations such as the European Union and other international agreements, and non-legal constraints such as economics and public opinion. The origins of law lie primarily in government policies, but are also supplemented by a vast number of reform and other public interest groups outside Parliament.

Bills may be Public, Private or Hybrid, and in addition there are Private Members' Bills. In addition to Primary Bills, there is secondary or delegated legislation which fills in the detailed rules and provisions of an Act of Parliament. Bills may be introduced into either House of Parliament, and the proceedings are similar in both Houses, with a formal first reading; a second reading, which deals with the principles of a Bill; a Committee stage, where the details of the Bills are scrutinised and amendments proposed; a report stage; and the formal third reading. The Royal Assent is required to make a Bill into an Act of Parliament.

As discussed in more detail in Chapter 16, the powers of the House of Lords are restricted by the Parliament Acts 1911 and 1949 which ensure that the elected House of Commons has priority (with limited exceptions) over the House of Lords.

---

59 Royal Assent Act 1967.

In addition to enacting law, Parliament must also scrutinise and approve the financing of government. The procedures designed to approve finance are complex and designed more to ensure openness and publicity rather than real control over finance, which is largely under government control.

Further Reading

Blackburn, R and Kennon, A, *Parliament: Functions, Practice and Procedures*, 2nd edn, 2003, London: Sweet & Maxwell.

Brazier, A, Flinders, M and McHugh, D, *New Politics, New Parliament? A Review of Parliamentary Modernisation Since 1997*, 2005, London: Hansard Society.

Cowley, P and Stuart, M, 'Parliament: a few headaches and a dose of modernisation' (2001) 54(3) *Parliamentary Affairs* 442.

Oliver, D, 'Improving the scrutiny of bills: the case for standards and checklists' [2006] *Public Law* 219.

Oliver, D, 'Reforming the United Kingdom Parliament' in J Jowell and D Oliver (eds), *The Changing Constitution*, 7th edn, 2011, Oxford: Oxford University Press.

Silk, P and Walters, R, *How Parliament Works*, 6th edn, 2006, London: Longman.

Chapter **15**

Scrutiny of the Executive

Chapter Contents

Learning Objectives

By the end of this chapter you should be able to:

- [ ] explain the relationship between the government and Parliament, particularly the House of Commons;
- [ ] explain the doctrine of collective and individual ministerial responsibility (discussed in Chapter 10);
- [ ] discuss the various parliamentary procedures which facilitate scrutiny of policy and administration;
- [ ] discuss the role of Select Committees and public inquiries in the scrutiny of government;
- [ ] discuss, briefly, the significance of the Freedom of Information Act;
- [ ] explain, in outline, the role and scope of judicial review of administrative action (discussed in detail in Chapters 23 to 25).

Introduction

The structure of central government, the concept of ministerial responsibility and the composition of the House of Commons are considered in Chapters 9, 10 and 13 respectively. It will be recalled that the Commons comprises Her Majesty's Government, which is drawn from the political party winning the largest number of seats at a general election, government backbenchers, Her Majesty's Loyal Opposition, comprising the Leader of the Opposition and Opposition spokesmen, who comprise the shadow Cabinet, and Opposition backbenchers and Members of other minority political parties.

In this chapter, the procedures by which the House of Commons scrutinises government action are discussed. Consistent with the doctrine of responsible government, the accountability of government towards the democratic legislature is of fundamental importance in ensuring that the government acts under the law and in accordance with the principles of constitutionalism and democracy. In order to evaluate the role of Parliament in ensuring compliance with these constitutional doctrines, the procedural mechanisms of the House must be examined.

It should be noted that scrutiny of both legislation and government administration is also undertaken in the House of Lords. The House of Lords' procedures are discussed in the following chapter.

Question Time[1]

Question Time in the House of Commons is one of the most publicised features of Parliament and represents one of the principal means by which information is obtained from Ministers by Members of Parliament and the public, and of underpinning individual ministerial responsibility.

Standing Orders provide that from Monday to Thursday the first hour of business is set aside for Question Time.[2] On these days, Ministers from several Departments may answer questions, appearing on a rota, determined by the government,[3] which ensures that Departments feature in Question Time approximately every five weeks. Questions selected for the day are determined by 'the shuffle', a computerised system.

The Speaker calls the first Member listed on the Order of Business. The Minister then answers the question, and the Member is able to ask a supplementary question. When that has been answered, the Speaker may then call on other Members to ask their supplementary questions. The time allocated to supplementary questions is within the Speaker's discretion. Currently, about 15 to 20 questions are answered orally on each day. The effect of the supplementary is that a Member is able to pose a question for which no notice has been given.

Questions may be put to Ministers for either oral or written answers.[4] Questions requiring written answers, which are to be printed in the *Official Journal*, are marked with a 'W' and are subdivided into ordinary written questions and 'Named Day' questions. Ordinary questions do not have to be answered within a specific time, but by convention they will be answered within seven days. 'Named Day' questions must receive an answer on the date specified by the Member. Those questions tabled for oral answer are printed on the Order Paper of the day. Only a few of the many questions put forward will receive an oral reply. However, those that do not receive an oral reply will receive a written reply published in

---

1 See Griffith and Ryle, 2003; Erskine May, 2011.
2 No question shall be taken after 3.30 p.m., other than where the Speaker deems it to be a matter of urgency relating to matters of public importance or to the arrangement of business of the House.
3 HC Deb 898 (1975–1976), London: HMSO. See Erskine May, 2011, Chapter 16.
4 Standing Order No. 21.

the Official Report of the House. The number of questions which an individual Member of Parliament may have pending at any one time is eight during a period of ten sitting days, and not more than two on any one day, of which not more than one may be addressed to any one Minister.[5] Answers to questions may be refused on the grounds of national security or commercial confidentiality or on the basis of their disproportionate cost.[6]

The last quarter of each oral session of parliamentary questions is set aside for Topical Questions. The question to be asked is not submitted in advance and this allows for questions to be put on recent events or developments. Members are selected for Topical Questions by a 'shuffle'.

In relation to ordinary questions for written or oral answer, Question Time is not a spontaneous affair, and it should not necessarily be criticised for not being so. Members wishing to ask questions other than Topical Questions are required to give up to three sitting days' notice.[7] This time span for notice is designed to ensure both that there is adequate opportunity for Ministers to prepare answers and that the issue being raised is still fresh and relevant. Changes to Question Time agreed by the Commons and implemented in the 2002–2003 session included limiting the number of questions which may be put by a Member on any one day, reducing the number of questions for oral answer printed on the Order Paper, electronic tabling of questions (in the 2013–2014 session 84.9 per cent of questions were e-tabled) and oral questions being put to junior Ministers in Westminster Hall.

From 2003, cross-cutting questions have been introduced. These take place in Westminster Hall and cover issues which are the responsibility of more than one government Department. An example is Youth Policy, which falls under the responsibility of the Department of Culture, Media and Sport, the Department of Education, the Department of Health and the Home Office.

On occasion – and particularly near the end of a parliamentary session – questions may be answered in the form of 'I will write to the Honourable Member …' rather than receiving an oral response. Such replies have not been published in *Hansard* in the past, but placed in the House of Commons' Library for Members' use. These 'Will Writes' have attracted criticism from the Select Committee on Public Administration as being used to avoid answering questions.[8]

Prime Ministerial Question Time

Prime Minister's Question Time takes place on Wednesdays at noon, when the Prime Minister answers questions for 30 minutes.[9] Questions put to the Prime Minister simply request that the Prime Minister list his engagements for the day. Over 100 such questions may appear on the Order Papers; on occasions, this number has risen to over 200. The open question also avoids the possibility – given the rules of notice for questions – that a subsequent question put to the Prime Minister will be politically stale. The open question, therefore, provides a neutral peg on which to hang a supplementary, and real, question. Only two supplementary questions per Member are allowed. Supplementary questions may concern any matter for which the Prime Minister carries responsibility or matters which do not fall within any individual Minister's responsibility. For example, if a question is addressed to the Prime Minister which should

---

5 Erskine May, 2011.
6 The current limit for written questions is £850. There is no cost limit for oral questions. The average cost of a written question is £164; the average cost of an oral question is £450.
7 The period of notice for questions to the Northern Ireland, Scottish and Welsh Secretaries of State is four working days.
8 See the Committee on Public Administration Second Special Report, HC 853. The Committee also monitors responses to requests for information under the Freedom of Information Act 2000.
9 See HC Deb Vol. 295 Col. 349, 4 June 1997.

be addressed to the Secretary of State for Social Security, the Prime Minister will decline to answer and suggest that the matter be referred to the responsible Minister. Generally, however, the issue raised will be one of general government policy in relation to matters such as the economy, unemployment and European or other international affairs. The strength of Prime Ministerial Question Time lies in the lack of notice given and the need for the Prime Minister to demonstrate his competence across the full range of government policy.

The Leader of the Opposition does not table questions for oral answer to the Prime Minister. Instead, he is entitled to ask up to six questions to the Prime Minister and may raise virtually any aspect of government policy. For the observer, this is frequently Parliament at its best, providing the opportunity – for Question Time is televised – to witness the leaders of the two main political parties in oral combat. As Griffith and Ryle observe:

> here is experienced the direct confrontation of the Prime Minister and the Leader of the Opposition in its most concentrated and highly charged form. It is an oppor-tunity no Leader of the Opposition can afford to neglect. It is also the occasion when the Prime Minister can be most critically tested, and various commenta-tors or experienced observers have testified to how carefully the Prime Minister has to prepare for this ordeal. Success or failure on these occasions can greatly strengthen or seriously weaken the political standing of the two protagonists. [2003, pages 501–502]

See further
Chapter 13.

The rules concerning questions have been developed over time by the Speaker of the House, who is responsible for enforcing them. Only questions on matters which are directly within a Minister's responsibility may be put forward and in addition, by convention, there exists a range of issues which may not form the subject of questions in the House. The following matters are not subject to Question Time:

(a)   questions bringing the Sovereign directly before Parliament, or questions reflecting on the Sovereign;
(b)   questions concerning issues on which the Prime Minister has given advice to the Crown in relation to the royal prerogative: the grant of honours, ecclesiastical patronage, appointment and dismissal of Privy Counsellors;
(c)   questions not relating to the individual responsibility of the relevant Minister. Accordingly, questions relating to organisations under the control of authorities other than Parliament (for example, the Stock Exchange, trade unions and nationalised indus-tries) are not permitted;[10]
(d)   questions concerning matters which have been devolved to Northern Ireland, Scotland or Wales.

The following subjects are also excluded:

● local authorities and nationalised industries;
● personal powers of the monarch;
● internal affairs of other countries;
● questions which have previously been put forward, or on which a Minister has previ-ously refused to answer, or to which the answer is a matter of public record;
● defence and national security;

---

10 Erskine May, 2011, Chapter 16.

- Cabinet business, and advice given to Ministers by civil servants;
- questions seeking legal advice;
- questions which raise issues so broad as to be incapable of reply within the time constraints;
- trivial or irrelevant questions;
- questions aiming to criticise judges;
- questions on matters which are *sub judice*;
- questions posed in unparliamentary language.[11]

The volume of parliamentary Questions

In the 2016 to 2017 session, a total of 39,133 Questions were put down. Of these, 34,711 were for written answer and 4,422 for oral answer (of which 3,362 received an answer in the House). Figures such as these emphasise one of the most important functions of Question Time: the accountability of government. A superficial observation of Question Time may prompt scepticism about its value. The charge is frequently made that Question Time is no more than a theatrical occasion, with Ministers fully briefed by the Civil Service giving prepared answers to questions posed within the rules relating to notice and substance. Questions are not limited to the Opposition parties and may, accordingly, come from the government's own supporters. This feature leads to the comment that questions are planted by government supporters in order to give a Minister the opportunity to promote the government's views or boast about its achievements. To exaggerate such claims would be to miss a point of prime importance about Question Time: the provision of information. Every answer given, oral or written, becomes a matter of public record, thus providing a wealth of data about the workings of government.

Urgent questions

An Urgent Question[12] is an oral question put to a Minister without the need to observe the normal rules as to notice. Standing Orders define Urgent Questions as raising matters which are 'in the Speaker's opinion, of an urgent character, and relate either to matters of public importance or to the arrangement of business'.

Such questions enable a matter of urgency to be raised for immediate discussion in the period following Question Time. Because Urgent Questions take priority over other parliamentary business, rules provide that a Member who wishes to put such a question must give notice to the Speaker before noon on the day he seeks to put the question, and the Speaker has absolute discretion as to whether to allow or disallow the question to be put.[13] Many applications for an Urgent Question are made, but few are granted. In the 2016 to 2017 session there were 74 Urgent Questions put.

Emergency Debates

Under Standing Orders,[14] any Member of Parliament may apply to the Speaker to raise an urgent matter for debate.[15] If granted, the matter will be raised immediately after Question

---

11 Erskine May, 2011, Chapter 17.
12 Urgent Questions were previously termed Private Notice Questions.
13 See Erskine May, 2011.
14 Dating from 1967.
15 See Erskine May, 2011, Chapter 16(3).

Time and Private Notice Questions, if any. At that time, the matter is briefly introduced and a substantive three-hour debate will be arranged for the following day. Because emergency debates disrupt the parliamentary timetable, they are confined to matters deemed to be of urgent national importance, and applications are sparingly granted (normally only one or two per session).

Daily Adjournment Debates

At the close of the parliamentary day, under Standing Orders, the opportunity is provided for backbenchers to initiate a short debate on a matter of their choosing. Competition for a debate is keen and Members take part in a ballot held in the Speaker's Office for the opportunity. If successful, the Member may speak for 15 minutes on the chosen subject and the relevant Minister is given 15 minutes for reply. The subject matter for debate is as varied as are Members' interests. The matter raised may be one of relevance solely to the Member's constituency, or the matter may be related to a particular source of general concern.

 Pause and Reflect

Do you think that parliamentary questions are, or are not, a valuable constitutional tool for ensuring the accountability of government? Give reasons for your answer.

Early Day Motions

Behind this curious colloquial term lies one of the least well-known or evaluated parliamentary processes. An Early Day Motion (EDM) is a written motion tabled in Parliament requesting a debate 'at an early day'. Any Member of Parliament may table an EDM, on any subject matter, subject to a few procedural rules.[16]

Early Day Motions originated in the mid-nineteenth century. Before that time, the parliamentary timetable was relaxed and Members had adequate opportunity to raise matters for subsequent debate in the House. As pressure for time in the House increased, the practice developed of Members giving notice that they intended to raise a particular matter for debate at some future, unspecified, date. These notices were formally recorded from 1865 in the daily papers of the House and today appear on the Motions Notice Paper, which forms part of the daily 'Vote Bundle' – the working papers of the House.

The purpose of tabling an EDM is not only to express a view and request a debate, but also to test the strength of feeling in the House over the matter involved. An EDM may be tabled by one Member or by several, and other Members may add their names in support. Some EDMs are tabled by the Leader of the Opposition: for example, EDM No. 351 of 1978–1979, supported by five other senior Conservative Members, led to a debate on 28 March 1979, which resulted in the resignation of the government and the subsequent general election.

Once tabled, an EDM remains current for the duration of the parliamentary session and may or may not attract considerable support within the House. Between 1948–1949 and 1990–1991, 29 EDMs attracted over 300 signatures.

The rules and restrictions on EDMs are few, and are consistent with the general rules concerning motions. Thus, the motion must be worded in parliamentary language, must not

---

16 See Griffith and Ryle, 2003, Chapters 6 and 10.

relate to a matter which is *sub judice* and is limited to 250 words. Within these limits, a Member may table an EDM on any subject. Many EDMs are tabled by Members of all parties on a particular issue, and provide an important outlet for the expression of views across party lines.[17]

In terms of the number of debates which flow from EDMs, their success rate must be regarded as low. The EDM censuring the government tabled by the Rt Hon Mrs Thatcher in 1979 is a rarity, both in terms of securing a debate and in the dramatic effect of signalling the fall of a government. The occasional success of the EDM was again seen in 1988 in relation to the Education Reform Bill 1988. There, two senior Conservative frontbench Members, Norman Tebbit and Michael Heseltine, tabled a motion calling for the abolition of the Inner London Education Authority, a matter which was contrary to the then policy of the Secretary of State for Education, Kenneth Baker. The EDM was supported by 120 other Conservative backbenchers and caused the Secretary of State to amend the Bill.[18]

Notwithstanding such rare examples of EDMs having important political and legal effects, the overall significance of the EDM should not be underestimated. Depending on the volume of support a particular EDM attracts, it represents an expression of the mood of the House across a whole spectrum of issues which places pressure on the government to respond. Furthermore, where the rules of the House prevent a Member from expressing a view in debate, perhaps because he cannot catch the Speaker's eye, or by means of a question, perhaps because of ministerial responsibility or because the subject matter falls within one of the excluded categories, the EDM may represent the only vehicle for expression.

Select Committees of the House of Commons

Select Committees in the House of Commons are of some antiquity, although the current structure of committees dates back to 1979. They take several forms and fulfil a number of different functions.[19] Some Select Committees relate to the running of the House of Commons itself and others relate to the procedures employed by the House, while a third class – the departmentally related Select Committees – fulfils an investigative and reporting function. In addition there may at any time be ad hoc Select Committees established to investigate and report on a specific matter. At any one time there will be a number of Joint Committees in existence, comprising Members from the House of Commons and House of Lords, which will examine specific topics, or give pre-legislative scrutiny to Bills. Three permanent Joint Committees exist: the Joint Committee on Human Rights; the Joint Committee on National Security Strategy; and the Joint Committee on Statutory Instruments (delegated legislation).

The 'domestic' committees include the following: Accommodation and Works, Administration Committee, Broadcasting Committee, Catering Committee, and Finance and Services Committee. The committees relating to procedures include the Modernisation Committee, Procedure Committee, Liaison Committee and the Information Committee. While the Procedure Committee keeps all Commons' procedures under review, the Modernisation Committee is specifically charged with examining and recommending changes to procedures. The Information Committee advises the Speaker on information technology. The Liaison Committee is made up of the Chairpersons of all the Select Committees and works to ensure that there is an efficient distribution on the workload of departmentally related committees (on this committee see below).

---

17 In the 2013–2014 session, there were 1,336 EDMS tabled.
18 EDM 563; Notices of Motions, 1987–1988, p. 3519.
19 For Select Committees in the House of Lords, see Chapter 16.

Scrutinising the efficiency and effectiveness with which government Departments and other public bodies have used their resources is the Public Accounts Committee.[20] The Public Administration Committee has the task of examining the reports of the Parliamentary Commissioner for Administration and the Health Service Commissioners for England, Scotland and Wales, and the Parliamentary Ombudsman for Northern Ireland. Additionally, the Public Administration Committee also considers matters relating to the Civil Service. Monitoring the privileges of Parliament and the conduct of Members of Parliament is the Committee on Standards and Privileges, discussed in Chapter 17. Examining delegated legislation is the task of the Select Committee on Statutory Instruments, which works closely with the Joint Committee on Statutory Instruments discussed in Chapter 14. There is a European Scrutiny Committee which scrutinises European Union documents, decides which issues require debate and monitors the activities of UK Ministers in the European Council. There is also an Environmental Audit Committee, which has the task of monitoring the contribution made by government Departments and public bodies towards environmental protection and sustainable development.

Powers and functions of Select Committees

The functions of departmentally related Select Committees are defined as being to examine matters within the Department and to report to the House. To fulfil their tasks, committees have the following powers:

(a)   to send for persons, papers and records;
(b)   to sit notwithstanding any adjournment of the House;
(c)   to adjourn from place to place;
(d)   to appoint specialist advisers, either to supply information which is not readily available or to elucidate matters of complexity within the committee's terms of reference.

Most Select Committees have 11 members. The scope of power granted to Select Committees is very broad. It is for the committee to determine, within the confines of the work of the Department, what subject matter to examine and to determine what evidence the committee needs to assist in its examination. To facilitate the working of Select Committees, each has a permanent staff of some three to four, and some committees have the power, under Standing Orders, to establish sub-committees.

The Liaison Committee

The task of coordinating the work of Select Committees falls to the Liaison Committee, first established in 1967, the membership of which comprises all the Chairmen of the departmentally related Select Committees, and the Chairmen of the Public Accounts Committee and the European Legislation Select Committee. Its role is defined as being:

(a)   to consider general matters relating to the work of Select Committees; and
(b)   to give such advice relating to the work of Select Committees as may be sought by the House of Commons Commission.

---

20 See further p. 377.

In 2003 the Prime Minister agreed to meet twice a year with the Liaison Committee to discuss matters of mutual concern.

Membership of Select Committees

Membership of Select Committees, unlike that of standing committees, lasts for the life of a Parliament, thus providing stability of membership and the opportunity for Members to develop a degree of expertise in the subject matter. Membership is largely limited, by convention, to backbenchers. The only Ministers who are Members are the Leader of the House,[21] the government Deputy Chief Whip[22] and the Financial Secretary to the Treasury.[23] Opposition frontbench spokesmen are not appointed to Select Committees.

Competition for membership of Select Committees is keen, particularly for the high-profile committees. With effect from 2010, members of Select Committees are elected by their political parties, using a secret ballot 'by whichever transparent and democratic method they choose'.[24]

Committee chairmanship

The chairs of Select Committees may be from government or opposition parties. The House of Commons' Reform Committee recommended that Chairs should be directly elected by Members of Parliament, rather than chosen by the Party Whips as previously. The majority of Select Committee chairs are now elected by fellow MPs. Candidates may be elected unopposed. If there is a contest, election is by secret ballot using the Alternative Vote system.

The significance of the sharing of chairs between government and opposition parties lies in the attempt to minimise party-political conflict, in order to increase the effectiveness and efficiency of the scrutiny to be brought to bear on government Departments. Once appointed, the chairman acts with complete impartiality. Select Committees are designed to operate on the basis of broad consensus as to aims and objectives, and to produce a single authoritative report to Parliament as a whole. It is not usual for the committee to vote on party lines, although, in highly controversial matters, this may occasionally be inevitable. If the committee intends to be critical of the government in its report, it is necessary for at least one Member of the government party to agree with the criticism(s).

The work of Select Committees illustrated

The inquiries undertaken by Select Committees are both broad ranging and in depth. It is entirely a matter for the committee to determine what subject to investigate and, accordingly, every aspect of government administration is potentially susceptible to inquiry. In the past, for example, Select Committees have inquired into the conduct of the Falklands War[25] and the banning of trade union membership at the Government Communication Headquarters (GCHQ).[26] The committees have investigated such matters as the Westland Helicopter affair, arms to Iraq, salmonella in eggs and the loss of the Maxwell pension funds, on which see

---

21 Services Committee.
22 *Ibid.*
23 Public Accounts Committee.
24 House of Commons Resolution, HC Deb Col. 1095, 4 March 2010. See House of Commons Library Standard Note SN/PC/3719, *Nominations to Select Committees*, 2010.
25 HC 11 (1984–1985), London: HMSO.
26 HC 238 (1983–1984), London: HMSO.

further below. The wide-ranging nature of inquiries undertaken is illustrated in the subject matter chosen by the Home Affairs Committee in 2091–2020:

Home Affairs Committee inquiries (a sample)
- Government preparation for Covid-19 (coronavirus);
- MacPherson Report: 21 years on;
- Channel crossings: migration and asylum-seeking routes through the EU;
- Police conduct and complaints.

The cooperation of government
It has been seen above that committees have the power to send for 'persons and papers'. The work of Select Committees would be much impaired if the committee was obstructed in its attempt to gain access to evidence. The Select Committee on Procedure had suggested, *inter alia*, that there should be power to compel Ministers to attend and to give evidence. That recommendation was rejected by the government, on the basis that Select Committees should not have power to issue orders to Ministers – such a power lay with the House alone. Accordingly, there is no formal requirement that the government cooperate with Select Committees. However, the Leader of the House has undertaken that: 'every Minister, from the most senior Cabinet Minister to the most junior Under Secretary, will do all in his or her power to co-operate with the new system of committees and to make it a success'.[27] For the most part, governments do cooperate with the committees, but limits to this cooperation can be perceived through an examination of three instances.

The Westland affair
In the aftermath of the Westland Helicopter affair, during which both the Secretary of State for Defence, Michael Heseltine, and the Secretary of State for Trade and Industry, Leon Brittan, resigned,[28] three Select Committees inquired into the matter.[29] When the Select Committee on Defence announced its intention to inquire into the matter, the government refused to allow witnesses from the Department of Trade and Industry, in particular the Director of Information, to whom a leak of the Solicitor General's letter had been attributed, to give evidence to the committee. The government's justification for this refusal was that the giving of evidence by a senior civil servant to a parliamentary committee would have major implications for the conduct of government and for relations between Ministers and their civil servants. This refusal had two implications. First, it meant that Parliament was unable to check the accuracy of statements made by the Prime Minister in the House, or those made by Leon Brittan in relation to the leaked letter. The second implication was that the civil servants concerned were neither able to explain nor defend their actions.

Salmonella in eggs
In 1988, a junior Health Minister, Edwina Currie, resigned office, subsequent to public comments made about alleged contamination of eggs. Her remarks that 'most eggs produced in the country' were infected with salmonella had an immediate impact on the sale and consumption of eggs, causing financial damage to egg producers. The Select Committee on Agriculture invited Mrs Currie to give evidence to the committee, but she declined. Following

---

27 HC Deb Col. 45, 25 June 1979; Col. 1677, 16 January 1981.
28 See the discussion in Chapter 8. See also Hennessy, 1986a; Oliver and Austin, 1987; Linklater, Leigh and Mather, 1986, Chapter 11; Marshall, 1986a.
29 Defence Committee, HC 518, 519 (1985–1986), London: HMSO; Trade and Industry Committee, HC 176 (1986–1987), London: HMSO; Treasury and Civil Service Committee, HC 92 (1985–1986), London: HMSO.

an exchange of letters which involved the Select Committee chairman insisting that it was for the committee, and not Mrs Currie, to decide whether or not she should give evidence, Mrs Currie grudgingly agreed to appear. In the event, her evidence proved, as she had indicated that it would, unhelpful.

The Maxwell pension fund

During the 1991–1992 session, the Social Services Select Committee was inquiring into the mismanagement of pension funds by the Mirror Newspaper Group's recently deceased Chairman, Mr Robert Maxwell. Mr Maxwell's sons, both holding prominent positions in the Group before their father's death, and subsequently assuming control of the companies, were summoned to give evidence. The Maxwells refused, relying on a claimed right to silence in the light of imminent criminal charges and the risk of jeopardising their own fair trial. The committee chairman wanted the Maxwells to be charged with contempt of Parliament (see Chapter 17), but no action was taken.

Reform of parliamentary evidence rules

There is a problem with witnesses who attend but who give evidence which is either untruthful or which paints only half the picture. Since 1997, persons giving evidence are required to take a formal oath. Anyone found to have lied to Parliament may be reported to the Crown Prosecution Service with a view to prosecution for perjury, which, in the event of conviction, could lead to a maximum prison sentence of seven years. Where the person is a Member of Parliament, the committee will ask the Commons to vote to remove the Member's immunity from prosecution.

Select Committee reports

At the conclusion of a Select Committee inquiry, a report will be drawn up. The committee aims to produce an authoritative, unanimous report which is presented to Parliament. The degree of consensus over a particular issue within the committee membership will dictate the extent to which unanimity can be achieved.

Approximately one-third of all reports published will be debated on the floor of the House. This fact is one which also gives rise to criticism of Select Committee effectiveness, although it must be conceded that the time given for debate on reports has increased in recent years. Parliamentary procedure does not make specific provision for debate on reports. The Procedure Committee has suggested that eight days per session should be devoted to such debates but this proposal has not been acted upon. Sufficient, but not too much, weight should be attached to this alleged defect, and four arguments may be advanced which limit its impact. The first relates to the commitment undertaken by successive governments to respond to Select Committee reports. Such an undertaking does not, of itself, ensure that the recommendations of the committee will be implemented but it does ensure that the government will react to any criticisms made and proposals put forward. Members of the committee and other interested Members of Parliament, particularly the Opposition, will be slow to let an opportunity to criticise government pass. The second argument centres on the information gained through the process of the inquiry. It has been seen that Ministers may decline or refuse to answer questions fully, and that they can restrict the extent to which civil servants may give evidence. Where a Minister refuses to cooperate with a Select Committee he will inevitably find media attention focused upon him, and some cogent justification for his reticence will have to be forthcoming. For the most part, evidence suggests that there is a high degree of ministerial cooperation with committees; this need not be seen as being necessarily willing participation but, rather, a matter of political prudence.

Third, it must be recognised that the reports emanating from Select Committee inquiries are matters of public record, available both to Members of Parliament and to the interested press and public. The information gathered in the course of an inquiry becomes public information, information which, before the introduction of the new committee structure, was often hidden from the public gaze. Finally, the absence of debate on the floor of the House in many cases will be justified by the pressure on the parliamentary timetable. It may well be the case that debate on all reports is desirable in principle. However, on many matters, opening debate to all Members of the House may involve a duplication of effort, with non-specialist Members of Parliament inexpertly attempting to re-analyse the information examined by the more specialised Select Committee Members.

 Pause and Reflect

To what extent do backbenchers have adequate opportunities to participate in the scrutiny of (a) government policy and (b) the administration of government?

Evaluation

An evaluation of the work of Select Committees in relation to the fundamentally important question concerning the accountability of government must be approached with caution. The outcome of an appraisal is inevitably related to the expectations which the appraiser holds and, as a consequence, the evaluation of one commentator may not be the same as another's. Caution is also urged against the making of sweeping generalisations as to the effectiveness of Select Committees, which are diverse in nature and operation. Many factors are involved in the analysis: the extent to which media, and hence public, attention is focused on a particular enquiry; the sensitivity of the subject matter; the degree of political consensus within the committee; the extent to which governments are prepared to make time on the floor of the House to debate Select Committee reports; the extent to which Select Committee inquiries result in improved efficiency in government; and the extent to which government and other witnesses cooperate with the committees in the provision of information. All of these factors, and more, must be put in the balance before any reasoned conclusions can be reached.

Griffith and Ryle state that:

> there are clear indications that the existence of select committees has affected the way government business is conducted. [2003, 11–054]

> General assessment of the relative success or failure of select committees ... depends on differing expectations. On one matter, however, opinion is almost unanimous: select committees since 1979 have increased the flow of information coming out of Whitehall [i.e. government Departments] and this has resulted to some extent in debates being better informed both inside and outside Parliament. [2003, 11–056]

At the heart of any evaluation must lie the recognition of the inherent tension – already stressed in Chapter 14 in relation to the scrutiny of legislation – between the legitimate right of the government to govern and the equally legitimate right of Parliament as a whole to ensure the collective accountability of government and the individual responsibility of Ministers.

As seen above, failures within government Departments may be examined by Select Committees. They may also be subject to investigation by the Parliamentary Commission for Administration, on whose role and powers see Chapter 27. Alternatively, the government may establish a formal statutory or non-statutory inquiry into a matter, on which see Chapter 26. Judicial scrutiny may be effected through proceeding for Judicial Review, discussed in Chapters 23 to 25. The National Audit Office plays an important role in monitoring departmental finances. Finally, a government Department may initiate an inquiry into a particular matter.

 Pause and Reflect

How effective are Select Committees in the scrutiny of government policy and administration? What are the limitations, if any, to their effectiveness?

Government Openness and Government Secrecy

The issue of the confidentiality of Cabinet papers has been discussed in Chapter 2. More generally, the issue of confidentiality of government papers gives rise to questions about the extent to which the government in the United Kingdom operates with an unnecessary degree of secrecy. Secrecy in government raises important questions for the individual citizen concerning the right of access to personal information stored by the government and also to the right of access of citizens more generally to documents concerning government of the state and of access to information about the policies and standards of service of public bodies.

Access to information[30]

The balance to be struck between the right of authorities to maintain confidential records and the right of individuals to access to that information is increasingly a matter of concern. There is no general right of access to data stored by the state, for example records maintained by the Police, Inland Revenue, National Health Service and Department of Social Security. Under the Official Secrets Act 1989, categories of information can never be disclosed. A limited right of access to personal files is granted under the Data Protection Act 1984.[31] Citizens in the United Kingdom are entitled to access to official records in certain categories of cases.[32] The information which can be disclosed is currently confined to computerised records – in other words, excluding manually created files, although access to these will be introduced in the future.

In any heavily regulated state, government Departments will have access to large amounts of personal data on its citizens. Tax authorities, social security offices, local authorities and driving licence authorities are but four major holders of personal information. The individual has two interests in personal records. The first is that information held about the individual should be accessible to him or her. The second is that the individual should be protected against disclosure of such personal data to third parties.

---

30 See Savage and Edwards, 1985; Reed, 2011.
31 As extended by the Data Protection (Subject Access Modifications) Health Order, SI 1987/1903.
32 On current proposals for greater access to information, see further below.

The protection of personal data

A range of statutes prohibit the unauthorised disclosure of personal data to third parties. Local authority records (relating to, *inter alia*, adoption, education, child support, housing, medical records and social security) are protected. Equally, in the finance industry, there is protection given to confidential information. In relation to such information, the government does not accept that there is a need to relax the restrictions on disclosure.

Access to personal data

The Data Protection Act 1984 provided that computer-held personal information should be made available to individuals, in order that the person concerned may check the accuracy of the data. The Data Protection Act 1998 replaced and repealed the 1984 Act. The Act applies only to personal data, defined in section 1(1), and confers the right to be informed of whether data is being held and to have that data communicated to the subject. The data covered by the Act is wider than under the 1984 Act and relates to both computer-held records and manual files. Disclosure may be refused where it would, *inter alia*, damage national security, or be counter to the interests of the prevention or detection of crime or the apprehension or prosecution of offenders (sections 28 and 29). The Information Commissioner supervises the operation of the Act, and may issue enforcement notices on any data controller who is not acting in accordance with the principles of the Act (see section 4 and Schedule 1). The Commissioner lays an annual report before Parliament. The Access to Personal Files Act 1987 provides that individuals have the right to inspect records relating to social services and housing tenancies. Medical records prepared for insurance or employment purposes are accessible under the Access to Medical Reports Act 1988. The Access to Health Records Act 1990 gives patients the right to see records held by general practitioners, health authorities or NHS trusts.

Access to public records

The Public Records Acts 1958 and 1967 provide for the inspection of public records at the Public Records Office after 30 years, unless there is justification for withholding them. The Lord Chancellor also has the power under the Act to order the release of documents at an earlier period if in the public interest. Under section 5 of the 1958 Act, records may be kept closed for a longer period.[33] The main classes of information not disclosed relate to population census returns, Ministry of Pensions First World War war pensions awards files and the Inland Revenue Stamps and Taxes Division registered files.

The Freedom of Information Act 2000 (FoIA)

In 1997, the incoming Labour government promised to inject greater openness into the machinery of government. Towards this end, a White Paper, *Your Right to Know: White Paper on Freedom of Information*, was published in December 1997.[34] The government intended that, for the first time, citizens should have a legal right to information and to the records in which that information is contained. In addition, an independent Information Commissioner would be appointed, who would be answerable not to Parliament, but to the courts. The right

---

33 Only 1 to 2 per cent of records remain closed for longer periods.
34 Cm 3818, London: HMSO.

applies throughout the public sector, as well as to some private organisations carrying out duties on behalf of government and privatised utilities. Citizens are entitled to information, subject to 'harm tests'. The Freedom of Information Act supersedes the Code of Practice on Access to Government Information and amends the Data Protection Act 1998 and the Public Records Act 1958. The Act was fully implemented in 2005, and applies to central government with effect from November 2002. The Act is the culmination of years of attempting to open up the processes of government. There are, however, a number of restrictions imposed on the right to information. In addition to the FoIA 2000, access to environmental information is provided for under the Environmental Information Regulations 2004 (EIR) which give effect to the EU Council Directive 2003/4/EC.

The FoIA for the first time confers on citizens a general right of access to data held by public authorities (section 1), including local government, National Health Service bodies, schools and colleges, the police and others. Freedom of information is a devolved matter and changes to the 2000 Act require the consent of the Welsh government and Assembly and the Northern Ireland Executive and Assembly. Scotland has its own Freedom of Information (Scotland) Act 2002. The Constitutional Reform and Governance Act 2010 amends section 37 of the 2000 Act to make communications with the Sovereign and Heir to the Throne, with effect from 2011, absolutely exempt.

Requests for information must be in writing, and the authority is under a duty to respond to the request within 20 working days of its receipt. A fee is payable and the duty to disclose does not arise until the fee is paid. The Act is regulated by the Information Commissioner (IC) to whom the public has a right of direct access (section 18; see further below).

The Act provides a list of exempted information, which considerably weakens the general principle of a 'right to know'. In total there are 24 exemptions to the general right of access. Information which is exempt from disclosure falls into two categories: that which is absolutely exempt and other information which requires the balancing of the public interest in maintaining the exemption and the public interest in disclosure. The exemptions are:

- Section 21: information accessible by other means;
- Section 22: information intended for future publication;
- Section 22A: information obtained in the course of, or derived from, a pre-publication research programme;
- Section 23: information supplied by, or relating to, bodies dealing with security matters;
- Section 25: information which must be exempt for the purpose of safeguarding national security;
- Section 26: information that would, or would be likely to, prejudice defence;
- Section 27: information that would, or would be likely to, prejudice international relations;
- Section 28: information prejudicial to relations between administrations within the UK;
- Section 29: information prejudicial to the economy;
- Section 30: information held for the purpose of an investigation or bringing proceedings;
- Section 31: information prejudicial to law enforcement;
- Section 32: information held within court, tribunal or public inquiry records;
- Section 33: information prejudicial to audit functions;
- Section 34: information prejudicial to the privileges of Parliament;
- Section 35: information relating to the formulation of government policy, Ministerial communications, advice by Law Officers or the operation of any Ministerial private office;
- Section 36: information prejudicial to the conduct of public affairs;

- Section 37: information relating to communications with the Royal Family and Household and honours;
- Section 38: information likely to endanger health or safety;
- Section 39: information within the scope of Environmental Information Regulations;
- Section 40: information which is personal data;
- Section 41: information which could lead to an actionable breach of confidence;
- Section 42: information to which a claim to legal professional privilege could be maintained;
- Section 43: information prejudicial to commercial interests or trade secrets;
- Section 44: information the release of which is prohibited by law.

A public authority may decline to provide information where the cost exceeds the 'appropriate limit' (section 11; the limits are prescribed and may be changed). The cost (in 2016) is £600 for central government Departments and £450 for other public bodies.

Where a request is refused, the requestor can appeal to the IC. The IC's Annual Report 2014–2015 states that the IC issued 1,305 decisions notices, of which 62 per cent (809) upheld the decision of the public authority and 14 per cent (189) were partially upheld; in 24 per cent (307), the decision of the public authority was overturned. Approximately 75 per cent of cases stop at the IC stage. Where the IC upholds the decision of the public authority, the requestor can appeal to the First-tier (Information Rights) Tribunal. Where the IC overturns the decision of the public authority, the authority can appeal to the Tribunal. If an appeal is unsuccessful, appeals on points of law can be heard by the Upper Tribunal, the Court of Appeal and ultimately the Supreme Court. In Northern Ireland appeals lie to the High Court of Justice; in Scotland, to the Court of Session. Decisions of the IC are subject to judicial review.

The Freedom of Information Act 2000 provides that a Cabinet Minister may overrule a decision of the IC, or a reviewing court or tribunal, on 'reasonable grounds'. The veto power is subject to judicial review. On this power see **R (Evans) v Attorney General** (2015) discussed below.

In **Independent Parliamentary Standards Authority v Information Commissioner** (2015) the Court of Appeal considered the meaning of 'information' within the context of section 1 of the FoIA 2000. Section 1(1) provides:

> Any person making a request for information to a public authority is entitled – (a) to be informed in writing by the public authority whether it holds information of the description specified in the request, and (b) if that is the case, to have that information communicated to him.

A journalist had requested the Independent Parliamentary Standards Authority (IPSA) to release original receipts submitted by three named MPs in respect of three specific claims for reimbursement of official expenditure. IPSA confirmed that it held the information and sent a transcript of redacted information contained in the receipts, in accordance with its policy not to publish images of receipts or invoices supporting claims. The journalist complained to the IC. The Commissioner upheld the complaint and required IPSA to provide the journalist with copies of the invoices on the basis that the information supplied did not contain all the recorded information to which the journalist was entitled under the Act. The First-tier Tribunal and the Upper Tribunal dismissed IPSA's appeal. On appeal to the Court of Appeal, the Court dismissed the appeal, holding that 'information' was an 'ordinary English word' to be construed as liberally as possible in accordance with the purpose of the Act. Presentational aspects of the information, including logos and letterheads, constituted information relevant to the identity of the supplier and genuineness of the document and fell within the definition of 'information' to which the journalist was entitled.

Interpretation of the scope of exemptions ultimately falls to the courts (on appeals see below). For example in **British Broadcasting Corporation v Sugar (No 2)** (2012), the Supreme Court interpreted section 7(1) of and Part VI of Schedule 1 to the Act which provided that the BBC was under a duty to disclose information on request only if it was 'held for purposes other than those of journalism, art or literature'. The applicant had sought disclosure of an internal report on the quality of its coverage of a particular area of news reporting. The Supreme Court ruled that if material was held to 'any significant degree for the purposes of journalism' and was also held for some other purpose, there was no duty of disclosure. In **Kennedy v Information Commissioner** (2014), the Supreme Court examined the exemption from disclosure relating to a statutory inquiry undertaken by the Charity Commission into a particular charity. Section 32(2) of the 2000 Act provides that information is exempt information 'if it is held only by virtue of being contained in (a) any document placed in the custody' or '(b) any document created by … for the purposes of the inquiry'. The Supreme Court, by a majority of five to two, ruled that the material remained exempt following the conclusion of the inquiry. However, the Supreme Court also ruled that while there was no remedy under the Freedom of Information Act, there was a common law principle of transparency, and that this formed the basis of a requirement of disclosure unless disclosure was 'demonstrably outweighed by any countervailing arguments that may be advanced'. Lord Pannick QC stated that if Article 10 of the European Convention on Human Rights confers a right of access to official information in addition to receiving and imparting information, then the 'blanket protection in section 32 needs to be amended'.[35]

The Act specifies the investigative and enforcement powers of the Commissioner. Where the Commissioner decides that a public authority has failed to communicate information, or to provide confirmation or denial, in a case where it is required to do so, the Commissioner may issue a decision notice specifying the steps which must be taken by the authority in order to comply (section 49(4)). The Commissioner may also issue enforcement notices requiring the authority to take, within a specified time, such steps as are required to comply. Where the Commissioner has issued a decision or enforcement notice in respect of the disclosure of information under section 13, a certificate may be issued by an 'accountable person' as defined in the Act, the effect of which is that a public authority need not comply with the Commissioner's notice (section 52). If an authority fails to comply with the Commissioner's notice, the Commissioner may so certify to the High Court or, in Scotland, the Court of Session, and the court may, having conducted a hearing, deal with the authority as if it had committed a contempt of court (section 53).

In **Browning v Information Commissioner** (2014) the Court of Appeal ruled that the First-tier Tribunal, when hearing an appeal against a decision of the Information Commissioner, was entitled to adopt a closed material procedure in which both a party to the proceedings and his legal representatives were excluded. That a party to proceedings could be excluded was clear from the 2009 Rules. What was unclear was whether his legal representatives could also be excluded. In ruling that this was lawful, the Court nevertheless stressed the importance of minimising the disadvantage to which the excluded persons were put by disclosing as much information as was consistent with them being able to make submissions to the tribunal, and by providing reasoned written decisions.

---

35 See 'Why right to freedom of information needs Strasbourg consideration', *The Times*, 20 November 2014.

In **R** *(Evans)* **v** *Attorney General* (2015) the issue was whether the decision of the Attorney General to issue a certificate under section 53(2) of the FoIA, which had the effect of overriding a decision of the Upper Tribunal, was lawful. The appellant was a journalist. He sought disclosure under the FoIA and EIR of a number of written communications between the Prince of Wales and various government Departments. The Departments refused to disclose the information and the IC backed the Departments. Mr Evans appealed. The Upper Tribunal, after six days of hearings, ruled that the communications (the 'advocacy correspondence') should be disclosed. The Attorney General then issued a certificate to render the Upper Tribunal's decision ineffective on the basis that it was in the public interest to do so. The Divisional Court dismissed Mr Evans' appeal, but the Court of Appeal upheld the decision of the Upper Tribunal, ruling that the Attorney General had failed to demonstrate reasonable grounds for his decision. The fact that the Attorney General disagreed with the decision of the Upper Tribunal was not sufficient; something more was required. Examples would include a material change of circumstances since the decision, or that the tribunal had made an error of fact or law. Here, the Attorney General 'simply disagreed with the evaluation made by the UT [Upper Tribunal]' and that was insufficient to amount to reasonable grounds. The matter then went to the Supreme Court. Dismissing the Attorney General's appeal, the Supreme Court, by a majority of five to two, held that the Attorney General was not entitled to issue the certificate as he did and that it was invalid. The Attorney General could not override a decision of a judicial tribunal or court on the basis that he disagreed with it. He had reached his decision on the basis of findings 'which differed radically from those made by the Tribunal' and he had not 'engaged closely' with the closely reasoned analysis of the Tribunal.

On constitutional principles and section 53 of the FoIA, Lord Neuberger PSC stated:

> A statutory provision which entitles a member of the executive (whether a Government Minister or the Attorney General) to overrule a decision of the judiciary merely because he does not agree with it would not merely be unique in the laws of the United Kingdom. It would cut across two constitutional principles which are also fundamental components of the rule of law.
>
> First, subject to being overruled by a higher courts or (given Parliamentary supremacy) a statute, it is a basic principle that a decision of a court is binding as between the parties, and cannot be ignored or set aside by anyone, including (indeed it may fairly be said, least of all) the executive. Secondly, it is also fundamental to the rule of law that decisions and actions of the executive are, subject to necessary well established exceptions (such as declarations of war), and jealously scrutinised statutory exceptions, reviewable by the court at the suit of an interested citizen. Section 53, as interpreted by the Attorney General's argument in this case, flouts the first principle and stands the second principle on its head. It involves saying that a final decision of a court can be set aside by a member of the executive (normally the minister in charge of the very department against whom the decision has been given) because he does not agree with it. [at paragraphs 51–52]

Amendments relating to public records

Part VI of the Act provides a statutory regime for access to public records, replacing the provisions of the Public Records Act 1958 relating to discretionary disclosure. It also provides for increased access to information contained in records more than 30 years old.

The independent Commission on Freedom of Information Report 2016

In 2015, the government established an independent, cross-party Commission on Freedom of Information. Its terms of reference were to review the working of the 2000 Act and to consider whether there is a satisfactory balance between access to information, the need for confidentiality and the burden imposed on public authorities by the Act. The Report on the operation of the Act was largely favourable. Recommendations made include strengthening the powers of the IC in relation to prosecution of offences relating to the destruction of information requested under the Act and increased penalties for the offence. It is also recommended that where an authority needs an extension of time for answering a request, that this should be restricted to a statutory period of 20 working days. On the executive's power of veto, the Commission recommended that the veto, i.e. the power to overturn the decision of the IC, should be exercisable where the executive takes a different view on the public interest requirement. Where the IC upholds a decision of the authority, the executive should have the power to issue a confirmatory veto and the only available challenge to that should be by way of judicial review. On appeals, the Commission found that there was duplication and that the role of the First-tier Tribunal should be removed. The IC should be the final decision-maker, subject to an appeal to the Upper Tribunal on a point of law.

On the application of the Act, the Commission recommended that it should apply to bodies providing public services under contract, but limits its extension to new contracts, and only those contracts where the annual value is £5 million or above.

Scrutiny of National Finance[36]

Any evaluation of Parliament's effectiveness in scrutinising government must incorporate discussion of the extent to which, and means by which, Parliament controls national finance, in terms of both taxation and expenditure. From a constitutional standpoint, the control over expenditure may be viewed as control over the government of the day and its policies. As WE Gladstone[37] remarked, 'expenditure flows from policy – to control expenditure one must control policy'. Constitutionally, therefore, Parliament's role in relation to spending is but one part of its wider role of scrutinising and calling the government to account. Hence, general debates, Question Time and select committees are all germane to this matter. The responsibility for expenditure lies with the Chancellor of the Exchequer. The manner in which Parliament scrutinises public expenditure is through the Public Accounts Select Committee, which examines reports of audits conducted by the Comptroller and Auditor General, who is head of the National Audit Office.[38]

Expenditure (supply)

Historically, the need to summon Parliament arose from the financial needs of the Crown.[39]

---

36 Note that the Budget Responsibility and National Audit Act 2011 imposes a duty on the Treasury in relation to the formulation and implementation of fiscal policy, and establishes the Office for Budget Responsibility (OBR) to examine and report on the sustainability of public finances. It produces economic and fiscal forecasts, for which the Chancellor of the Exchequer was formerly responsible. The OBR is independent of government. The Act also modernises the governance of the National Audit Office.

37 Prime Minister 1868–1874; 1880–1885; 1886; 1892–1894.

38 National Audit Act 1983.

39 See Chapters 5 and 6 on the historic struggles between Crown and Parliament.

The authority of the House of Commons sprang from, and is based on, its power to approve both the raising of taxation and expenditure. The governing maxim was, and remains, that 'the Crown demands, the Commons grant and the Lords assent to the grant of monies'.[40] The Bill of Rights 1689, Article IV, declared that raising money for the use of the Crown without Parliament's consent was unlawful.

Nowadays, for the 'Crown', must be inserted 'Ministers of the Crown'. Two propositions flow from this situation. First, that all charges – that is, proposals for the expenditure of monies – must be demanded by the Crown before they can be considered by Parliament. The demand for approval of monies comes today from Ministers, not backbenchers. Second, all charges must be considered by the House of Commons before they are approved. The proposals for charges come before the House in the form of resolutions which, once approved, must be embodied in legislation originating in the House of Commons but approved by both Houses.[41]

National revenue to cover the cost of government is derived from three main sources: taxation, borrowing and revenue from Crown lands. All revenue, of whatever kind, is credited to the Exchequer Account at the Bank of England in the form of the Consolidated Fund. All withdrawals must be authorised by statute. Under the Consolidated Fund Acts, approximately one-third of expenditure is authorised in permanent form and does not require annual parliamentary approval. Charges which are immune from this scrutiny are those payments for service which it is deemed should not be constantly drawn into the political arena for debate. For example, payment of interest on the national debt; salaries of judges of superior courts, the Speaker of the House of Commons, Leader of the Opposition, Comptroller and Auditor General and Parliamentary Commissioner for Administration; and payments to meet European Union obligations all fall under Consolidated Fund Services.

In contrast to Consolidated Fund Services are Supply Services. These cover the bulk of annual public expenditure and cover the needs of all government Departments and the cost of the armed forces. Provision for Supply Services requires annual approval. The following requirements must be satisfied. The government must lay before the House of Commons each year its estimates for the forthcoming financial year, in the form of resolutions. Once approved, these are translated into Bills – the Consolidated Fund Bills and Appropriation Bills. Money must be appropriated for specific purposes in the same session as that in which it is required by the government; thus, monies voted for one financial year cannot be applied to a subsequent year.

The Voting of Supply is announced in the Queen's Speech at the opening of the parliamentary session: 'Members of the House of Commons, estimates for the Public Service will be laid before you'. The Chancellor's Statement is made to Parliament, preceded by preparation of estimates by each government Department for the forthcoming financial year, and the Budget announced in the spring. The timing of the Budget is not, however, fixed and may be timetabled for spring or autumn.

Estimates

Government Departments assess the level of finance they require for the forthcoming financial year. The Treasury, however, will determine the sum a Department will receive.

Prior to estimates being settled, the Public Expenditure Survey Committee, under the responsibility of the Chief Secretary to the Treasury, will have reported on anticipated needs

---

40 Erskine May, 2011, and see Standing Order No. 46.
41 Subject to the Parliament Acts 1911–1949.

of Departments, and settled any disagreements between Departments. Its confidential report is sent to the Cabinet, which formalises expenditure plans.

Following parliamentary debate and approval, the Appropriation Bill will be drafted authorising withdrawal from the Exchequer Fund. In most parliamentary sessions, three regular Consolidated Fund and Appropriation Bills (and, where necessary, extra Consolidated Fund Bills) are put to Parliament for approval.

It will have been noticed that parliamentary approval for these financial Bills is 'without amendment or debate'. Thus far, there seems to be a virtual abandonment of Parliament's role in assenting to the 'demands of the Crown'.

Limited time for the scrutiny of expenditure estimates is provided under Standing Orders, which provide for five days per session to be allocated for the consideration of estimates. The estimates to be considered are selected by the Liaison Committee. The estimates selected for debate will generally be those into which the Select Committee has inquired and reported. Amendments may be tabled, including the reduction in the estimates.

Aside from this limited opportunity, any control which Parliament exercises is through the control of policy and the normal parliamentary mechanisms for the scrutiny of government policy and administration.

As the Public Accounts Committee Report to the House in 1987 admitted, 'Parliament's consideration of annual estimates – the key constitutional control – remains largely a formality'.[42] The Public Accounts Committee was established in 1861, for the purpose of examining accounts of Departments following the submission of reports from the National Audit Office.[43]

Taxation (ways and means)

In relation to taxation – ways and means – the role of parliamentary scrutiny is rather different. The initiative in tax policies lies with the Treasury, under the political direction of the Chancellor of the Exchequer.[44]

The starting point for the annual cycle is the Chancellor's Budget in the spring or autumn, in which, as Erskine May points out, 'the Chancellor develops his views of the resources of the country, communicates his calculations of probable income and expenditure and declares whether the burdens upon the people are to be increased or diminished'.

The Budget[45]

The Budget is the annual statement of tax proposals for the forthcoming year, together with the government's expenditure plans for the following three years. At the end of the Budget speech, the ways and means resolutions are tabled. These resolutions form the basis for the main debate on the Budget, which lasts for between three and five days. The Finance Bill is then introduced and, within three to four weeks, will receive its second reading. The Bill then stands committed, in part, to a Committee of the Whole House and to a standing committee. The size of the standing committee for consideration of the Finance Bill is larger than the normal composition, and will have about 30 to 40 Members.

---

42 HC 98 (1986–1987), London: HMSO, para. 2, cited in Griffith and Ryle, 2003.
43 See HC 634 (1974–1975), London: HMSO.
44 Nominally, the Prime Minister as First Lord of the Treasury.
45 The name derives from French: the *bougette*, or 'little bag'.

Income tax rates are effective only until the end of the tax year and require annual renewal under the Finance Act. The authority to collect taxes expires on 5 April each year. The Finance Act becomes law in July.

In **Bowles v Bank of England** (1913), the legality of taxation was considered. On 2 April 1912, the House of Commons passed a resolution approving the income tax rate for the year beginning 6 April 1912. The plaintiff had purchased stocks. The Bank deducted income tax from dividends due on 1 July at the new tax rate before the Consolidated Fund Act authorising the new rate had been passed by Parliament. The plaintiff sought a declaration that the Bank was not entitled to deduct the tax until approved by Parliament. The court ruled that a resolution could have no legal effect. **Bowles v Bank of England** led to the Provisional Collection of Taxes Act 1913,[46] which gives statutory authority to resolutions, as if imposed by Act of Parliament.

In **Attorney General v Wilts United Dairies Ltd** (1921), the Food Controller had, under a regulation of 1919, established a pricing structure for the issue of licences for milk purchase. The company claimed that the Food Controller had no power to impose conditions of payment in granting licences and that the condition amounted to a tax, which could not be imposed without clear and distinct legal authority. The court agreed, Lord Justice Atkin declaring that in view of the 'historic struggle' of the legislature to secure to itself the sole power to levy tax on its subjects, Parliament could not have intended to entrust a Minister with 'undefined and unlimited powers' of imposing charges upon the subject.

Note that the Finance Act is not usually a Money Bill for the purposes of the Parliament Act 1911, since it deals with wider matters than those listed in section 1(2) of the Act. Accordingly, unless certified by the Speaker to be a Money Bill, the Finance Bill will pass through the Lords in the usual manner. By convention, however, in relation to a Finance Bill, the House of Lords has relinquished any effective role in relation to taxation or expenditure.

The Public Accounts Committee (PAC)

This committee was first established in 1861. It has the power to examine the accounts 'showing the appropriation of the sums granted by Parliament to meet the public expenditure, and of such other accounts laid before Parliament, as the committee may think fit'.[47] The committee consists of not more than 15 Members, of whom four represent a quorum. While the composition of the committee represents (as does that of all Select Committees) the party-political strength of the House, the PAC functions in a non-partisan manner. By convention, the PAC's Chairman is a Member of the Opposition. The committee has the power to 'send for persons, papers and records' and to report from time to time.[48] The PAC issues approximately 30 to 40 reports per session.[49]

The principal function of the committee is to ensure that money is spent for the purposes intended by Parliament, and that money is spent effectively and economically. The committee holds many meetings in public. One day per session is set aside for debate of its reports. By critically examining the expenditure of Departments and assessing the extent to which expenditure produces value for money, the PAC exerts considerable influence on government.

---

46 Now, Provisional Collection of Taxes Act 1968.
47 Standing Order No. 122.
48 Standing Order No. 122, para. 2.
49 In May 1995, the PAC issued a highly critical report concerning delays and overspending by the Ministry of Defence in relation to defence equipment.

The Comptroller and Auditor General (CAG) and National Audit Office (NAO)[50]

The CAG is an officer of the House of Commons, appointed by the Crown, and can be removed from office for misbehaviour only on the successful moving of an address to both Houses of Parliament. As head of the National Audit Office, the CAG's function is to examine the economy, efficiency and effectiveness with which bodies have used their resources in the pursuit of policy.[51] The CAG appoints his own staff, who are not civil servants. The reports of the National Audit Office[52] are recorded in the Weekly Information Bulletin of the House of Commons and are available to the public.

The CAG audits and certifies the accounts of government Departments and bodies. Three significant areas of administration lie outside his jurisdiction: nationalised industries, local authorities and private bodies. The independence of the CAG from government, backed by the non-partisan PAC, provides a powerful watchdog over the administration of government and the expenditure of public money. National Audit Office reports are presented to Parliament and published. Most reports are considered by the Committee of Public Accounts in hearings at which senior officials are questioned. The Public Accounts Committee then publishes detailed recommendations to which the government formally responds. The National Audit Office then monitors the implementation of recommendations.

Summary

The scrutiny of government policy and administration is one of the key functions of Parliament, ensuring that government is accountable both to Parliament and the people. The principal forum for scrutiny is the House of Commons, although the House of Lords also plays a significant role.

Aside from the scrutiny of legislative proposals discussed in the previous chapter, the procedures for scrutiny are several, ranging from debates in the Chamber, Question Time, Opposition Days and Select Committees. In addition, on controversial matters an independent Committee of Inquiry may be established to investigate and report. Of the parliamentary procedures, the most in-depth scrutiny is effected by the departmental Select Committees. Each government Department has a related Select Committee which comprises backbench Members of Parliament. The party-political composition reflects that of the Commons overall. Select Committees may choose their own area of inquiry, and the government is committed to cooperation with the committees and also to responding to their reports. Select Committees do not, however, have the power to compel the attendance of Ministers.

Where there are serious concerns over the conduct of government, a public inquiry may be held to determine the facts and any culpability (on these see Chapter 10). The extent to which government is required to divulge information is regulated by the Freedom of Information Act.

📖 Further Reading

Allen, TRS, 'Law, democracy and constitutionalism: reflections on *Evans v Attorney General*' (2016) 75 *Cambridge Law Journal* 38.

---

50 See the Budget Responsibility and National Audit Act 2011, Pt 2.
51 National Audit Act 1983, ss 6 and 7.
52 And the corresponding Office for Northern Ireland.

Birkinshaw, P, *Freedom of Information: the 'Law, the Practice and the Ideal'*, 2010, Cambridge: Cambridge University Press.

Judge, D, 'Whatever happened to parliamentary democracy in the United Kingdom?' (2004) 57(3) *Parliamentary Affairs* 682.

Leopold, P, 'Standards of conduct in public life' in J Jowell and D Oliver (eds), *The Changing Constitution*, 7th edn, 2011, Oxford: Oxford University Press.

Maer, L and Sandford, M, *Select Committees under Scrutiny*, 2004, London: Constitution Unit, UCL.

Oliver, D, 'The challenge for Parliament' [2001] *Public Law* 666.

Sandford, M, *The System of Parliamentary Questions*, House of Commons Library Briefing Paper No. 04148, May 2015.

Tomkins, A, 'What is Parliament for?' in M Bamforth and P Leyland (eds), *Public Law in a Multi-Layered Constitution*, 2003, Oxford: Hart Publishing.

Wright, T, *British Politics: A Very Short Introduction*, 2nd edn, 2013, Oxford: Oxford University Press.

Chapter 16

The House of Lords

Chapter Contents

Learning Objectives

By the end of this chapter you should be able to:

☐ briefly explain the history of the House of Lords and its membership;

☐ outline the contemporary composition of the House of Lords;

☐ discuss the current functions of the House of Lords, with particular emphasis on legislation;

☐ explain the Parliament Acts 1911 and 1949;

☐ discuss twentieth-century reforms and the ongoing debate about further reform;
☐ evaluate the advantages and disadvantages which would accrue from having an elected House of Lords;
☐ give your own view on the preferred composition and powers of the House of Lords.

Introduction

The majority of liberal democracies have bicameral legislatures, or legislatures with two 'chambers' or 'houses'.[1] In the United Kingdom, the second chamber, the Upper House – or House of Lords – is currently an unelected chamber which has judicial, legislative, scrutinising and debating functions.[2] The justifications for, and advantages of, a second chamber, irrespective of the merits of the actual second chamber, are twofold. First, a second chamber provides a forum for reflection, and for 'second thoughts' on policies and legislative proposals. A second chamber provides for a *diffusion* rather than *concentration* of power within Parliament. Second, depending on the allocation of power between the two chambers, the Upper House plays a valuable role in the revision of legislation which has passed through the Lower House. Such revision is of particular significance where the Lower House is dominated by a government with a strong majority and also when – irrespective of the political make-up of the Lower House – procedures for curtailing debate have been employed. The scrutiny, and amendment, of Bills is equally important in improving the quality of the statute book. As will be seen below, the House of Lords plays a major role in statute revision. On occasion, such revision is contrary to the wishes of the Commons, which may choose to acquiesce in the Lords' amendments rather than employ the Parliament Act procedure which regulates the respective powers of the two Houses of Parliament. On other occasions, however, the revision undertaken in the Lords is either at the instance of the government itself, which may choose to introduce amendments to Bills in the Lords, or by Members of the House of Lords in order to improve the drafting of the Act.

The origins of the House of Lords lie in the councils summoned by English Kings in the eleventh, twelfth and thirteenth centuries, in order to give advice, decide on appeal cases and, under certain circumstances, make financial grants to the King. These 'King's Councils' had developed into a form which is recognisable today by 1295, then being an assembly of the 'three estates of the realm', the clergy, barons and commons – 'those who pray, those who fight, those who work'. From the earliest times, both spiritual and secular hereditary peers formed the membership of the House of Lords, by which name it became known in the sixteenth century. The House of Lords, until 1999, comprised a majority of hereditary non-spiritual (secular or temporal) peers, along with life peers (nominated members) and 26 Archbishops and Bishops.

See Chapter 14.

In 1999, the right of most hereditary peers to sit and vote in the Lords was abolished, leaving the Lords with a majority of nominated and no democratically elected members. Only Canada and Ireland have a predominantly nominated second chamber. Before the 1997 general election, the Labour Party had pledged to reform the House of Lords, regarding the role of the unelected House as incompatible with modern democracy. Rather than introduce wholesale reform immediately, however, the government decided on a two-stage reform. The first, which is largely but not wholly accomplished, was to remove the right of the hereditary peers to participate in Parliament. The second, which remained for the future,

---

1 Denmark, Sweden and New Zealand have unicameral Parliaments.
2 See Bromhead, 1958; Morgan, 1975; Shell, 1992. Under the Constitutional Reform Act 2005, the judicial function will be physically removed from the House of Lords.

was to decide precisely what form of composition was needed – whether fully elected or partly elected and partly nominated – and the powers which the reformed second chamber should have. In order to reach this decision, the government established a Royal Commission to consider the issue and make recommendations. While nothing came of those proposals, the election of a Coalition government in 2010 prompted a return to a further attempt at reform. Details of the reforms, achieved and proposed, are discussed below.

The Composition of the House of Lords

The House of Lords is unelected. While this situation is anomalous, undemocratic and anachronistic in an otherwise democratic society, there are some advantages in the arrangement which are too often overlooked. In essence, the value of an unelected chamber paradoxically lies in its lack of accountability to either the government of the day or the electorate, giving it an independence without which the value of its work would be diminished. However, whether such advantages actually flow from the House of Lords can only be evaluated through examining the impact which the House has, in its revising role, on government legislation. Prior to the removal of the majority of hereditary peers from the House, they represented a majority of peers and, being dominated by Conservative Members, had the ability to act in a party-political preferential manner – both to support a Conservative government's legislation and to frustrate that of a Labour government. It was perceptions such as this which caused, in part, the former Labour government to act swiftly to remove the hereditary element as a first stage of reform. In the event, some 92 hereditary peers remained in the Lords, and will so remain until the second stage of reform takes place. The uncompleted reform has led to the criticism that the government holds, through its selection of appointees, excessive powers of patronage, capable of undermining the independence of the Lords. A further factor in the composition of the House, which renders evaluation of its work more complex, is the considerable proportion of independent peers, or 'cross-benchers', who owe no political allegiance to any party.

The House of Lords has, under the Parliament Act 1911, the power to block any Bill attempting to extend the life of a Parliament.[3] This may be seen as no more than a constitutional 'backstop' against a potential abuse of power by government, and the life of a Parliament has indeed been extended in recent history in times of national emergency.[4] Such extensions, however, have been with the consent of the Lords. Any attempt by a government to suspend elections in order to protect its own political power would be blocked by the Lords, without whose consent such a Bill could not become law. On the other hand, any advantages which flow from the current composition of the Lords must be weighed in the balance against the demands of democracy. While an unelected second chamber having no role in the passage of legislation might be acceptable to some, an unelected second chamber with real – although ultimately limited – legislative power represents an affront to the idea of democratic government. It is for this reason that the issue of reform of the House of Lords has been for so long on the political agenda.[5]

---

3 Limited to five years: Parliament Act 1911, s. 7, amending the Septennial Act 1715, previously regulated under the Meeting of Parliament Act 1694.
4 For example, during the two World Wars.
5 For previous attempts to reform the Lords, and current reform proposals, see below.

The office of Speaker

Prior to the Constitutional Reform Act 2005, the office of Speaker of the House of Lords was fulfilled by the Lord Chancellor, appointed by the Crown on the advice of the Prime Minister. With effect from 2006, the speakership was taken over by the Lord Speaker of the House of Lords, elected by Members of that House. The Lord Speaker is elected for a five-year term and may not serve for more than two terms. The functions of the Lord Speaker are:

- to offer procedural advice to the House;
- to chair the Committee of the Whole House;
- to act as an ambassador for the House of Lords both in the United Kingdom and abroad;
- to ensure the security of the House.

The Lord Speaker, unlike the Speaker in the House of Commons, does not fulfil the function of ensuring order in the House or calling Members to speak. Furthermore, whereas the Speaker of the House of Commons plays a role in the legislative process and may rule that certain proposed amendments cannot be debated (perhaps on grounds of relevance), the Lord Speaker does not exercise this function and the House of Lords may decide to debate any and all amendments to Bills.

The Lord Speaker is politically impartial and independent of government.

Hereditary peers

Hereditary peers are created under the prerogative of the Crown of the advice on the Prime Minister. A peerage is created either by a Writ of Summons to the House or, more recently, under Letters Patent from the Sovereign which will define the line of succession, which invariably falls to the male heirs. A peerage created by a Writ of Summons will devolve to all heirs, thus enabling female successors to the title. Disputes concerning succession to a title are resolved by the House of Lords, through the Committee for Privileges. The evidence of blood tests is admissible in evidence.[6] A peerage cannot be surrendered other than under the disclaimer for life under the Peerage Act 1963,[7] on which see below. The disclaimer does not prevent the conferment of a life peerage.

In January 1998, there were 759 hereditary peers, out of a total membership of 1,272, comprising just under 60 per cent of the total.[8] All this changed, however, in 1999. Under the House of Lords Act 1999, the rights of most hereditary peers were removed. While it had been intended to remove the rights of all hereditary peers to sit and vote, threats of opposition to the House of Lords Bill from the majority of Conservative hereditary peers persuaded the government to allow 92 peers to remain. In the deal brokered by Viscount Cranborne, the then Conservative Leader in the Lords, the remaining hereditary peers would be elected by the hereditary peers themselves. A further seven former hereditary peers were returned to the House of Lords as life peers.

Life peers

Non-judicial life peers were not introduced until the Life Peerages Act 1958. The award of a peerage is one of the highest honours conferred in the United Kingdom. Approximately

---

6 See *The Ampthill Peerage Case* (1977); *Barony of Moynihan* (1997).
7 *Re Parliamentary Election for Bristol South East* (1964).
8 This figure excludes the 78 peers who had applied for leave of absence and 86 who had not applied for Writs of Summons.

one-third of former government Ministers will receive life peerages. Some former Prime Ministers – such as Sir Winston Churchill and Sir Edward Heath – refused the award of a peerage in order to remain in the House of Commons. Others will decline on point of political principle. Twice a year – at New Year and on the Queen's birthday – honours are awarded. There are, occasionally, honours lists announced to mark special occasions. Honours are also awarded on the dissolution of Parliament and, if there is a change of government, the outgoing Prime Minister will draw up a special honours list.

Once appointed, life peers tend to be more active in the House of Lords – in terms of both attendance in the House and participation in debate – than hereditary peers. Indeed, former Prime Minister Tony Blair made it clear that the appointment of new Labour life peers carried with it the responsibility to attend the House regularly in order to ensure that the government gets its key legislation through Parliament. However, the ever-increasing membership of the Lords remains a problem: with over 800 members in 2020 (compared with the Commons membership of 659), there is inadequate physical space for all members, and serious questions are raised over the quality of some of the members and their ability to make a contribution to legislation and the scrutiny of government.

Judicial peers

In 1856, for the first time, a life peerage was granted to a retired judge, although he was allowed neither to sit nor to vote in Parliament. In 1876, the Appellate Jurisdiction Act provided that two Lords of Appeal in Ordinary could be appointed as life peers, with both sitting and voting rights. The Lords of Appeal in Ordinary were originally appointed to add legal expertise to the House. In their judicial capacity, the Judicial Committee of the House of Lords represented the highest domestic court for civil appeals in the United Kingdom and for criminal appeals from England, Wales and Northern Ireland.[9] The Law Lords also sat as Members of the Judicial Committee of the Privy Council which has jurisdiction to hear appeals from a limited number of Commonwealth countries. The Law Lords played a role in the legislative and other functions but, by convention, did not participate in purely political debate.

See Chapter 4.

The Constitutional Reform Act 2005 reformed the arrangement to reflect a better separation of powers between the legislature and judiciary. As discussed in more detail in Chapter 4, a Supreme Court has been established in a place physically separated from Parliament. Justices of the Supreme Court are not allowed to sit in the House of Lords, although they may do so following retirement.

Lords spiritual

In addition to the hereditary and life peers, 26 Archbishops and Bishops of the Church of England sit in the Lords. The explanation for the presence of Anglican Archbishops and Bishops is historical. As seen above, until the dissolution of the monasteries, spiritual peers represented a majority in the House of Lords. Today, their presence is explained both on the basis of tradition and on the basis of the close links between the established Church of England and the state. There are arguments for reform, but it should be recognised that the Spiritual Peers owe no allegiance to any political party and, while by convention not speaking or voting on purely political issues, make a significant contribution to debate on many,

---

9 No appeal lies from the highest Scottish criminal court, the High Court of Justiciary: Criminal Procedure (Scotland) Act 1887.

often sensitive, moral and social issues, such as housing, divorce, abortion, homosexuality, embryology and human fertilisation.

The oath of allegiance

Before becoming a full Member of the House, the new peer is formally introduced and takes the oath of allegiance to the Crown.[10]

Government members in the Lords

The government is represented in the House by the Leader of the House (Lord Privy Seal), Lord Advocate, Ministers and Under Secretaries of State, the Chief Whip and Deputy Chief Whip and whips.

Disqualification from membership of the Lords

Aliens

Aliens are disqualified from membership of the Lords under section 3 of the Act of Settlement 1700. The British Nationality Act 1981, Schedule 7, amends the Act of Settlement to the effect that Commonwealth citizens or citizens of the Republic of Ireland are excluded from its provisions.

Persons under the age of 21

While the age of majority has been reduced from the age of 21 to the age of 18 years by section 1 of the Family Law Reform Act 1969, no person succeeding to a peerage below the age of 21 may take his or her seat in the House.[11] Technically, persons under the age of 21 are not disqualified, but merely ineligible to take their seats until they reach the age of 21.

Bankrupts

Under the Bankruptcy and Insolvency Acts,[12] no peer may sit whilst adjudicated bankrupt. The disqualification ceases in accordance with the Acts.[13] It is a breach of privilege to sit whilst disqualified.

Treason

Any peer convicted of treason is disqualified from sitting or voting as a Member of the House unless and until he has either completed his term of imprisonment or received a pardon.

The disclaimer of hereditary peerages[14]

Under the Peerage Act 1963, it became possible to disclaim a peerage. A peer who disclaims his or her title does so irrevocably, but the disclaimer will not affect the succession of the title. Under the Act, a peer succeeding to a title before the passing of the Act had 12 months

---

10 Promissory Oaths Act 1868, s. 2; Oaths Act 1978, s. 1.
11 Standing Order No. 2, 1685.
12 Bankruptcy Disqualification Act 1871; Bankruptcy Act 1883; Bankruptcy Act 1890; Bankruptcy (Scotland) Act 1913; Bankruptcy Act 1914; Insolvency Act 1986.
13 Insolvency Act 1986, s. 427.
14 See Hailsham, 1975; *Report of Joint Committee on House of Lords Reform*, HL 23 (1962–1963) and HC 38 (1962–1963), London: HMSO.

in which to disclaim the title. Peers succeeding to titles subsequently have one year within which to disclaim succession, or, in the case of a person under the age of 21, a year from the date of attaining the age of 21. One exception exists to this rule. If the successor is a Member of the House of Commons, or a candidate for election to the House of Commons, at the date on which he inherits the title, the period for disclaimer is one month (section 2 of the Peerage Act 1963).

Leave of absence

Leave of absence from the House of Lords may be granted at any time during a Parliament by applying to the Clerk of the Parliaments. At the start of each new Parliament, peers who have previously obtained leave of absence will be asked whether they wish it to continue. Where leave of absence is granted, it is expected that the peer will not attend the House. Should he or she wish to do so, he may give one month's notice of his intention to attend. However, there is no mechanism by which the House can exclude a peer who has leave of absence but nevertheless attends the House.

Attendance in the House

All peers are entitled to attend and vote in the House. Before becoming eligible to sit in the Lords, it is necessary to apply for and receive a Writ of Summons. It is expected that Lords who have not taken leave of absence will attend as regularly as possible. The average daily attendance in 2018–2019 was 471.

Resignation and expulsion

On this see the House of Lords Act 2014 and House of Lords (Expulsion and Suspension) Act 2015, discussed under Reform below.

Membership of the House of Lords: April 1998 prior to reform in 1999	
Archbishops and Bishops	26
Peers by succession	750 (16 women)
Hereditary peers of first creation	9
Life peers under the Appellate Jurisdiction Act 1876	26
Life peers under the Life Peerages Act 1958	462 (80 women)
Total	**1,273***

Note

* This figure included 68 Lords without Writs of Summons and 60 peers on leave of absence.

Membership of the House of Lords: June 2020	
Archbishops and Bishops	25
Peers under House of Lords Act 1999	89
Life peers	672
Total	**797**

Membership of the House of Lords by Gender: June 2020			
	Men	Women	Total
Bishops	20	5	25
Judicial Life Peers	10	1	11
Hereditaries	89	0	89
Life peers	459	213	672

Lords' expenses

No salary is payable to Members of the House of Lords. Members are entitled to expenses to cover the cost of travel, overnight accommodation, subsistence and secretarial and other expenses pertaining to their parliamentary duties. One question which remains for future decision is whether, when the final stage of reform takes place, there should be more substantial remuneration for parliamentary work.

Salaried Members of the House of Lords

The Lord Speaker, the Chairman and Principal Deputy Chairman of Committees, government Ministers and whips are salaried. The Leader of the Opposition and the Chief Opposition Whip also receive salaries.

Functions of the House of Lords

Until 1911, the powers of the Lords were equal to those of the Commons, with the exception that the Lords recognised – by convention – the supremacy of the Commons in relation to financial matters and accepted that they had no right to initiate or amend Bills relating to finance. The Lords nevertheless claimed the power to reject outright financial legislation, a power which, when exercised, led to a curtailment of their powers.

In the White Paper of 1968[15] which formed the basis for the Labour government's attempt further to reform the House of Lords, the following functions of the House of Lords were recorded:

(a)   the provision of a forum for debate on matters of public interest;
(b)   the revision of Bills brought from the House of Commons;
(c)   the initiation of Public Bills and Private Members' Bills;
(d)   the consideration of delegated legislation;
(e)   the scrutiny of the executive;
(f)   the scrutiny of private legislation;
(g)   Select Committee work;
(h)   the Supreme Court of Appeal (now reformed: see Chapter 4).

To this list must now be added the scrutiny and reporting of Bills and draft Bills for their compatibility with Convention rights protected under the Human Rights Act 1998.

---

15 *House of Lords Reform*, Cmnd 3799, 1968, London: HMSO, para. 8.

The House of Lords contains a wealth of specialism and experience which is unmatched by the House of Commons. It is in part the introduction of life peers which explains the revival of the House of Lords. Perhaps the major factor explaining the resurgence of activity in the Upper House lies in the sheer volume of legislative work introduced by governments in recent years.

The majority of time in the Lords is devoted to the scrutiny of legislation, both primary and secondary, which in an average session will occupy over 60 per cent of the time.

Procedure in the House of Lords

To some extent, the procedure in the House of Lords mirrors that of the Lower House, although significant differences must be noted. The control of procedure lies within the Privileges of the House (see Chapter 17), and is regulated by the Leader of the House, the government Chief Whip and by the House as a whole. As noted above, the Lord Speaker of the House has no formal powers to control the House. The Leader of the House is a political appointment in the hands of the Prime Minister, and the Leader of the House is a Member of Cabinet. It is his or her principal duty to advise on matters of procedure and order. The government Chief Whip is responsible for the arrangement of government business and consultation with other parties as to its arrangement. As with the Whip in the Commons, the Chief Whip sends out a weekly indication of the need for Members' attendance at particular items of business.

Having examined the composition of the House, the allocation of time and the principal officials of the House, we can now turn our attention to examining the actual business of the House.

General Debates

The importance of debates in the House of Lords, although occupying a decreasing percentage of the time of the House, should not be underestimated. Wednesdays are generally devoted to debates on matters of general public importance. One Wednesday per month is set aside for two short debates limited to two-and-a-half hours, when the subject matter is chosen by back-bench peers selected by ballot. Other debates take place as a result of consultation between the political parties, and will be generally timetabled to last for a maximum of either five hours or two-and-a-half hours.

The subject matter for debate is wide-ranging, and it is often commented that the quality of debate in the House of Lords attains a higher standard than that in the House of Commons. In part, this is due to the less partisan nature of the House of Lords and, paradoxically, their very lack of accountability enhances their capacity for independence and openness. Since the introduction of life peers in 1958, the quality of debate has been enriched by the diverse backgrounds and experience of Members.

Questions in the House of Lords

Four types of questions are provided for under Standing Orders: starred, unstarred, written and private notice questions.

The daily business of the House commences with up to four starred questions addressed to the government on four days per week. Notice must be given of the question to be asked, and each peer is restricted to two questions per day. The purpose of the question is not to initiate debate but to secure information from the government. Unstarred questions are asked at the end of the day's business and may initiate debate. They may be likened to daily adjournment debates in the Lower House. These are popular with Members, providing an opportunity to initiate debate on a matter of public interest. Questions for written answer are printed on the Order Paper of the day and a government Minister will reply within 14 days. The questions and replies are printed in *Hansard*, the official journal of the House. There is no limit on the number of questions which may be asked.

Private notice questions fulfil the same function as in the Lower House, that is, to raise matters for urgent debate without the need to observe the strict rules of notice for other questions. Notice must be given to the Leader of the House by noon on the day on which the question is to be put, and the Leader has absolute discretion as to whether to allow the question to be put.

The Scrutiny of Legislation

The scrutiny of legislation occupies the largest, and an increasing, proportion of the time of the House. Bills, other than financial Bills, which fall within the exclusive powers of the House of Commons, can be introduced in either the Commons or the Lords. The majority of government Bills will be introduced in the Commons and, having passed the Commons' stages of scrutiny, will be passed to the House of Lords, although many Bills are introduced in the Lords. The pre-legislative scrutiny of Bills by Joint Select Committees is now a regular process. The process of scrutiny in the Lords in some respects mirrors that in the Commons, and Bills receive a formal first reading, followed by the second reading debate and then 'stand committed' for the committee stage, after which the Bill is reported back to the House and then receives its third reading.

Legislative committees in the House of Lords

There are some differences between the two Houses in the scrutiny of legislation. First, in the House of Lords there is no regular use of Public Bill Committees. The House of Lords did make provision for Bills to be read off the floor of the House in Grand Committees. All peers are entitled to attend and participate. The measure facilitates greater efficiency by freeing time in the chamber itself. The introduction of Public Bill Committees was also favourably considered in relation to a limited number of Bills and was first used in the 1994–1995 session. A limited period of time is set aside for consideration of the Bill, where the committee takes written and oral evidence on the provisions of the Bill. The committee then examines the Bill clause by clause. The committees are used to scrutinise Law Commission Bills which are introduced in the House of Lords. Note that Select Committees may also be used for the committee stage,[16] although this is rare and generally reserved for sensitive issues. Once considered by the committee, the Bill is then recommitted to a committee of the whole House.

Since 2001 there has been a Constitution Committee designed to 'examine the constitutional implications of all Public Bills coming before the House; and to keep under review the operation of the constitution'. The House of Lords also scrutinises Bills for their compatibility with Convention rights.

---

16 House of Lords Procedure Committee, *Third Report*, 1993–1994.

Curtailment of debate

A further difference between procedure in the Commons and the Lords lies in the absence of procedures in the Lords for the curtailment of debate. The absence of the Closure Motion or the Allocation of Time Motion (Guillotine) in the Lords ensures that the contents of Bills are fully debated.

Party discipline in the House of Lords

There exists a system of 'whipping' which ensures some party political control over Members, although the extent of that control is far less than the control exerted by the whips in the Commons. The House of Lords is generally a far less party-political forum than the elected House of Commons. It must also be remembered that the House of Lords contains nearly 200 cross-benchers, or independents, who do not owe allegiance to any particular political party. This group represents a potentially significant force in so far as the way in which cross-benchers will vote cannot necessarily be foreseen in advance, let alone guaranteed. These factors, together with the independence of the House and not being accountable to an electorate, result in a scrutinising body which can review legislation in depth and largely free from the political and procedural controls which are prevalent in the House of Commons.

The Amendment of Legislation

The House of Lords has the power to delay enactment of a Bill under the Parliament Act 1911, as amended, but not to veto a Bill. As will be seen, the democratically elected Lower House has the ultimate right to enact legislation in the face of opposition from the Upper House. The House of Lords does, however, have the power to propose amendments to Bills, and it is their success or otherwise in this regard which requires examination. At the outset, it must be recognised that amendments proposed are of differing types and are put forward in response to a variety of circumstances. Not all amendments proposed in the Lords and accepted by the House of Commons stem from principled opposition in the House of Lords.

Some amendments are purely technical, amounting to tidying up of statutory language. Others will be the result of government undertakings to implement a proposed Commons amendment in the Lords. Amendments also arise out of the government's willingness to rethink an aspect of a Bill in light of consideration in the Commons or within the Department concerned with the legislation. The Lords here acts as a convenient forum for proposing the relevant amendments.

It may be the case that there has been opposition in the Commons to a particular proposal which the government has resisted, and has used its majority to that effect. If the government is prepared to concede a point, particularly where it foresees opposition in the Lords, it may prefer to give way than to risk losing part of the Bill on a vote in the Lords. Negotiations will frequently take place between the government Department and those intending to oppose the measure in order to secure a satisfactory compromise which will ensure the smooth passage of the Bill into law.

The House of Lords is both very active in relation to legislation and makes a substantial impact on many legislative proposals. Most often, the House of Commons will give way to the Lords and accept their amendments, rather than risk losing a Bill for lack of parliamentary time. It must be remembered that, if a Bill fails to pass all of its stages within a session, the Bill will generally be lost and the government must make time to reintroduce it in the next session. Accordingly, the later in a session a Bill is considered by the Lords, the greater will be the inclination of the House of Commons to accept Lords' amendments.

The House of Lords following the 1999 Act

When parliamentary business resumed in January 2000, the majority of hereditary peers had been ousted. It soon became clear, however, that the 'new' House of Lords was not prepared to be more acquiescent towards government legislative proposals. Even before the new year started, the Lords were proclaiming their renewed 'legitimacy' as a revising chamber, and soon made an impact on the government's legislative programme. An example of this was seen in relation to the Criminal Justice (Mode of Trial) Bill, which in part removed the right of defendants charged with 'either way offences', such as theft and burglary, to choose their mode of trial, and which was introduced in the Lords. The Parliament Act procedures do not apply to Bills introduced in the Lords, thus making it easier for the Lords to press home its objections to the Bill successfully. The Lords rejected the Bill, forcing the government to reintroduce the Bill in the Commons where at second reading the government secured a substantial majority. The House of Lords again rejected the Bill and it was withdrawn.

The House of Lords and delegated legislation

The House of Lords participates in the Joint Committee on Statutory Instruments (JCSI). In addition the House of Lords' Secondary Legislation Scrutiny Committee (SLSC) considers the merits of SIs and highlights those which are politically or legally important, or give rise to issues of public policy or are in some way an inappropriate use of delegated legislation.

The House of Lords' Delegated Powers and Regulatory Reform Committee's principal concern is to scrutinise Bills with a view to establishing the extent of legislative powers which Parliament intends to delegate to government Ministers. The role of the Committee is 'to report whether the provision of any Bill inappropriately delegates legislative power, or whether they subject the exercise of legislative power to an inappropriate degree of parliamentary scrutiny'. The committee reports to the House, which decides whether or not to accept the committee's recommendations. The committee has eight members and meets as needs require. The committee hears oral evidence in public, and takes evidence in writing on each Public Bill from the relevant government Department.

The committee, in the examination of a Bill, considers four principal matters. First, it considers whether the power to make delegated, or secondary, legislation is appropriate, or whether the grant of power is so important that it should only be granted in primary legislation. Second, the committee pays special attention to 'Henry VIII powers'.[17] Third, the committee considers which form of parliamentary scrutiny of delegated legislation is appropriate, and in particular whether the power specifies the use of the affirmative or negative resolution procedure.[18] Fourth, the committee considers whether the legislation should provide for consultation in draft form before the regulation is laid before Parliament, and whether its operation should be governed by a Code of Conduct.

 SELF-TEST QUESTIONS

List four categories of persons who sit in the House of Lords.

List at least four functions of the House of Lords.

Giving reasons for your answer consider whether a second chamber is necessary under the UK constitution.

---

17 The power conferred on Ministers to amend primary legislation.
18 See further Chapter 14.

The Balance of Power between the House of Lords and the House of Commons

The Parliament Acts 1911 and 1949

Before the Parliament Act 1911, the House of Lords enjoyed equal power with the Commons over legislation, with the exception of financial measures which, by convention, the Lords recognised as falling under the authority of the elected Lower House. However, in 1909, the Finance Bill containing Lloyd George's Budget was rejected, in breach of convention, by the House of Lords. As a consequence, the House of Commons passed a Resolution declaring that there had been a breach of the constitution and a usurpation of the rights of the Commons, and calling for the power of the House of Lords to be restricted. King Edward VII was called upon to create sufficient new peers to guarantee the passage of the Finance Bill but refused to do so until the Budget was approved by the electorate. Parliament was dissolved and, in the election of January 1910, the government secured a majority of seats only with the help of minor parties. The House of Lords then passed the Finance Bill.

This conflict between the House of Commons and House of Lords resulted in the Parliament Act 1911, passed by both Houses of Parliament but with the House of Lords being threatened with the creation of more peers to ensure the Bill's safe passage. The Act abolished the Lords' right to reject Money Bills,[19] and imposed a one-month time limit during which the Lords may consider such Bills and suggest amendments. If the Bill has not been approved without amendment within one month, provided it has been sent to the Lords within one month before the end of the session, the Bill will proceed to receive the Royal Assent without the approval of the Lords. Not all financial Bills are Money Bills. Where a Bill contains provisions dealing with other subjects it will not be a Money Bill. The Finance Bill is not automatically a Money Bill, and over half of the Finance Bills sent to the Lords since the 1911 Act have not been certified as Money Bills. While the purpose of the 1911 Act is to prevent amendment or delay in Money Bills, should the Lords propose amendments, these can be either accepted or rejected by the Commons.

Regarding non-Money Bills, the power of the House of Lords was curtailed, their right to reject legislation replaced by a power to delay Bills for a two-year period spread over three parliamentary sessions.

Conflict between the two Houses resurfaced over the Labour government's nationalisation programme following the Second World War. The Labour government, fearful that the Lords would reject the Iron and Steel Bill, introduced the Parliament Bill in 1947. In 1948, a conference between party leaders from both Houses met to attempt to reach agreement on the terms of the Parliament Bill. In the event, the conference broke down and the Parliament Bill was rejected by the House of Lords at second reading, only to be passed by the Commons under the Parliament Act 1911. The 1949 Act reduced the House of Lords' power of delay over non-Money Bills from two years over three sessions to one year over two sessions. No amendment was made to the provisions of the Parliament Act 1911 regarding Money Bills.

Exclusions from the Parliament Acts

The Parliament Acts do not apply to Private Bills, Bills originating in the House of Lords, Bills containing financial measures but not certified as Money Bills (because they contain other non-money provisions), statutory instruments or Bills purporting to extend the life

---

19 Bills certified by the Speaker as Money Bills, defined by the Parliament Act 1911, s. 1(2).

of a Parliament beyond the five years laid down in the Septennial Act 1715, as amended by section 7 of the Parliament Act 1911.

The use of the Parliament Acts

It is notable that the Parliament Acts have been used infrequently. Aside from the Parliament Act 1949, which was passed under the 1911 Act, the Government of Ireland Act 1914, the Welsh Church Act 1914, the War Crimes Act 1991, the European Parliamentary Elections Act 1999, the Sexual Offences (Amendment) Act 2000 and the Hunting Act 2004 were passed under this procedure. The explanation for the usually low use of the procedure lies largely in conventional practices regulating the relationship between the two Houses. First, as has been seen above, the House of Commons accepts a great many Lords amendments, for a variety of reasons. Second, the House of Lords exercises its delaying powers with some caution. In debate on the War Damage Bill 1965, Lord Salisbury stated that the House of Lords should insist on amendments under two circumstances:

(a)   if a matter raises issues important enough to justify such 'drastic' action;
(b)   if the issue is such that the electorate can understand it and express approval for the House of Lords' position. In this regard, the House of Lords acts as a 'watchdog of the people'.[20]

Third, if the House of Lords strongly disapproves of a measure but does not wish to defeat the Bill, it may move a resolution deploring parts of the Bill, as occurred in relation to the Immigration Bill 1971 and the British Nationality Act 1981. Fourth, many disagreements between the House of Commons and the House of Lords will be resolved by negotiations between the two Houses which generally will result in the avoidance of ultimate deadlock. Finally, the Parliament Act procedure may be avoided under the amendment procedure laid down in section 2(4) of the Parliament Act 1911. Under that section, the Acts may only be used if the House of Lords, over two successive sessions, rejects the same Bill. A Bill will be deemed to be the same Bill if it is identical with the former Bill 'or contains only such alterations as are certified by the Speaker to be necessary owing to the time which has elapsed since the date of the former Bill, or to represent any amendments which have been made by the House of Lords in the former Bill in the preceding session'.[21] If amendments have been made which are not agreed to by the Commons, the Bill is deemed to be rejected. This formulation facilitates agreements between the two Houses, yet preserves the ultimate possible use of the Parliament Act procedure.

The Parliament Act procedure and validity

As **Pickin v British Railways Board** (1974) illustrates, the courts are – mindful of Parliament's sovereign right to determine its own composition and procedure – reluctant to look at the procedure employed in enacting law. However, the case of **Jackson v Attorney General** (2005) provided an opportunity for the House of Lords to consider the validity of an Act which had been passed under the Parliament Act procedure. The claimants argued – unsuccessfully – that the Hunting Act 2004 was invalid because it had been passed under the Parliament Act 1949, which was also invalid. The reason for claiming that the 1949 Act was invalid was

---

20 See also HL Deb Vol. 365 Col. 1742, 11 November 1975 (Lord Carrington).
21 Erskine May, 2004.

because it had been passed under the Parliament Act 1911 without the consent of the House of Lords, a position which contrasts with the 1911 Act, which could only be amended with the consent of the House of Lords.[22]

Central to the argument was whether the Parliament Act 1949 was primary legislation or delegated legislation. It was argued that legislation is not 'primary' where it depends for its validity on a prior enactment. If it was in fact delegated legislation, then the principle came into play that a body which had been delegated power could not, without there being express permission in the delegating (parent) Act, enlarge its own powers. Applying that argument to the Parliament Acts 1911 and 1949, it was argued that the 1911 Act delegated power to the Crown and Commons to enact legislation, under specified circumstances and subject to stated exceptions, without the consent of the House of Lords. It followed that when the Parliament Act 1949 was enacted without the consent of the Lords and reduced the time period during which the Lords could delay legislation, it increased the powers delegated to the Crown and Commons and thereby infringed the principle that a delegate cannot increase its powers. Lord Bingham rejected the view that the 1911 Act delegated legislative power to the House of Commons. The overall objective of the Act, he stated, 'was not to delegate power: it was to restrict, subject to compliance with the specified statutory conditions, the power of the Lords to defeat measures supported by the majority of the Commons'.[23]

The House of Lords also took the opportunity to consider the precise *scope* of the power delegated to the Crown and Commons and this in turn entailed two issues. Section 2 of the 1911 Act states two types of Bills which are expressly excluded from passage under the Parliament Act procedure: Money Bills or Bills extending the life of Parliament beyond five years. The first question was whether the procedure could be used to amend section 2 itself and thereby extend the life of a Parliament.

The Court of Appeal had concluded that there was power under the 1911 Act to make a 'relatively modest and straightforward amendment' to the Act, including the amendment made by the 1949 Act, but not to making 'changes of a fundamentally different nature to the relationship between the House of Lords and the Commons from those which the 1911 Act had made'. Lord Bingham of Cornhill stated in the Lords that that was a proposition which could not be supported in principle. He went on to state that it was unnecessary to resolve the issue whether the 1911 and 1949 Acts could be relied on to extend the maximum duration of Parliament beyond five years. However, he did accept that, however academic the point might be, the Attorney General was right in submitting that the 1911 Act and 1949 Act could be used to amend or delete the reference to the maximum duration of Parliament in section 2(1) and that a further measure could then be introduced to extend the maximum duration. The issue was also considered by Lord Nicholls of Birkenhead. He accepted that the express language of the Act prevented the prolonging of the duration of a Parliament beyond five years. On whether the Commons could succeed by a two-stage process as considered by Lord Bingham, Lord Nicholls took the view that it could not be done, stating that the

> express exclusion carried with it, by necessary implication, a like exclusion in respect of legislation aimed at achieving the same result by two steps rather than one. If this were not so the express legislative intention could readily be defeated.

The second, and related, issue was whether the Parliament Act procedure could be used to effect other fundamental constitutional reform, given that section 2 only made two

22 See also **R (Countryside Alliance) v Attorney General** (2007).
23 At p. 745.

stipulated exclusions from the use of the procedure: Money Bills and Bills to extend the life of a Parliament. In other words, could other exclusions be implied into section 2? Lord Bingham rejected that suggestion. The House of Lords ruled that the purpose of the Parliament Act 1911 was not to enlarge the powers of the House of Commons or to delegate powers to it, but to restrict the powers of the House of Lords to defeat measures supported by the House of Commons. The 1911 Act stated that legislation made under it 'became an Act of Parliament on the Royal Assent being signified' and that there was nothing doubtful or ambiguous about that term.

On a proper interpretation of the 1911 Act, it created a parallel route by which, subject to certain exceptions, 'any' Public Bill introduced into the Commons could become an Act of Parliament. The term 'any' was to be construed according to its ordinary meaning. There were stated exceptions expressly stated in section 2(1) and there was no scope for introducing or implying further exclusions. Moreover there was no constitutional principle or principle of statutory construction which prohibited a legislature from altering its own constitution. Baroness Hale was forthright, rejecting the Court of Appeal's view that the 1911 procedure could not be used to effect fundamental constitutional change, stating that 'the 1911 Act procedure can be used to effect any constitutional change, with the one exception stated'.

More generally on the contemporary interpretation of parliamentary sovereignty, Lord Steyn, having alluded to the European Union and the European Convention on Human Rights, stated that:

> [T]he classic account given by Dicey of the doctrine of the supremacy of Parliament, pure and absolute as it was, can now be seen to be out of place in the modern United Kingdom. Nevertheless, the supremacy of Parliament is still the general principle of our constitution. It is a construct of the common law. The judges created this principle.

Suspension Motions

The Suspension Motion is a device currently available in relation to Private Bills which facilitates their passage through Parliament. Where the Suspension Motion is agreed by the House of Commons, a Private Bill may be carried over from one session to another, without the loss of that Bill.

The House of Commons Procedure Committee and House of Lords Procedure Committee agreed to extend the procedure to Public Bills. Where a Bill is in the Commons at the end of one session, and a Suspension Motion is agreed, that Bill will be able to continue its life into the next session. However, the procedure is not designed to 'rescue' contentious Bills over which the two Houses disagree.[24] Rather, the procedure will apply to those Bills which the government notifies to the House of Commons as candidates for the 'carry-over' procedure.[25] It will be for the Commons to agree the motion to suspend the Bill, should the need arise.

Select Committees in the House of Lords

The House of Lords has no structured system of Select Committees as exists in the House of Commons. The House may establish ad hoc committees to consider a matter of public

---

24 For example, the Crime and Disorder Bill 1998, which provided for the lowering of the age of consent for sexual intercourse between men.
25 The Financial Services and Markets Bill 1999 was passed under the carry-over procedure.

importance.[26] Domestic Select Committees exist to consider matters of procedure and privileges of the House. In addition, as has been seen, Bills may be committed to Select Committee for in-depth consideration and report.

A number of sessional committees exist. Significant among these are the Science and Technology Committee and the Economic Affairs Committee. In the 2000–2001 session, three new sessional committees were established. The Select Committee on the Constitution has two main functions. First, it examines the constitutional implications of all Public Bills coming before the House: the scrutiny function. Second, it keeps under review the operation of the constitution: the investigative function. The Committee has 12 members and is assisted by a Legal Adviser. When examining Bills, the Committee considers whether the Bill raises issues of principle affecting the constitution. If it does, the Committee may request information or clarification from the Minister responsible for the Bill or seek other advice. The Committee reports its evidence to the House and publishes any conclusion it has reached. If a Bill is subject to pre-legislative scrutiny, the Constitution Committee may communicate its views on the draft Bill to the Committee. In exercising its investigative function, the Committee may engage specialist advisers, take oral evidence and receive written evidence. The Committee publishes a report, and the government is obliged to respond to the report.

A Joint Committee on Human Rights was also established, having six members from the House of Lords and five from the House of Commons.[27] The Committee's terms of reference are wide. It has power to consider 'matters relating to human rights' (but not individual cases); to consider proposals for remedial orders, draft remedial orders and those laid before Parliament and to consider whether the attention of the House should be drawn to any aspect of them. The Committee has expressed a preference for law reform to be accomplished by primary legislation rather than remedial orders wherever possible in order to ensure adequate parliamentary scrutiny.[28]

The Economic Affairs Committee, having a membership of 13 and supported by a Clerk, a Secretary and a part-time Specialist Adviser, examines economic matters with which Parliament should be concerned. The Committee works through formal investigative enquiries hearing oral evidence and examining written evidence following which a report will be published, to which the government must formally respond.

Joint Committees, with members from both the House of Commons and House of Lords, have been established. There is a Joint Committee on House of Lords Reform and a Joint Committee on Human Rights. In addition, Joint Committees may be established to consider particular Bills.

The Steering Committee

In order to coordinate better the work of committees in the Lords, there is a Steering Committee which serves functions similar to those of the Liaison Committee in the Commons – namely, deciding on subjects for investigation by ad hoc Select Committees, allocating resources between differing Select Committees and monitoring the work of the committees.

---

26 For example, Unemployment (1979–1982), Overseas Trade (1984–1985), Murder and Life Imprisonment (1988–1989).
27 See Feldman, 2002.
28 See HL 58/HC 473 of 2001–2002.

Members' Interests in the House of Lords

In November 1995, a Register of Members' Interests was established, in which a number of interests must be recorded. The requirements are that three categories of interests must be registered, namely:

(a) consultancies or other similar arrangements involving payment or other incentive or reward for providing parliamentary advice or services. Registration under this category is mandatory;

(b) financial interests in businesses involved in parliamentary lobbying on behalf of clients. This requirement is also mandatory;

(c) other particulars relating to matters which the Lords consider may affect the public perception of the way in which they discharge their parliamentary duties. Registration under this category is discretionary.

Interests should be declared in debate whenever Members have a direct financial interest in a subject, along with any other interest which might affect the judgment of the House. The Committee on Lords' Interests has power to investigate allegations of failure to comply with the requirements. The register is published annually.

The 2009 scandal over MPs' allowances and expenses is discussed in Chapter 17. Similar charges were levelled against some Members of the House of Lords and some were under investigation by the police. The Independent Parliamentary Standards Authority, established under the Parliamentary Standards Act 2009 to investigate and regulate allowances and expenses in the House of Commons, does not extend to the House of Lords. However, in 2010 a new Code of Conduct for Members of the House of Lords came into effect. Furthermore, a Lords Commissioner for Standards was appointed in 2010. The Commissioner investigates alleged breaches of the new Code, including breaches of the rules relating to financial interests.

 Pause and Reflect

If you had to design an ideal second chamber for the United Kingdom, what would be its composition and what powers would it have?

Reform of the House of Lords

With a perfect Lower House it is certain that an Upper House would be scarcely of any value ... But though beside an ideal House of Commons the Lords would be unnecessary, and therefore pernicious, beside the actual House a revising and leisured legislature is extremely useful.[29]

---

29 Bagehot, 1867, pp. 133–134.

Parliament Acts 1911 and 1949
– giving primacy to the Commons, limiting the power of the Lords to revision and (limited) delay instead of rejection of Bills, no veto of Money Bills

Life Peerage Act 1958
– creating merit-based peerages, letting in 'the great and the good' from various backgrounds of expertise and experience and ending the exclusively hereditary (and male-dominated) composition

Peerage Act 1963
– entitling a peer to renounce title (and thus be eligible to stand for the Commons)

House of Lords Act 1999
– ending voting rights of hereditary peers (including 'Royals') and reducing their number to 92

Constitutional Reform Act 2005
– enhance separation of powers by replacement of judicial House of Lords with a new Supreme Court sitting in separate, new building

'Completion' of post-1997 reforms
– Royal Commission 2000 ('Wakeham Report'); agreement not reached; further all-party talks; Government Paper 2007
– 'Agenda':
– democratic legitimacy – composition – voting rights – functions and powers
– balance with Commons – primacy of Commons, Salisbury Convention
– difference (from Commons) – hybrid composition; different method of election to House and for a different term

House of Lords Reform Act 2014
– made provision for the resignation and expulsion of Members

House of Lords (Expulsion and Suspension) Act 2015

Both the Labour and Liberal Democrat Parties have long had proposals to reform the House of Lords. As seen above, the former Labour government proposed a phased reform, as a first step removing the right of the majority of hereditary peers to sit and vote. In the past, the Labour Party has advocated total abolition of the Upper House. Much of the antagonism to the Lords stems from basic principles of democracy, its opponents focusing on the fundamental paradox of a sophisticated democratic state having, as part of its legislative body, an unelected and democratically unaccountable institution. The preamble to the Parliament Act 1911 envisaged replacing the House of Lords with an elected House: 'And whereas it is intended to substitute for the House of Lords as it at present exists a Second Chamber constituted on a popular instead of hereditary basis, but such substitution cannot be immediately brought into operation'.

This did not represent the first proposal to reform the House of Lords. As early as 1886 and 1888, debate took place in the House of Commons on the desirability or otherwise of a hereditary element in the legislature. As has been seen above, the constitutional conflict between the House of Lords and Commons in 1908–1910 resulted in the restriction on the Lords' powers and the intention to replace the House of Lords.

In 1917, a conference comprising 15 Members of each House was established, under the chairmanship of Viscount Bryce, to consider the composition and powers of the Upper House. Reporting in 1918, the conference recommended that the Upper House should consist of 246 Members indirectly elected by Members of Parliament grouped into regional units, plus 81 Members chosen by a joint standing committee of both Houses of Parliament. The conference regarded the appropriate functions of this revised chamber to be the examination and revision of Commons Bills, the initiation of non-controversial Bills, the discussion of policy and the 'interposition of so much delay (and no more) in the passing of a Bill into law as may be needed to enable the opinion of the nation to be adequately expressed upon it'. No action was taken on the recommendations.

In 1922, the government put forward proposals for a House of Lords made up of 350 Members. The majority of these were to be either directly or indirectly elected 'from the outside', with the remainder comprising some hereditary peers elected by peers, plus Members nominated by the Crown. In 1949 the Parliament Act, discussed above, was passed by the Labour government and remains the basis for the relationship between the Houses of Commons and Lords today.

The Life Peerage Act 1958

The Life Peerage Act 1958 reinvigorated the Lords. This Act enabled the Crown, on the advice of the Prime Minister, to confer peerages for life on men and women who have reached prominence in public life. The Act provided an increased resource of specialisation and experience. By convention, life peerages are conferred on Members of any political party, and on those who have no particular political affiliation. Towards this end, the leaders of the major political parties put forward nominations to the Prime Minister on an annual basis. The Labour Party in the 1980s refused to make any nominations at all, basing their refusal on principled objection to the elitist nature of the House of Lords. This stance has proven to be something of an 'own goal' for the Labour Party, whose membership of the House of Lords is now smaller than it might otherwise have been. Note that since 2000 nominations for peerages are considered by the independent Appointments Commission (see further below).

The Peerage Act 1963

In 1963, a more limited, but nonetheless important, reform was implemented. The Peerage Act 1963 has its origins in the succession to a peerage by Anthony Wedgwood-Benn (as he then was), a Member of the House of Commons. As a result of succeeding to the title of Viscount Stansgate, Tony Benn, the Member for Bristol South East,[30] was barred from taking his seat in the Commons. A joint committee of the Houses of Commons and Lords reported on this matter in 1962 and recommended reform. As noted earlier, the Peerage Act 1963 provides that a person succeeding to a peerage may disclaim his peerage within one year of his succession,[31] and that a Member of the House of Commons may disclaim within a one-month period from succession. The disclaimer is irrevocable, but operates only for the lifetime of the peer disclaiming the title: the title will devolve to his heir upon his death. Section 6 of the Peerage Act 1963 provides for the first time that peeresses in their own right are entitled to sit and vote in the House of Lords.

---

30 See **Re Parliamentary Election for Bristol South East** (1964).
31 Or on attaining the age of majority.

The 1968 reform proposals

The Labour government of 1967–1969 again turned its attention to reform of the composition of the House of Lords. The party manifesto of 1966 declared the intention to introduce reforms to safeguard measures approved by the House of Commons against delay or defeat in the House of Lords. An all-party conference took place in 1967–1968, at which substantial cross-party agreement was reached on the proposals for reform. The resultant government White Paper of 1968[32] proposed that there should be a two-tier House. The first tier would consist of 230 voting peers who satisfied a test of attendance on a regular basis. The second tier would consist of peers who remained entitled to attend and to participate in debate, but would not be entitled to vote. The right to a seat in the House of Lords by virtue of succession to a peerage would be removed, but existing peers (who did not satisfy the attendance criteria) would either become non-voting peers or might be conferred a life peerage with entitlement to vote. It was recommended that the government of the day should have a small, but not overall, majority of voting peers in the House. The White Paper also recommended that the power of delay by the House of Lords be reduced to a six-month period.

The government proceeded to introduce the Parliament (No 2) Bill 1968 to give effect to the White Paper, but after extensive consideration the government withdrew the Bill.

The 1997 Labour government's reform agenda

The first commitment made in relation to the House of Lords by the Labour Party before its election to office in 1997 was to abolish, as a first measure, the voting rights of hereditary peers. This was accomplished under the House of Lords Act 1999. A Royal Commission was established to consider the next phase in reform and to make recommendations. All reform of the House of Lords is problematic. The 1968 reforms failed to be implemented, not because of opposition in the House of Lords, but through opposition in the House of Commons, which crossed party lines. The opposition arose from the Commons' perception that removing the right of hereditary peers to vote would enhance the authority of the House of Lords, and would risk the Lords becoming more bold in its dealing with the House of Commons. One key question for the Royal Commission and the government, therefore, was how to move forward to the second reform stage in order to produce an effective and valuable second chamber without threatening the supremacy of the democratically elected House of Commons.

The problem of legitimacy remained after the removal of the hereditary peers' right to vote. Life peers have no more constitutional legitimacy than do hereditary peers. Thus, removing the hereditary peers from the House of Lords did not effect any constitutional change of real value, and certainly did not mark a move towards greater democratic legitimacy, but represented no more than a starting point for further, largely undefined, future reform.

The Royal Commission Report *A House for the Future* was published in January 2000. To the disappointment of those advocating radical reform, the Commission recommended that the Upper House, having around 550 Members, comprise a majority of nominated Members and a minority of selected or elected Members representing regional interests. However, despite widespread consultation, the Commission reached no consensus on the most difficult issue: the number of selected or elected Members and the method by which Members would be selected.

In 2000, a non-statutory House of Lords Appointments Commission was established as an interim measure, which has the function of making recommendations for non-party-political

---

32 Cmnd 3799, 1968, London: HMSO.

peerages in the House of Lords.[33] In addition, the Committee vets all nominations for peerages from political parties with a view to assessing their propriety. The government signalled its acceptance in principle of the Report. However, the White Paper published in November 2001 made clear that only a minority of peers would be elected.[34] Once again, no further reform was achieved.

The House of Lords Act 2014 and House of Lord (Expulsion and Suspension) Act 2015

The House of Lords Act 2014[35] for the first time makes provision for the resignation or expulsion of Members. A Member of the House of Lords may now retire or resign by giving written notice to the Clerk of the Parliaments. The notice must specify a date from which the resignation is to take effect and be signed by the peer and a witness. The resignation takes effect on the day notified, and may not be rescinded (section 1). Non-attendance is a ground for removing a peer from the House. Under section 2, if the Speaker certifies that the peer has not attended the House during a session and did not have leave of absence in that session, the Member of the House will cease to be a Member of the House from the beginning of the following session.

The conviction of a serious offence is also a ground for removal. Under section 3, if the Speaker certifies that a peer has been convicted of a serious offence and sentenced or ordered to be imprisoned or detained for more than one year, the peer ceases to be a Member of the House. If the peer appeals against conviction successfully and the conviction has been quashed or the sentence reduced to less than one year, the Lord Speaker must issue a certificate which nullifies the original certificate.

Under section 4, a person who ceases to be a Member may no longer attend the House. The former Member is no longer disqualified from voting at election to the House of Commons or being elected to the House of Commons.

The House of Lords (Expulsion and Suspension) Act 2015 provides that the House of Lords may expel or suspend a member. If expelled the person ceases to be a member; if suspended the person may not attend the House during the period of the suspension.

 Pause and Reflect

There have been many attempts to reform the composition of the House of Lords to make it an elected chamber. All have so far failed. Discuss the reasons why, and offer your view on future reform.

Further reform proposals

The Coalition government formed in 2010 proposed to introduce a wholly or mainly elected Upper House on the basis of proportional representation. The Bill was withdrawn in 2012 following opposition from a significant number of Conservative MPs, without whose

---

33 HL Deb Vol. 60 Col. WA179, 25 January 2000.
34 *The House of Lords: Completing the Reform*, Cmd 5291, London: HMSO. See also the Labour government's White Paper, *The House of Lords: Reform*, published in 2007.
35 Royal assent 14 May 2014.

support the Bill was unlikely to be passed. Yet another attempt to reform the House of Lords failed.

In October 2017 the Lord Speaker's committee on the size of the House reported.[36] The main proposals, on which no action has been taken, were as follows:

- the reduction in numbers should be achieved without legislation, through the cooperation of political parties and existing members;
- membership of the House should be reduced to 600, a reduction to be achieved within 11 years;
- the guiding principle should be 'two-out, one-in' until the target is reached, thereafter 'one-out, one-in';
- once the target is reached the number of new members joining will be limited to the number of vacancies arising;
- all new members should serve a fixed term of 15 years;
- new political appointments would be shared between the parties in line with the preceding general election (being defined as the average of a party's percentage share of Commons seats and its percentage share of the national vote);
- no political party would be allowed to take an absolute majority of political seats in the House;
- cross-bench peers would make up the same proportion of the House as at present (23.38 per cent). In a House of 574 peers (600 minus 26 Bishops) this would be 134 cross-bench members;
- Supreme Court Justices should be made life peers on appointment to the Court and granted a seven-year fixed term in the House upon retirement from the bench;
- the number of Bishops will remain the same;
- consideration should be given as to whether the current system of by-election for hereditary peers should continue. Any change would require primary legislation;
- a new form of peerage would be introduced whereby an individual could receive an honour but was not entitled to sit in the House of Lords.

Summary

The House of Lords is the unelected second chamber, or Upper House of Parliament. Its membership comprises a small number of hereditary peers, a majority of Life Peers appointed under the Life Peerage Act 1958, retired Law Lords or Supreme Court Justices (judges) and 26 Archbishops and Bishops.

The House of Lords scrutinises proposals for legislation. Legislative proposals (Bills) may be introduced in either House of Parliament and the procedure in each House is similar. The powers of the House of Lords are, however, limited by the Parliament Acts 1911 and 1949. The Constitutional Reform Act 2005 provided for reform of the office of Lord Chancellor, who formerly acted as Speaker of the House of Lords. The Lord Speaker is now elected by the House of Lords. The 2005 Act also improved the separation of powers by removing the Appellate Committee of the House of Lords (the highest domestic court) from Parliament, establishing a Supreme Court now staffed by Justices of the Supreme Court, who may no longer participate in the legislative work of the House of Lords while sitting as judges in the Supreme Court.

---

36 *Report of the Lord Speaker's committee on the size of the House*, 31 October 2017.

Reform of the composition of the House of Lords has been on the agenda for over a century. The House of Lords Act 1999 removed the right of all but 92 hereditary peers to sit in the House of Lords. While successive governments declare their intention to reform the House of Lords, little progress has been made as a result of concerns over the balance of power between the two Houses following reform.

Further Reading

Bingham of Cornhill, Lord, 'The House of Lords: its future?' [2010] *Public Law* 261.

Bogdanor, V, 'Reforming the Lords: a sceptical view' (1999) 70 *Political Quarterly* 375.

Hansard Society, *The Future of Parliament: Reform of the Second Chamber*, 1999, London: Hansard Society.

Russell, M, *Reforming the House of Lords: Lessons from Overseas*, 2000, Oxford: Oxford University Press.

Russell, M and Cornes, R, 'The Royal Commission on the House of Lords: a House for the future?' (2000) 64 *Modern Law Review* 82.

Wakeham, Lord, 'A House for the Future: Royal Commission on the House of Lords' Cm4534, 2000, London: HMSO.

Chapter **17**

Parliamentary Privilege

Chapter Contents

Learning Objectives

By the end of this chapter you should be able to:

- ☐ explain the constitutional justification for parliamentary privilege;
- ☐ explain the historical and contemporary threats to the independence and integrity of Parliament and its Members;
- ☐ outline the principal collective and individual privileges;
- ☐ explain the difference between parliamentary privilege and contempt of Parliament;
- ☐ discuss the importance and scope of freedom of speech in Parliament;
- ☐ discuss the question of Members' outside financial and other interests and their control;
- ☐ explain why it was necessary to introduce the Independent Parliamentary Standards Authority;
- ☐ discuss the procedures for the enforcement of privileges, and sanctions for breach of privilege;
- ☐ discuss whether any further reforms are necessary.

Introduction

The privileges of the United Kingdom Parliament are those rules of both Houses of Parliament which offer protection from outside interference – from whatever source – to the Houses collectively, and to individual Members. The focus of this chapter is on the UK (Westminster) Parliament, but note that privileges also protect the workings of the Northern Ireland Assembly, Scottish Parliament and Welsh Senedd.[1] Parliamentary privilege also entails the right of Parliament to regulate its own composition and procedure: it is an aspect of Parliament's sovereignty or supremacy. Parliamentary privilege has a long history, dominated before 1688 by conflicts between Crown and Parliament. The constitutional settlement of 1688 settled that conflict in Parliament's favour.

The parliamentary authority Erskine May defines privilege as being:

> the sum of the peculiar rights enjoyed by each House collectively as a constituent part of the High Court of Parliament, and by Members of each House individually, without which they could not discharge their functions, and which exceed those possessed by other bodies or individuals. Thus, privilege, though part of the law of the land, is to a certain extent an exemption from the general law. [1997, page 69]

Parliamentary privilege provides protection for Members of Parliament against accusations of defamation from outside Parliament and also protects the individual Member – in the exercise of his or her freedom of speech – from the executive.

Parliamentary privilege presents some intriguing constitutional issues. In some respects, privilege may be compared with the royal prerogative, in so far as both privilege and the prerogative represent a unique aspect of legal power reserved exclusively for a special class of persons. Moreover, parliamentary privilege is a legal power in respect of which the courts – mindful of the doctrine of separation of powers – will be cautious in accepting jurisdiction to regulate. By asserting special powers and immunities for Parliament as a whole, and for its Members individually, Parliament throws around itself a cloak of protection which provides rights and immunities not accorded to individual citizens. The balance which is – and ought to be – struck between legitimate and necessary safeguards for Parliament and its Members in the exercise of parliamentary duties and the rights of individuals to the protection of the general law is not always satisfactorily achieved.

The law and practice of privilege reveals the extent to which individual Members and Parliament as a body are free from outside pressure – whether from interest groups, sponsoring bodies and institutions or the media – a freedom which is central to ensure an independent Parliament. However, as Marshall and Moodie point out: 'the boundary lines between free comment, legitimate pressure, and improper interference are obviously not easy to formulate in principle' (1971, page 112).

The law and custom of Parliament

The privileges enjoyed form part of the 'law and custom of parliament' – *lex et consuetudo parliament* – and, as such, it is for Parliament to adjudicate on matters of privilege, not the courts.[2] Privileges are embodied in rules of the Houses of Parliament. The United Kingdom Parliament, however, is not free to extend existing privileges by a mere resolution of the

---

1 Section 50 of the Northern Ireland Act 1998, s. 41 of the Scotland Act 1998 and s. 42 of the Government of Wales Act 2006.
2 Coke, 1 Inst 15.

House: only statute can create new privileges.[3] Privileges derive from practice and tradition; they are thus customary in origin. Nevertheless, they are recognised as having the status of law, being the 'law and custom of parliament'. Parliament itself can – in the exercise of its sovereign power – place privileges on a statutory basis. For example, in 1770, the Parliamentary Privilege Act withdrew the privilege of freedom from arrest from servants of Members of Parliament. Further, in 1689, Article IX of the Bill of Rights gave statutory recognition to the freedom of speech in Parliament. In 1868, Parliament ended its own jurisdiction to determine disputed elections, conferring jurisdiction on the courts by way of the Administration of Justice Act.

The role of the courts

The role of the courts in matters of privilege is confined to determining whether a privilege exists, and its scope. If the court rules that a disputed matter falls within parliamentary privilege the court will decline jurisdiction. This relationship between Parliament and the courts may be viewed in two ways. First, it could be viewed as the courts giving recognition to the supremacy – or sovereignty – of Parliament. Historically, Parliament was established as the High Court of Parliament, having legislative *and* judicial powers.[4] Accordingly, it was appropriate for the ordinary courts of law to defer to the highest court in the land. Nowadays, this justification is less well founded. It is unconvincing to portray Parliament, except when exercising its judicial function in enforcing and upholding privilege, as a judicial body.[5] The relationship between Parliament and the courts may also be explained by reference to the doctrine of the separation of powers. For the judiciary to rule on the legality of actions of Members of Parliament acting in their parliamentary capacity or on the actions of the House as a whole would, under current constitutional arrangements, place judges in a potentially dangerous position, exercising a controlling power over both the legislature and the executive within it.

Baron Mereworth v Ministry of Justice (2011) illustrates the approach of the courts. In this case, the Chancery Division ruled that the court does not have jurisdiction to determine whether a peer is entitled to receive a Writ of Summons which would entitle him to sit in the House of Lords. Such decisions are for Parliament alone to determine. Lord Mereworth succeeded to the title in 2002. In 2010 he requested Her Majesty to issue him a Writ of Summons which would entitle him to sit in the House of Lords. The Crown Office refused, stating that Lord Mereworth was not entitled to a writ as a result of section 1 of the House of Lords Act 1999. Making reference to the separation of powers and Article 9 of the Bill of Rights 1689, Lewison J stated that 'Existing in parallel with Article 9 is the principle of exclusive cognisance', a phrase explained by Lord Phillips of Worth Matravers PSC in **R v Chaytor** (2011) as follows:

> This phrase describes areas where the courts have ruled that any issues should be left to be resolved by Parliament rather than determined judicially. Exclusive cognisance refers not simply to Parliament, but to the exclusive right of each House to manage its own affairs without interference from the other or from outside Parliament.

---

3 **Stockdale v Hansard** (1839).
4 See McIlwain, 1910.
5 See below for a discussion of recent criticism of the Committee of Privileges and the decision-making process of the House of Commons in disciplining members.

The Principal Privileges

The principal individual privileges are freedom of speech in Parliament and freedom of Members from arrest in civil matters. The collective privileges of Parliament include the exclusive right to regulate composition and procedure, right of access to the Sovereign and the right to the 'favourable construction' by the Sovereign in relation to its actions. These are formally claimed by the Speaker, in the form of a Speaker's Petition to Her Majesty, at the opening of each new parliamentary session.

See Chapter 4.

The privileges are substantially the same for both Houses of Parliament (though see below on the 'privilege of peerage'). Each House has the sole right to regulate the privileges it enjoys – although neither House is free to extend its own privileges other than by statute – and, as a result, some minor differences may be discerned between the two Houses.

The Current Scope and Role of Privilege

Freedom from arrest

For Members of the House of Commons, the freedom extends for 40 days before the start of and 40 days after the end of the session. For peers, the privilege protects from arrest in civil matters at all times. The freedom from arrest does not extend to criminal charges or convictions.[6]

Where the criminal law is concerned, there is no immunity, and the re-arrest of a Member of the House of Commons who had escaped from prison, in the Chamber of the House, was not contrary to privilege.[7] In 1939, a Member of Parliament – Captain Ramsay – was detained under defence regulations. His detention did not amount to a breach of privilege, although it would have done so had he been detained for words spoken in Parliament.[8]

In order to protect his or her privacy, if a Member is arrested on a criminal charge, his or her name will not be disclosed in Parliament before the police conclude their investigations. If a Member is detained on grounds of mental illness under the Mental Health Act 1983 then – following specialists' reports to the Speaker confirming the Member's illness and detention – his seat will be declared vacant.

Nowadays, the freedom from arrest relates only to civil matters and is generally of little significance, given that, with one important exception, imprisonment for debt has been abolished. The exception concerns the availability of imprisonment as a penalty for the non-payment of financial provision during marriage, upon divorce and for children born outside marriage. In 1963, in the case of **Stourton v Stourton**, a Member of the House of Lords was able to escape the sanction of prison for maintenance default by pleading privilege. It is anomalous that Members of Parliament should be immune from the law in even this limited manner. The Committee on Parliamentary Privilege recommended, in 1967, that the freedom be abolished,[9] but no action was taken. A Joint Committee on Parliamentary Privilege, reporting in 2013, recognised that legislation was needed but concluded that the privilege was of little 'practical significance' and that legislation was therefore not a priority. The government agreed.[10]

---

6 4 Rot Parl 357; 1 Hatsell 17–22, **Thorpe's Case** (1452), cited in Erskine May, 1997, p. 75; **John Wilke's Case** (1760–1764).

7 Lord Cochrane, 1815: CJ (1814–1816) 186; Parl Deb (1814–1815) 30, c. 309, 336; Colchester ii, 534, 536, cited in Erskine May, 1997, p. 95.

8 HC 164 (1939–1940), London: HMSO.

9 HC 34 (1967–1968), London: HMSO, p. xxix.

10 See *Report on Parliamentary Privilege*, HL Paper 30/HC 100, July 2013 and Government Response Cm 8771, 2013.

Freedom of speech and 'proceedings in Parliament'

At present, it is more important to notice that this freedom of speech holds good not only against the Crown, but also against private individuals. A Member speaking in either House is quite outside the law of defamation: 'He may accuse any person of the basest crimes, may do so knowing that his words are false, and yet that person will be unable to take any action against him'.[11]

The most important privilege claimed by Parliament is freedom of speech. Article IX of the Bill of Rights 1689 provides that 'freedom of speech and debates in proceedings in Parliament ought not to be impeached or questioned in any court or place outside of Parliament'. It has been seen above that, if a matter falls within the privileges of Parliament, the courts will have no jurisdiction over the matter, other than to determine whether or not a matter of alleged privilege falls within the ambit of privilege. If a positive determination is made, jurisdiction to rule on the matter falls to Parliament and not the courts. In order to make such a determination in relation to freedom of speech, the courts are obliged to interpret Article IX of the Bill of Rights, and the phrase 'proceedings in Parliament'.

Some matters are settled. The Bill of Rights makes clear that freedom of speech in debate is protected from legal action and redress under the law of defamation. Debates and questions on the floor of the House and in standing and Select Committees are therefore clearly protected. Other situations are, or have been, less straightforward. For example, what is the situation where a Member of Parliament is discussing parliamentary matters outside the precincts of Parliament, or where a Member of Parliament writes to a Minister on such a matter? Moreover, what is the position where a Member writes to the Minister or another Member with regard to a matter which he wishes to raise in Parliament, or which involves allegations made against bodies or persons outside Parliament, on which he requires further information before raising the issue in Parliament? Despite numerous suggestions for reform to inject greater clarity into the law, many matters remain unclear. In order to clarify the meaning of proceedings in Parliament, the case law is instructive.

- In **Rivlin v Bilainkin** (1953), the plaintiff in an action for defamation had been granted an interim injunction to restrain the defendant from repeating the alleged defamation. The defendant repeated the defamatory remarks in letters and took them to the House of Commons, giving one to a messenger to deliver to a Member of Parliament and posting the other four, addressed to other Members, in the House of Commons' post office. In an action for an order committing the defendant for a breach of the injunction, the defendant argued that publication of the repetition of the libel was committed within the precincts of the House of Commons and was accordingly not actionable in a court of law. Mr Justice McNair declared himself: 'satisfied that no question of privilege arises, for a variety of reasons, and particularly I rely on the fact that the publication was not connected in any way with any proceedings in that House'.

- In the **Duncan Sandys** case (1937–1938), Mr Duncan Sandys had sent to the Secretary of State for War the draft of a parliamentary question in which he drew attention to a shortage of military equipment. Within the draft, Mr Sandys quoted figures which, in the view of the War Office, could have been obtained only as a result of a breach of the Official Secrets Acts 1911–1920. The Attorney General interviewed Mr Sandys, who later complained that he was being threatened with prosecution – in breach of privilege – for failing to disclose the source of his information. A Select Committee was established to

---

11 Maitland, 1908, p. 375. On the Defamation Act 1996 see further below, p. 412.

consider the relevance of the Official Secrets Acts to Members acting in their parliamentary capacity. The Committee Report considered Article IX of the Bill of Rights, and it observed that:

> the privilege is not confined to words spoken in debate or to spoken words, but extends to all proceedings in Parliament. While the term 'proceedings in Parliament' has never been construed by the courts, it covers both the asking of a question and the giving written notice of such question, and includes everything said or done by a Member in the exercise of his functions as a Member in a committee of either House, as well as everything said or done in either House in the transaction of parliamentary business.

The Committee ruled that if it were necessary, in order to prove the charge alleged, to produce evidence of what the defendant had said in the House it was 'in the power of the House to protect him by withholding permission for the evidence to be given'.[12]

● The response of the House differed markedly in the case of **Strauss and the London Electricity Board** in 1958.[13] At issue was whether or not communication in written form between a Member of Parliament and a Minister was protected by privilege. George Strauss MP had forwarded a letter from a constituent to the relevant Minister, in which criticism was made of the manner in which the Board disposed of scrap metal. The Minister passed the letter to the Board for comment, whereupon the Board threatened to sue Mr Strauss for libel. The Member believed that this was a matter concerned with his parliamentary duties and that he should be covered by privilege. The Committee of Privileges concluded that the letter written was a proceeding in Parliament and that, accordingly, the Board had committed a breach of the privilege of the House. The committee was undecided as to whether the Parliamentary Privilege Act 1770 (which provides that legal action taken against Members is in itself a breach of the privilege of the House) applied. It was recommended that the House seek a ruling from the Judicial Committee of the Privy Council on the matter. The Judicial Committee ruled that the Act referred only to legal action taken against a Member in his private capacity, and not as a result of his conduct as a Member of Parliament. The committee so reported to the House which, following debate, surprisingly rejected the finding of the committee. The London Electricity Board subsequently withdrew its action for libel, and an independent inquiry set up by the Minister exonerated the Board.[14]

Strauss raises two important questions for consideration. First, a great many important negotiations and communications take place through informal discussion between Members outside the precincts of the House. Much of this business is as important as matters raised for formal debate in the House, yet it is not covered by parliamentary privilege unless so closely associated to actual or pending proceedings in Parliament as to be brought within that phrase.

Second, many of the matters dealt with by Members of Parliament involve, as did the **Strauss** case, alleged grievances reported by constituents against government Departments and associated public bodies. Inevitably, such grievances may entail actual or potentially libellous statements, but they are not protected by privilege. Where such a matter falls within the

---

12 Report from the Select Committee on the Official Secrets Act, HC 146 (1938–1939), London: HMSO.
13 HC 305 (1956–1957), HC 227 (1957–1958), 591, HC Official Report, 5th Ser, Col. 208, London: HMSO; Re Parliamentary Privilege Act 1770 (1958); Cmnd 431, 1958, London: HMSO; Denning, 1985.
14 Cmnd 605, 1958, London: HMSO.

jurisdiction of the Parliamentary Commissioner, protection is now afforded by section 10(5) of the Parliamentary Commissioner Act 1967, which provides that such communications are absolutely privileged.[15] Uncertainty remains, however, where it is unclear as to whether or not the matter falls within his jurisdiction. It is unsatisfactory that neither members of the public, nor of Parliament, are clear as to the potential scope of liability under the law of defamation.

Four further cases illustrate the scope of the privilege.

- **R v Rule** (1937) involved a letter written by a constituent to his Member of Parliament complaining about the conduct of a police officer and a magistrate. In an action for libel the court held that, where a communication was one made under a duty or common interest, the matter would attract qualified privilege: that is to say, it would be protected from liability unless malice were proven.

- A similar conclusion was reached in **Beech v Freeson** (1972), where a Member of Parliament was sued by a firm of solicitors, concerning whom the Member had received complaints from a constituent and forwarded the letter, with a covering letter, to the Lord Chancellor and the Law Society. That the letters were defamatory was not contested, but the court nevertheless held that publication of the letters (to the Lord Chancellor and Law Society) was protected by qualified privilege on the basis of public interest.

- The protection of privilege does not attach to criminal activities of Members of Parliament. The Court of Appeal so ruled in **R v Chaytor**, **R v Morley**, **R v Devine** and **R v Hanningfield** (2010). The appellants attempted, unsuccessfully, to use privilege to protect themselves from prosecution on charges of false accounting in respect of their claims for expenses.

- In **Buchanan v Jennings** (2004)[16] the Privy Council considered the protection from defamation under Article IX of the Bill of Rights 1689.[17] The defendant had made defamatory statements in debate in the New Zealand House of Representatives: these were absolutely privileged and therefore not actionable. Subsequently, however, the defendant was interviewed by a newspaper journalist and stated that he 'did not resile'[18] from the claims made in Parliament. The plaintiff sued: such words were not covered by privilege. Further, nothing in the law of privilege prevented the plaintiff from relying on a record of what was said in Parliament as evidence to support an action against the Member based on what he had said outside the House. At common law every republication of a libel was a new libel and a new cause of action. Accordingly, the Member of Parliament could be held liable in defamation if he later adopted or confirmed the original statement, without repeating it, outside Parliament.

Buchanan v Jennings may be contrasted with **Makudi v Baron Triesman of Tottenham** (2014). In **Makudi** the defendant had made defamatory statements about the claimant to a parliamentary committee of the House of Commons. The claimant was a member of the Executive of the International Federation of Association Football (FIFA). The parliamentary committee requested that the defendant give evidence in the form of a witness statement and oral evidence to a barrister who was conducting a review of the allegations made. The claimant then brought proceedings in defamation and malicious falsehood. The judge held that the extra-parliamentary statements were not covered by privilege. On appeal, the Court of Appeal ruled that in exceptional circumstances privilege would extend to extra-parliamentary

---

15 On the jurisdiction of the Commissioner, see Chapter 26.
16 See Geddis, 2005.
17 Note that decisions of the Privy Council are persuasive rather than binding on the domestic courts.
18 Meaning that he stood by what he had said previously.

speech. Here there was a public interest in the inquiry to which the defendant had given evidence and there was a close nexus between the evidence given in Parliament and the extra-parliamentary evidence. However the Court of Appeal cautioned that there had to be a very strong case before the protection of Article 9 could extend to extra-parliamentary speech.

The protection granted by privilege was considered by the European Court of Human Rights in **A v United Kingdom** (2002). The applicant argued that defamatory remarks made about her and her children in a debate about housing policy which had been reported in local and national newspapers, which she could not challenge in court because of Article IX, violated Article 6 (right to a fair trial), Article 8 (right to respect for private life) and Article 13 (the right to an effective remedy) of the European Convention on Human Rights. The Court of Human Rights found the statements unnecessary and reference to her home 'regrettable', but nevertheless ruled that there was no violation of Convention rights. The rules on privilege were necessary to protect free speech in Parliament. Moreover, the British rules were narrower than those operating in several other states.

In **R (Miller) v The Prime Minister, Cherry v Advocate General for Scotland** (2019) (on which see Chapters 5 and 8), one question raised was whether the prorogation of Parliament was a proceeding in Parliament within Article 9 and therefore protected from challenge before the courts. The Supreme Court ruled that it was not. The essential reason for this was that although prorogation:

> takes place in the House of Lords in the presence of Members of both Houses, it is not a decision of either House of Parliament. Quite the contrary: it is something which is imposed upon them from outside. It is not something upon which the Members of Parliament can speak or vote. The Commissioners are not acting in their capacity as members of the House of Lords but in their capacity as Royal Commissioners carrying out the Queen's bidding. They have no freedom of speech. This is not the core or essential business of Parliament. Quite the contrary: it brings that core or essential business of Parliament to an end.[19]

The question whether a Report of an Inquiry, established by a Minister, is covered by privilege came before the court in **Foreign and Commonwealth Office v Warsama** (2020). In 2014 the Foreign and Commonwealth Office appointed a criminal barrister to chair an inquiry into allegations of serious child sex abuse and corruption on the island of St Helena. The Wass Inquiry was not set up under the Inquiries Act 2005 (on which see Chapter 26) which specifically protects reports as privileged. The Report contained serious criticism of two social workers who had made the allegations of abuse and which the Inquiry held to be unfounded. The claimants issued a claim against the FCO and the chair of the Inquiry, alleging that their reputations had wrongly been damaged and that there were serious inaccuracies and irregularities in the Report. The initial question before the Court of Appeal was whether the Report was protected by parliamentary privilege. In technical terms the Report was published under the Unopposed Returns procedure. Essentially this is a means whereby Parliament calls for the production of papers, reports or information from the government by means of a motion for a Return. By convention this is never opposed. The relevant Minister 'returns' the report to Parliament through publication. It was accepted that had the Minister read the report to Parliament it would have been covered by Article 9 as a proceeding in Parliament. Publishing

---

19 At paragraph 6.

the Report and making it available was a time-saving alternative device. The motion put to the House of Commons, and approved, was for the Report (the 'Return') to be laid before the House, and the Report was published by Parliament in 2015. The Court of Appeal had no doubt that the Report was covered by privilege:

> we have no doubt that the Unopposed Return is a proceeding in Parliament for the purposes of article 9 of the Bill of Rights 1689 and does confer on the content of the Report the protection of Parliamentary privilege.[20]

The Report was an essential part of the accountability of Ministers to Parliament.

 SELF-TEST QUESTIONS

Write a brief definition of parliamentary privilege.

Write a brief sentence explaining the meaning of the term 'proceedings in Parliament'.

Defining Privilege: The New Zealand Parliamentary Privilege Act 2014[21]

Section 10 of the New Zealand 2014 Act defines proceedings in Parliament as follows:

(1) Proceedings in Parliament, for the purposes of Article 9 of the Bill of Rights 1688, and for the purposes of this Act, means all words spoken and acts done in the course of, or for the purposes of or incidental to, the transacting of the business of the House or of a committee.

(2) The definition in subsection (1) must be taken to include the following:
   (a) the giving of evidence (and the evidence so given) before the House or a committee;
   (b) the presentation or submission of a document to the House or a committee;
   (c) the preparation of a document for purposes of or incidental to the transacting of any business of the House or of a committee;
   (d) the formulation, making, or communication of a document, under the House's or a committee's authority (and the document so formulated, made, or communicated);
   (e) any proceedings deemed by an enactment to be (or a thing said or produced, or information supplied, in an inquiry or proceedings, if an enactment provides the thing or information is privileged in the same way as if the inquiry or proceedings were) for those purposes proceedings in Parliament.

(3) In determining under subsection (1) whether words are spoken or acts are done for purposes of or incidental to the transacting of the business of the House or of a committee, words spoken or acts done for purposes of or incidental to the transacting of reasonably apprehended business of the House or of a committee must be taken to fall within subsection (1).

(4) In determining under subsection (1) whether words are spoken or acts are done for purposes of or incidental to the transacting of the business of the House or of a committee, no necessity test is required or permitted to be used.

---

20 At paragraph 60.
21 See also the Australian Parliamentary Privileges Act 1987, s. 16.

(5) Necessity test includes, but is not limited to, a test based on or involving whether the words or acts are or may be (absolutely, or to any lesser degree or standard) necessary for transaction of the business.

(6) Subsections (2) and (3) do not limit subsection (1).

Freedom of speech: its use and misuse

In the Committee of Privileges report of 1986–1987,[22] the Committee had endorsed the view expressed by the Speaker[23] that: 'We should use our freedom of speech ... with the greatest care, particularly if we impute any motives or dishonourable conduct to those outside the House who have no right of reply'. The Committee recognised that there is 'no clear dividing line between statements which represent a legitimate exercise of freedom of speech, on the one hand, and those which constitute an abuse, on the other' and called on members to exercise self-restraint.

- In 1955, Kim Philby was named in the House as a Soviet spy, an allegation which surely would not have been made without the protection of privilege. In the 1960s, the Minister of War's association with Christine Keeler, who also had a relationship with a Soviet Attaché, was revealed under the cloak of privilege.
- Also in the 1960s, a London property racketeer, Peter Rachmann, was identified in the House.
- In 1980, Jeff Rooker MP made a number of false accusations against a Director of Rolls-Royce: the allegations were withdrawn only after the lapse of five weeks.
- In the 1985–1986 session, Ministers were accused in Parliament of improper involvement with the Johnson Matthey Bank following its collapse.
- In 1986, Geoffrey Dickens MP accused an Essex doctor of the sexual abuse of children, following a decision of the Director of Public Prosecutions not to prosecute the doctor on the basis that there was insufficient evidence to secure a conviction.
- In 2011, John Hemming MP disclosed in the Commons that a former Chief Executive of the Bank of Scotland had been granted a 'superinjunction' by the court. A superinjunction means that the media is not only prohibited from disclosing factual matters but is also prevented from reporting that the injunction exists. The disclosure in Parliament undermined the court order.[24]
- In 2012 Tom Watson MP used Prime Minister's Questions to press the Metropolitan Police to 'investigate clear intelligence suggesting a powerful paedophile network linked to Parliament and No 10'.[25] The police inquiry, Operation Midland, named nine prominent people, some of whom had already died, as suspects. The inquiry was later abandoned, no evidence having been found.
- In June 2015 a Labour MP used privilege to allege that a Member of the House of Lords was guilty of sexual offences against children. The Crown Prosecution Service decided not to prosecute the peer on the ground that he was unfit to stand trial.
- In 2018 Lord Hain used privilege in the House of Lords to name a person whose identity had been protected by a temporary court injunction prior to legal proceedings, thereby undermining an order of a court. Lord Pannick QC stated that it was 'an abuse of privilege

22 Third Report of the Committee of Privileges 1986–1987, HC 604 (1995–1996), London: HMSO.
23 HC 110, Official Report, Col. 1084.
24 See the Report of the Committee on Super-Injunctions, 2011.
25 Hansard, 24 October 2012, Col. 923.

for one member of Parliament to set themselves up as a Supreme Court to override the judgment of the Court of Appeal'.[26]

Which of these exercises of freedom of speech represented a legitimate exercise of the freedom and which represented an abuse is a matter for individual judgment.

The House relies heavily on the notion of the self-restraint of its Members, and is slow to use its disciplinary powers against offending Members. The Committee on Procedure in its First Report urged Members to exercise caution, and to avoid misusing their freedom. Where Members insist on using privilege as a protective device and cause damage to the reputations and livelihoods of citizens, the advice of the Procedure Committee will give little comfort.[27] Individuals may try to rebut any allegations, may petition Parliament and may try to persuade a Member of Parliament to retract a damaging allegation, but such forms of redress are wholly unsatisfactory in comparison with the right to legal redress.

A Joint Committee on Parliamentary Privilege issued its First Report in 1999. In relation to members of the public, the Committee considered whether a 'right of reply' should be introduced but decided against it. A right of reply would do nothing to prove the truth or falsity of any allegation and no financial redress could be made, nor would a statement published in *Hansard* attract the same degree of publicity as the offending allegation.

The courts and privilege

More case law further illustrates the meaning of Article IX and the role of the courts in relation to matters of privilege. In **Rost v Edwards** (1990), a Member of Parliament sued the *Guardian* newspaper for alleged libel.[28] The *Guardian* article had stated that the Member, who was a member of the Energy Select Committee and a nominee for selection to the standing committee, considering an Energy Bill, had not registered his interests – as a consultant with two organisations concerned with energy. Subsequent to publication of the article, the Member was informed that he was no longer being considered for membership of the standing committee and, further, that he had not been given the chair of the Energy Select Committee. The Member instituted libel proceedings, which were adjourned by the court in order to determine the issue of parliamentary privilege. The Member wished to adduce evidence before the court which comprised correspondence between himself and a clerk of the House and the Register of Members' Interests.

Mr Justice Popplewell ruled that the correspondence could not be submitted in evidence: that clearly fell within the exclusive domain of Parliament and not the court. As to the Register, the judge took the view that it was a public document and, accordingly, could be put in evidence. Mr Justice Popplewell, recognising the respective jurisdictions of Parliament and the courts, declared that the courts should nevertheless be slow to refuse to admit in evidence documents which could affect the outcome of legal proceedings and hence individual rights. **Rost v Edwards** was considered by the Joint Committee on Parliamentary Privilege which reported in 1999. The report stated baldly that 'we are in no doubt that if this decision is correct, the law should be changed'.[29] In the Committee's opinion, it is quite wrong for a court of law to be free to investigate and adjudicate upon matters relating to the Register. If there are allegations of wrongful failure to register, that matter should be 'a matter for Parliament alone'. The Committee recommended that legislation be introduced to make

---

26 'Parliamentarians who think they are Solomon abuse their privilege', *The Times* 8 November 2018.
27 Given that 'advice' is less compelling than binding rules.
28 See Leopold, 1991.
29 First Report of the Joint Committee on Parliamentary Privilege, 1999, para. 123.

clear that the Register and matters relating thereto are 'proceedings in parliament'. The Joint Committee on Parliamentary Privilege, reporting in 2013, also expressed concern over the ruling. The government agreed, stating that its view was that 'the Registers in both Houses should be considered proceedings of Parliament'. However, the government did not feel that legislation was needed.[30]

Rost v Edwards was doubted by the Privy Council in **Prebble v Television New Zealand Ltd** (1994). In **Prebble**, a member of the New Zealand House of Representatives sued the television company for libel for publishing an article alleging that state assets had been sold off, contrary to stated policy, and that the Member had been involved in a conspiracy to effect the sale. In its defence, the company wished to introduce in evidence parliamentary papers which substantiated its claim. The Member pleaded privilege. The House of Representatives ruled that it had no power to waive its own privileges and thereby allow the papers to be considered in court. The Privy Council ruled that to adduce such evidence – without the House's waiver of privilege – contravened privilege and the protection given to parliamentary proceedings under Article IX of the Bill of Rights 1689.

In **Pepper v Hart** (1993),[31] the question considered by the House of Lords was whether judges may refer to *Hansard* as an aid to the interpretation of statutes. This issue has long been one of some controversy, and the orthodox view has hitherto been that judges may not under any circumstances refer to *Hansard*. In **Davis v Johnson** (1979), Lord Denning MR stated openly that he privately referred to *Hansard* as an aid to interpretation, only to be criticised for so doing by the House of Lords. However, in **Black-Clawson International Ltd v Papierwerke AG** (1975), all five judges in the House of Lords had agreed that official reports could be consulted to discern the 'mischief' with which the legislation was intended to deal, although their Lordships differed over the extent to which they could be used. Further, in **Pickstone v Freemans** (1988), three Members of the House of Lords made reference to a parliamentary speech of the Secretary of State (the other two judges were silent on this matter).

In **Pepper v Hart** (1993), six of the seven judges hearing the case ruled in favour of admitting parliamentary debates before the court in some circumstances (the Lord Chancellor dissented on this point). Arguments were advanced by the Attorney General against such a decision – not least that, by consulting parliamentary debates, the courts would be acting contrary to Article IX of the Bill of Rights 1689, which prohibits the courts from questioning proceedings in Parliament. The court rejected those views, concluding that there were no constitutional reasons which outweighed the merits of a 'limited modification' of the rule. Lord Browne-Wilkinson, giving the leading judgment of the court, stated that the rule should be relaxed where:

(a)   legislation is ambiguous or obscure, or leads to an absurdity;
(b)   the material relied on consists of one or more statements by a Minister or other promoter of the Bill together, if necessary, with such other parliamentary material as is necessary to understand such statements and their effect; and
(c)   the statements relied on are clear.

The House of Lords in **Pepper v Hart** revealed a marked change in attitude, although the right to refer to *Hansard* is not an unqualified right. The significance of this judgment from the point of view of parliamentary privilege lies in the court's consideration of the scope of Article IX of the Bill of Rights 1689. The Attorney General had argued strongly before the court that for judges to refer to *Hansard* infringed Article IX, amounting to an inquiry into the proceedings

---

30 Cm 8771, 2013.
31 See Oliver, 1993.

in Parliament. This submission was rejected by the court, Lord Templeman declaring that reference to *Hansard*, under limited circumstances, involved no questioning of Parliament, but merely clarification as to Parliament's intention.[32]

The case of **Prebble v Television New Zealand Ltd** (1995) was reconsidered in **Allason v Haines** (1995). Joe Haines, a political journalist, and Mr Richard Stott, editor of the newspaper *Today*, applied to have a libel action brought against them by the plaintiff, Mr Rupert Allason MP, stayed. The court held that where, in order to defend a libel action, it was necessary to bring evidence of a Member of Parliament's behaviour in the House of Commons, and such a defence would be in breach of parliamentary privilege, the action would be stayed, for it would be unjust to deprive the defendants of their defence. The defendants had sought to show that Early Day Motions were inspired by improper motives. Such evidence would be in contravention of Article IX of the Bill of Rights 1689. To enforce parliamentary privilege in this case would be to cause injustice to the defendants. A stay was granted.

Reference to *Hansard* was again considered in **Wilson v First County Trust** (2003). In this case the Court of Appeal referred to *Hansard* not, as in **Pepper v Hart**, to identify the intention of Parliament in order to give effect to it, but rather to understand the reason which led Parliament to enact a particular provision in the form that it took and to identify whether the statute was compatible with Convention rights. Unusually, legal representation on behalf of the Speaker of the House of Commons and the Clerk of the Parliaments gave evidence concerning the use of *Hansard* by the courts. Lord Nicholls of Birkenhead addressed the constitutional issue in the following way: 'This House sitting in its judicial capacity is keenly aware, as indeed are all courts, of the importance of the legislature and the judiciary discharging their constitutional roles and not trespassing inadvertently into the other's province' (page 584).

The House of Lords ruled that:

> it is a cardinal constitutional principle that the will of Parliament is expressed in the language used by it in its enactments. The proportionality of legislation is to be judged on that basis. The courts are to have due regard to the legislation as an expression of the will of Parliament. The proportionality of a statutory measure is not to be judged by the quality of the reasons advanced in support of it in the course of parliamentary debate, or by the subjective state of mind of individual ministers or other members.

Article 9 of the Bill of Rights was raised before the Supreme Court in **R (HS2 Action Alliance Ltd and others) v Secretary of State for Transport** (2013). In judicial review proceedings the issues involved aspects of decision making in relation to the high-speed rail link from London to the north, HS2, and whether the procedures adopted were compliant with two European Union Directives. One of the issues was whether the decision should be taken by Parliament rather than through the normal planning process. The Supreme Court considered the case law of the Court of Justice of the European Union (CJEU) and in particular submissions by two Advocates General to the CJEU to the effect that the national courts had to be satisfied that the parliamentary procedures satisfied the requirements of EU law. The Supreme Court rejected any such suggestion as contrary to the Bill of Rights. An inquiry into the adequacy of parliamentary proceedings was not a matter for a court of law. As Lords Neuberger and Mance stated: 'Scrutiny of the workings of Parliament and whether they satisfy externally

---

32 In **Three Rivers District Council v Bank of England (No 2)** and **(No 3)** (1996), it was held that references to Ministers' speeches in *Hansard* may be made not only to construe a particular statutory provision whose meaning was ambiguous or unclear, but also in a case where the purpose or object of the statute as a whole is in issue. See also **R v Deegan** (1998).

imposed criteria clearly involves questioning and potentially impeaching (i.e. condemning) Parliament's internal proceedings, and would go a considerable step further than any United Kingdom court has ever gone' (at paragraph 206).

Speaking extra-judicially, Lord Neuberger referred to the Supreme Court's concern over the suggestion that the court should examine parliamentary procedures and the concern that 'a fundamental aspect of the separation of powers was being questioned, indeed undermined, almost by a European sidewind'. Lord Neuberger commented that while the issue did not have to be decided in the **HS2** case 'it may be waiting there to be decided in another case'.[33] In 2013 the government stated that the 'current situation whereby the courts can use proceedings in Parliament so long as they are not questioned or impeached' was satisfactory, but that if there was any increase in 'inappropriate judicial questioning of proceedings in Parliament', as suggested in evidence to the Joint Committee on Parliamentary Privilege, the government would 'revisit' the issue.[34]

 Pause and Reflect

Explain the law on privilege in the following circumstances, using case law where relevant.

A back-bench MP, Jones, is presenting a Bill to Parliament in the near future. The Bill seeks to criminalise gambling in city centres. Jones asks a Minister, in a corridor of the House of Commons, whether his Bill has a chance of success and says that he hopes that it will put Mr Y – who he believes has been unlawfully fixing machines to deny customers their entitled pay-outs – out of business. A passing cleaner, hearing the conversation, telephones a national tabloid newspaper which publishes the allegation against Mr Y. Mr Y wishes to sue Jones in defamation. Is Jones protected by parliamentary privilege?

The Defamation Act 1996 and Article IX of the Bill of Rights

The Defamation Act 1996, section 13 provides that a person may waive, for the purpose of defamation proceedings in which his conduct in relation to proceedings in Parliament is in issue, the protection of any enactment or rule of law which prevents proceedings in Parliament being impeached or questioned in any court or place outside Parliament. As a result, a Member of Parliament may bring an action for defamation to defend his or her actions, provided that he or she waives the Article IX protection and thereby enables the defence to adduce evidence which otherwise would be excluded on the basis of privilege. If, however, the Member of Parliament is not willing to waive the Article IX privilege, then, on the authority of **Prebble v Television New Zealand Ltd**, the defamation action may be stayed in order to enable the newspaper to adduce evidence which proves the truth of its allegation.

In **Hamilton v Al Fayed** the House of Lords ruled that the effect of section 13 was that the defendant's waiver of his parliamentary protection in relation to the parliamentary inquiry into his conduct overrode any privilege belonging to Parliament as a whole and thus allowed the parties in the libel proceedings to challenge the veracity of evidence given to the parliamentary committee.[35] The Deregulation Act 2015 removes Section 13 from the 1996 Act.[36]

---

33 Conkerton Lecture 2014, Liverpool Law Society, 'The Supreme Court and the Rule of Law', 9 October 2014, para. 25.
34 Cm 8771, 2013.
35 *Hamilton v Al Fayed (No 1)* (1999) and *(No 2)* (2000).
36 See Schedule 23, para 44.

The composition and procedure of Parliament

The Houses of Parliament have an inherent right to regulate their own composition and procedure: 'exclusive cognisance'. The purpose of exclusive cognisance is to protect each House of Parliament from 'interference from any outside body'. This includes 'the conduct of its Members, and of other participants such as witnesses before Select Committees'.[37]

- In **Ashby v White** (1703), the plaintiff – a qualified voter – had been denied the right to exercise his vote by the Mayor of Aylesbury. The House of Lords awarded Ashby damages. The case gave rise to a significant constitutional conflict between Parliament and the courts. The House of Commons – which at the time had jurisdiction to hear matters on disputed elections – regarded the decision of the House of Lords as interfering with the exclusive right of the House of Commons to adjudicate on disputed elections. Other voters, similarly denied the right to vote, instigated legal proceedings and were committed to prison by the House of Commons. They brought an application for habeas corpus to test the legality of their detention. In **Paty's Case** (1704) the court refused the writ of habeas corpus. Counsel for the applicants, intending to appeal to the House of Lords, was committed to prison. The majority of the court refused to grant the application, deferring to the Commons.
- In **Bradlaugh v Gosset** (1884), Bradlaugh had been duly elected as a Member of Parliament. On arriving to take his seat, Bradlaugh refused to swear the required oath on the Bible, offering instead to swear an oath of allegiance to the Crown. The House of Commons resolved to exclude Bradlaugh from the House. The plaintiff sought a declaration from the court that the resolution was invalid and an injunction to prevent the House of Commons from excluding him. The Court of Queen's Bench declared that it had no jurisdiction to interfere with a matter concerning the internal regulation of Parliament's procedures.
- The right of the House to regulate its own procedures is further demonstrated in the case of **British Railways Board v Pickin** (1974). There the court declined to inquire into the manner of the passage of a Bill even though the plaintiff alleged that he had been denied his right to make representations on a matter adversely affecting his rights in breach of convention. The Court of Appeal held that the procedure used in relation to a Private – but not Public – Bill could be examined. Lord Denning MR took a bold approach, arguing that it was for the court to ensure that:

> the procedure of Parliament itself is not abused, and that undue advantage is not taken of it. In so doing, the court is not trespassing on the jurisdiction of Parliament itself. It is acting in aid of Parliament and, I might add, in aid of justice.

The House of Lords disagreed and adopted its traditional stance: the court will not look 'behind the Parliamentary Roll'.[38]

- On a lighter note, the exclusive rights of the Commons were tested in **R v Campbell ex parte Herbert** (1935). Three members of the Kitchen Committee of the House of Commons were accused of breaching the licensing laws. The action failed, the court holding that the House was not governed by the ordinary laws relating to licensing, which would only

---

37 Parliamentary Privilege, Cm 8318, 2012, London: TSO, p. 8.
38 Following, inter alia, **Edinburgh and Dalkeith Rly Co v Wauchope** (1842); **Lee v Bude and Torrington Junction Rly Co** (1871).

apply if it could be shown that they were expressly intended to apply to Westminster. It is for this reason that the House remains free to open its bars at any time of day or night. Sir AP Herbert once speculated whether the immunity conceded in **R v Campbell ex parte Herbert** could be extended by analogy to permit other licentious behaviour in the Commons.

An early conflict between Parliament and the courts

In **Stockdale v Hansard** (1839), a prison inspector made a written report to the Secretary of State alleging that 'improper books' were being circulated in Newgate prison. The report was subsequently published by *Hansard*, on order of the House of Commons. Stockdale, the publisher of the 'improper book', sued *Hansard* as publishers of the report, which he regarded as being libellous. In defence, *Hansard* argued that the publication had been by an order of the House of Commons and was, accordingly, covered by the privilege of the House. The Court of Queen's Bench ruled that such publication was not covered by privilege and, moreover, that the House of Commons could not by a resolution deprive the courts of jurisdiction to protect the rights of individuals. Stockdale was awarded damages. The Sheriff of Middlesex levied execution on *Hansard*'s property to satisfy the award of damages to Stockdale and the House of Commons responded by passing a resolution to commit the Sheriff for breach of privilege and contempt of Parliament. The Sheriff applied for a writ of habeas corpus to test the legality of his detention.[39] The Serjeant at Arms produced a certificate from the Speaker stating simply that the Sheriff was 'guilty of a contempt and a breach of the privileges of this House'. The court refused to examine the lawfulness of the Sheriff's detention, stating that, since the Speaker's warrant did not specify the facts justifying the detention, it was not for the court to inquire into Parliament's business. Accordingly, the court conceded jurisdiction to the House of Commons and rendered itself powerless to provide a remedy for an individual who, acting as an agent for the courts in enforcing the court's order for damages, found himself incarcerated on the order of the Commons. While such an outcome hardly inspires confidence in the judicial system, it nevertheless illustrates clearly the judges' reluctance to cross the boundary into matters of privilege.

 Pause and Reflect

Is parliamentary privilege an entirely anachronistic concept in a modern, democratic legislature?

Breach of privilege and contempt of Parliament

A breach of privilege is conduct offending against one of the known privileges of Parliament. Contempt is a far wider concept than this and has been defined as:

> any act or omission which obstructs or impedes either House of Parliament in the performance of its functions, or which obstructs or impedes any Member or Officer of the House in the discharge of his duty or which has a tendency, directly or indirectly, to produce such results. [Erskine May, 1997, Chapter 9]

---

39 **Sheriff of Middlesex's Case** (1840).

The main types of contempts dealt with by the House of Commons, with illustrations, are listed by Erskine May as being:

(a) misconduct in the presence of the House or its committees;
(b) disobedience to rules or orders of the House or its committees;
(c) presenting a forged or falsified document to the House or its committees;
(d) misconduct by Members or officers as such;
(e) constructive contempts: such as speeches or writing reflecting on the House; wilful misrepresentation of debates; premature disclosure of committee proceedings of evidence; other 'indignities' offered to the House;
(f) obstructing Members in the discharge of their duty;
(g) obstructing officers of the House while in the execution of their duty;
(h) obstructing witnesses.

Members' Interests and Members' Independence

Freedom from interference in Parliament's work is a foundational principle of privilege. Accordingly, it is essential that all Members of Parliament are under no external pressure which could pose an actual or potential threat to their independence. However, from a constitutional standpoint, this issue represents one of the most troublesome aspects of privilege. It remains a topic of much contemporary significance and raises difficult questions. In 1994, this issue came to the fore and, as a result of a number of allegations concerning Members' interests, an inquiry headed by Lord Justice Nolan was established by the Prime Minister to examine the issue.[40] The findings of the inquiry are discussed below.

A majority of Members of the House of Commons are in paid employment in addition to being salaried Members of the House.[41] Many Members are also sponsored by outside bodies who contribute to their election expenses and may contribute towards the cost of secretarial and/or research staff employed by a Member.[42] It may be argued as a point of principle that Members of Parliament should not receive any financial or other assistance from any outside party, whether a company or a trade union, since the very fact of receipt of such support potentially undermines the independence and integrity of the recipient.[43] This is not, however, the view adopted by the House of Commons itself although, from time to time, the House is troubled by such issues. The traditionally accepted view is that such sponsorship or remuneration is perfectly proper, provided that it does not impede the Member's independence in the actual exercise of his parliamentary duties.

However, there is a fine line to be drawn between legitimate payments to Members and payments designed to impede a Member's independence, which may amount to bribery and corruption.

Rules regulating Members' interests

In 1695, by a resolution of the House, the 'offer of money or other advantage' to a Member of Parliament for the purpose of persuading him or her to promote any matter in Parliament

40 Committee of Inquiry on Standards in Public Life.
41 Non-ministerial salaries have only been payable since 1911. For the background, see Erskine May, 1997, Chapter 1.
42 The trade unions have a statutory right to sponsor Members of Parliament from separate political funds (Trade Union and Labour Relations (Consolidation) Act 1992).
43 A view expressed by Dennis Skinner MP: 'One Member, one salary' (BBC Television News, 20 April 1995).

was ruled to be 'a high crime and misdemeanour'. Further, in 1858, a resolution declared it to be 'improper for any member to promote any matter' in relation to which he or she had received a financial reward.[44] Specifically in relation to the asking of parliamentary questions, the Committee of Privileges in 1945 ruled that it was a breach of the privileges of the House to 'offer money or other advantage' to induce Members to take up questions with Ministers.[45] Members of Parliament found guilty of corruption may be expelled from the House.

When speaking in debate or in any proceedings in the House or its committees, or when communicating with other Members or Ministers, a resolution of 1974 requires that Members shall disclose 'any relevant pecuniary interest or benefit ... whether direct or indirect, that he may have had, may have or may be expecting to have'.[46]

In 1947, the Committee of Privileges had the opportunity to examine the issue of contracts made between Members and outside bodies. Mr WJ Brown was elected the Member for Rugby in 1942. He had previously held the post of General Secretary of the Civil Service Clerical Association and, following his election, agreed to become its Parliamentary General Secretary. Following disagreements between Mr Brown and the Association, it was resolved that Mr Brown's appointment should be terminated. The matter was raised in the Commons, the argument being advanced that the Association's threat to terminate Mr Brown's contract was calculated to influence the Member in the exercise of his parliamentary duties and, accordingly, amounted to a breach of privilege.

On the facts of the case, the Committee ruled that the making of such payments in itself did not involve any breach of privilege, and that:

> On the other hand, your committee regard it as an inevitable corollary that if an outside body may properly enter into contractual relationships with and make payments to a Member as such, it must in general be entitled to terminate that relationship if it lawfully can where it considers it necessary for the protection of its own interest so to do. What, on the other hand, an outside body is certainly not entitled to do is to use the agreement or the payment as an instrument by which it controls, or seeks to control the conduct of a Member or to punish him for what he has done as a Member.[47]

A further instance of alleged improper pressure being brought to bear on Members of Parliament occurred in 1975. The Yorkshire Area Council of the National Union of Mineworkers, who sponsored a number of Labour Members of Parliament, resolved that it would withdraw its sponsorship from any Member who voted in the House in a manner which conflicted with Union policy. The Committee of Privileges found this threat to be a serious contempt of the House, amounting as it did to an attempt to force a Member to vote in a particular way and thus threatening a Member's freedom of speech.[48] In the event, the National Executive of the Union nullified the resolution and no action was taken against the Union.

---

44 CJ (1857–1858) 247.
45 **Henderson's Case**, HC 63 (1944–1945), London: HMSO.
46 Adopting recommendations of the Select Committee on Members' Interests (Declaration), HC 57 (1969–1970), London: HMSO.
47 See HC Deb 15 Col. 284, July 1947; HC 118 (1946–1947), London: HMSO.
48 See HC 634 (1974–1975), London: HMSO.

The Register of Members' Interests

On the wider question of the financial interests of Members of Parliament, under the rules of the House, all Members are required to declare their interests, these being recorded in the Register of Members' Interests. A resolution of the House of Commons provided that:

> in any debate or proceeding of the House or its committees or transactions or communications which a Member may have with other Members or with Ministers or servants of the Crown, he shall disclose any relevant pecuniary interest or benefit of whatever nature, whether direct or indirect, that he may have had, may have or may be expecting to have. [22 May 1974]

The Register of Members' Interests is published annually. The following classes of interests are required to be registered:[49]

(1)   remunerated directorships of companies, public or private;
(2)   remunerated employments, trades, professions, offices or vocations;
(3)   the names and details of clients in relation to which a Member plays a parliamentary role;
(4)   sponsorships, donations/support;
(5)   gifts, benefits or hospitality received;
(6)   overseas visits;
(7)   overseas benefits and gifts;
(8)   land and property;
(9)   shareholdings;
(10)   controlled transactions within section 7A Political Parties Elections and Referendums Act 2000 (loans; credit arrangements);
(11)   miscellaneous;
(12)   family members employed and paid in respect of parliamentary duties.

Failure to register an interest may be regarded as a contempt of the House. The only Member who consistently refused to enter any interests on the Register was Mr Enoch Powell. Mr Powell adopted the constitutional stance that, since only statute could impose legal duties on individuals, the House could not – through the use of resolutions – lawfully require him to register. The Select Committee, having tried persuasion and inviting the House to take action to enforce the duty to register, took no further action.

The rules relating to Ministers are stricter than those relating to ordinary Members of Parliament. The 2005 Ministerial Code required that Ministers must resign any directorships they hold when they take up office.[50] This requirement, however, is absent from the Code published in 2018. In its place is a restatement of the general principle that Ministers must ensure that no conflict arises between their public duties and their private interests, and procedures designed to ensure that no actual or potential conflict arises.[51]

---

49 With effect from June 2009.
50 Paragraph 5.20.
51 *Ministerial Code*, 2018, Cabinet Office, chapter 7.

Cash for questions[52]

The cash for questions affair began in 1993, when political lobbyist Ian Greer allegedly advised Mohamed Al Fayed to bribe Members of Parliament to pursue his interests in Parliament. In 1994, Al Fayed publicly claimed that Tory MPs were paid to plant questions. The *Guardian* newspaper pursued the story, leading to a libel action by Mr Hamilton and Mr Greer. That action was dropped when it became apparent that the *Guardian* had damning evidence which would cause the action to fail.[53]

In 1994, a number of allegations were made against Members of Parliament in relation to accepting money for the tabling of parliamentary questions to Ministers. Allegations were also made in relation to improper payments being accepted by Members from outsiders, in the form of payment for hotel bills. Further allegations were made in respect of the failure of a number of Members of Parliament who allegedly failed to record benefits received and other relationships in which Members received financial reward for services in the Register of Members' Interests. In 1994, two Parliamentary Private Secretaries resigned (from the government but not from Parliament) following allegations that they had received money in exchange for tabling parliamentary questions. The matter was referred to the Committee of Privileges. The rapidly accelerating and intensifying atmosphere of suspected corruption – or 'sleaze' – in public life caused the Prime Minister to appoint a judicial inquiry to be carried out by the Committee on Standards in Public Life.[54]

The Committee on Standards in Public Life: the Nolan Inquiry

The Committee on Standards in Public Life, chaired by Lord Nolan, was established as a standing body, with membership being held for three years. The Committee's terms of reference were:

> To examine current concerns about standards of conduct of all holders of public office, including arrangements relating to financial and commercial activities, and to make recommendations as to any changes in present arrangements which might be required to ensure the highest standards of probity in public life.

Individual allegations of impropriety do not fall within the committee's terms of reference.[55]

The First Report (the Nolan Report) of 1995 stated that while 'there is no evidence ... of a growth in actual corruption' (paragraph 6), there was a widespread loss of public confidence in the probity of Members of Parliament.

The committee set out the general principles of conduct which apply to public life as being selflessness, integrity, objectivity, accountability, openness, honesty and leadership.

Members of Parliament

The Nolan Report recorded that the 1995 Register of Members' Interests suggested that almost 30 per cent of Members of Parliament held some form of consultancy agreement and that almost 70 per cent of Members of Parliament (excluding Ministers and the Speaker) had some form of financial relationship with outside bodies.

---

52 See also Chapter 10 on fitness for public office.
53 For an entertaining account, see Leigh and Vulliamy, 1997.
54 In May 2014 Patrick Mercer MP resigned his seat after being suspended for six months from the Commons for deliberately evading parliamentary rules and lobbying for personal gain.
55 See Doig, 2002. In this chapter, the findings relating to Members of Parliament are discussed. The conduct of Ministers and civil servants is considered in Chapter 10.

Despite the evidence of witnesses and persons writing to the committee, the committee did not conclude from this evidence that such arrangements should be banned. Indeed, the involvement of Members of Parliament in outside work was regarded by the committee as a benefit to Parliament as a whole. As the committee viewed the matter: 'a Parliament composed entirely of full time professional politicians would not serve the best interests of democracy. The House needs if possible to contain people with a wide range of current experience which can contribute to its expertise' (paragraph 19).

The committee was also concerned that a ban on outside financial interests would act as a deterrent to people who would otherwise stand for election to Parliament. The committee recommended, therefore, that Members of Parliament should continue to have the right to engage in outside employment. The matter which remained was how best to protect the integrity of Members and the House as a whole in light of such continuing outside employment.

Having reviewed the early resolutions of the House, and the later resolution of 1947, and the rules regulating the registration of Members' interests, the committee found that the Register had worked unsatisfactorily. The committee invited the House of Commons to review the statement of principle which governed the registration of interests.

Paid consultancies

Three-fifths of all Members of the House have arrangements with clients or sponsors. While appreciating that paid consultancies enable 'many entirely respectable, and in some cases highly deserving, organisations' to 'gain a voice in the nation's affairs',[56] the committee recognised that there was a fine – and difficult – line to be drawn between paid advice and paid advocacy, the latter of which is a matter of concern. To remove the right to engage in such arrangements would be 'impracticable' and was, accordingly, not recommended. There was, however, one area – the issue of 'general consultancies' – in which the committee wanted to see firm and immediate action.

General consultancies

Public relations and lobbying firms are engaged in acting as advisers and advocates to a wide range of clients, all of which pursue their own objectives in terms of exerting pressure on Parliament. The problem posed by such companies is that registration of an agreement with the company does not necessarily disclose the actual client for whom, in fact, the member is acting in a parliamentary capacity. The committee recommended that there be an immediate ban introduced on such relationships; Parliament did not act specifically on this proposal but, rather, tightened the rules relating to registration and the declaration of interests.

Clarifying the Register of Members' Interests

Members are now required to deposit in full any contracts which involve the Member acting in a parliamentary capacity on behalf of any organisation, and these contracts are available for public inspection. In addition, Members are required to reveal their annual remuneration, and also estimated monetary benefits received of any kind. Furthermore, all agreements which do not involve the Member acting in a parliamentary capacity for an organisation and, therefore, do not need to be deposited, should contain clear terms stating that the agreement does not involve the Member acting for the organisation in a parliamentary capacity.[57]

---

56 Nolan Report, para. 46.
57 Ibid., para. 70.

The committee also emphasised the requirement that Members of Parliament disclose their interests on 'each and every occasion when a member approaches other members or ministers on a subject where a financial interest exists'.[58] The onus is on the Members to disclose the interest, and he or she should not assume that the interest is one known about by the other party.

Gifts and hospitality

In relation to gifts and hospitality, the committee found that the rules set out in *Questions of Procedure for Ministers*[59] were sufficiently detailed and that no further elaboration was required. The committee endorsed the important principle set out in *Questions of Procedure*: 'It is a well established and recognised rule that no Minister or public servant should accept gifts, hospitality or services from anyone which would, or might appear to, place him or her under an obligation'.[60]

Enforcing Members' obligations

The committee proposed the appointment of an independent Parliamentary Commissioner for Standards, responsible for maintaining the Register of Members' Interests and for providing guidance on standards of 'conduct, propriety and ethics'. The Commissioner fulfils a similar function to that of the Comptroller and Auditor General and the Parliamentary Commissioner for Administration.[61] The Commissioner has power to receive and investigate complaints concerning Members' conduct.[62]

In relation to Ministers, the Nolan Report was critical of the position whereby Ministers may leave government office and assume senior positions with – in particular – companies which have recently been privatised by the government.

In response to aspects of the Nolan Report, the House approved a Code of Conduct, incorporating the key principles of conduct in public life.[63] The House of Commons passed a resolution, now incorporated in the Code of Conduct for MPs, making it clear that any payment for promoting any matter in Parliament is not allowed.[64] The House also resolved to clarify the rules on declaration of interests when participating in parliamentary proceedings.

MPs' expenses and allowances

In 2009 it was revealed that MPs had been abusing the system of allowances and expenses. The revelation came following a request under the Freedom of Information Act 2000 and a decision of the High Court ruling that MPs were not exempt from disclosures under the Act.[65]

Many of the wrongful claims had been approved by the Commons' Department of Resources, the 'Fees Office', fuelling the demand for parliamentary reform. An inquiry was undertaken by an independent auditor, Sir Thomas Legg. As a result of his inquiry many MPs were ordered to repay monies which were regarded as wrongly claimed. The scandal also led to the forced resignation of the Speaker of the House of Commons, Michael Martin, who had

---

58 *Ibid.*, para. 63.
59 *Ibid.*, paras 80–81. Now known as the Ministerial Code.
60 At para. 126. See Chapter 3, para. 40 of the report.
61 See Chapters 15 and 27, respectively.
62 In **R v Commissioner for Standards and Privileges ex parte Al Fayed** (1998) the Court of Appeal ruled that the court had no jurisdiction to review decisions of the Commissioner, on the basis that the Commissioner was concerned with activities within Parliament, and the Commissioner was accountable to a Select Committee in the House of Commons, which alone had the power to perform supervisory functions over the Commissioner.
63 HC 688 (1995–1996).
64 HC 816 (1994–1995).
65 **Corporate Officer of the House of Commons v The Information Commissioner** (2008).

lost the confidence of MPs. The Speaker is Chairman of the Members' Estimates Committee, which oversees the *Green Book* which sets out the principles to which MPs are to adhere when making claims against allowances. He became the first Speaker to be forced out of office since 1695, leaving office following unprecedented cross-party calls for his resignation.

The scandal led to the rapid introduction and passage of the Parliamentary Standards Act 2009, which had the support of all political parties. The Act created an Independent Parliamentary Standards Authority (IPSA) to regulate the system of pay and allowances, to formulate rules to deal with financial interests and to prepare a code of conduct on financial interests.

Section 1 of the Act ensures that parliamentary privilege is unaffected, providing that: 'Nothing in this Act shall be construed by any court in the United Kingdom as affecting Article IX of the Bill of Rights 1689'.

Constitutionally the Parliamentary Standards Act raises a number of issues. The Act for the first time established a body outside Parliament to regulate Parliament's affairs. Questions relating to Parliament's sovereignty and privileges inevitably arose. There was the question of who would oversee the working of IPSA and whether it would be subject to judicial review, giving rise to a potential difficulty in the relationship between Parliament and the courts. Concerns over the working of the Act, so hastily drafted and passed by Parliament, led to the insertion of a 'sunset clause' – a provision stating that sections of the Act would cease to have effect at the end of a period of two years (see section 15).[66]

The Constitutional Reform and Governance Act 2010, Part 3, amended the Parliamentary Standards Act 2009. The Act imposes a general duty on IPSA to promote efficiency, cost-effectiveness and transparency in the discharge of its functions and provides that IPSA is to determine MPs' pay.

Section 3 of the Parliamentary Standards Act (as amended) provides for the establishment of a Compliance Officer for IPSA. The Compliance Officer may review decisions of IPSA to refuse an expenses claim or allow only part of the claim, and subject to rights of appeal, IPSA must make adjustments necessary to comply with the Compliance Officer's findings. The Compliance Officer may conduct investigations into payments made under the allowances scheme if he or she has reason to believe that the payments should not have been allowed.[67] Investigations may be undertaken on the Compliance Officer's own initiative, at the request of IPSA, at the request of an MP or in response to a complaint by an individual. Following investigation, the Compliance Officer must prepare a statement of findings (see section 9(5) and 9(6)). Section 9A of the Parliamentary Standards Act 2009 provides that IPSA must determine the procedures to be followed, and that these procedures must be 'fair'. A Member of Parliament has the right of appeal against a decision of the Compliance Officer to the First-tier Tribunal (see section 6A).

The Compliance Officer may provide the Parliamentary Commissioner for Standards with any information connected with an investigation, including action taken to enforce a decision.[68] In relation to other bodies, section 10A provides that the IPSA and Compliance Officer must prepare a joint statement setting out how they will work with the Parliamentary Commissioner for Standards, the Director of Public Prosecutions, the Commissioner of Police of the Metropolis and any other person the IPSA and Compliance Officer consider appropriate.

---

[66] A further inquiry into MPs expenses was undertaken in 2009 by Sir Christopher Kelly, Chair of the Committee on Standards in Public Life. The Report, *Report on MPs Expenses and Allowances: Supporting Parliament, Safeguarding the Taxpayer*, Committee on Standards in Public Life, Cm 7724, November 2009.
[67] Parliamentary Standards Act 2009, s. 9.
[68] Parliamentary Standards Act 2009, s. 9B.

The IPSA published the new scheme for the reimbursement of expenses applicable from May 2010. The detailed scheme is available at www.parliamentary-standards.org.uk.[69] Note that the IPSA's jurisdiction does not extend to the House of Lords.

Lobbying

Ministers, other Members of Parliament and peers in the House of Lords and all-party groups in Parliament are targeted by individuals and organisations which seek to influence the opinions of Members of Parliament. There is no statutory register of lobbyists, no parliamentary regulation and little transparency in their operations. In 2009 the Public Administration Select Committee published a report, *Lobbying: Access and Influence in Whitehall* and in 2010 the incoming Coalition government committed itself to regulating the lobbying industry.[70] As the government explained:

> Lobbying – seeking to influence public policy, government decisions or legislation – can improve results by ensuring that those developing and considering the options are better informed about the consequences of the available options. Lobbying is a perfectly legitimate activity that has been carried out for many years in many different forums by a wide variety of individuals and groups of all sorts. However, where lobbying is not transparent, it can undermine public confidence in the decision-making process and its results.[71]

The Transparency of Lobbying, Non-party Campaigning and Trade Union Administration Act 2014 provides for a register of professional lobbyists and a Registrar of Consultant Lobbyists to supervise and enforce the registration requirements. It is a criminal offence to function as a consultant lobbyist when not registered. A consultant lobbyist is a person who is engaged in a commercial business and communicates personally in writing or orally with: 'UK government ministers or Permanent Secretaries, about government policy, legislation, contracts, licences or other benefits, on behalf of another person, in return for payment'.[72]

A Registrar of Consultant Lobbyists is introduced. The Registrar is under a duty to maintain the Register and ensure that it is up to date. Registered lobbyists must update their entry each quarter. The Register is published online and in any other format the Registrar thinks appropriate.

The Act provides for both civil and criminal penalties. It is a criminal offence to carry on the business of consultant lobbyist without an accurate and up-to-date entry in the Register. It is also an offence to fail to supply information to the Registrar. The offences are triable in either the Magistrates' Courts or the Crown Court. The Registrar may choose to impose civil penalties for lesser offences. The civil penalty may not exceed £7,500. There is a right of appeal to a Tribunal.

Penalties for breach of privilege and contempt

Historically, the most important power available to the House was to commit the offender to prison. Erskine May describes this power as the 'keystone of parliamentary privilege', but it is little used and has not been used since **Bradlaugh**'s case in 1884.[73] The House can vote

---

69 CJ (1970–1971).

70 See *Introducing a Statutory Register of Lobbyists*, Cm 8233, January 2012.

71 *Introducing a Statutory Register of Lobbyists*, p. 9.

72 Exceptions are provided for in Sched. 1.

73 The Joint Committee on Parliamentary Privilege recommended in 1999 that the power to imprison should be abolished, except for the power to detain persons temporarily who disrupt the proceedings of either House.

to allow the offender to be prosecuted by the police, as happened in 1970, when a stranger threw a CS gas canister into the Chamber.[74] The most regularly employed sanction is the reprimand. The House may order that a Member be suspended from the House or expelled. In 1948, Garry Allighan MP was found to have lied to a committee, falsely accusing other Members of taking money. The House ordered his expulsion from Parliament.[75] In 1988, Ron Brown MP was suspended from the House for the contempt of damaging the Mace. In 1994, the House suspended two Members, with loss of salary, for 20 days and ten days respectively, for accepting payment for putting down parliamentary questions. Following a report from the Standards and Privileges Committee,[76] a Member of Parliament, the Member for Liverpool (Mr Wareing) was also suspended for failing to register a shareholding interest in the Register of Members' Interests. In 2004 a Labour Minister was required by the Standards and Privileges Committee to apologise to the House of Commons for failing to register her earnings as a presenter of a television show.

The House of Lords has the power to impose fines on offenders. Curiously, the House of Commons does not have that power although, historically, it did. The last occasion on which a fine was imposed was in 1666.[77] The power to impose fines was denied in **R v Mead** (1762). Recommendations of the Select Committee on Parliamentary Privilege in 1967 and 1977 that such a power be introduced by statute have not been implemented. Where newspapers breach the rules of privilege or commit contempt of Parliament, the editor may be called to the Bar of the House to explain and apologise, and journalists may be excluded from the precincts of the House for a specified period.

With regard to maintaining order in the House, the Speaker has a range of available disciplinary powers. The Speaker will first warn a Member about his conduct. If this does not ensure order, the Speaker may request the Member to leave the Chamber. If the Member refuses to leave, the Speaker may direct him to withdraw immediately, and the Member must leave the precincts of Parliament for the remainder of the day. In the rare event that a Member refuses to comply with the order to withdraw, the Speaker may formally 'name' the Member and put down a motion that the Member be suspended from the service of the House. The suspension on a first offence will last for 5 sitting days, on a second occasion for 20 sitting days and on any subsequent occasion for as long as the House shall determine.

There has always been uncertainty over whether the bribery of a Member of either House is an offence under common law which is enforceable by the courts.[78] The Public Bodies (Corrupt Practices) Act 1889 and the Prevention of Corruption Act 1916 apply.[79]

The Parliamentary Commissioner for Standards

The office of Parliamentary Commissioner was introduced to advise Members of Parliament and to investigate allegations relating to the Register of Members' Financial Interests and complaints relating to the Code of Conduct. The Commissioner reports to the Committee for Standards and Privileges. If a prima facie case is disclosed, the committee, following its examination, will report to the Commons. The final decision on the matter lies with the House of Commons. The Commissioner produces an Annual Report.

---

74 CJ (1970–1971).

75 HC Deb Vol. 443 Cols 1094–1198, 30 October 1947.

76 HC 182 (1997–1998), London: HMSO; and see the MP's complaint concerning procedure, HC Deb Vol. 299 Col. 1051, 30 October 1997.

77 **White's Case** (1666).

78 Upholding Integrity: The Prevention of Corruption – the Government's Proposals for Reform of the Criminal Law of Corruption in England and Wales, Cm 4759. See also the Report of the Joint Committee on Parliamentary Privilege, HL 43, HC 214 (1998–1999).

79 See **R v Greenaway** (1998). Parliamentary privilege did not protect an MP guilty of accepting a bribe. The court had no need to inquire into any parliamentary proceeding.

The Commissioner does not have the power to investigate the conduct of Ministers. Ministers are regulated by the Ministerial Code, which is enforced by the Prime Minister. One area of concern relates to the appointment of former Ministers to appointments or employment which may appear to have been influenced by their former position in government. The Ministerial Code 2007 makes it compulsory for Ministers to seek the advice of the independent Advisory Committee on Business Appointments before accepting positions.

The Code of Conduct for Members of Parliament

The Code of Conduct sets out the general principles to guide Members on standards of conduct that the House and the public have a right to expect, together with a *Guide to the Rules relating to the Conduct of Members*.[80] These include matters relating to the registration of interests and their declaration and the advocacy rule. Where Members have entered into agreements which are relevant to their parliamentary duties, these are to be deposited with the Parliamentary Commissioner for Standards in addition to being registered. Where an informal, unwritten agreement has been entered into, it must also be deposited with the Commissioner in written form. In relation to paid advocacy, this is banned in relation to a number of important matters. In particular, paid advocacy is banned in relation to initiating parliamentary proceedings, including the presentation of Bills, presentation of petitions, the asking of parliamentary questions, tabling or moving motions or moving amendments to Bills.

The procedure for determining issues of privilege and contempt

If an allegation of breach of privilege or contempt is made, the complaint is communicated to the Speaker. The Member will be given written notice of the complaint. The Speaker must be satisfied, first, that the matter is one involving privilege and, second, that the complaint is substantial. If he or she so finds, the Speaker advises the complainant that he may put down a Motion which will be debated the following day. For the most part, the matter will then be referred by the House to the Committee on Standards and Privileges (formerly the Committee of Privileges). The committee is made up of 11 senior Members of the House from all political parties, chaired by the Leader of the House. The Committee has the power to call for persons, papers and records. It also has the power to compel Members to attend. Although acting in a quasi-judicial capacity, the committee is not bound to follow strict rules of procedure. The legal rules of evidence do not apply and there is normally no legal representation. The Committee sits in private (but may sit in public).[81] If the Committee finds that there has been a breach, it will make recommendations as to punishment, but has no power to apply the sanction: that is for the House as a whole, who will vote on the matter following a debate. The House is not bound by the Committee's recommendations and may, as happened in the case of **Strauss** (1958), reject them.

The manner in which Parliament regulates aspects of privilege gives rise to questions concerning the right to fair trial protected under Article 6 of the European Convention on Human Rights, incorporated under the Human Rights Act 1998. Parliament is exercising a form of penal jurisdiction when punishing Members.[82]

---

80 HC Deb Vol. 282 Col. 392, 24 July 1996.

81 Demands by the Rt Hon Tony Benn MP that the Committee sit in public were rejected in 1994. Moreover, his announced intention to disclose details of the Committee's hearings resulted in his deselection from the Committee.

82 See Report of the Joint Committee on Parliamentary Privilege, HL 43-I, HC 214-I (1998–1999), paras 271–314.

SUMMARISING THE REGULATION OF PARLIAMENT AND ITS MEMBERS

I The House of Commons

1. The Parliamentary Commissioner for Standards:

   - established in 1995 by the House of Commons;
   - the Commissioner is appointed by resolution of the House of Commons and holds office for a fixed five-year term;
   - the Commissioner maintains and monitors the Register of Members' Financial Interests,[83] the Register of Journalists[84] and the Register of All-Party Groups;[85]
   - the Commissioner investigates and reports on complaints concerning breaches of the MPs' Code of Conduct, the Register of Financial Interests and donations to individual Members;
   - works with the Electoral Commission and Independent Parliamentary Standards Authority in areas of mutual or overlapping concern.

2. The Committee on Standards and Privileges:

   - considers the reports of the Commissioner for Standards and makes recommendations to the House of Commons regarding sanctions.

3. The Speaker's Committee on the Electoral Commission:

   - is the parliamentary body to which the Electoral Commission is accountable.

II The House of Lords

1. The Lords' Commissioner for Standards:

   - was established in 2009;
   - has a role equivalent to the House of Commons' Commissioner for Standards.

2. The House of Lords' Committee for Privileges and Conduct rules on matters relating to parliamentary alleged breaches of the Code of Conduct and rules relating to financial interests and makes recommendations to the House of Lords regarding sanctions.

III The Committee on Standards in Public Life

The Committee:

   - was established in 1994 by the House of Commons as an independent body;
   - has ten members appointed for up to three years;
   - advises government on ethical standards across the whole of public life in the United Kingdom;
   - has reviewed MPs' expenses and allowances and the funding of political parties.

---

83 The Register is published fortnightly during the parliamentary year.
84 Journalists who are accredited and have access to Parliament.
85 Over 500 All-Party Groups are registered. The majority are subject-specific, the remainder groups focusing on a country or region.

IV The Independent Parliamentary Standards Authority (IPSA)

Established under the Parliamentary Standards Act 2009, amended by the Constitutional Reform and Governance Act 2010:

- IPSA has responsibility for MPs' salaries, pensions, allowances and expenses;
- the Compliance Officer of IPSA investigates and reports on complaints concerning alleged breaches of the rules relating to expenses and allowances.

V The Electoral Commission

Established under the Political Parties, Elections and Referendums Act 2000, as amended by the Electoral Administration Act 2006 and the Political Parties and Elections Act 2009.

The Electoral Commission:

See further
Chapter 12.

- is an independent body set up by statute;
- maintains the Register of Political Parties;
- maintains and monitors donations and loans to political parties;
- investigates alleged breaches of the rules relating to donations;
- draws on the Register of Members' Interests for data on donations;
- oversees the conduct of elections and referendums.

The Commission is accountable to Parliament through the Speakers' Committee, chaired by the Speaker of the House of Commons and has one member appointed by the Prime Minister and five members appointed by the Speaker of the House.

Publication of Parliamentary Proceedings

The publication of proceedings in Parliament is covered by the same rules as the reporting of proceedings in court. The underlying principle is that publication is in the public interest and generally outweighs any disadvantage to individuals.

On the extent to which the reporting and publication of parliamentary proceedings is protected, section 1 of the Parliamentary Papers Act 1840 provides that, where civil or criminal proceedings are commenced, the defendant may present to the court a certificate stating that the publication in question was made under the authority of the House of Lords or House of Commons, and that the 'judge or court shall thereupon immediately stay such civil or criminal proceeding'.

Section 2 provides that similar protection exists for correct copies of official reports and authorised papers. Section 3 provides that extracts or abstracts from such reports or papers, for example in newspapers, are protected provided that such extracts are published *bona fide* and without malice. Thus papers of the House, or papers ordered to be published by the House, plus fair and accurate, but unauthorised, reports of proceedings are covered by qualified privilege, and an action for damages for injury allegedly caused by their publication would only lie if malice could be proven.

The Parliamentary Papers Act was passed as a direct result of two cases in which the courts and Parliament came into conflict, namely *Stockdale v Hansard* (1839) and the *Sheriff of Middlesex's Case*. While the passing of the Parliamentary Papers Act 1840 gives statutory authority to publication of official papers and authorised reports, uncertainty still remains as to the scope of the protection.

Where a newspaper reports parliamentary proceedings and goes beyond the mere publication of a Member of Parliament's speech and includes material of its own, in order to determine whether the whole article is protected by privilege it is necessary for the court to determine first what was said in debate, then decide whether any extraneous material added by the newspaper made the report unfair or inaccurate and thereby removed any privilege from the report.[86]

The Joint Committee on Parliamentary Privilege, reporting in 2013, recognised that there is a lack of clarity in the law relating to the reporting and broadcasting of parliamentary proceedings and recommended that the law should be modernised. New statutory provisions should be introduced to confirm that broadcasts made under the authority of Parliament, including online publication, enjoy absolute privilege. Furthermore there should be a statutory provision to establish that all 'fair and accurate' media reports enjoy privilege unless they had been motivated by malice.[87] The Joint Committee recommended the repeal of the 1840 Act. The government, in response, stated that it would consider whether to repeal or amend the Act.[88]

Publications which reflect on the dignity of the House as a whole are classified as 'constructive contempts', as are reflections on individual Members.[89] Illustrations of adverse comments published in the press include that of the *Sunday Express* which, in 1953, commented that two Members were asleep during an all-night sitting of the House. Further, in 1956, the *Sunday Express* criticised Members of Parliament for exempting themselves from the petrol rationing which had been imposed as a result of the Suez crises. The report of the Committee of Privileges held that the editor had been:

> guilty of a serious contempt in reflecting upon all Members of the House and so upon the House itself by alleging that Members of the House had been guilty of contemptible conduct in failing, owing to self interest, to protest at an unfair discrimination in their favour. Such an attack on Members is calculated to diminish the respect due to the House and so to lessen its authority.[90]

The issue of media pressure again fell for consideration by the Committee of Privileges in 1956. A Member of Parliament, Mr Arthur Lewis, gave notice of a forthcoming Prime Ministerial parliamentary question, which asked:

> whether he will arrange for part of the money contributed by the government for relief in Hungary to be allocated to the relief of the several thousand Egyptian people who have been rendered homeless and destitute by British shelling and rocket fire in Egypt.

In a scathing editorial in the *Sunday Graphic*, readers were invited to telephone Mr Lewis and give him their views. To assist this task, the newspaper published the Member's telephone number. As a consequence, the Member received thousands of irate telephone calls before the Post Office was able to change his number. In both cases, the editors were called to the Bar of the House and apologised.

---

86 **Curistan v Times Newspapers Ltd** (2007).
87 Report of the Joint Committee, HL Paper 30/HC 100, July 2013.
88 Cm 8771, 2013.
89 Erskine May, 1997, p. 121.
90 *Second Report from the Committee of Privileges*, HC 38 (1956–1957), London: HMSO.

Unauthorised disclosure of parliamentary proceedings

The unauthorised disclosure of proceedings conducted in private and of draft reports of committees which have not been reported to the House is governed by a resolution of the House of 1837, as amended in 1980. The resolution makes such disclosure a contempt of the House.[91] The House resolved in 1978 that its penal jurisdiction should only be used where the action complained of was likely to cause a 'substantial interference' with a committee's work.[92] The Committee of Privileges recommended in its 1985 report that 'substantial interference' with regard to leaked documents should be confined to confidential or classified information or deliberate attempts to undermine the work of the committee.[93]

Privilege and interests in the House of Lords

Privilege in the House of Lords

The House of Lords enjoys the same privilege of freedom from arrest[94] and freedom of speech as the Commons. Freedom of access to the Sovereign is enjoyed by the House collectively and by each peer individually. This privilege of peerage extends to all peers, irrespective of whether they sit in the House of Lords. The House of Lords has the same right as the Commons to determine its own procedure. In the event of a disputed peerage, the House of Lords has jurisdiction to determine the matter.[95] The House of Lords has the power to commit persons for breach of privilege or contempt and also the power to impose fines. The House of Lords may also summon judges to attend in order to give advice on points of law.

Members' interests

In 1996, in response to increased concerns over Members' interests, a Register of Members' Interests was established in the House of Lords. In addition, the House has approved a motion that Lords should always act on their personal honour and should never accept any financial inducement as an incentive or reward for exercising parliamentary influence. Members are regulated by a Code of Conduct.

Peers are no longer permitted to act as advocates for companies or organisations from whom they receive remuneration. They are, however, allowed to act as advisers to outside groups. Peers are no longer free to ask questions or to table amendments where their sponsoring organisation stands to gain benefit.

On Members' interests, the House of Lords agreed in 2011 to include in the Register of Interests 'the precise source of each individual payment made in relation to any directorship and the nature of the work carried on in return for that payment'. Transitional rules are in place to enable Members to regulate their relationships with outside bodies in compliance with the amended Guide to the Code of Conduct. From March 2013, any Member unable or unwilling to comply with the revised Code must take leave of absence.[96]

Enforcing the rules

In 2010 the House of Lords appointed a Lords Commissioner for Standards to investigate alleged breaches of the Code of Conduct or rules regulating Members' financial interests. The

---

91 See Leopold, 1980.
92 HC Deb Vol. 943 Col. 1198, 6 February 1978.
93 *Second Report from the Committee of Privileges: Premature Disclosure of Proceedings of Select Committee*, HC 555 (1984–1985), London: HMSO, paras 51–55; see Griffith and Ryle, 2003.
94 Sunday Times, 16 July 1995.
95 See **Stourton v Stourton** (1963).
96 See the Privileges and Conduct Committee, HL Paper 15, First Report, June 2012.

Commissioner reports to the Sub-Committee on Lords' Conduct. The Sub-Committee, where appropriate, recommends a disciplinary sanction to the Committee for Privileges and Conduct. The Member concerned has a right of appeal to the Committee for Privileges and Conduct against the Commissioner's findings and any recommended sanction. The Committee reports its recommendations to the House, which has the final decision. Members are under a duty to cooperate with any investigation.

Summary

The purpose of parliamentary privilege (which is enjoyed by both Houses of Parliament), both collective and individual, is to protect the independence and integrity of Parliament from outside influence and interference. To protect the separation of powers between the judiciary and Parliament, the courts may rule on the existence and scope of privilege, but once a matter is deemed to be within parliamentary privilege, the matter is left to Parliament to determine.

The collective privileges include the right to determine its own composition and procedure, and to discipline its Members (but note the Parliamentary Standards Act 2009). Individual privileges include freedom from arrest for civil matters for 40 days before and after a parliamentary session and, most importantly, freedom of speech in proceedings in Parliament which is protected under Article IX of the Bill of Rights 1689.

Members of Parliament have always been permitted to have employment outside Parliament and to enter into contracts for services with outside bodies. In recent years, the issue of the financial interests of both Members of Parliament and Members of the House of Lords has caused damage to the integrity of Parliament. Most recently with the abuse of MPs' expenses and allowances, Parliament finally agreed to establish an independent body and Commissioner to regulate MPs' pay and expenses, under the Parliamentary Standards Act 2009, as amended by the Constitutional Reform and Governance Act 2010.

 Further Reading

Denning, Lord, 'The Strauss Case' [1985] *Public Law* 80.

Doig, A, 'Sleaze fatigue: the house of ill-repute' (2002) 55 *Parliamentary Affairs* 389.

Geddis, A, 'Parliamentary privilege: quis custodiet ipsos custodes?' [2005] *Public Law* 696.

Leopold, P, 'Proceedings in Parliament: the grey area' [1991] *Public Law* 475.

Leopold, P, 'Free speech in Parliament and the courts' (1995) 15 *Legal Studies* 204.

Leyland, P, 'Freedom of information and the 2009 parliamentary expenses scandal' [2009] *Public Law* 675.

Parpworth, N, 'The Parliamentary Standards Act 2009: a constitutional dangerous dogs measure?' (2010) 73 *MLR* 262.

Chapter 18

The Protection of Human Rights

Chapter Contents

Learning Objectives

By the end of this chapter you should be able to:

☐ explain the theoretical approaches to the existence of human rights such as natural law and social contact theories;

☐ discuss the traditional piecemeal approach to civil liberties and human rights under the UK constitution;

☐ explain the origins and scope of the European Convention on Human Rights and Fundamental Freedoms and, with reference to case law, its impact on UK law;

☐ explain why the United Kingdom did not incorporate Convention rights into domestic law before the Human Rights Act 1998;

☐ explain in outline the procedure for making an application under the European Convention on Human Rights;

☐ explain the principal aspects of the Human Rights Act 1998;

☐ discuss the ways in which the Human Rights Act preserves parliamentary sovereignty and the separation of powers;

☐ evaluate the manner in which and extent to which the Human Rights Act promotes the rule of law;

☐ consider whether the Human Rights Act should be reformed, and the options for reform.

On the philosophy of rights see the companion website and see Chapter 3 for an introduction to social contract theory.

Introduction

The protection of the rights and freedoms of citizens and others within their jurisdiction is a fundamental duty of the state. In the majority of democratic states, fundamental rights are defined and protected by law under a written constitution. Under the United Kingdom's largely unwritten (or uncodified) constitution, rights and freedoms have traditionally been protected either by individual Acts of Parliament passed to meet a particular need[1] or by the judges in developing the common law.

One response to the ravages of the Second World War was the formation of the Council of Europe. Under its authority the European Convention on Human Rights and Fundamental Freedoms was designed to guarantee the protection of basic rights against the state. The majority of Member States (formally High Contracting Parties) – of whom there are now 47 – either had a written constitution which protected rights or they had incorporated the Convention rights into their law. For reasons discussed below, the British government remained reluctant, until 1997, to make Convention rights directly enforceable before the domestic courts. Accordingly, Convention rights could only be enforced before the Court of Human Rights in Strasbourg.[2] In 1997 the incoming government was committed to making Convention rights enforceable in the domestic courts, a commitment achieved under the Human Rights Act 1998.

The Emergence of the Constitutional Protection of Rights

The attempt to protect human rights on an international level began with the founding of the League of Nations after the First World War and the imposition of certain safeguards of human rights in peace treaties negotiated after the war for the protection of minorities. It was not, however, until after the Second World War that the international community became convinced of the real and pressing need to protect and promote human rights as an integral and essential element for the preservation of world peace and cooperation. The United Nations[3] provided the appropriate forum for international quasi-legislative activity. In 1948, the Universal Declaration on Human Rights was adopted, supplemented by two implementing international covenants in 1966: the International Covenant on Civil and Political Rights and the International Covenant on Economic, Social and Cultural Rights. Taken together, these documents represent an international Bill of Human Rights. Inspired by the United Nations Declaration and Covenants, many other regional conventions were drafted, for example the European Convention on Human Rights and Fundamental Freedoms 1950, the American Convention on Human Rights 1969 and the African Charter of 1987.[4]

---

1 For example the Race Relations Acts prohibiting discrimination. See further Chapter 19.
2 The Human Rights Act 1998 came into effect in Northern Ireland and Scotland in 1998, in England and Wales in 2000.
3 Which superseded the League of Nations in 1945.
4 See also the Hong Kong Bill of Rights based on the UN Covenant on Civil and Political Rights.

Rights and freedoms in Britain

It has long been a paradox that the United Kingdom – viewed as a liberal democratic state – should have no comprehensive written Bill of Rights.[5] This is especially so given that the United Kingdom has been responsible for restoring independence to many former colonies and dominions and, in so doing, has conferred upon those states both a written constitution and a Bill of Rights. The Human Rights Act 1998 marks a significant constitutional change in relation to citizens' awareness about rights, and their protection by judges in the domestic courts.[6] The Act and its implications are considered later in this chapter. Prior to incorporation of Convention rights, the judges used the Convention as an aid to interpretation to assist in resolving ambiguities in domestic law. However, given the supremacy of Parliament, the judges previously had no jurisdictional basis on which they could employ the Convention to protect rights. The Human Rights Act confers this jurisdiction, requiring the courts not only to protect Convention rights, but to make 'declarations of incompatibility' wherever domestic law is judicially seen to conflict with Convention rights. By this means, Parliament preserves its supremacy over changes in the law which may be required by judicial evaluation of domestic law against the provisions of the Convention. Before considering the Human Rights Act, however, it is necessary to understand the status and working of the European Convention and the scope and application of the Convention rights which the Act incorporates.

PART A: THE EUROPEAN CONVENTION ON HUMAN RIGHTS AND FUNDAMENTAL FREEDOMS

Introduction

Europe was one of the principal theatres of the Second World War, following which there was felt to be a great need for European political, social and economic unity. Those objectives were perceived to be promoted, in part, by the adoption of a uniform Convention designed to protect human rights and fundamental freedoms. In 1949, the Council of Europe was established and the Convention on Human Rights ratified by signatory states (formally High Contracting Parties) in 1951, coming into force in 1953.[7] Despite having been instrumental in the drafting of the text of the Convention, the British government had strong reservations about the Convention and its impact on British constitutional law. As a result of such reservations, it was not until 1965 that the government gave individuals the right to petition under the Convention.

The influence of the Convention before the Human Rights Act 1998[8]

The attitude of the United Kingdom courts towards the Convention was, in the past, the traditional one adopted in relation to treaties. Treaties form part of international law and have no place within the domestic legal order unless and until incorporated into law.[9] The courts regarded the Convention as an aid to interpretation but had no jurisdiction directly to enforce

---

5   The Bill of Rights 1689, it will be recalled, was concerned with constitutional arrangements between the Crown and Parliament, not with the rights of individuals.

6   See the Consultation Paper, *Bringing Rights Home: Labour's Plans to Incorporate the European Convention on Human Rights into United Kingdom Law*, 1996, London: Labour Party. Note that technically the Human Rights Act 1998 does not incorporate the Convention, but rather makes Convention rights enforceable before the domestic courts.

7   For a succinct history of the Convention, see Lester (Lord), 'European human rights and the British constitution', in Jowell and Oliver, 2000.

8   See Browne-Wilkinson, 1992; Bingham, 1993; Laws, 1993.

9   See **Kaur v Lord Advocate** (1980).

the rights and freedoms under the Convention.[10] This could, however, of itself be significant. For example, in **Waddington v Miah** (1974), Lord Reid stated – having referred to Article 7 of the Convention which prohibits retrospective legislation – that 'it is hardly credible that any government Department would promote, or that Parliament would pass, retrospective criminal legislation'.[11]

R v Secretary of State for the Home Department ex parte Brind (1991) also illustrates the influence of the Convention. The Home Secretary had exercised his discretionary power under section 29(3) of the Broadcasting Act 1981 to issue a notice prohibiting the broadcasting on television or radio of the voices of any person speaking on behalf of an organisation proscribed under the Prevention of Terrorism (Temporary Provisions) Act 1974. The words used could be reported through the medium of an actor, provided that the voice of the spokesperson was not broadcast. The challenge to this prohibition was, in the House of Lords, based primarily on the argument that it was contrary to the United Kingdom's obligations under Article 10 of the Convention, guaranteeing freedom of expression. It was argued that the Home Secretary should have had regard to the Convention in exercising his discretion under the Broadcasting Act.

The House of Lords was prepared to accept that there was a presumption that Parliament would enact laws that were in conformity with the Convention. Accordingly, it was accepted that where a statute permits two interpretations, one in line with the Convention, the other contrary to it, the interpretation which fitted with the Convention should be preferred. In **Brind**, the court could find no ambiguity in section 29(3) of the Broadcasting Act.[12] The only basis for challenge therefore was that the Home Secretary's decision was unreasonable in the **Wednesbury**[13] sense: that the decision was so irrational or unreasonable that no rational or reasonable person could have reached the same decision.

A rather different approach to the Convention was adopted in **Derbyshire County Council v Times Newspapers Ltd** (1993), concerning the question of whether a local council could bring an action in libel against newspapers (see further below). In the Court of Appeal, Butler-Sloss LJ was forthright in declaring that 'where there is ambiguity, or the law is otherwise unclear as so far undeclared by an appellate court, the English court is not only entitled but … obliged to consider the implications of Article 10'. The House of Lords, however, while arriving at the result achieved in the Court of Appeal – namely that local authorities enjoyed no standing to sue in defamation – did so without relying on Article 10 of the Convention, but relying on the common law.

Accordingly, there existed (before the Human Rights Act 1998 came into force) no obligation on courts to rely on the Convention if a source of authority could be found within domestic law. Increasingly, however, it appeared that – within certain limits – the judiciary expressed willingness to protect individual liberties and, where a statute was ambiguous, or silent, to construe the statute strictly and in favour of the liberty of the citizen.

However, there were limits to the extent to which judges were able to protect rights, as the case of **R v Inland Revenue Commissioners ex parte Rossminster Ltd** (1980) revealed.[14] In **Rossminster**, the House of Lords ruled that, where the meaning of a statute is clear and unambiguous, the court possessed no jurisdiction to go against its unambiguous words, and was under a duty to uphold the will of Parliament by giving effect to its words.[15] In both **Attorney**

---

10 **Waddington v Miah** (1974).
11 See further below for the (retrospective) War Crimes Act 1991.
12 On the post Human Rights Act 1998 position and ambiguity, see Lord Irvine, 1998.
13 **Associated Provincial Picture Houses Ltd v Wednesbury Corporation** (1948). See further Chapter 24.
14 See also **R v Kelly, R v Sandford** (1998); **R v Secretary of State for the Home Department ex parte Hussain Ahmed** (1998).
15 See also **R v DPP ex parte Kebeline** (1999).

General v *BBC* (1981) and *Attorney General* v *Guardian Newspapers (No 2)* (1990), however, the House of Lords confirmed that it was the duty of the courts to have regard to the international obligations assumed under the Convention, and to interpret the law in accordance with those obligations.

Institutions and procedure under the Convention

The Council of Europe, under which the Convention operates, is constitutionally distinct from the European Union. The Council was founded in 1949, inspired by the United Nations' Universal Declaration of Human Rights of 1948. The Committee of Ministers is the political body, consisting of one representative from each state government (Foreign Ministers). The Parliamentary Assembly of the Council of Europe (PACE) has 636 members representing the countries belonging to the Council of Europe. The Assembly has power to investigate human rights issues, to make recommendations and to advise. Its work is valuable and bodies such as the Parliament of the European Union and other European Union institutions refer to its work. The Assembly elects the Secretary General of the Council of Europe and the judges of the Court of Human Rights. The Court of Human Rights represents the judicial body. Judges are elected for a renewable six-year term of office, and need not be drawn exclusively from the judiciary. To qualify for appointment, a person must be 'of high moral character' and must either possess the qualifications required for appointment of high judicial office or be a jurisconsult of recognised competence.

The right of application

Applications may be brought by states or by individuals. The right of individual petition to a body outside the jurisdiction of states was a constitutional innovation. As noted above, the British government was exceedingly cautious about conceding such a right and only in 1965 did the right of individual application become available to citizens of the United Kingdom. Applications may come from individuals, groups of individuals or non-governmental organisations. The applicant(s) must be personally affected by the issue: complaints involving alleged conduct which does not personally affect the individual complainant are not admissible.[16]

With the Human Rights Act 1998 fully in force, individuals will only make an application to the Court of Human Rights if they fail to secure an effective remedy before the domestic courts.

The procedure
Exhaustion of domestic remedies

Any domestic remedies which are available must be exhausted.[17] Thus, if a remedy is available within domestic law, it must first be sought. Only where there exists no remedy in law, or where the pursuit of a remedy would be unequivocally certain to fail,[18] may an individual lodge a petition.

---

16 *X* v *Norway* (1960). See also *Vijayanathan* v *France* (1991).
17 ECHR, Article 35.
18 For example, where there are strong precedents established.

The time limit

The application must be made within six months of the final decision of the highest court having jurisdiction within the domestic legal system.[19] The time limit will be reduced to four months once Protocol 15 comes into force. On this see Reform below.

Admissibility

A number of hurdles face the applicant in having his application declared admissible:

> The Court may only deal with a matter after all domestic remedies have been exhausted. The Court shall not deal with any application that is:
>
> (a)   anonymous; or
> (b)   substantially the same as a matter that has already been examined by the Court and contains no relevant new information.

An individual application will be declared inadmissible where it is incompatible with the Convention or its Protocols, manifestly ill-founded or an abuse of the right of application; or where the applicant has not suffered a significant disadvantage. An application may not be dismissed on the basis of no significant disadvantage if it has not been considered by a domestic court. The Court may reject an application which it considers inadmissible at any stage of the proceedings.

Under Protocol 15, which has yet to be ratified by all state parties, the test of 'substantial disadvantage' has been amended to delete the proviso that the case has been duly considered by a domestic tribunal. This is intended to ensure that the Court deals only with significant matters.

Once an application is declared admissible, the examination of the merits will commence. The complainant has a limited right to appear where the Court requires further evidence. The Court's decision must be reasoned and, if not unanimous, individual judges may give a separate opinion. Under Article 43(1) of the Convention, any party to the case may, within three months from the date of the judgment of a Chamber (effectively the 'court of first instance' hearing the case), request that the case be referred to the Grand Chamber. If it is not so referred, the judgment becomes final. Alternatively, if referred, the judgment of the Grand Chamber is final (Article 44) and states undertake to abide by the decision of the Court. Compensation can be awarded by the Court.

Enforcing the judgment

As noted above, under Article 46, states are under an obligation to comply with the judgment of the Court of Human Rights. The task of ensuring that the judgment is complied with lies with the Committee of Ministers: the matter is thus returned to the political arena. If a state refuses to comply with the judgment, its membership of the Council of Europe can be suspended or, ultimately, it may be expelled from the Council. Where exercised, this ultimate power has regrettable implications and would remove the protection of the Convention from individuals within the state and thus further damage the protection of rights. Greece withdrew from the Council of Europe following five allegations of persecution against it between 1967 and 1970. In 1974, a new Greek government ratified the Convention once

---

19 ECHR, Article 35.

more. However, failure to comply with a judgment will cause adverse publicity for the state and there is thus great political pressure to conform.[20]

The 'margin of appreciation'

In respect of almost all Articles of the Convention, there is an area of discretion as to the means by which they protect the substantive rights. This margin of appreciation is necessary in order that the Convention can apply in a workable fashion in very diverse societies. It also means, however, that application of the Convention will not be uniform throughout the legal systems and that states may be able to deviate from the protection given.

Whether the state has a margin of appreciation – and the scope of it – is a matter to be determined under the Convention. The doctrine is unpredictable in operation and has become, over the years, applicable to all Articles. Accordingly, it is a concept which is capable of significantly undermining the protection given by the Convention, and has been criticised for so doing.[21]

Derogation and reservation

Where a state finds it impossible or undesirable to comply with specific Articles, it is possible for the state to derogate, or enter a reservation as to the matter. No derogation is permitted in relation to Article 2 (the right to life), other than in war situations. Derogation is not allowed in respect of Articles 3 (freedom from torture), 4(1) (slavery or servitude) and 7 (freedom from retrospective criminal liability).[22] The right of derogation is limited. Article 15 provides that:

> In time of war or other public emergency threatening the life of the nation any High Contracting Party may take measures derogating from its obligations under this Convention to the extent strictly required by the exigencies of the situation, provided that such measures are not inconsistent with its other obligations under international law.

A challenge can be made to the lawfulness of derogation. Following the United Kingdom's derogation after the decision in **Brogan v United Kingdom** (1988), a challenge was lodged, but failed when it was held that the situation in Northern Ireland did amount to a public emergency[23] and was thus within the terms of Article 15.

Article 17: the prohibition of abuse of rights

Article 17 prohibits the state or any 'group or person' from engaging in any activity which is aimed at the destruction of rights and freedoms protected under the Convention, or from limiting the rights and freedoms to a greater extent than is provided for in the Convention.

---

20 On derogation from Convention right, see below.
21 See Van Dijk and Van Hoof, 1990, p. 604.
22 But see the War Crimes Act 1991, which provides for the prosecution of war crimes committed during the Second World War.
23 **Brannigan and McBride v United Kingdom** (1993).

The Convention Protocols

In addition to the substantive Articles of the Convention, there exists a series of Protocols on matters ranging from the right to peaceful enjoyment of possessions (First Protocol, Article 1),[24] education (First Protocol, Article 2),[25] the holding of regular free elections (First Protocol, Article 3), freedom of movement (Fourth Protocol), abolition of the death penalty (Sixth Protocol), appeals in criminal cases and sexual equality (Seventh Protocol), procedural matters under the Convention (Ninth Protocol) and minority rights (Tenth Protocol). The Eleventh Protocol abolished the Commission and provided new procedures for applying directly to the court. The United Kingdom is not a party to the Fourth or Seventh Protocols. In relation to Article 2 of the First Protocol, the government has entered a reservation to the effect that the rights of parents to determine the education of their children are respected in the United Kingdom only to the extent that such respect is compatible with the requirements of the Education Acts.[26]

Reform

Political concerns over the role of the Court of Human Rights led to three conferences of the Committee of Ministers of the Council of Europe, held at Interlaken, Switzerland in 2010, Izmir, Turkey in 2011 and Brighton, England in 2012. The outcome was Protocol 15, adopted by the Committee of Ministers in May 2013. The Protocol will come into force three months after ratification by all 47 state parties.

Protocol 15 amends the Preamble to the Convention, adding a reference to the principle of subsidiarity and doctrine of margin of appreciation. This is intended to enhance the transparency of these concepts and to be consistent with the margin of appreciation accorded to state parties. The margin of appreciation is intended to reflect the fact that national authorities are in principle the better safeguards of individual rights than an international court.

Protocol 15 also amends Article 30 so that the parties to a case may no longer object to a Chamber relinquishing a case in favour of the Grand Chamber. This is designed to accelerate proceedings before the Court particularly where there is an important question regarding the interpretation of the Convention or the Protocols or there is a potential departure from existing case law.

As noted above, the time limit for applications is reduced from six to four months, and the test of serious disadvantage has been amended.

Convention violations 2018

In 2018 the European Court of Human Rights handed down a total of 2,738 judgments. Of these, the Court found at least one Convention violation in 880 cases. The state with the highest number of judgments was the Russian Federation with 248 judgments. The total number of judgments relating to the United Kingdom was two, with a violation being found in one case.[27]

---

24 See **Stretch v United Kingdom** (2003).
25 See **Belgian Linguistics Case (No 2)** (1968).
26 On 4 November 2000, Protocol 12 opened for signature. Protocol 12 introduces an independent right to equality, stating that the 'enjoyment of any right set forth by law shall be secured without discrimination, on any arbitrary ground'.
27 For the full list of violations by Article and by respondent State in 2015 see the Annual Report of the European Court, pp. 199–200.

PART B: THE HUMAN RIGHTS ACT 1998

The incorporation of Convention rights into domestic law under the 1998 Act put an end, finally, to the debate over whether or not to incorporate – a debate which had endured for decades. That long-running debate focused on three principal concerns, namely: the criticism that the Convention was outdated and not tailored specifically to British conditions; that the judiciary was ill equipped to assume the mantle of guardian of individual rights in the face of executive power and the concept of parliamentary sovereignty;[28] and concerns over the manner in which 'incorporation' would affect the conventional balance of power between judges and Parliament. There was also the argument that the House of Commons, as the democratically elected representative of the people, was best equipped to respond to the better protection of rights.

The effect of the Act is such that three avenues for challenging public bodies arise:

- first, a failure to comply with Convention rights now forms the basis for legal action;
- second, a new ground for judicial review has been introduced, namely the alleged breach of human rights; and
- third, Convention rights may in some circumstances be used as a defence to actions brought by public bodies.

The Act provides a charter of rights now enforceable before the domestic courts. The effectiveness of the Human Rights Act 1998 rests on three foundations:

- the willingness of the judges robustly to defend rights and to interpret Convention rights in a manner favouring individual protection against governmental encroachment;
- Parliament's willingness to amend the law to ensure compliance with declarations of incompatibility with Convention rights; and
- the energy with which individual citizens are prepared to assert their rights in courts of law.

The manner in which the Act was drafted raised a number of questions:

- the meaning of 'public authorities' for the purposes of the Act;
- whether the Act had solely 'vertical' effect – binding only those bodies for which the state is accountable to Strasbourg – or is capable of also having 'horizontal' effect, and being enforceable against bodies for which the state is not accountable to Strasbourg;
- the extent to which judicial interpretative techniques relating to statutes have changed, and the extent to which the judges have developed the common law to give effect to Convention rights.

As will be seen below, the case law is clarifying these issues.

The territorial reach of the Convention

Article 1 of the Convention provides that signatory states 'shall secure to everyone within their jurisdiction the rights and freedoms defined in … this convention'. The question which has arisen is the scope of the state's jurisdiction. It is clear that jurisdiction relates to the

---

28 See Griffith, 1997; but cf. Lester, 1994 and 1997.

country itself, but it is less clear as to whether it extends to territory or property abroad but under the control of the signatory state. One case considering the scope of the Convention was **R (Al Rawi) v Secretary of State for Foreign and Commonwealth Affairs** (2006), in which the Court of Appeal considered allegations of discrimination on the part of the Foreign Office between British nationals and non-nationals; the scope of responsibility of the state for non-nationals and the justiciability of the conduct of foreign affairs. The claimants were imprisoned by the United States authorities at Guantanamo Bay and sought judicial review of the Secretary of State's refusal to make diplomatic representations requesting their release and return to Britain, alleging discrimination on grounds of nationality and a violation of their rights under the European Convention. The Court of Appeal ruled that the difference in treatment between the claimants and British citizens in the same position was that the claimants, as non-nationals, were not persons the United Kingdom was under a duty to protect. On the issue of the justiciability of foreign policy, the court reiterated the principle that matters of 'delicate policy' were for the executive and not the courts.

The question of whether the Convention applies to territories in which British troops are operating is a complex and controversial issue which has been considered by the European Court of Human Rights and the domestic courts. A number of claims have been made against the British government in relation to the Iraq War, some involving allegations of unlawful imprisonment by British troops, others involving allegations of ill-treatment by British troops, others demanding that the government establish independent inquiries into the deaths of Iraqi citizens. In **Al-Saadoon v Secretary of State for Defence** and **Rahmatullah v Secretary of State for Defence** (2016) Lloyd Jones LJ stated that there were 1,282 public law claims whereby claimants sought orders requiring the Secretary of State to investigate alleged human rights violations and approximately 646 claims for compensation for alleged Convention violations in war time pending, with 257 claims having been settled. In 2016 the Defence Secretary announced that in future conflicts the government intended to derogate from the Convention. However, Article 15 makes it clear that derogation is only allowed in relation to a 'time of war or other public emergency threatening the life of the nation' and is only allowed 'to the extent strictly required by the exigencies of the situation'. Furthermore, derogation is not permitted from Article 2 – the right to life (except in respect of deaths resulting from lawful acts of war) – or to Article 3 – protection from torture, degrading or inhuman treatment. Derogating, therefore, would not protect British troops from allegations of violations of Articles 2 or 3 in war time.

The issue was considered by the House of Lords in **R (Al-Skeini and Others) v Secretary of State for Defence** (2007) in relation to acts of the armed forces overseas. The Court referred to the general rule that every statute was to be interpreted, 'so far as language permitted', so as not to be inconsistent with the established rules of international law and the comity of nations. Following the jurisprudence of the European Court of Human Rights,[29] the House of Lords ruled that the Convention reflected an essentially territorial notion of jurisdiction and that the extra-territorial exercise of jurisdiction was exceptional and required justification. The Court ruled that the Convention operates extra-territorially first in circumstances where the state has – as a consequence of military occupation or the consent of the government of that country – effective control of the relevant country. Second, the Convention operates in relation to diplomatic embassies/consulates and on-board craft and vessels registered or flying the flag of that state.[30] It does not, however, operate in relation to armed forces serving overseas when they are not in premises which are under state control. In **R (Smith) v Secretary**

---

29 See **Bankovic v Belgium** (2001); **Drozd v France** (1992); **Issa v Turkey** (2004).
30 On territorial reach, see also **R (Al-Saadoon) v Secretary of State for Defence** (2009).

of State for Defence (2010) the Supreme Court confirmed that the Convention did not operate in relation to armed forces serving overseas when not on premises which are under state control. Third, in **Al-Skeini and Others v United Kingdom** (2011) the Court of Human Rights ruled that the European Convention on Human Rights applied in southern Iraq at the time when Britain was the occupying power in that region. This decision represented a departure from earlier case law and extends the reach of the Convention into previously excluded territory. The European Court of Human Rights' interpretation of territorial reach is broader than either the House of Lords or its successor, the Supreme Court. Contracting states are now required to comply with the Convention 'whenever a State through its agents exercises control and authority over an individual'. The **Al-Skeini case** was brought by relatives of five Iraqis, four of whom were shot by British forces, one of whom drowned. In each case there should have been a full investigation into the circumstances surrounding the deaths by an expert and independent investigator. The Military Special Investigation Branch (SIB) was not independent and therefore was not an appropriate investigator: there was a violation of Article 2 of the Convention.

In **Smith (and Others) v Ministry of Defence** (2013) the Supreme Court considered several issues which have wide-ranging implications for the liability of government for soldiers on active service. The case arose out of the deaths of three servicemen and serious injuries of two other servicemen serving in Iraq. The first set of claims (the Challenger claims) arose from a 'friendly fire' incident. The action was brought in negligence and alleged that the Ministry of Defence (MOD) had failed to equip the tanks properly and to give adequate training. The second set of claims (the Snatch Land Rover claims) arose from the deaths of two soldiers by the detonation of improvised explosive devices (IEDs). It was alleged that the MOD had failed in its duty under Article 2 to protect the lives of soldiers required to patrol in the Land Rovers. In its defence the MOD argued that the soldiers were not within the UK's jurisdiction, that accordingly there was no duty under Article 2 and that in relation to the negligence claims these should be struck out on the basis of combat immunity and that it would not be 'fair, just or reasonable' to impose a duty of care on the MOD in the circumstances.

The first issue was whether soldiers serving overseas were within the territorial reach of the European Convention on Human Rights and therefore entitled to the protection of Convention rights. If they were within the jurisdiction of the UK (the first issue), the second issue was whether Article 2 imposed positive obligations on the UK to prevent the deaths of its soldiers in active operations. Third, in relation to allegations of negligence on the part of the Ministry of Defence, should those claims be struck out on the basis that they fell within the concept of 'combat immunity' or that it would not be 'fair, just or reasonable' to impose a duty to protect against death or injury in the circumstances of the case. The Supreme Court held, unanimously, that the soldiers were within the UK's jurisdiction for the purposes of the Convention. The Court ruled, by four votes to three, that the claims should not be struck out on the ground that they were not within Article 2 and that they should not be struck out on the basis of 'combat immunity' or that it would not be 'fair, just or reasonable' to extend the MOD's duty of care to those cases.

The protection of the Convention may, however, be unavailable where action taken by British forces overseas were acts of an 'inherently governmental nature in the conduct of foreign military operations by the Crown'. In **Mohammed v Ministry of Defence** (2017) the claimant, an Afghan national, had been captured by British troops and transferred into Afghan custody. He was subsequently convicted of offences relating to the insurgency in Afghanistan. He sought damages from the British government. The Supreme Court ruled that the alleged mistreatment and alleged unlawful detention of the claimant were Crown acts of state for which the government could not be liable. However, the Court also ruled that the doctrine of acts of state must be narrowly confined to a class of acts which are governmental in nature, committed abroad and so closely connected to policy as to be necessary. It could not apply to acts of torture or maltreatment of detainees.

Military operations in Iraq between 2003 and 2009 and in Afghanistan in 2002 to 2017 gave rise to an unprecedented number of legal claims for damages and non-compliance with the ECHR.[31] The Overseas Operations (Service Personnel and Veterans) Bill 2019 - 2021 provides a statutory presumption against prosecution and the requirement to give particular weight to specified factors when considering whether or not to prosecute in criminal cases. The measures will apply only to events that took place more than five years ago, the period being calculated from the date of the alleged conduct. The government claims that nothing in the Bill will prevent the prosecution of those guilty of serious criminal offences, but that it will stop the 'wave of vexatious claims' that UK service personnel and veterans have had to endure. Separate legislation will be introduced in relation to Northern Ireland. The Bill also contains a derogation provision.

Clause 12 inserts a new section 14A into the Human Rights Act and provides that in relation to any 'significant' overseas operations, the Secretary of State must consider whether it would be appropriate to derogate from the Convention, A 'significant operation' is one defined as being an overseas operation in the course of which members of British forces may come under attack or face the threat of attack or violent resistance. The duty is ongoing: the Secretary of State must keep the question of derogation under review throughout the whole operation.

The status of the Human Rights Act

As discussed in Chapter 6, under the constitution of the United Kingdom, and consistent with the doctrine of parliamentary sovereignty, legislation cannot be entrenched. That is to say, it cannot be given a 'special' or 'higher' status than other Acts of Parliament. This traditional doctrine has been preserved in relation to the Human Rights Act. In its White Paper, the government announced that it did not intend to permit the courts to strike down Acts of Parliament, whether that legislation preceded the Act or was introduced subsequently. Thereby, Parliament's sovereignty and, to the extent possible, the separation of powers, are preserved. The Act, in the government's view, was 'intended to provide a new basis for judicial interpretation of all legislation, not a basis for striking down any part of it'.[32]

However, notwithstanding the careful drafting of the Human Rights Act in order to preserve sovereignty, the judges have developed the concept of the 'constitutional statute',[33] one consequence of which is that the doctrine of implied repeal does not operate and only an express intention to amend or repeal the Act will have effect.

The meaning of public authorities[34]

The Human Rights Act 1998 provides that public authorities exercising executive powers must comply with the requirements of the Convention. The European Convention imposes responsibilities on signatory states to protect rights, and as such it is the state and its agencies

---

31 Including 1,400 applications for judicial review and 900 civil claims for compensation and findings that the UK was in breach of ECHR requirements.
32 White Paper, *Rights Brought Home: The Human Rights Bill*, Cm 3782, 1997, London: HMSO, para. 2.14. However, the courts are given power over delegated, or secondary, legislation.
33 See **R v Secretary of State for the Home Department ex parte Simms** (2000); **Thoburn v Sunderland City Council** (2002).
34 See Oliver, 2004; Sunkin, 2004.

which are the defendants in allegations of Convention violations before the Court of Human Rights. The emphasis on public bodies/authorities under the Human Rights Act reflects this now traditional form of state liability.[35] As will be seen, however, the impact of the Human Rights Act is extending beyond the sphere of public bodies for which the state is responsible.

Section 6(3)(b) of the Act provides that a public authority includes 'any person certain of whose functions are functions of a public nature'. The test, therefore, is not state ownership, funding or control per se but rather the functions which a body performs. The position is complicated by section 6(5), which provides that a person is not a public authority (applying the functions test) 'if the nature of the act is private'. Accordingly, the Act recognises that some authorities may, notwithstanding their ownership or control or funding by the state, be public on the functions test, but will not be treated as public bodies in relation to some actions which are deemed to be private. An example given in debate was that of Network Rail, which is a public authority when exercising its function as a safety regulator, but acts privately in its role as property developer.[36]

The definition of 'public body' was considered by the Court of Appeal in **R (Heather) v Leonard Cheshire Foundation** (2002). The Foundation is a private charity which provides accommodation for the disabled, some of which is funded by the local authority pursuant to its statutory duty under the National Assistance Act 1948, as amended. The court made it clear that residents of the home funded by the local authority could rely on their Convention rights against the authority but not against the charity, since it was not exercising public functions. Aside from the funding being provided by the state, there was no other evidence 'of there being a public flavour to the functions of the foundation or the foundation itself. The foundation was not standing in the shoes of the local authorities'.[37] In **Aston Cantlow and Billesley Parochial Church Council v Wallbank** (2003), the House of Lords ruled that a Parochial Church Council which had statutory duties to enforce parish church repairs was not a public authority for the purposes of the Human Rights Act. The Court ruled that although the Church of England had special links with central government and performed certain public functions, it was not a core public authority.

The 'functions test' which is central to whether a body is a public body and therefore bound by the Human Rights Act was considered by the House of Lords in **YL v Birmingham City Council and Others** (2007).[38] The case involved the rights of a resident in a private care home who had been placed there by her local authority, which paid the fees[39] save for a small top-up fee paid by her relatives. The Court ruled, Lord Bingham of Cornhill dissenting, that the company acted as a private, profit-earning company. Lord Bingham in his dissent, however, stated that this situation was 'precisely the case which section 6(3)(b) was intended to embrace'.[40] The unsatisfactory outcome of this decision, which left an estimated 300,000 elderly people living in private care homes unprotected by the Human Rights Act, was essentially caused by the undefined dividing line between public and private functions. The law was reformed. The Health and Social Care Act 2008, section 145, states that those providing accommodation under the National Assistance Act 1948 or equivalent Scottish and Northern Ireland statutes are exercising functions of a public nature.

---

35 See Oliver, 2000.
36 See HC Deb Vol. 314 Cols 406–414, 17 June 1998, and Col. 1231, 16 November 1997. The Home Secretary in debate stated that the British Broadcasting Corporation is a public authority but that independent television companies are not, whilst the Independent Television Commission is: *Hansard* Col. 778, 16 December 1998.
37 See also **Poplar Housing and Regeneration Community Association Ltd v Donoghue** (2001): a housing association performing functions analogous to the local authority was a public authority for the purposes of the Act.
38 The decision was reached by a majority of three to two.
39 Pursuant to its duty under s. 21 of the National Assistance Act 1948 as amended by s. 195 of and para. 2 of Sched. 23 to the Local Government Act 1989.
40 At p. 118, para. 20. Baroness Hale echoed this approach: see p. 132, para. 73.

However, the classification of bodies (public or private) does not exhaust the potential for the Act to develop the protection of human rights, because according to section 6 the courts themselves are public authorities and are under a statutory duty to give effect to Convention rights. Accordingly, the courts may, in complying with their section 6 duty, enforce Convention rights against private – or non-state – bodies.[41]

Section 2: The European Court of Human Rights and domestic courts

In **R (Osborn) v Parole Board** (2013) the Supreme Court considered the relationship between the common law, the Human Rights Act 1998 and the European Convention on Human Rights. In a summary of the conclusion reached, Lord Reed JSC explained that relationship in the following manner:

> In order to comply with common law standards of procedural fairness, the board should hold an oral hearing before determining an application for release, or for a transfer to open conditions, whenever fairness to the prisoner requires such a hearing in the light of the facts of the case and the importance of what is at stake. By doing so the board will also fulfil its duty under section 6(1) of the Human Rights Act 1998 to act compatibly with article 5.4 of the European Convention for the Protection of Human Rights and Fundamental Freedoms, in circumstances where that article is engaged. [paragraph 2]

Lord Reed stated that the correct starting point for the analysis of rights is the common law. The rights guaranteed under the European Convention (as with much of international law) are expressed in very broad terms, and in order to be enforced must be translated into detailed rules in domestic law:

> The values underlying both the Convention and our own constitution require that Convention rights should be protected primarily by a detailed body of domestic law. The Convention taken by itself is too inspecific to provide the guidance which is necessary in a state governed by the rule of law. [at paragraph 56]

On the Human Rights Act 1998, Lord Reed emphasised that although it is an Act of great importance, it does not supersede the protection of human rights under the common law or statute. Lord Reed set out several examples from the case law to demonstrate that the analytical starting point is the common law, not the jurisprudence of the European Court of Human Rights. In **R (Daly) v Secretary of State for the Home Department** (2001) Lord Bingham of Cornhill adopted the approach of Lord Cooke of Thorndon who said that:

> It is of great importance, in my opinion, that the common law by itself is being recognised as a sufficient source of the fundamental right to confidential communication with a legal adviser for the purpose of obtaining legal advice. Thus the decision may prove to be in point in common law jurisdictions not affected by the Convention. Rights similar to those in the Convention are of course to be found in constitutional documents and other formal affirmations of rights elsewhere. **The**

---

41 See Wade, 2000, p. 223; cf. Hunt, 1998. There is an analogy here with Article 10 of the EC Treaty, which the CJEU has used to great effect in extending the liability of Member States. See further Chapter 8.

truth is, I think, that some rights are inherent and fundamental to democratic civilised society. Conventions, constitutions, bills of rights and the like respond by recognising rather than creating them. [at paragraph 58; emphasis added]

Citing also **R (Sturnham) v Parole Board** (2013) Lord Reed stated that:

the ordinary approach to the relationship between domestic law and the Convention was described as being that the courts endeavour to apply and if need be develop the common law, and interpret and apply statutory provisions, so as to arrive at a result which is in compliance with the UK's international obligations, **the starting point being our own legal principles rather than the judgments of the international court.** [emphasis added]

The judicial focus on the common law is increasingly apparent. Paul Craig cites, in addition to **Osborn** and **Daly**, the case of **R (West) v Parole Board** (2005) in which the right to an oral hearing was held to derive from common law principles, not from either Articles 5 or 6 of the Convention.[42] Also discussed is the case of **R (Anufrijeva) v Secretary of State for the Home Department** (2003) in which the House of Lords ruled that the notice of a decision adversely affecting the claimant had to be given before the decision could take effect was a principle derived from common law. Equally, the House of Lords' rejection of evidence obtained by torture is based on common law principles, not statute.[43]

In **Kennedy v Charity Commission** (2014) the common law principle of open justice underpinned the requirement of disclosure of information. Lord Toulson JSC discussed the relationship between the Human Rights Act and the common law in the following manner:

The analysis set out above is based on common law principles and not on Article 10, which in my view adds nothing to the common law in the present context. This is not surprising. What we now term human rights law and public law has developed through our common law over a long period of time ... The growth of the state has presented the courts with new challenges to which they have responded by a process of gradual adaption and development of the common law to meet current needs. This has always been the way of the common law and it has not ceased on the enactment of the Human Rights Act 1998, although since then there has sometimes been a baleful and unnecessary tendency to overlook the common law. It needs to be emphasized that it was not the purpose of the Human Rights Act that the common law should become an ossuary.[44]

Section 2 of the Human Rights Act 1998 requires the court to 'take into account the judgments, decisions, declarations or advisory opinions' of the European Court of Human Rights, Commission and Committee of Ministers. This does not, however, mean that the courts are bound to follow slavishly such judgments. The issue was central to the case of **Kay v Lambeth LBC; Leeds City Council v Price** (2006), in which the House of Lords considered both sections 2 and 6 of the Human Rights Act 1998. In the **Leeds** case before the Court of Appeal, the court concluded that the decision of **Connors v United Kingdom** (2004) was inconsistent with the earlier decision of the House of Lords in **Harrow LBC v Qazi** (2004) and that they

---

42 See also **Guardian News v City of Westminster Magistrates' Court** (2012).
43 See **A v Secretary of State for the Home Department** (2004), discussed below.
44 At para. 133.

were bound to follow the House of Lords. Lord Bingham of Cornhill recognised that effective implementation of the Convention depended upon 'constructive collaboration' between the Court of Human Rights and national courts. He also, however, insisted that adherence to precedent was a 'cornerstone of the legal system' which ensured a degree of certainty. In **R v Horncastle, R v Marquis** (2009), the Supreme Court made an important statement of principle concerning the duty to follow the case law of the Court of Human Rights. In this case, the applicants argued that their right to fair trial had been violated, based on the decision of the Court of Human Rights in **Al-Khawaja and Tahery v United Kingdom** (2009). Rejecting that argument, Lord Phillips of Worth Matravers PSC stated that on rare occasions the domestic court might have concerns that the Court of Human Rights had not 'sufficiently appreciated or accommodated particular aspects of the domestic process'. In those circumstances the domestic court could decline to follow the Strasbourg decision, giving reasons for doing so. That could then lead to a 'valuable dialogue' between the domestic and Strasbourg courts.

A starting point for considering the issue is **R (Ullah) v Secretary of State for the Home Department** (2004), in which it was stated that the case law of the European Court was not strictly binding but must be followed unless special circumstances dictated otherwise. Lord Bingham in **Ullah** stated that 'The duty of the courts is to keep pace with the Strasbourg jurisprudence as it evolves over time: no more, but certainly no less' and that no national court should 'without strong reason dilute or weaken the effect of the Strasbourg case law'. This was interpreted to mean that the national courts were obliged to follow Strasbourg.

In **Pinnock v Manchester City Co** (2010), Lord Neuberger JSC stated that:

> This Court is not bound to follow every decision of the EurCtHR. Not only would it be impractical to do so: it would sometimes be inappropriate, as it would destroy the ability of the Court to engage in the constructive dialogue with EurCtHR which is of value to the development of Convention law. Of course, we should usually follow a clear and constant line of decisions by the EurCtHR …

> Where, however, there is a clear and constant line of decisions whose effect is not inconsistent with some fundamental substantive or procedural aspect of our law, and whose reasoning does not appear to overlook or misunderstand some argument or point of principle, we consider that it would be wrong for this Court not to follow that line. [at paragraph 48]

The **Pinnock** case must be considered in the light of **R v Horncastle & Ors** (2009). In that case, Lord Phillips of Matravers PSC stated that the domestic courts were not obliged to follow the jurisprudence of the European Court of Human Rights where that Court insufficiently appreciated domestic law. The Court could depart from the Strasbourg case law, provided it gave reasons for doing so. In adopting that approach a dialogue between the domestic courts and Strasbourg would be facilitated.

In 2011, giving evidence to the Joint Committee on Human Rights, Lord Judge, the Lord Chief Justice, put forward the view that it was 'at least arguable' that 'what Lord Bingham said in **Ullah** went too far'. Lord Phillips of Worth Matravers, President of the Supreme Court, amplified this by stating that Lord Bingham was talking about a 'settled line of Strasbourg jurisprudence', not a single case.

In **R (Children's Rights Alliance) v Secretary of State for Justice** (2013) Laws LJ, in the Court of Appeal, called for the **Ullah** principle to be revisited. He stated that:

> There is no doubt that in this court we are bound by the *Ullah* principle. It has been repeatedly affirmed in the House of Lords …

But perhaps I may be forgiven for stating, with great deference to the House of Lords and the Supreme Court, that I hope the *Ullah* principle may be revisited. There is a great deal to be gained from the development of a municipal jurisprudence of the Convention rights, which the Strasbourg court should respect out of its own doctrine of the margin of appreciation, and which would be perfectly consistent with our duty to take account of (not to follow) the Strasbourg cases. [paragraphs 63 and 64]

Disagreement with the position of the European Court of Human Rights arose in **Attorney General's Reference No 69 of 2013; R v McLoughlin; R v Newell** (2014). The European Court of Human Rights has held that for a life sentence to be compatible with Article 3 there must be a legal regime in place for a review of that sentence in place at the time the sentence is passed.[45] Under Section 30 of the Crime (Sentences) Act 1997 the Secretary of State has the power to order the release of a prisoner on compassionate grounds. This the Grand Chamber had held in **Vinter** (2012), was insufficiently clear and that there was a lack of clarity in the domestic law. The Court of Appeal disagreed: the Secretary of State had to exercise his powers by considering all the relevant circumstances; he could not fetter his discretion and his decision was subject to scrutiny by judicial review. Accordingly, the law of England did offer 'hope' or the 'possibility of release' 'where exceptional circumstances rendered the just punishment originally imposed no longer justifiable' (paragraph 35).

In **R (Kaiyam) v Secretary of State for Justice** (2013) when faced with the question of the relevant precedent case, rather than consider the merits of the cases in detail, the Court of Appeal decided to grant permission to appeal to the Supreme Court to determine the issues and also to decide whether the jurisprudence of the European Court of Human Rights or that of the Supreme Court should be followed. As Lord Dyson MR said:

The issue of whether the Supreme Court should follow either or both of the Strasbourg decisions in preference to its own (relatively recent) decisions is one pre-eminently for it to determine. Our courts are required by section 2(1) of the Human Rights Act 1998 to do no more than 'take into account' the relevant Strasbourg jurisprudence. In these circumstances, whether the Supreme Court decides to follow Strasbourg raises policy questions of some delicacy. [paragraph 12]

The Supreme Court in **R (Kaiyam and Others) v Secretary of State for Justice** (2014) ruled that it was not bound to follow the European Court's precedent case (**James v United Kingdom**) on the basis that the express wording of Article 5(1) or 5(4) did not create a duty – as the European Court had held – to provide prisoners with a reasonable opportunity to progress their rehabilitation and release. There was, however, an implied ancillary duty to facilitate prisoners' rehabilitation and release, and breach of that duty, while not affecting the lawfulness of the detention, would entitle the prisoners to damages.

In **Poshteh v Royal Borough of Kensington and Chelsea** (2017), the Supreme Court again considered the relationship between its precedent decisions and those of the Court of Human Rights. In this case, which turned on the right to accommodation under the Housing Act 1996, the Court held that it would not depart from its previous unanimous decision in **Ali v Birmingham City Council** (2010) in order to follow the decision of the Strasbourg Court in **Ali v United Kingdom** (2016). The ECtHR's decision was from a Chamber of the Court and it had not

---

45 **Kafkaris v Cyprus** (2009).

addressed in any detail the Supreme Court's reasoning or its concerns over the 'judicialisation' of the welfare services. In this case, the Supreme Court would await a decision of the Grand Chamber before considering whether to depart from its previous decision. In **Brown v The Parole Board for Scotland** (2017), at issue was the requirement for prisoners to be provided with a rehabilitation course, a requirement which had been held to be an intrinsic part of the right to liberty guaranteed under Article 5 of the Convention. Reviewing the authorities, the Supreme Court held that the domestic case law imposed a higher duty on prison authorities than that imposed by the European Court. Accordingly, the Supreme Court should now adopt the same approach as the European Court in **James v United Kingdom** and cease to treat the obligation to provide rehabilitation facilities as an intrinsic part of Article 5.

Section 3: the interpretative duty

Section 3 of the Human Rights Act 1998 requires that primary and secondary legislation, whenever enacted, must be interpreted and applied in a manner consistent with Convention rights. However, section 3(2) makes it clear that this requirement does not affect the validity, continuing operation or enforcement of any incompatible primary legislation, and does not affect the validity, continuing operation or enforcement of incompatible subordinate legislation, if the primary legislation prevents removal of the incompatibility.[46] The definition of primary legislation is provided in section 21 of the Act, which in part provides that primary legislation includes any 'public general Act, local and personal Act, private Act ... and Order in Council made in exercise of Her Majesty's Royal Prerogative'. It was seen in Chapter 5 that Acts of Parliament have always been deemed to have superior force to acts of the prerogative,[47] and that where a claimed prerogative power is held to exist, if it is not expressly overruled by statute, it will be held to be 'in abeyance' and the statute will prevail. The Human Rights Act 1998, however, appears to elevate Orders in Council to the same status as Acts of Parliament, thereby making them immune from invalidation by the courts. Accordingly, whereas the courts may set aside secondary legislation which is incompatible with the Convention – unless the parent Act makes this impossible – Orders in Council regulating the exercise of the prerogative may not be so set aside.[48]

Declarations of incompatibility are regulated under section 4, which provides that if a court is satisfied that a provision of primary or subordinate legislation is incompatible with one or more Convention rights, it may make a declaration of incompatibility. The courts with the jurisdiction to make declarations of incompatibility are the House of Lords, the Judicial Committee of the Privy Council, the Courts-Martial Appeal Court; in Scotland, the High Court of Justiciary, sitting as a court of criminal appeal, or the Court of Session; and, in England, Wales and Northern Ireland, the High Court or Court of Appeal. Section 4(6), however, contains a vital limitation, in that a declaration of incompatibility does not affect the validity, continuing operation or enforcement of the provision in question, and is not binding on the parties to the proceedings in which it is made. However, where the court finds a violation of a Convention right, it has the power under section 8 to grant a remedy to the victim. The power to amend the law has thereby been preserved for the government and Parliament.[49]

In **Wilson v First County Trust Ltd (No 2)** (2003), the House of Lords took the opportunity to examine the structure and workings of the Human Rights Act. The House of Lords ruled that

---

46 See Feldman, 2002.
47 See **Attorney General v de Keyser's Royal Hotel Ltd** (1920); **R v Secretary of State for the Home Department ex parte Fire Brigades' Union** (1995).
48 See Allen and Sales, 2000.
49 See below on declarations made under the 1998 Act.

there was no power to grant a declaration under section 4 of the Human Rights Act unless the interpretative duty under section 3 had been engaged. There was a powerful presumption against the retrospective application of the Act, and, in relation to transactions which had taken place prior to the coming into force of the Act, there could be no question of interpretation under section 3 and accordingly no power to grant a declaration under section 4.

Proportionality

In the exercise of the interpretative duty under section 3 of the Human Rights Act 1998, the courts have rapidly adapted to the approach of the European Court of Human Rights in employing the concepts of *proportionality* and *necessity*, which give greater scope for the protection of rights than the conventional concepts employed in judicial review under the umbrella of the **Wednesbury**[50] unreasonableness test.

Proportionality is discussed in more detail in Chapter 24 at pages 708–716.

Proportionality is a concept central to continental European legal systems, its recent origins lying in German law. Proportionality is now enshrined in the European Union treaty.[51] Within the context of the European Convention on Human Rights, proportionality is inextricably linked to the margin of appreciation – the area of discretion left to Member States in relation to the interpretation and application of Convention rights.

The essence of proportionality is that the means adopted to achieve an objective must be no more than is necessary. In the context of the Convention on Human Rights, most of the Articles set out a particular right in broad terms in the first paragraph and then provide, in the second paragraph, a list of factors which justify the restriction of the exercise of that right. Common factors are that the restrictions must be in accordance with law and are 'necessary in a democratic society' on the basis of national security, public safety etc. It is for the legislature to make the law, but if there is a challenge to that law on Convention grounds, then it is for the courts of law to determine whether that law is necessary and proportionate.

On proportionality, Lord Reed JSC stated in **Bank Mellat v HM Treasury (No 2)** (2013) that: 'inherent in the whole of the Convention is a search for a fair balance between the demands of the general interest of the community and the requirements of the protection of the individual's fundamental rights', and that: 'An assessment of proportionality inevitably involves a value judgment at the state at which a balance has to be struck between the importance of the objective pursued and the value of the right intruded upon'.[52]

In **Manchester City Council v Pinnock** (2010) *supra* it was held that where a public authority sought a possession order for property against an occupier it was open to the occupier to raise the question of whether the making of the order was proportionate. However, the Supreme Court made clear in **McDonald v McDonald** (2016) that a court was not required to consider the proportionality of evicting a tenant where the possession order was sought by a private-sector landlord. To do so would alter the contractual obligations of landlord and tenant, and would interfere with the landlord's rights under Article 1 of the First Protocol (the right to peaceful enjoyment of possessions).

Even before the Human Rights Act 1998 came into effect, the courts were developing a more vigorous approach to the protection of rights. In **R v Ministry of Defence ex parte Smith** (1996), it was recognised that in judicial review proceedings, where human rights were in issue, the courts should 'anxiously scrutinise' executive decisions. That approach, however, did not satisfy the interpretative duty according to Lord Steyn in **R (Daly) v Secretary of State for the Home Department** (2001), where he stated that while there was an overlap between the

---

50 *Associated Provincial Picture Houses Ltd v Wednesbury Corporation* (1948).
51 Article 5(4) EU Treaty.
52 At paras 70, 71.

traditional **Wednesbury** grounds for review and the proportionality approach, there was nevertheless 'a material difference between the **Wednesbury** and **Smith** grounds of review and the approach of proportionality applicable in respect of review where Convention rights are at stake'.

Lord Steyn cited Lord Clyde's approach in **De Freitas v Permanent Secretary of Ministry of Agriculture, Fisheries, Lands and Housing** (1999), namely that in considering whether a restriction on a right is 'arbitrary' or 'excessive', the court should ask itself:

whether:

(i) the legislative objective is sufficiently important to justify limiting a fundamental right;
(ii) the measures designed to meet the legislative objective are rationally connected to it; and
(iii) the means used to impair the right or freedom are no more than is necessary to accomplish the objective.

In Lord Steyn's analysis there are three 'concrete differences' between the traditional grounds for judicial review and the proportionality test, namely:

First, the doctrine of proportionality may require the reviewing court to assess the balance which the decision maker has struck, not merely whether it is within the range of rational or reasonable decisions.

Secondly, the proportionality test may go further than the traditional grounds of review inasmuch as it may require attention to be directed to the relative weight accorded to interests and considerations.

Thirdly, even the heightened scrutiny test developed in *R v Ministry of Defence, ex P Smith* (1996) is not necessarily appropriate to the protection of human rights.

A v Secretary of State for the Home Department (2004), the Belmarsh case, discussed further below, illustrates how proportionality is considered. At a time of heightened fears of terrorist attacks Parliament passed the Anti-Terrorism, Crime and Security Act 2001 (ATCSA). Section 23 of that Act provided that foreign terrorist suspects (but not British suspects) who could neither be put on trial nor deported[53] could be detained indefinitely. The government derogated from Article 5 in respect of ATCSA on the basis that the terrorist threat amounted to 'an emergency threatening the life of the nation' as required by Article 15 of the Convention. The detainees challenged their continued detention on the basis of a violation of Articles 5 and 14 (non-discrimination in the enjoyment of Convention rights) and the case went to the House of Lords (now the Supreme Court). The Court had to consider the proportionality of section 23: was the government right to claim that there was a threat to the life of the nation and so justified in derogating from Article 5, and was the indefinite detention of the foreign suspects (but not British suspects) necessary and proportionate? A majority of the House of Lords found that the derogation was not strictly required, while also accepting that in matters of national security the views of the government carried great weight. However, on the issue of whether it was *necessary* to detain the foreign suspects, the Court was clear. Lord Scott of Foscote stated

---

53 They could not be put on trial because the evidence relied on could not be disclosed in open court for national security reasons. They could not be deported because to do so would have infringed Article 3 of the Convention.

that the government had failed to meet the necessity test, since it had not been shown that measures other than indefinite detention would not have averted the terrorist threat. Lord Rodger of Earlsferry pointed out that if the detention of British terrorist suspects was not necessary to protect against terrorist acts, the detention of foreign suspects could not be necessary either. Baroness Hale of Richmond put it succinctly: if it was not necessary to lock up the nationals it could not be necessary to lock up the foreigners.

Another illustrative case is that of **Bank Mellat v HM Treasury (No 2)** (2013), which is discussed further in Chapter 21. The Treasury made a Financial Restrictions (Iran) Order 2009[54] which had the effect of prohibiting all those in the financial sector from dealing with Bank Mellat, a major Iranian commercial bank. The basis for the Order was that the Treasury believed that the development or production of nuclear weapons in Iran posed a significant threat to the security of the United Kingdom. The Bank challenged the Order on the basis, among other claims, that the requirements imposed were disproportionate to the national interests of the United Kingdom and that there was a breach of Article 6 and Article 1 of the First Protocol to the Convention.

The Supreme Court ruled, by a majority, that although the Order had a rational connection with the objective of frustrating Iran's weapons programme, the singling out of Bank Mellat from other Iranian banks was irrational and disproportionate.

On occasion proportionality will be the key issue to be decided. For example, in **R (Catt) v Commissioner of Police of the Metropolis** (2015) an application for judicial review was lodged to challenge the retention of personal data by the police. The applicant, who was 91, had committed no crime, but had been a peaceful demonstrator with a group, some members of which were associated with violent crime. It was agreed by all Justices of the Supreme Court that the retention of data by the police was clearly an interference with the right to privacy (Article 8). What was at issue therefore was whether the retention was justified under Article 8(2). For it to be justified, its retention had to be proportionate: in other words it had to be necessary to achieve a legitimate objective. In this case, the data was disclosable and used only by the police and the material was regularly reviewed for deletion according to a Code of Conduct and Guidelines. It was therefore proportionate. Lady Hale, DPSC, stated, however, that to have retained the data on Mr Catt indefinitely, given that he has committed no crime and was unlikely to be involved in criminal activity himself, would have been disproportionate.

Convention rights, section 3 and statute[55]

Section 3 of the Human Rights Act requires the courts to interpret primary and subordinate legislation in a way which is compatible with Convention rights, 'so far as it is possible to do so'.[56] The House of Lords in **R v A (Complainant's Sexual History)** (2002)[57] gave guidance as to the correct approach. At issue was whether the statutory restrictions on the admissibility of evidence prejudiced the right to fair trial.[58] The Court ruled that it first had to consider whether a legislative provision interfered with a Convention right. If there was an interference, then the court had to look at the legislative purpose of the provision and employ the concept of proportionality. Three issues had to be considered:

- first, was the legislative objective sufficiently important to justify limiting a fundamental right?

---

54 Under the Counter-Terrorism Act 2008, s. 62 and Sched. 7.
55 See Klug and Starmer, 2001.
56 See Bennion, 2000.
57 On the joinder of the Home Secretary under s. 5 see **R v A** (2001).
58 Under consideration was the Youth Justice and Criminal Evidence Act 1999, s. 41(3)(c), which precluded evidence and questioning about a complainant's sexual history in an attempt to redress the problems of low conviction rates and outmoded stereotypes of women.

- second, were the measures adopted to meet that objective rationally connected to it?
- third, the court must be satisfied that the means used to impair the right or freedom were no more than necessary to accomplish the objective (the proportionality test).

Section 3 of the Human Rights Act 'went further than requiring the court to take the Convention into account: the court had a duty to strive to find a possible interpretation compatible with Convention rights'. Lord Steyn stated that this might even require the courts 'to adopt an interpretation which may appear linguistically strained'.[59]

Section 3 provided the basis for the reinterpretation of a statutory provision to make it compatible with Convention rights in **Ghaidan v Godin-Mendoza** (2004). The Rent Act 1977[60] provided that on the death of a protected tenant his or her surviving spouse, if then living in the house 'as his or her wife or husband', became a statutory tenant by succession. The House of Lords in **Fitzpatrick v Sterling Housing Association Ltd** (2001) had ruled that this provision did not include same-sex relationships. In **Ghaidan**, however, the House of Lords used Article 3 as a remedial section and reinterpreted the provision to read 'as if they were his wife or husband' and thereby protected the tenancy. Lord Steyn stated that it was necessary 'to emphasise that interpretation under section 3(1) is the prime remedial remedy and that resort to section 4 must always be an exceptional course'.

The interpretative duty was clear in the case of **Principal Reporter v K (Scotland)** (2010). In that case an unmarried father had been denied the opportunity to participate in discussion concerning his natural child's future, on the grounds that he was not a 'relevant person' under section 93 of the Children (Scotland) Act 1995. The Supreme Court ruled that there was an incompatibility between section 93 and Article 8, but that the incompatibility could be 'cured' by reading in words to the statute to make the natural father a 'relevant person'.

The limits of interpretation

Strive as the judges may to interpret statutes compatibly, there are limits. First, it is clear that the 1998 Act is not retrospective. For example, in **R v Kensal (No 2)** (2001), the House of Lords ruled that it should follow its previous decision notwithstanding that a majority of the House now believed the precedent case to have been wrongly decided. Note, however, that this case involved a pre-Human Rights Act precedent. The court ruled that if Parliament had intended convictions valid before the Act came into force to be re-opened on the basis of rights conferred by the 1998 Act, it would have said so clearly.[61]

In **Pearce v Governing Body of Mayfield School** (2001), the Court of Appeal considered the issue of gender orientation in relation to discrimination under the Human Rights Act 1998. Disruptive pupils abused a lesbian teacher at the school in the early 1990s. Such conduct was not discriminatory under the Sex Discrimination Act 1975. Since the Human Rights Act was not in force at the time of the conduct in question, the applicant could not seek compensation under that Act. In **Secretary of State for the Home Department v Wainwright** (2002), the Court of Appeal affirmed that there was no tort of invasion of privacy at common law, and that because the conduct complained of occurred in 1997, before the Human Rights Act came into force, section 3(1) of the Act did not apply to introduce a right to privacy retrospectively. Mrs Wainwright and her son had been strip-searched by prison officers,[62] having been told that they were under suspicion of bringing drugs into the prison when visiting an inmate.

---

59 See also **R v Ashworth Special Hospital Authority ex parte N** (2001) and **R v Secretary of State for the Home Department ex parte Mellor** (2001), discussed below.
60 Schedule 1, para. 2(2).
61 See also **R v Secretary of State for the Home Department ex parte Mahmood (Amjad)** (2001).
62 Under r. 86(1) of the Prison Rules (SI 1964/388), made pursuant to the Prison Act 1952, s. 47.

They consented to the searches. The county court judge ruled that the tort of trespass to the person had been committed and awarded damages. The claimants relied on section 3 of the 1998 Act, arguing that once the Act was in force the court had the duty to comply with it even though the matters complained of took place before the Act came into force.[63] The Lord Chief Justice stated that the 1998 Act could not change substantive law by introducing a retrospective right to privacy which did not exist at common law.

The second limitation lies in the distinction between legitimate interpretation and the 'redrafting' of statutes. For example, in **In re W and B (Children: Care Plan)** (2002), the Court of Appeal considered the interpretive duty and held that the duties of local authorities under the Children Act 1989 should be subject to a system of 'starred milestones' which require authorities to implement care plans within time limits. No such provision had been made by Parliament in the Children Act. In the House of Lords Lord Nicholls ruled that section 3 of the 1998 Act maintained the constitutional boundary between interpretation by the courts and the enactment and amendment of statutes by Parliament, and that an interpretation of an Act which departed from an essential feature of an Act of Parliament was likely to have crossed the boundary. Here, Parliament had entrusted local authorities with responsibility for looking after children in care. The House of Lords ruled that the Court of Appeal's interpretation went beyond the boundary of interpretation and exceeded its judicial jurisdiction.[64] Although the line between legislating and interpreting may appear to be fine, it is nevertheless understood by the judges.

Convention rights, interpretation and common law

The Lord Chancellor in debate stated that:

> it is right as a matter of principle for the courts to have the duty of acting compatibly with the Convention not only in cases involving other public authorities but also in developing the common law in deciding cases between individuals. Why should they not?[65]

While section 3 does not refer to common law, as seen above, the Act requires that the common law be developed consistently with Convention rights, and section 6, which includes courts and tribunals as public bodies, underpins the jurisdiction. Development of the common law has been seen most clearly in relation to privacy, which engages three issues. First, there is no common law right to privacy: as Glidewell LJ stated in **Kaye v Robertson** (1991), 'It is well-known that in English law there is no right to privacy'. Second, privacy rights under common law derive from a relationship of confidence and breach of that confidentiality. Third, Article 8 protects privacy rights in relation to family life, the home and correspondence. In **Venables v News Group Newspapers Ltd** (2001), an injunction was granted which prevents, indefinitely, the media from revealing the identity and whereabouts of the applicant. Butler-Sloss LJ recognised that the defendant newspapers were not within the definition of public authorities, but nevertheless asserted that the court – as a public authority – must itself act compatibly with the Convention. Article 8 of the Convention thus prevailed over Article 10 (freedom of expression) and was applied against a private body, thereby giving horizontal effect to the right.[66]

---

63 **R v Kensal (No 2)** (2001) did not decide this point.
64 See **Poplar Housing and Regeneration Community Association Ltd and Secretary of State for the Environment v Donoghue** (2001).
65 *Hansard* 583 HL Deb 783, 24 November 1997. And see Lord Irvine, 1998, in which the Lord Chancellor stated that 'the Convention rights must pervade all law and all court systems' (at p. 232).
66 See also **Campbell v MGN Ltd** (2002) and **Douglas v Hello! Ltd** (2002), and Chapter 19.

The doctrines of proportionality and necessity, developed by the Court of Human Rights, have been accepted as judicial tools in the enforcement of Convention rights. In **R (Daly) v Secretary of State for the Home Department** (2001), for example, in the House of Lords, in declaring the prison policy of requiring prisoners to leave their cells for the purpose of searches, including searches of privileged legal correspondence, unlawful, Lord Bingham of Cornhill stated that his conclusions had been reached 'on an orthodox application of common law principles' but stated that the same result would yield by reliance on the Convention. However, he recognised that this coincidence between common law and Convention might not always occur. Lord Steyn was more explicit regarding the requirements of proportionality. Citing Lord Clyde in **De Freitas v Permanent Secretary of Ministry of Agriculture, Fisheries, Lands and Housing** (1999), Lord Steyn declared that the criteria to be applied are 'more precise and more sophisticated than the traditional grounds of review', and that under the proportionality approach 'the intensity of review is somewhat greater'. Where there has been an infringement of a right, it must be established that the limitation of the right 'was necessary in a democratic society, in the sense of meeting a pressing social need, and the question whether the interference was really proportionate to the legitimate aim being pursued'.

Section 5 of the Human Rights Act

Section 5 of the Human Rights Act 1998 confers on a Minister the right to be heard. The purpose of section 5(2) is to ensure that the appropriate Minister has an opportunity to address the court on the objects and purposes of the legislation in question and any other matters which might be relevant. In **R v A (Joinder of Appropriate Minister)** (2001), the House of Lords ruled that where an issue was raised in criminal proceedings which might lead to the House of Lords considering making a declaration of compatibility, it was appropriate to join the Crown in advance of the appeal hearing. Where the Crown was already represented by the Director of Public Prosecutions, his role as prosecutor was different from that of a government Minister in the discharge of executive responsibilities. The House granted the application for joinder made by the Home Secretary, who bore responsibility for promotion of the legislation in question. See also **Wilson v First County Trust Ltd (No 2)** (2003) (discussed above) in which the Attorney General appeared on behalf of the Speaker of the House of Commons and the Clerk of the Parliament intervened.

Declarations of incompatibility

Where the superior courts[67] are unable to interpret statutes in a manner which makes them compatible with Convention rights, a declaration of incompatibility may be issued. This puts the government and Parliament 'on notice' that the statute requires amendment.[68]

By October 2019 the total number of declarations made by the UK courts since the Human Rights Act came into force in October 2000 was 42. Of these ten were overturned on appeal; a further two were subject to appeal. Sixteen were addressed by primary or secondary legislation and six were addressed by Remedial Order. Others remained under consideration.

There are a number of explanations for the relatively low number of declarations. First, as **Wilson v First County Trust Ltd** (2003) makes clear, the power to make a declaration only arises where the duty of interpretation is engaged, and that cannot be engaged where the facts occurred before the Human Rights Act came into force. Second, there have been several

---

67 The High Court and above.
68 See **R (D) v Secretary of State for the Home Department** (2002).

cases in which the High Court has issued a declaration but this has been overturned on appeal. Third, where there are defects in procedures or administrative practices, the courts will generally hold that these are cured by the supervisory jurisdiction of the courts. Fourth, the Court of Appeal ruled that a declaration should not be granted to a claimant who had not been, and could not be, adversely affected by impugned legislation in **Lancashire County Council v Taylor** (2005). Finally, there is emerging from the case law a 'doctrine of deference'.

The doctrine of deference[69]

It is apparent from the case law that the judges are very conscious of the invisible boundary line between those matters on which they regard themselves as competent to adjudicate and those matters which should be left for the democratically elected government. This is the doctrine of deference. The doctrine may be compared with that of justiciability under judicial review. The principal distinction lies in the fact that whereas courts will rule on justiciability in order to decide whether to review, with deference the courts conduct an examination and then decide that they should defer to the elected government and/or Parliament on the grounds of competence and/or democratic principle. The concept is also similar to the concept of margin of appreciation, which is used by the Court of Human Rights and which confers on states an area of discretion with which the Court will not interfere.[70] 'Deference' may also be expressed in the form of competence – in the form of the question: 'Is this matter within the competence of the courts to decide or for Parliament and/or the executive?' Underlying the concept is the desire to preserve the separation of powers between the judiciary, executive and legislature and to protect the judges from charges that they are interfering in another institution's legitimate sphere of power. Notwithstanding the legitimacy of the objective, there is a fine line to be drawn between deferring to another institution and failing adequately to protect human rights – the duty which has been conferred on the judges by the Human Rights Act. The case law is considered in Chapter 24.

Making an application under the Act

Standing

Section 7(3) of the Act provides that an individual may make an application to the courts if, and only if, he or she 'is, or would be, a victim of an unlawful act'.[71] A person claiming that a public authority has acted, or proposes to act, in a way made unlawful by section 6(1) may bring proceedings against the authority, or may rely on the Convention right concerned in any legal proceedings. In relation to judicial review proceedings, the victim test is also applied, giving a narrower meaning to 'sufficient interest' (or 'standing') than that applied under other judicial review proceedings.

The definition of standing follows the approach of the Court of Human Rights. A victim or potential victim has standing, as does a person who, while not the immediate victim of an alleged violation, is nevertheless affected. An example is a family member of a person deported or threatened with deportation where this violates the Article 8 right to family life. The position of third parties who are not directly affected is more complex and gives rise to differing tests to be applied depending on the type of proceedings being brought. The sufficient interest – or standing – requirements in judicial review proceedings allow 'public

---

69 See Jowell, 2003; Jowell, 'Judicial deference and human rights: a question of competence', in Craig and Rawlings, 2003; Edwards, 2002; Oliver, 2003, Chapter 6; Steyn, 2005.
70 The margin of appreciation is a concept derived from international law: it has no application within domestic law.
71 On the interpretation of victim see **Lancashire County Council v Taylor** (2005).

interest' organisations to bring proceedings. Help the Aged, the Child Poverty Action Group and the Joint Council for the Welfare of Immigrants have all been taken to have standing.[72] Standing for the purposes of the Human Rights Act, however, excludes interest groups unless they can establish that their members are actual or potential victims. Interest groups whose members are not victims, but who have special expertise in an area (for example, environmental groups such as Greenpeace or Friends of the Earth), will not have standing. They will, however, be permitted to make submissions to the court on matters within their expertise. In debate, the Lord Chancellor, referring the practice before the Court of Human Rights, stated that 'our courts will be ready to permit amicus written briefs from non-governmental organisations; that is to say briefs, but not to treat them as full parties', and further that 'I dare say that the courts will be equally hospitable to oral interventions, provided that they are brief'.[73]

The question of standing was central to **In the matter of an application by the Northern Ireland Human Rights Commission for Judicial Review** (2018).[74] Under the law in force at the time[75] it was a criminal offence for a woman to have an abortion in Northern Ireland unless it was necessary to preserve the life of the mother or to prevent her becoming a 'mental or physical wreck'. Proceedings were brought by the Northern Ireland Human Rights Commission, challenging the compatibility of the law of Northern Ireland with Articles 3, 8 and 14 of the Convention. A panel of seven Justices heard the appeal.

On the question of standing, by a majority of four to three, the Court held that the Northern Ireland Human Rights Commission did not have standing. Section 7 of the Human Rights Act requires that the applicant must be a 'victim' of the alleged violation of rights. Because of the decision on standing, the Court was unable to grant a Declaration of Incompatibility.

Time limits

Proceedings must be brought within one year of the date on which the act complained of took place, but this limit may be extended by the court if it considers it 'equitable', having regard to any stricter time limit imposed on the proceedings in question (section 7(5) of the Act). 'Legal proceedings' is defined to mean proceedings brought by a public authority and appeals against the decision of a court or tribunal (section 7(6)).

Remedies

Article 13 of the Convention, which provides that everyone shall have an effective remedy before a national authority, has not been incorporated. Instead, section 8 of the Human Rights Act regulates remedies. Section 8 provides that, where a court finds that a public authority has acted unlawfully, it may grant 'such relief or remedy, or make such order within its jurisdiction as it considers just and appropriate'. Accordingly, courts and tribunals may only award a remedy which is within their statutory powers.

Damages may only be awarded by a court which has power to award damages or to order the payment of compensation in civil proceedings, and no award of damages is to be made unless, taking into account all the circumstances of the case and any other relief or remedy available, the court is satisfied that the award is necessary to afford just satisfaction to the complainant. The court must take into account the principles applied by the Court of

---

72 See **R v Sefton Metropolitan Borough Council ex parte Help the Aged** (1997); **R v Secretary of State for Social Security ex parte Joint Council for the Welfare of Immigrants** (1997); and **R v Lord Chancellor ex parte Child Poverty Action Group** (1998).

73 Hansard HL Deb Col. 834, 24 November 1997.

74 Reference by the Court of Appeal in Northern Ireland under para. 33 of Sched. 10 to the Northern Ireland Act 1998 (Abortion).

75 Sections 58 and 59 of the Offences Against the Person Act 1861 and s. 25(1) of the Criminal Justice Act (NI) 1945.

Human Rights in relation to the award of compensation under Article 41. In many instances, a finding of a violation may be deemed to be a sufficient remedy. However, the full range of remedies – declarations, injunctions and the prerogative orders (quashing orders, mandatory orders and prohibitory orders) – are also available to those courts and tribunals with the power to grant them.

One question which arises is the issue of whether or not section 8 provides an adequate remedy according to the jurisprudence of the European Court of Human Rights.[76] The courts are under a duty, under section 2, to take into account the case law developed in Strasbourg. Accordingly, there is the potential for considerable case law on the relationship between section 8 of the Human Rights Act 1998 and Article 13 of the Convention.

Where it is alleged that a decision of a court violates a Convention right, the decision must be challenged by an appeal or by an application for judicial review. This is the effect of section 9 of the Human Rights Act which was considered in **Mazhar v Lord Chancellor** (2019). In that case a judge had authorised the removal and detention of the claimant to hospital because there were no carers available to look after him at home. The claimant sought a declaration that the authorisation was unlawful, and claimed damages. The Court of Appeal ruled that there was no jurisdiction to make a declaration or award damages: section 9 was clear that the only way to challenge a judicial act was via an appeal against the decisions or by way of judicial review.

Ensuring legislative conformity with Convention rights

Ensuring that domestic legislation conforms to Convention requirements involves two procedures. The first relates to the enactment of legislation generally, and the second relates to legislative action taken after a declaration of incompatibility has been issued by the courts.

In relation to legislative proposals, the Act provides for declarations to be made to Parliament that the proposed legislation conforms to Convention requirements. Section 19 requires that a Minister in charge of a Bill in either House of Parliament must, before second reading, make a statement to the effect that either a Bill does comply with Convention rights or that, although such a statement cannot be made, the government nevertheless wishes to proceed with the Bill.

In relation to remedial legislation, the Act introduces a special legislative procedure for reform. While this mechanism preserves the principle that it is Parliament, as the democratically elected legislature, which is sovereign in making and reforming law, it also opens the door to the possibility that governments of differing political persuasions may react with greater or lesser enthusiasm to declarations of incompatibility. The extent to which successive governments respond to the ruling of the courts thus lies in the *moral* rather than *legal* authority of the Convention.

The fast-track legislative procedure

Where a higher court[77] makes a declaration of incompatibility, or where the Court of Human Rights in Strasbourg declares that the Convention has been violated, the relevant government Minister will have power to enact amending legislation by Order in Council (a 'remedial order'). Other than where it is necessary for the Order to have immediate effect, the Order

---

76 See **Chahal v United Kingdom** (1996).
77 As interpreted by the Human Rights Act 1998, s. 6.

will be subject to the approval of both Houses of Parliament, and will only come into effect once approval has been secured. Section 10 and Schedule 2 regulate remedial action and remedial orders.

Two procedures are provided for. Under the standard procedure,[78] a draft of the order must be laid before Parliament for a 60-day period before it is approved by resolution of each House. When laying the draft instrument, the Minister must also provide the 'required information', which entails an explanation of:

> the incompatibility which the proposed order seeks to remove, including particulars of the court declaration, finding or order which caused the minister to propose a remedial order; and a statement of the reasons for proceeding under section 10 and for making an order in the terms proposed.[79]

During the period in which the draft is laid before Parliament, representations may be made to the Minister, either by Parliament or by any other person. If representations are made, the draft must be accompanied by a statement containing a summary of the representations and details of any changes introduced into the proposed order as a result of the representations.[80] Section 10 and Schedule 2 also provide that, if a Minister considers that there are 'compelling reasons', he may make such amendments to legislation as he considers necessary to remove the incompatibility, by means of a statutory instrument. The power applies to both primary and subordinate legislation, thus conferring on the executive potentially wide law-making power – subject ultimately to Parliament's approval. In debate on the Bill, the Lord Chancellor stated that 'if legislation has been declared to be incompatible, a prompt parliamentary remedy should be available'.[81]

Derogations and reservations

The Human Rights Act 1998 makes provision for derogations and reservations in sections 14 to 17.

In relation to reservations, section 15 provides in part that:

> (1) In this Act, 'designated reservation' means:
>> (a) the United Kingdom's reservation to Article 2 of the first protocol to the Convention [the right to education in conformity with parents' religious and philosophical convictions]; and
>> (b) any other reservation by the United Kingdom to an Article of the Convention or of any protocol to the Convention, which is designated for the purposes of this Act in an order made by the Secretary of State.

Reform of the Human Rights Act 1998

In 2011 the Commission on a Bill of Rights, an independent Commission set up by the government, published a Discussion Paper designed to begin a period of public consultation on

---

78 Human Rights Act 1998, Sched. 2.
79 Ibid., Sched. 2, para. 3.
80 Ibid., Sched. 2, para. 2.
81 Hansard HL Col. 1231, 3 November 1997.

the question of whether the United Kingdom should have a Bill of Rights. The Commission failed to reach a unanimous conclusion and no action was taken. In December 2020 the government announced that it was setting up an independent review of the working of the Human Rights Act. By way of introduction, the government states that it remains committed to 'upholding the UK's stature on human rights'. There are two principal issues outlined in the terms of reference. The first is the relationship between domestic courts and the European Court of Human Rights; the second is the impact of the HRA on the relationship between the judiciary, the executive and the legislature.[82] The review will also consider the manner in which the HRA applies to acts of public authorities taking place outside the territory of the UK.[83] The inquiry will not examine the substantive rights protected under the Convention and HRA. The Review Panel is due to report in the summer of 2021, with options for reform.

SELF-TEST QUESTIONS

What is the test to be applied when considering whether a body is a 'public body' for the purposes of the Human Rights Act 1998?

What do you understand by a Bill of Rights? In what respects does the Human Rights Act 1998 differ from a Bill of Rights?

Under the UK constitution, do you think it is possible to introduce a Bill of Rights without also introducing a written constitution?

What do you understand by the doctrine of 'deference'? Under what circumstances will the doctrine come into play?

Summary

The European Convention on Human Rights has provided vital protection for citizens against the power of the state. As has been seen, the case law against the United Kingdom is substantial and, in many instances, has led to considerable reform of the law. The Convention has for the most part, and despite its limitations in scope, served individuals well in the protection of fundamental rights. Nevertheless, the right of individual petition, conferred in 1965, meant long delays and high costs for litigants. The incorporation of Convention rights into domestic law under the Human Rights Act 1998 was a logical step forward for a government seriously committed to individual rights and freedoms and represents a significant extension of the rule of law. Incorporation may also change the traditional public conception of individual freedoms in favour of rights, and bring a greater clarity to the law relating to both civil liberties and human rights. The Act preserves the traditional balance in the constitution – ensuring that Parliament alone can reform the law but enabling judges of the higher courts to grant a Declaration of Incompatibility where a violation of a right which cannot be remedied by interpretation of the relevant domestic law is found. The Declaration does not invalidate the offending law but puts government and Parliament on notice that reform is called for.

The case law under the Human Rights Act is discussed on the Companion Website.

---

82 In part, prompted by government fury at the **Miller** decision favouring parliamentary control over the dissolution of parliament rather than the prerogative.

83 Underlying concerns include the imposition of liability on the state for actions taken by armed forces personnel overseas.

Further Reading

Amos, M, 'The impact of the Human Rights Act on the UK's performance before the European Court of Human Rights' [2007] *Public Law* 655.

Buxton, R, 'The future of declarations of incompatibility' [2010] *Public Law* 213.

Craig, P, 'The courts, the Human Rights Act and judicial review' (2001) 117 *Law Quarterly Review* 589.

Edwards, R, 'Judicial deference under the Human Rights Act' (2002) 65 *Modern Law Review* 859.

Ewing, K, 'The futility of the Human Rights Act' [2004] *Public Law* 829.

Fenwick, H, 'Marginalising human rights: breach of the peace, "kettling", the Human Rights Act and public protest' [2009] *Public Law* 737.

Fredman, S, 'Human rights transformed: positive duties and positive rights' [2006] *Public Law* 498.

Gearty, C, 'Reconciling parliamentary democracy and human rights' (2002) 118 *Law Quarterly Review* 248.

Gearty, C, *Can Human Rights Survive?* 2006, Cambridge: Cambridge University Press (Hamlyn Lectures).

Grieve, D, 'Can a bill of rights do better than the Human Rights Act?' [2016] *Public Law* 223.

Harris, DJ, 'Human rights or mythical beasts' (2004) 120 *Law Quarterly Review* 428.

Harvey, C, 'Talking about human rights' [2004] *European Human Rights Law Review* 500.

Hickman, TR, 'Between human rights and the rule of law' [2005] *Modern Law Review* 655.

Hoffmann, Lord, 'The universality of human rights' (2009) 125 *Law Quarterly Review* 416.

Irvine of Lairg, Lord, 'The impact of the Human Rights Act: Parliament, the courts and the executive' [2003] *Public Law* 308.

Jowell, J, 'Judicial deference and human rights: a question of competence' in P Craig and R Rawlings (eds), *Law and Administration in Europe*, 2003, Oxford: Oxford University Press.

Kavanagh, A, 'Judging the judges under the Human Rights Act: deference, disillusionment and the "war on terror"' [2009] *Public Law* 287.

Kavanagh, A, 'Defending deference' (2010) 126 *LQR* 222.

Klug, F, 'A bill of rights: do we need one or do we already have one?' [2007] *Public Law* 701.

Lester, A, 'The utility of the Human Rights Act: a reply to Keith Ewing' [2005] *Public Law* 249.

Malleson, K, 'The evolving role of the UK Supreme Court' [2011] *Public Law* 754.

Nicol, D, 'Law and politics after the Human Rights Act' [2006] *Public Law* 722.

Oliver, D, 'Functions of a public nature and the Human Rights Act' [2004] *Public Law* 329.

Redmayne, M, 'Hearsay and human rights: *Al-Khawaja* in the grand chamber' (2012) 75 *Modern Law Review* 865.

Responding to Human Rights Judgments: Government Response to the Joint Committee on Human Rights' Thirty-first Report of Session 2007–08, *Cm7524*, 2009.

Rooney, JM, 'A legal basis for non-arbitrary detention: *Mahammed v Secretary of State for Defence*' [2016] *Public Law* 563.

Sales, P, 'Rights and fundamental rights in English law' [2016] 75 *Cambridge Law Journal* 86.

Steyn, Lord, 'Deference: a tangled story' [2005] *Public Law* 346.

Young, AL, 'A peculiarly British protection of human rights' (2005) 68 *Modern Law Review* .

Young, AL, 'In defence of due deference' (2009) 72 *MLR* 554.

Young, AL, 'Is dialogue working under the Human Rights Act 1998?' [2011] *Public Law* 773.

Chapter 19

Freedom of Expression and Privacy

Chapter Contents

Learning Objectives

By the end of this chapter you should be able to:

☐ explain the constitutional importance of freedom of expression;
☐ discuss the impact of the Human Rights Act on freedom of expression;
☐ discuss the lawful restrictions on freedom of expression and their justifications;
☐ explain, in outline, the law of confidence;
☐ discuss privacy under the Human Rights Act 1998;
☐ explain how the courts have developed the law of confidence to establish a right to privacy under domestic law;
☐ explain the importance of press freedom, and any legitimate restrictions on that freedom.

Introduction

In this chapter we examine the scope of freedom of expression and the lawful restrictions which may be imposed upon it together with the law relating to breach of confidence and privacy.

Freedom of Expression

Freedom of expression entails many aspects: an individual's freedom to express any view he or she wishes, however offensive to others, in private or public; freedom of the press to express any view; freedom of authors to write and publish; and freedom of film makers to record and distribute films/videos for private and public consumption. From the standpoint of democracy, freedom of speech is crucial to the exchange of political ideas and to the formation of political opinions. The freedom of speech guaranteed to Members of Parliament under Article IX of the Bill of Rights 1689 reflects the constitutional importance of political debate, as does the right of newspapers and broadcasters to publish fair and accurate reports of parliamentary proceedings.[1] Freedom of expression is essential in a free and democratic society, and restrictions which inhibit criticism of public authorities, in particular, undermine the potential for scrutiny of official action. For this reason, in **Derbyshire County Council v Times Newspapers** (1993), the House of Lords ruled that neither local nor central government had standing to sue for defamation. Lord Keith stated that 'it is of the highest importance that a democratically elected governmental body ... should be open to uninhibited public criticism'.[2]

Freedom of Expression and the Human Rights Act

In the United Kingdom, before the Human Rights Act 1998 there was no right to free speech but, in a negative way, there was a freedom of expression subject to the limitations imposed by law. Freedom of expression is now regulated under Article 10 of the European Convention on Human Rights, incorporated into domestic law under the Human Rights Act 1998. However, the right is limited by restrictions.

Freedom of expression under Article 10 includes the 'freedom to hold opinions and to receive and impart information and ideas without interference by public authority and regardless of frontiers'.[3] The right is subject to such legal restrictions as are 'necessary in a democratic society in the interests of national security or public safety, for the prevention of disorder or crime, for the protection of health or morals or for the protection of the rights and freedoms of others'. Legal restrictions on the exercise of the right by members of the armed forces, police or administration of the state are permitted. The effect of Article 10 is that all restrictions on the right must be justified, in common with other restricted Articles, according to these criteria: they must be both *necessary* and *proportionate*.[4]

---

1 The Parliamentary Papers Act 1840. See Chapter 17.
2 Note that both the Freedom of Information Act 2000 and the Data Protection Act 1998, as amended, discussed in Chapter 10, are central both to the availability of information and to the protection of privacy of the individual.
3 Article 10 does not prevent state licensing of broadcasting, television or cinemas.
4 On the meaning of these terms, see Chapter 18.

The Article 10 right is also regulated by section 12 of the Human Rights Act 1998, which was drafted so as to prevent claims to privacy[5] restricting freedom of the press. Section 12(4) provides that:

> The court must have particular regard to the importance of the Convention right to freedom of expression and, where the proceedings relate to material which the respondent claims, or which appears to the court, to be journalistic, literary or artistic material (or to conduct connected with such material), to –
>
> (a)   the extent to which –
>
>   (i)   the material is, or is about to, become available to the public;[6] or
>
>   (ii)   it is, or would be, in the public interest for the material to be published;
>
> (b)   any relevant privacy code.[7]

The House of Lords upheld the right of prisoners to freedom of expression in **R v Secretary of State for the Home Department ex parte Simms** (1999). The court ruled that an indiscriminate ban on all visits to prisoners by journalists or authors in their professional capacity was unlawful. A prisoner had a right to seek, through oral interviews, to persuade a journalist to investigate his allegations of miscarriage of justice in the hope that his case might be re-opened. The applicants were serving life sentences for murder and, having had their renewed applications for leave to appeal against conviction turned down, continued to protest their innocence. The Home Office had adopted a blanket policy that no prisoners had a right to oral interviews with journalists. Lord Steyn stated that the applicants wished to challenge the safety of their convictions, and that, 'in principle, it was not easy to conceive of a more important function which free speech might fulfil'. His Lordship was satisfied that it was administratively workable, and consistent with prison order and discipline, to allow prisoners to be interviewed for the purpose here at stake. The Home Secretary's policy and the governor's administrative decisions pursuant to that policy were unlawful.

Freedom of expression was also at issue in **R (Nilsen) v Governor of Full Sutton Prison** (2004). The Court of Appeal ruled that a prison rule preventing a prisoner from publishing material about his offences did not violate the right to freedom of expression and its application was proportionate and justified on the facts. In 1983 Nilsen had been sentenced to six life sentences for six murders, the details of which were horrifying. He intended to publish details in an autobiography. The Home Secretary had exercised powers under the Prison Act 1952 to withhold the work. The restriction was a legitimate exercise of power: it could not be argued that a prisoner should be permitted to publish an article 'glorifying in the pleasure

---

5 Protected under Article 8.

6 In *Attorney General v Times Newspapers* (2001) the government lost its appeal to restrain publication of Richard Tomlinson's *The Big Breach: From Top Secret to Maximum Security*, which the government alleged would damage national security. The Court of Appeal ruled that if the material was already in the public domain, whether at home or abroad (the book had been published in Moscow), then there should be no restraint on freedom of expression.

7 See *R v Advertising Standards Authority Ltd ex parte Matthias Rath BV* (2001), in which adjudications published by the Advertising Standards Authority under its non-statutory code were held to be 'prescribed by law' within the meaning of Article 10. The Codes of Advertising and Sales Promotion had the 'underpinning' of subordinate legislation which gave recognition to the means of dealing with complaints. The Code of Practice was readily accessible and therefore prescribed by law, its provisions being sufficiently clear and precise to enable any person to know the acceptable limits of advertisements and the consequences of infringing the provisions. The rights of children to freedom of expression and participation in family life was recognised by the Court of Appeal in *Mabon v Mabon* (2005). The Court recognised that in the case of articulate teenagers, it must accept that their rights outweighed the paternalistic judgment of the welfare of the child. 'There was a growing acknowledgment of the autonomy and consequential rights of children'. See also *Ferdinand v MGN Ltd* (2011).

that his crime had caused him'. The restriction was not disproportionate and it was legitimate to have regard to the effect the exercise of freedom of expression would have in the world outside the prison. The right of the state to restrict the distribution of pornography was considered in **Belfast City Council v Miss Behavin' Ltd** (2007) in which the House of Lords ruled that the Council was entitled by statute to restrict the company's rights. The restrictions only prevented the company from using unlicensed premises: it did not prohibit the exercise of a right. The state had a wide margin of appreciation in relation to controlling pornography, and provided that a local authority exercised its powers rationally and in accordance with statute 'it would require very unusual facts for it to amount to a disproportionate restriction on Convention rights'.[8]

Freedom of expression does not necessarily include the right to access to information. In **R v Secretary of State for Health ex parte Wagstaff; R v Secretary of State for Health ex parte Associated Newspapers Ltd** (2001), the High Court ruled that the holding in private of the inquiry into the multiple murders committed by Dr Harold Shipman contravened Article 10. It constituted unjustified governmental interference with the reception of information that others wish or may be willing to impart. Compare **R (Persey) v Secretary of State for Environment, Food and Rural Affairs** (2002), in which the High Court distinguished **Wagstaff** and ruled that Article 10 did not impose a positive obligation on government to provide an 'open forum'. The applications related to the Secretary of State's decision to hold three separate, independent inquiries into the outbreak of foot and mouth disease with the evidence for the most part to be heard in private. The court distinguished between the right to freedom of expression and access to information: Article 10 prohibited interference with freedom of expression, it did not require its facilitation. Equally, the High Court ruled in **R (Hard) v Secretary of State for Health** (2002) that there was no presumption one way or the other as to whether an inquiry should be held in public. There was no right of access to information conferred by Article 10. However, in **Open Door Counselling and Dublin Well Woman v Ireland** (1992), the Court of Human Rights ruled that restrictions – an injunction – placed on the dissemination of any information regarding the availability of abortion advice and treatment represented an unlawful restriction and was therefore contrary to Article 10.

In **MGN Ltd v United Kingdom** (2011) the European Court of Human Rights ruled that a court order requiring the losing party to legal proceedings to pay legal costs amounting to over £1,000,000 in total and including success fees agreed between the successful party and her lawyers was disproportionate to the aim of the success fee system. That system was intended to facilitate access to law for those who would otherwise not be able to afford legal representation. Accordingly, there was a violation of Article 10. The Legal Aid, Sentencing and Punishment of Offenders Act 2012, section 44, reforms the law.

Article 10 was also considered by the Court of Human Rights in **Animal Defenders International v United Kingdom** (2013). The applicant was an organisation which campaigned on behalf of animal welfare. It wished to screen a television advertisement. The Broadcast Advertising Clearance Centre refused permission on the ground that its transmission would breach the prohibition on political advertising in section 321(1) of the Communications Act 2003. The Court held that the restrictions imposed on political advertising were justified. In particular the Court attached weight to the fact that there had been considerable cross-party parliamentary support for the ban, and that the domestic courts had given careful consideration to the jurisprudence of the Court of Human Rights. There were alternative outlets for the applicant to use to publicise their case. Furthermore, there was no consensus concerning political broadcasts among contracting states, a factor which pointed towards allowing a

---

8 See para. 1426.

wider margin of appreciation than normally afforded to restrictions on freedom of expression on matters of public interest.

One of the statutory justifications for restricting freedom of expression – the need to 'maintain the authority and impartiality of the judiciary' – was considered in **A v British Broadcasting Corporation** (2014). A was subject to a deportation order following his conviction for sexual offences. He claimed that if his identity became known in his country of origin he would be at risk of death or serious harm. A court order made under section 11 of the Contempt of Court Act 1981 prohibited disclosure of his identity. The British Broadcasting Corporation challenged the order as being contrary to the right to freedom of expression. The Supreme Court ruled that if the order was lifted, it would undermine all the proceedings which had taken place since 2007. Protection of A's identity was essential to the ability to deport without violating A's Article 3 rights. The exception to the principle of open justice, and restriction of the right of the BBC to disclose A's identity was justified by Article 10.2 – the need to protect the authority and impartiality of the judiciary.

Restrictions on Freedom of Expression

Defamation[9]

Defamation – slander or libel – may be defined as the publication, whether oral or written, of a falsehood which damages the reputation of the person concerned and lowers the victim's reputation in the eyes of 'right thinking members of society generally'.[10] Slander is defamation in the form of the spoken word; libel is defamation in some permanent form, such as publication in books or newspapers. Publication via radio or television broadcasting, or in the course of public theatre performances, is defined as libel rather than slander.[11] Technological developments such as electronic mail (email) and the internet raise new questions for the law.

Defamation poses difficult questions concerning the extent to which freedom of expression is to be balanced against protection of the reputation of others – whether individuals or organisations.

The technological advances in communications have prompted further regulation. Defamatory statements in newsgroup postings, emails or on web pages are regarded as libel.[12] Defamatory statements made in the course of internet relay chat, internet phone or video teleconferencing are regarded as slander. The Court of Appeal considered a libel claim brought against Google in **Tamiz v Google Inc.** (2013). The Court ruled that although some of the comments posted on a blog were defamatory, Google was not a publisher for the purpose of section 1 of the Defamation Act 1996. Google had not issued the defamatory comments, but was rather the provider of access to a communications system for the use of others.

The law relating to defamation has hitherto comprised common law, the Defamation Act 1952 and the Defamation Act 1996. The Defamation Act 2013 represents a major reform of aspects of the law of defamation.

In order to prevent frivolous cases, and reflecting the trend for the courts to require a 'threshold of seriousness',[13] section 1 of the Act provides that a statement is not defamatory

---

9 For details, see textbooks on the law of tort. Note that the common law offence of criminal libel has been abolished: Coroners and Justice Act 2009, s. 73.
10 **Sim v Stretch** (1936), p. 671.
11 Theatres Act 1968, s. 4; Broadcasting Act 1990, s. 166.
12 For libel to be established, there must be publication. However, in relation to articles on the internet there is no presumption of publication and the claimant in a libel action bears the burden of proving that the material in question has been accessed and downloaded: **Al Amoudi v Brisard and another** (2006).
13 See **Thornton v Telegraph Media Group Ltd** (2010).

unless its publication has caused or is likely to cause serious harm to the reputation of the claimant. In relation to commercial enterprises, the concept of serious harm relates to serious financial loss. The concept of serious harm was considered by the Supreme Court in **Lachaux v Independent Print Ltd** (2019).[14] Establishing whether a statement had caused serious harm involved assessing 'the inherent tendency of the words to cause harm and their actual impact on those to whom they were communicated'. That exercise called for an investigation into the actual impact of the statement. The Court therefore came down in favour of freedom of information over the privacy of the individual.

The 2013 Act also aims at restricting the use of the English courts for actions in defamation brought against persons not resident in the United Kingdom. Section 9(2) provides that a court shall not have jurisdiction to hear an action unless it is satisfied that, of all the places in which an allegedly defamatory statement has been published, England and Wales is the most appropriate place to bring an action. The 2013 Act introduces the 'single publication rule'. Formerly, each publication of defamatory material gave rise to a separate cause of action. The single publication rule is designed to prevent an action being brought in respect of the same material being republished after the one-year limitation period has passed. It does not apply if the manner of the subsequent publication is materially different from the first.

Under section 69 of the Senior Courts Act 1981 and section 66 of the County Courts Act 1984 there is a right to trial by jury in defamation cases unless the court considers that trial requires the prolonged examination of evidence which cannot 'conveniently be made with a jury'. Section 11 of the 2013 Act removes this presumption in favour of trial by jury. Defamation cases will in future be held without a jury unless the court orders otherwise.

Defences to an action for defamation
Unintentional defamation

The Defamation Act 1996 provides that the unintentional, or innocent, publication of statements which are defamatory may be defended. It must be shown that the publisher of the defamation has genuinely tried to make amends either by way of an apology or by correcting the false statement.

Absolute privilege

See Chapter 17.

Some speech is absolutely privileged. That is to say, the words, however libellous, are protected from the law of defamation. An example of such protection is parliamentary privilege. As we have seen, Article IX of the Bill of Rights 1689 gives absolute protection to words spoken in proceedings in Parliament. Statements made in the course of judicial proceedings also attract absolute privilege, as do statements by the Parliamentary Commissioner for Administration.[15] In **Buckley v Dalziel** (2007) it was held that absolute privilege and immunity from suit were available to a person who provided information to the police to set in motion the process of an inquiry into possible illegality. The Court, following **Taylor v Director of the Serious Fraud Office** (1999) ruled that it was necessary to protect those who provided evidence to the police in the course of an inquiry and that public policy considerations relating to the legal process applied equally to those who were witnesses and to those who were initial complainants.

---

14 [2019] UKSC 27; times LR 8 July 2019.
15 Parliamentary Commissioner Act 1967, s. 10(5).

The defence of truth

Section 2(1) of the Defamation Act 2013 provides that it is a defence for the defendant to show that the imputation conveyed by the statement complained of is substantially true. The common law defence of justification is abolished, and section 5 of the Defamation Act 1952 (justification) is repealed.

Honest opinion

This defence is important in giving limited protection to the publication of comments about public figures whose actions are matters of public interest.[16] In **Spiller v Joseph** (2010) Lord Phillips of Worth Matravers suggested that there should be a review of the law, and stated that the common law defence of 'fair comment' should in future be known as 'honest comment'. Section 3 of the 2013 Act adopts the phrase 'honest opinion'. Section 3(8) provides that the common law defence of fair comment is abolished, and that section 6 of the Defamation Act 1952 (fair comment) is repealed.

Publication on matter of public interest

Section 4 creates a new defence of publication on a matter of public interest. This is based on the defence of qualified privilege. Qualified privilege is a defence to an action for defamation in relation to statements on a matter of public interest made without malice. Qualified privilege arises under common law and statute. It has been held to attach to a communication between a Member of Parliament, who forwarded a constituent's complaint, and the Lord Chancellor and the Law Society where the matter was in the public interest.[17] Qualified privilege also applies to newspapers, radio and television broadcasts. The Defamation Act 2013, section 7 amends the Defamation Act 1996 which provides protection to fair and accurate reports of judicial proceedings and international organisations, legislatures or governments anywhere in the world and other public bodies. Section 7(9) of the 2013 Act extends the law to provide protection for fair and accurate reports of proceedings of scientific or academic conferences held anywhere in the world, and reports of its publications.

The common law defence of qualified privilege was considered in **Reynolds v Times Newspapers** (1999). In **Reynolds** the former Prime Minister of the Republic of Ireland brought libel proceedings against The Times newspaper in relation to an article which, he alleged, suggested that he had lied to Parliament and to Cabinet colleagues. No account of the Prime Minister's explanation was given. The House of Lords ruled, inter alia, that the article had made serious allegations without giving the former Prime Minister's explanation, and the defence of qualified privilege was not made out and could not be relied on by the defendants. In **Jameel (Mohammed) v Wall Street Journal sprl** (2006) the House of Lords ruled that a trading corporation was entitled to sue in respect of defamatory matters which could damage its business. The Court also held that a 'necessary precondition' of reliance on qualified privilege is 'that the matter should be one of public interest'. Furthermore, it was important that the publisher had taken reasonable steps to verify the material to be published. Where a matter was in the public interest and the publisher had sought to verify its contents, then qualified privilege applied. The public interest was also central in **Flood v Times Newspapers Ltd** (2012). The Times had published an article in which it alleged that a police officer, whom it named, had accepted bribes in exchange for confidential information. Was the newspaper entitled to the public interest defence? The Supreme Court ruled that it was. The story, if true, was of high public interest. There was no evidence that the police were conducting an investigation into

16 See **Silkin v Beaverbrook Newspapers Ltd** (1958); **Slim v Daily Telegraph Ltd** (1968).
17 **Beech v Freeson** (1972).

the allegation and there was circumstantial evidence that the allegation was true. The public interest lay in the fact that the allegation had been made and the publishers did not have to verify the substance of the allegation.

Section 4(1) of the Defamation Act 2013 provides it is a defence to an action for defamation for the defendant to show that:

(a)   the statement complained of was, or formed part of, a statement on a matter of public interest; and

(b)   the defendant reasonably believed that publishing the statement complained of was in the public interest.

In determining whether the defendant has established the matters set out above, the court must 'have regard to all the circumstances of the case'. The reform is intended to codify the common law defence, and accordingly section 4(6) provides that the common law defence known as the Reynolds defence is abolished. The Supreme Court confirmed that the section 4 defence had replaced the Reynolds defence in **Serafin v Malkiewicz** (2020).[18] The Court also ruled that it was inappropriate to regard the Reynolds decision as providing a 'check list' in relation to section 4.

Incitement to disaffection and treason[19]
Incitement to disaffection

The Incitement to Disaffection Act 1934 provides that it is an offence intentionally to attempt to dissuade a member of the armed forces from complying with his duty. It is also an offence to aid, counsel or procure commission of the principal offence. In **R v Arrowsmith** (1975), the defendant was accused and convicted for distributing leaflets to soldiers urging them not to serve in Northern Ireland, and the conviction was upheld by the Court of Appeal.[20] A similar offence exists in relation to causing disaffection within the police force.[21] There also remains on the statute book the Aliens Restriction (Amendment) Act 1919, as amended, section 3 of which prohibits aliens from causing sedition or disaffection among the population and the armed forces, and makes it a summary offence to cause industrial unrest in an industry in which one has not been employed for two years.

Treason

The Treason Act 1351 made it a capital offence to give 'aid and comfort to the King's enemies'. In **Joyce v Director of Public Prosecutions** (1946), William Joyce was convicted of making propaganda broadcasts on behalf of the Nazis during the Second World War. The death penalty for treason and piracy with violence was abolished by the Crime and Disorder Act 1998, section 36. Section 21(5) of the Human Rights Act 1998 abolishes the death penalty for military offences.

Racial hatred and hatred on grounds of sexual orientation

The first attempt at protecting persons from racial hatred was contained in the Race Relations Act 1965. The justification for restricting offensive racist speech – and hence freedom of

---

18 [2020] UKSC 23.
19 The common law offence of sedition was abolished by the Coroners and Justice Act 2009, s. 73.
20 An application under the European Convention on Human Rights failed: see **Arrowsmith v United Kingdom** (1978).
21 Police Act 1996, s. 91.

expression – lies in the greater need to protect individual minority groups from demeaning and discriminatory speech. Incitement to racial hatred is now regulated under sections 17 to 23 of the Public Order Act 1986. Section 17 defines racial hatred as meaning 'hatred against any group of persons in Great Britain defined by reference to colour, race, nationality (including citizenship) or ethnic or national origins'.

There are two basic requirements which relate to the offences in the Act. First, that the words used, or behaviour, must be 'threatening, abusive or insulting'. Second, the words or behaviour must either have been intended to incite racial hatred or be likely to do so. Under the Act, it is an offence to use words or behaviour, or display written material, which have the above elements. Publication of or distributing such material is also an offence.[22] The performance of plays, showing of films or videos or playing of records or broadcasts intended to or likely to incite racial hatred is an offence.[23] The Act, in section 23, also creates the offence of possession of such materials. Prosecutions may only be commenced with the consent of the Attorney General. Section 29AB of the Public Order Act 1986 criminalises the use of threatening words or behaviour or the display of any written material which is threatening with the intention of stirring up religious hatred or hatred on the grounds of sexual orientation.

Racial abuse at football matches is a criminal offence.[24] The Crime and Disorder Act 1998 extends the law to include racially aggravated offences,[25] a reform prompted by the findings of the inquiry into the death of Stephen Lawrence.[26] The offences of racially aggravated assault, criminal damage, public disorder and harassment are created. In addition, higher sentences may be imposed in relation to any other offences found to be racially motivated.

The Communications Act 2003, section 127, makes it an offence to send a 'message or other matter that is grossly offensive or of an indecent, obscene or menacing character' via a public telecommunications system. The offence is committed when a grossly offensive message is sent and the person sending the message intended his/her words to be grossly offensive. It is for the court to determine, 'applying the standards of an open and just multiracial society' to determine whether a message was grossly offensive.[27] In **R (Miller) v College of Policing and Chief Constable of Humberside** (2020) the police had warned the claimant against further tweeting of his views on transgenderism. The court held that his tweets did not 'even come close' to the offence and that no reasonable person would have regarded them as grossly offensive. The court considered Article 10 of the European Convention and the justified restrictions under Article 10(2), namely the prevention of crime and protection of others. Here there was no risk of the claimant committing a criminal offence; there was no evidence of anyone being upset by them. Freedom of speech was one of the fundamental rights in a democratic society: restrictions had to be both strictly necessary and proportionate. In this case there was no justification for the police's action and their treatment of the claimant disproportionately interfered with his right to freedom of expression.

The Racial and Religious Hatred Act 2006[28]

The Racial and Religious Hatred Act 2006 amends the Public Order Act 1986. Part IIIA of the Public Order Act defines religious hatred as being 'hatred against a group of persons defined by reference to religious belief or lack of religious belief'. It is an offence to use threatening

---

22 Public Order Act 1986, s. 19.
23 Ibid., ss 20–22 and also Broadcasting Act 1990, s. 164(1).
24 Football (Offences) Act 1991, s. 3 and also Football (Offences and Disorder) Act 1999, s. 9.
25 Sections 28–32 and also Anti-terrorism Crime and Security Act 2001, s. 39.
26 *The Macpherson Report*, Cmnd 4262.
27 **Director of Public Prosecutions ve Collins** (2006).
28 The Act does not extend to Northern Ireland or Scotland.

words or behaviour, or to display any written material which is threatening, if the person intends to stir up religious hatred. It is also an offence to publish or distribute written material which is threatening if the person intends to stir up religious hatred.[29] The 2006 Act also makes it an offence to present or direct a play which involves the use of threatening words or behaviour if there is intent to stir up religious hatred. The distribution, showing or playing of a recording of visual images or sounds which are threatening is also an offence. It is also an offence to have such materials in one's possession if there is the intention to stir up religious hatred.[30] No proceedings may be brought without the consent of the Attorney General.

The concerns of those who opposed the Bill on the grounds that it would restrict freedom of expression by criminalising discussion or criticism or ridicule of religions or beliefs or practices were met with the insertion of section 29J to the Public Order Act 1986, which now provides that:

> Nothing in this Part shall be read or given effect in a way which prohibits or restricts discussion, criticism or expressions of antipathy, dislike, ridicule, insult or abuse of particular religions or the beliefs or practices of their adherents, or of any other belief system or the beliefs or practices of its adherents, or proselytising or urging adherents of a different religion or belief system to cease practising their religion or belief system.

Incitement to terrorism

The Terrorism Act 2006, section 1, makes it a criminal offence to publish material intended to encourage members of the public, directly or indirectly, to commit acts of terrorism. Section 2 makes it an offence to disseminate such material. A 'publication' includes printed material as well as internet material. On conviction, the penalty is up to seven years' imprisonment.

Obscenity, indecency, censorship and pornography[31]
The Obscene Publications Act 1959

The Obscene Publications Act 1959 creates the offence of publication of an obscene article, whether or not for gain. Further, it is an offence to have such articles in ownership, possession or control for the purpose of publication for gain or with a view to publication.[32] An article[33] is 'obscene' if 'its effect ... is ... such as to tend to deprave and corrupt persons who are likely, having regard to all relevant circumstances, to read, see or hear the matter contained or embodied in it'.[34]

An article will be 'published', according to section 1(3), if a person:

(a) distributes, circulates, sells, lets on hire, gives or lends it, or who offers it for sale or for letting on hire; or

(b) in the case of an article containing or embodying matter to be looked at or a record, shows, plays or projects it.

---

29 Sections 29A, 28B and 29C respectively of the Public Order Act 1986.
30 Racial and Religious Hatred Act 2006, inserting ss 29D, 29E and 29F to the 1986 Act.
31 See Robertson, 2001, Chapter 5. On feminist arguments against pornography, see Smart, 1989, especially Chapter 6; Itzin, 1992; Barnett, 1998, Chapter 12.
32 Obscene Publications Act 1959, s. 2(1), as amended.
33 Which covers books, pictures, films, records, video cassettes, CDs, DVDs etc.
34 Obscene Publications Act 1959, s. 1(1).

The Criminal Justice and Public Order Act 1994 amends section 1(3) by adding the words 'or where the matter is stored electronically, transmits that data'.[35] The Court of Appeal, in **R v Smith (Gavin)** (2012) allowed an appeal by the prosecution against a ruling of a Crown Court that there was no case to answer to charges of publishing obscene material contrary to section 2(1) of the Obscene Publications Act 1959 on the basis that communication to only one person could not amount to publication. The defendant had sent an obscene comment in an internet relay chat with an unknown person. Richards LJ stated that section 1(3), as amended by the Criminal Justice and Public Order Act 1994,[36] provided that communication, including the transmission of electronically stored data to only one person, sufficed to constitute publication.

The tendency to 'deprave and corrupt'

It is not sufficient that an article disgusts, or is 'filthy', 'loathsome' or 'lewd'.[37] What must be established is that the article will 'deprave or corrupt'.[38] Nor is it sufficient that the article is capable of depraving or corrupting just one person: the test is whether or not a significant proportion of persons likely to read or see the article would be depraved or corrupted by it.[39] The fact that the persons likely to read the article regularly read such materials is irrelevant to whether or not the material can deprave or corrupt,[40] although the same argument may not hold if the likely audience is police officers experienced with dealing with pornography.[41]

In **Handyside v United Kingdom** (1976),[42] in which a publication entitled *The Little Red Schoolbook* had been seized under the Obscene Publications Act 1959, the Court of Human Rights ruled that there was no violation of Article 10.[43] The publishers claimed that the Obscene Publications Act represented a violation of Article 10 in several respects. The Court ruled that there was no breach of the Convention. The 'protection of morals' clause in Article 10(2) entitled the government to impose restrictions on freedom of expression, provided that the restrictions were proportionate to the aim pursued. It was for the Court to decide whether the restrictions were necessary and sufficient. In this case, the book was aimed at under-18-year-olds and encouraged promiscuity.

There exists a defence of public good[44] but the defence is interpreted narrowly.[45] For example, in **Director of Public Prosecutions v Jordan** (1977),[46] where the defendant argued the psychotherapeutic benefit of 'soft porn' for the consumer, the judge rejected the defence, holding that what was for the public good was art, literature or science. It is an offence to send or attempt to send indecent or obscene materials through the post.[47] It is also an offence to import indecent or obscene materials. Such materials may be forfeited.[48]

---

35 Criminal Justice and Public Order Act 1994, s. 84. See **R v Fellows and Arnold** (1997).
36 Section 168(1) and para. 3 of Sched. 9 to the 1994 Act.
37 **R v Anderson** (1972).
38 **R v Martin Secker and Warburg** (1954).
39 **DPP v Whyte** (1972), per Lord Wilberforce.
40 **Shaw v DPP** (1962).
41 **R v Clayton and Halsey** (1963).
42 See also **Muller v Switzerland** (1991).
43 See also **Wingrove v United Kingdom** (1996) and **Otto-Preminger Institut v Austria** (1994) on the law of blasphemy. On public order, see **Steel v UK** (1998) and **Hashman and Harrup v UK** (2000).
44 Obscene Publications Act 1959, s. 4.
45 See e.g. **R v Penguin Books Ltd** (1973).
46 And see **Attorney General's Reference (No 3 of 1977)** (1978).
47 Postal Services Act 2000, s. 85(3), (4).
48 Customs Consolidation Act 1876, Customs and Excise Act 1952 and Customs and Excise Management Act 1979, s. 49.

Indecency and pornography

While offences relating to obscenity require proof relating to its tendency to 'deprave and corrupt', indecency requires no such proof and is of a lesser order. Lord Parker in **R v Stanley** (1965) stated that indecency was 'something that offends the ordinary modesty of the average man ... offending against recognised standards of propriety at the lower end of the scale'.[49]

Pornography is not a legal concept. There is no legal prohibition against pornography as such – rather prosecutions will be brought under the headings of obscenity and/or indecency. Pornography does, however, raise a number of issues which are of particular concern to feminists and the literature is now extensive. The pornography industry is both global and vast. Concerns about pornography include the protection of women who work in the industry, and the impact that pornographic representations of women have on the status of women in society. However, the attempt in the United States to outlaw pornography on the grounds – inter alia – that it undermines women's equality, failed: freedom of expression prevailed.[50]

The Criminal Justice and Immigration Act 2008 increases penalties for offences under the Obscene Publication Act to five years. It also creates a new offence of possession of extreme pornographic images.

Broadcasting, cinemas, theatres and video recordings

Section 2 of the Theatres Act 1968 prohibits obscenity in theatrical performances. The law relating to obscenity applies to live performances, subject to the defence of public good. Legal regulation of live performances also exists in the form of section 20 of the Public Order Act 1986, which prohibits the use of threatening, abusive or insulting words or behaviour intended or likely to stir up racial hatred. Section 6 of the Theatres Act prohibits words or behaviour likely to cause a breach of the peace. In order to avoid frivolous or censorious legal action, the consent of the Attorney General is required in relation to prosecutions under the Theatres Act, Public Order Act and Sexual Offences Act.

The Broadcasting Act 1990 and Video Recordings Act 1984 each prohibited obscenity on local radio services, television and video. In relation to broadcasting, the British Broadcasting Corporation (BBC), established under the royal prerogative,[51] is under a duty not to adopt its own political stance on current affairs, and may only broadcast party political programmes with the consent of the major political parties.

Impartiality in broadcasting is promoted by the prohibition on political broadcasting. In **R (London Christian Radio Ltd) v Radio Advertising Clearance Centre** (2013) the Court of Appeal held that the term 'political' in section 321(2)(b) of the Communications Act 2003 was not to be given a narrow interpretation since that would frustrate the statutory aim. It was lawful for the Radio Advertising Clearance Centre to refuse to allow an advertisement which was designed to reduce or eliminate the 'marginalisation' of Christians in the work place. The advertisement was of a political nature and directed towards a political end.

The Office of Communications (Ofcom)[52]

The Office of Communications Act 2002 established Ofcom in preparation for the transfer of regulatory functions from the former broadcasting regulators.[53] The Communications Act

---

49 See Robertson, 1979, Chapter 7.
50 See Dworkin, 1981.
51 The BBC was established by Royal Charter. Its chairman and governors are appointed by the Crown on the advice of the Prime Minister. The BBC operates under licence from the government issued under the Wireless Telegraphy Act 1904–1967.
52 See Office of Communications (Ofcom), *Annual Report 2011–12*, HC 237, London: TSO.
53 See the White Paper, *A New Future For Communications* (Cm 5010).

2003 provided for the transfer of functions from five bodies or office holders to Ofcom. With effect from 1 October 2011, Ofcom assumed responsibility for postal services.[54]

The general duties of Ofcom are set out in section 3 of the Communications Act 2003. Ofcom's principal duty is to further the interests of the public and to further consumer interests where appropriate through promoting competition. Ofcom is required to ensure a wide availability of a range of television and radio services and maintain a sufficient plurality of providers. It is also required to protect members of the public from offensive and harmful material and to apply standards in television and radio services which protect people from unfair treatment and infringements of privacy. In exercising its functions, Ofcom is to have regard to the principles of transparency, accountability and proportionality.

Ofcom is under a duty to publish a Broadcasting Code for television and radio, covering 'standards in programmes, sponsorship, product placement in television programmes, fairness and privacy'. The Code must be read in light of the European Convention on Human Rights.[55]

Film and video

The regulation of films falls to the British Board of Film Classification (BBFC), and their availability for viewing by the public controlled by local authorities. The BBFC operates a system of classification by age: 'U' for general circulation, 'PG' (parental guidance), 12, 12A (children under 12 accompanied by an adult), 15 and 18 certificate films and R18 films which are for restricted viewing only on segregated premises. The BBFC may refuse a certificate if the film contravenes the Obscene Publications Act 1959, and may insist on cuts to a film before a certificate is granted. Local authorities exercise control through the granting of licences for a particular film to be shown in its area.[56]

The BBFC also classifies videos, DVDs and Blu-ray discs for private viewing. The Video Recordings Act 1984 requires that the BBFC should have 'special regard to the likelihood of video works being viewed in the home' (section 4). The BBFC must also pay 'special regard' to the harm caused to potential viewers by the depiction of criminal activity, illegal drugs, violence and sexual behaviour.[57] The growth of the internet led to the transmission of electronically stored data being included within the Obscene Publications Act 1959 definition of 'publication'.[58] In 2009 it became apparent that the 1984 Act was legally unenforceable, having been enacted in breach of an EC Technical Standards Directive which required draft legislation to be notified to the European Commission for consultation. The Video Recordings Act 2010 re-enacts the provisions and came into force on receiving the Royal Assent.

Conspiracy to corrupt public morals

Under the common law, publishers may be liable for the offence of conspiracy to corrupt public morals. In **Shaw v Director of Public Prosecutions** (1962), Shaw, the publisher of a directory giving the names and details of prostitutes, was prosecuted for conspiracy to corrupt public morals.[59] The House of Lords (Lord Reid dissenting) held that the courts have a 'residual power to enforce the supreme and fundamental purpose of the law, to conserve not only the safety and order but also the moral welfare of the state'.[60]

---

54 Postal Services Act 2011.
55 See **R (Gaunt) v Office of Communications (Ofcom)** (2011).
56 Under the Cinemas Act 1985.
57 Under the Criminal Justice and Public Order Act 1994, s. 90.
58 Criminal Justice and Public Order Act 1994, s. 168.
59 Shaw was also found guilty of an offence under the Obscene Publications Act 1959. See further above.
60 Seaborne Davies, 1962.

Shaw v Director of Public Prosecutions was upheld in **Knuller Ltd v Director of Public Prosecutions** (1973). The publishers had produced a magazine containing advertisements for male homosexuals. The House of Lords, upholding **Shaw**, rejected as a defence the fact that the Sexual Offences Act 1967 provided that homosexual acts between adult males, in private, were no longer an offence. The use of this common law offence is rare; nevertheless, it remains an available offence which enables the state to avoid statutory offences which provide defences such as that of the 'public good'.[61]

Blasphemy and blasphemous libel[62]

Blasphemy was a common law offence which prohibited words abusing Christ or denying or attacking the established Church which caused outrage to the feelings of a Christian. Long criticised as being discriminatory, the Law Commission recommended in 1985 that the offence be abolished. However, it was not until 2008 that the government acted and section 79 of the Criminal Justice and Immigration Act 2008 states that: 'The offences of blasphemy and blasphemous libel under the common law of England and Wales are abolished'.

Contempt of court

The law relating to contempt of court developed in order to protect the judiciary and judicial proceedings from actions or words which impede or adversely affect the administration of justice, or 'tends to obstruct, prejudice or abuse the administration of justice'.[63] Contempt of court, under English but not Scottish law, may be criminal or civil. In relation to criminal contempt, which may be dealt with in both the civil and criminal courts, the action relates to conduct which is designed to interfere with the administration of justice, which may of itself involve a criminal offence. The court has the power to rule on the existence of a contempt and to punish the guilty party. Where the judge finds the person guilty of contempt, he may commit the person instantly to prison. Two principal forms of criminal contempt exist.

Contempt in the face of the court[64]

Conduct in court which impedes the judicial process may be a contempt. A demonstration which interrupts proceedings,[65] or insulting behaviour, or refusal of a witness to answer questions or give evidence or comply with a court order to disclose information, may amount to contempt.[66]

Publications prejudicing the course of justice

The balance to be struck between freedom of expression and the protection of judicial proceedings is a matter for debate. The Contempt of Court Act 1981, which reformed the common law of contempt, sought to achieve the appropriate balance. Before that Act, the law relating to contempt proved capable of inhibiting freedom of the press for an extensive period of time, where judicial proceedings became protracted. The leading case which presaged reform of the law is that of **Sunday Times v United Kingdom** (1979). In 1974, the House of Lords restored

---

61 Obscene Publications Act 1959, s. 4.
62 See Kenny, 1992.
63 Report of the Phillimore Committee on Contempt of Court, Cmnd 5794, 1974, p. 2. See Dhavan, 1976.
64 Note that the common law offence of scandalising the judiciary was abolished in England and Wales by s. 33 of the Crime and Courts Act 2013.
65 See **Morris v Crown Office** (1970).
66 See **Attorney General v Mulholland and Foster** (1970); **British Steel Corporation v Granada Television Ltd** (1963).

an injunction[67] prohibiting the *Sunday Times* from publishing articles relating to the drug thalidomide, manufactured by Distillers Ltd, which, it was alleged, caused serious deformities in babies. The parents of the affected children intended to sue Distillers for compensation. The company entered into protracted negotiations with the families' solicitors. The injunction restrained any further publication on the matter by the newspaper. The *Sunday Times* made an application under Article 10 of the European Convention on Human Rights, which protects freedom of expression, alleging that the common law of contempt violated Article 10. The European Court of Human Rights held that there had been a violation of Article 10. As a result, the Contempt of Court Act 1981 was enacted, clarifying the law on pre-trial publicity.[68]

The Contempt of Court Act 1981

Section 1 of the Contempt of Court Act provides for the 'strict liability rule'. The rule is defined as 'the rule of law whereby conduct may be treated as a contempt of court as tending to interfere with the course of justice in particular legal proceedings *regardless of intent to do so*' (emphasis added). In order for the strict liability rule to be established, a number of issues need to be satisfied. First, the test relates only to publications falling within section 2 of the Act. Publications are defined in section 2(1) as including 'any speech, writing [programme included in a programme service][69] or other communication in whatever form, which is addressed to the public at large or any section of the public'. Second, the publication must be such that it 'creates a substantial risk that the course of justice in the proceedings in question will be seriously impeded or prejudiced'.[70] Third, the strict liability rule applies only if the proceedings in question are 'active', as defined by Schedule 1 to the Act. In relation to appellate proceedings, these are active from the time they are commenced, by an application for leave to appeal or apply for review, or by notice of appeal or of application to review or by other originating process, 'until disposed of or abandoned, discontinued or withdrawn'. In relation to criminal proceedings, the starting point is the issue of a warrant for arrest, arrest without warrant or the service of an indictment. The end point is acquittal, sentence, any other verdict or discontinuance of the trial. In relation to civil proceedings, the start point is when the case is set down for a hearing in the High Court. The end point is when the proceedings are disposed of, discontinued or withdrawn.[71]

In **Attorney General v MGN Ltd** (2012) an application for the committal of newspaper publishers for contempt of court was granted on the basis that articles which vilified a suspect in a murder case were a potential impediment to the course of justice within section 2(2) of the 1981 Act. This was held even though the suspect was subsequently released without charge and would therefore never face trial.

It is a defence to prove that, at the time of publication, or distribution of the publication, the defendant does not know, and has no reason to suspect, that relevant proceedings are active.[72] Fair and accurate reports of legal proceedings, held in public and published 'contemporaneously and in good faith' do not attract the strict liability rule.[73] In addition, if publication is made as, or as part of, a discussion in 'good faith of public affairs or other matters of

---

67 **Attorney General v Times Newspapers Ltd** (1974). The injunction had been discharged by the Court of Appeal.
68 See further Chapter 20 on Article 10 and rights of protest.
69 Added by the Broadcasting Act 1990, s. 203.
70 See **Re Lonrho** (1990).
71 See **Attorney General v Hislop and Pressdram** (1991).
72 Contempt of Court Act 1981, s. 3(1), (2).
73 *Ibid.*, s. 4.

general public interest', it is not to be treated as contempt of court, 'if the risk of impediment or prejudice to particular legal proceedings is merely incidental to the discussion'.[74]

Section 10 of the Contempt of Court Act regulates the disclosure of sources. The court may not require disclosure, and a person will not be guilty of contempt as a result of non-disclosure unless the court is satisfied that 'disclosure is necessary in the interests of justice or national security or for the prevention of disorder or crime'. The leading case is **X Ltd v Morgan Grampian** (1991), in which the House of Lords ruled on the decision-making process entailed in section 10. In that case, a confidential plan was stolen from the plaintiffs and information from the plan given to a journalist. The plaintiffs applied for an order requiring the journalist, William Goodwin, to disclose the source and sought discovery of his notes of the telephone conversation in order to discover the identity of the source. The House of Lords, in balancing the competing interests – the applicant's right to take legal action against the source and the journalist's interest in maintaining confidentiality with the source – held that the interests of the plaintiffs outweighed the interests of the journalist. This decision led to an application under Article 10 of the European Convention – the right to freedom of expression. In **Goodwin v United Kingdom** (1996), the Court ruled that the order against the journalist violated his right to freedom of expression which was central to a free press.[75]

It is for the court to determine whether a particular decision-making forum is a 'court' for the purposes of the law of contempt of court. In **General Medical Council v British Broadcasting Corporation** (1998), the Court of Appeal ruled that the Professional Conduct Committee (PCC) of the General Medical Council was not part of the judicial process of the state and accordingly was not subject to the Contempt of Court Act 1981. The PCC was a statutory committee under the Medical Act 1983, which exercised a sort of judicial power, but it was not the judicial power of the state. It had a recognisable judicial function, but was not part of the judicial system of the state.

Contempt of court and Article 10 of the European Convention

The impact of the Human Rights Act 1998 is being felt in this area of law. In **Ashworth Security Hospital v MGN Ltd** (2002), the Mirror newspaper had published verbatim extracts from hospital medical records of information concerning a convicted murderer who was detained at the hospital. The information had been supplied to the newspaper, in breach of confidence and breach of contract, by a hospital employee through an intermediary. The Contempt of Court Act 1981, section 10, provided for orders of disclosure of sources of information only where it was established that 'disclosure is necessary in the interests of justice or national security or for the prevention of disorder or crime'. The hospital had failed to identify the informant and sought an order that MGN identify the intermediary as the only likely means of discovering the source's identity. MGN argued that such an order would contravene Article 10 of the Convention. The Court of Appeal ruled that unless the source was identified and dismissed, there was a significant risk that there would be further selling of confidential information, and that such disclosures amounted to an attack on confidentiality which should be safeguarded in any democratic society. Where a person against whom disclosure was sought – in this case the intermediary – had 'become mixed up in wrongful, albeit not tortious, conduct that infringed a claimant's legal rights', the court had jurisdiction to order disclosure. The

---

74 See *Attorney General v English* (1983); *Attorney General v TVS Television*; *Attorney General v HW Southey & Sons* (1989); *Pickering v Liverpool Daily Post and Echo Newspapers plc* (1991). See also the Public Interest Disclosure Act 1998, which amends the Employment Rights Act 1996 and provides protection for employees who disclose wrongdoing by his or her employer.

75 See also *John v Express Newspapers* (2000) but cf. *Camelot Group plc v Centaur* (1999). The public interest in the protection of journalists' sources was sufficient to outweigh any threat of damage through future dissemination of a company's confidential information or any possibility of obtaining damages for past breaches of confidence. The Court of Human Rights so held in *Financial Times Ltd v United Kingdom* (2006).

decision was affirmed by the House of Lords. In **Interbrew SA v Financial Times** (2002), the court declared itself bound by the decision in **Ashworth**. A claimant was entitled to an order for delivery up of leaked and partly forged documents held by publishers in order to enable him to ascertain the proper defendant to a breach of confidence action. The 'public interest in protecting the source of a leak was not sufficient to withstand the countervailing public interest in letting Interbrew seek justice in the courts against the source'.[76]

However, the importance of protecting journalistic sources was recognised in **Mersey Care NHS Trust v Ackroyd** (2006), the sequel to **Ashworth Hospital Authority v MGN Ltd** (*supra*). The Hospital Trust had commenced an action against the journalist identified as a result of the order of disclosure, Mr Ackroyd, in an attempt to compel the journalist to reveal the source of his information. The High Court ruled that in balancing conflicting rights – the right to privacy and the right to freedom of expression – it was necessary to apply the guidelines set out in **Campbell v Mirror Group Newspapers plc** (2004).[77] Applying those guidelines, the court came to the opposite conclusion to that reached in the **Ashworth Hospital** case. Here an order for disclosure would not be proportionate to the hospital's legitimate aim to seek redress against the source, given 'the vital public interest in the protection of a journalist's source'.[78]

In **Attorney General v Punch Ltd** (2002), the former editor of *Punch* magazine, and the publishers, had been fined for being in contempt of court. At issue was the publication by *Punch* of an article by David Shayler, the former MI5 officer. The Attorney General had been granted injunctions on the basis that revelations by Shayler about matters relating to his employment would be contrary to national security. The question was, where a court ordered that specified material was not to be published, would a third party who, with the knowledge of the order, published the specified material automatically commit a contempt of court, or would contempt only occur if the third party thereby knowingly defeated the purpose for which the order was made? The House of Lords ruled that the editor must have known that by publishing the article he was doing 'precisely what the court order was intended to prevent, namely, pre-empting the court's decision on the confidentiality issues relevant to trial'.

In **In re S (A Child) (Identification: Restrictions on Publication)** (2004), the House of Lords considered the basis of the courts' jurisdiction to restrain publicity to protect a child's private and family life by way of injunction. The Court ruled that jurisdiction derived from Convention rights rather than the inherent jurisdiction of the High Court. At issue here was the conflict between the child's right to private and family life under Article 8 and the right of freedom of expression (of the press) under Article 10.

The House of Lords stated that:

> neither Article as such had precedence over the other, the correct approach being to focus on the comparative importance of the specific rights claimed in the individual case, with the justifications for interfering or restricting each right being taken into account and the proportionality test applied to each.

On the fact of this case, the Court declared that:

> although the ordinary rule was that the press could report everything that took place in a criminal court, it was the duty of the court to examine with care each

---

76 The restriction on publication of information which would lead to the identification of an HIV healthcare worker (here a dentist) was justified under Article 10(2) according to the Court of Appeal in **H v N (A Health Authority); H v Associated Newspapers Ltd** (2002).
77 Discussed below at p. 508.
78 See **Financial Times Ltd v United Kingdom** (2006).

> application for a departure from the rule by reason of Article 8, but in so doing the court was not ... to create further exceptions by a process of analogy save in the most compelling circumstances.

The freedom of the press to report criminal proceedings would be inhibited by an extension of the protection of Article 8 and there should be no injunction granted.

The law of confidence

At common law, where information is received in a situation where the recipient knows or ought to know that the information is confidential and therefore not to be disclosed to others, that information is protected by law and any unauthorised disclosure of that information – by whatever means – will be actionable. The law of confidence therefore protects information which an individual does not want disclosed while simultaneously restricting the freedom of expression of the recipient of that information.

Originally, actions for breach of confidence were relevant mainly to trade secrets, unfair competition and industrial espionage. However, the law has expanded into many other areas, proceeding on a case-by-case basis. The disclosure of information may amount to breach of confidence if the relationship is based on marriage,[79] contracts of employment, consultancies and potentially any situation involving a 'confidential relationship'.

Where there is a breach of the common law duty of confidence, or an anticipated breach, an injunction may be granted by the court, prohibiting publication or further publication of the information.[80] An example of this is seen in **Schering Chemical v Falkman Ltd** (1981). In **Schering**, a Thames Television documentary about a pregnancy drug was scheduled for transmission. The programme revealed material obtained by the producer in his role as a consultant to the company. The court held that an enforceable duty of confidence existed. A further example is seen in the proposal, in 1987, by the BBC to transmit a documentary *My Country Right or Wrong* in which former security officers were interviewed. An injunction was granted on the basis that there had occurred a breach of confidence in the course of the interviews.[81] *Spycatcher*, a book written by a former member of the Security Services, was also restrained by way of an injunction based on breach of confidence.[82] One difficult aspect of the use of such prior restraint is that there exists no trial of the facts until a future date, when it may transpire that there has been an unjustified, and often lengthy, restriction on freedom of expression.

 SELF-TEST QUESTION

What are the principal restrictions on freedom of speech?

Defences to an action for breach of confidence
Staleness

In **Attorney General v Jonathan Cape Ltd** (1976) (the **Crossman Diaries** case) the information disclosed in breach of confidence was some ten years old and no harm would follow from its

---

79 **Duke of Argyll v Duchess of Argyll** (1967).
80 Injunctions may be used for several different purposes. We are concerned here solely with injunctions as a remedy for breach of confidence.
81 *The Times*, 5 and 18 December 1987.
82 See further Chapter 22.

publication. Accordingly, the court held that, in the absence of a breach of national security, further restraint was not justified. However, in the *Spycatcher* case, **Attorney General v Guardian (No 2)** (1990), while the injunction was eventually lifted, the government claimed that the duty of former Security Service personnel is lifelong and that no publication of any matter concerning their employment may be disclosed. Section 1 of the Official Secrets Act 1989 now reflects this duty and imposes criminal sanctions on any unauthorised revelations made in relation to security matters.

The material is in the public domain

While there may be found to be a duty of confidence, this duty does not necessarily result in an injunction being permanently imposed to restrain publication. In addition to the material being 'stale', it may be that the material has already been published elsewhere, and is thus in the 'public domain'. In relation to the book *Spycatcher*, this matter weighed with the court. The book had been published in Australia and the United States of America and was, in fact, freely available anywhere outside the United Kingdom. In **Attorney General v Times Newspapers Ltd** (2001) the Court of Appeal ruled that it was the responsibility of the newspaper's editors to form a judgment about whether material had been brought sufficiently into the public domain. The editor was not required to seek confirmation from either the Attorney General or the court that this was the case. Such an approach, the court ruled, was 'consonant with Article 10 of the European Convention on Human Rights and section 12 of the [Human Rights] Act'.

Revealing true information to correct falsity

Irrespective of the existence of a duty of confidence, there may be situations where material has been published which is false and which justifies a breach of confidence in order to rectify the falsehood. In **Woodward v Hutchins** (1977), for example, a falsehood concerning a pop star had been published. Notwithstanding a duty of confidence, there was a justified and legitimate need for rebuttal of the untruths.

Iniquity: to reveal evidence of crime/fraud

Breach of confidence may be excused by the court if the defence of revealing criminal or fraudulent activities is made out.

Public interest

The defence of public interest was considered in **Lion Laboratories v Evans and Express Newspapers** (1984). The *Express* newspaper revealed information concerning faulty intoximeters used to measure the extent of alcohol in an individual's bloodstream. Deficiencies in the breathalyser equipment could have resulted in wrongful convictions for driving under the influence of alcohol. The disclosure of confidential information was justified. There was no question of the manufacturer having been guilty of any 'iniquity' or wrongdoing. However, the matter was one of public interest which overrode any claim to confidentiality of the information. Public interest disclosures by employees are now protected under the Public Interest Disclosure Act 1998 which amends the Employment Rights Act 1996.

Privacy

The idea that individuals have a 'right to privacy' has a strong and intuitive hold on the popular imagination: the autonomous human being claims a protective personal and family sphere into which others may not intrude without permission. Privacy is inextricably linked to liberty: the freedom from restriction on lawful activities whether by the state, its agents or private bodies or individuals. As John Stuart Mill wrote in *On Liberty*:

> the sole end for which mankind are warranted, individually or collectively, in inter-fering with the liberty of action of any of their number, is self-protection. [That] the only purpose for which power can be rightfully exercised over any member of a civilised community, against his will, is to prevent harm to others. His own good, either physical or moral, is not a sufficient warrant.

However, there has never been either a common law or statutory right to privacy as such.[83] In place of a right to privacy there are numerous provisions which restrict individuals and state officials from intruding on areas of a person's privacy. However, there are equally numerous provisions which permit intrusions into privacy, provided they are carried out under law-ful authority. The principal reason for this lies in the difficulties in defining the full scope of privacy and its relationship with competing concepts and interests. The privacy of the individual, for example, competes with the right to freedom of expression of the press.[84] The need for the state to keep official records also competes with individual privacy. Privacy may compete also with the powers of the police to investigate crime and the powers of the secu-rity forces to combat terrorism. Increasingly as criminal activities such as drug trafficking, trafficking in human beings and international money laundering are globalised, there is a need for the police and security agencies to cooperate with European and international forces.

Examples of the legal protection of aspects of privacy include the following:

- The right to personal safety and the enjoyment of personal possessions is reflected in the law relating to offences against the person and the law of theft.
- The right to exclude uninvited visitors from one's home is reflected in laws relating to trespass (see **Entick v Carrington** (1765)) and the requirements of lawful authority to enter private property.
- The right to protect one's reputation is provided by the law of defamation.
- Private information which is disclosed to another in a situation of confidence is protected by the law of breach of confidence.[85]
- The right to express one's sexual identity, in private, is recognised in the laws legalising homosexuality and in laws prohibiting discrimination on grounds of gender.
- Surveillance, investigations and interception of communications by the police and secu-rity forces require statutory authority.[86]
- The law regulating the storing of individual data by the state requires authorisation and provides safeguards.[87]

The European Convention on Human Rights and the Human Rights Act 1998

Prior to the Human Rights Act 1998, Article 8 of the European Convention protected privacy and provided the legal means by which to challenge domestic law. Article 8 provides:

---

83 See, for example, *Kaye v Robertson* (1991) discussed below at p. 513.
84 On the regulation of the press see *Report of the Younger Committee*, Cmnd 5012, 1972; *Report of the Committee on Privacy and Related Matters*, Cmnd 1102, 1990; *Review of Press Self-Regulation*, Cmnd 2135, 1993.
85 See the discussion above and the case law below.
86 Police and Criminal Evidence Act 1984, Regulation of Investigatory Powers Act 2000.
87 See, *inter alia*, the Data Protection Act 1984 and Freedom of Information Act 2000.

> Everyone has the right to respect for his private and family life, his home and his correspondence.
>
> There shall be no interference by a public authority with the exercise of this right except such as is in accordance with the law and is necessary in a democratic society in the interests of national security, public safety or the economic well-being of the country, for the prevention of disorder or crime, for the protection of health or morals, or for the protection of the rights and freedoms of others.

The law of confidence, discussed above – now interpreted in light of the Human Rights Act 1998 – has proven central to extending the legal protection of aspects of privacy. Key factors in recent developments include the following:

- Section 6 of the Human Rights Act, which requires the courts, as a public body, to comply with Convention rights and thereby enables the courts to give horizontal effect to Convention rights;[88]
- Article 8 of the Convention: the right to respect for private and family life, home and correspondence;
- Article 10 of the Convention: the right to freedom of expression which includes restrictions on that right expressed as follows:

> The exercise of these freedoms, since it carries with it duties and responsibilities, may be subject to such formalities, conditions, restrictions or penalties as are prescribed by law and are necessary in a democratic society ... **for preventing disclosure of information received in confidence**. [emphasis added]

- Section 12 of the Human Rights Act, which provides that where there is an application to a court to restrain in advance the publication of information, or prevent further publication of information to which confidentiality applies: '(3) No relief [affecting the exercise of freedom of expression] is to be granted so as to restrain publication before trial unless the court is satisfied that the applicant is likely to establish that publication should not be allowed'.

The manner in which the courts have developed the law relating to breach of confidence in light of the Human Rights Act has ensured that privacy claims are now being given greater protection than was the case prior to the Act. For example, in **Douglas v Hello! Ltd** (2001), the Court of Appeal ruled that individuals had a right of personal privacy which was grounded in the equitable doctrine of breach of confidence.[89] Michael Douglas and Catherine Zeta-Jones had granted OK! magazine exclusive rights to publish photographs of their wedding. Hello! magazine had obtained photographs of the wedding and had been subjected to an interim injunction restraining publication before the trial of the substantive issues. In this case, the claimants had lessened the degree of privacy concerning their wedding by allowing OK! magazine to publish photographs, thereby affecting the balance between their rights (to privacy) and the rights of others to freedom of expression. The court discharged the injunction. However, in a strong statement of principle, Sedley LJ said that 'we have reached a point at

---

88 Meaning that private bodies are required to comply with the Convention: see further Chapter 18.
89 See also **Earl Spencer v United Kingdom** (1998), in which the Court of Human Rights stated, inter alia, that the claim to breach of privacy could have been adequately protected under the common law of breach of confidence.

which it can be said with confidence that the law recognises and will appropriately protect a right of personal privacy'.

In **Campbell v Mirror Group Newspapers (MGN) Ltd** (2004), the model Naomi Campbell was awarded damages, albeit minimal, by the High Court for the disclosure of information relating to her attending meetings for the treatment of drug addiction. By a majority of three to two, the House of Lords held that the 'broad test' to be applied was 'whether disclosure of the information ... would give substantial offence to a reasonable person of ordinary sensibilities assuming that the person was placed in similar circumstances'. Lord Hope stated that the right to privacy (which lies at the heart of an action for breach of confidence) had to be balanced against the right of the media to publish information. Conversely, the media's freedom of expression had to be balanced against the respect which had to be given to private life. In this case, Lord Hope said that had it not been for the publication of photographs of Ms Campbell leaving the place of treatment, the balance between the competing rights would have been 'about even'. However, the photographs 'added greatly' to the intrusion of the claimant's private life and their publication outweighed the defendants' right to freedom of expression.[90]

In the House of Lords, Lord Nicholls of Birkenhead stated that:

> The time has come to recognise that the values enshrined in Articles 8 and 10 are now part of the cause of action for breach of confidence ... [and] are as much applicable in disputes between individuals or between an individual and a non-governmental body such as a newspaper as they are in disputes between individuals and a public authority.[91]

Campbell established the correct approach to privacy cases. This involves a two-stage test. The first stage is to ask 'whether in respect of the disclosed facts in question the person had a reasonable expectation of privacy'. If they did have such an expectation then the court has to conduct a 'balancing exercise' between the Article 8 right and the Article 10 right to freedom of expression.

Campbell may be compared with **A v B plc** (2002). The Court of Appeal ruled that any interference with freedom of the press had to be justified, and could not be limited because there was no identifiable public interest in the material being published. The court distinguished between the confidentiality which attached to sexual relations within marriage 'or other stable relationships' and the confidentiality which attached to transient relationships. Here, a footballer, A, had had sexual relationships with C and D. He did not want his wife to find out. C and D, however, had no interest in maintaining confidentiality. The Lord Chief Justice recognised that the Convention provided 'new parameters within which the court would decide in an action for breach of confidence whether a person was entitled to have his privacy protected', or 'whether the intrusion into freedom of information which such protection involved could not be justified'. In this case, it was not obvious why an injunction should be granted: A's relationships were not in the categories of relationships which the court should be astute to protect when other parties did not want them to remain confidential. Freedom of the press should prevail, and regulation of reporting in the press should be a matter for the Press Council, not the courts.

---

90 **Campbell** was considered in **Murray v Express Newspapers plc** (2007) in which it was held that celebrities enjoy no special right to privacy and that going about their ordinary daily activities such as walking down the street or shopping did not attract an expectation or right to privacy. Leave to appeal was granted. See **Murray v Big Pictures (UK) Ltd** (2008).

91 At para. 17.

The Court of Appeal extended the right to privacy – through its interpretation of the scope of confidence – in **McKennitt v Ash** (2006). Buxton LJ stated that the first question for the court to ask was whether the information was 'private in the sense that it was in principle protected by Article 8. If it was not, that was the end of the case'. However, if the answer was 'yes', then the court had to consider whether, in all the circumstances, the interests of the owner of the private information had to give way to the right of freedom of expression conferred by Article 10. It was the balance between these two Articles which was crucial. Applying **Von Hannover v Germany** (2005) the matters disclosed were of a private nature and Article 8 was engaged.[92]

In **HRH Prince of Wales v Associated Newspapers Ltd** (2007), a former member of the Prince's staff disclosed to the defendant copies of travel journals written by the Prince. These were intended to remain confidential and were not intended for publication. Lord Phillips of Worth Matravers CJ laid emphasis on section 3 of the Human Rights Act 1998, stating that:

> The English court has been concerned to develop a law of privacy that provides protection of the rights to 'private and family life, his home and his correspondence' recognised by Article 8 of the Convention. To this end the courts have extended the law of confidentiality so as to protect Article 8 rights in circumstances which do not involve a breach of a confidential relationship.[93]

This introduces artificiality into the law: the law of confidentiality now appears to have been extended to cover situations where the court considers that privacy should be protected. In **Campbell v MGN** (2002), discussed above, Lord Nicholls of Birkenhead had recognised the difficulty in this way:

> the law imposes a 'duty of confidence' whenever a person receives information he knows or ought to know is fairly and reasonably to be regarded as confidential … The continuing use of the phrase 'duty of confidence' and the description of the information as 'confidential' is not altogether comfortable. Information about an individual's private life would not, in ordinary usage, be called 'confidential'. The more natural description today is that such information is private. The essence of the tort is better encapsulated now as misuse of private information.[94]

The result of these developments is that the law of confidentiality now encompasses not only pre-existing relationships but also situations where no previous relationship of confidence exists but the information has been improperly obtained and used (as in the **Prince of Wales** case).

The Court of Appeal returned to its analysis of breach of confidence and privacy in **Lord Browne of Madingley v Associated Newspapers Ltd** (2007). The claimant, the group chief executive of a major international company, had obtained an interim injunction restraining the defendant newspaper from publishing information concerning his private life and business activities. The Master of the Rolls stated that the Court should first decide whether Article 8 is engaged; then consider whether Article 10 is engaged and then proceed to decide whether

---

92 The Court rejected the argument that it would be a defence to establish that the information disclosed was in fact untrue.
93 The Court ruled that Prince Charles had 'an unanswerable claim for breach of privacy. When the breach of a confidential relationship is added to the balance, the case is overwhelming': para. 74.
94 At para. 14. Cited in the **Prince of Wales** case at para. 26, emphasis added.

the applicant 'has shown that he is likely to establish at a trial that publication should not be allowed within the meaning of section 12(3)'.[95]

In **Max Mosley v News Group Newspapers** (2008) the court considered the applicant's right to privacy (Article 8) and the newspaper's right to freedom of expression (Article 10). Mr Mosley is a public figure. The cause of action was breach of confidence and/or the unauthorised disclosure of personal information allegedly infringing the complainant's right to privacy. It was argued that the content of the material (the portrayal of sado-masochistic activities) was inherently private in nature and that there had been a pre-existing relationship of confidentiality between the complainant and the five participants. The material had been secretly video-recorded by one of the participants and published in the newspaper and on the internet.

The newspaper claimed that, even if there was an infringement of Article 8, there was a public interest in the disclosure of the material, one aspect of which was the allegation that the activities represented Nazi or concentration camp role-play (Mr Mosley is the son of Sir Oswald Mosley, the British wartime fascist leader).

The newspaper's public interest defence was rejected and it was held that there had been a violation of the complainant's right to privacy. In considering the question of damages, the court considered the extent to which the complainant's own conduct had contributed to his distress and loss of dignity and observed that his behaviour could be regarded as 'reckless and almost self-destructive'. A relatively modest sum in damages was awarded (see further below).

In **Mosley v United Kingdom** (2011), the European Court of Human Rights ruled – unanimously – that Article 8 of the Convention on Human Rights does not impose a legal duty on newspapers to notify the subjects of intended publications in advance so as to give them an opportunity to seek an injunction to prevent publication.

Mr Mosley argued that damages alone were not an adequate remedy for the breach of his rights, on the basis that damages could not restore his privacy. He accordingly argued that newspapers should be under a legal duty to notify those who were to be the subject of damaging articles in order to allow them to seek to prevent publication. The European Court of Human Rights accepted that there had been a 'flagrant and unjustified invasion' of Mr Mosley's private life. However, the Court considered that to introduce a pre-notification requirement would affect political reporting and serious journalism (in addition to the sensationalist reporting at issue in Mr Mosley's case).

In conclusion, the Court ruled that a pre-notification requirement risked having a 'chilling effect' on freedom of expression which was protected under Article 10 of the Convention. Furthermore, given the wide margin of appreciation afforded to the United Kingdom in relation to the right to privacy, Article 8 did not require a legally binding pre-notification requirement.

In **Cream Holdings Ltd v Banerjee** (2004) the claimants sought an interim injunction to restrain publication of confidential information supplied by a former employee of the claimants who had obtained the information without permission. This raised the issue of the freedom of the press in relation to section 12(3) of the Human Rights Act 1998, which, as noted above, provides that no injunctive relief should be granted so as to restrain publication unless the court is satisfied that the applicant is likely to establish that publication should not be allowed. The House of Lords ruled that the principal purpose for which section 12(3) was

---

95 The Court ruled that it should be slow to make interim orders where the claimant had not satisfied the court that he was more likely than not to succeed at trial.

enacted was to protect freedom of speech by setting a higher threshold for the granting of interlocutory injunctions against the media.

The House of Lords ruled that to construe the word 'likely' as to mean 'more likely than not' in all situations would impose too high a test; that there could be no single rigid standard governing all applications and some flexibility was needed. All the circumstances of the case had to be taken into consideration. Generally, the court should not make an interim restraint order unless it was satisfied 'that the applicant's prospects of success at trial were sufficiently favourable to justify the order being made in the light of all the other circumstances of the case'. In the instant case, the disclosures were matters of serious public interest and the claimants' prospects of success at trial were not sufficiently high to justify making an interim order.[96] The Court of Appeal has ruled that it is not necessary for the court to state the precise degree of probability of success at trial: if there is a 'sufficient likelihood that claimants will defeat a public interest defence at trial', that entitles the court to grant an interim injunction restraining publication.[97]

Article 8 came into conflict with Article 10 once more in **In re Guardian and Media News Ltd and Others** (2010). The Supreme Court ruled that the general public interest in publishing a report of legal proceedings in which individuals had been named overrode the claimants' Article 8 rights. The claimants were subject to asset-freezing orders on the ground of suspicion of actually or potentially facilitating terrorist acts[98] and anonymity orders had been granted to protect them from identification in the media. While lifting the anonymity orders would undoubtedly have a direct effect on the individuals' private life, there was a 'powerful general public interest' in identifying parties to such proceedings which justified curtailing Article 8 rights.[99]

In **JIH v News Group Newspapers Ltd** (2011) the Court of Appeal recognised the difficulties in balancing the rights in Articles 8 and 10. Granting an anonymity order until trial or further order, the Court stated that in general where anonymity was ordered the nature of the information was to be disclosed, but, conversely, if the claimant was identified the nature of the information should not be disclosed.

Increasingly, celebrities have sought injunctions from the courts to prevent the disclosure of personal information. A recent trend has been for 'super-injunctions' to be granted. This form of injunction not only prevents the disclosure of information relating to an individual but also prevents disclosure of the fact that an injunction exists. Public concern over this development led to the Culture, Media and Sport Select Committee inquiring into their use.[100] Following that report, a committee, chaired by Lord Neuberger MR, was established to investigate and report. The Committee Report, 'Report of the Committee on Super-injunctions, 2011', concluded that the use of such injunctions had been reduced, and they were now being granted only for very short periods, and only where the level of secrecy they effect is 'necessary to ensure that the whole point of the order is not destroyed'.[101]

The Supreme Court upheld an interim injunction restraining publication of the name of a celebrity before trial in **PJS v News Group Newspapers Ltd** (2016). This was despite the fact that the identity of the person had already been disclosed in the press in the United States and Scotland and on social media. The Supreme Court recognised that it was faced with a 'difficult choice'. It was highly likely on the facts that at trial the claimant would establish that

---

96 On prior restraint see also **Martha Greene v Association Newspapers Ltd** (2004).
97 **ABC v Telegraph Media Group Ltd** [2018] EWCA Civ 2329.
98 Terrorism (United Nations Measures) Orders (SI 2006 Nos 2652 and 2957).
99 The Supreme Court quashed SI No. 2657: see Chapter 24. See also **Independent News and Media Ltd v A** (2010).
100 Culture, Media and Sport Select Committee Report, 24 February 2010.
101 On freedom of speech in Parliament see Chapter 17.

publication would involve further tortious invasions of privacy of the rights of the claimant, his partner and their children. On the other hand, those interested in the story would be able to access it on the internet and the court would be criticised for giving undue protection to a 'tawdry story'. However, the Court ruled, there was no public interest – in the legal sense – in the story and not to grant an injunction would add to further disclosure and breaches of privacy. Accordingly, on balance, continuation of the interim injunction was the best outcome.

The welfare of children will be given special consideration in relation to privacy. Two cases illustrate the position. In **Murray v Express Newspapers** (2009) the newspaper published images of the children of a well-known author and her husband, without the consent of their parents. The family was on a private outing at the time. At first instance, the action on behalf of the child was struck out, the Court holding that a child had no arguable case based on privacy. This the Court of Appeal held was wrong. A child does not have a guarantee of privacy, but he or she does have a reasonable expectation of privacy, an expectation which is then tested against the publisher's right to freedom of expression.[102]

In **Richards v British Broadcasting Corporation** (2018) it was held that the claimant had a legitimate expectation of privacy in respect of a police investigation by South Yorkshire Police and in relation to a search of his home. Where information got into the hands of a media organisation it retained its private quality and the claimant therefore had an expectation of privacy against that organisation.

In 2014 the claimant, a well-known entertainer, became the subject of a police investigation into historic child abuse. A BBC reporter heard of the investigation and intended search of the claimant's home and given notice of when that was to occur. As a result, wide publicity was given to the investigation and search. In 2016 the police decided that no charges would be brought against the claimant who, in a settlement with the police, was awarded damages of £400,000 plus legal costs.

The BBC relied on its right to freedom of expression under Article 10. The Court had to conduct a balancing exercise between the competing rights of Articles 8 and 10. In this case there was no legitimate public interest in publicising the identity of the claimant. The claimant had done nothing to diminish his right to privacy: his expectation of privacy outweighed the broadcaster's right to freedom of expression.

Closely related to breach of confidence is the civil tort of Misuse of Private Information, first recognised in 2014.[103] This was at the centre of the case of **HRH the Duchess of Sussex v Associated Newspapers** (2021). While there are similarities between the two causes of action, Misuse of Private Information relates to information which is of an essentially personal and private nature. It does not have to be disclosed within an expectation of confidentiality (as with breach of confidence). The court will consider two issues: firstly does the claimant have a reasonable expectation of privacy and secondly whether the right to privacy (Article 8) outweighs the right to freedom of expression under Article 10. In the **Sussex case** the unauthorised publication of a private letter from the Duchess to her estranged father was a Misuse of Private Information.

 Pause and Reflect

Following the introduction of the Human Rights Act 1998, the law of confidence has been extended far beyond its original scope. Making reference to case law, explain this evolution.

---

102 See also *Weller v Associated Newspapers Ltd* (2016).
103 See *Vidal-Hall v Google Inc* (2014).

GDPR and Data Protection Act 2018

The right to privacy and personal data

The right to privacy encompasses several facets. The European Convention on Human Rights, Article 8, protects the right to respect for private and family life, home and correspondence: this is discussed in Chapter 18. As discussed above, domestic law recognises the doctrine of confidentiality, breach of which is actionable in law and breach of confidence has been extended by the courts to develop a right to privacy.

Personal data acquired and processed by the state is also an aspect of privacy. The individual has three interests in personal data. The first is that data should only be collected and processed if authorised by law for specified purposes. The second interest is in the protection of personal data lawfully held against unauthorised disclosure. The third interest is that an individual is entitled to know, subject to limited exceptions, whether or not personal data has been acquired and processed by the state and to have a right of redress against the unlawful processing of data.

Access to personal data

Government departments and agencies collect and store vast amounts of personal data and the right to do so needs regulation by law to ensure that the privacy of the individual is protected from misuse.[104] Tax authorities, social security offices, local authorities and driving licence authorities are but four major holders of personal information. The police and security services also have access to and a right to retain personal data, subject to law.

Today the electronic storage and transmission of personal data exists in an international environment and there needs to be regulation at an international level. The European Union General Data Protection Regulation (GDPR)[105] sets standards for EU-wide regulation of data storage and processing. The GDPR, however, does not apply to the processing of personal data by the police and other law enforcement agencies in relation to the detection etc. of crime and threats to public security. The EU Law Enforcement Directive (LED) was introduced to cover this aspect of data processing.[106] In addition, the Council of Europe established the Convention for the Protection of Individuals with regard to Automatic Processing of Personal Data (Convention 108) in 1981 which covers intelligence services processing. Convention 108 has been updated with effect from 2018.

The Data Protection Act 2018 reflects the requirements of the EU GDPR and LED and the Council of Europe's Convention 108. Having left the EU, the EU GDPR is incorporated into domestic law under the EU (Withdrawal) Act 2018.

The Data Protection Act (DPA) 2018:

- governs the working of the GDPR (Parts 2, Chapters 2 and 3);
- provides data protection rules for law enforcement agencies (Part 3: sections 29–81 and Schedules 7–8);
- provides data protection rules in relation to national security and defence (Part 4; sections 82–113 and Schedules 9–11); and
- sets out the Information Commissioner's functions and powers.

---

104 Note that medical records prepared for insurance or employment purposes are accessible under the Access to Medical Reports Act 1988 a/a Data Protection Act 2018. The Access to Health Records Act 1990 a/a Data Protection Act 2018 gives patients the right to see records held by general practitioners, health authorities or NHS trusts.
105 EU 2016/679. As a Regulation it has direct effect in domestic law.
106 Under Article 16 TFEU: EU 2016/680. As a Directive, the LED is not directly applicable EU law. The DPA 2018 transposes the LED into domestic law.

The Data Protection Act principles

The GDPR sets out a number of principles, many of which were reflected in previous domestic law, which govern the working of data processing. These principles have been incorporated into the Data Protection Act 2018 as follows.

(1)   Lawfulness: personal data shall be processed lawfully, fairly and in a transparent manner in relation to the data subject (section 35).

(2)   Purpose: personal data shall be collected for specified, explicit and legitimate purposes (section 36).

(3)   Minimisation: personal data processed for any law enforcement purposes shall be adequate, relevant and limited to what is necessary in relation to the purposes for which they are processed (section 37).

(4)   Accuracy: personal data processed for any law enforcement purposes shall be accurate and any inaccuracies removed without delay (section 38).

(5)   Storage: personal data processed for any law enforcement purposes shall be stored for no longer than necessary unless stored solely for purposes in the public interest, scientific or historical research or statistical purposes (section 39).

(6)   Security: personal data processed for any law enforcement purposes must be processed in a way that ensures appropriate security, including protection against unauthorised process or loss (section 40).

(7)   Accountability: there must be an accountable controller responsible for compliance with the above purposes (the Information Commissioner fulfils this role: sections 115 and 116 DPA).

The data subject's right of access to information concerning personal data is governed by section 45 DPA. An individual who makes a written request for information about personal data is entitled to that information within one month (exceptionally three months) without the payment of a fee unless the request is unreasonable or repetitive. The information to be disclosed is confirmation whether or not personal data is being processed, and where it is, the following information:

Section 45.2(1):

(a)   the purpose of and legal basis for the processing;

(b)   the categories of personal data concerned;

(c)   the recipients to whom the data has been disclosed;

(d)   the period for which it is envisaged that the data will be stored, or where that is not possible, the criteria used to determine that period;

(e)   the existence of the right to request rectification or erasure;

(f)   the existence of the right to complain;

(g)   communication of the data and any available information as to its origin.

The information must be given without 'undue delay' and within time limits set under section 54. Exceptions to the right include necessary and proportionate measures to avoid obstructing official or legal inquiries; avoid prejudicing inquiries into criminal activities; the protection of public and/or national security and the protection of rights and freedoms of others. Where information rights are restricted the data subject is entitled to be informed of this and the reasons for the restriction. Detailed provision is made for the right to rectification and/or erasure of personal data (sections 46 to 48). There is a right to complain to the Information Commissioner, and where a complaint is upheld, an enforcement notice may be issued (section 52). Failure to comply with an enforcement notice may lead to a referral to the High Court or Scottish Court of Session for a finding of contempt of court. An appeal against the decision of the Information Commissioner lies to the Information Tribunal with a further appeal on a point of law from the Upper Tribunal to the Court of Appeal (sections 57 to 59).

In relation to national security, section 79 of the DPA provides that a Minister may issue a certificate certifying that a restriction on information is a necessary and proportionate measure to protect national security. A person 'directly affected' by the issuing of a certificate may appeal to the Tribunal. If the Tribunal finds, applying judicial review principles, that the Minister did not have reasonable grounds for issuing the certificate the tribunal may quash the certificate.

In *Catt v United Kingdom* (2019), the keeping of records by the police was scrutinised by the European Court of Human Rights. The applicant had participated in various demonstrations and attended a Trade Union Congress Conference. The object of some of the demonstrations was a company opposed by a group which included some who resorted to 'extreme tactics'. The applicant himself had no record of violence and although he had been arrested twice had not been convicted of any offence. The police had recorded his attendance on a database (the extremism database maintained by the National Public Order Intelligence Unit of the police) established under common law powers rather than statute. The applicant asked the Association of Chief Police Officers (ACPO) to remove his data from the database and when it refused sought judicial review of that decision. The Court of Appeal held that the inclusion of the applicant's personal data was an interference with his Article 8 (right to respect for private and family life etc.) which was not justified. The Supreme Court, however, allowed the appeal of the Police Commissioner and ACPO, agreeing that Article 8 was applicable but that the interference was in accordance with the law. Lord Toulson dissented. In his view there was no justification for keeping information for many years on someone who was not violent and who was exercising his right to peaceful protest – a right protected under the Convention on Human Rights, Articles 10 and 11.

The European Court of Human Rights expressed concern over the 'ambiguity' (the vagueness of the criteria of 'extremism') of the non-statutory legal base for the collection of data and the fact that the data could potentially be retained indefinitely. The question of whether the collection, retention and use of personal data was in accordance with the law was closely related to the issue of whether the interference (with the Article 8 right) was 'necessary in a democratic society'. It was clear that the database pursued a legitimate aim. However, the nature of the data retained was sensitive data (political opinion), a special category attracting a heightened level of protection. The Court accepted that there was a need to collect data about the applicant, and that the police were justified in monitoring the activities of a group which engaged in violent protest. But there was no pressing need to retain the applicant's data and there were no clear safeguards to prevent the indefinite retention of the data. There was a violation of Article 8.[107]

The 'right to be forgotten'

In 2010 a Spanish citizen, Mario Costeja Gonzalez, lodged a complaint with the national Data Protection Agency against a Spanish newspaper and Google Spain and Google Inc., complaining that information concerning him breached his right to privacy. On a reference for a

---

107 See also **MM v UK**, Application 24029/07; **S & Marper v UK**, Applications 30562/04 and 30566/04.

preliminary ruling,[108] the Court of Justice of the European Union had to consider three main questions:

- first, whether the EU 1995 Data Protection Directive (95/46/EC) applied to a search engine such as Google;
- second, whether the Directive applied to Google Spain, given that the company's data processing server was in the United States;
- third, whether an individual has the right to request that his or her personal data be removed from accessibility via a search engine.

The Court ruled that the activity of a search engine and making it available to internet users had to be classified as 'processing of personal data' within the meaning of Article 2(b) of the Directive. On the second question, that of territorial scope, the Court ruled that where a company has a subsidiary in a Member State, it is therefore an 'establishment' within the meaning of the Directive. On the third question, an individual has the right – which is not unlimited – to ask search engines to remove links with personal information about them. In its Press Release the Court stated that:

> However, inasmuch as the removal of links from the list of results could, depending on the information at issue, have effects upon the legitimate interest of internet users potentially interested in having access to that information, the Court holds that a fair balance should be sought in particular between that interest and the data subject's fundamental rights, in particular the right to privacy and the right to protection of personal data. The Court observes in this regard that, whilst it is true that the data subject's rights also override, as a general rule, that interest of internet users, this balance may however depend, in specific cases, on the nature of the information in question and its sensitivity for the data subject's private life and on the interest of the public in having that information, an interest which may vary, in particular, according to the role played by the data subject in public life.

Furthermore, an individual has the right to the removal of personal data where the data appears to be inadequate, irrelevant or no longer relevant, or excessive in relation to the purposes for which they were processed in light of the time that has elapsed. Where an individual requests the operator of a search engine to remove personal data, that request must be examined on its merits. Where the operator refuses, the individual may then bring the matter before a supervisory body or a court. The European Commission pointed out that the right to have data removed is not new: Article 12 of the 1995 Directive makes clear that 'rectification, erasure or blocking of data' is required where the data is incomplete or inaccurate. Having left the EU, the extent to which EU law and decisions of the CJEU apply in the UK will depend on Parliament and the Supreme Court.

Press Freedom and Privacy

Blackstone, in his *Commentaries*, said of freedom of the press that:

> the liberty of the press is indeed essential to the nature of a free state. Every free man has an undoubted right to lay what sentiments he pleases before the

---

108 *Google Spain SL, Google Inc. v Agencia Espanola de Proteccion de Datos*, Case C-1311/12.

public; to forbid this is to destroy the freedom of the press; but if he publishes what is improper, mischievous or illegal, he must take the consequences of his own temerity.

The invasion of privacy by the media has become a matter of rising concern. In 1953, the Press Council was established.[109] This self-regulatory body proved woefully inadequate at controlling the press, not least because it had no powers to fine newspapers. In 1972, the Younger Committee was established to consider reforms in relation to press freedom. The Committee recommended that a tort of disclosure of information unlawfully acquired and a tort and crime of unlawful surveillance by technical devices be introduced.[110] The proposed reforms were not implemented. Concern over intrusions into individual privacy increased with the media attention given to the Royal Family in recent years. The case of **Kaye v Robertson** (1991) heightened public interest in the respective right of an individual to privacy and the right of the public to information. In **Kaye**, journalists entered a hospital room in which the well-known actor, Gorden Kaye, was being treated for severe injuries sustained in a car accident. Kaye agreed neither to be photographed nor interviewed. An injunction was sought, and granted, to restrain the newspaper from publishing the 'interview' and photographs. On appeal, the Court of Appeal ruled that there was no right to privacy under English law which could found the basis for an injunction.

In 1990, the Committee on Privacy and Related Matters (the Calcutt Committee) was established, which led to the creation of another self-regulatory body in 1991, the Press Complaints Commission.[111] A review of the workings of the Commission by Sir David Calcutt[112] found the protection accorded to individuals to be inadequate. The Commission closed in 2014. Further revelations relating to press conduct – allegations concerning phone hacking, intrusions into privacy, concerns over the relations between the press and the police and the press and politicians – led to the appointment of Lord Justice Leveson to inquire into and make recommendations concerning the future regulation of the press. The key issue from a constitutional point of view is how the freedom of the press can be maintained while at the same time protecting the rights of individuals whose lives or reputations may be harmed by the press. Another key question is whether, and how, the law could or should be used to regulate the press.

Lord Justice Leveson recognised the importance of a free press, stating in his Report that:

I know how vital the press is – all of it – as the guardian of the interests of the public, as a critical witness to events, as the standard bearer for those who have no one else to speak up for them ... The press, operating properly and in the public interest is one of the true safeguards of our democracy.[113]

Moreover:

There are truly countless examples of great journalism, great investigations and great campaigns. The exposure of thalidomide, the campaign to bring the killers

---

109 The Broadcasting Complaints Commission plays a similar role in relation to broadcasting: Broadcasting Act 1990, s. 142.

110 *Report of the Younger Committee*, Cmnd 5012, 1972; and see MacCormick, 1973.

111 *Report of the Committee on Privacy and Related Matters*, Cmnd 1102, 1990. See Munro, 1991.

112 *Review of Press Self-Regulation*, Cmnd 2135, 1993, London: HMSO.

113 The Leveson Report, *An Inquiry into the Culture, Practices and Ethics of the Press: Executive Summary*, HC 779, November 2012, London: TSO. www.official-documents.gov.uk/document/hc1213/hc07/0779/0779.pdf.

of Stephen Lawrence to justice, the exposure of abuse in the operation of MPs expenses are but the best known in a long list.[114]

The purpose of the Leveson Inquiry was to expose malpractices by the press, as revealed in evidence to the Inquiry, and to make recommendations for reform.[115] Key to the proposed new system of regulation was the establishment of a new independent regulator governed by an independent Board, with members being appointed in an open and transparent way without any influence from industry or government. There should be no serving editors of newspapers on the Board. The Board should have the power to investigate complaints against the press, to order 'appropriate remedial action' and to impose 'appropriate and proportionate sanctions'.

In order to ensure that the regulatory body fulfils its functions and ensure its independence (of the press, Parliament and government), the Report recommends that legislation be introduced to underpin the new body. The law should also, Leveson recommended, impose a clear duty on the government to uphold the freedom of the press. The Prime Minister was swift in his expressing his reservations about using legislation. The Deputy Prime Minister and Leader of the Opposition supported Leveson. An official Press Recognition Panel was established in 2014, and funding by the government guaranteed for three years. The Panel is to approve newspaper regulators and ensure that they comply with the Royal Charter agreed by the main political parties in 2013. A majority of newspaper and magazine editors have refused to be regulated under the Charter on the basis that it would interfere with press freedom. In the alternative, in September 2014 a self-regulatory Independent Press Standards Organisation (Ipso) was introduced. The Board comprises 12 members, seven of whom are independent of the media and five representatives of newspapers and magazines. It is chaired by a former Court of Appeal judge, Sir Alan Moses. It has the power to impose fines of £1 million for the most serious breaches of the Editors' Code of Conduct. There is a Complaints Committee to adjudicate on individual complaints. Ipso's website is at www.ipso.co.uk/IPSO/index/html.

 SELF-TEST QUESTIONS

What is the constitutional importance of freedom of the press?

What constitutional principles does it underpin?

Should there be increased controls over the press? If so, what form should these take?

Summary

Freedom of expression, under English law, has traditionally been regarded as a freedom which could be exercised subject to any restrictions imposed by law (for example defamation, the prohibition of race hate speech, speech likely to cause a breach of the peace, the unauthorised disclosure of confidential information). It is therefore necessary to understand the legal restrictions before any evaluation of the scope of freedom of expression can be undertaken.

114 The Leveson Report, para. 8.
115 See www.levesoninquiry.org.uk.

Freedom of expression is now also governed by Article 10 of the European Convention on Human Rights, Article 10.2 of which imposes a number of restrictions. With the incorporation of Article 10 into domestic law, the domestic courts have increasingly been faced with the apparent conflict between freedom of expression and the right to privacy protected under Article 8 of the European Convention. Privacy, however, has never been recognised as a distinct legal entity under domestic law. The emerging case law suggests that the courts are interpreting Article 8 to expand the law relating to breach of confidentiality in a manner which suggests extending an individual's right to privacy.

Freedom of expression must also be considered in conjunction with freedom of assembly and association discussed in the next chapter.

 ## Further Reading

Bailey, S and Taylor, N, *Bailey, Harris & Jones: Civil Liberties: Cases, Materials and Commentary*, 2009, Oxford: Oxford University Press.

Barendt, E, *Freedom of Speech*, 2nd edn, 2005, Oxford: Oxford University Press.

Fenwick, H, *Civil Liberties and Human Rights*, 5th edn, 2011, Abingdon: Routledge-Cavendish.

Morgan, J, 'Privacy in the House of Lords again' (2004) 120 *Law Quarterly Review* 563.

Wragg, P, 'The legitimacy of press regulation' [2015] *Public Law* 290.

Chapter 20

Freedom of Association and Assembly and Police Powers

Chapter Contents

Learning Objectives

By the end of this chapter you should be able to:

- [ ] define what is meant by 'assembly' and 'association';
- [ ] with reference to case law, discuss the indirect restrictions on freedom of assembly;
- [ ] explain the law relating to public protest and the restrictions which can be imposed;
- [ ] discuss whether the law achieves the correct balance between public order and freedom of assembly;
- [ ] in outline discuss the various public order offences;
- [ ] explain the powers of the police in relation to arrest and detention, search and seizure.

Introduction

While the detection and prosecution of crime and the preservation of public order are of first importance in any state, the extent to which police powers reflect a legitimate interference with the liberty and security of citizens is a problematic question which involves evaluating the balance struck between the rights of the individual and the powers of the police. In this chapter, the manner in which law regulates associations and assemblies – whether meetings or processions – is examined. In addition, it is necessary to consider the manner in which law regulates an individual's freedom to move around, and the conditions under which it is or is not lawful to enter into and remain on land, both private and public.

The law of association and assembly must be evaluated against Article 11 of the European Convention on Human Rights, incorporated under the Human Rights Act 1998. Article 11 provides that 'everyone has the right to freedom of peaceful assembly and to freedom of association with others, including the right to form and to join trade unions for the protection of his interests'. Article 11, however, is subject to a number of lawful exceptions. The rights may be restricted on the basis that they are 'necessary in a democratic society in the interests of national security or public safety, for the prevention of disorder or crime, for the protection of health or morals or for the protection of the rights and freedoms of others'. In addition, Article 11 does not prevent lawful restrictions being imposed by the state on members of the armed forces, or the police or the civil service. Accordingly, while all domestic law must be compatible with Article 11, a great deal of discretion is accorded to the state.

Freedom of assembly and association, protected by Article 11, must also be viewed in relation to freedom of expression guaranteed by Article 10 of the Convention and is considered in the previous chapter.

Freedom of Association

While citizens are generally free to join any club, society or trade union, two statutory restrictions exist. The first restriction relates to membership of military or quasi-military organisations. The Public Order Act 1936 provides, in part, that the wearing of uniforms in public with the intention of promoting a political objective is unlawful, and that membership of groups organised and trained for the purpose of displaying physical force is unlawful. To be a member of such a group, or to solicit or invite financial or other support for the group, is an offence.

See further Chapter 21.

In **R v Jordan and Tyndall** (1963), the defendants were members of a fascist group, Spearhead. They exercised in military fashion and were known to be storing chemicals capable of being used for the manufacture of bombs. They were convicted under section 2(1)(b) of the Public Order Act 1936. In **Director of Public Prosecutions v Whelan** (1975), the defendants were charged under section 1 of the 1936 Act. Participating in a Sinn Féin march in Northern Ireland, the defendants wore black berets, dark clothing and carried the Irish flag. It was held that the wearing of similar clothing could amount to a 'uniform'. Specific groups are proscribed under the Terrorism Acts.

As noted above, the right of peaceful assembly and association includes the right to belong to a trade union (**Young, James and Webster v United Kingdom** (1981)) or political party. The European Court of Human Rights reconsidered this right in **Redfearn v United Kingdom** (2012). In this case, the applicant was a member of the British National Party (BNP), a right-wing political party. As a result of his membership he was dismissed from his employment, on the basis that his employment would cause problems in an area in which there was a high concentration of non-white families. He was unable to claim unfair dismissal because he had not been in the post for the qualifying one-year period. His claim that he had been discriminated against on grounds of race contrary to the Race Relations Act 1976 were dismissed by the Court of Appeal. The Court ruled, by four votes to three, that the United Kingdom government was under a duty to take 'reasonable and appropriate measures' to protect employees from dismissal on grounds of political opinion or affiliation. The legislation was 'deficient' in providing no remedy and there was, accordingly, a violation of Article 11.

The Terrorism Act 2000 makes it a criminal offence to belong to and participate in the activities of proscribed organisations. For details, see Chapter 21 pages 581 to 582.

Freedom of Assembly

> [I]t can hardly be said that our constitution knows of such a thing as any specific right of public meeting.[1]

An individual is free to assemble peacefully with others to the extent that the law does not prohibit such assemblies or the assembly does not involve unlawful actions. In 1885, Dicey was to record that 'the police have with us no special authority to control open air assemblies'. Today much has changed. Under common law, a number of restraints were placed on this freedom, and the Public Order Acts 1936 and 1986 and the Criminal Justice and Public Order Act 1994 restrict rights of assembly. While there is a general freedom to assemble on private property or on public land, in the case of the former, it will be a trespass to do so without the consent of the landowner. In relation to land to which the public have a right of access, the right of assembly is controlled by local authority bylaws, and a criminal offence is committed if these are breached. Further, the right of assembly may be controlled by statute. By way of example, the right to assemble in Trafalgar Square is regulated under statute, under which permission must be granted by the Secretary of State for the Environment.[2] Hyde Park is equally regulated.[3]

The duty to facilitate meetings

The constitutional importance of freedom of expression and involvement in civic life is reflected in the right to use schools and other public rooms for meetings in local elections, by-elections and general elections.[4] In addition, under the Education (No 2) Act 1986, the governing bodies of universities and colleges are under a duty to 'take such steps as are reasonably practicable to ensure that freedom of speech within the law is secured for members, students and employees of the establishment and for visiting speakers'.[5] This requirement gave rise to a challenge in **R v University of Liverpool ex parte Caesar-Gordon** (1991). In that case, the university had refused permission for a meeting at which two diplomats from the South African Embassy were due to speak. The decision was based on the fear that the meeting would cause public unrest in the surrounding area. The Divisional Court ruled that the

---

1 Dicey, 1885, p. 271.
2 SI 1952/776. See also the Metropolitan Police Act 1839, s. 52, which provides for police enforcement of access to Parliament by its members.
3 Royal and Other Parks and Gardens Regulations 1988, SI 1988/217, and see **Bailey v Williamson** (1873).
4 Representation of the People Act 1983, as amended by the Representation of the People Act 1985 and Greater London Authority Act 1999, s. 17.
5 Education (No 2) Act 1986, s. 43.

university had acted *ultra vires* its powers. The university authorities were not entitled to take into account threats of violence outside its precincts. Only where the risk of violence would relate to university precincts, would the university be justified in imposing restrictions.

The meaning of 'public meeting' was considered by the House of Lords in **McCartan (Turkington Breen) v Times Newspapers Ltd** (2000). At issue was whether a meeting, in this case a press conference, held on private premises, to which members of the press had been invited and others also attended without an invitation but without any restriction, was a 'public meeting'.[6] A meeting was public if those who arranged it opened it to the public, or by issuing a general invitation to the press showed an intention that the proceedings of the meeting should be communicated to a wider public.

Indirect Restrictions on Freedom of Assembly

A number of indirect means may be employed in order to restrain public meetings. Such means include breach of the peace, obstruction of police officers and obstruction of the highway.

Breach of the peace

In **Beatty v Gillbanks** (1882), the Salvation Army met knowing that there would be an opposing meeting being held. The magistrates' court issued an order preventing the Salvation Army meeting. When the meeting assembled in defiance of the order, the police ordered the meeting to disband and arrested one of the members. On the defendant's appeal against conviction, the Queen's Bench Division refused to accept the restriction on freedom of assembly based on the threatened unlawful acts of others. A person acting lawfully was not responsible for the unlawful reaction of others. Where, however, participants in a meeting engage in unlawful conduct which provokes others and results in a breach of the peace – or a reasonable apprehension of a breach of the peace – the meeting may be held to be unlawful. Further, if the meeting is conducted lawfully and yet provokes an actual breach of the peace, the police may order the meeting to disband. Failure to comply with an order to leave an assembly on the grounds of an officer's reasonable belief that it is necessary to avoid a breach of the peace is a criminal offence.[7]

Breach of the peace is a concept which traditionally has involved a degree of proximity and immediacy between the conduct of individuals and the anticipated breach of the peace. However, in **Moss v McLachlan** (1985), in the course of the miners' strike of 1984–1985, the defendants were ordered to turn back on a journey to another colliery some four miles away. The police suspected that they were intending to join the picket line in support of fellow miners and that a breach of the peace might occur. When the miners refused to obey the order to turn back, they were arrested for obstruction. The judge conceded a wide discretion to the police and ruled that, provided a senior police officer 'honestly and reasonably formed the opinion' that there was a real risk of a breach of the peace, in an area proximate to the point of arrest, they could take whatever measures were reasonably necessary to prevent it. This decision, whilst understandable from the police's point of view, is regrettable for it introduces a dangerous breadth to the offence. Furthermore, uncertainty is created as to the precise scope of the police's power to interfere with freedom of movement.

---

6 For the purposes of a claim to privilege under the Defamation Act (Northern Ireland) 1955, s. 7.
7 **Duncan v Jones** (1936): see below.

The **Beatty v Gillbanks** principle has been undermined in a number of cases. In **Jordan v Burgoyne** (1963), the court ruled that a person addressing an audience would be found guilty of a breach of the peace if his or her words were likely to inflame the audience and lead to violence. Equally, in **Percy v Director of Public Prosecutions** (1995), the court ruled that conduct which was not itself unlawful could amount to a breach of the peace if the words spoken were likely to cause disorder among those listening, even if members of the audience had attended with the express intention of causing trouble. Further, in **Morpeth Ward Justices ex parte Ward** (1992), the issue was not so much the conduct of the protesters but, rather, whether or not the conduct had the effect of provoking violent behaviour, even where the reaction to the protest was unreasonable. However, in **Nicol v Director of Public Prosecutions** (1996), the court adopted a more restrictive approach. The protest in question concerned an attempt to stop anglers from fishing. The protesters blew horns and provoked the anglers. It was held that, although there was nothing unlawful in the protesters' actions, the provocation of the anglers was likely to cause a breach of the peace because it was unreasonable action.

A more liberal approach was taken in **Redmond-Bate v Director of Public Prosecutions** (1999). Three women preachers, who were preaching on the steps of a cathedral, were approached by a police constable and warned not to stop people. Later, he returned to find that a crowd had gathered, some of whom were hostile to the speakers. The constable asked the women to stop preaching, and when they refused arrested them for a breach of the peace. They were convicted of obstructing a police officer in the execution of his duty. On appeal, it was held that there was no lawful basis for the arrest. Free speech, provided that it did not tend to provoke violence, irrespective of its content (unless contrary to law), was to be respected. There were no grounds on which the constable could apprehend a breach of the peace, much less one for which the preachers would be responsible.

The European Convention on Human Rights is making an impact on the law of protest, in terms of both the right to liberty (Article 5) and the right to freedom of expression (Article 10). In **Hashman and Harrup v United Kingdom** (2000), the issue was freedom of expression relating to hunt saboteurs. The applicants were bound over 'to be of good behaviour' for one year. The applicants claimed that the concept of behaviour *contra bona mores* was so broadly defined that it did not comply with Article 10(2) of the Convention, the requirement that any interference with freedom of expression be 'prescribed by law'. The Court of Human Rights ruled that the definition of *contra bona mores*, as behaviour which was 'wrong rather than right in the judgment of the majority of contemporary fellow citizens', was particularly imprecise and failed to give the applicants sufficiently clear guidance as to how they should behave in future. Accordingly, the interference with freedom of expression was not 'prescribed by law' and there had been a violation of Article 10.[8]

In **Appleby v United Kingdom** (2003), the Court of Human Rights ruled that campaigners against building on a playing field did not suffer a deprivation of their right to freedom of speech or assembly when the owners of a shopping centre prevented them from meeting on their premises to exchange information and ideas about the proposed building plans. While freedom of expression was an important right it was not unlimited. Nor was it the only Convention right at stake. Regard must also be given to the property rights of the owner of the shopping centre under Article 1 of Protocol 1. In the present case the restriction on the applicants' ability to communicate their views was limited to the entrance areas and passageways of the shopping centre. It did not prevent them from expressing their views elsewhere, including the public access paths into the area.

---

8 See also **Steel v United Kingdom** (1998).

The House of Lords considered police powers in respect of demonstrations in **R (Laporte) v Chief Constable of Gloucestershire** (2006). The claimant was a member of an activist group travelling in three coaches from London to an air force base at which a demonstration was planned. The Chief Constable considered that a breach of the peace would occur if the protesters were allowed to join the demonstration. He ordered the driver of the coach to return to London, escorted by police riders who prevented the coaches from stopping, in effect 'imprisoning' the passengers for two-and-a-half hours.

In a powerful judgment, the House of Lords ruled that the actions of the police were unlawful, not being prescribed by law and disproportionate. Lord Brown of Eaton-under-Heywood stated that 'if any power to prevent entirely innocent citizens' from taking part in a demonstration exists then the 'power can only be conferred by Parliament. It is not to be found in the common law'. By contrast in **R (Hicks) v Commissioner of Police for the Metropolis** (2017) the Supreme Court ruled that the temporary detention (between 2.5 and 5.5 hours) and release without charge did not breach Article 5 of the European Convention on Human Rights (the right to liberty). The police had arrested four individuals on the grounds that they reasonably believed an imminent breach of the peace was about to occur on the day of the wedding of the Duke and Duchess of Cambridge. The Court held that Article 5 should not be 'interpreted in such a way as to make it impracticable for the police to perform their duty to maintain public order and protect the lives and property of others'.

The balance to be struck between the right to liberty and the power of the police to protect public order was considered in the House of Lords in **Austin v Commissioner of Police of the Metropolis** (2009). Some 3,000 people had assembled in central London as part of a May Day demonstration. The police were aware that a demonstration was planned, but the organisers had refused to inform the police of their plans. The police imposed a cordon around the area with the effect that thousands were detained for several hours.[9] The stated intention of the police was to prevent a breach of the peace and to control the crowd in order to effect an orderly dispersal of the crowd. On the legality of the action by the police, the Court ruled, *inter alia*, that measures of crowd control must 'be resorted to in good faith and must be proportionate to the situation which has made the measures necessary'. Provided that these requirements are met, measures of crowd control that are undertaken in the interests of the community will not infringe the Article 5 rights of individual people in the crowd.[10] In **Austin v United Kingdom** (2012) the Grand Chamber of the European Court of Human Rights upheld the decision of the House of Lords (now Supreme Court). In a situation of potential violence and risk of injury and damage to property the 'kettling' by the police did not amount to a deprivation of liberty. Notwithstanding its conclusion, the Court emphasised that such measures should not be employed to stifle or discourage protest which was of fundamental importance to freedom of expression.

Freedom of expression and freedom of assembly and association were considered in **Tabernacle v Secretary of State for Defence** (2009). The Women's Peace Camp had been established at Aldermaston (the Atomic Weapons Establishment at which nuclear weapons were designed, tested and built) for some 23 years. A local bylaw prohibited camping. In answer to the claim that the state had violated the right to freedom of expression, association and assembly, the Secretary of State submitted that the restriction was on the 'manner and form' in which the right could be exercised, not a restriction on the right itself. The Court of Appeal disagreed. The manner and form in which a right might be exercised might constitute the very nature and quality of the protest in question. Here the manner and form – the protest

---

9 A practice known as 'kettling'.
10 See also **R (Moos and McClure) v Commissioner of Police of the Metropolis** (2012).

on the prohibited site – was the protest itself. Moreover the Secretary of State's arguments were weak: the camp represented no more than a nuisance rather than a threat. There was a violation of Articles 10 and 11.

 Pause and Reflect

In what ways has the offence of breach of the peace changed in recent years? Do you think that the offence is now too broadly defined?

Obstructing the police

Under the Police Act 1996,[11] it is a criminal offence to obstruct the police in the execution of their duty. Section 89 provides that:

(1) Any person who assaults a constable in the execution of his duty, or a person assisting a constable in the execution of his duty, shall be guilty of an offence ...

(2) Any person who resists or wilfully obstructs a constable in the execution of his duty, or a person assisting a constable in the execution of his duty, shall be guilty of an offence.

In **Duncan v Jones** (1936), the defendant had intended to hold a public meeting at a place previously used for that purpose. The police, aware that a disturbance had previously occurred in that place, instructed Mrs Duncan to hold the meeting on an alternative site. Mrs Duncan refused and started the meeting on the highway. She was arrested and charged under section 51 of the Police Act. The defendant could have been charged with obstruction of the highway (see below) or with inciting a breach of the peace. However, in the alternative the police charged her with obstructing a police officer. The court held that, once the police officer reasonably considered that a breach of the peace could occur, any action which impeded him in the course of preventing such an occurrence amounted to an obstruction of the police. In **Piddington v Bates** (1960), in the course of an industrial dispute, the police directed that no more than two pickets should be allowed at each entrance to the factory. The defendant joined the picket line in defiance of the order, regarding the restriction as unreasonable, and was charged with obstruction. On appeal, the Divisional Court upheld his conviction.

Obstructing the highway: the Highways Act 1980

A citizen is free to move along the highway. It is, however, a criminal offence to obstruct the highway. Obstructing the highway also represents a public nuisance, which may be prosecuted on indictment under common law.[12] Under section 137 of the Highways Act 1980, 'if a person, without lawful authority or excuse, in any way wilfully obstructs the free passage along a highway he is guilty of an offence'. In **Hirst v Chief Constable for West Yorkshire** (1986), animal rights demonstrators protesting outside a store selling animal fur products were charged with obstructing the highway. The magistrates' court convicted them of obstruction. However, on appeal, the Divisional Court held that the justices should have considered the reasonableness of the action and weighed in the balance the right to protest and demonstrate

---

11 Formerly, Police Act 1964, s. 51.
12 **R v Clark (No 2)** (1964).

and the need for public order. The magistrates' court had failed to consider this and, accordingly, failed to respect the freedom to protest on matters of public concern. This approach was echoed in **Director of Public Prosecutions v Jones** (1999), in which the House of Lords ruled that – provided a highway was not in fact obstructed – it could be lawful to use it for protest.

The granting of a possession order and the removal of a protest camp was not an unjustified interference with the protesters' rights to freedom of expression and assembly under Articles 10 and 11 of the European Convention on Human Rights. The Queen's Bench Division so ruled in **The Mayor, Commonality and Citizens of the City of London v Samede and Others** (2012). The camp – consisting of up to 200 tents – occupied highway land and open land owned by the Church of England. The relief claimed was not disproportionate and was 'entirely lawful and justified', both at common law and under statute.

Public Order

The Public Order Act 1986 was passed after growing concern over demonstrations, industrial disputes, riots and football hooliganism.[13] The Act had two principal objectives. The first was to provide a comprehensive code as to the organisation and control of processions and demonstrations. The second was to provide a code relating to disorderly conduct, which can range from behaviour which causes alarm or distress to riot. In addition, the Act created offences relating to football hooliganism and to control of persons unlawfully camping on private land.

The law relating to public order was further reformed substantially by the Criminal Justice and Public Order Act 1994.[14] This Act made major reforms across a wide spectrum of criminal justice matters and matters relating to sexual offences. New sentences for young offenders were introduced, the right to silence of defendants was curtailed and the powers of police to take body samples increased. In relation to public order, the Act increased the powers of the police and local authorities in respect of trespass, 'rave parties', squatters and campers, and marked a significant shift away from individual liberties towards increasing state regulation in favour of maintaining public order. The Crime and Disorder Act 1998 introduces new criminal offences where conduct contrary to public order is racially aggravated.[15]

The regulation of processions

A procession is not defined in the Public Order Act. Processions were originally regulated under the Public Order Act 1936 and the powers were extended under the Public Order Act 1986. In **Flockhart v Robinson** (1950), a procession was said to be 'not a mere body of persons: it is a body of persons moving along a route'. Accordingly, a procession must involve more than one person. To be regulated by the Act, a procession must be public. A public place is defined in section 16 as being:

(a) any highway ...; and
(b) any place to which at the material time the public or any section of the public has access, on payment or otherwise, as of right or by virtue of express or implied permission.

---

13 See *Report on the Red Lion Square Disorders*, Cmnd 5919, 1975, London: HMSO; *Report on the Brixton Disorders*, Cmnd 8427, 1981, London: HMSO; *Criminal Law: Offences Relating to Public Order*, Law Com No 123, 1983, London: HMSO; *Review of Public Order Law*, Cmnd 9510, 1985, London: HMSO.
14 *Implementing the Report of the Royal Commission on Criminal Justice*, Cmnd 2263, 1993, London: HMSO.
15 The Anti-Social Behaviour Act 2003 amends both the 1986 and 1994 Acts.

The requirement of notice

Under section 11, notice must be given to the police of a procession which is designed to express or oppose the views of another, to publicise or encourage support for a campaign, or to commemorate an event. Processions which are regularly held within a particular area need not be notified to the police. Where it is impracticable to give notice in advance, the requirement may be waived. This exception enables spontaneous demonstrations to take place.

Six clear days' notice must be given, except where it is impracticable to do so.[16] Failure to give notice, or organising a procession different from the one notified, is a summary offence. In Scotland, similar requirements exist. Where a ban is imposed on a particular march, a right of appeal exists.

Under section 11(2) of the Public Order Act 1986 there is no requirement to give notice of processions which are 'commonly or customarily held' in an area. Examples would include the annual Remembrance Day service and the judges' annual procession to the courts of law at the start of the new term. The House of Lords had an opportunity to examine section 11(2) in **R (Kay) v Commissioner of Police of the Metropolis** (2008). The Court ruled that monthly cycle rides through London, which had no formal organisation, but started from the same point each time and on each occasion followed a different route, did not require notice to be given under section 11. The cycle rides had sufficient common features to amount to a 'procession' 'commonly or customarily held' and were therefore exempt from the notification requirement.

The power to impose conditions

Where notice has been given in accordance with section 11, then a senior police office (Chief Constable or Commissioner) may impose conditions, under section 12. If a procession is under way, then a senior officer on the scene may impose conditions. The basis on which conditions may be attached include situations where the senior police officer reasonably believes that a procession may result in serious public disorder, serious damage to property or serious disruption of the life of the community.[17] An alternative basis for conditions is where it is reasonably believed that the procession is taking place for an illegitimate purpose. Intimidation, for example, would be an 'illegitimate purpose'. Under section 14 of the Act, conditions may also – on the same grounds as those stated in section 12 – be imposed on assemblies.

If the requirements for the imposition of conditions are met, the senior officer has a wide discretion as to the conditions which may in fact be imposed. Section 12(1) merely states that he may impose conditions 'as appear to him necessary'. Under section 12, there is power to impose conditions as to the route to be followed, and to prohibit entry into particular public places. Failure to comply with the conditions, or to incite others not to comply, is an offence.[18] However, with the Human Rights Act 1998 in force, the powers of the police are now subject to the requirements of the European Convention on Human Rights. As seen in the case of **Austin v Commissioner of Police** (2009), discussed above, this superimposes the requirements of proportionality on to the exercise of police power, enabling the courts to evaluate the justification for police action against the necessity for such action in the particular circumstances. In other words, the court will assess whether the action taken by the police was a proportionate response to the circumstances.

---

16 Public Order Act 1986, s. 11(6).
17 Ibid., s. 12(1).
18 Public Order Act 1986, s. 12(4), (5).

The power to ban processions

Under section 13(2), the Chief Officer of Police[19] may issue a banning order, which may only be issued if the power to impose conditions is insufficient to prevent serious public disorder. In London, the banning order must have the consent of the Home Secretary, and elsewhere the consent of the local authority. The power to ban processions represents a power to ban all processions, rather than to ban a particular procession, and can cover all or part of a police area and last for up to three months.[20] Organising or participating in, or inciting participation in, a banned procession is a summary offence.[21]

The power to enter meetings on private premises

Where a private meeting is held, the police have power to enter and remain on the premises under certain circumstances. A meeting is defined as a private meeting if it is held in entirely enclosed premises. Thus, even if the meeting is held in publicly owned and managed premises, such as a school or town hall, it will be a private meeting. In **Thomas v Sawkins** (1935), a police officer entered a private meeting which was held to protest against the Incitement to Disaffection Bill. The organiser of the meeting brought an action based on trespass, and argued that, as a result of trespass by the police, he had the right to evict the officers. The meeting had not given rise to a breach of the peace. However, the court held that notwithstanding its peaceful nature, the police had grounds for reasonably suspecting that a breach of the peace might occur and were therefore entitled to enter and remain on the premises.

The regulation of public assemblies[22]

While there is power to regulate a public assembly, there was no power to issue a banning order under the 1986 Act. A public assembly is defined as 'an assembly of two or more persons in a public place which is wholly or partly open to the air'.[23] However, an individual who disobeys an order, even where he or she does not actually join the assembly, is liable under the Act.[24] The basis on which the conditions which may be attached[25] are the same as those for conditions imposed on processions. Intimidation, as a ground for imposing a condition, has been interpreted to mean more than 'causing discomfort'.[26]

The definition of a public assembly and the lawfulness of conditions attached came under consideration in **Jones v The Commissioner of Police for the Metropolis** (2019).[27] The claimant sought judicial review of the decision of the Commissioner to impose conditions on the Extinction Rebellion Autumn Uprising (XRAU) under section 14 of the Public Order Act 1986. XRAU coordinated separate gatherings or events at different times and places around London. One of the (several) legal questions raised was whether the Commissioner had the legal power to impose conditions on the basis that XRAU was one public assembly for the purpose of section 14 POA 1986: it was a matter of statutory interpretation. The section 16 definition required that a public assembly must be in a location to which the public has access and must be wholly or partly open to the air. Section 14 refers to the meaning of the senior officer

---

19 In London, the Commissioner for the City of London or Commissioner for the Metropolis.
20 The power to ban a procession is subject to judicial review: **Kent v Metropolitan Police Commissioners** (1981).
21 Public Order Act 1986, s. 13(7), (8), (9).
22 See Bonner and Stone, 1987.
23 Public Order Act 1986, s. 16, as amended by the Anti-Social Behaviour Act 2003, s. 57.
24 **Broadwith v Chief Constable of Thames Valley Police** (2000).
25 Public Order Act 1986, s. 14(1).
26 **Police v Reid** (1987).
27 [2019] EWHC 2957 (Admin).

who is entitled to impose conditions as being 'the most senior in rank of the police officers present at the scene'. To the court, the phrase 'at the scene' clearly indicated one location – not a number of locations around London. On this analysis, the Commissioner had no power to impose conditions: the XRAU protests were not a 'public assembly'. The conditions imposed were therefore unlawful and quashed.

Special rules apply to demonstrations in the vicinity of Parliament. The Police Reform and Social Responsibility Act 2011, sections 142–148, authorise the police to direct a person not to start, or to cease, doing a 'prohibited activity', defined as including the operation of amplified noise equipment or the erecting of a tent or other structure in the area of Parliament Square. Section 143 confers power to seize prohibited items. Under section 144 a direction may be given requiring a person to cease doing, or not to start doing, a prohibited activity. The direction may not be longer than 90 days.

Trespassory assemblies

Section 70 of the Criminal Justice and Public Order Act 1994 inserted section 14A into the 1986 Act, which provided a power to ban trespassory assemblies.

A Chief Officer of Police may apply for a banning order if he reasonably believes that an assembly is likely to involve trespass or might result in serious disruption to community life or cause damage to buildings and structures. This power must be seen within the context of section 14C of the Public Order Act 1986,[28] which confers power on the police to stop persons within a five-mile radius of the assembly, if the police reasonably believe that they are on their way to the assembly, and the assembly is subject to a section 14A order.

In **Director of Public Prosecutions v Jones** (1999), section 14 was considered. A section 14A order had been issued, which prohibited the holding of a trespassory assembly within a four-mile radius of Stonehenge. The assembly was heading for Stonehenge, and was within the four-mile radius, and on the public highway. The court held that the highway was for passing and repassing only, and that assembling on the highway was outside the purpose for which the implied licence to use the highway was granted. The respondents argued that they were both peaceful and not obstructive and were making 'reasonable use' of the highway. The House of Lords ruled, by a majority of three to two, that the public had the right to use the highway for such reasonable and usual activities, inter alia including peaceful assembly, as was consistent with the primary use for passage and repassage. It was a question of fact and degree in each case whether the user was reasonable and not inconsistent with that primary right.

The right to move freely along the highway, for a minority group such as Gypsies, entails the need for a lawful place to stop. While local authorities had been under a duty to provide sites under the Caravan Sites Act 1968,[29] that statutory duty has now been removed.[30] This is of particular concern, given that Gypsies – a recognised racial group protected under the Race Relations Act 1976 and under international law[31] – traditionally travel with caravans from area to area, usually in search of seasonal work.

The problems encountered in the 1970s and 1980s with groups of New Age Travellers meeting for the summer solstice at Stonehenge and the problems caused by 'rave parties' resulted in the criminalisation of trespass for the first time under English law. The Criminal Justice and Public Order Act 1994 provides that the police may remove from land persons who are in fact trespassing, irrespective of whether or not they entered the land lawfully

---

28 Inserted by the Criminal Justice and Public Order Act 1994, s. 71.
29 Caravan Sites Act 1968, s. 6.
30 Criminal Justice and Public Order Act 1994, s. 80.
31 **Commission for Racial Equality v Dutton** (1989).

or as trespassers.[32] The 1994 Act also provides that the power of removal applies in relation to persons having six vehicles on land, as opposed to 12 under the 1986 Public Order Act. Furthermore the 1994 Act extended the land to which the provisions apply. Common land[33] is now included, as are footpaths, bridleways, byways, public paths and cycletracks.[34] Section 62 of the 1994 Act gave the police new powers to remove 'vehicles and other property' on land. The police must be satisfied that there are alternative caravan sites available to the trespassers to move to.[35] The power to seize vehicles and property arises where the trespasser fails to comply with a direction to leave within a reasonable time. Reasonableness is an objective test and will depend on all the circumstances of the case, including the roadworthiness of vehicles.[36]

 Pause and Reflect

Making reference to statute and case law, consider whether the law strikes an appropriate balance between the right to demonstrate and the need for public order.

Rave parties

The Criminal Justice and Public Order Act 1994 introduced new police powers to order persons to leave gatherings, created a new criminal offence of failing to leave within a reasonable time and provided for arrest without warrant. The provisions govern open-air gatherings of 20 or more persons, where amplified music is played at night time.[37] Failure to comply with a police direction may result in the power to seize and remove vehicles and sound equipment.[38]

The Act gives the police power to regulate the movement of persons to a gathering. Where a direction has been made under section 63, the police may stop persons and order them not to proceed to the gathering. The exercise of this sweeping power is confined to an area within a five-mile radius of the gathering.

Note that the 2019–2020 Coronavirus pandemic gave rise to emergency powers being conferred on the police to control the movement and assembly of people. The legislation is discussed in Chapter 21.

Other public order offences under the 1986 Act

The Act replaces a number of common law offences. The Law Commission considered, for example, that the offence of breach of the peace was too vague a concept and that it should be replaced with more specific offences. In its place, the concept of unlawful violence is used, which encompasses a number of situations. Violent conduct is defined as meaning any violent conduct, whether or not intended to cause injury or damage.[39]

---

32 Criminal Justice and Public Order Act 1994, s. 61(2).
33 As defined in the Commons Registration Act 1965, s. 22.
34 Criminal Justice and Public Order Act 1994, s. 61(9)(b)(i).
35 Ibid., s. 62A, as amended by the Anti-Social Behaviour Act 2003, s. 60.
36 See **Krumpa v Director of Public Prosecutions** (1989).
37 Criminal Justice and Public Order Act 1994, s. 63, as amended by the Anti-Social Behaviour Act 2003, s. 58.
38 Ibid., s. 64.
39 Public Order Act 1986, s. 8.

Riot

Riot is the most serious offence under the Act. 'Riot' is defined in section 1 as being where 12 or more persons who are present together use or threaten unlawful violence for a common purpose and the conduct of them (taken together) is such as would cause a person of 'reasonable firmness' present at the scene to fear for his personal safety; each of the persons using unlawful violence for the common purpose is guilty of riot.

Under section 1, a riot may be committed in private as well as public places. The common purpose may be inferred from the conduct, and does not need to be articulated. The purpose itself need not be unlawful – a perfectly legitimate demonstration may turn into a riot if the conditions for a riot are satisfied, namely the use of unlawful violence for a common purpose which is such as to cause persons of reasonable firmness present to fear for their personal safety, although it is not necessary that such persons actually be present at the scene. The mental element required for liability, under section 6(1), is that a person 'intends to use violence or is aware that his conduct may be violent'. The seriousness with which the offence is viewed is reflected in the requirement of trial on indictment (trial by jury) and liability on conviction to imprisonment for a term not exceeding ten years or a fine, or both.[40]

Violent disorder

Section 2 of the Public Order Act 1986 created a new statutory offence of violent disorder, which replaced the common law offence of unlawful assembly. The offence shares similarities with the offence of riot, but differs in several respects. First, for the offence to be committed, there need to be only three people, rather than 12 as required for a riot, involved in the violent conduct. Second, there needs to be no common purpose, as is required for the offence of riot. It is sufficient for an offence of violent disorder to be committed that the persons be involved in the use or threat of violent conduct. It is necessary that the conduct be such that it causes a person 'of reasonable firmness' to 'fear for his personal safety', although such persons need not actually be present.[41] The offence can be committed in private or in public.[42] The mental element required under section 6 is that the person intends to use or to threaten violence, or is aware that his conduct may be violent or threaten violence. Self-induced intoxication, other than through prescribed medication in a course of medical treatment, is not an excuse.

The requirement of three persons' involvement in the violent disorder has caused difficulties. In **R v Fleming** (1989), for example, four persons were charged, one was acquitted and the jury failed to reach a decision on a second. Accordingly, the conviction of the remaining two defendants was quashed.[43] The Court of Appeal in **Fleming** noted that it was possible for fewer than three persons to be convicted where, for example, there was sufficient evidence as to the involvement of more than three persons but some of the greater number evaded arrest or lacked the required mental element for the offence. The jury must be correctly directed on the matter, and failure to direct appropriately will cause a conviction to be quashed. This occurred in **R v Whorton** (1990), where there was evidence that eight to ten people were involved in the violence, but only four were charged and only two convicted. Their appeal against conviction was successful, on the basis that the judge had not directed the jury that they could only convict if there were either three defendants before them or, if a lesser number, a greater number had in fact been involved in the violent disorder.

---

40 Ibid., s. 1(6).
41 Public Order Act 1986, s. 2(3).
42 Ibid., s. 2(4).
43 See also **R v Abdul Mahroof** (1988).

The offence is triable on indictment (by the Crown Court) or summarily (by a magistrates' court), and carries a term of imprisonment of up to five years on indictment, a fine or both and, on summary conviction, imprisonment of up to six months or a fine, or both.[44]

Affray

A person is guilty of an affray if he uses or threatens unlawful violence towards another and his conduct is such as would cause a person of reasonable firmness present at the scene to fear for his personal safety.[45]

Two or more persons may be involved in the offence, in which case it is necessary that their conduct be considered together for the purpose of section 3. A verbal threat of unlawful violence is not sufficient for the offence to be committed. The offence may take place in private or in public and, again, the test for unlawful violence is whether a person of reasonable firmness, who need not in fact be present, is put in fear of his personal safety. The mental element is the same as that required for violent disorder. Police constables may arrest without warrant, and the offence is triable on indictment or summarily. On indictment, the offence carries a term of imprisonment not exceeding three years or a fine or both; on summary conviction, there is liability to imprisonment of up to six months or a fine or both.[46]

The definition of affray was considered by the Court of Appeal in **R v Sanchez** (1996). On the charge of affray, the trial judge directed the jury on the requirement for a 'person of reasonable firmness' and said that the victim was such a person and that he was to be believed when he said that he was frightened. The Court of Appeal held that there was a misdirection, in that the judge's directions overlooked the need to direct the jury to consider not only the victim but also the putative third person, the hypothetical bystander; affray was a public order offence and there were other offences for the protection of persons at whom the violence was aimed.

Fear or provocation of violence

Under section 4 of the Public Order Act 1986, a person is guilty of an offence if he:

(a) uses towards another person threatening, abusive or insulting words or behaviour; or

(b) distributes or displays to another person any writing, sign or other visible representation which is threatening, abusive or insulting, with the intent to cause that person to believe that immediate unlawful violence will be used against him or another by any person, or to provoke the immediate use of unlawful violence by that person or another, or whereby that person is likely to believe that such violence will be used or it is likely that such violence will be provoked.

The offence is one which may be committed by a single person. For a prosecution to succeed, it is necessary to establish that threatening, abusive or insulting words or behaviour have been directed towards a specific person. Rude or offensive words or behaviour may not necessarily be insulting, and swearing may not be abusive.[47] It is also necessary to establish that the person affected is caused to believe that immediate unlawful violence is about to be used against him. In **Horseferry Road Metropolitan Stipendiary Magistrate ex parte Siadatan** (1990), it was

---

44 Public Order Act 1986, s. 2(5).
45 Ibid., s. 3.
46 Ibid., s. 3(7).
47 **R v Ambrose** (1973).

held that the violence feared must be both immediate and unlawful.[48] A threat of violence at some future time will not suffice for this offence to be proven. The mental element required under section 6 is that the person intends his words or behaviour (or signs, etc.) to be threatening, abusive or insulting or that he is aware that it may be threatening, abusive or insulting.

Harassment, alarm or distress[49]

Under sections 4A[50] and 5 of the Act, a person is guilty of an offence if he:

(a) uses threatening, abusive or insulting words or behaviour, or disorderly behaviour; or
(b) displays any writing, sign or other visible representation which is threatening, abusive or insulting, thereby causing ... harassment, alarm or distress or within the hearing or sight of a person likely to be caused harassment, alarm or distress thereby.

The introduction of these offences, and the use to which they are put by the police, raise controversy. The offence was designed to provide powers to deal with relatively minor acts of anti-social, unruly or disorderly conduct which, while of itself not serious, causes fear in others. In its White Paper, the government illustrated the sort of behaviour that was being targeted:[51]

(a) hooligans on housing estates causing disturbances in the common parts of blocks of flats ...;
(b) groups of youths persistently shouting abuse and obscenities or pestering people waiting to catch public transport or to enter a hall or cinema; someone turning out the lights in a crowded dance hall, in a way likely to cause panic;
(c) rowdy behaviour in the streets late at night which alarms local residents.

For the offence to be proven, it is necessary that the words or behaviour, or signs etc., are uttered or displayed within the sight of a person who is likely to be harassed or alarmed or distressed – it is not necessary to prove actual harassment, alarm or distress. However, the mental element required is that the person using the words, behaviour or signs either intended his conduct to be threatening, abusive or insulting or was aware that it might be. Thus, words uttered in a public place (for example, by demonstrators or persons attending football matches) which might in fact be threatening or abusive, and might in fact cause alarm or distress to someone hearing the words, will not be sufficient for a prosecution to succeed.[52] No offence occurs if the prohibited conduct occurs inside a dwelling used as a person's home or at other living accommodation.[53] A person detained in a police cell does not occupy it as a home or other living accommodation: see **R v Francis** (2006).

In **Jordan v Burgoyne** (1963), the accused made an inflammatory racist speech in Trafalgar Square. He was prosecuted under the forerunner to section 4 of the Public Order Act 1986, section 5 of the Public Order Act 1936. It was held that the speech went beyond the limits of tolerance. The defendant could not argue that the words used were not likely to cause ordinary persons to commit breaches of the peace. The defendant had to 'take his audience

---

48 See further below. On the Racial and Religious Hatred Act 2006 see Chapter 19.
49 See *Criminal Law: Offences Relating to Public Order*, Law Com No. 123, 1983, and Williams, 1984. See Geddis, 2004.
50 Introduced by s. 154 of the Criminal Justice and Public Order Act 1994.
51 *Review of Public Order Law*, Cmnd 9510, 1985, London: HMSO, para. 3.22. On Anti-Social Behaviour Orders see 11th edn, Chapter 21.
52 See **Director of Public Prosecutions v Clarke** (1992); **Harvey v DPP** (2011) C 81HC B1 (admin).
53 Public Order Act 1986, s. 4A(2).

as he found them'. If the words used were likely to provoke that audience, or part thereof, to commit a breach of the peace, the defendant was guilty of an offence.

Insulting words were the subject of judicial scrutiny in **Brutus v Cozens** (1973). In **Brutus**, the defendant and other anti-apartheid protesters interrupted play at a Wimbledon tennis match. The audience resented the interruption. Brutus was charged with insulting behaviour likely to cause a breach of the peace. In the Divisional Court, it was held that an offence occurred where the behaviour affronted other people, and reflected a contempt for their rights. The House of Lords, however, allowed Brutus' appeal. Not all speech or conduct fell within the meaning of the section. It must be conduct or speech which the ordinary person would recognise as insulting – a term which was deemed incapable of precise definition. The mere resentment of the crowd, as opposed to violence, did not suffice to make the actions insulting. 'Insulting words or behaviour' as an offence have been abolished: section 57 of the Crime and Courts Act 2013 amends section 5 of the Public Order Act to remove the offence.

The issue of violent reaction to provocative words was considered in **R v Horseferry Road Magistrates ex parte Siadatan** (1991). The case concerned Salman Rushdie's novel, *The Satanic Verses*. In an application laid against the publishers and the author, it was argued that distribution of the book offended against section 4 of the 1986 Act, in so far as it contained abusive and insulting language which was likely to provoke violence amongst devout Muslims. The magistrates refused to issue a summons. The issue went to the Divisional Court for judicial review. It was there held that the violence which was apprehended by the words must be immediate violence, not some distant act of violence.

In **R v Stephen Miller** (1999), the defendant appealed against sentence for racially aggravated threatening words. The defendant had pleaded guilty to two offences: first, aggravated threatening words and behaviour contrary to section 4 of the Public Order Act 1986, as amended by section 31 of the Crime and Disorder Act 1998; and, second, travelling on a railway without a ticket. He was sentenced to 18 months' imprisonment, and appealed. The Court of Appeal dismissed his appeal. His conduct towards the conductor on the train was particularly bad. The sentence was designed to reflect public concern about conduct which damaged good racial relations within the community.[54]

The mental element on the part of the accused must be satisfied. KA Ewing and CA Gearty provide illustrations of the uses to which section 5 has been put.[55] The Act has been used to curb the wearing of obscene T-shirts and hats, to suppress a satirical poster of the former Prime Minister Mrs Thatcher and to prosecute protesters outside abortion clinics in Ireland.[56] In Gearty and Ewing's assessment, section 5 of the Act represents a 'mechanism for punishing non-violent non-conformity for the crime of being itself'.[57] It must be conceded that section 5 represents a serious, and hitherto uncontemplated, limitation of freedom of expression and an alteration of the balance between individual liberty and the legitimate expectations of citizens to be protected from the consequences of another person's words and actions.

However, Article 10 proved constructive in relation to section 5 of the Public Order Act 1986 in **Percy v Director of Public Prosecutions** (2002). In this case, Ms Percy had been convicted under section 5 in relation to her protest against American military policy at an American air base. In the course of her protest Ms Percy defaced and trampled on an American flag. On appeal, it was held that too much reliance had been placed by the trial judge on the fact that her behaviour towards the flag – which was insulting to Americans at the base – was

---

54 In **R v Rogers (Philip)** (2007), the House of Lords ruled that using the words 'bloody foreigners' was capable of amounting to the offence of using racially aggravated abusive or insulting words with the intent to cause fear or provoke violence.

55 Ewing and Gearty, 1990, Chapter 4.

56 **Director of Public Prosecutions v Fidler** (1992); **Director of Public Prosecutions v Clarke** (1992).

57 Ewing and Gearty, 1990, p. 123.

avoidable, at the expense of the defendant's right to freedom of expression. Her conviction was incompatible with Article 10 and was quashed. See also **Ajit Singh Dehal v Crown Prosecution Service** (2005).

Harassment

The Protection from Harassment Act 1997 makes it a criminal offence to pursue a course of conduct which amounts to harassment of another and which that person knows amounts to harassment of the other.[58] Section 3 provides a civil remedy which enables an individual to seek an injunction against a person who is harassing them or may be likely to do so. In addition, damages may be awarded for any anxiety caused by the harassment and any financial loss resulting from the harassment.[59] In order to secure a conviction under section 2, the following requirements must be met:

- there must be a 'course of conduct';
- the conduct must take place on at least two occasions;[60]
- the course of conduct must take place against 'another person';
- the conduct must harass or alarm another or cause that person distress.

Section 1(3) provides exceptions to liability under section 1, which does not apply if the person accused of harassment can show that:

(a) the conduct in question was pursued for the purpose of preventing or detecting crime;
(b) the conduct in question was pursued under any enactment or rule of law or to comply with any condition or requirement imposed by any person under any enactment; or
(c) in the particular circumstances the pursuit of the course of conduct was reasonable.

Section 1(3)(a) was considered by the Court of Appeal in **Hayes v Willoughby** (2013). In this case, the defendant had waged a 'lengthy and persistent campaign of correspondence and investigation' into the affairs of the claimant. His defence was that the conduct fell within section 1(3)(a). The Supreme Court ruled that a purely subjective belief in the mind of the harasser that he was preventing or detecting crime was not enough, and that Parliament intended there should be limits to the conduct falling within the defence. In this case the defendant's conduct had become irrational and he could not rely on section 1(3)(a).

Where a course of conduct causes fear, on at least two occasions, that violence will be used against another a criminal offence is committed. On conviction the court may, in addition to sentencing the offender, issue a restraining order prohibiting the offender from doing anything which amounts to harassment or causes a fear of violence.[61] A similar power exists in relation to a person who is acquitted of an offence.[62] A restraining order may be made for a specified period or may have effect until further order. The date of expiry of the order is variable.[63]

In **Dalichi UK Ltd v Stop Huntingdon Animal Cruelty** (2004), the High Court ruled that the Protection from Harassment Act 1997 was intended to protect individuals and not corporate

58 Protection from Harassment Act 1997, s. 2. The exercise by an individual of his right to freedom of expression and the instigation of secret surveillance of another person were capable of constituting a course of conduct amounting to harassment: **Howlett v Holding** (2006).
59 On this see **Jones v Ruth** (2011).
60 See **Banks v Ablex Ltd** (2005).
61 Protection from Harassment Act 1997, s. 5.
62 Ibid., s. 5A.
63 See **Director of Public Prosecutions v Hall** (2005).

victims of harassment. However, individuals who were non-corporate claimants were entitled to protection. Stop Huntingdon Animal Cruelty was an unincorporated association whose stated objective was the closure of laboratories run by Huntingdon Life Sciences, which conducted research using live animals. As a result of a campaign of harassment and intimidation, Huntingdon Life's insurance brokers had ceased to act for them. In addition, its auditors withdrew their services. The claimants, their directors and employees had 'unquestionably been subject to harassment of a very serious nature intended to intimidate and terrify'. Granting the injunctive relief, Owen J ruled that the 'balance of justice and convenience weighed heavily in favour of granting interlocutory injunctive relief' bearing in mind 'the rights to freedom of speech and of assembly and association'.[64]

The courts have interpreted the 1997 Act strictly, requiring that 'another person' be a specific individual. As a result, it was unclear whether protection could be given to the employees of an organisation who had not been personally harassed, even though another employee had been. The Serious Organised Crime and Police Act 2005 (SOCPA) amends the 1997 Act to cover this situation. Section 125 SOCPA amends section 1 of the 1997 Act. Section 1A of the 1997 Act provides (in part) that:

A person must not pursue a course of conduct –

(a) which involves harassment of two or more persons, and
(b) which he knows or ought to know involves harassment of those persons, and
(c) by which he intends to persuade any person –

(i) not to do something that he is entitled to do, or
(ii) to do something that he is not under any obligation to do.

The provision is not intended to criminalise peaceful protesting but will be engaged where there are threats and intimidation which seek to force others to do something or not to do something. Section 125(5) SOCPA inserts a new section 3A into the 1997 Act which allows for an injunction to be sought where there is an actual or apprehended breach of section 1(1A). Section 125(7) amends the definition of course of conduct in section 7(3) of the 1997 Act stating that in the case of conduct in relation to two or more persons, a course of conduct means conduct on at least one occasion in relation to each person.[65]

The Crime and Disorder Act 1998

Sections 28 to 32 of the Crime and Disorder Act 1998 extend the law to encompass racially aggravated offences. It is an offence under sections 4 and 5 of the Public Order Act 1986 (fear of provocation of violence, intentional harassment, alarm or distress) to engage in racially aggravated conduct. Section 32 makes it an offence to act in a racially aggravated manner in relation to sections 2 and 4 of the Protection from Harassment Act 1997. Under section 28(1), an offence is racially aggravated if:

(a) at the time of committing the offence, or immediately before or after doing so, the offender demonstrates towards the victim of the offence hostility based on the victim's membership (or presumed membership) of a racial group; or

---

64 See also *Hall v Save Newchurch Guinea Pigs (Campaign)* (2005). An employer can be vicariously liable under s. 3 of the 1997 Act for breach of a statutory duty imposed only on his employee for harassment committed by one of its employees in the course of his or her employment. The Court of Appeal so ruled in *Majrowski v Guy's and St Thomas's NHS Trust* (2005).
65 On harassment of a person in his or her home see SOCPA 2005, s. 126. On harassment in employment see also the Equality Act 2010.

(b) the offence is motivated (wholly or partly) by hostility towards members of a racial group based on their membership of that group.[66]

Section 28(3) provides that: 'It is immaterial … whether or not the offender's hostility is also based, to any extent, on – (a) the fact of presumption that any person or group of persons belongs to any religious group'. Under section 82, the court may impose a higher penalty for racially aggravated offences.

> **Pause and Reflect**
>
> With reference to case law, explain the impact of Convention rights on freedom of assembly and association.

The Anti-Social Behaviour, Crime and Policing Act 2014

The Anti-Social Behaviour, Crime and Policing Act 2014 is a wide-ranging Act with provisions relating to anti-social behaviour which causes harassment, alarm or distress, new police powers relating to dispersal.[67] In addition it contains various measures relating to policing, extradition and compensation following a miscarriage of justice. In relation to freedom of assembly this may be restricted by the use of dispersal powers. Section 34 provides that a senior police officer may authorise the use of dispersal powers only if satisfied on reasonable grounds that the use of the powers may be necessary for removing or reducing the likelihood of (a) members of the public in the locality being harassed, alarmed or distressed, or (b) the occurrence in the locality of crime and disorder. When considering whether to authorise dispersal, the officer must have 'particular regard to the rights or freedom of expression and freedom of assembly'. The order may require a person to leave an area and not to return to that area (section 35). The exclusion notice may not last more than 48 hours. Restrictions apply. A direction may not be made in relation to a person under the age of ten years, or in relation to a place of employment, or a place where the individual is expected to attend for the purpose of education or training or for receiving medical treatment. Where a direction is given, an officer may direct the person to surrender any item which has been used or is likely to be used in behaviour that causes harassment, alarm or distress. See also the Coronavirus Act, the Public Health Act 1984 and associated Regulations which regulate police powers to control public gatherings discussed in Chapter 21.

Police Powers in Relation to the Detection and Investigation of Crime

Questioning by the police

It is a fundamental rule that the citizen is not obliged to answer police questions, unless there is lawful justification for official interference with the citizen's liberty. The rule was endorsed in **Rice v Connolly** (1966). There, the appellant was questioned by the police. He refused to

---

66 In **DPP v M** (2004), the High Court ruled that the use of the phrase 'bloody foreigners' was contrary to s. 28(1)(a) in that the word 'foreigners' was capable of describing a racial group and the word 'bloody' was capable of demonstrating hostility.
67 And amendments to the Dangerous Dogs Act 1991, the Sexual Offences Act 2003 and Criminal Justice and Immigration Act 2008.

answer questions and was, accordingly, arrested for obstructing a police officer in the execution of his duty contrary to section 51(3) of the Police Act 1964.[68] On appeal, Lord Parker CJ stated that a citizen has every right to refuse to answer questions; generally the citizen has a 'right to silence'.

In **Kenlin v Gardiner** (1967), the issue in question concerned whether a person could lawfully be stopped in the street by the police. Police officers attempted to question two boys. One of the boys tried to run away, whereupon a police constable tried physically to stop him and a scuffle broke out. The boys were charged with assaulting a police constable in the execution of his duty. There was no question that an assault on the police had occurred. The question for decision was whether the assault by the boys was justified. The Divisional Court held that the attempt to restrain the boy amounted to an assault by the police officer, and was, accordingly, an unlawful attempt to detain him. As such, the police officer was not acting in the course of his duty and, as a result, the boys were not guilty of assaulting a police officer 'in the execution of his duty'. A distinction must be made between a refusal to answer questions and conduct which amounts to obstruction of the police; see further below.

There are, however, situations in which a citizen is under a duty to answer questions. For example, under road traffic law, there is a duty to give one's name and address, and a refusal to do so and to give up one's driving licence and other motoring documents is an offence. There is also a duty to provide police with the name of the person driving the car at a particular time. Other than under statutory authority, however, there is a right to silence.[69]

Power exists to stop motorists on any ground, and failure to stop is an offence.[70] A police officer is entitled to immobilise a car by removing the ignition keys. The vehicle owner may be detained in order to allow the officer sufficient time to determine whether an arrest is to be made, to effect arrest and to give reasons for the arrest. Moreover, the police have the power to detain a motorist in order to administer a breathalyser test. Powers also exist under the Official Secrets Act 1911 whereby the Home Secretary can grant the police permission to question suspects. Refusal to answer questions in respect of inquiries made in respect of investigations into fraud and drug trafficking can amount to a criminal offence, as can refusal to disclose information under the Terrorism Acts.[71]

Helping the police with inquiries

In law, the police have no power to detain a person in order to make inquiries. Section 29 of the Police and Criminal Evidence Act 1984 (PACE) clarifies this rule. A person is either free to leave a police station where he voluntarily attends to assist the police, or the police must arrest him. If a person is detained by the police, he must be informed immediately that he is under arrest and be given reasons for the arrest, the absence of which may render the arrest unlawful.

The identification of suspects

One of the principal causes of wrongful conviction lies in the wrongful identification of suspects. Identification may take place by witnessing, or by fingerprinting and the taking of bodily samples. Code of Practice D governs the procedures to be followed. Identification by identity parade is the most reliable means of identification, and will be carried out if the

---

68 Now Police Act 1996, section 89.
69 **Lodwick v Sanders** (1985).
70 Road Traffic Act 1988, a/a by Serious Organised Crime and Police Act 2005.
71 See Chapter 21.

defendant requests it or consents to it. If it is impracticable to hold an identity parade, perhaps because there are a large number of suspects or because there are insufficient people with similar characteristics to the suspect, the police may then turn to alternative means of identification. Identification by witness may be effected by arranging for the witness to see the suspect in a group, generally in a public place away from the police station. The consent of the suspect is required, but his or her failure to consent does not prohibit the use of group identification. Alternatively, video identification may be used. Face-to-face confrontation of the witness and accused may take place provided identification is not possible by any other means.

Stop and search powers

Under the Police and Criminal Evidence Act 1984 (PACE), the police have been given the power to stop and search a person reasonably suspected of carrying prohibited articles such as offensive weapons and/or housebreaking equipment or stolen goods. A record of the search must be made, either on the spot or as soon as practicable thereafter.[72] The police also have the power to set up road blocks if there are reasonable grounds for suspicion that a person in the area has committed an offence (see further below), or that an offence is about to be committed, or that a person is unlawfully 'at large'. Section 60 of the Criminal Justice and Public Order Act 1994 provides that powers may be given to the police, by a police officer of the rank of superintendent or above, to stop and search persons and vehicles, where that officer reasonably believes that incidents involving serious violence may take place in any locality in his area, and that it is expedient so to do to prevent their occurrence. The authorisation lasts for up to 24 hours. Section 60 also authorises stop and search for 'dangerous instruments or offensive weapons' that are being carried without good reason, whether or not there are reasonable grounds for suspecting that a person is carrying them. This power was challenged in **R (Roberts) v Commissioner of Police of the Metropolis** (2015). A police officer had searched Mrs Roberts' handbag in order to establish her identity. Mrs Roberts alleged (among other things) that this violated her right to privacy under Article 8 and that the power was incompatible with the Convention. The Supreme Court dismissed her appeal: section 60 required an officer to give reasons for the authorisation and for the stop and search. This was a sufficient safeguard to enable a judgment to be made on whether the power had been exercised lawfully. The Terrorism Acts also confer powers of stop and search: see further Chapter 21. The European Court of Human Rights has confirmed that the use of these powers to stop and search people without grounds for suspicion is unlawful. The Protection of Freedoms Act 2012 reformed the law: see Chapter 21.

Before 1984, there was considerable doubt about the breadth of power to search an arrested person. The police had a common law power to search a person if they reasonably believed that he was carrying a weapon or evidence relevant to the crime of which he was suspected. Resisting a lawful search would amount to obstruction of the police.

Under section 32 of PACE, where a person is arrested at a place other than a police station, a police constable may search the arrested person for anything which might assist him to escape from lawful custody or for anything which might be evidence relating to an offence, and to enter and search any premises in which he was when arrested or immediately before he was arrested for evidence relating to the offence for which he has been arrested (s 32(2)). The power is subject to the requirement that the 'constable has reasonable grounds

---

72 PACE section 3.

for believing that the arrested person may present a danger to himself or others' (s 32(1)). The power to search is limited to what is 'reasonably required' for the purpose of discovery (s 32(3)). Search of the person is restricted: a person may not be required to remove any of his or her clothing in public, other than an outer coat, jacket or gloves, and the search may only be conducted if the constable 'has reasonable grounds for believing' that the person concerned has concealed on his or her person anything for which a search is permitted (s.32(4)(5)). If the permitted search discloses anything which might be used to cause physical injury to the person or any other person, the officer may seize and retain anything found, other than an item subject to legal privilege, if there are reasonable grounds for believing that the item may be used to assist escape from lawful custody, or is evidence of an offence, or has been obtained in consequence of the commission of an offence (s 32(8)(9)).

Intimate body searches are also permitted under the 1984 Act. The search must be carried out by a doctor, unless a senior officer believes that that is impracticable. The search may only be made for articles which may cause injury or for class 'A' drugs. The powers to search the person and take personal samples were extended by the Criminal Justice and Public Order Act 1994, section 58, which defines both intimate and non-intimate samples.

The Criminal Justice Act 2003 extended police powers, authorising the police to take electronic fingerprints and a DNA sample. Electronic fingerprinting enables the police to confirm the identity of a suspect within minutes where that person's fingerprints are already held on the National Fingerprint Database. The DNA sample will be entered onto the National DNA Database. Both databases enabled speculative searches to be made to see whether a suspect is linked to any unsolved crime.

The Protection of Freedoms Act 2012, Part 1, now regulates the retention and destruction of fingerprints, footwear impressions and DNA samples and profiles. Section 63D of the Police and Criminal Evidence Act 1984 provides that fingerprints and DNA profiles ('section 63D material') must be destroyed if they were taken unlawfully. If they were taken lawfully, they must be destroyed unless the Act provides the power to retain the section 63D material in new sections 63E to 63P.

The Act distinguishes between two principal classes of person. Material taken from persons arrested for or charged with a minor offence will be destroyed following either a decision not to charge or following acquittal by a court (section 63E). Fingerprints and DNA profiles of persons charged with, but not convicted of, a 'qualifying offence' offence may be retained for three years. A single two-year extension may be available on the application of the police to a District Judge. The Act also regulates material taken from persons convicted outside England and Wales, persons under the age of 18 convicted of a first minor offence and persons given a penalty notice. The Act also makes special provision for material given voluntarily and material retained with consent (s 63N, 63O). Where a chief officer of police determines that section 63D material needs to be retained for national security purposes, the determination must be in writing, and has effect for a maximum, renewable term of two years (s 63M PACE). The Act makes detailed provision relating to the destruction of section 63D material, and restrictions on the use of retained material.

Intercepts

Article 8 of the European Convention on Human Rights provides for respect for private and family life, home and correspondence. Surveillance operations and interception of communications are intrinsic aspects of policing. Prior to the Human Rights Act 1998, there being no common law or statutory right to privacy under domestic law, such techniques were not unlawful, as confirmed by Sir Robert Megarry VC in **Malone v Metropolitan Police Commissioner** (1979). However, in **Malone v United Kingdom** (1984) the Court of Human Rights ruled that there was insufficient protection given by law. The Interception of Communications Act 1985 was passed to remedy the defects in domestic law. The legal framework is now set out in the Regulation of Investigatory Powers Act 2000 (on which see Chapter 21). The Police Act 1997 placed the power of the police to interfere with property and plant surveillance devices on a statutory basis. Modelled on the Interception of Communications Act 1985, the Act provides that authorisation for the bugging of property may be given on the basis that it would facilitate the 'prevention and detection of serious crime' which cannot 'reasonably be achieved by other means' (s 93(2)). No exemptions from the provisions are made: thus, solicitors' offices, doctors' surgeries and even Roman Catholic confessionals may fall victim to bugging by the police. Authorisation must be given by the Chief Officer of Police (s 93(3)) or, if he is unavailable, by an officer of Chief Constable rank (s 94). Written authorisations remain in effect for three months, whereas, in cases of emergency, oral authorisation may be made which will remain in force for 72 hours. Following opposition to the Bill, the government accepted that independent commissioners should review the authorisations. Such review does not, however, necessarily precede police action on the warrant. In cases where private dwellings, hotel bedrooms or offices are involved, a commissioner's prior approval for the authorisation is required. Prior approval is also required where the surveillance may result in the revealing of confidential personal information, confidential journalistic material or matters which are subject to legal privilege (s 97).

Property searches

In **Semayne's Case** (1605),[73] the principle that an 'Englishman's home is his castle' was judicially declared. Two early cases reveal judicial boldness in the protection from unlawful entry into property. In **Wilkes v Wood** (1763),[74] an Under Secretary of State, accompanied by police, entered Wilkes's home, broke open his desk and seized papers. In an action for trespass against the Under Secretary, Lord Pratt CJ stated that the power claimed would affect 'the person and property of every man in this kingdom, and is totally subversive of the liberty of the subject'. Moreover, such action, being without justification and unlawful, was 'contrary to the fundamental principles of the constitution'.

In the seminal case of **Entick v Carrington** (1765), the Secretary of State, under a general warrant, authorised the entry into property and the seizure of property belonging to Entick, who was suspected of publishing seditious literature. In an action for trespass against Carrington, the court ruled that the Secretary of State's action was unlawful: a specific warrant was needed to legitimise entry into a citizen's property.

Freedom from arbitrary intrusion into property is – in the absence of a written guarantee of rights – subject always to the sovereignty of Parliament. The principle that 'a man's home is his castle' has many exceptions. For example, statutory rights of entry are conferred on employees of public authorities. In addition to rights of physical entry into property, the issue of warrants to intercept communications authorises a non-physical but nevertheless real intrusion into a person's private property.

Rights of entry and search under common law

At common law, the police had no right to enter private property without a warrant. Accordingly, if they so entered and were asked to leave – even where reasonable force was

---

73 (1605) 5 Co Rep 91a.
74 (1763) 19 St Tr 1153.

used to evict them – the police were not acting in the execution of their duty and an individual could not be convicted for assaulting a police officer executing his duty. The common law responded to this problem with a series of complex conditions. With the exception of rights of entry relating to a breach of the peace or for preventing a breach of the peace, common law rights of entry are abolished and now regulated under the PACE 1984.

Rights of entry and search under statute

The Police and Criminal Evidence Act 1984 (PACE) and Code of Practice B on the Searching of Premises and Seizure of Property regulate the power of the police.

The grounds on which a warrant may be issued are specified in section 8 of PACE, which provides, in part, that a justice of the peace 'is satisfied' [from the application made by the police] that 'there are reasonable grounds for believing':

- that an indictable offence has been committed;
- that there is material likely to be of substantial value to the investigation of the offence;
- that material is likely to be relevant evidence;
- that it does not consist of or include items subject to legal privilege (for example, communications between a legal adviser and client), or excluded material or special procedure material (for example confidential records; journalistic material held in confidence);
- that any of the conditions below applies.

The conditions include the fact that it is impracticable to communicate with any person entitled to grant entry to the premises or grant access to the evidence or that entry will be denied unless a warrant is produced or that the purpose of the search will be frustrated or seriously prejudiced unless an officer can secure immediate entry to them (PACE s. 81(1)). Once a search is authorised, a constable may seize and retain any evidence relating to the search (PACE s. 19).

Problems are encountered by the police in the seizure of materials which might be legally privileged, namely correspondence between a client and his or her lawyer. Where the police seize such material and the owner claims that it is privileged, the position of the police had proved uncertain. In order to remedy the difficulties, the Criminal Justice and Police Act 2001 provides statutory authority for the removal of property for examination elsewhere and authorises the removal of material which is intrinsically related (such as computer disks), where it is not reasonably practicable for the property to be separated from that which it would otherwise be unlawful to remove. Where property is found to be privileged, it must be returned as soon as is practicable (CJ&PA 2001, s. 54). Any person from whom property is seized may apply to the Crown Court for the return of the property (ibid. s. 59).

As noted above, the police have special powers of entry and search under PACE. For the most part, entry is authorised under a warrant authorised by a magistrate.[75] Where a warrant is issued, any constable may execute it and any person authorised to accompany a constable has the same powers as that constable (PACE s. 16). A warrant must be executed within one month and entry and search must be undertaken at a reasonable time, unless the purpose of the search would be frustrated by entry at a reasonable time. Over and above entry under warrant, however, there exists a class of cases under which the police may enter without warrant under sections 17 and 18 of the Act. Included in this class is entry to arrest for an indictable offence or for offences under the Public Order Act 1936, or Criminal Law Act 1977.

---

75 PACE s. 8 as amended by SOCPA s. 113.

Entry without warrant is also lawful if exercised to recover a prison, court or mental hospital detainee and to save life or prevent serious damage to property.

The Protection of Freedoms Act 2012, Part 3, confers powers on ministers to repeal, by order, unnecessary powers of entry to land or other premises. Each Cabinet Minister is under a duty to review existing powers of entry.

The conditions of interviews

The Code of Practice on the Detention, Treatment, and Questioning of Persons by Police Officers (Code C) provides that a suspect should be given eight hours in any 24 hours free of questioning. Breaks for refreshment should be given regularly (every two hours), unless such breaks would adversely affect the inquiries. Persons who are mentally disordered and children should be interviewed in the presence of a competent adult. The detention must be reviewed regularly, the first taking place after six hours from the time of lawful detention; subsequent reviews to be conducted at intervals of no more than nine hours.

Tape recording of interviews

The tape recording of police interviews acts as protection for the person being questioned, and as protection for the police against accusations of oppression. Tape recording is regulated by a Code of Practice. Both the defence and prosecution have the right to listen to tape recordings, although the police provide summaries of the recordings. The police must maintain proper records of any interview, including the time of commencement and ending and any breaks in questioning. The person interviewed must be allowed to read the record.

The caution

The caution to be administered is set out in Code of Practice C, paragraph 10.5:

> You do not have to say anything. But it may harm your defence if you do not mention when questioned something which you later rely on in Court. Anything you do say may be given in evidence.

Arrest

A lawful arrest is an arrest for which there is legal authority. Three categories of lawful arrest exist: arrest under warrant, arrest without warrant under common law and arrest without a warrant under statute. Where a person has been wrongly arrested and detained under statute,[76] the person detained is entitled to damages: **Roberts v Chief Constable of Cheshire Constabulary** (1999); **Woodward v Chief Constable, Fife Constabulary** (1998).

Arrest under warrant

Section 1(1) of the Magistrates' Courts Act 1980 provides that a warrant for arrest may be made on the basis that a 'person has, or is suspected of having, committed an offence'. The warrant should not be issued unless the offence is indictable (i.e. triable by jury in the Crown Court) or punishable by imprisonment (Magistrates Courts Act 1980, s. 1). The warrant is issued by a magistrate after a written application by a police officer has been

---

76 PACE s. 34 and Criminal Justice (Scotland) Act 1980.

substantiated on oath. The warrant may be executed even if the police officer does not have it in his or her possession at the time, but the warrant must be shown to the person arrested as soon as possible. When an arrest warrant has been issued, a constable may enter and search premises to make the arrest, using such reasonable force as is necessary. Where a constable executes a warrant in good faith believing it to be valid, he or she is protected from liability under the Constables' Protection Act 1750. The magistrate may endorse the warrant for bail.

Arrest without warrant: common law

The only common law power to arrest without warrant is where there are reasonable grounds for suspicion that a breach of the peace is about to occur, or has been committed and is likely to continue or to reoccur. If violence has occurred or is about to occur to persons or property, a police officer may reasonably believe that a breach of the peace is about to occur. If a breach of the peace has occurred, but has ceased, the power to arrest ceases.

In **Foulkes v Chief Constable of Merseyside Police** (1998), the Court of Appeal considered the issue of reasonable grounds in law for the arrest and subsequent detention of a person in relation to an apprehended breach of the peace. The police officer had arrested the appellant in the course of a domestic incident, honestly believing that arrest was necessary to prevent a breach of the peace. The Court of Appeal ruled that, where there was no actual breach of the peace but only an apprehended breach, the power of arrest was only to be exercised in the clearest of circumstances where the officer was satisfied that a breach of the peace was imminent. The arresting officer in this case acted honestly but did not have reasonable grounds for the arrest. Arrest was an inappropriate management of a dispute between husband and wife in the family home.

An apprehended breach of the peace was also central to the decision in **Bibby v Chief Constable of Essex Police** (2000). A bailiff had gone to a debtor's premises for the purpose of seizing assets due under a liability order issued by a magistrates' court. The debtor threatened to call his friends to prevent the removal of goods. Fearing a breach of the peace, a police constable, who had been called to the premises, ordered the bailiff to leave. When the bailiff refused, he was arrested and led away to the police station in handcuffs. He was later released without charge. The bailiff sued the police for assault and wrongful imprisonment. The Court of Appeal ruled that the bailiff was acting lawfully but although the constable reasonably came to the conclusion that a breach of the peace was imminent, he had failed to consider where the threat was coming from. Accordingly, neither the arrest nor the use of handcuffs was justified.[77]

Arrest without warrant under statute

The powers of arrest provided under PACE are based on the concept of the seriousness of the offence in question. Sections 110 and 111 of the Serious Organised Crime and Police Act 2005 (SOCPA) amend these powers. Section 110 provides a replacement section 24 of PACE. The power of arrest without warrant for an 'arrestable offence' is replaced with the power of arrest without warrant for an 'offence'. Under the new section 24(1), a constable has the power of arrest without a warrant in relation to:

(a)   anyone who is about to commit an offence;
(b)   anyone who is in the act of committing an offence;

---

77 See also **Redman-Bate v DPP** (1999).

(c)   anyone whom he has reasonable grounds for suspecting to be about to commit an offence;

(d)   anyone whom he has reasonable grounds for suspecting to be committing an offence.

Under section 24(2) a constable may arrest without a warrant anyone whom he has reasonable grounds to suspect is guilty of an offence which the constable has reasonable grounds to suspect has been committed. If an offence has been committed, a constable may arrest without warrant anyone who is guilty of the offence or anyone whom he has reasonable grounds for suspecting to be guilty of it (section 24(3)). However, the power of arrest under subsections (1), (2) or (3) is exercisable only if the constable has reasonable grounds for believing that it is *necessary* to arrest the person in question for any of the reasons specified in subsection (5). These are:

- to enable the name of the person in question to be ascertained (in the case where the constable does not know, and cannot readily ascertain, the person's name, or has reasonable grounds for doubting whether a name given by the person as his name is his real name);

- correspondingly as regards the person's address;

- to prevent the person in question –

    (i)   causing physical injury to himself or any other persons;

    (ii)   suffering physical injury;

    (iii)   causing loss of or damage to property;

    (iv)   committing an offence against public decency (subject to subsection (6)); or

    (v)   causing an unlawful obstruction of the highway;

- to protect a child or other vulnerable person from the person in question;

- to allow the prompt and effective investigation of the offence or of the conduct of the person in question;

- to prevent any prosecution for the offence from being hindered by the disappearance of the person in question.

Section 24 was considered by the Court of Appeal in **Hayes v Chief Constable of Merseyside Police** (2011). The claimant had been arrested but not charged, and released. It was not in dispute that the constable had reasonable grounds for suspecting that an offence had been committed and that the claimant was guilty of it. As to section 24(4) and (5)(e), the claimant argued that the constable had to consider all alternatives to arrest. The Court of Appeal rejected that argument: it was sufficient for an arrest to be lawful that the officer believed the arrest to be necessary and that the belief was reasonable. Contrast that case with **Richardson v Chief Constable of West Midlands Police** (2011), in which the arrest and detention of the claimant was declared unlawful. The claimant had attended the police station voluntarily and the police had failed to consider the necessity of his arrest in light of that attendance. Section 24A of PACE relates to the power of persons other than police constables to make an arrest without a warrant. That right is now limited to the power of arrest for indictable offences, and the power may only be exercised on the basis of *necessity*, and in the absence of a constable who could make the arrest. The reasons that make an arrest necessary are stipulated as being to prevent the person in question:

(a)   causing physical injury to himself or any other person;
(b)   suffering physical injury;
(c)   causing loss of or damage to property; or
(d)   making off before a constable can assume responsibility for him.

Giving reasons for the arrest

A failure to give reasons for an arrest will cause the arrest to be unlawful. In **Christie v Leachinsky** (1947), the House of Lords ruled that a person must be told of the fact of his or her arrest and the grounds for arrest, although this need not be done if the circumstances are obvious or it is difficult to communicate with the arrested person. Section 28 of PACE places the requirements on a statutory basis and makes them more stringent. Subject to a person escaping before the information can be communicated, section 28 requires that:

(a)   the person making the arrest must inform the arrested person of the fact of, and reasons for, arrest, either immediately or as soon as is reasonably practicable afterwards;
(b)   a police officer making an arrest must inform the person arrested of these matters even if they are obvious.

No particular form of words need be used, but they must be in sufficient detail to enable the arrested person to understand the issue and, if possible, to deny the allegation and be released. Where it is not possible to state reasons immediately, for example because the arrestee is reacting violently, reasons must be stated as soon as practicable. This requirement is illustrated in **Director of Public Prosecutions v Hawkins** (1988). In that case, a violent struggle prevented reasons being given immediately. However, when the arrestee was subdued, reasons for the arrest were still not given. The arrest became unlawful when the opportunity to give reasons arose, and reasons were not given. A sympathetic attitude to the arresting authorities was seen in **Lewis v Chief Constable of the South Wales Constabulary** (1991). There, two people were arrested and not immediately informed of the reasons for arrest. In an action for false imprisonment, the Court of Appeal upheld the decision of the circuit judge: that the arrests were unlawful until the reasons were given but, once the reasons were given, the arrests became lawful.

The giving of reasons for arrest is also a requirement under the European Convention on Human Rights. In **Fox, Campbell and Hartley v United Kingdom** (1990), the applicants were arrested on suspected terrorist offences, but were not informed of the reason for the arrest, although they were told they were being arrested under a specified statutory provision. When later interviewed, they were asked about specific criminal offences. The Court of Human Rights held that paragraph 5(2) of Article 5 had not been satisfied at the time of the arrest, but that the defect was later rectified. In **Murray v United Kingdom** (1996), the Court again found no breach of Article 5. Although the applicant was denied reasons for some half an hour, she was eventually informed of the reason for arrest during interrogation.

Detention following arrest

Once a person has been arrested, he or she may be detained by the police for questioning before a charge is laid. There exists a fine balance to be achieved here between permitting the police to question a suspect in order to determine whether there exist sufficient grounds on which to make a charge, and the need to protect persons from unwarranted detention by the police. As a general rule, where a person has been charged with an offence he or she must be brought before a magistrates' court 'as soon as practicable'. This provision gives effect to the requirements of the European Convention on Human Rights. The Police and Criminal Evidence Act 1984, as amended, provides that a person may be detained, under the authority of a superintendent, for a maximum of 36 hours for any indictable offence. The time runs from the time of the person's arrest or, in the case of a person's arrest outside the relevant police area, from the time he arrives in the police station (PACE s. 42).

The period is extendable. The grounds on which extended detention may be authorised are as follows. For authorisation by a senior officer of police, there must be reasonable grounds for believing that the detention is necessary in order to secure or preserve evidence or obtain evidence by questioning; that the offence in question is indictable; and that the police investigation is being conducted 'diligently and expeditiously' (s 42). A review of detention must be made after 24 hours (s 42(4)). The police may apply to a magistrates' court for a further period of detention which, if granted, may extend the period of detention to a possible maximum of 96 hours (s 43).

Bail

The Criminal Justice Act 2003 amends the Bail Act 1976 in order to ensure that the law is compliant with Article 5 of the European Convention on Human Rights. Article 5(3) specifically provides for entitlement to trial within a reasonable time or to release pending trial.

Section 41(7) provides that, if a person has not been charged at the expiry of 36 hours, he shall, subject to sub-section 8, be released, either on bail or without bail. The time limit does not apply to persons whose extended detention has been authorised by a senior officer (s 42) or where a successful application has been made to a magistrates' court by the police for continued detention (s 43). The maximum period a person may be detained is 96 hours. Any time spent on bail is not counted as part of the allowable detention period (s 34, 47).

Bail may be subject to conditions, such as reporting to a police station. Exceptionally – as in the case of a Class A drug user whose drug-taking contributed to the offence or where he or she has been assessed and refuses to undergo treatment – bail may be denied.[78] The Criminal Justice Act 2003 enables the police to make an immediate grant of bail ('street bail') where there is no need to deal with the arrested person at a police station. Sections 114–115 Coroners and Justice Act 2009 make the granting of bail more difficult for those charged with imprisonable offences.

---

78 Bail Act 1976, s. 3.

Conditions of detention

The Codes of Practice detail the conditions under which persons may be held. These include no more than one person in a cell, access to toilet and washing facilities, the provision of adequate food and daily exercise. The police may not use more than 'reasonable force' in relation to detainees in preventing escape or causing damage to property. Appropriate medical treatment must be given where necessary. Article 3 of the European Convention on Human Rights, incorporated into domestic law under the Human Rights Act 1998, prohibits torture and inhuman or degrading treatment or punishment.

In *R v Commissioner of Police of the Metropolis* (1999), the House of Lords ruled that authorities, such as the police or prison service, who were entrusted with holding prisoners in custody, had a duty to take reasonable care to prevent them from harming themselves or committing suicide. Where there was a breach of that duty and a suicide occurred, the authorities were not entitled to rely on the defences of *volenti non fit injuria* or *novus actus interveniens* in an action for negligence brought by the estate of the deceased.

The right to legal advice

Under section 58(1) of PACE 'a person arrested and held in custody in a police station or other premises shall be entitled, if he so requests, to consult a solicitor privately at any time'. The right to legal advice is also protected under Article 6 of the European Convention on Human Rights. The right to legal advice under Article 6 arises once suspicion begins to fall on a person being questioned, because that is the point at which the need for protection against self-incrimination comes into play: *Ambrose v Harris; HM Advocate v G; Same v M* (2011). Delay in complying with a request to consult a lawyer is only permitted where the person is being held in connection with an indictable offence and where a senior officer has authorised the delay. The grounds on which delay may be authorised include reasonable grounds for believing that there will be interference with or harm to evidence; that exercising the right would lead to alerting other suspects who have not yet been arrested; or that exercising the right would hinder the recovery of any property obtained as a result of the offence (PACE s. 58(8)).

Legal representation may be crucial to the protection of the suspect from oppressive questioning by the police. Where confessions are obtained by oppression, a guilty verdict may subsequently be set aside.

The right of access to a legal advice is not confined to questioning while in police custody. The question of precisely when a person is entitled to access to a lawyer, and the related question concerning the admissibility of evidence gained through questioning prior to the presence of a lawyer, was considered by the Supreme Court in *Ambrose v Harris (Procurator Fiscal, Oban) (Scotland)* (2011). Having reviewed domestic and Strasbourg jurisprudence, Lord Hope stated that:

> in principle the line as to when access to legal advice must be provided before the person is questioned should be drawn as from the moment that he has been taken into police custody, or his freedom of action has been significantly curtailed. (at para 55)

When a person has been arrested and is being held in custody at a police station, he or she has the right to communicate with one other person 'as soon as practicable' (PACE s. 56).

A delay is only permitted where an officer of the rank of superintendent authorises it, on the basis that 'he has reasonable grounds to believe' that the communication will lead to interference with evidence connected with an indictable offence, or physical injury to other persons, or will lead to alerting of other suspects connected with the offence, and will hinder the recovery of property obtained as a result of the offence (s 56(5)). Section 58(1) also provides that a person who is in police detention 'shall be entitled, if he so requests, to consult a solicitor privately at any time'. Under PACE Code of Practice C, a detainee is to be informed of the right to legal advice, and given the name of a duty solicitor if he or she requires it. The detainee is also entitled to have a solicitor present during questioning. However, where a person is arrested for an indictable offence, and an officer of the rank of superintendent or above so authorises, access to a solicitor may be delayed for up to 36 hours. Under section 56(5A) PACE such a delay may be authorised where the officer is concerned that there is a risk to witnesses or to evidence relating to the case, or where immediate access would hinder the recovery of any property obtained as a result of the offence. The Court of Appeal initially construed section 58(8) narrowly. In **R v Samuel** (1988), it was held that delay in access to legal advice can only be justified on specific grounds which must be substantiated to the satisfaction of the court. However, recent changes under the Proceeds of Crime Act 2002 do suggest that if the person has benefited from their criminal conduct then delay may be more defensible.

The right to inform someone of arrest and detention

A person held in a police station is entitled to inform a relative or friend 'or other person concerned with his welfare' of his arrest without delay, unless such notification would prejudice the investigation of crime or the arrest of other suspects.

The right to silence

In relation to the right to silence, the position of a person who has been arrested is different from that of a citizen before arrest. The reforms introduced under the Criminal Justice and Public Order Act 1994 were amongst the most controversial reforms to the protection of an accused for many years. Those who opposed a weakening of the right to silence based their arguments on the relative vulnerability of the accused, and the need to protect the accused from making statements which might falsely incriminate him or her. Against this concern must be set the argument that when individuals are permitted to remain silent when questioned by the police, advantage of this right is taken by 'professional criminals' who are familiar with the process. The concern has been that such persons will conceal information under questioning and then 'ambush' the prosecution by revealing the information in court.

Sections 34 to 38 of the Criminal Justice and Public Order Act 1994 effected the reforms. Under section 34, where an accused is being questioned under caution and fails to mention any fact later relied on in his evidence or, where the accused has been officially charged with an offence or officially informed that he might be prosecuted for it, he fails to mention any fact which in the circumstances existing at the time 'the accused could reasonably have been expected to mention' when questioned, charged or informed, then the court, in determining whether there is a case to answer, and the court of jury, in determining whether the accused is guilty of the offence charged, may 'draw such inferences from the failure as appear proper'. Following the case of **Murray v United Kingdom** (1996), such inferences may only be drawn when the accused has consulted a lawyer before exercising the right to silence.

Section 35 relates to the accused's silence at trial. If the accused then chooses not to give evidence, or without good cause refuses to answer questions, it is permissible for the court or jury to draw such inferences 'as appear proper from his failure to give evidence or his refusal, without good cause, to answer any question'.

Section 37 relates to the accused's failure to account for his or her presence at a particular place. If a person arrested by a constable was found at a place where the offence was committed, and the officer reasonably believes that his presence was attributable to participation in the offence, and the constable requests him to account for his presence, then, if that person fails to do so, a court, or court or jury, in circumstances (a), (b) and (c) in relation to section 36, may draw 'such inferences from the failure or refusal as appear proper'.

The reliability of evidence[79]

It is central to the protection of the individual that evidence is obtained in a lawful manner. The question arises as to how the law can secure a balance between ensuring that the police operate within the law and the Codes of Practice which supplement the law, and allowing evidence to be used which may have been obtained in a manner not strictly in accordance with the rules but which does prove that a suspect committed a particular crime. If evidence is made inadmissible on the basis of a procedural irregularity, a guilty suspect may go free. On the other hand, if the evidence – however obtained – is admitted, and proves false, there is a danger of innocent suspects being wrongfully convicted. The use of telephone intercepts by the police is authorised under the Police Act 1997, which makes it clear that such intercepts are lawful provided they are authorised under the Act. In addition, the Regulation of Investigatory Powers Act 2000 provides statutory authority for interceptions by the security forces. On intercepts see Chapter 22.

Prior to PACE 1984, the admissibility of evidence was regulated under the common law. A distinction was drawn between illegally obtained evidence which was admissible, and involuntary confessions which were inadmissible on the basis that they might be unreliable. PACE placed the admissibility of evidence on a statutory basis. In relation to confessions, there are four criteria to be employed in determining whether they should be admissible in court. Section 76 regulates confessions. Confessions are admissible into court unless the confession has been obtained by (a) oppression or (b) in consequence of anything said or done which was likely, in the circumstances existing at the time, to render unreliable any confession which might be made by him in consequence thereof. In those circumstances, the court 'shall not allow the confession to be given in evidence against him except in so far as the prosecution proves to the court beyond reasonable doubt that the confession (notwithstanding that it may be true) was not obtained as aforesaid'. Moreover, in any case where the prosecution proposes to give in evidence a confession, the court may, of its own motion, require the prosecution to prove that the confession has not been obtained in the circumstances above. However, where a confession has been partly or wholly excluded on the grounds above, that fact does not affect the admissibility in evidence (a) of any facts discovered as a result of the confession, or (b) where the confession is relevant as showing that the accused speaks, writes or expresses himself in a particular way, of so much of the confession as is necessary to show that he does so.

---

79 The law of evidence is complex: this is no more than a brief introduction.

In relation to the exclusion of 'unfair evidence', section 78 of PACE provides that:

> In any proceedings, the court may refuse to allow evidence on which the prosecution proposes to rely to be given if it appears to the court that, having regard to all the circumstances, including the circumstances in which the evidence was obtained, the admission of the evidence would have such an adverse effect on the fairness of the proceedings that the court ought not to admit it.

Section 78 of PACE is far wider than section 76, and may be relevant to confessions obtained which do not fall within the requirements of section 76. Thus, for example, if a confession is fabricated, the defence will argue that the accused did not make a confession and, accordingly, that 'confession' could not fall under section 76. The power to refuse to allow evidence is discretionary. Where there has been a breach of the rules under the Police and Criminal Evidence Act, and that breach is substantiated to the satisfaction of the court, the question to be determined is whether the breach is substantial or significant, other than where the police have acted in bad faith. Having established whether a breach of the rules is substantial or significant, the court will then look to the nature of the rule in question in relation to the circumstances of the case. Thus, for example, the right to have a legal adviser present will be deemed the more important in relation to a vulnerable suspect who could be easily confused by police questioning.

Summary

Under domestic law, the law relating to assembly and association encompasses a number of different situations: the right to peaceful protest through a gathering or procession and restrictions imposed by the law relating to breach of the peace, obstruction of the police and obstructing the highway. The law seeks to achieve a balance between the right of the individual and group to demonstrate and the right of other citizens to a secure and peaceful society through public order law which confers on the police the power to control assemblies and processions.

Domestic law must be measured against Article 11 of the European Convention on Human Rights, incorporated into domestic law under the Human Rights Act 1998. The domestic courts are required to evaluate the legality of reactions to public disorder according to the European concept of proportionality.

The public order offences such as riot, affray, provocation of violence and harassment must also be considered in relation to public order law.

The powers of the police in relation to arrest and detention and the search and seizure of property are heavily regulated by statute and influenced by the European Convention on Human Rights, particularly Articles 5 (the right to liberty), 6 (the right to fair trial), 8 (the right to privacy) and 11 (the right relating to freedom of association).

Further Reading

Fenwick, H, 'Marginalising human rights: breach of the peace, "kettling", the Human Rights Act and public protest' [2009] *Public Law* 737.
Fenwick, H, *Civil Liberties and Human Rights*, 5th edn, 2011, Abingdon: Routledge-Cavendish.

Nicolson, D and Reid, K, 'Arrest for breach of the peace and the ECHR' [1996] *Criminal Law Review* 764.

Stone, R, The Law of Entry, Search and Seizure, 5th edn, 2013, Oxford: Oxford University Press.

Williams, DGT, 'Processions, assemblies and the freedom of the individual' [1987] *Criminal Law Review* 167.

Williams, V, *Surveillance and Intelligence Law Handbook*, 2006, Oxford: Oxford University Press.

Zander, M, *The Police and Criminal Evidence Act 1984*, 5th edn, 2005, London: Sweet and Maxwell.

Zander, M, *The Police and Criminal Evidence Act 1984. First Supplement to the Fifth Edition*, 2006, London: Sweet and Maxwell.

Chapter 21

State Security

Chapter Contents

Learning Objectives

By the end of this chapter you should be able to:

☐ explain the changing nature of threats to the security of the state;
☐ explain the role/functions of the principal agencies of state/national security;
☐ explain the statutory framework of state security law;
☐ explain the law relating to official secrets;
☐ explain the law relating to interception of communications and communications data;

☐ discuss the definition of terrorism;

☐ explain the issues in the case of **A v Secretary of State for the Home Department** (2004);

☐ explain the role of the Special Immigration Appeals Commission and the concept of closed material proceedings;

☐ evaluate whether the law strikes an appropriate balance between protecting the security of the state and the human rights of individuals;

☐ explain in outline the need for emergency powers and evaluate the exceptional powers granted under the Coronavirus Act 2020 and associated legislation.

Introduction

The security of the state is of the utmost importance to the integrity and well being of a nation and to individual citizens whose rights and freedoms are protected by the security of the state. On the other hand, the rights of citizens may be adversely affected by the exercise of such powers and there exists the potential for governments to hide behind the doctrine of national security in order to prevent scrutiny of executive action. Two principal constitutional questions arise from state security. The first concerns the extent to which arrangements secure some form of balance between the competing needs of state security and protection of the individual. The second issue relates to the manner in which – and extent to which – the government is held accountable for powers exercised in the name of state security, either through supervision of the courts or through the democratic process.

Legal regulation of state security matters is relatively recent. Although the original Official Secrets Act dates from 1911, it has only been since the mid-1980s that statute has regulated the interception of communications,[1] and the Security and Intelligence Services, MI5 and MI6, and the government's signals intelligence organisation, Government Communications Headquarters (GCHQ). Incorporation of Convention rights under the Human Rights Act 1998 necessitated further clarity in the law to ensure that relevant investigatory powers are used in accordance with human rights.

The threat to national security has changed dramatically over the past few decades. In the government's words:

> Our predecessors grappled with the brutal certainties of the Cold War – with an existential danger that was clear and present, with Soviet armies arrayed across half of Europe and the constant threat of nuclear confrontation between the super-powers. Today, Britain faces a different and more complex range of threats from a myriad of sources. Terrorism, cyber attack, unconventional attacks using chemical, nuclear or biological weapons, as well as large scale accidents or natural hazards – any one could do grave damage to our country.[2]

In 2010 the government set up the National Security Council (NSC) and appointed a National Security Adviser.[3] The NSC comprises Ministers and military and intelligence chiefs. It meets weekly and is chaired by the Prime Minister. The NSC is responsible for developing a National Security Strategy (NSS), the first of which was published in 2010.[4] In addition, the govern-

---

1 Interception of Communications Act 1985, Security Services Act 1989, Intelligence Services Act 1994, Regulation of Investigatory Powers Act 2000.
2 Foreword, *A Strong Britain in an Age of Uncertainty: The National Security Strategy*, Cm 7953, 2010. See also *Securing Britain in an Age of Uncertainty: The Strategic Defence and Security Review*, Cm 7948, 2010.
3 The first National Security Adviser was Sir Peter Ricketts, Permanent Under-Secretary at the Foreign and Commonwealth Office.
4 See the National Security Strategy 2015.

ment has published its Strategic Defence and Security Review which sets out how the armed forces, police and intelligence agencies are to be equipped to deal with current and future threats to national security. A parliamentary Joint Committee has been established to review the NSS and the work of the NSC and National Security Adviser.[5] In 2016 a new National Cyber Security Centre (NCSC) was established to focus on combating the cyber threats to security.

The security of public telecommunications networks came to the fore in 2020 with the government decision to prohibit UK communications network providers from buying 5G equipment from the Chinese phone-maker Huawei. The Communications Act 2003 provides the existing legal framework for the regulation of telecommunications by Ofcom, the independent regulator of communications.[6] The Telecommunications (Security) Bill 2019–2021 amends the 2003 Act, introducing a new security framework for the telecoms sector and conferring additional powers on Ofcom to regulate the system.[7] Through recent assessments from the NCSC, the government has identified those countries representing a threat to the UK's security. The Telecommunications Bill gives new national security powers to the government to control communications networks in light of such threats to national security.

In this chapter we consider first the role and powers of the security services and their regulation; then the law relating to official secrets, the interception of communications, emergency powers and the law relating to terrorism.

The Security Services

The terminology

The United Kingdom's internal Security Service is known as MI5 (MI stands for Military Intelligence). The Security Service dealing with matters overseas is the Secret Intelligence Service, or MI6. The government's signals intelligence-gathering headquarters is Government Communications Headquarters, or GCHQ. Special Branch is part of the police forces and has special duties in relation to public order, the gathering of intelligence and combating subversion and terrorism. The operations of MI5 and MI6 are coordinated by the Intelligence Coordinator, based in the Cabinet Office. In addition, there is the armed forces wing of military intelligence which, nowadays, is operative overseas.

The Security Service (MI5)

Until 1989, MI5 was unknown to law. It was not regulated by statute and did not enjoy any special common law powers. MI5 was established in 1909[8] under the royal prerogative as part of the defence forces of the realm. The Service is headed by a Director General who is responsible to the Secretary of State for the Home Office. It is not, however, formally a part of the Home Office and thus occupies a curious constitutional status. The Director General has access to the Prime Minister on matters of importance. Since the ending of the Cold War, approximately 70 per cent of MI5's resources have been devoted to gathering intelligence about terrorism. Moreover, the Security Service Act 1996 now extends the role of MI5 in relation to investigations relating to 'serious crime', particularly the drugs trade.

---

5 See the First Report of the Joint Committee, 2010–2012, HL Paper 265, HC 1384, March 2012.
6 See Part 2.
7 The Bill applies to the whole of the UK. Telecommunications and national security are both reserved matters under the devolution Acts.
8 As part of the War Office. MI5 was originally known as MO5.

Functions of the Service

In 1952, the then Home Secretary, Sir David Maxwell-Fyfe, issued a directive to the Director General outlining the functions of the Service:

> The Security Service is part of the defence forces of the country. Its task is the defence of the Realm as a whole, from external and internal dangers arising from attempts at espionage and sabotage, or from actions of persons and organisations whether directed from within or without the country, which may be judged to be subversive of the state.[9]

The Profumo affair[10]

In 1963 the Secretary of State for War, the Rt Hon John Profumo, resigned from office as a result of him lying to the House of Commons over press disclosures concerning an alleged affair with Christine Keeler, who had associations with a Russian Naval Attaché. The Prime Minister, Harold Macmillan, appointed Lord Denning to inquire into the security aspects of the affair. In his report, Lord Denning stressed that the function of the Security Service:

> is to defend the Realm from dangers which would threaten it as a whole, such as espionage on behalf of a foreign power, or internal organisations subversive of the state. For this purpose it must collect information about individuals and give it to those concerned. But it must not, even at the behest of a Minister or a government department, take part in investigating the private lives of individuals except in a matter bearing on the defence of the Realm as a whole.[11]

Further judicial expression of the role of MI5 is found in the judgment of Taylor J in **R v Secretary of State for the Home Department ex parte Ruddock** (1987).

> The function of the Security Service is the defence of the realm as a whole from, *inter alia*, the actions of persons who and organisations which may be subversive of the state ... A warrant to intercept should only issue where there is reasonable cause to believe that major subversive activity is already being carried on and is likely to injure the national interest. The material reasonably likely to be obtained by the interception must be of direct use to the Security Service in its functions ...
>
> Normal methods of investigation must either have failed or be unlikely to succeed. Interception must be strictly limited to what is necessary to the Security Service's defined functions and must not be used for party political purposes.

Despite such strictures, there have been many charges made against MI5 from journalists and from members of MI5 itself.[12]

---

9 Reproduced in Lord Denning MR's judgment in **R v Home Secretary ex parte Hosenball** (1977).
10 See Denning, 1980, Chapter 3.
11 The *Report on the Security Aspects of the Circumstances Leading up to the Resignation of Mr JD Profumo*, Cmnd 2152, 1963, London: HMSO, caused disquiet. One outcome was the establishment of the Security Commission in 1964. See Leigh and Lustgarten, 1991.
12 See, *inter alia*, Pincher, 1981; West, 1983.

The Security Service Act 1989[13]

The Act defined the functions of MI5 and placed the issuing of warrants under statutory authority. Section 3 of the Act empowered the Home Secretary to issue warrants authorising 'entry on or interference with property'. This power is now contained in sections 5 and 6 of the Intelligence Services Act 1994. The Act also provided, for the first time, a complaints procedure for individuals who are aggrieved by actions of MI5 and a Commissioner charged with the task of reviewing the procedure by which the Home Secretary issues warrants. Section 1 defines the functions of MI5 as being:

> (2) the protection of national security and, in particular, its protection against threats from espionage, terrorism and sabotage, from the activities of agents of foreign powers and from actions intended to overthrow or undermine Parliamentary democracy by political, industrial or violent means.

> (3) It shall also be the function of the Service to safeguard the economic well being of the United Kingdom against threats posed by the actions or intentions of persons outside the British Islands.

In 1992, MI5 assumed responsibility for terrorism related to Northern Ireland. This had previously been under the jurisdiction of Special Branch.

MI5 itself is not defined in the Act. The Secret Intelligence Service – MI6 – did not fall under the control of the Act. Other agencies, such as Special Branch, which carries out many of the functions of MI5 (see below), and GCHQ, are not mentioned in the Act.[14] National security is not defined in the Act. In debate on the Bill, the Home Secretary stated that the 'phrase refers – and can only refer – to matters relating to the survival or well being of the nation as a whole, and not to party-political or sectional or lesser interests'.[15]

The duties of the Director General of MI5 are set out in section 2. These are primarily the responsibility 'for the efficiency of the Service', and for ensuring that the Service collects only information necessary for the proper discharge of its functions, and that it does not take any action to further the interests of any political party. The Director General is required to report annually to the Prime Minister and the Secretary of State for the Home Department, and may otherwise report to them at any time the Director General so decides.

While the Director General is under a duty to report to the Prime Minister, there is no duty imposed on the Prime Minister to lay that report before Parliament. There is thus no parliamentary scrutiny of the Director General's exercise of power. Attempts in both the House of Commons and the House of Lords to introduce such scrutiny failed. However, the Intelligence Services Act 1994,[16] for the first time, introduced parliamentary scrutiny to the work of the Security Services – both MI5 and MI6 – and to GCHQ. Under the Act, a Parliamentary Intelligence and Security Committee was established. On the Committee see further below.

The 1989 Act also introduced a Security Services Commissioner to keep under review the procedure by which warrants were issued by the Home Secretary. That role is now undertaken by the Investigatory Powers Commissioner established under the Investigatory Powers Act 2016. See further below.

---

13 See Leigh and Lustgarten, 1989.
14 This omission is remedied by the Intelligence Services Act 1994, on which see further below.
15 *Hansard*, HC Vol. 143 Col. 1113; see also Vol. 145 Col. 217, and see HL Vol. 357 Col. 947.
16 See Supperstone, 1994.

The Security Service Act 1996

The Security Service Act 1996 extended the function of MI5 to matters concerning 'serious crime'. The government's objective was to enable MI5 to investigate 'organised crime' and 'drug trafficking, money launderers and racketeers'. MI5 acts in a supportive role, and the principal responsibility lies with the conventional law enforcement agencies.[17] However, 'serious crime' is not itself defined in the Act. Nor is the scope of MI5's jurisdiction entirely clear. Moreover, it remains under the operation control of the Director General, and is not accountable to local police authorities, nor are its operations supervised by the Police Complaints Authority.

Authorisation of surveillance and human intelligence sources

Part II of the Regulation of Investigatory Powers Act 2000 (RIPA) provides a statutory basis for the authorisation and use of covert surveillance agents, informants and undercover officers. It is intended to regulate the use of such techniques and 'safeguard the public from unnecessary invasions of their privacy'.

The Covert Human Intelligence Sources (Criminal Conduct) Bill 2019–2021 amends RIPA[18] to provide for the authorisation of criminal conduct in the course of or in connection with the conduct of covert human intelligence sources (CHIS). An authorisation may not be given unless the relevant person believes that it is proportionate and necessary on one of the grounds specified in subsection (5). These grounds are that the authorisation is necessary:

(a)   in the interests of national security;
(b)   for the purpose of preventing or detecting crime or of preventing disorders or
(c)   in the interests of the economic well-being of the UK.

Authorisation may be given by a range of bodies including any police force, the National Crime Agency and Serious Fraud Office; any of the intelligences services or the armed forces; HM Revenue and Customs; the Department of Health and Social Care, the Home Office and the Ministry of Justice and other regulatory bodies.[19] The Investigatory Powers Commissioner must keep the exercise of the power to grant authorisations under review and report on the use of the power in his annual and other reports.[20] The Home Secretary stated that the Bill was compliant with the Human rights Act 1998. The Act will apply to the whole of the UK.

The Secret Intelligence Service (MI6)[21]

MI6 is the branch of the Security Services which deals with information gathering and operations outside the United Kingdom. Whereas a degree of openness has been established concerning the work of MI5, the work of MI6 remains closely guarded. It was only in 1992 that the Prime Minister acknowledged publicly for the first time that MI6 existed. It is MI6 operations – together with military intelligence and the work of GCHQ – which gathers intelligence from around the world through espionage and covert action. In times of war – whether 'hot' or 'cold' – the Service is of inestimable value to the protection of the state against outside

---

17 See HL Deb Cols 398–399, 14 May 1996.
18 Section 26 inserting new subsection 8A and section 29, inserting new section 29B.
19 Competition and Markets Authority, Environment Agency, Financial Conduct Authority, Food Standards Agency and Gambling Commission.
20 Clause 4.
21 See West, 1981; Bloch and Fitzgerald, 1983.

threats.[22] MI6 is under the control of the Foreign and Commonwealth Office, and requires its approval before launching operations. Any politically sensitive matters require the personal approval of the Foreign Secretary. While, in theory, MI6 is confined to operations outside the United Kingdom, and hands responsibility over to MI5 once a matter becomes 'internal', there have been doubts expressed as to whether the boundaries are, or indeed can be, so clearly drawn.

The functions of MI6

The Intelligence Services Act 1994 defined, for the first time, the statutory functions of MI6. Section 1 provides that its function is to obtain and provide information relating to the actions or intentions of persons outside the British Islands, and to perform other tasks relating to the actions or intentions of such persons. Such actions must be related to the objectives defined in the Act, namely in the interests of national security 'with particular reference to defence and foreign policies', in the interests of the nation's economic well being, and assisting in the 'prevention or detection of serious crime'.[23] The Intelligence Services Act 1994 provides for the issue of warrants. Authorisation given by the Secretary of State excludes criminal or civil liability for acts done under the authorisation. The Secretary of State may only grant an authorisation if he is satisfied that the operation is necessary for the 'proper discharge of a function of the Intelligence Service or GCHQ'. The authorisation may relate to particular acts or acts undertaken in the course of a specified operation. It may be limited to a particular person or persons and be subject to conditions. The authorisation must be signed by the Secretary of State or, in an urgent case, a senior official where the Secretary of State has expressly authorised it to be given. Where the authorisation is signed by the Home Secretary it will expire at the end of a six-month period, subject to renewal by the Home Secretary for a further six-month period. Any other authorisation ceases to have effect at the end of the second working day following the day on which it was given.

Operations are authorised by the Secretary of State for Foreign and Commonwealth Affairs, and agents' activities are regulated by administrative internal rules. Where action within the British Islands is required, MI5 may apply to the Home Secretary for a warrant to carry out operations on behalf of MI6. The Terrorism Act 2006 amends the 1994 Act to extend protection for action taken within the British Islands under a warrant authorising action in relation to property outside the British Islands where the property is believed to be outside the British Islands or where there is a mistaken belief as to whether it is within the British Islands and action is taken in respect of that property within five days from the day on which the presence of the property became known.[24]

Government Communications Headquarters (GCHQ)[25]

GCHQ at Cheltenham[26] was established under the royal prerogative, as part of the Foreign and Commonwealth Office.[27] The principal tasks of GCHQ include the security of military and official communications and the provision of signals intelligence (SIGINT) for the government. GCHQ has an annual budget of about £500 million and a staff of some 4,500 personnel, making it the largest of the three intelligence services in the United Kingdom.

---

22 It was with MI6 that Paul Henderson, Managing Director of Matrix Churchill, worked during the Iran–Iraq War – a matter which led to a judicial inquiry. See further Chapter 10.
23 Intelligence Services Act 1994, s. 2.
24 Terrorism Act 2006, s. 31.
25 See Andrew, 1985; West, 1986; Lustgarten and Leigh, 1994.
26 GCHQ has stations abroad including Cyprus.
27 Its original title was the Government Code and Cipher School.

Legal authority for the interception of international communications was first provided under the Official Secrets Act 1920, section 4 of which provided for the interception of 'telegrams' under the warrant of the Home Secretary on the basis of the public interest. The Intelligence Services Act 1994 placed GCHQ on a statutory basis.[28] The statutory duty of MI6 and GCHQ is to exercise its functions:

> in the interests of national security, with particular reference to the defence and foreign policies of Her Majesty's government in the United Kingdom; in the interests of the economic well being of the United Kingdom in relation to the actions or intentions of persons outside the British Islands; or in support of the prevention or detection of serious crime.[29]

The Director of GCHQ is responsible for the 'efficiency of the agency'[30] and has a right of access to the Prime Minister and Secretary of State for Foreign and Commonwealth Affairs. The Director is under a duty to report annually to the Prime Minister.

The Intelligence Services Act 1994, sections 5 to 7, provides statutory authority for warrants issued by the Secretary of State. No warrant may be issued for interference with individual communications within the United Kingdom, unless the interception is designed to uncover information relating to the prevention or detection of terrorism. GCHQ cooperates in signals intelligence matters with its counterparts in Australia, Canada, New Zealand and the United States.

From 1947 until 1984, employees at GCHQ were entitled to belong to trade unions. In January 1984, the Foreign Secretary announced, without warning, that this right was to be removed. GCHQ had experienced disruption for some two years, with a loss of 10,000 working days. In 1983, a GCHQ employee, Geoffrey Prime,[31] was arrested and convicted of spying for the Soviet Union. Both factors – and the government's general desire to curb the power of trade unions – contributed to the banning of unions at GCHQ.[32] The legal outcome of the exercise of the prerogative[33] in banning union membership at GCHQ led to **Council of Civil Service Unions v Minister for the Civil Service** (1985), in which the House of Lords ruled in favour of the government on the basis of national security.[34]

Special Branch[35]

Established in 1883 to deal with problems of security in relation to Ireland, Special Branch rapidly expanded to deal with many security matters. Originally, Special Branch was confined to the Metropolitan Police Force; from 1945, other police forces established Special Branches. Nowadays, each provincial force has its own Special Branch. Special Branch is staffed by ordinary police officers under the direction of the Chief Constable. Much of

---

28 The Australian and Canadian equivalents, the Defence Signals Directorate and Communication Security Executive respectively, remain regulated under the prerogative.

29 Intelligence Services Act 1994, ss 1(2)(a) and also Scotland Act 2012, s. 12(4); and 3(2)(a).

30 Ibid., s. 4.

31 See *Report of the Security Commission: GA Prime*, Cmnd 8876, 1981, London: HMSO.

32 See Young, 1989, Chapter 16.

33 Under the Civil Service Order in Council 1982, Article 4, which empowers the Minister to make regulations and issue instructions regarding the conditions of service of civil service employees. See Forsyth, 1985; cf. Wade, 1985.

34 See further on this case, Chapters 5 and 18. In 1995, the government amended the terms and conditions of employment of staff at GCHQ. Staff are to be restricted to membership of a body whose officers and representatives are appointed from, and answerable only to, GCHQ staff. The conditions of service continue to exclude any form of industrial action: HL Deb Vol. 567 Col. 147, 20 December 1995. Note that in 1997 the Labour government restored trade union rights to employees at GCHQ.

35 See Bunyan, 1977; Allason, 1983.

their work is related to Security Service matters. The principal task of Special Branch is to counter threats of terrorism. In 2005 the Metropolitan Police Special Branch merged with the Anti-Terrorist Branch to form Counter-Terrorism Command (CTC). Other Special Branch functions include jury vetting in cases involving national security or terrorism, providing personal protection and assisting with immigration matters, including keeping watch at airports and seaports.

Military intelligence and the armed forces

In 1940, the Special Operations Executive (SOE) was formed to supplement the work of MI5 and MI6, which were geared principally to work in peace time. Subsequently, the need for special units to operate under military command, and under cover, became perceived as imperative. Originally known as L Detachment, Special Air Service Brigade and, later, simply SAS, the service was introduced on the initiative of David Stirling of the Scots Guards, and approved by the Commander-in-Chief. Members of the SAS were recruited primarily from commandos. A parallel organisation, the Special Boat Service (SBS), was established to complement the work of the SAS.

The SAS has been involved in many operations overseas, in Northern Ireland and on the mainland, principally working against terrorism. It was, for example, the SAS which stormed the Iranian Embassy in London in 1980 to free hostages from terrorists who had occupied the Embassy and, as discussed below, it was the SAS which was dispatched to Gibraltar to arrest suspected IRA terrorists.

The SAS is controlled at both a political level and a practical, operational level. In relation to terrorism, a special committee, COBRA, chaired by the Home Secretary, meets with representatives from the Ministry of Defence, MI5, the Foreign and Commonwealth Office and the SAS to decide the appropriate political and military response. In relation to operational matters, a special unit within the Ministry of Defence, the Joint Operations Centre (JOC), comprising the Foreign Office, Home Office, intelligence services and the SAS, activates the SAS at home or overseas. Exceptionally, the Prime Minister may personally activate the SAS, as in the Iranian Embassy siege. When the SAS is operational, it exercises the powers of the police, although formal authority remains with the police, and the police resume their normal functions once the operation is complete.

Defence intelligence

The Ministry of Defence has its own Defence Intelligence Staff, DIS, which is the main provider of strategic defence intelligence to the Ministry of Defence and the armed forces. The Chief of DIS, a serving three-star officer drawn from any of the three services, reports to the Chief of the Defence Staff and the Permanent Secretary of the Ministry of Defence, and is a member of the Joint Intelligence Committee (on which see further below). DIS is divided into two main parts: the Defence Intelligence Analysis Staff (DIAS) and the Intelligence and Geographic Resources Staff (IGRS). DIAS is responsible for providing global defence intelligence assessments and strategic warning, and draws on classified information provided by GCHQ. IGRS has six discrete policy branches, including the Joint Air Reconnaissance Intelligence Centre, and the Defence and Security Centre and Military Survey.

DIS analyses GCHQ's signals intelligence with a view to assessing the strength of foreign armies and weaponry, including chemical weapons. Defence attachés at foreign embassies act as information gatherers in the field. During the Cold War, the role of DIS was principally intelligence analysis. In times of war, however, that function changes from intelligence gathering and analysis to the provision of information for use of troops on the ground.

The Joint Intelligence Committee[36]

The Joint Intelligence Committee (JIC) coordinates the work of MI6 and GCHQ, and agrees intelligence requirements. The head of the JIC reports to the Cabinet Secretary and, through him, to the Prime Minister. The JIC has around 30 members, drawn on secondment from the Foreign Office and Ministry of Defence. Membership of the JIC includes the Director of GCHQ, the Chief of MI6, Chief of Defence Intelligence Staff and the Director General of MI5. Divided into geographic areas and by functions, the JIC meets weekly to review assessments.

MI5 contributes intelligence to the JIC on national matters. The JIC also makes international assessments, drawing on intelligence from other agencies such as the United States' Central Intelligence Agency (CIA). The intelligence requirements are reviewed annually by the Intelligence Coordinator. Close links are maintained between the JIC and MI5, with its Director General being a member of JIC. MI5 and MI6 also cooperate to avoid duplication and their financial resources in some areas are shared. MI5 also contributes intelligence to the JIC Assessments Staff, and is a major customer for intelligence produced by MI6 and GCHQ, particularly in relation to terrorism.

Interception of Communications and Communications Data[37]

The government's response to the outcome of **Malone v United Kingdom** (1984), in which the absence of statutory authority for intercept warrants was held to have violated Article 8 of the Convention on Human Rights, was to pass the Interception of Communications Act 1985. The Interception of Communications Act 1985 made it a criminal offence to intentionally intercept a communication and provided statutory power to the Secretary of State to issue warrants 'in the interests of national security, or for the purpose of preventing or detecting serious crime or for the purpose of safeguarding the economic well-being of the United Kingdom'.

The provisions relating to interception of communications under the 1985 Act were repealed and replaced by the Regulation of Investigatory Powers Act 2000 (RIPA), which also amended the Police Act 1997 and the Intelligence Services Act 1994. The 2000 Act was prompted by two major concerns. The first was that the 1985 Act regulated intercepts of communications transmitted via mail and by a public telecommunications system, which at the time of the legislation covered most data transmissions. Technological advances since 1985, however, have expanded communications systems – through the internet and email and through telecommunication systems not provided by public telecommunications providers. Also falling outside the 1985 Act was data which was 'encrypted' and required a 'key' to unlock it. The second motivation for reform was the influence of the European Convention on Human Rights and the Human Rights Act 1998. As discussed in more detail in Chapter 18, cases such as **Halford v United Kingdom** (1997) and **Khan v United Kingdom** (2000) had successfully challenged domestic law.

While the interception of communications has been regulated by law since 1985, the question of gaining access to data about communications is more recent. Communications data is the term relating to the time and duration of communications, the email addresses of

---

36 See Adams, 1994, and Urban, 1997.
37 See Report of the Committee on the Interception of Communications (the Birkett Report), Cmnd 283, 1957, London: HMSO; The Interception of Communications in Great Britain, Cmnd 7873, 1980, London: HMSO; The Interception of Communications in Great Britain (the Diplock Report), Cmnd 8191, 1981, London: HMSO; Williams, 1979; Lambert, 1980; The Interception of Communications in the United Kingdom, Cmnd 9438, 1985, London: HMSO; Leigh, 1986; Interception of Communications in the United Kingdom, Cm 4368, 1999, London: HMSO.

the sender and recipient of communications, and the location of the device from which the communication was sent. Communication Service Providers (CSPs) store this data for business and related purposes. For the police and security services, gaining access to that data is critically important in combating crime and terrorism, claiming that it has been a vital factor in 97 per cent of counter-terrorism, serious and organised crime and online child abuse investigations.[38] However, gaining access to communications data has proven controversial with allegations that proposals to regulate access amount to a 'snoopers' charter'.

The law governing the interception of communications, the acquisition and retention of communications data, equipment interference and the acquisition of bulk data is now provided under the Investigatory Powers Act 2016.

The Investigatory Powers Act 2016[39]

The Investigatory Powers Act (IPA) is a complex and wide-ranging Act introduced in response to the review of existing laws relating to investigatory powers by David Anderson QC, and reviews undertaken by the Intelligence and Security Committee (ISC) and the Royal United Services Institute. The IPA updates the legal framework relating to communications and data about communications, although it does not amount to a consolidation of the law.

Section 1 sets out duties and consideration to which public authorities must have regard when taking decisions relating to actions under the Act. Privacy and proportionality are built into section 2: the authority must consider whether the objective sought could be achieved by less intrusive means and the public interest in the protection of privacy. Section 3 makes it an offence to intentionally intercept a communication without lawful authority. The offence applies to communications in the course of transmission via a public or private telecommunications system, or a public postal service.[40] Section 6 defines 'lawful authority'. This includes interceptions authorised by a warrant (see below), or interception with consent, or other lawful interceptions covered under the Act (see sections 44 to 52).

Section 15 regulates warrants. There are three types of warrant: a targeted interception warrant, a targeted examination warrant and a mutual assistance warrant. A targeted interception warrant authorises the person to intercept communications described in the warrant and secondary data. A targeted examination warrant authorises the person to whom it is addressed to select the content of intercepts for examination. A mutual assistance warrant authorises the provision of assistance in relation to intercepts to authorities outside the UK where there is an international mutual assistance agreement.

The authorities who may apply for a warrant include the heads of the three intelligence agencies (MI5, MI6, GCHQ), the National Crime Agency, the Police Services of Northern Ireland and Scotland, HM Revenue and Customs and the Chief of Defence Intelligence. Warrants are issued by the Secretary of State or Scottish Ministers: section 19. The grounds on which a warrant can be issued are the interests of national security, for the purpose of detecting or preventing serious crime, in the interests of the economic well being of the UK or giving effect to a mutual assistance agreement: section 20. The Secretary of State must consider that a warrant is 'necessary' and 'proportionate'. Before the warrant can be issued it must be approved by a Judicial Commissioner: section 23. Section 24 makes provision for urgent cases.

---

38 See Alan Travis, 'Snooper's charter or justified safeguard?' *Guardian*, 10 July 2014.
39 The Act came into force on 31 December 2018.
40 For definitions, see s. 261 IPA.

The Act provides special safeguards in relation to interceptions relating to Members of Parliament and items subject to legal privilege. In relation to MPs, the Secretary of State may not issue a warrant without the approval of the Prime Minister: section 26. In relation to items subject to legal privilege, there must be exceptional and compelling circumstances justifying the warrant: section 27. Protection is also given to confidential journalistic material and the journalistic sources: section 28.

Part 4 of the IPA relates to the retention of communications data, replacing section 1 of DRIPA. Part 5 deals with equipment interference – interfering with computer equipment to obtain communications, information or equipment data. This power was previously regulated under the Intelligence Services Act (ISA) 1994 and in relation to police powers, the Police Act 1997.

Part 6 relates to powers of the security and intelligence agencies to conduct equipment interference and obtain bulk communications data. Where the communications are overseas-related the Act allows the interception in bulk. 'Bulk data' includes two forms of data: 'bulk personal datasets' and 'bulk communications data'.[41] Bulk personal datasets are sets of personal information about a large number of people, most of whom are of no interest to the security services. Examples include the electoral roll, telephone directories and travel-related data. The only data that will be examined relates to those of interest to the services. Bulk communications data is data about communications, not the substance of those communications. Examples include the subscriber to a telephone service or an itemised bill.

Part 8 provides a new oversight regime. The four existing Commissioners – the Intelligence Services Commissioner, the Interception of Communications Commissioner, the Chief Surveillance Commissioner and the Investigatory Powers Commissioner for Northern Ireland – has been replaced by a single new Commissioner: the Investigatory Powers Commissioner (IPC). The IPC has greater powers and resources than previous commissioners. The IPC is a senior judge, supported by a number of Judicial Commissioners (also senior judges) undertaking authorisation or oversight and inspection functions. It is the new system for overseeing the work of the security and intelligence agencies which is the most significant aspect of the Investigatory Powers Act. Although issuing warrants remains in the hands of the executive, for the first time there will be judicial scrutiny and approval of warrants.

The Investigatory Powers Tribunal

The Investigatory Powers Tribunal (IPT) was established under the Regulation of Investigatory Powers Act 2000, section 65. Formerly, the only challenge which could be brought against its decisions was to the European Court of Human Rights. The Investigatory Powers Act 2016 now provides for a right of challenge to the Court of Appeal in England and Wales and the Court of Session in Scotland: section 242. Leave to appeal must be granted either by the IPT or the appellate court, and leave must not be granted unless the appeal would raise an important point of principle or practice or 'there is another compelling reason for granting leave' (section 242 IPA inserting section 67A to RIPA 2000). Decisions of the IPT are amenable to judicial review: the Supreme Court so ruled in **R (Privacy International) v Investigatory Powers Tribunal** (2019).[42] On this see further Chapter 23.

The Tribunal has a duty to investigate allegations against the Security Services and to hear and determine any proceedings brought. The Tribunal is not under a duty to hear or

---

41 Prior to the Act, such data was acquired under s. 94 of the Telecommunications Act 1984.
42 [2019] UKSC 22.

determine any complaint which is frivolous or vexatious. Complaints must be brought within one year after the taking place of the conduct to which it relates, but the Tribunal may, if it is equitable to do so, extend the time. The Tribunal has the power to make an award of compensation. In addition, the Tribunal may order the quashing or cancelling of any warrant or authorisation and/or the destruction of any records of information. The Commissioner assists the Tribunal in connection with the investigation of any matter by the Tribunal. The Tribunal is the only tribunal to which proceedings under section 7 of the Human Rights Act 1998 may be brought against any of the intelligence services, or any other person in relation to conduct by or on behalf of any of those services.[43] The conduct in question must have been conduct by or on behalf of a person holding any office, rank or position with any of the intelligence services, any of Her Majesty's forces, any police force or the National Crime Agency. All persons employed by the Security and Intelligence Services and police are under a duty to disclose or provide to the Commissioner all documents and information as he or she may require for the purposes of an investigation. The Commissioner makes an annual report to the Prime Minister, which is to be laid before each House of Parliament. If it appears to the Prime Minister, after consultation with the Commissioner, that the publication of any matter in an annual report would be contrary to the public interest or prejudicial to national security, the prevention or detection of serious crime or the economic well being of the United Kingdom, the Prime Minister may exclude that matter from the report laid before each House.

The adequacy of the system of the authorisation of warrants and the complaints procedure before the IPT was considered by the European Court of Human Rights in **Kennedy v United Kingdom** (2010).[44] The Court ruled that the system provided sufficient safeguards against abuse, and that the IPT was an independent and impartial body whose members must hold or have held high judicial office or be experienced lawyers and its procedures could not be held to violate the right to fair trial (Article 6). The jurisdiction of the IPT was considered in judicial review proceedings in **R (A) v Director of Establishments of the Security Service** (2009). The Supreme Court ruled that section 65 of RIPA did not amount to an ouster of the jurisdiction of the courts, but rather an allocation of an exclusive jurisdiction by Parliament to the Tribunal. In **Liberty s v Government Communications Headquarters and Others** and **Amnesty International Ltd v Security Service** (2014) the IPT ruled that the law relating to the interception of communications was compliant with human rights law (in particular Article 8, the right to privacy, and Article 10, the right to freedom of expression). The law 'gives individuals an adequate indication as to the circumstances in which and the conditions upon which the Intelligence Services are entitled to resort to interception, or make use of intercept' (at paragraph 159). Claimants were more successful in **Privacy International v Secretary of State for Foreign and Commonwealth Affairs** (2018) in which the IPT held that bulk personal data and bulk communications data had been unlawfully held by GCHQ, MI5 and SIS (MI6).[45]

Parliamentary Scrutiny of the Security Services

National security and the work of the Security Services have traditionally been matters on which governments have declined to provide information to Parliament. Parliamentary Committees repeatedly have been denied the right to investigate MI5[46] although, since 1979,

---

43 Section 7 proceedings relate to applications brought by victims of an alleged violation of Convention rights by a public authority.
44 On this case see also Chapter 18. See also **Knaggs v United Kingdom** (2009).
45 In **Big Brother Watch v UK** (2018) the Court of Human Rights found that aspects of the law in RIPA 2000 violated Article 8 and 10. The case was prior to the IPA 2016 which amends the law. See **Privacy International v Information Commissioner (Dismissed),** [2019] UKFTT 2018_0164 (GRC) 20 December 2019.
46 See HC 773 (1979–1980); HC 242 (1982–1983); HC Deb Col. 444, 12 May 1983.

the Defence Committee has considered aspects of security. In 1994 the Intelligence and Security Committee (ISC) was established, under the Intelligence Services Act, with limited powers to investigate security matters. The ISC, which has a membership of nine, is established to 'examine the expenditure, administration and policy of the Security Service, the Intelligence Service and GCHQ'. Membership is confined to non-ministerial Members of the House of Lords and House of Commons. Members are appointed by the Prime Minister, after consultation with the Leader of the Opposition.[47] The ISC makes an annual report to the Prime Minister, which must be laid before Parliament. A Government Response is published. The annual reports are debated in both Houses of Parliament.

The Committee determines its own procedure. Where the Committee requests information from the Director General of MI5, the Chief of MI6 or the Director of GCHQ, that information must be supplied unless the relevant person informs the Committee that it cannot be disclosed on the basis of sensitivity,[48] or where the Secretary of State has determined that it should not be disclosed.[49]

The Justice and Security Act 2013 strengthens the powers of the Intelligence Security Committee. Its role is expanded to include overseeing aspects of security[50] beyond the remit of the three security services and it also has the power to scrutinise, retrospectively, operational activities of the Agencies. In addition, the Committee has the power to require information from the Agencies which can only be vetoed by the Secretary of State rather than, as at present, by the Heads of the Agencies.

As noted above, currently the ISC makes an annual report to Parliament. Before submitting the Report, it must be sent to the Prime Minister. Matters may be excluded from the Report if the Prime Minister, in consultation with the ISC, considers that the matter would be 'prejudicial to the continued discharge of the functions' of MI5, MI6 or GCHQ.[51]

Official Secrets[52]

The Official Secrets Acts 1911–1989

The first Official Secrets Act arrived on the statute book in 1889. The latest Act is that of 1989. The 1911 Act – which survived virtually untouched until 1989 – was passed through Parliament with one hour's debate and within 24 hours. Motivation for the 1911 Act lay in alleged enemy agent activity in the country.[53] The motives behind the 1989 Act were formed largely from the failure of the earlier Act. As will be seen, section 2 of the 1911 Act provided for numerous offences based on vague criteria of disclosure of information and juries have on occasion refused to convict, even where it was clear from the facts and the law that a guilty verdict should have been returned.[54] Official inquiries into the working of the Act revealed deficiencies.[55]

The **Spycatcher** case also provided motivation for the government to reform the law. In the government's view, members and ex-members of the Security Services should be under

---

47 Intelligence Services Act 1994, s. 10(3).
48 Sensitive information is defined in s. 5 of the Justice and Security Act 2013.
49 Justice and Security Act 2013, s. 4.
50 Such as the Joint Intelligence Organisation, the Office for Security and Counter-Terrorism in the Home Office and Defence Intelligence in the Ministry of Defence.
51 Justice and Security Act 2013, s. 3.
52 See Robertson and Merrills, 1993; Hooper, 1988; Ewing and Gearty, 1990.
53 See Andrew, 1985; French, 1978; Le Queux, 1915.
54 See **R v Ponting** (1985), discussed in Chapter 3, p. 61.
55 See *Departmental Committee on Section 2 of the Official Secrets Act 1911*, Cmnd 5104, 1972, London: HMSO; White Paper, *Reform of Section 2 of the Official Secrets Act 1911*, Cmnd 7285, 1978, London: HMSO.

a life-long duty of confidentiality in respect of their work. One defect in the 1911 Act lay in the duty of – and hence liability for – non-disclosure enduring only for the duration of employment.

Section 1 of the 1911 Act provides penalties for spying. It is an offence to enter into top-secret establishments or to collect, publish or communicate any official document (which includes official code words, passwords, sketches, plans, models, articles or notes) or information which might be useful to a potential enemy, if the actions are carried out 'for any purpose prejudicial to the safety or interest of the state'. The accused has no 'right to silence' and a trial may be held in secret, or partly in secret. Section 2 of the Act reversed the normal burden of proof from the prosecution to the defence. It was not necessary for the prosecution to prove that the accused was guilty of any particular act 'tending to show a purpose prejudicial to the safety or interest of the state'. Guilt could be established if 'from the circumstances of the case, or his conduct, or his known character as proved, it appears that his purpose was a purpose prejudicial to the safety or interest of the state'. Moreover, any information or document handed over to another person, without lawful authority, could 'be deemed to have been made, obtained, collected, recorded or communicated for a purpose prejudicial to the safety or interests of the state unless the contrary is proved'. Penalties for espionage are swingeing. George Blake, a former MI6 officer convicted of espionage, was sentenced to 42 years' imprisonment.[56] In 1985, Michael Bettany, a former MI5 officer, was convicted of attempting to pass official information to the Russians and sentenced to 23 years' imprisonment. Geoffrey Prime was sentenced to 35 years for disclosing material while employed at GCHQ.[57] Not all offences will lead to a prosecution. Neither Kim Philby nor Anthony Blunt was prosecuted. Instead, each was offered immunity from prosecution in return for a confession, an offer declined by Kim Philby, who fled to Moscow.

Section 2 of the 1911 Act (now reformed under the Official Secrets Act 1989) prohibited the disclosure of any official information without authorisation to anyone not authorised to receive it, and covered some one million public servants and a further one million government contractors. It also covered the retention of any document by a person not entitled to retain the same, failure to take reasonable care of a document and receiving any document without authority. Section 2 was capable of generating over 2,000 different criminal offences, including the disclosure of the number of cups of tea consumed in the MI5 canteen.[58]

Reform of the Official Secrets Act 1911[59]

In 1971 a Committee of Inquiry, headed by Lord Franks, was established to review the working of section 2. Reporting in 1972, the Committee was highly critical of section 2 and recommended that it be reformed.[60] It was not, however, until 1989 that reform took place.[61]

---

56 Blake subsequently escaped from prison after 25 years, with the help of friends.
57 **R v Prime** (1983).
58 *Departmental Committee on Section 2 of the Official Secrets Act 1911*, Cmnd 5104, 1972, London: HMSO, para. 16, and see Robertson and Merrills, 1993. See **Chandler v Director of Public Prosecutions** (1964); **R v Aitken** (1971). For an account, see Aitken, 1971.
59 See, *inter alia*, Hooper, 1988; White Paper, *Reform of Section 2 of the Official Secrets Act 1911*, Cm 408, 1988, London: HMSO. See also the White Paper, *Open Government*, Cm 2290, 1993, London: HMSO, discussed in Chapter 10.
60 *Departmental Committee on Section 2 of the Official Secrets Act 1911*, Cmnd 5104, 1972, London: HMSO.
61 See the White Paper, *Reform of Section 2 of the Official Secrets Act 1911*, Cmnd 7285, 1978, London: HMSO; Green Paper, *Freedom of Information*, Cmnd 7520, 1979, London: HMSO; White Paper, *Reform of Section 2 of the Official Secrets Act 1911*, Cm 408, 1988, London: HMSO.

The major provisions of the Official Secrets Act 1989

Section 2 of the Official Secrets Act 1911 was repealed and replaced by the 1989 Act. Rather than the catch-all section 2 of the 1911 Act, the 1989 Act created offences directed to specific groups of people and information. In relation to most areas, the prosecution must prove both that the information has been unlawfully transmitted and that the disclosure of the information is 'damaging'. The concept of 'damaging disclosure' has, however, not been incorporated into section 1, which relates to security and intelligence matters. With this exception, there is a presumption of harm built into the Act. A further exception relates to those who are not Crown servants or government contractors in relation to whom the prosecution will have to prove – in addition to the harm test – that the defendant knew or had good reason to know that the specific harm was likely to have been caused. In relation to such information, the disclosure in itself is an offence. There is no longer a defence of 'public good' which applied under section 2 of the 1911 Act.

Security and intelligence

Under section 1 of the 1989 Act, any person who is, or has been, a member of the Security and Intelligence Services, and any other person who is informed that the provision of the Act applies to him, is guilty of an offence if 'without lawful authority' he discloses 'any information, document or other article related to security or intelligence'. The offence is committed irrespective of whether or not the disclosure is damaging. A person who is, or has been, a Crown servant or government contractor will be guilty of an offence if he makes a 'damaging disclosure of any information, document or other article relating to security or intelligence'. In **R v Shayler** (2001), the House of Lords ruled that a former member of the Security Services was not entitled to rely on the defence that the disclosure was made in the public or national interest. There was no contravention of Article 10 of the European Convention through the restriction of members and former members of the security forces disclosing information.[62]

Security and intelligence are defined as being the work of, or work in support of, the Security and Intelligence Services. A disclosure is defined as damaging if 'it causes damage to the work of, or of any part of, the Security or Intelligence Services' or if unauthorised disclosure would be likely to cause such damage. A charge may be defended if the person in question can prove that, at the time of the alleged offence, 'he did not know, and had no reasonable cause to believe' that the unauthorised disclosure related to security or intelligence or, in the case of an offence under subsection (3), he did not know, or had no reasonable cause to believe, that the disclosure would be damaging.

Defence

Any unauthorised damaging disclosure of information, documents or other articles relating to defence is an offence.[63] A disclosure is damaging if:

> it damages the capability of any part of the armed forces, or leads to loss of life or injury to the forces, or endangers the interests of the United Kingdom abroad, or obstructs the promotion or protection of those interests, or is likely to have any of these effects.

---

62 In **R (A) v Director of Establishments of the Security Service** (2009), the Court of Appeal ruled that the Investigatory Powers Tribunal (IPT) was the 'only appropriate tribunal' for the purposes of proceedings under s. 7(1)(a) of the Human Rights Act 1998 brought against one of the intelligence services (the claimant was a former member of the Security Service who had been refused permission to publish a book relating to his work).
63 Official Secrets Act 1989, s. 2.

It is a defence to prove that the person did not know, and had no reasonable cause to believe, that such disclosure would be damaging.

Section 4 defines 'defence' as including the

> size, shape, organisation, logistics, order of battle, deployment, operations, state of readiness and training of the armed forces of the Crown; weapons, stores or other equipment of those forces; defence policy and strategy, and military planning and intelligence; and plans and measures for the maintenance of essential supplies and services that are, or would be, needed in time of war.

International relations

Under section 3 of the 1989 Act, an unauthorised damaging disclosure, by a person who is or has been a Crown servant or government contractor, of any information, document or other article relating to international relations, or confidential information obtained from another state or international organisation is an offence. A disclosure is damaging if it 'endangers the interests of the United Kingdom abroad, or seriously obstructs the promotion or protection of those interests or endangers the safety of British citizens abroad', or 'is likely to have any of those effects'. It is a defence to prove that the accused did not know, and had no reasonable cause to believe, that the information fell within subsection (1), or that its disclosure would be damaging.

In **R v Keogh** (2007) the Court of Appeal considered the burden of proof relating to unauthorised disclosures contrary to sections 2 and 3 of the Official Secrets Act 1989. The defendant, employed in the government communications centre, photocopied a letter which recorded discussions between the Prime Minister and the President of the United States relating to political, diplomatic and defence issues relating to Iraq, and showed it to his co-defendant who was a researcher for a Member of Parliament who opposed the Iraq war. The co-defendant placed the photocopy in the MP's papers. The section 2(3) defence, given its ordinary meaning, reverses the burden of proof. Lord Phillips of Worth Matravers CJ cited Lord Bingham in **R v Sheldrake** (2005): 'The task for the court is never to decide whether a reverse burden of proof should be placed on a defendant, but always to assess whether a burden enacted by Parliament unjustifiably infringes the presumption of innocence'. The Court of Appeal concluded that the 1989 Act could operate effectively without the imposition of the reverse burden of proof which 'would be disproportionate and unjustifiable'. Those sections were incompatible with Article 6 of the Convention and should be 'read down' to make them compatible.

Crime and special investigation powers

Section 4 of the Act makes it an offence to disclose, without lawful authority, information, documents or other articles which result in the commission of an offence, or facilitate an escape from legal custody or impede the prevention or detection of offences or the apprehension or prosecution of suspected offenders, or disclosures which are likely to have those effects. It is a defence to a charge to prove that the person did not know, and had no reasonable cause to believe, that the disclosure related to prohibited materials or that disclosure would have any of the damaging effects mentioned.

Authorised disclosures under the Act

A disclosure by a Crown servant (or other notified person) is authorised if it is made with lawful authority and if (and only if) the disclosure is made in accordance with a person's official duty.[64] In relation to government contractors, a disclosure is lawful only if it is made with

---

64 Official Secrets Act 1989, s. 7.

official authorisation or for the purposes of his functions relating to the contract and without contravening an official restriction. In relation to any other person, a disclosure is lawful only if it is made to a Crown servant for the purposes of his functions as such, or in accordance with official authorisation. It is a defence to a charge to prove that, at the time of disclosure, the person believed that he had lawful authority to make the disclosure in question.

The duty to safeguard information

Under section 8, Crown servants and government contractors are under a duty to protect any information, document or other article which it would be an offence to disclose under the Act. It is an offence for a Crown servant to retain an article contrary to his or her official duty, and for a government contractor to fail to comply with a request for the return or disposal of the information or document, or to fail to take such care of the information or document as 'a person in his position may be reasonably expected to take'. It is a defence for a Crown servant to prove that he believed he was acting in accordance with his official duty and 'had no reasonable cause to believe otherwise'.

Prosecutions

No prosecution may be instituted other than with the consent of the Attorney General.[65]

Penalties

A person convicted of an offence under the Act, other than under section 8(1), (4) or (5), shall, on indictment, be liable to imprisonment for a two-year term, or a fine, or both. On summary conviction, a person is liable to up to a six-month term of imprisonment, or a fine, or both. A person convicted under section 8(1), (4) or (5) is liable, on summary conviction, to a term of imprisonment of up to three months, or a fine, or both.

The catch-all nature of section 2 of the Official Secrets Act 1911 has thus been reformed. Whether, in fact, the 1989 Act is less swingeing in scope is another matter. Geoffrey Robertson QC states that the scope of the 1989 legislation, 'while not the theoretical dragnet of the old section 2, is none the less considerable'.[66]

 ## SELF-TEST QUESTIONS

Outline the role and functions of MI5, SIS (MI6) and GCHQ. Which statutes regulate the three agencies?

Explain the concept of 'damaging disclosure' under the Official Secrets Act 1989. To what extent is this an improvement on the 1911 Official Secrets Act?

Restrictions on the media: defence advisory notices[67]

The Official Secrets Acts of course apply to information which might be revealed by the press, and the doctrine of breach of confidence also represents a fetter on freedom of information. A further restriction on press freedom is the Defence and Security Media Advisory (DSMA) Notice system. The aim of the DSMA system is 'to prevent inadvertent public disclosure of

---

65 Official Secrets Act 1989, s. 9.
66 Robertson and Merrills, 1993. See also Palmer, 1990.
67 See *The 'D' Notice System*, Cmnd 3312, 1967, London: HMSO; *Report of the Committee of Privy Councillors Appointed to Inquire into 'D' Notice Matters*, Cmnd 3309, 1967, London: HMSO; *Third Report of the Defence Committee: The 'D' Notice System*, HC 773 (1979–1980), London: HMSO; *Ministry of Defence: The Defence Advisory Notices: A Review of the 'D' Notice System*, MOD Open Government Document 93/1993.

information that would compromise UK military and intelligence operations and methods; or put at risk the safety of those involved in such operations; or lead to attacks that would damage the critical national infrastructure and/or endanger lives'.[68] The basis for the system is entirely extralegal and voluntary. No formal sanction exists for failure to comply with a DA Notice. The system was established in 1912. A Defence Advisory (DA) Notice Committee was established, chaired by a Permanent Under Secretary of the Ministry of Defence, which comprised both newspaper editors and civil servants.[69] Today the Defence and Security Media Advisory Committee is chaired by the Director General Security Policy, Ministry of Defence. There are four members representing Government departments (Home Office, Ministry of Defence, Foreign and Commonwealth Office and the Cabinet Office). In addition, there are 17 members nominated by the media, including representatives from the press, broadcasting and publishers. Compliance with a DA Notice will not affect any right to bring legal action against a newspaper,[70] and neither will non-compliance. The system was reviewed in both 1962 and 1980, when retention of the system was recommended. Further reviews were conducted in 2000 and 2015. In the 2015 review the importance of the wider concept of security was recognised and the name changed from the Defence Advisory system to the Defence and Security Media Advisory system. There are five Standing Notices. The current DA Notices cover Military Operations, Plans and Capabilities; Nuclear and Non-nuclear Weapons and Equipment; Military Counter-Terrorist Forces, Special Forces and Intelligence Agency Operations, Activities and Communication Methods and Techniques; Physical Property and Assets; Personnel and their Families who work in Sensitive Positions.

Judicial attitudes to pleas of national security

Where national security is pleaded by the government in judicial review proceedings, the courts are exceedingly reluctant to challenge the executive. Whilst this is, *prima facie*, regrettable from the point of view of the aggrieved citizen, it is explained – although not necessarily justified – by the relationship between the executive, legislature and judiciary. As seen in Chapter 4, the doctrine of separation of powers, whilst not strictly adhered to under the United Kingdom's constitution, is respected by the courts. In no area of policy is this respect more clearly demonstrated than in matters of national security, which will frequently, but not inevitably, be linked to the exercise of the royal prerogative. In Chapter 5, the judiciary's cautious approach to review of the prerogative was examined, and it was there seen that the prerogative ensures for the executive a wide and inadequately defined area of power which is largely immune from judicial review. It will be recalled that in **Council of Civil Service Unions v Minister for Civil Service** (1985) (the **GCHQ** case) the House of Lords ruled that the courts have jurisdiction to review the exercise of executive power irrespective of whether the source of power was statutory, or under the common law prerogative.

Notwithstanding that claim, the House of Lords conceded that matters of national security fell within the class of powers deemed 'non-justiciable' by the courts (by which is meant that the subject matter is one more appropriately controlled by the executive accountable to Parliament rather than the courts of law).[71] However, the incorporation of Convention rights under the Human Rights Act 1998 extends judicial protection. The Convention protects, *inter alia*, the right to liberty and the right to fair trial. In **A v Secretary of State for the Home Department**

---

68 https://dsma.uk/how-the-system-works/.
69 Then known as the Admiralty, War Office and Press Committee; now the Defence Press and Broadcasting Advisory Committee.
70 As occurred in 1970 when *The Sunday Telegraph* was prosecuted under the Official Secrets Act 1911 for disclosure of material supplied by Jonathan Aitken.
71 On the definition of harm to national security see **Secretary of State for the Home Department v Rehman** (2001).

(2004) the House of Lords took a robust approach to the power of the executive to detain non-British terrorist suspects, declaring that the relevant statutory provision was incompatible with the right to liberty protected under Article 5 (see further page 579).

Detention in wartime

In **Liversidge v Anderson** (1942), the House of Lords refused[72] to review the Home Secretary's power of detention under the Defence of the Realm Acts. It will be recalled from Chapter 5 that the regulation provided that the Minister had power to order the detention of persons whom he 'had reasonable cause to believe' to be of hostile origin or associations and 'in need of subjection to preventative control'.[73]

Emergency Powers

While, in peace time, the responsibility for maintaining order and detecting crime lies with the police forces, in times of emergency, further assistance will be needed if order is to be restored.

The Civil Contingencies Act 2004

The Civil Contingencies Act 2004 confers on the executive wide-ranging powers to deal with emergency situations. The Act is separated into two main parts: Part 1 making provision for local arrangements for civil protection and Part 2 providing for emergency powers. An 'emergency' is broadly defined.[74] In relation to Part 1 of the Act, it is defined as 'an event or situation' which threatens serious damage to human welfare, serious damage to the environment of a place in the United Kingdom, or war or terrorism which threatens serious damage to the security of the United Kingdom. In relation to Part 2, an emergency is defined in the same way but relates to emergencies in the United Kingdom or in a part or region rather than a 'place'. In both Parts of the Act, an event or situation which threatens damage to human welfare only if it involves loss of human life; human illness or injury; homelessness; damage to property; disruption of a supply of money, food, water, energy or fuel; disruption of a system of communication; disruption of facilities for transport; or disruption of services relating to health. An event or situation threatening damage to the environment involves contamination of land, water or air with biological, chemical or radioactive matter, or disruption or destruction of plant life or animal life.

The Act confers on the executive the power to amend the definition of an emergency by amending, by order, the list of events or situations which may threaten damage to human welfare. Any such orders are subject to the affirmative resolution procedure. Under Part 2, section 20, emergency regulations may be made by Order in Council if the conditions in section 21 are satisfied. Those conditions are that an emergency has occurred, is occurring or is about to occur, that it is necessary to make provision for the purpose of preventing, controlling or mitigating an aspect or effect of the emergency, and that the need for such provision is urgent. Emergency regulations lapse 30 days after they are made unless an earlier date

---

72 Lord Atkin dissenting. Note that Lord Atkin's dissent was accepted as a correct statement of common law in **R v Inland Revenue Commissioners ex parte Rossminster Ltd** (1980).

73 On deportation see further below. On extradition see Chapter 18.

74 Civil Contingencies Act 2004, ss 1 and 19.

is specified. The regulations are renewable.[75] They must be laid before Parliament as soon as reasonably practicable and lapse at the end of seven days unless each House of Parliament passes a resolution approving them.

The Act imposes duties on public authorities to assess and make provision for emergencies, and to provide information and assistance to the public.

The use of the armed forces in times of unrest

The use of troops in 1911 in South Wales is the only occasion on which troops have been brought in to assist the police. During the miners' strike 1984–1985, the troops were not called in. Instead, the police forces coordinated their operations in order to contain the situation successfully. Where troops are deemed necessary to aid the police, it is the Home Secretary, acting on the request of the Chief Officer of police, who has responsibility. As was seen in Chapter 5, the Home Secretary has the power to issue weapons to police forces for the quelling of civil disturbance.[76]

In time of war

The Defence of the Realm Act 1914–1915 conferred wide powers on the Crown to make regulations for ensuring public safety and defence of the realm. The courts have ruled that these broad powers include the power to detain a person without trial on the basis of his or her hostile associations.[77] The power to regulate supplies does not, however, include the power to impose a tax upon produce.[78] Specific power to impose charges in relation to matters regulated under Defence Regulations was conferred under the Emergency Powers (Defence) Act 1939. Under the regulations, the Home Secretary was given power to detain persons whom he had reasonable cause to believe came within certain categories. The power was regarded by the courts as reviewable.[79] Under the Emergency Powers (Defence) (No 2) Act 1940, powers were conferred compulsorily to direct labour in support of the war effort. Compulsory military service was introduced under National Service Acts.

Terrorism

The United Kingdom strategy for countering terrorism is CONTEST. This strategy is based around four main areas of work:

- Pursue: the investigation and disruption of terrorist attacks.
- Prevent: work to stop people becoming terrorists or supporting terrorism and extremism.
- Protect: improving protective security to stop a terrorist attack.
- Prepare: working to minimise the impact of an attack and to recover from it as quickly as possible.

---

75 Ibid., s. 26.
76 See **R v Secretary of State for the Home Department ex parte Northumbria Police Authority** (1988).
77 See **R v Halliday ex parte Zadig** (1917).
78 See **Attorney General v Wilts United Dairies Ltd** (1921) and the War Charges Validity Act 1925.
79 See **Liversidge v Anderson** (1942).

The Terrorism Act 2000 reformed and extended existing terrorist legislation.[80] Whereas the Prevention of Terrorism (Temporary Provisions) Act 1989 required annual renewal, the Terrorism Act has permanent status.

The terrorist attacks on New York and Washington in September 2001 prompted a swift response from the British government. The Anti-Terrorism, Crime and Security Act 2001 built on existing legislation in order to ensure that the security forces have the necessary powers to combat terrorist threats to the United Kingdom. The 2001 Act aimed to cut off terrorist funding and to enable government Departments and agencies to collect and share information in the attempt to avert threats. The Act also altered immigration procedures, and provided additional powers for the detention of suspected international terrorists who have been certified by the Secretary of State as a threat to national security. In *A v Secretary of State for the Home Department* (2004) a panel of nine Law Lords (Lord Walker dissenting) ruled that measures empowering the Home Secretary to detain indefinitely, without charge or trial, non-nationals whom he suspected of international terrorist activity, but whom he could not deport, were incompatible with the United Kingdom's European Convention obligations. The House of Lords made a declaration of incompatibility under section 4 of the Human Rights Act that section 23 of the Anti-terrorism, Crime and Security Act 2001 was incompatible with Articles 5 and 14 of the Convention.

The 2001 Act also enhanced the security of nuclear and aviation industries and aimed to improve the security of dangerous substances which may be used by terrorists. It extended police powers and facilitated greater cooperation between police forces. Controversially, the Act also provided for extended powers of disclosure of information by public authorities to the police and security agencies involved in criminal investigations.

See further
Chapter 18.

The law relating to terrorism must be seen within the wider geographical context as the world seeks to counter the globalisation of terror. In 2001 the United Nations (UN) adopted Security Council Resolution 1373 on the fight against terrorism and there are 12 UN terrorism conventions setting standards for international action:

- to prevent and combat terrorist acts such as bombing, hijacking and hostage-taking;
- to prevent and combat terrorist financing, recruitment and supply of weapons; and
- to extradite or prosecute terrorists and deny them safe haven.

Within the European context, both the Council of Europe and the European Union have been active. In 2003 the Council of Europe set up the Committee of Experts on Terrorism (CODEXTER) with the responsibility of coordinating and monitoring terrorism. Under the auspices of the Committee of Experts two new Conventions against terrorism have been drafted and opened for signature by Member States: the *Council of Europe Convention on the Prevention of Terrorism* and the *Council of Europe Convention on the Laundering, Search, Seizure and Confiscation of the Proceeds from Crime and on the Financing of Terrorism*.[81] In 2002 the Council of the European Union adopted the Council Framework Decision on Combating Terrorism.[82] Article 1 of the Framework Decision requires all Member States to take the necessary action to ensure that terrorist acts committed with the aim of seriously intimidating a population, or unduly compelling a government or international organisation to perform or abstain from performing any act, or

---

80 It repealed the Prevention of Terrorism (Temporary Provisions) Act 1989, the Prevention of Terrorism (Additional Powers) Act 1996, the Northern Ireland (Emergency Provisions) Act 1996 and the Northern Ireland (Emergency Provisions) Act 1998, and made minor amendments to other relevant Acts. See Inquiry into *Legislation Against Terrorism*, Cm 3420, 1996, London: Stationery Office; *Legislation Against Terrorism*, Cm 4178, 1998, London: Stationery Office.
81 Council of Europe Treaty Series 196 and 198 respectively (2005).
82 2002/475/JHA.

seriously destabilising or destroying the fundamental political, constitutional, economic or social structures of a country or international organisation are defined as criminal offences under domestic law. In December 2020 a security agreement was reached with the EU covering a wide range of security and law enforcement measures.

Defining terrorism

Whereas under the Prevention of Terrorism (Temporary Provisions) Act 1989, terrorism was defined as the 'use of violence for political ends, and included the use of violence for the purpose of putting the public or any section of the public in fear',[83] section 1 of the Terrorism Act 2000[84] adopted a wider definition, namely:

(1)   In this Act 'terrorism' means the use or threat of action where –

    (a)   The action falls within subsection (2),

    (b)   the use or threat is designed to influence the government or an international governmental organization or to intimidate the public or a section of the public, and

    (c)   the use or threat is made for the purpose of advancing a political, religious, racial or ideological cause.

(2)   Action falls within this subsection it if –

    (a)   involves serious violence against a person,

    (b)   involves serious damage to property,

    (c)   endangers a person's life, other than that of the person committing the action,

    (d)   creates a serious risk to the health or safety of the public, or a section of the public, or

    (e)   is designed seriously to interfere with or seriously to disrupt an electronic system.

Action includes action outside the United Kingdom, and references to any person or to property mean any person or property wherever situated, and a reference to the public includes a reference to the public of a country other than the United Kingdom.[85] This definition is intended to cover not just terrorism for political ends but terrorism undertaken for religious or ideological motives, which, while not necessarily violent in themselves, are capable of having widespread adverse effects. Examples cited are of disruption to key computer systems or interference with the supply of water or power where life, health or safety may be put at risk. In *Secretary of State for the Home Department v Rehman* (2002), it was held that the promotion of terrorism against any state by an individual in the United Kingdom was capable of being a threat to the national security of the United Kingdom, and accordingly deportation in the interests of national security for terrorist activities which were not targeted against the

---

83 Prevention of Terrorism (Temporary Provisions) Act 1989, s. 20.
84 As amended by s. 34 of the Terrorism Act 2006 and s. 75 of the Counter-Terrorism Act 2008.
85 Terrorism Act 2000, s. 1(2).

United Kingdom or its citizens was lawful under the Immigration Act 1971. Lord Hoffmann expressed the view that judges should respect the decisions of Ministers of the Crown in relation to whether national security is threatened. In **R v Gul** (2013) the Supreme Court considered the definition of terrorism. In the Court of Appeal it had been stated that the definition included those who encouraged terrorism by glorifying attacks on the armed forces. On appeal it was argued that the definition was so broad that exceptions should be read into it. For the Crown it was argued that terrorism could not be narrowly defined and the Parliament had deliberately adopted a very broad definition and that the requirement of the consent of the Director of Public Prosecutions (or for conduct abroad the Attorney General) protected against improper prosecutions. The Supreme Court accepted that a wide interpretation 'accords with the natural meaning of the words used' in the Acts. The Court nevertheless expressed concerns over the broad discretion conferred in relation to prosecutions and the wide power conferred on the police and security services. It was, however, for Parliament – not the Court – to decide whether there should be a narrowing of the definition.

Proscribed organisations

The Terrorism Act 2000 governs proscribed organisations, listed under Schedule 2. Part II of the Terrorism Act 2006 amends the 2000 Act to cover organisations which promote or encourage terrorism. The 2006 Act also provides that an organisation listed in Schedule 2 which is operating under a different name shall be treated as the listed organisation (section 22). The Secretary of State may add or remove an organisation from the list, but may only add an organisation if he believes that the organisation is concerned in terrorism.[86] An organisation is concerned in terrorism if it commits or participates in acts of terrorism, prepares for terrorism, promotes or encourages terrorism or is otherwise concerned in terrorism.[87] The Act introduces a Proscribed Organisations Appeal Commission (POAC),[88] to which individuals or organisations may appeal, having first applied to the Secretary of State for de-proscription and been refused.[89]

The Commission must allow an appeal if it considers that the Secretary of State's decision was flawed when considered in the light of the principles applicable on an application for judicial review.[90] If the appeal is allowed, the Secretary of State must lay a draft order before Parliament or, in urgent cases, make an order removing the organisation from the list.[91] Appeals from the POAC, on a question of law, lie to the Court of Appeal, Court of Session or Court of Appeal in Northern Ireland. An appeal may only be brought with the consent of the Commission or, where the Commission refuses permission, with the permission of the relevant court.[92] If an appeal to the POAC is successful, and an order made de-proscribing the organisation, any individual convicted of an offence in relation to the organisation, provided the offence was committed after the date of the Secretary of State's refusal to de-proscribe, may appeal against his conviction to the Court of Appeal or Crown Court.[93] In order that individuals seeking de-proscription should not be deterred from

---

86 Terrorism Act 2000, s. 3.
87 Ibid., s. 3(5).
88 Ibid., s. 5, as amended by s. 22 of the Terrorism Act 2006.
89 *Terrorism Act 2000*, s. 4, as amended by s. 22 of the Terrorism Act 2006.
90 See Chapter 23. See **Alton v Secretary of State for the Home Department** (2008).
91 Terrorism Act 2000, s. 5.
92 Ibid., s. 6.
93 Ibid., s. 7, as amended by s. 22 of the Terrorism Act 2006. Section 8 makes equivalent provision for Scotland and Northern Ireland. Section 9 makes provision for the Human Rights Act 1998, s. 7, to apply to appeal proceedings brought before the POAC, in relation to s. 5(4) and (5), ss 6 and 7 (appeals to a court of law from a decision of the POAC), and paras 4–8 of Sched. 3 (relating to procedure before the POAC).

pursuing an appeal or from instituting proceedings under section 7 of the Human Rights Act 1998, through a risk of prosecution for offences in relation to a proscribed organisation, section 10 of the Terrorism Act provides that evidence cannot be relied on in criminal proceedings for such an offence except as part of the defence case. In **R v Z (Attorney General for Northern Ireland's Reference)** (2005) the House of Lords considered the definition of a proscribed organisation under the 2000 Act. Z and others had been charged with belonging to a proscribed organisation, being an organisation listed in Schedule 2 or, by section 3(1)(b) one that operated 'under the same name as an organisation listed in that Schedule'. Z belonged not to the Irish Republican Army listed in the Schedule, but to the Real Irish Republican Army, a splinter group formed in 1997, and was convicted. The Court of Appeal dismissed Z's appeal, ruling that in the interpretation of a controversial provision in a statute, it had to be read in the context of the statute as a whole and the historical context of the situation which led to its enactment. Faced with rival claims as to who represented the IRA, a blanket description had been adopted to embrace all 'emanations, manifestations and representations of that organisation': accordingly the term 'IRA' encompassed the Real Irish Republican Army.

Sections 11 to 12 relate to offences concerning membership of and support for a proscribed organisation. A person guilty of an offence under these sections shall be liable, on conviction on indictment, to a term of imprisonment not exceeding ten years, to a fine or to both, and, on summary conviction, to a term of imprisonment not exceeding six months, to a fine not exceeding the statutory maximum or to both. It is a defence for a person charged with an offence under section 11(1) to prove that the organisation was not proscribed on the last occasion on which he became a member or began to profess to be a member, and that he has not taken part in the activities of the organisation at any time while it was proscribed. Section 12 relates to the support for a proscribed organisation and makes it an offence to invite support and/or to arrange, manage or assist in arranging or managing a meeting and/or to address such a meeting. A 'meeting' means a meeting of three or more persons, whether or not the public are admitted.

The wearing of an item of clothing, or wearing, carrying or displaying an article in a public place, in such a way or in such circumstances as to arouse reasonable suspicion that that person is a member or supporter of a proscribed organisation is an offence. On summary conviction, a person guilty under section 13 is liable to six months' imprisonment, a fine not exceeding level five on the standard scale or both. In **Pwr v Director of Public Prosecutions** (2020) the court ruled that section 13 created an offence of strict liability, and did not constitute an interference with the right to freedom of expression under Article 10 of the European Convention on Human Rights. The language of section 13 was clear and unambiguous and gave practical effect to Parliament's intention to ban proscribed organisations. Section 13 restricted the right to freedom of expression (ECHR Article 10). However, that restriction was justified. It pursued a legitimate aim and was necessary in a democratic society on national security grounds and did not amount to a disproportionate interference with Article 10 rights.

Terrorist property

Part III of the Terrorism Act 2000 relates to terrorist property, defined under section 14 to mean money or other property which is likely to be used for the purposes of terrorism (including the resources of a proscribed organisation) and proceeds of acts of terrorism. It is an offence to partake in fundraising for the purposes of terrorism. In relation to inviting support from others or receiving money or other property, there must be an intention that it should be used, or reasonable cause to suspect that it may be used, for terrorist purposes. Part III of the 2000 Act introduced powers for the police, customs officers and immigration officers to seize cash at borders and to seek forfeiture of cash in civil proceedings. The Anti-Terrorism, Crime and Security Act 2001 extended the law in order to prevent terrorists gaining access to their money.

More recently, in **A v HM Treasury** (2010), the Supreme Court ruled that Orders in Council were *ultra vires* and unlawful. The United Kingdom, as a member of the United Nations, was required to give effect to decisions of the UN Security Council. Security Council Resolutions were made to combat terrorism, in part by freezing financial assets and other economic resources of terrorists. The United Nations Act 1946, section 1, provided that in order to give effect to Security Council Resolutions, 'His Majesty may by Order in Council make such provision as appears to Him necessary or expedient for enabling those measures to be effectively applied'. Unlike other forms of delegated legislation which are subjected to parliamentary proceedings, the Orders in Council came into effect following their laying before Parliament. The effect of this was to leave the content of the Orders entirely in the hands of the executive. Two Orders in Council were made, each of which laid down conditions which had to be satisfied before the Treasury could 'designate' a person and freeze his or her financial assets or economic resources. One condition was that the Treasury 'have reasonable grounds for suspicion that the person is or may be' involved in terrorism.

The four appellants in **A v HM Treasury** argued that the Orders were *ultra vires* the 1946 Act. The power conferred by section 1 was for measures which were 'necessary or expedient'. The Terrorism Order (TO) and the Al-Qaeda and Taliban Orders (AQO) were so widely drawn as to deprive the designated person of any resources whatsoever. Lord Hope of Craighead DPSC approved the *dictum* of Sedley SJ in the Court of Appeal that designated persons 'are effectively prisoners of the state'. In adopting the test of 'reasonable suspicion' the Orders went beyond what was 'necessary or expedient' to comply with the Security Council Resolutions and were accordingly beyond the scope of section 1 of the 1946 Act.

The Terrorist Asset-Freezing Act 2010 now regulates asset-freezing.[94]

Terrorist investigations

Part IV of the Terrorism Act 2000 regulates powers in relation to terrorist investigations, defined to include the commission, preparation or instigation of acts of terrorism, an act which appears to have been done for such purposes, the resources of a proscribed organisation, the possibility of making a proscription or de-proscription order under section 3(3), or the commission, preparation or instigation of an offence under the Act.[95] Sections 33 to 36 give power to the police to designate and demarcate a specified area by cordons for the purposes of a terrorist investigation. It is an offence to fail to comply with an order.

Under section 39, it is an offence to disclose to another anything which is likely to prejudice a terrorist investigation or to interfere with material which is likely to be relevant to the investigation.[96]

---

94 See also **R (Youssef) v Secretary of State for Foreign and Commonwealth Affairs** (2013).
95 Terrorism Act 2000, s. 32.
96 Terrorism Act 2000, s. 39(7). It is also an offence for a person to collect, make a record of, publish, communicate or attempt to elicit information which is useful to a person committing or preparing an act of terrorism, or to possess a document or record containing information which would be useful (*ibid.*, s. 103). The offence is confined to a person who is or has been a constable, a member of Her Majesty's Forces, the holder of a judicial office, an officer of any court or a full-time employee of the prison service in Northern Ireland. It is a defence to prove that he had a reasonable excuse for his action or possession.

The 2000 Act also conferred wide powers of stop and search on the police under sections 44 to 47 of the Act (now repealed by the Protection of Freedoms Act 2012 on which see further below). Section 44 conferred power on a senior police officer to authorise a police officer the power to stop and search a pedestrian in any area if he or she considered that 'it was expedient for the prevention of acts of terrorism'. The power required no doctrine of necessity nor an assessment of the proportionality of the action. Held to be a lawful power in **R (Gillan) v Commissioner of Police of the Metropolis** (2006), it was held by the European Court of Human Rights to be a violation of Article 8 (the right to respect for private and family life). The powers of authorisation and stop and search were neither sufficiently circumscribed nor subject to adequate legal safeguards against abuse. They were not, therefore, 'in accordance with law'.[97]

Section 59 of the Protection of Freedoms Act 2012 (PFA) repealed sections 44 to 47 of the 2000 Act. Section 61 PFA provides for authorisations to stop and search specified areas or places where the power is both necessary and proportionate to prevent acts of terrorism.[98]

Terrorism overseas

The Terrorism Act 2000 also regulates terrorism overseas. Under section 59, it is an offence to incite another person to commit an act of terrorism wholly or partly outside the United Kingdom, if that act would constitute an offence listed in subsection (2) in England and Wales, namely, murder, wounding with intent and offences involving poison, explosions and endangering life by damaging property. A person found guilty shall be liable to any penalty to which he would be liable on conviction of the relevant offence. Sections 60 and 61 make equivalent provision in relation to Scotland and Northern Ireland. Section 62 regulates acts of terrorism outside the United Kingdom involving causing explosions[99] and the use of biological or chemical weapons, and provides that a person committing such an act is guilty of an offence. Equally, it is an offence to do anything outside the United Kingdom which would amount to an offence under sections 15 to 18 if it had been done in the United Kingdom. See further the Counter-terrorism and Security Bill 2015, discussed below.

Port and border controls

Section 53 and Schedule 7 to the Terrorism Act 2000 regulate border controls. An 'examining officer', being a constable, immigration officer or customs officer designated for the purposes of Schedule 7 by the Secretary of State and Commissioners of Customs and Excise, has the power to stop, question and detain a person, at an airport, port or border area, for the purposes of determining whether he or she is a person suspected of being concerned in the commission, preparation or instigation of acts of terrorism.[100]

A person questioned is required to provide any information requested, and produce a valid passport or other document establishing his or her identity. A person may be removed from a ship, aircraft or vehicle for the purpose of detaining for questioning. A person detained

---

97 *Gillan and Quinton v United Kingdom* [2010] ECHR 28.

98 Note that the Counter-Terrorism and Sentencing Bill 2019–2021 increases custodial sentences for terrorist offences.

99 An offence under the Explosive Substances Act 1883, ss 2, 3 or 5; an offence under the Biological Weapons Act; 1974, s. 1; an offence under the Chemical Weapons Act 1996, s. 2.

100 Defined in the Terrorism Act 2000, s. 40(1)(b) and 40(2), as including a person who has been, whether before or after the passing of the Act, concerned in the commission, preparation or instigation of acts of terrorism within the meaning given in s. 1.

for questioning must be released no later than the end of a six-hour period beginning with the time when the questioning begins, unless otherwise detained under any other power.[101]

Powers of search are granted to examining officers. The examining officer may 'for the purpose of satisfying himself whether there are any persons who he may wish to question' search a ship or aircraft, a person and/or his possessions. Schedule 7 to the 2000 Act empowers a police officer to question a person at an airport for the purpose of determining whether he is a person falling within section 40(1)(b) of the 2000 Act, namely a person who was concerned in the commission, preparation or instigation of acts of terrorism as defined in section 1 of the Act. This power was central to the case of **R (Miranda) v Secretary of State for the Home Department** (2016). Before the Court of Appeal there were two principal grounds of appeal. The first related to the use of the Schedule 7 powers and whether on the facts it was proportionate, the second to the claim that the power was incompatible with the right to freedom of expression guaranteed under Article 10 of the European Convention on Human Rights in relation to journalistic material in that it was not subject to satisfactory safeguards against its arbitrary exercise.

The Master of the Rolls, Lord Dyson, ruled that the use of the Schedule 7 power was lawful and dismissed the appeal on that ground. However, in relation to the Article 10 ground, the appeal was allowed in part: the use of Schedule 7 in relation to journalistic material did not have sufficient safeguards.

On proportionality Lord Dyson took as his starting point the need for 'a substantial degree of deference' to the police acting in the interests of national security. The police have both 'the institutional competence and the constitutional responsibility to make such assessments and decisions'.[102] On conducting the balancing exercise between individual rights and the interests of the community, Lord Dyson recognised that the greater the potential harm, the greater the weight that should be given to community interests. In the instant case the potential harm caused by disclosure was 'very substantial'.

On the Article 10 ground of appeal, the Court recognised that there were constraints on the exercise of the power: the need for proportionality and good faith, the limits on the definition of terrorism in the Terrorism Act and the fact that the power could only be exercised at a port or border area and that the power of detention was limited to nine hours. There could also be a *post factum* challenge to the use of the powers by judicial review.

On the latter point, Lord Dyson held that the availability of judicial review, after the event, could not cure a breach of Article 10 and was not an adequate safeguard. What was required in relation to journalistic material was prior judicial or other independent and impartial oversight, or immediate *post factum* oversight in urgent cases. That was the 'natural and obvious safeguard against the unlawful exercise of the Schedule 7 powers in cases involving journalistic freedom'.[103]

The Court declared that the stop power in Schedule 7, paragraph 2(1) was incompatible with Article 10 in that it was not subject to adequate safeguards against its arbitrary exercise. It was for Parliament to provide the protection.

On further controls and the Counter-Terrorism and Border Security Act 2019 see further below.

---

101 The period under Sched. 7 was originally nine hours. The period was reduced to six hours under the Anti-Social Behaviour, Crime and Policing Act 2014, s. 148. In **Beghal v DPP** (2015) the Supreme Court had ruled that the detention power was lawful. The Court took into account the amendment to the law. In **Beghal v UK** (2019), the European Court of Human Rights ruled that the law as it stood at the time Ms Beghal was detained was not in accordance with the law.
102 At para. 79.
103 See paras 113 and 114.

The Prevention of Terrorism Act 2005

The Prevention of Terrorism Act 2005 was a response to the House of Lords' decision in *A v Secretary of State for the Home Department* (2005). The 2005 Act provided for the making of 'control orders' over terrorist suspects. These were preventative in nature and imposed any conditions necessary to prevent or restrict an individual's further involvement in terrorist-related activities. Controversy over control orders led to reform.[104] In a Ministerial Statement in 2011,[105] the Home Secretary announced that legislation was to be introduced to provide for a less restrictive system than control orders, but that the control order system would continue to operate until replacement measures were in force.[106] The Terrorism Prevention and Investigation Measures Act 2011 reforms the law and abolishes the Prevention of Terrorism Act 2005. On the 2011 Act see further below.

The Terrorism Act 2006

The Terrorism Act 2006 was introduced to tighten the law following two attacks on London in July 2005. The Act introduced new criminal offences in relation to terrorism, amended the definition of terrorism, increased the penalties available, extended the grounds for detention and extended the period of detention and made other miscellaneous changes to the law.[107] Section 36 provides that the Secretary of State must appoint a person to review the operation of the Terrorism Act 2000 and Part I of the 2006 Act. The review must be carried out every 12 months and the report made to the Secretary of State must be laid before Parliament.

The definition of terrorism is extended to include actions and threats or using noxious substances or things to influence a government or to intimidate international governmental organisations.[108] Section 1 creates the offence of encouragement of terrorism, and applies to a statement

> that is likely to be understood by some or all of the members of the public to whom it is published as a direct or indirect encouragement or other inducement to them to the commission, preparation or instigation of acts of terrorism or Convention offences.

It is an offence to publish such a statement, or cause another to publish such a statement with the intention that members of the public 'be directly or indirectly encouraged to commit, prepare or instigate acts of terrorism or Convention offences'.[109] It is also an offence to be 'reckless as to whether members of the public will be directly or indirectly encouraged etc'. An indirect encouragement is defined as being a 'statement describing terrorism in such a way that the listener would infer that he should emulate it'. Section 2 creates the offence of disseminating a terrorism publication with the intention, or being reckless, of directly or indirectly encouraging or inducing the commission, preparation or instigation of acts of terrorism.[110] The criminal offences under sections 1 and 2 extend to internet activity.[111]

---

104 See *Control Orders in 2011: Final Report of the Independent Reviewer on the Prevention of Terrorism Act 2005*, 2012, London: TSO.
105 *Hansard* Col. 27 WS, 17 March 2011.
106 See Sched. 8 to the Terrorism Prevention and Investigation Measures Act 2011.
107 The Terrorist Offenders (Restriction of Early Release) Act 2020 introduced longer sentences for terrorist offences and provided that the rules on early release from a sentence are changed in order that early release will not be considered until two-thirds (rather than half) of a sentence has been served.
108 Amending s. 1(1)(b) of the Terrorism Act 2000 and s. 113(1)(c) of the Anti-Terrorism, Crime and Security Act 2001.
109 Convention offences are those listed in Sched. 1 to the Act.
110 The Terrorism Act 2006, s. 28 provides for warrants to enter and search and seize terrorist publications and for forfeiture.
111 Terrorism Act 2006, s. 3.

The Act extends the law to cover *any* conduct undertaken in preparation for committing, or assisting another to commit, acts of terrorism. Conviction carries a sentence of life imprisonment. Providing training or instruction for, or receiving instruction or training in, skills relating to terrorism is a criminal offence carrying a sentence on conviction on indictment to a term of imprisonment of up to ten years or a fine, or both. If tried summarily, the offences carry a term of imprisonment of up to 12 months, a fine not exceeding the statutory maximum, or both.[112] The same penalties apply to the offence of attendance at a place used for terrorist training.[113] The making and possession of radioactive material or devices, or the misuse of devices or material, or demands or threats relating to such items are criminal offences punishable with life imprisonment.[114] Conduct outside the United Kingdom is a criminal offence in the United Kingdom if it would amount to an offence listed in section 17(2). Prosecutions may be instituted in England and Wales only with the consent of the Director of Public Prosecutions and in Northern Ireland with the consent of the Director of Public Prosecutions for Northern Ireland.

The Terrorism Act 2006 extended the period in which a terrorist suspect may be held in detention without charge to 28 days. That period has been reduced to 14 days by section 57 of the Protection of Freedoms Act 2012.

The Counter-Terrorism Act 2008

The Counter-Terrorism Act 2008 amended the definition of terrorism to make it clear that advancing a racial cause, in addition to a political, religious or ideological cause, is within the definition. The Act also made provision for the gathering and sharing of information for counter-terrorism purposes; and introduced a number of extensions to police powers in respect of entry, search and seizure.[115]

The Terrorism Prevention and Investigation Measures Act 2011

The Terrorism Prevention and Investigation Measures Act 2011 (TPIMA) repeals the Prevention of Terrorism Act 2005. Replacing control orders are Terrorism Prevention and Investigation Measures (TPIMs), defined as 'requirements, restrictions and other provisions' which may be imposed. Schedule 1 to the 2011 Act sets out the details, which include overnight residence requirements, travel restrictions and exclusions from specified areas or places, restrictions on financial services and property transfers, restrictions on possession or use of electronic communications devices, restrictions on employment or studies, and reporting and monitoring requirements.

A TPIM may be imposed on an individual if the conditions specified in section 3 are met. These conditions are as follows:

(a) that the Secretary of State reasonably suspects that the individual is, or has been, involved in terrorism-related activity (the 'relevant activity');
(b) that some or all of the relevant activity is new terrorism-related activity;

---

112 In Scotland or Northern Ireland, on summary conviction to imprisonment for a term not exceeding six months or a fine not exceeding the statutory maximum, or both.
113 Terrorism Act 2006, s. 8.
114 Ibid., ss 9–11.
115 Section 1 of the 2008 Act is amended by s. 56 of the Crime and Security Act 2010.

(c) that the Secretary of State reasonably considers that it is necessary, for purposes connected with protecting members of the public from a risk of terrorism, for TPIMs to be imposed on the individual;

(d) that the Secretary of State reasonably considers that it is necessary for the specified TPIMs to be imposed;

(e) that:
    (i) the court gives the Secretary of State permission under section 6, or
    (ii) the Secretary of State reasonably considers that the urgency of the case requires TPIMs to be imposed without obtaining permission of the court.

Terrorism-related activity is defined under section 4(1) as including the commission, preparation or instigation of acts of terrorism, conduct which facilitates or encourages acts of terrorism and conduct which gives support or assistance to individuals known or believed to be involved in terrorism.

The Counter Terrorism and Sentencing Bill 2020 amends the 2011 Act and extends the length of time a TPIM notice lasts from two years to an indefinite period. The 2020 Bill also extends terrorist provisions to those under the age of 18. The Bill creates a new type of sentence for the most serious terrorist and terrorism-related offences with a minimum term of 14 years and the removal of the possibility of early release from custody for those convicted of serious terrorist offences. The Secretary of State may vary the measures specified in a TPIM notice, and the individual may apply for a variation of the notice (section 12). A TPIM may be revoked at any time and a notice may also be revived (section 13).

A TPIM may be quashed in 'TPIM proceedings'. The individual may appeal to the court in relation to the extension, variation or revival of measures. Further, if the individual has applied unsuccessfully to the Secretary of State for variation or revocation of measures, the individual may appeal to the court. An appeal also lies against a decision by the Secretary of State in relation to matters requiring permission. The court only has the power to quash the extension or revival of the TPIM notice, quash measures in the notice or give direction to the Secretary of State for revocation or variation of measures, or give directions in relation to permissions (section 16). Section 17 makes clear that TPIM decisions are not to be questioned in any legal proceedings other than TPIM proceedings.

The Secretary of State is under a duty to report to Parliament, on a three-monthly basis, on the operation of the Act (section 19). In addition, the Secretary of State must appoint an independent reviewer to carry out an annual review of the working of the Act. The review must be laid before Parliament by the Secretary of State (section 20). The Secretary of State's TPIM powers expire at the end of five years from the date on which the Act was passed. However, the powers may be extended, by statutory instrument, for a further five-year period. Before making such an order the Secretary of State must consult the independent reviewer, the Intelligence Services Commission and the Director-General of the Security Service. An order may not be made unless a draft has been laid before Parliament and approved by a resolution of each House (section 21).

During the period when Parliament is dissolved,[116] the Secretary of State has the power to make a temporary enhanced TPIM order (section 26). These may only be made if the Secretary of State considers it is 'necessary to do so by reason of urgency' and is satisfied, on the balance of probabilities, that an individual is or has been involved in terrorism-related activity.

---

116 From the date of dissolution until the date of the Queen's Speech at the opening of a new Parliament.

Pause and Reflect

Control Orders were introduced under the 2005 Prevention of Terrorism Act, only to be replaced by Terrorism Prevention and Investigations Measures under the Terrorism Prevention and Investigation Measures Act 2011. Explain why it was necessary to abandon Control Orders. How different are TPIMs from Control Orders?

The Protection of Freedoms Act 2012

The Protection of Freedoms Act (PFA) reduces the period for which a suspected terrorist may be detained from 28 to 14 days (section 57). In an emergency situation, section 58 permits a temporary extension of that period to 28 days. The stop and search powers in sections 44 to 47 of the Terrorism Act 2000 are repealed and the 2000 Act amended to provide a replacement regime (see section 60). Section 62 provides that the Secretary of State must publish a Code of Practice on stop, search and seizure powers. Section 1 of the Act sets out a replacement regime for the retention and destruction of fingerprints and DNA samples.

The Protection of Freedoms Act 2012 also provides for increased control over the use of surveillance devices operated by the police and local authorities. The PFA amends the Regulation of Investigatory Powers Act 2000 so as to require local authorities to obtain judicial approval for the use of covert investigatory techniques.

The Counter-Terrorism and Security Act 2015

In 2014 the Joint Terrorism Analysis Centre (JTAC) raised the UK national terrorist threat level from substantial to severe. The government considered that additional powers were needed to deal with individuals who travel overseas to engage in terrorism and then seek to return to the United Kingdom. By January 2015 there were reported to be approximately 550 individuals 'of interest to the police and security services' who had travelled from the UK to Syria and the region and an estimated 50 per cent of these had returned to the UK.

The Counter-Terrorism and Security (CTS) Act, section 1 and Schedule 1, provides mechanisms to stop people travelling from the UK to fight for terrorist organisations overseas. Where a police officer has reasonable grounds to believe that a person intends to become involved in terrorism overseas, he or she may stop and search the person (Schedule 1, paragraph 2), and reasonable force may be used (paragraph 2(7)(b)). The person concerned must be informed of the officer's suspicion. The constable may give directions to customs or immigration officers for the retention of a passport or ticket for travel. The travel document may be retained for a short period in order to allow the Secretary of State to consider whether to cancel the person's passport, consider whether or not to charge the person with an offence or consider whether to make the person subject to an order to protect the public from a risk of terrorism (paragraph 5). A review of the decision to retain the document must be undertaken after 72 hours (paragraph 6). The documents may not be retained for more than 14 days, unless the period is extended by a judge to a total period not exceeding 30 days (paragraph 8). The person concerned may be legally represented and has a right to make oral or written representations to the court. The court may exclude that person or his or her representative from the hearing (paragraph 10). Where a person is unable to leave the UK as a result of the retention of his or her travel document the Secretary of State may make 'whatever arrangements' in relation to that person as she thinks appropriate (paragraph 14). A Code of Practice regulates the operation of these powers.

Temporary exclusion orders (TEOs) are provided for under section 2. The purpose of the order is to prevent a person from returning to the UK unless their return is in accordance with a permit from the Secretary of State. A TEO may only be made where the Secretary of State reasonably suspects that the individual is or has been involved in terrorism-related activity outside the UK, and reasonably believes that the imposition of the order is necessary to protect the public in the UK from a risk of terrorism and the permission of a court has been given (section 3). The function of the court is to determine whether the decision of the Secretary of State is 'obviously flawed'. If it is not, the court must give permission (section 37). Section 2(7)(b) provides that if the Secretary of State reasonably believes that there is an urgent need to impose a TEO it may be imposed without the permission of the court. In such circumstances the Secretary of State must, immediately after giving notice of the imposition of the TEO to the individual concerned, refer the matter to the court (Schedule 2, paragraph 3). The function of the court is to determine, within seven days of the TEO being imposed, whether her decision was 'obviously flawed'. If it was flawed, the TEO will be quashed by the court (Schedule 2, paragraph 4(1)). If it is not, the court must confirm the order. Where a TEO is imposed, it comes into effect on notification of its imposition, and is in force for a period of two years, unless revoked or brought to an end earlier (section 4(3)).

Where a TEO is made, the passport of a British citizen is invalidated (section 4(9)). A person subject to the TEO may be granted permission to return. If the individual applies for permission to return it must be granted unless the Secretary of State requires the individual to attend an interview with a police officer or immigration officer and the individual fails to attend the interview (section 6(2)). Permission to return may be subject to reporting requirements and attendance at appointments which may include de-radicalisation programmes (sections 5 to 9).

The CTS Act 2015 amends the Terrorism Prevention and Investigation Measures Act 2011 (TPIM), reinstating the power to order a person to live in a specified locality (section 16). If there are premises that are the individual's own residence, premises more than 200 miles away may only be specified if they are in an agreed locality (section 16(3)).

The Counter-Terrorism and Security Act 2015 includes measures designed to prevent people from being drawn into terrorism. Section 26 provides that specified authorities (as listed in Schedule 6) 'must, in the exercise of its functions' have due regard to the need to 'prevent people from being drawn into terrorism'. The Secretary of State has the power to issue guidance to authorities (section 29). If an authority has failed to comply with the Act the Secretary of State may give directions 'for the purpose of enforcing the performance of that duty' (section 3(1)). In relation to universities and colleges of further education, section 31 provides that when carrying out its duty under the Act, the authority must have particular regard to its duty to ensure freedom of speech, and the importance of academic freedom. In order to identify and support individuals who are vulnerable to being drawn into terrorism, section 36 provides that every local authority must have a panel of persons to assess individuals who are referred to it by the police. In addition to assessments the panel must draw up support plans with a view to preventing the person being drawn into terrorism.

The operation of the Act is subject to review by the Independent Reviewer of terrorist legislation (section 44). Part 5 of the Act extends to England, Wales and Scotland, the rest of the Act applies to the whole of the United Kingdom.

The Counter-Terrorism and Border Security Act 2019 updates and strengthens the legal powers and capabilities of the law enforcement and intelligence agencies. It does so against the background of the heightened terrorist threat to the United Kingdom and the government's updated counter-terrorism strategy published in June 2018.

The Act amends the law to ensure that it is capable of dealing with new threats in the digital age and to reflect changing patterns of radicalisation. It also provides a new power to strengthen the UK's border defences against hostile state activity, as evidenced in the poisoning of Sergei and Yulia Skripal in March 2018 by suspected Russian agents. Part 2 of the 2019 Act provides the power to stop, question, search and detain individuals at a UK port or the Northern Ireland border area to determine whether they are, or have been, involved in activity that threatens the UK's national security.

In order to deal with the problem of individuals travelling overseas to engage in terrorist activity the 2019 Act creates a new criminal offence. Under section 4 (amending the Terrorism Act 2000: see section 58B) it is a criminal offence to enter into or remain in an area outside the UK that has been designated by the Home Secretary. Section 58B(4) to (6) provide a number of exemptions from liability and there is a defence of reasonable excuse. The new offence carries a maximum penalty of ten years' imprisonment and/or an unlimited fine. The offence will not be retrospective.

The case of Shemima Begum gave rise to widespread publicity of the difficulties entailed in dealing with people who are radicalised and travel to support terrorist organisations overseas. Since birth Shamima Begum had held British citizenship because both her parents were settled in the UK.[117] She also had citizenship of Bangladesh through her father. In 2015, at the age of 15, Shamima Begum left the UK with two school friends and travelled to Syria via Turkey. Shortly after arriving in Syria she married an Islamic State (ISIL) fighter. Her whereabouts were unknown until February 2019 when she was found by journalists in a camp run by the Syrian Democratic Forces by whom she was detained. Since being in Syria Ms Begum had had three children, all of whom died. When found she was unrepentant about joining Islamic State and showed little remorse for her actions but expressed disillusionment with ISIL and indicated her wish to return to the UK.

In February 2019, the Home Secretary deprived Ms Begum of her British citizenship on the basis that she was a threat to national security.[118] Ms Begum's Bangladeshi citizenship meant that she would not be made stateless, which is unlawful under international law. Ms Begum appealed against her deprivation of citizenship. In July 2020 the Court of Appeal refused to allow her appeal and overturn the Home Secretary's deprivation order. Instead, the Court ruled that she should be allowed to return home in order to conduct her appeal against the Home Secretary's decision to refuse her leave to enter the UK, on the basis that she could not do so effectively from a war zone and that justice and fairness outweighed the national security concerns.[119] In **R (Begum) v Special Immigration Appeals Commission; Secretary of State for the Home Department** (2021) the Supreme Court dismissed Ms Begum's appeal against the refusal to allow her to enter the UK to pursue her appeal and her applications for judicial review. The Court of Appeal had given insufficient weight to the Home Secretary's assessment of the risk to national security and the right to a fair hearing did not 'trump' all other considerations, such as the safety of the public.

National security and the public interest

The state has the right to expel non-British citizens, subject to international obligations,[120] on the grounds of national security, namely that their presence is 'contrary to the public interest' or 'not conducive to the public good'. Prior to 1997 there was no right of appeal to a court of law against the government's decision to deport a person where national security was pleaded. Instead there was a right to a hearing before a panel of three advisers to the Home Secretary.[121]

---

117 British Nationality Act 1981, section 1(1).
118 Deprivation of citizenship is provided for under section 40 of the British Nationality Act 1981.
119 **Begum v Special Immigration Appeals Commission** (2020).
120 These include the Geneva Convention on Refugees 1951; the European Convention on Human Rights; and EU law.
121 A process which did not satisfy the requirements of Article 5 of the European Convention on Human Rights.

In 1962, Dr Soblen, an American citizen who had been convicted of espionage in the United States, fled from the country before being sentenced. While on an aeroplane Dr Soblen cut his wrists and was landed in London for hospital treatment. The Home Secretary issued a deportation order on the basis that his continued presence was 'not conducive to the public good'. When Dr Soblen applied for habeas corpus, the Court of Appeal ruled that Dr Soblen had no right to make representations, and that deportation was an administrative matter for the Home Secretary.[122]

In **R v Home Secretary ex parte Hosenball** (1977), two American journalists, Philip Agee and Mark Hosenball, were detained with a view to deportation, on the basis that their work involved obtaining and publishing information prejudicial to national security. There was no appeal against the Home Secretary's decision where national security was pleaded. Instead, there was a right to a hearing before a panel of three advisers to the Home Secretary. When Hosenball tried to challenge the Home Secretary's decision in the courts, the Court of Appeal upheld the deportation order. While recognising that the rules of natural justice[123] had not been complied with in the decision to deport Hosenball, the Court of Appeal nevertheless ruled that the requirements of national security prevailed and that, in matters of national security, the Home Secretary was responsible to Parliament, and not to the courts.

The case of **R v Home Secretary ex parte Cheblak** (1991) reveals the extensive powers of the Home Secretary to detain persons 'in the interests of national security'. During the Gulf War, 160 Iraqi and Palestinian citizens were detained with a view to deportation, on the basis that their presence was not 'conducive to the public good'. Abbas Cheblak and his family had been resident in the United Kingdom for 16 years. In an application for habeas corpus, the Court of Appeal accepted the Home Secretary's explanation that Cheblak had associations with an unspecified organisation which supported the Iraqi government, and refused to press the Home Secretary for further information.[124] The problem of trying to balance the need for judicial control over proposed deportations of those whose presence is deemed contrary to the public interest and the requirements of national security was met by the Special Immigration Appeals Commission Act 1997, establishing the Commission (SIAC) with jurisdiction to hear immigration appeals[125] where an order had been made on the ground that exclusion, departure or deportation on the basis that the person's removal was 'conducive to the public good' (on the Special Immigration Appeals Commission see below).

In **Rehman v Secretary of State for the Home Department** (2003), the House of Lords considered the Secretary of State's decision to refuse an application for indefinite leave to remain in the United Kingdom on the basis that the applicant represented a threat to national security, in that he was allegedly involved in an Islamist terrorist organisation. The Special Immigration Appeals Commission (SIAC) had ruled that the conduct relied on by the Secretary of State had to be conduct targeted at the United Kingdom or its citizens. The House of Lords upheld the Secretary of State's appeal: action against a foreign state could indirectly affect the security of the United Kingdom, and preventative or precautionary action might be justified. While there had to be material from which the Secretary of State could proportionately and reasonably conclude that there was a real possibility of actions harmful to national security, deciding whether deportation would be conducive to the public good was a matter of executive judgment.

---

122 See **R v Home Secretary ex parte Soblen** (1963). See also Thornberry, 1963.
123 See Chapter 26. The rules of natural justice apply to immigration decisions: **Re HK** (1967).
124 Mr Cheblak was subsequently released from detention following a hearing before the Home Secretary's panel. See also **R v Secretary of State for the Home Department ex parte Jahromi** (1995) and **Chahal v UK** (1997).
125 Relating to refusals of leave to enter, refusal of admission, deportation etc.: see s. 2(1).

In *RB (Algeria) v Secretary of State for the Home Department; U (Algeria) v Same; Othman v Same* (2009), the claimants appealed against the decision of the Secretary of State to deport them on the ground that their deportation would be conducive to the public good because they were a danger to national security. They argued that returning them to their country of origin would involve a real risk that they would be subjected to torture or to inhuman or degrading treatment or punishment, and that their right to fair trial would be breached.

SIAC had concluded that there were no substantial grounds for believing that the claimants would be exposed to treatment contrary to Article 3. It had considered closed as well as open material.[126] Section 7(1) of the Special Immigration Appeals Act 1997 limits review of SIAC's decisions to questions of law. SIAC's conclusions, therefore, could only be attacked on the grounds that it had failed to have due regard for some rule of law, had regard to irrelevant matters, failed to take into account relevant matters or that its procedures had failed to meet the requirements imposed by law, none of which were applicable in the instant case.

The UK Government's 2015 Prevent Strategy defines radicalisation as follows: 'Radicalisation' refers to the process by which a person comes to support terrorism[127] and extremist ideologies associated with terrorist groups.[128]

> 'Extremism' is the vocal or active opposition to fundamental British values, including democracy, the rule of law, individual liberty and mutual respect and tolerance of different faiths and beliefs. We also include in our definition of extremism calls for the death of members of our armed forces, whether in this country or overseas. Terrorist groups very often draw on extremist ideas developed by extremist organisations.[129]

The UK Government's counter-terrorism strategy is **CONTEST** of which the **Prevent** strategy is a part. According to the Government Guidance, the Prevent strategy has three specific objectives:

- to respond to the ideological challenge of terrorism and the threat we face from those who promote it;
- to prevent people from being drawn into terrorism and ensure that they are given appropriate advice and support;
- to work with sectors and institutions where there are risks of radicalisation that we need to address.

Public bodies are under a duty to 'have due regard to the need to prevent people from being drawn into terrorism', including non-violent terrorism.[130] The bodies include local authorities, prisons and young offenders' institutions, all schools, colleges and universities, the National Health Service and the Police. Preventing people becoming involved in terrorism 'requires challenge to extremist ideas where they are used to legitimise terrorism and are shared by terrorist groups'. The Prevent strategy is aimed at all kinds of terrorist threats to the UK. Particularly prominent are the threats caused by terrorist organisations in Syria and

---

126 Closed material being material which the Secretary of State relies on but cannot disclose to the appellant for reasons of national security or public interest.
127 Terrorism is defined in the Terrorism Act 2000, section 1. It is a criminal offence to belong to, support or display support for a proscribed (prohibited) organisation.
128 Prevent Duty Guidance for England and Wales, 2015.
129 Statutory Duty for Channel panel members and partners of local panels, 2015.
130 Counter-Terrorism and Security Act 2015, section 26 and Schedule 6.

Iraq and Al Qa'ida groups and also threats posed by extreme right-wing views: the 'white supremacist ideology'.

The success of the Prevent strategy depends on adequate training of staff to ensure awareness of the risks involved in extremist ideology and inter-agency cooperation. The Home Office has overall responsibility for issuing Guidance on the strategy. The Extremism Analysis Unit (EAU) is a Home Office unit which researches extremism in the UK and overseas. The Home Office is also responsible for drawing together data from the agencies involved.

A legal challenge to Home Office Prevent Guidance centred on the identification by the Extremism Analysis Unit (EAU) of Dr Salman Butt, the editor of Islam21C – a website dedicated to 'articulating Islamic beliefs in the 21st century' – as a 'hate speaker'. Dr Butt claimed that the collection and retention of data about his views was incompatible with Article 8 of the ECHR (the right to respect for privacy etc.), and that the Higher Education Prevent Duty Guidance (HEPDG) was incompatible with Article 10 ECHR (freedom of speech).[131] The Guidance stated that when considering whether to host a particular speaker, a Higher Education institution has to 'have regard to the need to prevent people from being drawn into terrorism'. However, higher education bodies are also under a duty to 'pay particular regard' to the duty to ensure freedom of speech.[132] If there is a perceived risk of people being drawn into terrorism, the institution should refuse to allow a speaker a platform unless the risk could be mitigated by either strong chairing of the meeting and by having speakers with opposing views on the platform. The Court of Appeal dismissed Dr Butt's appeal relating to the collection of data by the EAU, but allowed his appeal in relation to the Secretary of State's Guidance relating to freedom of speech: that part of the Guidance was unlawful and quashed (declared invalid). This was because the Secretary of State had failed to balance the risk that was posed by a particular speaker against the mitigating factors (i.e. chairing, platforming opposing views) and he had therefore not discharged his duty of balance under the Act. The challenge on Article 10 was dismissed: there was no evidence that the Secretary of State had actually prevented Dr Butt from speaking at universities.

Channel is the Government's programme for identifying and protecting children and adults from being drawn into terrorism.[133] A key part of the Channel strategy is early identification of potentially vulnerable children and adults and supporting them before they become victim to extremism and radicalisation and from there into involvement with terrorism. This requires inter-agency cooperation, with the police coordinating activity by requesting information from public bodies, assessing the vulnerability of people at risk and presenting this to a local multi-agency Panel with a view to developing a support plan for an individual. The Channel programme overlaps with the safeguarding duties of local authorities to protect children from harm.

Assessing vulnerability focuses on three factors: **engagement** with a group, cause or ideology; **intent to cause harm** and **capability to cause harm**. Indicators of engagement include:

- spending time with suspected extremists;
- changing personal style of dress or appearance to fit in with the group;
- day-to-day behaviour becoming increasingly focused on extremist ideology;
- loss of interest in friends or activities;

---

131 **Butt v Secretary of State for the Home Department** (2019).
132 Counter-Terrorism and Security Act 2015, section 26.
133 HM Government: *Channel Duty Guidance: Protecting vulnerable people from being drawn into terrorism*, 2015.

- possession of materials or symbols associated with an extremist cause (e.g. a Nazi swastika);
- attempts to recruit others to a group or cause;
- communications which suggest identification with a group or cause.

Indicators as to intention include:

- clearly identifying another group as threatening what they stand for;
- using insulting or derogatory language or labels for another group;
- speaking about the imminence of harm from the other group and the importance of action now;
- expressing attitudes that justify offending on behalf of the group, cause or ideology;
- condoning or supporting violence or harm towards others;
- plotting or conspiring with others.

Indicators as to capability of causing harm or contributing to terrorist acts include:

- having a history of violence;
- being criminally versatile and using criminal networks to support extremist goals;
- having occupational skills that enable acts of terrorism;
- having technical expertise, e.g. IT skills etc., that can be deployed in terrorist acts.

Channel is a voluntary programme and therefore requires the consent of participants: for children this requires the consent of parents or carers. Consent is required at two stages: for the sharing of information between agencies and in advance of support measures being put in place. Where parental consent is not given for participation in the support programme, consideration must be given to whether the child is a 'child in need' (Children Act 1989, section 17) of local authority support, and/or whether the child is at risk of significant harm (Children Act 1989, section 31(9)). In either case social services must be involved and statutory assessments made with a view to protecting the child under a Care or Supervision Order.[134]

For all the good intentions of the Prevent programme and Channel, it has to be recognised that there are serious criticisms which have been expressed by Parliamentarians, community groups and NGOs. The mention of 'British values' in the definition of extremism has attracted the accusation from Muslim commentators and rights groups that it is 'racist'. Muslim communities have repeatedly claimed that they are disproportionately targeted and that this violates their rights. The strategy is also criticised for having an adverse impact on freedom of speech and religion. Rights Watch UK claims that Prevent has led to 'a systematic breach of children's human rights in the school setting', leading to 'violations of the right to education, the right to freedom of expression, the right to freedom of religion, the right to privacy, the right to freedom from discrimination' and the fundamental principle that actions taken in relation to children must treat the child's best interests as a primary consideration.[135]

The reliance on teachers, health workers and social workers to identify those vulnerable to extremism and make referrals to Channel has been described as having a 'negative impact' on the fragile trust between communities and public services and has led to calls for it to be scrapped.[136] It has also allegedly led to significant increase in the number of referrals to

---

134 Under the Children Act 1989, section 17 or section 47.
135 Rights Watch UK: *Preventing Education: Human Rights and UK Counter-Terrorism Policy in Schools*, 2016.
136 UN Special Rapporteur Fionnuala Ni Aolain.

Prevent. In 2017–2018 over 7,000 people, including children, were referred, 95 per cent of whom did not require action under the Channel programme.

The Government is under a statutory duty to establish an independent review of its strategy for supporting those vulnerable to being drawn into terrorism.[137] In 2019, the Government appointed Lord Carlisle as the reviewer, but was forced to drop him after allegations that Lord Carlisle had a well-recorded bias in favour of the Prevent programme and Rights Watch (UK) threatened legal action. He was succeeded by Jonathan Hall QC. The next Review was originally scheduled to report by August 2020, but this date has now slipped to August 2021.

Terrorist trials and the principle of open justice

That trials should be held in public is a fundamental principle of justice. It will be seen below that proceedings before SIAC and the use of Closed Material Proceedings both represent a departure from that principle, a departure justified on national security grounds. In **Guardian News and Media Ltd v AB CD** (2014) the media appealed against a decision that a trial of two alleged terrorists should be held in *camera* (i.e. behind closed doors), the first part-secret trial held in the United Kingdom. Stressing the importance of the principle of open justice, the Court of Appeal (Criminal Division) nevertheless recognised that national security is itself a 'national interest of the first importance', and that national security may justify departure from the principle of open justice. However, Gross LJ stated that any departure from the principle of open justice must be both 'necessary and proportionate', and that no more than 'the minimum departure' from open justice would be countenanced. In the instant case, the Court modified the order of the court below, ruling that the core of the trial would be held in *camera*, on the basis that if some evidence were to be heard in open court the Crown would be deterred from continuing with the prosecution. Other aspects of the trial – procedural matters such as the reading of charges to the jury and the judge's introductory remarks and the verdicts – could be held in open court. The Court also ruled that the defendants should not be anonymised: to hold a criminal trial in *camera* and to allow the anonymisation of the defendants was too great a departure from open justice.

The jury failed to reach a verdict. The defendants, Erol Incedal and Mournir Rarmoul-Bouhadjar (formerly known as AB and CD), now face a retrial. In his Annual Press Conference the Lord Chief Justice, Lord Thomas of Cwmgiedd, deplored the idea of secrecy in trials and called for clearer rules to govern the area. He was forthright in opposing the anonymity of defendants, saying that he hoped 'we will never, ever see [it] again in our courts' and that 'justice that is not open is not good justice'.[138]

On the principle of open justice, see further Chapter 22.

The right to trial by jury has long been regarded as an intrinsic element in the right to fair trial. However, in exceptional circumstances, trials may be undertaken without a jury. For example in **In the matter of an application by Dennis Hutchins for Judicial Review (Northern Ireland)** (2019)[139] the Supreme Court dismissed an appeal against the issuing of a certificate directing that a person be tried by a judge sitting alone without a jury.[140] The Act provided that a certificate could be issued where there was a risk that the administration of justice might be harmed if there was a jury trial. In this case, the trial was for the alleged attempted murder of a person suspected of involvement with terrorist activity by the Provisional Irish Republican Army in

---

137 Counter-terrorism and Border Security Act 2015, section 20.
138 On the principle of open justice in relation to extradition proceedings, see **R (B) v Westminster Magistrates' Court** (2014).
139 [2019] UKSC 26.
140 Under the Justice and Security (Northern Ireland) Act 2007, section 1.

Northern Ireland in 1974. The case turned on the interpretation of one of the conditions for issuing a certificate under the Act: namely that the offence was committed in relation to 'religious or political hostility' towards another person or group of persons. The Supreme Court ruled that the DPP had acted lawfully. The right to jury trial was not an absolute right and in certain circumstances could be antithetical to a fair trial.

The Special Immigration Appeals Commission

The Special Immigration Appeals Commission (SIAC) (a superior court of record) was established to provide a forum for appeals in situations where the normal principle of open justice cannot operate without risking damage to the security of the state.[141] SIAC deals with appeals where the Secretary of State for the Home Department exercises his or her power to deport a person, or refuses to admit a person to the UK, on national security or other public interest grounds.[142]

The Commission comprises three persons, one of whom must have held high judicial office, one a present or former legally qualified member of the Asylum and Immigration Tribunal (AIT) and a third member with experience of national security matters.

Closed Material Proceedings (CMP)

SIAC considers both 'open' and 'closed' material. Neither the applicants nor their legal advisers are entitled to see the closed material. Instead, the closed material is disclosed to one or more 'Special Advocates' appointed by the Solicitor General to act on behalf of each of the applicants. During closed sessions before SIAC, the Special Advocate can make submissions on behalf of the applicant. However, from the time at which the Special Advocate had sight of the closed material, he is not permitted any further contact with the applicant and his representatives, unless permission to do so is given by SIAC. Note that the CMP cannot be used in ordinary civil claims for damages without statutory authority. The Supreme Court so held, by a majority, in **Al Rawi and others v Security Service** (2011).

In **Yam v United Kingdom** (2020)[143] the European Court of Human Rights ruled that closed proceedings did not breach the right to fair trial. The applicant was on trial for murder, and some of the proceedings were closed on grounds of national security. The applicant had seen all the evidence on which the reasons for the prosecution's request had been based, and he had taken part in the hearing leading to the decision (and that decision had been reviewed on appeal). The judge had balanced the need for openness against the national security interests and was satisfied that the trial would be fair. The UK had not failed to comply with its obligations under the Convention.

The Special Advocate's role is to cross-examine witnesses, make written submissions and make submission at a hearing from which the appellant is excluded.[144] Appeals from SIAC lie to the Court of Appeal on points of law.

- The need to appoint a Special Advocate to assist a claimant was considered in **R (AHK and others) v Secretary of State for the Home Department** (2009). The Secretary of State had refused an application for British citizenship, on the ground that the applicant had failed to

141 See the Special Immigration Appeals Act 1997.
142 SIAC also deals with appeals against decisions refusing a person citizenship under the British Nationality Act 1981 as amended.
143 Application No 31295/11; ECHR 25 March 2020.
144 SIAC Procedure Rules 2003.

demonstrate good character.[145] The legal burden of establishing good character is on the claimant, as is the burden of showing that the decision of the Secretary of State is wrong in law. The Secretary of State was unwilling to disclose the relevant material on public interest grounds. The Court considered the case of Malik (2008), and Lord Bingham's opinion that the appointment of a Special Advocate must be necessary and will 'always be exceptional, never automatic; a course of last and never first resort'. In the instant case, the Court of Appeal ruled that a Special Advocate should be appointed 'where it is just, and therefore necessary, to do so in order for the issues to be determined fairly' (see paragraph 37).

- In **RB (Algeria) v Secretary of State for the Home Department**; U **(Algeria) v Same**; **Othman v Same** (2009) the House of Lords considered the grounds on which a decision of SIAC could be challenged. The claimants appealed against the decision of the Secretary of State to deport them on the ground that their deportation would be conducive to the public good because they were a danger to national security. SIAC had concluded that there were no substantial grounds for believing that the claimants would be exposed to treatment contrary to Article 3 or Article 6. It had considered closed as well as open material. Section 7(1) of the Special Immigration Appeals Act 1997 had limited review of SIAC's decisions which the Court of Appeal could undertake to questions of law. Accordingly, SIAC's conclusions could only be attacked on the grounds that it had failed to have due regard for some rule of law, had regard to irrelevant matters, failed to take into account relevant matters or that its procedures had failed to meet the requirements imposed by law.

The use of closed material was considered by the Court of Appeal in **AT v Secretary of State for the Home Department** (2012). AT was alleged to be a 'significant and influential member' of a terrorist group. The allegation was general and any determinative evidence was in closed material which had not been disclosed to AT. Accordingly he could not refute the allegation. The Court of Appeal allowed his appeal. Carnworth LJ, following the reasoning of the European Court of Human Rights in **A v United Kingdom** (2009), stated that:

> Where reliance is placed on closed material to determine an issue of significance, that needs to be made clear in the judgment, and the judge needs to satisfy himself that the subject has had adequate notice of the points against him. [at paragraph 51]

Where a witness, subject to a deportation order, appeared before SIAC and feared reprisals, it is open to the Commission to make an irrevocable non-disclosure order, without prior notice to the Home Secretary, to protect the identity of that witness. Such orders should be exceptional. They had the effect of preventing the Home Secretary from examining the evidence and explaining or refuting it. They were justified, however, on the basis that SIAC needed as much evidence as possible in order to reach the correct decision. The Supreme Court so ruled in **W (Algeria) and Others v Secretary of State for the Home Department** (2012).

The difficulties caused by the disclosure of sensitive evidence in open court are dealt with by the Justice and Security Act 2013. Public Interest Immunity (PII) is a claim that material should not be disclosed to the court. It is a common law principle, the use of which is controlled by the courts. PII operates in relation to national security, international relations and the prevention or detection of crime. Where a Minister claims PII, on the basis that the

---

145 As required by the British Nationality Act 1981.

disclosure of evidence would cause harm to the public interest, there is no guarantee that a court will uphold that claim – despite the general willingness of the courts to defer to Ministers on matters of national interest. A clear, if rare, example of the court rejecting such a claim occurred in **R (Binyam Mohamed) v Secretary of State for Foreign and Commonwealth Affairs** (2010). In 2008 Binyam Mohamed brought judicial review proceedings against the Foreign Secretary. He sought disclosure of evidence to assist his defence before a US military commission. The Foreign Secretary argued that disclosure should not be ordered on the basis that it would harm the relationship between the US intelligence agencies and the UK. The Foreign Secretary claimed PII in relation to sensitive information contained in the judicial review proceedings. The Court of Appeal rejected the Foreign Secretary's claim for PII. In a civil action for damages against the UK Government, alleging complicity in his rendition, detention and torture, the government, without admitting liability, agreed a settlement rather than risk the disclosure of intelligence damaging to national security.

The **Binyam Mohamed** case highlights the difficulties faced by government in ensuring the maximum openness and transparency in the interests of the rule of law while simultaneously trying to protect state security. The Justice and Security Act 2013 broadens the scope of CMPs to remedy the problem of a court refusing to uphold a claim for PII. The proposals are controversial and have attracted many criticisms. However, the government's stated intentions are to ensure that, rather than abandoning a case for fear of revealing sensitive information, CMP will enable all the evidence to be considered by a court of law without the risk of harm to national security.

Section 6 of the Act provides that the Secretary of State may apply to a court hearing a civil case for a declaration that the case is one in which CMP ('section 6 proceedings') may be used. Where it is used, non-government parties, who will be represented by special advocates, leave the court while sensitive material is heard. The use of CMP is to be confined to civil proceedings before the High Court, Court of Appeal, Court of Session or the Supreme Court. Where the court agrees to CMP it may require the person withholding the information to provide a summary of it to other parties to the proceedings and their legal representatives, providing that the summary would not damage national security.

 Pause and Reflect

Under what circumstances is it necessary for Closed Material Proceedings to be used? What safeguards are there for the defendant?

In 2009 HM Treasury had imposed sanctions (under section 62 and Schedule 7 to the Counter-Terrorism Act 2008) on Iran's largest commercial private bank, Bank Mellat, alleging that the Bank's activities supported Iran's nuclear programme. In **Bank Mellat v Her Majesty's Treasury (No 2)** (2013) the claimant applied to set aside the order on the grounds that (1) the reasons for making the order were based on irrelevant considerations and factual errors, (2) that the restrictions imposed were disproportionate to the risk posed to the national interests of the UK and (3) that in failing to provide an opportunity to make representations before the order was made, the Treasury acted in breach of the rules of natural justice and of Article 6.1 and Article 1 of the First Protocol of the European Convention on Human Rights.

In the course of the appeal it was argued by the Treasury that a closed session could make a difference to the outcome of the appeal. The Supreme Court ruled that it had jurisdiction to use a CMP. However, in a highly critical judgment the Supreme Court made it clear that in this case the Treasury had misused the procedure and that there was nothing gained by its use. Lord Hope of Craighead stated that:

> The most obnoxious feature of the closed material procedures at the stage of an appeal is the possibility that the appellate court may have to give the whole or part of its reasons for the disposal of the appeal in a judgment to which the state only, and not the other party to the appeal or anyone else, has access. [at paragraph 98]

On the substantive appeal, the Supreme Court, by a majority, ruled that the Order was unlawful and would be quashed. The decision to make the order was irrational and disproportionate: there was no basis for singling out Bank Mellat from other banks. Furthermore, the common law duty to give an opportunity to make representations had been breached.

In addition to CMP, the Justice and Security Act 2013, section 17, prevents a court from ordering the disclosure of sensitive information under its residual disclosure jurisdiction, generally referred to as the **Norwich Pharmacal** jurisdiction (derived from **Norwich Pharmacal Co v Customs and Excise Commissioners** (1974)). A Norwich Pharmacal order is one which requires a third party to release information if a party has been involved in an alleged wrongdoing: it assists the individual in bringing or defending proceedings overseas (as in the **Binyam Mohamed** case). The restriction on disclosure would relate to sensitive national security information held by the security services, the armed forces or Ministry of Defence intelligence activities.

The government considers that the provisions of the Justice and Security Act 2013 are compatible with the European Convention on Human Rights.

Summary

The law relating to state, or national, security spans a number of different issues.

For many years the role and powers of the security services were formally unrecognised and unregulated by statute. From 1989, however, Acts of Parliament have been passed to regulate the services: the Security Services Act 1989, Intelligence Services Act 1994 and Regulation of Investigatory Powers Act 2000. In addition to the security services, the related matter of the interception of communications and its regulation are central to the balance to be struck between the rights of individuals to be free from state interference and the requirements of national security.

The law relating to official secrets is also vital to state security. The Official Secrets Act 1911 provided an absolute prohibition on the unauthorised disclosure of official information and was reformed by the Official Secrets Act 1989 which introduces the concept of harmful disclosure in relation to much, but not all, confidential information.

The law relating to terrorism has become an increasingly important area of the law. Until recent years, the law was directed towards protecting against terrorism relating to the situation in Northern Ireland. With the resolution of that conflict, new threats to security have emerged from extremist groups outside and within the United Kingdom. Organised crime, national and international, also increasingly engages the security forces and requires cooperation with security forces both in Europe and worldwide.

Further Reading

Anderson, DQC, *Control Orders in 2011: Final Report of the Independent Reviewer on the Prevention of Terrorism Act 2005*, 2012, London: TSO.

Anderson, DQC, 'The Independent Review of Terrorism Law' [2014] *Public Law* 403.

Arden, M, 'Human rights in the age of terrorism' (2005) 121 *Law Quarterly Review* 609.

Blackbourn, J and Walker, C, 'Interdiction and indoctrination: the Counter-terrorism and Security Act 2015' (2016) 79 *Modern Law Review* 840.

Bonner, D, 'Terrorism, human rights and the rule of law: 120 years of the UK's response to terrorism' [2004] *Criminal Law Review* 981.

Dickson, B, 'Law versus terror: can law win?' [2005] *European Human Rights Law Review* 12.

Feldman, D, 'Proportionality and discrimination in anti-terror legislation' [2005] *Cambridge Law Journal* 271.

Feldman, D, 'Human rights, terrorism and risk: the roles of politicians and judges' [2006] *Public Law* 364.

Gearty, C, 'Counter terrorism and the Human Rights Act' (2005) 32(1) *Journal of Law and Society* 18.

Gearty, C, 'Human rights in an age of counter terrorism: injurious, irrelevant or indispensable?' (2005) 58 *Current Legal Issues* 25.

Ip, J, '*Al Rawi, Tariq*, and the future of closed material procedures' (2012) 75 *MLR* 606.

Kavanagh, A, 'Judging the judges under the Human Rights Act: deference, disillusionment and the "war on terror"' [2009] *Public Law* 287.

Murphy, MH, 'Transparency and surveillance' [2016] *Public Law* 9.

Supperstone, M, 'The Intelligence Services Act 1994' [1994] *Public Law* 329.

Tomkins, A, 'Readings of *A v Secretary of State for the Home Department*' [2005] *Public Law* 259.

Walker, C, 'The legal definition of "terrorism" in United Kingdom law and beyond' [2007] *Public Law* 331.

Walker, C, 'The threat of terrorism and fate of control orders' [2010] *Public Law* 4.

White Paper, 'Counter terrorist powers: reconciling security and liberty in an open society' Cm6147, 2004.

Wilkinson, N, *Secrecy and the Media – The Official History of the D Notice System*, 2009, Oxford: Routledge.

Zedner, L, 'Security liberty in the face of terror: reflections from criminal justice' (2005) 32(4) *Journal of Law and Society* 507.

Part 7

Judges and the Legal System

Chapter 22

Judges and the English Legal System

Chapter Contents

Learning Objectives

By the end of this chapter you should be able to:

- ☐ discuss the constitutional role of judges;
- ☐ explain the importance of judicial independence;
- ☐ discuss judicial accountability;
- ☐ explain the different categories of law;
- ☐ discuss the hierarchy of civil and criminal courts;
- ☐ discuss judicial techniques of statutory interpretation and the doctrine of precedent.

Introduction

The rule of law, discussed in Chapter 3, is one of the fundamental principles of the United Kingdom constitution. The rule of law protects the rights of the individual against arbitrary power and ensures that those with power exercise their powers according to law. The task of upholding the rule of law lies with both Parliament and the judiciary. Through the settlement of disputes according to law, interpreting Acts of Parliament and applying the doctrine of precedent, judges develop the law, usually incrementally, occasionally boldly, and supplement Parliament's law-making role. In this chapter the role of the judges, the differing categories of law and the court structure are discussed, together with an introduction to the doctrine of precedent and statutory interpretation. Of central constitutional importance is the independence of the judiciary: independence from the government and freedom from any external influences which could compromise that independence. In Chapter 4 the separation of powers was discussed: in this chapter we look further at the laws and conventions which uphold judicial independence and consider the question of judicial accountability.

There is no single unified legal system within the United Kingdom. England and Wales share one system, while Scotland and Northern Ireland each has its own distinctive system. Following devolution (see Chapter 11), Scotland, Northern Ireland and Wales also have their own law-making Parliament or Assembly with its powers defined in an Act of the United Kingdom (UK) Parliament. Paradoxically, England is the only country in the United Kingdom which does not have its own law-making body. By convention, the UK Parliament will not legislate on matters which have been devolved to a national Assembly or Parliament. However, in relation to non-devolved matters, the UK Parliament continues to legislate for the whole of the United Kingdom. Supplementing statute law is the common law – the law derived from judicially decided cases. In addition, during the UK's membership of the EU, the law of the European Union (EU) entered into domestic law under the European Communities Act 1972 and the Human Rights Act 1998 enables rights protected under the European Convention on Human Rights to be enforced in the domestic courts. As a result, the law is a mixture of statute law made by the UK Parliament and the devolved legislatures, the common law and European law.

The Ministry of Justice paper **Transforming Our Justice System** 2016 sets out its vision for the future of the court and tribunal system. In response to technological advances the system is currently undergoing significant change. While traditionally cases have been heard in a court of law or a tribunal before a judge, modern communications technology enables cases to be started online, and many to be completed online while others will be scheduled for physical hearings. Many courts have already been closed: research having shown that in 2014–2015, 48 per cent of courts and tribunals were used for less than half the available time. The closure of courts enables investment in fewer more modern buildings. The principles guiding reforms are that the court and tribunal system should be open, proportionate and accessible.

In relation to criminal justice, the whole system is being digitised. Already most of the Magistrates' Court work is transferred digitally between the police and Crown Prosecution Service. The aim is to provide an online process to manage criminal cases from start to finish. In relation to non-imprisonable offences where there is no victim involved (e.g. rail ticket evasion), defendants will be able to plead online and choose to be dealt with by an automated system which could impose a conviction online and impose a fine and costs. Witnesses are already able to give evidence over a video link and the aim is to increase the number of locations from where victims and witnesses can give their evidence.

In relation to the civil courts, the aim was to automate and digitise the process of civil money claims, claims which make up over four-fifths of 1.6 million claims issued in the County Courts and High Court each year. Further reforms are designed to promote different ways of resolving disputes to minimise adversarial hearings, to reduce the time taken to settle disputes and to provide better controls over court costs.

PART A: THE JUDICIARY
The Constitutional Role of Judges

The judiciary is one of the three major institutions of the state, the others being the legislature and executive. Constitutionally, each of these institutions acts in the name of the Crown. The relationships between the three institutions were discussed in Chapter 4 under the separation of powers. It was seen there, that while there are many overlaps between the executive and legislature, the judiciary maintains a separation from both – a separation which ensures the independence of the judiciary and which is protected both by law and convention. Judicial independence is of fundamental importance to the rule of law: without independence the judges would not be able to keep the government within the law or to protect individual rights.

The United Kingdom constitution has traditionally been viewed as a constitution based on the fundamental principle of the supremacy, or sovereignty, of Parliament.[1] The relationship between the legislature and the judiciary is one characterised by the aphorism 'Parliament makes the law, judges interpret the law', thereby stressing the ultimate supremacy of the legislature over the judiciary. In constitutional terms this relationship manifests itself in the fact that Parliament has the power and right to overturn judicial decisions, that the judges will faithfully interpret and apply the intention of Parliament as expressed in statutes and will not challenge the validity of an Act of Parliament.

However, although theoretically correct, the above explanation is both too simple and misleading, masking the complex interaction between the three institutions of the state. This interaction between the executive, Parliament and the judiciary is also one which is undergoing change as successive governments implement constitutional reform. One major constitutional change of the last century was Britain joining the European Communities (now European Union) in 1972 (discussed in Chapters 7 and 8). With the Labour government elected in 1997 came further major constitutional changes, among them the devolution of law-making powers to Northern Ireland, Scotland and Wales (see Chapter 11), the Human Rights Act 1998 incorporating rights protected under the European Convention on Human Rights and Fundamental Freedoms (see Chapter 18) and the establishment of a Supreme Court under the Constitutional Reform Act 2005 (on which see below). Each of these developments has had a significant impact on the role of the judiciary.

Membership of the European Communities (now EU) from 1973 to 2020 entailed the acceptance of the body of law enacted in the Communities and the law developed by the Court of Justice of the European Union (CJEU). In order that EU law has the same meaning and applicability in all Member States of the Union, in addition to making EU law enforceable before the domestic courts, all Member States must accept that EU law takes priority over any conflicting domestic law. Judges in the domestic courts tried through statutory interpretation to make domestic law compatible with EU law. If there were doubts about the requirements of EU law, the domestic courts could refer a question to the ECJ seeking clarification on the requirements of EU law. Once the answer to the question was received back, the domestic court was obliged to follow EU law. The end result of this process, as seen most starkly in

---

1 On sovereignty see Chapter 6.

the **Factortame**[2] cases, is that where a domestic statute conflicted with the requirements of EU law, that statute must be 'set aside' and EU law applied. This is not to say that the judges held an Act of Parliament to be invalid: it remained technically valid until repealed by Parliament, but the Act could no longer be applied. The UK left the EU in January 2020. Until the end of 2020 there was a transition stage, during which the future relations between the EU and UK were to be finalised. The domestic courts no longer make references to the European Court of Justice of the EU, and it is for the government and Parliament to determine how much EU law is retained within the domestic legal system (see further Chapter 8). From the end of December 2020, the UK Parliament is once again 'fully' sovereign.

Devolution to the nations also has an impact on the role of judges. Whereas judges do not have the power to invalidate an Act of the United Kingdom Parliament, the position is different with an Act of a devolved legislature. Acts of the Northern Ireland, Scottish and Welsh Assemblies/Parliament are valid only if they fall within the power ('competence') devolved to that body by the UK Parliament. If there is a dispute about the scope of competence devolved the courts will resolve that conflict and the matter may ultimately go to the Supreme Court for judgment. If it is held that the relevant legislature lacked the competence to pass a particular measure, that measure will be held to be invalid. It has always been the case that secondary legislation can be invalidated by the courts if it falls outside the powers conferred by the parent Act. That, however, is uncontroversial in that the judges are upholding the will of Parliament. With devolution, however, for the first time the judges are ruling on the validity or invalidity of primary legislation (albeit of a devolved non-sovereign legislature). This gives to the courts a role very similar to that of a Supreme Court under a written constitution – a role very different from the conventional judicial role in the United Kingdom.

The Human Rights Act 1998 raises different, but no less significant, issues for the relationship between the judiciary, the government and Parliament. Under the Human Rights Act, judges are instructed to interpret domestic legislation 'so far as it is possible to do so' in a manner compatible with Convention rights.[3] Furthermore, the courts are defined as public bodies.[4] It is unlawful for public bodies to violate Convention rights (unless primary legislation makes it impossible for them to act in any other way). Accordingly, the judges must protect Convention rights. The combination of these provisions of the Act has led to a great deal of judicial creativity in developing the law. Two examples may briefly be offered. The first is the case of **Ghaidan v Godin-Mendoza** (2004) in which the House of Lords ruled that a housing Act designed to protect the occupation rights of a husband or wife on the death of the other spouse, should, in order to comply with Article 8 of the Convention, be interpreted to include within the meaning of 'spouse' a same-sex partner who had cohabited with the deceased for some time. The second example is the development of a right to privacy,[5] contrary to Parliament's intention. This was achieved by the judges, led largely by Eady J, extending the English law of confidence to protect the privacy of the individual as guaranteed by Article 8 of the European Convention on Human Rights. Essentially, the law of confidence provides a remedy for a person who has conveyed information to another in a situation where it is clear, or ought to be clear, that the information is confidential and hence not to be passed on or published to others. Article 8 of the Convention provides the 'right to respect for private life, family and correspondence'. One example from the case law illustrates the approach of the judges to the interplay between the law of confidence and the right to privacy under Article

---

2 See Chapter 8.
3 Human Rights Act 1998, s. 3.
4 Ibid., s. 6(3).
5 There has never been a substantive right to privacy under English law.

8. In **HRH Prince of Wales v Associated Newspapers Ltd** (2007)[6] a former member of the Prince's staff disclosed to the defendant copies of travel journals written by the Prince. They were confidential and not intended for publication. Lord Phillips of Worth Matravers emphasised the importance of section 3 of the Human Rights Act (the interpretative duty) in developing domestic law so as to give effect to Convention rights, in this case Article 8. He went on to say: 'To this end the courts have extended the law of confidentiality so as to protect Article 8 rights [i.e. the right to privacy] in circumstances which do not involve a breach of a confidential relationship'.

One further development which has brought the judiciary into sharper constitutional focus is the rapid expansion of judicial review. Applications for judicial review have risen considerably over recent decades, and they have done so particularly in areas of administration which attract critical media and public attention – most notably in immigration and terrorism. As discussed below, this has led to some public outbursts by Ministers which contravene the constitutional convention that the executive will not criticise judicial decisions which in turn has led to criticism of the judges in the press. The main thrust of these criticisms is that judges are 'interfering' in areas which should best be left to the executive and Parliament. What is ignored, however, is that the judges are doing no more, and no less, than applying the intention of Parliament as laid down in the Human Rights Act 1998, section 3 (the duty to interpret statutes in a manner compatible with Convention rights) and section 6 (as a public body the court is under a duty to protect Convention rights).

The constitutional effect of these developments has been to heighten interest in the constitutional position of judges. In particular, as discussed below, the issues of judicial independence and judicial accountability have moved to the forefront of constitutional debate. In addition, over recent years there has been a lively academic debate over whether the relationship between Parliament and the judges has changed, or is changing. This issue is discussed in some detail in Chapter 6. To summarise that debate, there have been statements made by a few members of the senior judiciary in the course of their judgments, and extra-judicially, to the effect that the concept of parliamentary sovereignty is undergoing change. The essence of the argument is that if Parliament passed legislation infringing fundamental human rights or fundamental constitutional principles such as access to a court of law (in particular the right to apply for judicial review) the judges – acting as guardians of the rule of law – might refuse to apply the statute. Such a view is, of course, contrary to the traditional doctrine of sovereignty which insists that no one, including a court of law, may challenge the validity of an Act of Parliament. Such a situation should be unlikely to arise provided that the democratic process remains sufficiently robust to restrain a government from abusing its power. However, expressions of judicial disquiet over the traditional doctrine of sovereignty, albeit from a minority of judges, do raise important constitutional questions. For legal constitutionalists the role of the judges is emphasised and the suggestion made that sovereignty is, or is becoming, shared between Parliament and the courts. As early as 1991 the flavour of the debate was captured in the statement of Lord Bridge of Harwich in **X Ltd v Morgan Grampian Ltd** that:

> The maintenance of the rule of law is in every way as important in a free society as the democratic franchise. In our society the rule of law rests upon twin foundations: the sovereignty of the Queen in Parliament in making the law and the sovereignty of the Queen's courts in interpreting and applying the law.

---

6 This and other cases are discussed further in Chapter 19.

For political constitutionalists the suggestion that sovereignty is 'shared' between Parliament and the courts is highly problematic. Judges do not have any democratic mandate and are not answerable to the electorate. Furthermore, as discussed below, the senior judiciary does not reflect society in terms of gender, age, race or class but remains essentially male, white, middle class, educated at public school and at Oxford or Cambridge University. For all these reasons, the idea that there is an emerging shared or 'bi-polar' sovereignty is one to be resisted. For further detail on the debate, see Chapter 6 and for discussion of the concept of constitutionalism see Chapter 1.

Judicial Functions

Dispute settlement

Law is the formal mechanism by which disputes in society are settled. It was seen in Chapter 3 when discussing the rule of law that in earlier times in traditional eastern states the settlement of disputes took place in systems of mediation rather than law, with recourse to law being seen as detrimental to society's cohesion. In complex societies, however, such mechanisms are inadequate and more formal, rule-based, procedures are needed. The court structure and law fulfil this need.[7] Disputes may be between individuals over matters of private law such as the validity of marriage or the validity of a contract or property transaction. Disputes may also involve public law matters where the individual is aggrieved by a decision or act of a public body and seeks to challenge that act or decision. Statistically, it is the criminal law which accounts for the majority of cases before the courts, with the state prosecuting a suspect for an alleged breach of the law.[8]

It is a fundamental requirement of the rule of law that the legal system ensures fairness in the decision-making process. This principle is reflected in Article 6 of the European Convention on Human Rights (ECHR) which guarantees the right to fair trial, requiring *inter alia* that there is a 'fair and public hearing' by an 'independent and impartial tribunal'. A key element of fairness at trial is the impartiality of the judge. On rare occasions this impartiality may be questioned as in **Serafin v Malkiewicz** (2020). This was a libel case in which Mr Serafin represented himself at trial. On appeal one of the arguments was that the conduct of the judge was such as to render the trial unfair. The Supreme Court found that the judge had 'directed a barrage of hostility' towards the claimant's case and the claimant, using 'immoderate, ill-tempered and at times offensive language' and had 'harassed and intimidated him'. Lord Wilson stated that the justice system had 'failed both sides' and 'with deep regret' ordered a full retrial.

Interpreting and applying the law

In the settlement of disputes, one of the principal functions of judges is applying the law as laid down in Acts of Parliament or by common law. This, for the most part, is straightforward, but when a case is appealed and reaches the higher courts it is because there is a dispute about the meaning of the law and how it should apply to a given factual situation. It is here that the judges must, through the process of statutory interpretation and the doctrine of precedent (for details of which see below) interpret what Parliament's intention was when passing the Act or interpret the precedent case law on a particular matter. In both cases the

---

7 There are, however, alternatives to courts. Tribunals are the major alternative, and in many respects increasingly act with the same formality as courts: see Chapter 26 on Tribunals. There are also different forms of mediation and conciliation which operate alongside the formal structure of law.
8 On categories of law, see further below.

process of interpretation and application results in the development of the law. On the interpretation and development of the law see further below at pages 627 to 637.

Judicial review of administrative action

Another major role of the judiciary is ensuring that public bodies who exercise powers conferred by Parliament are kept within those powers. Allied to this is the insistence by the courts that public bodies respect the rules of natural justice and fairness in the exercise of their powers. This jurisdiction is judicial review which is essential to the maintenance of the rule of law and enforcing Parliament's will. Judicial review is discussed in detail in Chapters 23 to 25.

Judicial Independence

Once appointed, the independence of the judiciary from the executive and from Parliament is protected both by statute and convention. Without independence from the other institutions of government, judges would be unable to carry out their duties in an impartial manner. Independence is both personal and collective. The individual judge must be protected from pressure from the other institutions of the state and from non-state institutions that might seek to exert influence. Collectively, the judiciary must also be protected from threats to its independence: public trust in the judges can only be sustained if the judiciary as a whole is seen to be impartial and independent. The Constitutional Reform Act 2005, section 3, provides for judicial independence as follows:

> (3) Guarantee of continued judicial independence
>
> > (1) The Lord Chancellor, other Ministers of the Crown and all with responsibility for matters relating to the judiciary or otherwise to the administration of justice must uphold the continued independence of the judiciary.
> >
> > ...
> >
> > (4) The following particular duties are imposed for the purpose of upholding that independence.
> >
> > (5) The Lord Chancellor and other Ministers of the Crown must not seek to influence particular judicial decisions through any special access to the judiciary.
> >
> > (6) The Lord Chancellor must have regard to –
> >
> > > (a) the need to defend that independence;
> > >
> > > (b) the need for the judiciary to have the support necessary to enable them to exercise their functions;
> > >
> > > (c) the need for the public interest in regard to matters relating to the judiciary or otherwise to the administration of justice to be properly represented in decision affecting those matters.

Equivalent statutory provisions are made in relation to Scotland and Northern Ireland under the Judiciary and Courts (Scotland) Act 2008, and the Justice (Northern Ireland) Act 2002.

Various aspects of individual and collective judicial independence are considered below before discussing the issue of accountability.

The appointment of judges

Appointment to the Supreme Court is by the Crown on the recommendation of the Prime Minister. The Prime Minister is under a statutory duty to recommend only that person who has been nominated by the Lord Chancellor.[9] It is the Supreme Court Selection Commission that selects the candidates, in consultation with senior judges who are not themselves candidates, the Lord Chancellor, the First Minister for Scotland, the Secretary of State for Northern Ireland and First Minister for Wales. Qualification for appointment is that a person has held judicial office for at least two years or has been a qualifying practitioner for at least 15 years.[10] Selection is based on merit, and the Commission may select only one person.[11] Having made its selection the Commission must report to the Lord Chancellor, stating who has been selected.

The Lord Chancellor will then engage in further consultation with senior judges etc., as above. Having consulted, the Lord Chancellor has the power to accept, reject or ask the Commission to reconsider its nomination. Once the selection is made, the Lord Chancellor reports to the Prime Minister who then advises the Queen.

The jurisdiction of the Supreme Court is that of final court of appeal from all courts in England and Wales and Northern Ireland, and the final court of appeal in relation to civil – but not criminal – cases from Scotland. Supreme Court Justices also act as judges in the Privy Council.

The Lord Chief Justice, Master of the Rolls, President of the Family Division, Vice Chancellor, Lord Justices of Appeal are appointed by the Queen.[12] For appointments to the High Court, the candidate must be a barrister of ten years' standing, or a solicitor with rights of audience in the High Court, or a circuit judge of two years' standing. For appointment to the Court of Appeal, the candidate must either be a barrister of ten years' standing, a solicitor with rights of audience in the High Court, or a current member of the High Court Bench.[13]

The Lord Chief Justice is the head of the judiciary assuming the additional title of President of the Courts of England and Wales and Head of the Judiciary of England and Wales.

The Judicial Appointments Commission

In England and Wales, the Judicial Appointments Commission (JAC) was established under the Constitutional Reform Act 2005. In Northern Ireland, the JAC, established under the Justice (Northern Ireland) Acts 2002 and 2004, has been in operation since 2005. The Commission recommends appointments to the Queen, via the Lord Chancellor. In Scotland, the Judicial Appointments Board has operated since 2002.[14] It makes recommendations to the Queen, through the First Minister. The focus here is on the English JAC, although the principles and procedures are common to all jurisdictions. Scotland and Northern Ireland each has its own JAC.

The JAC was established to assume responsibility for selecting candidates for judicial office, a responsibility which had previously lain with the Lord Chancellor. The principal objective in setting up the Commission was to make the appointment process more transparent and more accountable.

---

9 Constitutional Reform Act 2005, ss 26(3) and 29.
10 *Ibid.*, s. 25(1).
11 Constitutional Reform Act 2005, s. 27(10).
12 Senior Courts Act 1981, s. 10.
13 Courts and Legal Services Act 1990, s 71.
14 See now the Judiciary and Courts (Scotland) Act 2008.

The Commission is made up of 15 Commissioners, appointed by the Crown on the advice of the Lord Chancellor, through open competition, with the exception of three judicial members who are selected either by the Judges' Council or the Tribunals' Council.

Section 63 of the Constitutional Reform Act 2005 provides that selection to judicial office must 'be solely on merit' and that 'a person must not be selected unless the selecting body is satisfied that he is of good character'. The Commission is also required, under section 64, to 'encourage diversity in the range of persons available for selection for appointment'. This latter requirement is subject to section 63.

Disqualification from judicial office

Holders of full-time judicial appointments are barred from legal practice,[15] and may not hold paid appointments as directors or undertake any professional or business work. Judges are also disqualified from membership of the House of Commons.[16] Membership of the House of Commons does not, however, disqualify that person from appointment to the Bench.

Tenure and retirement

If judges are to fulfil their constitutional role they must be free from fear of dismissal on political grounds. The Act of Settlement 1700 secured a senior judge's tenure of office during 'good behaviour'. In relation to the Supreme Court, the Constitutional Reform Act 2005, section 33, now provides that: 'A judge of the Supreme Court holds that office during good behaviour, but may be removed from it on the address of both Houses of Parliament'. Judges can be removed by compulsory retirement if they are incapacitated or unable to resign through incapacity.

'Misbehaviour' relates to the performance of a judge's official duties or the commission of a criminal offence. Not every judge convicted of an offence will be dismissed: six judges have been convicted for driving with an excess of alcohol in their blood but have continued in office. In 1830, Sir Jonah Barrington was removed from office in Ireland under the Address procedure for the embezzlement of monies paid into court. Theoretically, a judge can also be removed by 'impeachment' for 'high crimes and misdemeanours', although this procedure has not been used since 1805 and is thought to be obsolete.[17] In Scotland, judges can only be removed on the grounds of misconduct.[18]

The Constitutional Reform Act 2005 established the Office for Judicial Complaints. The Lord Chief Justice and the Lord Chancellor can refer a matter to the Office for investigation and report. Any decision relating to further action lies with the Lord Chief Justice.

The Judicial Pensions and Retirement Act 1993 introduced the retirement age of 70, which may be extended to 75 if in the public interest. From 1959, the retirement ages were set at 75 for a High Court judge and 72 for a circuit judge, although judges appointed before this date were permitted to remain in office.[19]

---

15 Courts and Legal Services Act 1990, s. 75 and Sched. 11.
16 House of Commons Disqualification Act 1975, s. 1 and Sched. 1.
17 Impeachment is not obsolete in the United States of America, where President Nixon was threatened with impeachment and resigned in 1974 and President Clinton was acquitted in impeachment proceedings in 1999.
18 Claim of Right 1689, Article 13, *Mackay and Esslemont v Lord Advocate* (1937).
19 As did Lord Denning, who retired at the age of 83.

England and Wales: The Number of Judges and Qualifications		
Supreme Court Justices	12	High judicial office for 2 years or 15 years as a 'qualifying practitioner'
Court of Appeal judges	39	High Court judge or 10 years' right of audience in High Court
High Court judge	99	Circuit judge for 2 years or 10 years' right of audience in the High Court
Circuit judge (Crown Court and County Court)	1088	Recorder or 10 years' right of audience in Crown Court or County Court or other judicial office
Magistrates (England and Wales)	13,177	No formal qualifications
Tribunals	c.500	Salaried judges, plus specialist non-legal members Many salaried judges are legally qualified

Salaries

Judicial salaries are determined by the independent Senior Salaries Review Body (SSRB). The SSRB gives independent advice to the Prime Minister, Lord Chancellor, Defence, Health and Home Office Ministers on salaries for the senior civil service, judiciary, armed forces, some NHS posts and Police and Crime Commissioners. In order further to protect the judiciary from political debate, judicial salaries are charged on the Consolidated Fund. Judicial salaries are relatively high (but far lower than can be earned in successful legal practice), on the basis that it is in the national interest 'to ensure an adequate supply of candidates of sufficient calibre for appointment to judicial office'.[20]

Immunity from suit

All judges have immunity from legal action in the performance of their judicial functions. Provided that a judge acts within his or her jurisdiction, or honestly believes he is acting within his jurisdiction, no action for damages may lie. A judge is immune from the law of defamation and, even if 'actuated by envy, hatred and malice and all uncharitableness', he or she is protected. In **Sirros v Moore** (1975), Lord Denning MR and Ormrod LJ ruled that every judge – irrespective of rank and including the lay magistracy – is protected from liability in respect of his judicial function provided that he honestly believed that the action taken was within his jurisdiction. The Crown Proceedings Act 1947 also provides protection for the Crown from liability for conduct of any person discharging 'responsibilities of a judicial nature vested in him' or in executing the judicial process.[21]

Oath of allegiance/affirmation

On appointment, judges must take the Judicial Oath of Allegiance and the Judicial Oath, or to affirm. The oaths and affirmations provide that judges will bear 'true allegiance' to the

---

20 HC Deb Vol. 223 Cols 257–261.
21 Crown Proceedings Act 1947, s. 2(5).

Queen and her successors, and 'to do right to all manner of people after the laws and usages of this realm, without fear or favour, affection or ill will'.

The Oaths and Affirmations are adaptable for Hindu, Jewish, Muslim and Sikh members of the judiciary.

Bias or personal interest

A judge is under a duty not to adjudicate on cases in which he has either an interest – whether personal or financial – or where he may be influenced by bias. A fundamental doctrine of natural justice is that 'no man should be judge in his own cause': *nemo iudex in sua causa*. Judicial impartiality – or freedom from bias – is discussed in detail in Chapter 25.

See Chapter 25.

Two contrasting examples will suffice here. The first is the **Pinochet** case, **R v Bow Street Metropolitan Stipendiary Magistrate, ex parte Pinochet Ugarte (No 2)** (2000). Spain had requested the extradition of the former Head of State of Chile, Pinochet, to stand trial for war crimes. The panel of judges in the House of Lords included Lord Hoffmann who had links with Amnesty International. Amnesty, a charity which campaigns on behalf of political prisoners, had been permitted to give evidence to the court. Although there was no suspicion that Lord Hoffmann was actually biased, the fact that the public might perceive him to be biased was sufficient to have the decision set aside and a different panel of judges convened to re-hear the case.

Similar circumstances, but with a different result, arose in **Helow v Secretary of State for the Home Department** (2004). In this case, the appellant had applied for, but been refused, asylum in the United Kingdom. She was a Palestinian who had been actively involved with the Palestinian Liberation Organisation. It was discovered that one of the judges hearing her appeal was a member of the International Association of Jewish Lawyers and Jurists. Would a 'fair minded and informed observer' consider that the judge was biased? The House of Lords ruled that there was no bias: the Association had not been party to the proceedings (unlike Amnesty in **Pinochet**) and there was no basis on which 'the observer would conclude that there was a reasonable possibility that the judge was biased'.

Political neutrality

Once appointed, judges must not participate in any party political activity. The Judges' Council, *Guide to Judicial Conduct*, states that judges must 'forego any kind of political activity'. To engage with politics would compromise judicial independence and risk making a judge ineligible to adjudicate impartially on any issue that might come before a court. The Judicial Oath or Affirmation upholds this principle. The *Guide to Judicial Conduct* provides that judges may, however, engage in public debate, provided that it relates to 'the operation of the courts, the independence of the judiciary or aspects of the administration of justice'. They must avoid, however, saying anything which would 'cause the public to associate the judge with a particular organisation, group or cause'.[22]

Judges are careful to avoid any contact with government which could compromise their independence. When governments are developing policy, particularly over a sensitive area on which the courts are likely to have to rule, it is understandable that Ministers should seek the advice of the judges. An example given by Lord Phillips of Worth Matravers, the first President of the Supreme Court, is that of a former Home Secretary, Charles Clarke, inviting Lord Bingham, a Law Lord, to discuss how the government could lawfully deal with the

---

22 Paragraphs 8.2.1. and 8.2.4. respectively.

problem of terrorism. Lord Bingham declined. Lord Phillips stated that 'Such a conversation would have been inappropriate and infringed the separation of powers'.[23]

The *sub judice* rule prohibits discussion in Parliament of cases before the courts. However, once a case is concluded the rule no longer applies. More generally, constitutional conventions play an important role in protecting judicial independence, although as will be seen, their operation has not been uniform.

 Pause and Reflect

Why, from a constitutional point of view, is judicial independence so important?

A Diverse and Representative Judiciary?

It has long been recognised that judges are drawn from a narrow social and educational background and that greater diversity is needed if the judiciary is to be representative of the society it serves, and to command its respect. Although the judiciary is appointed rather than elected, there is nevertheless the question of how best the judges can serve society. Having a judiciary which is representative of a very narrow stratum of society does not inspire confidence in its ability to understand the rest of society. As Baroness Hale, the first female President of the Supreme Court, has written, judges are the link between government, Parliament and the people and also have the function of keeping the organs of the state within the law. Achieving diversity, however, has to date proved to be an elusive goal.

In *The Politics of the Judiciary* (1977),[24] Professor John Griffith (1918–2010) criticised the composition of the judiciary as being essential middle- and upper-class, middle-aged, white, predominantly male and dominated by people with a public school and Oxford or Cambridge University education. It was Griffith's thesis, in part, that as a result of their social backgrounds judges form part of the elite governing group in society. As such their attitudes coincide with others within the governing group of established authority, and judges will lean towards the maintenance of the status quo and have a distrust of those groups in society – trade unions, minorities, students, demonstrators – who might threaten the established order. In short, judges are not politically neutral. As Griffith explains:

> judges in the United Kingdom cannot be politically neutral because they are placed in positions where they are required to make political choices ... as determinations of where the public interest lies; that their interpretation of what is in the public interest and therefore politically desirable is determined by the kind of people they are and the position they hold in our society; that this position is a part of established authority and so is necessarily conservative and illiberal.[25]

Griffith supported his thesis by reference to numerous cases. Highly controversial at the time of first publication and widely criticised, the essence of Griffith's thesis remains important: the lack of diversity within the judiciary is a matter of continuing concern. The lack of diversity is, as Griffith explains, a product of the background of the senior judiciary who are drawn from middle-class, professional families, educated at independent schools and Oxford

---

23 Lecture: Judicial Independence, 8 February 2011, UCL.
24 1977. 4th edn, 1991.
25 *Politics of the Judiciary*, 4th edn, p. 319.

or Cambridge, and spend 'twenty to twenty-five years in successful practice at the Bar' in London before being appointed to the Bench. Even if candidates for appointment were to be drawn from state schools and redbrick universities, Griffith doubts that there would be a difference in outlook by the time of appointment: too many years have been spent in practice, absorbing the professional mores of the Bar.

In 2012 the House of Lords Select Committee on the Constitution in its Report, *Judicial Appointments*,[26] made the following observation regarding diversity:

> Justice, fairness and equality are central values in the law which should be reflected in the composition of the judiciary itself. Judges are independent of Parliament and the executive, but they should not stand apart from the society in which they adjudicate: the public must have confidence in the judges who make the decision which affect their day to day lives. [paragraph 73]

The central difficulty in achieving diversity in the judiciary lies in the conflict between the requirement that appointment be made 'on merit' and the need for diversity. Eligibility for appointment to judicial office has traditionally been tied in with rights of audience in the higher courts which entails experience of advocacy at the Bar. The Courts and Legal Services Act 1990 (CLSA) removed the exclusive right of audience of the Bar, thereby opening up opportunities for solicitors to be appointed to the bench. Baroness Hale of Richmond, then Deputy President of the Supreme Court, writing in 2001 questioned whether experience of litigation allied to the assumption that it was necessary 'to get to the top' in order to be considered for appointment was essential to judicial appointment,[27] pointing out that both disadvantaged women. Professor Kate Malleson, discussing the lack of diversity, has suggested that the use of quotas could be an effective way of achieving greater diversity – provided that it did not lead to unqualified candidates being appointed.[28] In *Rethinking the Merit Principle in Judicial Selection*, Malleson suggested that the concept of merit needed to be reconstructed to include qualifications other than successful advocacy.[29]

The government has accepted that there needs to be an improvement in diversity.[30] The Crime and Courts Act 2013 amends the Constitutional Reform Act (CRA) 2005 and includes two provisions designed to facilitate greater diversity. Schedule 13, Part I, introduces greater flexibility into appointments to the judiciary by replacing full-time judges with the maximum full-time equivalent number. Part 2 of the 2013 Act amends the Constitutional Reform Act 2005, section 63, by providing that the selecting body is not prohibited – when choosing between two candidates of equal merit – from preferring one candidate over another for the purpose of increasing diversity. A new section 137A is introduced into the CRA 2005, imposing a duty on the Lord Chancellor and Lord Chief Justice of England and Wales to take 'such steps as that office-holder considers appropriate for the purpose of encouraging judicial diversity'.

The proportion of court judges who were women increased from 24 per cent to 32 per cent in 2019 and 46 per cent of tribunal judges were women. In terms of Black, Asian and Minority Ethnic (BAME) representation in the judiciary seven per cent of court judges and 11 per cent of tribunal judges were BAME in 2019.[31]

---

26 25th Report, Session 2010–2012.
27 Hale, 2001.
28 Malleson, 2009.
29 Malleson, 2006.
30 Appointments and Diversity: A Judiciary for the 21st Century, 2012, Ministry of Justice.
31 See Ministry of Justice: Diversity of the Judiciary 2020 statistics: report, September 2020.

The appointment process for Justices of the Supreme Court has been criticised as creating a 'self-perpetuating oligarchy'.[32] The Selection Committee comprises the President and Deputy President of the Supreme Court, one representative of each of the statutory appointments commission and one layperson. The consultation process ensures that the senior judges and 'two or three laypersons' effectively determine selections with the inevitable consequence of candidates with the same background, experience and gender being selected. In 2011, Lord Phillips of Worth Matravers, first President of the Supreme Court stated that:

> the limited diversity in the senior ranks of the judiciary in its turn impacts on applications for appointment to the Supreme Court. It is not satisfactory that our twelve members include only one woman [now three] and that most of us have very similar backgrounds. We take decisions that are not bound by the precedents of the lower courts and which often raise questions of social values. It is plainly desirable that we should have a more even gender balance and better reflect the ethnic mix of our diverse population.[33]

The appointment process was examined by the House of Lords Select Committee on the Constitution in 2010 to 2012.[34] Acknowledging the increasingly widespread concerns over the process especially in light of the expanded and expanding role of judges (particularly in judicial review and the interpretation of law under the Human Rights Act 1998) the Committee took evidence on the desirability of introducing parliamentary pre- and post-selection hearings.[35] Jack Straw MP, a former Lord Chancellor, supported pre-selection hearings as a way to address the 'lack of mutual confidence between the senior judiciary and its broadening authority into areas that are inevitably political'. The majority of witnesses were, however, against the proposal. At the heart of the matter lay the preservation of judicial independence. It would be difficult to limit questions to 'matters of general judicial philosophy and approach' and a danger that questions would touch on matters which could come before the courts for adjudication. If the views of the candidates were known on such issues, it would be impossible for a Justice to sit on the case without giving rise to allegations of bias. Impartiality and independence would both be compromised. For these reasons the Committee rejected pre-appointment hearings:

> However limited the questioning, such hearings could not have any meaningful impact without undermining the independence of those subsequently appointed or appearing to pre-judge their future decisions. In the United Kingdom, judges' legitimacy depends on their independent status and appointment on merit, not on any democratic mandate.[36]

Post-appointment confirmation hearings were also rejected, in this case on the basis that they 'would serve no useful purpose'. A suggestion that parliamentarians should sit on selection panels was also rejected. Baroness Hale had argued that being elected (and therefore having democratic legitimacy) their involvement would be 'a small step towards increasing the democratic accountability of the process'. The Committee, however, favouring a clear separation

---

32 Stevens, 2002, p. 177 cited in Paterson, 2013, p. 309.
33 Lecture: Judicial Independence, 8 February 2011, UCL.
34 Judicial Appointments, 25th Report of Session 2010–2012, HL Paper 272, 2012.
35 See Clark, 2010.
36 Report, para. 46.

of powers, took the view that there was no 'useful role that parliamentarians could play that could not be played by lay members of selection panels'.[37]

Judicial Accountability

Should judges be accountable for the exercise of their duties? And, if so, what form should that accountability take and to whom should they be accountable? Judges exercise considerable power. They have the responsibility for interpreting Acts of Parliament, for developing the common law and for holding government Ministers and other public bodies and officials to account through judicial review of administrative action. The growth in judicial review in recent years and the introduction of the Human Rights Act 1998 give rise to the argument that the power of the judiciary – vis-à-vis both the executive and Parliament – has increased.

Bearing in mind the importance of judicial independence – which is supported by the judges' immunity from legal action in respect of their judicial duties – great care needs to be taken in formulating processes for accountability. Diane Woodhouse states that there are three forms of accountability: explanatory, amendatory and sacrificial.[38] Explanatory accountability is present in the form of reasoned judgments; amendatory accountability exists in the form of the right of appeal to a higher court.[39] Sacrificial accountability is present in the disciplinary system which enables judges to be removed for misconduct. On the relationship between the judiciary and Parliament, Professor Vernon Bogdanor has stated that judges should not be accountable to Parliament to justify their decisions but that they should 'answer to' Parliament through Committee appearances. They should be subject to 'explanatory' not 'sacrificial' accountability.[40]

One form of accountability is *internal* – it is embedded in the judicial process and the practices of the courts. The principle of open justice ensures that the courts of law are open to all. Judicial decisions of the lower courts can be upheld or overturned on appeal. Decisions of the Supreme Court are, however, not subject to appeal.[41] Departures from precedent – where that is possible – must be reasoned and fall within the accepted rules for departing from the precedent case (on which see below). The establishment of the Supreme Court has increased transparency with the Court welcoming members of the public to attend hearings and having a website which details the cases listed for hearing and the decisions reached in cases heard. The judgments of the Court are supplemented by Summaries designed to facilitate understanding of often complex decisions. Public lectures given by Justices of the Supreme Court give an insight into judicial thinking and approach are also available online.

Judges must give reasons for their judgment, thereby making appeals possible. Judicial decisions are recorded and published in the Law Reports, and are accessible to everyone in paper form and online. Traditionally (with the exception of the Court of Appeal Criminal Division) each judge on the panel will write his or her individual judgment for publication. Increasingly, however, particularly in the Supreme Court, where there is unanimity as to the outcome of a case single judgments are being produced. Where there is a majority decision, dissenting judgments will be published. In terms of individual accountability the publication of multiple judgments help the reader to understand the approach of the individual judge and what has led him or her to reach that particular conclusion. Single judgments mask

---

37 Report, para. 52.
38 Woodhouse, 2004.
39 And on occasion the need to form a new panel of judges to re-hear a case as in **Pinochet**.
40 See www.ukpac.org/bogdanor_speech.htm.
41 However, if no remedy is available under the Human Rights Act 1998, a dissatisfied litigant may take his or her case to the Court of Human Rights in Strasbourg.

individuality in judicial reasoning, suggesting a uniformity of approach which might be conducive to brevity and clarity but does nothing to promote individual accountability.

There is also a complex statutory disciplinary scheme for judges in England and Wales, established under the Constitutional Reform Act 2005. Disciplinary powers are exercisable by the Lord Chief Justice, acting with the agreement of the Lord Chancellor (see further above, under Tenure).

Other forms of accountability may be labelled *external*.

Section 5 of the Constitutional Reform Act 2005 provides that the Lord Chief Justice of England and Wales or Northern Ireland or the Lord President of the Court of Session in Scotland may lay written representations before Parliament. These may raise 'matters of importance relating to the judiciary or otherwise to the administration of justice'. Giving evidence to the House of Lords Select Committee on the Constitution the then Lord Chancellor described this as 'a rarely used power' and commented that it should only be used if the judiciary failed to get a satisfactory response through discussions with the executive.[42]

Judges may be invited to give evidence to parliamentary Committees. By convention, judges are prevented from commenting on several matters. These include the merits of government policy (other than in relation to the administration of justice), the merits of a particular case, comments on politicians or other public figures, and the meaning and likely impact of proposed legislation if that would call into question the judge's impartiality. In 2011 Lord Judge, Lord Chief Justice of England and Wales, and Lord Phillips of Worth Matravers, President of the Supreme Court, appeared before the Joint Committee on Human Rights answering questions on the relationship between the Supreme Court and the Court of Human Rights in Strasbourg.

Professor Andrew Le Sueur identifies three main schools of thought on judicial accountability: the opponents, the re-conceptualists and the radicals.[43] The opponents to judicial accountability adopt the position that a judge cannot be both independent and accountable. The re-conceptualists reconcile independence and accountability by arguing that the procedures in place (internal accountability, see above) are adequate to ensure effective accountability. The radicals by contrast call for more and new forms of accountability. From this perspective, the judicial appointments process should be made more transparent and some radicals would argue that there needs to be a parliamentary procedure for the confirmation of appointments.

Le Sueur distinguishes between the individual accountability of judges and their institutional accountability. Within the former are the disciplinary system, the requirement to give reasoned judgments and the explanation of views in public lectures and articles. Within the latter are annual reports, the requirement that courts sit in public, rights of appeal, consultation with government over proposed reforms, financial audit, responding to judgments from the CJEU and/or European Court of Human Rights and parliamentary debates on the judicial function. He also suggests that accountability can be formulated by distinguishing between content accountability, process accountability, performance accountability and probity accountability:

● content accountability is characterised by written judgments and contributions to law reviews and public speeches;

---

42 Sixth Report, Relations between the Executive, the Judiciary and Parliament, 2006–2007, paras 113–115.
43 Le Sueur, 2004.

- process accountability is found in the selection of cases for hearing and in the selection of judges to sit on particular cases;
- performance accountability concerns explanations for time taken to determine cases; while
- probity accountability comprises financial audit and systems for the registering of financial or other interests.

Judges, politicians and the media

By convention, Ministers of the Crown are not allowed to criticise judicial decisions. Two breaches of this convention were cited by Lord Phillips of Worth Matravers PSC in his lecture to the UCL Constitution Unit in 2011. The first relates to the then Home Secretary Charles Clarke, who, following the **Belmarsh** case,[44] publicly stated that: 'The judiciary bears not the slightest responsibility for protecting the public and sometimes seems utterly unaware of the implications of their decisions on our society'.

The second example cited was that of Lord Howard, a former Home Secretary and Conservative Party leader, who stated in a radio interview that:

The power of the judges, as opposed to the power of elected politicians, has increased, is increasing and ought to be diminished.

More and more decisions are being made by unelected, unaccountable judges, instead of accountable, elected Members of Parliament, who have to answer to the electorate for what has happened.

A decision by the courts in 2006 that nine Afghan hijackers should be granted indefinite leave to remain in the United Kingdom rather than be returned to their country of origin drew criticism from the Prime Minister when the decision was being appealed.[45] The *Daily Express* stated that:

Using the European Convention on Human Rights as cover, Mr Justice Sullivan made a ruling which many will regard as tantamount to a judicial coup against Parliament ... Britain's out of touch judges are increasingly using the Human Rights Act as a means of asserting their will over our elected representatives.[46]

In the same year a defendant convicted of the abduction and sexual assault of a three-year-old girl was sentenced to life imprisonment with a tariff of 12 years. This was misreported in the press as a sentence of six years. Media outcry followed and the Home Secretary called the sentence 'unduly lenient'. The Prime Minister backed the Home Secretary. More recently in 2010 the Home Secretary stated that the government was 'disappointed and appalled' by a Supreme Court decision, and the Prime Minister stated in Parliament that the idea of granting voting rights to prisoners, as required by the European Court of Human Rights, made him feel 'physically ill'.[47] His comments were televised and widely reported in the press.

---

44 *A v Secretary of State for the Home Department* (2004).
45 **R (S) v Secretary of State for the Home Department** (2006).
46 Leader, 11 May 2006, cited in House of Lords Select Committee on Constitution Sixth Report, 2007, at para. 145.
47 *Hansard*, HC Vol. 517 Col. 921, 3 November 2010.

The examples given above presumably stem from a misunderstanding of the judicial function. In relation to Acts of Parliament the judicial role is to give effect to Parliament intention. In other words the judges are complying with their constitutional duty. If politicians do not like particular judicial decisions, it is for them to persuade Parliament to change the law. When politicians criticise judges, their statements, repeated by the media, offend the separation of powers and damage judicial independence by lowering the image of judges in the eyes of the public. The judges themselves cannot react to such criticism. The Lord Chancellor has the responsibility, under the Constitutional Reform Act 2005, to defend judicial independence but there have been criticisms of his failure to react speedily to inaccurate media reporting.[48] Having discussed various ministerial outbursts regarding judicial decisions, Shetreet and Turenne comment that: 'These criticisms only underline the need for the Lord Chancellor to ensure that his Cabinet colleagues respect judicial decisions. Yet this is not happening'.[49]

More generally, the role of the media raises further issues. The accurate reporting of cases and informed comment are valuable contributions to democratic debate and enhance the accessibility and transparency of the judicial process. But as Shetreet and Turenne note in *Judges on Trial*, 'The press or media constructs public opinion as much as it channels public opinion'.[50] It is therefore critically important that the media coverage of judges and courts is accurate, objective and responsible.

To facilitate accurate media coverage, the Judicial Communications Office (JCO) was established in 2005. The then Lord Chief Justice, Lord Woolf, stated that the JCO's role was 'to increase the public's confidence in judges ... as part of an overall requirement to enhance public confidence in the justice system'.[51] The JCO has nine staff and provides the media with explanations of cases and comments on sentencing, a topic which is frequently misunderstood and misreported by the press. The House of Lords Select Committee on the Constitution recommended in 2007 that the JCO should be more active and assertive in its dealings with the media in order to represent the judiciary effectively.[52]

PART B: THE ENGLISH LEGAL SYSTEM
The Principle of Open Justice

The principle of open justice has been recognised since the seventeenth century. The principle was central to the case of **R (Guardian News and Media Ltd) v City of Westminster Magistrates' Court** (2012) in which a journalist appealed to the Court of Appeal against the refusal of his application for the disclosure of documents relating to extradition proceedings. In his judgment, allowing the journalist's appeal, Toulson LJ said of open justice:

> Open justice. The words express a principle at the heart of our system of justice and vital to the rule of law. The rule of law is a fine concept but fine words butter no parsnips. How is the rule of law itself to be policed? It is an age old question. *Quis custodiet ipsos custodies* – who will guard the guards themselves? In a democracy, where power depends on the consent of the people governed, the answer must lie

---

48 See Shetreet and Turenne, 2013, pp. 400–405.
49 Shetreet and Turenne, p. 404.
50 Ibid., pp. 390–391.
51 Cited in House of Lords Select Committee on Constitution Sixth Report, 2007, para. 161.
52 Ibid., at para. 171.

in the transparency of the legal process. Open justice lets in the light and allows the public to scrutinise the workings of the law, for better or for worse.

It has long been acknowledged that the principle of justice cannot be absolute, and that there are exceptions. However, the principle represents a starting point – a presumption – from which departures can be made as necessary. There can be no standard formula, as the Court recognised in the **Guardian** case. As Toulson, LJ stated:

> The court has to carry out a proportionality exercise which will be fact-specific. Central to the court's evaluation will be the purpose of the open justice principle, the potential value of the material in advancing that purpose and, conversely, any risk of harm which access to the documents may cause to the legitimate interests of others.

There may be the need to protect personal information relating to vulnerable people – children, battered spouses, the mentally disabled or the elderly and infirm where there is no public-interest reason in publicity.[53] The principle of open justice is compromised where for the safety of one of the parties to proceedings it is necessary not publicly to disclose the party's name. The principle is also compromised where Closed Material Proceedings are allowed in terrorist trials. What is important is that for the principle to be restricted there needs to be some justification which overrides open justice.

The **Guardian** case was considered by the Supreme Court in **Kennedy v Information Commissioner** (2014), discussed further in Chapter 10. In this case Duncan Kennedy, a journalist, made a request to the Charity Commission, under the Freedom of Information Act (FOIA) 2000, for the disclosure of information relating to statutory inquiries which it had carried out. The request was refused and, following four unsuccessful appeals, the matter eventually went to the Supreme Court. The Supreme Court upheld the decision of the Court of Appeal. However, while Kennedy lost under the FOIA, the Supreme Court recognised that the functioning of charities was a matter of public importance and legitimate interest and that the Charity Commission should accede to the request for information in the public interest, other than where there were 'countervailing arguments' which outweighed the principle of open justice. Lord Mance JSC was clear that while Kennedy could not succeed under the FOIA, the common law could require disclosure in the public interest under the principal of open justice.[54]

In **Guardian News and Media Ltd v R & Incedal** (2016), the Court of Appeal upheld reporting restrictions imposed in relation to the trial of terrorist suspect Erol Incedal. Incedal was convicted of having a bomb-making manual in his possession, but following a re-trial, was acquitted of a charge of plotting a terrorist attack in London. The Director of Public Prosecutions (DPP) had applied to the court for part of the proceedings to be heard in *camera*. Initially an anonymity order was granted, but that was lifted by the Court of Appeal following representations by the media. The trial was heard in three parts: open court sessions, closed (secret) sessions and sessions where designated journalists could attend but not report on the proceedings and were required to surrender their mobile phones and to hand their notebooks to police officers to ensure that no notes were removed from the court.

---

53 New Zealand Law Commission Report on Access to Court Records at para. 2.37, cited in the **Guardian** case.
54 See para. 135.

The Lord Chief Justice, Lord Thomas of Cwmgiedd, analysed the respective constitutional functions of the DPP and the courts in cases involving national security when an application is made to hear part of the evidence when the public and the media are excluded. The approach of the court, on hearing an application by the DPP, is that the 'principle of open justice is fundamental to the rule of law and to democratic accountability'. However, exceptions to the principle of open justice exist. In **Scott v Scott** (1913), Viscount Haldane LC stated that departure from the principle must be 'strictly necessary' and 'that by nothing short of the exclusion of the public can justice be done'. In national security cases, while it was for the court 'and the court alone' to determine if the stringent test had been met, the court would nevertheless pay 'the highest regard' to the view of the Secretary of State. As Lord Thomas expressed it: '[t]hat is because under our constitution the identification and delineation of national security interests is for the Executive branch of the state'.

On the three-part process adopted at the trial, Lord Thomas recognised that the presence of journalists made the conduct of the trial very much more difficult than would have been the case if proceedings had been either open or closed, and he concluded that a court should hesitate 'long and hard' before adopting the same procedure.

Another aspect of open justice is the question of when it will be appropriate for a court to grant anonymity to a party to legal proceedings. This issue arises in national security cases and terrorist trials (on which see Chapter 21), but it also arises in other cases. In civil proceedings in the High Court, for example, under Rule 39.2 of the Civil Procedure Rules, hearings should be held in public subject to certain classes of hearings, for example those relating to children, which should be heard in private. Rules for anonymity are provided for in relation to hearings under the Mental Health Act 1983, and in relation to the Court of Protection. One recent example is the case of **R (C) v Secretary of State for Justice** (2016). In this case the claimant had severe mental health problems. While on release from hospital in 1997 he committed murder. At the end of the tariff period of imprisonment[55] the claimant was transferred to a secure psychiatric hospital. In 2013 an application was made for unescorted community leave, a request which the Secretary of State refused. The claimant then sought judicial review and the High Court ordered that he should be granted anonymity. The anonymity order was later set aside and an appeal against the continuity of the anonymity order reached the Supreme Court. The Court allowed the appeal: an anonymity order was necessary in the interests of the patient. Years of treatment and reintegration into the community would not succeed without the order. Baroness Hale stated that there was no presumption in favour of an anonymity order. A balance had to be struck between the public's right to know and the right of a patient not to have his treatment jeopardised by the disclosure of his identity. The case of **Khuja (formerly PNM) v Times Newspapers** (2018)[56] also raised the difficult question of balance. In this case, a 'prominent figure' in the local area was arrested along with several other men in connection with an investigation into sexual offences against children. He was later de-arrested. He was referred to in evidence at the trial of the other accused. Khuja sought an injunction to restrain newspapers from publishing information which might reveal his identity. The matter went to the Supreme Court, which by five to two, dismissed his appeal. The appellant was seeking to prohibit matters discussed at a public trial and he could have no reasonable expectation of privacy: the principle of open justice prevailed.

---

55 The minimum period of imprisonment to be served under a life sentence.
56 See Craig, 2019.

The Court Structure: England and Wales

The Supreme Court
Final court of appeal for all United Kingdom civil cases, and criminal cases from England, Wales and Northern Ireland. Devolution issues.
The Privy Council
The Judicial Committee of the Privy Council is court of final appeal for overseas territories, Crown Dependencies and some Commonwealth countries. It also has jurisdiction in relation to professional bodies.

Court of Appeal

Criminal Division	**Civil Division**
Appeals from the Crown Court	Appeals from the High Court, tribunals and certain cases from County Court

High Court

Queen's Bench Division	**Family Division**	**Chancery Division**
Contract and tort Commercial Court Admiralty Court		Equity and trusts, Contentious probate, tax, partnerships, Bankruptcy and Companies Court, Patents Court
Administrative Division Supervisory and appellate jurisdiction overseeing legality of decisions and actions of inferior courts, tribunals, local authorities, Ministers and other public bodies and officials	**Divisional Court** Appeals from Magistrates' Courts	**Divisional** Appeals from County Court on bankruptcy and land
Crown Courts Trials of indictable offences, appeals from Magistrates' sentence		**County Courts** Majority of civil litigation subject to nature of the Courts, cases for claim
Magistrates' Courts Committals to Crown Court, and youth courts. Limited civil jurisdiction		**Tribunals** Pensions, tax and lands, employment, welfare, immigration etc.
Coroners' Court		**Courts Martial**

Source: Her Majesty's Court Service.

The interests of children might also affect the general principle of open justice. In **In re W (Children) (Care Proceedings: Publicity)** (2016), for example, the Court of Appeal held that the 'strong' presumption of open justice did not apply to proceedings relating to children which were held in private, and that the presiding judge had a wide margin of discretion when it came to allowing reporting of proceedings which might prejudice the interests of the children.

Categories of Law

Common law and statute

As seen in Chapter 2 common law is one of the principal sources of the United Kingdom constitution. The common law is the law created through judicial decisions over many centuries. The common law develops gradually, through the application of the rules of precedent, the guiding principle of which is that like cases must be treated alike, and, conversely, different cases must be treated differently.

Statute law is the law as made by the UK Parliament and the legislatures of Northern Ireland, Scotland and Wales which were established under the 1998 devolution acts.[57] Whereas the common law can be traced back to the Middle Ages at least, statute law only became a major source of law in the mid- to late nineteenth century and twentieth century when increasing industrialisation and urbanisation occurred, prompting the need for centralised law-making in relation to employment, health and housing.

Acts of Parliament made by the UK Parliament are the highest form of law: the expression of the will of the sovereign Parliament: the validity of an Act of Parliament cannot be challenged. Acts made by the devolved legislatures of Northern Ireland, Scotland and Wales are valid only if they fall within the sphere of competence devolved to that legislature by the relevant devolution Act. Disputes over jurisdiction will be resolved by the courts.

The United Kingdom Parliament continues to legislate for the nations of Northern Ireland, Scotland and Wales in relation to those matters which have not been devolved. Every Act of Parliament contains a statement about its territorial scope. Note that Acts of Parliament come into force either on the date of the Royal Assent being given, or at a later date to be determined by the relevant government Minister, and that different parts of Acts may come into force on differing dates.

Common law and equity

As the legal system developed, the right to a remedy in law was linked to using the correct procedure to get a matter before a court. Specific writs related to specific actions: if there was no writ, there could be no legal remedy. As a result of this rigidity, the practice arose whereby a person could petition the King for a remedy. That plea would be delegated to the Lord Chancellor who had the power – in the name of the Crown – to grant an equitable remedy. There then developed two distinct systems of law – common law and equity – each with its own courts, procedures and remedies. This reintroduced the rigidity which equity was designed to remedy. The two systems were finally merged by the Judicature Acts 1873–1875.

Civil law and criminal law

What is meant by the term 'civil law' is the law that regulates aspects of daily life and the relationships between individuals. The law of property ownership, the law of contract, law relating to marriage and the family are all aspects of civil law. Where a dispute arises between individuals, and it cannot be resolved without recourse to law, the civil courts are there to rule on an issue and provide an appropriate remedy. Unlike criminal law, the civil courts are not concerned with punishment (although compensation or damages may be awarded in some cases) but with restoring the correct balance between individuals and stating their legal

---

57 On devolution see Chapter 11.

rights. Civil law is a form of private law (see below) in that whether or not to pursue a legal action is a matter for the individual to decide, not the state.

Criminal law is defined by the state and regulates the behaviour of individuals, groups and organisations by laying down what is and what is not permissible conduct. Where the law is breached, the state may respond by prosecuting the offender and the courts will – if the offender is found guilty – impose a punishment. There are some crimes which are rooted in social morality and common to most legal systems: for example, laws against murder, theft of property and incest. Nowadays many offences are more to do with social regulation than morality: traffic offences, offences relating to taxation, hygiene standards and environmental matters are categorised as criminal by the state and attract criminal sanctions.

It is the state which determines into which category a certain matter will fall, and this may have important ramifications for an individual. Slapper and Kelly cite as an example the categorisation of domestic violence as civil law with remedies in civil law as detrimental to women in that it fails to emphasise the criminal nature of domestic violence.[58]

Public law and private law

Public law relates to the government and state institutions and the relationship between the individual and the state. Accordingly, constitutional law and administrative law are both major aspects of public law.

Private law, by contrast, relates to those relationships between individuals in which the state has no direct interest. As such, there is considerable overlap between the terms 'civil law' and 'private law'.

There is also some difficulty in distinguishing clearly between public and private law. For example, in relation to family law the qualifications for entering marriage, or dissolving a marriage, regulate the most personal of relationships and yet the state has a direct interest in setting out the framework for marriage and divorce in order to ensure that the status of individuals is clear and that there are accurate public records.

Developing the Law

In Chapter 4, the question of whether or not judges 'make law' was briefly discussed. Here the issue is explored a little further. Under the doctrine of parliamentary supremacy, the fiction long endured that judges merely apply Acts of Parliament in line with Parliament's intention, or, under common law, declare what the law 'has always been' (the declaratory theory) rather than openly developing the law. The fiction of judicial non-creativity served the purpose of showing deference to Parliament and protecting the separation of powers by preventing allegations that the judges were acting as legislators. The fiction, however, was not to hold. In a lecture in 1972, Lord Reid, the senior Law Lord in the Appellate Committee of the House of Lords said:

> There was a time when it was thought almost indecent to suggest that judges make law – they only declare it ... But we do not believe in fairy tales any more. So we must accept the fact that for better or worse judges do make law, and tackle the question how do they approach their task and how should they approach it.[59]

---

58 See 11th edn, p. 8.
59 Reid, 1972.

Statutory Interpretation: An Introduction

As has been seen, the constitutional position of judges is one of independence from both the executive and Parliament, but also paradoxically subordination to the sovereign legislature, the United Kingdom Parliament. The fundamental principle underlying the interpretation of Acts of Parliament is that the judges must interpret and apply the latest expression of Parliament's will. This task, however, is not straightforward. Statutes are complex: in 1975 a Committee on the Preparation of Legislation, the Renton Committee, reported four main difficulties with the drafting of statutes, namely that:

- the language used was obscure;
- the provisions were over elaborated;
- the structure was illogical; and that
- confusion arose from amendments of existing provisions.[60]

Judges, in interpreting statutes, traditionally employ three principal methods: the literal approach, the golden rule and the mischief rule.

The literal approach

The dominant conventional approach is the literal approach. This presupposes that the true meaning of the Act is to be found from the literal interpretation of the words used, by giving to the words their ordinary commonplace meaning, and nothing more. This approach may only be departed from if the meaning derived from an analysis of the words produces an absurd result, or a result which, while not absurd, is such that Parliament cannot have intended it. The constitutional advantage of the literal approach is that it best reflects the traditional view that judges are subordinate to Parliament and merely declare what Parliament intended, rather than making new law by attributing new meanings to the words used. The literal approach, where operable, also lends itself to a high degree of consistency in the law. If judges confine themselves to the literal approach, there should be no room for subjective opinions to creep in and alter the meaning that Parliament intended. On the other hand, judges can and do disagree as to what the 'plain meaning' of a word is, or if agreeing that the meaning of a word is 'plain' they may still differ as to its precise interpretation. This is unsurprising given the inherent fluidity of language.

Professor Herbert Hart addresses this linguistic feature when he speaks of words having a 'core of meaning' and a 'penumbra of doubt'.[61] For Hart, in order to attribute the appropriate meaning to a word, it is necessary to place that word within its context. For example, if a local authority bylaw prohibits 'vehicles' in a park, in order to understand the meaning of the word 'vehicle' it is necessary to step outside the word and consider it in relation to the objective and scope of the bylaw. While the word 'vehicle' may have a plain meaning for some purposes it may not for others. If the bylaw is intended to provide a safe play area for small children, the word 'vehicle' may be broad enough to cover the prohibition of rollerblades. On the other hand, if the purpose of the bylaw is to provide a recreation ground for teenagers, rollerblades may not be interpreted as prohibited vehicles. Or, yet again, if the purpose of the prohibition is to provide a peaceful relaxation area for elderly people, rollerblades would again fall within the confines of prohibited 'vehicles'.

---

60 Report, Cmnd 6053.
61 See Hart, 1961.

The Law Commission in 1969 criticised the literal approach in the following manner:

> To place undue emphasis on the literal meaning of the words of a provision is to assume an unattainable perfection in draftsmanship; it presupposes that the draftsmen can always choose words to describe the situations intended to be covered by the provision which will leave no room for a difference of opinion as to their meaning. Such an approach ignores the limitations of language, which is not infrequently demonstrated even at the level of the House of Lords [now Supreme Court] when Law Lords [now Justices of the Supreme Court] differ as to the so-called 'plain meaning' of words.[62]

Further problems arise when Parliament has not expressed itself clearly, or has left a particular situation uncovered. On the strict view, judges are not free to put words into an Act which Parliament did not enact, for this is to 'usurp the legislative function' of Parliament. Where the literal rule is incapable of achieving a result in line with Parliament's overall intention, the judges may adopt a less literal approach.

The golden rule

To remedy some of the defects of the literal approach, the judges developed the golden rule. This is intended to enable judges to avoid the worst excesses of absurdity by finding a meaning which makes sense of the legislation without departing from its intention. This is not to say that judges are free to decide that Parliament has created an absurdity and that accordingly they can depart from the clear meaning of the words used. There must be some genuine reasons justifying the departure from the literal approach. On occasion, the literal rule is no more than a choice exercised between two conflicting meanings, one of which would result in absurdity, the other of which would give effect to Parliament's intention. In other instances, the golden rule may be adopted to avoid an absurdity which would result from the literal rule being applied in circumstances which Parliament has not envisaged. For example, in **Re Sigsworth** (1935) the court interpreted legislation relating to inheritance in such a manner as to exclude from the beneficiaries the person who had murdered the testator by employing the maxim 'no one shall profit from his own wrong'. The literal rule would have enabled the murderer to inherit: an absurdity which the court refused to allow.

The 'mischief rule'

Where neither the literal rule nor the golden rule is capable of achieving a result in line with Parliament's overall intention, the judges may adopt the mischief rule. This rule can be traced to **Heydon's Case** of 1584. The mischief rule entails the court asking itself a series of questions in relation to the legislation, namely:

(a)   what the common law was before the statute was passed;
(b)   what the 'mischief' was which the common law did not cover;
(c)   what remedy Parliament attempted to provide; and, finally,
(d)   what was the reason for adopting that particular remedy?

---

62 The Interpretation of Statutes, para. 30.

Judges are required to understand the reasons for the legislation, both in terms of the former defect in the common law and in terms of the remedy Parliament chose to redress the defect. In order to achieve this judges use both intrinsic and extrinsic aids to interpretation.

Intrinsic aids

Intrinsic aids, as the name suggests, are those within the Act itself. For example, Acts have both long titles and short titles, there are marginal notes printed at the side of sections which act as a guide to the meaning of the section, and there are headings which precede a number of related sections and which reflect the overall topic to which the sections relate. Acts generally have a number of Schedules which are designed to amplify particular aspects of the Act. In addition, Acts contain interpretation sections designed to clarify the intended meaning of words and phrases. All of these may be used by the judges to aid interpretation, but not to the point of contradicting the words in the sections.

Extrinsic aids

More controversial is the question of using extrinsic aids. These include former legislation and judicial decisions on the subject in question, international conventions and treaties, background materials relating to the Act and the record of parliamentary proceedings relating to the passage of the Act. While reference to such extrinsic aids may be legitimate in guiding the court towards a correct interpretation, the court may not rely on such aids to such an extent that the meaning of the Act is distorted.

Judges are entitled to look at background materials such as Law Commission reports and Royal Commission reports. Until 1993 judges were not permitted to look at the verbatim reports of parliamentary debates recorded in *Hansard*. In the case of **Pepper v Hart** (1993) the arguments for and against the use of extrinsic aids were heard. In the leading judgment Lord Browne-Wilkinson stated that the:

> exclusionary rule should be relaxed so as to permit reference to parliamentary materials where (a) legislation is ambiguous or obscure, or leads to an absurdity; (b) the materials relied on consists of one or more statements by a minister or other promoter of the Bill together if necessary with such other parliamentary material as is necessary to understand such statements and their effect; (c) the statements relied on are clear.

In **Three Rivers District Council v Bank of England (No 2)** (1996) the rule was extended to cover unambiguous legislation in a situation in which it might nevertheless be ineffective in its intention to give effect to a European Community (now Union) Directive.

Presumptions

Judges also use a number of presumptions in interpretation, presumptions which may be rebutted in the course of proceedings. Among these is the rule that 'words take their meaning from their context': *noscitur a sociis*. For example, if a statute prohibits betting in a number of outdoor places, it is unlikely to prohibit betting indoors.[63] Where a statute gives examples of persons or objects covered by a particular provision the rule operates that a general class added to the end of specified examples must be interpreted in line with those examples:

---

63 **Powell v Kempton Park Racecourse** (1899).

ejusdem generis. The *expressio unius exclusio alterius* rule provides that where a statute lists those matters covered by it, anything not included in that list is excluded – for example, a reference to coal mines will exclude limestone mines.[64]

More generally, presumptions include the presumption that criminal statutes should be strictly construed in favour of the citizen, that *mens rea* – the intention to commit an offence – is required before criminal liability arises, and that a person's liberty and right to property should not be restricted save where clear words are used in a statute to that effect. There is also a presumption that statutes do not have retrospective effect. There is a presumption that statutes do not bind the Crown unless the intention to do so is clearly stated or the purpose of the Act would be frustrated if the Crown was not bound ('necessary implication'). For example, in **R (Black) v Secretary of State for Justice** (2016) the Court of Appeal ruled that a smoking ban imposed by Part 1 of the Health Act 2006 did not expressly or by necessary implication apply to the Crown. There was no express provision, the test for necessary implication was strict and here not satisfied. Part 3 of the Act relating to drugs and medicines bound the Crown thereby reinforcing the view that since there was no equivalent provision in Part 1 Parliament did not intend the Crown to be bound by that Part. A further presumption is that Parliament did not intend to oust the jurisdiction of the courts, and attempts to exclude the jurisdiction of the courts are most carefully scrutinised by the judges.

Other presumptions include the presumption that Parliament did not intend to change the common law, or to restrict fundamental rights, except where that intention is expressly stated. There is also the presumption that Parliament does not intend to legislate contrary to international obligations, and the courts will attempt to interpret domestic law in such a way as to make it consistent with international law.

Interpreting European law: the purposive approach

Whereas domestic Acts of Parliament are highly detailed, with the draftsman trying to cover every possible situation to which the law might apply, civil law countries adopt more generalised, less detailed, forms of drafting. Legislation will set out general principles, leaving interpretation to the courts of law. This requires the courts to step outside the actual words of the legislation and seek its meaning through looking at the purpose of the legislation.

Lord Bingham in **R (Quintavalle) v Secretary of State for Health** (2003) considered the purposive approach and stated that:

> The basic task of the court is to ascertain and give effect to the true meaning of what Parliament has said in the enactment to be construed. But that is not to say that attention should be confined and a literal interpretation given to the particular provisions which give rise to difficulty. Such an approach not only encourages immense prolixity in drafting, since the draftsman will feel obliged to provide expressly for every contingency which may possibly arise. It may also (under the banner of loyalty to the will of Parliament) lead to the frustration of that will, because undue concentration on the minutiae of the enactment may lead the court to neglect the purpose which Parliament intended to achieve when it enacted the statute ... The court's task, within the permissible bounds of interpretation, is to give effect to Parliament's purpose. So the controversial provisions should be read in the context of the statute as a whole, and the statute as a whole should be read in the historical context of the situation which led to its enactment.[65]

---

64 **R v Inhabitants of Sedgley** (1831).
65 **R (Quintavalle)**, at para. 118.

The Doctrine of Precedent

Justice requires that like cases are treated alike and that different cases are treated differently. It also requires that there is certainty in the law, in order that citizens may conduct themselves with confidence that their actions are lawful. These principles underpin the rules which the judges have developed in their interpretation and evolution of the common law through the doctrine of precedent.

The doctrine of binding precedent is that of *stare decisis* – keeping to the decisions of previous cases. However, if precedent was always and invariably binding there would be no evolution of the law. Accordingly, a number of rules have been formulated to achieve both certainty and a degree of flexibility in the law to accommodate new circumstances or changes in society.

Exactly what constitutes a 'precedent' is the subject of much debate. Not all aspects of a previous case and the judgment of the court will 'bind' a future decision. What is binding is the *ratio decidendi* of a precedent case: the central core of meaning. Slapper and Kelly define the *ratio* as 'the statement of the law applied in deciding the legal problem raised by the concrete facts of the case'.[66] This is to be distinguished from other principles, propositions and statements which are made in the court of a judgment known as *obiter dicta* which, while persuasive in the future, are not binding on a future court.

The system operates on the basis of the hierarchy of courts, the general rule being the higher the court the more binding its precedents, with the precedents of the Supreme Court binding all lower courts. A decision of the Supreme Court will bind future Supreme Court decisions. However, greater flexibility was injected into the system in 1966 with a Practice Statement which provided that the House of Lords (the predecessor to the Supreme Court) could depart from its own decisions, in exceptional cases, where it is right to do so. Because contradictory decisions would have an unsettling effect on the courts below, the power to depart from precedent is cautiously exercised. Professor Alan Paterson sets out the guidelines on the use of the Practice Statement provided by Lord Reid:

> the freedom to depart from a precedent of the House should be exercised sparingly and should rarely be used in situations where parliamentary reform would be more suitable, eg (1) where it would upset contracts or expectations based on the old decision, (2) where the precedent turned on statutory construction, (3) where the consequences of changing the law could not be estimated or (4) where the area was one which required comprehensive reform. However, a decision should be overruled if it caused great uncertainty to advisers or it was considered to be unjust or out of touch with modern conceptions of public policy.[67]

On overruling, Lord Judge, Lord Chief Justice giving evidence to the Joint Committee on Human Rights said of precedent and overruling:

> I do not think there is any doubt about it: the only court that can overrule itself is the Supreme Court. Indeed, if the Court of Appeal has a choice to make between what appears to be a Supreme Court or House of Lords decision, or indeed one of its own earlier decisions, and a decision of the European Court that appears to be

---

66 Slapper and Kelly, 2010, p. 133.
67 Paterson, 2013, p. 265.

clean contrary to it, we must follow our own Supreme Court. The only court that can then say its own decision has to be relooked at is the Supreme Court.[68]

An example of the Supreme Court departing from precedent cases is seen in **R v Jogee** and **Ruddock v The Queen (Respondent) (Jamaica)** (2016). These cases involved the mental element of intent which had to be proved when a defendant is accused of being a secondary party to a crime. Two previous cases, **Chan Wing-Siu v The Queen** (1985) and **R v Powell and English** (1999), were authority for the principle that a person who encourages or assists a person to commit a crime is also guilty of the offence committed by that other person: the mental element required of the secondary party was that he or she foresaw the possibility that the principal offender might commit the crime. In **Jogee** and **Ruddock** the Supreme Court ruled that the former cases had 'taken a wrong turning'. The relevant law was common law, and it was therefore for the courts to investigate if the law had taken a 'wrong turning'. The previous cases had departed from the well-established rule that the mental element required of a secondary party is an intention to assist or encourage the principal to commit the crime. The Court subsequently ruled that Jogee should be re-tried on the charge of murder and/or manslaughter. In **Ivey v Gaming Casinos (UK) Ltd** (2017)[69] the Supreme Court laid down a new test for dishonesty, overturning a precedent which had endured since 1982, but which the Court considered incorrect. The reasoning behind the decision was explained by Lord Hughes with whom the other Justices agreed. However, that explanation was *obiter* (i.e. unnecessary to the decision of the Court). In **R v Barton** (2020)[70] the question of the correct precedent to be applied came before the Court of Appeal. The Court ruled that, notwithstanding that the new test had been expressed *obiter*, it was binding on the Court of Appeal.

The doctrine of precedent in relation to the Judicial Committee of the Privy Council (JCPC) was considered by a panel of nine Supreme Court Justices in **Willers v Joyce (No 2)** (2016). Lord Neuberger PSC emphasised the importance of the doctrine of precedent, saying that 'in a common law system ... it is fundamental' and that without precedent 'the law becomes anarchic, and it loses coherence clarity and predictability'.[71] Explaining the position of the JCPC, Lord Neuberger stated that as a court determining appeals from overseas jurisdictions, the JCPC was not a court of any part of the United Kingdom. However, the JCPC 'almost always applies the common law' and the Privy Counsellors sitting on appeals are almost always Justices of the Supreme Court. Not being a court of the UK, the decisions of the JCPC cannot override any decision of the English courts. However, any decision of the JCPC 'should ... be regarded ... as being of great weight and persuasive value'. Courts in England and Wales would normally be expected to follow a decision of the JCPC, although 'they are not bound to do so as a matter of precedent'. However, a court should not follow a decision of the JCPC if that decision is inconsistent with the decision of a court which is otherwise binding on the court.[72] There is, however, an important exception to this rule. The exception lies in cases where a party to an appeal wishes to challenge the correctness of an earlier decision of the House of Lords or the Supreme Court. In such cases, the President of the JCPC can take into account the challenge when deciding on who should sit on the appeal and the number of Justices who will sit. That panel can then decide, if appropriate, that an earlier decision of the highest court (or the Court of Appeal) was wrong and give a direction that the domestic

---

68 Minutes of Evidence, HC 873-ii, 2011, uncorrected transcript of oral evidence, Q80.
69 [2018] AC 391.
70 [2020] EWCA Crim 575.
71 At para. 4.
72 At para. 16.

courts should treat the decision of the JCPC as representing the correct statement of the law of England and Wales.[73]

Decisions of the Court of Appeal will bind the courts below, and for the most part will bind itself in future cases. Exceptions to this rule exist. The exceptions were formulated by Lord Greene MR in **Young v Bristol Aeroplane Co Ltd** (1944):

(1)   The court is entitled and bound to decide which of two conflicting decisions of its own it will follow.

(2)   The court is bound to refuse to follow a decision of its own which, though not expressly overruled, cannot, in its opinion, stand with a decision of the House of Lords (now Supreme Court).

(3)   The court is not bound to follow a decision of its own if it is satisfied that the decision was given *per incuriam* (that is to say, it was decided in ignorance of a relevant statutory provision or common law)

The doctrine of binding precedent ensures stability and certainty in the law. On occasion, however, there is a need to depart from precedent in order to meet some new circumstance, or to reflect changing standards/morals in society. Two principal means by which courts can depart from precedent are through the processes of *overruling* and *distinguishing*.

Two cases discussed in Chapter 2, illustrate the courts' approach to *overruling*. In **R v R** (1992) the House of Lords ruled that – contrary to established authority – a husband could be found guilty of raping his wife, thereby overturning the historic legal immunity enjoyed by husbands. The court stressed, however, that it was not creating new law, but correcting a former misinterpretation of the law. In **Bellinger v Bellinger** (2003) the House of Lords issued a declaration of incompatibility in respect of section 11 of the Matrimonial Causes Act 1973, but declined to hold that previous authorities were wrong. Section 11 required that parties to a valid marriage must be respectively male and female. Under English law gender was fixed at birth and could not be altered. Accordingly, transgender people who had undertaken gender confirmation surgery and treatment could not marry. Parliament subsequently passed the Gender Recognition Act 2004 to give transgender people the right to marry.

To *distinguish* a case is to hold that there are material differences between the present case and the otherwise binding case, differences which justify reaching a different conclusion. Two examples from the law of contract illustrate distinguishing. In **Balfour v Balfour** (1919) the husband worked for the government in Sri Lanka (then Ceylon). His wife became ill and was advised to stay in England. The husband agreed to pay her £30 per month. He subsequently stopped the payment and the wife tried to enforce the agreement. It was held to be legally unenforceable on the basis that it concerned domestic relations and that there could be no intention to create legal relations between husband and wife. In **Merritt v Merritt** (1970), the husband and wife had separated and the husband went to live with another woman. He promised his wife £40 per month and that he would transfer the home to her if she continued to make the mortgage payments. She did so, but when the mortgage was paid off the husband refused to transfer the property to her. Was the agreement enforceable? Yes: the Court of Appeal distinguished the facts in **Merritt** from those in **Balfour**, ruling that the fact that the husband had left his wife for another woman took the agreement out of the 'domestic arena' and into the ambit of a legally enforceable contract.

---

73 Judgments of the Supreme Court are highly persuasive, but no more, in Scotland. Accordingly, decisions of the JCPC have the same authority as those of the Supreme Court.

Pause and Reflect

Explain what is meant by the 'declaratory theory' of statutory interpretation and why the judges insisted for so long that it explained their constitutional role.

Precedent and European law

Two sources of European law have a significant effect on the doctrine of precedent, but vary in application and binding force. The two sources are the law of the European Union and the law of the European Convention on Human Rights.

In relation to the law of the European Union (EU), during the UK's membership from 1973 to 2020, judges in the domestic courts were under a statutory duty to apply the decisions of the CJEU: section 2 of the European Communities Act 1972. If there were doubts as to the meaning of a particular EU law, the domestic courts could refer the matter to the CJEU for a ruling and EU law had to be applied to the case before the court. However, under the EU (Withdrawal) Act 2018, having left the EU, new decisions of the CJEU will no longer be binding on the domestic courts and the requirement to make a reference to the CJEU is abolished.

In relation to the European Convention on Human Rights the position is very different. Section 2 of the Human Rights Act 1998 requires judges to 'take into account' the jurisprudence of the Court of Human Rights in Strasbourg. There is no provision in the Act enabling the courts to request a ruling on a point of law from the European Court of Human Rights. In the past there has been a great deal of debate about the extent to which the courts are bound by the Strasbourg case law. Lord Bingham in **R (Ullah) v Special Adjudicator** (2004) stated that 'The duty of the courts is to keep pace with the Strasbourg jurisprudence as it evolves over time: no more, but certainly no less' and that no national court should 'without strong reason dilute or weaken the effect of the Strasbourg case law'. This was interpreted to mean that the national courts were obliged to follow Strasbourg. In 2011, giving evidence to the Joint Committee on Human Rights, Lord Judge, the Lord Chief Justice, put forward the view that it was 'at least arguable' that 'what Lord Bingham said in **Ullah** went too far'. Lord Phillips of Worth Matravers, President of the Supreme Court, amplified this by stating that Lord Bingham was talking about a 'settled line of Strasbourg jurisprudence', not a single case.

The relationship between the national courts and Strasbourg is one of partnership and the Court of Human Rights takes into account the views of the national courts thereby facilitating a dialogue between the two systems. Lord Phillips was very clear in his evidence to the Joint Committee in 2011, stating that 'In as much as we are not obliged to follow, as a matter of law, the Strasbourg jurisprudence domestically, we are supreme as a Supreme Court'.[74]

Judicial creativity versus judicial restraint

Setting out the 'rules' of statutory interpretation and explaining the doctrine of precedent does not address the fundamental question in relation to the role of the judiciary. Constitutionally, judges work within three key concepts: the rule of law, the supremacy of Parliament and the separation of powers. Critical to understanding the interrelationship between these concepts is the extent to which judges develop the law.

In the law reports there are numerous cases in which the courts have boldly departed from precedent or interpreted an Act of Parliament so as to change the law. The introduction

---

74 Uncorrected Transcript of Oral Evidence, Joint Committee on Human Rights, 15 November 2011.

of the Human Rights Act 1998 is one aid to reinterpretation, requiring the courts to interpret Acts of Parliament in a manner consistent with the rights protected under the European
Convention on Human Rights. A significant example of the impact of the Human Rights Act
can be seen in the case of **Ghaidan v Godin Mendoza** (2004), discussed briefly above.

In **Ghaidan** the principal issue was whether a same-sex partner who had lived with his
partner for 18 years could succeed to the tenancy of a property on the death of his partner.
The relevant Act, the Rent Act 1977,[75] provided that a 'surviving spouse' had the right of succession. The meaning of a 'surviving spouse' was 'a person who was living with the original
tenant as his or her wife or husband'. The task for the House of Lords (now Supreme Court)
was to decide whether the statutory definition was capable of including a same-sex partner:
could a same-sex partner be treated as a 'spouse'? The Court ruled that it could. It was clear
that a literal interpretation of the statute would have made it impossible for the tenant to
succeed. However, the courts are under a duty to apply the provisions of the Human Rights
Act 1998, section 6 of which provides that a public body (which includes a court of law)
must act compatibly with the Convention rights which had been incorporated under the Act.
Article 8 of the Convention requires, among other things, the courts to respect a person's
home. Article 14 requires the law to be applied without discrimination. The combined effect
of Article 8 and 14 required the Court to reinterpret the law to include the same-sex partner
within the meaning of a 'spouse'.

However, while seminal cases may be cited, it must be recognised that only the superior
courts have leeway to develop the law, and that for the most part there is judicial restraint
even at the highest level. Generalisations give false impressions: there may be periods in
which the courts may appear more creative than others, and issues over which the courts
may be more willing to act. The composition of the judicial bench in a particular case and
the influence of particular judges may have an enormous impact on the development of the
law and there is much academic literature on these factors.[76]

Alan Paterson, in *Final Judgment: The Last Law Lords and the Supreme Court*, examines the extent to
which the House of Lords Appellate Committee and now the Supreme Court departed from
precedent, as permitted under the 1966 Practice Direction discussed above. In his analysis the
Appellate Committee of the House of Lords resorted to the Practice Statement in only eight
decisions between 1966 and 1980 and almost 25 in the first 43 years (to 2009). The Supreme
Court, by contrast, has avoided using the Practice Statement, preferring to distinguish precedent cases in order to get around them. Paterson notes that: 'In short, the tendency of the
Supreme Court to date has been to pursue indirect methods of removing unhelpful precedents of the House rather than direct ones'.[77]

On judicial creativity, Paterson cites Lord Reid as identifying different areas of law to
which the judiciary react with differing degrees of creativity. The law relating to property,
trusts and the criminal law – areas which have an impact on wide sections of society – calls
for certainty in the law rather than flexibility. Contract, tort, restitution and public law lend
themselves to judicial law-making while controversial areas such as assisted dying and abortion were best left to Parliament to resolve through primary legislation.[78] What is at issue here
is the question of 'institutional competence': which branch of governance is best suited to
deal with a particular matter?

The question of institutional competence may also be tied in with Parliament's attitude
to a particular matter. If Parliament has been invited by the courts to act on a matter, and

---

75 Schedule 1, para. 2.
76 Duxbury, 2001; Paterson, 2013.
77 Paterson, 2013, p. 268.
78 See Paterson, 1982 and 2013, at p. 275.

fails to do so, the courts may then step in. This was mooted in **R (Nicklinson) v Secretary of State for Justice** (2014), the 'right to die' case, discussed in Chapter 18. In **Nicklinson** considering whether or not a declaration of incompatibility should be issued, four of the nine Justices ruled that the matter should be left to Parliament, five of the nine Justices ruled that the court had the right to get involved but three of those five ruled that Parliament should have the opportunity to rule on the matter before the Court made a ruling. Paterson identifies further cases where parliamentary activity or inactivity played an important role in the attitude of the court. In **Stack v Dowden** (2007) Baroness Hale stated that Parliament was not going to act on recommendations of the Law Commission and therefore the court would act. In **Airedale NHS Trust v Bland** (1993), **Pretty v DPP** (2001) and **Purdy v DPP** (2009) Parliament was unable (as a result of political opposition) to reform the law: the courts stepped in.[79]

Summary

In this chapter the issues identified under Learning Objectives have been discussed. In order to ensure that you have achieved the stated objectives, return to the first page of this chapter and check your knowledge against the objectives.

 Further Reading

Clark, M, 'Introducing a parliamentary confirmation process for new Supreme Court Justices' [2010] *Public Law* 464.

Griffith, JAG, *The Politics of the Judiciary*, 1997, London: Fontana.

Hale, Rt Hon. B, 'Equality and the judiciary: why should we want more women judges?' [2001] *Public Law* 489.

Hart, HLA, *The Concept of Law*, 1961, Oxford: Clarendon Press.

Le Sueur, A, 'Developing mechanisms for judicial accountability in the United Kingdom' [2004] *Legal Studies* 73.

Malleson, K, 'Rethinking the merit principle in judicial selection' [2006] *Journal of Law and Society* 126.

Malleson, K, 'Diversity in the judiciary: the case for positive action' [2009] *Journal of Law and Society* 376.

Ministry of Justice, *Appointments and Diversity: A Judiciary for the 21st Century*, 2012.

Paterson, A, *Final Judgment: The Last Law Lords and the Supreme Court*, 2013, Oxford: Hart Publishing.

Reid, Lord, 'The judge as law maker' [1972] 12 *Journal of the Society of Public Teachers of Law* 22.

Shetreet, S and Turenne, S, *Judges on Trial*, 2nd edn, 2013, Cambridge: Cambridge University Press.

Slapper, G and Kelly, D, *The English Legal System*, 15th edn, 2014, Abingdon: Routledge.

Stevens, R, *The English Judges*, 2013, Oxford: Hart Publishing.

---

79 See Paterson, 2013, p. 279.

Part **8**

Administrative Law

Chapter 23

Judicial Review: Introduction, Jurisdiction and Procedure

Chapter Contents

Learning Objectives

By the end of this chapter you should be able to:

☐ explain the constitutional role and purpose of judicial review;
☐ discuss the difference between an appeal and an application for judicial review;
☐ explain the statutory basis for judicial review;
☐ with reference to case law, explain the law on standing or sufficient interest;
☐ discuss the ways in which the law may attempt to restrict or limit judicial review, making reference to case law.

Introduction

Judicial review represents the means by which the courts control the exercise of governmental power. Government Departments, local authorities, tribunals, state agencies and agencies exercising powers which are governmental in nature must exercise their powers in a lawful manner. Judicial review has developed to ensure that public bodies which exercise law-making power or adjudicatory powers are kept within the confines of the power conferred. In one sense, therefore, judicial review is relevant to most aspects of the constitution. The Human Rights Act 1998 extends the scope of judicial review in that any failure on the part of a public body to respect human rights will be subject to review by the courts.

Judicial review is concerned with the legality of the decision made, not with the merits of the particular decision. Accordingly, the task of the judges is to ensure that the exercise of any power which has been delegated to Ministers and administrative and adjudicatory bodies is lawful according to the power given to that body by Act of Parliament and the common law principles developed by the judges. As will be seen in the next chapter, there is debate concerning the appropriate basis on which the courts exercise their supervisory jurisdiction.

The traditional view has been that the judge's task is to ensure that public bodies act within their powers – or *intra vires* – and that, provided that the body has acted within its powers as defined by statute, and according to common law principles the body's decision will not be challengeable under the public law process of judicial review. From this traditional perspective, judicial review is principally concerned with questions of jurisdiction and natural justice. The primary question to be asked is whether a particular person or body with delegated law-making or adjudicatory powers had acted *intra vires* or *ultra vires*, and whether the decision-making process entailed the application of natural justice. If the person or body was acting within its jurisdiction, and respecting the demands of natural justice, the courts would not interfere with the decision – even if the decision was in some respect wrong. Nowadays, although the judges still express their role in the traditional language of 'vires', the approach taken is more robust than before. If a public body, as defined in law, makes an error of law, the courts – through the process of judicial review – will intervene to ensure that the body in question reconsiders a matter and acts in a procedurally correct manner.[1] Furthermore, the Human Rights Act 1998 now requires that all public bodies comply with the right protected by the European Convention on Human Rights and judicial review proceedings may be brought to enforce that legal duty.[2]

Judicial review has traditionally been regarded as unconcerned with the merits of a particular case, or with the justice or injustice of the rules which are being applied. The principal concern is the manner in which decisions have been taken: has this decision maker acted within the powers given? Most of the rules applied by administrators will be statutory, but the courts have also – under common law – developed rules which will apply to decision makers over and above the statutory rules. Thus, decision makers must not only exercise their powers in the correct manner as prescribed by the statute and in accordance with human rights, but must also comply with the rules of reasonableness, natural justice and fairness.

In essence, the courts seek, by judicial review, to ensure four principal objectives:

(a)   that Acts of Parliament have been correctly interpreted;
(b)   that discretion conferred by statute has been lawfully exercised;
(c)   that the decision maker has acted fairly;
(d)   that the exercise of power by a public body does not violate human rights.

---

1 See Chapter 24 for further discussion of the concept of *ultra vires*.
2 See Human Rights Act 1998, s. 7.

The expanding role of judicial review causes controversy.[3] Simply expressed, in any society regulated by a complex administrative machinery, an essential feature of that society is that administrators have a sphere of power within which, in the interests of certainty and efficiency, they should be free to operate. The doctrine of ministerial responsibility ensures that accountability for policy and administration lies with the relevant Secretary of State, who is accountable to the electorate through Parliament. However, against that argument for non-interference with matters of administration must be set the demands of individual justice and fairness. If an individual, or a body of persons, is aggrieved by an administrative decision, and their rights adversely affected, there is a requirement that procedures exist whereby such decisions may be challenged in the courts. It is through judicial review that the requirements of legality of the exercise of powers by public bodies is tested. From this perspective, judicial review exemplifies the application of the rule of law[4] in a democratic society.[5] This raises a further question of constitutional significance. To what extent is it legitimate for a non-elected judiciary to intervene to correct the administrative process which is controlled through powers granted by the democratically elected Parliament? One response to this question is that judicial review – with respect to the review of delegated law-making and adjudicatory powers – ensures that Parliament's will is observed, and judicial review may thus be regarded as an aspect of parliamentary sovereignty.[6]

See Chapter 6.

The balance to be struck between these contrasting views is usefully understood using the traffic light analogy introduced by Harlow and Rawlings.[7] 'Light-heartedly' called 'red light' theory, its adherents are generally suspicious of the executive and believe that the state should be controlled and prevented from interfering with individual rights and that the courts should control the power of the state.[8] Historically this approach is tied in with Dicey and his distrust of administrative discretion and insistence on the rule of law. Professor HWR Wade echoes Dicey:

See Chapter 10.

> The primary purpose of administrative law, therefore, is to keep the powers of government within their legal bounds, so as to protect the citizen from their abuse. The powerful engines of authority must be prevented from running amok. 'Abuse', it should be made clear, carries no necessary innuendo of malice or bad faith. Government departments may misunderstand their legal position as easily as may other people, and the law which they have to administer is frequently complex and uncertain. Abuse is therefore inevitable, and it is all the more necessary that the law should provide means to check it.[9]

The preference for legal control of administrative power underlies the judiciary's attitude to attempts to restrict judicial review. In Harlow and Rawlings' analysis this is seen most clearly in relation to 'ouster clauses' which are designed to prevent the courts from reviewing the exercise of administrative power:

> Judges have developed various strategies to emphasise their opposition to ouster. Ouster clauses are restrictively interpreted. A common law presumption has

---

3 See e.g. the differing views of Stephen Sedley J and Professor Ross Cranston expressed in Richardson and Genn, 1994, Chapters 2 and 3, respectively.

4 For an early expression of this view, see Dicey, 1885, Appendix 2.

5 See Allan, 2001.

6 See also Craig, 1999, and Jowell, 1999.

7 Harlow and Rawlings, 1984, see 3rd edn, 2009, p. 44.

8 Supporters of this view include Dicey and Hayek. Both wrote at different points in the history of constitutional law but both believed that any attempt to restrict access to the courts by the executive was pernicious and contrary to the rule of law.

9 HWR Wade and C Forsyth, *Administrative Law*, 2004, Oxford: OUP, pp. 4–5 cited in Harlow and Rawlings, 2009, p. 24.

evolved whereby access to the courts is not to be denied save by clear statutory words; equally, it may be proclaimed a 'constitutional' or 'fundamental' right.[10]

Opposing 'red light' theory, unsurprisingly, is 'green light' theory. This emerged during the inter-war period.[11] It argues that administrative law should be used as a way of facilitating the operation of the state rather than controlling it. As society has become more complex so it argued that the courts should endeavour to take a less restrictive view of administrative action. The courts should be less interventionist, and although the result may compromise an individual's rights, this is defended on the basis that it assists the functioning of the state, which necessarily has a wider commitment to society as a whole.

> To the lawyers, law is the policeman; it operates as an external control, often ret-rospectively. But a main concern of many green light writers was, as already sug-gested, to minimise the influence of the courts: courts, with their legalistic values, were seen as obstacles to progress, and the control that they exercise as unrepre-sentative and undemocratic.[12]

Supporters of 'green light' theory believe that political and democratic forms of accountabil-ity are preferable to the courts.[13] In response to these two schools of thought a third way has been advocated:[14] the 'amber light' theory. It lies between the 'red' and 'green' extremes and takes the view that the approach to be used will be determined by an individual case.

The 2019 Supreme Court decision over the prorogation of Parliament (discussed in Chapter 5) led to criticisms that the judges had ruled on a matter which properly lay within the political rather than judicial arena.[15] Lord Sumption, former Supreme Court Justice, cit-ing recent case law of the Supreme Court,[16] has been highly critical of senior judges who in his view:

> have developed a broader concept of the rule of law which greatly enlarges their constitutional role. They have claimed a wider supervisory authority over other organs of the state. They have inched their way towards a notion of fundamental law overriding ordinary processes of political decision-making.[17]

Concerns such as these have led to a formal inquiry into the role of judicial review being launched in July 2020. The terms of reference of the inquiry are:

(1) Whether the amenability of public law decisions to judicial review by the courts and the grounds of public law illegality should be codified in statute.
(2) Whether the legal principle of non-justiciability requires clarification and, if so, the identity of subjects/areas where the issue of the justiciability/non-justiciability of the exercise of a public law power and/or function could be considered by the Government.
(3) Whether, where the exercise of a public law powers should be justiciable: (i) on which grounds the courts should be able to find a decision to be unlawful: (ii) whether those

---

10 Ibid., p. 26.
11 Between 1918 and 1939.
12 Harlow and Rawlings, 2009, p. 37.
13 Ganz discussed in Harlow and Rawlings, 2009, p. 41.
14 Harlow and Rawlings, 2006, p. 127.
15 Miller v The Prime Minister (2019).
16 R (Unison) v Lord Chancellor (2017); R (Evans) v Attorney-General (2015).
17 Sumption J. [Lord], Trials of the State: Law and the decline of politics, London: Profile Books, 2019, pp. 34–35.

grounds should depend on the nature and subject matter of the power and (iii) the remedies available in respect of the various grounds on which a decision may be declared unlawful.

(4) Whether procedural reforms to judicial review are necessary in general to 'streamline the process', and, in particular: (a) on the burden and effect of disclosure in particular in relation to "policy decisions" in Government; (b) in relation to the duty of candour, particularly as it affects Government; (c) on possible amendments to the law of standing; (d) on time limits for bringing claims; (e) on the principles on which relief is granted in claims for judicial review; (f) on rights of appeal, including on the issue of permission to bring JR proceedings; and (g) on costs and interveners.

The inquiry is to be chaired by Lord Faulks, QC, a former Justice Minister. Lord Faulks has stated that 'it is reasonable to ask, has judicial review gone too far? The only question is where are the boundary lines? It is quite impossible that we will recommend the abolition of judicial review [as some suggest]'.[18] The inquiry reported at the end of 2020 and the government's response is awaited. However, given the broad terms of reference, there is the potential for a radical reform of judicial review. This could include clarifying – by placing on a statutory basis – the grounds for judicial review and the power to quash (nullify) decisions of administrative bodies, restricting the concept of standing to individual 'victims' and excluding claims by interest groups, restricting the concept of justiciability so as to exclude issues involving 'policy', rights of appeal and the burden of costs. The government's response will be discussed on the companion website to this text.

Judicial Review and the Human Rights Act 1998

As will be seen from the discussion in this and the following chapters, the Human Rights Act 1998 has had a major impact on judicial review. By way of introduction, the impact of the Act can be summarised as follows:

- public bodies – as defined by the courts – have a legal duty to act in accordance with Convention rights and failure to do so may result in proceedings for judicial review;[19]
- consistent with the procedural requirements of the European Convention on Human Rights, only 'victims' of a public body's unlawful act may apply for judicial review in relation to human rights claims;[20]
- an application for judicial review on human rights grounds must be made within a period of one year from the date on which the act complained of took place (for other judicial review proceedings the normal period is three months).[21] The one-year period may be extended by the court;[22]
- the Act was intended to operate vertically (binding only state bodies). However, because section 6(3) of the Act includes courts and tribunals in the definition of public bodies, the courts have a duty to comply with Convention rights and have been able to extend the operation of the Act to private bodies;

---

18 *The Times*, 10 September 2020, p. 56.
19 The definition of public bodies is linked to their function rather than formal legal status.
20 Section 7: this creates a different test of 'sufficient interest' or 'standing' from that required for other judicial review proceedings.
21 Part 54.5 Civil Procedure Rules 1998.
22 Section 7(5)(1),(b) Human Rights Act 1998.

- in addition to the remedies which a court may award in other proceedings, in judicial review proceedings based on human rights claims, the High Court and above may make a 'Declaration of Incompatibility' which – while having no effect on the parties to the case – may result in the law being reformed;[23]
- consistent with the interpretative method of the European Court of Human Rights, in addition to the usual techniques of interpretation, the courts now also employ the concept of 'proportionality';
- the Human Rights Act 1998 supplements the statutory and common law requirements of natural justice through incorporation of Article 6 of the Convention which stipulates the requirements of fair trial.

In **Secretary of State for the Home Department v Nasseri** (2009) the House of Lords explained the correct judicial approach to applications for judicial review based on an alleged infringement of a Convention right. Mr Nasseri, an Afghan national, had claimed asylum in Greece. That application was rejected and he travelled to the United Kingdom and again claimed asylum. Under an EC Regulation, where an asylum seeker enters a third country from another Member State, that Member State is solely responsible for determining the application. Accordingly, the Home Office notified the applicant that he would be returned to Greece on the basis that it was a safe country.[24] The applicant sought judicial review of the removal decision which was arguably incompatible with Article 3.

Lord Hoffmann stated that when a court is hearing an application for judicial review, its focus is on whether the decision maker reached a decision according to law: it is concerned with the decision-making process rather than the merits of the decision. However, when an application involves an alleged violation of a Convention right, the court's approach must differ. The focus is not on whether the decision-making process is defective, but on whether or not the applicant's Convention rights have been violated. Lord Hoffmann went on to state that: 'when breach of a Convention right is in issue, an impeccable decision-making process by the Secretary of State will be of no avail if she actually gets the answer wrong' [at paragraph 14].

The European Court of Human Rights has welcomed the domestic courts' willingness to 'develop and expand conventional judicial review grounds' beyond the traditional **Wednesbury unreasonableness** ground (in this case in light of Article 8). In **Kay v United Kingdom** (2010) the European Court found a violation of Article 8 in respect of procedures for seeking the repossession of property under English law.[25] In particular, the applicants had been dispossessed of their homes without any opportunity to have the *proportionality* of the measure determined by an independent tribunal.

The Growth in Public Administration[26]

Judicial review derives from the historical power of the courts to keep inferior bodies within their legal powers. While 'public administration' may be traced back to Elizabethan times,[27] it was in the mid-nineteenth century that government expanded its legislative and administrative functions into areas hitherto untouched. The growth in the nineteenth century of

---

23 Human Rights Act 1998, s. 4.
24 Deemed to be a safe country under Sched. 3 to the Asylum and Immigration (Treatment of Claimants, etc) Act 2004.
25 The case derives from **Kay v Lambeth LBC** (2006), and subsequent cases in which doubts over the correct interpretation of the law were expressed.
26 See, *inter alia*, Dynes and Walker, 1995.
27 For example, the Poor Relief Act 1601.

industrialisation resulted in central regulation, for example of town and country planning, the provision of housing and housing improvement,[28] public health, regulation of the railways and factory management, and schemes for compensation for injury.[29] One consequence of such regulation was the need for mechanisms for resolving disputes between individuals and the regulatory bodies. Statutory inquiries became the formal mechanism by which disputes were to be resolved.[30]

The early twentieth century laid the foundations for the Welfare State. The introduction of health insurance[31] and measures to combat unemployment[32] led to the establishment of tribunals of administration and adjudication. The major reform came with the publication of the Beveridge Report,[33] which set out radical proposals for extensive reforms in social welfare and led to the introduction of the National Health Service. The incoming Conservative government in 1979 embarked on a programme of privatisation of public authorities, including the denationalisation of major public bodies such as British Airways, British Coal, British Gas, British Rail and British Telecom. The further rolling back of state control came through the government divesting itself of its shares in such companies as Jaguar, Rolls-Royce and British Nuclear Fuels. However, while governments have continued to privatise, other bodies have been created to regulate certain bodies and others created as self-regulatory bodies. To portray succinctly the administrative system existing nowadays is not an easy task. As with so much of the institutional framework of the state, developments have proceeded in a pragmatic, ad hoc fashion. In 1980, the *Report on Non-Departmental Public Bodies*[34] classified administrative bodies into executive bodies, advisory bodies and tribunals. Today, numerous different tribunals exist, with jurisdiction over such diverse subject matters as commerce, economic matters, education, employment, Foreign Compensation, housing, physical and mental health, immigration, the National Health Service, pensions and residential homes.

The volume of judicial review applications

Between 2007 and 2012, the volume of applications for judicial review increased by 86 per cent. Much of this increase was explained by the vast increase in the number of Immigration and Asylum applications which showed an increase of 129 per cent during that period. In 2013, immigration and asylum claims were transferred from the High Court to the tribunal system. Once the Immigration and Asylum figures were removed, the increase in applications was very limited. However, the government considered that judicial review was being used as a means of delaying public decision making and initiated reform under the Criminal Justice and Courts Act 2015 (discussed below at pages 652 and 657 to 658).

In 2014, after the transfer of immigration and asylum to the tribunal system there was a marked decrease in applications to the High Court with the Ministry of Justice stating that the number had fallen by nearly 25 per cent. This downward trend continued into 2018 and 2019, with the number of applications in 2019 down by six per cent from 2018. The Official Statistics for 2019 show that the Ministry of Justice and the Home Office had the largest number of applications lodged against them: 1,100 applications (down seven per cent on 2018)

---

28 Artisans' and Labourers' Dwelling Improvement Act 1875; Housing of the Working Classes Act 1890.
29 Public Health Acts 1848, 1872, 1875; Factory Act 1833; Workmen's Compensation Acts 1897 and 1906, respectively.
30 Craig, 2008, pp. 283–301.
31 National Insurance Act 1911.
32 Labour Exchanges Act 1909 and National Insurance Act 1911.
33 *Social Insurance and Allied Services*, Cmnd 6404, 1942, London: HMSO.
34 Cmnd 7797, 1980, London: HMSO; see also *Report of the Committee on Administrative Tribunals and Enquiries*, Cmnd 218, 1957, London: HMSO.

and 976 (down 17 per cent) respectively. The third largest recipient of applications was Local Authorities, having 586 applications (down ten per cent).

What is a 'public body' for the purposes of judicial review?

Judicial review is only available to test the lawfulness of decisions made by public bodies. If judicial review is applied for, and the court rules that the body whose decision is being challenged is a private body, then the remedy of the aggrieved individual will lie in private law, not public law, proceedings. In determining whether or not the body whose decision is being challenged on an application for judicial review is a public as opposed to private body, the court will look at its functions. The test is not whether or not the authority is a government body as such but, rather, whether it is a body exercising powers analogous to those of government bodies. National public agencies have been a feature of administration since the Reform Act of 1832. The Poor Law Commissioners established in 1834, for whom there was no responsible Minister in Parliament (until 1847) are an early example of such an agency. The post-Second World War nationalisation programmes of the Labour government between 1945 and 1951 and the expansion of welfare provision, both then and subsequently, resulted in numerous public bodies being established which were not government bodies, nor were they part of local government. Examples of such bodies include the British Broadcasting Authority, Legal Aid Board (now the Legal Services Commission), Atomic Energy Authority and British Airports Authority. It was estimated that by 1991 there were some 1,444 public bodies which were not related to government Departments.[35] In 1979, the incoming Conservative government was firmly committed to privatisation. British Gas, British Airways, British Rail, British Telecom, the water supply industry and electricity industry were all privatised.[36] The drive towards privatisation and reduced state holdings in many other enterprises[37] has not, however, reduced the number of public bodies. Paralleling the privatisation movement has been the growth in standard-setting and regulatory bodies designed to ensure appropriate accountability of providers to consumers, many statutory, some established on a voluntary basis. One question which arises is how the courts determine whether a body — howsoever established — is a public body and thus amenable to judicial review of its decisions.

The Courts' Interpretation of Public Bodies

In **R v City Panel on Takeovers and Mergers ex parte Datafin Ltd** (1987), the Takeover Panel had dismissed a complaint made by a bidder of 'acting in concert' contrary to the rules on takeovers. The bidder applied for judicial review. The court declined to grant the application on the basis that there were no grounds for judicial review (on which, see below) but, nevertheless, rejected the claim made by the City Panel that the court had no jurisdiction to consider the application. The Panel was subject to judicial review, despite its lack of statutory or prerogative source of power, because it was a body exercising public functions analogous to those which could be, or could have been in the absence of the Panel, exercised by a government Department. Lord Justice Lloyd stated that, for the most part, the source of the power will be decisive. Accordingly, if a body is set up under statute or by delegated legislation, then the source of the power brings the body within the scope of judicial review. However, Lloyd LJ

---

35 *Public Bodies*, 1991, London: HMSO.
36 Gas Act 1986, Civil Aviation Act 1980, Water Act 1989, Electricity Act 1989.
37 For example, British Petroleum, British Nuclear Fuels Ltd, Cable and Wireless, Rolls-Royce, Jaguar.

also recognised that in some cases the matter would be unclear. Where that situation existed, it was necessary to look beyond the source of the power and consider the 'nature of the power' being exercised. In Lloyd LJ's view, '[i]f a body in question is exercising public law functions, or if the exercise of its functions have public law consequences, then that may be sufficient to bring the body within the reach of judicial review'.

By contrast with the **City Panel on Takeover and Mergers** case, in **R v Disciplinary Committee of the Jockey Club ex parte Aga Khan** (1993), the Aga Khan sought judicial review of the Jockey Club's decision to disqualify his winning horse from a race for failing a dope test. The court ruled that the relationship between racehorse owners and the Club, and the powers of the Club, derived from agreement between the parties and was a matter of private rather than public law.[38]

In **R (Julian West) v Lloyd's of London** (2004) the Court of Appeal ruled that decisions taken by Lloyd's of London were not amenable to judicial review either on the basis that it was performing a governmental function or because it was a public authority within the meaning of section 6(1) of the Human Rights Act 1998. The decisions were solely concerned with the commercial relationship between the applicant and Lloyd's and were governed by the contracts into which the applicant had entered. Accordingly the decisions were of a private and not a public nature. The same principle will be applied whenever a matter is regulated by contract between two private parties – the matter is one of private and not public law. There is a fine distinction to be drawn here. The regulation of a private school, for example, has been held to be a matter of private law, whereas the regulation of City Technical Colleges, non-fee-paying publicly funded institutions, is a matter of public law. However, where a pupil attends a private school under a publicly funded assisted places scheme, that school falls within the jurisdiction for judicial review in relation to the school's decision; in particular, the decision to expel a pupil.[39]

Under section 6 of the Human Rights Act 1998, public authorities are defined as including courts and tribunals and 'any person certain of whose functions are functions of a public nature'. In **Marcic v Thames Water** (2004), for example, a privatised water and sewerage company was held to be a public body for the purposes of the Act. The Act excludes both Houses of Parliament and those acting in connection with parliamentary proceedings. For the purposes of judicial review, section 7 provides that an applicant is only to have sufficient interest if he or she is a victim of the unlawful act. In relation to proceedings relating to judicial acts, these may be brought only by exercising a right of appeal or by an application for judicial review.[40]

In **R (Holmcroft Properties Ltd) v Financial Conduct Authority** (2018) the Court of Appeal upheld the decision of the Divisional Court that KPMG LLP, a private firm of accountants, was not amenable to judicial review. KPMG was appointed to report on redress arrangements as required by the Financial Services Authority (now Financial Conduct Authority). However, the Court also criticised the decision as 'focusing too narrowly on the source of the Independent Reviewer's power and stated that it should have taken a wider view of the regulatory position and factual context'. The Court cited with approval the following principles set out in the **Aga Khan** case:

> A body whose birth and constitution owed nothing to any exercise of governmental power *may* be subject to judicial review if it has been woven into the fabric of public

---

38 See also **R v Chief Rabbi ex parte Wachmann** (1993); and Barendt, Baron, Herberg and Jowell, 1993. See also **R (Mullins) v Appeal Board of the Jockey Club** (2004).

39 See **R v Governors of Haberdashers' Aske's Hatcham College Trust ex parte T** (1994), per Dyson J.

40 Human Rights Act 1998, s. 9.

regulation or into a system of governmental control (per Sir Thomas Bingham MR at pp 921C and 923H) or is integrated into a system of statutory regulation (per Hoffmann LJ at 932H) or is a surrogate organ of government (per Hoffmann LJ at p 932D) or but for its existence a governmental body would assume control (per Farquharson LJ at p 930B and Hoffmann LJ at p 932B).

The case law on the interpretation of public bodies for the purposes of the Human Rights Act 1998 is discussed in Chapter 18.

Review and appeal[41]

Judicial review must be distinguished from an appeal against a decision. The court and tribunal structure provides a more or less rational appeal structure for those aggrieved by a judicial decision. The appellate court will have the power to reconsider the case and to substitute its own decision for that of the lower court. An appeal may be made on both the law and the facts of the case, so that a full re-hearing may take place. Judicial review, by contrast, is concerned solely with the manner in which the decision maker has applied the relevant rules: it is thus procedural in nature. It is not for the court – in judicial review proceedings – to substitute its judgment for that of the decision-making body to which powers have been delegated but, rather, to ensure that the adjudicator has kept within the rules laid down by statute and the common law. In short, the role of the courts in judicial review is to exercise a supervisory, not an appellate, jurisdiction. Judicial review 'is not an appeal from a decision, but a review of the manner in which the decision was made'.[42]

Judicial review derives from the courts' inherent powers to keep decision-making bodies within the bounds of their powers, and to provide remedies for abuse of power, and its purpose is not to substitute a decision of the court for the decision of the administrative body.

It should be noted that seeking judicial review is not the only avenue for those complaining about public bodies. The case of **Marcic v Thames Water Utilities Ltd** (2004) illustrates the courts' approach. The appellant sought an injunction to restrain Thames Water from permitting the use of its sewerage system in such a way as to cause flooding to his property, and a mandatory order compelling Thames Water to improve the sewerage system, and damages. Thames Water operates its system under statutory powers and subject to statutory duties. The Water Industry Act 1991 provides for a Director General of Water Services with wide-ranging powers and duties, not least of which the power to make Enforcement Orders requiring providers to comply with the requirements of the Act. The House of Lords ruled that the appellant had chosen to side-step the statutory scheme by pursuing judicial review proceedings against the Secretary of State rather than seeking to enforce the statutory duty of the water authority. The House of Lords emphasised that the courts were ill-equipped to deal with statutory undertakings which involved large-scale capital expenditure: Parliament had entrusted that function to the Director.

The outcome of judicial review

Differences also exist in the respective outcomes of appeal and judicial review. In the case of appeals, where the appeal is successful, it will usually result in a new decision being

---

41 See **Chief Constable of the North Wales Police v Evans** (1982).
42 Per Lord Brightman in **Chief Constable of the North Wales Police v Evans** (1982), p. 1174.

substituted for the previous decision.[43] In the case of review, a successful case will usually result in the previous decision being nullified – or quashed – but no new decision will be put in its place. Instead, the body in relation to which a successful application for judicial review has been made will be directed to redetermine the case according to the correct rules and procedure, and it is by no means inevitable that the decision reached according to the lawful procedure will be more favourable to the individual than the original decision.

Furthermore, there is no automatic right to a remedy in judicial review proceedings: the remedy is discretionary. This matter is contentious.[44] In some cases, the court will decline to grant a remedy. The court may hold, for example, that while the decision-making process was defective, nevertheless the applicant has suffered no injustice, or that even if a remedy were granted, the decision maker would reach the same conclusion on the merits, or that the impact on administration would be too great if a remedy were granted.

The Basis for Judicial Review

The Senior Courts Act 1981[45]

The basis for review today lies in section 31 of the Senior Courts Act 1981 and the Civil Procedure Rules 1998.

Section 31 provides, in part, that:

(1) An application to the High Court for one or more of the following forms of relief, namely:

    (a) an order of mandamus, prohibition or *certiorari*;

    (b) a declaration or injunction under sub-section (2); or

    (c) an injunction under section 30 restraining a person not entitled to do so from acting in an office to which that section applies, shall be made in accordance with rules of court by a procedure to be known as an application for judicial review.

(2) A declaration may be made or an injunction granted under this subsection in any case where an application for judicial review, seeking that relief, has been made and the High Court considers that, having regard to:

    (a) the nature of the matters in respect of which relief may be granted by orders of mandamus, prohibition or *certiorari*;

    (b) the nature of the persons and bodies against whom relief may be granted by such orders; and

    (c) all the circumstances of the case, it would be just and convenient for the declaration to be made or for the injunction to be granted, as the case may be.

(3) No application for judicial review shall be made unless the leave of the High Court has been obtained in accordance with rules of court; and the court shall not grant leave to make such an application unless it considers that the applicant has a sufficient interest in the matter to which the application relates.

---

43 In some instances, a new trial may have to be ordered in order for a fresh decision to be reached.

44 See Bingham, 1991.

45 The Supreme Court Act 1981 was renamed the 'Senior Courts Act' under the Constitutional Reform Act 2005. See Sched. 11, Pt I.

Note that the Criminal Justice and Courts Act 2015 amends section 31, inserting the requirement that to be granted leave an applicant must be able to show that the alleged unlawful conduct has made a substantial difference to him or her. This is discussed further below at pages 657 to 658.

Under the Civil Procedure Rules 1998, an action must be brought within three months of the decision against which review is sought. However, shorter time periods may be specified in statute and these must be complied with.

Applying for permission for judicial review

It must be noted here that there is no unfettered right to judicial review. The aggrieved individual must seek permission to apply for judicial review, and a number of criteria, which are discussed below, govern the exercise of the discretion to grant or refuse the application for judicial review.

The requirement to seek permission for judicial review is controversial, and there are cogent arguments for its reform. For example, the JUSTICE-All Souls Report[46] argued for its repeal on the basis, first, that the permission requirement is discriminatory; second, that the justification for permission based on eliminating 'groundless, unmeritorious or tardy harassment' on the part of applicants can be dealt with in the same manner as in ordinary litigation;[47] and third, that the issue of standing is no longer finally determined at the stage at which the application for permission is considered; see further below. However, there is support for the view that, while the need to seek permission represents a procedural hurdle which does not exist in other areas of the law, there remains a need to filter out unmeritorious cases at an early stage. The Law Commission re-examined the question of application for permission and concluded that it remains 'essential to filter out hopeless applications for judicial review by a requirement such as leave'.[48]

When seeking permission to apply the application must be served on the defendant and unless the court orders otherwise, any person the claimant considers to be an interested party. Permission will be granted where an arguable case has been shown. Rule 54.12 of the Civil Procedure Rules (CPR) provides that where permission to apply for judicial review is refused, the claimant is entitled to request reconsideration of the application at an oral hearing (a 'renewal application'). Paragraph 7 of that Rule provides that 'where the court refuses permission to proceed and records the fact that the application is totally without merit ... the claimant may not request that decision to be reconsidered at a hearing'. The criteria by which permission should be granted is undefined in the Rules or the Tribunal Courts and Enforcement Act 2007 (which imposes permission requirements on the Upper Tribunal). In *Wasif v Secretary of State for the Home Department* (2016) the Court of Appeal examined the correct approach, stating that it was now generally accepted that the test was whether the application was 'arguable' or had 'a realistic prospect of success'. But was there a difference between that criterion and the criterion that an application was totally without merit and therefore bound to fail? The Court of Appeal ruled that there was a 'real' distinction, although it was not 'black and white'. It was possible that oral argument might persuade a judge who had refused permission on the papers that the application did in fact have a realistic chance of success. Where, however, the judge found that the claim was bound to fail, there was no chance that an oral hearing would make a difference and would simply prolong the process

46 *Administrative Law: Some Necessary Reforms*, 1988. See also Law Commission, *Administrative Law: Judicial Review and Statutory Appeals*, Consultation Paper No. 226/HC 669.
47 As provided for by RSC Ord. 18, r. 19.
48 Law Commission, *Administrative Law: Judicial Review and Statutory Appeals*, Consultation Paper No. 226/HC 669.

and waste the resources of the court. It was essential that a judge refusing permission to apply give reasons for the decision, and to give reasons for certifying an application as totally without merit separately from his or her reasons for refusing permission.

Where granting permission for an application for judicial review would make no difference to the circumstances of the claimant, the court was entitled to refuse permission to review. The Supreme Court so ruled in **R (O) v Secretary of State for the Home Department** (2016). 'O' had arrived in the UK illegally. She suffered from mental illness. Her claim for asylum and leave to remain was refused. She was later convicted of a criminal offence and on release from prison was detained pending deportation. She was released on bail and challenged the lawfulness of her detention. The judge refused permission for the claim to proceed and the Court of Appeal dismissed her appeal. The Supreme Court also dismissed her appeal. The Court found that the Secretary of State had not applied her policy in relation to the detention of mentally ill persons pending deportation correctly and as a result the decision to continue to detain O was procedurally flawed. However, if the Home Secretary had correctly applied the policy, it would not have resulted in O being released from detention any earlier than the date of her release on bail. If the application for judicial review was permitted to proceed it would result in nothing more than a declaration that her detention was unlawful and the award of nominal damages. Accordingly the judge was entitled to refuse the application.

Standing to Apply for Judicial Review

The 'sufficient interest' test[49]

Prior to 1977 the rules on standing were largely in the hands of judges and the way the rules operated largely depended on the remedy being sought.[50] The test was one of whether the person was 'aggrieved' and not a 'mere busybody'.[51] The 1977 Rules of the Supreme Court Order 53 rule 3(7) and the Senior Courts Act 1981 placed the test for standing on a statutory footing. The Senior Courts Act 1981 provides that the court must not grant permission for an application for judicial review 'unless it considers that the applicant has a sufficient interest [otherwise expressed as "standing" or locus standi] in the matter to which the application relates'. The justification for such a requirement lies in the need to limit challenges to administrative decision making to genuine cases of grievance and to avoid unnecessary interference in the administrative process by those whose objectives are not authentic. The applicant may be an individual whose personal rights and interests have been affected by a decision, or an individual concerned with official decisions which affect the interests of society as a whole. Alternatively, the application may be brought by an interest or pressure group desiring to challenge a decision which affects the rights and interests of members of that group or society at large. To limit access to the courts using a test for standing is controversial. On the one hand there are practical objections to opening the doors of the courts too wide for fear of vexatious litigants,[52] but at the same time public bodies should be held accountable for the decisions they make.

---

49 Senior Courts Act 1981, s. 31(3).
50 See *Ware v Regents Canal Company* (1858); *Boyce v Paddington Borough Council* (1903); *R v Thames Magistrates Court ex parte Greenbaum* (1957); *Thorne v British Broadcasting Corporation* (1967); *Blackburn v Attorney General* (1971); *Attorney General (ex rel McWhirter) v Independent Broadcasting Authority* (1973).
51 *R v Liverpool Corporation ex parte Liverpool Taxi Fleet Owners Association* (1972).
52 A vexatious litigant is someone who has been prevented by the court from bringing an action due to a history of bringing superfluous and largely irrelevant cases before the court.

The manner in which the test is applied

The test of 'sufficient interest' was provided in **R v Inland Revenue Commissioners ex parte National Federation of Self-Employed and Small Businesses** (1982). The House of Lords' approach was as follows. The question of whether there is standing should be examined in two stages. At the first instance, standing should be considered when permission to apply is sought. At that stage, the court is concerned, according to Lord Scarman, to ensure that 'it prevents abuse by busybodies, cranks and other mischief makers'. If permission is granted, the court may – at a second stage, when the merits of the case are known – revise its original decision and decide that after all the applicants do not have sufficient interest. The effect of this is to reduce the issue of sufficient interest and to elevate the question of the merits of the case.

Individual standing: personal rights and interests

Given the breadth of administrative decision making in a heavily regulated society, individuals may have their rights or expectations affected in multifarious ways, as has been seen above. Further examples from the case law illustrate the concept of individual standing. In **Schmidt v Secretary of State for Home Affairs** (1969), students who had entered the country as 'students of scientology' challenged the decision of the Home Office not to allow them to remain once the permitted period of stay had expired. The students had 'sufficient interest' for permission to be granted.

In the case of **R v Secretary of State for the Environment ex parte Ward** (1984) a Gypsy living on a caravan site was held to have standing to apply for an order requiring that the Secretary of State should direct the local authority to fulfil its statutory duty to provide an adequate site. Standing was also granted to Mrs Gillick, the mother of several daughters, who wished to challenge a Health Authority over its policy relating to contraception for young girls,[53] and to a journalist acting in the public interest.[54] By contrast, in **Holmes v Checkland** (1987) an opponent of cigarette smoking was deemed not to have standing to seek to restrain the BBC from broadcasting a snooker championship sponsored by a tobacco company on the ground that he had no more interest than any other member of the public and accordingly could only proceed with the aid of the Attorney General.[55]

In **R v Secretary of State for Foreign and Commonwealth Affairs ex parte Rees-Mogg** (1994), the applicant sought judicial review of the government's ratification of the Treaty on European Union without parliamentary consent. Rees-Mogg was held to have sufficient standing, but the application was dismissed on the basis that the issue was non-justiciable.[56]

The Human Rights Act 1998 introduced a new basis for 'standing'. Section 7 of the Act provides that only a 'victim' of an act of a public body may make a claim.[57] That test – which is the same as the test applied under the European Convention on Human Rights – is narrower than standing in other judicial review proceedings. It also excludes representative bodies and interest groups taking action on behalf of their members.[58]

---

53 *Gillick v West Norfolk and Wisbech Area Health Authority* (1986).
54 R v Felixstowe Judges ex parte Leigh (1987).
55 Note that the Attorney General's decision whether to bring a relator action cannot be challenged in court: **Gouriet v Union of Post Office Workers** (1978).
56 For the meaning of 'justiciability', see above. See also **Blackburn v Attorney General** (1971), wherein a challenge to accession to the Treaty of Rome was unsuccessful.
57 See *Adams v Lord Advocate* (2003); *Lancashire City Council v Taylor* (2005).
58 See R (Johnson) (Deceased) v SSHD & Cumbria County Council (Interested Party) (2006).

The standing of interest and pressure groups
Actions in defence of the group's own interests

A group may have its interests adversely affected by administrative decision making. By way of illustration, in **R v Liverpool Corporation ex parte Liverpool Taxi Fleet Operators' Association** (1972), Liverpool Corporation had the duty of licensing taxis and fixing the number of licences to be granted. When the Corporation announced that the number of licences was to be increased, without consulting the Operators' Association, leave to apply for judicial review was sought. The Association had sufficient standing. Equally, in **Royal College of Nursing v Department for Health and Social Security** (1981), the Royal College had standing to challenge a departmental circular concerning the role of nurses in abortions.

Both these cases involve organisations seeking to challenge decisions which affect their own members. Accordingly, the standing requirement is relatively easy to satisfy, since each of their members would have individual standing. The position is less straightforward where a group seeks to defend what it regards as the wider interests of society.

The standing of interest and pressure groups acting in the public interest

Inland Revenue Commissioners v National Federation of Self-Employed and Small Businesses (1982) provided the test for standing. The facts, in brief, entailed the employment of casual labour on newspapers, where the workers frequently adopted false names and paid no income tax. The Inland Revenue Commissioners (IRC) entered into an agreement with the relevant trade unions, workers and employers to the effect that if the workers filled in tax returns for the previous two years, the IRC would not pursue tax due for previous years. The National Federation (an association of taxpayers) argued that the IRC had no power to enter into this agreement and sought judicial review. The IRC defended the action on the basis that the National Federation did not have sufficient interest – or standing (*locus standi*) – to apply for judicial review. The court upheld the IRC's claim. The House of Lords ruled that the court had been correct in granting permission at the first stage, but that on the facts – the second stage – the National Federation lacked sufficient interest to challenge the legality of the agreement. The House of Lords ruled that there was no standing to challenge the particular wrongdoing alleged but that, if the Revenue had in fact been acting with impropriety, there would have been standing in a taxpayer to challenge its unlawful acts. In **R v Her Majesty's Treasury ex parte Smedley** (1985), the applicant for review sought to challenge the decision of the Treasury to pay a sum of money from the Consolidated Fund, without express parliamentary approval, to meet European Community obligations. Smedley was thus applying in his own interest and in the interests of all British taxpayers and electors.[59] The court held that he had standing, although the challenge failed on its merits. A case to be distinguished from the **National Federation** case is that of **R v Attorney General ex parte ICI plc** (1986). The application was based on a complaint that four competitor companies had been assessed at too lenient a rate, contrary to the Oil Taxation Act 1975. The court held that the company had standing: it had a genuine and substantial complaint.

The judges are, however, not united in their approach to the 'sufficient interest' test, which confers on the courts a great deal of discretion. In **R v Secretary of State for the Environment ex parte Rose Theatre Trust Company Ltd** (1990), Schiemann J cited a number of propositions which he deduced from the **IRC** case. The **Rose Theatre** case concerned the question of whether a company which had been incorporated for the purpose of campaigning to save the historic Globe Theatre site in London had sufficient interest, or *locus standi*. Included in the guidelines were: that the question of whether sufficient interest exists is not purely a matter within the

---

59 Per Sir John Donaldson MR.

discretion of the court; that sufficient interest did not necessarily entail a direct financial or legal interest; that the assertion of an interest by a person or a group does not mean that sufficient interest exists; and that, even where thousands of people joined together in a campaign, that was not conclusive that sufficient interest existed. The court ruled that the company did not have sufficient interest. However, in **R v Poole Borough Council ex parte BeeBee** (1991), the same judge ruled that two pressure groups, the World Wildlife Fund (WWF) and the British Herpetological Society (BHS), had sufficient interest to challenge a decision of the Council which had granted planning permission to itself for the development of a heathland with designated 'special scientific interest' status. The BHS had a financial interest in the site, and the WWF had undertaken to pay any legal costs if necessary.[60]

A liberal approach to sufficient interest was also taken in **R v Secretary of State for the Environment ex parte Greenpeace Ltd (No 2)** (1994). Greenpeace applied for judicial review to challenge the decision of the Inspectorate of Pollution to allow the siting of a nuclear reprocessing plant (THORP) at Sellafield in Cumbria. It was held that the Inspectorate had not abused its powers in varying British Nuclear Fuel plc's licence. However, while Greenpeace lost the case, the court nevertheless ruled that Greenpeace did have standing to challenge the decision. It was in the interests of justice to allow Greenpeace – an organisation with over 400,000 supporters in the United Kingdom – to bring an action on behalf of all concerned with the project. The court declined to follow the **Rose Theatre** decision, but warned that it should not be assumed that Greenpeace or other pressure groups would automatically be held to have sufficient interest in any future case.

Further cases involving successful challenges by pressure groups include **R v Secretary of State for Foreign and Commonwealth Affairs ex parte World Development Movement Ltd** (1995), **R v Secretary of State for Employment ex parte Equal Opportunities Commission** (1995) (the **EOC** case) and **R v Secretary of State for the Environment ex parte the Royal Society for the Protection of Birds** (the **RSPB** case) (1995). In the first case, the World Development Movement (WDM) sought judicial review of the Foreign Secretary's decision to grant financial aid to Malaysia for the building of the Pergau dam. The WDM argued that the Secretary of State had exceeded his powers. The court held that the WDM had sufficient interest. The WDM played a prominent role in giving advice and assistance in relation to aid and had consultative status with the United Nation's bodies. Further, it was unlikely that there would be any other person or body with sufficient interest to challenge the decision. In the **EOC** case, the Equal Opportunities Commission (EOC) sought a declaration that the United Kingdom was in breach of European Community law (now EU law) obligations in relation to Article 119 (now Article 141) of the EC Treaty and the Equal Pay and Equal Treatment Directives of the Community. The alleged breach concerned the Employment Protection (Consolidation) Act 1978, which discriminated between full-time and part-time employees in relation to redundancy pay and compensation for unfair dismissal. The House of Lords confirmed that the EOC had sufficient interest and, moreover, that English law was incompatible with the requirements of European Community law. In the **RSPB** case, the Royal Society had sufficient interest to challenge the decision of the Secretary of State affecting the development of land which had hitherto been a special site for the conservation of birds.

---

60 But for another decision denying sufficient interest to interest groups see **R v Darlington Borough Council ex parte Association of Darlington Taxi Owners** (1994).

SELF-TEST QUESTIONS

Why do you think it is necessary for a person or body to have 'sufficient interest' in a matter in order to apply for judicial review?

'Sufficient interest' is one of the restrictions on judicial review. What are the others (if any)?

The requirement of 'substantially different outcome'

Concern over what the government regarded as abuse of the judicial review process led to reform. The Criminal Justice and Courts Act 2015, section 84 amends section 31 of the Senior Courts Act 1981 to include the requirement that a court must refuse relief on an application for judicial review if it appears to the court 'to be highly likely that the outcome for the applicant would not have been substantially different if the conduct complained of had not occurred' (section 31(2)(2A)). The court may disregard that requirement if it appears to the court that there are reasons of 'exceptional public interest' for so doing (section 31(2B)). The High Court, of its own motion, considers whether the outcome would have been substantially different or not, and must consider that question if the defendant asks it to do so (section 31(2)(3C)).

Where the applicant cannot establish that the outcome would have been substantially different, the court must refuse to grant leave. The effect of this is that focus shifts from the central consideration of whether or not a public body has acted unlawfully to considering the impact of the alleged conduct on the applicant. The government claims that the reform 'will not stop the crucial role that judicial review plays', and that it is 'designed to tackle the large and growing number of unmeritorious judicial review applications which clog up our court system, put burdens on public services, and hold up reform'.[61] The difficulty with this provision is that where a person cannot establish that the outcome would have been 'substantially different', there is no mechanism whereby the courts can rule on the legality or otherwise of a public body's decision unless the 'exceptional public interest' exception can be satisfied.

The 2015 Act includes the requirement that the applicant provides the court with information about the financing of an application, including information about the 'source, nature and extent of financial resources available' to meet liabilities arising in connection with the application (section 85 amending section 31(3) of the Senior Courts Act 1981). The Criminal Justice and Courts Act 2015 also provides that the court may not order a party to the proceedings (whether the applicant or defendant) to pay the costs of an intervener, other than where the court considered there are 'exceptional circumstances' making it appropriate to do so (section 87). The court must order the intervener to pay any costs that have been incurred as a result of that intervention in the proceedings if certain conditions are met. Those conditions are that:

(a) the intervener has acted as the sole or principal applicant, defendant, appellant or respondent;
(b) the intervener's evidence and representations, taken as a whole, have not been of significant assistance to the court;

---

61 Criminal Justice and Courts Bill Fact Sheet: Reform of Judicial Review.

(c)   a significant part of the intervener's evidence and representations relates to matters that it is not necessary for the court to consider in order to resolve the Issues that are the subject of the stage in the proceedings; or that

(d)   the intervener has behaved unreasonably (section 87(6)).

The court is not required to make an order that the intervener pay costs if it considers that there are 'exceptional circumstances' that make it inappropriate not to do so (section 87(7)). The concern over this provision is that it has the potential to deter all but the wealthiest organisations from intervening in a case and assisting the court. The courts already have a discretion to order costs against third parties: this they rarely do which suggests that intervention by respected organisations is considered beneficial to the court.

The Existence of Alternative Remedies

The availability of alternative remedies is a relevant factor in deciding whether leave will be granted for judicial review. In **R v Inland Revenue Commissioners ex parte Preston** (1985), Lord Templeman stated that leave for an application for judicial review should not be granted 'where an alternative remedy was available'. Thus, by way of example, where Parliament has set up under statute a comprehensive appeals structure, judicial review cannot be used as a means of circumventing this.[62] Moreover, the statutory rights of appeal must be exhausted.[63] If, however, there are exceptional circumstances – for example if inordinate delays are experienced in the proceedings – the court may grant leave to apply for judicial review.[64]

A Matter of Public – Not Private – Law

Judicial review is confined to matters of public – as opposed to private – law. The courts will not seize jurisdiction to review an administrative action or decision if the matter involved is one of private law. Accordingly, the respondent must be a public authority, and the right at issue must be a public right. If the matter is one of public law, the aggrieved person must apply by way of judicial review and not under any other procedure.

The 'exclusivity principle'

In **O'Reilly v Mackman** (1983), the applicants had taken part in a prison riot at Hull gaol and the Board of Visitors (who exercise disciplinary powers over prisoners) reduced the remission of sentence as punishment. The applicants tried to establish that the Board of Visitors had acted contrary to the rules of natural justice. This they attempted to do by means of an originating summons or writ.[65] It was not contested that the issue was a matter of public law and that they could have employed the judicial review procedure, provided that they applied for leave within the requisite three months. No leave from the court is needed in relation to private law proceedings. The issue for the court was whether it was an abuse of the process of the court to use the alternative basis to bring the action. Lord Diplock stated:

> If what should emerge is that his complaint is not of an infringement of any of his rights that are entitled to protection in public law, but may be an infringement of

62   **R v Secretary of State for Social Services ex parte Connolly** (1986).
63   **R v Secretary of State for the Home Department ex parte Swati** (1986).
64   **R v Chief Constable of Merseyside Police ex parte Calveley** (1986).
65   The means by which private law proceedings are initiated.

his rights in private law and this is not a proper subject for judicial review, the court has power under rule 9(5), instead of refusing the application, to order the proceedings to continue as if they had begun by writ. [pages 283–284]

Referring to the procedural disadvantages which had existed prior to the reforms introduced in 1977 by Order 53,[66] Lord Diplock went on to state:

now that those disadvantages to applicants have been removed and all remedies for infringement of rights protected by public law can be obtained upon an application for judicial review, as also can remedies for infringements of rights under private law if such infringement should also be involved, it would in my view as a general rule be contrary to public policy, and as such an abuse of the process of the court to permit a person seeking to establish that a decision of a public authority infringed rights to which he was entitled to protection under public law to proceed by way of an ordinary action and by this means evade the provisions of Order 53 for the protection of such authorities. [page 285]

The decision in **O'Reilly** has been trenchantly criticised by Professor HWR Wade.[67] The 'exclusivity principle' – keeping public and private law rigidly distinct – was introduced by Lord Diplock in **O'Reilly**, notwithstanding the Law Commission's intention that procedural reforms introduced in 1977 were not intended to create a rigid distinction between public and private law proceedings.[68] Before that time, although the distinction between public and private law was drawn, the system was not exclusive. Professor Wade regards the exclusivity principle, declared in **O'Reilly**, as amounting to a 'serious setback for administrative law'. He goes on to state that:

it has caused many cases, which on their merits might have succeeded, to fail merely because of choice of the wrong form of action ... It has produced great uncertainty, which seems likely to continue, as to the boundary between public and private law, since these terms have no clear or settled meaning. [Wade and Forsyth, 1994, page 682]

Professor Wade regards this as an unnecessary restriction on access to the courts, a restriction which has been avoided in Scotland, Australia, New Zealand and Canada. His assessment of the House of Lords' decision in **O'Reilly** is that: 'the House of Lords has expounded the new law as designed for the protection of public authorities rather than of the citizen. Such are the misfortunes which can flow from the best intentioned reforms'.

Exceptions to the exclusivity principle

The harshness with which the exclusivity principle could operate led Lord Diplock in **O'Reilly** to state that exceptions to the rule would exist where the case involved both public and private law elements, particularly where the public law element was collateral (auxiliary or secondary) to the private law element. What is evident in this matter is that a balance needs to be struck between too rigid a rule, which denies individuals the protection of judicial review, and too lax an approach, which would enable individuals either to pursue a remedy

---

66 Now replaced by the Civil Procedure Rules 1998.
67 Wade and Forsyth, 2004.
68 Cmnd 6407, 1976, London: HMSO.

in judicial review when other procedures are in fact more appropriate or, conversely, to pursue other remedies when judicial review would be appropriate, in order to evade the requirements of judicial review. It is also evident that the judges are struggling to find the correct balance.

A public law issue used in defence in private law proceedings

In **Wandsworth London Borough Council v Winder** (1985), the House of Lords allowed a matter of public law (the lawfulness of the council's decision) to be used as a defence to private law proceedings (possession proceedings). Winder was a tenant of the local authority, which gave notice that rents were to be raised. Winder claimed that the increase was unreasonable and contrary to law. The local authority brought an action for possession of the premises. Winder defended this action on the basis that the rent increase was outside the powers of the local authority and void for unreasonableness. On appeal to the House of Lords, the question for the court was whether Winder could challenge the local authority's action by way of a defence based on judicial review grounds, or whether he should have instigated separate judicial review proceedings by way of an application to the High Court. The local authority submitted that Winder should have used judicial review but that, since he was by then out of time to do so, he could not challenge their decision by way of a defence to the possession proceedings.

Lord Fraser of Tullybelton, citing **O'Reilly**, acknowledged that it was in the interests of good administration to protect authorities from unmeritorious or late challenges, but that this factor had to be weighed in the balance against the argument for preserving the ordinary rights of private citizens to defend themselves against unfounded claims. In his opinion, Winder's action could not be described as an abuse of the process of the court. Winder had not selected the procedure, he was merely seeking to defend himself. If the public interest required that people should not have the right to defend themselves, then that was a matter for Parliament, not the courts.

Cases involving both public and private law issues

In **Roy v Kensington and Chelsea and Westminster Family Practitioner Committee** (1992) a further exception to the exclusivity principle emerged, whereby the House of Lords ruled that the principle did not apply where the proceedings involved matters of both public and private law. In **Roy**, a Family Practitioner Committee was responsible for making payments to general practitioners in respect of their National Health Service work.[69] Dr Roy's allowance was reduced by the committee on the basis that he had reduced the amount of his time spent on National Health Service work. Dr Roy litigated to recover the sum reduced. At first instance, the judge decided that the decision to reduce his payments was a matter of public law to be challenged under judicial review proceedings. On appeal to the House of Lords, it was held that, when a litigant had a private law right – in relation to a matter which involved an issue of public law – he was not precluded from pursuing his private law right. Accordingly, the fact that the public law issue could have been determined under judicial review proceedings was not held to deny him a remedy under private law. In **Andreou v Institute of Chartered Accountants in England and Wales** (1998), the applicant had been granted leave to bring judicial review to challenge the validity of a bylaw of the Chartered Institute, but failed to observe the time limit. He then commenced a private law action alleging breach of contractual duty to exercise its bylaw-making powers fairly and to act fairly in its disciplinary proceedings. The Court of Appeal ruled that the Institute was, in part, a public body. However, here it was appropriate to proceed under private law since there was a private law right at issue, even though there was also a public law issue involved.

---

69 Under the National Health Service (General Medical and Pharmaceutical) Regulations 1974.

In **R v Peter Edward Wicks** (1997), the House of Lords ruled that the validity of an enforcement notice under the Town and Country Planning Act 1990 could not be impugned in criminal proceedings, but only by the High Court on an application for judicial review. The defendant appealed against the Court of Appeal decision dismissing his appeal against conviction for failure to comply with the enforcement notice. So long as the enforcement notice was not a nullity or patently defective on its face, it was valid and would remain so until quashed. No criminal court had the power to quash, and it was not open to the defence to go behind the notice and seek to investigate its validity. The proper course to take was to apply for an adjournment of the criminal proceedings and apply to the High Court for judicial review in which the validity of the notice could be attacked.[70]

A challenge to the *vires* of subordinate legislation or an administrative act can be raised in criminal proceedings. The House of Lords so held in **Boddington v British Transport Police** (1998). The defendant, in criminal proceedings on charges of smoking a cigarette in a railway carriage where smoking was prohibited, sought to argue that the Network South Central's decision to post notices banning smoking was *ultra vires* its powers to bring the relevant bylaw into force. On appeal, the court had ruled that it was not open to the defendant to raise that public law defence in criminal proceedings against him. The House of Lords, however, stated that a defendant was so entitled, and that if the defendant managed to rebut the presumption in favour of the lawfulness of the subordinate legislation or administrative act, the legislation or act had no legal effect at all and could not found a prosecution. In the instant case, there was nothing in the bylaws or the relevant Act to rebut the presumption that the defendant was entitled to defend himself against a criminal charge on the basis of the validity of the decision to put no smoking notices in carriages. However, the manner in which the relevant bylaw had been brought into force was not *ultra vires* and accordingly the appeal was dismissed.

Broad versus restrictive approaches

O'Reilly and **Winder** were both considered extensively in **Roy v Kensington and Chelsea and Westminster Family Practitioner Committee** (above), in which Lord Lowry examined the 'broad' or 'liberal' approach to judicial review and the 'narrow' or 'restrictive' approach. A broad approach lessens the importance of the distinction between public and private law and would allow either the Order 53 procedure to be used or the pursuit of a private law remedy. A narrow approach, however, would dictate that if the matter is primarily a matter of private law then the judicial review procedure is inappropriate. While Lord Lowry 'disclaimed any intention of discussing the scope of the rule in **O'Reilly**', he nevertheless went on to make a case for a more liberal approach. Lord Lowry stated that:

> the Law Commission, when recommending the new judicial review procedure, contemplated the continued co-existence of judicial review proceedings and actions for a declaration with regard to public law issues …

> … this House has expressly approved actions for a declaration of nullity as alternative to applications for *certiorari* to quash, where private law rights were concerned: **Wandsworth London Borough Council v Winder** (1992), p. 655, per Robert Goff LJ.

---

70 See also **Steed v Secretary of State for the Home Department** (2000); **R v Falmouth and Truro Port Health Authority ex parte Southwest Water Ltd** (2000); **Wandsworth LBC v A** (2001).

Citing Goff LJ, Lord Lowry continued:

> The principle remains in fact that public authorities and public servants are, unless clearly exempted, answerable in the ordinary courts for wrongs done to individuals. But by an extension of remedies and a flexible procedure it can be said that something resembling a system of public law is being developed. Before the expression 'public law' can be used to deny a subject a right of action in the court of his choice it must be related to a positive prescription of law, by statute or by statutory rules. We have not yet reached the point at which mere characterisation of a claim as a claim in public law is sufficient to exclude it from consideration by the ordinary courts: to permit this would be to create a dual system of law with the rigidity and procedural hardship for plaintiffs which it was the purpose of the recent reforms to remove: *Davy v Spelthorn Borough Council* (1984), per Lord Wilberforce.

> In conclusion, my Lords, it seems to me that, unless the procedure adopted by the moving party is ill suited to dispose of the question at issue, there is much to be said in favour of the proposition that a court having jurisdiction ought to let a case be heard rather than entertain a debate concerning the form of the proceedings.

Lord Slynn advanced the argument for a more flexible approach to the choice of proceedings in **Mercury Communications Ltd v Director General of Telecommunications** (1996). In that case, the effect of **O'Reilly v Mackman** was further limited. A dispute arose between Mercury Communications and British Telecom (BT), both of which are public limited companies licensed by the Secretary of State under the Telecommunications Act 1984. Mercury Communications was dependent upon the rental of part of BT's network. The Director General, exercising powers under the 1984 Act, determined the dispute, and his decision affected the terms of the contract between Mercury and BT. Mercury initiated private proceedings in the Commercial Court by originating summons. At first instance, the Director General and BT failed to have the proceeding struck out, the court applying the **O'Reilly** principle. On appeal, however, it was argued, successfully, that this was an abuse of process. The case went to the House of Lords, which reversed the decision of the Court of Appeal. Lord Slynn emphasised that when determining the issue of the choice of private or public law proceedings, flexibility must be retained. It was recognised that the Director General had statutory functions and performed public duties. However, this did not eliminate the possibility of private law proceedings. Since the Director General's decision had been imposed as part of a contract, this could be regarded as a contractual dispute. Accordingly, the commencement of private law proceedings was equally well suited to determine the issue as judicial review proceedings. The issue of the appropriateness of proceedings was a matter to be determined by the courts on a case-by-case basis. Lord Slynn stated that:

> when it comes to a question of striking out for abuse of process of the court the discretion exercised by the trial judge should stand unless the arguments are clearly and strongly in favour of a different result to that to which he has come. [page 59]

The House of Lords reconsidered the question of the appropriate form of proceedings once more in **O'Rourke v Camden London Borough Council** (1997). In this case, the plaintiff had applied to the local authority for accommodation, under the Housing Act 1985, on his release from prison. Section 63(1) of the Housing Act provides that a local authority is under a duty to provide accommodation in respect of those who are 'homeless and [have] a priority need', and that includes persons who are 'vulnerable as a result of … physical disability or other special reason'. Initially, the authority refused him accommodation, but subsequently provided accommodation for a 12-day period, after which the plaintiff was evicted and no alternative accommodation offered. The plaintiff brought a private action against the council for wrongful eviction without providing alternative accommodation, and claimed damages. The House of Lords ruled that the question of whether section 63 of the Housing Act gave rise to public or private law proceedings depended on the intention of Parliament. The duty to provide accommodation was a matter of public law and the Act

> was a scheme of social welfare, intended on grounds of public policy and public interest to confer benefits at the public expense not only for the private benefit of people who found themselves homeless but also for the benefit of society in general.

The provision of accommodation, and the type of accommodation, was 'largely dependent on the housing authority's judgment and discretion'. Accordingly, it was 'unlikely' that Parliament had intended section 63 to give rise to a private action.

The issue of the choice between public and private proceedings returned to the courts in **Trustees of the Dennis Rye Pension Fund v Sheffield City Council** (1997). The plaintiffs were required by the local council to carry out repairs to certain houses to make them fit for human habitation,[71] and applied for improvement grants from the council under the Local Government and Housing Act 1989. When the work was complete, the council refused to pay the grant, on the basis that, inter alia, the repairs had not been carried out to the required standard. The plaintiff then commenced private law proceedings for recovery of the money due. The council, however, argued that if there were any grounds for complaint, the appropriate process was an application for judicial review. Accordingly, the council sought to have the plaintiff's claim struck out, on the grounds that the private law proceedings were an abuse of process. The issue went to the Court of Appeal. Lord Woolf MR regretted that the 'tactical' issue of the choice of proceedings had inevitably led to very substantial costs being incurred 'to little or no purpose'. He further criticised the narrow approach taken by the House of Lords in **O'Rourke v Camden London Borough Council**.

The Court of Appeal considered the choice between judicial review proceedings and other legal action against a public authority. In determining that question, the court should not be overly concerned with the distinction between public and private rights, but look to the practical consequences of pursuing the alternative actions. The court accepted that when a council was performing its role in relation to the making of grants, it was performing a public function which did not give rise to private rights. If the choice made had 'no significant disadvantages' for the parties, the public or the courts, it should not normally be regarded as an abuse of process. The court applied **O'Reilly v Mackman** (1982) and **Roy v Kensington and Chelsea and Westminster Family Practitioner Committee** (1992). Lord Woolf MR, after a consideration of these and other cases, ruled that as a general rule it is contrary to public policy, and as a result an abuse of the process of the court:

> to permit a person seeking to establish that a decision of a public authority infringed rights to which he was entitled to protection under public law to proceed by way of an ordinary action and by this means to evade the provisions of Order 53 for the protection of such authorities.

---

71 Under the Housing Act 1989, s. 189.

However, Lord Woolf made three 'pragmatic suggestions' and stated that it is to be remembered that:

> If it is not clear whether judicial review or an ordinary action is the correct procedure it will be safer to make an application for judicial review than commence an ordinary action since there then should be no question of being treated as abusing the process of the court by avoiding the protection provided by judicial review ...
>
> If a case is brought by an ordinary action and there is an application to strike out the case, the court should, at least if it is unclear whether the case should have been brought by judicial review, ask itself whether, if the case had been brought by judicial review when the action was commenced, it is clear leave would have been granted. If it would, then that is at least an indication that there has been no harm to the interests judicial review is designed to protect ...
>
> Finally, in cases where it is unclear whether proceedings have been correctly brought by an ordinary action, it should be remembered that, after consulting the Crown Office, a case can always be transferred to the Crown Office List as an alternative to being struck out.[72]

The more liberal approach to procedure was evident in **Clark v University of Lincolnshire and Humberside** (2000) in which a student sued her university for breach of contract after having been failed in her examination following unproven allegations of plagiarism. She was outside the three-month time limit for judicial review and the university argued that this would have been the appropriate form of proceeding. The Court of Appeal disagreed, stating that the distinction between judicial review and private actions was now limited and that a claim would not be struck out on the basis that the applicant had proceeded under contract rather than judicial review.

It must also be recognised that the courts are keen to ensure that the parties have made use of any alternative suitable remedies. In the case of **R (Cowl) v Plymouth City Council (Practice Note)** (2001) the Court of Appeal was critical of litigation which raised no point of legal principle but which the claimants nevertheless appealed against the decision of the Council. Lord Woolf CJ, having reviewed the facts and the alternative remedy of having the matter determined by a complaints panel, stated that:

> The courts should not permit, except for good reason, proceedings for judicial review to proceed if a significant part of the issues are limited. If subsequently it becomes apparent that there is a legal issue to be resolved, that can thereafter be examined by the courts which may be considerably assisted by the findings made by the complaints panel.
>
> This case will have served some purpose if it makes clear that the lawyers acting on both sides of a dispute of this sort are under a heavy obligation to resort to litigation only if it is really unavoidable. If they cannot resolve the whole of the dispute by the use of the complaints procedure they should resolve the dispute so far as is practicable without involving litigation.[73]

---

72 **Trustees of the Dennis Rye Pension Fund v Sheffield City Council** (1997), p. 755.
73 **R (Cowl) v Plymouth City Council (Practice Note)**, paras 14 and 27.

Limitations on Judicial Review

Justiciability

Justiciability is a concept which defines the judges' view of the suitability of the subject matter to be judicially reviewed.[74] There are some matters in relation to which the courts – mindful of the doctrine of separation of powers – prove to be exceedingly reluctant to review. Matters such as the exercise of prerogative power and, most importantly, issues of national security, and matters of high policy, the courts may regard as non-justiciable. However, the courts will not decline to review a matter simply because the source of the power exercised is the royal prerogative. The House of Lords made it clear in **Council of Civil Service Unions v Minister for Civil Service** (1985) that the source of the power was not determinative of whether the courts would review, but rather whether the subject matter of the application was justiciable or not.[75]

Matters of public policy not for judicial review

Where a matter complained of involves issues of high policy, the courts will decline to exercise a supervisory function over such decisions. Matters of public policy are for determination by the executive, and not the judiciary, and any purported attempt to control the decision will be regarded as a violation of the separation of powers and an intrusion into the proper decision-making sphere of the executive. For example, in **Nottinghamshire County Council v Secretary of State for the Environment** (1986), it was held that the court should not intervene to quash guidance drafted by the Secretary of State, on the authority of Parliament, setting limits to public expenditure by local authorities. Lord Scarman ruled that:

> Unless and until a statute provides otherwise, or it is established that the Secretary of State has abused his power, these are matters of political judgment for him and for the House of Commons. They are not for the judges or your Lordships' House in its judicial capacity.

Similarly, in **Hammersmith and Fulham London Borough Council v Department of the Environment** (1991), concerning the lawfulness of 'charge capping' local authorities (penalising local authorities for exceeding their budgets), the House of Lords ruled that the decision was not open to challenge on the grounds of irrationality 'short of the extremes of bad faith, improper motive or manifest absurdity'. Lord Bridge went on to rule that such decisions, relating to national economic policy, 'are matters depending essentially on political judgment' and that, in the absence of any evidence of bad faith or abuse of power, the courts would be 'exceeding their proper function if they presumed to condemn the policy as unreasonable'. In **R v Parliamentary Commissioner for Administration ex parte Dyer** (1994), Simon Brown LJ held that matters of national policy were not open to challenge before the courts other than on the basis of bad faith, improper motive or manifest absurdity. Matters of national economic policy were for political – not judicial – judgment.

Then in **R (Friends of the Earth) v Secretary of State for Business, Enterprise and Regulatory Reform; R (Help the Aged) v Secretary of State for Environment, Food and Rural Affairs** (2009) the Court of Appeal ruled that it was not unlawful for government Ministers to consider 'reasonable

---

74 See **Thorne v University of London** (1966); **R v Bristol Corporation ex parte Hendy** (1974).
75 See also **Attorney General v de Keyser's Royal Hotel Ltd** (1920); **Laker Airways v Department of Trade** (1977); **R v Secretary of State for the Home Department ex parte Fire Brigades' Union** (1995); **M v Home Office** (1993).

practicability', at least to some extent by reference to departmental budgets, when taking steps to implement specific targets, including eliminating fuel poverty.[76]

Under the Warm Homes and Energy Conservation Act 2000 the government's strategy targets were set for ending fuel poverty for vulnerable households by 2010, 'as far as reasonably practicable'. The government argued that it had done all it could to achieve the targets, given the overall spending priorities of government and the budgets allowed for ending fuel poverty. The claimants argued that the statutory duty must be complied with, irrespective of budgets. The statute provided that Secretaries of State were only obliged to take such steps as 'in their opinion' are necessary to implement the strategy. The Court of Appeal accepted that opinions could differ as to how best to implement such a policy and it was not for the court to adjudicate on the merits of the opinions formed, in the absence of a challenge as to its rationality. This is another example of the courts being careful not to trespass on areas more appropriately decided by the democratically accountable executive. As Maurice Kay LJ stated, if the position was otherwise 'the scene would be set for a wholly undesirable judicialisation of public spending priorities'.

The financial resources of local authorities are also a relevant consideration in judicial review proceedings. In **R (Hunt) v North Somerset Council** (2013), for example, the Court of Appeal ruled that it would not grant a remedy on the basis that to do so would in effect be to re-write the expired budget from a previous year, a move which would be 'highly impractical and detrimental to good administration'.

The doctrine of deference

It is apparent from the case law that the judges are very conscious of the invisible boundary line between those matters that they regard themselves as competent to adjudicate and those matters which should be left for the democratically elected government. This is the doctrine of deference. Closely related to the courts' self-imposed restrictions on jurisdiction by excluding matters of public policy from judicial review, judicial deference to the executive government is a distinctive manifestation of the concept of justiciability (or non-justiciability). The principal distinction lies in the fact that whereas courts will rule on justiciability in order to decide whether to review, with deference the courts conduct an examination and then decide that they should defer to the elected government and/or Parliament on the grounds of competence and/or democratic principle. The concept is also similar to the concept of margin of appreciation, which is used by the Court of Human Rights and which confers on states an area of discretion with which the Court will not interfere.[77] 'Deference' may also be expressed in the form of competence – in the form of the question: 'Is this matter within the competence of the courts to decide or for Parliament and/or the executive?' Underlying the concept is the desire to preserve the separation of powers between the judiciary, executive and legislature and to protect the judges from accusations that they are interfering in another institution's legitimate sphere of power. Notwithstanding the legitimacy of the objective, there is a fine line to be drawn between deferring to another institution and failing adequately to protect human rights – the duty which has been conferred on the judges by the Human Rights Act.

Deference by the judges to the executive protects the courts from accusations that they have intruded on a sphere of decision making which is more appropriately undertaken by the democratically elected and accountable government, and is an important feature of the

76 The claimants sought a declaration that the relevant Secretaries of State had unlawfully failed to perform their statutory duties under the Warm Homes and Energy Conservation Act 2000 and the UK Fuel Poverty Strategy, and a mandatory order that the defendants perform those duties.
77 The margin of appreciation is a concept derived from international law: it has no application within domestic law.

doctrine of separation of powers. The doctrine can be seen working in areas of law such as national security, particularly in relation to emergency situations such as war or terrorist threats. Foreign affairs (including treaties), immigration and deportation decisions are also areas where the judges exercise restraint, leaving an area of discretion to the executive. Difficult situations arise where individual human rights are pitted against the principle of deference. For example in **R v Ministry of Defence ex parte Smith** (1996) the Court of Appeal upheld the government's policy of not allowing homosexuals to serve in the armed forces. The European Court of Human Rights, however, found a violation of the right to respect for the claimants' private lives (Article 8) which could not be justified as being 'necessary in a democratic society'.[78]

The doctrine can be illustrated by reference to a number of cases. For example, in **R v Secretary of State for the Environment ex parte Holding and Barnes plc** (2001) (the **Alconbury** case) – in which it was argued that the Secretary of State's power to rule on planning matters contravened the requirements of a fair and independent tribunal – the House of Lords held that decisions relating to planning were best made by the executive. In **R v Lambert** (2001) Lord Woolf stated that the courts: 'should as a matter of constitutional principle pay a degree of deference to the view of Parliament as to what is in the interest of the public generally' when upholding the rights of the individual under the Convention. In **R v Lichniak** (2002) the House of Lords ruled that the imposition of a mandatory life sentence on all convicted murderers did not violate Articles 3 and/or 5 and was a matter of policy best determined by the democratically elected Parliament. In **R (Farrakhan) v Secretary of State for the Home Department** (2002) the Home Secretary had banned the entry of a preacher into the United Kingdom on the basis that his presence would threaten community relations and pose a threat to public order. This ban clearly infringed Farrakhan's freedom of speech (protected under Article 10 of the Convention on Human Rights) and the court therefore had to decide whether or not the prohibition fell within Article 10.2 – whether it was a *necessary* infringement. The Court of Appeal upheld the Home Secretary's decision, stating that he 'is far better placed to reach an informed decision as to the likely consequences of admitting Mr Farrakhan to this country than is the court'.[79]

In **International Transport Roth GmbH v Secretary of State for the Home Department** (2002) Lord Justice Laws, within the context of discussing parliamentary supremacy and the protection of fundamental rights, stated four principles relating to deference. These were:

- that greater deference is to be paid to an Act of Parliament than to a decision of the executive or subordinate legislation;
- that there is more scope for deference in relation to Convention rights which require a balance to be struck (between the right and the restrictions) than Convention rights which are unqualified;
- that greater deference will be due to the executive and/or Parliament where the subject matter is within their constitutional responsibility, and less where it is within the constitutional responsibility for the courts; and
- closely linked to the principle above, that 'greater or lesser deference' will be due where the subject matter lies within the actual or potential expertise of the executive and/or Parliament (for example, defence, macro-economic policy).

---

78 See **Smith and Grady v United Kingdom** (1999).
79 At para. 73.

In **ProLife Alliance v BBC** (2003) the House of Lords overturned the decision of the Court of Appeal which had ruled that freedom of political expression overrode the duty of the BBC not to broadcast material which was offensive. Lord Hoffmann argued that the decision was one 'within the proper competence of the legislature', not the courts. He was, however, to criticise the term 'deference' as being inappropriate to describe the relationship between Parliament, the government and the courts, stating that:

> In a society based upon the rule of law and the separation of powers, it is necessary to decide which branch of government has in any particular instance the decision-making power and what the legal limits of that power are. That is a question of law and must therefore be decided by the courts.

> This means that the courts themselves often have to decide the limits of their own decision-making power. That is inevitable. But it does not mean that their allocation of decision-making power to the other branches of government is a matter of courtesy or deference.

> ... when a court decides that a decision is within the proper competence of the legislature or executive, it is not showing deference. It is deciding the law.[80]

Viewed from that perspective, the issue of 'deference' becomes one of determining the scope of discretionary powers and the appropriate allocation of powers – a question of competence.

However, by viewing the allocation of powers as a question of law, Lord Hoffmann appears to be excluding from the courts wide areas of decision making. This Lord Steyn took issue with, preferring the view that when a court 'defers' to the executive or Parliament, it is exercising judicial discretion, and that the outcome of that exercise will depend on all the circumstances: the court's jurisdiction should not be constrained by a pre-determined view of the allocation of power.[81]

In **A v Secretary of State for the Home Department** (2004) both judicial 'deference' and the concepts of necessity and proportionality came into play. In **A**, foreign suspected terrorists (who could neither be put on trial nor deported) were detained indefinitely, pursuant to section 21 of the Anti-terrorism Crime and Security Act 2001 (ACTSA). The Act did not authorise the indefinite detention of suspected terrorists who were British nationals. The government had derogated from Article 5 on the basis that the terrorist threat constituted a 'public emergency threatening the life of the nation'. The House of Lords ruled that section 21 was incompatible with Article 5 (the right to liberty) of the European Convention on Human Rights and Parliament reformed the law. On 'deference' Lord Bingham stated:

> I would accept that great weight should be given to the judgment of the Home Secretary, his colleagues and Parliament on this question, because they were called on to exercise a pre-eminently political judgment ... I do not accept the full breadth of the Attorney General's argument on what is generally called the deference owed by the courts to the political authorities. It is perhaps preferable to approach this question as one of demarcation of functions or what Liberty in its written case called 'relative institutional competence'. The more purely political (in a broad or narrow sense) a question is, the more appropriate it will be for political

80 On this see Jowell, 2003; Jowell, 'Judicial Deference and human rights: a question of competence' in Craig and Rawlings, 2003.
81 See Steyn, 2005.

resolution and the less likely it is to be an appropriate matter for judicial decision. The smaller, therefore, will be the potential role of the court. It is the function of political and not judicial bodies to resolve political questions. Conversely, the greater the legal content of any issue, the greater the potential role of the court, because under our constitution and subject to the sovereign power of Parliament it is the function of the courts and not of political bodies to resolve legal questions. The present question seems to me to be very much at the political end of the spectrum.

The House of Lords while recognising that national security issues fell within the competence of the executive and Parliament, nevertheless ruled that section 21 infringed the applicants' right to liberty. On proportionality, the court ruled that permitting the indefinite, discriminatory, detention of foreign nationals was disproportionate to the threat posed. The government had not considered it necessary to detain British suspects: as Baroness Hale put it 'If it is not necessary to lock up the nationals it cannot be necessary to lock up the foreigners'.[82]

In **R (Lord Carlisle of Berriew and others) v Secretary of State for the Home Department** (2014) the Supreme Court considered the concepts of both deference and proportionality within the context of Convention rights. A dissident Iranian politician, resident in France, had been denied entry to the United Kingdom since 1997 on the ground that her exclusion was conducive to the public good. Members of the House of Commons and House of Lords invited her to meet them to discuss issues of human rights and democracy. Acting on the advice of the Foreign Secretary, the Home Secretary refused her entry on the basis that her presence would risk jeopardising the UK's economic interests and its diplomatic relationship with Iran and increase the risk of violence against property and people in Iran. Judicial review was sought on the grounds that the Home Secretary's reasons for maintaining the exclusion were disproportionate and her decision unlawful, and that the decision was an unjustified interference with their right to freedom of expression (Article 10).

The appeal was dismissed. The Court of Appeal had held that in matters of national security and foreign policy a review of the Secretary of State's decision was to be conducted on the basis of 'rationality, legality and procedural propriety' and that once the court was satisfied that the decision fell within the range of decisions that could lawfully be made, the Court was not required by proportionality to go further. This, the Supreme Court ruled, was the wrong approach. According to Lord Kerr JSC the process stated in *Aguilar Quila* (2012) applied. The questions which had to be asked were:

(a)   Is the objective sufficiently important to justify limiting a fundamental right?
(b)   Are the measures which have been designed to meet it rationally connected to it?
(c)   Are they no more than are necessary to accomplish it?
(d)   Do they strike a fair balance between the rights of the individual and the interests of the community?

In conducting this exercise, the court must exercise its own judgment. It is for the court, not the decision maker, to decide that the measures are no more than is required to achieve the objective and that a fair balance has been struck, i.e. that it is proportionate (at paragraph 137).

On the issue of institutional competence and deference, the Supreme Court ruled that where the executive's decision was based on factors 'where the court did not have the evidence, experience and institutional legitimacy to form its own view with confidence, its

---

82 At para. 231. For further discussion of *A* see Chapter 22.

interference could only be justified in exceptional circumstances'. In this case international relations, economic and diplomatic interests and the potentially harmful effects on the safety of individuals were matters which were entrusted to the executive which had the specialised experience, range of source material and the institutional competence to enable it to reach a decision which should be given 'great respect' by the courts.

Time limits and exclusion clauses

It is a first principle of justice and the rule of law that public bodies are required to act within the scope of the powers allocated to them by Parliament and, accordingly, in principle, judicial review should lie wherever the *vires* of administrative action is in question. However, that principle must be set in the balance against the needs of certain administration, and the necessary restrictions which may be imposed on individuals or bodies seeking to disrupt the administrative process, without good cause. The balance to be struck between these often-competing principles is a difficult matter. Where Parliament limits the availability of judicial review, the courts will adopt a restrictive interpretation to the statutory words, employing the presumption that Parliament did not intend – save in the most express manner – to exclude the jurisdiction of the courts. A number of different statutory means are employed in the attempt to limit the availability of judicial review. In summary, Parliament may adopt the following means:

(a) the general requirement that applications for judicial review are brought within three months of the challenged decision;
(b) clauses which are intended to prevent any challenge;
(c) clauses which are designed to limit review to a specified time period in relation to particular matters where delay needs to be avoided;
(d) 'conclusive evidence' clauses.

Time limits

Rule 54.5(1) of the Civil Procedure rules provides that a claim for judicial review must be made 'promptly' and in any event not later than three months after the ground to make the claim 'first arose'. Section 31(6) of the Senior Courts Act 1981 provided that where there had been undue delay in making an application, the court might refuse to grant permission or relief if it considered that the relief would be likely to cause substantial hardship to or substantially prejudice the rights of any person or be detrimental to good administration. The Court of Appeal interpreted the requirements in **R (Badmus) v Secretary of State for the Home Department** (2020).[83] To decide when the grounds 'first arose' it was necessary to identify what it was that was to be judicially reviewed. The Court held that the correct approach was that the grounds for making a judicial review claim first arose when the person was affected by the application of the challenged legislation, policy or practice. Precisely when a person became affected would depend on the facts and circumstances of each case.

In the attempt to protect administrative decisions from challenges which may impede or otherwise affect their implementation, statute may provide that there should be no challenge by way of judicial review other than within a specified time period. **Smith v East Elloe Rural District Council** (1956) illustrates the attitude of the courts to such time limits. In **Smith**, a challenge to the validity of a compulsory purchase order was limited, under statute, to a six-week period following the date of confirmation of the order. If not challenged within that period the order 'shall not ... be questioned in any legal proceedings whatsoever'. Mrs Smith did not

---

83 [2020] EWCA Civ 657.

challenge the order within the time limit but, some six years later, sought to challenge the order on the basis that the clerk to the council had acted in bad faith, and that bad faith was a ground on which – despite the clear wording of the time limit in the statute – the order's validity could be impugned. The House of Lords, by a majority, rejected this view. It was, however, unanimously agreed that Mrs Smith could proceed against the clerk to the council for damages, on the basis of bad faith in procuring the order. Viscount Simonds explained the attitude of the court:

> My Lords, I think that anyone bred in the tradition of the law is likely to regard with little sympathy legislative provisions for ousting the jurisdiction of the court ... But it is our plain duty to give the words of an Act their proper meaning, and ... I find it quite impossible to qualify the words ... in the manner suggested ... What is abundantly clear is that words are used which are wide enough to cover any kind of challenge which an aggrieved person may think fit to make. I cannot think of any wider words ... I come, then to the conclusion that the court cannot entertain this action in so far as it impugns the validity of the compulsory purchase order. [pages 750–752]

The Court of Appeal in **R v Secretary of State for the Environment ex parte Ostler** (1976) followed the reasoning in **Smith**. In **Ostler**, the Highways Act 1959[84] provided that an aggrieved person had the right to challenge the validity of a compulsory purchase order – on the basis of *ultra vires* – within six weeks from the date of publication of the order. Subject to that right, the order 'shall not be questioned in any legal proceedings whatsoever'. The proposed road-building scheme had two stages. The first involved the acquisition of the land for the main road; the second related to the acquisition of land for the side roads which would give access to the main road. Two public inquiries were held, at the first of which there were allegations that an officer of the Department of the Environment had given assurances that vehicular access would be gained by a widening of the access road during the second phase of the development. Ostler's business would be affected by the widening of the access road, but he was unaware of the assurance allegedly given at the inquiry and did not challenge the decision. At the second inquiry, Ostler wished to object to the road widening, and wanted to give evidence that he would have objected at the first inquiry had he known of the secret undertaking. He was refused permission to give evidence on the basis that his objection related to the first stage of the development. Ostler subsequently learned of the undertakings and sought to challenge the compulsory order on the ground that natural justice had been denied and that the order had been made in bad faith amounting to fraud. The court accepted that, had Ostler challenged the order within six weeks, the court would have considered his complaint. The court was faced with the question of whether **Anisminic** (discussed below) applied, or whether the decision in **Smith v East Elloe** (1956) was the relevant precedent. Lord Denning MR considered the two precedent decisions and distinguished between them in three respects. First, the limitation in the **Smith** case amounted to a time limitation for review, as opposed to a purported total ouster of jurisdiction as in **Anisminic**. Second, the decision by the Foreign Compensation Board in **Anisminic** was a 'truly judicial' decision, whereas that in **Smith** was an administrative decision. Third, in **Anisminic**, the court was required to consider the 'actual determination of the tribunal', whereas in **Smith** the court was considering the process by which the decision was reached. Lord Denning concluded:

> the policy of the 1959 Act is that when a compulsory purchase order has been made, then if it has been wrongly obtained or made, a person aggrieved should

---

84 Schedule 2, paras 2 and 3.

have a remedy. But he must come promptly. He must come within six weeks. If he does so, the court can and will entertain his complaint. But if the six weeks expire without any application being made, the court cannot entertain it afterwards. The reason is because, as soon as that time has elapsed, the authority will take steps to acquire property, demolish it and so forth. The public interest demand that they should be safe in doing so. [pages 95–96]

Time limits were reconsidered by the Court of Appeal in **R (Gerber) v Wiltshire Council** (2016). In this case planning permission had been granted for the building of a solar farm. The claimant was not consulted prior to permission being granted, on the basis that only those owners of properties adjacent to the site had to be consulted. The claimant was not aware of the planning permission and sought judicial review and an extension of time in which to bring proceedings. The Court of Appeal ruled that the planning authority had complied with its statutory duty on consultation and that the claimant had no legitimate expectation of being consulted. On the application for an extension of time the Court ruled that a balance had to be struck between the objector, the developer and the public. Very special circumstances would have to be present for an extension of time to be granted. Here the claimant had no legitimate expectation to be consulted and no legal basis for challenging the decision. The appeal was dismissed.

Exclusion clauses

Any attempt to exclude judicial review goes to the heart of the argument regarding the respective freedom of government to act and the right of the individual to seek the protection of his or her rights through the courts. In **R v Medical Appeal Tribunal ex parte Gilmore** (1957), the statute provided that 'the decision on any medical question by a medical appeal tribunal … is final'. Under an industrial injuries scheme, compensation for accidental industrial injuries was set under a tariff. Gilmore went blind in both eyes in two accidents and was assessed at a disablement of 20 per cent. The tariff provided that the loss of sight in both eyes entitled the applicant to a 100 per cent assessment. The tribunal had, accordingly, made an error of law. However, the opportunity for the court to redress the wrong turned on the exclusion of review in the statute. The Court of Appeal held that the jurisdiction of the court was not ousted by the statutory words, Denning LJ stating that:

> the remedy of *certiorari* is never to be taken away by any statute except by the most clear and explicit words. The word 'final' is not enough. That only means 'without appeal'. It does not mean 'without recourse to *certiorari*'. It makes the decision final on the facts, but not final on the law. Notwithstanding that the decision is by a statute made 'final', *certiorari* can still issue for excess of jurisdiction or for error of law on the face of the record. [page 583]

However, in **South East Asia Firebricks v Non-Metallic Mineral Products Manufacturing Employees' Union** (1981), an 'ouster clause' succeeded. The Malaysian Industrial Court, in a successful legal challenge by trade unions, had ordered employers to take back employees after a strike. Statute[85] provided that an award of the court was 'final and conclusive' and that 'no award shall be challenged, appealed against, reviewed, quashed or called into question in any court of law'.

---

85 Industrial Relations Act 1967, s. 29(3)(a).

The Privy Council, citing **Gilmore** with approval, nevertheless distinguished between an error which affected the jurisdiction of the court to make a determination[86] and decisions which, whilst in error, were not of such a fundamental nature as to deprive the court of jurisdiction. In this case, the error was within the jurisdiction of the court and, accordingly, the ouster clause was effective. According to Lord Fraser of Tullybelton:

> the Industrial Court applied its mind to the proper question for the purpose of making its award. The award was accordingly within the jurisdiction of that court, and neither party has contended to the contrary ... the error or errors did not affect the jurisdiction of the Industrial Court and their Lordships are therefore of the opinion that section 29(3)(a) effectively ousted the jurisdiction of the High Court to quash the decision by *certiorari* proceedings. [pages 373–374]

The seminal case on ouster clauses is **Anisminic v Foreign Compensation Commission** (1969). In 1956, property in Egypt belonging to an English company was sequestrated by the Egyptian authorities and subsequently sold to an Egyptian organisation, TEDO. Anisminic then sold to TEDO its mining business. In 1959, a Treaty signed by the United Kingdom and the United Arab Republic provided for the return of sequestrated property, other than property sequestrated in a period during which Anisminic's property was taken over. The Foreign Compensation Commission (FCC), established to make awards of compensation to companies adversely affected by sequestration of property, ruled that Anisminic did not qualify for compensation. The Foreign Compensation Order 1962,[87] Article 4(1)(b)(ii), provided that both the applicant and the successor in title be British nationals. TEDO – the successor in title – was not a British national and, accordingly, Anisminic's claim failed. The Foreign Compensation Act 1950 provided that the decisions of the FCC 'shall not be called in question in any court of law'.[88]

Anisminic sought judicial review of the FCC's decision. The question for the court was whether the phrase 'shall not be questioned' succeeded in ousting the jurisdiction of the courts, or whether, notwithstanding that section, the courts had the power to rule on the lawfulness of the FCC's decision. The House of Lords ruled that the jurisdiction of the courts was not ousted. Accordingly the court had power to review the FCC's decision, which it declared to be null and void. The FCC had acted outside its jurisdiction by misinterpreting the Order in Council and reached a decision based on a ground which it was not entitled to take into account, namely the nationality of the successor in title. The nationality of the successor in title, according to the House of Lords, was not a relevant consideration when the applicant was the original owner of the sequestered property. The House of Lords ruled unanimously that section 4(4) did not protect decisions which were taken outside jurisdiction.

Anisminic was considered by the Supreme Court in **R (A) v Director of Establishments of the Security Service** (2009). In **A**'s case section 65(2)(a) of the Regulation of Investigatory Powers Act 2000 (RIPA) provided that the Investigatory Powers Tribunal (IPT) was 'the only appropriate court or tribunal' in relation to proceedings under section 7(1)(a) of the Human Rights Act 1998 before which a claim by a member of the intelligence services could be made in relation to alleged abuses of human rights (in this case Article 10, freedom of expression). The Supreme Court ruled that section 65(2)(a) did not amount to an ouster of the jurisdiction

---

86 Relying on **Anisminic v Foreign Compensation Commission** (1968).
87 Egypt: Determination and Registration of Claims. An Order in Council.
88 Foreign Compensation Act 1950, s. 4(4).

of the courts, but rather the allocation, by Parliament, of an exclusive jurisdiction to the Tribunal.[89]

The **Anisminic** decision raises complex issues. The House of Lords appeared to destroy the distinction between errors of law within the jurisdiction of the decision-making body, which had previously been regarded as non-reviewable, and errors of law which took the decision maker outside its jurisdiction and were therefore reviewable. In effect, clauses which attempted to oust the jurisdiction of the courts appeared to have been rendered meaningless. The problem which remains is whether **Anisminic** provides clear guidelines as to how to distinguish between those elements of a tribunal's decision which, if decided incorrectly, cause the tribunal to exceed its jurisdiction, and those aspects of a tribunal's decision which, although decided incorrectly, do not cause the tribunal to exceed its jurisdiction – in other words the error is 'within jurisdiction'. The decision also reveals judicial emphasis on the rule of law – even in the face of apparently clear words that Parliament does not intend review to take place. In the view of Wade and Forsyth (2004), the judges in **Anisminic** have ensured that the courts are 'the exclusive arbiters on all questions of law'.

In **Pearlman v Keepers and Governors of Harrow School** (1979), the Court of Appeal ruled that the misinterpretation of provisions in the Housing Act 1974 by the county court amounted to a 'jurisdictional error' which nullified the court's decision. Lord Denning MR stated that the distinction between errors which entail an excess of jurisdiction and an error made within jurisdiction should be abandoned.

The question of exactly which errors of law are 'jurisdictional' was considered in **Re Racal Communication Ltd** (1981). In **Racal**, the Director of Public Prosecutions (DPP) sought an order of the court[90] in order to obtain evidence relating to an alleged offence. The order was refused. Section 441(3) of the Companies Act provided that no appeal lay from a decision of the judge hearing the application. Nevertheless the DPP appealed, and the Court of Appeal allowed the appeal, relying on **Anisminic** and **Pearlman**. Lord Denning ruled that the 'no appeal' clause was of no effect, for the judge had misconstrued the words in section 411 of the Act. The House of Lords overturned the Court of Appeal's decision, approving of Geoffrey Lane LJ's dissenting judgment in **Pearlman**, in which he had held that the judge had done nothing which was outside his scope of inquiry. A distinction was drawn between errors made by a tribunal or other administrative bodies, which would be reviewable, and errors made by a court of law. Lord Diplock, in **Racal**, supported the view expressed by Lord Denning MR in **Pearlman**, stating: 'The breakthrough made by **Anisminic** was that, as respects administrative tribunals and authorities, the old distinction between errors of law that went to jurisdiction and errors of law that did not was for practical purposes abolished' (page 383).

A further distinction, and limitation to the **Anisminic** principle, is to be seen in **R v Lord President of the Privy Council ex parte Page** (1992). There, the issue concerned a decision made by a university visitor, and whether such a decision was reviewable on the basis of **Anisminic**. The House of Lords ruled that it was not. The powers of visitors were established by the founder of the university, who had established a body of law and the office of visitor to enforce that 'domestic' law. Accordingly, per Lord Browne-Wilkinson, the visitor could not 'err in law in reaching his decision since the general law is not the applicable law'. Accordingly, the visitor could not act ultra vires by applying his interpretation of the rules of the university. Jurisdiction to review did lie in cases where the visitor acted outside his jurisdiction, or where he acted without regard to the rules of natural justice. However, there was no jurisdiction to review decisions taken within jurisdiction.

---

89 The claim that the IPT's procedures violated the right to fair trial was also rejected.
90 Under the Companies Act 1948, s. 411.

In **R (Privacy International) v Investigatory Powers Tribunal** (2019)[91] the Supreme Court ruled that the Investigatory Powers Tribunal (IPT) is in principle amenable to judicial review. Section 67(8) of RIPA provides that decisions of the IPT 'shall not be subject to appeal or be liable to be questioned in any court'. Did section 67(8) oust the supervisory jurisdiction of the High Court to quash a judgment of the IPT for error of law? No: following **Anisminic** (1969) the Supreme Court held by a majority that reference to a 'determination' was to be read as a reference only to a legally valid determination. There was a common law presumption against ousting the jurisdiction of the High Court, and the words of the statute had to yield to the principle that the words could not protect a legally invalid decision.

'Conclusive evidence clauses'

Parliament may effectively oust the jurisdiction of the courts by inserting a clause into statute which provides that a subordinate piece of legislation shall have effect 'as if enacted in this Act', or that confirmation of an order by a designated Minister shall be 'conclusive evidence that the requirements of this Act have been complied with, and that the order has been duly made and is within the powers of this Act'. Such clauses were strongly criticised in 1932 by the Committee on Ministers' Powers[92] but, nevertheless, they continue to be used and have been effective in ousting judicial review. In **R v Registrar of Companies ex parte Central Bank of India** (1986), for example, a clause in the Companies Act 1985 effectively ousted the jurisdiction of the courts. Nevertheless, the potential for their use, and their effectiveness, provides the basis for a damaging exclusion of judicial review.

The Freedom of Information Act 2000 and judicial review

As discussed in Chapter 10, the Freedom of Information Act gave legislative force to the Labour government's commitment to more open government. An Information Commissioner was appointed, with jurisdiction to investigate allegations that public authorities and bodies have failed to provide information and documents requested. The Act, it will be recalled, introduced the principle that information and documents will be disclosed, subject to a test of harm which justifies official non-disclosure. The Commissioner's decisions are published and are subject to judicial review. The effect of the Freedom of Information Act on judicial review will, however, arguably be to reduce the number of applications for judicial review, in particular on the basis of failure to give reasons.

Judicial review is concerned with the decision-making process rather than the merits of the decision, and provides a discretionary remedy, which requires the decision maker to reconsider the matter in accordance with the correct procedure. Provided that the decision-making process is in accordance with the requirements of law and the principles of natural justice, the decision will not be impugned. Under the Freedom of Information Act, however, where a public body – which is widely defined – fails to give reasons for its decision, recourse may be had to the Commissioner who has wide-ranging powers to investigate, and has the power to order disclosure. Where a public body refuses to supply, for example, reasons for its decision, and the Commissioner orders it to disclose reasons, should the public body then continue to refuse to disclose, with no justification, that refusal may be deemed to be analogous to contempt of court. Furthermore, should the body concerned reveal to the Commissioner that it had no rational basis for its decision, that decision may then be

See Chapter 10.

---

91 [2019] UKSC 22.
92 Cmd 4060, 1932, London: HMSO.

impugned on the basis of irrationality. The citizen may, accordingly, find a more efficient and effective remedy under the jurisdiction of the Commissioner than the courts.[93]

Remedies[94]

Introduction

The granting of a remedy in judicial review proceedings is at the discretion of the court. Even where the applicant establishes his or her case, the court may refuse a remedy if there has been a delay in commencing proceedings, or if the applicant has acted unreasonably, or where the public interest in efficient administration could be damaged by the granting of a remedy. The available remedies under public law are the 'prerogative remedies': quashing orders, prohibiting orders and mandatory orders. In addition, under private law there are the remedies of declaration and injunction, which may also be granted under judicial review proceedings. Historically claimants used to have to specify which of the remedies they required. Since 1978 the claimant now brings an action for judicial review and it is for the court to decide which remedy should be granted.

Quashing order (formerly *certiorari*)

This remedy overlaps with that of prohibition (below). A quashing order is one which 'quashes', or sets aside as a nullity, the original decision: accordingly it is both negative and retrospective in nature: **R v Criminal Injuries Compensation Board ex parte Lain** (1967); **O'Reilly v Mackman** (1983). The classic *dictum* is that of Lord Atkin:[95]

> whenever any body of persons having legal authority to determine questions affecting the rights of subjects, and having the duty to act judicially, act in excess of their legal authority, they are subject to the controlling jurisdiction of the King's Bench Division exercised in these writs.

If only part of a decision is *ultra vires* that part may be severed from the good and the order of *certiorari* granted to quash the bad part of the decision. A quashing order is similar to a prohibiting order, the quashing order operating retrospectively, the prohibiting order operating prospectively.

Prohibiting order (formerly prohibition)

Prohibition is an order which prevents a body from making a decision which would be capable of being quashed by *certiorari*. It is thus protective in nature. Neither quashing orders nor prohibiting orders lie against decisions of the higher courts.

Lord Atkin explained the relationship between *certiorari* and prohibition in the **London Electricity** case:

> I see no difference in principle between *certiorari* and prohibition, except that the latter may be invoked at an earlier stage. If the proceedings establish that the body

---

93 See Pitt-Payne and Kamm, 2009.
94 The orders were renamed under the Civil Procedure Rules 1999, r. 54.1. See Oliver, 2001.
95 **R v Electricity Commissioners ex parte London Electricity Joint Committee Company (1920) Ltd** (1924).

complained of is exceeding its jurisdiction by entertaining matters which would result in its final decision being subject to being brought up and quashed on *certiorari*, I think that prohibition will lie to restrain it from exceeding its jurisdiction.

Prohibition will prevent a public body from acting unlawfully in the future. It may also be used to prevent a body from implementing a decision which has already been taken which was itself *ultra vires*. A failure to comply with an order amounts to a contempt of court.

Mandatory order (formerly *mandamus*)

This order is one which compels an authority to act. A mandatory order does not lie against an authority which has complete discretion to act. A failure to comply with the order amounts to a contempt of court. Mandatory orders do lie against the Crown, and may be used to enforce action by a Minister or official, as for example in **Padfield v Minister of Agriculture Fisheries and Food** (1968) in which a Minister was compelled to refer a complaint to a statutory committee.

Whereas prohibition prevents a future unlawful act, a mandatory order prevents an unlawful failure to act. Whenever a public body is under a duty to act, and fails to comply with that duty, a citizen with sufficient interest may seek an order which compels the authority to act. A mandatory order and a quashing order may work together. For example, if an authority has abused its power, a quashing order may be issued together with a mandatory order requiring the authority to act according to law. On the other hand, a mandatory order alone implies that the authority has acted *ultra vires* and therefore operates like a quashing order to nullify the defective decision.

Declarations

A declaration is a statement of the legal position of the parties, and is not accordingly a remedy per se. Although lacking coercive force, public bodies will respond to a declaration and comply with its terms by rectifying their actions.[96] Declarations are available against the Crown.

Injunctions

Injunctions may be interim or permanent, and positive or negative. Injunctions may be used to prevent a Minister or administrative body from acting unlawfully. In **M v Home Office** (1993), the House of Lords held that injunctions could lie against Ministers of the Crown, and that breach of an injunction could lead to a Minister, in his official capacity as representative of the Crown, being held in contempt of court.

See further
Chapters 5 and 10.

Damages

An applicant for judicial review may be awarded damages in conjunction with one of the other remedies. Damages will only be awarded if they would have been recoverable had the applicant begun an action by writ (that is, a private law action).

---

96 See **Dyson v Attorney General** (1911); **Pyx Granite Co Ltd v Ministry of Housing and Local Government** (1958); **R v Secretary of State for the Home Department ex parte Salem** (1999).

Habeas corpus

See Chapter 18.

The writ of habeas corpus has long been used to challenge the legality of a decision to detain an individual. Literally meaning 'you shall have the body', habeas corpus enjoys a treasured position in English legal history.[97]

Default Powers

Statute may provide that a Minister has powers to act in order to oblige a decision-making body to comply with its statutory duty. For example, section 9 of the Caravan Sites Act 1968 provided that the Secretary of State had the power to give directions to local authorities to comply with their statutory duty to provide adequate sites for Gypsies residing in, or resorting to their area.[98] Other examples of similar powers are found in the Public Health Act 1936, the Education Act 1944, the National Health Service Act 1977, the Housing Act 1985, the Local Government Act 1985 and the Town and Country Planning Act 1990. In respect of the Housing Act provisions, in **R v Secretary of State for the Environment ex parte Norwich City Council** (1982), the Secretary of State had the power to act as he 'thinks necessary' to ensure that tenants are able to exercise their 'right to buy' from local authorities. His failure to enforce the local authorities' duty was itself subject to the control of the courts through judicial review. Default powers are a backstop, but an important weapon in ensuring that local authorities and other bodies comply with the requirements of statute.

Remedies and the Human Rights Act 1998

Section 8 of the Human Rights Act 1998 authorises a court to 'grant such relief or remedy, or make such order, within its powers as it considers just and appropriate'. Accordingly, any remedies which a particular court may award are available for breaches of Convention rights. Declarations, damages, injunctions or the prerogative orders are available. When awarding damages, the courts must take into account the principles applied by the European Court of Human Rights in relation to awards of compensation. Claims for damages do not lie against the decision of a court which has breached the Convention, even though courts are defined as public bodies under the Act. Section 9 of the 1998 Act requires that proceedings against a first instance court be brought by way of appeal or by judicial review. An exception to this is provided in section 9(3) and (4), which provide for awards of damages against the Crown where any judicial body has been guilty of a breach of Article 5 (the right to liberty). Where there has been a breach of a Convention right caused by an Act of Parliament, damages cannot be awarded. In this situation, the consequence will be the making of a declaration of incompatibility. Only the High Court and courts above have the power to issue declarations of incompatibility.

Summary

Judicial review of administrative action is the mechanism by which the judges ensure that those to whom powers are given by Parliament are kept within the scope of power granted.

---

97 See Farbey and Sharpe, 2011.
98 The duty to provide sites has been repealed: Criminal Justice and Public Order Act 1994, s. 80.

In judicial review proceedings the court is concerned with whether the decision maker reached the decision in accordance with the correct rules and principles, not with whether the decision was just or unjust, right or wrong. Accordingly, the judicial review process must be contrasted with that of a right of appeal, and the difference in outcome between an appeal and an application for judicial review.

An individual who is aggrieved by an administrative decision may apply for judicial review. The law relating to judicial review is both statutory and common law. In order to protect the administrative process from unmeritorious challenges, the law requires that applicants satisfy a number of criteria.

The matter complained of must be a matter of public, not private, law and be directed against a public, not private, body. The aggrieved individual must apply within three months of knowledge of the impugned decision. He or she must also have a 'sufficient interest' in the matter to justify the intervention of the courts, and the application must (with exceptions) be through the stipulated public law procedure.

There are a number of restrictions on judicial review. In order to protect the administrative process Parliament may insert clauses in a statute which preclude judicial review, or which restrict applications for judicial review to a shorter time period. Furthermore, the judges impose their own restrictions on judicial review through the concepts of justiciability and non-justiciability, which ensure that the courts do not trespass on the executive's sphere of decision making.

The law of judicial review has expanded with the Human Rights Act 1998, which makes it unlawful for a public authority to act contrary to Convention rights, other than where an Act of Parliament prevents the authority from acting differently. An application for judicial review under the Human Rights Act may only be made by a victim, or potential victim, of an allegedly unlawful act.

Further Reading

Blom-Cooper, L and Drabble, R, 'GCHQ revisited' [2010] *Public Law* 18.

Bondy, V and Sunkin, M, 'Settlement in judicial review proceedings' [2009] *Public Law* 237.

Cane, P, 'Accountability and the public/private distinction' in N Bamforth and P Leyland (eds), *Public Law in a Multi-Layered Constitution*, 2003, Oxford: Hart Publishing.

Cane, P, *Introduction to Administrative Law*, 5th edn, 2011, Oxford: Clarendon Press, Chapter 3.

Craig, P, 'Competing models of judicial review' [1999] *Public Law* 428.

Craig, P, 'The common law, shared power and judicial review' (2004) 24 *Oxford Journal of Legal Studies* 129.

Craig, P, 'Judicial review, appeal and factual error' [2004] *Public Law* 788.

Craig, P, *Administrative Law*, 8th edn, 2016, London: Sweet & Maxwell.

Craig, P, 'Judicial review and anxious scrutiny' [2015] *Public Law* 60.

Daly, P, 'Justiciability and the "political question"' [2010] *Public Law* 160.

Eliantoniom, M, 'Europeanisation of administrative justice? The influence of the ECJ's case law in Italy, Germany and England' (2010) 22(3) *European Review of Public Law* 681.

Harlow, C and Rawlings, R, *Law and Administration*, 3rd edn, 2009, Cambridge: Cambridge University Press.

Harlow, C and Rawlings, R, 'Administrative law in context' [2014] *Public Law* 28.

Jowell, J, 'Of *vires* and vacuums: the constitutional context of judicial review' [1999] *Public Law* 448.

Jowell, J, 'Beyond the rule of law: towards constitutional judicial review' [2000] *Public Law* 671.

Lever, A, 'Is judicial review undemocratic?' [2007] *Public Law* 280.

Mills, A, 'Reforms to judicial review in the Criminal Justice and Courts Act 2015' [2015] *Public Law* 583.

Wade, W and Forsyth, C, *Administrative Law*, 11th edn, 2014, Oxford: Oxford University Press.

Chapter 24

Grounds for Judicial Review I: The Substantive Grounds for Judicial Review

Chapter Contents

Learning Objectives

By the end of this chapter you should be able to:

☐ explain the concept of 'ultra vires';
☐ discuss the constitutional basis for judicial review and arguments against ultra vires as the basis for review;
☐ in outline explain the concepts of illegality, irrationality and procedural impropriety;
☐ with reference to case law discuss different aspects of illegality;
☐ with reference to case law discuss different aspects of irrationality;
☐ discuss the concept of proportionality, making reference to case law.

Introduction

With the procedural aspects of judicial review proceedings in mind, attention can now be turned to the grounds on which judicial review may be sought. Two principal classes of action may be pursued: those which allege that there has been a breach of statutory requirements, and those alleging that a decision has been reached in an unreasonable manner or in disregard of the rules of natural justice. These broad headings have traditionally been divided into a number of subheadings. In **Council of Civil Service Unions v Minister of State for Civil Service** (1985) (the **GCHQ** case), the House of Lords took the opportunity to offer a rationalisation of the grounds for judicial review and ruled that the bases for judicial review could be subsumed under three principal heads, namely illegality, irrationality and procedural impropriety.[1] It was accepted that further grounds for review such as 'proportionality' might emerge. Lord Diplock elucidated the concepts:

> By 'illegality' as a ground for judicial review, I mean that the decision maker must understand correctly the law that regulates his decision making power and give effect to it. Whether he had or not is par excellence a justiciable question to be decided, in the event of dispute, by those persons, the judges, by whom the judicial power of the State is exercisable.

> By 'irrationality', I mean what can now be succinctly referred to as **Wednesbury** unreasonableness.[2] It applies to a decision which is so outrageous in its defiance of logic or of accepted moral standards that no sensible person who had applied his mind to the question to be decided could have arrived at it. Whether a decision falls within this category is a question that judges by their training and experience should be well equipped to answer …

> I have described the third head as 'procedural impropriety' rather than failure to observe basic rules of natural justice or failure to act with procedural fairness towards the person who will be affected by the decision. This is because susceptibility to judicial review under this head covers also failure by an administrative tribunal to observe the procedural rules that are expressly laid down in the legislative instrument by which its jurisdiction is conferred, even though such failure does not involve any denial of natural justice.

> That is not to say that further development on a case by case basis may not in course of time add further grounds. I have in mind particularly the possible adoption in the future of the principle of 'proportionality' which is recognised in the administrative law of several of our fellow members of the European [Economic] Community. [pages 410–411]

The Traditional Doctrine of *Ultra Vires*

Ultra vires refers to action which is outside – or in excess of – powers of decision-making bodies. While judges continue to use the term *ultra vires*, it is nowadays too limited a term to encompass the whole ambit of judicial review. It may be preferable, therefore, to regard judicial review as the control of discretion and the regulation of the decision-making process by the courts. By way of example, in **R v Hull University Visitor ex parte Page** (1993), Lord Browne-Wilkinson adopted the traditional language of *ultra vires*: 'If the decision maker exercises his

---

1 Chapter 26 will consider procedural impropriety in more detail.
2 **Associated Provincial Picture Houses Ltd v Wednesbury Corporation** (1948). See further below.

powers outside the jurisdiction conferred, in a manner which is procedurally irregular or is **Wednesbury** unreasonable, he is acting ultra vires his powers and therefore unlawfully'.

In **R v Richmond upon Thames Council ex parte McCarthy and Stone Ltd** (1992), the local planning authority implemented a scheme of charging £25 for informal consultation between corporation officers and property developers. The House of Lords held that the imposition of the charge was unlawful. Such a charge was neither incidental to the planning function of the local authority, nor could a charge be levied on the public without statutory authority. The council had misconstrued its powers and, accordingly, acted ultra vires. Further, in **Hazell v Hammersmith and Fulham Council** (1992), the council attempted to increase its revenue through financial investments which, for success, were dependent upon the fluctuation in interest rates. The House of Lords ruled that the council had no power to enter into 'interest rate swaps' which were purely speculative in nature. Such speculation was inconsistent with the statutory borrowing powers conferred on local authorities and neither conducive to nor incidental to the exercise of those powers.[3]

In **R (Public Law Project) v Lord Chancellor** (2016) the Supreme Court, unanimously, held that subordinate legislation intended to amend Schedule 1 to the Legal Aid, Sentencing and Punishment of Offenders Act 2012 (LASPO) was ultra vires and invalid. Under the 2012 Act, Parliament had conferred on the Lord Chancellor a power to amend primary legislation by means of secondary legislation (a 'Henry VIII power'). The Lord Chancellor proposed to amend the 2012 Act so as to introduce a residency requirement into the qualifying criteria for legal aid. Such a criterion fell outside the scope of the Act which did provide for restrictions of the availability of legal aid but none of those restrictions – unlike the proposed residency requirement – related to the personal characteristics or circumstances of the claimant. According to Lord Neuberger the draft Order was: 'attempting to do something which the legislature never had in mind when enacting Part I of LASPO'.[4]

Difficulties with the traditional *ultra vires* doctrine

The ultra vires principle is consistent with the doctrine of parliamentary sovereignty and, to some extent, with the concept of the rule of law. However, there are objections to the courts holding so tenaciously to a concept which, in some respects, is inappropriate to describe what the courts actually do in the control of administrative powers. The judges cling to the ultra vires doctrine as a means of protecting their constitutional position. As has been seen in Chapters 4 and 6, the judges are not entrusted with constitutional powers to invalidate Acts of Parliament, and judicial decisions are susceptible to being overruled by Acts of Parliament.[5] With the supremacy of Parliament in mind, the judges exercise care to maintain a sufficient separation of powers. It is for this reason that judges are cautious about reviewing the exercise of prerogative powers and limit their role in relation to parliamentary privileges to ruling on the existence and scope of privilege. Keen awareness of this constitutional position explains the hold which the traditional doctrine of ultra vires has for judges. Ultra vires is entirely consistent with the supremacy of Parliament and the rule of law. However, the doctrine of ultra vires cannot explain adequately the judges' power to rule, as they do, on certain aspects of decision making. While the judges declare that matters of 'high policy' are not for them to decide,

---

3 More recently in **EN (Serbia) v Secretary of State for the Home Department; KC (South Africa) v Same** (2009) the Court of Appeal ruled that the Secretary of State had misunderstood the extent and purpose of the statutory power when formulating subordinate legislation. As a result he had exceeded his powers and the order was ultra vires and unlawful. The Court of Appeal stated that a tribunal had no power to quash delegated legislation but should have adjourned proceedings, where it considered that the instrument was ultra vires, in order to give the party challenging its lawfulness an opportunity to issue judicial review proceedings.

4 At para. 34.

5 See e.g. **Burmah Oil v Lord Advocate** (1965) and the War Damage Act 1965.

when judges rule on 'unreasonableness' or, as Lord Diplock classifies the concept, 'irrationality', the judges come close to ruling on the merits of a particular decision.

The Constitutional Basis for Judicial Review

For reasons such as these, the concept of *ultra vires* is nowadays regarded by many as an inadequate rationale for judicial review. There are now three principal lines of thought regarding the constitutional foundations of judicial review. The first holds to the *ultra vires* doctrine. The second, and competing, approach focuses on the common law and the principles developed by the judges. A third approach seeks a middle way through the conflicting claims of the *ultra vires* proponents and the common law advocates.

In 1987 Professor Dawn Oliver examined the basis for judicial review and argued that *ultra vires* was an inadequate concept to explain the breadth of judicial review. *Ultra vires* essentially rests on the premise that Parliament has conferred power on a public body by an Act of Parliament and that the task of the judges is to interpret the intention of Parliament as expressed in the statute to determine whether or not the decision maker has acted within the power conferred. However, while this is an appropriate approach in relation to Acts of Parliament it does not 'fit', as Oliver points out, with the common law power of the royal prerogative. The royal prerogative is inherent in the power of the Crown: it is not a power 'conferred' by Parliament. *Ultra vires* as an explanation for judicial review therefore does not make sense in the context of the prerogative, and yet the courts nowadays will review the royal prerogative, provided that the subject matter is justiciable. As stressed by Lord Diplock in the **GCHQ** case[6] the courts' power to review the exercise of the prerogative depends not on the source of power, but on the nature of the power.

Furthermore, the courts will assume jurisdiction to review the administrative action of bodies which are exercising a governmental function, but are not themselves part of the machinery of government. As discussed in Chapter 24, the courts will assume jurisdiction to review the actions of a non-governmental regulatory body (such as the City Panel on Takeovers and Mergers)[7] if that body is 'standing in the shoes of the government' and fulfilling a function which otherwise the government would have to undertake. Judicial review of such a body does not fall within the *ultra vires* doctrine, since there is no statute establishing the body and conferring upon it regulatory power. If the *ultra vires* doctrine cannot explain review of the exercise of the royal prerogative and actions/decisions of private regulatory bodies there must be some alternative doctrine which explains the constitutional foundations of judicial review.

For some the answer to these difficulties lies in the common law. There are a number of different strands to this approach. In 'Is the *Ultra Vires* Rule the Basis for Judicial Review?'[8] Professor Dawn Oliver argues that judicial review has progressed beyond *ultra vires*. While *ultra vires* remains a basis for judicial review, the courts may also hold that a body has acted unlawfully if that body uses its powers improperly, or unreasonably or in breach of the rules of natural justice. In her view, Parliament is presumed to have intended public administrators to act in accordance with the common law principles developed by the judges. As Oliver expresses the matter, 'judicial review has moved on from the *ultra vires* rule to a concern for the protection of individuals, and for the control of power'.[9] While this means that *ultra vires* is

---

6 **Council for Civil Service Unions v Minister for Civil Service** (1985).
7 **Council for Civil Service Unions v Minister for Civil Service** (1985).
8 Oliver, 1987.
9 Ibid.

not the basis for the jurisdiction of the courts in judicial review, it remains relevant but must be seen within the broader judicial review context which also incorporates common law principles and enables the courts to rule whenever there is an abuse of power.

Furthermore, it is argued by Sir John Laws that the principles of judicial review are judicial creations and do not owe their existence to the 'will of the legislature'. The insistence on the 'intention of Parliament' is a 'fig leaf to cover their true origins'.[10] Laws LJ concludes that 'We do not need the fig leaf any more'. Accordingly, it is the common law which constitutes the legal basis for judicial review and there is no need to relate judicial review to the intention of Parliament. Professor Christopher Forsyth, in response to Sir John Laws, accepts that the development of judicial review is attributable to the creativity of the judiciary. However, he argues that the judges did not develop judicial review in a 'constitution vacuum'. They did so 'against the background of a sovereign legislature that could have intervened at any moment'. And Parliament, aware of the development of judicial review, could be taken to give tacit approval to the role of the judges 'subject, crucially, to the recognition of legislative supremacy'.[11] To argue, as did Sir John Laws, that the basis for judicial review does not lie in the intention of Parliament but in the common law, is to ignore the constitutional reality that it is the sovereignty of Parliament which remains the key component of the constitution and that it is not for the unelected judges to attempt to change that constitutional fundamental.

Professor Paul Craig favours the common law, arguing that the foundations of judicial review were laid by the courts over 300 years ago.[12] In his analysis the relationship between Parliament and the courts, in judicial review, is one where Parliament is presumed to intend that 'legislation conforms to the basic principles of fairness and justice which operate in a constitutional democracy'. Parliament delegates power to the courts which in turn adjudicate in accordance with their conception of the rule of law. This relationship may be conceptualised as a 'modified *ultra vires* model' or a 'general legislative intent model'.

Professor Jeffrey Jowell also advances a common law justification for judicial review, but one which also acknowledges the limitations in judicial power. There are issues of both constitutional and institutional competence to be considered. Concepts such as the rules of natural justice and fairness owe nothing to the intention of Parliament. However, while a common law justification for judicial review is to be preferred, it is one which is tempered by the question of competence.[13] The recognition of the limits imposed by constitutional and institutional competence provides the explanation for those cases where the courts will either defer to the executive over a particular matter or rule that an issue is non-justiciable and therefore not subject to review by the courts. Examples of these limits are many and varied. Issues of national security and matters of public expenditure are two obvious key areas where the courts will set a clear boundary to their powers of review in favour of the democratically elected government.

Dr Mark Elliott also stresses the importance of recognising that judges do not have unlimited power and that there are boundaries which they will not, must not, cross.[14] Elliott argues for a middle way through the conflicting approaches to the basis for judicial review, stating that presenting the matter as a choice between 'two camps' is 'futile'. In his balanced assessment, both the will of Parliament and the creativity of judges have important roles to play in judicial review. He concludes that the *ultra vires* doctrine continues to provide the conceptual basis for judicial review, but also that the common law recognises the legislative

---

10 Laws, 1995.
11 Forsyth, 1996.
12 Craig, 1999.
13 Jowell, 1999.
14 Elliott, 1999.

sovereignty of Parliament and adopts the presumption that Parliament intends the rule of law to be upheld. In *The Constitutional Foundations of Judicial Review*[15] Elliott concludes that the basis for judicial review does not lie on a single foundation, but rather rests on 'a set of constitutional foundations'. The justification for judicial review is to be found within the context of the interaction of the three key principles of the constitution: the rule of law, the separation of powers and the sovereignty of Parliament.

In 'Constitutional Dialogue and the Justification of Judicial Review',[16] Professor TRS Allan also criticises the polarised approaches to judicial review, arguing that the 'choice between legislative intent and common law as the basis for judicial review is as arbitrary as the choice between parliamentary sovereignty and judicial supremacy'. In Allen's view in rejecting legislative intent as the basis for review, common law proponents such as Sir John Laws portray the matter as a stark contest between the two approaches. To reject the intention of Parliament is wrong: concepts such as irrelevant considerations or improper purpose depend on the interpretation of the statute in question. What is needed is the recognition that both Parliament and the courts have power: there is a 'shared sovereignty' or 'interdependent sovereignties' and it is this which provides a more convincing or better foundation for judicial review. This approach can lead to a modified *ultra vires* doctrine, one in which Parliament is taken to have the general intention that public bodies must exercise their powers in a manner consistent with the rule of law, the meaning of the rule of law being left to the courts.

Classificatory difficulties in judicial review

While Lord Diplock, in the **GCHQ** case, offered a rationalisation of the headings of review, the question of terminology and classification remains difficult and sometimes obscure. This problem should be recognised at the outset. It should also be borne in mind that the categories are by no means watertight and discrete: in many instances, there will appear overlaps between the headings. By way of illustration, a decision maker may act *ultra vires* by taking into account irrelevant considerations. Depending upon the magnitude of the irrelevant consideration, he or she may also be acting irrationally.

In **Boddington v British Transport Police** (1999)[17] Lord Irvine echoed Lord Diplock's concerns when he stated:

> Categorisation of types of challenge assists in an orderly exposition of the principles underlying our developing public law. But these are not watertight compartments because the various grounds for judicial review run together. The exercise of a power for an improper purpose may involve taking irrelevant considerations into account, or ignoring relevant considerations; and either may lead to an irrational result. The failure to grant a person affected by a decision to a hearing, in breach of principles of procedural fairness, may result in a failure to take into account relevant considerations.

Illegality

In the administrative process, which often entails a degree of discretion to be exercised by the decision maker, there is the potential for errors to occur. The decision maker may, for

---

15 Elliott, 2001.
16 Allan, 2003.
17 At p. 152.

example, misunderstand the law; may take into account irrelevant considerations or ignore relevant considerations, or adopt a rigid policy which prevents him or her from exercising the correct degree of discretion. Failure to comply with the rules of natural justice and fairness may also cause a decision to be held to be unlawful and the decision to be set aside by the courts in judicial review proceedings. The principal categories under which decisions may be challenged are discussed below.

Errors of law

The problem concerning the role of the courts and the extent to which it is appropriate for there to be judicial intervention in administration, discussed in Chapter 23, is clearly illustrated in relation to errors of law and errors of fact. The question for determination is whether, and to what extent, administrators enjoy a measure of discretion in decision making, which empowers them to make determinations of fact which are immune from judicial review. Before considering the courts' approach, it is necessary to define the terms 'error of law' and 'error of fact'.

An error of law may take several forms. An authority may wrongly interpret a word to which a legal meaning is attributed. For example, where an authority is under a duty to provide 'accommodation', the question arises as to whether the quality of what they have, in fact, provided amounts, in law, to accommodation. Does the accommodation have to be of a particular quality, or be particularly suited to what the applicant needs?[18] Questions may also arise as to whether there has been a legal exercise of power in relation to the objectives of relevant legislation, or whether a discretion has been properly exercised, or whether relevant considerations have been taken into account, or irrelevant considerations excluded from the decision-making process. The question of whether or not a body had acted in breach of its statutory duty arose in **R (Lumsden and Others) v Legal Services Board** (2014). The regulatory objectives of the Quality Assurance Scheme for Advocates (QASA), a body established to oversee the quality of advocacy at the Bar, were set out in section 1 of the Legal Services Act 2007. The claimants sought judicial review of the decision of the Legal Services Board to approve the introduction of QASA on the ground that the combined effect of elements of the scheme was such as to undermine the independence of the advocates. The Court of Appeal disagreed: neither individually nor cumulatively did those elements undermine the independence of advocates. On the correct test to be applied to review, the Court ruled that the heightened **Wednesbury** principles applied. Since the scheme did not involve any interference with fundamental human rights or constitutional principles, proportionality was not the correct test. Moreover, the Legal Services Board was the regulator given power by Parliament to assess advocacy quality and had a 'substantial margin of discretion'. It was not for the Court to substitute its own decision for that of the Board.

Historically, the judges have assumed the power to adjudicate on matters which are termed 'errors on the face of the record'. Errors on the face of the record – that is to say, evidence from the documentation that the decision maker has made a wrong decision in law – will cause the judges to rule that the decision was defective, even if the decision maker was acting inside jurisdiction (*intra vires*). Such a power does not sit easily alongside the concept of *ultra vires*, the very basis of which is to strike down decisions which have been taken *ultra vires* (outside jurisdiction).

As has been seen, if an authority is to act *intra vires*, it must conduct itself according to a correct interpretation of the law. However, what is of the essence in relation to error of law is

---

18 See **R v Hillingdon London Borough Council ex parte Pulhofer** (1986).

that the authority misinterprets or misunderstands the powers which it has been granted and, accordingly, acts *ultra vires* whereas, when an authority uses powers for the wrong purpose, the authority has correctly interpreted its powers but used them towards the wrong objective. As has been said, an error of law may manifest itself in several ways. It may be that an authority misinterprets its legal powers, as in **Perilly v Tower Hamlets Borough Council** (1973), where the local authority believed – erroneously – that it was obliged to consider applications for stall licences in a street market in the order in which they were received. The effect of this was to deny a licence to Perilly even though his mother, by then deceased, had held a licence for some 30 years. The licence granted to an incoming applicant in preference to Perilly was set aside by the court.

See further Chapter 23.

The seminal case is that of **Anisminic Ltd v Foreign Compensation Commission** (1969), discussed in Chapter 23. It will be recalled that the House of Lords held the decision of the Commission to be *ultra vires*. The decision made by the Commission was so wrong that, in law, it did not amount to a decision at all. As a result, the section preventing the questioning of the Commission's decision in a court of law was not relevant or binding on the court, for the ruling of the Commission – being so wrong in law – resulted in the Commission acting outside its jurisdiction, and nothing in the Act prohibited a court of law from reviewing what was, in law and in effect, a nullity.

The House of Lords ruled that:

> If the inferior tribunal, as a result of its misconstruing the statutory description of the kind of case in which it has jurisdiction to inquire, makes a purported determination in a case of a kind into which it has no jurisdiction to inquire, its purported determination is a nullity.

Anisminic Ltd v Foreign Compensation Commission destroyed the distinction between errors of law which 'went to jurisdiction' (that is, deprived the decision-making body of power to determine the question) and errors of law within jurisdiction. In **Anisminic**, the House of Lords ruled that, in effect, the old distinctions were obsolete in relation to the decisions of administrative and other bodies (but not necessarily inferior courts of law).[19] Lord Diplock reasserted his support for this view in **Re Racal Communications Ltd** (1981) and **O'Reilly v Mackman** (1983). In the former case, Lord Diplock confirmed the 'breakthrough' achieved in **Anisminic**. In **O'Reilly**, Lord Diplock went further and asserted that the distinction had been rendered obsolete in relation both to tribunals and inferior courts. This approach was confirmed by the House of Lords in **R v Hull University Visitor ex parte Page** (1993). Professor HWR Wade's evaluation of these cases is that 'it is clear now that they made an important extension of judicial review in English law'.[20]

The House of Lords returned to the questions of jurisdictional errors in **R v Monopolies and Mergers Commission ex parte South Yorkshire Transport Ltd** (1993). Under section 64(1)(a) of the Fair Trading Act 1973, the Secretary of State has power to refer a merger of companies to the Monopolies and Mergers Commission (MMC). The jurisdiction of the MMC was to consider mergers which result in more than 25 per cent of services being supplied by one company 'in a substantial part of the United Kingdom'. Two merged bus companies sought judicial review of the MMC's investigation, on the basis that the land area did not amount to a 'substantial part of the United Kingdom'. The court ruled that the MMC had directed itself properly as to the meaning of 'substantial'. However, it was also recognised that what

---

19 See Diplock, 1974; Wade, 1969; Gould, 1970; Gordon, 1971.
20 Wade and Forsyth, 2004.

amounted to 'substantial' could be interpreted in different ways, and that persons might reasonably disagree about that interpretation. Lord Mustill ruled that, in such a situation, a decision would only be ruled unlawful if the decision 'is so aberrant that it cannot be classed as rational'. Thus, where the statute provides broad criteria, over the meaning of which reasonable persons might reasonably disagree, the court will be slow to step in and substitute its judgment, unless the decision maker's decision falls outside what the court regards as a reasonable interpretation of a word which is essentially imprecise.[21]

Errors of fact[22]

An error of law will be reviewed by the courts. An error of fact is an error which the courts will be more reluctant to review. Administrators are given powers to exercise in relation to their specialised area, and it is the decision maker who has all the factual information to hand on which to base a decision. For the courts to intervene in this matter, would – unless some caution is exercised – amount to the courts taking over the very role of the administrators. Nevertheless, there may be some errors of fact which are of such a fundamental nature that they cause a decision to be unlawful.

When the court considers whether there has been an error of law, it is seeking to discover the correct definition of the legal words in the relevant statute. When the court is considering whether there has been an error of fact, the court is trying to determine whether the facts of the case 'fit' with the interpretation of the statute.

Errors of fact raise difficult questions. As has been seen, an error of law will be made when the decision maker acts contrary to the requirements of legality – or, in other words, he has broken one of the rules for lawful decision making. Errors of fact are more complex. If a decision maker bases his decision on a misunderstanding of the factual situation of the case, he will reach a decision which is wrong. The question which then arises is whether the courts will review such an error in judicial review proceedings. In general, the answer to that question is that the courts will be very cautious. After all, the courts will often not have the expertise to assess the factual situation, and may have great difficulty in deciding whether a factual error has resulted in the wrong decision. The courts have traditionally approached this matter by dividing errors of fact into two categories. The first relates to reviewable errors of facts, which are jurisdictional, and the other category is that of non-reviewable, non-jurisdictional facts.

Professor Wade illustrates a jurisdictional fact as follows:

> A rent tribunal ... may have power to reduce the rent of a dwelling house. If it mistakenly finds that the property is a dwelling house when in fact it is let for business purposes, and then purports to reduce the rent, its order will be ultra vires and void, for its jurisdiction depends upon the facts which must exist objectively before the tribunal has power to act. [Wade and Forsyth, 2004]

On the other hand, other mistakes will not have this effect. Professor Wade illustrates as follows:

> Many facts on the other hand will not be jurisdictional, since they will have no bearing on the limits of the power. A rent tribunal's findings as to the state of repair of

---

21 See also **R v Ministry of Defence ex parte Walker** (1999).
22 See Jones, 1990; Yeats, I, 'Errors of fact: the role of the courts law', in Richardson and Genn, 1994; Craig, 2004.

the property, the terms of the tenancy, and the defaults of landlord or tenant will probably not affect its jurisdiction in any way and will therefore be immune from jurisdictional challenge.

The question to be asked, therefore, is whether the mistake of fact is one which is central to the decision maker's power of decision. Only such crucial errors of fact will be reviewed by the court. In addition, if a decision is reached on the basis of facts for which there is no evidence, or based on essential facts which have been proven wrong, or been misunderstood or ignored, the court will quash the decision.

Two cases further illustrate the courts' approach to law and fact, and demonstrate that the judges will – depending upon the circumstances of the case – adopt either a strict approach or a more lenient approach to the matter. In **R v Secretary of State for the Home Department ex parte Khawaja** (1984), the House of Lords was required to rule on two questions. The first question was whether the phrase 'illegal immigrant' in the Immigration Act 1971 covered a person who had been granted permission to enter the country through fraud or deception as well as a person who secretly entered the country without any leave. On this point, the House of Lords held that it could. The second question concerned the standard of proof which the immigration officer had to apply. It was argued that the correct standard to be applied was whether the immigration officer had reasonable grounds for his decision. The House of Lords rejected that view, holding that, because the liberty of the person was involved, the standard of proof that deception had taken place was one of a high degree of probability.

In **R v Hillingdon London Borough Council ex parte Pulhofer** (1986), the House of Lords approached the matter rather differently. Under the Housing Act 1985,[23] local authorities are under a duty to provide accommodation for homeless persons as defined by the Act. For the purposes of their decision, the House of Lords had to interpret the meaning of 'accommodation'. The House of Lords adopted a very broad interpretation of the word, refusing to import a standard of reasonableness of accommodation which would protect the individual from being placed in unsuitable housing. Unlike the decision in **Khawaja**, where the House of Lords introduced a standard of proof which was protective of the individual against the administration, in **Pulhofer**, the court's ruling protected the administration – the housing authority – and not the individual. The Housing and Planning Act 1986 reverses the House of Lords' decision in **Pulhofer**, and requires that 'accommodation' be accommodation which it is reasonable for a person to continue to occupy. It can be seen from these two cases that the interpretation of the question of law can dictate a very different outcome, depending upon the judicial approach taken.

When the issue concerns individual rights, for example, the courts will be slow to adopt an approach which has the effect of delimiting those rights. **Tan Te Lam v Superintendent of Tai A Chau Detention Centre** (1996), decided by the Privy Council, illustrates the point well.[24] The applicants were detainees in Hong Kong, having arrived there by boat from Vietnam. They were detained in detention centres, pending decisions as to whether to grant or refuse permission to remain in Hong Kong, or, if a decision to refuse permission were made, pending their removal from Hong Kong and repatriation to Vietnam. They applied for writs of habeas corpus to test the legality of their detention. By the time the appeal reached the Privy Council, the applicants had been detained for long periods of time, the longest being 24 months, pending determination of refugee status, followed by a further 44 months. The Privy Council stated, first, that the power to detain could only be exercised during the period necessary, in all the circumstances, to effect removal; second, that if it becomes clear that removal is not

---

23 Originally, the Housing (Homeless Persons) Act 1977.
24 Following the transfer of sovereignty in 1997, appeals no longer lie to the Privy Council from the Hong Kong courts.

going to be possible within a reasonable time, further detention is not authorised; third, that the person seeking to exercise the power of detention must take all reasonable steps to ensure removal within a reasonable time.

In **Khawaja v Secretary of State for the Home Department** (1984), discussed above, the House of Lords had earlier considered the legality of a detention order pending removal, as an illegal immigrant, from the United Kingdom.[25] There was a dispute of fact as to whether the applicant had obtained leave to enter as a result of fraud. The House of Lords ruled that the issue of whether the applicant was an illegal immigrant was a matter which had to be established before it could be determined whether there was any power to detain with a view to deportation. That question 'was a precedent or jurisdictional fact which, in the case of deprivation of liberty, had to be proved to exist before any power to detain was exercisable at all'.

E v Secretary of State for the Home Department (2004) provided the opportunity for the Court of Appeal to reconsider the review of fact. The applicants claimed that the Immigration Appeal Tribunal (IAT) which had refused leave to appeal to the Court of Appeal had erred in not taking account evidence which had become available since the hearing before the IAT but before making the decision whether to allow an appeal. The evidence supported the applicants' claims that they would be at risk if returned to their country of origin. The Court of Appeal ruled that the IAT should reconsider the decision to take account of the evidence where there was a serious risk of injustice because the evidence had not been considered.

Onerous conditions attached to decision

A decision by an authority may also be unlawful if conditions are attached to the decision which are difficult or impossible to perform. For example, in **Pyx Granite Co Ltd v Ministry of Housing and Local Government** (1958), Lord Denning MR in the Court of Appeal held that planning conditions 'must fairly and reasonably relate to the permitted development' and must not be so unreasonable that it can be said that Parliament clearly cannot have intended that they should be imposed.

Accordingly, in the **Pyx Granite** case, the condition that permission be conditional upon the company constructing a road ancillary to the development at its own expense when so required by the authority and to grant a public right of passage over it was *ultra vires*. **Pyx Granite** was followed in **Hall and Co Ltd v Shoreham-by-Sea Urban District Council** (1964). The defendant council granted planning permission for a development, subject to conditions, which included the requirement to construct an ancillary road over the entire frontage of the site and subject to the right of public passage. While the objective of the council was viewed as 'reasonable', the terms of the conditions requiring the plaintiffs to construct a road at their own expense, for public use and without compensation, were not reasonable. The *ultra vires* conditions were fundamental to the whole planning permission which was, accordingly, void. Equally, in **R v Hillingdon London Borough Council ex parte Royco Homes Ltd** (1974), planning permission was also tied to conditions. The conditions were that Royco Homes make properties constructed available for occupation by those on the council's housing waiting list and, further, that for ten years the houses be occupied by persons subject to security of tenure under the Rent Acts. The conditions were *ultra vires*.

According to Lord Widgery CJ, the conditions represented:

> the equivalent of requiring the applicants to take on at their own expense a signifi-
> cant part of the duty of the council as housing authority. However well intentioned

---

25 The power to detain in **Khawaja** arose from the Immigration Act 1971, Sched. 2, paras 9 and 16.

and however sensible such a desire on the part of the council may have been, it seems to me that it is unreasonable. [page 732]

Where an authority makes a decision which is in part good, but in part bad – perhaps because of attaching onerous conditions to planning permission – the court may either invalidate the entire decision or sever the bad part of the decision from the good. The decision in **Agricultural Horticultural and Forestry Industry Training Board v Aylesbury Mushrooms Ltd** (1972) illustrates the principle. There, the Training Board was under a mandatory statutory duty to consult certain organisations and trade unions before reaching a decision. The Board failed to consult the Mushroom Growers Association. The court held that the decision was good, and could remain, in relation to those associations which had been consulted, but bad in relation to the Mushroom Growers Association, and that the Board had a duty to reconsider their decision after consultations with the Association.

In some cases, it will not be possible to sever a part of a decision from the whole decision, in which case the entire decision may be invalidated.[26] For example, in **Director of Public Prosecutions v Hutchinson** (1990), the local authority passed a bylaw which prohibited unauthorised access to Greenham Common air force base. The Act of Parliament, under which the authority purported to exercise its powers, provided that no bylaw should be passed which affected the rights of registered commoners in the area. In an action for trespass against anti-nuclear protesters, the defendants pleaded the invalidity of the bylaw. The House of Lords ruled that the bylaw was invalid and, as a result, the protesters escaped conviction for trespass. Conditions were held to be ultra vires in **Director of Public Prosecutions v Haw** (2007).[27] The police had imposed a number of conditions on Brian Haw's demonstration (which had been ongoing since 2001) in Parliament Square. Haw challenged the conditions as being either ultra vires or incompatible with Articles 10 and 11 of the European Convention on the grounds that they were unreasonable or insufficiently clear.[28] The Court ruled that the objective behind the conditions – which in part were designed to ensure others did not use the demonstration as a cover for terrorist activities – provided 'a perfectly reasonable and proportionate justification for imposing appropriate conditions'. However, as the conditions were unworkable they were ultra vires for lack of clarity.

Using powers for the wrong purpose

Powers conferred must be used for the purpose for which they were granted. In **Attorney General v Fulham Corporation** (1921), the authority was empowered under statute to establish wash-houses for the non-commercial use of local residents. The Corporation decided to open a laundry on a commercial basis. The Corporation was held to have acted ultra vires the statute. **Westminster Corporation v London and North Western Railway Company** (1905), however, represents a case where a charge of wrong purpose failed. The Corporation had power, under section 44 of the Public Health Act 1891, to provide public conveniences and had constructed them midway under the street with access gained by means of a subway. The Railway Company which owned stock in adjacent buildings claimed that the power had been used improperly. The House of Lords disagreed, stating that 'the primary object of the council

---

26 As in **Hall and Co Ltd v Shoreham-by-Sea Urban District Council** (1964) discussed above.

27 Also at issue was delegation of powers: it was held, following **Carltona v Works Commissioners** (1943) that the Commissioner of Police could not be expected personally to draft conditions and that delegation was not unlawful.

28 The conditions included restrictions on the size of the site, its supervision, ensuring that no items could be used to conceal other items and requirements to report to the police if 20 or more persons were to be present.

was the construction of the conveniences with the requisite and proper means of approach thereto and exit therefrom'.

Thus, where a public authority uses a power for the purpose intended by Parliament and reasonably provides a facility incidental to – or complementary to – the power conferred, the authority is acting within its powers. It can of course be argued that the Corporation's prime objective was, in fact, the provision of a subway; nevertheless, that objective – if it was the primary objective – did not invalidate the action.

The *Westminster Corporation* case was further considered in **R v Inner London Education Authority ex parte Westminster City Council** (1986), which provided an opportunity for the Divisional Court to consider the issue of two purposes being pursued under one power. On the facts of the case, it was held that, in pursuing two purposes in relation to education funding, the Council had allowed an 'irrelevant consideration' to dominate its decision making and that, accordingly, it had acted *ultra vires*.

The test which Professor Evans prescribes is:

> What is the true purpose for which the power was exercised? If the actor has in truth used his power for the purposes for which it was conferred, it is immaterial that he was thus enabled to achieve a subsidiary object.

Acting in a manner inconsistent with the purpose of an Act was seen in **Padfield v Minister for Agriculture, Fisheries and Food** (1968). Under the Agricultural Marketing Act 1958, a Committee of Investigation was established to make inquiries, if the Minister 'so directed', into complaints made to the Minister concerning the operation of, amongst other products, milk. South-eastern dairy farmers complained that the Milk Marketing Board had fixed prices in a manner prejudicial to farmers in the south-eastern region of the country. The Minister refused to refer the matter to the Committee of Investigation. The farmers challenged the Minister's decision. The House of Lords granted an order of mandamus, requiring the Minister to consider properly whether he should exercise his discretion to refer. The House of Lords ruled by a majority[29] that, while the Minister was not obliged to refer every complaint made, he did not have an unfettered discretion to refuse to refer a case. The result was something of a hollow victory for the farmers, since the incoming Minister, having referred the matter to the committee, which upheld the complaint, rejected the committee's recommendations.

R v Brixton Prison Governor ex parte Soblen (1963) also illustrates the problem of distinguishing between proper and improper motives. The United States of America had requested the return of Soblen to face criminal charges. The offence with which he was charged was not a legal basis for extradition. In judicial review proceedings, the Home Secretary argued that his deportation was on the basis that his continued presence in Britain was not 'conducive to the public good'. The Court of Appeal ruled that the Home Secretary's power to deport on that ground was not restricted by the fact that he was also responding to a request from the government of the United States.

In **R v Secretary of State for Foreign and Commonwealth Affairs ex parte World Development Movement** (1995), the government was held to have acted unlawfully in relation to aid money paid to Malaysia. In 1988, the United Kingdom Government signed an agreement with the Malaysian Prime Minister for the sale of arms valued at £1.3 billion. In 1989, Britain offered £234 million towards the building of the Pergau Dam. In 1991,[30] the deal went ahead, despite warnings from officials that the project was uneconomic and a waste of public funds. The monies were

---

29 Lord Morris of Borth-y-Gest dissenting.
30 Under the premiership of John Major.

paid out of the Overseas Development Administration (ODA) budget. Under international law, any linkage between aid monies and arms sales is prohibited. While the government denied any such link, a House of Commons Foreign Affairs Committee inquiry concluded that the government had, in effect, made such a link. Furthermore, under section 1 of the Overseas Development and Co-operation Act 1980, the Foreign Secretary is empowered to authorise payments only 'for the purpose of promoting the development or maintaining the economy of a country or territory outside the United Kingdom or the welfare of its people'. The High Court ruled that the Foreign Secretary had acted unlawfully, in part because the project was 'economically unsound', and also because the aid did not promote the development of a country's economy as required by law. As a result, some £55 million already spent on the project had to be returned to the ODA.[31]

In **Porter v Magill** (2002), the House of Lords ruled that the power to sell property to tenants in the hope of gaining party political advantage at an election was unlawful. It was argued that provided some proper purpose was being pursued, the decision was not unlawful. The House of Lords disagreed: the power had to be used for its intended purpose – and that was not to secure an electoral advantage.

Improper purpose was central to **R (Core Issues Trust) v Transport for London and Another** (2014). In 2012 Transport for London (TfL) decided not to allow an advertisement placed by Core Issues Trust, to appear on the side of London buses. The Advertising Policy of TfL stated that advertisements would not be approved if they were 'likely to cause widespread or serious offence' or which 'relate to matters of public controversy or sensitivity'. The advertisement in question implied that 'there could be some reversal of or recovery from homosexuality'. The Mayor, Boris Johnson, was Chairman of TfL, and he had made his opposition to the advertisement known to TfL. Counsel for the Core Trust alleged that the motivation behind TfL's case was the 'improper advancement of the Mayor's election campaign'. There was some dispute as to whether or not the decision was taken by the Head of Marketing or whether the Mayor had instructed TfL to withdraw the advertisement. It was accepted by the Court of Appeal that if the decision to disallow the advertisement was taken to advance Mr Johnson's election campaign rather than for the purpose of fulfilling the objectives of the Policy, that decision would have been unlawful. However, on the evidence before the Court, a decision as to purpose could not be made. The Court of Appeal therefore remitted the case for reconsideration the issue. In any event, if the decision was instructed by the Mayor or made for an improper purpose, it remained open to TfL to disallow the advertisement (i.e. remake the same decision) provided that it was not instructed by the Mayor or pursuing an improper purpose.

Frustrating the purpose of a statute was illustrated by **R (Rights of Women) v Lord Chancellor** (2016). In this case the Lord Chancellor had the power to make Regulations under the Legal Aid, Sentencing and Punishment of Offenders Act 2012 (LASPO). A Regulation amended in 2014 provided that in order to qualify for legal aid victims of domestic violence (save for certain exceptions) had to produce documentary evidence of violence within a 24-month period before applying for legal aid. Rights of Women, a charity specialising in gender-based violence, sought judicial review on the basis that, first, the Regulation was ultra vires the Act and, second, that it frustrated one of the purposes of the Act – namely that victims of domestic violence should be granted legal aid if they satisfied the financial need and merits requirements of the Act. The purpose of the Act was to make legal aid available to those in the most deserving categories, but also to save money by withdrawing legal aid from other types of case. The Court of Appeal held that the Regulation in question was within the power conferred by

---

31 See also **R v Secretary of State for the Environment ex parte Spath Holme Ltd** (2000).

Section 12 of LASPO and therefore not *ultra vires*. However, the Regulation had to be rationally connected to the purpose of the Act. Longmore LJ cited Lord Kerr of Tonaghmore JSC in **R (GC) v Commissioner of Police of the Metropolis** (2011) who stated that:

> a discretion conferred with the intention it should be used to promote the policy and objects of the Act can only be validly exercised in a manner that will advance that policy and those objects. More pertinently, the discretion may not be exercised in a way that would frustrate the legislation's objectives.

For the claimant it was argued that there were many instances where victims of violence were unable to provide the documentary evidence required by the Regulation, even though they satisfied the needs and merits test under the Act, a situation described by Longmore LJ as a 'formidable catalogue of areas of domestic violence not reached by a statute whose purpose is to reach just such cases' (at paragraph 44). In addition, the Regulation did not offer any 'safety valve' which would enable victims to explain why they had been unable to provide the documentation. The Court held that the Regulation frustrated the purpose of the Act in that it required documentation to be provided and further that it did not cater for victims of domestic violence who had suffered from financial abuse. Accordingly, the Court declared that the Regulation was invalid and would be quashed.

Relevant and irrelevant considerations in decision making

The following section considers relevant and irrelevant considerations which are taken into account in decision making. To a large extent, there is at best a fine line between using powers for the wrong purpose and the relevancy of considerations. Categorisation is a limited, although organisationally useful, device: the essential point to remember is that the heart of the matter lies in whether discretionary powers have been exercised lawfully or not, irrespective of the headings under which cases may be grouped. One case which straddles the boundaries of using powers for an improper purpose and taking irrelevant considerations into account is that of **R v Somerset County Council ex parte Fewings** (1995). The local authority decided to ban stag hunting on land owned by the council and designated for recreational purposes.[32] Laws J accepted that, in some circumstances, stag hunting could legitimately be banned – for example, where the hunt would damage rare flora, or if the animals themselves were rare. Here, however, the motivation behind the ban was the moral objection of the councillors to hunting. Laws J ruled that:

> If the activity in question is permissible under the general law, as is the practice of deer hunting, it is by no means to be prohibited on grounds only of the decision maker's distaste or ethical objection where the reach of his statutory function on its face requires no more than the making of objective judgments for the management of a particular regime. [page 530]

On appeal to the Court of Appeal, the decision was upheld, but on narrower grounds. The Court ruled that the Council's mind had not been directed to relevant statutory provisions, and it had not considered, as it was required to do, whether a ban of hunting would be for the general public benefit.

---

32 Under the Local Government Act 1972, s. 120.

A case which illustrates the intermingling of grounds for review is that of **Wheeler v Leicester City Council** (1985). In **Wheeler**, the House of Lords thoroughly examined the concepts of unreasonableness and of fairness, and here the interaction between bad faith, unreasonableness and procedural impropriety can be discerned. In 1984, the Rugby Football Union announced a tour to South Africa, with a team including three members of the Leicester Football Club. At the time, the government was opposed to any sporting links with South Africa. Leicester City Council – with a 25 per cent immigrant population – was virulently opposed to the proposed tour. The Leicester Club secretary attended a meeting with the leader of Leicester Council, at which he was asked to support the government's – and the council's – policy of opposition to the South African regime of apartheid. The club's response was to assert its opposition to apartheid but to stress that they were not constrained from playing in South Africa as a result of governmental opposition, which had neither made such tours illegal nor subject to sanctions on those who visited South Africa. As a result of the club's refusal to comply with the City Council's request that they withdraw from the tour, Leicester City Council resolved that the club would be suspended from using a local playing field for a 12-month period, the ban to be reviewed after a year and a new decision to be taken based on the club's attitude to South Africa at that time. The House of Lords ruled that a political policy – however morally justified – could not provide the lawful basis on which to deprive the club of engaging in its lawful activities.

As can be seen, the two purposes test involves the issue of irrelevant considerations. That is to say, a subsidiary or secondary purpose being pursued may – if it dictates the decision-making process – invalidate that process. Here, attention is turned to situations where an authority fails to take account of relevant considerations, or takes into account irrelevant considerations which materially affect the decision reached, and may be held to be acting *ultra vires*. Many of the cases involve the fiduciary duty which is owed by local authorities to their ratepayers. In **Roberts v Hopwood** (1925), for example, the local authority was empowered by statute to pay its workers 'as it thought fit'.[33] Nevertheless, when the council decided to pay wages which were higher than the national average and to pay men and women equally, it was held to have been acting beyond its powers. Its duty to its ratepayers overrode its desire to better the lot of its workers.[34] The court held that the council was pursuing a policy of 'philanthropic socialism' which was inconsistent with its duties to its ratepayers. Compare **Roberts v Hopwood** with **Pickwell v Camden London Borough Council** (1983), in which the council had paid additional monies to its manual workers in order to secure settlement of an industrial dispute. It was held that the payments were reasonable.

Similar considerations applied in **Bromley London Borough Council v Greater London Council** (1983). There, the Greater London Council, wishing to increase passenger numbers – and thereby reduce the traffic congestion on the roads – by decreasing fares on public transport, sought to pay for this by seeking a higher level of subsidy for London Transport by increasing the rates payable by ratepayers, the burden of which would fall on the residents of London boroughs. The House of Lords held the Greater London Council to be acting *ultra vires*. The House of Lords ruled that, whilst section 3 of the Transport (London) Act 1969 conferred a wide discretion on the authority, and that grants could be levied to supplement the income from transport fares, that discretion was limited by London Transport's basic obligation to run its operations on ordinary business principles, which their fare reduction policy contravened. As in **Roberts v Hopwood** (1925), the council could not use its grant-making powers to achieve a social policy which was inconsistent with those obligations: the Greater London

---

33 Under the Metropolis Management Act 1855, s. 62.
34 See also **Prescott v Birmingham Corporation** (1955); **Taylor v Munrow** (1960).

Council (GLC) was using its powers for the wrong purpose. Moreover, the rate reduction was also invalid insofar as it involved a breach of fiduciary duty owed by the council to its ratepayers. The fact that the policy had been part of an election mandate was not sufficient justification for the policy. The members of the council were representatives of the people, not delegates thereof. Accordingly, they were not irrevocably bound to fulfil election promises but, rather, must act in the interests of all constituents – not just those constituents who were users of London Transport.

This view on the doctrine of mandate – or responsibility to electors – may be contrasted with the decision in **Secretary of State for Education v Tameside Metropolitan Borough Council** (1977). The Labour-controlled Council in March 1975 proposed a scheme of comprehensive education to come into effect in 1976. In 1976, a Conservative Council was elected. The Party had conducted its election campaign in large part on the education platform. On entering office, the council reversed the education policy of the previous administration. The Secretary of State issued a direction under section 68 of the Education Act 1944, ordering the council to implement the comprehensive schooling policy of the previous local council. The House of Lords laid much emphasis on the wishes of the electorate. Lord Wilberforce declared:

> if he [the Secretary of State] had exercised his judgment on the basis of the factual situation in which this newly elected authority were placed – with a policy approved by the electorate, and massively supported by the parents – there was no ground, however much he might disagree with the new policy and regret such administrative dislocation as was brought about by the change, on which he could find that the authority were acting or proposing to act unreasonably.

Where an irrelevant consideration does not affect the outcome of a decision, the court may hold that the authority is acting *intra vires*. For example, in **R v Broadcasting Complaints Commission ex parte Owen** (1985), the Broadcasting Authority – with the statutory responsibility of ensuring fairness in the allocation of broadcasting time for political parties at election time – refused to consider a complaint that a political party had been given too little broadcasting time. That decision was challenged in the courts. However, while the Commission had some good reasons for not considering the complaint, it had also erred by giving weight to an irrelevant consideration, namely, that the task would be burdensome. The court nevertheless held that the Commission was acting within its lawful discretion.

Whether or not a local authority may take into account considerations relating to financial resources when assessing an individual's needs was considered by the Court of Appeal and House of Lords in **R v Gloucestershire County Council ex parte Barry; R v Lancashire County Council ex parte Royal Association for Disability and Rehabilitation** (1997).[35] Under the Chronically Sick and Disabled Persons Act 1970, a local authority is under the duty to identify the needs of disabled persons, and to meet such needs. The House of Lords ruled that the resources of the authority were a relevant consideration. Lord Nicholls of Birkenhead conceded that the argument put forward by Lord Lloyd, dissenting, that a person's needs were unaffected by local authority resources was an 'alluring argument', but one which he could not accept. The argument, he stated, was flawed by a 'failure to recognise that needs for services cannot sensibly be assessed without having some regard to the cost of providing them'.[36] The reasoning of the majority in the House of Lords in **Barry** was followed in **R v Sefton Metropolitan Borough Council ex parte Help the Aged** (1997). In that case, the needs of an elderly woman who was admitted to a

---

35 See also **R v Liverpool Crown Court ex parte Luxury Leisure Ltd** (1998).
36 Local authority resources were also significant in the case of **R (McDonald) v Kensington and Chelsea LBC** (2011). See Gordon, 2011.

nursing home, and the cost of meeting those needs, were in issue. Having considered the case of **Barry**, the Court of Appeal ruled that a local authority was entitled to have regard to its own limited financial resources. However, where a need existed, the authority was under a statutory duty to make arrangements to meet that need and lack of resources was no excuse. The authority could not, from the time that a person was assessed as being in need, fail to meet their statutory duty. Financial considerations were uppermost in the decision in **R v Cambridge Health Authority ex parte B** (1995), in which the Court of Appeal held that the courts could not make judgments about how health authorities decide to allocate a limited budget. The health authority had refused to fund further chemotherapy or a second bone marrow transplant for a ten-year-old girl with only a few weeks to live. Notwithstanding that decisions relating to human life had to be treated with the greatest seriousness, the court could not substitute its judgment about the allocation of financial resources for that of the authority.[37]

The Home Secretary was held to have taken irrelevant considerations into account, and failed to give weight to relevant considerations, in **R v Secretary of State for the Home Department ex parte Venables** (1997). In this case, when the Home Secretary decided to impose a tariff (the minimum sentence to be served to reflect retribution and deterrence) on the teenage killers of a young child, he took into account public opinion demanding that they be detained for life and failed to consider the progress which the killers had made in detention.

Medical Justice v Secretary of State for the Home Department (2017) is an example of the executive issuing unlawful statutory guidance, and policies, as a result of failing to adopt a correct definition. The case concerned the detention of individuals subject to immigration law. The Secretary of State had issued guidance (Adults at Risk in Immigration Detention, AARSG0)[38] intended to prevent those who were vulnerable (having been victims of torture) from entering detention, or removing them from it. Where the guidance 'went wrong' was in adopting a definition of torture that was so narrow that it covered only torture inflicted by state agents, and not torture inflicted by non-state actors. As a result aspects of the guidance were unlawful, the correct interpretation of torture not being adopted and as a result conflicting with the purpose of the statutory provision – a conflict for which there was no rational or evidential base.

Failure to take into consideration a statutory principle caused a prohibition on having tobacco products by detained patients, and related powers to search and confiscate such products, unlawful. The Supreme Court so ruled in **McCann v State Hospitals Board for Scotland** (2017). In instituting a comprehensive ban on tobacco products the Hospital's Board had failed to take into consideration the principle that it must discharge its functions in a manner that involves the minimum restriction on the freedom of a patient that is necessary in the circumstances.[39]

In **R (PK(Ghana)) v Secretary of State for the Home Department** (2018) the Court of Appeal held that the Secretary of State's guidance that a victim of trafficking should be granted discretionary leave to remain if his personal circumstances were 'compelling' failed to reflect the UK's obligation under the Council of Europe's Convention on Action against Trafficking in Human Beings 2005 (Cm 7465). The Convention required that a receiving country grant a renewable residence permit to a victim of trafficking where the authority considered that the stay was 'necessary owing to their personal situation'. The Secretary of State's guidance was silent as to the purpose for which it had to be 'necessary' for a victim to remain: it required no assessment of whether it was necessary to protect the victim. The imposition of the higher

---

37 See also **R v East Sussex County Council ex parte Tandy** (1998); **B v Harrow London Borough Council** (2000); **R v Camden and Islington Health Authority ex parte E** (2001).
38 Issued under section 59 of the Immigration Act 2016.
39 See also **R (Squire) v Shropshire Council** (2019). [2019] EWCA Civ 888.

threshold of 'compelling' risked the decision maker applying a difference and higher threshold than that required by the Convention. Accordingly the guidance was unlawful.

The failure by the Home Secretary to consider the requirements under the Data Protection Act 2018 resulted in the Supreme Court holding her decision unlawful: **Elgizouli v Secretary of State for the Home Department** (2020). Information had been transferred to the US concerning the appellant's son's alleged membership of a group of terrorists operating in Syria. Prosecution in the US could have led to the imposition of the death penalty and no assurances had been given to the Home Secretary that this would not be imposed. Under the Data Protection Act 2018 data cannot be transferred unless there are 'appropriate safeguards' or there are 'special circumstances'. Furthermore, as Lady Hale discussed, where fundamental rights and freedoms are concerned these override the public interest in the transfer of data. The right to life being fundamental, the law must be interpreted in a way that does not allow the transfer of data which could result in the death penalty. The state has a duty to investigate, prevent or protect an individual from trafficking.[40] This duty imposes a positive obligation to investigate, and in **MS (Pakistan) v Secretary of State for the Home Department** (2020) the Supreme Court held that the failure of the police to conduct an investigation breached that duty.

Acting in bad faith

To some extent, any decision which is *ultra vires* may involve 'bad faith' whenever there has been a failure to decide a case in the manner required by law. Some decisions, however, may have inadvertently breached the requirements of legality, whereas others will reveal an improper motive and unreasonableness, and more clearly demonstrate that the decision maker acted in 'bad faith'. An early judicial explanation of the limits of powers conferred upon public bodies is provided by Lord Macnaghten in **Westminster Corporation v London and North West Railway** (1905):

> It is well settled that a public body invested with statutory powers … must take care not to exceed or abuse its powers. It must keep within the limits of the authority committed to it. It must act in good faith. And it must act reasonably. The last proposition is involved in the second, if not in the first. [at page 430]

While the courts regularly use the language of 'good' and 'bad' faith, this usually means no more than that a decision maker must act 'reasonably' and must pursue the true objective of a statute. It seldom implies any moral wrongdoing on the part of the decision maker.

Fettering discretion

An authority may act *ultra vires* if, in the exercise of its powers, it adopts a policy which effectively means that it is not truly exercising its discretion at all. This principle is explained in **R v Port of London Authority ex parte Kynoch** (1919), in which it was held that an authority could not adopt a rigid policy which had the effect of ensuring that applications of a certain category would invariably be refused. In **Kynoch**, the applicant sought judicial review of the decision of the Port of London Authority to refuse him permission to construct a wharf on land he owned adjoining the River Thames. Permission was refused on the basis that the Authority

---

40 See the European Convention on Action against Trafficking in Human Beings (ECAT).

itself had a duty to provide the facilities. The challenge to the Authority's decision failed, on the basis that it appeared to the court that the Authority had given genuine consideration to the application on its merits.

Compare **Kynoch** with **British Oxygen Co v Board of Trade** (1971), in which **Kynoch** was judicially considered. In **BOC**, the House of Lords upheld the right of the Board of Trade to have a general policy, provided that the policy did not preclude the Board from considering individual cases. Lord Reid considered the scope of discretion, asserting that:

> There are two general grounds on which the exercise of an unqualified discretion can be attacked. It must not be exercised in bad faith, and it must not be so unreasonably exercised as to show that there cannot have been any real or genuine exercise of the discretion. But, apart from that, if the minister thinks that policy or good administration requires the operation of some limiting rule, I find nothing to stop him ... What the authority must not do is to refuse to listen at all.

The application failed. The Board of Trade had not adopted a rigid and invariable policy which rendered the consideration of applications a mere sham exercise in which there was no possibility of a fair consideration of the merits because of the adoption of a rigid policy.

However, in **H Lavender & Sons Ltd v Minister of Housing and Local Government** (1970), a different conclusion was reached. Lavender had applied for planning permission to extract sand and gravel from high-grade agricultural land. The local planning authority refused permission and Lavender appealed to the Minister of Housing and local government. The appeal was dismissed, the Minister of Housing and local government being persuaded by the Minister of Agriculture that such land should be preserved for agricultural purposes. Accordingly, the Minister ruled that:

> It is the minister's present policy that land should not be released for mineral working unless the Minister of Agriculture is not opposed. In the present case, the agricultural objection has not been waived and the minister has therefore decided not to grant planning permission for the working of the site.

The decision was set aside. The Minister was entitled to have a policy but, in reality, in this instance, the Minister's decision had been based solely on another Minister's objection. The Minister, therefore, did not open his mind to Lavender's application and thereby fettered his discretion. In reality, the decision to refuse planning permission was that of the Minister of Agriculture, who had no power to determine such matters.

In **Stringer v Minister of Housing and Local Government** (1970), the court considered the legality of a Minister's policy to restrict development of land which could interfere with the Jodrell Bank radio telescope. The court held that the Minister's general policy was lawful, provided that the policy did not result in him failing to take into account relevant issues in each individual application for planning permission. In **Sagnata Investments v Norwich Corporation** (1971), the council had a policy never to grant permits for amusement arcades in Norwich. There was no objection to Sagnata Investments itself; rather, no application – whatever its merits – would have succeeded because of the council's policy. The court held that the council had paid no regard whatsoever to the merits of the application. The council's decision was therefore quashed.[41]

---

41 See also **R (Nicholds) v Security Industry Authority** (2007).

In **R v Chief Constable of North Wales Police ex parte AB** (1997),[42] the Court of Appeal ruled that the policy of the North Wales police to disclose information to members of the public concerning the presence of a former paedophile offender was not unlawful. The court recognised that, in general, good public administration involved not disclosing damaging information about individuals unless there was sound justification for so doing. The applicants for judicial review, who were married, had both been convicted of serious sexual offences against children, and had served long prison sentences. The Lord Chief Justice recognised the tension between the rights of former offenders and the interests of the community. The police had not adopted a policy of blanket disclosure, but had carefully considered the case on its merits, and accordingly had not fettered its discretion.[43]

The House of Lords' decision in **R v Secretary of State for the Home Department ex parte Simms** (1999) is also significant in demonstrating the courts' refusal to allow a strict policy to undermine individual rights. The decision in **Simms** was reached on common law principles and before the Human Rights Act 1998 came into force, but nevertheless the approach taken is consistent with post-Human Rights Act cases. It may be compared with the House of Lords' decision in **Daly**, discussed below, in which a prison policy was held to violate a Convention right.[44] In **Simms**, the applicants had been convicted of murder but continued to plead their innocence; they had been refused permission to appeal against their convictions. The prisoners wished to pursue their claim to justice through the press. The Home Secretary had adopted a policy which imposed a blanket ban on journalists interviewing prisoners with a view to publication, on the basis that such publicity could undermine prison control and discipline. Lord Steyn concluded – in the language of proportionality and human rights[45] – that 'these provisions are exorbitant in width in so far as they would undermine the fundamental rights invoked by the applicants in the present proceedings and are therefore *ultra vires*'.[46]

In **R (Sandiford) v Secretary of State for Foreign and Commonwealth Affairs** (2014) the Supreme Court ruled that the Foreign Secretary's policy of refusing to provide funding for legal representation to UK nationals facing the death penalty abroad was lawful. The policy of not funding legal advice or representation for a national abroad was a blanket policy with no exceptions. The source of the Foreign Secretary's power was the royal prerogative, not statute, and the court's approach to the prerogative was different. Whereas under statute there could be an implication that a power was to be exercised differently under different circumstances, this was not the case with the prerogative. The royal prerogative was intrinsic to the Crown and it was 'for the Crown to determine whether and how to exercise them in its discretion'.[47] However, that did not mean that the exercise of a prerogative power 'should be immune from all judicial review',[48] and there was no reason why the exercise of a power or failure to exercise a power should not be reviewable on the grounds of irrationality or breach of other judicial review principles.

Dismissing the appeal, the Supreme Court found that on the facts the Foreign and Commonwealth Office had responded 'with appropriate urgency', and had put the appellant

---

42 See **R (H) v Ashworth Hospital Authority; R (Ashworth Health Authority) v Mental Health Review Tribunal for West Midlands and North West Region** (2002).

43 Reported as **R v Chief Constable of North Wales Police ex parte Thorpe** (1998). See also **R v Secretary of State for the Home Department ex parte Dinc** (1998); **R v North West Lancashire Health Authority ex parte A** (2000).

44 In **Daly**, the right in question was the right to privacy. In **Simms** – had it been heard after the Human Rights Act 1998 came into force – the issue would have been freedom of expression under Article 10.

45 On which see below.

46 See more recently a discussion of the scope of the rule against fettering in **R (on the application of Nicholds) v Security Industry Authority** (2007).

47 At para. 61.

48 At para. 65.

in contact with an experienced local lawyer. However, the Court stated that the appellant remained in urgent need of legal help and called on the government to review its policy.

There was nothing unlawful in the policy adopted by the Secretary of State to impose a time limit of three months on applications to reopen decisions on compensation following a finding of a miscarriage of justice. There was nothing unreasonable, irrational or unlawful in the imposition of the time limit. The Court of Appeal so ruled in **R (Ali) v Secretary of State for Justice** (2014).

Unauthorised delegation

Where powers are conferred by statute, the general rule is that they may not be delegated unless that delegation is authorised by law. Not all delegations will be unlawful. The courts will not hold, for instance, that a Minister must exercise each and every power personally. It is accepted that, where statute confers powers on Ministers, the powers are, in fact, exercisable on his behalf by the personnel of his Department. As explained in **Local Government Board v Arlidge** (1915), 'a minister cannot do everything himself'.[49] In **Arlidge** – an early and seminal case which ensured the conduct of government under the supervision of the courts – the court held that, whilst a Minister could lawfully delegate his power of determination to a subordinate, he, nevertheless, remained constitutionally and personally accountable to Parliament for the conduct of his Department.[50]

This principle was well illustrated in **Carltona v Works Commissioners** (1943). The Commissioners were given powers, under wartime regulations, to requisition property. Carltona's property was requisitioned, the order for requisition being signed, for and on behalf of the Commissioners, by a civil servant with the rank of assistant secretary. Lord Greene MR stated:

> It cannot be supposed that the particular statutory provision meant that in every case the minister in person should direct his mind to the matter. Constitutionally the decision of such an officer is the decision of the minister; the minister is responsible to Parliament. If the minister delegated to a junior official then he would have to answer to Parliament.

The decision in **Arlidge** may be compared with that of **Barnard v National Dock Labour Board** (1953). In **Barnard**, disciplinary powers delegated by statute to the London Dock Board were subdelegated to a port manager. That delegation was held to be *ultra vires*, on the basis that such a disciplinary function could not lawfully be delegated to another and must be exercised by the Board to whom the power was granted. Similarly, in **R v Talbot Borough Council ex parte Jones** (1988), where a local councillor applied for local authority housing. The housing tenancy committee resolved that the applicant should be given priority status and that her rehousing, subsequent to divorce, should be decided by the chairman and vice chairman of the committee, according to the Council's Standing Orders,[51] in consultation with the Borough Housing Officer. In 1986, the Housing Officer allocated her a house. In proceedings for judicial review, it was held that the decision to allocate housing could not lawfully be subdelegated from the chairman and vice chairman of the committee to the Housing Officer. The decision was also void on the grounds that irrelevant considerations had been taken

---

49 Note also that this case is an early authority for the proposition that the rules of natural justice do not necessarily require an oral hearing in every case: per Taylor LJ in **R v Army Board of the Defence Council ex parte Anderson** (1991).
50 See Dicey, 1885, Appendix 2.
51 Under the Local Government Act 1972, s. 101.

into account and that relevant considerations – the needs of others on the waiting list – had been ignored.[52] Also in relation to housing, it was held in **Credit Suisse v Waltham Forest London Borough Council** (1997) that a local authority with a statutory duty to provide housing for the homeless could not lawfully set up a company (with finance guaranteed by the Council) to purchase homes, but over which the Council would have little control. The Council could not lawfully delegate its powers in this manner.

The **Carltona** case was considered by the Supreme Court in **R (Bourgass and another) v Secretary of State for Justice** (2015). At issue was the legality of a decision to keep prisoners in solitary confinement. Under the Prison Rules a prisoner was not to be segregated for more than 72 hours without the authority of the Secretary of State. Bourgass was segregated for seven months, the other appellant for six months. The Supreme Court considered the legality of the decisions taken and whether the procedures met the requirements of fairness under the common law and, if applicable, Article 6 of the European Convention on Human Rights. It was argued that the decision of the 'operational manager' – a senior prison officer – was the decision of the Secretary of State by virtue of the *Carltona* principle. This argument the Supreme Court rejected. Prison officers were regulated by specific legislation and that was not 'readily reconcilable' with the idea that prison governors and officers are constitutionally indistinguishable from the Secretary of State. The *Carltona* principle therefore did not apply to the Prison Rules and a prison governor was not entitled to take a decision on the Secretary of State's behalf. As to procedural fairness the Court ruled that Article 6 did not apply, but that in any event judicial review met the requirements of fairness.

The *Carltona* principle also came under scrutiny in **R v Adams** (2020). The case concerned the legality of the detention without trial (internment) in Northern Ireland of persons where the Secretary of State considered that an individual was involved in terrorism. Mr Adams had been detained in 1973 under an Interim Custody Order (ICO) issued under the 1972 Order.[53] In 1975 he was convicted of attempting to escape from lawful custody. Government papers released under the 30-year rule[54] indicated that his case had not been personally considered by the Secretary of State. The question before the Supreme Court was whether the ICO was rendered invalid by the fact that it was made by a Minister of State and not personally by the Secretary of State. The Court ruled that the making of the ICO was invalid and his subsequent detention unlawful. The matter – which involved a 'power to detain without trial and potentially for a limitless period' – could not be delegated and should have been personally considered by the Secretary of State. Lord Sumption, the former Supreme Court judge, has criticised the decision, calling 'its ambit unclear and its reasoning unworldly, cursory and obscure'. In his view, the decision also 'makes the lawfulness of hundreds of thousands of past decisions by official and junior ministers subject to judicial review on principles so unclear as to leave rulings, in practice, to the discretion of the courts'.[55] The convictions for the offences of escaping from lawful custody were quashed.

Failure to act

An authority may be under a statutory duty to take action and, depending upon the specificity of that duty, may be held to be acting unlawfully if it fails to act. This is a difficult area

---

52 In **R v Home Secretary ex parte Oladehinde** (1991), the House of Lords ruled that the Immigration Act 1971 provided specific matters which could not be delegated by the Minister, and the court would not infer further restrictions.
53 Under Article 4 of the Detention of Terrorists (Northern Ireland) Order 1972.
54 Under which sensitive government papers are not released for 30 years.
55 Sumption, Lord, 'Supreme Court's Adams decision has left the law in an awful mess', *The Times*, 2 July 2020, page 52.

of law, in that some duties imposed by statute are clear and precise, and hence enforceable by the courts, whereas others may be of a general, non-specific nature and thus not court-enforceable: all will turn on the wording of the statute. Statute may stipulate the objective to be achieved but leave it to a local authority or other public body to determine the manner in which the objective should be achieved. Furthermore, in many cases, statute will provide that the Secretary of State shall have default powers, by the use of which he can compel a local authority to act should it fail so to do, in which case, the courts may be reluctant to permit the pursuit of an alternative remedy. In **R v Secretary of State for the Environment ex parte Norwich City Council** (1982), the authority had the duty to sell council housing to tenants[56] at a discounted rate. If a tenant exercised his or her right to buy, and the council did not respect that right, the Minister could exercise his powers to ensure compliance with the legislation, if satisfied that a tenant's right had 'not effectively and expeditiously' been recognised. The council argued that this policy was reasonable. However, the Court of Appeal rejected that argument, since the council had no discretion in light of the statutory right to buy. The failure of the council to implement the 'right to buy' legislation was to be controlled by the Minister. Should the Minister, in the exercise of his powers, act *ultra vires*, the court will control the exercise of power by judicial review. However, the courts may not be willing to rule against the Minister merely because the court takes a different view of the merits of the case (*per* Lord Denning).

Failure to comply with policy

The rule of law requires that there should be certainty and clarity in the law. However, in the administrative process, it is commonplace for there to be policies which supplement the legal rules. In relation to the powers of the police, for example, there exist Codes of Practice which guide the police in the exercise of their statutory duties. In relation to immigration law, there are Immigration Rules which similarly inform those applying the law. It is an established principle of public law that policy, while not law, must be adhered to unless there are justifiable reasons for departing from it.[57]

There are circumstances in which failure to comply with a published policy renders an otherwise lawful decision unlawful. An example of this is seen in **Shepherd Masimba Kambadzi v Secretary of State for the Home Department** (2011), a decision of the Supreme Court.[58] The appellant, a Zimbabwean national, had served a prison sentence at the end of which he was lawfully detained[59] pending deportation. The Home Secretary's published policy included the instruction that 'once detention has been authorised it must be kept under close review to ensure that it continues to be justified'. The system of review had not been complied with. Did this failure to comply with policy render the decision to detain unlawful? The Supreme Court ruled, by a majority of three to two, that it did. Lord Hope, while recognising that policy is not law, nevertheless endorsed the view expressed by Lord Phillips of Worth Matravers MR in **R (Saadi) v Secretary of State for the Home Department** (2002)[60] that the lawful exercise of statutory powers can be restricted, according to established principles of public law, by government policy and legitimate expectation to which such policy gives rise (at paragraph 34E). Furthermore, Lord Hope stated that a 'failure by the executive to adhere to its published policy without good reason can amount to an abuse of power which renders the detention

---

56 Housing Act 1980. The Housing Act 1985 confers default powers on the Minister to act where a local council fails to comply with the policy of the Act.
57 See **R (Hardial Singh) v Governor of Durham Prison** (1983) and **Nadarajah v Secretary of State for the Home Department** (2003).
58 Otherwise reported as **R (SK (Zimbabwe)) v Secretary of State for the Home Department** (2011).
59 Under the Immigration Act 1971.
60 At para. 7.

itself unlawful' (at paragraph 41). Of particular importance in this case was the deprivation of liberty of the individual protected under Article 5 of the European Convention on Human Rights. This case may be contrasted with the Supreme Court's decision in **R (Munir) v Secretary of State for the Home Department; R (Rahman) v Same** (2012). In **Munir and Rahman** the key issue was whether the Secretary of State's policy (Deportation Policy 5/96) was a statement of practice which fell within the meaning of section 3(2) of the Immigration Act 1971, and therefore required laying before Parliament. The Supreme Court ruled that it did not: the statement did no more than state that a rule might be relaxed if certain conditions were satisfied, but that whether it would be relaxed would depend on all the circumstances. As such it was highly flexible and could not be regarded as a statement of practice. In **R (Alvi) v Home Secretary** (2012), however, the Supreme Court ruled that section 3(2) of the Immigration Act 1971 required that statements of the rules and any changes to the rules be laid before Parliament and that failure by the Home Secretary to comply with this duty had the consequence that he could not rely on the statements in reaching an immigration decision. In this case the statements formed a part of the Immigration Rules and were determinative of the claimant's case.

Questions of the legality of decisions are also raised where an executive policy exists but remains unpublished: this is discussed in Chapter 25.

Irrationality: *Wednesbury* Unreasonableness

'Irrationality' is a concept which takes the courts further from reviewing the procedures by which a decision has been made and testing its legality, and closer to substituting the court's own view of the merits of the decision. The terms 'irrationality' and '**Wednesbury** unreasonableness' appear to be used at the judge's own preference.[61] Alternative expressions such as 'arbitrary and capricious', 'frivolous or vexatious' and 'capricious and vexatious' are also used on occasion to express the same concept.[62] 'Acting perversely' has also been used to express judicially the idea of unreasonableness.[63] The term 'unreasonableness' may thus be seen as an 'umbrella concept' which covers most of the major headings of review.

Early expression was given to the concept in two cases, **Rooke's Case** (1598) and **Keighley's Case** (1609). In **Rooke's Case**, Coke LJ proclaimed:

> and notwithstanding the words of the commission give authority to the commissioners to do according to their discretions, yet their proceedings ought to be limited and bound with the rule of reason and law. For discretion is a science or understanding to discern between falsity and truth, between wrong and right, between shadows and substances, between equity and colourable glosses and pretences, and not to do according to their wills and private affections.

The classic case of more recent times is that of **Associated Provincial Picture Houses Ltd v Wednesbury Corporation** (1948). The local authority had the power to grant licences for the opening of cinemas subject to such conditions as the authority 'thought fit' to impose. The authority, when granting a Sunday licence, imposed a condition that no children under the age of 15 years should be admitted. The applicants argued that the imposition of the condition was

---

61 See e.g. Lord Donaldson MR in **R v Devon County Council ex parte G** (1989), p. 577.
62 Per Wade and Forsyth, 2004 and references therein.
63 Per Lord Brightman in **R v Hillingdon London Borough Council ex parte Pulhofer** (1986). The test of **Wednesbury** unreasonableness is the foundation of the jurisdiction of university visitors, who should only intervene in academic matters in exceptional circumstances: **Jhamat v Inns of Court School of Law (Visitors to the Inns of Court)** (1999).

unreasonable and *ultra vires* the corporation's powers. The authority argued that there were no limits on the conditions which could be imposed in the statute. Lord Greene MR alluded to the many grounds of attack which could be made against a decision, citing unreasonableness, bad faith, dishonesty, paying attention to irrelevant circumstances and disregard of the proper decision-making procedure, and held that each of these could be encompassed within the umbrella term 'unreasonableness'. The test propounded in that case was whether an authority had acted, or reached a decision, in a manner 'so unreasonable that no reasonable authority could ever have come to it':

> a person entrusted with a discretion must, so to speak, direct himself properly in law. He must call his own attention to the matters which he is bound to consider. He must exclude from his consideration matters which are irrelevant to what he has to consider. If he does not obey those rules, he may truly be said, and often is said, to be acting 'unreasonably'. Similarly, there may be something so absurd that no sensible person could ever dream that it lay within the powers of the authority ...

> The court is entitled to investigate the action of the local authority with a view to seeing whether they have taken into account matters which they ought not to take into account, or, conversely, have refused to take into account and once that question is answered in favour of the local authority, it may still be possible to say that, although the local authority have kept within the four corners of the matters which they ought to consider, they have nevertheless come to a conclusion so unreasonable that no reasonable authority could ever have come to it. In such a case, again, I think the court can interfere. [page 229]

'Unreasonableness' was employed to challenge a bylaw which prohibited singing 'in any public place or highway within fifty yards of any dwelling house' although, on the merits of the case, the challenge failed.[64] In **Roberts v Hopwood** (1925), the council, in adopting a policy of paying higher wages than the national average for its workers, was unreasonable, for the discretion of the council was limited by law – it was not free to pursue a socialist policy at the expense of its ratepayers. The House of Lords ruled that, irrespective of the wording of the statute, the council had a duty to act 'reasonably'; its discretion was limited by law.[65]

The standard of reasonableness imposed by the courts is high: to impose too low a standard would in effect mean the substitution of judicial discretion for administrative discretion. It is for this reason that Lord Greene, cited above, states that a decision is unreasonable if it is 'so absurd that no sensible person could ever dream that it lay within the powers of the authority', and Lord Diplock, in **Council of Civil Service Unions v Minister for the Civil Service** (1985), regarded unreasonableness as entailing a decision 'so outrageous in its defiance of logic or of accepted moral standards that no sensible person who had applied his mind to the question to be decided could have arrived at it'.

In **Secretary of State for Education and Science v Tameside Metropolitan Borough Council** (1977), the Secretary of State for Education directed a newly elected local authority to implement plans, devised by the predecessor council, to introduce comprehensive schooling and abolish grammar schools.[66] At the election, there had been a change in the political composition of the council, which resulted in the change of policy. The Secretary of State's power was to

---

64 **Kruse v Johnson** (1898).
65 See Lord Wrenbury's judgment (1925) at p. 613.
66 Under powers conferred by the Education Act 1944, s. 68.

direct an authority as to the exercise of its powers if he was satisfied that the authority was acting unreasonably. The Secretary of State argued that the new council would not be able to organise the necessary system of selective entry required for grammar schools in time for the new academic year, and that the authority was therefore unreasonable.

The matter went to the House of Lords. The court had to determine the extent of the Secretary of State's discretion under section 68 of the Education Act. The wording of the section was subjective: 'if the Secretary of State is satisfied'. It fell to the court to determine whether, in the circumstances of the case, the Secretary of State had acted lawfully according to the court's interpretation of whether the Secretary of State did in fact have reasonable grounds for believing that the authority had acted unreasonably. Applying the **Wednesbury** reasonableness test to the decision of the local authority to retain grammar schools, the House of Lords ruled that the authority had not been unreasonable and, as a result, the Secretary of State's directions were unlawful.

Where human rights are concerned, the courts will subject decisions to a higher level of scrutiny than otherwise. In **R v Ministry of Defence ex parte Smith** (1996) Sir Thomas Bingham MR adopted the following as the correct approach to irrationality where human rights were in issue:

> The court may not interfere with the exercise of an administrative discretion on substantive grounds save where the court is satisfied that the decision is unreasonable in the sense that it is beyond the range of responses open to a reasonable decision-maker. But in judging whether the decision-maker has exceeded this margin of appreciation the human rights context is important. The more substantial the interference with human rights, the more the court will be required by way of justification before it is satisfied that the decision is reasonable in the sense outlined above.[67]

Irrationality was also central to **R (Rogers) v Swindon NHS Primary Care Trust** (2006). The applicant had been denied Herceptin treatment for breast cancer. She fell within the eligibility criteria, and the Trust did not deny funding on grounds of financial considerations.[68] However, the Trust had developed a policy which denied funding for treatment to any patient who could not show 'exceptional personal or clinical circumstances'. The Court of Appeal ruled that since financial considerations were irrelevant and the Trust had the resources to fund any treatment prescribed, to adopt a policy based on individual 'exceptional' circumstances was irrational.

In **R v Secretary of State for the Home Department ex parte Brind** (1991), the House of Lords re-examined the reasonableness of the exercise of the Home Secretary's discretion to issue a notice banning the transmission of speech by representatives of the Irish Republican Army and its political party, Sinn Féin. Despite the issue involving a denial of freedom of expression, the Court ruled that the exercise of the Home Secretary's power[69] did not amount to an unreasonable exercise of discretion.[70]

The courts continue to consider judicial review cases on the basis of irrationality. In **R (Limbu) v Secretary of State for the Home Department** (2008) a discretionary immigration policy was said irrationally to exclude material which would provide evidence which was imperative for the decision making involved. In **R (Ahmad) v Newham LBC** (2009) it was confirmed

---

67 At p. 554.
68 See **R v Cambridge Health Authority ex parte B** (1995).
69 Under the Broadcasting Act 1981. See further Chapter 18.
70 **R v Radio Authority ex parte Bull** (1995).

that a new scheme for the allocation of housing which in certain circumstances favoured those who had waited longest on the local authority list was not irrational as it involved prioritisation which was standard in such circumstances. In *Fargia Petitioner* (2008) the Court went as far as to say that proportionality was not a ground of review, preferring the language of irrationality when considering a cut-off date for the claiming of compensation.

 Pause and Reflect

Explain *Wednesbury* unreasonableness. Does the test of unreasonableness set too high a standard for review?

The Doctrine of Proportionality[71]

The doctrine of proportionality is one which confines the limits of the exercise of power to means which are proportionate to the objective to be pursued. Proportionality has a long history: in **Bank Mellat v HM Treasury (No 2)** (2013) Lord Reed JSC states that '[t]he idea that proportionality as an aspect of justice can be traced back via Aquinas to the *Nicomachean Ethics* and beyond'.[72] The doctrine has taken firm roots in the jurisprudence of, for example, the United States of America, Canada and the law of many continental European countries. Both the Court of Justice of the European Union (CJEU)[73] and the European Court of Human Rights[74] adopt proportionality as a test against which to measure the legality of actions of authorities.[75] To what extent the concept applies to judicial review cases beyond those concerning EU law and ECHR law is unclear: in **R v Home Secretary ex parte Brind** (1991), the House of Lords was not yet prepared to accept that the concept represented a separate and distinct head of judicial review. However, as will be seen from recent case law discussed below, proportionality is now being applied in the English courts and the issue is one which remains at the forefront of current academic and judicial debate.

In **Stoke-on-Trent City Council v B & Q plc** (1984), for example, Hoffmann J was prepared to adopt the ECJ's (now CJEU) proportionality test when considering the compatibility of the Shops Act 1950 and the free trade provisions of the EC Treaty.

It must be recognised at the outset that there is no single definition of or interpretation of proportionality and that its meaning varies according to the source of law. In particular, proportionality has a different interpretation under EU law from that under the ECHR. The concept arises under three broad headings:

● European Union law;
● human rights law under the European Convention on Human Rights and Fundamental Freedoms;
● judicial review of administrative action.

---

71 See the discussion on proportionality in Chapter 18. See Jowell and Lester, 'Proportionality: neither novel nor dangerous', in Jowell and Oliver, 1988; Jowell, 2000. On the status of the Convention before the Human Rights Act came into force, see Chapter 18. See also **R v Secretary of State for the Home Department ex parte Hussain Ahmed** (1999).
72 At para. 68.
73 See Chapters 7 and 8.
74 See Chapter 18.
75 See e.g. **Dudgeon v United Kingdom** (1982), discussed in Chapter 18.

The Human Rights Act 1998 provides for judicial review to extend to the review of administrative action to determine its compatibility with Convention requirements. As has been seen above, a fundamental concept utilised in domestic judicial review cases has conventionally been that of 'reasonableness'.[76] At issue is whether a public body, in its exercise of administrative discretion, has acted within the bounds of reasonableness conferred by the legislation, under which are subsumed the concepts of illegality, irrationality and procedural impropriety. Both the European Court of Justice of the European Union and the European Court of Human Rights – which are separate institutions and operate under separate jurisdictions[77] – have long employed the concept of 'proportionality', albeit with differing interpretations of the concept. As will be seen, the domestic courts have been less willing to adopt the principle and there remains uncertainty as to its scope of application. It is for this reason that Lord Carnwath JSC called in **R (Youssef) v Foreign Secretary** (2016), discussed below, for an 'authoritative review' of the issue in order 'to provide more structured guidance to the lower courts than such imprecise concepts as "anxious scrutiny" and "sliding scales"'.[78]

Proportionality and the Human Rights Act

Consistent with the requirements of the Convention, any action which prima facie violates protected rights must be justified on the basis that the infringement is justifiable on the grounds set out in the Convention Articles: thus, the action taken must be judged according to whether or not that action was proportionate to the objective behind the action. The Convention is replete with state discretion – the 'margin of appreciation' – allied to criteria such as

> necessary in a democratic society in the interests of national security, public safety or the economic well being of the country, for the prevention of disorder or crime for the protection of health or morals, or for the protection of rights and freedoms of others.[79]

The doctrine of proportionality has now been adopted in domestic courts of law. In **Brind**, Lord Ackner asked pithily whether the Secretary of State had 'used a sledgehammer to crack a nut'. In several pre-Human Rights Act cases, it is clear that the courts have been using the doctrine of proportionality but without making explicit references thereto. For example, in **R v Barnsley Metropolitan Borough Council ex parte Hook** (1976), a market stall holder had had his licence revoked for urinating in public. Lord Denning MR quashed the decision, partly on the basis that the penalty – the loss of the licence – was disproportionate to the 'offence'.[80]

Proportionality was also evident in **R v Chief Constable of Sussex ex parte International Trader's Ferry Ltd** (1999). In that case, judicial review had been sought regarding the Chief Constable's decision to restrict the deployment of police officers to assist the exporters, who were being obstructed by demonstrators. In the House of Lords, Lord Slynn stated that when answering the question of whether 'appropriate measures' had been taken, the correct approach was to ask 'whether the steps taken were proportionate', and that the Chief Constable had 'shown here that what he did in providing police assistance was proportionate to what was required'. In his judgment, Lord Cook took the opportunity to consider proportionality and the **Wednesbury** test of unreasonableness, stating that 'the European concepts of proportionality and margin

76 See *Associated Provincial Picture Houses Ltd v Wednesbury Corporation* (1948).
77 See further Chapter 7.
78 At para. 55.
79 ECHR, Article 8(2).
80 Also consider **Wheeler v Leicester City Council** (1985), discussed above.

of appreciation produce the same result as what are commonly called **Wednesbury** principles', and redefined the reasonableness test to the more simple formula of 'whether the decision in question was one which a reasonable authority could reach'.

See Chapter 18.

With the Human Rights Act 1998, proportionality moves centre stage. In interpreting the Act, section 2 requires that domestic courts and tribunals 'must take into account' the judgments and decisions of the Court of Human Rights. Under section 6, courts and tribunals are public authorities under the Act and are therefore under a duty not to violate Convention rights. Furthermore, most Convention rights are not absolute and unqualified, but allow states to impose limitations on specified grounds, commonly in the interests of 'public safety' or 'national security'. Restrictions on the exercise of rights – derogations – must also commonly be 'prescribed by law' and 'necessary in a democratic society'. The combined effect of these provisions necessitates that courts follow the reasoning of the Court of Human Rights, and that includes the doctrine of proportionality. The domestic courts have traditionally been wary of the doctrine, on the basis that it requires judges to go beyond an analysis of the legality of the decision-making process on the grounds of legality, rationality and procedural propriety, and to address a further question. That is, where a breach of a right is found to have occurred, was the offending action justified as being both necessary and proportionate to the objective being sought? This requires the courts not only to look at the processes involved in reaching decisions, but to evaluate whether on the facts the decision maker adopted the approach which least undermined the right in question. That exercise involves the judges looking to the merits of decisions, rather than the process of decision making – which has been the conventional concern of judicial review – and blurs the line between review and appeal. Constitutionally, that alters the position of the judges vis-à-vis the executive.

The decision of the House of Lords in **R (Daly) v Secretary of State for the Home Department** (2001) is also important in demonstrating the movement away from the traditional test of **Wednesbury** unreasonableness towards the doctrines of necessity and proportionality. The House of Lords ruled that the policy of excluding prisoners from their cells while prison officers conducted searches – which included scrutinising privileged legal correspondence – was unlawful. Lord Bingham stated that the conclusion had been reached according to common-law principles, but accepted that the same result could have been achieved if the analysis had proceeded on the basis of the European Convention.[81] Lord Cooke was explicit in recognising the limitations of the traditional **Wednesbury** approach, stating that before long it would be accepted that the **Wednesbury** case was an unfortunately retrogressive decision in English law. Proportionality was central to the decision in **R v Waya** (2012), a case involving a confiscation order made under the Proceeds of Crime Act 2002 and the relationship between that order and Article 1 of Protocol 1 (A1P1) of the European Convention on Human Rights. The Supreme Court, analysing this relationship, held that the effect of case law on A1P1 was that to be Convention compliant, a confiscation order must be proportionate.

In **R (Bibi) v Secretary of State for the Home Department** (2013) the Court of Appeal ruled that the requirement that a foreign spouse or partner of a British citizen or person settled in the UK produce a test certificate of knowledge of the English language prior to entering the UK was proportionate. The Home Secretary had amended the Immigration Rules to require foreign spouses to demonstrate a minimum knowledge of English. The objective was to facilitate the integration of non-English-speaking spouses. It was a benign measure and the state should be accorded a wide margin of appreciation. The requirement was proportionate to the objective and therefore not unlawful.

It is clear from the case law that in the exercise of the interpretative duty imposed by section 3 of the Human Rights Act 1998, the courts have adapted to the approach of the Court

---

81 The relevant Convention right being the right to privacy under Article 8.

of Human Rights in employing the concepts of *proportionality* and *necessity*, which give greater scope for the protection of rights than the conventional concepts employed in judicial review under the umbrella of the **Wednesbury** unreasonableness test. Even before the Human Rights Act 1998 came into effect, the courts were developing a more vigorous approach to the protection of rights. In **R v Ministry of Defence ex parte Smith** (1996), it was recognised that in judicial review proceedings, where human rights were in issue, the courts should 'anxiously scrutinise' executive decisions. That approach, however, did not satisfy the interpretative duty according to Lord Steyn in **R (Daly) v Secretary of State for the Home Department** (2001), where he stated that while there was an overlap between the traditional **Wednesbury** grounds for review and the proportionality approach, there was nevertheless 'a material difference between the **Wednesbury** and **Smith** grounds of review and the approach of proportionality applicable in respect of review where Convention rights are at stake'.

Lord Steyn cited Lord Clyde's approach in **De Freitas v Permanent Secretary of Ministry of Agriculture, Fisheries, Lands and Housing** (1999), namely that in considering whether a restriction on a right is 'arbitrary' or 'excessive', the court should ask itself:

whether:

(i)   the legislative objective is sufficiently important to justify limiting a fundamental right;
(ii) the measures designed to meet the legislative objective are rationally connected to it; and
(iii) the means used to impair the right or freedom are no more than is necessary to accomplish the objective.

In Lord Steyn's analysis there are three 'concrete differences' between the traditional grounds for judicial review and the proportionality test, namely:

First, the doctrine of proportionality may require the reviewing court to assess the balance which the decision maker has struck, not merely whether it is within the range of rational or reasonable decisions.

Secondly, the proportionality test may go further than the traditional grounds of review inasmuch as it may require attention to be directed to the relative weight accorded to interests and considerations.

Thirdly, even the heightened scrutiny test developed in **Smith** is not necessarily appropriate to the protection of human rights.

Lord Clyde's formulation of proportionality was criticised in **Huang v Secretary of State for the Home Department** (2007) on the basis that it omitted an important aspect of proportionality, namely, the need to balance the interests of society with those of individuals and groups. As stated in **R (Razgar) v Secretary of State for the Home Department** (2004) in relation to human rights, the judgment on proportionality:

must always involve the striking of a fair balance between the rights of the individual and the interests of the community which is inherent in the whole of the Convention. The severity and consequences of the interference will call for careful assessment at this stage.

The need to balance the rights of the individual and the interests of society as a whole is built into the structure of the many qualified Convention rights. A right is conferred in the first paragraph of the Convention Article. That right is then qualified by various factors provided in the second paragraph of the relevant Article (public order, health or morals, the protection of the rights and freedoms of others). In order to interpret the scope of the right conferred it is therefore essential to interpret the limits of that right. What unites the various qualifications to rights is that they are 'necessary in a democratic society'. If the state limits a right, under the second paragraph, then that limitation must be no more than is required to achieve the objective being sought: in other words, it must be *proportionate*.

The question of balancing the rights of the individual and the interests of society as a whole, discussed above, was considered by Laws LJ in **R (Miranda) v Home Secretary** (2014). In this case a person acting on behalf of a journalist was stopped and searched at Heathrow Airport under Schedule 7 of the Terrorism Act 2000 and material (which had been stolen from GCHQ) seized by the police.[82] The defence argued, *inter alia*, that the power used was disproportionate. Lord Justice Laws explained the origins of the 'balancing exercise' but stated that it 'should be approached with some care'. That is because in Laws LJ's words 'there is a real difficulty in distinguishing this from a political question to be decided by the elected arm of government'. Furthermore, in the instant case if there was a balance to be struck, it was 'between two aspects of the public interest': the public interest in press freedom and the public interest in national security.[83]

However, the question arises as to whether the doctrine of proportionality applies only where fundamental human rights are in issue, or whether it will come to pervade all aspects of judicial review. This issue was addressed by Lord Slynn in **R (Alconbury Developments Ltd) v Secretary of State for the Environment, Transport and the Regions** (2001), where he stated that:

> I consider that even without reference to the Human Rights Act the time has come to recognise that this principle [proportionality] is part of English law, not only when judges are dealing with [European] Community acts, but also when they are dealing with acts subject to domestic law. *Trying to keep the **Wednesbury** principle and proportionality in separate compartments seems to me to be unnecessary and confusing.* [emphasis added]

Whether proportionality will ultimately supersede the concept of reasonableness or rationality was also considered by Dyson LJ in **R (Association of British Civilian Internees Far East Region) v Secretary of State for Defence** (2003) in which he stated that:

> we have difficulty in seeing what justification there now is for retaining the **Wednesbury** test ...

> But we consider that it is not for this court to perform its burial rites. The continuing existence of the **Wednesbury** test has been acknowledged by the House of Lords on more than one occasion.

On the other hand, Professor Jowell QC has stated:

> The new constitutional approach will not affect all our judicial review. There will no doubt remain areas where traditional techniques of reasoning and justification

---

82 On which see further Chapter 22.
83 **Miranda**, at paras 45 to 46.

will suffice to ensure standards of legal, fair and reasonable administration based upon the practical morality familiar to our common law. [2000, page 682]

A former Lord Chancellor, Lord Irvine, moreover, has expressed constitutional objections to the introduction of proportionality:

it invites review of the merits of public decisions on the basis of a standard which is considerably lower than that of *Wednesbury* unreasonableness and would involve the court in a process of policy evaluation which goes far beyond its allotted constitutional role. [Irvine, 1996]

The difficulty with proportionality from the traditional approach to judicial review is that it comes close to ruling on the substance, or merits, of a case and thereby risks the judges becoming embroiled in the administrative process in a manner which might be seen as infringing on the separation of powers between the executive and the judiciary. It also, at a conceptual level, raises the question of whether – and under what circumstances – differing levels of judicial scrutiny are required. Unreasonableness and irrationality are terms imbued not only with familiarity but with the comfort of a degree of objectivity which can (generally) be applied without a deep analysis of the merits of the case in hand. Proportionality, on the other hand, is more sensitive to the context of the case and requires the court to consider whether the decision reached or action taken is restricted to what is strictly required (proportionate) to the objective being sought – a task it cannot do without considering both the policy and the means adopted to achieving it.

The importance of context was emphasised by Lord Mance in **Kennedy v The Charity Commission** (2014), who expressed the view, *obiter*, that proportionality could be relevant in judicial review 'even outside the scope of Convention and EU law'.[84] On context, Lord Mance stated that:

The common law no longer insists on the uniform application of the rigid test of irrationality once thought applicable under the so-called *Wednesbury* principle ... The nature of judicial review in every case depends on the context.

Lord Mance stated the advantages of proportionality in the following terms:

The advantage of the terminology of proportionality is that it introduces an element of structure into the exercise, by directing attention to factors such as suitability or appropriateness, necessity and the balance or imbalance of benefits and disadvantages. [at paragraph 54]

On whether proportionality had developed more generally into domestic public law, Lord Carnwath was doubtful, expressing the view that: 'it is at best uncertain to what extent the proportionality text, which is an essential feature of Article 10.2 as interpreted by the Strasbourg court, has become part of domestic public law' (at paragraph 246).

Four recent cases develop the analysis of proportionality further. In **Pham v Secretary of State for the Home Department** (2015), the issue was whether the Home Secretary could lawfully deprive the appellant of his British citizenship.[85] **R (Keyu) v Secretary of State for Foreign and Commonwealth Affairs** (2015) concerned a claim – which failed – that the United Kingdom

---

84 At para. 54.
85 Under s. 40(2) of the British Nationality Act 1981.

government was under a duty to hold a full investigation into the deaths of civilians in the State of Selangor in 1948. The third case, **R (Lumsdon) v Legal Services Board** (2015), involved a challenge to a quality assessment scheme (QASA) for advocates appearing before the criminal courts. The final case, **R (Youssef) v Secretary of State for Foreign and Commonwealth Affairs** (2016), concerned the legality of the appellant's inclusion in the United Nations Security Council's list of persons associated with terrorist organisations.

The Secretary of State's decision to deprive a person suspected of terrorist involvement of his British citizenship was upheld by the Supreme Court in **Pham v Secretary of State for the Home Department**. The Court accepted that citizenship was a fundamental human right and therefore of the highest importance under domestic, European and international law. Accordingly the standard of judicial review had, in Lord Mance's view, to be 'strict'. Proportionality would be an appropriate tool to be employed in such a case. In **Pham** it was Lord Sumption JSC (with whom Lord Mance agreed) who gave the most in-depth consideration to proportionality. Lord Sumption's starting point was the recognition that under both EU law and European human rights law, proportionality was an 'integral part of their test for legal justification', but that while the domestic courts had applied the proportionality test in cases having an EU or ECHR dimension, they had not accepted proportionality generally as a principle of English law. Nevertheless, he went on to argue, domestic law had 'for many years stumbled towards a concept which is in significant respects similar' (at paragraph 105). Lord Reed JSC also discussed the manner in which the courts adapt their reasoning in light of the factual context of the case. Arguing that proportionality is 'not a monolithic principle' and that it is not 'expressed and applied in a uniform way in different legal systems and in different contexts', Lord Reed stated that the intensity of review will vary depending 'on the nature of the right involved, the seriousness of the interference with that rights and the nature of the justification for that interference' (at paragraph 117). He went on to conclude that:

> One can infer ... that where Parliament authorises significant interferences with important legal rights, the courts may interpret the legislation as requiring that any such interference should be no greater than is objectively established to be necessary to achieve the legitimate aim of the interference: in substance, a requirement of proportionality.

In **Keyu** the Supreme Court ruled that the Secretary of State's decision not to hold an inquiry was reasonable and rational, and according to Lord Neuberger PSC, 'applying classic judicial review principles, I consider that the decision cannot be impugned'. However, the Court was invited to consider whether the time had come to reconsider the basis on which the courts review decisions of the executive and, per Lord Neuberger, whether 'in particular the traditional **Wednesbury** rationality basis for challenging executive decisions should be replaced by a more structured and principled challenge based on proportionality' (at paragraph 131). Lord Neuberger took the view that for the Court to adopt such an approach a re-hearing of the case would be necessary before a full panel of nine justices (here there were five). Lord Neuberger did not accept that this was necessary in this case because he considered that the result would have been the same even if it had been based on proportionality. On the implications of a move from rationality to proportionality, Lord Neuberger stated that:

> The move from rationality to proportionality ... would appear to have potentially profound and far reaching consequences, because it would involve the court considering the merits of the decision at issue; in particular, it would require the courts to consider the balance which the decision-maker had struck between competing interests (often a public interest against a private interest) and the weight to be accorded to each such interest.

His Lordship then referred to *dicta* in precedent cases (**Bank Mellat (No 2)**, **Kennedy v Information Commissioner**, **Pham**) and concluded that 'the domestic law may already be moving away to some extent from the irrationality test **in some cases**' (at paragraph 133, emphasis added).

Lord Kerr of Tonoghmore JSC also reflected on proportionality in **Keyu**. Accepting that the Supreme Court would have to address the issue 'sooner rather than later', Lord Kerr argued that the idea that a choice had to be made between proportionality and irrationality 'may be misplaced' (at paragraph 271), and that the difference between a rationality challenge and one based on proportionality is not 'as stark as it is sometimes portrayed' (at paragraph 273). Arguing that the instant case was not the correct occasion in which to review the authorities, Lord Kerr set out the issues which would need to be addressed in a future case. These were as follows:

- whether irrationality and proportionality are forms of review which are bluntly opposed to each other and mutually exclusive;
- whether intensity of review operates on a sliding scale, dependent on the nature of the decision under challenge and that, in consequence, the debate about a 'choice' between proportionality and rationality is no longer relevant;
- whether there is any place in modern administrative law for a 'pure' irrationality ground of review i.e. one which poses the question, 'could any reasonable decision-maker, acting reasonably, have reached this conclusion'; and
- whether proportionality provides a more structured and transparent means of review. (at paragraph 278)

R (Lumsdon) v Legal Services Board (2015) concerned a challenge by criminal law barristers, by way of judicial review, to the decision of the Legal Services Board (LSB) to approve a scheme of quality assessment for advocates (QASA) on the ground that it was contrary to Regulations which implemented an EU Directive. The Supreme Court held, *inter alia*, that the principle of proportionality varied according to context and that the way the principle was expressed or applied differed between the Court of Justice of the EU and the European Court of Human Rights.

The final case is **Youssef** (2016). The appellant sought judicial review of three decisions of the Secretary of State relating to his inclusion in the United Nations' Sanctions Committee asset-freezing list and the equivalent listing of the European Union on the basis of involvement with terrorism. One of the grounds for appeal was the standard of review. Lord Carnwath JSC considered proportionality and expressed the hope that an opportunity might arise in which a 'comprehensive review of the tests to be applied to administrative decisions generally' could be undertaken by the Supreme Court. Referring to Lord Reed's *dicta* in **Pham** (see above), Lord Carnwath reiterated his support for a more flexible approach where individual rights were at issue, but also made the point that in many cases, 'perhaps most' applying a proportionality test would not lead to a different result from the traditional grounds for judicial review – especially where national security was involved (because national security is an area where the courts are particularly slow to interfere in executive decisions).

The differences between proportionality under EU law and ECHR law
ECHR/Human Rights Act proportionality
Lord Reed JSC offered a succinct analysis of the requirements of proportionality in **Bank Mellat v HM Treasury (No 2)** (2013):

it is necessary to determine:

(1) whether the objective of the measure is sufficiently important to justify the limitation of a protected right;
(2) whether the measure is rationally connected to the objective;
(3) whether a less intrusive measure could have been used without unacceptably compromising the achievement of the objective; and
(4) whether, balancing the severity of the measure's effects on the rights of the persons to whom it applies against the importance of the objective, to the extent that the measure will contribute to its achievement, the former outweighs the latter.

In essence, the question at step four is whether the impact of the rights infringement is disproportionate to the likely benefit of the impugned measure (at paragraph 74).[86]

 Pause and Reflect

What do you understand by the concept of proportionality? What are the advantages and disadvantages of proportionality over the traditional ground of 'unreasonableness' or 'irrationality'? Is proportionality confined to cases involving EU law and human rights or does it apply more generally to judicial review?

What has become clear from the case law is that there are now differing levels of review being applied, depending on the nature of the case in hand, ranging from non-justiciable issues on which the courts will not adjudicate,[87] from areas of policy where the judges will defer to the executive,[88] the conventional reasonableness test,[89] EU law issues where the courts will follow the lead of the CJEU and human rights issues where the courts will give 'anxious scrutiny' to the matter[90] and apply a proportionality test which differs from that applied in cases involving EU law.[91] And still to be determined is the application of proportionality to judicial review cases not involving human rights or EU law. Note that the UK will no longer be subject when the UK leaves the EU.

Summary

The traditional focus of the courts in judicial review proceedings is that of *vires* – and the question whether a decision maker has acted inside (*intra vires*), or outside (*ultra vires*) his or her powers. However, these phrases are but a blanket expression or umbrella term for a number of ways in which an administrative body can 'go wrong'. In the **GCHQ** case (1985), Lord Diplock identified the headings for judicial review as being: illegality, irrationality or procedural impropriety, recognising that a further head of proportionality might be added in the future. Illegality, irrationality and procedural impropriety again cover a number of different,

---

86 Note that the concept of proportionality is now enshrined in the Treaty on European Union, Article 5(4): under the principle of proportionality, the content and form of Union action shall not exceed what is necessary to achieve the objectives of the Treaties.

87 As in **Council for Civil Service Unions v Minister for the Civil Service** (1985).

88 See, e.g. **A v Secretary of State for the Home Department** (2004).

89 See **Associated Provincial Picture Houses Ltd v Wednesbury Corporation** (1948).

90 **R v Ministry of Defence ex parte Smith** (1995).

91 **R v Secretary of State for the Home Department ex parte Daly** (2001). See Le Sueur, 2005 and Olley, 2004.

but often overlapping grounds and these and the case law must be studied. Judicial review on human rights grounds is a fertile and rapidly expanding area of the law. Here the courts are increasingly adopting the concept of proportionality to evaluate the legality of administrative action although there is no consensus on whether proportionality as a ground for review has expanded beyond the realms of human rights and EU law and entered into the broader areas of domestic public law. Procedural impropriety is discussed in Chapter 25.

📖 Further Reading

Allan, TRS, 'Judicial deference and judicial review: legal doctrine and legal theory' (2011) 127 *Law Quarterly Review* 96.

Craig, P, 'The nature of reasonableness' (2013) 66 *CLP* 131.

Feldman, D, 'Error of law and flawed administrative acts' (2014) 73 *Cambridge Law Journal* 275.

Hickman, TR, 'The reasonableness principle: reassessing its place in the public sphere' (2004) 63 *Cambridge Law Journal* 166.

Hickman, TR, 'The substance and structure of proportionality' [2008] *Public Law* 694.

Hilson, C, 'Judicial review, policies and the fettering of discretion' [2002] *Public Law* 111.

Hunt, M, 'Sovereignty's blight: why contemporary public law needs the concept of due deference' in N Bamforth and P Leyland (eds), *Public Law in a Multi-Layered Constitution*, 2003, Oxford: Hart Publishing.

Irvine of Lairg, Lord, 'Judges and decision makers: the theory and practice of *Wednesbury* review' [1996] *Public Law* 59.

Jowell, J, 'Beyond the rule of law: towards constitutional judicial review' [2000] *Public Law* 671.

Jowell, J, 'Judicial deference: servility, civility or institutional capacity' [2003] *Public Law* 592.

Kavanagh, A, 'Defending deference in public law and constitutional theory' (2010) 126 *LQR* 222.

Leigh, I, 'Taking rights proportionately: judicial review, the Human Rights Act 1998 and Strasbourg' [2002] *Public Law* 265.

Tomkins, A, *Public Law*, 2003, Oxford: Clarendon Press, Chapter 6.

Young, AL, 'In defence of due deference' (2009) 72 *MLR* 534.

Chapter 25

Grounds for Judicial Review II: Procedural Impropriety

Chapter Contents

Learning Objectives

By the end of this chapter you should be able to:

- ☐ explain what is meant by 'procedural impropriety';
- ☐ explain what is meant by natural justice;
- ☐ discuss the rules relating to bias, financial and otherwise;
- ☐ with reference to case law explain the test for bias;
- ☐ discuss the right to a fair hearing, and its various elements;
- ☐ explain the duty to give reasons;
- ☐ explain the concept of 'legitimate expectation';
- ☐ discuss the ways in which a legitimate expectation may be raised;
- ☐ with reference to case law explain the difference between procedural and substantive legitimate expectations.

Introduction

Having considered the substantive grounds for judicial review we now consider those grounds which are largely brought under the umbrella term of 'procedural impropriety'. It is important to note that although this is labelled as 'procedural' it covers aspects of natural justice which are deep rooted in the common law tradition and have significant theoretical importance within administrative law.[1] At the present time procedural impropriety could be said to cover the following aspects of judicial review:

- failing to comply with mandatory procedures;
- breach of natural justice;
- Article 6 of the European Convention on Human Rights;
- the rule against bias: *nemo iudex in causa sua*;
- the right to a fair hearing: *audi alteram partem*;
- the duty to act fairly;
- the duty to give reasons;
- legitimate expectations.

Procedural Impropriety under Statute

Failure to comply with procedures laid down by statute may invalidate a decision. The courts distinguish between those procedural requirements which are mandatory, the breach of which will render a decision void, and those which are directory, which may not invalidate the decision taken. In **London and Clydesdale Estates Ltd v Aberdeen District Council** (1979), the House of Lords emphasised the inherent vagueness in the distinction and stressed that the court would not draw a hard and fast line: it is all a matter of degree and the particular circumstances of the case must be examined.[2] However, in some cases, the requirement to adhere to procedural correctness is clear. For example, in **Bradbury v Enfield London Borough Council** (1967), the Education Act 1944 provided that, if a local education authority intends to establish new schools or cease to maintain existing schools, notice must be given to the Minister, following which, public notice must be given in order to allow interested parties to comment.[3] The Council breached the requirement of public notice and the plaintiffs sought an injunction. The Council claimed that educational chaos would occur if they were required to comply with the procedural requirements. That plea met with little sympathy in court. Lord Denning stated that:

> if a local authority does not fulfil the requirements of the law, this court will see that it does fulfil them ... I can well see that there may be a considerable upset for a number of people, but I think it far more important to uphold the rule of law. Parliament has laid down these requirements so as to ensure that the electors can make their objections and have them properly considered. We must see that their rights are upheld. [page 1324]

---

1 See Wade and Forsyth, 2004.
2 See also *Wang v Commissioner of the Inland Revenue* (1994).
3 Education Act 1944, s. 13.

Further, as has been seen earlier, in the **Aylesbury Mushroom** case,[4] the court ruled that the statutory requirements of consultation[5] with organisations or associations which represented substantial numbers of people could not be avoided by consultation with the largest representative body of all agricultural horticultural and forestry industry workers – the National Farmers' Union. For true consultation to take place in accordance with law, there must be communication with the representative organisations and the opportunity given of responding thereto, without which 'there can be no consultation'.

A consultation exercise was ruled to be unlawful by the Supreme Court in **R (Massey) v Haringey London Borough Council** (2014). Prior to 2013 central government operated a Council Tax Benefit scheme. Residents in local authority areas were relieved from paying council tax on a means-tested basis. The local authority was reimbursed in full by central government. For the year 2013 to 2014 the amount to be reimbursed to local authorities was reduced to 90 per cent of the sum received in the previous year. Each local authority was required to devise a Council Tax Reduction Scheme (CTRS) for those whom they considered to be in financial need.[6] Before making such a scheme the authority was under a statutory duty to 'consult such other persons as it considers are likely to have an interest in the operation of the scheme'. Haringey LBC published a draft scheme in 2012 proposing that the shortfall in central government funding would be met by a reduction in council tax relief for all Council Tax Benefit claimants other than pensioners. It did not explain the different options for making up the shortfall in revenue, such as raising council tax, reducing funding to council services or deploying capital reserves. Lord Wilson ruled that fairness demanded that the consultation document should refer to alternative methods of meeting the shortfall. The council assumed that the shortfall would be met by a reduction in council tax relief and no other option was presented. Lord Reed also ruled that the consultation was unlawful. However, he based his decision not on fairness but on the context in which the statutory duty was imposed. In this case, the duty was to ensure public participation in the decision-making process. Accordingly it was essential that those consulted should be provided 'with an outline of the realistic alternatives' and an indication of the main reasons for the authority's adoption of the draft scheme. However, while the consultation process was unlawful, the Court declined to order a fresh consultation, on the basis that that would be disproportionate.[7]

However, on occasion, although an authority is under a duty to act, and fails to act, the court may nevertheless uphold the decision made, provided that the decision-making process was otherwise fair and the failure to act does not affect the quality of the decision reached. This was the position in **Berkeley v Secretary of State for the Environment** (2000). In this case, in a planning application by Fulham Football Club to redevelop part of its land to provide apartments and a riverside walk, the Secretary of State was required[8] to consider the environmental impact of the proposed development, and to issue an 'environmental statement'. The Court of Appeal ruled that the Secretary of State's failure to act did not invalidate the decision. The planning application had been referred to the Secretary of State, who had appointed an inspector. A public hearing had been held, at which the applicant had been heard and at which the environmental impact of the proposed development had been fully considered. The court found that 'the procedures adopted, although flawed, had been thorough and effective [so as] to enable the inspector to make a comprehensive judgment on all the environmental issues'.[9] By contrast, in **R (Smith) v North Eastern Derbyshire Primary Care Trust** (2006) the Court of Appeal quashed a decision which had been taken without the consulta-

---

4 *Agricultural, Horticultural and Forestry Industry Training Board v Aylesbury Mushroom Ltd* (1972).
5 Under the Industrial Training Act 1964, s. 1(4).
6 Under the Local Government Finance Act 1992, para. 3(1)(c) of Sched. 1A as amended.
7 Compare **R (United Company Rusal plc) v London Metal Exchange** (2014).
8 Under the Town and Country Planning (Assessment of Environmental Effects) Regulations, SI 1988/1199, reg. 4.
9 See also **R v Secretary of State for the Home Department ex parte Jeyeanthan; Ravichandran v Secretary of State for the Home Department** (1999).

tion required by statute. If there had been proper consultation a different decision might have been reached. Accordingly the decision was unlawful.

When an individual is charged with an indictable offence[10] an indictment is drafted which contains a list of the charges that are being brought against the accused. The defendant then pleads either guilty or not guilty to that indictment. The jury can only try one indictment at a time. Once this indictment has been prepared it must be signed by an officer of the Crown Court in accordance with section 2(1) of the Administration of Justice (Miscellaneous Provisions) Act 1933. If there is no signature, any conviction flowing from the indictment will be nullified. In **R v Clarke and McDaid** (2008) the question for the House of Lords was whether the absence of a signed indictment at the outset of proceedings and during most of the trial had the legal effect of invalidating those proceedings. The Court also considered if that invalidity had been cured by the late signature of the indictment. The Court decided the proceedings were invalid and the convictions should be quashed.

However, despite the House of Lords' robust defence of the need for strict compliance with procedures in relation to criminal trials, the decision in **Clarke and McDaid** was in effect nullified by section 116 of the Coroners and Justice Act 2009.

Breach of Natural Justice

The rules of natural justice are common law rules – although, in many instances, their requirements may be made statutory. The fundamental dictate of justice is that those affected by decision makers should be dealt with in a fair manner. In order for this to be achieved, there may be several requirements which must be fulfilled. As Lord Lane CJ stated in **R v Commission for Racial Equality ex parte Cottrell and Rothon** (1980):[11]

> As has frequently been said, and there is no harm in repeating it, all that the rules of natural justice mean is that the proceedings must be conducted in a way which is fair … fair in all the circumstances.

That the rules of natural justice are not rigid and determinate is emphasised by Lord Bridge in **Lloyd v McMahon** (1987):

> the so-called rules of natural justice are not engraved on tablets of stone. To use the phrase which better expresses the underlying concept, what the requirements of fairness demand when any body, domestic, administrative or judicial, has to make a decision which will affect the rights of individuals depends on the character of the decision making body, the kind of question it has to make and the statutory or other framework in which it operates.

The principles of fairness have not been given either universal or consistent interpretations, nor should they be for – as judicially recognised – the requirements of fairness will vary according to the circumstances of the case. For example, in **McInnes v Onslow Fane** (1978), Megarry VC stated:

> the further the situation is away from anything that resembles a judicial or quasi-judicial decision, and the further the question is removed from what may reasonably be called a justiciable question, the more appropriate it is to reject an

---

10 Historically referred to as a serious arrestable offence.
11 At p. 1586.

expression which includes the word justice and to use instead terms such as 'fairness' or the 'duty to act fairly'. [page 1530]

In **Council of Civil Service Unions v Minister for the Civil Service** (1985), the House of Lords once again turned to the apparent differences in the concepts, Lord Roskill seemingly rejecting the phrase 'natural justice' in favour of the duty to 'act fairly'. Lord Roskill asserted that:

> The phrase [natural justice] might now be allowed to find a permanent resting place and be better replaced by speaking of a duty to act fairly. But the latter phrase must not in its turn be misunderstood or misused. It is not for the courts to determine whether a particular policy or particular decisions taken in fulfilment of that policy are fair. They are only concerned with the manner in which those decisions have been taken and the extent of the duty to act fairly will vary greatly from case to case as indeed the decided cases since 1950 consistently show. [page 414]

The principle of fairness can be clearly seen in the case of **Re HK (An Infant)** (1967), wherein it was held that, whilst immigration officers were not obliged to hold a hearing before deciding an immigrant's status, they were nevertheless under an obligation to act fairly. The duty to give a hearing will be higher if a 'legitimate expectation' has been created in the mind of the complainant by the public body concerned.[12] Legitimate expectations are discussed below at pages 739 to 743.

Fairness was at issue in **R (L) v West London Mental Health NHS Trust** (2014) a case concerning a patient with serious mental health problems who was detained under the Mental Health Act 1983. The managers of a medium-security hospital wanted to transfer the patient to a high-security hospital. Before he was transferred the patient sought judicial review on the basis that the procedure before the decision-making panel had been unfair. He had not been given the gist of the reasons for his transfer, or been allowed to see documents concerning his case or allowed to make representations to the panel. The Court of Appeal ruled that the common law duty of procedural fairness required that the patient be given the gist of the facts on which they relied and allowed to make written representations to the panel. In **R (Detention Action) v First-tier Tribunal (Immigration and Asylum Chamber)** (2015) the Court of Appeal ruled that the Fast Track Rules 2014 which governed asylum appeals was unlawful on the basis that they lacked justice and fairness. The Rules were intended to strike a balance between the need for administrative speed and efficiency and fairness and justice to the appellant. However, the time limits for preparing for an appeal were so tight that it was impossible for appeals to be given a fair hearing. Accordingly the Rules were *ultra vires* and unlawful.

Policies, consultation and publication

Administrative decision making is based upon policy, and every individual has the right to have his or her case considered according to the policy adopted by the decision maker – provided that the policy is lawful on public law grounds. The existence of policies gives rise to a number of considerations. Must there be consultation before a policy is adopted? And how widely must an administrative body consult? Must a policy be published? These

---

12 The courts are also concerned to ensure that government proposals which will affect individual citizens are fairly presented in order to enable objectors to address the issue in question. In **R v Secretary of State for Transport ex parte Richmond upon Thames London Borough Council (No 4)** (1994), the Court of Appeal ruled that the government's proposals to restrict night flights at Heathrow, Gatwick and Stansted had been fairly set out in consultation documents. On this issue see further Chapter 18. See also **R v National Lottery Commission ex parte Camelot Group plc** (2001).

questions may be answered by statute: and failure to comply with statutory requirements – as discussed above at pages 719 to 721 – may render decisions unlawful. As discussed in Chapter 24, the failure of a public body to comply with a published policy may also lead to illegality.

A key case on the requirements of publication is **R (Lumba) v Secretary of State for the Home Department** (2011). The two claimants, who were foreign nationals, had committed serious offences and served prison sentences. The Home Secretary notified them that they were to be deported. The Home Office's published policy stated that there was a presumption in favour of release pending deportation. In 2006, however, the Home Office adopted a policy, which remained unpublished, which amounted to a near blanket ban on release. The Supreme Court ruled that an unpublished policy, which conflicted with previously published policy, rendered their detention unlawful. It was immaterial that they could have been detained lawfully pending deportation. As Lord Dyson JSC explained:

> The individual has a basic public law right to have his or her case considered under whatever policy the executive sees fit to adopt provided that the adopted policy is a lawful exercise of the discretion conferred by the statute ... There is a correlative right to know what that currently existing policy is, so that the individual can make relevant representations in relation to it (at paragraph 35).

> The precise extent of how much detail of a policy is required to be disclosed was the subject of some debate between us. It is not practicable to attempt an exhaustive definition ... What must, however, be published is that which a person who is affected by the operation of the policy needs to know in order to make informed and meaningful representations to the decision-maker before a decision is made (at paragraph 38).

There is no common law duty to consult those who will be affected by the operation of policy (although statute will often stipulate the extent to which consultation must take place). However, common law does require consultation in circumstances in which a legitimate expectation (on which see below) may arise. Furthermore, as Lord Wilson JSSC stated in **R (Moseley) v Haringey LBC** (2014) (at paragraph 35, quoting Stephen Sedley QC (as he then was)) the common law requires that:

(1) consultation must be at a time when proposals are still at a formative stage;
(2) the proposer must give sufficient reasons for any proposal to permit of intelligent consideration and response;
(3) adequate time must be given for consideration and response; and
(4) the product of consultation must be conscientiously taken into account in finalising any statutory proposals.

Fairness, and the publication of policy, was central to the decision in **R (Bloomsbury Institute) v The Office for Students** (2020). The Bloomsbury Institute is a private educational establishment founded in 2002. Bloomsbury catered for students from disadvantaged backgrounds, and most were enrolled on four-year courses which included a foundation year (for those without A-level qualifications) prior to starting a degree programme. As an 'Alternative Provider' the Institute did not receive direct grants from the funding councils and needed to be 'designated' in order that students could access student loans. In 2018 Bloomsbury applied for designation. The Office for Students (OfS) issued an 'intention to refuse registration letter' and in January 2019 issued its provisional decision to refuse registration, that decision being confirmed in May 2019. The OfS did not consider that Bloomsbury had performed sufficiently well on two of its 'performance indicators': namely, the continuation rate from year one to year two and the progression rate to professional qualifications or post-graduate study.

The OfS was required, by statute,[13] to publish a 'regulatory framework' consisting of a statement as to how it performed its functions and guidance to higher education providers on the registration conditions. In addition to this, the OfS produced a confidential Decision Making Guidance (DMG) document for use by assessors setting out the way in which assessors would evaluate educational providers. While the Regulatory Framework was published, the DMG had not been published at the time Bloomsbury was refused registration, nor had there been any consultation prior to it being adopted. Neither the Regulatory Framework nor the DMG made it clear that no special allowance was made for courses involving a foundation year, an essential feature of Bloomsbury's courses. Not having been consulted, and the DMG being unpublished, Bloomsbury had no opportunity to make representations. The process was procedurally unfair: the DMG embodied an important policy decision and the OfS was under a duty to consult and to publish. The registration decision was quashed.

The Rule against Bias: *Nemo Iudex in Causa Sua*[14]

The requirements of fairness are reflected in Article 6 of the European Convention on Human Rights, enforceable in the domestic courts under the Human Rights Act 1998. Article 6 requires a 'fair and public hearing within a reasonable time by an independent and impartial tribunal established by law'.

The essence of justice lies in a fair hearing. The rule against bias is strict: it is not necessary to show that actual bias existed, the merest appearance or possibility of bias will suffice: 'justice should not only be done but should manifestly and undoubtedly be seen to be done'. The suspicion of bias must, however, be a reasonable one. Either financial or personal interest in a case may disqualify a person from adjudicating.

Financial bias

A financial interest in the outcome of a case will automatically disqualify a judge from hearing a case. In **Dr Bonham's Case** (1609), Lord Coke held that members of a board which determined the level of physicians' fines could not both impose and receive the fines, thus giving early judicial expression for the requirement of freedom from bias. An early expression of the absolute requirement not only to be impartial in fact, but also to be demonstrably and clearly free from the merest suspicion of bias, is found in **Dimes v Grand Junction Canal Ltd** (1852). In **Dimes**, Lord Cottenham LC held shares in the canal company involved in litigation. The House of Lords set aside the decision in which he had adjudicated despite the fact that:

> No one can suppose that Lord Cottenham could be in the remotest degree influenced by the interest ... It is of the last importance that the maxim that no man is to be judge in his own cause should be held sacred.

---

13 Under the Higher Education and Research Act 2017.
14 On the independence of the judiciary see Chapter 4.

Thus, the mere existence of a financial interest, even where it does not, in fact, result in actual bias but may present the appearance of bias, will be sufficient to disqualify a judge from adjudication.

In **R v Sussex Justices ex parte McCarthy** (1924), the applicant had been charged with dangerous driving and convicted. On discovering that the clerk to the magistrates' court was a solicitor who had represented the person suing McCarthy for damages, McCarthy applied for judicial review based on bias on the part of the clerk. The clerk had retired with the magistrates when they were considering their verdict. It was accepted that the magistrates neither sought advice nor were given advice by the clerk during their retirement. Nevertheless, McCarthy's conviction was invalidated on the basis of the possibility of bias.[15]

The question of financial bias again arose in **Metropolitan Properties Co v Lannon** (1969), where an application was lodged by a property company in order to challenge a decision of a rent assessment committee on the basis that Lannon, a member of the committee had, in his professional capacity as a solicitor, given advice to tenants of a close business associate of the property company. Lord Denning MR ruled that, while there was no actual bias:

> the court looks at the impression which would be given to other people. Even if he was as impartial as could be, nevertheless, if right minded persons would think that, in the circumstances, there was a real likelihood of bias on his part, then he should not sit. And, if he does sit, his decision cannot stand ...

> The court will not inquire whether he did, in fact, favour one side unfairly. Suffice it that reasonable people might think he did. The reason is plain enough. Justice must be rooted in confidence: and confidence is destroyed when right minded people go away thinking: 'The judge was biased'. [page 599]

A financial interest in a case which does not go beyond the financial interest of any citizen does not disqualify judges from sitting. Thus, for example, in **Bromley London Borough Council v Greater London Council** (1983), the fact that all the judges in the Court of Appeal were themselves both taxpayers and users of public transport in London did not disqualify them from hearing the case. The same position prevails in the United States of America[16] but there the issue of the financial interests of federal judges is expressly covered by statute. The Ethics in Government Act 1978 requires that Supreme Court and Federal judges must make a public declaration of 'income, gifts, shares, liabilities and transactions in securities and real estate'.[17]

Other bias

Judges — as with any other person — may exhibit bias by virtue of race, sex, politics, background, association and opinions.[18] When adjudicating, however, they must be demonstrably impartial. This impartiality involves: 'the judge, listening to each side with equal attention, and coming to a decision on the argument, irrespective of his personal view about the litigants' and, further, a requirement that: 'Whatever his personal beliefs, the judge should seek to give effect to the common values of the community, rather than any sectional system of values to which he may adhere'.[19]

---

15 See also **Virdi v Law Society** (2010).
16 28 USC S455(b).
17 See Cranston, 1979.
18 See Griffith, 1997; Devlin, 1978.
19 Bell, 1983, pp. 4 and 8.

Where a judge feels that he has a bias against one of the parties to litigation he may disqualify himself from sitting on the case, as did Lord Denning MR in **Ex parte Church of Scientology of California** (1978). There, counsel for the Church requested that he disqualify himself as a result of eight previous cases involving the Church on which he had sat. In **R v Bow Street Metropolitan and Stipendiary Magistrate ex parte Pinochet Ugarte** (1999), extradition proceedings against the former Chilean Head of State were challenged on the basis that one of the Law Lords, Lord Hoffmann, had links with Amnesty International, the charitable pressure group which works on behalf of political prisoners around the world, which had been allowed to present evidence to the court. It was accepted that there was no actual bias on the part of Lord Hoffmann, but there were concerns that the public perception might be that a senior judge was biased. As a result, the proceedings were abandoned and re-heard by a new bench of seven judges.

The Court of Appeal has jurisdiction to re-open proceedings if it is clearly established that a significant injustice has probably occurred and that there is no alternative effective remedy. Before exercising such a power, the court considers the effect of re-opening the appeal on others and the extent to which the complaining party is the author of his own misfortune. Where a remedy lies in an appeal to the House of Lords, the Court of Appeal will only give permission to re-open an appeal if it is satisfied that leave to appeal to the House of Lords will not be given.[20]

There has been uncertainty and inconsistency in the interpretation of 'bias'. In **R v Gough** (1993), opposing counsel presented two different tests for bias. The first suggested criterion was whether a reasonable and fair-minded person sitting in the court and knowing all the relevant facts would have had a reasonable suspicion that a fair trial of the defendant was not possible – the 'reasonable suspicion' test. The second suggested test was whether there was a real likelihood of bias. The question to be asked is whether there was a 'real danger' that a trial may not have been fair as a result of bias – the 'real likelihood' test.[21] The House of Lords declared that the correct test was whether there was a real likelihood, in the sense of a real possibility, of bias on the part of a justice or member of a tribunal. The **Gough** test must now be considered in light of **Porter v Magill** (2002, discussed below), which provides the definitive test.

The Court of Appeal reconsidered judicial bias in the **Locabail (UK) Ltd v Bayfield Properties Ltd** (2000) cases. The court distinguished the two rules relating to disqualification, the first being where the judge had an interest in a case which he decided, as in **Dimes v Grand Junction Canal** (1852), and where he would be automatically disqualified. The second rule was that based on examination of all the relevant circumstances, where there was a real danger or possibility of bias, as in **R v Gough** (1993). In relation to the circumstances surrounding **Timmins v Gormley**, one of the **Locabail** cases, which concerned the publication, by the Recorder who adjudicated in a personal injury case, of articles which were allegedly biased in favour of claimants and against insurers, the court ruled that, taking a broad common-sense approach, a lay observer with knowledge of the facts could not have excluded the possibility that the Recorder was biased. While it was not inappropriate for a judge to publish in his area of expertise, and that such contributions could further rather than hinder the administration of justice, nevertheless, it was always inappropriate for a judge to use intemperate language about subjects on which he had adjudicated or would have to adjudicate. The appeal was allowed and a retrial ordered.[22]

---

20 See **Taylor v Lawrence** (2002).
21 At p. 727; see also **R v Spencer** (1987).
22 See also **R v Local Commissioner for Administration ex parte Liverpool City Council** (1999).

In **Porter v Magill** (2002) the Leader of Westminster Council had allegedly adopted a policy of selling certain properties to tenants who would then be disposed to vote Conservative in a forthcoming election. The issue of bias arose through the role of the district auditor, Magill. There were allegations that the auditor had acted as investigator, prosecutor and judge. Moreover, it was alleged that he had prejudged the issue. The common law rule against bias came under fresh scrutiny. Uncertainty had arisen due to a divergence between the English and Scottish courts, the fact that some Commonwealth jurisdictions did not follow the **Gough** test, and that the test also diverged from the approach used by the Court of Human Rights in Strasbourg. Lord Hope stated that the question of bias should be phrased in the following manner: 'The question is whether the fair-minded and informed observer, having considered the facts, would conclude that there was a real possibility that the tribunal was biased'.[23,24]

The House of Lords considered the issue of bias in **Gillies v Secretary of State for Work and Pensions** (2006). A Disability Appeal Tribunal consists of a legally qualified chairman and two other members, including a medical member. The medical member of the tribunal in question was a doctor who for a number of years had been providing reports for the Benefits Agency as an examining medical practitioner. The appellant, whose application for renewal of a disability living allowance had been refused, argued that there was a reasonable apprehension that the medical member had been biased. Referring to **Porter v Magill** (2002) the House of Lords ruled that a fair-minded observer would have had no reason to suppose that the doctor would not act impartially towards the claimant. Her experience in the preparation of reports was an asset and the bringing of experience to bear when examining evidence and reaching a decision had nothing to do with bias.[25] However, in **Smith v Kvaerner Cementation Foundations Ltd** (2006)[26] the Court of Appeal, following **Metropolitan Properties v Lannon**, ruled that a litigant had the right not to have his case adjudicated by a judge who knew one of the witnesses. The applicant's counsel had advised that the judge was unlikely to be biased. The Court ruled that such advice should not have been given as it influenced the applicant's decision. The decision would be set aside.

Where there is a 'significant public interest' in an issue, funding may be required. This issue was explored in **R (Main) v Minister for Legal Aid** (2007). M's mother and sister had been killed in a rail accident. The coroner considered that legal aid funding was necessary to assist M on the grounds that rail safety issues were of significant public interest. The Minister for Legal Aid refused funding, despite a recommendation from the Legal Services Commission that it be granted. The decision was held to be **Wednesbury** unreasonable: the Minister should have given reasons for departing from the Commission's recommendations and had failed to take into account the potential benefit of representation for a party representing the travelling public.

In **R v Abdroikov** (2007) the House of Lords considered whether the possibility of bias was apparent where an employed Crown prosecutor were to sit as a juror in a prosecution which was brought by his own Crown prosecution authority. They decided in the majority that a fair-minded and reasonable observer would not have seen the possibility of bias in this case. This problem was considered again in **R v Khan (Bakish Alla)** (2008) where this time the composition of the jury included a serving police officer. It was decided that such issues should be dealt with prior to trial and the presence of a police officer on a jury would not automatically render a conviction unsafe.

23 See also **Secretary of State for Work and Pensions v Cunningham** (2004); **AWG Group Ltd v Morrison** (2006).
24 The test in **Porter v Magill** was applied in **Resolution Chemicals Ltd v H Lundbeck A/S** (2013).
25 See also **Ansar v Lloyds TSB Bank** (2006); **R (Paul) v Deputy Coroner of Queen's Household** (2007); **Helow v Advocate General for Scotland** (2007).
26 See also **AWG Group v Morrison** (2006).

In **El Faragy v El Faragy** (2007) a judge was asked to recuse himself (stand down) from a trial when it transpired that during a pre-trial review hearing he had made discriminatory racial comments about the second respondent. The Court held that he should have withdrawn from the case due to the real possibility of bias.[27]

The issue of decisions being made with a 'closed mind' was considered in **R (Lewis) v Redcar and Cleveland BC** (2008). The case concerned the granting of a planning application. It was claimed that the members of the planning committee made their decisions with political rather than legal issues in mind. It was held that as members of the planning committee were not exercising a judicial or quasi-judicial function they could consider matters of policy when making their decisions.

The issue of presumed bias was considered in **Helow v Advocate General for Scotland** (2008). In this case the judge in an immigration case (concerning a Palestinian petitioner) was a member of a Jewish association whose members, via their publications, expressed extreme views against Palestinian causes. The House of Lords took the view that the judge's membership did not itself imply that the judge shared or endorsed the views of the association. If the judge had expressed support for these extreme views then she would not have been eligible to hear the case, but she did not.

The Right to a Fair Hearing: *Audi Alteram Partem*

See also Chapter 18.

It is a fundamental requirement of justice that, when a person's interests are affected by a judicial or administrative decision, he or she has the opportunity both to know and to understand any allegations made, and to make representations to the decision maker to meet the allegations. As noted above, the right to fair trial is protected under Article 6 of the European Convention on Human Rights. The case law of the Court of Human Rights and the domestic courts is discussed in Chapter 18. By way of example, a fair determination of a case may involve one or more of the following:

(a)   the right to be given notification of a hearing;
(b)   the right to be given indications of any adverse evidence;
(c)   the right to be given an opportunity to respond to the evidence;
(d)   the right to an oral hearing;[28]
(e)   the right to legal representation at a hearing;
(f)   the right to question witnesses.

An early expression of the requirement of a hearing is to be found in **Cooper v Wandsworth Board of Works** (1893). There, Cooper had – without giving notice to the Board, as required by law – started to erect a house. The Board had the power to demolish buildings built without the requisite permission, and exercised its power so to do. Cooper applied for – and recovered – damages from the Board for trespass to his property. Byles J held that the plaintiff should have been given a hearing before the Board exercised its powers, even though there was no express statutory requirement that it do so: 'although there are no positive words in a

---

27 See also **JSC BTA Bank v Mukhtar Ablyazov** (2012).
28 This is closely linked to the right to be heard as in **R (Wright) v Secretary of State for Health** (2007) and **R (O'Connell) v Parole Board** (2007).

statute requiring that the party shall be heard, yet the justice of the common law shall supply the omission of the legislature'.[29]

Ridge v Baldwin (1964) represents a classic case which reveals judicial insistence on procedural fairness.[30] Ridge, the Chief Constable of Brighton, had been suspended from duty following charges of conspiracy to obstruct the course of justice. Despite Ridge having been cleared of any allegations against him, the judge made comments which were critical of Ridge's conduct. Subsequently, Ridge was dismissed from the force.[31] Ridge was not invited to attend the meeting at which the decision to dismiss him was reached, although he was later given an opportunity to appear before the committee which confirmed its earlier decision. Ridge appealed to the Home Secretary,[32] who dismissed his appeal. Ridge then sought a declaration that the dismissal was *ultra vires*, on the basis that the committee had violated the rules of natural justice. The following extract is taken from Lord Reid's judgment, in which the opportunity was taken to review the doctrine.

> The principle of *audi alteram partem* goes back many centuries in our law and appears in a multitude of judgments of judges of the highest authority. In modern times opinions have sometimes been expressed to the effect that natural justice is so vague as to be almost meaningless ... It appears to me that one reason why the authorities on natural justice have been found difficult to reconcile is that insufficient attention has been paid to the great difference between various kinds of cases in which it has been sought to apply the principle. What a minister ought to do in considering objections to a scheme may be very different from what a watch committee ought to do in considering whether to dismiss a chief constable. [page 64]

> I would think that the authority was wholly in favour of the appellant, but the respondent's argument was mainly based on what has been said in a number of fairly recent cases dealing with different subject matter. Those cases deal with the decisions of ministers, officials and bodies of various kinds which adversely affected property rights or privileges of persons who had no opportunity or no proper opportunity of presenting their cases before the decisions were given. [page 68]

There were echoes of **Ridge v Baldwin** in **R (Shoesmith) v OFSTED** (2011). The Director of a local authority's Children's Services was dismissed following the death of a child on the protection register. The Secretary of State made a direction appointing a new Director. The council dismissed Ms Shoesmith. No opportunity had been given to make representations. The Secretary of State's decision was unlawful, as was the dismissal which had been based on the Secretary of State's directions.

The right to a hearing founded a challenge in **Re Pergamon Press Ltd** (1971),[33] in which the directors of two companies refused to answer questions unless given a judicial-style hearing. The court ruled, however, that, although the inspectors appointed to investigate the

---

29 See **Steeple v Derbyshire County Council** (1984); but cf. **R v Amber Valley District Council ex parte Jackson** (1984). See also **R v Hendon Rural District Council ex parte Chorley** (1933).

30 See, on this point, **R v Hillingdon Borough Council ex parte Royco Homes Ltd** (1974); **R v Commission for Racial Equality ex parte Cottrell and Rothon** (1980).

31 Under the Municipal Corporations Act 1882, s. 191(4), which provides that a constable may be dismissed on the basis of either negligence in the discharge of his duty or being 'otherwise unfit' for duty.

32 Under the Police (Appeals) Act 1927.

33 See also **Maxwell v Department of Trade** (1974).

companies were under a duty to act fairly, this must be weighed against the interests of good administration.

Impartiality was scrutinised by the European Court of Human Rights in **Kingsley v United Kingdom** (2001). The Court ruled that the applicant's right to fair trial, guaranteed by Article 6, had been violated. The applicant had been refused a certificate to hold a management position in the gaming industry by the Gaming Board of Great Britain. He sought judicial review, alleging bias on the part of a supervisory board. The Court examined the composition of the panel which decided that the applicant was not a fit and proper person to hold a certificate, and concluded that it did not present the necessary appearance of impartiality to amount to an independent and impartial tribunal. However, the Court went on to assert that even where an adjudicatory body did not comply with the requirements of Article 6, there would be no breach of the Article if the proceedings were subject to 'subsequent control by a judicial body that had full jurisdiction and did provide the guarantees of Article 6(1)'. The Court of Appeal accepted that the applicant had an arguable case, and that there was a real risk of bias, but had concluded that the decision had to stand, since the decision could only be made by the board and could not be delegated to an independent tribunal. The Court of Human Rights ruled that where a complaint was made about a lack of impartiality, the concept of full jurisdiction required that the 'reviewing court not only considered the complaint but had the ability to quash the impugned decision and to remit the case for a new decision by an impartial body'. In the present case, the domestic courts were unable to remit the case to an impartial tribunal; neither the High Court nor the Court of Appeal had 'full jurisdiction' within the meaning of Article 6 and there was a violation of the Convention.

However, the Court of Appeal in **R (Beeson) v Dorset County Council** (2003) affirmed the view that the availability of judicial review satisfied the requirements of Article 6 of the European Convention on Human Rights regarding an independent and impartial tribunal. Even where the first instance decision maker lacked the necessary element of impartiality (here the tribunal had two members who were local councillors in a dispute over the now-deceased's entitlements regarding residential care and the value of his property), the availability of judicial review would remedy that defect 'unless there was some special feature of the case to show the contrary'. In the instant case there was no special feature and there was no evidence that the panel had not arrived at a fair and reasonable recommendation.

The Supreme Court examined the circumstances in which a prisoner was entitled to an oral hearing before the Parole Board in **R (Osborn) v Parole Board; R (Booth) v Same, In re Reilly** (2013). While recognising that there could be no exhaustive definition of when an oral hearing should be granted, the Court held that an oral hearing was required 'whenever fairness to the prisoner requires such a hearing in the light of the facts of the case and the importance of what is at stake'. This very broad test of fairness requires public bodies to consider each case on its facts to establish the appropriate form of hearing. In **Osborn** the Supreme Court also made important observations about the relationship between common law, statute and the European Convention on Human Rights. This aspect of the case is discussed in Chapter 18.

The right to make representations

Inevitably, the extent to which the individual is enabled to make representations to a decision-making body will be inextricably linked to the question of the right to a hearing. Where there exists no right to an oral hearing, the question becomes one of the extent to which – and means by which – the view of the individual can be put to the decision-making authority. It may well be the case that the opportunity to make written submissions will satisfy the requirements for justice and fairness. For example, in **Lloyd v McMahon** (1987), local government councillors were in breach of their statutory duty to set the level of local rates. When the district auditor came to determine the issue, the applicants claimed the right to an oral hearing, and that the absence of such a hearing amounted to a breach of the rules of natural justice and was, accordingly, *ultra vires*. The court disagreed, holding that, since the auditor had given notice of the case against them and had considered written representations from them, he had acted fairly and, accordingly, lawfully.

The requirements of fairness mean that where a body was exercising penal powers which involved the imposition of a penalty which was more severe than would normally be expected, it had to give the person affected the opportunity of making representations on the issue. The High Court so held in **R (Gutta) v General Medical Council** (2001). The Medical Council had found Dr Gutta guilty of serious professional misconduct and resolved to have her name erased from the register and that her suspension should take effect immediately, rather than after an appeal had been heard, as was normal. The Council was under a duty to give notice of its intention to make such an order, give the opportunity to make representations and give adequate reasons for reaching its conclusion.[34]

The right to question the 'other side'

It is not invariably the case that, where there is to be an oral hearing, it should be conducted according to the strict rules which would apply in a court of law. Accordingly, it should not be assumed that a party will be entitled to cross-examine the 'other side'. However, in **Errington v Wilson** (1995), it was made clear that Justices of the Peace must observe the rules of natural justice and, in particular, allow cross-examination under certain circumstances. A food authority had seized batches of cheese which it believed to be contaminated with *Listeria monocytogenes*. The authority then sought a destruction order from the justice of the peace. The magistrate refused to allow cross-examination of witnesses called by the authority. The court held that, given the nature of the proceedings, the magistrate was required to allow cross-examination if the proceedings were to be fair; and that, given the difference of opinion between experts on crucial points, Errington had been denied natural justice.

The admissibility of evidence and attendance of witnesses

In **R v Board of Visitors of Hull Prison ex parte St Germain (No 2)** (1979), prisoners who had been involved in a prison riot were charged with breaches of the Prison Rules. In the course of the hearing, hearsay evidence was given to the court on behalf of a number of officers who were unable to attend the hearing. The decision of guilt on the charges was challenged by judicial review proceedings, on the basis that the Board of Visitors had breached the rules of natural justice. Lane LJ, while not ruling that hearsay evidence could never be admissible, nevertheless ruled that, in the particular circumstance of the case, the Board should have ruled the hearsay evidence inadmissible. The decision of the Board was quashed by order of *certiorari*. Similar issues were under scrutiny in **R v Commissioner for Racial Equality ex parte Cottrell and Rothon** (1980). The Commissioner had received a complaint of unlawful discrimination by Messrs Cottrell and Rothon, a firm of estate agents. The company had been given the opportunity to make representations – both written and oral – to the commissioners. No witnesses were available at the hearing. Nevertheless, the Commission issued a non-discrimination notice. The company sought to have the decision quashed, relying in part on **R v Board of Visitors of Hull Prison ex parte St Germain (No 2)** (1979). Noting the absence of any statutory requirement to provide an opportunity to cross-examine witnesses in the course of

---

34 See also **R (D) v Bromley LBC** (2007).

a hearing, and distinguishing between the facts of **St Germain**, the Court of Appeal ruled that there was no breach in the rules relating to fairness.

In **R v Panel on Takeovers and Mergers ex parte Guinness plc** (1990), the Takeover Panel refused to grant an adjournment of the inquisitorial proceedings in order to allow witnesses to attend. The court expressed anxiety about this refusal, but declined to hold that the Panel had acted unlawfully.

A different conclusion was reached in **R v Army Board of the Defence Council ex parte Anderson** (1991). The applicant for judicial review had made allegations of racial discrimination[35] which resulted in him taking absence without leave. Members of the Board considered his allegation of discrimination on the basis of circulated papers, and did not meet for the purpose of reaching its decision. The complainant had requested, but been refused, an oral hearing, and had also requested, but been refused, the disclosure of documents relating to his case. The Board decided that whilst there was some *prima facie* evidence of discrimination, it was insufficient to warrant either an apology or an award of compensation. Anderson sought judicial review of the Army Board's decision. Counsel for the Board reverted to the distinction between administrative and judicial functions. Taylor LJ, in the course of ruling that such a distinction was unnecessary, held that, should the distinction have been a necessary one, he would characterise the role of the Army Board, in connection with the complaint, as judicial rather than administrative. Applying the principles established in **Lloyd v McMahon** (1987), Taylor LJ ruled that four principles applied to the standard of fairness required in a hearing such as that of the Board:

(1) There must be a proper hearing of the complaint in the sense that the board must consider ... all the relevant evidence and contentions before reaching its conclusion. This means, in my view, that the members of the Board must meet ...

(2) The hearing does not necessarily have to be an oral hearing in all cases ... Provided that they [the board] achieve the degree of fairness appropriate to their task it is for them to decide how they will proceed and there is no rule that fairness always requires an oral hearing ... What it [the board] cannot do ... is to have an inflexible policy not to hold oral hearings. The board fettered its discretion and failed to consider the requirements for an oral hearing in the present case on its own merits.

(3) The opportunity to have the evidence tested by cross-examination is again within the Army Board's discretion. The decision whether to allow it will usually be inseparable from the decision whether to have an oral hearing. The object of the latter will usually be to enable witnesses to be tested in cross-examination, although it would be possible to have an oral hearing simply to hear submissions.

(4) Whether oral or not, there must be what amounts to a hearing of any complaint under the 1976 Act. This means that the Army Board must have such a complaint investigated, consider all the material gathered in the investigation, give the complainant an opportunity to respond to it and consider his response.

On the duty of disclosure of documents, Taylor LJ ruled that:

Because of the nature of the Army Board's function pursuant to the 1976 Act ... I consider that a soldier complainant under that Act should be shown all the material seen by the board, apart from any documents for which public interest immunity can properly be claimed.

---

35 Race Relations Act 1976, s. 58(5).

The decision of the board was quashed.

The rights of prisoners have also been scrutinised in relation to the requirement that they have sufficient information in order to challenge a Home Secretary's decision as to their detention or release. Under the Criminal Justice Act 1991, the Home Secretary has a statutory duty to release, on the direction of the Parole Board, discretionary life prisoners after they have served a 'tariff period' (section 34). The period to be served is considered by the trial judge. In **R v Secretary of State for the Home Department ex parte Doody** (1993), the House of Lords ruled that the prisoner was entitled to know the length of the tariff period recommended by the trial judge, and other relevant factors, in order that he may make written representation to the Home Secretary concerning the date fixed for consideration by the Parole Board of his sentence.[36] The failure to respect the entitlement to know the period recommended in order to make written submissions led to the Home Secretary's decision being quashed.[37,38]

See Chapter 10 on public interest immunity.

The availability of legal representation

Whether or not legal representation is available as of right will also depend upon the nature of the hearing and the nature of the rights affected. There is no general right to legal representation and, in some cases, it may prove to be either unnecessary or counterproductive to the proceedings and, accordingly, the courts have been unwilling to concede a general right to representation.[39] Where the proceedings are before a tribunal, the right to be represented is at the discretion of the tribunal. The general principle, according to the Royal Commission on Legal Services, is that 'it is desirable that every applicant before any tribunal should be able to present his case in person or to obtain representation'.[40]

Whereas legal representation is rarely denied before tribunals,[41] such representation is inextricably linked to the financial means of the applicant or to the availability of Legal Aid (now referred to as Legal Help). It may be more appropriate, in many instances, for applicants to be represented by non-lawyers. A range of organisations offer representation. The Citizens Advice Bureaux, trade unions, social workers, specialist agencies,[42] the Free Representation Unit, friends or relatives may all be allowed to appear before tribunals. The essential criterion for representation is that the tribunal should not adopt a rigid policy, but rather should exercise a genuine discretion in relation to the availability of representation.[43]

In **Martin v Greater Glasgow Primary Care NHS Trust** (2009) the issue of legal representation was raised once more.[44] In this case the claimant argued that she had not had legal representation whilst the hospital trust, as respondent, had representation. The Court decided that in these circumstances the presence or not of legal representation would have made very little difference to the outcome of the case and the test continued to be whether the presentation of the case was unduly affected by the absence of legal representation.

---

36 Where the trial judge does not make a recommendation, the Home Secretary may certify the length of the period of sentence which must be served: Criminal Justice Act 1991, Sched. 12, para. 9. See **R v Home Department ex parte McCartney** (1993).

37 See also **R v Secretary of State for the Environment ex parte Slot** (1997); **R v Secretary of State for the Home Department ex parte McAvoy** (1998).

38 On the difficulties relating to evidence and representation entailed in terrorist trials see Chapter 22.

39 See, inter alia, **R v Secretary of State for the Home Department ex parte Tarrant** (1985); **R v Board of Visitors of HM Prison, The Maze ex parte Hone** (1988).

40 *Report of the Royal Commission*, 1979, Vol. I, para. 15.11, p. 169.

41 Proceedings before the Family Practitioner Committee is an exception; National Health Service (Service Committees and Tribunal) Regulations, SI 1974/455, reg. 7.

42 For example, the Child Poverty Action Group; the United Kingdom Immigration Advisory Service.

43 Per Lord Denning MR in **Pett v Greyhound Racing Association (No 2)** (1970).

44 Also see **R (Bhatt Murphy) v Independent Assessor** (2008).

In **Kulkarni v Milton Keynes Hospital NHS Trust** (2009) a hospital doctor who was subject to hospital disciplinary proceedings was denied legal representation as the published guidance on disciplinary proceedings did not permit it. The published guidance had been modified to indicate that legal representation was possible. However, it was held that he could require legal representation but that it could not be instructed independently and instead had to be nominated by his Union. The Court indicated that given the gravity of the proceedings Article 6 of the European Convention on Human Rights would have been engaged if this point had been raised before the court.

In **R(G) v X School Governors** (2009) a teaching assistant in a school had allegedly kissed a 15-year-old boy on work experience. No criminal charges were brought but following an internal investigation and a disciplinary hearing the teaching assistant (G) was dismissed on the basis of an abuse of trust. The governors reported their decision to the relevant authorities and the name of the teaching assistant was placed on a statutory register that prevented him from being allowed to work with children in the future. G applied for a judicial review of the decision by the governors on the basis they had decided not to allow him legal representation at the original disciplinary hearing or the appeal hearing. He claimed this violated his Article 6 rights. The Court of Appeal ruled that, given the severity of the case, G's right to a fair hearing under Article 6 included the right to legal representation.

The Duty to Give Reasons

In 1971 Lord Denning MR stated that the giving of reasons is 'one of the fundamentals of good administration'.[45] The rationale for the duty to give reasons lies in the fact that unless a decision maker provides adequate information as to the basis on which a decision has been reached, an individual is unable to understand a decision and has inadequate information to challenge the decision on appeal. However, while statutes may lay down the duty to give reasons, at common law there has in the past been doubt as to the nature and extent of the requirement.[46]

A decision-making body is under a 'general duty' to give reasons, and any departure from the requirement to give reasons will require sound justification. Where an authority fails to give reasons for a decision which is challenged subsequently by judicial review proceedings, the failure to give reasons may cause the court to consider that there were no good reasons whatsoever for the decision. Lord Keith expressed it thus:

> if all other known facts and circumstances appear to point overwhelmingly in favour of a different decision, the decision maker who has given no reasons cannot complain if the court draws the inference that he has no rational reason for his decision.[47]

The courts had developed a number of exceptions to the general rule that no reasons need be given at common law. The courts may hold, for example, that a failure to give reasons will prejudice an applicant's chances of successfully applying for judicial review,[48] or that a failure to give reasons amounts to arbitrariness,[49] or that legitimate expectations have been created

---

45 **Breen v AEU** (1971), p. 191.
46 Under the Tribunals and Inquiries Act 1992, there exists a statutory duty to give reasons, on request, where decisions are reached by tribunals, public inquiries or under specific statutes.
47 **R v Trade Secretary ex parte Lonrho plc** (1989), p. 620. See Bradley, 1986; and Herberg, 1991.
48 As in the **Doody** case (1993).
49 See **Padfield v Minister of Agriculture, Fisheries and Food** (1968).

which demand that any departure from that expectation be explained or, more sweepingly, that in the interests of fairness, reasons must be given.

In **R v Civil Service Appeal Board ex parte Cunningham** (1991), for example, the Court of Appeal, while again stating that there was no general duty to give reasons, held that the Civil Service Appeal Board – which determined the applicant's compensation for unfair dismissal – was under a duty to give reasons, for its powers were analogous to the judicial powers of an industrial tribunal. Fairness demanded that the Board give reasons, in the same manner as required for tribunals.[50]

The duty to give reasons was central to the House of Lords' decision in **R v Secretary of State for the Home Department ex parte Doody** (1993). As seen above, in **Doody**, the applicants, who were serving mandatory life sentences, sought information as to the basis on which the decision concerning the period for their mandatory detention had been reached. The House of Lords laid down two justifications for the requirement that information be given. First, if reasons were not given to the applicants, the possibility of them successfully applying for judicial review would be frustrated. Second, a failure to give reasons adversely affected the concept of fairness. Lord Mustill, while acknowledging that there remained no general duty to give reasons, stated that a duty would be implied under certain circumstances. Where, as in **Doody**, the applicant did not know the reasons for a decision, it was impossible to make any effective representations in support of his case. Without the knowledge of any case against him, the applicant was denied the very information which would found the basis of making representations in support of his case. The Home Secretary was, accordingly, under a duty to provide reasons both on the basis that the giving of reasons was a prerequisite to an application for judicial review, and on the basis of requirements of fairness.

In **R v Ministry of Defence ex parte Murray** (1998), the Divisional Court ruled that, although there was no general overriding principle of law which required decision makers to give reasons for their decisions, the duty of fairness required that reasons be given, where demanded by the circumstances of the case. The applicant had been convicted by court martial of wounding. The court martial reached its conclusion and passed sentence without giving reasons. The applicant's conduct, which was 'entirely out of character', and to which he pleaded guilty, was caused by ingestion of an anti-malarial drug. Where there was no explicit duty of fairness in statute, the courts would require that reasons be given where fairness demanded it. In this case, the applicant, his regiment and his family were entitled to reasons.

In **R v Criminal Injuries Compensation Authority ex parte Leatherland** (2000), the High Court ruled that the Criminal Injuries Compensation Authority was obliged as a matter of procedural fairness to provide proper reasons, together with at least the gist of any supporting evidence, for its decisions to reduce or refuse claims for compensation. A practice of withholding such material until the day of any appeal hearing was bad administration and unfair.

However, not all bodies will be under a duty to give reasons on the basis of fairness. In **R v Universities Funding Council ex parte Institute of Dental Surgery** (1994), for example, the Divisional Court ruled that the Higher Education Funding Council was not under a duty to give reasons as to why an academic institution was given a downgraded research grading which resulted in a loss to the Institute of research funds. Such matters were, in the court's opinion, matters of academic judgment, and a duty to give reasons for a decision could not, in this case, be founded on the requirements of fairness alone.[51]

---

50 See also **R v Parole Board ex parte Wilson** (1992); **Selvanathan v General Medical Council** (2001); **Baird v Thurrock Borough Council** (2005).
51 See also **R v University College London ex parte Idriss** (1999), in which it was held that it was 'very doubtful' whether a university's refusal to admit an applicant for entry to a course was susceptible to judicial review and that there was no duty to give reasons either at common law or under the university's own statutes.

Sedley J stated that there were two classes of case emerging. The first class was exemplified in the **Doody** case, where the nature of the process requires, in the interests of fairness, reasons to be given. The second class is illustrated by **Ex parte Cunningham** (1991), in which the majority of the court held that there was something peculiar to the case which required reasons to be given in the interests of fairness. In the **Institute of Dental Surgery** case, provided the decision was based purely on academic judgment, and did not involve any irrelevant or improper factors being taken into account, the decision would not be impugned on the basis that reasons had not been given for the decision. TRS Allan is critical of the decision. In his view, 'if the requirement of reasons, where it exists, reflects the demands of fairness and reasonableness, its denial in the present case must cause one to doubt whether the Institute was treated either fairly or reasonably' (1994, page 210).

The duty of the Crown Prosecution Service to give reasons for its decisions was considered by the Divisional Court in **R v Director of Public Prosecutions ex parte Manning** (2000). The applicant's brother had died of asphyxia while being restrained by prison officers whilst on remand in prison. At a coroner's inquest, the jury returned a verdict of unlawful killing. However, the Crown Prosecution Service concluded that, while there was a *prima facie* case against a prison officer, there was no realistic prospect of a successful prosecution. The applicant then requested the reasons for the Crown Prosecution Service's decision, but was refused. He then sought judicial review. It was held that while there was no absolute obligation on the Service to give reasons for a decision not to prosecute, a violent death in custody gave rise to great concern. Further, since a jury had returned a verdict of unlawful killing implicating an identifiable person, there was an expectation of a plausible explanation for the decision and of solid grounds to support the decision.

In **R v Secretary of State for the Home Department ex parte Al Fayed** (1997), the Court of Appeal ruled that the Home Secretary had a duty to indicate to the applicant the area(s) of concern on which he was basing his refusal to grant naturalisation in order that the applicant may have an opportunity to allay the Home Secretary's concerns. The Home Secretary's decision was quashed. In **R v Secretary of State for the Home Department ex parte Moon** (1995), the court ruled that the Secretary of State's refusal to explain his reasons for concluding that the entry of the Reverend Sun Myung Moon would not be conducive to the public good was unfair and contrary to the rules of natural justice. In **Stefan v General Medical Council** (1999), the health committee of the General Medical Council had suspended the applicant indefinitely because of her medical condition. No reasons were given. The court stated that the common law rule against a general duty to give reasons was changing and might have to be reconsidered in light of the Human Rights Act 1998. Although there was no general duty to give reasons, nevertheless, in light of the nature of the appeal and the importance for the practitioner, they ought to have done so.[52]

The duty of a judge to give reasons was upheld by the Court of Appeal in **Flannery v Halifax Estate Agencies Ltd** (2000).[53] In this case, the sole ground for allowing the appeal was that the judge had failed to give adequate reasons for his decision. Henry LJ explained the general duty to give reasons as follows:

(1) The duty is a function of due process, and therefore of justice. Its rationale has two principal aspects. The first is that fairness surely requires that the parties especially the losing party should be left in no doubt why they have won or lost. This is especially so since without reasons the losing party will not know whether the court has misdirected itself, and thus whether he may have an

---

52 See *Practice Direction* (1999).
53 See also **R (I) v Independent Appeal Panel for G** (2005).

available appeal on the substance of the case. The second is that a requirement to give reasons concentrates the mind; if it is fulfilled, the resulting decision is much more likely to be soundly based on the evidence than if it is not.

(2) The first of these aspects implies that want of reasons may be a good self-
standing ground of appeal. Where because no reasons are given it is impossible to tell whether the judge has gone wrong on the law or the facts, the losing
party would be altogether deprived of his chance of an appeal unless the court
entertains an appeal based on the lack of reasons itself.

(3) The extent of the duty, or rather the reach of what is required to fulfil it,
depends on the subject matter. Where there is a straightforward factual dispute whose resolution depends simply on which witness is telling the truth
about events which he claims to recall, it is likely to be enough for the judge
(having no doubt summarised the evidence) to indicate simply that he believes
X rather than Y; indeed there may be nothing else to say. But where the dispute
involves something in the nature of an intellectual exchange, with reasons and
analysis advanced on either side, the judge must enter into the issues can-
vassed before him and explain why he prefers one case over the other. This is
likely to apply particularly in litigation where as here there is disputed expert
evidence, but it is not necessarily limited to such cases.

(4) This is not to suggest that there is one rule for cases concerning the witnesses' truthfulness or recall of event, and another for cases where the issue
depends on reasoning or analysis (with experts or otherwise). The rule is the
same; the judge must explain why he has reached his decision. The question
is always, what is required of the judge to do so; and that will differ from case
to case. Transparency should be the watchword.

In **South Buckinghamshire District Council v Porter (No 2)** (2004) the House of Lords gave guidance
concerning the adequacy of reasons given in planning decisions. Summarising the law, Lord
Brown of Eaton-under-Heywood stated that:

The reasons for a decision must be intelligible and they must be adequate. They
must enable the reader to understand why the matter was decided as it was and
what conclusions were reached on the 'principal important controversial issues',
disclosing how any issue of law or fact was resolved. Reasons can be briefly stated,
the degree of particularity required depending entirely on the nature of the issues
falling for decision. The reasoning must not give rise to a substantial doubt as to
whether the decision-maker erred in law, for example by misunderstanding some
relevant policy or some other important matter or by failing to reach a rational
decision on relevant grounds ... A reasons challenge will only succeed if the party
aggrieved can satisfy the court that he has genuinely been substantially prejudiced
by the failure to provide an adequately reasoned decision.

The duty to give reasons was considered by the Court of Appeal in **Horada v Secretary of State
for Communities and Local Government** (2016). In this case the Secretary of State had departed
from a planning inspector's recommendation that a compulsory purchase order should be
refused. The appellants represented a number of traders. The inspector considered that the
rights of the traders were insufficiently protected by the agreement between the council
and the developer. The Court of Appeal stated that where the relevant Minister upheld a
planning inspector's recommendation, it was implicit that he or she adopted the reasoning of the inspector. Where, as here, the Minister took a different view it was essential that
he or she explained the reasons for the decision in terms which the affected citizen could

understand. The livelihoods of the traders were put at risk by the proposed development and the Minister had to give a proper and easy to understand explanation for rejecting the inspector's recommendation.[54]

The Supreme Court examined the duty to give reasons in **R (Lee-Hirons) v Secretary of State for Justice** (2016). The appellant suffered from mental disorders and had been convicted of arson and burglary. In light of his disorder he was detained in a secure hospital, from which he was released, subject to conditions, in 2012. Subsequently the Minister was asked to consider recalling the appellant on the basis that his mental health had deteriorated. This was the only reason given to the appellant. Fifteen days after his recall the appellant was provided orally with a full and adequate explanation for his recall, but not provided with a written explanation. The appellant claimed that this breached his common law right to reasons and violated Article 5 of the Convention. He alleged that the failure to give adequate reasons within three days, in line with Department of Health Guidelines, made his detention unlawful and/or gave rise to a declaration and damages. His appeal was dismissed. Although there was a breach of the Guidelines and the common law right to have the Department's policy properly applied, and a breach of Article 5(2) of the ECHR, the initial explanation for his recall satisfied the demands of the common law and Article 5. There was no link between the Minister's failure to give adequate reasons within three days and the legality of his detention. The appellant was not entitled to damages: no tort had been committed; he had suffered no financial loss and any distress he suffered was the result of the recall, not the failure to give reasons and was insufficiently grave to warrant an award of damages.

The giving of reasons, whether by courts or administrative bodies, assumes increased importance in light of the Human Rights Act 1998. Article 5 of the Convention (the right to liberty and security) expressly states that persons arrested shall be informed promptly, in a language which he or she understands, of the reasons for the arrest. Article 6 of the Convention protects the right to a fair trial in the determination of civil rights and obligations or of criminal charges. While the giving of reasons is not an explicit requirement in Article 6, it is implicit in facilitating the right of appeal.

The duty to give reasons was considered by the Court of Appeal in **Oakley v South Cambridgeshire District Council** (2017). An application had been made for the development of a football stadium on Green Belt land (land which is subject to special controls and subject to a National Policy Framework). The Council's senior Planning Officer made a detailed report in 2014 recommending that the application be rejected and permission refused. The Council's Planning Committee rejected the recommendation and gave approval in principle, subject to certain conditions being met. Planning permission was granted in April 2015, without giving reasons.

There had been a statutory duty to give reasons for all planning decisions between 2003 and 2013. This had been removed for planning approvals. However, that did not mean that there was no common law duty to give reasons.

Elias LJ accepted that there was no 'general obligation to give reasons at common law', as confirmed in the *ex parte Doody* case (1994). However, he also accepted that 'the tendency increasingly is to require them rather than not'. It was his conclusion that:

> it may be more accurate to say that the common law is moving to the position whilst there is no universal obligation to give reasons in all circumstances, *in general they should be given unless there is a proper justification for not doing so.* [emphasis added]

---

54 See also **R (Jedwell) v Denbighshire County Council** (2016).

The decision in **Oakley** was considered and the dictum of Elias LJ approved by the Supreme Court in **Dover District Council v CPRE Kent** (2017). Lord Carnwath stated that although planning law is largely a 'creature of statute', the proper interpretation of the statute was 'underpinned by general principles, properly referred to as derived from the common law'. Lord Carnwath addressed the criticism that there was some uncertainty in when the common law duty to give reasons arose. However, he stated that it would be wrong to be over-prescriptive and considered that it should not be difficult for councils and their officers to identify cases which called for a formulated statement of reasons, beyond the statutory requirements.

The Concept of Legitimate Expectations

A legitimate expectation will arise in the mind of the complainant wherever he or she has been led to understand – by the words or actions of the decision maker – that certain procedures will be followed in reaching a decision. The complainant may have been led to believe, for example, that there would be an oral hearing, or that he would be able to make formal representations. Where such expectations have been created, the decision maker is not free simply to ignore the procedures which have been indicated. Two considerations apply to legitimate expectations. The first is where an individual or group has been led to believe that a certain procedure will apply. The second is where an individual or group relies upon a policy or guidelines which have previously governed an area of executive action.

The principle of the protection of legitimate expectations was recognised under English law in the 1970s in **R v Liverpool Corporation ex parte Liverpool Taxi Fleet Operators' Association** (1972) (discussed below),[55] and it is one of the major principles of European Community law.[56] The concept is one which has given rise to judicial disagreement. The central difficulty with legitimate expectation is whether an individual affected by an administrative decision has a legitimate expectation that the correct procedure will be followed, or whether the expectation to be protected can also be substantive. The debate as to whether legitimate expectations are confined to procedure and do not extend to substance was considered in **R v Ministry of Agriculture ex parte Hamble Fisheries** (1995) in which Sedley J stated that the applicants had a legitimate expectation on the basis of the Ministry's previous policy and accepted that substantive as well as procedure legitimate expectations could be protected. Conversely in **R v Secretary of State for the Home Department ex parte Hargreaves** (1996), in the Court of Appeal Hirst LJ rejected Sedley J's approach and stated that in relation to matters of substance the test was that of **Wednesbury** unreasonableness – not legitimate expectation.

The Court of Appeal ruled in **R (Bibi) v Newham LBC** (2001) that a local authority which made promises which gave rise to legitimate expectations that the applicants would be provided with accommodation with security of tenure had to be honoured to the extent that the expectation was taken into account when allocating the applicants' position on the housing list. The applicants were refugees and accepted by the authority as homeless. The authority wrongly thought that it was under a duty to provide accommodation with security of tenure. However, the promise that such accommodation would be provided founded a legitimate expectation which had to be considered.[57]

However, while the concept of legitimate expectation has, according to the Court of Appeal, achieved an important place in developing the law of administrative fairness, whether such an expectation has been raised is dependent upon the circumstances in which

---

55 See also **Council for Civil Service Unions v Minister for Civil Service** (1984).
56 See Usher, 2005.
57 See also **Henry Boot Homes Ltd v Bassetlaw DC** (2002).

statements are made, and whether in an instant case they could be taken as propounding a policy or merely statements applicable to particular cases. In **R v Secretary for the Home Department ex parte Behluli** (1998), the Home Secretary had ordered the removal of the applicant to Italy under section 2 of the Asylum and Immigration Act 1996. The applicant argued that he had a legitimate expectation that his case would be dealt with in accordance with the Dublin Convention.[58] The Court of Appeal ruled, however, that the statements relied on by the applicant fell short of the requirements necessary to establish to the requisite degree of clarity and certainty that the Secretary of State would deal with all applications for asylum in accordance with the Convention and not in accordance with the Asylum and Immigration Act 1996 and rules made thereunder.

Legitimate expectations were again considered by the Court of Appeal in **R (Nadarajah) v Secretary of State for the Home Department, R (Abdi) v Same** (2005). Lord Justice Laws stated that the theme running through the legitimate expectation cases was that:

> where a public authority had issued a promise or adopted a practice which represented how it proposed to act in a given area, the law would require the promise or practice to be honoured unless there was good reason not to do so.

The principle underlying that requirement was one of good administration, which was a legal standard, which although not articulated in the Convention on Human Rights nevertheless took its place alongside such rights as the right to fair trial and no punishment without law. The principle of good administration would be undermined 'if the law did not insist that any failure or refusal to comply was objectively justified as a proportionate measure in the circumstances'. Moreover, that approach made 'no distinction between procedural and substantive expectations'.[59]

In **R (X) v Head Teacher and Governors of Y School** (2007) a claim was made for judicial review when a pupil was not allowed to wear the niqab (a form of Muslim dress). Her elder sisters had been allowed to wear the niqab when being taught by a male teacher but this policy had recently been changed. It was held there was no claim based on legitimate expectation as the school was entitled to make changes to its uniform policy.

In **R (Bapio Action Ltd) v Secretary of State for the Home Department** (2008) there had been a change in the rules for those wishing to get medical training in the United Kingdom and return to their own country. New guidance stated that offers of places (training posts) should only be made to international medical graduates if there were no suitable home candidates. It was deemed to be unlawful as it was not made in accordance with the Immigration Act 1971 and because it undermined legitimate expectations generated by Immigration Rules and the Home Office.[60]

The giving of assurances

In **Attorney General for Hong Kong v Ng Yuen Shiu** (1983), the applicant had been an illegal immigrant for some years. He was eventually detained and an order was made for his deportation. The Director of Immigration had given a public undertaking that illegal immigrants such as Ng Yuen Shiu would not be deported without first being interviewed. The assurance was also given that 'each case would be treated on its merits'. Lord Fraser of Tullybelton in the Privy

---

58 Relating to the removal of persons to safe third countries.
59 See also **R (Greenpeace Ltd) v Secretary of State for Trade and Industry** (2007); **R (Bapio Action Ltd) v Secretary of State for the Home Department** (2008).
60 And see discussion of **R (Bancoult) v Secretary of State for Foreign and Commonwealth Affairs** (2008) as discussed in Chapter 5.

Council ruled that there was no general right in an alien to have a hearing in accordance with the rules of natural justice. Nevertheless, a 'legitimate expectation' had been created in the mind of the immigrant and, accordingly, breach of the requirement of fairness justified the order for his removal from Hong Kong to be quashed.[61] A public body cannot give undertakings which conflict with its statutory duty. In **R v Inland Revenue Commissioners ex parte Preston** (1985),[62] the House of Lords ruled that if it should do so, it was in principle entitled to go back on its undertaking. However, if the authority made an assurance and then exercised its statutory power in a manner which caused unfairness, that exercise could be viewed as an abuse of power and the undertaking upheld by the courts.

Fairness may involve the due consultation of interested parties before their rights are affected by decisions. For example, in **R v Liverpool Corporation ex parte Liverpool Taxi Fleet Operators Association** (1972), the corporation had given undertakings to the taxi drivers to the effect that their licences would not be revoked without prior consultation. When the corporation acted in breach of this undertaking, the court ruled that it had a duty to comply with its commitment to consultation.[63]

The Court of Appeal in **R v North and East Devon Health Authority ex parte Coughlan** (1999)[64] ruled that a decision by a health authority to close a home for the severely disabled at which the applicant resided, and to transfer her to the care of a local authority, was unlawful. The applicant had been assured by the predecessor to the health authority that the home was her home for life, thus creating a legitimate expectation which no public interest overrode. Furthermore, under Article 8 of the Convention on Human Rights, everyone had a right to respect for his home and the judge had been entitled to treat the case as one in which there would be an unjustifiable breach of Article 8. Lord Woolf MR explained the concept as follows:

> Where the court considers that a lawful promise or practice has induced a legitimate expectation of a *benefit which is substantive*, not simply procedural, authority now establishes that here too the court will in a proper case decide whether to frustrate the expectation is so unfair that to take a new and different course will amount to an abuse of power. Here, once the legitimacy of the expectation is established, the court will have the task of weighing the requirements of fairness against any overriding interest relied upon for the change in policy. [at paragraph 57]

The **Coughlan** decision has significant implications for judicial review. The Court of Appeal moved beyond the traditional test of procedural impropriety, thereby developing the law relating to legitimate expectations. The Court identified three differing situations which would give rise to differing approaches to review. The first related to a public body which had to consider previous policy or representations before changing that policy. Here, review on **Wednesbury** grounds was appropriate. The second class of case concerned the legitimate expectation of being consulted, in which case the court would look closely at the reasons

---

61 See also **R (Zegiri) v Secretary of State for the Home Department** relying on **R v Secretary of State for the Home Department ex parte Besnik Gashi** (1999).

62 See also **R v Inland Revenue Commissioners ex parte MFK Underwriting Agencies Ltd** (1990).

63 See also **R v Ministry of Defence ex parte Walker** (2000) in which the House of Lords ruled that a soldier injured in action in the former Yugoslavia was not entitled to compensation under the Criminal Injuries Compensation Scheme. A policy adopted in 1994 excluding compensation for death or injury resulting from war operations or military action in peacekeeping operations in Bosnia was not irrational. The applicant had been given no assurances and the only legitimate expectation he had was that the Ministry of Defence would apply the policy in force at the time of his injury.

64 See Craig and Schonberg, 2000; Roberts, 2001; Elliott, 2000; Hilson, 2002.

for the change of policy and whether that decision was fair. The third class of case is where a promise by a public body had brought about a 'substantive legitimate expectation' on the part of the applicant. Here the court's approach would be more intensive. Accordingly, there are two standards of review, one where the decision was irrational in the **Wednesbury** sense, and one on the basis of abuse of power, which was for the court to determine. Policy changes on the part of public authorities are not unusual or unlawful in the general case, nor should the courts, as the Court of Appeal recognised, jeopardise 'the important principle that the executive's policy making powers should not be trammelled'. Where, however, a substantive legitimate expectation has arisen – as in **Coughlan** – through the express promise made in precise terms, and was relied on by the applicant, the decision was unlawful.[65]

Coughlan was reconsidered by the Privy Council in **Paponette v Attorney General of Trinidad and Tobago** (2010). The applicants were members of an association who owned and operated public service vehicles. They were persuaded to move the site of their taxi stand on reliance on government assurances that, *inter alia*, they would not be under the control or management of the owners of the new site, and that the management of the site would, within six months, be transferred to the association. In breach of this undertaking the government introduced new regulations giving control over the site to the landowners. There was no doubt that the assurances had created a legitimate expectation of a substantive benefit. At issue was whether the government was entitled to frustrate the legitimate expectation. This it could only do if there was a sufficient public interest to override the legitimate expectation and in this case the government was unable to do so.

Acting in a manner so as to create an expectation

A public body may act in a manner which creates an expectation in the mind of a person or body. For example, in **R v Secretary of State for Health ex parte US Tobacco International Inc** (1992), the company had opened a factory in 1985, with a government grant, for the production of oral snuff. The government made the grant available notwithstanding its awareness of the health risks of the product. In 1988, however, the government – having received further advice from a committee – announced its intention to ban snuff. The company sought judicial review, relying on a legitimate expectation based on the government's action. The court ruled, however, that, even though the applicant had a legitimate expectation, that expectation could not override the public interest in banning a harmful substance.

The Court of Appeal also considered the concept of 'legitimate expectation' in **R (Patel) v General Medical Council** (2013). Under the Medical Act 1983 the General Medical Council (GMC) was responsible for registering and regulating doctors within the United Kingdom. The claimant had undertaken a long course of study at an overseas university. He had sought, and been given, assurances from the GMC that he would be entitled to registration on completion of all the clinical requirements. However, the GMC later changed its policy and refused to register the claimant. The Court of Appeal accepted that the GMC was entitled to change its policy. However, the claimant had been given 'a clear, unequivocal and unqualified assurance', and it was not now open to the GMC to refuse to recognise his qualification.

---

65 See cases post-**Coughlan**: R v Secretary of State for Education and Employment, ex parte Begbie (2000); Henry Boot Homes Ltd v Bassetlaw District Council (2003); Nadarajah v Secretary of State for the Home Department (2008); R (S) v Secretary of State for the Home Department (2007).

The existence of policies and/or guidance

In **R v Secretary of State for the Home Department ex parte Asif Mahmood Khan** (1984), the Home Office had published a circular stating the criteria to be used for determining whether a child could enter the United Kingdom. When the applicant sought to bring his nephew into the United Kingdom from Pakistan, entry was refused. In judicial review proceedings, it was established that the immigration rules did not specify any particular criteria, but that the Home Department's circular did so specify. It was also established that the criteria used in determining whether to allow the child into the country were different from that provided under the circular. The Home Secretary had acted *ultra vires*: he had created legitimate expectation and was not free to employ different criteria.[66]

A further challenge to the powers of the Home Secretary can be seen in **R v Secretary of State for the Home Department ex parte Ruddock** (1987). The Home Secretary had authorised the interception of telephone calls without statutory authority.[67] The basis on which the Home Secretary decided to intercept calls was provided in a circular. The applicant claimed that the Home Secretary had failed to follow the criteria laid down in the circular. The court held that the applicant had a legitimate expectation that the criteria would be followed but, nevertheless, the applicant lost the case because it was held that the Minister could have come to the judgment that the criteria were applied and that he was not acting unreasonably. The decision, which appears to weaken the binding nature of legitimate expectations, is explainable in light of the alleged national security aspects of the case. The applicant had been a leading member of the Campaign for Nuclear Disarmament, which the government feared was being influenced by the Communist Party.

A change made to a policy which had been embedded in an agreement between prison inmates and prison authorities was considered by the Court of Appeal in **R v Secretary of State for the Home Department ex parte Hargreaves** (1996). The agreement stated that prisoners could apply for home leave after serving one-third of their sentence, subject to good behaviour. The Secretary of State decided, however, that only prisoners who had served half their sentence could apply for home leave. Hargreaves and others unsuccessfully applied for judicial review. They subsequently appealed to the Court of Appeal.

The Court of Appeal held that the agreement between the prison inmates and the prison authorities did not give rise to a legitimate expectation which could be enforced by judicial review. Furthermore, the Home Secretary's decision to change the policy was not to be tested against the overall fairness of that decision, but rather whether the policy was unreasonable in the *Wednesbury* sense. On that test, the Home Secretary's decision was not unlawful. The Court of Appeal expressed regret, however, that the documents on which the prisoners relied were 'other than completely clear and unambiguous', and called for greater clarity in the future.

 SELF-TEST QUESTION

Explain the difference between procedural and substantive legitimate expectations, making reference to case law.

---

66 Cf. **Re Findlay** (1985), wherein the doctrine was limited merely to an expectation that prisoners would have their cases individually considered according to whatever policy the Minister chose to adopt.

67 The case was decided before the Interception of Communications Act 1985 was implemented.

Summary

Breach of natural justice, which includes an aspect of procedural impropriety, is an increasingly important concept in ensuring fairness in the administrative process. Originally a common law requirement, it is often, but not always, incorporated into statute. Natural justice covers a very broad range of issues including the right to a fair hearing, the rule against bias, legitimate expectations and the giving of reasons for decisions.

Further Reading

Ahmed, F and Perry, A, 'The coherence of the doctrine of legitimate expectations' (2014) 73 *Cambridge Law Journal* 61.

Bell, J, 'The doctrine of legitimate expectations: power-constraining or right-conferring legal standard?' [2016] *Public Law* 437.

Clark, D, 'Natural justice: substance or shadow' [1975] *Public Law* 27.

Craig, P, 'The common law, reasons and administrative justice' [1994] *Cambridge Law Journal* 282.

Elliott, M, 'Has the common law duty to give reasons come of age yet?' [2011] *Public Law* 56.

Forsyth, C, 'The provenance and protection of legitimate expectations' [1988] *Cambridge Law Journal* 238.

Ganz, G, 'Legitimate expectation: a confusion of concepts' in C Harlow (ed.), *Public Law and Politics*, 1986, London: Sweet & Maxwell.

Harris, BV, 'The continuing struggle with the nuanced obligation on judges to provide reasons for their decisions' (2016) 132 *LQR* 216.

Malleson, K, 'Judicial bias and disqualification in the Pinochet Case' [1999] *Public Law* 391.

Malleson, K, 'Judicial bias and disqualification after Pinochet (No 2)' [2000] *Modern Law Review* 119.

Mullan, D, 'Fairness: the new natural justice' [1975] *University of Toronto Law Journal* 280.

Murray, P, 'Escaping the wilderness: *R v Bolton* and judicial review for error of law' (2016) 75 *Cambridge Law Journal* 333.

Olowofoyeku, A, 'The *Nemo Judex* rule: the case against automatic disqualification' [2000] *Public Law* 456.

Williams, R, 'The multiple doctrines of legitimate expectations' (2016) 132 *Law Quarterly Review* 639.

Chapter 26

Tribunals and Inquiries

Chapter Contents

Learning Objectives

By the end of this chapter you should be able to:

- ☐ explain why tribunals were introduced;
- ☐ explain the differences between courts and tribunals;
- ☐ discuss the organisation of tribunals;
- ☐ explain proposed changes to the tribunal system;
- ☐ explain why statutory or non-statutory inquiries are established;
- ☐ explain the differences between non-statutory and statutory inquiries;
- ☐ discuss the main features of statutory inquiries and their advantages over non-statutory inquiries.

PART A: TRIBUNALS

Introduction

A tribunal, like a court of law, is a forum in which disputes are settled by an impartial adjudicator. A network, or system, of tribunals – each focusing on a particular area of law – forms part of the civil justice system and represents an important part of administrative law.

It was the twentieth-century expansion of the role of the state and the growth in government Departments – in relation to taxation, the provision of welfare benefits, the National Health Service, transport, planning and public housing, immigration and asylum – which explains the expansion of tribunals. Disputes between the individual and the day-to-day administration of government are inevitable, and mechanisms were needed to deal with such disputes. While access to courts of law is open, it is also costly, time-consuming and formal, with strict rules of procedure and evidence. What was needed was a less formal, but nevertheless specialist and authoritative forum to deal with the large volume of complaints and/or appeals against departmental decisions.[1] Historically tribunals were operated by the government Department which had undertaken the decision being challenged by the citizen. Government Ministers appointed tribunal members and the Department took responsibility for the administration of the process.

Tribunals not only span a wide range of specialist areas of law, but also differ in their degree of specialism and formality. Some, for example the Lands Tribunal,[2] operate in a formal manner, hardly distinguishable from a court of law. For the most part, however, tribunals are intended to offer a less formal atmosphere in which the issues can be resolved. These tribunals do not necessarily consist of lawyers although more recent developments have required tribunal chairmen/women to be legally qualified. Lay membership has long been a common feature of tribunals and where the subject matter requires it, specialists from other disciplines may be appointed.[3] The appointment and training of tribunal judiciary is undertaken by the Judicial Appointments Commission established under the Constitutional Reform Act 2005.

The earliest examples of tribunals can be said to date back to the early nineteenth century. These dealt with issues concerning income tax.[4] As the range of areas for adjudication by tribunals developed over the next century it became clear that reliance on tribunals was useful because of the advantages they posed over the normal court process. As government became more complex and the level of administration grew, tribunals could be used to dispense quick and effective justice outside the court system. With their *ad hoc* development, the number and types of tribunals expanded without being organised in any formalised system.

The common features of a tribunal (although not applicable to all) are that they:

- should be able to make final and legally enforceable decisions which are subject to review and appeal;
- should be independent of any Department of government;
- should hold oral hearings in public;
- should have sufficient expertise to deal with specialist matters;
- should be under a duty to give reasons for decisions taken.

---

1 See Genn, 1993.
2 Established under the Lands Tribunal Act 1949 to determine complex aspects of property law.
3 For example a medical doctor is required for a mental health review tribunal.
4 Richardson and Genn, 2007.

In addition an appeal on a point of law should be available to the courts of law and judicial review of tribunal decisions should be available.

Within the tribunal system administrative justice hearings outnumber the combined total of civil justice and criminal justice hearings and trials.[5] Over 400,000 claims a year go to tribunals, the majority of which will be to the First-tier Tribunal (Social Security and Child Support), the First-tier Tribunal (Employment) and the First-tier Tribunal (Immigration and Asylum).

The working of the tribunal system is changing, alongside changes to the court system.[6] The aim is to modernise the entire system with the aim of ensuring that it is just, proportionate and accessible. Central to this process is the use of technology. While the resolution of disputes has traditionally been in a physical courtroom before a judge, technology now enables large amounts of case preparation, adjudication and resolution to be completed online. The aim is for all cases to be started online. Some will be completed online, while others will be scheduled for physical hearings in a court or tribunal.

The Range of Tribunals

There are over 70 tribunals in England and Wales, although few of these hear more than 500 cases a year. All tribunals are established by statute under which their jurisdiction, membership and procedure are defined. Tribunals include Agriculture, Aviation, Data Protection, Education, Employment, Fair Trading, Financial Services, Foreign Compensation, Immigration, Land, Misuse of Drugs, National Health Service, Pensions, Property and Taxation. In addition to the above, the following sample illustrates the wide-ranging subject matter of tribunals.

The First-tier Tribunal (Social Security and Child Support)

As seen above, the most heavily used tribunal at the current time is the Social Security and Child Support Tribunal. This tribunal is responsible for the resolution of disputes concerning an assessment of the wide variety of social security benefits offered by the welfare state.[7] The objective of this tribunal is:

> To bring together the parties to the appeal, and the judiciary, with all appropriate resources for the fair and independent delivery of decisions. We will do this in a way that best meets the expectations of all parties to the appeal and the demands of the public purse. [Social Security and Child Support Tribunal, 2010]

The First-tier Tribunal (Mental Health)

In contrast the Mental Health Review Tribunal has less than ten per cent of the case load of the Social Security and Child Support Tribunal. This tribunal makes decisions, *inter alia*, on

---

5 Public Administration Select Committee Report, 2010–2012, Future Oversight of Administrative Justice.

6 See **Transforming our Justice System**, Ministry of Justice 2016.

7 At the present time it is responsible for resolving disputes concerning Job Seekers Allowance, Income Support, Incapacity Benefit, Employment Support Allowance, Disability Living Allowance, Attendance Allowance and Retirement Pensions. It is also responsible for dealing with disputes concerning Child Support, Tax Credits, Statutory Sick Pay, Statutory Maternity Pay, Compensation Recovery Scheme, Road Traffic (NHS) Charges, Vaccine Damage and decisions made concerning Housing Benefit and Council Tax allowance.

whether an individual detained under the Mental Health Act 1983[8] should be released from hospital supervision.

The Investigatory Powers Tribunal[9]

The Investigatory Powers Tribunal (IPT) is equally specialist, its jurisdiction being confined to the investigation of complaints against the security services (MI5, MI6 and GCHQ).[10] It was formed to ensure that the UK provided an effective domestic remedy as required by Article 13 of the European Convention on Human Rights.[11] The IPT replaced the Interception of Communications Tribunal, the Security Service Tribunal, the Intelligence Services Tribunal and the complaints provision under the Police Act 1997 relating to police interference with property. The tribunal has eight Members – all are experienced lawyers. The President and Vice-President are High Court judges. The tribunal only investigates complaints relating to interception, intrusive surveillance, entry on to or interference with property or wireless telegraphy, directed surveillance or the use of agents. The function of the tribunal is to consider whether conduct authorised under the Act has been properly authorised and carried out in accordance with appropriate guidelines. The IPT is the only tribunal to investigate complaints against the Security Services.

See also Chapter 21.

The IPT has unique characteristics distinguishing it from other courts and tribunals. It has adjudicative functions, but is primarily an investigatory body. It is able to order, receive and consider evidence; can protect the identity of complainants and give anonymity to witnesses. It may sit in open court, but given the nature of its jurisdiction, more often will not and there is limited information concerning hearings and findings. Under the Regulation of Investigatory Powers Act 2000, the only avenue for an appeal was to the European Court of Human Rights. The Investigatory Powers Act 2016 now provides for a right of appeal, subject to leave being given, to the Court of Appeal or the Court of Session in Scotland. Appeals may only be granted leave if there are compelling reasons to do so.[12]

Reforming the System

By the 1950s concerns had been raised over the lack of supervision of decisions made by tribunals. The Committee on Administrative Tribunals and Enquiries (the Franks Committee)[13] was set up to review the operation of tribunals. The Committee stated that: 'statutory tribunals are an integral part of the machinery of justice in the state and not merely administrative devices for disposing of claims and arguments conveniently'[14] and that tribunals should be: 'open, impartial and fair'.[15]

A series of recommendations followed which commented on the values that tribunals should share, their constitutional make-up and the procedure which should be devised and supervised by a newly created Council on Tribunals. There was no proposal for a unitary tribunals system. The Committee recommended that tribunal chairmen/women should usually be legally qualified. Chairpersons should be appointed by the Lord Chancellor and the Council of Tribunals should take responsibility for appointing other members. The Franks

---

8 As amended by the Mental Health Act 2007.
9 See also Chapter 21.
10 The tribunal was established under the Regulation of Investigatory Powers Act 2000, Pt IV.
11 In 2015 the IPT received over 250 complaints against the intelligence services.
12 Section 242 IPA 2016. See further Chapter 21.
13 Report of the Committee on Administrative Tribunals and Enquiries, Cmnd 218, 1957.
14 As discussed by Wade and Forsyth, 2004.
15 Report of the Committee on Administrative Tribunals and Enquiries, Cmnd 218, 1957, para. 42.

Committee also recommended changes to the procedure for setting up and supervising tribunals to be undertaken by the Council of Tribunals.

Many of the recommendations were implemented in the Tribunals and Inquiries Act 1958.[16] The Council of Tribunals[17] was established to provide an advisory and supervisory function over existing tribunals. The Committee accepted that it was necessary for tribunals to be connected to government Departments and executive decision making, but insisted that they should remain firmly committed to impartiality and independence.

By 2000 it had become clear that the practices of tribunals were still disparate and lacked cohesion. The Council of Tribunals had also been criticised. Initially it was thought that the Council would advise, supervise and champion the merits of tribunals but it became clear that it had failed to meet these expectations. As the Council was composed of part-time members they had insufficient time to devote to the envisaged activities of the Council. It also had no opportunity to evaluate its practices through research. As a result it was suggested that the Council of Tribunals' work was unable to provide effective supervision of the way that tribunals were operating.

The Legatt Report

A review of tribunals was commissioned by the Lord Chancellor in 2000,[18] chaired by Sir Andrew Legatt and reporting in 2001.[19] The Report, *Tribunals for Users: One System, One Service*, noted that:

> The present collection of tribunals has grown up in an almost entirely haphazard way. Individual tribunals were set up, and usually administered by departments, as they developed new statutory schemes and procedures. The result is a collection of tribunals, mostly administered by departments, with wide variations of practice and approach, and almost no coherence. The current arrangements seem to us to have been developed to meet the needs and convenience of the departments and other bodies which run tribunals, rather than the needs of the user.

There also existed a concern that although tribunals were serving a crucial function, their working practices were often old-fashioned and daunting to users. Information technology resources and training practices were criticised and as cases had become more complex the required levels of expertise had not been matched by the necessary level of training and support. The most important criticism made of tribunals was that they were not independent of the Departments that sponsored them. The Report therefore recommended that a system be put in place within a clearly organised Tribunal Service which was 'independent, coherent, professional, cost effective and user friendly'.[20]

The Legatt Report led to the White Paper, *Transforming Public Services: Complaints, Redress and Tribunals*.[21] The White Paper echoed many of the recommendations made by the Legatt Report but went further. It proposed that a newly created unified tribunals system would become a new type of organisation which was not simply a 'federation of existing tribunals'.[22] It would stimulate improved decision making and the leadership of this system would be expected to innovate and to re-engineer existing processes as a way of eradicating poor decision making.

---

16 See also the Tribunals and Inquiries Act 1992.
17 Having at least ten members and not more than 15.
18 There had already been a reorganisation of social security appeals after the Social Security Act 1998.
19 Report of the Review of Tribunals, 16 August 2001.
20 *Tribunals for Users: One System, One Service*, p. 16. For further discussion see Wade and Forsyth, 2004, p. 906.
21 Cm 624.
22 *Transforming Public Services: Complaints, Redress and Tribunals*, para. 6.1–4, also see www.justice.gov.uk/about/hmcts.

In addition the Council of Tribunals would be replaced by a new Administrative Justice Council which would not only have a supervisory role for tribunals but would also provide advisory services for the whole of the administrative justice sector.

The Tribunals, Courts and Enforcement Act 2007

The Tribunals, Courts and Enforcement Act 2007 brought some unity to tribunals which had thus far not existed.[23] The new Tribunals Service was created as an Executive Agency of the Ministry of Justice and was operated under the responsibility of the Secretary of State, who is accountable to Parliament. The Tribunal Service had responsibility for the management and allocation of tribunal resources. It shared resources with the existing Courts Service and was responsible for the administration of the system. The Tribunals Service and Courts Service are now combined as Her Majesty's Courts and Tribunals Service (HMCTS), on which see below.

Section 3 of the Tribunals, Courts and Enforcement Act 2007 created two new generic tribunals into which the existing tribunal jurisdictions were transferred. The first of these is the First-tier Tribunal and the second is the Upper Tribunal. The Upper Tribunal is an appellate tribunal from the First-tier Tribunal although it may have other functions.[24]

The Act establishes a series of 'chambers' to accommodate the wide-ranging subject matter dealt with by tribunals. The Upper Tribunals are made up of the Lands Chamber, Immigration and Asylum Chamber, Tax and Chancery Chamber and Administrative Appeals Chamber. First-tier Tribunals are organised under seven Chambers, each headed by a judge as president: the General Regulatory Chamber; the Social Entitlement Chamber; Health, Education and Social Care Chamber; War Pensions and Armed Forces Compensation Chamber; Tax Chamber; Immigration and Asylum Chamber and the Property Chamber. Employment tribunals are outside this structure.

Her Majesty's Courts and Tribunals Service (HMCTS)

HM Courts and Tribunals Service is responsible for the administration of the criminal, civil and family courts and tribunals in England and Wales, and non-devolved tribunals in Scotland and Northern Ireland. HMCTS was established in 2011 as an executive agency sponsored by the Ministry of Justice. HMCTS operates on the basis of a partnership between the Lord Chancellor and Lord Chief Justice, neither of whom are involved in the Service's administration. The overall leadership and direction of the Service lies with its Board, and responsibility for administration lies with the Chief Executive. The Service:

> provides the system of support, including infrastructure and resources, for the administration of the business of the courts in England and Wales and those tribunals throughout the United Kingdom for which the Lord Chancellor is responsible. The agency provides the support necessary to enable the judiciary, tribunal members and magistracy to exercise their judicial functions independently.[25]

The objectives of HMCTS are to:

● provide the supporting administration for a fair, efficient and accessible courts and tribunal system;

---

23 Endicott, 2009, p. 435.
24 Endicott, 2009, p. 463.
25 Lord Chancellor and Secretary of State for Justice, HM Courts and Tribunals Service Framework Document, Cm 8882, July 2014, para. 1.6.

- support the independent judiciary in the administration of justice;
- drive continuous improvement of performance and efficiency across all aspects of the administration of the courts and tribunals;
- collaborate effectively with other justice organisations and agencies, including the legal professions, to improve access to justice;
- work with government Departments and agencies, as appropriate, to improve the quality and timeliness of their decision making in order to reduce the number of cases coming before tribunals and courts.

The membership of the Board comprises an independent non-executive Chair, the Senior Presiding Judge for England and Wales and two further judicial representatives, the agency Chief Executive and three Executive Directors and three Non-executive Directors. HMCTS employs some 18,000 staff and the HMCTS estate consists of around 500 courts and tribunals buildings with approximately 3,000 courtrooms.

The administrative work of HMCTS is subject to the jurisdiction of the Parliamentary Commissioner for Administration (Ombudsman). The Chief Executive and the Permanent Secretary may be asked to appear before the Committee for Public Accounts. Invitation to appear before other parliamentary committees will be considered by the Chief Executive, in consultation with the Lord Chancellor and Lord Chief Justice as appropriate.

Reviewing administrative justice

The Administrative Justice and Tribunals Council (AJTC) replaced the Council on Tribunals and was a non-departmental public body until its abolition in 2013. The AJTC was designed to be a 'powerful ally in the reform programme, and an independent guardian of the objectives of the service'.[26] The AJTC was headed by a chairman, and had a membership of 14 acting on a part-time basis. The Parliamentary Commissioner for Administration was also a member of the Council.[27] The Council's role was to 'cover the whole process from initial decision until final resolution at whatever level'.[28] The AJTC had a statutory duty to:

- keep the overall administrative justice system[29] under review;
- keep under review the constitution and working of specified tribunals, including the First-tier and Upper Tribunals;
- keep under review the constitution and working of specified statutory inquiries.

The Coalition government formed in 2010 decided to abolish the AJTC as part of its cost-cutting programme. It was abolished by Order under the Public Bodies Act 2011, with effect from August 2013. The Ministry of Justice took the view that the AJTC was an advisory body whose functions were 'either no longer required' – because of the establishment of HMCTS – or, in terms of its policy functions, was something which could be 'more properly performed by the government itself'.[30]

Recognising the need to understand the user perspective in the administrative justice system, the government established the Administrative Justice Advisory Group in 2012. Following the abolition of the AJTC, this became the Administrative Justice Forum (AJF). The

---

26 Sir Robert Carnwath quoted in Harlow and Rawlings, 2009.
27 See ss 44 and 45 and Sched. 7 to the Tribunals, Courts and Enforcement Act 2007.
28 The Senior President of Tribunals' Annual Report, February 2010, para. 96.
29 Defined as 'the overall system by which decisions of an administrative or executive nature are made in relation to particular persons, including the procedures, the law, and systems for resolving disputes'. Ibid.
30 See Government Response to the Public Administration Select Committee Report on the Future Oversight of the Administrative Justice System, Cm 8354, 2012.

AJF is an independent body, the membership of which is drawn from bodies active in the administrative justice system, including organisations representing users. Its aims are:

- to gauge how the administrative justice and tribunals system is working, and identify any areas of concern or good practice, and
- to provide early, informal testing of policy initiatives.[31]

The Senior President and membership of Tribunals

Section 2 of the Tribunals, Courts and Enforcement Act 2007 creates the office of Senior President of Tribunals, appointed by the Crown on the recommendation of the Lord Chancellor following consultation with senior judges or the Judicial Appointments Commission.[32] The first Senior President was Sir Robert Carnwath who was subsequently appointed to the Supreme Court.[33] The Senior President holds office 'during good behaviour' and is removable from office subject only to an address to both Houses of Parliament. The Senior President reports to the Lord Chancellor, may make practice directions and has a duty to maintain arrangements for the welfare and training of tribunal members. The Senior President of Tribunals gives tribunal judges the representation they previously lacked, being under a statutory duty to represent the view of tribunal members to Parliament, the Lord Chancellor and Ministers of the Crown in general.[34] The Senior President is required to report annually to the Lord Chancellor in relation to tribunal cases.[35]

In carrying out his functions the Senior President is required to have regard to:

- the need for tribunals to be accessible;
- the need for proceedings before tribunals to be fair and to be handled quickly and efficiently;
- the need for members of tribunals to be experts in the subject matter of, or the law to be applied in, cases in which they decide matters; and
- the need to develop innovative methods of resolving disputes that are of a type that may be brought before tribunals.[36]

Tribunal members are now appointed by the Judicial Appointments Commission rather than the Lord Chancellor, and the appointments process has greater independence from the executive than previously. Under section 1 of the Tribunals, Courts and Enforcement Act 2007 there is a guarantee of continued judicial independence for all tribunal members, thereby emphasising the independence of tribunals from government Departments.

Judges and members who sat under the former system have been transferred into the new structure. For example specialist surveyor members of the Lands Tribunal have transferred into the Lands Chamber and continue to sit as previously. In addition judges of the High Court in England and Wales, and of the Court of Session in Scotland and of the High Court in Northern Ireland may also sit as full-time or part-time judges in the Upper Tribunal. First-tier judges require a legal qualification and five years' post-qualification experience,

---

31 Ministry of Justice, Annual Administrative Justice and Tribunals Performance Report, Cm 8873, 2013–2014 and see Ministry of Justice, Administrative Justice and Tribunals: A Strategic Work Programme 2013–2016.
32 Tribunals, Courts and Enforcement Act 2007, Sched. 1, Pts 1 and 2.
33 See Carnwath, 2009.
34 Tribunals, Courts and Enforcement Act 2007, Sched. 1, para. 14.
35 Section 43, Tribunals, Courts and Enforcement Act 2007.
36 Section 2(3), Tribunals, Courts and Enforcement Act 2007.

while Upper-tier judges must be legally qualified and have seven years' post-qualification experience.

Non-lawyer members are retained in the new tribunal structure. However, there is no purely lay category of members, but rather non-lawyer members are appointed and allocated to tribunals on the basis of their expertise. Judges have long felt that non-lawyer members are a crucial addition to any tribunal.[37] The role of non-legal members is to be kept under review to ensure that new members with the skills and experience necessary are appointed.[38]

Procedure

The Tribunals, Courts and Enforcement Act 2007 also revises the procedural rules for tribunals. Historically tribunals had their own procedural rules which were usually drafted by the Lord Chancellor or Secretary of State in consultation with the Council on Tribunals. The procedural rules concerned such matters as the right to know that an application to a tribunal is possible and the right to a hearing and the process that the hearing may adopt. Legal representation was possible and after the hearing some tribunals had to provide reasons for the decisions taken. Many of the rules were governed by the Tribunals and Inquiries Act 1992.

The 2007 Act creates the Tribunal Procedure Committee to make procedural rules for each Chamber. Procedure is now governed by section 22 of the Tribunals, Courts and Enforcement Act 2007 and secondary legislation with the view to providing a more consistent and coherent approach to the procedural rules operating in any given tribunal. There exists a statutory duty to ensure that these new arrangements are efficiently and effectively administered.[39]

The procedure rules for the First-tier General Regulatory Chamber, for example, provide that the tribunal (with stipulated exceptions) must hold a hearing, unless each party consents to the matter being determined without a hearing and the tribunal is satisfied that it can properly determine the issues without a hearing.[40] Each party is entitled to attend any hearing that is held and make written representations to the tribunal and to the other party prior to the hearing. The tribunal must give reasonable notice of the time and place of any hearing. All hearings must be held in public, unless the tribunal directs that it is to be held in private.[41]

Hearings and mediation

In addition to the usual hearings, the rules provide for judicial mediation – a form of alternative dispute resolution which attempts to reach a settlement of a dispute without going to court – thereby giving the parties a key role in reaching a settlement.[42] Where mediation has been agreed between the parties the judges in the First-tier Tribunal and Upper Tribunal will act as mediators. The Senior President's Annual Report states that where mediation is offered, the success rates are in excess of 65 per cent and that those parties who have experienced mediation 'have generally been positive about it'.

---

37 See Lord Hope in *Gillies v Work and Pension Secretary* (Scotland) (2006).
38 The Senior President's Annual Report recognises that it is difficult to recruit sufficient medical members. One factor in recruitment of non-legal members is the level of remuneration.
39 See s. 22(4) of the Tribunals, Courts and Enforcement Act 2007.
40 Oral hearings are important and it has been suggested that complainants are more likely to be successful when they appear before the Tribunal as they tend to be more articulate in person than on paper.
41 Tribunal Procedure (First-tier) (General Regulatory Chamber) Rules 2009, 2009 No. 1976 (L. 20).
42 Section 24, Tribunals, Courts and Enforcement Act 2007.

Legal representation

In relation to legal representation, the government White Paper favoured its reduction in tribunal hearings.[43] The practice in recent years has been for participants in tribunals to partake of legal representation where the issues were potentially complex or there was a need for skilled advocacy. Legal representation is generally permitted, but, with the exception of certain tribunals,[44] state-funded legal assistance is not available to meet the costs of representation. However, given that all public authorities (the definition of which includes courts and tribunals)[45] are required to comply with the Human Rights Act 1998, the right to representation – depending on the seriousness of the case – is an aspect of the right to fair trial which includes the right to a 'fair' hearing 'in the determination of his [or her] civil rights'.

Reasons

Tribunal practice has long supported the giving of reasons which are essential in order to enable the parties to understand the decision and also form the basis for any appeal which may be undertaken. The Procedure Rules regulating the General Regulatory Chamber, for example, provide that the tribunal may give a decision orally at a hearing and subject to limited exceptions must provide each party 'as soon as practicable' with a decision notice stating the tribunal's decision, the written reasons for the decision and notification of any right of appeal, time limits for appeal and the manner in which a right of appeal may be exercised.

Review and appeal

The new system offers a range of mechanisms for checking the decisions made by the tribunals.[46] These include:

- Self review: under sections 9 and 10 of the 2007 Act, both First-tier Tribunals and Upper Tribunals have the jurisdiction to review their own decisions. If the First-tier Tribunal does review and set its own decision aside then it can either re-decide the issue or refer it to the Upper Tribunal. If the Upper Tribunal decides to set aside its own decision then it has to re-decide that decision itself.
- A right of appeal: with limited exceptions[47] a right of appeal on a point of law from the First-tier Tribunal to the Upper Tribunal is permitted. If there has been an error of law then the Upper Tribunal may set aside the decision of the First-tier Tribunal, remit the case back to the First-tier Tribunal for decision or make its own decision on the case.[48]

An appeal on a point of law lies to the Court of Appeal. Leave (i.e. permission) to appeal is required. Section 13(6) of the Tribunals, Courts and Enforcement Act 2007 and Article 2 of the Appeals from the Upper Tribunal to the Court of Appeal Order 2008[49] provides that permission to appeal was not to be granted unless the Upper Tribunal or the Court of Appeal

See further
Chapters 23–25.

---

43 The White Paper, *Transforming Public Services: Complaints, Redress and Tribunals*, Secretary of State for Constitutional Affairs, Cm 6243, July 2004.
44 Employment Appeals Tribunals, Mental Health Tribunals, the Lands Tribunal and Revenue Commissioners.
45 See s. 6 Human Rights Act 1998 and Chapter 18.
46 See Craig, 2008, p. 266.
47 See s. 13(8) Tribunals, Courts and Enforcement Act 2007.
48 Under s. 13 the right of appeal can be exercised to the Court of Appeal from the Upper Tribunal if permission has been granted. There are time limits governing this process which can be found in the Civil Procedure Rules.
49 SI 2008 No. 2834.

consider that (a) a proposed appeal would raise some important point of principle or practice; or (b) there is some other compelling reason for the Court of Appeal to hear the appeal. The Court of Appeal may remit the case to the Upper Tribunal for reconsideration[50] or it can make the decision itself.

The power of judicial review lies with the High Court. Section 15 of the Tribunals, Courts and Enforcement Act 2007 also grants the power of judicial review to the Upper Tribunal (on this see **R (Cart) v Upper Tribunal** (2011), discussed below). Now able to grant mandatory, prohibition and quashing orders along with declarations and injunctions, the Upper Tribunal takes on many of the existing powers of the High Court. The Upper Tribunal applies the principles currently governing judicial review by the High Court which means that permission is required and a sufficient interest will need to be demonstrated before judicial review will be made available. The powers granted to the Upper Tribunal are subject to four conditions.[51] These are:

- that the relief sought can be obtained from the Upper Tribunal;
- that the activities of the Crown Court are not called into question;
- that the action falls within a specified class under section 18(6) Tribunals, Courts and Enforcement Act 2007;
- that a High Court or Court of Appeal judge in England, Wales and Northern Ireland or Court of Session in Scotland is presiding.

The Supreme Court considered the 2007 Act and judicial review in **R (Cart) v Upper Tribunal; R (MR (Pakistan)) v Same** (2011). At issue was the question of whether, and if so according to what criteria, judicial review was available of the decision of the Upper Tribunal (UT) to refuse permission to appeal to itself, a decision from which there is no statutory right of appeal. In the High Court, the judge held that refusal of permission to appeal by the Upper Tribunal was not amenable to judicial review. It was accepted by the Supreme Court that the Tribunals, Courts and Enforcement Act 2007 did not contain clear words ousting or excluding judicial review. However, it was also accepted that the 2007 Act established a 'new and in many ways enhanced tribunal structure which deserves a more restrained approach to judicial review than has previously been the case' (per Lord Phillips at paragraph 57). There was discussion of the rule of law and the need to ensure that decisions of tribunals were made according to law. Baroness Hale stated that the real question at issue in this case was 'what level of independent scrutiny outside the tribunal structure is required by the rule of law', and that in deciding that question there must be a 'principled but proportionate approach' (at paragraph 55).

Three approaches to the issue were considered. The first was the government's own approach, that judicial review should be available only in 'exceptional circumstances'. Set against this was the argument for unrestricted judicial review. Neither of these approaches was accepted by the Supreme Court. The exceptional circumstances criteria would be too stringent, while the unrestricted right to judicial review would ignore the standing of the Upper Tribunal as a superior court of record and create undue pressure on the system. Furthermore, according to Lord Dyson JSC, 'unrestricted judicial review of unappealable

---

50 Section 14, Tribunals, Courts and Enforcement Act 2007.
51 Section 18, Tribunals, Courts and Enforcement Act 2007.

decisions of the UT, is neither proportionate nor necessary for maintaining the rule of law' (at paragraph 122).

What was required were criteria which fell between these two approaches, and that adopted in relation to second appeals before the ordinary courts,[52] namely that (a) the proposed appeal would raise some important point of principle or practice; or (b) there is some other compelling reason for the relevant appellate court to hear the appeal.[53]

Summary

The changes to the organisation of tribunals since 2007 have been substantial in form. For the first time, there now exists a rational tribunal *system* as opposed to miscellaneous tribunals, established under statute as necessary, each with its own rules and procedures. The creation of the First-tier and Upper-tier Tribunals and Chambers within which various tribunals are organised creates a coherent structure. The arrangements for the appointment of legally qualified judges and lay members emphasises the judicial independence of tribunal members from the executive.

 Further Reading

Adler, M, 'Lay tribunal members and administrative justice' [1999] *Public Law* 616.

Adler, M, 'Tribunal reform: proportionate dispute resolution and the pursuit of administrative justice' (2006) 69 *MLR* 958.

Bradley, AW, 'The Council on Tribunals: time for a broader role?' [1991] *Public Law* 6.

Cane, P, *Administrative Tribunals and Adjudication*, 2009, Oxford: Hart Publishing.

Cane, P, 'Judicial review in the age of tribunals' [2009] *Public Law* 479.

Cane, P, *Administrative Law*, 5th edn, 2011, Oxford: Clarendon Press.

Carnwath, R, 'Tribunal justice: a new start' [2009] *Public Law* 48.

Craig, P, *Administrative Law*, 7th edn, 2012, London: Sweet & Maxwell.

Elliott, M, 'Has the common law duty to give reasons come of age yet?' [2011] *Public Law* 56.

Endicott, T, *Administrative Law*, 3rd edn, 2015, Oxford: Oxford University Press.

Foulkes, D, 'The Council on Tribunals: visits policy and practice' [1994] *Public Law* 564.

Genn, H, 'Tribunals and informal justice' (1993) 56 *Modern Law Review* 3.

Harlow, C and Rawlings, R, 'Tribunals in transition' in *Law and Administration*, 2009, Cambridge: Cambridge University Press.

Machin, D and Richardson, G, 'Judicial review and tribunal decision making: a study of the mental health review tribunal' [2000] *Public Law* 494.

Nason, S, 'Regionalisation of the Administrative Court and the tribunalisation of judicial review' [2009] *Public Law* 440.

Richardson, G and Genn, H, 'Tribunals in transition: resolution or adjudication?' [2007] *Public Law* 116.

Wade, W and Forsyth, C, *Administrative Law*, 11th edn, 2014, Oxford: Oxford University Press.

---

52 See s. 55(1) Access to Justice Act 1999 and s. 13(6) of the Tribunals, Courts and Enforcement Act 2007.

53 On compelling reasons, see **PR (Sri Lanka) v Secretary of State for the Home Department** (2012); **JD (Congo) v Secretary of State for the Home Department** (2012).

PART B: INQUIRIES

Introduction

Formal public inquiries are established to examine and report on a disaster or situation giving rise to public concern and are an important feature of government.[54] The role and function of public inquiries have been summarised by Lord Howe as follows:

- to establish the facts;
- to learn from events and thereby help prevent their recurrence;
- to provide an opportunity for reconciliation and resolution;
- to rebuild public confidence;
- to hold people and organisations to account;
- political considerations: the need to demonstrate that action has been taken or providing the impetus for change.[55]

Inquiries may be statutory (established under specific Acts of Parliament or under the Inquiries Act 2005) or non-statutory. The essential function of inquiries is fact-finding and the making of recommendations with a view to avoiding a recurrence of a situation, or establishing improved procedures which would apply in the event of a recurrence. Inquiries also contribute to transparency and accountability and to public confidence in a particular body. Inquiries do not establish civil or criminal liability (Inquiries Act 2005, section 2) or impose penalties or award compensation. They are therefore distinguishable from courts and tribunals. Since 1990 there have been over 40 public inquiries.[56] Inquiries in recent years include the following:

- Transport disasters such as the rail crash outside Paddington Station, London in 1999, the inquiry being chaired by the Rt Hon Lord Cullen PC; and the sinking of the Thames pleasure-boat *Marchioness*, also in 1999, the inquiry being chaired by Lord Justice Clarke.[57]
- Allegations of wrongdoing or injustices caused by the armed forces gave rise to two inquiries into the shooting of civilians on Bloody Sunday in Northern Ireland 1972. The first was established immediately after the shooting and chaired by Lord Widgery, who reported within three months. The second was established in 1998 under the 1921 Tribunals of Inquiry Act and chaired by Lord Saville of Newdigate. The inquiry finally reported in 2010.[58]
- The circumstances surrounding the racist murder of Stephen Lawrence led to an Inquiry which reported in 1999.[59]
- Failures in the national health system have given rise to several inquiries. The deaths of child patients at the Bristol Royal Infirmary were investigated,[60] and the removal of organs from deceased children without parental consent at the Royal Liverpool Children's Hospital was also subject to a formal inquiry.[61]

---

54 Inquiries are also established as part of the process of planning permission in respect of property or major developments. These do not fall within the Inquiries Act 2005.
55 Howe, 1999.
56 See www.publicinquiries.org.
57 *The Thames Safety Report*, 2000.
58 *Principal Conclusions and Overall Assessment of the Bloody Sunday Inquiry*, HC 30 (2010–2011): www.bloody-sunday-inquiry.org.
59 *The Stephen Lawrence Inquiry Report*, CM 4262-I, 1999, London: TSO.
60 *Learning from Bristol: Report of the Public Inquiry into Children's Heart Surgery at the BRI 1984–95*, Cm 5207, 2001.
61 See respectively, *Learning from Bristol: Report of the Public Inquiry into Children's Heart Surgery at the BRI 1984–95*, Cm 5207, 2001; *The Royal Liverpool Children's Hospital (Alder Hey) Inquiry*, HC 12 (1998–1999).

- The 'Arms to Iraq' Inquiry, reporting in 1996, examined allegations concerning the export of defence equipment to Iraq.
- The death of government scientist David Kelly.[62]
- Intelligence data on weapons of mass destruction 2004.
- Government decision making prior to the Iraq War 2003.
- The inquiry into the death of Iraqi civilian Baha Mousa, who was detained and tortured and died in the custody of British troops. Chaired by Sir William Gage, the Report was published in 2011.[63]
- Allegations of widespread 'phone hacking' by the media led to the Media Inquiry into the 'culture, practices and ethics of the press' chaired by Lord Justice Leveson, which reported in 2012.[64]
- The inquiry into deaths and injuries at Hillsborough Football ground in 1989. Established in 2010 and chaired by the Bishop of Liverpool, the Report revealed basic flaws in policing and the response of the emergency services.[65]

Non-Statutory Inquiries

Non-statutory inquiries may be established to examine a particular issue, and may be preferred by the government on the basis that there can be greater flexibility in procedures. Examples include the BSE Inquiry which reported in 2000 and which examined the crisis in agriculture caused by the bovine spongiform encephalopathy (BSE, or 'mad cow disease') outbreak which led to the slaughter of some 200,000 cattle.[66] The Paddington Rail Crash Inquiry, chaired by Lord Cullen, was also non-statutory. The Scott inquiry into the export of equipment capable of being transformed into weaponry in Iraq, the Hutton inquiry into alleged weapons of mass destruction in Iraq, the inquiry into the circumstances surrounding the death of government scientist Dr David Kelly chaired by Lord Hutton and the Chilcot inquiry, chaired by Sir John Chilcot, into the circumstances leading to the decision to go to war in Iraq were also examples of non-statutory inquiries. However, non-statutory inquiries have disadvantages. There is no power, for example, to compel witnesses to give evidence or to compel the disclosure of documents as is the case with inquiries under the 2005 Act.[67] On the other hand, where the subject matter is sensitive or controversial, witnesses may be more likely to cooperate with a non-statutory inquiry than an inquiry under the 2005 Act in which coercive powers are available. As noted above, if the government feels that a non-statutory inquiry would be more effective if undertaken under statute, it can be 'converted' into a statutory inquiry under section 15 of the 2005 Act.

The Coalition government formed in 2010 has made good use of inquiries. The Leveson Inquiry, chaired by Lord Justice Leveson, into the culture, practices and ethics of the media was established in 2011 (see Chapter 19). In 2012 there was a Commission on a Bill of Rights, established in 2011, to consider whether the United Kingdom needs a Bill of Rights to supplement the Human Rights Act 1998 (see Chapter 18). There was also the McKay Commission, established in 2012, to examine the consequences of devolution on the House of Commons

---

62 *Report of the Inquiry into the Circumstances Surrounding the Death of Dr David Kelly*, HC 247 (2003–2004).
63 *The Baha Mousa Public Inquiry Report*, HC 1452-1 (2011), London: TSO.
64 *The Leveson Report: An Inquiry into the Culture, Practices and Ethics of the Press*, HC 779 (November 2012), London: TSO.
65 *The Report of the Hillsborough Independent Panel*, HC 581 (2012), London: TSO.
66 The BSE Inquiry was chaired by Lord Phillips, and cost £30 million.
67 Inquiry Act 2005, s. 21; and see s. 35 on penalties for non-compliance.

(see Chapter 11). The privileges of Parliament have also been subject to extensive review, not through a formal inquiry, but via the publication of a consultation paper.[68]

Statutory Inquiries

Many Acts of Parliament confer the power to establish tribunals of inquiry. The most common form of inquiry is that into planning applications, where a public inquiry may be ordered under section 20 of the Town and Country Planning Act 1990. Outside planning matters, other inquiries include that into the *Marchioness* disaster, in which a pleasure cruiser on the River Thames sank, causing many deaths: the inquiry was set up under the Merchant Shipping Act 1995. The inquiry into the circumstances surrounding the death of Stephen Lawrence which reported in 1999 was established under section 49 of the Police Act 1996.[69] The Health and Safety at Work Act 1974 and the National Health Service Act 1977 are further examples of legislation conferring power to establish inquiries. Inquiries into the conduct of the prisons may be set up under the Prisons Acts.

Prior to the Inquiries Act 2005, the principal Act for general statutory tribunals of inquiry was the Tribunals of Inquiry Act 1921. The 1921 Act, however, required a formal Resolution of both Houses of Parliament before an inquiry could be established. While this had the merit of ensuring a link between inquiries and Parliament, it restricted the scope of inquiries. The 1921 Act had other disadvantages. First, there was no provision for procedural rules. Second, there was no provision to control the cost of inquiries. The example set by the Bloody Sunday Inquiry, set up under the 1921 Act – 12 years and a cost of £192 million – was one not to be followed in the future.

The 2005 Act repeals the 1921 Act and confers on government Ministers a great deal of discretion in establishing tribunals of inquiry, their terms of reference and procedure.

Common issues and concerns

Irrespective of the basis for the inquiry, there are a number of common issues which may be summarised as follows:

- the discretion which the government has in relation to whether to establish an inquiry;[70]
- whether the inquiry should be held in public or private;
- the independence of inquiries from government;
- the chairmanship of inquiries;
- the procedure to be followed;
- the anonymity of witnesses;
- the disclosure of evidence;
- the government's and Parliament's response to inquiries.

One of the most difficult issues lies in the choice between a public inquiry and an inquiry conducted in private. That is a decision for the government to take, but is one that may be challenged by proceedings for judicial review. Two examples of inquiries conducted in private – and challenges made to them – are the inquiry into the murder of elderly patients by

68 Cm 8318, London: TSO 2012.
69 See the *Stephen Lawrence Inquiry*, Report of an Inquiry by Sir William Macpherson of Cluny, Cm 4262, 1999.
70 There is no legal duty to establish an inquiry. See **Keyu v Secretary of State for Foreign and Commonwealth Affairs** (2012); **R (Mousa) v Secretary of State for Defence** (2011).

Dr Harold Shipman and the inquiry into the 2001 outbreak of foot and mouth disease (FMD) in cattle.

In 2000 Dr Shipman was found guilty on 15 counts of murder. The Secretary of State decided to establish an inquiry under the National Health Service Act 1977 and that the hearings should be in private but that the inquiry would publish its findings and a final report. In his statement to Parliament the Minister stated that there would be an 'independent inquiry' that would be 'comprehensive and inclusive'. In judicial review proceedings challenging the legality of the Minister's decision, the decision was set aside on grounds of irrationality.[71] In September 2000 the Secretary of State announced that the Inquiry would be held in public under the terms of the Tribunals of Inquiry (Evidence) Act 1921. Explaining the basis for the finding of irrationality, Simon Brown LJ in **Persey v Secretary of State for Environment, Food and Rural Affairs** (2002) cited five principal reasons: that the Secretary of State had mistakenly thought that the families of victims did not want a public inquiry; that the terms of reference were exceedingly wide; that a misunderstanding had arisen as a result of the Minister's statement to the House of Commons; that there was no body of opinion in favour of closed hearings; and that there was no reason why a public inquiry should take longer than one conducted in private.

Nevertheless, this does not mean that there is a presumption in favour of public inquiries, still less that there is a 'right' to a public inquiry or to a particular form of inquiry. As Simon Brown LJ remarked in **Persey**: 'Inquiries, in short, come in all shapes and sizes and it would be wrong to suppose that a single model – a full-scale open public inquiry – should be seen as the invariable panacea for all ills' (at paragraph 42).

Persey v Secretary of State for Environment, Food and Rural Affairs (2002) was a challenge to the government's decision to set up three separate independent inquiries to examine the circumstances surrounding and response to the outbreak of FMD in cattle in 2001. The inquiries – the Lessons Learned Inquiry, the Scientific Inquiry and the Policy Commission – were to receive evidence, mostly in private. The claimants' challenges focused on the Lessons Learned Inquiry and their principal contention was that as a matter of law the inquiry should be held in public. The Court found that the main factors influencing the government's decision were (a) the need to learn lessons as rapidly as possible, (b) the expectation that witnesses would be more open and forthcoming in private, as opposed to public hearings, (c) that there would be a saving in financial and human resources. After examining the several grounds of challenge, the Court found they lacked substance and the Minister's decision was lawful.

The Inquiries Act 2005

The Inquiries Act 2005 was passed to give effect to the [then] Department of Constitutional Affairs consultation paper, *Effective Inquiries*,[72] which had concluded that defects in the current law necessitated reform. As noted above, the 1921 Act made no provision for rules of procedure, nor was there any power to control the costs of an inquiry: the Bloody Sunday Inquiry had lasted 12 years and cost £192 million. In the words of the Ministry of Justice's Memorandum to the Justice Select Committee, *Post-Legislative Assessment of the Inquiries Act 2005*, the 2005 Act: 'aimed to make inquiries swifter, more effective at finding facts and making practical recommendations, and less costly whilst still meeting the need to satisfy the public expectation for a thorough and wide ranging investigation' (paragraph 6). It also: 'codified

---

71 **R v Secretary of State for Health ex parte Wagstaff** (2000).
72 Following on from the House of Commons' Public Administration Select Committee investigation, *Government by Inquiry*, HC 51 (2005).

best practice from previous statutory and non-statutory inquiries such as the need to ensure that those conducting inquiries are impartial and have appropriate expertise'.

The Act applies across the United Kingdom, providing a uniform structure. There is also provision for joint inquiries to be conducted across national administrations. Inquiries are not empowered to rule on any person's civil or criminal liability (section 2, 2005 Act): they are not courts of law. Also distinguishing inquiries from courts of law is the fact that while proceedings in courts are *adversarial*, a tribunal of inquiry acts in an *inquisitorial* manner.

Concerns over the inquisitorial process and in particular concerns over procedural aspects of one judicial inquiry, that of Lord Denning into the Profumo affair,[73] led to a Royal Commission on Tribunals of Inquiry, chaired by Lord Justice Salmon. Reporting in 1966, the Salmon Report laid down six basic principles of fair procedure for tribunals of inquiry. These are:

- before any person becomes involved in an inquiry, the tribunal must be satisfied that there are circumstances which affect them and which the tribunal proposes to investigate;
- before any person who is involved in an inquiry is called as a witness, they should be informed of any allegations made against them and the substance of the evidence in support of them;
- they should be given an adequate opportunity to prepare their case and of being assisted by legal advisers and their legal expenses should normally be met out of public funds;
- they should have the opportunity of being examined by their own solicitor or counsel and of stating their case in public at the inquiry;
- any material witnesses they wish to call at the inquiry should, if reasonably practicable, be heard;
- they should have the opportunity of testing by cross-examination conducted by their own solicitor or counsel any evidence which may affect them.

These principles, when applied, bring the inquiry process closer to the adversarial model of legal proceedings, injecting a greater degree of formality. However, it is for the chairman of an individual inquiry to decide whether or not, and to what extent, the Salmon principles should apply.

Power to establish an inquiry

The power to establish an inquiry is conferred on a United Kingdom Minister, Scottish Ministers or a Northern Ireland Minister. The power is conferred under section 1, where 'it appears to him that':

(a) particular events have caused, or are capable of causing, public concern; or
(b) there is public concern that particular events may have occurred.

The decision whether or not to establish an inquiry can prove controversial and may lead to a legal challenge. This occurred in relation to the death in custody of a young offender, Zahid Mubarek, who had been placed in a cell with a known violent and racist offender. The Home Secretary refused to establish an inquiry into his death. This refusal was challenged in judicial review proceedings, in which the House of Lords ruled that his refusal violated the duty under Article 2 of the European Convention on Human Rights not only to protect the

---

73 See *Lord Denning's Report*, Cmnd 2152, 1963, London: TSO.

life of those in custody of the state but also, where death occurred, to investigate that death.[74] A judicial inquiry was established and its findings were highly critical of the Prison Service.[75]

In **R (Litvinenko) v Secretary of State for the Home Department** (2014) the widow of a Russian agent, Alexander Litvinenko, murdered in London in 2006 sought judicial review of the Secretary of State's refusal to establish a statutory inquiry into his death, as requested by the Coroner. The Secretary of State had not ruled out an inquiry but had adopted a 'wait and see' approach. The deceased had been murdered with polonium, and *prima facie* evidence suggested that the murder was committed on the orders of officials of the Russian state. The Secretary of State gave six reasons for declining to accede to the Coroner's request. Three of these were found to be inadequate or incorrect; two raised 'concerns' but were of subsidiary importance to the claim and one was found to be wrong, but immaterial. Taken together, the Court ruled that there was a strong case for setting up a statutory inquiry and that taken together the 'reasons given by the Secretary of State do not provide a rational basis for the decision not to set up a statutory inquiry'. The deficiencies in the reasons given were so substantial that the decision could not stand and a quashing order would be granted. Richards LJ went on to rule that the Secretary of State needed to offer better reasons for not holding an inquiry than those provided in order to provide a rational basis for her decision. However, her discretion under section 1(1) of the Inquiries Act 2005 was very broad. Accordingly the Court did not feel that it could say that the Secretary of State 'has no rational option but to set up a statutory inquiry now'.[76] The Home Secretary then decided to establish an Inquiry, under the Inquiries Act 2005. The Inquiry opened in January 2015, chaired by former High Court judge, Sir Robert Owen.

Power to suspend or terminate an inquiry

Under section 13 of the Inquiries Act 2005, Ministers are given the power to suspend an inquiry, following consultation with the chairman, on the grounds that it is necessary to allow for the completion of other investigations into any of the matters to which the inquiry relates, or the determination of any civil or criminal proceedings arising out of matters to which the inquiry relates. This was the situation in January 2012 when the Justice Secretary announced the suspension of the Detainee Inquiry chaired by Sir Peter Gibson. The Inquiry had been established to examine the alleged role of MI5 and MI6 in the torture and rendition of detainees after the September 2001 terrorist attacks.

The power to terminate an inquiry is conferred under section 14 of the 2005 Act. An inquiry will come to an end on the date on which the chairman notifies the Minister that the inquiry has fulfilled its terms of reference unless an earlier date is specified to the chairman by the Minister.

Converting other inquiries into a 2005 Act inquiry

The Inquiries Act 2005, sections 15 to 16 enable a Minister to convert a non-statutory or statutory inquiry into a 2005 Act inquiry provided that he or she is satisfied that the matter being investigated falls within the scope of a 2005 Act inquiry. This precludes other forms of inquiry, such as planning inquiries, from being converted into 2005 Act inquiries. Where a non-statutory inquiry has been established and there is found to be a need for a greater

---

74 See **R (Amin) v Secretary of State for the Home Department** (2003).
75 *Report of the Zahid Mubarek Inquiry*, HC 1082 (2005–2006).
76 At para. 75.

degree of formality or control over potential costs, that inquiry may be converted into a 2005 Act inquiry. The power to convert an inquiry into an inquiry under the 2005 Act arises only where the Minister considers that there is public concern over an issue. Before exercising the power under section 15 the Minister must consult the chairman of the original inquiry. The terms of reference of the converted inquiry may differ from those of the original inquiry.

The terms of reference

Under section 5 of the 2005 Act, the Minister must set out the terms of reference of the inquiry. The terms of reference are defined in section 5(6) as being:

- the matters to which the inquiry relates;
- any particular matter as to which the inquiry panel is to determine the facts;
- whether the inquiry panel is to make recommendations;
- any other matters relating to the scope of the inquiry that the Minister may specify.

The terms of reference may be amended if the Minister considers that the 'public interest so requires' (section 5(3)).

Chairing the inquiry

It is for the Minister to decide who should chair an inquiry. Most inquiries will be chaired by a senior judge, former senior civil servant or an academic with expertise in the matter to be considered. High-profile and controversial inquiries chaired by judges include the Security Inquiry chaired by Lord Denning in 1963 and the inquiry into the riots in Central London in 1981, chaired by Lord Scarman. The Arms to Iraq Inquiry, the Inquiry into Weapons of Mass Destruction and the circumstances surrounding the death of Dr David Kelly were also chaired by judges, as was the Media Inquiry (Lord Leveson). The inquiry into intelligence data relating to weaponry in Iraq was chaired by a former Cabinet Secretary, Lord Butler. The Iraq Inquiry established in 2009 was chaired by a former senior civil servant, Sir John Chilcot.

There are arguments for and against the use of judges as chairs of inquiries. On the one hand, by training and expertise, judges are well qualified both to ensure impartiality and to evaluate evidence. On the other hand, the higher the public profile, and the more political the subject matter under examination, the greater the danger of drawing judges into the political arena which they are so careful to avoid. It may also be argued that judges are not best qualified to make judgments on matters of policy.[77] Recognising the potential drawbacks, the 2005 Act provides that when a Minister proposes to appoint a senior judge as a member of an inquiry panel, he or she must first consult, as relevant, the Lord Chief Justice of England and Wales, the Lord President of the Scottish Court of Session or the Lord Chief Justice of Northern Ireland.[78]

The inquiry panel

An inquiry may be undertaken by the chairman alone, or by a chairman with one or more other members (section 3, 2005 Act). Panel members are appointed by the Minister, in

---

77 Note the care with which judges avoid issues of high policy in judicial review proceedings: see the concept of justiciability discussed in Chapter 23.
78 Section 10, Inquiries Act 2005.

consultation with the person appointed, or to be appointed as chairman. In making appointments, the Minister is under a statutory duty to ensure that the panel has the necessary expertise to undertake the inquiry, and that the composition of the panel is balanced (section 8). The impartiality of panel members is a fundamental requirement. No one may be appointed who has a direct interest in the matters to which the inquiry relates or who has a close association with any interested party (section 9).

In addition to the chair and panel members, assessors may be appointed to assist the inquiry (section 11).

Procedure

The procedure to be followed (subject to the 2005 Act and subordinate legislation) is for the chairman of the inquiry to establish (section 17). In particular the chairman may decide whether or not to take evidence on oath: section 17(2). In exceptional circumstances, the chairman may also admit evidence anonymously, if the evidence would otherwise not be available to the Inquiry. Section 17(3) imposes a statutory duty on the chairman to act 'with fairness and with regard also to the need to avoid any unnecessary cost'.

Hearings in public

There is a presumption that proceedings will be open to members of the public (section 18) and that the public will have access to the record of evidence and documents before the inquiry. This presumption is subject to a 'restriction notice' given by a Minister to the chairman 'at any time before the end of the inquiry', or by the chairman during the course of the inquiry (sections 19–20).

Evidence

While the hearings will be public, witnesses may be permitted to give evidence in private. This is generally the case where the material to be disclosed would cause harm to the public interest, often on the grounds of national security and international relations. Where evidence is given in private, that evidence may be published by the inquiry, subject to redactions or summarising where necessary in accordance with the inquiry's Protocol for Witnesses. Evidence may also be published anonymously. Some evidence may consist of classified documents. In relation to the Iraq Inquiry, for example, there was established a Protocol between the Inquiry and Her Majesty's government regarding documents and other written and electronic information detailing the arrangements for the giving of evidence. In relation to classified documents, the Inquiry has sought declassification by the government prior to publication of its report.

Anonymity of witnesses

The giving of evidence by some witnesses, particularly those from the military or security forces, may bring the principle of open justice into conflict with the duty of the state to protect life under Article 2 of the European Convention on Human Rights. This situation has given rise to legal challenges. In **Re Officer L (Respondent) (Northern Ireland)** (2007) the House of Lords stated that the correct test to be applied to a request for anonymity is to ask the question whether the risk to life would be materially increased if the potential witness were required to give evidence without anonymity. Anonymity was also challenged in relation to the Leveson Inquiry, where Lord Justice Leveson allowed journalists who feared for their jobs or reputations, if their evidence was attributed to them, to give evidence anonymously.[79]

---

79 See **R (Associated Newspapers Ltd) v Leveson** (2012).

Legal representation

The Inquiry Rules 2006[80] provide that 'core participants', defined in Rule 5 as a person who has played or may have played a significant role in relation to the matter under investigation, or a person with a significant interest, or a person who may be subject to explicit or significant criticism during the inquiry or in its report(s), and witnesses, are entitled to legal representation.

Counsel to the Inquiry may be appointed to advise on the law and to question witnesses.

The report

The findings of the inquiry are to be reported to the Minister, together with recommendations of the panel (where the terms of reference require recommendations to be made): section 24. The report of the inquiry should be unanimous, but if there are disagreements within the panel, those disagreements must be made clear in the report. The Minister is under a duty to arrange for inquiry reports to be published, unless that duty has been conferred on the inquiry chairman: section 25.

Material may be withheld from publication if disclosure is prevented by any rule of law or on the basis of public interest. In deciding whether to withhold material, the person concerned must consider the following matters:

(a) the extent to which withholding material might inhibit the allaying of public concern;
(b) any risk of harm or damage that could be avoided or reduced by withholding any material;
(c) any conditions as to confidentiality subject to which a person acquired information that he or she has given to the inquiry.

The report must be laid before Parliament or the relevant Assembly 'at the time of publication or as soon afterwards as is reasonably practicable': section 26 Inquiries Act 2005.

Where criminal proceedings are taken against any person in relation to matters covered by the inquiry, publication of the report into the inquiry will be postponed until those proceedings are concluded. This situation arose in respect of the Inquiry into the death of Robert Hamill, who was murdered in Northern Ireland in 1997, when charges of perverting the course of justice were made against officers serving in the Royal Ulster Constabulary.[81]

In its *Memorandum to the Justice Select Committee: Post-Legislative Assessment of the Inquiries Act 2005*,[82] the Ministry of Justice gave a favourable overall assessment of the 2005 Act, stating that it operates 'well in practice' although minor amendments may be needed. The *Memorandum* notes, however, that the Act can only work well in ensuring a timely conclusion and without excessive costs if the chairman and inquiry team have the necessary expertise. Particular features of the Act selected for favourable comment include the rules relating to disclosure of evidence, the ability to convert another inquiry into a 2005 Act inquiry and the duty imposed on the chairman to act with fairness and with regard to the need to avoid any unnecessary costs.[83]

---

80 SI No. 1838 2006.
81 The Secretary of State for Northern Ireland announced the delay in publishing the report in a Ministerial Statement to the House of Commons on 31 January 2011.
82 Cm 7943, 2010, London: TSO.
83 Paragraphs 41–44.

Summary

Inquiries are an important feature of the democratic process, promoting transparency and accountability. The form they take may be statutory or non-statutory. Commissions may also be established by government to consult and make recommendations on various aspects of governance: the McKay Commission on the impact of devolution on the House of Commons and the Commission on a UK Bill of Rights are examples of these.

 Further Reading

Beatson, J, 'Should judges chair public inquiries?' (2005) 121 *Law Quarterly Review* 221.

Denning, Lord, *Lord Denning's Report*, Cmnd2152, 1963, London: TSO.

Drewry, G, 'Judicial inquiries and public reassurance' [1996] *Public Law* 368.

Endicott, T, *Administrative Law (italicised)*, 3rd edn, 2015, Oxford: Oxford University Press.

Howe, G, 'The management of public inquiries' (1999) 70 *Political Quarterly* 294.

Scott, R, 'Procedures at inquiries: the duty to be fair' (1995) 111 *Law Quarterly Review* 596.

Steele, I, 'Judging judicial inquiries' [2004] *Public Law* 738.

Thomas of Cwmgiedd, Lord, 'The future of public inquiries' [2015] *Public Law* 225.

Chapter **27**

Commissioners for Administration: Ombudsmen

Chapter Contents

Learning Objectives

By the end of this chapter you should be able to:

☐ explain the range of Ombudsmen and the advantages of the system;
☐ explain why there was a need to introduce a Parliamentary Ombudsman;
☐ discuss her jurisdiction;
☐ explain which areas are excluded from the Ombudsman's jurisdiction;

- [ ] explain the MP 'filter' and its justification;
- [ ] define the concept of 'maladministration';
- [ ] give examples of major enquiries undertaken by the Ombudsman;
- [ ] name the Departments most frequently subject to Ombudsman's enquiries;
- [ ] discuss the government's response to Ombudsman's Reports;
- [ ] explain the role of the Public Administration Select Committee.

Introduction

In the United Kingdom recent years have seen a major expansion in mechanisms for citizens to complain against government Departments and other public bodies. When a citizen has a complaint against the administration of government, that complaint could be pursued in courts or tribunals or through Parliament via the constituency Member of Parliament. However, these means for the redress of grievances have been proven inadequate and, as a result, alternative and additional mechanisms have been introduced.

The word 'ombudsman' is Swedish, and means a representative of the people. In Sweden, the office of *Justitieombudsman* was established in 1809. Finland introduced a similar office in 1919, as did Denmark in 1955. In 1963, Norway followed, with a parliamentary ombudsman, the model which had been adopted by New Zealand in 1962. During the 1970s, countries throughout the world adopted some form of office of ombudsman.

Commissioners for Administration in the United Kingdom

The existing scheme of Commissioners for Administration is given below. Note that, in addition, there exist a number of ombudsmen in the private sector, for example the Banking Commissioner, Building Societies Commissioner, Corporate Estate Agents Commissioner, Pensions Commissioner,[1] Personal Investment Authority Ombudsman, Prisons Ombudsman, Investment Commissioner, Insurance Commissioner, Commissioner for Trade Union Members and the press and media and telephone information services.

---

1 It has been held that the Pensions Ombudsman is required to observe the statutory procedure within the Pensions Schemes Act 1993 and the rules of natural justice: see **Seifert v Pensions Ombudsman**; **Lynch v Pensions Ombudsman** (1997). See also **Miller v Stapleton** (1996); **Hamar v Pensions Ombudsman** (1996).

Commissioners for Administration	Date of Introduction
Parliamentary Commissioner for Administration[2]	1967
Parliamentary Commissioner for Administration[3] Complaints and Commissioner (Northern Ireland)[4]	1969
Ombudsman (Northern Ireland) Order	1996
Health Service Commissioners: England, Wales and Scotland[5]	1972
Local Government Commissioners: England, Wales[6] and Scotland[7] (Scotland 1975)	1974
Legal Services Commissioner[8]	1990
European Union and Community Ombudsman[9]	1992
Scottish Parliamentary Commissioner[10]	1998
Scottish Public Services Ombudsman	2002
Welsh Administration Ombudsman[11]	1998
Public Services Ombudsman for Wales	2005
Housing Ombudsman	2013

The Parliamentary and Health Services Ombudsman[12]

[T]he Parliamentary Ombudsman has a constitutional role that cannot simply be confined to the function of dispute resolution, important though that is; that the Ombudsman system of justice is distinctive yet integral to a broader administrative justice system as a whole, and that the framework of values within which the work of the Ombudsman can be located is that of the protection and promotion of citizens' rights.[13]

The movement towards establishing a Parliamentary Commissioner for Administration (hereafter Ombudsman) began in 1959. In that year, the British section of the International Commission of Jurists, JUSTICE, established an inquiry into grievances against the administration. The resultant report[14] advocated setting up an additional avenue for the redress of grievances, the office being modelled on the same lines as those of the ombudsmen in Scandinavian jurisdictions. As the report stated, there appeared to be:

a continuous flow of relatively minor complaints, not sufficient in themselves to attract public interest, but nevertheless of great importance to the individuals

---

2 Parliamentary Commissioner Act 1967. As amended by the Parliamentary and Health Service Commissioner Act 1987; Parliamentary Commissioner Act 1994.
3 Parliamentary Commissioner (Northern Ireland) Act 1969.
4 Commissioner for Complaints (Northern Ireland) Act 1969.
5 National Health Service (Scotland) Act 1972; National Health Service Reorganisation Act 1973; Parliamentary and Health Service Commissioners Act 1987; Health Service Commissioners Act 1993; Health Service Commissioners (Amendment) Act 2000.
6 Local Government Act 1974; Local Government and Housing Act 1989, s. 23.
7 Local Government (Scotland) Act 1975.
8 Courts and Legal Services Act 1990.
9 EC Treaty, Article 195, introduced under the Treaty on European Union 1992.
10 Scotland Act 1998. See Scotland Act 1998 (Transitory and Transitional Provisions) (Complaints of Maladministration) Order 1999, SI 1999/1351.
11 Government of Wales Act 1998.
12 See Pugh, 1978. See also Clothier, 1984.
13 A. Abraham, 'The Parliamentary Ombudsman and Administrative Justice', JUSTICE, Tom Sargent Memorial Lecture, 2011.
14 *The Citizen and the Administration* (the Whyatt Report), 1961.

concerned, which give rise to feelings of frustration and resentment because of the inadequacy of the existing means of seeking redress.[15]

The existing machinery was found wanting: parliamentary Question Time was inadequate to deal with the volume of problems arising; if a complaint was made directly to the government Department, the Department investigated the complaint; if a Member of Parliament attempted to investigate, he could not gain access to all departmental documentation. Accordingly, the report advocated establishing a permanent office, independent of the executive and accountable only to Parliament, removable from office only after a successful address had been moved to both Houses of Parliament. The report recommended that a Select Committee should be established to consider the Ombudsman's reports and to give parliamentary authority to the work of the Ombudsman. The report also recommended that the Parliamentary Ombudsman's office should be one which supplemented, rather than undermined, existing procedures for complaint. Complaints, at least initially, concerning maladministration[16] should be routed through Members of the House of Commons, rather than directly addressed to the Parliamentary Ombudsman. This would preserve to Members of Parliament the opportunity to resolve a matter of complaint but, failing their ability to do so, confer the right to refer the matter to the Parliamentary Ombudsman for investigation and report.

The government's response to the report was cautious. Concern was expressed as to the interference in the running of government,[17] and that the Ombudsman's role would be incompatible with the doctrine of ministerial responsibility. Furthermore, the government felt that: 'there is already adequate provision under our constitution and Parliamentary practice for the redress of any genuine complaint of maladministration, in particular by means of the citizen's rights of access to Members of Parliament'.[18] The incoming Labour government, however, accepted the need for an office to complement the existing complaints machinery.[19] Thus, in 1967, the Parliamentary Commissioner Act was passed. Being a constitutional innovation, the provisions as to procedure, jurisdiction and powers of enforcement were restrictive.

Appointment

The Parliamentary Ombudsman is appointed by the Crown on the advice of the government, following consultation with the Chairman of the House of Commons' Public Administration Select Committee. The post is held 'during good health and behaviour' and is effectively until retirement.

The National Health Service (Scotland) Act and National Health Service Reorganisation Act 1973 introduced separate Health Service Commissioners for England, Wales and Scotland. These offices are now combined with the office of Parliamentary Ombudsman formally called the Parliamentary and Health Service Ombudsman.

---

15 Ibid., para. 76.
16 On which, see below.
17 Lord Chancellor, HL Deb Vol. 244 Cols 384–385.
18 Attorney General, 666 HC, Col, 1125.
19 *The Parliamentary Commissioner for Administration*, Cmnd 2767, 1965, London: HMSO.

The constitutional position of the Ombudsman

By 1983, the office of Parliamentary Ombudsman had been operative for 15 years, and the Ombudsman[20] took the opportunity to review the working of his office in his annual report. He described his office in the following manner:

> The office of Parliamentary Commissioner stands curiously poised between the legislature and the executive, while discharging an almost judicial function in the citizen's dispute with his government, and yet it forms no part of the judiciary. It is from the centre of that triangle that I have been able to appreciate the virtues of our unwritten and therefore flexible constitutional arrangements and still more the goodwill of those men and women, legislators and administrators who govern us.

Aims and objectives

The purpose of the Office of Parliamentary and Health Service Ombudsman (OPHSO) is:

(a)   to consider and resolve complaints impartially and promptly and to achieve appropriate redress of grievances;

(b)   to report the results to complainants, Members of Parliament and the bodies complained about; and

(c)   to promote improvements in public services by feeding back the lessons learned from casework to policy makers and providers.[21]

The complaints procedure

Complaints must be in writing, and made to the constituency Member of Parliament (i.e. a Member of the House of Commons).[22] The complaint must be made within 12 months of the day on which the person became aware of the matters alleged, unless the time period is extended by the Ombudsman, on the basis that an investigation is necessary.[23] There is no charge involved in making a complaint, or for any investigation which is undertaken. The complaint must relate to maladministration and not the merits of a decision or the policy being pursued.

The requirement that complaints be made initially to Members of Parliament reinforces the view that the Ombudsman is a supplement to the parliamentary process rather than a substitute. This restricted right of access, however, causes difficulties for complainants, and is not a model adopted elsewhere.[24] Of the 100 plus national ombudsmen around the world, the Parliamentary Ombudsman is unique in having no powers of initiative and being dependent upon references from MPs. Moreover, this filter mechanism has not been adopted in relation to the Commissioners for Local Government or the Complaints Commissioner for Northern Ireland.[25] Ann Abrahams, a former Parliamentary Ombudsman, has called for the MP filter to be removed, as has the Select Committee for Public Administration. In 2020 Ombudsman Rob Behrens stated that the filter was preventing too many people from reaching the service

---

20 Sir Cecil Clothier, who held office from 1979 to 1985.
21 OPHSO, *Business Plan 2003–04*.
22 Parliamentary Commissioner Act 1967, s. 5(1)(a).
23 *Ibid.*, s. 6(3).
24 See the JUSTICE Report, *Our Fettered Ombudsman*, 1977, and the Select Committee Report, *Parliamentary Commissioner for Administration (Review of Access and Jurisdiction)*, HC 615 (1978–1979), London: HMSO.
25 There is, however, a 'filter' procedure for the Parliamentary Commissioner for Northern Ireland.

and called for the MP filter to be abolished, describing the legislation requiring the filter 'outdated'.

There are arguments for and against the MP filter. On the positive side, the filter emphasises that the Ombudsman – while independent of Parliament – is nevertheless part of the parliamentary machinery. The filter ensures that MPs are engaged in the complaints process and given the opportunity to attempt to resolve a constituent's grievance. Only where that fails (and MPs unlike the Ombudsman have no legal power to compel government bodies to produce witnesses or evidence), will a referral to the Ombudsman be made. Former Ombudsman Ann Abrahams has made the point that there was an 'urgent need to re-engage the interest of MPs in the work of the Ombudsman' and to make MPs aware of the importance of Ombudsmen inquiries in relation to the process of holding government to account.[26] The filter also reduces the pressure on the Ombudsman and concern has been expressed that if the filter were removed, the Ombudsman would be overwhelmed with complaints. This point does not stand up well against the Ombudsman's own research finding that in 2014 public awareness of the Ombudsman's office stood at 19 per cent.

Against the filter is the argument that it is an unnecessary barrier to the Ombudsman who is dependent upon MPs' referrals. As noted above, the Ombudsman has no right to initiate investigations. Maintaining the MP filter is also out of line with other public service Ombudsmen in the United Kingdom – none of whom is restricted by a filter. Concerns about the involvement of MPs could be addressed by requiring the Ombudsman to notify MPs about inquiries being undertaken. Removing the filter would also facilitate raising public awareness of the Ombudsman's role.

 Pause and Reflect

Reviewing the arguments for and against the 'MP filter' do you think that it should be retained or removed? Give reasons for your answer.

Jurisdiction

Section 5(1) of the Parliamentary Commissioner Act 1967 provides that a member of the public may make a complaint and the Ombudsman may investigate that complaint where, subject to the rules on jurisdiction, the person 'claims to have sustained injustice in consequence of maladministration'.[27] Before examining that concept, it must be noted that there are a number of restrictions to the jurisdiction of the Parliamentary Ombudsman, which result in a large number of complaints each year not being investigated.

The office of Ombudsman suffers from a number of drawbacks. As noted above, individuals have – unlike in most other jurisdictions – no right of direct access to the Parliamentary Ombudsman. The concept of maladministration is relatively narrow and is linked to injustice suffered as a result of a decision. Furthermore, while the 1987 Act has extended the bodies into which the Ombudsman has jurisdiction to investigate, as seen below, there remain a significant number of matters outside his or her jurisdiction. Many of these relate to matters which fall under the royal prerogative, which, as has been seen (Chapter 5), is subject to inadequate parliamentary scrutiny and to limited judicial review.

26 Abrahams, 2008b, pp. 542–543.
27 See below for the meaning of 'maladministration'.

Excluded matters

The work of the police,[28] of nationalised industries, the Cabinet Office, Prime Minister's Office, Parole Board, tribunals, Bank of England, Criminal Injuries Compensation Board and government commercial and contractual transactions are all excluded.[29] The Ombudsman may not investigate any matter where the complainant has a right of 'appeal, reference or review' to a tribunal, or a remedy in any court of law, unless it would be unreasonable to expect the complainant to have to resort to such a remedy.[30] The Ombudsman thus has a discretion as to whether or not a complaint should be accepted. It has been indicated that, where the legal process would be too cumbersome, slow or expensive in relation to the objective to be gained, the complaint will be accepted.[31]

The interaction between legal proceedings and complaints to the Ombudsman was well illustrated in 1975. The government decided to increase the licence fee for television sets. In advance of the fee increase, people renewed their licences at the existing rate. The Home Office then decided to revoke the 36,000 licences issued at the cheaper rate. A number of complaints were referred to the Ombudsman, who found maladministration on the part of government, *inter alia*, for not giving sufficient warning of the increases and for inefficiency. The Ombudsman, however, ruled that the government was acting on legal advice and therefore should not be sanctioned. In **Congreve v Home Office** (1976) the Home Secretary's decision was challenged in judicial review proceedings. as a result of which the complainants established a legal remedy.[32] It may be argued that the Ombudsman was wrong in exercising his discretionary jurisdiction in this case, since it should have been foreseen that an action in judicial review would lie. Both the Law Commission and the Administrative Justice and Tribunal Council (AJTC) have argued that the statutory bar which precludes the Ombudsman from investigating a complaint if the complainant has or had recourse to a legal remedy before a court or tribunal should be relaxed, and that there should be greater flexibility for the transfer of cases between the courts and the Ombudsman.[33]

The Departments and matters which the Ombudsman is precluded from investigating are wide ranging. Schedule 3 to the Parliamentary Commissioner Act 1967 sets out the excluded matters, the most significant of which are:

- action taken in matters certified by a Secretary of State or other Minister of the Crown to affect relations or dealings between the government of the United Kingdom and any other government or any international organisation of states or government;
- action taken in connection with the administration of the government of any country or territory outside the United Kingdom which forms part of Her Majesty's dominions or in which Her Majesty has jurisdiction;
- action taken by the Secretary of State under the Fugitive Offenders Act 1967 or the Extradition Act 1989;
- action taken by or with the authority of the Secretary of State for the purposes of investigating crime or of protecting the security of the state, including action so taken with respect to passports;
- the commencement or conduct of civil or criminal proceedings before any court of law in the United Kingdom;

---

28 Which has its own internal complaints procedures.
29 See HC 322 (1983–1984), London: HMSO.
30 Parliamentary Commissioner Act 1967, s. 5(2).
31 See McMurtie, 1997.
32 **Congreve v Home Office** (1976).
33 Administrative Justice and Tribunal Council, The Developing Administrative Justice Landscape, September 2009, para. 43.

- any exercise of the prerogative of mercy;
- action taken in matters relating to contractual or other commercial transactions … being transactions of a government Department;
- action taken in respect of appointments or removals, pay, discipline, superannuation or other personnel matters, in relation to the armed forces, any office or employment under the Crown;[34]
- the grant of honours, awards or privileges within the gift of the Crown, including the grant of Royal Charters.

Departments and matters within the Commissioner's jurisdiction

Schedule 2 to the Act lays down those Departments subject to the jurisdiction of the Ombudsman. The Parliamentary and Health Service Commissioners Act 1987 extended the Ombudsman's jurisdiction to cover some non-departmental bodies, and the complete list of Departments and bodies within the Ombudsman's jurisdiction is now found in Schedule 1 to the 1987 Act, as amended by the Parliamentary Commissioner Act 1994. The Health Service Act 1977 provided that regional, district and special health authorities, family health services authorities, Mental Health Act Commission, Dental Practice Board and National Health Service Trusts are all subject to investigation by the Ombudsman. The Ombudsman may investigate any matter relating to an alleged failure to provide a service it is meant to provide, and any other action taken by or on behalf of the authority. The jurisdiction is thus much broader than 'maladministration'. However, the complaint must be one which involves injustice or hardship suffered as a result of failures under the two headings for complaint. Individuals have the right of direct access to the Ombudsman. Originally excluded from investigation by the Ombudsman, the Health Service Commissioners (Amendment) Act 1996 extended the jurisdiction of Ombudsmen to include clinical judgments of medical practitioners.

The Ombudsman's discretion

Where a matter falls within the Ombudsman's jurisdiction, the Ombudsman has discretion as to whether to accept the complaint.[35] Section 5(5) provides that the Ombudsman shall act 'in accordance with his own discretion'. However, while the Ombudsman's discretion is broad, it is not unlimited and is subject to judicial review. In **Re Fletcher** (1970), the applicant sought an order of *mandamus* to force the Ombudsman to investigate a complaint. The House of Lords refused, relying on the broad discretion conferred on the Commissioner by statute. In **R v Parliamentary Commissioner for Administration ex parte Dyer** (1994), the applicant sought judicial review of the Ombudsman's investigation into her complaints against the Department of Social Security. The applicant was dissatisfied with a report of the Ombudsman and sought judicial review on four grounds. The allegations were, first, that the Ombudsman had not investigated all her complaints; second, that she had not been given the opportunity to comment on the draft reports; third, that the Ombudsman, having heard her complaints, refused to reopen the investigations; and, fourth, that the Ombudsman was wrong in holding that he could not reopen the inquiry. The Queen's Bench Division held that it had jurisdiction to review the work of the Ombudsman. Lord Justice Simon Brown declared that he could see nothing in the Ombudsman's role or the statutory framework in which he operated which

---

34 Commissioner for Complaints (Northern Ireland) Act 1969, s. 5(1), provides that the Commissioner has jurisdiction over matters of employment in the public sector.
35 Parliamentary Commissioner Act 1967, s. 5(1).

is 'so singular as to take him wholly outside the purview of judicial review'. Nevertheless, the court would be slow to review given the breadth of discretion conferred under the Act.[36]

The meaning of 'maladministration'

Maladministration is the key concept relating to the Ombudsman's jurisdiction, but it is not defined in the Act. The concept derives from the Whyatt Report of 1961, where it was described as a term which 'was not of precise meaning'. The failure to define the concept in the Act was deliberate. The Minister responsible for introducing the legislation, Mr Richard Crossman, felt that the Act was of such an innovatory nature that time would be needed to adjust to the Act's introduction and that no rigid criteria should be set. In the House of Commons, Mr Crossman described maladministration as including 'bias, neglect, inattention, delay, incompetence, ineptitude, perversity, turpitude, arbitrariness and so on'.[37]

The meaning of maladministration can best be understood when placed in the context of actual investigations undertaken by the Ombudsman. Among its many cases undertaken in one year, the *Annual Report 2004–2005: A Year of Progress* presents the following examples:

> The Ombudsman found that a General Practitioner had failed to provide an adequate standard of care and treatment through delay and obstruction.

> The Ombudsman upheld a complaint concerning informed consent to surgery. The patient required treatment for cancer of the oesophagus. The Ombudsman found that the brief 'mention' of the surgery procedure was unacceptable and meant that informed consent was not given. Poor documentation was also found. It was also unacceptable that the task of obtaining signed consent was given to a junior doctor.

> Jobcentre Plus had incorrectly advised a couple over their eligibility to income support. The couple had moved in together and the man had reduced his working hours as a result of the advice. They then suffered a loss of income. They complained to Jobcentre Plus which admitted the mistake but refused to pay any compensation for their loss which was exacerbated by the man's deterioration in health as a result of stress.

> The Ombudsman found maladministration on the part of the Legal Services Commission which had failed to provide an appropriate level of service; as a result of the mistakes interest had accrued on her statutory charge liability. The Commission apologised and arranged for her statutory charge account to be reimbursed and for an *ex gratia* payment to compensate for the distress suffered as a result of the Commission's failings.

The courts have examined the concept of maladministration in relation to the work of Local Government Ombudsmen. For example, in **R v Commissioners for Local Administration ex parte Bradford Metropolitan Borough Council** (1979), maladministration was described as 'faulty administration' and 'bad administration', whereas, in 1980, Lord Donaldson MR explained that maladministration is primarily concerned with the manner in which authorities reach or implement decisions, and is not concerned with the quality of the decision itself.[38] In **R v**

---

36 Cf. **R v Parliamentary Commissioner for Administration ex parte Balchin** (1998) and **Balchin (No 2)** (2000), in which judicial review was granted, and the Parliamentary Commissioner found to have fallen into error.

37 *Official Report*, HC 734 Col. 51.

38 **R v Commissioners for Local Administration ex parte Eastleigh Borough Council** (1980).

Local Commissioner for Administration ex parte Liverpool City Council (1999), the Court of Appeal ruled that the failure of local councillors to follow the National Code of Local Government Conduct, and failure to observe the requirement to declare financial interests when taking part in decisions relating to planning, was maladministration.

Maladministration is a more restrictive concept than is employed in other jurisdictions. In Denmark, for example, the ombudsman may examine 'mistakes' and 'unreasonable decisions' and, in Norway, the ombudsman can investigate decisions which are 'clearly unreasonable'. In the United Kingdom, being tied to the concept of maladministration, the Ombudsman is not concerned with the merits of any decision taken, or the fairness or otherwise of the rules governing any situation, but rather with the manner of the application of the rules.

 Pause and Reflect

What do you understand by the concept of 'maladministration'? What reform, if any, would you propose?

The principles of good administration

In the quest for an improvement in public service provision, the Ombudsman has published its *Principles of Good Administration, Principle of Good Complaint Handling* and *Principles for Remedy.*[39] The *Principles of Good Administration* include:

- Getting it right: acting in accordance with the law and with regard for the rights of those concerned; acting in accordance with the public body's policy and guidance; taking proper account of established good practice; providing effective services, using appropriately trained and competent staff; taking reasonable decisions, based on all relevant considerations.
- Being customer focused: ensuring people can access services easily; informing customers what they can expect and what the public expects of them; keeping to its commitments, including any published service standards; dealing with people helpfully, promptly and sensitively, bearing in mind their individual circumstances; responding to customers' needs flexibly, including, where appropriate, coordinating a response with other service providers.
- Being open and accountable: being open and clear about policies and procedures and ensuring that information and advice is clear, accurate and complete; stating its criteria for decision making and giving reasons for decisions; handling information properly and appropriately; keeping proper and appropriate records; taking responsibility for its actions.
- Acting fairly and proportionately: treating people impartially, with respect and courtesy; treating people without unlawful discrimination or prejudice and ensuring no conflict of interest; dealing with people and issues objectively and consistently; ensuring that decisions and actions are proportionate, appropriate and fair.
- Putting things right: acknowledging mistakes and apologising where appropriate; putting mistakes right quickly and effectively; providing clear and timely information on how

---

39 See www.ombudsman.or.uk.improving-public-service/ombudsmanprinciples-of-good-administration.

and when to appeal or complain; operating an effective complaints procedure, which includes offering a fair and appropriate remedy when a complaint is upheld.

- Seeking continuous improvement: reviewing policies and procedures regularly to ensure they are effective; asking for feedback and using it to improve services and performance ensuring that the public body learns lessons from complaints and uses these to improve services and performance.

Judicial review and Ombudsmen

In **Law Debenture Trust Group plc v Pensions Ombudsman** (1999), the Chancery Division allowed an appeal against a finding of maladministration by the Pensions Ombudsman. The complainant had applied to trustees of his pension scheme for early retirement following an injury. The trustees concluded, on the basis of video surveillance, that he was not incapacitated. The court ruled that the only basis available to the Ombudsman for overturning the decision of the trustees was on the ground of perversity, and that such a finding would have to be expressed in clear terms in the Ombudsman's decision, which had not been done. Further, a finding of perversity could only be made after consideration of the **Wednesbury** criteria with respect to unreasonableness. The Ombudsman was wrong to find that surveillance per se amounted to maladministration.

In the **Balchin** cases no fewer than three decisions of the Ombudsman were struck down by the courts in judicial review proceedings. In **R v Parliamentary Commissioner for Administration ex parte Balchin** (1998) the Ombudsman had found maladministration in relation to property blighted by a road scheme in Norfolk, but following judicial review his decision was quashed on the basis that the Ombudsman had failed to take into account a relevant consideration. A second Ombudsman investigated the matter. The second decision included fresh findings based on new evidence. It was disputed whether the Ombudsman had made a finding as to whether, if there had been any maladministration, that had caused any injustice to the applicants. The court held that the decision on maladministration was flawed since his reasoning was insufficient to support his conclusions. A third investigation followed. On this occasion the Ombudsman's decision was struck down on the basis that there had been a failure to give adequate reasons for findings on the principal controversial issues. The **Balchin** cases have been criticised on the basis that, in part, the courts were usurping the Ombudsman's role and that excessive control by the courts risks undermining the breadth of discretion given to the Ombudsman in conducting inquiries and the absence of formalistic procedures.[40]

Commenting on the **Balchin** cases, Ann Abrahams, former Parliamentary Ombudsman, made the point that while she had been able to investigate complaints into central government Departments, there were restrictions on her ability to work with the Local Government Ombudsman who was also investigating aspects of the case.[41] The Regulatory Reform Order 2007 empowers Commissioners to conduct joint investigations, to share information and to issue joint reports.[42] It also provides power to appoint a mediator to assist in the resolution of a case. The purpose of the reform was to facilitate cooperation over complaints which affect the jurisdiction of more than one Commissioner.

The Court of Appeal struck down an Ombudsman's finding in **Cavanagh v The Health Service Commissioner** (2005). In **Cavanagh** a complaint had been made to the Health Service Commissioner

---

40 See Giddings, 2000.
41 See Parliamentary Ombudsman Case No. C57/94, Redress in the Round: Remedying Maladministration in Central and Local Government, 2005.
42 SI No. 1889. The Order amends the Parliamentary Commissioner Act 1967, the Local Government Act 1974 and the Health Service Commissioner Act 1993.

concerning medical treatment which had been terminated when a doctor refused to take responsibility for the patient's overall care. The complaint raised no issue of clinical judgment or practice. The Ombudsman's investigation was to be 'into the arrangements for monitoring and treating [the patient]'. In undertaking her inquiry, however, the Ombudsman's investigation 'had become an investigation into the clinical justification for these arrangements, and thence into the professional standards and conduct of the two doctors responsible for them' (at paragraph 35). Sedley LJ examined the role for the Commissioner and stated that:

> First, the Commissioner's functions are limited to the investigation of complaints: she has no power of investigation at large. Secondly, the statutory discretions which she possesses, while generous, go to (a) whether she should embark upon or continue an investigation into a complaints (s.3(22)) and (b) how an investigation is to be conducted (s.11(3)). They do not enable her to expand the ambit of a complaint beyond what it contains, nor to expand her investigation of it beyond what the complaint warrants. [at paragraph 16]

> This does not mean that the ambit of every complaint or the scope of every inquiry is a question of law: it is for the Commissioner not only to decide what constitutes a discrete complaint but to decide what questions it raises and to investigate them to the extent she judges right. But there are legal limits. One may well be … that if she does not elect to discontinue an investigation she cannot truncate it. Another is that how she investigates a complaint is subject not only to the express requirement of notice to those directly implicated (s.11(1)) but to the common law's requirements of fairness in so far as the statute itself does not restrict them. A third, central to these appeals, is that a point may come at which the pursuit of an investigation goes beyond any admissible view either of the complaint or of what the statutory purpose of the investigation will accommodate. [at paragraph 17]

The Court ruled that the Report exceeded the Commissioner's statutory powers 'not technically or marginally but so substantially as to vitiate it in its entirety' (at paragraph 45).

In **R (Bradley) v Secretary of State for Work and Pensions** (2008) the Court of Appeal held that the Secretary of State was not free to reject the findings of the Ombudsman without 'cogent reasons'. In fact, the government decided, belatedly, to accept the main findings of the Ombudsman. Nevertheless, **Bradley** establishes an important point of principle – namely that while a body may with good reason fail to accept the findings and recommendations of the Ombudsman, it may not do so without good reason.

The Ombudsman's investigation and report

In the exercise of his or her jurisdiction, the Ombudsman is vested with strong powers by the Parliamentary Commissioner Act 1967. The Ombudsman has the same powers as a court in respect of requiring the attendance of witnesses and the right of examination, and the production of documents, subject to the protections of Cabinet proceedings and documents and such information as a person would not be compelled to disclose to a court of law (section 8). To obstruct the Ombudsman in the performance of his duties under the Act, without lawful excuse, may be certified as a contempt. Nevertheless, there are significant differences between the Ombudsman system and a court of law. The procedure for investigation lacks the formality of a court. The Ombudsman has a wide discretion in the conduct of proceedings. The service is free; witnesses are not legally represented and do not give 'evidence' under oath. The Ombudsman's findings are not legally binding and cannot be enforced by the Ombudsman. Furthermore, there is no right of appeal against the findings of the Ombudsman.

Under section 10, where the Ombudsman accepts jurisdiction and investigates a complaint, a report of the findings is sent to the complainant and the principal officer of the Department concerned. If the matter has not been remedied, or is unlikely to be, he or she may lay a special report before each House of Parliament. The Ombudsman's *Annual General Report* is laid before Parliament. The Ombudsman has no power to grant a remedy or to grant compensation. He or she does, however, make recommendations as to the appropriate remedy, and as to levels of suitable compensation.

The volume of complaints[43]

The evidence indicates that, whilst a high number of complaints are rejected (either because they relate to matters not within the Ombudsman's jurisdiction, whether relating to an excluded Department or relating to matters of policy, or because they reveal no *prima facie* case of maladministration), once a complaint is admitted for investigation, the prospect of a finding of maladministration – at least in part – is high.

The PHSO *Annual Report 2017–2018* reveals that just over 20 per cent of complaints were about government Departments, agencies and other public organisations compared with 76 per cent about the NHS in England. The government Departments with the most complaints accepted for formal investigation were the Ministry of Justice, the Home Office (including the UK Border Agency), the Department for Work and Pensions and HM Revenue and Customs. Of the various health bodies, the most complaints investigated were in relation to NHS hospitals. In 2019–2020 the PHSO received 103,965 enquiries, and handled 30,895 complaints. Recommendations made included 507 formal apologies; 297 payments for financial loss, altogether totalling £626,288; 491 improvements to services and 71 'other remedial' actions.

Major inquiries+
Sachsenhausen

The first major investigation arising out of a number of complaints was into the non-payment of compensation by the Foreign Office to 12 persons who had been prisoners of war in the Sachsenhausen camp.[44] Monies had been made available by the German government and distributed by the Foreign Office to former detainees. The Ombudsman found there had been maladministration[45] and the government awarded compensation to the complainants.

Barlow Clowes

The Barlow Clowes affair resulted in hundreds of complaints being made to the Ombudsman concerning the collapse of the Barlow Clowes company.[46] In 1988, the group of companies collapsed, causing significant losses to shareholders. The Department of Trade and Industry has responsibility for licensing such investment companies.[47] Following the company's collapse, numerous shareholders complained to Members of Parliament, 159 of whom referred the complaints to the Parliamentary Ombudsman. The Ombudsman made five findings of maladministration on the part of the Department of Trade and Industry, including errors, lack of information before making decisions, delay in instigating a formal inquiry, a failure

---

43 Cf. **R v Parliamentary Commissioner for Administration ex parte Balchin** (1998) and **Balchin (No 2)** (2000), in which judicial review was granted, and the Parliamentary Commissioner found to have fallen into error.
44 See Bradley, 1992b.
45 *Third Report of the Parliamentary Commissioner for Administration*, HC 54 (1967–1968), London: HMSO; and see Gregory and Drewry, 1991, Pts I and II.
46 See Gregory and Drewry, 1991, Pts I and II.
47 Under the Prevention of Fraud (Investment) Act 1958; now Financial Services Act 1986.

to appreciate that auditors would not find the relevant information and insufficient rigour in exercising its regulatory role – all of which resulted in injustice.

The government initially rejected the Ombudsman's findings and recommendations as to compensation, arguing both that no investment is free of risk and that those with larger amounts of money should accept a higher level of responsibility and therefore loss. The Ombudsman expressed disappointment that the government did not unreservedly accept his report. His recommendation was that compensation should be payable to investors at a rate of 90 per cent for losses incurred under £50,000, and 85 per cent for losses under £100,000. The Secretary of State for Trade and Industry accepted the recommendations, but maintained that the government had no legal liability to compensate investors, and claimed that the Department's handling of the case was 'within acceptable range of standards reasonably to be expected of regulators'. The Secretary of State went on to say that compensation was being made only because of the Ombudsman's recommendations.[48]

Salmonella in eggs

The losses caused to egg manufacturers over allegations made by officials concerning *Salmonella* infection resulted in charges of maladministration and compensation of £600,000 being paid by the Ministry of Agriculture, Fisheries and Food.[49] The Animal Health Act 1981[50] provided that, where the *Salmonella* virus was found in flocks, the flock should be slaughtered and compensation paid for the loss of the healthy birds. No compensation was payable for the diseased birds. The Ministry fixed the level of compensation – irrespective of the proportion of the flock infected by the virus – at 60 per cent of the value of the healthy birds. On investigation, the Ombudsman found that inadequate compensation had been paid.[51]

The Channel Tunnel Rail Link

The Channel Tunnel Rail Link (the CTRL) is a stretch of railway line designed to take high-speed cross-channel trains. The government's original intention was that the CTRL would be financed by the private sector. However, when private funding was not forthcoming, the project could not proceed. In 1990, the Secretary of State for Transport announced that the route was to be reconsidered. The project was thus kept alive, but uncertainty surrounded the area of southeast England in which it was to be built. As a result, thousands of properties were 'blighted' and owners were unable to sell their homes. The route was finally decided in 1994.

In February 1995, the Ombudsman[52] laid a special report before the House.[53] The special report was only the second such report to be made in the history of the office of Ombudsman.[54] The basis for the laying of a special report is that the Ombudsman considers that injustice has been caused to persons as a result of maladministration and that the injustice has not been, or will not be, remedied. In the Ombudsman's report on the CTRL project, the Ombudsman considered that maladministration had occurred in the Department of Transport between June 1990 and April 1994. The Ombudsman's view was that the Department of Transport 'had a responsibility to consider the position of … persons suffering exceptional or extreme hardship and to provide for redress where appropriate'[55] and that the government had a duty to consider the position not just of all citizens, but also of individual citizens harmed by its action. The Ombudsman found that 'no special consideration was given to that aspect of good

---

48 In total, £150 million was paid in compensation.
49 HC 947 (1992–1993), London: HMSO.
50 Animal Health Act 1981, Sched. 3, para. 5(2).
51 *Fourth Report: Compensation to Farmers for Slaughtered Poultry*, HC 519 (1992–1993), London: HMSO.
52 Mr William Reid CB.
53 Pursuant to the Parliamentary Commissioner Act 1967, s. 10(3).
54 The first was in 1977–1978, which also involved the Department of Transport.
55 *Fifth Report of the PCA: The Channel Tunnel Rail Link and Blight*, HC 193 (1994–95), London: HMSO, para. 46.

administration and it is on that basis that I criticise the department'.[56] The Ombudsman recommended that individuals who had suffered exceptional hardship should receive compensation from the government. The government's reaction was to state that it was not its policy to compensate those affected by generalised blight, and that, in relation to those individuals who had suffered exceptional hardship, it was too difficult to define criteria to identify such individuals. With this, the Ombudsman disagreed. While he accepted that there were definitional difficulties, he did not 'accept at all that it is technically beyond a government department's capabilities' to establish the relevant criteria.[57]

The Ombudsman's report and the government's response was considered by the Select Committee (see further below). In its report,[58] the committee agreed with the Ombudsman's assessment of the evidence. The committee stated that:

> The department failed to provide any material to contradict this finding when invited to do so by the committee. At no point was direct and comprehensive consideration given to the question of whether it was either desirable or possible to offer ex gratia compensation to those exceptionally afflicted by the generalised blight of the CTRL project.

The committee considered that at the heart of the matter lay the definition of maladministration. In his annual report for 1993, the Ombudsman included in his definition 'failure to mitigate the effects of rigid adherence to the letter of the law where that produces manifestly inequitable treatment'.[59] Endorsing this definition, the committee stated that the definition implies:

> an expectation that when an individual citizen is faced with extraordinary hardship as a result of strict application of law or policy, the executive must be prepared to look again and consider whether help can be given. That the department did not do. It never considered the possibility of distinguishing cases of extreme hardship from the mass of those affected adversely by blight.[60]

The committee concluded that:

(1) (i) ...the Department of Transport should have considered whether any ex gratia payments were due when the CTRL project entered the period of uncertainty caused by problems of funding between June 1990 and April 1994;

(ii) ... it is desirable to grant redress to those affected to an extreme and exceptional degree by generalised blight, in line with the principle that maladministration includes a failure to mitigate the effects of rigid adherence to the letter of the law where that produces manifestly inequitable treatment;

(ii) ... it should be possible to distinguish a small number of cases of exceptional hardship.

---

56 Ibid., Q 1.
57 Ibid.
58 Sixth Report of the PCA: The Channel Tunnel Rail Link and Exceptional Hardship, HC 270 (1994–1995), London: HMSO.
59 Report of the Parliamentary Commissioner for Administration: Annual Report for 1993, HC 345 (1993–1994), London: HMSO, para. 10.
60 Sixth Report, fn. 58, para. 20.

This highly critical report on the actions of the Department of Transport and the government's failure to respond positively to the Ombudsman's report represents a landmark case in the complex tri-partite constitutional relationship between the Ombudsman, his or her Select Committee and Parliament, and the executive. In 1997, the government finally agreed to pay compensation of £5,000 to property owners whose property value had been adversely affected by the delay in reaching decisions over the routing of the CTRL.[61]

Equitable Life

Equitable Life, the world's oldest mutually owned insurance company, having more than 1,500,000 members, suffered a decline in profitability as a result of which it was forced to reduce the costs of guaranteed rate pensions. In 2001 it made major policy value cuts, as a result of which pension payments were reduced, causing hardship. Initial allegations of maladministration by the regulators – the Financial Services Authority, the Department of Trade and Industry (as it was then) and Government Actuary's Department – were rejected by the Ombudsman. However, in 2004 the Ombudsman undertook a second investigation into the regulation of Equitable Life.

In July 2008 the Ombudsman's Report, *Equitable Life: A Decade of Regulatory Failure*, was published. The Ombudsman, Ann Abrahams, made ten findings of maladministration leading to injustice. She made two recommendations. First that the government should apologise to those who had suffered as a result of the maladministration and second that the government should establish a compensation scheme with a view to assessing individual cases and providing compensation. The level of compensation was recommended to be such as to return the individual to the position they would have been in had the maladministration not occurred.

In December 2008 the Public Administration Select Committee published its Report, *Justice Delayed: The Ombudsman's Report on Equitable Life*, which endorsed the two recommendations made by the Ombudsman. The government's response, *The Prudential Regulation of the Equitable Life Assurance Society: the Government's Response to the Report of the Parliamentary Ombudsman's Investigation*, was published in January 2009.[62] Ministers apologised to the policyholders for the maladministration which the government accepted had occurred. However, the government decided not to accept the recommendation regarding compensation. Instead, it decided to ask a former judge, Sir John Chadwick, to advise the government of the losses suffered, and what factors should be taken into account in determining whether some *ex gratia* payments should be made. No timetable was set for the completion of this review.

In May 2009 the Ombudsman then issued a Special Report under section 10(3) of the Parliamentary Commissioner Act 1967: *Injustice Unremedied: The Government's Response on Equitable Life*.[63] She concluded that:

> In this case, I am satisfied that the injustice I found in my report to have resulted from maladministration on the part of the public bodies responsible for the prudential regulation of the Society has not so far been remedied. I am also satisfied,

---

61 See James and Longley, 1996. The Child Support Agency also attracted a significant volume of complaints. The number of complaints was such that, in 1994, the Commissioner took the 'unprecedented step of declining to investigate fresh individual complaints' other than where they concerned aspects of the Agency's work which the Commissioner had not yet inquired into. In 1995, complaints against the Child Support Agency amounted to one-quarter of all cases referred to the Commissioner. See *Sixth Report*, paras 17–18 and *Parliamentary Commissioner for Administration Annual Report for 1995*, Cm 296; and see HC 193 (1994–1995), London: HMSO.

62 Cm 7538.

63 HC 435 (2008–2009).

for the reasons I have given, that it will not be so remedied whatever the outcome of the work yet to be done by Sir John Chadwick.[64]

In judicial review proceedings, **R (Equitable Members Action Group) v HM Treasury and Others** (2009) the High Court ruled that the government had failed to give adequate reasons for rejecting three of the six findings regarding maladministration. However, on the issue of the government's refusal to award compensation as recommended, the Court ruled that:

It is not in dispute, as we understand it, that the question whether to establish a compensation scheme in any particular context, and the limits of such a scheme, is a matter for the Government, reporting to Parliament, and not reviewable in the courts save on conventional irrationality grounds.

As to the particular criticism, they fall significantly short of making out a case of irrationality.[65]

The Public Administration Select Committee issued its Second Report of 2008–2009,[66] *Justice Delayed: The Ombudsman's Report on Equitable Life*, endorsing the Ombudsman's finding that the members of Equitable Life were seriously let down by the regulators, and stating that it shared: 'both a deep sense of frustration and continuing outrage that the situation has remained unresolved for so long'.

It has been seen above that the government is, in general, prepared to accept the findings of the Ombudsman and to implement his or her recommendations. In December 1991, the Financial Secretary to the Treasury[67] stated that:

I am not aware of any circumstances in which [the Parliamentary Ombudsman's] recommendations have been ignored. This is the basis on which the government has tended to work – and has, as far as I am aware, always worked – in that we do accept and implement the recommendations that are made.[68]

This commitment was reiterated by the Chancellor of the Duchy of Lancaster[69] in 1993, when he stated that 'invariably, in the end, [the government] accepted the Ombudsman's say-so'.[70] Equitable Life, however, reveals that the government may well resist the recommendation for compensation when financial loss is suffered as a result of maladministration.

HS2 Ltd[71]

The High Speed 2 (HS2) is a planned high-speed railway link between London, the Midlands and the North of England, to be constructed in two phases.

Residents who were likely to be affected by the scheme – whether through compulsory purchase or loss of value of their homes as a result of the rail link – could apply for compensation to HS2 Ltd. A group of six families lived in a hamlet of 12 properties which were

---

64 Report, at para. 72.
65 At paras 132, 133.
66 HC 41-1.
67 Mr Francis Maude MP.
68 Second Report from the Select Committee on the PCA: The Implications of the Citizen's Charter for the Work of the Parliamentary Commissioner for Administration, HC 159 (1991–1992), London: HMSO, Q 11.
69 Then the Rt Hon William Waldegrave MP.
70 First Report from the Select Committee on the PCA: The Powers, Work and Jurisdiction of the Ombudsman, HC 33 (1993–1994), London: HMSO, Q 733.
71 Report of an Investigation into a Complaint about HS2 Ltd, November 2015.

to be seriously affected by the rail link, with some properties to be demolished and some not. The families wanted to keep their community intact and for all the properties to be relocated rather than to have the properties purchased and receive compensation. HS2 Ltd failed to respond promptly to their proposal and the families suffered prolonged uncertainty over their future. The families complained to HS2 over their treatment but were not satisfied with the way in which this was dealt with. They then complained to the PHSO. Following investigation into HS2 Ltd's communications and engagement with the group, the PHSO found that 'overall HS2 Ltd's actions fell below the reasonable standards we would expect, so much so that they constituted maladministration'. The PHSO recommended that HS2 Ltd apologise to the group within four weeks of the publication of the Report, and that compensation should be paid to the families. The PHSO also recommended that HS2 appoint an independent reviewer to monitor the handling of communications and complaints and to make recommendations. HS2 Ltd should also publish the outcome of the implementation of any recommendations.

The Public Administration and Constitutional Affairs Committee examined the PHSO's Report and was highly critical of HS2 Ltd, stating that it 'remained unconvinced that the necessary changes, identified some time ago, in the way HS2 Ltd engages with the public, have ever taken place'.

The Select Committee

The Parliamentary Commissioner is aided by the Public Administration and Constitutional Affairs Committee (PACAL) which considers the annual and special reports of the Parliamentary and Health Service Ombudsman and takes evidence from the Ombudsman and others, including government Departments and health authorities, on matters arising from reports in order to ensure that all reasonable efforts are made to tighten up procedures, prevent the repetition of faults and provide any appropriate remedies.

The Select Committee represents the formal link between the Ombudsman and Parliament. The committee is able to exert pressure on government Departments to comply with the recommendations of the Ombudsman.

In its Annual Report on the Parliamentary and Health Services Ombudsman for 2016–2017[72] the PACAC acknowledged that the time taken to complete investigations was unacceptable and that a new Service Charter included the systematic monitoring of complaints. It also recognised the challenges faced as a result of a 24 per cent cut in spending required by HM Treasury.

The Parliamentary Ombudsman and ministerial responsibility

See further
Chapters 1 and 10.

One aspect of the office of Ombudsman which caused concern when the office was proposed was the relationship between the Ombudsman and Ministers, and the impact of the Ombudsman's office on the doctrine of ministerial responsibility.

Ministerial responsibility is a fundamental constitutional principle. Separated into the collective responsibility of the Cabinet and the individual responsibility of Ministers for their conduct and that of their Department, the concept underpins the idea of governmental accountability to Parliament and to the electorate. Accordingly, where a person has a grievance against a government Department or other public body which is not resolved to the complainant's satisfaction, responsibility falls on the relevant Minister and it is for the

---

72 HC 1388.

Minister to account to Parliament for any wrongdoing by a body under his responsibility. The view of the government at the time was that ministerial responsibility and the office of the Ombudsman were irreconcilable. As noted above, in the Attorney General's view, there already existed 'adequate provision' under the constitution for the redress of grievances.

JUSTICE replied:

> The Commissioner would help to make ministerial responsibility more effective. He would penetrate the screen which Ministers interpose between Members of Parliament and government departments and he would keep Parliament informed about administrative practices which were open to criticism. The responsibility of the Minister would remain as it is – neither more nor less.

The government's policy of making administration more open and accessible has an impact on the work of the Parliamentary Ombudsman. Three major developments reflected this commitment. The Citizen's Charter provided that public bodies must state their objectives, must publicise the standards of service to be expected by consumers and establish complaints procedures for dissatisfied customers. Specific services must publish their own individuated Charter. The establishment of 'Next Step Agencies',[73] the task of which is to achieve greater efficiency in the delivery of public services, also affects the role of the Ombudsman. The setting up of Agencies, the head of which are responsible for operational matters and accountable to Parliament through Select Committee inquiries, has the effect of reducing the size of the central Civil Service and introducing greater management efficiency and accountability. The Minister remains responsible to Parliament for policy matters. In relation to the Parliamentary Ombudsman,[74] his powers of investigation, report and recommendation continue to extend to Agencies. However, complaints made by the public to Members of Parliament about operational matters are to be directed to the chairman of the board of the Agency. Complaints regarding matters of policy remain within the political domain and the responsibility of Ministers.

See Chapter 5.

Ombudsmen for Northern Ireland, Scotland and Wales

Northern Ireland, Scotland and Wales each have a Parliamentary Ombudsman with similar powers and functions as the United Kingdom Parliamentary Ombudsman. In Northern Ireland there is also a Police Ombudsman.[75]

In Northern Ireland the office of Ombudsman[76] is regulated under the Ombudsman (Northern Ireland) Order 1996.[77] A complaint must relate to 'injustice in consequence of maladministration', and be made in writing to a member of the Assembly. The Assembly Member may refer the matter to the Ombudsman, with the consent of the complainant, with a request to investigate the matter.

Following a review of the offices, a Northern Ireland Public Services Ombudsman Bill is to be introduced in the Assembly in 2015. If enacted, the Bill will establish a single office of Northern Ireland Public Services Ombudsman combining the present offices of Assembly Ombudsman and the Commissioner for Complaints.

---

73 See *Improving Management in Government: The Next Steps*, 1988, London: HMSO.
74 And Commissioner for Local Administration.
75 Respectively, Parliamentary Commissioner (Northern Ireland) Act 1969; Scotland Act 1998; Government of Wales Act 1998; Police (Northern Ireland) Act 1997.
76 Originally established under the Northern Ireland Constitution Act 1973.
77 SI No. 1298 1996 (NI8).

In Scotland section 91(1) of the Scotland Act 1998 provides for the establishment of a body to investigate complaints of maladministration. A Transitional Maladministration Order[78] made temporary arrangements for the investigation of complaints by the Scottish Parliamentary Commissioner for Administration from the public where they had suffered injustice as a result of maladministration. The Scottish Public Services Ombudsman Act 2002[79] now regulates the office of the Public Services Ombudsman. The Ombudsman now has responsibility for investigations previously undertaken by the Parliamentary Commissioner in addition to the Health Service Commissioner, the Commissioner for Local Administration, the Housing Association, Mental Welfare and complaints against the Scottish Enterprise and Highlands and Islands Enterprise. The Ombudsman is supported by up to three deputy Ombudsmen.

In Wales the office of Ombudsman was provided for under section 111 of the Government of Wales Act 1998. The Public Services Ombudsman (Wales) Act 2005 now regulates the office, which combines the offices of Welsh Administration Ombudsman, Health Service Commissioner, Social Housing Ombudsman and Commission for Local Administration in Wales. A member of the public may complain on the basis that he or she has 'sustained injustice or hardship' as a result of maladministration, an alleged failure in service provision or an alleged failure to provide a service. Complaints may be made directly to the Ombudsman, in writing within a period of one year.[80] Complaints may also be made to a 'listed authority' and referred to the Ombudsman for investigation. Schedule 3 lists the authorities subject to investigation: the list may be amended by the Assembly.

Complaints against the police

In England and Wales complaints against the police are considered by the Independent Police Complaints Commission (IPCC).[81] This is discussed in Chapter 21.

As noted above, in Northern Ireland there is a separate Police Ombudsman for Northern Ireland.[82] Complaints against the police may not be investigated by the police themselves, but must be referred to the independent Police Ombudsman's Office. The Ombudsman may investigate complaints about the conduct of police officers which have occurred in the previous 12 months. Historical allegations relating to police conduct during the period of civil unrest (1968 to 1998) may also be investigated.

In Scotland the office of Police Complaints Commissioner for Scotland (PCCS) was created by the Police, Public Order and Criminal Justice (Scotland) Act 2006. The PCCS does not investigate complaints against the police but rather investigates how the police force has handled complaints. It is therefore a reviewing body rather than one with investigative powers.

Local Government Ombudsmen[83]

The Local Government Act 1974 established Ombudsmen for Local Administration for England and Wales. England is divided into three areas, each represented by one or more

---

78 Transitory and Transitional Provisions (Complains of Maladministration) Order 1999, SI 1999/1351.
79 At p. 11.
80 Section 5, Public Services Ombudsman (Wales) Act 2005.
81 Police Reform Act 2002.
82 See the Police (Northern Ireland) Acts 1998 and 2000.
83 Recommended by the JUSTICE Report, *The Citizen and His Council: Ombudsmen for Local Government?* 1969; and see the White Paper, *Reform of Local Government in England*, 1970, London: HMSO.

Ombudsmen.[84] The Scottish system was established under Part II of the Local Government (Scotland) Act 1975. Ombudsmen are appointed by the Crown and hold office 'during good behaviour'.

Jurisdiction

The Ombudsmen have jurisdiction to investigate any complaint of maladministration or failure in service provision by council committees, their members and officers of the council. Police authorities, water boards, development corporations and those bodies with whom the council has partnership arrangements for the provision of services are also within the Ombudsmen's jurisdiction.[85]

Since 1989 the public has had the right of direct access to the Ombudsman, a reform which led to a significant increase in complaints.

Maladministration causing injustice

The concept of maladministration used for the Parliamentary Ombudsman is adopted for the Local Government Ombudsmen. Maladministration resulting in injustice has been found to include incomplete record keeping and the failure to give reasons for decisions, and a finding of maladministration may be made where an authority fails to have adequate complaints procedures. Inadequate school places, and unreasonable delays in processing applications for improvement grants, have also been found to amount to maladministration. Shortages of staff and financial resources will not excuse a council from a finding of maladministration.

Section 31 of the Act provides that an authority need only consider an Ombudsman's report if it has been found that the maladministration in question has resulted in injustice. Mere maladministration is not enough.

Remedies

Where a finding of maladministration resulting in injustice has been made, section 31 of the Local Government Act 1974 imposes a duty on authorities to consider the report and to advise the Ombudsman of any action taken to comply with the findings, or proposed action. Section 31 of the 1974 Act has been amended to provide that authorities may make 'any payment' to the aggrieved person that it thinks appropriate.

Not every decision of the Ombudsman will be accepted. In 1986, for example, the Select Committee noted that 19 per cent of local authorities who had adverse reports made by the Ombudsmen had ignored the recommendations.[86] The Local Government and Housing Act 1989 provides that local authorities have three months in which to respond to the Ombudsman's report and that they should notify the Ombudsman of any action taken, or action which they are proposing to take in response to his report.[87] If the Ombudsman is not satisfied with the response he may issue a further report. Where the local authority proposes not to act in response to the report, the matter must be referred to a full council meeting.

---

84 Local Government Act 1974, s. 23.
85 Local Government and Public Involvement in Health Act 2007, s. 172.
86 *Third Report from the Select Committee on the Parliamentary Commissioner for Administration: Local Government Cases: Enforcement of Remedies*, HC 448 (1985–1986), London: HMSO.
87 Local Government and Housing Act 1989, s. 26(2)–(2)(c).

Excluded matters

Schedule 5 to the Local Government Act excludes matters relating to the internal regulation of schools, personnel matters, action taken concerning the commencement of legal proceedings and criminal investigations. The general exclusion of commercial and contractual matters has been replaced by a list of particular excluded matters.[88]

Complaints

A complaint may be made by a person who claims to have sustained injustice as a result of the local authority's failure, or a person authorised to act on behalf of that person.[89] Where a complaint is made to a public authority over whom the Ombudsman has jurisdiction, a member of that authority may refer the complaint to the Ombudsman.[90] Complaints must be in writing unless the Ombudsman disapplies this requirement.[91] The permitted period for bringing a complaint is 12 months from the day the person was affected or his or her personal representative had notice of the matter, although these requirements may be set aside by the Ombudsman.[92]

The Ombudsmen have the power to initiate an investigation into possible maladministration or service failure affecting persons other than the original complainant where this emerges in the course of an investigation.[93]

Housing matters form the basis for approximately 40 per cent of complaints each year, with complaints about planning accounting for approximately 30 per cent of complaints. Education, social services, local taxation and environmental health each comprise approximately 5 per cent of complaints.

The Information Commissioner

The Freedom of Information Act 2000 represents a step in the direction of more open government by conferring on citizens a legal right, subject to limited exceptions, to access to information held by public bodies. On this see Chapter 10.

See further
Chapter 10.

The Legal Services Ombudsman

The Legal Services Ombudsman was established under the Courts and Legal Services Act 1990. The Legal Services Act 2007 established the Office for Legal Complaints (OLC) which now regulates the Ombudsman scheme. The OLC is responsible for the appointment of the Chief Ombudsman and one or more others as Assistant Ombudsmen. The Chief Ombudsman must be a layperson. Complaints against members of the legal profession must first be directed to the relevant professional body. If that body fails to investigate the complaint adequately, a complaint may then be made to the Ombudsman.

88 Local Government and Public Involvement in Health Act 2007, s. 173.
89 Section 26A Local Government Act 1974, inserted by s. 174 Local Government etc Act 2007.
90 Section 26C Local Government Act 1974, inserted by s. 174 Local Government etc Act 2007.
91 Complaints may now be made electronically: Local Government etc Act 2007, s. 178.
92 Section 26B Local Government Act 1974, inserted by s. 174 Local Government etc Act 2007.
93 Section 26D Local Government Act 1974, inserted by s. 174 Local Government etc Act 2007.

The Housing Ombudsman

The Housing Ombudsman started work in 2013, with jurisdiction to resolve disputes between tenants and landlords in the social housing sector.[94] It was originally established under the Housing Act 1996.

Reforming the Ombudsman Service

In 2011 the Law Commission published its report on Public Services Ombudsmen making recommendations to improve access to the Ombudsmen. It also recommended that the government undertake a wide-ranging review of public services Ombudsmen and their relationship with other bodies such as courts and tribunals.[95] In 2014 the Public Administration Select Committee (PASC) published its report, *Time for a People's Ombudsman Service*.[96] The Report states that the Ombudsman is impeded by out-dated legislation and as a result unable to meet the standards set by Scotland, Wales, Northern Ireland and elsewhere.

The PASC recommended that the MP filter should be abolished, and the requirement that complaints be in writing removed. Requiring complaints to go through an MP was 'a denial of equal access to administrative justice and is an anachronism which is at odds with the expectations of today's citizens'. Citizens should be able to complain by telephone, online or in person.

Furthermore, the Ombudsman should have the power to investigate a matter on her own initiative without having received a specific complaint. The Public Administration Select Committee (PASC, the forerunner to the PACAC) also recommended that a single public services Ombudsman for England would be beneficial, bringing together the Parliamentary and Health Service Ombudsman, Local Government Ombudsman and Housing Ombudsman. The Committee recognised, however, that devolution complicates the matter, since the Ombudsman deals with complaints regarding non-devolved matters in Scotland and Wales. That suggests that there needs to be a UK-wide Ombudsman service for non-devolved matters, as well as a single Public Services Ombudsman for England. Whatever the organisation, the PHSO stressed that what was needed from the point of view of service providers is a consistent service, not one where there are potentially different decisions made by different Ombudsman services. A Draft Bill uniting the PHSO and Local Government Ombudsman under a single Public Service Ombudsman was published in 2016, but did not survive the 2017 general election.

Summary

It became recognised in the 1960s that there was inadequate provision for the investigation and resolution of citizens' complaints against government Departments. Adopting the *Ombudsmen* concept from Scandinavian countries, Parliament enacted the Parliamentary Commissioners Act 1967. This established the office of Parliamentary Ombudsman, a post independent of Parliament and the executive, with wide-ranging powers to investigate complaints based on 'maladministration'.

---

94 Established under the Housing Act 1996, s. 51 and Sched. 2.
95 Law Commission, Public Service Ombudsmen, HC 1136 (2011–2012).
96 Fourteenth Report of 2013–2014, HC 655.

Complaints must be made to the citizen's Member of Parliament who may attempt to resolve the matter or refer it to the Ombudsman. As discussed, there is no 'MP filter' applying to other Ombudsmen. The Ombudsman has a discretion whether to investigate a complaint. He or she makes an annual Report to Parliament and is supported by a Select Committee. The Ombudsman makes recommendations but cannot compel a body to accept those recommendations or grant a remedy.

Further Reading

Abraham, A, 'The ombudsman as part of the UK constitution: a contested role?' (2008) 61(1) *Parliamentary Affairs* 601.

Abraham, A, 'The ombudsman and individual rights' (2008) 61 *Parliamentary Affairs* 370.

British and Irish Ombudsman Association website. www.ombudsman.org.uk.

Gregory, R and Giddings, P, *The Ombudsman, the Citizens and Parliament*, 2002, London: Politico's Publishing.

Kirkham, R, 'Challenging the authority of the ombudsman: the parliamentary commissioner's special report on wartime detainees' (2006) 69 *Modern Law Review* 792.

McMurtie, SN, 'The waiting game: the parliamentary commissioner's response to delay in administrative procedures' [1997] *Public Law* 159.

Seneviratne, M, *Ombudsmen: Public Service and Administrative Justice*, 2002, Oxford: Oxford University Press.

Bibliography

Abraham, A, 'The ombudsman and individual rights' (2008) 61 *Parliamentary Affairs* 370 (2008a).

Abraham, A, 'The ombudsman and the executive: the road to accountability' [2008] *Parliamentary Affairs* 535 (2008b).

Abraham, A, 'The ombudsman as part of the UK constitution: a contested role?' (2008) 61(1) *Parliamentary Affairs* 601 (2008c).

Abraham, A, 'The parliamentary ombudsman and administrative justice' JUSTICE, *Tom Sargent Memorial Lecture*, 2011.

Adams, J, *The New Spies: Exploring the Frontiers of Espionage*, 1994, London: Hutchinson.

Adler, M, 'Lay tribunal members and administrative justice' [1999] *Public Law* 616.

Adler, M, 'Tribunal reform: proportionate dispute resolution and the pursuit of administrative justice' (2006) 69 MLR 958.

Ahmed, F and Perry, A, 'The coherence of the doctrine of legitimate expectations' (2014) 73 CLJ 61.

Ahmed, F and Perry, A, 'The quasi-entrenchment of constitutional statutes' (2014) CLJ 514.

Aitken, J, *Officially Secret*, 1971, London: Weidenfeld & Nicolson.

Alan Travis, 'Snooper's charter or justified safeguard?' *Guardian*, 10 July 2014.

Alderman, RK and Carter, N, 'A very Tory coup: the ousting of Mrs Thatcher' (1991) 44 *Parliamentary Affairs* 125.

Alderman, RK and Smith, MJ, 'Can prime ministers be pushed out?' (1990) 43 *Parliamentary Affairs* 260.

Allan, T, 'The rule of law as the rule of reason: consent and constitutionalism' (1999) 115 *Law Quarterly Review* 221.

Allan, T, *Constitutional Justice: A Liberal Theory of the Rule of Law*, 2001, Oxford: Oxford University Press.

Allan, T, 'Law, democracy and constitutionalism' (2016) 75 CLJ 38.

Allan, TRS, 'Legislative supremacy and the rule of law: democracy and constitutionalism' [1985] CLJ 111 (1985a).

Allan, TRS, 'The limits of parliamentary sovereignty' [1985] PL 614 (1985b).

Allan, TRS, 'Law, convention, prerogative: reflections prompted by the Canadian constitutional case' [1986] CLJ 305.

Allan, TRS, *Law, Liberty and Justice*, 1993, Oxford: Clarendon Press.

Allan, TRS, 'Requiring reasons for reasons of fairness and reasonableness' [1994] CLJ 207.

Allan, TRS, 'Parliamentary sovereignty: law, politics and revolution' (1997) 113 LQR 443.

Allan, TRS, *Constitutional Justice: A Liberal Theory of the Rule of Law*, 2001, Oxford: Oxford University Press.

Allan, TRS, 'Constitutional dialogue and the justification of judicial review' (2003) 23(4) OJLS 563.

Allan, TRS, 'Judicial deference and judicial review: legal doctrine and legal theory' (2011) 127 *Law Quarterly Review* 96.

Allason, R, *The Branch: A History of the Metropolitan Police Special Branch 1883–1983*, 1983, London: Secker & Warburg.

Allen, CK, *Law and Orders*, 3rd edn, 1965, London: Stevens.

Allen, R and Sales, P, 'The impact of the Human Rights Act 1998 upon subordinate legislation promulgated before October 2, 2000' [2000] PL 358.

Allison, JWF, *The English Historical Constitution: Continuity, Change and European Effects*, 2007, Cambridge: Cambridge University Press.

Amos, M, 'The impact of the Human Rights Act on the UK's performance before the European Court of Human Rights' [2007] *Public Law* 655.

Andenas, M and Fairgrieve, D, 'Reforming Crown immunity: the comparative law perspective' [2003] PL 730.

Anderson, DQC, *Control Orders in 2011: Final Report of the Independent Reviewer on the Prevention of Terrorism Act 2005*, 2012, London: TSO.

Anderson, DQC, 'The Independent Review of Terrorism Law' [2014] PL 40403.

Andrew, C, *Secret Service: The Making of the British Intelligence Community*, 1985, London: Heinemann.

Anson, W (Sir), *Law and Custom of the Constitution*, 4th edn, 1933, Oxford: Clarendon Press.

Archbold, *Criminal Pleading, Evidence and Practice*, 2014, London: Sweet & Maxwell.

Arden, M, 'Human rights in the age of terrorism' (2005) 121 LQR 609.

Aristotle, *The Politics*, 1962, TA Sinclair (trans.), Harmondsworth: Penguin.

Arnull, A, 'National courts and the validity of Community acts' (1988) 13 European Law Review 125 (1988a).

Arnull, A, 'The scope of Article 177' (1988) 13 European Law Review 40 (1988b).

Arnull, A, 'The uses and abuses of Article 177 EEC' (1989) 52 MLR 622.

Arnull, A, 'References to the European Court' (1990) 15 European Law Review 375.

Ashworth, A, 'Involuntary confessions and illegally obtained evidence in criminal cases: part I' [1963] Criminal Law Review 15 (1963a).

Ashworth, A, 'Involuntary confessions and illegally obtained evidence in criminal cases: part II' [1963] Criminal Law Review 77 (1963b).

Ashworth, A, 'Excluding evidence and protecting rights' [1977] Criminal Law Review 723.

Atkins, E and Hoggett, B, *Women and the Law*, 1984, Oxford: Basil Blackwell.

Aubert, V, *In Search of Law*, 1983, Oxford: Martin Robertson.

Austin, J, *The Province of Jurisprudence Determined* (1832), 1954, London: Weidenfeld & Nicolson.

Austin, R, 'The new powers of arrest: plus ça change: more of the same or major change?' [2007] CLR 459.

Bacon, F, *Advancement of Learning* (1605), 1951, Oxford: Oxford University Press.

Bagehot, W, *The English Constitution* (1867), 1993, London: Fontana.

Bailey, S and Taylor, N, *Bailey, Harris & Jones: Civil Liberties: Cases, Materials and Commentary*, 2009, Oxford: Oxford University Press.

Bailey, SH, Taylor, NW and Ching, JPL, *Smith, Bailey and Gunn on The Modern English Legal System*, 5th edn, 2007, London: Sweet & Maxwell.

Baldwin, R and Houghton, J, 'Circular arguments: the status and legitimacy of administrative rules' [1986] PL 239.

Barber, NW, 'Privacy and the police: private right, public right or human right? R v Chief Constable of the North Wales Police ex parte AB' [1998] PL 19.

Barber, NW, 'Laws and constitutional conventions' (2009) 125 LQR 294.

Barendt, E, 'Separation of powers and constitutional government' [1995] Public Law 599.

Barendt, E, 'Is there a United Kingdom constitution?' (1997) 17 Oxford JLS 137.

Barendt, E, *Freedom of Speech*, 2nd edn, 2005, Oxford: Oxford University Press.

Barendt, E, Baron, A, Herberg, JW and Jowell, J, 'Public law' (1993) 46 CLP Annual Review 101.

Barker, R, *Political Legitimacy and the State*, 1990, Oxford: Clarendon Press.

Barnett, H, 'Reflections on the Child Support Act' (1993) 5 Journal of Child Law 77.

Barnett, H, 'A privileged position? Gypsies, land and planning law' [1994] Conveyancer 454.

Barnett, H, 'The end of the road for Gypsies?' (1995) 24 Anglo-American Law Review 133.

Barnett, H, 'Buckley v United Kingdom: landmark or signpost?' (1996) 146 NLJ 1628.

Barnett, H, *Introduction to Feminist Jurisprudence*, 1998, London: Cavendish Publishing.

Barron, A and Scott, C, 'The citizen's charter programme' (1992) 55 MLR 526.

Bates, St JT, *Devolution to Scotland: The Legal Aspects*, 1997, Edinburgh: T & T Clark.

Beatson, J, 'Should judges chair public inquiries?' (2005) 121 LQR 221.

Beatson, J, 'Reforming an unwritten constitution' (2010) 126 LQR 48.

Beattie, K, 'Control orders and ASBOs: taking liberties?' [2005] Legal Action, April.

Bebr, G, 'The reinforcement of the constitutional review of Community acts under Article 177 EEC Treaty' (1988) 25 Common Market Law Review 667.

Beith, A, 'Prayers unanswered: a jaundiced view of the parliamentary scrutiny of statutory instruments' (1981) 34 Parliamentary Affairs 165.

Bell, J, *Policy Arguments in Judicial Decisions*, 1983, Oxford: Clarendon Press.

Bell, J, 'The Doctrine of Legitimate Expectations: power – constraining or Right-conferring Legal Standard?' [2016] PL 437.

Bell, JB, *The Secret Army: The IRA 1916–79*, 1979, Dublin: Academy.

Bellamy, R, 'Political constitutionalism and the Human Rights Act' (2011) 9 *International Journal of Constitutional Law* 86.

Benn, T, 'The case for a constitutional premiership' (1980) 33 *Parliamentary Affairs* 7.

Bennion, F, 'What interpretation is "possible" under section 3(1) of the Human Rights Act 1998?' [2000] PL 77.

Bindman, G, '*Spycatcher*: judging the judges' (1989) 139 NLJ 94.

Bingham (Lord), 'The rule of law' (2007) 66 CLJ 67.

Bingham (Lord), *The Rule of Law*, 2010, London: Penguin.

Bingham (Lord), 'The House of Lords: its future?' [2010] PL 261.

Bingham, TH (Sir), 'Should public law remedies be discretionary?' [1991] PL 64.

Bingham, TH (Sir), 'The European Convention on Human Rights: time to incorporate' (1993) 109 LQR 390.

Birch, D, 'The pace hots up: confessions and confusions under the 1984 Act' [1989] *Criminal Law Review* 95.

Birch, D, 'Excluding evidence from entrapment: what is a "fair cop"?' (1994) 47 CLP 73.

Birkenhead (Lord), *Points of View*, Vol. 1, 1922, London: Hodder & Stoughton.

Birkinshaw, P, 'Constitutions, constitutionalism and the state' (2005) 11 *European Public Law* 31.

Bishop, P and Maillie, E, *The Provisional IRA*, 1987, London: Heinemann.

Blackbourne, J and Walker, C, 'Interdiction and Indoctrination: the Counter-terrorism and Security Act 2015' (2016) 79 MLR 840.

Blackburn, R, 'Monarchy and the personal prerogatives' [2004] PL 546.

Blackburn, R, *King and Country: Monarchy and the Future King Charles II*, 2007, London: Politico's Publishing.

Blackburn, R, *King and Country: Monarchy and the Future King Charles III*, 2008, London: Politico's Publishing.

Blackburn, R, 'The prerogative power of dissolution of Parliament: law, practice and reform' [2009] PL 766.

Blackburn, R, 'The 2010 General Election outcome and formation of the Conservative-Liberal Democrat coalition government' [2011] PL 30.

Blackburn, R and Kennon, A, *Parliament: Functions, Practice and Procedures*, 2nd edn, 2003, London: Sweet & Maxwell.

Blackburn, RW, *Constitutional Studies*, 1992, London: Mansell.

Blackburn, RW and Kennon, A, with Wheeler-Booth, Sir Michael, *Parliament: Functions, Practice and Procedures*, 2nd edn, 2003, London: Sweet & Maxwell (referred to as Griffith and Ryle, 2003 in the text).

Blackstone, W (Sir), *Commentaries on the Laws of England (1765–69)*, 2001 edn, W Morrison (ed), London: Cavendish Publishing.

Blake (Lord), *The Office of Prime Minister*, 1975, Oxford: Oxford University Press.

Bloch, J and Fitzgerald, P, *British Intelligence and Covert Action*, 1983, Brandon: Dingle, Co Kerry.

Blom-Cooper, L and Drabble, R, 'GCHQ revisited' [2010] PL 18.

Blom-Cooper, L and Drewry, G, *Final Appeal*, 1972, Oxford: Clarendon Press.

Blom-Cooper, L and Munro, C, 'The Hutton Report' [2004] PL 472.

Bogdanor, V, 'The forty per cent rule' (1980) 33 *Parliamentary Affairs* 249.

Bogdanor, V, *The People and the Party System*, 1981, Cambridge: Cambridge University Press.

Bogdanor, V, *Multi-Party Politics and the Constitution*, 1983, Cambridge: Cambridge University Press.

Bogdanor, V (ed), *Constitutions in Democratic Politics*, 1988, London: Policy Studies Institute.

Bogdanor, V, *Power and the People*, 1997, London: Gollancz.

Bogdanor, V, 'Reforming the Lords: a sceptical view' (1999) 70 *Political Quarterly* 375.

Bogdanor, V, *Devolution in the United Kingdom*, 2001, Oxford: Oxford University Press.

Bogdanor, V, 'Our new constitution' (2004) 120 LQR 242.

Bogdanor, V and Butler, D, *Democracy and Elections*, 1983, Cambridge: Cambridge University Press.

Bogdanor, V and Vogenauer, S, 'Enacting a British constitution: some problems' [2008] PL 38.

Bolingbroke, H, *Remarks on the History of England*, 3rd edn, 1748, London: Franklin.

Bondy, V and Sunkin, M, 'Settlement in judicial review proceedings' [2009] PL 237.

Bonner, D, 'Terrorism, human rights and the rule of law: 120 years of the UK's response to terrorism' [2004] CLR 981.

Bonner, D and Stone, R, 'The Public Order Act 1986: steps in the wrong direction' [1987] PL 202.

Bowen, CD, *The Lion and the Throne*, 1957, London: Hamish Hamilton.

Boyle, K, Hadden, T and Hillyard, P, *Law and State*, 1975, Oxford: Martin Robertson.

Boyron, S, 'Proportionality in English administrative law: a faulty translation?' (1992) 12 OJLS 237.

Bracton, H, *The Laws and Customs of England* (1200–68), 1968–1977, SE Thorne (trans.), Cambridge, MA: Harvard University Press.

Bradley, AW, 'Openness, direction and judicial review' [1986] PL 508.

Bradley, AW, 'The Council on Tribunals: time for a broader role?' [1991] PL 6.

Bradley, AW, 'Good government and public interest immunity' [1992] PL 514 (1992a).

Bradley, AW, 'Sachsenhausen, Barlow Clowes – and then' [1992] PL 353 (1992b).

Bradley, AW, 'Relations between Executive, Judiciary and Parliament: an evolving saga?' [2008] PL 470.

Bradley, AW, 'The sovereignty of Parliament: form or substance?' in J Jowell and D Oliver (eds), *The Changing Constitution*, 7th edn, 2011, Oxford: Oxford University Press.

Bradley, AW and Ewing, KD, *Constitutional and Administrative Law*, 16th edn, 2014, Harlow: Longman.

Bradney, A, 'The judicial activity of the Lord Chancellor 1946–87' (1989) 16 JLS 360.

Brazier, A, Flinders, M and McHugh, D, *New Politics, New Parliament? A Review of Parliamentary Modernisation Since 1997*, 2005, London: Hansard Society.

Brazier, M, 'Judicial immunity and the independence of the judiciary' [1976] PL 397.

Brazier, R, 'Choosing a prime minister' [1982] PL 395.

Brazier, R, 'Government and the law' [1989] PL 64.

Brazier, R, *Constitutional Texts*, 1990, Oxford: Clarendon Press.

Brazier, R, 'Reducing the power of the prime minister' (1991) 44 Parliamentary Affairs 453.

Brazier, R, 'The downfall of Margaret Thatcher' (1991) 54 MLR 471.

Brazier, R, 'Regulating ministers' and ex-ministers' finances' (1992) 43 NILQ 19.

Brazier, R, 'Ministers in court: the personal legal liability of ministers' (1993) 44 NILQ 317.

Brazier, R, 'It is a constitutional issue: fitness for ministerial office in the 1990s' [1994] PL 431.

Brazier, R, 'The Scottish government' [1998] PL 212.

Brazier, R, *Constitutional Practice*, 3rd edn, 1999, Oxford: Clarendon Press.

Brazier, R, *Constitutional Reform*, 3rd edn, 2008, Oxford: Clarendon Press.

Brazier, R, Finders, M and McHugh, D, *New Politics, New Parliament? A Review of Parliamentary Modernisation Since 1997*, 2005, London: Hansard Society.

Bridges, L, Meszaros, G and Sunkin, M, 'Regulating the judicial review caseload' [2000] PL 651.

Bromhead, PA, *The House of Lords and Contemporary Politics*, 1958, London: Routledge & Kegan Paul.

Brookfield, FM, 'The courts, Kelsen, and the Rhodesian revolution' (1969) 19 Toronto ULJ 326.

Browne-Wilkinson (Lord), 'The independence of the judiciary in the 1980s' [1988] PL 44.

Browne-Wilkinson (Lord), 'The infiltration of a Bill of Rights' [1992] PL 405.

Bulloch, J, *MI5: The Origin and History of the British Counter-Espionage Service*, 1963, London: Arthur Barker.

Bunyan, T, *The History and Practice of the Political Police in Britain*, 1977, London: Quartet.

Burns, P, 'The law and privacy: the Canadian experience' (1976) 54 Canadian Bar Review 1.

Butler, D, 'The Australian crisis of 1975' (1976) 29 Parliamentary Affairs 201.

Butler, D, *Governing Without a Majority: Dilemmas for Hung Parliaments in Britain*, 1983, London: Collins.

Butler, D, *British General Elections Since 1945*, 1989, Oxford: Blackwell.

Butler, D and Ranney, A (eds), *Referendums Around the World*, 1994, Basingstoke: Macmillan.

Butterworths European Information Services, *Butterworths' Annual European Review*, 1994, London: Butterworths.

Buxton, R, 'The future of declarations of incompatibility' [2010] PL 213.

Byrne, A, *Local Government in Britain*, 7th edn, 2000, Harmondsworth: Penguin.

Cabinet Office, *An Independent Review of Government Communications* (The Phillis Report), 2004, London: The Cabinet Office.

Cain, M and Hunt, A, *Marx and Engels on Law*, 1979, London: Academic.

Callaghan, J, *Time and Chance*, 1987, London: Collins.

Calvert, H, *Constitutional Law in Northern Ireland*, 1968, London: Stevens.

Campbell, D and Young, J, 'The metric martyrs and the entrenchment jurisprudence of Lord Justice Laws' [2002] PL 399.

Cane, P, 'Accountability and the public/private distinction' in N Bamforth and P Leyland (eds), *Public Law in a Multi-Layered Constitution*, 2003, Oxford: Hart Publishing.

Cane, P, 'Judicial review in the age of tribunals' [2009] PL 479.

Cane, P, *Administrative Tribunals and Adjudication*, 2009, Oxford: Hart Publishing.

Cane, P, *Introduction to Administrative Law*, 5th edn, 2011, Oxford: Clarendon Press.

Carnwath, R, 'Tribunal justice: a new start' [2009] PL 48.

Chambers, G, *Equality and Inequality in Northern Ireland, Part 2: The Workplace*, 1987, London: Policy Studies Institute.

Chandler, JA, 'The plurality vote: a reappraisal' (1982) 30 *Political Studies* 87.

Chester, N and Bowring, N, *Questions in Parliament*, 1962, Oxford: Oxford University Press.

Chitty, J, *Law of the Prerogatives of the Crown*, 1820, London: Butterworths.

Clark, D, 'Natural justice: substance or shadow' [1975] PL 27.

Clark, M, 'Introducing a Parliamentary confirmation process for new Supreme Court Justices' [2010] PL 464.

Clarke, DN and Feldman, D, 'Arrest by any other name' [1979] *Criminal Law Review* 702.

Clayton, R, 'Regaining a sense of proportion: the Human Rights Act and the proportionality principle' [2001] EHRLR 504.

Clayton, R and Tomlinson, H, *Civil Actions against the Police*, 3rd edn, 2005, London: Sweet & Maxwell.

Clothier, C (Sir), 'Legal problems of an ombudsman' (1984) 81 *Law Soc Gazette* 3108.

Coke, E (Sir), *Institutes of the Laws of England: Concerning the Jurisdiction of the Courts*, 1644.

Collins, H, *Marxism and Law*, 1982, Oxford: Clarendon Press.

Colvin, M and Cooper, J, *Human Rights in the Investigation and Prosecution of Crime*, 2009, Oxford: Oxford University Press.

Connolly, M and Loughlin, J, 'Reflections on the Anglo-Irish Agreement' (1986) 21 *Government and Opposition* 146.

Convery, J, 'State liability in the United Kingdom after Brasserie du Pêcheur' (1997) 34 *Common Market Law Review* 603.

Cooke (Lord), 'The law lords: an endangered heritage' (2003) 119 LQR 49.

Coppel, J, 'Horizontal effect of directives' [1997] *Industrial LJ* 69.

Cornes, R, 'Devolution and England: what is on offer?' in N Bamforth and P Leyland (eds), *Public Law in a Multi-Layered Constitution*, 2003, Oxford: Hart Publishing.

Cornford, T and Sunkin, M, 'Bowman, access and the recent reforms of judicial review procedure' [2001] PL 11.

Cotterrell, RBM, 'The impact of sex discrimination legislation' [1981] PL 469.

Cowen, DV, *Parliamentary Sovereignty and the Entrenched Sections of the South Africa Act*, 1951, Cape Town: Juta.

Cowley, P and Stuart, M, 'Parliament: a few headaches and a dose of modernisation' (2001) 54(3) *Parliamentary Affairs* 442.

Craig, P, 'Sovereignty after Factortame' (1991) 11 YNEL 221.

Craig, P, 'Constitutional foundations, the rule of law and supremacy' [2003] PL 92 (2003a).

Craig, P, 'Judicial review, appeal and factual error' [2004] PL 788.

Craig, P, 'The common law, shared power and judicial review' (2004) 24 *Oxford JLS* 129.

Craig, P, 'The Treaty of Lisbon, process, architecture and substance' (2008) 33 *European Law Review* 137.

Craig, P, 'Britain in the European Union' in J Jowell and D Oliver (eds), *The Changing Constitution*, 7th edn, 2011, Oxford: Oxford University Press.

Craig, P, 'The nature of reasonableness' (2013) 66 CLP 131.

Craig, P, 'Judicial Review and Anxious Security' [2015] PL 60.

Craig, P, *Administrative Law*, 8th edn, 2016, London: Sweet & Maxwell.

Craig, P and de Búrca, G, *Text, Cases and Materials on EU Law*, 6th edn, 2015, Oxford: Oxford University Press.

Craig, PP, 'Dicey: unitary, self-correcting democracy and public law' (1990) 106 LQR 105.

Craig, PP, 'Sovereignty of the United Kingdom after *Factortame*' (1991) 11 YBEL 221.

Craig, PP, 'The common law, reasons and administrative justice' [1994] CLJ 282.

Craig, PP, 'Directives: direct effect, indirect effect and the construction of national legislation' (1997) 22 *European Law Review* 519.

Craig, PP, 'Competing models of judicial review' [1999] PL 428.

Craig, PP, 'The courts, the Human Rights Act and judicial review' (2001) 117 LQR 589.

Craig, PP, 'The Human Rights Act, Article 6 and procedural rights' [2003] PL 753 (2003b).

Craig, PP, *Administrative Law*, 8th edn, 2016, London: Sweet & Maxwell.

Craig, PP. and Rawlings, R (eds), *Law and Administration in Europe*, 2003, Oxford: Oxford University Press.

Craig, PP and Schonberg, S, 'Substitute legitimate expectations after *Coughlan*' [2000] PL 684.

Craig, R, 'The end of innocence: open justice, free speech and privacy in the modern constitution – *Khuja v Times Newspapers Ltd*' [2019] Public Law xxx.

Cranston, R, 'Disqualification of judges for interest or opinion' [1979] PL 237.

Crossman, R, *The Diaries of a Cabinet Minister*, 1977, London: Jonathan Cape.

Crossman, R, *Introduction to the English Constitution*, 1993, London: Fontana.

Curtin, D, 'The province of government: delimiting the direct effect of directives in the common law context' (1990) 15 *European Law Review* 195.

Curtin, D, 'The constitutional structure of the Union: a Europe of bits and pieces' (1993) 30 *Common Market Law Review* 17.

d'Entrèves, AP, *Natural Law*, 2nd edn, 1970, London: Hutchinson.

Daintith, T and Page, A, *The Executive in the Constitution*, 1999, Oxford: Oxford University Press.

Dale, W, *The Modern Commonwealth*, 1983, London: Butterworths.

Daly, P, 'Justiciability and the "political question" doctrine' [2010] PL 160.

Dauses, M, 'The protection of fundamental right in the Community legal order' (1985) 10 *European Law Review* 398.

David, R and Brierley, JEC, *Major Legal Systems*, 3rd edn, 1985, London: Sweet & Maxwell.

de Búrca, G, 'A community of interests? Making the most of European law' (1992) 55 MLR 346 (1992a).

de Búrca, G, 'Giving effect to European Community directives' (1992) 55 MLR 215 (1992b).

de Búrca, G, 'The principle of subsidiarity and the Court of Justice as an institutional actor' (1998) 36(2) JCMS 217.

de Búrca, G and Scott, J (eds), *From Uniformity to Flexibility*, 2000, London: Hart.

de Smith, SA, *The New Commonwealth and its Constitutions*, 1964, London: Stevens.

de Smith, SA and Brazier, R, *Constitutional and Administrative Law*, 8th edn, 1998, Harmondsworth: Penguin.

de Smith, SA, Woolf, H and Jowell, J, *Judicial Review of Administrative Action*, 5th edn, 1995, Harmondsworth: Penguin.

Deacon, R, *A History of the British Secret Service*, 1969, London: Frederick Muller (updated, 1980, London: Panther).

Denning (Lord), *Lord Denning's Report*, Cmnd2152, 1963, London: TSO.

Denning (Lord), *The Discipline of Law*, 1979, London: Butterworths.

Denning (Lord), *The Due Process of Law*, 1980, London: Butterworths.

Denning (Lord), *What Next in the Law?* 1982, London: Butterworths.

Denning (Lord), 'The Strauss case' [1985] PL 80.

Devlin (Lord), 'Judges, government and politics' (1978) 41 MLR 501.

Dhavan, R, 'Contempt of court and the *Phillimore Committee Report*' (1976) 5 *Anglo-American Law Review* 186.

Dias, RWM, 'Legal politics: norms behind the *grundnorm*' [1968] CLJ 233.

Dicey, AV, *Introduction to the Study of the Law of the Constitution* (1885), 10th edn, 1959, London: Macmillan.

Dickson, B, 'Northern Ireland's emergency legislation: the wrong medicine' [1993] PL 592.

Dickson, B, 'Law versus terror: can law win?' [2005] EHRLR 12.

Diplock (Lord), 'Administrative law: judicial review reviewed' [1974] CLJ 223.

Doherty, M, 'Prime ministerial power and ministerial responsibility in the Thatcher era' (1988) 41 *Parliamentary Affairs* 49.

Doig, A, 'Sleaze fatigue: the house of ill-repute' (2002) 55 *Parliamentary Affairs* 389.

Donaldson, F, *The Marconi Scandal*, 1962, London: R Hart-Davis.

Dougan, M, 'Case comment' (2001) 38 *Common Market Law Review* 1503.

Dougan, M, 'The Treaty of Lisbon 2007: winning minds, not hearts' (2008) 45 *Common Market Law Review* 617.

Doukas, D, 'The verdict of the German federal constitutional court on the Lisbon Treaty: not guilty, but don't do it again' (2009) 34 *European Law Review* 866.

Downes, A, 'Trawling for a remedy: state liability under Community law' [1997] LS 286.

Drake, S, 'Twenty years after Von Colson: the impact of "indirect effect" on the protection of the individual's community rights' (2005) 30 *European Law Review* 329.

Dremczewski, A, 'The domestic application of the European Human Rights Convention as European Community law' (1981) 30 *ICLQ* 118.

Drewry, G, 'The Lord Chancellor as judge' (1972) 122 *NLJ* 855.

Drewry, G (ed), *The New Select Committees*, 1989, Oxford: Oxford University Press.

Drewry, G, 'Judicial inquiries and public reassurance' [1996] PL 368.

Drewry, G, 'The executive: towards accountable government and effective governance?' in J Jowell and D Oliver (eds), *The Changing Constitution*, 7th edn, 2011, Oxford: Oxford University Press.

Drewry, G and Butcher, T, *The Civil Service Today*, 1988, Oxford: Blackwell.

Duxbury, N, *Jurists and Judges*, 2001, Oxford: Hart Publishing.

Dworkin, A, *Pornography: Men Possessing Women*, 1981, London: Women's Press.

Dworkin, R, *Taking Rights Seriously*, 1977, London: Duckworth.

Dworkin, R, *Taking Rights Seriously*, 1978, Cambridge, MA: Harvard University Press.

Dworkin, R, *A Matter of Principle*, 1985, Oxford: Oxford University Press.

Dworkin, R, *Justice for Hedgehogs*, 2011, Cambridge, MA: Harvard University Press.

Dynes, M and Walker, D, *The Times Guide to the New British State: The Government Machine in the 1990s*, 1995, London: Times Books.

Dyrberg, P, 'Current issues in the debate on public access to documents' (1999) 24 *European Law Review* 157.

Easton, S, 'Electing the electorate: the problem of prisoner disenfranchisement' (2006) 69(3) MLR 443.

Editorial, 'The Treaty of Amsterdam: neither a bang nor a whimper' (1997) 34 *Common Market Law Review* 767.

Edwards, R, 'Judicial deference under the Human Rights Act' (2002) 65 MLR 859.

Electoral Commission: *The Funding of Political Parties: Report and Recommendations*, 2004.

Eleftheriadis, P, 'The direct effect of Community law: conceptual issues' (1996) 16 YBEL 205.

Eleftheriadis, P, 'On rights and responsibilities' [2010] PL 31.

Eliantoniom, M, 'Europeanisation of administrative justice? The influence of the ECJ's case law in Italy, Germany and England' (2010) 22(3) *European Review of Public Law* 681.

Elliott, M, 'The ultra vires doctrine in a constitutional setting: still the central principle of administrative law' (1999) 58(1) CLJ 129.

Elliott, M, '*Coughlan*: substantive protection of legitimate expectations revisited' (2000) 5 JR 27; (2000) 59 CLJ 421.

Elliott, M, *The Constitutional Foundations of Judicial Review*, 2001, Oxford: Hart Publishing.

Elliott, M, 'United Kingdom: parliamentary sovereignty under pressure' (2004) 2 *International Journal of Constitutional Law* 545.

Elliott, M, 'Has the common law duty to give reasons come of age yet?' [2011] PL 56.

Emiliou, N, 'Subsidiarity: an effective barrier against "the enterprises of ambition"?' (1991) 17 *European Law Review* 383.

Endicott, T, *Administrative Law*, 3rd edn, 2015, Oxford: Oxford University Press.

Erskine May, T, *Parliamentary Practice*, 24th edn (also see previous editions 1997 and 2004), 2011, London: Butterworths.

Esher, RBB, *The Influence of King Edward: And Essays on Other Subjects*, 1915, London: John Murray.

European Commission, 'Report from the Commission on monitoring the application of Community law' [2003] 21st Annual Report Com (2004) 839.

Ewing, KD, *The Funding of Political Parties*, 1987, Cambridge: Cambridge University Press.

Ewing, KD, 'The futility of the Human Rights Act' [2004] PL 829.

Ewing, KD, *The Cost of Democracy: Party Funding in Modern British Politics*, 2007, Oxford: Hart Publishing.

Ewing, KD and Gearty, CA, *Freedom Under Thatcher*, 1990, Oxford: Clarendon Press.

Fairgrieve, D, 'Pushing back the boundaries of public authority liability: tort law enters the classroom' [2002] PL 288.

Farbey, J and Sharpe, RJ, *The Law of Habeas Corpus*, 3rd edn, 2011, Oxford: Oxford University Press.

Farmer, J, *Tribunals and Government*, 1974, London: Weidenfeld & Nicolson.

Fawcett, J, *The Application of the European Convention on Human Rights*, 1987, Oxford: Clarendon Press.

Feldman, D, 'Parliamentary scrutiny of legislation and human rights' [2002] PL 323.

Feldman, D, 'Proportionality and discrimination in anti-terror legislation' [2005] CLJ 271.

Feldman, D, 'Human rights, terrorism and risk: the roles of politicians and judges' [2006] PL 364.

Feldman, D, 'Error of law and flawed administrative acts' (2014) 73 CLJ 275.

Fenwick, H, 'Marginalising human rights: breach of the peace, "kettling", the Human Rights Act and public protest' [2009] PL 737.

Fenwick, H, *Civil Liberties and Human Rights*, 5th edn, 2011, Abingdon: Routledge-Cavendish.

Finders, M, 'The enduring centrality of individual ministerial responsibility within the British constitution' (2000) 6 *Journal of Legislative Studies* 73.

Fine, R, *Democracy and the Rule of Law: Liberal Ideals and Marxist Critiques*, 1984, London: Pluto.

Finer, SE, 'The individual responsibility of ministers' (1956) 34 *Public Administration* 377.

Finer, SE, *Anonymous Empire*, 1958, London: Pall Mall.

Finer, SE, *Adversary Politics and Electoral Reform*, 1975, London: Anthony Wigram.

Finer, SE, *The Changing British Party System*, 1980, Washington: AEI Studies.

Finnis, JM, *Natural Law and Natural Rights*, 1980, Oxford: Clarendon Press.

Forsyth, C, 'Judicial review, the royal prerogative' (1985) 36 NILQ 25.

Forsyth, C, 'The provenance and protection of legitimate expectations' [1988] CLJ 238.

Forsyth, C, 'Of fig leaves and fairy tales: the ultra vires doctrine, the sovereignty of Parliament and judicial review' (1996) 55 CLJ 122.

Foster, RF (ed), *The Oxford History of Ireland*, 1989, Oxford: Oxford University Press (1989a).

Foster, RF, *Modern Ireland 1600–1972*, 1989, Harmondsworth: Penguin (1989b).

Foulkes, D, 'The Council on Tribunals: visits policy and practice' [1994] PL 564.

Franklin, M and Norton, P, *Parliamentary Questions*, 1993, Oxford: Clarendon Press.

Fredman, S, *Women and the Law*, 1997, Oxford: Clarendon Press.

Fredman, S, 'Human rights transformed: positive duties and positive rights' [2006] PL 498.

French, D, 'Spy fever in Britain 1900–15' (1978) 21 *Historical Journal* 355.

Fry, GK, 'The Sachsenhausen concentration camp case and the convention of ministerial responsibility?' [1970] PL 336.

Fuller, L, 'Positivism and fidelity to law: a reply to Professor Hart' (1958) 11 *Harvard Law Review* 630.

Fuller, L, *The Morality of Law*, 1964, New Haven: Yale University Press.

Galligan, DJ, 'The nature and functions of policies within discretionary power' [1976] PL 332.

Ganz, G, 'Legitimate expectation: a confusion of concepts' in C Harlow (ed) *Public Law and Politics*, 1986, London: Sweet & Maxwell.

Ganz, G, *Quasi-legislation: Some Recent Developments in Secondary Legislation*, 1987, London: Sweet & Maxwell.

Garton Ash, T, *The File: A Personal History*, 1997, London: HarperCollins.

Gearty, C, *Terror*, 1991, London: Faber & Faber.

Gearty, C, 'Reconciling parliamentary democracy and human rights' (2002) 118 LQR 248.

Gearty, C, 'Counter terrorism and the Human Rights Act' (2005) 32(1) *Journal of Law and Society* 18.

Gearty, C, 'Human rights in an age of counter terrorism: injurious, irrelevant or indispensable?' (2005) 58 *Current Legal Issues* 25.

Gearty, C, *Can Human Rights Survive?* 2006, Cambridge: Cambridge University Press (Hamlyn Lectures).

Geddis, A, 'Free speech martyrs on unreasonable threats to social peace' [2004] PL 853.

Geddis, A, 'Parliamentary privilege: *quis custodiet ipsos custodes?*' [2005] PL 696.

Gee, G, 'The political constitutionalism of JAG Griffith' (2008) 28 *Legal Studies* 20.

Gee, G, 'What are Lord Chancellors for?' [2014] PL 11.

Genn, H, 'Tribunals and informal justice' (1993) 56 MLR 3.

Giddings, P, 'Ex parte Balchin: findings of maladministration and injustice' [2000] PL 201.

Gilvarry, E, 'Selection changes to be urged' (1991) 88 Law Soc Gazette 6.

Goodhart, AL, Essays in Jurisprudence and the Common Law, 1931, Cambridge: Cambridge University Press.

Goodhart, AL, 'Thomas v Sawkins: a constitutional innovation' [1936–38] CLJ 22.

Gordon, DM, 'What did the Anisminic case decide?' (1971) 34 MLR 1.

Gordon, K, 'Counting the votes: a brief look at McDonald' (2011) 14 CCLR 337.

Gordon, M, 'The conceptual foundations of parliamentary sovereignty: reconsidering Jennings and Wade' [2009] PL 519.

Gould, BC, 'Anisminic and judicial review' [1970] PL 358.

Gregory, R and Drewry, G, 'Barlow Clowes and the ombudsman: part I' [1991] PL 192 (1991a).

Gregory, R and Drewry, G, 'Barlow Clowes and the ombudsman: part II' [1991] PL 408 (1991b).

Gregory, R and Giddings, P, The Ombudsman, the Citizens and Parliament, 2002, London: Politico's Publishing.

Greive, D, 'Can a Bill of Rights Do Better Than The Human Rights Act?' [2016] PL 223.

Griffith, JAG, 'The political constitution' (1979) 42 MLR 1.

Griffith, JAG, 'Crichel Down: the most famous farm in British constitutional history' (1987) 1 Contemporary Record 35.

Griffith, JAG, The Politics of the Judiciary, 5th edn, 1997, London: Fontana.

Griffith, JAG, 'The brave new world of Sir John Laws' (2000) 63 MLR 159.

Griffith, JAG, 'The common law and the political constitution' (2001) 117 LQR 42.

Griffith, JAG and Ryle, M, Parliament: Functions, Practice and Procedures, 2nd edn, 2003, London: Sweet & Maxwell.

Guest, AG (ed), Oxford Essays in Jurisprudence, 1961, Oxford: Oxford University Press.

Gwynn, SL, The Life of Walpole, 1932, London: Butterworths.

Hadfield, B, 'The Anglo-Irish Agreement 1985: blue print or green print' (1986) 37 NILQ 1.

Hadfield, B, The Constitution of Northern Ireland, 1989, Belfast: SLS.

Hadfield, B, 'The Belfast agreement' [1998] PL 599.

Hadfield, B, 'Judicial review and the prerogative powers' in M Sunkin and S Payne (eds), The Nature of the Crown, 1999, Oxford: Oxford University Press.

Hadfield, B, 'The nature of devolution in Scotland and Northern Ireland: key issues of responsibility and control' [1999] Edinburgh Law Review 3.

Hadfield, B, 'Devolution, Westminster and the English question' [2005] PL 286.

Hailsham (Lord), The Door Wherein I Went, 1975, London: Collins.

Hailsham (Lord), The Dilemma of Democracy, 1978, London: Collins.

Hailsham (Lord), 'The quest for equal treatment' [2005] PL 571.

Hale, B (Dame), 'Equality and the judiciary: why should we want more women judges?' [2001] PL 489.

Hale, M (Sir), The History of the Pleas of the Crown, 1736, S Emlyn (ed), London: E and R Nott and R Gosling.

Hamilton, E and Cairns, H (eds), Plato's Collected Dialogues, 1989, Ewing, NJ: Princeton University Press.

Hanks, PJ, Constitutional Law in Australia, 2nd edn, 1996, Sydney: Butterworths.

Hansard Society, Report of the Commission on Electoral Reform, 1976, London: Hansard Society.

Hansard Society Commission, The Financing of Political Parties, 1981.

Hansard Society, Making the Law, 1993, London: Hansard.

Hansard Society, The Future of Parliament: Reform of the Second Chamber, 1999, London: Hansard Society.

Harlow, C (ed.), Public Law and Politics, 1986, London: Sweet & Maxwell.

Harlow, C, 'European governance and accountability' in M Bamforth and P Leyland (eds), Public Law in a Multi-Layered Constitution, 2003, Oxford: Hart Publishing.

Harlow, C and Rawlings, R, 'Accountability and law enforcement: the centralised EU infringement procedure' (2006) 31 European Law Review 447, 226 and 228 EC.

Harlow, C and Rawlings, R, 'Tribunals in transition' [2009] Law and Administration 508.

Harlow, C and Rawlings, R, 'Tribunals in transition' in *Law and Administration*, 2009, Cambridge: Cambridge University Press.

Harlow, C and Rawlings, R, *Law and Administration*, 3rd edn, 2009, Cambridge: Cambridge University Press.

Harlow, C and Rawlings, R, 'Administrative Law in Context' [2014] PL 28.

Harris, BV, 'The Continuing Struggle with the Nuanced Obligation on Judges to Provide Reasons for Their Decisions' (2016) 132 LQR 216.

Harris, DJ, 'Human rights or mythical beasts' (2004) 120 LQR 428.

Harris, DJ, O'Boyle, M and Warbrick, C, *Law of the Convention on Human Rights*, 3rd edn, 2014, Oxford: Oxford University Press.

Harris, J, *Legal Philosophies*, 1980, London: Butterworths.

Hart, HLA, 'Positivism and the separation of law and morals' (1958) 71 *Harvard Law Review* 593.

Hart, HLA, *The Concept of Law*, 1961, Oxford: Clarendon Press.

Hartley, T, 'The European Court, judicial objectivity and the constitution of the European Union' (1996) 112 LQR 411.

Hartley, T, *The Foundations of European Union Law*, 8th edn, 2014, Oxford: Clarendon Press.

Harvey, C, 'Talking about human rights' [2004] EHRLR 500.

Harvey Cox, W, 'The Anglo-Irish Agreement' (1987) 40 *Parliamentary Affairs* 80.

Hayhurst, JD and Wallington, P, 'The parliamentary scrutiny of delegated legislation' [1988] PL 547.

Hazell, R, 'Freedom of information in Australia, Canada and New Zealand' (1989) 67 *Public Administration* 189.

Hazell, R, 'Reinventing the constitution: can the state survive?' [1999] PL 84.

Headey, BW, *British Cabinet Ministers: The Roles of Politicians in Executive Office*, 1974, London: Allen & Unwin.

Hennessy, P, 'Helicopter crashes into Cabinet: Prime Minister and constitution hurt' (1986) 13 JLS 423 (1986a).

Hennessy, P, *Cabinet*, 1986, Oxford: Blackwell (1986b).

Hennessy, P, *Whitehall*, 1990, London: Fontana.

Hennessy, P, *The Hidden Wiring*, 1995, London: Gollancz.

Herberg, JW, 'The right to reasons: palm trees in retreat?' [1991] PL 340.

Heuston, RFV, *Essays in Constitutional Law*, 2nd edn, 1964, London: Stevens (1964a).

Heuston, RFV, *Lives of the Lord Chancellors, 1885–1940*, 1964, Oxford: Clarendon Press (1964b).

Heuston, RFV, *Lives of the Lord Chancellors, 1940–1970*, 1987, Oxford: Clarendon Press.

Hewart, CJ, *The New Despotism*, 1929, London: Benn.

Heydon, JD, 'Illegally obtained evidence' [1973] *Criminal Law Review* 690.

Hickman, TR, 'The reasonableness principle: reassessing its place in the public sphere' (2004) 63 CLJ 166.

Hickman, TR, 'The uncertain shadow …' [2004] PL 122.

Hickman, TR, 'Between human rights and the rule of law: indefinite detention and the derogation model of constitutionalism' [2005] MLR 655.

Hickman, TR, 'The substance and structure of proportionality' [2008] PL 694.

Hilson, C, 'Judicial review, policies and the fettering of discretion' [2002] PL 111.

HMSO, 'Your region, your choice, revitalising the English regions' [2002], CM 5511.

HMSO, *Review of Intelligence on Weapons of Mass Destruction: Report of a Committee of Privy Counsellors*, 2004, London: The Stationery Office, HC898.

Hobbes, T, *The Leviathan* (1651), 1973, London: JM Dent.

Hodson, D, and Peterson, J, *Institutions of the European Union*, 4th edn, 2017, Oxford: Oxford University Press.

Hoffmann (Lord), 'The universality of human rights' (2009) 125 LQR 416.

Hogg, PW and Monahan, P, *Liability of the Crown*, 3rd edn, 2000, London: Carswell.

Holdsworth, W, 'The treaty making power of the Crown' (1942) 58 LQR 177.

Holt, J, *Magna Carta*, 1965, Cambridge: Cambridge University Press.

Hooper, D, *Official Secrets: The Use and Abuse of the Act*, 1988, Sevenoaks: Coronet.

Hope of Craighead (Lord), 'Voices from the past: the Law Lords' contribution to the legislative process' (2007) 123 LQR 547.

Hough, B, 'Ministerial responses to parliamentary questions: some recent concerns' [2003] PL 211.

House of Lords Select Committee on the Constitution, 6th Report of 2014–2015, *The Office of Lord Chancellor*, HL Paper 75, London: TSO.

House of Lords' European Union Report, 'Withdrawing from the EU' [2016] HL Paper 138.

House of Lords' Constitution Committee, 'The Union and Devolution' [2016] HL Paper 149.

Howe, G, 'The management of public inquiries' (1999) 70 *Political Quarterly* 294.

Hughes, M, *Ireland Divided: The Roots of the Modern Irish Problem*, 1994, Cardiff: Wales University Press.

Hume, D, *Political Discourses* (1752), 1769, Edinburgh: Kineald & Donaldson.

Hume, D, *An Enquiry Concerning the Principles of Morals* (1751), 1957, Indianapolis, IN: Bobbs-Merrill.

Hunt (Lord), 'Access to a previous government's papers' [1982] PL 514.

Hunt, M, 'The "horizontal effect" of the Human Rights Act' [1998] PL 423.

Hunt, M, 'Sovereignty's blight: why contemporary public law needs the concept of due deference' in N Bamforth and P Leyland (eds), *Public Law in a Multi-Layered Constitution*, 2003, Oxford: Hart Publishing.

Hutchinson, A and Petter, A, 'Private rights/public wrongs: the liberal lie of the Charter' (1988) 38 *Toronto ULJ* 278.

Hutchinson, AP and Monahan, P (eds), *The Rule of Law: Ideal or Ideology*, 1987, Toronto: Carswell.

Identity Cards, *A Summary of Findings from the Consultation on Entitlement Cards and Identity Fraud*, 2003, London: TSO, Cm6019.

Identity Cards, *The Next Steps*, 2003, London: TSO, Cm6020.

Ip, J, 'Al Rawi, Tariq, and the future of closed material procedures' (2012) 75 MLR 606.

Irvine (Lord), 'The development of human rights under an incorporated Convention on Human Rights' [1998] PL 221.

Irvine (Lord), 'The impact of the Human Rights Act: parliament, the courts and the executive' [2003] PL 308.

Irvine of Lairg (Lord), 'Judges and decision-makers: the theory and practice of Wednesbury review' [1996] PL 59.

Irvine of Lairg (Lord), 'The impact of the Human Rights Act: parliament, the courts and the executive' [2003] PL 308.

Itzin, C (ed.), *Pornography: Women, Violence and Civil Liberties*, 1992, Oxford: Oxford University Press.

Iyer, TKK, 'Constitutional law in Pakistan: Kelsen in the courts' (1973) 21 AJCL 759.

Jackson, P and Leonard, P, *Constitutional and Administrative Law*, 8th edn, 2001, London: Sweet & Maxwell.

Jacob, JM, 'From privileged Crown to interested public' [1993] PL 121.

Jaconelli, J, 'The "D notice" system' [1982] PL 37.

Jaconelli, J, 'The nature of constitutional conventions' (1999) 19 *Legal Studies* 24.

Jaconelli, J, 'Do constitutional conventions bind?' (2005) 64 CLJ 149.

Jalland, P, *The Liberals and Ireland: The Ulster Question in British Politics to 1914*, 1980, Hemel Hempstead: Harvester.

James, R and Longley, D, 'The Channel Tunnel rail link, the ombudsman and the select committee' [1996] PL 38.

Jennings, I (Sir), *Cabinet Government*, 3rd edn, 1959, Cambridge: Cambridge University Press (1959a).

Jennings, I (Sir), *The Law and the Constitution*, 5th edn, 1959, London: Hodder & Stoughton (1959b).

Jennings, I (Sir), *Parliament*, 2nd edn, 1969, Cambridge: Cambridge University Press.

Joint Committee on Human Rights Draft Bill of Rights for the UK, HL Paper 165-I; HC 150-I, 2008, London: TSO.

Jones, G (ed), *The New Government Agenda*, 1997, Hemel Hempstead: ICSA.

Jones, T, 'Mistake of fact in administrative law' [1990] PL 507.

Jones, T and Williams, J, 'The legislative future of Wales' (2005) 68 MLR 642.

Jones, T, Turnbull, J and Williams, J, 'The law of Wales or the law of England and Wales?' [2005] *Stat LR* 135.

Joseph, P, 'Parliament, the courts, and the collaborative enterprise' [2004] *King's College Law Journal* 321.

Jowell, J, 'Of *vires* and vacuums: the constitutional context of judicial review' [1999] PL 448.

Jowell, J, 'Beyond the rule of law: towards constitutional judicial review' [2000] PL 671.

Jowell, J, 'Judicial deference: servility; civility or institutional capacity?' [2003] PL 592.

Jowell, J, 'Judicial deference and human rights: a question of competence' in P Craig and R Rawlings (eds), *Law and Administration in Europe*, 2003, Oxford: Oxford University Press.

Jowell, J, 'Parliamentary sovereignty under the new constitutional hypothesis' [2006] PL 562.

Jowell, J, 'The rule of law and its underlying values' in J Jowell and D Oliver (eds), *The Changing Constitution*, 7th edn, 2011, Oxford: Oxford University Press.

Jowell, J and Oliver, D (eds), *New Directions in Judicial Review*, 1988, London: Stevens.

Jowell, J and Oliver, D (eds), *The Changing Constitution*, 2000, Oxford: Oxford University Press.

Jowell, J and Oliver, D (eds), *The Changing Constitution*, 7th edn, 2011, Oxford: Oxford University Press.

Jowell, J and Oliver, D (eds), *The Changing Constitution*, 8th edn, 2015, Oxford: Oxford University Press.

Judge, D, 'Whatever happened to parliamentary democracy in the United Kingdom?' (2004) 57(3) *Parliamentary Affairs* 682.

Kafka, F, *The Trial*, E Muir and W Muir (trans.), 1956, London: Secker & Warburg.

Kavanagh, A, 'Judging the judges under the Human Rights Act: deference, disillusionment and the "war on terror"' [2009] PL 287.

Kavanagh, A, 'Defending deference in public law and constitutional theory' (2010) 126 LQR 222.

Keedy, ER, 'R v Sinnisiak: a remarkable murder trial' (1951) 100 *Pennsylvania UL Review* 48.

Keith, B, *The King, the Constitution, the Empire and Foreign Affairs: Letters and Essays 1936–37*, 1936, London: Longmans, Green.

Keith-Lucas, B and Richards, PG, *A History of Local Government in the Twentieth Century*, 1979, London: Allen & Unwin.

Kelsen, H, *The General Theory of Law and State*, 1961, New York: Russell.

Kelsen, H, *The Pure Theory of Law*, 1967, Berkeley, CA: California University Press.

Kenny, CS, 'The evolution of the law of blasphemy' [1992] CLJ 127.

Kent, SK, *Sex and Suffrage in Britain 1860–1914*, 1987, Ewing, NJ: Princeton University Press (rep 1990, London: Routledge).

King, ML, *Why We Can't Wait*, 1963, New York: Signet.

Kingsford-Smith, D and Oliver, D (eds), *Economic with the Truth: The Law and Media in a Democratic Society*, 1990, Oxford: Oxford University Press.

Kirkham, R, 'Challenging the authority of the ombudsman: the parliamentary commissioner's special report on wartime detainees' (2006) 69 MLR 792.

Klug, F, 'A bill of rights: do we need one or do we already have one?' [2007] PL 701.

Klug, F and Starmer, K, 'Incorporation through the "front door": the first year of the Human Rights Act' [2001] PL 654.

Klug, F and Starmer, K, 'Standing back from the Human Rights Act: how effective is it five years on?' [2005] PL 716.

Knight, CJS, 'Bi-polar sovereignty restated' (2009) 68 CLJ 361.

Krämer, L, *The EEC Treaty and Environmental Protection*, 1992, London: Sweet & Maxwell.

Lambert, J, 'Executive authority to tap telephones' (1980) 43 MLR 59.

Lardy, H, 'Prisoner disenfranchisement: constitutional rights and wrongs' [2002] PL, 524.

Laski, H, *Reflections on the Constitution*, 1951, Manchester: Manchester University Press.

Laslett, P (ed.), *Philosophy, Politics and Society*, 1975, Oxford: Blackwell.

Laws, J (Sir), 'Is the High Court the guardian of fundamental constitutional rights?' [1993] PL 60.

Laws, J (Sir), 'Law and democracy' (1995) 95 *Public Law* 72.

Le Queux, W, *German Spies in England*, 1915, London: S Paul.

Le Sueur, A, 'Developing mechanisms for judicial accountability in the United Kingdom' [2004] *Legal Studies* 73.

Le Sueur, A, 'The rise and ruin of unreasonableness' [2005] *Judicial Review* 32.

Le Sueur, A, 'Gordon Brown's new constitutional settlement' [2008] PL 21.

Leach, P, 'Birth certificates, privacy and human rights' (1998) 142 SJ 628.

Leach, S, Stewart, J and Walsh, K (eds), *The Changing Organisation and Management of Local Government*, 1994, Basingstoke: Macmillan.

Lee, HP, 'Reforming the Australian Constitution: the frozen continent refuses to thaw' [1988] PL 535.

Lee, JJ, *Ireland 1912–85: Politics and Society*, 1990, Cambridge: Cambridge University Press.

Lee, S, 'The limits of parliamentary sovereignty' [1985] PL 633.

Lee, S, 'And so to school' (1987) 103 LQR 166.

Lee, S, *Judging Judges*, 1989, London: Faber & Faber.

Legal Studies Special Issue, *Constitutional Innovation: The Creation of a Supreme Court for the United Kingdom; Domestic, Comparative and International Reflections*, 2, 3, 5, 7, 8, 9, 10, 2004.

Legg, T (Sir), 'Judges for the new century' [2001] PL 62.

Leigh, D, *Betrayed: The Real Story of the Matrix Churchill Trial*, 1993, London: Bloomsbury.

Leigh, D and Vulliamy, E, *Sleaze: The Corruption of Parliament*, 1997, London: Fourth Estate.

Leigh, I, 'A tapper's charter?' [1986] PL 8.

Leigh, I, '*Spycatcher* in Strasbourg' [1992] PL 200.

Leigh, I, 'Matrix Churchill, supergun and the Scott Inquiry' [1993] PL 630.

Leigh, I, 'Taking rights proportionately: judicial review, the Human Rights Act 1998 and Strasbourg' [2002] PL 265.

Leigh, I, 'By law established? The Crown, constitutional reform and the Church of England' [2004] PL 266.

Leigh, I, 'Local Government and Political Constitutionalism' [2014] PL 43.

Leigh, I and Lustgarten, L, 'The Security Services Act 1989' (1989) 52 MLR 801.

Leigh, I and Lustgarten, L, 'The Security Commission: constitutional achievement or curiosity?' [1991] PL 215.

Lenaerts, K, 'The rule of law and the coherence of the judicial system of the EU' (2007) 44 *Common Market Law Review* 1625.

Leopold, P, 'Leaks and squeaks in the Palace of Westminster' [1980] PL 368.

Leopold, P, 'Freedom of speech in Parliament: its misuse and proposals for reform' [1981] PL 30.

Leopold, P, '"Proceedings in Parliament": the grey area' [1991] PL 475.

Leopold, P, 'Free speech in Parliament and the courts' (1995) 15 *Legal Studies* 204.

Leopold, P, 'Standards of conduct in public life' in J Jowell and D Oliver (eds), *The Changing Constitution*, 7th edn, 2011, Oxford: Oxford University Press.

Lester (Lord), 'Fundamental rights' [1994] PL 70.

Lester (Lord), 'First steps towards a constitutional Bill of Rights' (1997) 2 EHRLR 124.

Lester, A, 'The utility of the Human Rights Act: a reply to Keith Ewing' [2005] PL 249.

Lever, A, 'Is judicial review undemocratic?' [2007] PL 280.

Lewis, T, 'Animal Defenders International v UK: sensible dialogue or a bad case of Strasbourg jitters?' (2014) 77 MLR 460.

Leyland, P, 'Freedom of information and the 2009 parliamentary expenses scandal' [2009] PL 675.

Linklater, M, Leigh, D with Mather, I, *Not Without Honour: The Inside Story of the Westland Scandal*, 1986, London: Sphere.

Locke, J, *Two Treatises of Government* (1690), 1977, London: JM Dent.

Lockyer, R, *Tudor and Stuart Britain 1471–1714*, 2nd edn, 1985, Harlow: Longman.

Loughlin, M, 'Constitutional theory: a 25th anniversary essay' (2005) 25 Oxford JLS 183.

Lustgarten, L, *The Legal Control of Racial Discrimination*, 1980, London: Macmillan.

Lustgarten, L, 'Racial inequality and the limits of law' (1981) 44 MLR 68.

Lustgarten, L, 'Socialism and the rule of law' (1988) 15 JLS 25.

Lustgarten, L and Leigh, I, *In From the Cold: National Security and Parliamentary Democracy*, 1994, Oxford: Clarendon Press.

Lysaght, CE, 'Irish peers and the House of Lords' (1967) 18 NILQ 277.

MacCormick, DN, 'A note on privacy' (1973) 84 LQR 23.

MacCormick, N, 'Does the United Kingdom have a constitution? Reflections on *MacCormick v Lord Advocate*' (1978) 29 NILQ 1.

MacCormick, N, *Questioning Sovereignty*, 2001, Oxford: Oxford University Press.

Macdermott (Lord), 'Law and order in times of emergency' [1972] *Juridical Review* 1.

Machin, D and Richardson, G, 'Judicial review and tribunal decision making: a study of the mental health review tribunal' [2000] PL 494.

Mackay (Lord), *The Administration of Justice*, 1994, London: Stevens.

Mackenzie, R, *Free Elections*, 1967, London: Allen & Unwin.

Mackintosh, JP, *The British Cabinet*, 3rd edn, 1977, London: Stevens.

MacMillan, CA, 'Burying treasure trove' (1996) 146 NLJ 1346.

Macmillan, H, *At the End of the Day (1961–63)*, 1973, London: Macmillan.

Maer, L and Sandford, M, *Select Committees under Scrutiny*, 2004, London: Constitution Unit, UCL.

Maitland, FW, *The Constitutional History of England*, 1908, Cambridge: Cambridge University Press.

Malleson, K, 'Judicial bias and disqualification in the Pinochet Case' [1999] PL 391.

Malleson, K, 'Judicial bias and disqualification after Pinochet (No 2)' [2000] MLR 119.

Malleson, K, 'Rethinking the merit principle in judicial selection' (2006) 33(1) *Journal of Law and Society* 126.

Malleson, K, 'Diversity in the judiciary: the case for positive action' [2009] *Journal of Law and Society* 376.

Malleson, K, 'The evolving role of the UK Supreme Court' [2011] PL 754.

Mancini, G and Keeling, D, 'From CILFIT to ERTA: the constitutional challenge facing the European Court' (1991) 11 YBEL 1.

Markesinis, BS, *The Theory and Practice of Dissolution of Parliament*, 1972, Cambridge: Cambridge University Press.

Marsh, D and Read, M, *Private Members' Bills*, 1988, Cambridge: Cambridge University Press.

Marsh, NS, 'The declaration of Delhi' (1959) 2 *Journal of the International Commission of Jurists* 7.

Marshall, G, *Parliamentary Sovereignty and the Commonwealth*, 1957, Oxford: Clarendon Press.

Marshall, G, *Constitutional Theory*, 1971, Oxford: Clarendon Press.

Marshall, G, *Constitutional Conventions*, 1984, Oxford: Clarendon Press.

Marshall, G, 'Cabinet government and the Westland affair' [1986] PL 181 (1986a).

Marshall, G, 'The Queen's press relations' [1986] PL 505 (1986b).

Marshall, G (ed.), *Ministerial Responsibility*, 1989, Oxford: Clarendon Press.

Marshall, G, 'The end of prime ministerial government?' [1991] PL 1.

Marshall, G, 'The referendum: what? when? how?' (1997) 50 *Parliamentary Affairs* 307.

Marshall, G and Moodie, G, *Some Problems of the Constitution*, 5th edn, 1971, London: Hutchinson.

Martin, FX (ed.), *Leaders and Men of the Easter Rising: Dublin 1916*, 1967, London: Methuen.

Mathijsen, PSRF, *A Guide to European Union Law*, 11th edn, 2013, London: Sweet & Maxwell.

McAuslan, P, 'The Widdicombe Report: local government business or politics?' [1987] PL 154.

McAuslan, P and McEldowney, JF, *Legitimacy and the Constitution: The Dissonance between Theory and Practice in Law*, 1985, London: Sweet & Maxwell.

McConville, M and Baldwin, J, 'Confessions: the dubious fruit of police interrogation' (1980) 130 NLJ 993.

McConville, M and Hodgson, J, *Custodial Legal Advice and the Right to Silence*, RCCJ Research Study No 16, 1993, London: HMSO.

McCrudden, C, 'Northern Ireland and the British constitution since the Belfast Agreement' in J Jowell and D Oliver (eds), *The Changing Constitution*, 6th edn, 2007, Oxford: Oxford University Press.

McGarry, J, 'The Anglo-Irish Agreement and the prospects for power sharing in Northern Ireland' (1988) 59 *Political Quarterly* 236.

McIlwain, CH, *The High Court of Parliament and its Supremacy*, 1910, New Haven, CT: Yale University Press.

McIlwain, CH, *Constitutionalism Ancient and Modern*, 1947, London: Cornell University Press.

McMurtie, SN, 'The waiting game: the Parliamentary Commissioner's response to delay in administrative procedures' [1997] PL 159.

Mendelsen, M, 'The European Court of Justice and human rights' (1981) 1 YBEL 126.

Miers, DR and Page, AC, *Legislation*, 2nd edn, 1990, London: Sweet & Maxwell.

Mill, JS, *Representative Government* (1861), 1958, Indianapolis: Bobbs-Merrill.

Mill, JS, *On Liberty* (1859), 1989, Cambridge: Cambridge University Press.

Mill, JS, *The Subjection of Women* (1869), 1989, Cambridge: Cambridge University Press.

Millar, E and Phillips, P, 'Evaluating anti-discrimination legislation in the United Kingdom: some issues and approaches' (1983) 11 *International Journal of Society Law* 417.

Millett (Lord), 'The right to good administration in Europe' [2002] PL 309.

Mills, A, 'Reforms to Judicial Review in the Criminal Justice and Courts Act 2015' [2015] PL 538.

Ministry of Justice, *Election Day: Weekend Voting CO 13/08*, 2008, London: TSO.

Ministry of Justice, *An Elected Second Chamber: Further Reform of the House of Lords*, 2008, London: TSO, Cm7438.

Ministry of Justice, *Appointments and Diversity: A Judiciary for the 21st Century*, 2012.

Mitchell, JDB, 'Sovereignty of Parliament: yet again' (1963) 79 LQR 196.

Mitchell, JDB, *Constitutional Law*, 2nd edn, 1968, Edinburgh: Green.

Montesquieu, C, *De l'Esprit des Lois* (1748), 1989, Cambridge: Cambridge University Press.

Morgan, J, 'Privacy in the House of Lords again' (2004) 120 LQR 563.

Morgan, JP, *The House of Lords and the Labour Government 1964–1970*, 1975, Oxford: Oxford University Press.

Morrison (Lord), *Government and Parliament*, 3rd edn, 1964, Oxford: Oxford University Press.

Morton, G, *Home Rule and the Irish Question*, 1980, Harlow: Longman.

Mosley, RK, *The Story of the Cabinet Office*, 1969, London: Routledge & Kegan Paul.

Mullan, D, 'Fairness: the new natural justice' [1975] *University of Toronto Law Journal* 280.

Mummery, DR, 'The privilege of freedom of speech in Parliament' (1978) 94 LQR 276.

Munday, R, 'Inferences from silence and European human rights law' [1996] *Criminal Law Review* 370.

Munro, CR, 'Laws and conventions distinguished' (1975) 91 LQR 224.

Munro, CR, 'Press freedom: how the beast was tamed' (1991) 54 MLR 104.

Munro, CR, 'Power to the people' [1997] PL 579.

Munro, CR, *Studies in Constitutional Law*, 2nd edn, 1999, London: Butterworths.

Munro, CR, 'Privilege at Holyrood' [2000] PL 347.

Murkens, JEK, 'The quest for constitutionalism in UK public law discourse' (2009) 29 *Oxford JLS* 427.

Murphy, C, 'An effective right to cross-border healthcare? Comment on Elchinov' [2011] *European Current Law Yearbook* cxv.

Murphy, C, *EU Counter-Terrorism Law*, 2012, London: Hart Publishing.

Murphy MH, 'Transparency and Surveillance...' [2014] PL 9.

Murray, P, 'Escaping The Wilderness: R v Bolton and Judicial Review to Error of Law [2016] CLJ 333.

Naffine, N, 'Windows on the legal mind: evocations of rape in legal writing' (1992) 18 *Melbourne UL Review* 741.

Naffine, N, 'Possession: erotic love in the law of rape' (1994) 57 MLR 10.

Nason, S, 'Regionalisation of the Administrative Court and the tribunalisation of judicial review' [2009] PL 440.

Neumann, F, *The Rule of Law: Political Theory and the Legal System in Modern Society*, 1986, Leamington Spa: Berg.

Newburn, T, *The Settlement of Claims at the Criminal Injuries Commission Compensation Board*, Home Office Research Study No 112, 1989, London: HMSO.

Newton, K and Karran, TJ (eds), *The Politics of Local Expenditure*, 1985, London: Macmillan.

Nicol, D, 'Law and politics after the Human Rights Act' [2006] PL 722.

Nicolson, D and Reid, K, 'Arrest for breach of the peace and the ECHR' [1996] CLR 764.

Nicolson, IF, *The Mystery of Crichel Down*, 1986, Oxford: Clarendon Press.

Norton, P, *Parliament in the 1980s*, 1985, Oxford: Blackwell (1985a).

Norton, P, *The Commons in Perspective*, 2nd edn, 1985, Oxford: Blackwell (1985b).

Norton, P, 'Televising the House of Commons' (1991) 44 *Parliamentary Affairs* 185.

Norton, P, *Does Parliament Matter?* 1993, Hemel Hempstead: Harvester.

Norton-Taylor, R, *Truth is a Difficult Concept: Inside the Scott Inquiry*, 1995, London: Fourth Estate.

Nozick, R, *Anarchy, State and Utopia*, 1974, Oxford: Blackwell.

Nugent, N, *The Government and Politics of the European Union*, 2010, Basingstoke: Macmillan.

O'Cinneide, C, 'The Race Relations (Amendment) Act 2000' [2001] PL 220.

O'Connor, U, *The Troubles: The Struggle for Irish Freedom 1912–1922*, 1989, London: Mandarin.

O'Halpin, E, *The Decline of the Union: British Government in Ireland 1892–1920*, 1987, Dublin: Gill & Macmillan.

O'Keefe, D and Twomey, PM (eds), *Legal Issues of the Maastricht Treaty*, 1994, London: Chancery.

Oliver, D, 'Reform of the electoral system' [1983] PL 108.

Oliver, D, 'Is the *ultra vires* rule the basis of judicial review?' [1987] PL 543.

Oliver, D, '*Pepper v Hart*: a suitable case for reference to Hansard?' [1993] PL 5.

Oliver, D, 'The frontiers of the state: public authorities and public functions under the Human Rights Act' [2000] PL 476.

Oliver, D, 'The challenge for Parliament' [2001] PL 666.

Oliver, D, 'Public law procedures and remedies: do we need them?' [2001] PL 91.

Oliver, D, *Constitutional Reform in the United Kingdom*, 2003, Oxford: Oxford University Press.

Oliver, D, 'Functions of a public nature under the Human Rights Act' [2004] PL 329.

Oliver, D, 'Improving the scrutiny of bills: the case for standards and checklists' [2006] PL 219.

Oliver, D, 'Reforming the United Kingdom Parliament' in J Jowell and D Oliver (eds), *The Changing Constitution*, 7th edn, 2011, Oxford: Oxford University Press.

Oliver, D and Austin, R, 'Political and constitutional aspects of the Westland affair' (1987) 40 *Parliamentary Affairs* 20.

Olley, K, 'Proportionality at common law' (2004) 9 *Judicial Review* 197.

Olowofoyeku, AA, 'The *nemo judex* rule: the case against automatic disqualification' [2000] PL 456.

Owen Dixon, J, 'The law and the constitution' (1935) 51 LQR 611.

Ozin, P, Norton, H and Spivey, P, *PACE: A Practical Guide to the Police and Criminal Evidence Act 1984*, 3rd edn, 2013, Oxford: Oxford University Press.

Paine, T, *Rights of Man* (1791, Pt I), 1984, rep. 1998, H Collins (ed), New York: Penguin.

Paine, T, *Rights of Man* (1792, Pt II), 1984, rep. 1998, H Collins (ed), New York: Penguin.

Palley, C, 'The evolution, disintegration and possible reconstruction of the Northern Ireland Constitution' (1972) 1 *Anglo-American Law Review* 368.

Palley, C, *The United Kingdom and Human Rights*, 1991, London: Sweet & Maxwell.

Palmer, S, 'Tightening secrecy law' [1990] PL 243.

Pannick, D, *Sex Discrimination Law*, 1985, Oxford: Clarendon Press.

Parpworth, N, 'The Parliamentary Standards Act 2009: a constitutional dangerous dogs measure?' (2010) 73 MLR 262.

Parpworth, N, 'Succession to the Crown Act 2013: modernising the monarchy' (2013) 76 MLR 2070.

Party Funding Review Report, *Strengthening Democracy: Fair and Sustainable Funding of Political Parties*, March 2007.

Paterson, A, *The Law Lords*, 1982, London: Macmillan.

Paterson, A, *Final Judgment: The Last Law Lords and the Supreme Court*, 2013, Oxford: Hart Publishing.

Peers, S, 'Finally "fit for purpose"? The Treaty of Lisbon and the end of the third pillar legal order' (2008) 27 *Yearbook European Law* 47.

Pennock, JR and Chapman, JW (eds), *Political and Legal Obligation*, 1970, New York: Atherton.

Pescatore, P, 'The "doctrine of direct effect": an infant disease of Community law' (1983) 8 *European Law Review* 155.

Peterson, J and Shackleton, M (eds), *The Institutions of the European Unions*, 3rd edn, 2012, Oxford: Oxford University Press.

Petite, M, *The Treaty of Amsterdam*, http://centers.law.nyu.edu/jeanmonnet/archive/papers/98/98-2-.html.

Philby, K, *My Silent War*, 1968, London: MacGibbon & Kee.

Phythian, M and Little, W, 'Parliament and arms sales: lessons of the Matrix Churchill affair' (1993) 46 *Parliamentary Affairs* 293.

Pincher, C, *Their Trade is Treachery*, 1981, London: Sidgwick & Jackson.

Pitt-Payne, T and Kamm, R, 'Freedom of Information: the story so far' [2009] *Judicial Review* 239.

Plamenatz, J, *Man and Society*, 1963, New York: Longman.

Plucknett, TFT, 'Dr Bonham's Case and judicial review' (1926) 40 *Harvard Law Review* 30.

Poole, KP, 'The Northern Ireland Commissioner for Complaints' [1972] PL 131.

Poole, T, 'Tilting at windmills? Truth and illusion in "the political constitution"' (2007) 70 MLR 250.

Powell, E and Wallis, K, *The House of Lords in the Middle Ages*, 1968, London: Weidenfeld & Nicolson.

Priestley, J, *An Essay on the First Principles of Government; and on the Nature of Political, Civil, and Religious Liberty, Including Remarks on Dr Brown's Code of Education, and on Dr Balguy's Sermon on Church Authority*, 2nd edn, 1771, London: J Johnson.

Prosser, T, 'Poverty, ideology and legality: supplementary benefit appeal tribunals and their predecessors' (1977) 4 *British Journal of Law and Society* 59.

Pugh, I (Sir), 'The ombudsman: jurisdiction, power and practice' (1978) 56 *Public Administration* 127.

Rainey, B, Wicks, E and Ovey, C, *The European Convention on Human Rights*, 6th edn, 2014, Oxford: Clarendon Press.

Ramsay, P, 'What is anti-social behaviour?' [2004] *Criminal Law Review* 908.

Ranelagh, J, *A Short History of Ireland*, 1983, Cambridge: Cambridge University Press.

Rasmussen, H, 'The European Court's acte clair strategy in CILFIT' (1984) 9 *European Law Review* 242.

Rasmussen, H, 'Between self-restraint and activism; a judicial policy for the European Court' (1988) 13 *European Law Review* 28.

Rasmussen, H, 'Present and future European judicial problems after enlargement and the post-2005 ideological revolt' (2007) 44 *Common Market Law Review* 1661.

Rawlings, HF, *Law and the Electoral Process*, 1988, London: Sweet & Maxwell.

Rawlings, R, 'Hastening slowly: the next phase in Welsh devolution' [2005] PL 824.

Rawls, J, *A Theory of Justice*, 1973, rev. edn 1999, Oxford: Oxford University Press.

Raz, J, 'The rule of law and its virtue' [1977] LQR 93.

Raz, J, *The Authority of Law*, 1979, Oxford: Oxford University Press.

Redmayne, M, 'Hearsay and human rights: *Al-Khawaja* in the grand chamber' (2012) 75 MLR 865.

Reed, C (ed.), *Computer Law*, 7th edn, 2011, Oxford: Oxford University Press.

Reid (Lord), 'The judge as law maker' [1972] JSPTL 22.

Report of the Independent Commission on the Voting System (Jenkins Report), 1998, London: HMSO, Cm4090.

Richardson, G and Genn, H (eds), *Administrative Law and Government Action*, 1994, Oxford: Oxford University Press.

Richardson, G and Genn, H, 'Tribunals in transition: resolution or adjudication?' [2007] PL 116.

Riddell, P, 'Quality control deficiency that lets down the law' [1994] *The Times*, 16 December.

Ridley, FF, 'There is no British constitution: a dangerous case of the Emperor's clothes' (1988) 41 *Parliamentary Affairs* 340.

Robert, S, *The English Judges*, 2002, Oxford: Hart Publishing.

Roberts, M, 'Public law representations and substantive legitimate expectations' (2001) 64 MLR 112.

Robertson, AH and Merrills, JG, *Human Rights in Europe*, 3rd edn, 1993, Manchester: Manchester University Press.

Robertson, G, *Obscenity*, 1979, London: Weidenfeld.

Robertson, G, *Freedom, the Individual and the Law*, 7th edn, 2015, Harmondsworth: Penguin.

Roberts-Wray, K, *Commonwealth and Colonial Law*, 1966, London: Stevens.

Robilliard, St J, 'Offences against religion and public worship' (1981) 44 MLR 556.

Rogers, R and Walters, R, *How Parliament Works*, 5th edn, 2004, London: Pearson.

Rooney, JM, 'A Legal Basis for Non-arbitrary Detention' [2016] PL 563.

Rose, R, 'Law as a resource of public policy' (1986) 39 *Parliamentary Affairs* 297.

Ross, M, 'Beyond Francovich' (1993) 56 MLR 55.

Rousseau, J, *The Social Contract and Discourses* (1762), 1977, London: JM Dent.

Rowbottom, J, 'The Electoral Commission's proposals on the funding of political parties' [2005] PL 168.

Russell, M, *Reforming the House of Lords: Lessons from Overseas*, 2000, Oxford: Oxford University Press.

Russell, M and Cornes, R, 'The Royal Commission on the House of Lords: a House for the future?' (2000) 64 MLR 82.

Ryle, M and Richards, G (eds), *The Commons Under Scrutiny*, 3rd edn, 1988, London: Routledge & Kegan Paul.

Sadurski, W, 'Solange, chapter 3: constitutional courts in Central Europe – democracy – European Union' (2008) 14 *European Law Journal* 1.

Sales, P, 'Rights and Fundamental Rights in English Law' [2016] CLJ 86.

Sales, P and Steyn, K, 'Legitimate expectations in English public law: an analysis' [2004] PL 564.

Sampford, CJG, '"Recognize and declare": an Australian experiment in codifying constitutional conventions' (1987) 7 OJLS 369.

Samuals, A, 'Anti-social behaviour orders: their legal and jurisprudential significance' (2005) 69 *Journal of Criminal Law* 223.

Sandford, M, *The System of Parliamentary Questions*, House of Commons Library Briefing Paper No D4148.

Savage, N and Edwards, C, *A Guide to the Data Protection Act 1985*, 1985, London: Financial Training.

Sawer, G, *Australian Federalism in the Courts*, 1967, Melbourne: Melbourne University Press.

Sawer, G, *Federation Under Strain*, 1977, Melbourne: Melbourne University Press.

Schermers, HG, *Judicial Protection in the European Community*, 4th edn, 1987, Dordrecht: Kluwer.

Schermers, HG, 'The European Community bound by fundamental human rights' (1990) 27 *Common Market Law Review* 249.

Schutz, R and Tierney, S (eds), *The UK and the Federal Idea*, 2018, Oxford: Hart Publishing.

Schutze, R, 'Cooperative federalism constitutionalised: the emergence of complementary competences in the EU legal order' (2006) 31 *European Law Review* 167.

Schutze, R, 'From Rome to Lisbon: "executive federalism" in the (new) European Union' (2010) 47 *Common Market Law Review* 1385.

Schwarze, J, *European Administrative Law*, 1992, Luxembourg: Office for Official Publications of the European Communities.

Scott, J, *Development Dilemmas in the EC: Rethinking Regional Development Policy*, 1995, Milton Keynes: OU Press.

Scott, J, *European Community Environmental Law*, 1998, London: Longman.

Scott, R, 'Procedures at inquiries: the duty to be fair' (1995) 111 LQR 596.

Scott, R (Sir), 'Ministerial accountability' [1996] PL 410.

Seaborne Davies, D, 'The House of Lords and the criminal law' (1962) 6 JSPTL 104.

Sedley, S (Sir), 'The sound of silence: constitutional law without a constitution' (1994) 110 LQR 270.

Sedley, S (Sir), 'Human rights: a twenty-first century agenda' [1995] PL 386.

Seneviratne, M, *Ombudsmen: Public Service and Administrative Justice*, 2002, Oxford: Oxford University Press.

Sharpe, LG, 'Theories and values of local government' (1970) 18 *Political Studies* 153.

Shaw, J, *Law of the European Union*, 3rd edn, 2000, Basingstoke: Palgrave.

Shaw, J, 'Europe's constitutional future' [2005] PL 132.

Shell, D, 'The House of Lords and the Thatcher government' (1983) 38 *Parliamentary Affairs* 16.

Shell, D, *The House of Lords*, 2nd edn, 1992, London: Harvester.

Shetree, S and Turenne, S, *Judges on Trial: The Independence and Accountability of the English Judiciary*, 2nd edn, 2013, Cambridge: Cambridge University Press.

Silk, P and Walters, R, *How Parliament Works*, 6th edn, 2006, London: Longman.

Simmonds, KR, 'The British Islands and the Community: II Isle of Man' (1970) 7 CMLR 454.

Simmonds, KR, 'The British Islands and the Community: III Guernsey' (1971) 8 CMLR 475.

Simon Brown LJ, 'Public interest immunity' [1994] PL 579.

Slapper, G and Kelly, D, *The English Legal System*, 11th edn, 2010, Abingdon: Routledge.

Slapper, G and Kelly, D, *The English Legal System*, 15th edn, 2014, Abingdon: Routledge.

Slapper, G and Kelly, D, *The English Legal System*, 16th edn, 2015, Abingdon: Routledge.

Slot, PJ, 'Case C-194/94: CIA Security International SA v Signalson SA and Securitel SPRL' (1996) 33 *Common Market Law Review* 1035.

Slynn, G, 'The Court of Justice of the European Community' (1984) 33 ICLQ 409.

Smart, C, *Feminism and the Power of Law*, 1989, London: Routledge.

Smith, ATH, 'Dicey and civil liberties: comment' [1985] PL 608.

Smith, DJ, 'Policy and research: employment discrimination in Northern Ireland' (1988) 9(1) *Policy Studies* 41.

Snyder, F, 'Enhancing EU democracy, constituting the EU' (2005) 11 *ELJ* 131.

Somek, A, 'Postconstitutional treaty' (2007) 8 *German Law Journal* 1121.

Spalin, E, 'Abortion, speech and the European Community' [1992] *Journal of Social Welfare and Family Law* 17.

Spjut, RJ, 'Internment and detention without trial in Northern Ireland' (1986) 49 MLR 712.

Stanton, J, 'Local Democracy, Economic Development and Construction Act 2009: a reinvigorated local democracy?' [2010] PL 1.

Steele, I, 'Judging Judicial Inquiries' [2004] PL 738.

Steiner, J, 'From direct effects to *Francovich*: shifting means of enforcement of Community law' (1993) 18(3) *European Law Review* 3.

Steiner, J, *Enforcing EC Law*, 1995, London: Blackstone.

Stephens, L, *The Science of Ethics* (1882), 1972, Newton Abbot: David & Charles.

Stevens, R, *The English Judges*, 2013, Oxford: Hart Publishing.

Stewart, J and Stoker, J (eds), *The Future of Local Government*, 1989, Basingstoke: Macmillan.

Steyn (Lord), 'The case for a supreme court' (2002) 118 LQR 382.

Steyn (Lord), 'Deference: a tangled story' [2005] PL 346.

Steyn (Lord), 'Civil liberties in modern Britain' [2009] PL 228.

Stubbs, W, *The Constitutional History of England: In its Origin and Development*, 1880, Oxford: Clarendon Press.

Sunkin, M, 'Crown immunity from criminal liability in English law' [2003] PL 716.

Sunkin, M, 'Pushing forward the frontiers of human rights protection' [2004] PL 643.

Sunkin, M and Payne, S (eds), *The Nature of the Crown: A Legal and Political Analysis*, 1999, Oxford: Clarendon Press.

Supperstone, M, 'The Intelligence Services Act 1994' [1994] PL 329.

Supperstone, M and Cavanagh, J, *Immigration*, 3rd edn, 1994, London: Longman.

Szyszczack, E, 'Sovereignty: crisis, compliance, confusion, complacency?' (1990) 15(6) *European Law Review* 483.

Tebbitt, N, *Upwardly Mobile*, 1988, London, Weidenfeld & Nicolson.

Temple-Lang, J, 'Community constitutional law: article 5 EC Treaty' (1990) 27 *Common Market Law Review* 645.

Temple-Lang, J, *The European Commission: Safeguard for Member States*, 5 June 1995, European Law Lecture, Queen Mary, University of London.

Thatcher, M, *The Downing Street Years*, 1993, London: HarperCollins.

Thomas of Cwmgiedd, Lord, 'The Future of Public Inquiries' [2015] PL 225.

Thompson, WI, *The Imagination of an Insurrection: Dublin, Easter 1916*, 1967, Oxford: Oxford University Press.

Thoreau, HD, *Resistance to Civil Government* (1848), 2nd edn, W Rossi (ed.), 1992, London: Norton.

Thornberry, CHR, 'Dr Soblen and the alien law of the United Kingdom' (1963) 12I CLQ 414.

Thorne, SE, 'Dr Bonham's case' (1938) 54 LQR 543.

Thornton, GC, *Legislative Drafting*, 3rd edn, 1987, London: Butterworths.

Tomkins, A, 'Public interest immunity after Matrix Churchill' [1993] PL 650.

Tomkins, A, 'Government information and Parliament: misleading by design or by default?' [1996] PL 472.

Tomkins, A, *The Constitution after Scott: Government Unwrapped*, 1998, Oxford: Clarendon Press.

Tomkins, A, 'What is Parliament for?' in M Bamforth and P Leyland (eds), *Public Law in a Multi-Layered Constitution*, 2003, Oxford: Hart Publishing.

Tomkins, A, *Public Law*, 2003, Oxford: Clarendon Press.

Tomkins, A, 'Readings of *A v Secretary of State for the Home Department*' [2005] PL 259.

Tomkins, A, *Our Republican Constitution*, 2005, Oxford: Hart Publishing.

Toth, AG, 'The principle of subsidiarity in the Maastricht Treaty' [1992] *Common Market Law Review* 1079.

Trench, A, 'The Government of Wales Act 2006: the next step in devolution for Wales' [2006] PL 687.

Trevor-Roper, H, *The Philby Affair: Espionage, Treason and Secret Service*, 1968, London: Kimber.

Tur, R and Twining, W (eds), *Essays on Kelsen*, 1986, Oxford: Clarendon Press.

Turnbull, M, *The Spycatcher Trial*, 1988, London: Heinemann.

Twomey, A, 'Changing the rules of succession to the throne' [2011] PL 378.

Uglow, S, *Criminal Justice*, 2002, London: Sweet & Maxwell.

Urban, M, *UK Eyes Alpha: The Inside Story of British Intelligence*, 1997, London: Faber & Faber.

Usher, J, 'The reception of general principles of Community law in the United Kingdom' (2005) 16 *European Business Law Review* 489.

Van Dijk, P and Van Hoof, G, *Theory and Practice of the European Convention on Human Rights*, 2nd edn, 1990, Deventer: Kluwer.

van Sliedregt, E, 'The European Arrest Warrant: between trust, democracy and the rule of law: introduction. The European Arrest Warrant: extradition in transition' (2007) 3 *European Constitutional Law Review* 244.

Van Zyl Smith, J, *The New Purposive Interpretation of Statutes: HRA Section 3 after Ghaidan v Godin-Mendoza*, 2007.

Vile, MJC, *Constitutionalism and the Separation of Powers*, 1967, Oxford: Clarendon Press.

von Hayek, F, *The Constitution of Liberty*, 1960, London: Routledge & Kegan Paul.

von Hayek, F, *The Road to Serfdom* (1944), 1994, London: Routledge & Kegan Paul.

Wade, ECS, 'Act of state in English law' (1934) 15 BYIL 98.

Wade, HWR, 'The basis of legal sovereignty' [1955] CLJ 172.

Wade, HWR, 'Constitutional and administrative aspects of the *Anisminic* case' (1969) 85 LQR 198.

Wade, HWR, 'Procedure and prerogative in public law' (1985) 101 LQR 180.

Wade, HWR, *Constitutional Fundamentals*, rev. edn, 1989, London: Stevens.

Wade, HWR, 'What has happened to the sovereignty of Parliament?' (1991) 107 LQR 1.

Wade, HWR, 'Sovereignty: revolution or evolution' (1996) 112 LQR 568.

Wade, HWR, 'Horizons of horizontality' [2000] LQR 217.

Wade, W and Forsyth, CF, *Administrative Law*, 11th edn, 2014, Oxford: Oxford University Press.

Wagner, A and Squibb, GD, 'Precedence and courtesy titles' (1973) 89 LQR 352.

Wakeham (Lord), *A House for the Future: Royal Commission on the House of Lords*, 2000, London: HMSO, Cm4534.

Walker, C, 'Review of the prerogative' [1987] PL 63.

Walker, C, 'The legal definition of "terrorism" in United Kingdom law and beyond' [2007] PL 331.

Walker, C, 'The threat of terrorism and fate of control orders' [2010] PL 4.

Walker, D, 'Beyond the unitary conception of the United Kingdom constitution' [2000] PL 384.

Walker, D, 'The idea of constitutional pluralism' (2002) 65 MLR 317.

Walker, N, 'European constitutionalism and European integration' [2005] PL 266.

Wallington, P (ed.), *Civil Liberties*, 1984, Oxford: Martin Robertson.

Walsh, D, *The Use and Abuse of Emergency Legislation in Northern Ireland*, 1983, London: The Cobden Trust.

Wasserstrom, R, 'The obligation to obey the law' [1963] *California UL Review* 780.

Watkins, A, *A Conservative Coup*, 1992, London: Duckworth.

Watson, J, 'Experience and problems in applying Article 177 EEC' (1986) 23 *Common Market Law Review* 207.

Watt, D, 'Fallout from treachery: Peter Wright and the Spycatcher case' [1988] *Political Quarterly* 206.

Weatherill, S and Beaumont, P, *EU Law*, 3rd edn, 1999, Harmondsworth: Penguin.

Webb, P, 'Parties and party systems: modernisation, regulation and diversity' (2001) 54 *Parliamentary Affairs* 308.

West, N, *MI5: British Security Service Operations 1909–45*, 1981, London: Bodley Head.

West, N, *A Matter of Trust: MI5 1945–72*, 1983, London: Hodder & Stoughton.

West, N, *GCHQ: The Secret Wireless War 1900–86*, 1986, London: Weidenfeld & Nicolson.

Wheare, KC, *The Constitutional Structure of the Commonwealth*, 1960, Oxford: Clarendon Press.

Wheare, KC, *Federal Government*, 4th edn, 1963, Oxford: Oxford University Press.

Wheare, KC, *Modern Constitutions*, 2nd edn, 1966, Oxford: Oxford University Press.

Wheeler, CJ, 'Royal Assent in the British Constitution' (2016) 132 LQR 495.

White, F and Hollingsworth, K, 'Public finance reform: the Government Resources and Account Act 2000' [2001] PL 50.

White Paper, *A New Future for Communications*, 2000, London: TSO, Cm5010.

White Paper, *Respect and Responsibility: Taking a Stand against Anti-Social Behaviour*, 2003, London: TSO, Cm5778.

Wicks, E, 'A new constitution for a new state? The 1707 union of England and Scotland' (2001) 117 LQR 109.

Williams, DGT, *Not in the Public Interest*, 1965, London: Hutchinson.

Williams, DGT, 'Telephone tapping' [1979] CLJ 225.

Williams, DGT, 'Public order and common law' [1984] PL 12.

Williams, DGT, 'Processions, assemblies and the freedom of the individual' [1987] CLR 167.

Williams, G, *Learning the Law*, ATH Smith (ed.), 15th edn, 2013, London: Sweet & Maxwell.

Williams, L, 'Defining a sufficiently serious breach of Community law: the House of Lords casts its net into the waters' (2000) 25(4) *European Law Review* 452.

Williams, R, 'The Multiple Doctrines of Legitimate Expectations' (2016) 132 LQR 639.

Williams, V, *Surveillance and Intelligence Law Handbook*, 2006, Oxford: Oxford University Press.

Wilson, H, *The Labour Government 1964–70: A Personal Record*, 1971, London: Weidenfeld & Nicolson.

Wilson, H, *The Governance of Britain*, 1976, London: Weidenfeld & Nicolson.

Wilson, R (Sir), *The Civil Service in the New Millennium*', unpublished speech, May 1999.

Wilson, R, 'The robustness of conventions in a time of modernisation and change' [2004] PL 407.

Winter, T, 'Direct applicability and direct effect: two distinct and different concepts in Community law' (1972) 9 *Common Market Law Review* 425.

Wolf-Phillips, L, 'A long look at the British constitution' (1984) 37 *Parliamentary Affairs* 385.

Woodhouse, D, 'Ministerial responsibility in the 1990s: when do ministers resign?' (1993) 46 *Parliamentary Affairs* 277.

Woodhouse, D, 'Ministerial responsibility: something old, something new' [1997] PL 262.

Woodhouse, D, 'The constitutional and political implications of a United Kingdom Supreme Court' (2004) 24(1–2) *Journal of Law and Society* 134.

Woods, L and Watson, P, *Steiner and Woods' EU Law*, 12th edn, 2014, Oxford: Oxford University Press.

Wormald, J, 'James VI and I: two kings or one?' (1983) 68 *History* 187.

Wragg, P, 'The Legitimacy of Press Reputation' [2015] *Public Law* 290.

Wright, P, *Spycatcher: The Candid Autobiography of a Senior Intelligence Officer*, 1987, New York: Viking.

Wright, T, *British Politics: A Very Short Introduction*, 2nd edn, 2013, Oxford: Oxford University Press.

Young, AL, 'A peculiarly British protection of human rights' (2005) 68 MLR 858.

Young, AL, 'In defence of due deference' (2009) 72 MLR 554.

Young, AL, 'Is dialogue working under the Human Rights Act 1998?' [2011] PL 773.

Young, H, *One of Us*, 1989, London: Macmillan.

Young, H, *The Crossman Affair*, 1976, London: Hamish Hamilton.

Zander, M, *Cases and Materials on the English Legal System*, 9th edn, 2003, London: Butterworths.

Zedner, L, 'Security liberty in the face of terror: reflections from criminal justice' (2005) 32(4) *Journal of Law and Society* 507.

Zellick, GJ, 'Government beyond law' [1985] PL 283.

Zuckerman, AAS, 'Public interest immunity: a matter of prime judicial responsibility' (1994) 57 MLR 703.

Websites

Government

www.cabinetoffice.gov.uk
www.cabinetoffice.gov.uk/news/coalition-documents
www.homeoffice.gov.uk
www.ombudsman.org.uk

Case law

www.baillii.org
www.criminallawandjustice.co.uk

Devolution and local government

www.assemblywales.org
www.bcomm-wales.gov.uk
www.directgov.uk
www.lga.gov.uk
www.niassembly.gov.uk
www.northernireland.gov.uk
www.scotland.gov.uk
www.scottish.parliament.uk
www.wales.gov.uk

Elections and referendums

www.electoralcommission.org.uk

Public inquiries

www.bloody-sunday-inquiry.org
www.detainteeinquiry.org.uk
www.iraqinquiry.org.uk
www.levesoninquiry.org.uk
www.publicinquiries.org
www.the-hutton-inquiry.org.uk
www.the-shipman-inquiry.org.uk

European Union

www.europa.eu/index_en.htm

Index